For Review material in a printed format . . .
Ask your bookstore for the
Study Guide

Study Guide
for use with

LEGAL ENVIRONMENT
OF BUSINESS
In the Information Age

David L. Baumer
J. C. Poindexter

Prepared by
Evan Sheffel

In it you'll find:

- The Learning Objectives from the chapter revisited.
- A detailed outline that reviews the important concepts of each chapter.
- Multiple Choice and True/False questions to quiz yourself on material.
- Issue Development and Essay questions to help you think through key legal situations and arguments, just like you'll have on exams.
- Answers at the back of the guide to provide you with quick access to the information and mobile study opportunities.

Legal Environment of Business in the Information Age

David L. Baumer
North Carolina State University

J. C. Poindexter
North Carolina State University

Boston   Burr Ridge, IL   Dubuque, IA   Madison, WI   New York   San Francisco   St. Louis
Bangkok   Bogotá   Caracas   Kuala Lumpur   Lisbon   London   Madrid   Mexico City
Milan   Montreal   New Delhi   Santiago   Seoul   Singapore   Sydney   Taipei   Toronto

The McGraw·Hill Companies

McGraw-Hill
Irwin

LEGAL ENVIRONMENT OF BUSINESS IN THE INFORMATION AGE

Published by McGraw-Hill/Irwin, a business unit of The McGraw-Hill Companies, Inc., 1221 Avenue of the Americas, New York, NY, 10020.

domestic   1 2 3 4 5 6 7 8 9 0 DOW/DOW 0 9 8 7 6 5 4 3
international 1 2 3 4 5 6 7 8 9 0 DOW/DOW 0 9 8 7 6 5 4 3

ISBN   0-07-244115-1

Editor in chief: *John E. Biernat*
Senior sponsoring editor: *Andy Winston*
Senior developmental editor: *Christine Scheid*
Marketing manager: *Lisa Nicks*
Producer, Media technology: *Anthony Sherman*
Senior project manager: *Kari Geltemeyer*
Production supervisor: *Debra R. Sylvester*
Lead designer: *Matthew Baldwin*
Cover image: *© Masterfile*
Senior supplement producer: *Susan Lombardi*
Senior digital content specialist: *Brian Nacik*
Typeface: *10/12 Times Roman*
Compositor: *Interactive Composition Corporation*
Printer: *R. R. Donnelley*

Library of Congress Cataloging-in-Publication Data

Baumer, David L.
   Legal environment of business in the information age / David L. Baumer, J.C.
Poindexter.—1st ed.
     p. cm.
   Includes index.
   ISBN 0-07-244115-1 (alk. paper)
   1. Electronic commerce—Law and legislation—United States. 2. Business
enterprises—Law and legislation—United States. 3. Internet—Law and legislation—United
States. I. Poindexter, J. Carl (Julius Carl), 1943—II. Title.
KF889.B328 2004
346.73'065—dc21

                           2003052665

www.mhhe.com

About the Authors

David L. Baumer is an associate professor of law and technology at the College of Management, North Carolina State University. He received a B.A. in Economics from Ohio University, J.D. from the University of Miami, and a Ph.D. in Economics from the University of Virginia. Baumer is a licensed attorney in the state of North Carolina and has been a litigation consultant and expert witness in numerous antitrust, intellectual property, contract, wrongful death, and medical malpractice cases. He is the Director of the Cyberlaw Initiative at NCSU, which is a partnership between the NCSU College of Management and corporations that have substantial Internet presences.

J. C. Poindexter is an associate professor of economics and finance in the College of Management, North Carolina State University. He received a B.S. from the University of Virginia and a Ph.D. in economics from the University of North Carolina at Chapel Hill. He has more than two decades of experience as a consultant in litigation, encompassing a wide swath of the legal perils faced by businesses today, ranging from employment discrimination to antitrust violations. He has been the author or co-author of a number of widely used textbooks.

Preface

Significant changes in society are often closely followed by significant legal changes. The changes in the U.S. and world economies during the last 10 years are, by any measure, significant. Arguably, most of these changes are due to advances in technology, particularly information technology. Broadly defined, more than one-third of the GDP in the United States is attributable to *information technology* and that figure is expected to exceed one-half by 2006. A large proportion of the laws that compose the legal environment of business will change and the pace of the change is likely to be quick. It is hoped that this book will enable business students to focus on the legal issues that have the most significant impacts on them and their businesses in the twenty-first century. This book targets future managers who will be dealing with information technology in some way.

Business pedagogy involves recognition that there are many issues that are basically *cross-functional*. Managers in each functional area of business already have had to deal with new challenges created by technology, advances in information systems, and, we believe, law. There are legal issues in every functional area of business, and many of them were hardly (or not) taught to business students 10 years ago. We are at the beginning of a new era in business and many of the more traditional concepts will have considerably less significance for business managers of the future. On the other hand, many new legal issues have emerged and are occupying center stage. Compared to other legal environment textbooks, we devote significantly more attention to e-commerce contract law and legal protection of intellectual property. We place an emphasis on the manner in which regulatory law deals with changes in technology. The Internet has significantly affected regulatory law dealing with consumer protection, securities, and antitrust among other issues. We hope that we provide a stimulating and relevant presentation of the significance of law in this exciting Information Age.

In this book, we have eschewed some of the traditional approaches to introducing business students to law. Many of the preliminary topics commonly covered in depth in the first chapter of legal environment textbooks, such as legal theory, the structure of the legal system in the United States, legal, vocabulary, ethics, and social responsibility of business, are integrated into the discussion in Chapters 2–6. Business students generally begin their training in business with an overall process course that provides integrated discussion of the major functions of business: marketing, production, finance, human resource management, and information systems. The plan in this book is to reinforce the latest trends in business education by providing a similar experience with law. In this textbook, and in real life, law is a cross-functional factor that affects the decision-making environment of managers in every functional area.

PEDAGOGICAL FEATURES

Emphasis on the Modern Legal Environment of Business

We have made a concerted effort in this textbook to focus on the present, the recent past, and the future. Most of the cases reviewed are recent. We take for granted that business students have more than a rudimentary knowledge of computers and the Internet. We do not explain each and every Internet term such as cookies, hyperlinks, and MP3 in detail, and we make frequent use of high-tech terminology and situations.

Use of Mathematics and Statistics

Mathematics and statistics are required in virtually all business management programs. In many contexts, mathematical and statistical concepts such as present value illustrate points much more cogently than long-winded discussions of vague trade-offs and concepts. We assume throughout the textbook that students have a working knowledge of algebra, calculus, present value, statistical significance, and other standard business management terms and concepts. The integration of law and quantitative analysis already has taken place at a number of law schools and in legal scholarship generally, and it is overdue in business law and legal environment textbooks.

The Cases Are Recent and Use the Language of the Courts

In most chapters, there are from three to five cases, most of which have dates after 1980 and many of which were decided after 1998. The electronic environment that current business management students will inherit imposes a premium on selecting cases that deal with issues they are likely to encounter. Students are not likely to deal with the "mailbox" rule when fax machines and online contracting are the norm. Some of the cases are longer because they are more complicated factually and technically than when a farmer named Sherwood is selling a cow that becomes pregnant after the contract is signed.

Many of the cases deal with highly technical issues that courts tackle with admirable persistence. After teaching some of this material to students, undergraduates and graduates, for several semesters, we are convinced that students are easily capable of comprehending information age legal issues such as those associated with the Internet privacy protection. We provide what are intended to be thought-provoking questions at the end of each case to test students' understanding of the case.

Management Suggestions and Recommendations Are Part of the Message

Both authors have a great deal of experience as expert witnesses in high-tech cases. We have observed, up close and personal, management mistakes attributable to either ignorance of the legal environment or deliberately ignoring the legal environment. Also we both have Ph.D.s in economics, which enables us to view legal mistakes, evident in some of the cases, from a perspective of incentives, constraints, and principles of equilibrium. At times we make use of a law and economics approach that has been so influential in legal journals and in actual cases.

FEATURED BOXES

Cyberlaw Developments

In virtually every area of law, from contracts and torts to regulatory law, cyber considerations are very much in evidence. In most chapters, we attempt to bring in the flavor of legal issues that courts are dealing with that are created by cyberspace situations. Many of the issues dealt within the "Cyberlaw Developments" boxes have not been resolved to date, but are likely to require attention from legislatures or de novo examinations by the courts. Virtually all of the "Cyberlaw Developments" boxes would have been unfathomable to legal authorities as recently as 10 years ago because the technology did not exist that gave rise to the legal issue in cyberspace.

International Perspective

Certainly, the impact of globalization is reflected in business management curricula throughout the United States. The impact of globalization also has been evident in business law and legal environment textbooks for some time. Originally, most textbooks devoted a single chapter to international law issues, but the trend more recently has been to integrate international issues throughout most areas of law. We follow the latter trend and integrate international considerations into chapters with an emphasis on "International Perspective" boxes. We also devote a separate chapter to international law issues, mainly jurisdiction and enforcement of intellectual property rights.

Nutz and Boltz

Pictures, tables, and Internet inserts are placed throughout the textbook in boxes entitled "Nutz and Boltz." For many subjects, visual aids enhance narrative discussions. For many legal avenues, the legal system is a process that more resembles a decision tree with numerous options along the way. We provide a large number of charts, tables, graphs, and other visual aids that are all subsumed under the rubric of "Nutz and Boltz."

Ethical Challenges

We also provide boxed inserts that illustrate ethical challenges that have confronted business and government leaders. Certainly recent events surrounding the collapse of Enron and other corporations illustrate the continuing significance of business ethics. We devote part of one chapter exclusively to ethics, but intersperse "Ethical Challenge" boxes throughout the textbook. Many of the most significant ethical challenges in business take place in cyberspace and involve privacy and property rights issues.

END-OF-CHAPTER MATERIAL

Each chapter concludes with rich end-of-chapter material, including the following:

- *Summary by learning objectives.*
- *Key terms with definitions.* The key terms are found in the margins throughout each chapter. The list at the end of the chapter gives the page on which the defined term can be found.
- *Questions for Review and Analysis.* These questions review concepts and can be used as class discussion jump-starters.
- *If you really understood this chapter, you should be able to provide informed commentary on the following.* The title is self-explanatory.
- *Using the Internet to Your Advantage.* At the end of each chapter, we list a number of websites that enable students to dig deeper into the material discussed in the chapter. These websites can facilitate term projects or simply illustrate the text in the chapter. It is hoped that these websites will enable the student to be less intimidated by the prospect of legal research and to recognize that with the Internet, in most cases, there is no need to visit a bricks-and-mortar law library.

ACKNOWLEDGMENTS

We have benefited mightily from two sources: (1) the McGraw-Hill staff and (2) reviews by our law colleagues. The McGraw-Hill staff of Andy Winston, Christine Scheid, and others have worked tirelessly to assist and prod when necessary. Their patience has been an important factor in the creation of this book and we appreciate their encouragement and assistance. We'd like to thank the following colleagues for their thoughtful reviews of our manuscript:

Karen Barr
Penn State University–Beaver Campus

Bruce Batterson
Peru State College

Ron Cereola
James Madison University

Amy Chataginer
Mississippi Gulf Coast Community College–Gautier

Linda Christiansen
Indiana University–New Albany

Angelo Ciotti
Mt. San Jacinto College

Gerald Conway
Wayne State College

Jan Davison
Jefferson Davis Community College

Gary Greene
Manatee Community College

Mark Hall
Auburn University–Montgomery

Earl Clayton Hipp Jr.
Wake Forest University

James Hunt
Mercer University

Deborah Kottel
University of Great Falls–Great Falls

Rita Lambrecht
Northeastern Junior College

Robert Mitchum
Arkansas State University–Beebe Branch

Gary Patterson
California State University–San Bernardino

Sarah Pitts
Christian Brothers University

Roger Reinsch
University of Wisconsin–LaCrosse

Mitchell Sherr
Indiana University/Purdue University– Fort Wayne

Ken Taurman
Indiana University–New Albany

Maurice Tonissi
Quinsigamond Community College

Tom Tuytschaevers
Northeastern University

The faculty reviewers have been brutally honest in their assessments and ultimately very complimentary. We have worked with a belief that business law and the legal environment are interesting and even humorous. A number of our reviewers have endorsed this view and have tremendously assisted us in writing and rewriting the chapters in this book as well as pointing out numerous opportunities to eliminate errors and improve our exposition.

ANCILLARY MATERIALS

Instructor's CD-Rom (007-244119-4)

This is state-of-the-art technology that provides a single resource for faculty to customize in-class presentations. It includes

1. *Instructor's Manual.* Developed by Michael Katz, Delaware State University. The Instructor's Manual includes many valuable tools for teaching a legal environment course, including expanded chapter outlines and teaching suggestions, answers to case questions and discussion questions, "hypotheticals," additional scenarios for further illustrations of topics, and much more.

2. *Test bank and computerized testing.* Written by Judy Spain, Eastern Kentucky University, the Testbank includes a minimum per chapter of 75 questions. The question format incorporates multiple choice, true/false, short answer "fact patterns," and essay problems.

3. *PowerPoint presentation slides.* Developed by David Baumer, the PowerPoint slides are derived directly from the directives of his course. Baumer has been teaching business law, legal environment, sports law, and cyberlaw courses for 23 years. He has compiled his lecture notes for this book on PowerPoint slides. He has erred on the side of too much inclusiveness, recognizing that many who teach this course will not need to rely so heavily on these PowerPoint slides. Regardless of how heavily instructors rely on PowerPoint, it is believed that these slides will dramatically reduce preparation time. Experienced teachers can review the book and be assured that the main points in each chapter will appear in the PowerPoint slides. Over the years, Baumer has had to hire a number of part-time instructors on short notice who were able to step in and do a

credible job with the aid of PowerPoint slides. He believes that adopters of this textbook, armed with these PowerPoint slides, will have a similar experience.

Videos (007-288543-2)

The videos provide current footage to enhance chapter topics.

Student Print Study Guide (007-288542-4)

Available for packaging with the text, the Study Guide includes an outline with tips for understanding difficult topics and quiz questions. Evan Sheffel of California State University–Northridge developed the material.

Online Learning Center with PowerWeb

The OLC is a warehouse of information and activities for both professors and students. The Instructor's area includes electronic versions of the Instructor's Manual, PowerPoint presentations, and other teaching aides. Students have the ability to test their vocabulary knowledge with flash cards, topic knowledge with quizzes, and much more. With the latest addition of direct feeds from PowerWeb and *The New York Times,* current articles and information are available at the touch of your mouse. Ask your McGraw-Hill/Irwin sales representative for ISBN: 007-294-313-0 if you want your students to have access to these features within their OLC.

Student-Focused Learning Features

Baumer/Poindexter is not about throwing legal environment terms and topics at the student to juggle and understand. It's about helping students grasp the legal environment within the scope of business, and the changes that technology is thrusting upon it daily.

> "In this textbook, and in real life, law is a cross-functional factor that affects the decision-making environment of managers in every functional area."
>
> *David Baumer and J. C. Poindexter*

Text Written with Your Student in Mind

I like the authors' writing. They seem to have a sense of humor and seem to want to be more in touch with the reader than other books I have examined.

Karen Barr
Pennsylvania State University,
*   Beaver Campus*

You doubtless already have experience with *negotiation*—negotiation of how you will divide the telephone bill with your roommates, negotiation of who prepares what for the party you're having this weekend, and negotiation of the price of a used computer you've bought or sold. Negotiation, as you know, involves the presentation of information, the delivery of offers and counteroffers, and any other activity that leads to an agreement. In a business setting, virtually all contracts are formed after negotiations. Our immediate negotiations focus, however, is on reaching agreements (settlements) when there is a legal conflict to be resolved without resort to the courts.

Learning Objectives

A topical guide for the student, Learning Objectives tell them what they should and will know after completing the Chapter.

Learning Objectives

After completing this chapter, you should

1. Know the basic components and structures of federal and state court systems.
2. Understand the differing roles of trial and appeals courts.
3. Be able to explain the nature and importance of jurisdiction and venue concepts.
4. Know the roles the Supreme Court plays in our legal system.
5. Be able to work with and explain the concepts of standing and justiciability.

Nutz and Boltz

Nutz and Boltz encompass a wide variety of charts, graphs, and tables expressly singled out to highlight "road maps" for students to easily grasp the topic.

Nutz and Boltz What Is a Magistrate in the Federal Court System and What Do They Do?

According to the website for the U.S. judiciary (http://www.uscourts.gov),

> A U.S. magistrate judge is a judicial officer of the district court and is appointed by majority vote of the active district judges of the court to exercise jurisdiction over matters assigned by statute as well as those delegated by the district judges. The number of magistrate judge positions is determined by the Judicial Conference of the United States, based on recommendations of the respective district courts, the judicial councils of the circuits, and the Director of the Administrative Office of the U.S. Courts. A full-time magistrate judge serves a term of eight years. Duties assigned to magistrate judges by district court judges may vary considerably from court to court.

On the criminal side, one of the main tasks of magistrates is to sign *search and arrest warrants* upon a showing of probable cause by a law enforcement officer. In civil procedure, magistrates perform a number of tasks including conducting a civil trial, if both parties agree. Mainly, magistrates are in a subordinate position relative to federal district court judges and assist as requested. The Federal Rules of Civil Procedure (discussed in Chapter 3) refer to "magistrates" 46 times.

International Perspectives

With the heightening importance of global issues, the International Perspective boxes highlight the impact of these topics. Again, the text also includes an entire chapter devoted to jurisdiction and enforcement of intellectual property rights.

International Perspective

The fact that U.S. law under the CDA exempts ISPs from most liability associated with republishing defamatory material does not resolve the issue of ISP liability for defamation. A businessman in Australia alleges he was defamed by the Dow Jones and Co. based on an article that appeared in the business periodical *Barron's* and on the Internet. The highest court in Australia refused to dismiss the case. The defendant, Dow Jones Co., claims that if this suit can go forward, it is possible that it will be liable for defamation [suits in locales spanning the globe] from Afghanistan to Zimbabwe. The fact that the Internet is a worldwide [communications vehicle] may make actions that were formerly local now carry worldwide legal liability throughout 190, and counting, nations.

defamation—could set a precedent and affect publishers and Web sites that post articles in the 190 nations that allow defamation cases.

"This is a significant ruling in that it could push publishers into having to consider every conceivable defamation law in the world before posting something online," said **CBSNews.com Legal Analyst Andrew Cohen.** "On the other hand, it still is enormously difficult to collect upon a foreign judgment even if these Internet plaintiffs win, so the news isn't all that dire for online sites."

The High Court of Australia unanimously dismissed an appeal by Dow Jones & Co. aimed at stopping a defamation suit in Australia by mining magnate Joseph Gutnick.

Cyberlaw Developments

Cyberlaw Developments spotlight emerging and ongoing legal issues due to the influence of technology and the internet.

The following is an excerpt of a thought-provoking article by Robert Plotkin on the issue of using online and electronic resources to make more efficient some basic litigation activities.

ELECTRONIC COURT FILING: PAST, PRESENT, AND FUTURE

by Robert Plotkin, *lexisONE*^{sm} Contributor, November 2000

Despite the growing use of computers in the legal profession, authoring and filing legal pleadings remains a labor-intensive process that has yet to fully benefit from the potential for automation offered by recent advances in computer technology. Efforts are underway, however, to computerize virtually every aspect of court filing and case management.

Several courts and government agencies have already begun to supplement or replace their paper-based filing systems with electronic filing systems that allow pleadings to be filed over the Internet. Some systems also allow parties to access their case files and the court's docket over the Internet. These early systems, although rudimentary, are already facilitating interactions with the courts and are allowing attorneys and courts to recognize significant cost savings. The electronic filing systems of tomorrow will further automate the filing process and integrate computer systems for filing, case management, docketing, storage, and security.

Ethical Challenges

Although one entire chapter is devoted to the subject of ethics, these boxes are interspersed throughout each chapter to bring the issue home within the context of the chapter discussion.

CONFIDENTIAL SETTLEMENTS

In the year 2000, the Firestone/Bridgestone Tire Company engaged in a massive recall of tires it had manufactured and sold for several years prior to the recall. This was a consequence of a tire separation problem that had resulted in a large number of accidents, which in turn had resulted in many serious injuries and deaths. Firestone/Bridgestone was the target of numerous suits over this problem, producing litigation that is still ongoing, with the public widely informed of the defective tire problems this manufacturer was experiencing. A not surprising result of this information was a dramatic decline in tire sales enjoyed by this manufacturer.

Later in the year, there were indications that Goodyear Tire Company had experienced some of the same problems that Firestone/Bridgestone had, but that Goodyear had quietly settled the cases that resulted from its tire failures, including in all settlements confidentiality requirements that prevented any release of information on a tire failure, a resulting accident, or any settlement reached. Goodyear also had been successful in having court records sealed and kept secret in the few tire failure cases that had not settled but had gone to court.

Goodyear was accused of engaging in a "secret recall" of its allegedly defective tires, with generous replacement policies on those tires, and of hiding from the public information on dangers from certain of its tires. Near the end of the year (2000), two groups, the Trial Lawyers for Public Justice (TLPJ) and Consumers for Auto Reliability and Safety (CARS), sought public access to sealed records on Goodyear tire failure cases. A TLPJ spokesman said that "This is the latest disturbing example of court secrecy being used to hide potential dangers to the public" and "Dozens of people were killed or maimed before Firestone's and Bridgestone's tires were recalled because protective orders prevented the public and the government from learning the truth." TLPJ's challenge to make sealed records of cases public was part of its "Project ACCESS," a campaign against court secrecy.

1. How do you suppose Goodyear sales fared in 2000 relative to those of Firestone?
2. What role would confidentiality clauses have played in protecting Goodyear's market position?
3. Is it fair to the public to restrict the availability of information on potentially dangerous conditions by requiring confidentiality in settled cases involving products that could be safety threats?
4. Explain the difference in what you may think is legal for a firm in requiring confidentiality and what is ethical.
5. Is it possible that outlawing secrecy in settlements would result in fewer voluntary settlements and more trips to court? Explain.

Almost every one is a great addition to the chapter. I began to look forward to them at the end of the chapter.

Linda Christiansen
Indiana University Southeast

Key Terms and Marginal Definitions

The key terms of the chapter can be found in the margins defined, and listed at the end of the chapter with page numbers signifying their placement in the chapter.

Power of Eminent Domain

government takings
An action of the government in which private property is taken from a citizen.

eminent domain
The power of government to take private land for public use upon paying fair compensation.

Both state and federal governments have the power to take property from citizens, but only if the **government taking** is for public use with just compensation provided to the property owner. At the federal level, the Fifth Amendment states, ". . . nor shall private property be taken for public use without just compensation." A state or the federal government can force property owners to part with their property in a condemnation, or **eminent domain**, proceeding, but there are constitutional constraints to ensure that

1. The acquisition of property is for the public good.
2. The property owner is not individually oppressed by, in effect, having to pay for public improvements.

So, if a government decides to build a public road or highway and someone's property is in the way, the government can condemn the property and build the road over the property. Landowners can challenge condemnation proceedings on either of two grounds: first, that

---

I do like the "Sidebar Terms" at the end of the chapter. Students are more apt to read these than go to the glossary if they don't understand a certain term.

Kenneth Taurman
Indiana University Southeast

Questions for Review and Analysis

A useful review tool, students can use these for review purposes, or professors can assign them as homework, or even to initiate class discussion.

Questions for Review and Analysis

1. Discuss the economic factors that increasingly cause firms to make use of ADR relative to court litigation.
2. Why does the act of structuring negotiations often create a climate conducive to achieving a settlement?
3. Explain how the line can get blurred between assisted settlement negotiations and outright mediation?
4. Explain why it is both good and bad that (a) arbitrators are not bound by precedent and (b) their decisions are not appealable in many situations.

Instructor Supplements

Instructor's Resource CD-Rom

Contains everything you need to organize an effective classroom experience—Instructor's Manual, Computerized Testbank, and PowerPoint slide presentation. See the Preface for further information on what's inside these supplements.

VHS Video Collection

You Be the Judge Videos put your students in a live legal argument with no script. These 10 hypothetical cases are supplemented by additional material on the Online Learning Center where you will find evidence, background, and questions to help you generate a verdict on the case. To get the videos and material as an interactive experience for your student, ask your sales representative about the You Be the Judge DVD.

Online Learning Center www.mhhe.com/ baumerLEOB

A one-stop shopping website with additional course materials, supplements, links, and exercises found chapter-by-chapter. With the addition of our newly-integrated PowerWeb feature, students and professors alike have access to peer-reviewed content, including up-to-date articles from leading periodicals and journals, current news, and weekly updates with accompanying assessments, exercises, and study tips. Ask your sales representative how you can obtain access to the PowerWeb feature for your students.

Student Supplements

Student Study Guide

A compelling study tool for your students, the Study Guide revisits the Learning Objectives from the text, offers a chapter outline with tips and questions to highlight certain difficult or confusing topics, and reviews chapter material with multiple choice, fill-in-the-blanks, and "issue development" essay questions.

Online Learning Center www.mhhe.com/ baumerLEOB

As explained before, the OLC is a one-stop shopping website with additional course materials, quizzes, links, and exercises found chapter by chapter. With the addition of our newly integrated PowerWeb feature (a great term project resource), students have access to peer-reviewed content, including up-to-date articles from leading periodicals and journals, current news, and weekly updates with accompanying assessments, exercises, and study tips.

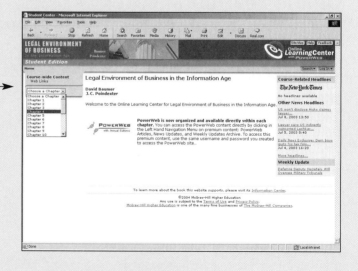

Brief Contents

Contents

Chapter 14
Business Organization and Cybercompanies   435

PART THREE
GOVERNMENT REGULATION   475

Chapter 15
Agency, Electronic Agents, and Employment at Will   476

List of Cases

The following cases can be found within *Legal Environment of Business in the Information Age*

The Structure of the Legal Environment

Chapter One

The Legal Environment of Business in the Information Age

Learning Objectives

With completion of this chapter, you should

1. Be able to provide a conceptual explanation of the meaning(s) of law.
2. Have an appreciation for the evolution of common law and the distinctions between common law and other sources of law.
3. Know the importance of law in protecting competitive advantages that are provided by ownership of intellectual property.
4. Understand the system of checks and balances that limit concentration of power in any branch of government.
5. Be familiar with a number of important classifications of law.

While sharing an order of fries at the student union cafeteria, Meg asked, "Ben, do you remember the guys who won the Management School's business plan competition here two years ago with the customer service software package?"

"Sure, they had a great combination of technology and a marketing strategy," replied Ben. "I'll bet that package is making a lot of money right now."

Half-smiling, half-frowning, Meg said, "Yes, I think it is doing very well. Unfortunately, though, their business plan is making the money for someone else! Apparently the guys made a marketing presentation that revealed a lot of operating details to an enterprise software company, and that company replicated the software and took it to market without any agreement with our guys. At least, that's what Greg Smith told me when I saw him at the Pub last night. He was one of the computer science guys on the team. He said there's been a lawsuit filed asking for an injunction against the pirate firm's offering the software and demanding damages. Unfortunately, he said, their lawyer has told them that their technology and marketing was better than their legal work, so he isn't sure they'll prevail in court. They're hoping to get some settlement offer, even if it's only $20,000, while the pirates make millions from their ideas."

"Gosh," said Ben, "I remember some stories similar to that from the legal environment course all of us business majors have to take. At the time, though, I figured those were such rarities I'd never run into anything like it."

"Apparently, Greg and the other guys on the team thought the same thing," Meg exhorted. "He says they all wish the business majors on the team had pushed them harder to get proper nondisclosure agreements and to have all their copyrights in place before they had any discussions with possible investors in their technology."

Is this just a hypothetical scenario? Absolutely it is not. Both "potential" companies and actual, often well-established companies have costly experiences like the one discussed by Meg and Ben, as reflected in the real world case presented below.

Case 1-1

Whelan Associates, Inc. v. Jaslow Dental Laboratory, Inc.

U.S. Court of Appeals, Third Circuit 797 F.2d 1222 (3rd Cir. 1986)

CASE BACKGROUND AND FACTS

This case illustrates the need for managers to be reasonably knowledgeable about copyright law and the consequences of ignorance of law in general and copyright law in particular.

Jaslow Dental Laboratory hired the Strohl Company to produce a software program that would improve Jaslow's billing and accounting system. Jaslow had tried earlier to develop its own software program but was unsuccessful. Elaine Whelan was the point person for Strohl and developed the needed software in EDL (Event Driven Language). The resulting software was called Dentalab. When it was registered with the Copyright Office, the author was listed as Elaine Whelan. Whelan subsequently opened her own firm and Strohl assigned its rights to Dentalab to that firm, Whelan Associates.

Jaslow thought, logically, if the software he had paid to have written would help his dental firm, it could help other firms too. Originally, Jaslow contracted with Whelan to act as Whelan's marketing agent, while Whelan would strive to improve Dentalab. However, Mr. Jaslow had acquired a good bit of knowledge in his two-year association with Whelan. He also knew that most computers at dental laboratories were not equipped to accept EDL, so he rewrote Dentalab software in BASIC (computer language), calling the new software program Dentcom.

With this accomplished, Jaslow broke off relations with Whelan Associates and began marketing Dentcom. When Whelan sued for copyright infringement, Jaslow took the position that the Dentalab software was his, as he had hired first Strohl and then Whelan to write the software. When this issue came to court, however, the court ruled that Whelan retained full ownership of the software. Jaslow, who paid for the creation of the dental software, was forbidden from selling both Dentalab and Dentcom, given the similarities between Dentalab and Dentcom software. Although the underlying computer code was different in Dentcom and Dentalab, both programs were judged to have the same "look and feel." The court ruled that Whelan had a valid copyright that prevented Jaslow from marketing a product (Dentcom) that had the same look and feel as did Dentalab.[1]

What to Focus on in the *Jaslow* Case

Because of his ignorance of basic copyright law, Jaslow committed critical and costly mistakes. Later in this text, we'll see additional situations in which the hiring of an outsider, an

---

[1] This case is most widely known for its discussion of the "look and feel" test, which is sometimes used by the courts to decide whether an allegedly infringing computer program infringes even though the computer code is dissimilar. The significance of this case and the "look and feel" test is discussed in more detail in Chapter 13.

independent contractor to perform a task, is not the same legally as having your own employees perform that task. A manager who is aware of the harsh requirements of the legal environment would not make the mistake of hiring an outsider to develop software without requiring the software developer to sign a contract that assigns copyrights to the software to the manager's company. Managers should know at least enough about legal risks to determine when they need expert legal help.

WHAT LIES AHEAD IN THIS TEXTBOOK

In this initial foray into "case law," we don't expect readers to feel that they are in command of the legal issues explored. Hopefully, however, this brief case illustration will serve to arouse interest and concern about what "the law" is, how the body of law now in place came to be, how it is applied, and how you can use knowledge of the law to avoid legal and management problems. To address these and other questions, following this introductory chapter the text discusses the court system (in Chapter 2), basic rules of the trial process (in Chapter 3), and alternative means of resolving disputes (in Chapter 4). Chapter 5 and forward, then, provide detailed looks at laws and regulations that form the legal environment of business. This chapter attempts to get your thinking about the legal environment of business started by briefly exposing you to a buffet of "law" topics. The brief discussions below of various areas of law are not intended to give you anything approaching a complete overview of these legal topics. We are, however, trying to instill a sense of the pervasiveness of the law in the business arena and a sense of what law, as it exists in our system, strives to accomplish.

The Pervasiveness of Law in Business

Your company, prospective or well-established, may have world-class product development; a finance group skilled at maximizing firm value; a marketing staff that excels at product design, placement, and promotion; enlightened human resource management personnel; and highly efficient production and transportation. And, yet, making legal mistakes can thwart the collective benefit of high skill levels in all of these functional levels.

There Is No Escape from the Law in Business

The *Whelan* case above provides an illustration of just one of the wide assortment of costly legal problems firms can confront. In addition to various legal problems involving intellectual property (which includes copyright law), there also exists a mine field of legal challenges in the areas of contracts, torts, product liability, consumer protection, employee protection, environmental law, securities regulation, credit regulation, international, and antitrust law. Clearly, every functional area of business management entails potential legal problems that can threaten a company's financial viability. Managers need to have a broad understanding of the restrictions and demands imposed by the law as they seek to address the wants, needs, and claims of customers, the business community, workers, and government.

THE LAW—WHAT IS THE LAW ANYWAY?

From your own life experiences and perhaps from other sources as well, you no doubt have some sense of the meaning of *the law*. Even so, you might find writing out a coherent description of the meaning of this phrase difficult as, indeed, scholars have found it to be. There can be numerous definitions of law offered, most of which do not add importantly to the understanding of law needed by business management majors. Many commentators

law
A collection of enforceable rules of conduct, aimed at controlling, or at least placing acceptable limits on, human behavior.

would agree, though, with Oliver Wendell Holmes that "Law is a statement of the circumstances, in which the public force is brought to bear . . . through the courts." The application of this broad statement leads to the conclusion that the law is composed of rules that must be obeyed, if not voluntarily, then through the use of public forces, generally the police, to compel compliance. Clearly, law is a formal collection of rules of conduct that are aimed at controlling human behavior, both personal and business. Through the enforcement of laws, government authority attempts to provide predictability and uniformity of acceptable limits on individual and business activities.

The Law Is Not Just Words on Pieces of Paper

The law involves much more than simply determining the meaning of words that are written in a legal document, like our Constitution, or in a collection of statutes. In fact, it is useful to think of law as providing *predictions* about how courts will resolve disputes as, with this mind-set, it is possible to comprehend the claim that the law is an evolving entity that changes in important ways over time. This phenomenon is illustrated by evolution of the way the First Amendment has been interpreted by the courts (constitutional law is discussed in Chapter 5). The First Amendment, adopted in 1791, reads in part as follows: "Congress shall make no law . . . abridging the freedom of speech, or of the press. . . ." Even though the First Amendment appears absolute in its prohibition of laws by Congress "abridging" freedom of speech, the Framers of the Constitution and composers of the First Amendment never intended to prevent Congress from enacting statutes (laws created by legislatures, Chapter 2) that outlaw treason, obscenity, or inciting a riot. Abridgments of free speech had specific meaning to the Framers (of the Constitution) and they could predict with reasonable accuracy which types of abridgments of free speech were in fact constitutional and which were not.

"I Can't Define What Is Obscene, but I Know It When I See It."[2]   Since 1791, a number of laws (statutes) enacted by Congress (and the states) have been declared unconstitutional based on court interpretations of the First Amendment. The application of the First Amendment to obscenity laws, however, has been particularly contentious because defining obscenity is a challenge. Many of the world's great visual works of art depict people in various stages of undress, which is, at least superficially, a basis often used in the past to declare various forms of expression obscene. Fifty years ago stores that sold magazines showing females' breasts were raided under state obscenity laws, and the works of the authors Henry Miller and James Joyce were both banned as being obscene.

Since the 1950s, however, society's view of what is "obscene" apparently has evolved and court decisions have reflected this evolution. Over the lengthy time span from 1791 to the present, the text of the First Amendment has not changed at all. Yet, there have been profound changes in what statutes the courts view as permissible constraints on freedom of expression. First Amendment scholars in the 1990s could confidently predict that there were changes in what the U.S. Supreme Court and other courts would or would not declare obscene. In 1996, when Congress passed the Communications Decency Act (CDA), which made it illegal to make available to minors on the Internet any obscene or "indecent" messages, "free speech" advocates were ready to act. One week after passage of the CDA, the America Civil Liberties Union (ACLU) challenged its constitutionality and was ultimately successful in having much of the CDA declared unconstitutional.[3] The courts held that the prohibitions of the CDA were overly broad and thus unconstitutional under the First Amendment.

---

[2] Paraphrase of a remark made by a U.S. Supreme Court justice after dealing with numerous obscenity cases and being unable to elucidate a definition of what made a particular picture or movie "obscene."

[3] *American Civil Liberties Union v. Reno,* 521 U.S. 844 (1997).

The Law Changed but the Words Did Not   Virtually no constitutional scholar was surprised that the courts struck down the CDA. Although the text of the First Amendment had not changed in over 200 years, First Amendment law had. Laws used to suppress obscene or indecent material that were upheld in the 1950s against First Amendment challenges are now declared unconstitutional. What has happened is that court interpretation of the First Amendment has changed since the 1950s. The demise of the CDA as it was applied to the Internet made these changes dramatically evident.

There have been similar, though less dramatic, evolutions of the law in countless other areas. The main point is that it is a mistake to view "the law" as simply words on a piece of paper. Laws written on pieces of paper are defined, interpreted, enriched, and modified over time by court decisions, which doubtless reflect the changing mores of society and changes in technology.

TECHNOLOGY AND THE LAW

precedent
A case decision that is used to determine decisions in subsequent cases that have similar sets of facts.

An important focus of this text is on the legal issues that frequently confront managers today and that promise (threaten?) to do so with increasing frequency in the future as we rapidly progress from the *industrial age* of the twentieth century to the *information age* of the twenty-first century. Technological change/progress has always impacted the law and vice versa, both through court interpretations of existing statutes and through the creation of wholly new statutes. Also, courts serve as important sources of legal innovation when they confront novel legal issues created by new technology. Confronted with new technological realities, courts have had to modify existing case law, creating new legal rules (called **precedents**) in many areas of law. From the perspective of firms, recent modifications of patent and copyright statutes and of court rulings interpreting those statutes have significantly changed the legal environment (particularly for high-tech businesses). In anticipation of the importance attached in this text to the interface between technology and the law, several aspects of that interface are briefly discussed below. Each of the topics introduced will receive more attention in later chapters.

Intellectual Property

intellectual property
Unlike land or a building, intellectual property is an asset that has no physical (tangible) existence. It is the product of a creative (intellectual) process.

Many companies in the information age are valued mainly for the **intellectual property** (IP) they own. Intellectual property is described as intangible, meaning that it has no *physical* existence. There are four basic forms of legal protection for IP (discussed in detail in Chapters 12 and 13):

- Some firms such as the Coca-Cola Company keep some of their important IP in the form of *trade secrets*. The Coca-Cola Company has never applied for a patent on the secret formula used to make Coca-Cola but, instead, has relied upon keeping the formula hidden from rivals.
- For many firms, *patents* protect innovations. Patent law explicitly grants to the patentee (the person receiving the patent) exclusive rights to make, use, or sell the patented process, product, machine, or composition of matter.
- *Copyright* law provides legal protection for authors of original compositions such as books, music, and computer software. Unauthorized reproductions are *infringements*, which entitle the copyright owner to collect damages from infringers.
- *Trademark* law allows manufacturers to identify their goods with a distinguishing symbol or mark and provides for punishment of infringers who deliberately or unintentionally imitate registered trademarks.

International Perspective

The following is an article about the Intellectual Property Institute of Canada, a professional organization that is dedicated to increased intellectual property law protection for Canadian innovators. As with many issues, Canadians are concerned about being overshadowed by the United States.

CANADA SEEKS TO INCREASE PATENT PROTECTION

In light of the challenges to protection of intellectual property in the rapidly changing world we face, legal organizations throughout the world are actively involved in the creation and modification of laws and regulations that affect IP protection. Illustratively, within the American Bar Association (ABA), there is a "section" (working group) that focuses its attention specifically on IP law. In the January 2001 website message from the chair of this ABA section (see http://www.abanet.org/intelprop/jan01chair.html), Canadian concerns were included as one of a number of items of interest in the IP protection arena.

Per the chair's observations: Canada is behind other major industrialized countries in securing patent protection, says the newly elected president of the Intellectual Property Institute of Canada (IPIC). Hence, raising awareness of IP protection needs among Canadian businesses, researchers, and others is targeted as a goal of the new IPIC president. "Compared to the rest of the world, the number of patents filed in Canada is not high enough, even though our costs to file are among the lowest," according to the IPIC president. "Without this protection, Canadian innovations, processes, and inventions are at high risk of moving into the public domain, with no return to investors or inventors." The IPIC president is also described as indicating that his organization intends to be active in international forums dealing with evolving treaties between nations on the handling of patents to protect IP internationally.

Source: Intellectual Property Institute of Canada, http://www.ipic.ca/english/general/what.cfm.

Electronic Commerce and Contract Law

While IP law may be the most obvious point of legal impact for technological advances, it certainly is not the only such impact area. Electronic commerce (e-commerce) is growing rapidly and, yet, is likely in the infancy of its growth trajectory. As with other types of sales, a company that makes substantial e-commerce sales must rely on solid "contractual agreements" both with other businesses and with ordinary consumers who are likely to be customers (e-commerce contract law is discussed in Chapter 9). Existing *contract* law, such as that codified in the Uniform Commercial Code (UCC) (discussed in Chapter 8), rests heavily on a notion of "objective intent" exercised by contracting parties (humans) in determining whether a contract has been formed. E-commerce contracts often rely on electronic agents. Determining the "intent" of electronic agents is a *non sequitur;* machines do not possess "intent" to do anything. So technical innovation and the growth of e-commerce can be expected to force extensive modification of commercial contract law in the years ahead.

With regard to successfully navigating commercial linkages provided by the Internet and e-commerce, managers certainly should have knowledge of basic contract law (Chapter 7), supplemented with recognition of the differences that operating in a technology-driven setting entails. Maintaining this knowledge is a challenge, as this body of law is rapidly evolving, requiring managers to regularly update their knowledge of the legal environment in which they operate. Illustratively, significant revisions of the UCC, dealing mainly with electronic contracting and the licensing of IP for Internet applications, were on the threshold of adoption as this chapter was being written. In the future, new "uniform" laws such as the Uniform Computer Information and Transactions Act (UCITA) and the Uniform Electronic Transactions Act (UETA) may rival the UCC in their importance to business managers.

Tort Law and Invasions of Privacy

tort
A civil wrong, not involving a contract, that results in injury (physical or economic). A tort results from violation of a legal duty rather than a contract duty.

A **tort** is committed when a plaintiff (the victim) is *wrongfully* harmed by a defendant (the alleged victimizer). Basic tort law is discussed in Chapter 10. Ordinarily, tort and contract law involve different issues but, in cyberspace, they frequently overlap (Chapter 11). Because personal signatures are not easily accomplished in e-commerce, Internet vendors must gather information from their customers to prevent fraud. The information those websites gather to prevent fraud also has value for market research purposes. Internet companies gather additional information by attaching "cookies" to the browsers of visitors to their websites. Cookies extract information (such as the identity of other websites visited) from these visitors or customers, often without the knowledge or consent of customers. Practices of this sort raise privacy concerns that have mushroomed as increased reliance on e-commerce and the Internet have occurred. Tort law, which includes invasions of privacy, has recently been augmented by a growing number of federal statutes that make more explicit what companies can and cannot do in the way of extracting and sharing information on the Internet.

Security, Encryption, and Cybercrime

Computer system privacy and security issues have spawned the birth of an entire new industry. Increasingly, firms are relying on encryption software to protect transactions and communications over the Internet. In addition, industrial espionage through computers and system invasions by pranksters, sometimes spreading viruses, has required firms to invest heavily in system security. Computer and cybercrime are now major areas of crime and have attracted the attention of Congress and the U.S. Department of Justice (see Chapter 22). Information revealed subsequent to the September 11, 2001, attacks that the terrorists coordinated some aspects of their attacks using the Internet has served to accentuate the importance of cybercrime. Security measures involve a firm's human resource department (HRM) as well as the information technology (IT) staff. Good and effective security requires a commitment from management and company employees, up-to-date security equipment and software, and technical skill in deploying and maintaining security technology. In spite of precautions, nearly every firm and person are vulnerable to penetration through access to computerized records that can uncover another firm's proprietary information or invade a person's privacy.

Constitutional Law

To the general public, constitutional law (http://www.access.gpo.gov/congress/senate/constitution/toc.html) may be viewed as being esoteric and primarily of interest to law professors. That, however, is not accurate. Under the broad shadow cast by constitutional law, there are a number of legal issues that are of immediate interest to business, a fact that has been accentuated by recent advances in information technology, particularly the creation and migration toward mass use of the Internet.

Federal versus State Law

constitutional law
At the federal level, law based on the U.S. Constitution; at the state level, law based on state constitutions.

The Constitution delineates a set of broad and general powers, largely regulating what restrictions (on the use of power) government must respect and what rights are enjoyed by the citizenry. In application, a great deal of federal **constitutional law** has dealt with conflicts between businesses on the one hand and state governments or the federal government on the other. Quite often, state governments have tangled with businesses over *interstate* commerce issues (see Chapters 2 and 5). Many state officials have sought to protect in-state businesses by erecting *trade barriers* to out-of-state businesses or by subjecting multistate businesses to *higher taxes* than purely in-state businesses. Relying on constitutional law, the U.S. Supreme Court has been very vigilant in paring back state-erected trade barriers to interstate commerce or any form of tax-based discrimination against multistate businesses.

Taxes and Jurisdiction, Nationally and Internationally

With the growing importance of the Internet and e-commerce, many of the Supreme Court rulings that in the past were relied on to limit the ability of states to tax out-of-state businesses are being used by Internet firms to escape state taxation altogether. When the federal Internet Tax Freedom Act expires in 2005, new constitutional law will be made as states seek to impose taxes on e-commerce sales. Already, estimates of lost sales tax revenue for states stemming from the increasing popularity of e-commerce transactions are in the millions and the "national tax" issues that accompany e-commerce sales are likely to be dwarfed by international jurisdictional issues (see Chapter 23). International jurisdictional issues in law generally are among the most important and vexing developments attributable to the Internet with no satisfactory answer in sight to the question of which of a nation's laws apply to many transactions that occur in cyberspace.

Regulatory Law in the Information Age

Numerous activities, both of individuals and businesses, are regulated in the United States—that is, they are constrained by regulatory law. Different sets of laws focus on different targets, as reflected in the several brief encounters below.

Consumer Protection

consumer protection law
Body of law intended to protect consumers in their ordinary usage of financial institutions, their interactions with other sales vendors, the privacy of their records, and their use of computers.

Consumer protection laws and regulations (discussed in Chapter 18) are, as the name indicates, designed to protect buyers. A large volume of **consumer protection law** dealing with credit, finance, and liability for fraud is interrelated with computers and electronic commerce. Credit reports have been computerized for at least 30 years. For many years, banks and finance companies, in their loans to consumers and businesses, have routinely made use of computerized transactions. In the not-too-distant future, online pharmacies will become prevalent, heightening concerns for illicit sales of prescription medications. The privacy of medical records is also an issue that is becoming more urgent, again due to the computerization of medical records (cybermedicine and online pharmacies are discussed in Chapter 22).

Antitrust

antitrust law
Law that protects commerce from illegal restraints on trade that businesses may impose, attempting to assure the public of access to competitive pricing and quality.

Antitrust laws, aimed at protecting competition and hence the public's access to products and services with competitive pricing and quality, evolved out of industrial-age *trust-busting* efforts. The resulting "smokestack" concepts of "products" and "geographic markets," when applied to information-age antitrust cases, have required considerable extensions and stretches and have resulted in rulings that are controversial (see Chapter 19). Traditional markets, which accommodate the purchase and sale of tangible goods, have geographic boundaries. Critics of the application of traditional antitrust analysis to cyberspace markets suggest that geographic boundaries may be less relevant (for most purposes) in cyberspace. Still, there are many analysts who claim that the basic laws of economics also operate in cyberspace—that a successful monopolist in cyberspace still has to control all, or most, alternative suppliers of competing services or get competitors to agree not to compete—and that there is no reason not to apply standard antitrust reasoning to cyberspace companies. Certainly this point was made repeatedly by attorneys representing the U.S. Department of Justice in its suit against Microsoft Corporation.[4]

---

[4] *Microsoft Corp. v. United States,* 534 U.S. 952, 122 S. Ct. 350, 151 L. Ed. 2d 264 (2001).

Securities Law

Online initial public offerings (IPOs) of company stock have created new investment opportunities for the public, but also have inspired substantive changes in regulations promulgated by the Securities and Exchange Commission (SEC) to protect investors. In the past, securities laws (discussed in Chapter 20) were aimed at requiring full disclosure for public offerings. Regulations issued by the SEC and generally accepted accounting principles (GAAP) prescribe precise methodologies for valuing assets. The rules appropriate for valuing "bricks and mortar" companies, however, may not apply to the valuation of cyber companies that sometimes have been valued in the billions by investors, even when they have never made a profit. Witness Amazon.com, which only recently realized a small profit, but which has a capitalized market value in the billions of dollars. It will be important to consider the new legal issues being created by online trading and cyber companies that have physical assets with values that are trivial relative to their market value.

Digital and Other Trash

The word *trash* is commonly used to refer to material we would prefer to do without. Environmental pollution fits into that category as does much of what appears on the Internet.

Atomic Trash

The environmental protection movement has been very successful, both in terms of securing legislation (discussed in Chapter 21) and in terms of winning the hearts and minds of citizens. Public awareness and support for statutes that protect the environment are strong, even though most people recognize that environmental regulations are costly to enforce. The trend in environmental legislation is to attempt to require the generators of pollution to pay the full cost that their emissions impose on society and the environment.

Advances in biotechnology have created new and exotic challenges as modern-day commercial nutrients, pesticides, and genetically engineered plants offer enhanced production efficiencies and product diversity, but also act as major sources of land and water pollution. The law must balance benefits and costs in regulations applied to these technological advances.

In some areas of regulation, the auto industry providing a prominent case in point, environmental regulations appear likely to cause significant product design changes. Low-pollution, energy-efficient electric cars, guided by computers, are technically feasible today and could become economical in the near future. Their development is spurred by the threat of onerous environmental protection and safety regulations.

Digital Trash and Waste

With the well-known "free speech" protection of the First Amendment to the U.S. Constitution, content providers on the Internet are virtually unregulated (Chapter 22). Cybertrash in the form of SPAM (unsolicited email advertisements), fraudulent get-rich-quick schemes, pornography, and other Internet "pollution" continues to trouble legislators. Internet service providers (ISPs) are the portals through which purveyors of the aforementioned *products* gain access to their "customers," and ISPs have even been sued by SPAMers demanding increased access to users of the ISPs' services. Government attempts at regulation of cybertrash so far have been largely unsuccessful, with efforts in that direction often declared unconstitutional. The federal government has been more successful in protecting the privacy of certain records, particularly those involving children, finance, and medical files.

Human Resource Management

Part of an effective program to protect IP is apt to involve incentives to keep secrets. Employment contracts that reward workers who invent or discover things of value to their firms are a standard feature of IP protection efforts. Nondisclosure agreements, noncompete agreements, and other employment contract components also may be used to protect trade secrets and other elements of a company's intellectual property. An additional set of issues appears when a firm outsources software development or some other process that may involve IP. As illustrated by the *Whelan* case at the beginning of this chapter, losses of important IP rights can result from oversights that easily could be avoided. Of course, human resource management (HRM) operations will have many things to deal with other than the implementation of reward systems that encourage the protection of IP. Certainly, HRM also must deal with worker safety (Chapter 16), nondiscrimination legal standards (Chapter 17), agency agreements, and employment at will (Chapter 15).

The following case illustrates the unfortunate consequences that can result from a human resource management breakdown. In this case, an ex-employee was marketing a product that competed with his former employer's product. According to the former employer, the ex-employee was able to do this only by using the former employer's *trade secrets,* and doing so is illegal. You also may want to know that this case is used in the appendix to this chapter as a model for a discussion of how to brief a case. A lot of the legalese present in the following, very typical case is explained in the appendix.

Case 1-2

Barr-Mullin, Inc. v. Douglas M. Browning and Primavera Systems, Ltd.

*Court of Appeals of North Carolina 108 N.C. App. 590
(N.C. Ct. App. 1993)*

COURT STATEMENT OF FACTS, CALLED A SYLLABUS

Plaintiff instituted this action seeking both injunctive relief and damages alleging defendants misappropriated its trade secrets. Plaintiff is a corporation engaged in selling lumber processing equipment to customers in the woodworking industry. COMPU-RIP, a "lumber optimization system," is one of the processing systems sold by plaintiff. This system has a computer software program which acts as the "brain," taking in data regarding the approaching lumber and instructing the mechanical handling components as to how to guide the lumber through the saw. COMPU-RIP was first offered for sale in 1986 and has received the Challengers Award, an honor recognizing significant developments in the woodworking industry.

From March 1985 through December 1986, plaintiff employed Douglas Browning (defendant) as an independent consultant to develop the computer software for the COMPU-RIP system. In December of 1986, Browning was employed by plaintiff as its vice president of engineering. From 1987 through 1989 Browning played a role in installing COMPU-RIP systems at various plant sites; his duties included installing the COMPU-RIP software and providing assistance to customers once the systems were installed.

In January of 1990, Browning informed plaintiff of his intention to resign from plaintiff's employ. Shortly thereafter, Browning incorporated defendant Primavera Systems. Around this same time, Browning entered into negotiations with plaintiff whereby defendant proposed to remain associated as an independent consultant authorized by plaintiff to render computer systems service to COMPU-RIP owners. These negotiations failed and Browning resigned effective 23 August 1990.

After Browning's resignation, defendants began developing a lumber optimization system known as LumberScan. In addition, defendants also began to provide technical assistance to COMPU-RIP purchasers by customizing the COMPU-RIP computer software to meet the individual needs of the owner. Plaintiff filed the present suit alleging that the computer software used in COMPU-RIP is its trade secret and that the aforementioned activities of defendants constitute misappropriation of a trade secret in violation of G.S. 66-152, et seq.

On 19 July 1991, the trial court entered a temporary restraining order enjoining defendants from selling or licensing any software product which uses the trade secrets of plaintiff and further enjoined defendants from modifying the COMPU-RIP software. At the preliminary injunction hearing, the trial court, after considering the pleadings, affidavits and arguments of counsel, entered an order on 30 August 1991 granting plaintiff's motion for preliminary injunction. By means of this order, defendants were prohibited from:

1. *Marketing, offering for sale or license any software product relating to computer assistance or control of the operation of a gang rip saw;*
2. *Modifying in any manner any software product which has been sold by the Plaintiff to any third party, or offering to perform such services; and*
3. *Disclosing or attempting to disclose to any third party any information related to the software products of the Plaintiff, including, but not limited to the Plaintiff's product COMPU-RIP.*

The trial court further ordered an injunction bond in the amount of $10,000. On 5 September 1991, defendant made a Motion for Reconsideration and Motion to Dissolve Preliminary Injunction. The trial court denied this motion by order entered 14 October 1991.

Opinion by Judge Walker

* * *

Under the North Carolina Trade Secret Protection Act, a trade secret is defined as follows:

[B]usiness or technical information, including but not limited to a formula, pattern, program, device, compilation of information, method, technique, or process that:

a. Derives independent actual or potential commercial value from not being generally known or readily ascertainable through independent development or reverse engineering by persons who can obtain economic value from its disclosure or use; and

b. Is the subject of efforts that are reasonable under the circumstances to maintain its secrecy.

G. S. 66-152(3). "Misappropriation" occurs when there is:

[A]cquisition, disclosure, or use of a trade secret of another without express or implied authority or consent, unless such trade secret was arrived at by independent development, reverse engineering, or was obtained from another person with a right to disclose the trade secret.

G.S. 66-152(1). In the present case, defendants contend the COMPU-RIP software is not a trade secret and that even if it is a trade secret, defendants' actions do not constitute "misappropriation."

According to defendants, the COMPU-RIP software is not a trade secret since it is (1) not subject to reasonable efforts to maintain its secrecy and (2) defendants reverse engineered this software. In order to answer the question of whether plaintiff took reasonable efforts to maintain the secrecy of the COMPU-RIP software, it is necessary to be familiar with the form in which this software was distributed. The COMPU-RIP software is contained in the form of "programmable read-only memory chips" (PROMS) imbedded in the COMPU-RIP machinery. These PROMS contain only the "object code" version of the computer program. This is the version of the computer software which is "read" by the computer's machinery. Computer programmers do not write computer software in object code; rather, the software is written in "source code" and then translated into object code so that the computer can execute the program. . . . Since the COMPU-RIP software was sold in PROM form, the source code was not available to the general public. At least one court has found that as regards computer software, the secrecy component of a trade secret is not compromised when only the object code version of the software is distributed to customers. *Q-CO Industries, Inc. v. Hoffman,* 625 F. Supp. 608, 617–618 (S.D.N.Y. 1985).

* * *

Defendants next argue that plaintiff was not entitled to a preliminary injunction since it has not established misappropriation of its trade secret. A *prima facie* case of misappropriation is established where plaintiff presents substantial evidence that (1) defendant knows or should have known of the trade secret; and (2) defendant has had a specific opportunity to acquire the trade secret. G.S. 66-155. Here, a *prima facie* case of misappropriation exists since defendant Browning helped to develop the COMPU-RIP software during his employ with plaintiff and Browning had access to copies of the COMPU-RIP source code prior to his resignation. Further, according to its president, plaintiff invested eight man-years in the development of the COMPU-RIP system. Toombs and Ruggles stated in their affidavits that in order to make modifications to the COMPU-RIP software, access to the source code is required; it is practically impossible to make any substantial modification to COMPU-RIP possessing only the object code. After reviewing the record from the preliminary injunction hearing, we find plaintiff has shown a likelihood of success on the merits of its case.

* * *

Decision and Outcome

The North Carolina Court of Appeals basically affirmed the decision of the trial court to place an injunction on the defendant, preventing him from marketing his competing software product.

Questions for Analysis

1. In ordinary English, what is a trade secret in North Carolina? What security measures did the plaintiff take to prevent the trade secret from becoming known generally?

2. The court takes note of the difference between source and object code. If a software program is distributed as object code, does that distribution make all the secrets of the software program apparent? What about if the software is distributed as source code?

3. Why were this court and the trial court skeptical of the defendant's contention that he reverse engineered the plaintiff's software and then the defendant created his own software in the form of LumberScan?

Other Topics Visited and Not Visited

As advertised, the topics discussed above are just snapshots of some areas of law that are analyzed in more detail in various chapters. The list of topics above is not complete; other areas of law discussed in various chapters of this textbook include the structure of the court system (Chapter 2), civil procedure (Chapter 3), alternative dispute resolution (Chapter 4), administrative law and ethics (Chapter 6), and business organization (Chapter 14). The subject of "business law" is even more extensive than the topics presented in this textbook. Other business law topics could have been discussed, such as debtor–creditor relationships and bankruptcy law, but it is unlikely that all the chapters in this book can be taught in one course, let alone these additional topics. We think the textbook provides a good foundation for understanding the most important law affecting the legal environment of business.

A PRIMARY GOAL: LEGAL ISSUE RECOGNITION

It is essential for managers in every enterprise to be mindful of the legal pitfalls that can confront their companies. As acknowledged at the beginning of this chapter, then illustrated with snapshot looks at "legal issues," every functional area in the business world has legal exposure. The focus of this text is on those areas of exposure that are most critical to managers in modern, technology-based, information-age companies. In the "new economy," in addition to "old economy," the law dealing with everything from contracts to antitrust enforcement presents challenges to management. A manager needs to know the basics of law in all the functional areas of business and be able to recognize potentially explosive legal issues without benefit of attorneys. Moreover, as all of the functional areas of business are impacted by technological change, which in turn creates the need for continuing adaptation of existing statutes and court precedents, knowledge of law must be updated over time.

SOURCES OF LAW IN THE UNITED STATES

Common Law

common law
Law developed by "court" decision rather than by legislative creation. Early U.S. common law was based on English custom and judicial decision, with continuing development from U.S. court decisions.

Common law was created in England when disputes were settled in a court of law instead of by violence. The common law first emerged sometime around the end of the eleventh century and was used mainly to resolve disputes between private citizens. The early courts, called the King's Courts, were an important unifying factor creating the nation-state of England.

Precedent

At the beginning of Norman rule in England, Parliament was not an important force in law making in England. There were few *statutes,* or laws created by a legislative body, such as a parliament. Instead, most law was *created* through the resolution of disputes between private citizens. As an example, assume that two farmers who occupied property adjacent to each other went to court to determine who was liable when, say, a fire that started on the property of one farmer (A) crossed property lines and burned down a dwelling on the other farmer's (B) property. Let us assume that the fire started because hay stacked by A on his property burst into flames due to lightning. Let us also assume that before the fire started, B warned A that hay was flammable and that if a fire started, his (B's) house was in peril.

Most Likely Consequence   After the fire occurred, most likely B would have picked up a stick and gone over to A's house to trash A. A in turn, knowing that this action was likely to occur, would have armed himself and perhaps called together some of his sons and brothers to aid in his defense. B would have known about A's defense preparations and would have assembled his own gang. A violent outcome would not be a surprise, but the victor would not have solved anything substantive except perhaps creating animosity between A's and B's families that might last for generations.

A Better Dispute Resolution Mechanism   Alternatively, if B knew that, at common law, whoever first breached the peace was in the wrong and instead decided to complain *at court* about A's behavior, the resolution of this dispute might be expected to be a peaceful one. B would be the complaining party or the *plaintiff* and A would try to defend himself as the *defendant.* If, after hearing the case, the court decided that A was in the wrong and was

FIGURE 1.1
Property Line Dispute

Source: Corel (clipart).

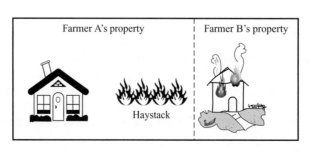

Farmer A's property | Farmer B's property

Haystack

negligent in not moving the hay to a different location, this decision would create a *precedent* that could be used by other courts dealing with similarly situated parties.

The Value of a Precedent   If another situation subsequently occurred involving farmers C and D who had adjacent property lines, D, the owner of the dwelling, could warn C to remove the flammable materials next to his house, citing the case between A and B. D could say not only that C's haystack was a fire hazard, but also that if a fire started and consumed his (D's) house, C would be liable for the fair market value of the house. Of course, two cases might not be identical, even though common elements exist that can provide a tie to existing precedent (case law). Instead of hay, suppose that C had stacked logs next to the property line, close to D's house. Logs are flammable but not nearly so easily as hay. It is also likely to take more work to move logs than hay.

New Precedents   If the logs somehow ignited into flame and damaged D's dwelling, a trip to court is a likely result. In this situation, it is possible that the defendant could prevail, perhaps because the chance of logs igniting is so much less than with hay, so that C's actions would not be deemed negligent. The court would have to decide. With the court's decision, a new precedent would be created and this process would continue with many other variations. You might ponder a situation in which Farmer F built his house next to Farmer E's property line *after* E's hay was already sitting on the ground. It should be noted that the availability of reasonable court remedies for harms suffered served, in our examples, to alter human behavior, first prompting interested parties to rely on "civilized" (court system) means of settling disputes in place of physical gang confrontations, and also providing incentives for avoiding the actions that result in legal liability. Lawsuits provide powerful disincentives to engaging in violent or destructive actions.

Source: Copyright © 2002, Tribune Media Services, Inc. All Rights Reserved.
Reprinted with permission.

Stare Decisis

The precedent-creating process occurs in many types of disputes among citizens. As precedents build up over a point of law, such as the responsibilities of adjacent landowners to each other, a rule of law is created that becomes like a statute (law) passed by a legislature. Parties knowledgeable about the line of cases, usually attorneys, can advise clients as to potential liability for various actions. As such rules of law accumulate in multiple areas of human activity, many of which involve commerce and economic relationships between various citizens, and between citizens and the state, a legal system emerges. In such a system, judges tend to follow precedents decided by other judges faced with similar facts unless underlying conditions in society change. If a judge does decide that a dispute among citizens is very similar to a dispute dealt with previously, with the court decision recorded, then the judge will most likely apply the doctrine of **stare decisis,** which means the judge has decided to apply the reasoning from a previously decided case.

stare decisis
The common law standard under which judges (courts) are bound to follow decisions set by precedents from prior court decisions.

Overturning Precedents

Changes in technology are a major force creating the conditions for overturning precedents. At one time most landlord–tenant relationships were between land "lords," who were literally lords, and tenant-farmers, who were serfs. Economically it made sense for the serfs, rather than the landlords, to be responsible for the maintenance of the leased premises. Serfs generally possessed more expertise and more incentive to maintain their dwellings in habitable condition. A precedent allocating responsibility for maintaining the leased dwellings in habitable condition to tenants became common in England and traveled to colonial courts in North America.

During the twentieth century as apartments became more common, *precedents* that required tenants to look after the upkeep of the leased property became unrealistic. Slowly but steadily, judges in virtually all the states overturned the *precedent* that required tenants to be responsible for the habitability of leased apartments. A host of other examples could be cited. Many changes in precedent are due to evolutions in societal mores such as views on racial segregation. Precedents enforcing certain conditions attached to deeds, such as prohibitions on African Americans ever owning a deeded property, have been overturned by courts as not being in the public interest (and possibly not constitutional!). So, we see, the common law is an evolving body as there are many forces, including changing technology and changing social norms, that make accepted legal standards in one era inappropriate in another.

Adoption in the United States of the Common Law Tradition

When England established the colonies in what was later to become the United States, colonial courts in each of the "separate" colonies routinely applied English common law, each generating its own evolving history of precedents. Since the United States is a union of *sovereign* states, there are now 50 bodies of common law in the United States, in addition to the body of common law followed by federal courts based on decisions reached in those courts. State courts frequently, though not invariably, refer to decisions of courts made in other states for guidance and precedent reference. The fact that there are occasions when states do not follow precedents created in other states makes for substantive differences in the common laws of the separate states.

Some of the most significant legal changes that have occurred in the latter half of the twentieth century have been due to the "uniform" movement, which is dedicated to elimination of idiosyncrasies of state law that built up under the common law. One of the most prominent results of unifying efforts, particularly for businesses, is the Uniform Commercial Code (UCC) that governs commercial contract law (discussed in Chapter 8).

Application to Modern Law

Any court that writes an opinion on a case contributes to the common law. State trial courts as well as the U.S. Supreme Court can create common law precedents. When the courts are confronted with novel situations such as the meaning of obscenity on the Internet and the enforceability of decency acts passed by Congress, their decisions establish precedents. The recent explosion in the production of high-tech products and methods of communication, including, most prominently, the Internet, has created an unprecedented number of novel legal situations and resulting precedents. It is probably true that the Internet has been responsible for more, new and different invasion-of-privacy laws and precedents in the last five years than have occurred during the previous 50 years.

What Does Monopolization Mean Legally?   Common law is also created when courts interpret statutes (laws), such as antitrust statutes, that are written ambiguously but are reasonably precise in application given the common law decisions that provide a history of court interpretation of the statutes. As discussed earlier, the Department of Justice recently charged Microsoft with "monopolization." Monopolization can only be clearly defined in light of previous court precedents that have resulted from other cases in which large firms were similarly charged.

This process of creating common law decisions regarding the meaning of statutes occurs at both the state level and the federal level. At the federal level, it has been said that the U.S. Constitution is what the U.S. Supreme Court says it is. Such statements are a testament to the importance of common law decisions by all courts, from the trial courts to supreme courts, in both the state and the federal court systems.

Court of Equity and Equitable Remedies

legal remedy
A court remedy generally providing monetary compensation.

In law a "remedy" is what the courts dispense to compensate plaintiffs for the wrongful actions of defendants. So far, we have been discussing "legal remedies." Illustratively, for a breach of contract, the typical **legal remedy** allows the plaintiff, the party suing because of the breach, to receive a *monetary award* that is supposed to equal the damages that the plaintiff incurred as a result of the breach. In most "court cases," plaintiffs go to court to seek a legal remedy, which is typically dispensed as a monetary judgment. This is not always a suitable remedy.

Consider a contract dispute over the agreement for a sale of land about which the plaintiff tells the judge, "Your honor, I don't want money; I want the thing the defendant promised to sell me. The defendant promised to sell me a parcel of land that has been in my family for more than 100 years. I want the land promised me in the contract as it is priceless to me for sentimental reasons. Furthermore, your honor, after agreeing to sell me the land in question, the defendant has opened up a mine on that land that he promised to sell me. If the mining activity is not stopped at once, irreparable harm will take place to my beloved land." In English common law courts, the only legal remedies available at law were money or property. There existed no means for stopping the "mining" plaintiff described as capable of destroying the value of the land to the plaintiff.

equitable remedy
A court remedy, seeking fairness, when monetary awards are not adequate to achieve that goal.

specific performance
A contract remedy in which the court awards the plaintiff what was promised in the contract by the defendant.

injunction
A court order to a party to stop doing something that could cause irreversible harm to the other party.

Equitable Remedies   To deal with this sort of conundrum in England, a system of **equitable remedies** grew in response to petitions to the king for remedies that were not provided by courts of law. Courts of equity evolved from these petitions to the king, who referred the petitions to a chancellor, which later evolved into courts of chancery or equity. Chancery courts were characterized by their emphasis on "fairness." Of course, the concept of "fairness" may be vague and arguable, but courts of chancery (or equity) were allowed to be creative in forming new remedies. In the hypothetical case above, a chancery court might decide that the plaintiff is entitled to **specific performance** on the contract, which means that he would receive the land rather than a monetary award. In addition, a court of equity or chancery might grant the plaintiff an **injunction,** a court order imposing an immediate stoppage on the defendant's mining action, so that irreparable damage to the land would not take place.

For a long period of time, there were two parallel court systems in England—courts of law and courts of equity—and plaintiffs actually had to choose whether to bring an action at law or an action in equity. This parallel system of courts was also part of the legal system of the American colonies and, thence, of the states when the United States gained independence from England. Today courts of law and equity have merged, but the remedies are still distinct. So, in our modern court system, there are legal remedies and there are equitable remedies. Most of this book and the vast bulk of civil litigation involve plaintiffs going to court and seeking legal remedies, though in some cases equitable remedies are still significant.

Equitable Remedies and Contract Law   Most applications of equitable remedies occur in connection with contract law, which is discussed in some detail in Chapter 8. In addition to the equitable remedies of *specific performance* and *injunction* described above, there is a third frequently applied equitable remedy in contract disputes called **rescission,** which involves returning the parties to a contract to the positions they occupied before the contract was formed. Under rescission, each party to a contract generally gets back whatever money or property was transferred to the other party pursuant to the contract. In broad terms, equitable remedies are applicable when monetary damages are inadequate to fully compensate a plaintiff. This situation typically occurs when the plaintiff in a breach of contract case, for good reason, values the consideration (things of value) promised in the contract significantly higher than fair market value. A plaintiff in a breach of contract case may value a work of art at more than its appraised fair market value and may seek specific performance if a seller of the art work breaches a contract and refuses to transfer the work.

rescission
A contract remedy in which each party to the contract must give back what was transferred in the contract.

Constitutional Law

At the apex of each legal system in the United States, state or federal, there is a constitution. Each state has its own constitution and our nation as a whole has the U.S. Constitution, which is the *supreme law* of the land. It is important to note that legal interpretation of the U.S. Constitution is a job for the federal courts and, ultimately, the U.S. Supreme Court. Laws, broadly defined to include state and federal statutes, regulations of administrative agencies, and other official acts taken by members of the executive branches of government, must not conflict with the U.S. Constitution. Any laws that conflict with a constitution are said to be "unconstitutional" and thus null and void. The determination of the constitutionality of either state or federal laws is mainly a judicial function, except when Congress and state legislatures amend the U.S. Constitution.

U.S. Constitution

Revolutionaries who had recently overthrown despotic colonial rule that was unresponsive to their wishes wrote the U.S. Constitution. Although most of the Framers of the Constitution were of English origin, they were also strongly influenced by French political philosophers such as Montesquieu and Rousseau. Together with John Locke and others among English *progressives,* the Framers believed in limited government and protection of certain "inalienable" rights of ordinary citizens. Rights are *inalienable* when governments cannot take them away from someone. Among the inalienable rights that the colonist/revolutionaries thought important were freedom of speech, freedom to bear arms, freedom from unreasonable searches and seizures, the right to due process, and so on. These inalienable rights are memorialized in the **Bill of Rights,** which is composed of the first 10 amendments to the U.S. Constitution.

Bill of Rights
The first 10 amendments to the U.S. Constitution. Fundamentally important personal rights are included.

Checks and Balances

At the time the Constitution was being developed, it was clear in the minds of the Framers that the greatest threat to freedom was government. In order to protect peoples' inalienable rights from the despotism of a strong and unresponsive central government, the Framers created the system of *checks and balances* that are the hallmark of government structure in the United States. The Ninth and Tenth Amendments reserve all rights not delegated to the federal government to the sovereign states and their citizens. The powers of the federal government were limited to enumerated powers, among which are included the powers to coin money, to regulate interstate commerce, and to declare war.

Separation of Powers

It was clearly the determination of our nation's founding fathers to prevent the emergence of an excessively powerful executive branch of federal government. The *checks and balances* established to avoid this possibility are reflected in the division of federal governmental functions into three branches: executive, legislative, and judicial. To a great extent, each of these branches of government has an ability to limit the power of each of the other branches.

Under our Constitution, only Congress (the legislative branch) has the power to raise taxes, but the president (the executive branch) has a veto power over this right. The U.S. Supreme Court (the judicial branch) can declare a law unconstitutional, but amendments to the Constitution, which originate in the legislative branch, can overturn such rulings. The president, like most chief executive officers running companies, can order actions taken. However, Congress can refuse to fund programs, agencies, and actions proposed or supported by the president. Under extreme circumstances, the Congress has the power to remove a president through impeachment and conviction.

The legislative branch is further divided between two branches (Senate and House). Some specific tasks are allocated individually to each branch of Congress, while other tasks are jointly assigned to the two branches of Congress.

Hierarchy of Law in the United States

The Supremacy Clause in the U.S. Constitution states that "This Constitution, and the Laws of the United States which shall be made in Pursuance thereof; and all Treaties made, or which shall be made under the Authority of the United States, shall be the supreme Law of the Land. . . ." The impact of the Supremacy Clause is that all *state* laws, including those in state constitutions, are subordinate to federal law, whether the *federal* law be constitutional, statutory, or regulatory.

As long as they do not conflict with federal law, state constitutions are the supreme law within the states. Hence, laws passed by a state legislature must not be in conflict with the state constitution. State constitutions differ to a degree that prevents a generalized discussion of their nature. It is notable, however, that all 50 states have three branches of government: legislative, executive, and judicial.

Statutory Law and Legislative Bodies

Unlike a *common law,* which is judge-made law, a statute is a law passed by a legislature. Congress is an example of a legislative body as are the 50 state legislatures that function within the states. To be legal, a state statute must not conflict either with the state's own constitution or with the federal constitution. Some states, such as California, are known for the significant state legislation that is enacted directly by the electorate through referenda and initiatives. Proposition 209, which prohibits racial preferences by any state agency in the state of California, was made part of statutory California law by a statewide ballot.

At the federal level, *statutes* begin as *bills* (proposed legislation) that are introduced to either the House or the Senate (note that only the House can initiate tax increases). Typically, bills are assigned to an appropriate committee for processing. Not surprisingly, bills often fail to emerge from the congressional committee as a consequence of lack of general support within the committee. Generally the same bill is introduced in both the House and the Senate. However, by the time the parallel bills are passed by each body, amendments to the bills are apt to make them differ to a degree that requires a unifying conference to end up with a bill that can be acceptable to both houses of Congress.

---

executive, legislative, and judicial branches
The three branches of the federal government, each of which has its own duties and powers. The legislative branch (Congress) writes our laws, the judicial branch (courts) interpret laws, and the executive branch (headed by the president) handles the government's administrative tasks including the enforcement of laws.

supremacy
The constitutional standard under which federal law is the law of the land, with any state-created laws subordinate to federal laws so that state laws that conflict with federal law are invalid.

statute
Law enacted by a legislative body. Federal statutes are enacted by Congress and state statutes by state legislatures.

Nutz and Boltz   The Supreme Court and Constitutional Interpretation

The following article, available at the U.S. Supreme Court website, describes some of what the U.S. Supreme Court does.

"EQUAL JUSTICE UNDER LAW"—These words, written above the main entrance to the Supreme Court Building, express the ultimate responsibility of the Supreme Court of the United States. The Court is the highest tribunal in the Nation for all cases and controversies arising under the Constitution or the laws of the United States. As the final arbiter of the law, the Court is charged with ensuring the American people the promise of equal justice under law and, thereby, also functions as guardian and interpreter of the Constitution.

The Supreme Court is "distinctly American in concept and function," as Chief Justice Charles Evans Hughes observed. Few other courts in the world have the same authority of constitutional interpretation and none have exercised it for as long or with as much influence. . . . The unique position of the Supreme Court stems, in large part, from the deep commitment of the American people to the Rule of Law and to constitutional government. The United States has demonstrated an unprecedented determination to preserve and protect its written Constitution, thereby providing the American "experiment in democracy" with the oldest written Constitution still in force.

The Constitution of the United States is a carefully balanced document. It is designed to provide for a national government sufficiently strong and flexible to meet the needs of the republic, yet sufficiently limited and just to protect the guaranteed rights of citizens; it permits a balance between society's need for order and the individual's right to freedom . . .

The complex role of the Supreme Court in this system derives from its authority to invalidate legislation or executive actions which, in the Court's considered judgment, conflict with the Constitution. This power of "judicial review" has given the Court a crucial responsibility in assuring individual rights, as well as in maintaining a "living Constitution" whose broad provisions are continually applied to complicated new situations. . . .

Chief Justice Marshall expressed the challenge which the Supreme Court faces in maintaining free government by noting: "We must never forget that it is a *constitution* we are expounding. . . . intended to endure for ages to come, and consequently, to be adapted to the various *crises* of human affairs."

Source: This brief description is excerpted from a longer document accessible at http://www.supremecourtus.gov. The excerpts are located at http://a257.g.akamaitech.net/7/257/2422/14mar20010800/www.supremecourtus.gov/about/constitutional.pdf.

Once passed by Congress, a bill goes to the president for signature. The president can *sign the bill into law,* at which time the bill becomes a statute. On the other hand, the president can *veto* any bill passed by Congress. Vetoes, however, can be overridden by a two-thirds vote of both houses of Congress. Even supported and approved by Congress and the president, a newly passed statute can be challenged in court and declared unconstitutional. The chart in the "Nutz and Boltz" box provides a schematic representation of the route typically followed by a bill from proposal until it becomes law or is vetoed by the president.

State Statutes

Similar processes take place at the state level, though there are numerous differences in detail state by state. In some states, such as North Carolina, the governor does not have veto power. In some states, being a legislator is a full-time job, while in others the job is specifically designed for citizen-legislators who only work part time as state legislators.

States have been called "laboratories for democracy," reflecting the fact that individual states can "experiment" with different laws that, generally, do not have national

Nutz and Boltz   The Route Followed from Proposed Law to Law

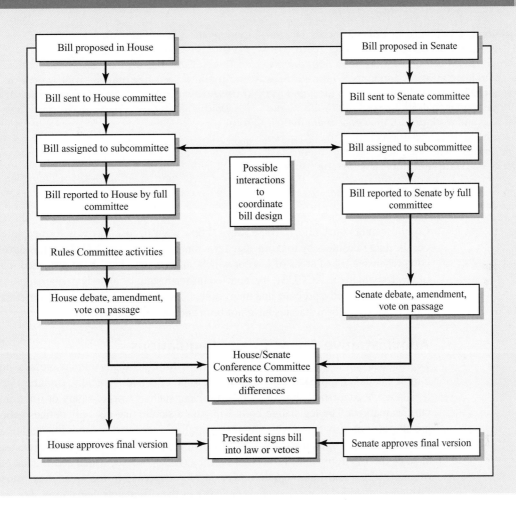

consequences. Many federal laws began as experiments at the state level. For example, federal securities (stocks and bonds) regulation was preceded by about 30 years by state *blue-sky laws*. State blue-sky laws superceded common law fraud actions in the sale of securities (stocks and bonds) and replaced them with a standard that made it much easier for *defrauded* investors to sue and get money back from poor investments in misrepresented ventures, even if they are unable to prove that the sellers of the ventures (securities) *intentionally* lied in order to make sales, which is required for success in common law fraud actions.

Unifying State-by-State Differences in Statutory Laws

Although states have a degree of freedom for legal experimentation, differences among state laws can have national consequences that are detrimental to businesses that operate in more than one state. Businesses that operate in several states have to be familiar with the idiosyncrasies of the laws in the various states in which they do business. To counteract the negative consequences of legal differences among the states, the National Conference of

Nutz and Boltz   National Conference of Commissioners

The National Conference of Commissioners on Uniform State Laws (NCCUSL) is now in its 108th year. The organization comprises more than 300 lawyers, judges, and law professors appointed by the states as well as the District of Columbia, Puerto Rico, and the U.S. Virgin Islands to draft proposals for uniform and model laws and work toward their enactment in their legislatures. Since its inception in 1892, the group has drafted more than 200 acts, among them such bulwarks of state statutory law as the Uniform Commercial Code, the Uniform Probate Code, and the Uniform Controlled Substances Act.

The NCCUSL has an extensive, informative, and user-friendly website that is well worth a visit (**http://www.ncculs.org**). Notice the number of laws for which there are efforts to make state laws uniform.

Source: http://www.nccusl.org/.

Commissioners on Uniform State Laws (http://www.nccusl.org) was formed to ease the cost of doing business by making state laws more uniform. The NCCUSL has developed a comprehensive list of areas of law for which uniform laws have been proposed. The areas of law for which the NCCUSL has enacted uniform statutes include partnerships, athletes-agents, child custody, probate, and many others. Except for the Uniform Commercial Code, most of these uniform statutes have not been adopted by all the states.

Administrative Agencies and Regulations

Legislatures can define legal and illegal actions for individuals and businesses, but often a more hands-on approach has been shown to be effective. Typically, Congress or a state legislature is concerned about a specific problem such as worker safety or fraud in the securities markets. The legislative body will pass a statute that not only defines actions that are illegal, but also may create an administrative agency to enforce the statute and develop additional regulations consistent with the statute. Federal administrative agencies such as the Environmental Protection Agency (EPA), the Securities and Exchange Commission (SEC), and innumerable others develop expertise in the areas they oversee and fashion regulations that are more detailed than the originating legislation. For example, the Internal Revenue Service has issued a body of regulations that is about five times as voluminous as the Internal Revenue Code, which is the codified set of tax statutes passed by Congress.

Regulations

Regulations issued by administrative agencies are by far the most voluminous source of law. When businesses complain about government red tape, it often reflects their concern that administrative agencies, particularly federal agencies, create excessive volumes of regulations. The Occupational Safety and Health Administration (OSHA), for example, has regulations that deal with how far off the floor commode seats in workers' bathrooms are to be (between 12 and 18 inches). This agency's recently issued regulations dealing with repetitive motion syndrome occupy 610 pages of the Code of Federal Regulations.[5]

---

[5] The OSHA regulations dealing with repetitive stress syndrome were issued by President Clinton during his last days in office but were withdrawn by President Bush.

Legal Actions by Administrative Agencies

Administrative agencies generally have their own courts, headed by administrative law judges (ALJs). Typically, an agency enforces its regulations through legal actions before ALJs in procedures like those in trial courts. Administrative agencies, especially at the federal level, are highly visible to the businesses under their purview, and often influence those businesses by the threat of an investigation or other actions that would create negative publicity for such businesses. Needless to say, the legal environment for businesses is heavily influenced by the actions of administrative agencies, both at the federal and state levels.

Alternative Dispute Resolution (ADR)

Courts are widely perceived by business as being too slow, too risky, and too public. Alternative dispute resolution (ADR) is a group of noncourt techniques for resolving disputes that have the potential to become lawsuits. Some common features of ADR are that it is quick, relatively inexpensive, and can be made confidential. We devote Chapter 4 to the main techniques of alternative dispute resolution, which include negotiation, mediation, and arbitration. ADR, especially arbitration agreements, which are agreements to take disputes before an arbitrator rather than a judge, is especially prevalent in international trade, because each company fears appearing before the courts in another country.

USEFUL LEGAL CLASSIFICATIONS

As you go forward through the rest of the chapters assigned, you will be expected to develop a firm understanding of the applications of law presented. A key element of achieving the needed understanding is development of an ability to compartmentalize. Illustratively, it makes no sense to apply *criminal law* concepts to *civil* suits. Once the type of law that applies is determined, comprehension of a case and prediction of its legal outcome become much easier. A firm grasp of the following basic classifications in law will ease your journey through the text.

Substantive versus Procedural Law

substantive law
Law that spells out the rights and duties of parties to a lawsuit.

The legal principles dealt with in this text are, by and large, what can be described as **substantive law.** Substantive law is concerned with the rights and responsibilities of the parties to a lawsuit. In the case of two farmers who have adjacent property lines, substantive law determines whether one farmer has a responsibility to the other farmer to clear out fire hazards next to the other farmer's dwelling. Substantive law addresses the question of whether government can fashion legislation that censors content on the Internet and still be constitutional under the First Amendment. Managers need a solid understanding of substantive law.

procedural law
Law that provides the rules for conducting the courtroom and related procedures in the event of a lawsuit.

Procedural law pertains to the rules of the contest when two parties go to court to resolve a dispute. To lean on a sports analogy, the winner of a football game is like the substantive winner of a court case, but the rules of the football game are akin to procedural law (and referees, who are supposed to be neutral, are like judges). Procedural law dictates how courtroom proceedings and related litigation activities take place. Parties that seek to introduce evidence that does not conform to *procedural law* requirements will be penalized by the exclusion of such evidence. Other procedural law issues pertain to motions made by either party, instructions to the jury, and other minutiae needed for proper execution of litigation. Unless you intend to represent yourself (or your company) in litigation without the assistance of legal counsel, you don't need to learn a great deal of procedural law. Lawyers, of course, need a solid understanding of procedural law.

Nutz and Boltz Public and Private Law

Public Law	Private Law
Administrative law	Contract law
Antitrust law	Corporate law
Constitutional law	Nuisance law
Criminal law	Partnership law
Environmental law	Property law
Patent and copyright law	Tort law
Consumer protection law	Trade secret law

Public versus Private Law

public law
Law governing the relationship between government and citizens.

Public law deals with the relationship between government and citizens (including business). **Private law** deals with disputes between citizens. When a party alleges that another trading partner has breached a contract, it is private law (contract law) that is used to resolve the dispute. In most public law disputes, the government is the plaintiff while the defendant is a private entity such as a business or individual, though there are public law disputes in which a citizen or business sues the government or one branch of government goes to court opposing another branch of government

private law
Law governing disputes between citizens.

In the public law arena, the government often has intervened and modified (corrected) free-market agreements that citizens and businesses can make among themselves. Illustratively, the government has declared that employment discrimination based on race, sex, and national origin is illegal under the Civil Rights Act of 1964, subjecting companies to civil damage claims and other penalties for discriminatory employment conditions they permit to exist (even if they can get "voluntary" acceptance of jobs at discriminatory compensation levels).

When two companies that compete with each other agree to charge the same price, Section 1 of the Sherman Antitrust Law is violated. The two colluding companies are subject to sanctions, including (but not limited to) the value of damages inflicted by the companies' collusive actions. Both antitrust violations and discriminatory (by race, sex, national origin, age, or disability) employment conditions involve public law. Other examples of public law include criminal law, constitutional law, and administrative law that comes into play when an administrative agency takes a business to court. By volume, the applications of law in this textbook are roughly equally divided between public and private law. The table in the "Nutz and Boltz" box is not exhaustive of all categories of either public or private law.

civil law
Public and private laws dealing with public and private rights, as opposed to criminal actions. Redress usually involves monetary awards.

Civil versus Criminal Law

For most businesses **civil law** is far more important than **criminal law,** although there certainly are activities that can be engaged in by business managers that will earn active prison time. Most public and private law is civil. A notable difference between civil and criminal law is that, if the defendant loses a civil case, the sanction against the defendant is generally monetary. In contrast, a defendant who loses a criminal case can be fined, but also can be imprisoned or even executed.[6] In a criminal case, the defendant is prosecuted on behalf of society or the public.

criminal law
Law that deals with crimes—i.e., with wrongful acts that violate society's rules for which criminal punishments, including jail or even execution, are required.

[6] In some civil cases the plaintiff seeks an injunction that is a court order directing the defendant to do or not to do something. If the defendant fails to abide by an injunction, the court can order the defendant to jail.

Nutz and Boltz

Civil Law	Criminal Law
Contract Law	**Misdemeanor Offenses**
Sale of goods	Most traffic violations
Employment contracts	Drunk and disorderly conduct
Purchase and sale of real estate	Theft of small amounts of property
Lease of intellectual property	Theft of computer services
Tort Law	**Felonies**
Battery	Murder
False imprisonment	Kidnapping
Defamation	Child pornography
Trespass	Burglary

Criminal and civil procedural law also differ significantly. In a criminal case, the state has the responsibility to prove *beyond a reasonable doubt* that the defendant is guilty (under substantive criminal law). In a criminal case, the defendant cannot be made to testify. Criminal cases are often subdivided into felonies and misdemeanors. Felonies are more serious offenses, in which the defendant can receive a sentence exceeding one year in jail. Misdemeanors are less serious offenses where the maximum imprisonment is less than one year.

In a civil case, the plaintiff tries to prove by a *preponderance of the evidence* that the defendant was responsible for a civil wrong that entitles the plaintiff to a monetary recovery or some kind of injunctive relief. The courts have resisted mathematical comparisons between the *beyond a reasonable doubt* and the *preponderance of the evidence* standards. It is the authors' opinion that the former standard is akin to a Type I error of .05 or less, while the latter implies that the probability the plaintiff's version of the truth is superior to the defendant's is greater than .5. In other words, in a criminal case where the *beyond the reasonable doubt* standard is used, the jury must have a less than one in 20 chance (of Type I error) in their minds that the defendant is not guilty when the jury finds the defendant guilty. *Preponderance of the evidence* is synonymous with the statement that "it is more likely than not that the defendant did the deeds that entitle the plaintiff to a monetary recovery." It should be emphasized that courts do not use mathematics to explain the difference between beyond a reasonable doubt and preponderance of the evidence. Instead judges orally make use of examples and anecdotes to illustrate the difference between the two standards.

A CAUTION REGARDING THE OVERLAY OF ETHICS AND LAW

Students should be careful not to confuse law and ethics. The interplay between the two is discussed more fully in Chapter 6. Although there may be general societal agreement on an ethical issue, compliance with a generally accepted ethical standard is optional unless the law requires compliance. Pharmaceutical companies have been accused of using Third World countries for development of drugs because their legal standards for the marketing of new drugs are less stringent than those in the United States. Should a pharmaceutical company market drugs in Third World countries that have been rejected by the U.S. Food and Drug Administration? It may be considered unethical by some, but it is not illegal for a corporation to market such drugs in Third World countries. Technology certainly works to expose us to new ethical issues, as well as legal issues. With limits on pages and expertise, this book must focus primarily on legality rather than ethics.

Summary

Impact of Law and Technology on the Conduct of Business

- The law relates to everyday experiences. Business students should be keenly aware of the importance of law. A legal mistake can be potentially fatal to any business or business plan.
- The legal environment of business is rapidly changing with the rise in the use of the Internet and the explosive growth of many high-tech enterprises, the principal assets of which are in the form of *intellectual property* (IP).
- The rapid evolution of technology and the development of e-commerce have caused the law to change significantly, particularly in the areas of contract and intellectual property law, the latter including patent, copyright, trademark, and trade secret law.
- The Internet has introduced a whole new way of doing business, but traditional *tort* law continues to be relevant. In particular, extractions of information without the consent of users or customers can be an invasion of privacy tort.
- Businesses face threats from industrial espionage and from hackers bent on mischief. In response, computer security consultants use a wide variety of tools to protect businesses. Encryption is relied on to scramble communications to avoid interception of transmissions of valuable information.
- Although the Founding Fathers could not have envisioned the Internet, the Internet impacts several key constitutional issues. The taxation of Internet sites is an important revenue issue for states. Pornography and other fringe activities provide an avenue for exploring the limits of the First Amendment, which protects freedom of expression.
- The Internet also creates new challenges for government regulation of businesses. Consumer protection, antitrust, and securities laws all have adapted and are continuing to adapt to new situations created by the Internet.

What Is the Law, What Are Its Functions, and How Does It Provide for Change?

- The primary goal of this textbook is to enable students to recognize legal issues.
- The legal exposures you need to be concerned about encompass both traditional legal issues and new issues brought about by the advance of technology.
- The law is more than words on a piece of paper. It is a set of rules enforced by public forces, generally the police. The law evolves according to societal changes and technological evolution.
- The common law was created when parties to a dispute came to court for judicial resolution of conflict. The common law is built through precedents and *stare decisis*. The common law originated in England and was the legal system used by the colonial courts.
- The law provides both *legal remedies* and *equitable remedies*. Legal remedies usually provide for monetary compensation. Equitable remedies are applicable when monetary awards are inadequate to provide equity.
- The common law continues to redefine law in a modern context, adapting to changes in society and technology.

Sources of U.S. Law and Alternatives for Dispute Resolution through Arbitration

- *Constitutional law* sits at the apex of our legal system. A primary function of the U.S. Constitution is protection of citizens' rights as memorialized in the Bill of Rights. The *Supremacy Clause* in the U.S. Constitution requires that federal law prevail in conflicts with state law.
- *Statutes* are laws passed by legislative bodies. In order to be enforceable, a statute must not conflict with a state constitution or with the U.S. Constitution. There are 51 legislatures in the United States: Congress plus 50 state legislatures.
- Congress and the states often create *administrative agencies* to enforce regulatory statutes and devise regulations consistent with regulatory statutes. The largest body of law, by volume, is the assemblage of regulations from administrative agencies.

- Increasingly, commercial parties are bypassing courts and engaging in dispute resolution through arbitration. Arbitration is generally faster and cheaper than court litigation. At the international level, arbitration clauses are very common.

Legal Classifications

- It is useful to classify law into various categories.
- The focus of this textbook is *substantive law*, but students should know a few basics of *procedural law*.
- Other useful classifications include civil versus criminal law and public versus private law.

Key Terms

antitrust law, *9*
Bill of Rights, *18*
civil law, *24*
common law, *14*
constitutional law, *8*
consumer protection law, *9*
criminal law, *24*
equitable remedy, *17*
executive, legislative, and
   judicial branches, *19*

injunction, *17*
intellectual property, *6*
law, *5*
legal remedy, *17*
precedent, *6*
private law, *24*
procedural law, *23*
public law, *24*
rescission, *18*
specific performance, *17*

stare decisis, *16*
statute, *19*
substantive law, *23*
supremacy, *19*
tort, *8*

Questions for Review and Analysis

1. Describe a technological change you are familiar with that has changed a law.
2. What is the difference between common law and statutory law?
3. When a law is said to be "unconstitutional," what does that mean?
4. How does the law facilitate planning by businesspersons?
5. What is the difference between substantive law and procedural law?

If You Really Understood This Chapter, You Should Be Able to Comment on the Following:

1. **The Impact of Technology on Law.** With the Internet, all websites are equally accessible, regardless of where a site's business sponsor is located. As a result, foreign websites are accessible to Internet cruisers. Suppose a foreign website sells drugs that are not approved by regulatory authorities to citizens in another country. Does that website have the obligation to be familiar with drug laws throughout the world? Have the owners of that website committed a crime?

2. **Interpretation of the Constitution.** Interpretation of the U.S. Constitution has inspired a debate that is nearly as old as the Constitution itself. On the one hand, there are those who believe that the U.S. Constitution should be interpreted as the Framers of the Constitution intended (these folks often are called strict constructionists and tend to be conservatives). On the other hand, some liberal jurists contend that the Constitution is a "living" document that should be interpreted in light of changes that have occurred since 1787 when the Constitution was signed. Does the Internet put more pressure on the interpretations of the strict constructionists or those who believe that the Constitution should be interpreted with reference to societal and technological changes? As the pace of change increases, is it more important than ever to have something stable, such as an unchanging interpretation of the Constitution to rely upon, or is it imperative to imagine how the Framers of the Constitution would have dealt with modern problems and not be constrained by the literal language of the Constitution? Creative comments are welcome.

3. **Advantages and Disadvantages of Common Law Precedents.** Each state has its own court system that is independent of that of other states in the sense that a common law precedent laid down by the supreme court in one state does not bind the courts in other states. The independence of the courts in each state allows each state to tailor its court rulings to the facts of the cases that are heard in the state. For example, recalling the hypothetical case between two farmers who shared a property line, the facts of the case could vary in an infinite number of ways, as suggested by some

of the discussion of the case. It is possible that the precedents established by the fact patterns that appear in one state will be different from the precedents established in another state. Over time, what harm is created by state-by-state differences in common law precedents?

4. **Legal Technicalities.** The general public and businesspeople in particular often become exasperated with "legal technicalities." The popular notion is that a defendant in civil or criminal cases is able to escape conviction or liability because of some legal technicality and that justice is retarded because of reliance on the technicalities. It could be argued, however, that most of the legal technicalities are there for a reason. Procedural law is full of technicalities about how evidence can be presented and is there to allow parties to present their case so that the winner will prevail on the substance, or merits, of the case. If an attorney for a party to litigation makes a technical procedural error, it may cause that party to lose a suit, but that is not an argument for getting rid of procedural law requirements. Think of a legal technicality that you have seen in a TV show that appeared to enable the guilty party to walk free or escape legal liability. Discuss the rationale for retaining the legal technicality. One possible hint: Suppose the prosecution could present evidence obtained without benefit of a search warrant. Knowing this rule of evidence would not be enforced, how many police would bother to obtain search warrants?

5. **International Law and the Internet.** The World Trade Organization (WTO) has been much in the news lately. Most people are only vaguely aware of what the WTO does and its relevance to everyday life for most people in the world. Since you are currently in the United States, focus on the WTO and U.S. law. Go to the WTO website (http://www.wto.org) and work backward to U.S. law. Peruse the WTO website and see if you can eventually identify something the WTO does that affects U.S. law and may affect you. *Hint:* Go to the A–Z List or the Site Map. After visiting several WTO web pages, can you see why more and more of the legal environment of businesses is international?

Social Responsibility and Ethics in a High-Tech World

Pills and Patents. There are millions of AIDS sufferers in Africa who are dying. There are patented pills that can significantly alleviate the symptoms of AIDS and slow or stop its progression. Some of these pills cost about a nickel to make (marginal cost) but sell for about $10 per pill. Given the cost of treating AIDS with patented pills, most of the AIDS sufferers in Africa will go untreated. Naturally, groups representing AIDS sufferers have made pleas to the companies that own the patents for free (or almost free) access to medication, but those pleas have largely gone unanswered. According to the patent owners, millions of dollars went into the research and development of those patented pills and, if they are given away at the cost of production, those investments are lost. In the longer term, it's argued, companies will not be motivated to do the pathbreaking research necessary to develop treatments and cures for diseases such as AIDS if their investments are wiped out based on "humanitarian" considerations. As future businesspeople, how do you feel about the issue? Should property rights in compelling cases such as the AIDS epidemic in Africa be cause for ignoring intellectual property rights? Suppose some African nations pay scientists to produce infringing copies of the patented pills used to treat AIDS patients. Should the United States visit trade sanctions on those very poor nations for violating the intellectual property rights of U.S.-based pharmaceutical companies?

Using the Internet to Your Advantage

The Internet has made legal research vastly easier. In the past, legal research involved (1) going to a law library and (2) finding the appropriate book by trying to follow the arcane conventions of legal citation. For many nonlaw students, at both the undergraduate and graduate levels, legal research was an overwhelming task. Today there are a number of websites that offer "free" access to legal research that eliminates (1) and a lot of (2) above. Fasten your seatbelts and let's cruise the Internet!

1. The Legal Information Institute at the Cornell Law School has put together an easy-to-use system for locating various laws, from the U.S. Constitution to regulations of administrative agencies (http://www.law.cornell.edu). Just for practice, suppose you were to try to find the following:

   a. Article I, Section 8 of the U.S. Constitution enumerates the legislative powers granted to Congress. See if you can find them.

b. Go to the search engine at the top of the page and type in a topic of interest. Maybe you are interested in the antitrust laws that were used by the U.S. Department of Justice in its recent suit against Microsoft Corporation. With a few clicks you should be able to find a page that gives you an overview of the antitrust laws, provides a hyperlink to the antitrust laws themselves in the U.S. Code, and also provides a portal to recent Supreme Court and U.S. Court of Appeals antitrust decisions. If your legal environment course requires a legal research project, a lot of your research is already done if you select the government's suit against Microsoft as your topic.

2. Today, most colleges and universities have access to Lexis-Nexis, which enables students to do legal research. Using an on-campus computer, go to Academic Universe, click with your mouse, and you will see Legal Research. Click on it. Since we are exploring a legal action by the U.S. government against the Microsoft Corporation for possible antitrust violations, click on "Get a Case" and insert *Microsoft v. United States* next to Party Name and hit Enter. Amazing! Since the United States has sued Microsoft more than once, and since resulting decisions were appealed several times, there are more than 30 separate reports of various cases involving these two parties.

a. There are two cases in this chapter. Find these cases by (1) putting in the case names and (2) putting in the citations. For example, in the first case, *Whelan Associates, Inc. v. Jaslow Dental Laboratory, Inc.,* put in the names of the parties in the same slots for Party Name. Notice that there are three cases retrieved. You are interested in just the case that is cited with the numbers 797 F.2d 1222, which is volume 797 of the *Federal Reporter,* Second Edition, page 1222. Delete the Party Names and insert those numbers in that order next to Citation and hit Enter. This time you get Case 1.1! Now you know how to look up cases!

b. Do the same thing for Case 1.2 to confirm your new skills.

c. While you are at the Lexis-Nexis site, click on Law Reviews and enter "antitrust" as a Keyword and "Microsoft" to Narrow Search and hit Enter. There are over 100 articles written on this topic in the last six months! What more do you need in the way of research ability? Now, go do the work!

3. Go to a search engine provided by Netscape, AOL, or Microsoft and insert the words "USA Patriots Act," which is the name of the bill that was introduced shortly after the events of September 11, 2001, to combat terrorists attacking the United States. It is a safe bet that you will encounter H.R. 3162, which stands for House Resolution 3162, the bill number for the USA Patriots Act. Go to the Library of Congress using http://www.loc.gov, and click on the Thomas Locator (named in honor of Thomas Jefferson). At the top of the web page is "Bill Number." Enter H.R. 3162 (for the 107th Congress) and notice that the text for the USA Patriots Act is shown.

4. Finally, there are commercial websites that provide excellent opportunities to do legal research, including http://www.findlaw.com. The Internet has opened up the legal world to nonlawyers. With a little patience, ingenuity, and persistence, you can do legal research on virtually any topic. Ignorance of the law really is not an excuse any longer!

Appendix **A**

How to Brief a Case and What Does All That Stuff Mean?

Reprinted below is Case 1-2. Immediately after the case, we examine the case in detail. Endnotes are used to provide brief descriptions of elements of the case presentation. Please note that this case description is only an excerpt and that real-world cases can get much more lengthy and complicated. This exposition gives you the tools to examine cases in subsequent chapters with more understanding though, in reading cases, practice makes perfect. Reasonably soon, with effort you will get a "feel" for reading cases and will come back to this appendix and chuckle. Initially, however, reading and briefing a case is a challenge.

Case 1-2

Barr-Mullin, Inc. v. Douglas M. Browning and Primavera Systems, Ltd.[1]

Court of Appeals of North Carolina[2] 108 N.C. App. 590 (N.C. Ct. App. 1993)[3]

COURT STATEMENT OF FACTS, CALLED A SYLLABUS[4]

Plaintiff instituted this action seeking both injunctive relief and damages alleging defendants misappropriated its trade secrets.[5] Evidence in the record discloses that plaintiff is a corporation engaged in selling lumber processing equipment to customers in the woodworking industry.[6] COMPU-RIP, a "lumber optimization system," is one of the processing systems sold by plaintiff. This system has a computer software program which acts as the "brain," taking in data regarding the approaching lumber and instructing the mechanical handling components as to how to guide the lumber through the saw. COMPU-RIP was first offered for sale in 1986 and has received the Challengers Award, an honor recognizing significant developments in the woodworking industry.

From March 1985 through December 1986, plaintiff employed Douglas Browning (defendant) as an independent consultant to develop the computer software for the COMPU-RIP system.[7] In December of 1986, Browning was employed by plaintiff as its vice president of engineering. From 1987 through 1989 Browning played a role in installing COMPU-RIP systems at various plant sites; his duties included installing the COMPU-RIP software and providing assistance to customers once the systems were installed.

In January of 1990, Browning informed plaintiff of his intention to resign from plaintiff's employ. Shortly thereafter, Browning incorporated defendant Primavera Systems. Around this same time, Browning entered into negotiations with plaintiff whereby defendant proposed to remain associated as an independent consultant authorized by plaintiff to render computer systems service to COMPU-RIP owners. These negotiations failed and Browning resigned effective 23 August 1990.

After Browning's resignation, defendants began developing a lumber optimization system known as LumberScan. In addition, defendants also began to provide technical assistance to COMPU-RIP purchasers by customizing the COMPU-RIP computer software to meet the individual needs of the owner. Plaintiff filed the present suit alleging that the computer software used in COMPU-RIP is its trade secret and the aforementioned activities of defendants constitute misappropriation of a trade secret in violation of G.S. 66-152, et seq.

On 19 July 1991, the trial court entered a temporary restraining order enjoining defendants from selling or licensing any software product which uses the trade secrets of plaintiff and further enjoined defendants from modifying the COMPU-RIP software.[8] At the preliminary injunction hearing, the trial court, after considering the pleadings, affidavits and arguments of counsel, entered an order on

30 August 1991 granting plaintiff's motion for preliminary injunction. By means of this order, defendants were prohibited from:[9]

1. *Marketing, offering for sale or license any software product relating to computer assistance or control of the operation of a gang rip saw;*
2. *Modifying in any manner any software product which has been sold by the Plaintiff to any third party, or offering to perform such services; and*
3. *Disclosing or attempting to disclose to any third party any information related to the software products of the Plaintiff, including, but not limited to the Plaintiff's product COMPU-RIP.*

The trial court further ordered an injunction bond in the amount of $10,000. On 5 September 1991, defendant made a Motion for Reconsideration and Motion to Dissolve Preliminary Injunction.[10] The trial court denied this motion by order entered 14 October 1991.[11]

Opinion by Judge Walker[12]

* * *[13]

Under the North Carolina Trade Secret Protection Act, a trade secret is defined as follows[14]:

[B]usiness or technical information, including but not limited to a formula, pattern, program, device, compilation of information, method, technique, or process that:

a. Derives independent actual or potential commercial value from not being generally known or readily ascertainable through independent development or reverse engineering by persons who can obtain economic value from its disclosure or use; and
b. Is the subject of efforts that are reasonable under the circumstances to maintain its secrecy.

G.S. 66-152(3).[15] "Misappropriation" occurs when there is:

[A]cquisition, disclosure, or use of a trade secret of another without express or implied authority or consent, unless such trade secret was arrived at by independent development, reverse engineering, or was obtained from another person with a right to disclose the trade secret.

G.S. 66-152(1).[16] In the present case, defendants contend the COMPU-RIP software is not a trade secret and that even if it is a trade secret, defendants' actions do not constitute "misappropriation."

According to defendants, the COMPU-RIP software is not a trade secret since it is (1) not subject to reasonable efforts to maintain its secrecy and (2) defendants reverse engineered this software.[17] In order to answer the question of whether plaintiff took reasonable efforts to maintain the secrecy of the COMPU-RIP software, it is necessary to be familiar with the form in which this software was distributed. The COMPU-RIP software is contained in the form of "programmable read-only memory chips" (PROMS) imbedded in the COMPU-RIP machinery. These PROMS contain only the "object code" version of the computer program. This is the version of the computer software which is "read" by the computer's machinery. Computer programmers do not write computer software in object code; rather, the software is written in "source code" and then translated into object code so that the computer can execute the program. *See* Comment, *The Incompatibility of Copyright and Computer Software: An Economic Evaluation and a Proposal for a Marketplace Solution*, 66 N. C. L. Rev. 977, 979 n.14 (1988).[18] Since the COMPU-RIP software was sold in PROM form, the source code was not available to the general public. At least one court has found that as regards computer software, the secrecy component of a trade secret is not compromised when only the object code version of the software is distributed to customers. *Q-CO Industries, Inc. v. Hoffman*, 625 F. Supp. 608, 617–618 (S.D.N.Y. 1985).[19]

* * *

Defendants next argue that plaintiff was not entitled to a preliminary injunction since it has not established misappropriation of its trade secret.[20] A *prima facie* case of misappropriation is established where plaintiff presents substantial evidence that (1) defendant knows or should have known of the trade secret; and (2) defendant has had a specific opportunity to acquire the trade secret.[21] G.S. 66-155. Here, a *prima facie* case of misappropriation exists since defendant Browning helped to develop the COMPU-RIP software during his employ with plaintiff and Browning had access to copies of the COMPU-RIP source code prior to his resignation. Further, according to its president, plaintiff invested eight man-years in the development of the COMPU-RIP system. Toombs and Ruggles stated in their affidavits that in order to make modifications to the COMPU-RIP software, access to the source code is required; it is practically impossible to make any substantial modification to COMPU-RIP possessing only the object code. After reviewing the record from the preliminary injunction hearing, we find plaintiff has shown a likelihood of success on the merits of its case.[22]

* * *

The North Carolina Court of Appeals basically affirmed the decision of the trial court to place an injunction on the defendant, preventing him from marketing his competing software product.

BRIEFING A CASE

Most cases are much longer than the excerpts that are reproduced in this textbook. The idea behind "briefing" a case is to cut right to the essence of the legal issues at stake in the case and strip away as much other discussion as possible. A case is *briefed* when

1. **There is a brief statement of the relevant facts.** In Case 1-2 the facts are italicized and are taken from a court syllabus. In most of the rest of the cases presented in this textbook, the facts will be a combination of material from the case itself and some paraphrasing from the authors.
   a. In briefing the facts of the case, it is a good idea to identify the parties by status. Is the plaintiff a customer, a government, a purchaser? Is the defendant a seller, a corporation, a foreign national?
   b. From the excerpt provided, try to get in the habit of summarizing the facts in two or three sentences. It is not possible to do this in all cases, but it is a good goal to work toward.

Sample Statement of Facts

Plaintiff/Barr-Mullin was in the business of selling lumber processing equipment that makes use of software programs that provide a lumber optimization system for customers in the wordworking industry. One of plaintiff's software programs was called COMPU-RIP, which was developed by defendant/Browning, who was an independent software developer, but who later became employed by plaintiff. Plaintiff distributed his software in object code, which means that it could be read by computers but not by computer programmers. In 1990 defendant informed plaintiff that he wished to establish his own company and shortly thereafter he began selling a lumber optimization system known as LumberScan and also was hired as a consultant by a number of plaintiff's former customers to work on customizing COMPU-RIP for their companies. Plaintiff filed suit and sought a temporary restraining order to prevent defendant from selling his computer program that plaintiff claims was the result of a misappropriation of the plaintiff's trade secrets.

2. **There is an issue that is phrased as a one-sentence question.**
   a. The issue should be stated as narrowly as possible. In virtually every case the issue is whether the defendant is liable to the plaintiff, so a broad statement of the issue is not appropriate. In some opinions the court will explicitly state what the issue is and in others it is for the student to determine.
   b. The issue should originate from the facts that the student considers relevant.

Sample Statement of the Issue

The court dealt with two issues in this case: Did the plaintiff use adequate security to protect COMPU-RIP as a trade secret? and (2) did it make out a prima facie case for its contention that the defendant misappropriated its COMPU-RIP trade secret?

3. **A discussion that states who wins the case, the holding in the case, and the rationale for the decision.** The court's decision involves a mix of facts and the law to arrive at a conclusion.
   a. The conclusion should answer the question posed in the issue generally with a rule of law that is often labeled a "holding" by the court.
   b. Just because a party is successful in this case does not mean that the party enjoys ultimate success. Often, the plaintiff is appealing the granting of a motion to dismiss. If the plaintiff is successful on appeal, it does not mean that the plaintiff wins the case but simply that the granting of the motion to dismiss is reversed and the case goes to trial.

Sample Decision with Winner, Holding, and Rationale

Decision   *The plaintiff wins this case, which is an appeal by the defendant of a decision of the trial court that the plaintiff is entitled to a preliminary injunction, pending a verdict on the merits when the case goes to trial. As a result of this decision, the defendant is prohibited from marketing any software program relating to the control of a gang rip saw, marketing any software program offered by the plaintiff, or* *offering to service same, and from disclosing to any third party pertinent information relating to the plaintiff's software.*

Holding   *The North Carolina Court of Appeals* **held** *that plaintiff provided adequate security for its software by distributing the software only in the form of object code.*

Rationale   *Firms that sell software licenses typically protect the secrecy of their software by distributing the software only as object code so that it cannot be operated on by other programmers. To require more measures to protect secrecy is unreasonable. Requiring more security would make it impossible for software developers to license their products.*

Holding   *The North Carolina Court of Appeals also* **held** *that the defendant knew or should have known that the plaintiff's software program was a trade secret and that the defendant had access to COMPU-RIP source code prior to his resignation. Thus, a prima facie case of trade secret misappropriation was made out and the preliminary injunction was appropriate.*

Rationale   *Since COMPU-RIP was distributed as object code, only the defendant's access to the source code while he was an employee explains how the defendant was able to develop his own program that competed with plaintiff's product. Thus, it was reasonable to place the burden on defendant to show that he did not misappropriate the plaintiff's trade secrets.*

As mentioned above, briefing a case is challenging at first, but once that skill is achieved, it is not generally forgotten. Try to be as narrow as possible in defining the issue in a case and use as much legalese as is appropriate, because legalese provides an efficient way of communicating in a court setting. Good luck!

Endnotes

1. The first line of a case excerpt lists the parties. The order of the parties does not indicate whether the party is the plaintiff or the defendant.

2. The second line identifies the court that is hearing the case. In this case, it is the North Carolina Court of Appeals. The vast majority of the cases in this or any textbook are appellate cases that have been appealed from a trial court. Basically, the "facts" of a case are established at the trial court level and the appeal is based on a point of law.

3. This line in the brief is what is known as the citation. The citation enables researchers and students to look up the case. Many universities have Lexis-Nexis, which allows students to *Get a Case* by inserting these numbers into a legal search engine. The first digits in the citation (cite) is the volume number, 108 in this case. The middle abbreviations are the name of the court reporter, which is the court reporter for the North Carolina Appeals Courts. The final number is the page number. With the citation a stu-

dent could go to a law library and look up a paper copy of the entire case. With Lexis-Nexis or Westlaw (another electronic law library), students can bring up the entire case by inserting the aforementioned citation into a legal search engine.

4. For most cases in this book, the Statement of Facts will be composed by the authors with liberal paraphrasing of the facts of the case as stated by the judge in the case. In this case, we simply reproduced the court Syllabus because it states the facts so directly that there was no need to paraphrase.

5. The plaintiff's claim for injunctive relief means that the plaintiff is seeking an equitable remedy in addition to monetary compensation for damages allegedly incurred as a result of the trade secret misappropriation (legalese for taking without justification).

6. Notice how the court identifies the plaintiff by status.

7. Notice how the court identifies the defendant by status.

8. A temporary restraining order (TRO) is a temporary injunction. If the plaintiff wins at trial, the injunction can become permanent.

9. The substance of the injunction is described in (1)–(3) below in the text.

10. The defendant made a motion to the trial court to reconsider the trial court's granting of the plaintiff's motion for a temporary injunction until trial.

11. The trial court denied the motion to reconsider and the defendant is appealing that denial.

12. The judge writing the opinion is Judge Walker.

13. Three stars indicate that something from the opinion, in this case the beginning, has been deleted. Remember that the cases you see in this textbook are only excerpts. To get the full case, go to a law library or use Lexis-Nexis.

14. The North Carolina Trade Secret Protection Act is a state statute passed by the North Carolina State Legislature.

15. G.S. stands for General Statutes. G.S. 66-152(3) means that a *trade secret* is defined by the 66th Chapter, Section 152(3) of the North Carolina General Statutes.

16. This section of the North Carolina General Statutes defines "Misappropriation."

17. The contentions advanced by the parties appealing, often called the appellants, are often the key to correctly identifying the relevant issues in the case. In this case the defendants contend that (1) the materials they used were not trade secrets and (2) even if they were trade secrets, they (the defendants) obtained these trade secrets honestly and legally.

18. This is a law review article that the court is relying on for technical information and to bolster the contention that the release of object code does not constitute a release of trade secrets.

19. This North Carolina court is citing a New York court precedent as support for the proposition that release of a

computer program in the form of object code does not constitute release of the trade secrets embedded in the program.

20. The opinion is now dealing with the second contention advanced by the defendants in note 17 above.

21. A prima facie case means that the plaintiff has presented enough evidence to avoid having this case dismissed. Once a prima facie case has been established, the burden of producing evidence shifts to the defendant to rebut the inference that the plaintiff is entitled to a judgment.

22. The injunction is appropriate because the trial court is entitled to use its discretion in granting the motion once a prima facie case in favor of the plaintiff has been shown. The facts reviewed in the paragraph clearly establish a prima facie case that (1) the defendant knew or should have known that plaintiff did have trade secrets wrapped up in his software and (2) the defendant had access to those trade secrets. Without an injunction, irreparable harm could occur to the plaintiff, because distribution of the defendant's product would make the plaintiff's trade secret no longer secret.

Chapter Two

The Court System and Jurisdiction

Learning Objectives

After completing this chapter, you should

1. Know the basic components and structures of federal and state court systems.
2. Understand the differing roles of trial and appeals courts.
3. Be able to explain the nature and importance of jurisdiction and venue concepts.
4. Know the roles the Supreme Court plays in our legal system.
5. Be able to work with and explain the concepts of standing and justiciability.

THE COURT SYSTEM—OVERVIEW

In recent years, television shows that feature courtroom drama have been quite popular, with large audiences watching *L.A. Law, Law and Order,* and *Judging Amy.* Most of the court proceedings (litigation) featured on television deal with criminal law, are dramatic, and are neatly resolved in one hour. Most litigation that affects businesses is concerned with civil law, is not dramatic, and, unfortunately, often takes place over a long period of time, sometimes several years, with outcomes not nearly so tidy as hoped for.

The court system in the United States where actual litigation takes place is unique in a number of ways, as explored below. In general, the structure of American court systems can be visualized as triangular (or as a pyramid). Trial courts, by far the greatest in number, are at the bottom of the triangle, above which are appellate courts, that are far fewer. At the apex of the court structure triangle is a *supreme court.* The triangular model, illustrated in the "Nutz and Boltz" box, applies to both federal and state court systems.

An important practical consideration in court procedures, and one that is largely ignored in television dramas, involves **jurisdiction.** Specific courts have specific assigned "turf," or jurisdiction, largely based on geography but, in some cases, based on subject matter. If a website located in New Mexico could be hauled into court in New Hampshire for an allegedly defective product, its potential legal liability is radically different than if the New Hampshire consumer has to travel to New Mexico to sue the owner of the website. How important these alternative forms of jurisdictional burdens are is sensitive to the amount at stake in a lawsuit and the significance of jurisdiction. If potential damages are large, say several million dollars, then plaintiffs are less reluctant to sue defendants, even if the plaintiff has to travel to the defendant's home state. On the other hand, the fact that a plaintiff has

jurisdiction
Authority over the persons and subject matter of litigation, entitling a court to hear and adjudicate a specific action.

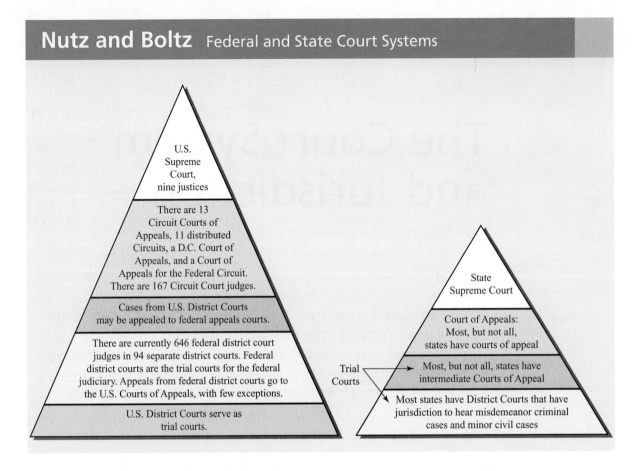

Nutz and Boltz   Federal and State Court Systems

to travel to the defendant's state to sue often makes lawsuits whose damages are moderate uneconomical. Needless to say, jurisdiction issues are of considerable importance in legal disagreements involving businesses. Hence, part of this chapter must be spent on exploring mechanisms for determining jurisdiction.

THE FEDERAL COURT SYSTEM

As indicated in the diagram above, the federal court *system* includes district courts, appellate courts, and the U.S. Supreme Court.

District Courts

federal district courts
District courts are trial courts in the federal court system. As trial courts, district courts serve as the finders of fact in federal court cases.

The U.S. Constitution authorizes creation of the U.S. Supreme Court and "such inferior Courts as the Congress may from time to time ordain and establish."[1] Congress has authorized *trial courts* in the federal system, called **federal district courts,** for which there are currently 94 federal district courthouses and 646 district court judges if all positions were filled, as indicated in the "Nutz and Boltz" box. Trial courts have *original*

[1] U.S. Constitution, art. III, § 1.

jurisdiction, which means that *evidence is presented in district courts* and *district courts find the facts* in the case at trial. Based on the evidence presented, either through a jury verdict or with the district court judge operating as both judge and jury if the parties waive their rights to a jury, district courts endeavor to apply the law to the facts presented to produce a trial result (verdict). During the process of finding facts, trial court judges in district courts must make rulings on procedural issues, such as admissibility of evidence and various motions by plaintiffs and defendants.[2] In general, it is the *legal decisions* made by the trial court judge that form the basis for appeals. Many of the legal decisions made by trial court judges that can be appealed involve *procedural* law such as rules for admission of evidence. Many of the other legal decisions that a trial court judge makes, however, concern both procedural and substantive law, such as jury instructions and rulings on motions: to dismiss, for a summary judgment, and for a directed verdict.[3] Virtually all of the cases explored in this textbook are based on appeals of decisions of trial courts, with many focused on flawed decisions judges made on various aspects of procedural and substantive law.

Federal Appellate Courts

courts of appeals
Courts above trial courts to which trial court decisions can be appealed if the appellant believes the trial court committed reversible error in its application of procedural law.

As illustrated in Figure 2.1, there are eleven U.S. **courts of appeals,** geographically dispersed across the United States, plus another "standard" appeals court for the District of Columbia. There is also a Court of Appeals for the Federal Circuit (CAFC) that deals with appeals involving IP, such as patents, copyrights, and trademarks. The entire United States is divided into 11 circuits, and there is a federal court of appeals for each circuit (see Figure 2.1 for a map of the United States divided up into federal circuits). Appeals, or *appellate,* courts handle appeals that come not only from rulings made by district courts, but also from "court-like" rulings issued by some administrative agencies such as the Patent and Trademark Office, the Federal Trade Commission, and the National Labor Relations Board. Generally, cases on appeal are heard by a three-judge panel, though in some cases the entire court (the court of appeals *en banc*) hears an appeal. The number of judges on the federal courts of appeals varies from 6 in the First Circuit to 28 in the Ninth Circuit (see Figure 2.1 for the location of the First and Ninth Circuits) and is largely linked to the volume of litigation work needed.

What Appellate Courts Do and Don't Do

As discussed above, federal district courts are *trial courts* and they are expected to find the facts in cases brought to court. Judges in these trial courts are supposed to supervise and ensure the fair and orderly presentation of evidence from both plaintiffs and defendants. In parallel fashion, administrative agencies have their own administrative law judges who conduct "trials" (usually called *hearings*) and also make findings of fact, rendering judgments based on applying relevant substantive law to the facts revealed. In general, an appeal to appellate courts, including U.S. courts of appeals, based on a dispute over the factual findings of district courts or administrative agencies does not have a strong foundation for a successful appeal. Since the evidence in a case is presented at a trial or hearing before a jury or a trial court judge, they (a jury or trial court judge) are in a better position than appellate judges to evaluate the evidence. For example, unlike a jury or trial

---

[2] Motions are discussed in some detail below and are a major topic in Chapter 3. The movant is the party making the motion, which is a request to the judge to rule in a certain way on a discretionary matter before the judge.

[3] All of these motions are discussed in detail in Chapter 3.

FIGURE 2.1
U.S. Courts of Appeals Circuits

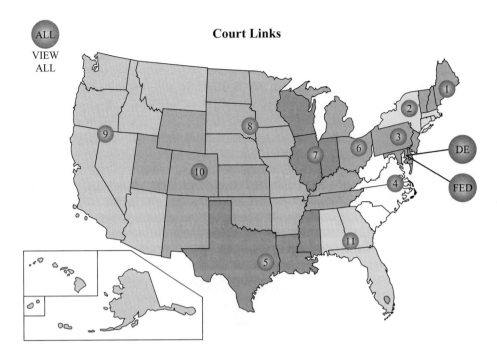

court judge, appellate court judges do not get to see the demeanor of witnesses testifying, which can be a large clue as to the veracity of witnesses. To successfully appeal a factual decision made by a jury or judge about the evidence, the appealing party generally has to show that some outside factor, such as jury tampering, influenced the decision of the jury, or that the factual findings of the trial court judge were "clearly erroneous."[4]

Appeals Based on Errors of Law

At the trial court level, there are a multitude of rules that govern the presentation of evidence and correctly interpreting those rules is not always simple or straightforward. For example, in many cases, a defendant will make a *motion* to have the case dismissed because the defendant contends that the evidence is too weak to merit a trial. If the defendant's motion to dismiss is granted, the case is over and the only option for the plaintiff is to appeal [to an appellate court] the decision of the trial court judge to grant the motion to dismiss. Alternatively, if the motion to dismiss is denied by the trial court judge, and the case does go to trial, the defendant can appeal the denial of the motion to dismiss to the appropriate court of appeals. Granting or not granting a motion to dismiss by the trial court judge is a potential *error of law* that can be appealed (to a court of appeals) for review and is a frequent source of the cases used in this textbook.

Potential errors of law also are committed when the trial court judge issues instructions to juries, rules on other motions, and makes decisions to admit or not admit certain evidence. To merit a hearing at the appellate level, the claimed legal error must be of sufficient magnitude to potentially, *materially alter* the verdict reached by a trial court. Only prospectively **reversible error** provides a basis for appeal.

reversible error
An error in the application of procedural law of sufficient importance in a trial to form a basis for appeal of the trial outcome.

---

[4] Factual findings of trial court judges or administrative law judges are sometimes overturned by courts of appeals when the factual findings of the trial courts or administrative law judges are "clearly erroneous."

U.S. Supreme Court

U.S. Supreme Court
The highest court in the land, serving primarily as an appeals court, but also as a trial court for disputes between states.

The **U.S. Supreme Court** is staffed by nine justices, headed by the Chief Justice (biographical sketches of the currently seated Supreme Court justices are available at http://www.supremecourtus.gov/about/biographiescurrent.pdf). Except for rare cases involving litigation between states, the Supreme Court is primarily an appellate court.[5] So the Supreme Court spends nearly the entirety of its time and effort determining whether lower level courts made errors of law, either at the trial court level or at the level of courts of appeals, in which opinions affirming or reversing decisions of trial courts are made. In cases appealed to the Supreme Court, there is no fact testimony or other fact evidence presented as the focus is on proper interpretation and application of the law. A highly important aspect of this Court's function as the arbiter of the supreme law of the land is the issuance of *Supreme Court opinions,* which explain the Court's reasoning and, in many cases, set legal standards for subsequent related cases.

Case Selection of the Supreme Court: Writs of Certiorari

writ of certiorari
Official written notice of a higher court decision that it wishes to receive the lower court's record of a case. Such a writ serves as notice that the higher court will review the identified case from the lower court.

The U.S. Supreme Court receives vastly more requests for case review than it is possible to hear. In 1999 alone, there were some 7,000 appeals to the Supreme Court. So, this court is highly selective in the cases it chooses to hear, having rendered decisions in only about 100 cases annually in recent years. A request to the Supreme Court for review of a case is called a *petition for certiorari*. If the Supreme Court agrees to hear a case appeal, it provides official notice of that decision in the form of granting a **writ of certiorari.** In general, the Supreme Court will choose to render a decision on a case if at least four justices recommend that the case be added to the Supreme Court docket. If the Supreme Court refuses to grant a writ of certiorari, the prior decision in that particular case is final. A Supreme Court decision to refuse a writ of certiorari does not mean that the Court agrees with the prior (district court or appeals court) decision. It can simply mean that the Supreme Court at that point in time attaches a higher priority to other cases it has been asked to hear. The fact that the case was appealed to the U.S. Supreme Court and the Supreme Court refused to hear the case *does not create a precedent* that the Supreme Court agrees with the decision of the lower courts.

The Supreme Court tends to accept appeals of

- Cases that involve constitutional issues of law.
- Cases in which the Supreme Court can resolve significant differences in rulings by different courts of appeals.
- Cases that are considered *ripe*—that is, representative cases of a kind appearing in appeals courts in significant volume, indicating that guidance from the Supreme Court in trial court adjudication of such cases is needed.

The Supreme Court, then, is continuously hearing high-profile cases involving hotly debated issues. In recent years, the Court has ruled in cases involving abortion rights; rights of defendants in criminal cases; citizens' rights to protection from government snooping with heat-sensing, imaging technology; and even voters' rights in a presidential election. As technology (making possible thermal imaging, and so on) and societal mores (acceptance of diversity, among others) change, there is accompanying pressure on existing law to

---

[5] In impeachment proceedings involving the president, the Chief Justice of the U.S. Supreme Court presides over the proceedings.

Nutz and Boltz

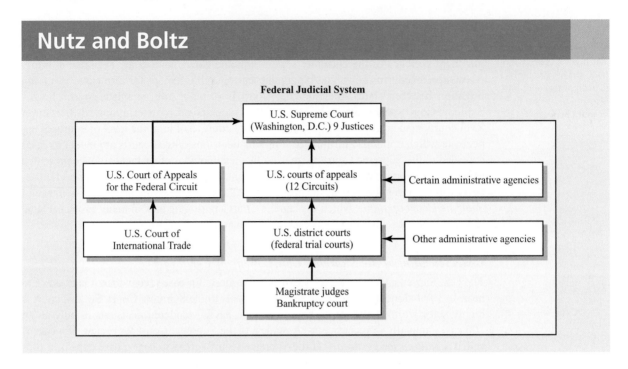

Federal Judicial System

change. Technological and societal pressures often result in acceptance of appeals by the Supreme Court when the Court considers such cases ripe for resolution.

Opinions of the Supreme Court

In Court decisions, each of the nine justices on the Supreme Court, including the Chief Justice, has an equal vote. Of course, with nine justices, there can be differing opinions on cases reviewed. Still, some Supreme Court decisions are *unanimous,* with all nine justices in agreement. *Such decisions set precedent for later cases.* Many other case outcomes are determined by *majority decision.* In such cases, there is a majority opinion written describing the court's decision and the majority reasoning that provides the basis for that decision. *Majority opinions also set precedent for subsequent cases.* In majority opinion cases, there also can be one or more *dissenting opinions* published. In addition, a justice who agrees with a decision, but has a rationale for the decision that differs from that of other justices, can write a *concurring opinion* that explains his or her reasoning. If a majority of the justices agree on a case decision, but cannot agree on the reasoning that supports the decision, the Court has delivered a *plurality decision.* The decision reached resolves the particular case, but *does not set precedent* for subsequent cases. If for some reason, such as the illness and absence of a justice, a tie decision is reached on a case, the lower court's ruling (which was appealed) is affirmed, with no presumption regarding precedent (just as if the case had not been accepted for review).

Other Federal Courts

For a variety of purposes, additional *specialized courts* exist at the federal level. So, there are a federal Tax Court, a federal bankruptcy court, a Court of Veterans Appeals, military courts, a U.S. Court of Federal Claims, and a Court of International Trade. In addition, as mentioned above, there are various federal administrative agencies with some court-like

Nutz and Boltz   What Is a Magistrate in the Federal Court System and What Do They Do?

According to the website for the U.S. judiciary (http://www.uscourts.gov),

A U.S. magistrate judge is a judicial officer of the district court and is appointed by majority vote of the active district judges of the court to exercise jurisdiction over matters assigned by statute as well as those delegated by the district judges. The number of magistrate judge positions is determined by the Judicial Conference of the United States, based on recommendations of the respective district courts, the judicial councils of the circuits, and the Director of the Administrative Office of the U.S. Courts. A full-time magistrate judge serves a term of eight

years. Duties assigned to magistrate judges by district court judges may vary considerably from court to court.

On the criminal side, one of the main tasks of magistrates is to sign *search and arrest warrants* upon a showing of probable cause by a law enforcement officer. In civil procedure, magistrates perform a number of tasks including conducting a civil trial, if both parties agree. Mainly, magistrates are in a subordinate position relative to federal district court judges and assist as requested. The Federal Rules of Civil Procedure (discussed in Chapter 3) refer to "magistrates" 46 times.

duties. Appeals from U.S. Bankruptcy Court go to federal district courts. Appeals from a number of administrative agencies' decisions are directed toward the U.S. courts of appeals, while appeals from other administrative agencies go to U.S. district courts.

STATE COURT SYSTEMS

Trial Courts

state court systems
Paralleling the federal court system, state court systems have trial courts (generally designated as district, superior, or circuit courts), courts of appeals, and state supreme courts.

For most states, the structure of the **state court system** resembles the federal structure. Thus, at the bottom of the state court system triangle there are numerous trial courts as well as some specialized courts such as small claims, probate, and juvenile. In many states trial courts are divided between district courts and superior courts. Typically, state *district* courts deal with civil litigation when the amount in dispute is fairly modest (less than $10,000 to $20,000, varying by state) and with *misdemeanors* on the criminal side. Superior Courts handle larger-value civil cases and criminal *felony* cases. Among the states, there is a good deal of variation in court systems; for example, some states have circuit courts instead of district and superior courts, but there are also a number of fundamental regularities common across states. As with the federal court system, the functions of state trial courts and other specialized courts at the state level are to determine the facts in disputes between litigants and, by ensuring the fair application of the law to those revealed facts, to provide resolutions of cases brought to trial.

Appellate Courts

In about one-fourth of the states, the only appellate court is the state supreme court. In the other, generally larger, states, there are intermediate courts of appeals that dispose of most appeals from trial courts. State supreme courts are called "courts of last resort," which they are as long as the point of law upon which an appeal is brought only involves *state law*. As an example, consider a contract law dispute between private citizens or companies involving the sale of goods. Since all 50 states have passed the Uniform Commercial Code, which governs the sale of goods, there is no such thing as federal contract law that involves sale-of-goods contracts between citizens. Contract law addressing the sale of goods is based on a state statute—in this example, the Uniform Commercial Code. If a case involving a point of contract law was appealed to the *state* supreme court, it would be the court of last resort for the appellant (the party filing the appeal, either the plaintiff or defendant). If the appellant was unsuccessful in his appeal to the state supreme court, he could not appeal to federal courts unless, somehow, federal law was involved in his contract claim or defense, which is very unlikely.

On the other hand, in a case involving *federal law* (constitutional, statutory, or regulatory), the decision of a state supreme court is not final. It is common for appeals from state supreme courts to federal courts to occur in

1. The prosecution of criminal actions, particularly in capital (death penalty) cases.
2. Cases involving state laws that interfere with interstate commerce.
3. Cases applying state laws that involve fundamental constitutional issues also involving race, abortion, and due process.

Appeals in these cases generally involve federal constitutional law, over which the U.S. Supreme Court has final say.

Specialized State Courts

In all states, there are specialized courts that only handle certain kinds of cases. It is common for states to have a *juvenile court* to deal with underage criminal offenders. State *small claims courts* are common for disputes that do not involve enough money to justify hiring an attorney. Most states also have *probate courts* that supervise the disposition of assets of deceased people and resolve disputes between beneficiaries of a deceased's will. Some states have separate *domestic courts* that deal with divorce, child support, and custody disputes. In most cases, appeals from these specialized courts go to district or superior courts in that state.

JURISDICTION

As is the case with many legal terms, *jurisdiction* is a term derived from Latin. Jurisdiction literally means *to speak the law*. If a court does not have jurisdiction (the right to speak the law) over a dispute and the persons involved, it is not able to resolve that dispute. In general, jurisdictional disputes involve attempts by the defendant(s) to resist the jurisdiction of a court in which a plaintiff has filed a complaint. There are several dimensions to jurisdiction and determination of jurisdiction is aided by proper categorization of disputes.

Jurisdiction Terminology

Original and Appellate Jurisdiction

A trial court hears evidence from the litigants (plaintiff and defendant), makes factual determinations with the aid of a jury or by a judge alone with litigant's approval, and renders a verdict. In the course of this process, trial courts are said to have *original jurisdiction*. When a case is appealed to the appellate courts, the jurisdiction of appellate courts is called *appellate jurisdiction*. U.S. courts of appeals and the U.S. Supreme Court have appellate jurisdiction, as do state supreme courts and state courts of appeals.

Subject Matter and Personal Jurisdiction

Other important dimensions of jurisdiction are labeled *subject matter jurisdiction* and *jurisdiction over the person*. A plaintiff must select a court that is viewed as having dominion over *both* of these dimensions of jurisdiction. A case begins when a plaintiff files a complaint in a court that he or she believes has jurisdiction over the defendant. Defendants can resist jurisdiction by filing a *motion to dismiss* for lack of jurisdiction. The trial court can agree with the defendant and dismiss a case by granting the motion. Of course, by failing to grant the motion (denying the motion), the court affirms the plaintiff's choice of jurisdiction. The trial court's decision on the defendant's motion may be appealed to an appellate court, which could overturn the trial court's decision regarding jurisdiction over the defendant.

Subject Matter Jurisdiction   Recall that there are a number of specialized courts at both the state and federal levels. These courts only have subject matter jurisdiction over their designated area of specialization, so the jurisdiction of specialized courts is strictly limited. Federal bankruptcy courts do not have subject matter jurisdiction over cases that involve violations of federal criminal law. If the amount in dispute exceeds more than $1,000 to $5,000 (depending on the state), state small claims courts do not have subject matter jurisdiction over the dispute. Subject matter jurisdiction is generally clear and is not a major source of litigation.

General Jurisdiction   At both the federal and state levels, trial courts have *general jurisdiction* over a wide variety of cases. These courts, called district, superior, or circuit courts at the state level, have original jurisdiction over both civil and criminal cases. In some cases, appeals from specialized courts go to district courts and, under some circumstances, these cases are tried again in front of such trial courts. At the federal level, as we know, the district courts are trial courts and, as such, they have original jurisdiction over civil and criminal disputes—they have general jurisdiction.

Jurisdiction over the Person: State Courts

With regard to *jurisdiction over the person,* the sovereignty of a state's authority extends to the borders of the state. A court in the state of Florida cannot adjudicate a dispute between New York City and a citizen of New Jersey. The general rule is that state courts only have jurisdiction to decide disputes that arise within the borders of the state, though this general rule is subject to a number of exceptions. Illustratively, state courts can exercise jurisdiction over not only citizens of the state but also residents of the state (who are not citizens). State courts also can exercise jurisdiction over an out-of-state business that does business within the state. What determines whether a firm is "doing business" within a state for jurisdictional purposes is subject to argument, and is addressed in litigation by application of a legal doctrine referred to as the "minimum contacts" rule.

long-arm statutes
State laws that allow states to exercise jurisdiction over non-residents if certain qualifying conditions, usually the existence of minimum contacts, are met.

minimum contacts
Indicators of whether a nonresident (to a state) firm has taken advantage of the benefits of having a presence of some type within a host state, enabling the host state to exert jurisdiction over the nonresident firm.

Long-Arm Statutes

Many states have enacted **long-arm statutes** that enable them to exercise jurisdiction over nonresident people and businesses if certain conditions are present. For nonresident *persons,* long-arm statutes enable state courts to have jurisdiction over nonresidents that either (1) commit a within-the-state tort (a legal wrong, such as injuring a state resident while driving negligently on an in-state road) or (2) form a contract within the state. For *businesses,* the **minimum contacts** test is applied to activities of out-of-state businesses in order to determine whether a state court has jurisdiction. Certainly, if a business is incorporated within a state or has a branch of its operations within a state, it is subject to the jurisdiction of that state. In general, courts look at whether the out-of-state business has *purposely availed* itself of the benefits of operating within the state. If the out-of-state business owns property within the state, sends employees to the state, or even directs advertising to the specific state, it is subject to jurisdiction of that state's courts.

Limits of State Long-Arm Statutes   The rationale for long-arm statutes is this: if an out-of-state entity is going to take advantage of the benefits of state enforcement of property rights, then it also should be subject to the jurisdiction of state courts. Typically, when the issue of jurisdiction is unclear, state courts have been inclined to rule that they have jurisdiction over businesses that have some contact with their state. A number of cases involving this issue have been appealed to the U.S. Supreme Court, which often has scaled back the reach of long-arm statutes applied by state courts. Notably, in several cases involving state sales taxes on sales by out-of-state businesses to in-state residents, the Supreme Court has ruled that mail order companies are *not* subject to the jurisdiction of remote state courts if the only contact of the mail order companies with the state is sending catalogs and taking orders.[6] The Supreme Court also has ruled that mere knowledge that a firm's product will end up in a state is not a sufficient basis for the exercise of state jurisdiction. If a hardware store sells shingles to a builder who has frequent construction jobs out of state, the hardware store is not subject to these other states' jurisdiction (say, for faulty shingle claims) on that basis alone.

Long-Arm Statutes and the Internet   Internet websites must be concerned with the exercise of jurisdiction by state courts (and the courts of other countries because sales could be made to residents of other countries). Websites are, of course, accessible anywhere in the world. If accessibility were the criteria, then every website would be subject to the jurisdiction of every state court in the United States. In concept, it can be argued that a website is not much different from a mail order catalog vendor. This analogy appears apt at this point in time as courts have agreed that merely being accessible to residents of a state (online) is not enough to subject a website to the jurisdiction of such a state. However, there have been cases that have held that, if a website supplements its contact with residents of states through emails and phone calls, such additional activity is enough to give a state jurisdiction over the website. Given the newness of e-commerce and the Internet, hard-and-fast rules have not been established as to just when website interaction with residents of a state gives that state power to exercise jurisdiction over the website whose owners do not reside within the state. Consider the following case and what factors the courts used to determine whether the minimum contacts test was satisfied.

[6] *National Bella Hess, Inc. v. Dept. of Revenue of the State of Illinois,* 386 U.S. 753 (1967).

Case 2-1

David Mink, Plaintiff-Appellant, v. AAAA Development LLC

United States Court of Appeals, Fifth Circuit
190 F.3d 333 (5th Cir. 1999)

BACKGROUND AND FACTS

David Mink is a Texas resident who works in the retail furniture business. In January 1997, Mink claims that he began to develop a computer program, the Opportunity Tracking Computer System (OTC), designed to track information on sales made and opportunities missed on sales not made. On May 13, 1997, Mink submitted a patent application for the computer software and hardware that he developed to the United States Patent and Trademark Office. He also submitted a copyright application for the

OTC to the United States Copyright Office. Mink claims that AAAA Development and David Middle-brook infringed his copyright and patent. AAAA Development is a Vermont corporation with its principal place of business in Vermont. Middlebrook is a Vermont resident. Neither AAAA Development nor Middlebrook own property in Texas. Mink is silent concerning where his contacts with the defendants occurred. The company has advertised in a national furniture trade journal and maintains a website advertising its sales management software on the Internet.

Opinion by: Robert M. Parker, Circuit Judge

The sole issue on appeal is whether the district court erred in dismissing defendants AAAA and Middlebrook for a lack of personal jurisdiction. The district court's determination of the exercise of personal jurisdiction over a defendant is a question of law subject to de novo review. [References deleted] When a nonresident defendant challenges personal jurisdiction, the plaintiff bears the burden of establishing the district court's jurisdiction over the defendant.

* * *

The "minimum contacts" aspect of the analysis can be established through "contacts that give rise to 'specific' personal jurisdiction or those that give rise to 'general' personal jurisdiction." Specific jurisdiction exists when the nonresident defendant's contacts with the forum state arise from, or are directly related to, the cause of action. General jurisdiction exists when a defendant's contacts with the forum state are unrelated to the cause of action but are "continuous and systematic." Because we conclude that Mink has not established any contacts directly related to the cause of action required for specific jurisdiction, we turn to the question of whether general jurisdiction has been established.

* * *

Courts addressing the issue of whether personal jurisdiction can be constitutionally exercised over a defendant look to the "nature and quality of commercial activity that an entity conducts over the Internet." The *Zippo* decision [a prior case involving a domain name dispute] categorized Internet use into a spectrum of three areas. At the one end of the spectrum, there are situations where a defendant clearly does business over the Internet by entering into contracts with residents of other states which "involve the knowing and repeated transmission of computer files over the Internet. . . ." In this situation, personal jurisdiction is proper. At the other end of the spectrum, there are situations where a defendant merely establishes a passive website that does nothing more than advertise on the Internet. With passive websites, personal jurisdiction is not appropriate. In the middle of the spectrum, there are situations where a defendant has a website that allows a user to exchange information with a host computer. In this middle ground, "the exercise of jurisdiction is determined by the level of interactivity and commercial nature of the exchange of information that occurs on the Website."

Applying these principles to this case, we conclude that AAAA's website is insufficient to subject it to personal jurisdiction. Essentially, AAAA maintains a website that posts information about its products and services. While the website provides users with a printable mail-in order form, AAAA's toll-free telephone number, a mailing address and an electronic mail ("e-mail") address, orders are not taken through AAAA's website. This does not classify the website as anything more than passive advertisement which is not grounds for the exercise of personal jurisdiction.

* * *

This case does not fall into the spectrum of cases where a defendant clearly conducted business over the Internet nor does it fall into the middle spectrum of interactivity where the defendant and users exchange information through the Internet. There was no evidence that AAAA conducted business over the Internet by engaging in business transactions with forum residents or by entering into contracts over the Internet.

We note that AAAA's website provides an e-mail address that permits consumers to interact with the company. There is no evidence, however, that the website allows AAAA to do anything but reply to e-mail initiated by website visitors. In addition, AAAA's website lacks other forms of interactivity cited by courts as factors to consider in determining questions of personal jurisdiction.

For example, AAAA's website does not allow consumers to order or purchase products and services on-line.

* * *

We conclude the district court did not err in dismissing the defendants for lack of personal jurisdiction.

Decision and Outcome

The U.S. Court of Appeals for the Fifth Circuit held that the district court did not err in dismissing the infringement suit against the defendants for lack of jurisdiction because the plaintiff's website was not interactive enough with residents of the state of Texas to justify the exercise of jurisdiction over the defendant.

Questions for Analysis

1. What actions does the court indicate would create jurisdiction in Texas for this Vermont corporation?
2. Does this case stand for the proposition that if a website does not provide an opportunity to buy something, then it escapes jurisdiction of other state courts? How many websites have you visited that do not offer an opportunity to buy something?

Increasingly, websites are anticipating the liability created by expansive state court interpretations of state long-arm statutes and have countered with browse-wrap agreements. Sophisticated websites claim that by browsing through their Web pages, you have entered into a contractual relationship with the website and are bound by the Terms of Service agreement that is hyperlinked at the bottom of the page. Generally the Terms of Service agreement states that by browsing and making use of the website that you also agree to the jurisdiction of courts of the home state of the website owners. Whether browse-wrap agreements are enforceable is questionable, but it is the current tactic being used by most commercial websites.

Jurisdiction of State Courts over Property

Even if a nonresident entity, individual or business, does not have minimum contacts with a state, if the nonresident owns property in a state, courts of that state can exert jurisdiction over the property. Consider a resident of Kansas who dies in Kansas but who owns real estate in the state of Texas. If a potential heir to the Texas property files a claim contesting the disposition of the property by the state of Kansas, the heir can claim that Texas courts have *in rem jurisdiction* over the property located in Texas. The location of the property gives Texas courts jurisdiction over the property even though they did not have jurisdiction over the deceased or the executor of his or her will.

Jurisdiction of Federal Courts

Federal Question

For federal courts, jurisdiction is based on two criteria: (1) the case involves a *federal question* or (2) the case involves parties from *diverse states.* Federal question jurisdiction is present when a case involves federal law, including the U.S. Constitution, a federal statute, or regulation of a federal administrative agency, such as the Environmental Protection Agency. Under such circumstances, a plaintiff is entitled to file a lawsuit in federal court. As an illustration, the Securities Act of 1933 prohibits the sale of unregistered securities (stocks or bonds). Under this act, a resident in any state can file a suit in federal district court based on a claim that (s)he was sold a security that was not registered with the Securities and Exchange Commission.

Diversity Jurisdiction

Diversity jurisdiction is applicable when the parties to a lawsuit reside in separate states and the amount in dispute in the lawsuit exceeds more than $75,000. In diversity claims, there must be no overlap among plaintiffs and defendants in the same state. If there are co-defendants, one residing in the plaintiff's state and one not, diversity jurisdiction is not applicable. A contract dispute between residents of two different states, with an amount in dispute exceeding $75,000, would enable the plaintiff to file the case in federal district court, even if the defendant did not have minimum contacts with the plaintiff's state.

Jurisdictional Relationship between Federal and State Courts

Federal Rules of Civil Procedure   Regardless of whether a federal district court is applying federal or state civil law to a dispute, federal courts use the Federal Rules of Civil Procedure (FRCP), most recently updated in December 2000, to resolve procedural issues.[7] The FRCP govern the details of pleadings, discovery, trial procedures, and motions made by the parties, all of which are discussed in some detail in the next chapter.

The FRCP were enacted as a reaction against complicated common law procedural rules that frequently got in the way of a straightforward presentation of evidence. The philosophy of the FRCP is to direct the court's focus on the essence of what is in dispute while avoiding the waste of time on highly technical exceptions that have crept into procedural law used by many states. Since the FRCP were enacted, many states have substantially modified their own rules of civil procedure to closely imitate the FRCP. State courts use their own procedural rules when a claim is filed in their courts, regardless of whether the claim is based on state or federal law. In spite of the advances that the FRCP created by reducing procedural complexity, highly technical procedural disputes are still common in federal and state courts, which explains in part the increasing popularity of alternative dispute resolution, particularly arbitration (discussed in Chapter 4).

Exclusive and Concurrent Jurisdiction between Federal and State Courts

There are some cases over which state courts have *exclusive jurisdiction,* and the same is true of the federal courts. If a dispute involves state law and both the plaintiff and defendant are residents of a single state, the case must be tried in the courts of that state. There are some types of cases in which state courts have exclusive jurisdiction including probate, domestic law cases dealing with divorce and custody, and juvenile court. If a dispute is between two citizens of separate states, and the dispute involves state law (as in the case of a contract dispute), only state courts have jurisdiction if the amount in dispute is less than $75,000. If the amount in dispute exceeds $75,000, then the plaintiff can choose to file in either state court or federal court.

Exclusive Federal Jurisdiction   Because of language in intellectual property statutes, federal courts have exclusive jurisdiction in cases involving such assets: patents, copyrights, and the like. Other areas of law in which federal courts have exclusive jurisdiction include antitrust, bankruptcy, and trademark suits that involve federal registration. So, if the U.S. Justice Department brings an antitrust suit against Microsoft, that suit will be under the

---

[7] The Federal Rules of Civil Procedure can be accessed at http://www.law.cornell.edu/rules/frcp/overview. htm#chapter_i. Also note that procedural rules in criminal cases are much different.

Nutz and Boltz

Jurisdiction		
Federal Exclusive	**Federal/State Concurrent**	**State Exclusive**
Federal crimes	Any claim based on diversity	Domestic relations
Patents, copyrights, federal trademarks	Federal statutes that do restrict enforcement to federal courts	Juvenile court
Bankruptcy		State contract, tort, and property claims when diversity does not apply
Antitrust		
This list is not exhaustive		This list is not exhaustive

exclusive jurisdiction of a federal court. All criminal prosecutions based on violations of federal law also must begin in federal courts. Despite the existence of what appear to be broad areas of federal court dominion over litigation, the reservation of exclusive jurisdiction to the federal courts for enforcement of a federal statute is the exception, not the norm. Most federal statutes do not prohibit state courts from providing the forum for litigating claims based on federal law; hence, the jurisdiction is *concurrent*.

Consequences of Concurrent Jurisdiction   If a dispute between residents of separate states involves state contract law and the conditions for diversity jurisdiction are present, a federal court hearing the case would be responsible for interpreting and applying *state* law. In like fashion, there are many claims filed by plaintiffs in state courts based on federal law. Unless a federal statute contains language that exclusively allocates jurisdiction for the statute to federal courts, a state court could be responsible for interpreting and applying the federal statute. It is common in employment discrimination suits for plaintiffs to sue under both the 1964 Civil Rights Act (a federal statute) and state antidiscrimination statutes. State courts have been responsible for creating many important precedents involving the Civil Rights Act as a result of such cases. Of course, any ruling of a state court involving a federal question can be appealed to federal courts.

Right of Removal to Federal Court   As discussed above, there are many instances in which plaintiffs can choose between suing in federal court or state court because jurisdiction is concurrent. Being able to choose in which court to file a suit, federal or state, can give plaintiffs a significant advantage in some cases. When a case involves a federal question or diversity jurisdiction, the defendant has the *right to remove* the case to federal court if the plaintiff had filed the claim in state court. The rationale for removal authority is based on suspicion that in-state residents may fare better in their state's courts than will an out-of-state defendant. If the plaintiff is able to haul an out-of-state defendant into the state court of the plaintiff, it is possible that the plaintiff has an edge because some state courts may favor in-state residents. Defendants can neutralize that advantage if they have the power to remove the case to the federal courts when the grounds for federal jurisdiction exist.

Conflicts of Law between States

There are frequent disagreements over what state laws apply to a case. Consider a contract formed in one state but performed in another state. Faced with a contract dispute in

Nutz and Boltz

The following chart exposes some of the jurisdictional intersections between federal and state courts.

Scenario	Courts	Consequence(s)	
A sues B, but B does not have minimum contacts with A's state. The claim is based on state law.	A must pursue litigation in the state courts of B except	If the amount in dispute exceeds $75,000, A can sue in federal court under diversity jurisdiction.	If the amount in dispute does not exceed $75,000, A's only remedy is to sue B in B's state courts.
A sues B, but B does have minimum contacts with A's state. The claim is based on state law.	A can sue B in A's state court	If the amount in dispute exceeds $75,000, B can remove the case to federal court.	If the amount in dispute does not exceed $75,000, B must defend against A's claim in A's state courts.
A sues B, but B does not have minimum contacts with A's state. The claim is based on a federal question.	A can sue in federal court or in B's state courts		
A sues B, but B does have minimum contacts with A's state. The claim is based on a federal question.	As long as federal jurisdiction is concurrent, A can sue B in either federal court or A's state courts	If A sues B in A's state courts, B can remove the case to the federal courts.	If federal jurisdiction is exclusive, then A must sue B in federal courts.
A and B live in the same state and the claim is based on state law.	A must sue in state court		
A and B live in the same state and the claim is based on a federal question.	A can sue B in	Federal or state court if jurisdiction is concurrent.	Only federal court if jurisdiction is exclusive.

this situation, many states apply mechanistic rules to determine jurisdiction (applicable law), with the assignment determined by identifying in which state the contract was made or performed, or by determining which state is most significantly affected by the contract. In tort law, it is generally the state in which the tort occurs that has jurisdiction. In a contract involving a business, a clause within the contract can specify what state laws apply. Such clauses are almost always respected by courts. Needless to say, legally sophisticated businesses seek to incorporate choice-of-state-law clauses in the contracts they enter, both to enjoy the benefit of possibly more favorable law and to avoid extra litigation over choice-of-law issues in the event of contract disputes. In the absence of choice of law clauses in contracts, the state that has the most significant relationships with the parties or the events that give rise to the litigation is the state whose laws determine the outcome of the case.

VENUE

venue
The physical location of
the courthouse where a
suit will be heard.

Venue is the physical location of the courthouse that will hear a case. If both parties to litigation are located within a state, the venue of the case is normally in the county where either the defendant or the plaintiff resides. At the federal level, the plaintiff can only select a federal district court where the plaintiff or defendant lives, or where the events occurred that gave rise to the litigation. There are rare situations in which pretrial publicity makes getting a fair trial in a particular venue difficult or impossible. Such situations generally involve high-profile criminal cases, but on some occasions can affect civil litigation as well. In such situations, a defendant can move for a change of venue because of presumed prejudice of the potential jury pool that has been affected by events giving rise to the litigation. The Timothy McVeigh case was tried outside Oklahoma because of the large number of Oklahomans who had relatives or friends injured or killed when the federal building, the Arthur Murrah building, was bombed by McVeigh.

FORUM NON CONVENIENS

The inconvenience of litigation is recognized by court officials and it is proper for a defendant to make a motion to dismiss a case based on inconvenience. When a party to litigation, presumably the defendant, files a *forum non conveniens* motion to move the trial to another location, the presiding judge will consider locations of the parties, locations of witnesses, and whether that particular court will create an unfair burden on a party in the suit. A *forum non conveniens* motion has effects similar to those following a motion to change venue. With either petition, if the motion is granted, the physical location of the litigation is changed. However, in state courts, a granted motion to change venue moves the court site to an equivalent court within the same state, whereas a *forum non conveniens* is a motion to change jurisdiction either to another state entirely or to a federal court. When the motion is made at the federal level, it is a motion to change states—obviously a venue change still leaves a case within federal jurisdiction in the federal court system.

STANDING TO SUE

U.S. court systems, federal and state, are *adversarial systems* applying law based in large part on precedents. The basis of an adversarial system is the belief that justice will emerge from competition between parties that have *real current interests* at stake in litigation. A party has a real current interest at stake if the party's freedom or property rights (values) depend on the outcome of the case. A party has *standing* to sue if he or she has a legally protected interest at stake in proposed litigation. For example, a person who has been the victim of a breach of contract has a protected interest at stake in ensuing litigation.

In most cases, standing is not a significant issue, as it is clear that the litigants have stakes in case outcomes (say, involving property disputes, clashes with government regulators over business conduct rules, or personal injury claims). In some types of cases, however, standing has been a critical issue. Public interest advocacy groups that challenge government actions can routinely expect standing challenges. In general, suits by citizens attacking government policies, such as the amounts of money spent on "homeland security," will be dismissed if the plaintiff's standing is solely based on the impact of the policy on his or her tax bill. Courts have refused to allow themselves to be used as platforms for promoting political and social causes.

Environmental Advocacy Group Suits to Protect the Environment

In some situations, courts have allowed parties to bring suit though their personal interests in the suit are limited. Perhaps most notably, environmental groups have been allowed to sue on behalf of stands of trees, claiming that at least one of their group's members actually takes walks in the affected area and has his or her aesthetic sensibilities adversely affected by the cutting of trees in the area at issue.

Do Tree Lovers Have Standing?

The issue of who stands up for trees and other features of the environment has been the subject of frequent litigation. The typical setting finds an environmental group that claims to represent the trees or some other aspect of the environment, challenging a specific government policy or action. To bring suit, the advocacy group must claim that a member of the group has been personally affected by the challenged activity. In a case involving the Sierra Club, the club brought suit in a dispute with Rogers Morton, then Secretary of the Interior, representing a stand of trees based on its widely recognized position as a reputable environmental group.[8] This case was dismissed by the Supreme Court based on a lack of standing. However, the Supreme Court indicated that its decision would have been different—that is, standing for the Sierra Club would have been established if the Sierra Club had claimed that (1) some of its members walked in the area set out by the secretary for a ski resort and (2) their aesthetic interests would be irreparably harmed by cutting down the trees. Subsequent to the *Sierra Club* case, environmental groups attacking government decisions that detrimentally affected the environment, in their view, have made a practice of alleging that some or all of their members would be personally affected by the contemplated changes because, for example, they walked in the areas affected by those policies.

   The following case is typical of many suits brought by environmental groups that claim harm to aesthetic interests resulting from government policies or actions. In this case, the Supreme Court seems concerned about opening the floodgates to a waterfall of litigation based on claims of "perceptible harm" stemming from any decision or action that affects an endangered species or any other facet of the environment.

[8] *Sierra Club v. Morton*, 411 U.S. 920; 93 S. Ct. 1545 (1973).

Case 2-2

Lujan v. Defenders of Wildlife

Supreme Court of the United States 504 U.S. 555 (1992)

BACKGROUND AND FACTS

Section 7(a)(2) of the Endangered Species Act (ESA) requires each federal agency to consult with the U.S. Secretary of the Interior to ensure that any action authorized, funded, or carried out by such agency is not likely to jeopardize the continued existence of any endangered or threatened species. In 1978, the Fish and Wildlife Service and the National Marine Fisheries Service, on behalf of the Secretary of the Interior and the Secretary of Commerce, respectively, promulgated a joint regulation stating that the obligations imposed by section 7(a)(2) extended to actions taken in foreign nations. However, a revised joint regulation (50 C.F.R. § 402.01), promulgated in 1986, reinterpreted section 7(a)(2) to require consultation only for actions taken in the United States or on the high seas.

Organizations dedicated to wildlife conservation and other environmental causes filed an action against the Secretary of the Interior in the U.S. District Court for the District of Minnesota to seek (1) a declaratory judgment that the regulation was in error as to the geographical scope of section 7(a)(2) and (2) an injunction requiring the secretary to promulgate a new regulation restoring the initial interpretation.

The district court granted the Secretary's motion to dismiss for lack of standing (658 F. Supp. 43). On appeal, the U.S. Court of Appeals reversed and remanded (851 F.2d 1035). The court of appeals said that the organizations' standing was supported by (1) an affidavit, filed by a member of one of the organizations, stating that the member had traveled to Egypt to observe the habitat of the endangered Nile crocodile and intended to do so again, and that she would suffer harm as a result of the role of the United States in overseeing and developing water projects in Egypt; (2) another member's affidavit, which stated that (a) the member had traveled to Sri Lanka to observe the habitat of endangered species such as the Asian elephant and the leopard, (b) a development project funded by a U.S. agency might severely shorten the future of these species, and (c) this threat harmed the member because she intended to return to Sri Lanka in the future in an attempt to see these species; and (3) a showing that the organizations had suffered a "procedural injury" based on the Secretary's failure to follow the consultation procedure required by section 7(a)(2) (911 F.2d 117).

Opinion by Scalia

Over the years, our cases have established that the irreducible constitutional minimum of standing contains three elements. First, the plaintiff must have suffered an "injury in fact"—an invasion of a legally protected interest which is (a) concrete and particularized . . . [References deleted] Second, there must be a causal connection between the injury and the conduct complained of—the injury has to be "fairly . . . trace[able] to the challenged action of the defendant, and not . . . the result [of] the independent action of some third party not before the court." Third, it must be "likely," as opposed to merely "speculative," that the injury will be "redressed by a favorable decision."

* * *

When the suit is one challenging the legality of government action or inaction, the nature and extent of facts that must be averred (at the summary judgment stage) or proved (at the trial stage) in order to establish standing depends considerably upon whether the plaintiff is himself an object of the action (or forgone action) at issue. If he is, there is ordinarily little question that the action or inaction has caused him injury, and that a judgment preventing or requiring the action will redress it. When, however, as in this case, a plaintiff's asserted injury arises from the government's allegedly unlawful regulation (or lack of regulation) of *someone else,* much more is needed. In that circumstance, causation and redressability ordinarily hinge on the response of the regulated (or regulable) third party to the government action or inaction—and perhaps on the response of others as well. The existence of one or more of the essential elements of standing "depends on the unfettered choices made by independent actors not before the courts and whose exercise of broad and legitimate discretion the courts cannot presume either to control or to predict." Thus, when the plaintiff is not himself the object of the government action or inaction he challenges, standing is not precluded, but it is ordinarily "substantially more difficult" to establish.

* * *

Respondents' other theories are called, alas, the "animal nexus" approach, whereby anyone who has an interest in studying or seeing the endangered animals anywhere on the globe has standing; and the "vocational nexus" approach, under which anyone with a professional interest in such animals can sue. Under these theories, anyone who goes to see Asian elephants in the Bronx Zoo, and anyone who is a keeper of Asian elephants in the Bronx Zoo, has standing to sue because the Director of the Agency for International Development (AID) did not consult with the Secretary regarding the AID-funded project in Sri Lanka. This is beyond all reason. Standing is not "an ingenious academic exercise in the conceivable," but as we have said requires, at the summary judgment stage, a factual showing of perceptible harm.

Decision and Outcome

The U.S. Supreme Court held that the environmental group Defenders of Wildlife did not have standing to sue because the harm incurred was too ephemeral to enable the group to have standing to challenge the actions of the secretaries of Interior and Commerce as they affect wildlife in Sri Lanka and Egypt.

Questions for Analysis

1. Justice Scalia is voicing a concern over whether standing requirements are too liberal. What is that concern? Using the plaintiff's proposed elastic standards for standing, what sort of mischief could occur with respect to the functioning of government?

2. Since the plaintiffs in this case fell short on demonstrating standing to sue, what additional facts does Justice Scalia suggest would be required to achieve standing? Should academics be able to get into court and challenge actions of a federal agency just because they study the species that is arguably affected by a change in government policy?

JUSTICIABILITY OF DISPUTES

justiciable
A conflict that is real and of sufficient consequence to be triable. Courts refuse to hear cases that are trivial, moot, political, or merely hypothetical.

In general, courts will not allow parties to sue on behalf of *hypothetical* disputes that may occur in the future. Similarly, if a dispute has already been resolved, at law the dispute is considered *moot* and therefore not **justiciable.** Courts do not want to be used for academic or political purposes and therefore will refuse to hear defenses based on a claim that discretionary decisions made by Congress or the president are illegal. During the Vietnam War, many draft resisters refused to serve in the armed forces claiming that the war was unconstitutional. The decision to go to Vietnam was a *political* decision, and the courts were not about to let draft resisters defend their refusal to serve in the armed forces because of a claim that the Vietnam War was somehow illegal. Courts also refuse to hear disputes they regard as *trivial.* A few years ago, the college national championship in football was arguably altered because officials in an important game gave a football team five downs instead of the customary four. An ensuing lawsuit was thrown out of court because officiating at a sporting contest is considered trivial and thus not justiciable.

Exceptions sometimes occur. As with most legal principles, courts can and do make exceptions to these standards. In a contract dispute, suppose one party believes that its proposed course of action is not in breach of a contract while the other side believes it is. When there is a lot at stake, courts will occasionally issue *declaratory judgments,* which inform both parties that, if a particular proposed course of action is taken, it is or is not a breach of contract. Many court decisions have immense political implications. This certainly was true of the 1954 *Brown v. Board of Education* case in which the Court ruled that segregation of public schools is a violation of the Fourteenth Amendment to the U.S. Constitution.[9]

In abortion cases, by the time women challenging state prohibitions on choosing abortions got to the appellate courts, the issue was moot (for the challengers). The women had either given birth to babies or experienced pregnancy terminations. In the famous *Roe v. Wade* case, the U.S. Supreme Court allowed a woman to claim that not only was she pregnant at the time she challenged the state statute prohibiting abortion, but also that she could get pregnant in the future and be similarly oppressed by the statute.[10]

[9] *Brown v. Board of Education,* 347 U.S. 483 (1954).
[10] *Roe v. Wade,* 410 U.S. 113 (1973).

Courts have no reluctance to dismiss cases in which a party does not have standing to sue or in which the dispute is not justiciable. Yet, as reflected in the cases above, courts have gladly stretched traditional concepts of standing and justiciability in order to deal with important legal (and social) issues. In parallel fashion, we've seen that courts have been willing to use some mechanisms of long standing, such as declaratory judgments, that allow parties to resolve disputes before the damages are done, so to speak, particularly in looming contract disputes, in lieu of going into litigation.

JUDICIAL OFFICIALS

The primary responsibility of judges is to be impartial to the outcome of cases brought before their courts. The highest achievement of a judge is to be fair to the litigants, regardless of likeability, wealth, political connections, notoriety, and other extraneous characteristics. A hallmark of American judicial heritage is the delivery of a high level of fairness, to those both great and small. When judges are not impartial, it undermines respect for the law.

Federal Judges

Federal judges are appointed for life, so long as they exhibit good behavior. Judges are nominated by the president and must be approved by a majority of the U.S. Senate. Judges can be impeached for treason, bribery, and other high crimes and misdemeanors. A judge is impeached when articles of impeachment are passed in the House of Representatives. The impeachment then moves to the Senate, which must vote by a two-thirds majority for impeachment for a judge to be removed. Impeachment convictions of federal judges are rare and most judges retire or die while in office. At present, there are about 1,200 federal judges.

Under the Constitution, Congress has the power to decide the jurisdiction of federal courts under the U.S. Supreme Court. Congress cannot reduce the pay of federal judges who remain in office. The writers of the U.S. Constitution were very familiar with dealing with corrupt judges—judges from England who did not accord equal treatment to the colonists. Even so, they permitted lifetime appointments for federal judges, conditional upon good behavior, to attempt to insulate judges from political processes and pressures. Even though judges are appointed through a political process, once appointed, many judges exhibit independence from their benefactors. Earl Warren, a Republican, was appointed by President Eisenhower. His opinions and influence were among the most liberal on the U.S. Supreme Court.

State Judges

At the state level, many judges are elected. In some states all judges are elected except for those few appointed by the governor of the state when sitting judges retire before the expiration of their terms or die in office. In some states, judges are appointed by the governor from a panel of qualified candidates recommended by the state bar association. In many states, judicial elections are partisan, which means judge candidates run as representatives of their political parties. In other states judicial elections are officially nonpartisan. In all states where judges are elected, the bulk of their campaign contributions come from attorneys who, as a group, are sure to be involved in cases that will be presided over by the same beneficiaries of campaign contributions. There certainly is a concern that *elected* state judges may be more politically attuned in their rulings. However, studies of this issue have not revealed statistical differences between rulings of elected and appointed judges. States are often characterized as "laboratories of democracy" because of the variety of features of operations fostered by our 50 separate states. Variability across states in the mechanisms for selecting judges is almost certain to continue.

Judicial Immunity

To further augment judicial impartiality, the common law principle of judicial immunity is prevalent throughout the United States. Judicial immunity shields judges from liability when they make mistakes, defame people, or act in ways that many would claim is malicious. Judges are not immune from prosecution if they are found guilty of taking bribes, but they are immune from suit for their courtroom behavior. At the same time, every state bar has a code of ethics for judges and state bars can recommend that a judge be removed from office. There have been a number of judges who have been removed from office for sexual harassment of female attorneys, for abusive behavior, and for other related reasons.

Summary

Structure, Function, and Modus Operandi of Courts, Including the U.S. Supreme Court

- The structure of both *federal* and *state* court systems is triangular. At the base are numerous *trial courts* and at the apex is a *supreme court*. At the federal level, trial courts are called *district courts,* while the appellate courts include the federal circuit courts of appeals and the U.S. Supreme Court.

- The function of trial courts is to determine the facts, applying existing law to those facts. Factual determinations are arrived at by juries, or by judges if both parties waive their rights to a jury. For the most part, the function of trial court judges is to fairly administer the rules of civil procedure.

- Appellate courts evaluate whether legal errors were made by the judge in the trial court. In most cases, judges at the trial court level correctly administer the rules of civil procedure, though in a number of cases appellate courts determine that the trial court judge did make an error and thus the verdict of the trial court is reversed in part or whole.

- The U.S. Supreme Court is composed of nine justices who serve on the highest court in the land. With very few exceptions, the U.S. Supreme Court is an appellate court. Since more cases are appealed to the U.S. Supreme Court than it could possibly hear, the Supreme Court must prioritize its selection of cases. In general, the Supreme Court hears cases that have constitutional implications, are important cases socially, or are cases that can be used to resolve differing rulings among the circuit courts of appeals.

- When the Supreme Court issues an opinion on a case, a single justice writes a *majority opinion.* Sometimes other justices agree with the outcome of the case but not the reasoning of the majority opinion and so will write a *concurring opinion.* Justices who disagree with the opinion or outcome of the majority can write *dissenting opinions.*

- The state court system has similarities and differences with the federal system. At the state level, trial courts are often subdivided between superior courts and district courts, depending on the importance of cases handled. Felonies and civil cases involving more than certain amounts of money are tried in superior courts, while misdemeanors and smaller civil cases are heard in district courts.

- In most states there is both a court of appeals and a state supreme court. In cases that only involve state law, such as contract disputes, the state supreme court is the court of last resort.

- At both the federal and state levels, there are specialized courts with jurisdiction restricted to such areas of law as taxes, probate, juveniles, or bankruptcy.

Jurisdiction over the Person and Subject Matter, State and Federal Courts

- *Jurisdiction* is the power a court has over a party to litigation and the power to decide the case. If a court does not have jurisdiction, then the person is not bound by the judgment of the court.

- From the perspective of plaintiffs, it is optimal to be able to sue defendants in courts located in the plaintiff's home state.

- Specialized courts, such as small claims courts, have limited jurisdiction, whereas district and superior courts have general jurisdiction to hear all disputes.

- Jurisdiction over the person can be exerted by a state court based on residency, contacts with the state, or commission of a tort within the state. State *long-arm statutes* allow states to exert jurisdiction over out-of-state corporations based on *minimum contacts* with the state. Long-arm statutes are being used to exert jurisdiction over out-of-state websites.

- Jurisdiction in federal courts is based on diversity of citizenship among the litigants or the presence of a federal question.

- Diversity jurisdiction requires that the amount in dispute exceed $75,000 and that the parties live in different states.

- A federal question exists when the claim of the plaintiff or the defense of the defendant involves federal law.

- Regardless of whether the dispute involves federal or state law, civil procedure in federal courts is based on the *Federal Rules of Civil Procedure.* In most cases, the jurisdiction of the federal courts is concurrent with the states; unless a federal statute specifically allocates jurisdiction to the federal courts, it can be enforced in either state or federal courts.

- Some statutes, such as antitrust, patent, copyright, and worker safety acts, can only be enforced through federal courts.

- If the plaintiff chooses a state court in a case in which federal courts also have jurisdiction, the defendant can remove the case to federal court.

Conflicts of Law, Venue, Standing to Sue, Justiciability, and Impartiality and Conduct of Judges

- A separate type of legal conflict exists when the laws of one or more states could be involved in resolving a dispute. Choice-of-law disputes are resolved on a case-by-case basis by looking at where the significant relationships are located.

- *Venue* is the physical location of the court that will resolve the dispute. In most cases, venue is established as close to the parties as possible for convenience purposes. In a few cases, venue is changed based on pretrial publicity or when the location of the court would be particularly inconvenient for one of the parties.

- Parties to suits have *standing* to sue based on whether the parties have a real current interest at stake. If the outcome of the dispute could affect the property, freedom, or life of a party to the suit, that party has standing to sue.

- A dispute is not *justiciable* if it is hypothetical, moot, political, or trivial. There are exceptions in that sometimes courts will resolve hypothetical disputes and many court rulings have political implications.

- Judicial officials are supposed to be fair and impartial. Federal judges are appointed for life, while some state judges are appointed and some are elected.

- Federal judges can be impeached for misconduct.

- In general, at common law judges are entitled to immunity for actions that take place in connection with a court case.

Key Terms

courts of appeals, *37*	long-arm statutes, *43*	U.S. Supreme Court, *39*
federal district courts, *36*	minimum contacts, *43*	venue, *50*
jurisdiction, *35*	reversible error, *38*	writ of certiorari, *39*
justiciable, *53*	state court systems, *41*	

Questions for Review and Analysis

1. If a case has a jury, the trial court judge makes legal rulings and the jury finds the facts. Explain why most appeals are based on the decisions of the trial court judge but not of the jury.

2. The U.S. Supreme Court mainly hears cases that have significant legal implications. Peruse this or any chapter for Supreme Court cases, select one, and identify why the case is significant.

3. What is the underlying rationale for diversity jurisdiction? Do you think that rationale is still relevant today?

4. State three types of cases over which both state and federal courts have concurrent jurisdiction. State three types of cases that are exclusively within the jurisdiction of state courts. Now do the same thing for the federal courts.

5. Why is it important that a person initiating a suit have standing to sue? What mischief could occur if standing requirements were significantly relaxed?

If You Really Understood This Chapter, You Should Be Able to Comment on the Following:

1. **Standing for Financial Institutions.** It would seem that the U.S. Supreme Court has "bent" the rules to allow environmental groups to take legal action with regard to actions of the federal government that substantially impact the environment. What about other regulatory actions of the federal government—can they be challenged by commercial groups affected by changes in government regulations? Suppose you operated a commercial bank and the agency that regulated credit unions changed those regulations in a way that enabled credit unions to compete more directly with commercial banks. Do commercial banks have standing to challenge regulations of an agency that does not regulate them directly but does regulate potential competitors? [*National Credit Union Administration v. First National Bank & Trust Co.*, 118 S.Ct. 927 (1998).]

2. **Ripeness for Consideration by the U.S. Supreme Court.** Consider the following case and see if you think this case is ripe for resolution by the U.S. Supreme Court. A Nebraska statute criminalized the performance of any "partial birth abortion" that was not necessary to save the life of the mother. The statute defined (a) "partial birth abortion" as a procedure in which one "partially delivers vaginally a living unborn child before killing the unborn child and completing the delivery" and (b) "partially delivers vaginally a living unborn child" as intentionally delivering into the vagina a living unborn child, or a substantial portion thereof. A live delivery procedure known as dilation and extraction (D&X) was ordinarily associated with the term "partial birth abortion." However, the most common abortion procedure, which was known as dilation and evacuation (D&E), sometimes involved live delivery of at least some bodily part. A Nebraska physician who performed abortions in a clinical setting filed a lawsuit in the U.S. District Court for the District of Nebraska (1) seeking a declaration that the statute violated the federal Constitution and (2) asking for an injunction forbidding enforcement of the statute. The district court held that the statute was unconstitutional and the U.S. Court of Appeals for the Eighth Circuit affirmed. Why does the uncertainty created by this state statute virtually compel the U.S. Supreme Court to resolve this case with a decision? [*Don Stenberg, Attorney General of Nebraska, et al. v. Leroy Carhart*, 530 U.S. 914 (2000).]

3. **Minimum Contacts.** In mid-1994, Fleet Bank of Albany, New York, issued two credit cards to "Ronald Aylward," allegedly of East Moriches, New York, who used both the plaintiff's name and his Social Security number in applying for the cards. The plaintiff, however, has lived in Missouri all his life. The accounts became delinquent within a short time in the amount of approximately $5,500 and Fleet Bank notified several credit reporting agencies about the delinquency. Fleet Bank's contacts with Missouri consist of three telephone calls and one letter within seven months. The plaintiff's complaint, filed in state court in Missouri, alleges that Fleet Bank defamed the actual Mr. Aylward, interfered with his business expectancy "to be extended credit as necessary for his personal and professional endeavors," committed fraud, and made negligent misrepresentations by communicating "derogatory credit references"—"false statements of fact"—to credit reporting agencies and then failing to correct those references, knowing that they would eventually be seen by others. The defendant, Fleet Bank, moved to dismiss for lack of personal jurisdiction. Does Fleet Bank of Albany have to go to Missouri to defend itself against the defamation charges filed by Mr. Aylward? [*Ronald L. Aylward, Appellant v. Fleet Bank, Appellee*, 122 F.3d 616 (8th Cir. 1997).]

4. **Minimum Contacts in Cyberspace.** The standard for State A to exert jurisdiction over a website that is owned by persons who live and work in another state seems to be accessibility "plus" something else. If the website is accessible by residents of State A and there is interaction with State A citizens, say in the form of e-mails and phone calls, then State A can (or may be able to) exert jurisdiction over the website from another state. On the other hand, mail order and catalog companies have relied on the *Bellas Hess* case to insulate them from liability if all they do is send catalogs to residents of other states and respond to orders. Surely in the mail order business there must be customer problems that require contact with the customer in the form of phone calls. If

the mail order company also has a website that allows for e-mail, does this added capability make the mail order company/website subject to jurisdiction of another state? [*GTE New Media Services, Inc., Appellee v. BellSouth Corporation, et al.,* 339 U.S. App. D.C. 332, 199 F.3d 1343 (DC Cir. 2000).]

5. *Forum Non Conveniens* **and Political Cases.** There are some cases in which it seems clear that the litigation was initiated as a vehicle to advance a political agenda rather than advance the claims of particular plaintiffs. In such cases, the defendants are generally high-profile while the plaintiffs are often people who inspire great sympathy. The goal for defendants is to have the case dismissed before trial so that plaintiffs cannot wash the defendants' "dirty laundry" in public. Imagine a case that involves allegations of sexual abuse against women located in an African country, with that abuse sanctioned and encouraged by large oil companies in collusion with local governmental officials. See what you think. [*Ken Wiwa, individually and as Administrator of the Estate of His Deceased Father et al. v. Royal Dutch Petroleum Company, and Shell Transport and Trading Company, P.L.C., Defendants-Appellees-Cross-Appellants,* 226 F.3d 88 (2nd Cir. 2000).]

6. **Throwing Out Jury Verdicts.** Suppose one juror is a know-it-all and cajoles and intimidates other jurors, making such claims as, "people who sue in personal injury claims are deadbeats and don't want to work for a living." Do the courts have to accept the fact that some jurors have more intense personalities than others and that it is best not to interfere or should a trial court judge consider complaints of other jurors about the conduct of one juror? What if the obnoxious juror had brought in outside material after jurors were warned not to consider anything but their life experiences and evidence presented at trial? [*Caterpillar Tractor Co. v. Hulvey,* 353 S.E. 747 (Sup. Ct. Va. 1987).]

Social Responsibility and Ethics in a High-Tech World

7. **Borking, Clarence Thomas, and Examination of Judicial Appointees.** When Robert Bork was nominated by the first President Bush, opponents of his nomination somehow obtained records of the videos he rented in an effort to embarrass him. Ultimately, Robert Bork's nomination to the U.S. Supreme Court was rejected, hence the term "borking," which refers to successful sabotage of a court nominee. Of course, in the case of Clarence Thomas's nomination to the U.S. Supreme Court, a number of alleged incidents were dragged up by opponents of his nomination to the U.S. Supreme Court, including testimony by Anita Hill, who claimed she was sexually harassed by Mr. Thomas. As information technology becomes more advanced, there will be more electronic trails of a person's life, so that foolish actions that took place during a person's teens or 20s may make the person vulnerable to being "borked" later in life. Some people regret this aspect of electronic records because electronic records are potentially eternal. For a different point of view, consider the article by Randall Kennedy, a law professor from Harvard University, who uses the term "borking" as a verb: http://www.prospect.org/print/V12/12/kennedy-r.html.

   a. Should there be some kind of automatic expungement of electronic records?

   b. Should the fact that a candidate for a judicial post once visited websites of white supremacy advocates be part of the public record if it occurred 10 years ago? What about 30 years ago?

   c. What about the fact that a judicial candidate was once treated for a venereal disease at a public health office? Again, with the computerization of records, these kinds of records are nearly cost-free to store and retrieve.

Using the Internet to Your Advantage

1. **Internet Access to the Courts.** The U.S. federal courts have developed a new system called Public Access to Court Electronic Records (PACER), which is an electronic public access service that allows users to obtain case and docket information from federal appellate, district, and bankruptcy courts and from the U.S. Party/Case Index. The PACER website is located at http://pacer.psc.uscourts.gov/pacerdesc.html. As the prevalence of the Internet grows, electronic access to the courts should become increasingly easy.

2. **U.S. Federal Courts.** The Internet has made legal research vastly easier. Using standard search engines from ISPs such as AOL or using Microsoft's Internet Explorer or Netscape's range of search engines, most legal topics can be explored easily. Why don't we begin with U.S. Courts? Let's insert "U.S. Courts" into a search engine and see what turns up. Using the AOL search en-

gine, the entry entitled "The Federal Judiciary" appears with the URL for the website: http://www.uscourts.gov. An enormous amount of information is packed into that website. Notice that the website offers to register you with PACER (Public Access to Court Electronic Records).

3. **U.S. Courts of Appeals.** Another entry on the AOL search engine is http://www.law. emory.edu/FEDCTS/. This URL allows you to examine each of the 11 Circuits of the U.S. Courts of Appeals, plus the D.C. Circuit and the Court of Appeals for the Federal Circuit. Clicking on any region of the United States, visitors are able to glean the latest opinions that have emanated from each circuit.

4. **Crime Statistics.** Another interesting website is from the U.S. Department of Justice, which makes available crime statistics at its Web page for the Bureau of Justice Statistics: http://www.ojp.usdoj.gov/bjs/. Although criminal law is not the focus of this textbook, there are statistics that are of interest. Computerized records are increasingly being enlisted to aid in law enforcement. The Bureau of Justice Statistics, for example, has a hyperlink to 62 million criminal history records (Criminal Record Systems Statistics that assist in enforcing the Brady Bill, which prohibits the sale of firearms to those convicted of certain crimes (http://www.ojp.usdoj. gov/bjs/crs.htm). It is likely that computers will continue to become more important in efforts to deal with repeat sex offenders and providing background checks for those who are trying to purchase guns.

5. **U.S. Supreme Court.** There are a host of websites that focus on the U.S. Supreme Court. For example, Northwestern University has a well-recognized website that links Supreme Court justices to the opinions that they have written: http://oyez.nwu.edu/. The Oyez project website makes use of multimedia in an effort to bring visitors "up close and personal" with Supreme Court justices. Biographies, pictures, and other information for each member of the U.S. Supreme Court are available at http://oyez.nwu.edu/justices/justices.cgi.

6. **State Courts.** In terms of volume, most litigation takes place at the state level. Again using the AOL search engine and inputting the words "state courts," the National Center for State Courts becomes available: http://www.ncsconline.org/. The National Center for State Courts is a nonprofit organization that provides electronic access to the courts in all 50 states. Like the other websites listed above, the National Center for State Courts website is a huge resource.

7. **History of the Federal Courts.** For those who are interested in the history of the federal courts, the Federal Judicial Center (http://www.fjc.gov/) provides the names and biographies of each district, circuit, or Supreme Court judge who has occupied office since the beginning of the federal courts in 1789.

8. **Instant Access to Federal Court Opinions.** For those who are used to checking the Sports Center on ESPN to hear about the latest scores in various sports, the same sort of access to federal court opinions is available at http://vls.law.vill.edu/Locator/fedcourt.html.

The sophistication and comprehensiveness of commercial, yet free, search engines are assets for legal research that should not be overlooked. In most situations, simply inputting the words of interest is sufficient to locate a website that has a wealth of information on the topic of interest. Searching the Internet for "legal research" is a skill that is easy to develop and could be very valuable in your future careers.

Chapter **Three**

The Litigation/Trial Process

Learning Objectives

After completing this chapter, you should

1. Be familiar with the trial process for civil cases.
2. Understand the roles of discovery and of motions in litigation.
3. Be familiar with the costliness of litigation and the resulting attractiveness of avoiding litigation or finding means of resolving disputes that avoid trials.
4. Understand the roles of damage awards in civil litigation.
5. Have a significantly expanded vocabulary of terms applicable to disputes that enter the court system.

THE TRIAL PROCESS

Overview

It has been said that corporate attorneys fail any time their clients have to go to court, even if their client wins. The thought behind those comments is that corporate executives should be working on strategy, new product development, and other business matters rather than litigation. Also behind those comments is the notion that the courtroom is much more uncertain than the business environment. If a corporation is a defendant, with litigation under way, the corporation may be just one inflamed jury away from bankruptcy. In addition to class-action product liability claims involving asbestos, breast implants, tobacco, DES,[1] misplaced auto gas tanks, and defective tires, hundred million and even billion dollar judgments against corporations have resulted from antitrust, securities, and sexual harassment suits. In addition to monetary losses in courtrooms, the cost firms face in preparing for litigation is quite high. In complex business litigation, attorney bills in the $100 million range are unusual, but not unheard of. IBM reportedly spent over $200 million defending itself from a Department of Justice antitrust suit—a suit that the government later dropped, conceding that the case no longer had merit.

---

[1] DES is a drug whose formal name is diethylstilbestrol. It is a synthetic hormone prescribed to pregnant women between 1940 and 1971 that is associated with abnormally high rates of cancer in the daughters and granddaughters of such women.

Adverse Publicity

When companies go to court, they not only risk losing huge judgments, tying up executive time, and having to fork over large fees to attorneys and others involved in developing their case, but also face the risk of embarrassing and financially damaging adverse publicity. An orange juice company in California was investigated because its customers became sick with diseases that are normally transmitted through human urine. Consider what publicity about this kind of problem would do for your juice packaging company.

People with Axes to Grind

Any time a company addresses a safety feature of a product, in design, packaging, or elsewhere, if the company fails to select the most effective means of preventing accidents tied to the product, legal challenges may be raised. This is so even if selecting the most effective safety feature prices the product out of the market. Disgruntled ex-employees often find sympathetic ears in reporters hungry for stories on company shortcomings.

Avoidance of Court Litigation

Needless to say, companies like to avoid having any "dirty laundry" aired in public. So they often seek to resolve litigation through settlements that keep issues, often including terms of settlement, confidential. Confidentiality is also one of the reasons for increasing popularity among businesses of reliance on **alternative dispute resolution (ADR),** generally in the form of binding arbitration. Increasingly, company contracts with employees, clients, and others call for arbitration of disputes rather than permitting the rolling of dice in court. Besides the lack of publicity, there are other reasons for businesses to prefer ADR, typically including increased speed in resolving disputes, lower variance in awards, and less cost generally. ADR is discussed extensively in the next chapter.

The Adversarial System

As any television watcher knows, courtroom contests sometimes resemble a nonviolent battle zone. Later in this chapter we discuss the rules of the contest, but, from the start, it must be recognized that litigation is a contest between parties with *real current interests* at stake.[2] As a result of such contests, court precedents are created and wealth is redistributed. As described in Chapter 2, a tenet of the **adversarial system** is the belief that justice and truth will emerge in the competition between adversaries in the courtroom. Unlike judges in many countries in the rest of the world, U.S. judges play a largely passive role in the courtroom (for a discussion of the virtues of the common law relative to civil law systems, see the "International Perspective" box). Judges do not present evidence, nor do they investigate facts. Judges are like umpires in a baseball game; as with good umpires, judges are impartial to the outcome and often stay in the background.

Burden of Proof   In most civil litigation, the overall burden of establishing a *cause of action,* and thus a favorable verdict, is borne by the plaintiff. In some cases, defendants have the burden of proving affirmative defenses (discussed later in the chapter). Generally, at the end of a trial, a judge will tell jury members that if they find that they are equally persuaded or unpersuaded by the plaintiff's evidence and that of the defendant, they should find for the defendant. In the most frequently encountered forms of civil cases, a plaintiff has the burden of showing, by a **preponderance of the evidence,** that it is more likely

alternative dispute resolution (ADR)
Means for resolving legal disputes without pursuing litigation remedies in the traditional judicial system. Negotiation, arbitration, and mediation are examples of ADR.

adversarial system
A judicial system, like that in the United States, that permits each side in litigation to have its best factual and/or expert opinion case presented to a court in the belief that courts (juries) will be able to determine truth and deliver justice with vigorous cases presented by both sides.

preponderance of the evidence
Evidence standard under which judgment is to be determined based on whether a claim is *more likely than not* to be valid.

---

[2] If a party has a real current interest at stake that party has "standing" to sue as was discussed in the previous chapter.

International Perspective   Is the Common Law Good for Capitalism Relative to Civil Law Systems?

THE LEGAL DNA OF GOOD ECONOMIES

By David Wessel

The World Economy is putting modern capitalism through another stress test. Like tests that physicians do for people with heart disease, this one highlights the system's weaknesses and brings forth various prescriptions for treating symptoms.

But, just as with heart disease, the stress test raises intriguing questions about genetic advantages: Do some economies have institutions, laws, and commonly accepted business norms that produce a stronger strain of capitalism, one better adapted to withstand shocks and improve its people's prosperity?

Specifically, why do the U.S. and Britain have bigger stock markets and more shareholding citizens than Germany and France, and does that make their economies more flexible? Why do more companies go public in India than in Brazil? Why do American businesses use private arbitration more than others to resolve corporate disputes? Why are U.S. governments more comfortable settling trade disputes one case at a time than their continental counterparts?

To a remarkable degree, the answers can be traced to the different legal traditions that emerged in England and France in the 12th century and spread through their colonies. Nine hundred years later, these traditions still influence business, investors, and government. And as globalization steadily erodes national boundaries, the differences are causing unavoidable strains.

Western commercial law comes from two traditions: the common law, with roots in England, and the civil law, rooted in ancient Rome and refined later by continental Europeans. Common-law countries, including the U.S. and other former British colonies, rely on independent judges and juries and legal principles supplemented by precedent-setting case law.

In civil-law countries, which include much of Latin America, judges often are lifelong civil servants who administer legal codes packed with specific rules. Case law matters less. Civil-law countries distrust judges and arbitrators; common-law countries venerate and empower them. Rule-laden civil-law countries aren't well-adapted to cope with change; the case-law approach makes common-law countries inherently more flexible.

All this has long fascinated law professors. After the early failures at building capitalism in Russia following communism's collapse, the issue also attracted a band of economists, led by Harvard's Andrei Shleifer. They sought to identify conditions essential for functioning markets and private property. Whatever they were, Russia didn't have them.

Examining 49 countries from Argentina to Zimbabwe, the economists discerned a distinct pattern in both rich and poor countries: "Civil-law countries exhibit heavier regulation, weaker property-right protection, more-corrupt and less-efficient governments, and less political freedom than do common-law countries," Mr. Shleifer puts it. As France well illustrates, civil law "more easily accommodates the expansion of government intervention in economic and social life."

Investors in civil-law countries, Mr. Shleifer and colleagues argue, are less certain that their property rights will be enforced. One symptomatic example: Civil-law countries more frequently require shareholders to attend meetings to vote instead of voting by mail. In these countries, few people own stock, bond and stock markets are smaller, and more companies are controlled by a few big holders. In the past decade, this has proved a significant constraint on investment and economic growth. The law matters—and it matters a lot.

There remains a chicken-and-egg dispute about which came first: The law, as Mr. Shleifer and allies argue, or the rise of an independent business-investor class that demanded legal protection, as Columbia law professor John Coffee Jr. sees it.

In either case, the lesson of history is sharp: Markets and the prosperity they can provide do not exist independent of the law and the institutions of government but are intertwined with them. Well-functioning financial markets, in particular, rest on clear and enforced protections for investors. And when a changing economy requires new rules—for auctioning radio spectrum, modernizing stock markets, regulating new financial products, enforcing intellectual property rights—it's wise to remember that the economic impact is long-lived.

Ethical Challenges   Threat of Lawsuits by Large Businesses

Imagine that you become aware of a small high-tech business that specializes in developing business process improvements that has developed a promising innovation for which it has received a process patent. Suppose further that you are affiliated with a large business that tries to purchase patent rights from the small firm because your firm has been working on developing a similar process and you do not want marketing efforts for your firm derailed by an infringement suit by the smaller firm. You begin negotiations with the management of the smaller firm, but they prove unreasonable (in your view), so you decide to (1) apply for a patent on the process your firm has been working on and (2) risk a lawsuit. If a lawsuit follows, your firm has the financial resources to wage a protracted legal battle and, regardless of the merits of the case, the other firm will not be able pursue the litigation because it does not have adequate financial resources.

Is it ethical for a large firm to throw its weight around simply because it can afford expensive legal contests? Suppose you were convinced that (1) your firm had infringed a patent of a smaller firm but (2) the smaller firm simply did not have the financial resources to win a patent case in federal court (note that legal fees for a typical patent case in federal court exceed $1 million on each side). Would you continue marketing your business process knowing that it infringes on the business process of the smaller firms, but also knowing that you were unlikely to be sued because the other firm could not afford costly litigation? As a future business manager, is it your job to ignore such ethical issues and just advance the interests of your firm?

than not that the facts he or she alleges are true.[3] Only by doing so does a plaintiff become entitled to a favorable verdict.

Business Litigation

The rules of civil procedure do not change just because both the plaintiff and the defendant are businesses. There is, however, increased complexity in suits involving business litigants. Both parties are apt to be well represented by experienced counsel and they sometimes employ legal strategies that make litigation more expensive for the other side as a means of encouraging settlements. In some states there are now separate **business courts** (or the equivalent), that have jurisdiction limited to complex business cases. Among the types of cases that give rise to complex business litigation are breach of contract cases; infringement cases involving IP that may be protected by patents, copyrights, and trademarks; antitrust claims; claims of fraud in connection with the sale of securities; and misappropriation of trade secrets, among others.

business courts
Specialized courts that have subject matter jurisdiction only over "business" cases.

Distinguishing Characteristics of Business Litigation

Keep Your Cards Close to the Vest: Don't Reveal Too Much Too Soon   In a nutshell, business litigation is likely to take longer, be more expensive, and tie up more resources than does nonbusiness litigation. Given the costs and risks of business litigation, it is obviously in the interests of the parties involved to dispatch such cases quickly and efficiently through settlements. Of course, if a firm is a defendant in a business case, the downside risk is such that it may be forced to defend itself vigorously. In this effort, it may not be the best strategy for the defendant firm to go into a settlement mode right away as the plaintiff may then assume that the defendant's case is weak, prompting the plaintiff to press for a settlement figure greater than would be considered reasonable in the face of a

---

[3] In some settings, the standard of proof is "clear and convincing," indicating that the evidence is deemed to make it highly probable that the claim is true or, for the defense, highly probable that any affirmative defense offered is true.

Nutz and Boltz

In North Carolina, the home state of the authors of your book, recognition of the unique challenges brought to courts by business litigation resulted in 1995 in creation of a "business court" whose case docket includes only complex business cases. With this action, our state has joined what appears to be a growing trend for adoption of specialized courts for business issues. In North Carolina, as in other states, it has been a concern of businesses, especially larger businesses, that there is a lack of specialization and accompanying skill levels in the judiciary. Indeed, in North Carolina as in most states, judges do not remain assigned to cases throughout their course and the judge who hears preliminary motions is likely to have moved to another venue by the time the case is tried.

Businesses also are concerned with the time and dollar costs of litigation. To expedite the disposition of business litigation, North Carolina also adopted rules for the rapid handling of most business cases. For commercial cases involving amounts in controversy over $500,000, and where the parties waive a jury trial and any claim of punitive damages, cases are tried on an expedited basis. Discovery is limited and expedited, summary judgment is unavailable, and short time limits are set for discovery, briefing, trial, and the court's decision.

It is expected that business court judges will develop expertise, experience, and knowledge and that cases will be handled more efficiently because a single judge will be involved from beginning to end. Also, specialized business court judges will render more consistent and predictable decisions. By requiring opinions to be written, a body of law should develop in North Carolina that will enable lawyers to give more helpful advice and businesses to order their legal affairs with greater confidence.

Outside of business population centers such as Manhattan; Dover, Delaware; Chicago; and so on, local jurisdictions seldom have enough complex business cases to permit specialization within an administrative unit. Therefore, in most jurisdictions, the only practical means of achieving the critical mass of experience in a judge or judges is at the state level. The model for specialized business courts may be attributed to Delaware, with its 200-year-old chancery court, which provides expert adjudication of business disputes. With some half of the Fortune 500 incorporated in Delaware, the specialization and high expertise of the chancery court cannot be easily duplicated elsewhere. Delaware also has instituted a specialized business litigation panel that provides summary proceedings for business cases involving $1 million or more.

Illinois has a unified court system, which includes a chancery court, and Cook County has judges assigned to hear only commercial cases. In 1993, New York City established four specialized "Commercial Parts" to hear complex business cases in Manhattan. Subsequently, a panel of the New York State Bar Association has recommended the adoption of a business court in the state.

Various other states have considered or are in the process of pursuing creation of a business court. This includes current activity in Wisconsin, Hawaii, Michigan, Minnesota, Ohio, and Texas. Notably, proposals to create such courts have stalled in other states, including Pennsylvania, Massachusetts, and California. How successful the movement to establish specialized state business courts will be remains to be seen.

For a more complete discussion of this topic, see "World Reports," *Lex Mundi Doing Business Guides* 8, no. 3 (November 1996), http://www.hg.org/1444.html.

---

strong defense. The job of attorneys representing a business defendant is, of course, to punch holes in the plaintiff's case and create uncertainty as to the verdict and amount of damages recoverable. Many times, the willingness to settle on the part of one or both parties radically changes depending on the performance of a key witness at a deposition (depositions are discussed later in this chapter).

Federal and State Civil Procedure: Differences

The next section examines the steps required and the nature of the rules to be followed in typical civil litigation. At the federal level, civil litigation can be discussed with more certainty because all federal courts use the Federal Rules of Civil Procedure (FRCP).[4] State courts exhibit more variability in their procedures, so the discussion in the next section can best be described as generally accurate for most state courts. There are, however, differences in civil procedure among state courts, many of which are due to history and events that no one can remember, but which still leave these differences in place.

PROCEDURE IN CIVIL LITIGATION

Overview

litigation
The processes through which the legal system is used to resolve legal disputes.

Litigation refers to the entire process through which the legal system is used to resolve disputes. Although court statistics reveal an increasing use of courts by businesses and individuals, court statistics alone do not reveal the true extent of litigation. The *threat* of a trip to court frequently inspires monetary settlements in which one business pays another in return for an agreement not to pursue a claim at court. Moving to the next stage of seriousness, the vast majority of *lawsuits that are filed are nevertheless settled before a trial.* Many additional legal claims are resolved as a result of ADR (alternative dispute resolution) in which the parties have waived their right to go to court but, instead, have agreed to have the claims "judged" by an arbitrator. Below, we take you through the various stages of litigation through court trial, and beyond, assuming the parties do not settle and have not already agreed to arbitrate the dispute.

Stages of Litigation

Litigation has certain distinct stages, beginning with *pleadings,* then proceeding through *motions* made by either party, *discovery, pretrial conferences,* the actual *trial, appeals* to higher courts, and, finally, if the plaintiff is successful, to *enforcement of a judgment.* Although civil procedure may appear to be a linear process proceeding in an orderly fashion, in fact there are many instances in which the parties can be recycled through various stages of the litigation process, sometimes more than once. Cases that are *reversed and remanded* require the parties to go through a trial again with added directions from an appeals court as to how the trial court should rule on particular matters. Cases that are dismissed at the motion stage in litigation can be reinstated if the granting of a motion to dismiss by the trial court is overturned on appeal. A trial court can declare a mistrial, at the end of a trial or even during a trial, if the judge knows he or she made a mistake during the trial that is likely to be reversed on appeal. Appellate decisions can be reversed by higher appellate courts and decisions of trial courts can be reinstated. Although relatively rare, some court cases go on and on, occasionally lasting for 10 years or more.

Described in the "Nutz and Boltz" box is a garden-variety version of litigation that does proceed in an orderly fashion from pleadings to jury verdict. For some classes, this will provide all the necessary summary understanding of the litigation process that your instructor wants you to have in this course. For others, the remainder of the chapter adds a lot of detail on the many component parts of the overall litigation process.

In reality, the litigation journey from alleged wrong to the collection of damages is generally accompanied by many twists and turns along the road, with most cases settled at some point along the path to trial. Our schematic representation of the litigation process begins with an assumed wrongful act.

---

[4] The FRCP can be accessed at: http://www.law.cornell.edu/rules/frcp/overview.htm.

Nutz and Boltz

An alleged negligent act causes an injury.

↓

The injured party hires an attorney.

↓

The injured party's (plaintiff's) attorney files a complaint.

↓

Pleadings stage of litigation:
 (complaint, answer, & followup
 responses from each side)

Defendant's attorney responds to the complaint.

↓

Additional responses may occur.

↓

Attorneys make pretrial motions to the court.

↓

Discovery stage of litigation:
 (interrogatories and depositions
 used to establish facts, admissions
 sought)

Each side's attorney(s) seek(s) to determine what evidence will show, looking for information that supports their client's point of view and refutes the opposing party's case.

↓

Additional pretrial motions

↓

Pretrial:
 [conference(s) with judge;
 informal negotiations for
 settlement; possibility of
 using formal, "structured"
 mechanisms for seeking
 a settlement]

Pretrial conference(s) involving the judge and both sides' attorneys. Conference will be used to clarify and limit the issues for trial, to plan the trial sequence, and to encourage settlement.

↓

Settlement negotiations may be occurring. Pressure for the use of methods of settling other than going to court may be exerted by the assigned judge.

↓

Additional pretrial motions

↓

The trial:
 (jury is selected, opening statements are
 made by each side, evidence is presented
 by plaintiff, evidence is presented by
 defendant, closing arguments are made)

The trial takes place: the trial court has the task of establishing the facts proved by the evidence, having the appropriate law properly applied to the facts revealed, and rendering a verdict. During this sequence, additional motions may be made.

↓

Post-verdict motions

↓

Enforcement of the verdict:

Post-trial, the winning party will pursue performance in conformance with the trial verdict, unless the trial court verdict is appealed.

↓

Appeal to a higher court:

If one party is dissatisfied with the outcome, believes that the disappointing result is due to error made in the trial, and/or thinks additional litigation is economically justified, that party can appeal.

↓

Enforcement of the verdict:

At the completion of the appeals process, the prevailing party will seek perfomance of the court verdict.

Pleadings

The Complaint

The modern theory of pleadings is that they are the documents that provide *general notice* to the other party in litigation of what will be alleged in the courtroom. The **pleadings** are composed of a **complaint** filed by the plaintiff with the court and an **answer** filed by the defendant within the time allowed by that jurisdiction or court. Under the Federal Rules of Civil Procedure, a complaint is a short statement of facts that

1. Allege jurisdiction.
2. Allege the facts necessary for the plaintiff to be entitled to court remedy.
3. Provide a prayer for relief or a remedy—in other words, indicate the amount of money or other remedy to which the plaintiff claims he or she is entitled.

A sample or example complaint is provided in the "Nutz and Boltz" box. In this complaint, the plaintiff is lodging legal claims against a driver and the company for which the driver was working at the time of an accident that injured the plaintiff.

The Summons

Once the complaint is filed with the court, the defendant is then *summoned* to trial with a *service of process*. In some cases it is difficult to locate the specific defendant. Most jurisdictions allow a defendant to be served by leaving the **summons** with a responsible adult, someone at least 18 years of age, residing at the plaintiff's residence. The summons gives the defendant a time period in which to respond to the complaint, and the complaint is part of the summons. It is possible for defendants to evade litigation by evading process servers and/or by not coming into the jurisdiction of the court.

Defendant's Responses: Answer and Motions

In most cases a defendant who is served will file an *answer.* If a defendant does not file an answer within 20 to 30 days, that defendant loses the case by *default.* Once a default occurs, the only issue that would remain would be the amount of damages that the plaintiff is able to obtain. In most cases, a defendant files an answer and also files a *motion to dismiss.* A **motion** to dismiss is a petition to the court to dismiss the suit because of the defendant's contention that even if the facts alleged in complaint were proved, the defendant is still not liable to the plaintiff.

Motion to Dismiss   What the plaintiff alleges in a complaint is a *cause of action.* In most causes of action, there are several components, as is the case with a cause of action for *defamation.* A plaintiff is entitled to a remedy for defamation if the defendant made false statements about the plaintiff, the false statements were heard or seen by third parties, and the statements held the plaintiff up to ridicule or hate.

In contrast, if the complaint alleged that the defendant made false statements about the plaintiff in his office, without anyone else within earshot, a motion to dismiss by the defendant should be granted because, based on the facts alleged, even if true, the defendant is not liable to the plaintiff for defamation as a matter of law (it's not illegal to say bad things about someone if those statements are not communicated to anyone else). So, if facts are not subject to dispute, courts make motion to dismiss decisions *based on the law.* It certainly would make no sense in this example situation, in which there is no dispute over facts, to take up trial time, including time for a judge to instruct a jury on what the law says and have the jury apply that law, when the judge can quickly and efficiently apply the same

pleadings
The complaint, answer, and accompanying documents in litigation. The pleadings document the claims, alleged facts, and defenses to be offered in trial.

complaint
The first document filed to initiate a lawsuit. The complaint provides notice to the opposing side in litigation that they have been sued and indicates what will be claimed in the ensuing litigation.

answer
A defendant's response to a complaint naming the respondent as a (the) defendant in a lawsuit. Answers are often accompanied by motions filed with the court.

summons
Written notification to a named defendant that a legal proceeding has been started that requires the defendant to come to court at a specified time and location if the named defendant wishes to offer a defense against the claims lodged.

motions
Requests made to the court by the parties involved in litigation that are ruled on by the court, not by jurors.

Nutz and Boltz

STATE OF NORTH CAROLINA
SUPERIOR COURT

ORANGE COUNTY

Civil Action No. _____

Betty Matthews,
  Plaintiff

JURY TRIAL DEMANDED

v.

William Petty and Speedy-Delivery Pizza
Defendant

COMPLAINT

Now comes the plaintiff and for his cause of action against the defendant states that:

1. She is a citizen of Orange County, North Carolina.
2. Defendant William Petty is a resident of Orange County, North Carolina.
3. Defendant Speedy-Delivery Pizza is a corporation incorporated under the laws of the state of North Carolina, conducting business in Orange County, North Carolina.
4. On July 28, 2000, defendant William Petty, while driving a pizza delivery vehicle, negligently failed to yield the required right-of-way to plaintiff, colliding with plaintiff's automobile.
5. At the time of this incident, defendant William Petty was operating a pizza delivery vehicle in the service of Speedy-Delivery Pizza.
6. As a result of the collision caused by defendant's negligent actions, plaintiff suffered the total loss of her automobile, suffered significant bodily injury, suffered very substantial pain in body and mind, incurred expenses for medical care and hospitalization, and was deprived of 3 months of employment.
7. The costs plaintiff incurred included: $15,000 lost value of her automobile; $25,000 in medical expenses; $12,000 in lost earnings; and $250,000 in pain and suffering.

WHEREFORE, plaintiff Betty Matthews demands judgment against defendants William Petty and Speedy-Delivery Pizza in the sum of $302,000.

By
[signature]
Charles P. H. Jones
Attorney for Plaintiff
Chapel Hill, N.C.

motions for judgment on the pleadings
Requests (motions) by either party to a lawsuit asking that the court resolve the legal issue being contested on the basis of information provided in the pleadings, without proceeding to trial. This can be done if there are no facts in dispute in the case.

law. Trials are for cases in which there are legitimate questions of fact—hence the emphasis on trial courts being "finders of facts."

Some of the cases reviewed in this textbook are appeals from decisions of trial courts to grant **motions for judgment on the pleadings.** A motion for a judgment on the pleadings is essentially the same as a motion to dismiss when filed by the defendant.

The following case discussion focuses on the handling of a motion to dismiss a suit brought against a company that allocates domain names in cyberspace.

Case 3-1

Bruce Watts, Plaintiff-Appellant v. Network Solutions, Inc., Defendant-Appellee

United States Court of Appeals for the Seventh Circuit
1999 U.S. App. LEXIS 28884 (1999)

BACKGROUND AND FACTS

Watts is suing NSI (Network Solutions Incorporated), a private company that registers Internet domain names pursuant to a government contract, because NSI refused to register the domain name "birthdayballoons.com" to him. Watts alleged that he was the first person to use the name "BIRTHDAY BALLOONS" in interstate commerce as part of his business of marketing gift packages. He further alleged that the name is distinctive, that it has become a "famous" mark, and that he has applied to register the name with the United States Department of Commerce's Patent and Trademark Office. Watts alleged that NSI informed him that it could not register the domain name "birthdayballoons.com" to him, because it was already registered to another individual, Steve Schwab. NSI told Watts that he could pursue relief against Schwab. In addition, NSI's Director of Business Affairs, David M. Graves, stated in a declaration pursuant to 18 U.S.C. § 1746 that NSI does not make independent determinations of an applicant's right to use a particular domain name. Instead, it merely registers domain names on a first-come, first-served basis. Graves further explained that NSI has a dispute resolution policy under which the holder of a federally registered trademark may challenge another's use of an allegedly infringing domain name, but he added that Watts had not presented NSI with any proof that he had a federally registered trademark in "BIRTHDAY BALLOONS" so as to trigger the policy.

Judges

Before Hon. Harlington Wood, Jr., Circuit Judge, Hon. Joel M. Flaum, Circuit Judge, Hon. Terence T. Evans, Circuit Judge.

OPINION: ORDER

We review the dismissal of the Sherman Act claims ***, drawing all reasonable inferences from the complaint in favor of Watts. [Citations deleted] In dismissing these claims, the district court held that Watts could not sue NSI because NSI is immune from antitrust liability as a federal instrumentality. Although NSI is responsible for domain name registration pursuant to a government contract, NSI does not therefore possess automatic government instrumentality immunity. As the D.C. Circuit recently observed, "A contractor might be free to perform the contract in any number of ways, only one of which is anticompetitive." Therefore, rather than decide the complex issue of whether NSI enjoys antitrust immunity, we choose to affirm on another ground supported by the record, namely, that Watts failed to state a claim because he alleged no antitrust injury.

In order to maintain an antitrust action under the Sherman Act, a private plaintiff must establish that he has suffered an antitrust injury and that he is the proper plaintiff to maintain an antitrust action with respect to the relevant market. An antitrust injury is the type of injury that "the antitrust laws were intended to prevent . . . The injury should reflect the anticompetitive effect either of the violation or of the anticompetitive acts made possible by the violation." Watts maintains that NSI has a monopoly in the domain-name registering business. However, he does not argue that he was injured as a consumer by, for example, being forced to pay higher prices or by being forced out of the market of registering domain names himself. Instead, Watts contends that his "injury" is his inability to register the name "birthdayballoons.com" because NSI already registered that name to Schwab. This is not an antitrust injury; NSI is not preventing Watts from competing in his business of selling gift packages because NSI does not compete with Watts in the sale of gift packages. Accordingly, the Sherman Act claims were properly dismissed.

Decision and Outcome

The U.S. Court of Appeals for the Seventh Circuit dismissed both of plaintiff's complaints. As to the antitrust claim, the court dismissed the complaint for failure to state a claim that is recognized as an antitrust injury.

Questions for Analysis

1. Was the plaintiff contesting any factual allegations made in this case?
2. What did the plaintiff allege in his complaint that was allegedly an antitrust complaint? Why did the court dismiss his complaint under the antitrust laws?
3. Give a coherent explanation of why the court, relying on existing law, would dismiss this suit rather than allowing it to proceed to trial where a jury could apply the law.

Answers to Complaints   Answers by defendants are supposed to address the allegations contained in the complaint. If the defendant does not contest jurisdictional allegations, then the defendant must deny some of the other allegations made in the complaint. Otherwise, a judgment is entered for the plaintiff (assuming, of course, that the defendant's motion to dismiss is denied). In most answers, the defendant will deny some of the facts alleged in the complaint or will issue a *general denial* of all the factual allegations contained in the complaint. If facts alleged in the complaint are denied by the answer, the case moves on toward trial, though other motions by either party could terminate the litigation before the case gets to trial.

affirmative defenses
Affirmative defenses are those that rely on facts or conditions that absolve a defendant of liability, even if the facts alleged in a complaint are true.

Affirmative Defenses   In addition to answers that deny generally the allegations made in the complaint or deny parts of what is alleged, a defendant can file an answer that incorporates **affirmative defenses.** In an affirmative defense, the defendant does not deny the allegations contained in the complaint, but asserts there are additional facts that exonerate the defendant. Illustratively, if the defendant is charged by the plaintiff with battery, the defendant could allege that the plaintiff consented to be battered by virtue of putting on a uniform and playing football. Tackling someone standing on a street corner is likely to be a battery, but if the tackling occurs in connection with a football game in which all the players voluntarily participated, the contact is legal and not actionable. Note, however, that recent examples from the worlds of both professional and amateur hockey indicate that unusual violence (battery) has a significant risk of being actionable.[5] In a NHL game in the year 2000, Donald Brashear of the Vancouver Canucks was hit in the head with a hockey stick brandished by Marty McSorley of the Boston Bruins. Knocked out, Mr. Brashear suffered a concussion from the blow. McSorley was charged with assault and tried in a Vancouver Court. (See http://abcnews.go.com/sections/sports/DailyNews/mcsorley000926.html.) In Waukegan Illinois, a 16-year-old hockey player accepted a plea agreement that found him guilty of battery after he used his hockey stick to push an opposing high school team player into the boards a second after the buzzer sounded ending a rough junior varsity game. The pushed player suffered a paralyzing injury from the impact experienced. (See http://abcnews.go.com/sections/us/DailyNews/hockey000807.html.)

Often, in contract cases involving large companies, the defendant firm accused of breaching a contract might claim that the contract it voluntarily signed with the plaintiff is

---

[5] The issue of when violence in a sporting contest gives rise to legal action is discussed in an article by Rich Harrow, "Violence in Sports: Aggressive or Excessive?" at http://CBSsportsline.com/&/sage/pressbox/0,1328,53817,680.

illegal because it violates some law, perhaps an antitrust law or a state unfair trade practice law. To succeed with such a maneuver, the defendant may have to prove that actions of the plaintiff were illegal, with the contract at issue an element of the alleged illegal activities, justifying the defendant in breaking the contract.

Counterclaims   In some cases, a defendant may allege that not only does he not owe the plaintiff any money or other remedy at law, but that the defendant is entitled to collect from the plaintiff for a legal wrong that the plaintiff committed. Among business litigants, **counterclaims** are common. When breach of contract is alleged by a plaintiff, the defendant frequently alleges, in the alternative, that (1) it did not breach the contract, but that, in fact, (2) the plaintiff breached the contract and the defendant is entitled to collect damages from the plaintiff for breach of contract. In contract breach cases with relatively large firms, as noted above, the defendant may defend its breach of contract by claiming that the contract was illegal under several provisions of the antitrust laws, then file a counterclaim to collect for being a "victim" of these antitrust violations.

counterclaims
Claims filed by a defendant in a civil suit claiming wrongdoing and resulting liability (to the defendant) on the part of the party who had filed the original complaint against the defendant.

Reply   If a defendant files a counterclaim, the plaintiff is required, at least under the Federal Rules of Civil Procedure, to file a *reply,* which has the same characteristics as an answer. The reply could deny some or all of the allegations contained in the counterclaim and it can also contain affirmative defenses.

Multiple Parties   It is important to know that, in many cases, there are multiple parties, possibly both co-plaintiffs and co-defendants. Sometimes the interests of the multiple parties on the same "side" of the case are adverse. When that is the situation, a plaintiff may file a cross-claim against a fellow plaintiff, and the same action can occur on the defendants' side. In sales contract cases in which a plaintiff alleges that a product is defective and the cause of her injuries, the plaintiff is entitled to sue every party up and down the marketing chain and join them as co-defendants. The co-defendants might include a retailer, a distributor, and a manufacturer. The retailer could file a *cross-claim* against the manufacturer, claiming, in effect, that "Yes, while I am technically liable, the manufacturer is primarily liable because he built the defective product." In many instances, cases are straightforward; a single plaintiff sues a single defendant. Other cases, however, are made much more complex by the presence of multiple parties. In such cases, cross-claims between co-defendants and co-plaintiffs are not uncommon.

If a party files a cross-claim against a co-defendant or co-plaintiff, the co-defendant or co-plaintiff is required to file an answer and all the characteristics and permutations of answers discussed above apply. As before, an answer can be in the form of a general denial, partial denial, or affirmative defense. To further complicate matters, a co-defendant or co-plaintiff can answer with a counterclaim and, of course, also can file motions to dismiss.

Motion for Judgment on the Pleadings   In making this motion, the defendant is claiming that the complaint, even if true, does not entitle the plaintiff to a remedy at law. If this motion is filed by the plaintiff, it could be, for example, a motion to strike an affirmative defense by the defendant as legally insufficient to excuse his behavior. Suppose the plaintiff claims he is a victim of a battery and defendant claims that they had agreed to fight in a bout that was not sanctioned by a boxing commission. Under those circumstances, the affirmative defense by the defendant—that he was just defending himself—is legally insufficient as an affirmative defense.

The following is an excerpt of a thought-provoking article by Robert Plotkin on the issue of using online and electronic resources to make more efficient some basic litigation activities.

ELECTRONIC COURT FILING: PAST, PRESENT, AND FUTURE

by Robert Plotkin, *lexisONE*[sm] Contributor, November 2000

Despite the growing use of computers in the legal profession, authoring and filing legal pleadings remains a labor-intensive process that has yet to fully benefit from the potential for automation offered by recent advances in computer technology. Efforts are underway, however, to computerize virtually every aspect of court filing and case management.

Several courts and government agencies have already begun to supplement or replace their paper-based filing systems with electronic filing systems that allow pleadings to be filed over the Internet. Some systems also allow parties to access their case files and the court's docket over the Internet. These early systems, although rudimentary, are already facilitating interactions with the courts and are allowing attorneys and courts to recognize significant cost savings. The electronic filing systems of tomorrow will further automate the filing process and integrate computer systems for filing, case management, docketing, storage, and security.

Electronic filing systems have the potential to:

- Simplify and standardize the process of filing court documents
- Greatly reduce the amount of resources devoted to paper file generation, manipulation, storage, and retrieval
- Reduce errors in copying and transcription
- Facilitate access to and sharing of court documents

A large and growing number of legal and computer professionals have recognized the benefits that would result from the widespread adoption of electronic court filing systems, and are actively working on developing nationwide open—non-proprietary and publicly accessible—technological standards for electronic court filing. And the success of such efforts will require the continued and growing involvement of all segments of the legal profession.

* * *

Advantages of Electronic Filing

A fully electronic filing system holds the promise of benefiting all constituents of the justice system: parties, their attorneys, the courts, and the public. Such a system would benefit parties and their attorneys by reducing the costs of printing, copying, mailing, courier services, travel, and storage associated with paper documents. Parties also would benefit from the ability to electronically access and search through court files and dockets from any location.

Courts that adopt electronic filing systems will benefit from a drastic reduction in the amount of physical space required to store case files. By one conservative estimate, paper court documents currently stored using 500 linear feet of shelf storage space (about 50 four-drawer file cabinets) could be stored on a single shelf using currently available and relatively inexpensive hard disk drive technology.

The amount of time spent by court staff searching for and handling case files would be greatly reduced with an electronic filing system. Data entry time would also be drastically reduced because information could be automatically extracted from documents submitted.

Electronic filing could benefit pro se plaintiffs by reducing overall filing costs and by simplifying the process of filing court documents. Courts that adopt electronic filing will, however, need to ensure that those without computer access are not disadvantaged by the adoption of electronic filing systems. Courts could, for example, provide public access through computer kiosks. Members of the public also should be able to access electronic filing systems from Web-connected computers at libraries and community resource centers.

* * *

Although development of standards for electronic filing and the implementation of actual systems that comply with such standards may appear to be daunting tasks, initial efforts demonstrate that such standards and systems can be developed incrementally to facilitate development and mitigate costs—and that their advantages by far outweigh their disadvantages.

Robert Plotkin is an intellectual property attorney specializing in high technology law. He is a member of Legal XML, a nonprofit organization that develops and promotes electronic filing standards for the legal profession. He can be reached at rplotkin@rplotkin.com or on the Web at http://www.rplotkin.com.

Reprinted with permission from the *Boston Bar Journal,* a publication of the Boston Bar Association.

Source: From "Electronic Court Filing" by Robert Plotkin. Reprinted with permission of the *Boston Bar Journal,* a publication of the Boston Bar Association.

Discovery

After the pleadings are in and follow-up motions are filed and rejected, litigation moves to the next stage, which is **discovery**.

discovery
Part of the litigation process in which the plaintiff(s) and defendant(s) obtain information both from each other and possibly from third parties who can provide information relevant to the issues to be tried.

Purposes of Discovery

Discovery is aptly named; it is the stage of litigation in which each side can use various tools to learn the evidence on both sides of a case and what the other side will likely present at trial. During discovery, evidence may be uncovered that causes parties to the litigation to radically reassess the value of their case. The modern view of litigation is that a trial is the forum for presenting evidence when both sides have detailed knowledge of what the other side is going to present. If the plaintiff is going to use an expert witness to discuss why the defendant's product contained a defect, the defendant is entitled during discovery to be apprised of the name of the expert and to question the expert as to the basis for his or her likely testimony. If what the expert says during a deposition varies from what he or she says during testimony at trial, the defendant's attorney can impeach the testimony of the expert by pointing out discrepancies. In many cases, witnesses who can offer evidence that is potentially relevant to the litigation may be unavailable for trial. Discovery allows a litigant to question such witnesses and their sworn testimony may be read at trial or a tape of the deposition replayed in trial with video equipment.

Other Important Uses of Discovery

motion for summary judgment
A request (motion) of the court that it render a decision without completing the trial process, generally submitted based on the pleadings and other evidence not in the pleadings when no material facts are in dispute.

During discovery, one side or the other may discover that their evidence is weak. Hence, discovery is a process that encourages settlements. In many cases, if an expert witness or a key witness such as a chief executive officer does well or poorly during a deposition, it forms a basis for reassessment of the value of a case, which may lead to a settlement or dismissal of the case. In other cases, when one party to litigation becomes aware through discovery of how weak the other side's case is, a **motion for summary judgment** may be filed and granted. In general, discovery is a mechanism that apprises one party of the other party's evidence and allows each party an opportunity to assess with considerable accuracy the strength of the other side's case. Where the evidence is overwhelmingly on one side or the other, a case is very likely to be disposed of either by settlement or through court acceptance of a motion for summary judgment.

Motion for Summary Judgment (MSJ)

In the course of discovery, it sometimes becomes apparent that one side or the other asserts alleged "facts" for which it has no credible proof. When a party moves for a *summary judgment,* the moving party is claiming that there is no genuine issue of fact and that the court should render a judgment based on the pleadings supplemented by affidavits. An affidavit is a sworn statement of a witness or a party. When a defendant moves for summary judgment, the criterion for granting it is similar to that of a motion to dismiss. The defendant is claiming that, based on the facts alleged in the complaint that have been made clearer by discovery, the claim of the plaintiff lacks essential components so that the proper course for the court is to dismiss the case. Pursued by the plaintiff, a motion for summary judgment would claim that the defendant's case relies on affirmative defenses for which there is no credible proof so that the case should be decided by the judge in the plaintiff's favor.

Tools of Discovery

During discovery, litigants can make use of various tools that enable them to investigate facts known to witnesses aligned with the other side. Under the Federal Rules of Civil Procedure, there are six tools that can be used in discovery:

deposition
Sworn testimony of parties to lawsuits or witnesses, taken before trial.

- **Depositions** are an out-of-court questioning of a witness by attorneys. Deposition testimony is taken under oath, which means that the witness is subject to criminal prosecution for lying. In a typical product liability case, attorneys representing the plaintiff may depose engineers who worked for the defendant and who assisted in the design of the product in question. Depositions allow one side to determine the likely testimony of witnesses who may be called to testify at trial. A deposition becomes part of the court record and, as indicated earlier, be used to impeach or contradict the testimony of a witness who says something different at trial.

interrogatory
Written questions submitted to opposing parties or witnesses in litigation, requiring written answers sworn to by the party answering.

- Written **interrogatories** are out-of-court written questions directed to a party in a suit. When received, written interrogatories require the party to answer in written form. In answering interrogatories, most parties confer with the attorney(s) with whom they are working to prepare responses. Answers prepared in response to written interrogatories are available to the opposing side for impeachment at trial if the party's testimony at trial appears to be different. The scope of written interrogatories can be quite broad and simultaneously precise as the party can be asked questions that rely extensively on document and record details. In an oral deposition, it is often unrealistic to expect a fact party deponent (the party being asked the written questions) to intelligently answer detailed questions that require a lot of sifting through documents.

- *Subpoena Duces Tecûm* are court order to produce documents. As discussed above, in many cases documents play a large role in determining the outcome of a case. In a product liability case, if the defendant's employees (generally its engineers and chief executive officers) were aware of safety features of a product that injured the plaintiff and the plaintiff was injured in ways that were a concern of these employees, the defendant is likely in big trouble legally. Generally, there are few "smoking guns" of the kind just described, but production of documents, through *subpoena duces tecûm,* allows the other side to "build" its case and search for such documents.

- *Requests for admissions* are written questions asked of the opposing party in litigation, focusing on facts that they may be willing to concede. Requests for admissions are limited by the Federal Rules to requests by one party in the lawsuit to another party to the suit. Illustratively, in a product liability case, the plaintiff may ask of the defendant whether the defendant made and sold the product that injured the plaintiff. If an admission to that effect is not agreed to by the defendant, then the plaintiff has the burden of proving in court that the defendant did, indeed, make and sell the product(s) that injured the plaintiff. A request for admissions allows the parties to focus on facts that are really in dispute and not waste their time, or the court's time, on matters that are obviously true. There is no real need to prove in court that IBM manufactures computers or that Firestone makes tires.

- *Physical and mental examinations* are appropriate when the physical or mental condition of a party is in dispute. If a plaintiff alleges that, as a result of being injured by a product produced by the defendant, he will never walk again, the defendant is entitled to have the plaintiff examined by a doctor selected by the defendant. If the plaintiff further alleges depression as a result of his impaired physical condition, the defendant is entitled to have the plaintiff examined by a psychiatrist or psychologist. In some cases, the mental or physical condition of employees of the defendant is at issue and so, while generally it is the defendant who requests this type of examination, it is sometimes the reverse.

Sanctions for Failing to Respond to Discovery Requests

The Federal Rules provide for severe consequences if one party is uncooperative when *good faith* discovery requests are made by the opposing party. If one party fails to respond to a subpoena or request for a deposition, the other party can petition the court for a court order requiring the other party to comply with the request for information under one of the discovery tools. Costs are likely to be borne by the party whose conduct necessitated the court order. The consequences for ignoring a court order can be even more severe as the trial court can treat such mischief as a contempt of court and impose criminal sanctions. In addition, the failure of a party to cooperate with legitimate discovery requests allows the court to strike possible claims by or defenses of that party, or to deny that party the right to present evidence in court on the point of law at issue.

Pretrial Conference

At the close of discovery, a pretrial conference is held with the judge. The focus of the pretrial conference is twofold: (1) to *encourage a settlement* or, failing that, (2) to gain *agreement on stipulations of facts* and the conduct of the trial. At the pretrial conference, the judge, who often has seen many similar cases, will try to get the parties to agree to a settlement. The judge may indicate to the defendant that the evidence clearly indicates he has a small chance of escaping liability for some or all of the wrongs alleged in the complaint. The judge may turn to the plaintiff and contend that some of the legal claims made in the complaint have little merit and that, for the claims that do have some merit, the damages requested are exorbitant.

If the judge is unsuccessful in persuading the parties to settle, then he or she will be active in trying to get the parties to agree on or *stipulate* to facts that are not really instrumental in the outcome of the case. Facts that are stipulated to by the parties do not have to be proved or refuted at trial, streamlining and shortening the trial process. The more facts agreed to (stipulated to), the less time the trial will take, which is a significant positive in the minds of judges.

The Trial

A major event in civil litigation is getting a trial date scheduled. Federal and state judges are required to make room on their dockets for criminal cases, in part because of constitutional guarantees of a "speedy trial" for criminal defendants. When a civil case is finally placed on the court docket, sometimes two or three years after the case is filed, a number of decisions must be made.

Can and Should a Jury Be Requested?

In federal courts, either party can request a jury trial if the amount at issue exceeds $20 and the dispute involves a common law claim. The kinds of court cases that are of concern to businesses generally meet the requirements for having a jury trial if the parties want that form of trial.[6] There are some civil claims brought against businesses by government units that are based on regulatory statutes in which the right to a jury is excluded, but these cases are relatively rare. In some state courts, the minimum amount in dispute must exceed a set amount, such as $1,000. Of course, this minimum amount varies from state to state.

While either litigant can request a jury, having a jury is not always desirable. Jury trials take far longer than trials before just a judge, adding to court costs. In addition, in complicated cases, the judge's ability to assimilate complex facts is often greater than that of most jurors. Jurors may fall asleep during testimony about subjects that they have had little or no exposure to or have little interest in.

Voir Dire *and Jury Selection*

If a party does request a jury, then both sides have an opportunity to assist in jury selection through a process known as *voir dire.* Attorneys representing the litigants can question prospective jurors about various matters and can request that a juror be excused if the attorney believes the juror is so biased that he or she cannot make a reasoned judgment. If a juror had previously been the victim of a defective product, that juror might have a tough time being objective when another case involving product liability, and a possibly defective product, is the case at hand. Other grounds for jury exclusions *for cause* exist when a juror knows one of the parties or makes comments during *voir dire* that reveals prejudice in the kind of case to be tried. Attorneys are not limited in the number of challenges to prospective jurors that they file for cause.

Peremptory Challenges

Attorneys also are given a limited number of peremptory challenges, say 6 to 12 depending on the jurisdiction, in which they do not have to provide a reason for the challenge and exclusion of a particular prospective juror. In high-profile and complex cases, attorneys often hire jury consultants who assist in predicting which jurors are likely to be more inclined to accept their client's point of view.

Trials

In general terms, it is a basic constitutional guarantee for U.S. citizens to have a right to trial. Although television trials are normally resolved in dramatic fashion about seven minutes before the end of the hour, often with surprise elements producing a usually happy ending, the modern concept of actual trials is that they provide an orderly presentation of evidence with few surprises. In general, each party to litigation must provide any opposing party with a list of prospective witnesses and, by trial, the discovery process will have allowed each party to discover the likely testimony of witnesses. Surprise witnesses and documents are the exception in civil litigation.

There are some differences between jury and nonjury trials in terms of trial procedure. However, the fundamental procedural elements are common to trials both with and without juries. The typical pattern follows:

Opening Statements

The courtroom segment of litigation begins with *opening statements.* In opening statements each attorney, beginning with the plaintiff, lays out his or her basic theory of the case. The plaintiff's attorney will discuss what the plaintiff's evidence is intended to

---

[6] Some types of cases, most of which are not of interest to businesses, cannot have jury trials. These include cases involving divorces, child custody, adoption, etc. We'll have more to say about this a bit later.

prove in order to hold the defendant liable and will preview the damages to be claimed. The defendant's attorney will then discuss key evidence that will be presented to rebut the plaintiff's evidence. Generally, opening statements in front of a jury are limited to 20 minutes.

Trial Procedures: Testimony

After opening statements, the plaintiff presents its case in the form of direct evidence. Plaintiffs have the burden of proof to show that it is more likely than not that the allegations of fact contained in the complaint took place. Generally, the plaintiff will call witnesses and present evidence through testimony of the witnesses. At the end of each witness's **direct testimony,** the defendant's attorney(s) is (are) entitled to *cross-examine* the plaintiff's witness. At the conclusion of the **cross-examination,** in which the defendant's attorney has tried to undermine testimony from the witness, the plaintiff's attorney may try to restore any loss of credibility by re–direct examination of the witness. If there is a re–direct examination, then the defendant's attorney is entitled to re-cross-examine the witness.

When the plaintiff is done presenting testimony and any other evidence, the defendant gets the turn to call witnesses and directly examine its witnesses, attempting to present evidence that tends to refute the evidence offered by plaintiffs. Symmetrically with the sequence described above, the plaintiff's attorneys have the right to cross-examine the defendant's witnesses. There is also a possibility that the defense will request re–direct examination and, of course, the plaintiff is entitled to re-cross-examine any witness who has testified on re–direct examination.

After direct testimony, each side, beginning with the plaintiff, is allowed to offer rebuttal evidence. Rebuttal evidence is presented through witnesses and is designed to contradict or impeach the credibility of witnesses who earlier testified on behalf of the opposing party's case. In a product liability case, if the plaintiff uses an expert witness to testify about a product defect, the defense may offer its own expert to testify that the plaintiff's expert did not examine key factors or does not have the training to scientifically make such a determination.

Motion for a Directed Verdict

At the conclusion of the plaintiff's presentation of evidence and with the jury momentarily excused, it is common for the defendant to move for a *directed verdict* in its favor. As with other motions presented to the judge, the defendant is claiming in this motion that the plaintiff has offered no credible evidence (or proof) on certain points necessary to make out a case for liability of the defendant. When both sides have completed their presentation of evidence, it is common for the defendant to reassert the **motion for a directed verdict,** again based on the same grounds, namely that there is no proof of an essential element of the plaintiff's claim. The plaintiff also could launch a motion for a directed verdict at this time, claiming that the defendant has not offered credible evidence to rebut the plaintiff's evidence or that the defendant has not successfully borne the burden of proof with respect to an affirmative defense.

As with the other motions we have discussed, if a motion is granted, it can stop the case from going forward to the jury. In this event, the case is over, unless the nonmoving party appeals to a higher court. If the nonmoving party wins on appeal, the case is remanded to the trial court for another trial. Also, if the judge does not grant a motion for a directed verdict and the defendant loses a jury verdict, the defendant can appeal that failure to grant the motion.

Slip and fall cases are brought against businesses in large numbers, and such cases are often greeted by defendants' motions for directed verdicts. In slip and fall cases, the facts are often sparse. We know the plaintiff fell, we know the claimed cause of the fall, but

---

direct testimony
For the plaintiff, evidence provided by testimony of plaintiffs and witnesses for plaintiffs in response to questions asked by plaintiff's attorney or attorneys. For the defendant, evidence provided by testimony of the defendant and witnesses for the defendant in response to questions asked by defendant's attorney(s).

cross-examination
The questioning of witnesses by the opposing party's attorney(s) for the purpose of undermining a witness's direct testimony.

motions for a directed verdict
Requests (motions) to the court (the judge) to issue a verdict, based on information available to the court, without allowing the jury to deliberate or reach a jury verdict.

beyond that it is anyone's conjecture as to whether the defendant was negligent, or whether the plaintiff was also negligent. In the next case, the defendant filed a motion for a directed verdict following the plaintiff's presentation of evidence that he slipped and fell while walking downstairs in the defendant's store. The plaintiff claimed he slipped on a pencil that was on the stairs, while the defendant claims in its motion that there was no way it could be responsible for knowing that there was a pencil on the stairs.

In many personal injury cases, juries side with victims (plaintiffs) because the members of the jury often identify with individuals rather than businesses. Knowing the biases of jurors, defendants rely heavily on motions to dismiss and motions for directed verdicts because, if the case between a business and an injured party goes to jury, the defendant is at significant risk of losing.

Case 3-2

Bobby Simmons, and Wife Sheila Simmons, Appellants v. Sears, Roebuck and Co., Appellee

Supreme Court of Tennessee, at Knoxville
713 S.W.2d 640 (1986)

BACKGROUND AND FACTS

This is an action to recover damages for injuries sustained by plaintiff, Bobby E. Simmons, in a fall on steps located on premises of the defendant, Sears, Roebuck and Company. The trial court directed a verdict for the defendant at the close of the plaintiffs' proof. A divided Court of Appeals affirmed. The Supreme Court of Tennessee granted an appeal to determine whether the evidence, when considered in the light most favorable to the plaintiffs, makes out a prima facie case of liability against the defendant.

The record shows that at about 6:00 P.M. on May 19, 1980, the plaintiff accompanied his friend, John Cooper, to Sears to purchase some small tools. The tools were displayed and sold in the basement of Sears. The stairway leading to the basement is located near the Pearl Street entrance to Sears. There is a concession stand near the head of the stairway, where customers can purchase soft drinks, peanuts, popcorn, and the like for consumption within the store. It is not uncommon for there to be debris on the floor from the concession purchases.

Defendant's employees thoroughly sweep or vacuum the entire store each day before opening. After 1:00 P.M., the maintenance staff is reduced to one man who is on call to clean up spills in addition to other duties assigned to him. The maintenance man also attempts to visit each department of the store during the afternoon and evening hours for cleanup purposes.

The stairway to the basement consists of 10 terrazzo steps from the building's main floor to a landing and 10 to 12 more steps to the basement. Plaintiff and his friend negotiated the first set of stairs and the landing without incident, though they did note considerable debris on the stairs. When plaintiff reached the second or third step of the second flight of stairs, he "stepped on something" with his right foot and his foot "rolled completely out from under [him]." When this happened, plaintiff lost his balance and "fell on the lower part of [his] back and bounced down the steps." The plaintiff did not undertake to identify the object or objects that caused his fall other than referring to it as "something" that rolled under his foot.

After plaintiff fell, a pencil was found on the stairs at the approximate location of plaintiff's fall. There is nothing in the record to indicate who dropped the pencil or whether it is of the type used by employees of Sears, nor is there any direct evidence to show how long the pencil had been on the stairway. Noting this, the trial court and the majority of the Court of Appeals concluded that the plaintiff had failed to carry his burden of showing that Sears had actual or constructive knowledge of the dangerous condition of the stairs in sufficient time to rectify the condition, and directed a verdict for the defendant.

Opinion by Cooper, Justice

The duty owed a customer by a proprietor of a place of business "is to exercise reasonable care to keep the premises in a reasonably safe and suitable condition, including the duty of removing or warning against a dangerous condition traceable to persons for whom the proprietor is not responsible . . . if the circumstances of time and place are such that by the exercise of reasonable care the proprietor should have become aware of such condition." *Allison v. Blount National Bank,* 54 Tenn. App. 359, 390 S.W.2d 716, 718 (1965).

A customer confirmed the finding of the pencil on the steps. He also testified as follows:

Q. And you went back up those steps?

A. Yes, sir.

Q. And you say you saw popcorn?

A. Yeah, I did. There was debris on the stairs.

Q. Well, tell us what you saw there.

A. Popcorn—

Q. How much popcorn?

A. Peanuts. Oh—

Q. How many peanuts?

A. Oh, seven or eight peanuts, maybe twenty or thirty pieces of popcorn, like a kid spilled some popcorn or something.

Q. Do you know how long it had been there?

A. No, sir. It was dirty. I mean, you know, it had been walked on.

Q. It could have been walked on by the people that just went up ahead of you?

A. Yes, sir.

Q. Just seconds before you went up?

A. No, I wouldn't think so. It was dirtier than that.

Q. Where was this popcorn and these peanuts?

A. It was all over the steps. It was like—you know, if you drop something in an aisle where people walk, after they walk on it, it will go to the sides. There wasn't too much of it in the middle.

The customer further testified that he had observed several of Sears' employees going up and down the stairway during the fifteen minute period preceding plaintiff's fall, and that "the debris, the peanuts, the popcorn bags, the cups" were obvious to those employees.

* * *

In our opinion, as we view the evidence, a trier of fact could reasonably conclude that Sears had constructive knowledge of the condition of the stairs in sufficient time to have removed the debris or have warned customers using the stairway of its condition and, in failing to do so, was guilty of negligence that proximately caused plaintiff to fall and be injured. It follows that a directed verdict for the defendant was error.

Decision and Outcome

The judgment for defendant based on the granting of a motion for a directed verdict by the trial court judge is reversed and the cause is remanded to the trial court for trial.

Questions for Analysis

1. Why was it important that the defendant knew or should have known that there were obstructions on the steps?

2. On remand to the trial court, what must the plaintiff show in order to get this case before a jury? If the case does go before a jury, what crucial issue must the jury decide?

Source: Copyright © 2002 Stu (www.stus.com).
Reprinted with permission.

Closing Arguments

At the end of the presentation of evidence and rulings on motions to dismiss, both parties will give closing arguments. In spite of extensive planning for the orderly presentation of evidence, events often occur at trial that were not foreseen. Sometimes, witnesses who appeared very credible in depositions before the trial turn out to be much less credible on the witness stand and vice versa. Attorneys have a feel for what went over well with the jury and will emphasize the evidence and testimony that appeared favorable to their case. In general, plaintiffs have the right to make some of their closing arguments both before and after the defendant's closing arguments.

Jury Instructions

After closing arguments, the judge will instruct the jury. The judge will request sample instructions from each side before selecting text for jury instruction. Each party to the litigation will suggest jury instructions that are worded in a manner slightly favorable to their positions in the case. As long as the attorney-recommended instructions are not too one-sided, the judge will select language from each party's recommendations. In the jury instructions, the judge tells jurors what they need to do in order to arrive at a verdict. In a product liability case, the judge may tell jurors that they are to decide if the product in question contained a *defect,* to determine whether the defect was the *proximate (legal) cause* of the plaintiff's injuries, and to determine the extent of the damages. Jurors will be instructed that if they do not find the product defective, then there is no need to consider the other issues.

Jury instructions can be a basis for appeal. Under the Federal Rules, a judge is required to inform the parties beforehand what the jury instructions will be. If one side objects, the objection must be made before the jury begins deliberations and it must explain with particularity the basis for the objection. If a party objects to a jury instruction and subsequently loses a jury verdict, that party can appeal the verdict based on the allegedly unfair jury instruction. If the losing party prevails on appeal, the case will be remanded back to the trial court for a new trial.

The appropriateness of jury instructions provided at trial is the core issue of the following case.

Case 3-3

State of Indiana and Indiana State Highway Department, Appellants-Defendants v. James R. Eaton, Shirley Eaton, as Legal and Natural Guardians of Jeffrey J. Eaton, Appellees-Plaintiffs

Court of Appeals of Indiana 659 N.E.2d 232 (1995)

BACKGROUND AND FACTS

On October 2, 1981, a state highway maintenance crew was continuing the work it began the day before, "clipping" the shoulder of U.S. Highway 421 ("Highway") for drainage. [Record cite omitted] When clipping a highway's shoulder, a grader pulls up dirt, gravel, and other materials along the edge of the road onto the road. Dust is created when a highway is clipped. A loader loads the dirt onto a dump truck, which hauls the debris away. Normally, a sweeper makes several passes to clear away much of the dirt and gravel left on the roadway.

Warning signs were posted in the vicinity of the area in which the crew was clipping. The crew was clipping the Highway from south to north, and much dust was generated by its activities. At approximately 2:30 P.M. on October 2, 1981, the plaintiff, Jeffrey Eaton ("Jeffrey"), then a high school senior, was driving his motorcycle home from school on the Highway, traveling in a northerly direction. Jeffrey noticed dirt and dust on the Highway. As he came up over a slight rise in the Highway, he slowed down from his speed of forty (40)–forty-five (45) miles per hour.

A semi-tractor trailer was traveling on the Highway in front of Jeffrey. The evidence is unclear regarding whether the trailer was slowing down, stopped, or beginning to move after stopping, but the driver stated that he was following a flagman's directions in the area of the Highway being clipped. The trailer's driver remembers hearing a bang and seeing something in the roadway in his rearview mirror. Upon exiting the trailer's cab, the driver discovered Jeffrey, who had apparently run into the rear of the trailer. Jeffrey, who suffered severe neurological injuries as a result of the accident, does not clearly remember the day's events, but it appears that Jeffrey's motorcycle collided with the rear end of the trailer.

In the trial, the jury returned a verdict in the Eatons' favor. The jury awarded the Eatons Four Hundred Forty-nine Thousand Two Hundred Eighty Dollars ($449,280.00) as Jeffrey's legal guardians for Jeffrey's personal injuries, and awarded them One Hundred One Thousand One Hundred Seventy-eight Dollars and Sixty-four Cents ($101,178.64) as Jeffrey's natural guardians for loss of Jeffrey's services. The trial court reduced the larger award to Three Hundred Thousand Dollars ($300,000.00) in accordance with the Indiana Tort Claims Act, but allowed the loss of services award to stand. This appeal ensued in due course.

Opinion by Rucker, Judge

The State first contends the trial court erred in instructing the jury on Jeffrey's duty of care as a motorist on a public highway. The jury was instructed that Jeffrey had a duty to use ordinary care. In so doing the court refused the State's tendered instruction which would have advised the jury that Jeffrey was required to use extraordinary care. In support of its contention the State points out that at the time of the collision Indiana Code § 9-4-1-33 then in effect provided in relevant part:

    a. No driver of a vehicle or motorman of a street car shall disobey the instructions of any official traffic control device placed in accordance with the provisions of this chapter, unless at the time otherwise directed by a police officer.

b. When traffic control devices or flagmen are utilized at worksites on any public highway for traffic control, all motorists shall exercise extraordinary care to secure the mutual safety of all persons and motorists at the worksite.

The State's tendered instruction tracked the language of the foregoing statute; and the State argues the court erred in rejecting it because the instruction was a correct statement of the law, supported by the evidence, and not covered by any other instruction.

The giving of jury instructions is a matter within the trial court's discretion, and we review only for abuse. *Weller v. Mack Trucks, Inc.* (1991), Ind. App., 570 N.E.2d 1341, 1343. The refusal of a tendered instruction constitutes reversible error when: (a) the instruction is shown to correctly state the law, (b) the instruction is supported by the evidence, (c) the instruction is not covered by others which were given, and (d) there is a reasonable probability substantial rights of the complaining party have been adversely affected. *Transport Ins. Co. v. Terrell Trucking, Inc.* (1987), Ind. App., 509 N.E.2d 220, 224.

Whether the State was entitled to an instruction that Jeffrey had a duty to use extraordinary care depends in part at least on whether there was evidence in the record showing the collision occurred at a worksite. This is so because ordinarily there are no degrees of care in Indiana, *Neal v. Home Builders, Inc.* (1953), 232 Ind. 160, 111 N.E.2d 280, *reh'g denied,* and absent a statute requiring otherwise, the proper standard is ordinary care. At the time of the collision the term "worksite" was defined as "[a] location or area upon which a public purpose construction or maintenance activity, or a private purpose construction or maintenance activity which is properly authorized by a governmental agency, is being performed on a public highway." Ind. Code § 9-4-1-19.5. The location or area comprising a worksite depends on the facts and circumstances of each case. Here, the only evidence of whether the collision occurred at a worksite was provided by the Eatons in their case in chief. Doctor Jack Humpries, a professor emeritus in civil engineering at the University of Tennessee, was qualified by the trial court as an expert in the field of highway safety. Without objection he testified, among other things, that the worksite "is the area where physically work is taking place. It doesn't include the entire stretch of roadway from the first sign to the last sign. . . ." Record at 989–990. According to Doctor Humpries the location of the "flagmen" in this case established the outer boundaries of where work was physically taking place on the roadway. The record shows the collision occurred at some distance away from the flagmen and thus not at the worksite. Because the collision did not occur at or within a worksite, Jeffrey was only required to use ordinary care while driving his motorcycle. The State's instruction concerning extraordinary care was not supported by the evidence and was therefore properly rejected. We find no error on this issue.

Decision and Outcome

The Indiana Court of Appeals rejected the appeal of the defendants who claimed that jury instructions were improper because the jury was not told that the plaintiff had an obligation to use "extraordinary" care near a road construction site. The Court of Appeals noted that the accident took place some distance from that actual construction site.

Questions for Analysis

1. If the jury instruction proffered by the State of Indiana had been accepted, would the jury have nevertheless found for Jeffrey Eaton? Is there any way of telling whether the changed jury instruction would have changed the ultimate jury verdict? Is it clear why an improper jury instruction requires the appellate court to not only reverse the verdict of the trial court, but also remand it back to the trial court for a new trial?

2. What fact made the jury instruction that the state wanted unnecessary? Should it matter where the road construction takes place? Is it reasonable that the care required of drivers in a worksite where construction is taking place immediately requires motor vehicle drivers to increase their level of care?

The Verdict

verdict
The outcome of a trial.

When a jury adjourns to determine its **verdict,** it will be instructed that if there is indecision on an essential element of the claim, it should find for the defendant because the plaintiff must prove his or her case by a *preponderance of the evidence.* In the federal courts, juries range from 6 to 12 members. Juries composed of fewer than 12 jurors are quite common at the state level, and in many cases, less than unanimous verdicts are allowed. The Federal Rules allow for less than unanimity in jury verdicts, but only if both sides agree.

hung jury
A jury that, based on the evidence presented in trial, is unable to agree on a verdict.

A hung jury exists if the jurors cannot reach a verdict, either because there is dissent in a trial that requires unanimity or because the required majority is not reached in a case that allows less than unanimity. Trials are expensive and time-consuming affairs, so a hung jury is an unsatisfactory result. Judges often will ask juries that report that they cannot reach a verdict to go back and deliberate some more. If the judge gives up and decides that there is no point in further deliberation by the hung jury, a mistrial will be declared.

Post-Trial Motions

Motion for a New Trial

After the jury verdict is recorded, parties to the litigation can file post-trial motions. The losing party in the litigation can *move for a new trial* on the grounds that the trial court judge obviously made a mistake. This plea continues with the argument that, with such error, there is no reason to wait for the case to be appealed and for the decision of the trial court to be reversed on appeal. A common mistake that would justify granting a motion for a new trial is the admission of evidence that should not be admitted (such as the fact that the defendant is being represented by an insurance company). In general, juries might be more disposed to find for the plaintiff if they know that the defendant is represented by an insurance company and the judgment is not coming out of the defendant's pocket. There are other grounds for granting a motion for a new trial, particularly when misconduct of the parties or their attorneys has occurred.

Motion for Judgment Notwithstanding the Verdict

motion for a judgment notwithstanding the verdict (J.n.o.v.)
A request of the court, provided by either party, for rejecting a jury verdict and deciding the case in the favor of the party making the request.

The losing party, typically the defendant, can file a motion for a judgment notwithstanding the verdict, often referred to as a J.n.o.v. It is appropriate to grant a J.n.o.v. in the defendant's favor on the same grounds as for a motion for a directed verdict, namely that there was not sufficient proof to bring the case to jury for a decision. The question may be asked, how can a judge deny a motion for a directed verdict and then grant a J.n.o.v?

Denying a motion for a directed verdict and granting a J.n.o.v. makes perfect sense when you consider what could happen on appeal. Undoubtedly, the losing side (in this situation the plaintiff) will appeal the decision of a trial court judge to grant a J.n.o.v. for the defendant. If the decision of the trial court to grant the J.n.o.v. is affirmed on appeal, then the case is over and the defendant wins the case. If the appellate court reverses the decision of the trial court by reversing the granting of the J.n.o.v. by the trial court, then there is no need to remand to the trial court for a new trial because there is already a jury verdict. By denying a motion for a directed verdict and granting a J.n.o.v., the judge is able to hedge his bet and conserve valuable trial time instead of having to go through the entire trial again.

Remedies: Monetary Damages

settlement
Agreement between litigants to settle their dispute without proceeding through trial, usually accompanied by consideration from both sides to the dispute.

Most cases that are filed with a court do not end up in a trial. Most are settled before the case gets to trial. In a settlement, the plaintiff signs a paper that releases the defendant from claims she or he may have had against the defendant, who, in return, will pay an agreed-upon sum of money to the plaintiff. Settlements make sense when both sides have about the same assessments of the value of the case as the settlement enables the parties to avoid many of the costs associated with litigation, not only attorney fees, but also executive time, uncertainty, and unwanted publicity. In tort claims, attorneys for the plaintiff generally work on contingency, which means they get a percentage of the damages awarded or agreed to. Attorneys working under a contingent fee arrangement are motivated to settle cases because a settlement enables them to get their percentage of the monetary damages without having to incur the expenses of going to trial or enduring the uncertainty of a jury verdict.

Monetary damages generally can be classified as compensatory, punitive, and nominal.

Compensatory Damages

Example: Contract Damages   If a case goes to trial and the plaintiff wins, the most common remedy is the payment of compensatory damages. As discussed above, civil litigation is weighted against full compensation for losses incurred by a plaintiff because courts will not allow recovery of monetary damages that are "speculative." Moreover, the costs of litigation, including attorney fees, generally are not recoverable. For most plaintiffs in contract or tort litigation, the theory of compensatory damages is to make the plaintiff "whole" again. In contracts, jurors are asked to imagine if the contract was performed by both sides, what would be the financial condition of the plaintiff. Assume the plaintiff is a buyer and the seller defaulted on his obligation to ship goods conforming to what was agreed to in the contract. One component of compensatory damages is the higher price the injured party, the buyer, had to pay for goods purchased on the market rather than at the contract price. In equation form, this component of compensatory damages is

$$D = (P_m - P_k)Q_k$$

where P_m is the market price and P_k and Q_k are contract price and quantity.

When the seller defaults on delivery of the goods, it can generally be assumed that the market price, P_m, will exceed the contract price, P_k. If there are quantifiable costs associated with going out on the market to obtain conforming goods, then the plaintiff is entitled to recover those incidental costs, in addition to any higher prices paid. In addition, if plaintiff expected to make profits using the goods that are the subject matter of the contract, then (s)he is entitled to prove that (s)he would have made those profits but for the default by the defendant. Again it should be emphasized that recovery for lost profits requires substantial proof rather than just generalized statements about profitability. There are other components of monetary damages associated with contract breaches and these are discussed more fully in later chapters.

Tort Damages   In tort claims, the theory is, again, that the court should make the plaintiff whole—that is, restore the plaintiff to the position (s)he occupied before (s)he was a tort victim. Suppose Howard was driving the speed limit and on his side of the road when he was hit and severely injured by Tom, whose driving was impaired by alcohol. Before the tort occurred, Howard was a healthy 30-year-old man who enjoyed participating in sporting contests and was earning a good living as an electrician. If the automobile wreck caused Howard to lose one of his arms, his **tort damages** should encompass the following:

tort damages
Compensation in cases involving injury intended to restore the victim to his or her pre-injury state.

- Howard may be able to recover for the value of his arm. Since Howard probably cannot continue working as an electrician, he would be entitled to a recovery equal to his lost wages, which generally would be based on the difference between pre- and post-injury wage rates available to Howard, all reduced to present value. In many cases of serious injury, there may be no post-injury earning capacity.

- Howard should be able to recover for all his medical bills. If he suffers mental depression as a result of his injuries, he should be compensated for bills for treatment for that condition also.

- Howard also should be able to recover for the pain and suffering that is attributable to the accident.

- Howard should be able to receive compensation for the tasks that he previously did around the house that, because of his lost arm, he can no longer perform and for which he may now have to hire outside help.

Even this listing of damages is incomplete. Obviously, tort claims require valuation of things that most people would prefer not to value. Let us assume that Howard is awarded $250,000 as compensation for his lost arm. After the injury occurred, if you asked Howard whether he would rather have his arm back or the $250,000, for most people, the answer is obvious, even though the conceptual intent of tort damage awards is "to make the injured party whole again." Some tort claims involve wrongful deaths. In these cases, it certainly is not possible through any monetary award to make the victim of the tort "whole" (unless, perhaps, the victim is Lazarus).[7]

Punitive Damages

punitive damages
Court-awarded damages intended to punish or make an example of a defendant in order to deter wrongful conduct.

As the label implies, the intent of **punitive damages** is to punish the defendant for his outrageous behavior and to make an example of the defendant so as to deter similarly situated defendants from doing the same potentially injurious things in the future. In some states punitive damages are called *exemplary* damages, further emphasizing the deterrent purpose of such damages. Given the purpose of punitive damages, it is a remedy reserved for defendants who act *intentionally* to harm others. Plaintiff's attorneys, however, have an incentive to blur the distinction between intentional and accidental harm. In the case immediately above, it might be accurate to say that Tom had no specific intent to harm Howard. However, driving while impaired shows a *reckless disregard* for the safety of others on the road. If Tom had been stopped before for driving under the influence of alcohol and if his blood alcohol score was, say, .20, it could be said that Tom was grossly negligent, which is probably enough for the imposition of punitive damages.

Relationship of Punitive Damages to Compensatory Damages   In some tort claims in which the defendant is a large corporation, juries have awarded punitive damages that are many times the amount of compensatory damages. In one case involving a repainted BMW, a jury in Alabama awarded the plaintiff $4,000 in compensatory damages and $4,000,000 in punitive damages, a multiple of 1,000 to 1.[8] The Alabama Supreme Court let the verdict stand but reduced the punitive damage award to $2,000,000. The U.S. Supreme Court struck down this judgment as being at odds with due process. Courts have not fashioned a hard and fast rule as to how much is too much when comparing punitive damages to compensatory damages, leaving juries with wide discretion over punitive awards. Needless to say, one of the reasons businesses are so fearful of litigation is the possibility of harsh punitive damage awards. Because of the perceived excessiveness of some punitive damage awards, 30 states have posted some form of cap on punitive damages. Some of the caps limit punitive damage awards to a multiple (say three or four) of compensatory damages.

Appeals to Higher Courts

appeals
Requests to a higher court that a case tried in a lower court be reviewed and its outcome altered, based on the claim that errors of law were committed in the trial court.

Most **appeals** are unsuccessful. The judicial system has a stake in resolving disputes at the trial court level and most trial court judges know their job well and avoid making egregious legal errors. Even when errors are made, not every error of law made by a trial court is appealable; only *material* errors of law—that is, errors of law that could have affected the

---

[7] In the Bible, Jesus caused Lazarus to rise from the dead even though he was presumed dead for three days. Since most folks would choose life over a monetary award, regardless of the amount of the damage award in a tort claim, there is really no way to make a wrongful death victim "whole."

[8] *BMW of North America v. Gore,* 517 U.S. 559 (1996).

outcome of the case—are subject to appeal. Within the judicial system, there certainly is recognition of the value of closure, which trial courts normally provide.

The arguments made by attorneys representing the parties before appellate court judges can be both oral and written. Written appellate briefs lay out the litigants' positions on whether the trial court did or did not make an error of law while oral arguments enable the appellate court judges to question the attorneys about points that may not have been adequately discussed in the written briefs. Generally, at courts of appeal in the federal system, three judges hear a case, though, for important cases, the entire group of judges at the appellate court may be involved in the decision.

Options Available to Appellate Courts

In general, appellate courts can *affirm, reverse,* or *reverse and remand* cases appealed from trial courts. Of course, if the appellate court is the supreme court in the jurisdiction, it can affirm or reverse a decision of a lower court of appeals, in most cases the circuit court of appeals. Appellate courts do not have to explain their reasoning in cases they review and, with some frequency, cases reviewed that are affirmed get a one-word opinion: "Affirm." In most cases, however, appellate courts do discuss the reasoning applied in coming to their decisions, no matter whether the appellate court affirms or reverses the decision of the trial court. If the decision of the appellate court judges is not unanimous, a *majority opinion* is written, as well as a *dissenting opinion.* In addition to the majority opinion, there are sometimes *concurring opinions* in which some judges agree with the outcome reached by the majority, but disagree to some degree with the bases for the decision.

In some cases appellate courts simply *reverse* decisions reached at the trial court level, while, in other situations, appellate courts *reverse* the decision of the trial court *and remand* the case back to the court for a trial on all or some part of the core issues contested in the original trial. If the appeal of the losing party is based on an improper jury instruction, and the appellate court reverses the trial court, holding that the jury instruction was improper, the case must be remanded for a new trial because the appellate judges do not know what jurors would have ruled if their instructions were not flawed. If the appellate court reverses a trial court decision to grant a motion to dismiss, then the case is remanded back to the trial court for a trial. If the trial court's granting of a J.n.o.v. is reversed, there is already a jury verdict, so there is no need to remand the case to the trial court.

Judgments

Once all appeals are resolved, a final judgment is entered, detailing the compensation that must be delivered to the plaintiff. Given the substantial stake the judicial system has in closure, there are rules that prevent litigation of the same case more than once. *Res judicata* means that the thing has been decided, and the concept of *res judicata* prevents a case from being reinstated once all appeals have been exhausted and a final judgment entered. If a losing plaintiff initiated essentially the same suit against the defendant in another state, the defendant could move to have the case dismissed based on the principle of *res judicata.* States accord *comity* to judicial decisions of the courts of sister states, meaning that a judgment earned in one state can be enforced in another state without allowing the defendant to relitigate issues of liability and damages in the second state.

Enforcement of Judgments

In most cases, the objective of a plaintiff's lawsuit is winning a monetary judgment. In many cases, after all appeals are exhausted, the defendant will write a check to satisfy the judgment. In other cases, the plaintiff has to chase down the assets of the defendant and may need the assistance of law enforcement to enforce the judgement it has won. A plaintiff can obtain a *writ of execution,* which, in simple terms, is a command to the sheriff to seize property of the defendant. It is much easier to seize bank accounts than real property. In some cases, because of homestead laws, defendants cannot be dispossessed of their homes. Hence, plaintiffs put liens on the defendant's real estate, which means that, if the real estate is sold, the defendant is entitled to some of the proceeds after prior mortgagees (generally held by banks or other financial institutions) are paid. Other assets that can be used to satisfy a judgment include wages (garnishments are used) and specific property such as automobiles that may have been collateral for the loan the plaintiff made to the defendant.

Summary

Factors the Parties Must Take into Account in the Decision to Litigate

- Litigation is a very expensive process. Not only are large sums of money spent in attorney fees and damages, but also there are less visible costs, particularly those accompanying the time demands placed on executives.

- Our system of justice is based on an *adversarial process* in which parties with *real, current interests* at stake try to prove their case in front of neutral judges and juries.

- The burden of proof in civil cases is borne by the plaintiff. In order to win, the plaintiff must show by a *preponderance of the evidence* that the facts the plaintiff alleges are true.

- Business plaintiffs should look at litigation as an investment and value it using basic principles of finance, present value, and risk. Business plaintiffs should be aware that litigation rarely compensates for the full losses associated with a legal wrong. Various rules of evidence have the effect of limiting recoveries to less than actual losses.

- Plaintiffs are generally not entitled to recover for attorney fees, the opportunity cost of executive time, and impairment of relations with trading partners as a result of litigation. Also, since damages are recoverable only after the defendant has finished with appeals, the estimated value of a case should be reduced to reflect the present value of money to be received in the future. Litigation is risky and there is apt to be a wide variance associated with estimated values of a case. Most businesses are *risk averse*, further diminishing the value of a case.

- Business defendants bear most of the same costs of litigation that are borne by the plaintiff. The higher the costs of litigation, the greater the potential gains from negotiation and settlement.

- Business litigation is likely to be especially expensive because of the large number of documents involved, the opportunity cost of executive time, the expense and uncertainty of reliance on expert witnesses, and the possibility of truly huge damage awards. Also, large damage awards inspire time-consuming appeals and delays.

Stages of Litigation before the Trial: Pleadings, Motions, Discovery, and Pretrial Conference

- It is possible to classify litigation by stages. The sequence of events (both likely and possible) in a typical injury case that goes to trial are as follows:

- The first stage is the *pleadings*. In the pleadings, the parties basically lay out what they contend the facts are and what they intend to prove in a courtroom. With multiple parties, pleadings can become complicated by counterclaims, replies, cross-claims, and more answers.

- Once the pleadings are filed, it is common for the defendant to file a *motion to dismiss* or a *motion for a judgment* on the pleadings. With these motions, the defendant generally contends that, even if the facts alleged in the complaint are accurate, that (s)he is not liable to the plaintiff.

- During discovery, each party can use various tools such as *depositions* and *subpoenas* to obtain relevant information. Failure to respond appropriately to legitimate requests for information or failure to preserve relevant information can result in severe sanctions or dismissal of the case or of defenses in the case.

- Often the parties reevaluate the value of their case during discovery and settle as a result. Alternatively, one side may conclude that the other side's case is so weak that he files a motion for a summary judgment, when it is concluded that there is no genuine issue of fact.

- The purpose of a *pretrial conference* is to promote settlements and, failing that, to obtain stipulations as to facts so that the trial can be expedited.

- Before the trial, a jury is selected unless both parties waive that right. During *voir dire,* attorneys for both sides question jurors for possible prejudice and can discharge jurors without citing a reason by using their *peremptory challenges.*

The Trial: Voir Dire, Presentation of Evidence, Motions, Jury Instruction, and Verdict	• During the trial, each party is allowed to make an *opening statement,* to call witnesses, and to present evidence to prove his or her side of the case or to rebut evidence presented by the other side. Each party can directly *examine* his or her witnesses and can *cross-examine* witnesses presented by the other party.
	• During the trial, either side can move for a *directed verdict* if proof offered by the other side is so weak that no rational jury could find for that side. If the motions for directed verdict are not granted, each side is allowed to make a *closing statement* before the case goes to a jury.
	• The language the judge uses to charge the jury with its tasks is a frequent source of appeals. Juries can find for either the plaintiff or the defendant or a jury could be *hung* in the case that they cannot decide. Jury verdicts need not be unanimous if both sides agree to less than unanimity.
	• After the jury verdict, or the decision of the judge when there is no jury, *post-trial motions* are common such as a motion for a new trial or a *motion for a judgment notwithstanding a verdict.*

Remedies and Appeals: Most Remedies Are Monetary and Compensatory, but Punitive Damages Are Reserved for Intentional Wrongs; Appeals Are Based on Errors of Law by the Trial Court	• In most cases, the plaintiff is seeking monetary compensation. *Compensatory damages* compensate the plaintiff for the harm incurred as a result of the defendant's legal wrongs. In many cases, money is used to compensate for assets that are hard to value such as body parts, life, and loss of future opportunities.
	• *Punitive damages* are designed to punish the defendant and to deter future defendants who may be in a similar situation. Punitive damages are reserved for intentional wrongs. The relationship between the amounts of punitive damages relative to compensatory damages is a source of controversy. Many states have fashioned various means to cap punitive damage awards.
	• When a case is *appealed,* the appellate court can *affirm* the decision of the trial court, *reverse* that decision, or *reverse* the decision *and remand* the case back to the trial court for a new trial.
	• In most cases, a defendant who loses a case and has exhausted options for appeal will write out a check to satisfy the judgment. In some cases, the plaintiff must get a *writ of execution* to enforce the judgment.

Key Terms

adversarial system, *61*
affirmative defenses, *70*
alternative dispute resolution (ADR), *61*
answer, *67*
appeals, *85*
business courts, *63*
complaint, *67*
counterclaims, *71*
cross-examination, *77*
deposition, *74*
direct testimony, *77*

discovery, *73*
hung jury , *83*
interrogatory, *74*
litigation, *65*
motion for a judgment notwithstanding the verdict (J.n.o.v.), *83*
motion for summary judgment, *73*
motions, *67*
motions for a directed verdict, *77*

motions for judgment on the pleadings, *68*
pleadings, *67*
preponderance of the evidence, *61*
punitive damages, *85*
settlement, *83*
summons, *67*
tort damages, *84*
verdict, *82*

Questions for Review and Analysis

1. Compare and contrast the following motions: motion to dismiss, motion for a summary judgment, motion for a directed verdict, and motion for a judgment notwithstanding the verdict.
   a. When does each of these motions occur in the litigation process?
   b. What does each of these motions have in common with the others?
   c. How is each of these motions dissimilar to the others?

2. Discuss the factors that a business has to take into account when deciding whether to litigate. How might a rational business want to evaluate the decision to sue?

3. Discuss how the various stages in litigation are designed to prevent a surprise at the trial from occurring and from determining the outcome of the case.

4. Explain the difference between an appellate court reversing a decision of a trial court and that court both reversing the decision of a trial court and remanding the case back to the trial court for a new trial.

If You Really Understood This Chapter, You Should Be Able to Provide Informed Commentary on the Following:

1. **Hidden Costs of Litigation.** Dollar Rent-a-Car (Dollar) sued the Ford Motor Company for alleged antitrust violations because Ford gave preferential prices to Hertz and Avis but not Dollar. In seeking to provide evidence of an alleged antitrust violation, Dollar sought to depose several Ford executives, but Ford resisted producing these high-level executives on the grounds that Dollar was requesting depositions for the purpose of harassing its executives and not for the purpose of proving its case. Dollar contended that deposing high-level executives is the only way of uncovering who in the Ford organization authorized the differential pricing policies that Dollar contends harmed it and caused Ford to be in violation of the antitrust laws. Is there anything that can be done when a much smaller company demands the time of high-level executives in a very large company? Dollar filed a motion in federal district court requesting that the court order Ford to produce the executives on the Dollar list. To find out the disposition of this motion, see *Travelers Rental v. Ford Motor Co. et al.,* 116 F.R.D. 140 (D. Mass. 1987).

2. **Service of Process.** In order for the plaintiff's case to proceed, the plaintiff, or his or her representative, must serve the defendant with a summons that apprises the defendant of the lawsuit and the claims made by the plaintiff. Service of a summons to the defendant is a separate issue, however, from the issue of personal jurisdiction. In order to contest jurisdiction, the defendant has to appear in court with his or her lawyer. Suppose a defendant, who has not been served with a summons, nevertheless appears in court to contest whether the court in which the plaintiff has filed a claim against him has jurisdiction over him. Suppose, further, at his appearance contesting jurisdiction, the plaintiff serves the defendant with a summons. Is it legal for a plaintiff to serve a defendant whose only reason to appear in court is to contest jurisdiction? [*Northern Light Technology, Inc. v. Northern Lights Club, Jeffrey K. Burgar,* 236 F.3d 57 (1st Cir. 2001).]

3. **Motion for Summary Judgment.** As you know, a motion for summary judgment occurs after the pleadings but before trial. The record of events in this case is that, from December 1993 to June 1996, Medina Rene, an openly gay man, was employed by the MGM Grand Hotel in Las Vegas, Nevada, and worked as a butler on the 29th floor, which was reserved for high-profile and wealthy guests. All of the employees assigned to the floor were male. Rene's responsibilities included responding to the requests of guests staying on that floor. Rene provided extensive evidence that from approximately February 1994 to February 1996, his supervisor, Tang Lam, and several of his co-workers subjected him to a hostile work environment. According to Rene, the harassment took place "practically every day" and comprised a panoply of markedly crude, demeaning, and sexually oriented activities. Rene sues, claiming that he is a victim of sex discrimination and is entitled to recover under the 1964 Civil Rights Act. The 1964 Civil Rights Act does not protect gays from discrimination in employment based on the fact that they are gay. Rene claims he was discriminated against because he was a male homosexual, but the defendant moves for a summary judgment. Are any of the facts in dispute and therefore should the motion be granted? [*Medina Rene v. MGM Grand Hotel, Inc.,* 243 F.3d 1206 (9th Cir. 2001).]

4. **Jury Instructions and Appeals.** If jury instructions are appealed by one party, who subsequently lost when the case went to the jury, the best the appellant can hope for is that the decision of the trial court is reversed. With such an appeal won, there is no guarantee that the appellant will prevail in the new trial when new, and presumably correct, jury instructions are delivered at the end of the new trial. Often parties appeal jury instructions on seemingly minute points of law, such as whether the jury was instructed to base its decision on "objective" or "subjective" intent in contract disputes. As you will learn later in this book, it is objective intent, that is, what the words and actions of a party to a contract mean to a reasonable man, not subjective intent, the "real" feelings of the parties, that is important. The losing party at the trial court level challenged the following jury instruction in their contract dispute because it contended that the instruction asked the jury to determine "subjective intent," which is not the standard used in contract law:

   To decide what their intent [the parties] was you should first examine the language of that quotation. You may also consider the circumstances under which Ronan made and NESCO received the quotation, *and what the parties themselves believed the terms of the quotation meant* as shown by the evidence. You may also consider the past dealings of the parties and the language of previous quotations.

Should this instruction cause a jury verdict in a contract case to be overturned? [*National Environmental Service Company v. Ronan Engineering Company,* 256 F.3d 995 (10th Cir. 2001).]

Social Responsibility and Ethics in a High-Tech World

5. **Punitive Damages.** There is a fear among many businesspeople that going to court is very risky because of the threat of seemingly capricious punitive damage awards—recall the BMW case discussed in which a jury awarded the victim of a faulty paint job $4 million. The evidence, however, suggests that such awards are rare and that there are safeguards within the system to avoid such contingencies. According to Mary Alice McLarty, an attorney,

> Punitive damages are awarded in less than 5 percent of civil jury verdicts, according to a 1990 American Bar Foundation study of 25,000 jury verdicts in 11 states over a four-year period. Between 1965 and 1990, there were only 355 such awards in products liability cases, according to a study by law professor Michael Rustad of Suffolk University in Boston. And more than half of those awards were reduced or overturned on appeal. The rarity of punitive damages helps to explain why such awards often have news value. Moreover, the U.S. Supreme Court has mandated that courts carefully scrutinize such awards.
>
> A 1995 U.S. Department of Justice study analyzing civil jury cases over a 12-month period in the nation's 75 most populous counties found that juries awarded punitive damages in just 6 percent of all successful suits, and that approximately half of these punitive damage awards were for $50,000 or less.

The provocative article by Ms. McLarty can be accessed at http://www.maryalice.com/reform/punitive.html. Ms. McLarty makes the comment that,

> Americans would be much worse off if they were not able to hold wrongdoers accountable. The makers of asbestos certainly did not voluntarily assume responsibility for the harm they caused. The A.H. Robins Company did not offer to compensate the thousands of women injured by the Dalkon Shield. It is only the civil justice system and punitive damages that have placed accountability where it belongs—at the door of the wrongdoer.

What do you think? Are doctors being driven from the practice of medicine by lawyers or is this claim an urban legend?

Using the Internet to Your Advantage

1. As was discussed at the end of the previous chapter, a number of universities have taken the lead in assembling large amounts of useful legal information and have made this information accessible electronically. The Federal Rules of Civil Procedure, used in the federal courts in the United States, are available thanks to the Cornell Law School Legal Information Institute at http://www.law.cornell.edu/rules/frcp/overview.htm. The same institute at Cornell also has compiled the Federal Rules of Evidence at http://www.law.cornell.edu/rules/fre/overview.html.

2. If you are willing to pay money, *California Civil Practice Electronic Textbook: Cases, Statutes, Forms & Other Materials* by William R. Slomanson (2001) is a reference site that purports to have all of California's civil procedure on line at http://home.att.net/~slomansonb/ccpCsePg.html.

3. Online electronic discovery services are now available, for example, http://www.forensics.com/html/electronic_overview .html. According to Computer Forensics, Inc., which makes use of what it terms *Electronic Discovery:* "To start, we can help you determine whether certain information may exist, and if it does, where it might be located. The timing of requests is also critical. Parties may unintentionally destroy evidence or simply overwrite files in their normal course of business. We can help you move quickly to preserve and collect evidence."

4. AAERT is the American Association of Electronic Reporters and Transcribers (http://www.aaert.org/). This website has a large amount of use links with virtual law libraries at Indiana University

(http://www.law.indiana.edu:80/law/v-lib/lawindex.html) and Stanford University (http://vlib. stanford.edu/Overview.html) as well as access to expert witness associations in various disciplines. So, again, with a little creativity in your search activities, the Internet can provide a wealth of information about virtually any topic discussed in Chapter 3, whether it be the Federal Rules of Civil Procedure, the latest techniques used in discovery, or any other topic covered in the chapter. It may be worthwhile to conduct your own searches on some facet of law that has always interested you or about which you wanted to know the answer. The information is just a few clicks away!

Chapter **Four**

Alternative Dispute Resolution

Learning Objectives

On completing this chapter, you should

1. Have a firm understanding of the high monetary and opportunity costs of litigating disputes.
2. Appreciate the roles of and distinctions between negotiation, mediation, and arbitration.
3. Be familiar with specific mechanisms, such as minitrials, used in the pursuit of dispute resolution outside of the court system.
4. Understand the critical need for well-designed alternative dispute resolution (ADR) agreements in contracts involving international commerce.
5. Have a working knowledge of online dispute resolution procedures.

MARKET ALTERNATIVES TO COURT LITIGATION

It is a virtual certainty that most varieties of litigation will chew up large amounts of company resources and expose the defending company to potentially large downside risks—possibly unreasonable, but sustainable, large jury awards or government sanctions. Hence, there are powerful incentives for avoiding litigation. Of course, the ideal solution is to avoid those situations and those actions that result in legal disputes. Since that will not always be possible, means of settling disputes without going to court have become increasingly popular. These alternatives, labeled logically as *alternative dispute resolution* (ADR) mechanisms, have become commonplace in business contracts, though there continue to be situations in which ADR cannot be used. This chapter deals with the situations in which ADR is used, which, for starters, can only occur when both parties to a dispute agree to use ADR instead of court litigation.[1] These alternative (to court) mechanisms now have a significant history of usage both within the United States and in international settings.

ADR: International and Cyberspace

There are "extra" reasons for ADR to have become a prominent part of international transactions. Fear of biased and unfamiliar courts by both U.S. and foreign firms has caused most countries throughout the world to agree to operate in accordance with the 1958 United

---

[1] There are some limited circumstances when ADR is "mandatory," as discussed below.

Nations Convention on the Recognition and Enforcement of Foreign Arbitral Awards. With virtually unanimous adherence to the Foreign Arbital awards treaty among nations, many contracts involving companies in different countries make use of clauses that call for arbitration of disputes between two companies at a neutral site, often the International Chamber of Commerce.[2] Like practices are now being extended into the new "geographic" arena often referred to as cyberspace. We'll take a detailed look at these practices later in this chapter.

Dispute Resolution outside the Courts

There are three categories of ADR: *negotiation, mediation,* and *arbitration.* Of the three, negotiations are used most often, generally for the good reason that they are successful in a sizeable proportion of conflicts with low costs. Most businesspeople are reasonable and would rather compete in the marketplace than in a courtroom. Mediation, defined and discussed below, has traditionally been used to resolve labor disputes but has become increasingly popular a means of solving all kinds of disputes. Surveys of the parties involved in disputes that have been mediated indicate that mediation has the highest post-dispute satisfaction ratings because, in mediation, there is no clearly defined "winner" or "loser." For more "serious" disputes that would probably go to trial in the absence of an agreement, arbitration is generally viewed as the cleanest and most decisive method of alternative dispute resolution. From a business perspective, arbitration offers the advantages of being quick, confidential, relatively inexpensive, and generally nonappealable—so long as it is clear that the parties agreed to resolve their dispute through arbitration.[3]

AVOIDANCE OF LITIGATION: NEGOTIATION AND SETTLEMENTS

You doubtless already have experience with *negotiation*—negotiation of how you will divide the telephone bill with your roommates, negotiation of who prepares what for the party you're having this weekend, and negotiation of the price of a used computer you've bought or sold. Negotiation, as you know, involves the presentation of information, the delivery of offers and counteroffers, and any other activity that leads to an agreement. In a business setting, virtually all contracts are formed after negotiations. Our immediate negotiations focus, however, is on reaching agreements (settlements) when there is a legal conflict to be resolved without resort to the courts.

Settlements

Business firms in conflicts generally recognize the potential high costs of court litigation. Even government agencies, including the U.S. Department of Justice, have finite budgets and recognize that alternatives to court litigation are often more cost-efficient and capable of producing results that are preferable to those reached in court. It is notable that even after parties file a court suit, the vast majority—some 90 percent cases filed—*settle* before they actually go to trial. In many instances, cases are settled before the expenses of discovery are incurred. A *settlement* occurs when both parties agree that the dispute is over, resolved by an agreement that each side is willing to honor. Generally, the terms of a settlement include the payment of money from one party to the other in return for an enforceable agreement

---

[2] About 120 nations of the world have signed the United Nations Convention on the Recognition and Enforcement of Foreign Arbitral Awards. http://www.jus.uio.no/lm/un.arbitration.recognition.and. enforcement.convention.new.york.1958/doc.html.

[3] There are other situations, discussed below, when arbitration agreements and awards will not be enforced by the courts.

Ethical Challenges   Should Settlements Be Secret?

CONFIDENTIAL SETTLEMENTS

In the year 2000, the Firestone/Bridgestone Tire Company engaged in a massive recall of tires it had manufactured and sold for several years prior to the recall. This was a consequence of a tire separation problem that had resulted in a large number of accidents, which in turn had resulted in many serious injuries and deaths. Firestone/Bridgestone was the target of numerous suits over this problem, producing litigation that is still ongoing, with the public widely informed of the defective tire problems this manufacturer was experiencing. A not surprising result of this information was a dramatic decline in tire sales enjoyed by this manufacturer.

Later in the year, there were indications that Goodyear Tire Company had experienced some of the same problems that Firestone/Bridgestone had, but that Goodyear had quietly settled the cases that resulted from its tire failures, including in all settlements confidentiality requirements that prevented any release of information on a tire failure, a resulting accident, or any settlement reached. Goodyear also had been successful in having court records sealed and kept secret in the few tire failure cases that had not settled but had gone to court.

Goodyear was accused of engaging in a "secret recall" of its allegedly defective tires, with generous replacement policies on those tires, and of hiding from the public information on dangers from certain of its tires. Near the end of the year (2000), two groups, the Trial Lawyers for Public Justice (TLPJ) and Consumers for Auto Reliability and Safety (CARS), sought public access to sealed records on Goodyear tire failure cases. A TLPJ spokesman said that "This is the latest disturbing example of court secrecy being used to hide potential dangers to the public" and "Dozens of people were killed or maimed before Firestone's and Bridgestone's tires were recalled because protective orders prevented the public and the government from learning the truth." TLPJ's challenge to make sealed records of cases public was part of its "Project ACCESS," a campaign against court secrecy.

1. How do you suppose Goodyear sales fared in 2000 relative to those of Firestone?
2. What role would confidentiality clauses have played in protecting Goodyear's market position?
3. Is it fair to the public to restrict the availability of information on potentially dangerous conditions by requiring confidentiality in settled cases involving products that could be safety threats?
4. Explain the difference in what you may think is legal for a firm in requiring confidentiality and what is ethical.
5. Is it possible that outlawing secrecy in settlements would result in fewer voluntary settlements and more trips to court? Explain.

by the other party not to sue the original party on the basis of some credible legal claim. It is common in settlements to have anti-publicity clauses that impose substantial penalties for disclosure of the terms of the settlement, protecting the parties from adverse publicity that could be injurious to their businesses.

An example of a simple form of settlement is provided by a personal injury case. Consider a case involving an electrician who was injured and disabled when the SUV he was driving rolled over after the tread separated from his left front tire. Without any admission of guilt or, indeed, any public revelation of the tire failure, the defendant tire manufacturer could pay a sum (say, $500,000) to the injured electrician, who would agree, in turn, not to sue the manufacturer and to keep confidential the resolution of his dispute.

B2B Settlements

In business-to-business conflicts, a settlement can be and usually is much more complicated. There may be a series of questionable acts on both sides of a contract that may be actionable in court. Business parties may have the expectation of continuing in a contractual relationship, but want a settlement to remove the uncertainty associated with possible liability for actions that took place in the recent past. In negotiations dealing with IP in which patents or copyrights may be involved, one side may serve notice that it is considering suing the other side for possible infringement. It is not uncommon in this situation for a negotiated settlement of the potential conflict to emerge under which the purported infringer becomes a licensee of the patent or copyright owner and agrees to pay royalties for continued IP usage.

A Settlement Is Not an Admission of Liability

A rule of law firmly adhered to is that parties to settlement negotiations are not bound by the arguments and concessions they make during negotiations if negotiations break down and court litigation follows. So a business that willingly concedes in settlement negotiations that it breached its contract with the other business is not bound to admit to that concession if litigation subsequently takes place. Neither would the other party be permitted to offer testimony that during settlement negotiations such an admission was made. That is, parties are forbidden to introduce as evidence at a trial positions taken by their adversaries in settlement negotiations. Quite obviously, the parties in settlement negotiations are likely to be more candid if they know they are not going to be bound by statements made during those negotiations.

Source: Reprinted with permission of Erik Holland.

Value of Attorneys in Negotiations

In many cases, executives from separate companies can negotiate between themselves and work out a dispute resolution. In other cases, attorneys assist executives in successful negotiations.

Sometimes it is said that "Once the lawyers get involved . . . ," goodwill is gone and a competitive spirit to argue on behalf of clients eliminates the opportunity for amicable settlements. An alternative view suggests that attorneys are often less emotional than their corporate clients (represented by executives) and that attorneys have training and experience in structuring settlements that is a benefit to negotiations. Corporate attorneys know that their clients do not want to go to court if it can be avoided. Attorneys also have expertise at assessing the probability of winning cases and the expected value of damage awards. If corporations could do better negotiating without attorneys, those corporations that handle all conflicts on their own would make more money, word would get out, and there would be a lot of unemployed corporate attorneys. The fact that there are many fully employed corporate attorneys strongly indicates that they are valuable in dealing with corporate legal issues, including the resolution of conflicts that otherwise would propel firms into courts. The legal knowledge corporate attorneys possess also helps them avoid unwise settlements that would seriously interfere with their corporate clients' pursuit of their business objectives.

Settling at All Costs Could Be Really Costly

This is not to say that attorneys are flawless in the work they do for corporations or that settlements are always preferable to litigation. There certainly have been monumentally bad settlements hammered out by attorneys on behalf of their clients. Arguably, the Microsoft Corporation owes much of its success to its attorneys. In 1980, when Microsoft was still a small, obscure software company, it negotiated a very favorable contract with the dominant computer firm at the time, International Business Machines (IBM). In its contract with IBM, Microsoft *negotiated* a very favorable royalty arrangement that allowed it to sell the same operating system to manufacturers of IBM clones. This contract was a critical foundation element in Microsoft's path to a position of dominance in the market for operating systems.

There also was a time, in the mid-1980s, when the Apple Computer Company was widely viewed as having the best operating system among personal computer makers. At that time, users of IBM PCs and their clones used a clunky operating system, called MS DOS, developed by Microsoft. When Apple came out with its revolutionary icon-based (Windows-like) operating system, it became apparent that the days of MS DOS were numbered. Microsoft introduced an initial crude version of the Windows operating system that bore more than a passing resemblance to the highly popular and distinctive MacIntosh operating system. Apple was tempted to file suit against Microsoft for infringement, but ultimately negotiated a settlement in which it licensed Microsoft's continued use of the Windows operating system.

As subsequent versions of Windows were dramatically improved, in the process becoming more and more like Apple's operating system, Apple did sue Microsoft for copyright infringement.[4] When the case between Apple and Microsoft went to trial, Apple executives and attorneys representing Apple discovered to their horror that their earlier settlement with Microsoft prevented them from successfully suing Microsoft over Windows 3.1. The rest of the story is history—a history in which a licensing agreement led to market dominance for Microsoft and a minor market position for Apple.

Structured Forms of Settlement Negotiations

A large proportion of the negotiations aimed at settling disputes between firms takes place on an informal basis, as would be the case when the parties to a dispute and their attorneys get together in a conference room to discuss their disagreements and ways they might go about resolving them. There are, however, significantly more formal or structured ways to pursue ADR settlements, a few of which are described here.

Minitrials

Two parties with a conflict that is headed toward litigation often have unrealistic perspectives of how their case(s) will be handled by courts. It is common for angry litigants to mentally demonize their adversaries and, in their fury, to take excessively adversarial positions. In

---

[4] *Apple Computer, Inc. v. Microsoft Corp.*, 35 F.3d 1435 (1994).

Cyberlaw **Developments** A Potentially Big Cyberspace Lawsuit Settled

There have been many successful settlements that have avoided costly litigation. In March of 2000 some of the major players in the computer interactive entertainment, Sega America, Electronic Arts, and Nintendo of America had good evidence that Yahoo! subscribers were illegally selling counterfeit video products from the Yahoo! website. According to one company representative, "Yahoo! has created a virtual flea market for thieves to sell stolen property." A 1999 survey found that 60 percent of the software sold at auctions was counterfeit and that the percentage was increasing in 2000. Industry estimates of annual losses due to software piracy had reached over $10 billion by the turn of the century.

The suit, filed against Yahoo! by the three video companies on March 29, 2000, in U.S. District Court for the Northern District of California, sought an injunction against Yahoo! and damages of $100,000 per copyright violation, plus $2,500 for the sale of hardware devices to copy the games, which were being offered by Yahoo! subscribers on Yahoo! Auctions and Yahoo! Classifieds web pages.

Less than 13 months later, the lawsuit against Yahoo! was settled, thus avoiding a costly and time-consuming trial and appeals. Yahoo! general counsel Joh Sobel indicated that working together rather than litigating was best for all four companies, in part because the courts operate too slowly for today's fast-moving technology. For its part, the plaintiffs pledged to work with Yahoo! to counteract counterfeit sales after Yahoo! developed software that was designed to screen and block counterfeit video sales. The Yahoo! screening software also prohibits the sale of Nazi memorabilia and other "hate" materials on its site but its main use was to block the sale of counterfeit video games at its auctions and classifieds web pages. The willingness of Yahoo! to cooperate and develop a plan to combat counterfeit sales by its subscribers rather than contesting in court obvious counterfeit sales of video games and copying devices avoided costly litigation that could have resulted in enormous damages.

minitrial
A private (out-of-court), structured process in which each party to a dispute presents its "case," along with supporting information, before a neutral third party in the pursuit of a settlement without going to a court trial.

such cases, experience indicates that it is very helpful to bring in an outside neutral observer for a reality check, and to engage the warring parties in a tightly structured process to advance a settlement agenda. To this end, there has been growing reliance on **minitrials** in such settings. Minitrials are not really trials at all. They are simply structured processes for the pursuit of dispute settlements in which agendas are carefully arranged so that the parties do not get bogged down on a few contentious issues. Minitrials are one of the services provided by the American Arbitration Association (see http://www.adr.org).

Before an actual minitrial hearing (called an *information exchange*), the parties will agree not only on the desirability of conducting a minitrial, but also on specific rules to be applied in that setting. Typically, the parties agree to rules providing that (1) the proceedings are confidential, (2) tight limits are imposed on discovery, and (3) each party exchanges information on what position they will take, key documents, and other relevant information.

During the information exchange, which is like a hearing or trial, executives from both sides are present while their attorneys make arguments on behalf of their companies (because of the expense, minitrials are almost always used for disputes between two companies that can afford to share the costs). Most of the procedural formalities required for presentation of evidence in a court are relaxed so that the parties can focus on what they perceive to be the contentious issues in the case. The purpose of the information exchanges is to apprise a neutral third party of the evidence each litigant possesses in a "trial-like" setting, in order to get an objective view of the likely outcome of the case in court based on the decision of the neutral party, though that decision is *nonbinding*. The neutral party can be supplied by an arbitrator's association or can be a retired judge who has heard many cases of the same type. Although minitrial decisions are nonbinding, such "verdicts" are generally accorded great weight by the parties in conflict, who often find it in their interests to compromise and reach a settlement after this exercise is completed, if not before.

In fact, experience indicates that settlements of disputes often occur before the minitrial process is completed. Throughout the minitrial process, the neutral party can function as a mediator, working to get the parties in agreement on a settlement that each can accept. The very act of getting the parties together to agree on the simplified rules of engagement often has the beneficial effect of fostering trust between the businesses involved in the dispute, leading to dialogues that result in settlements.

Summary Jury Trial

summary jury trial
A process in which summary evidence from discovery is presented to an "advisory" jury that renders a nonbinding jury decision as an aid in the pursuit of dispute resolution without going to a court trial.

A parallel example of ADR in federal district courts is provided by **summary jury trials.** In a summary jury trial, at the conclusion of discovery, an abbreviated version of evidence that could be taken into trial is presented by attorneys for the parties involved to six "advisory" jurors. These jurors are allowed to consider the evidence and render a verdict in the case, without knowing that the verdict they render is *not binding*. Witnesses do not normally testify at summary jury trials. With the resulting streamlined presentation of what the evidence is, summary jury trials are typically concluded in one day. When a verdict is reported, it is expected that serious settlement negotiations between the disputants will begin. In one court that kept statistics on the process, over 95 percent of summary jury trials resulted in settlements. In the 5 percent that proceeded to trial, most of the trial verdicts were consistent with those rendered in the summary jury trial. Of course, if one side is unhappy with the advisory verdict reached by the jury in the summary jury trial, it can simply refuse to settle and retain the right to take the case to a regular trial in federal court.

Rented Judges

Well-heeled parties can buy their way to the head of the line when it comes to obtaining judicial resolution of disputes. If two large companies are unwilling to wait until their case appears on the docket of their assigned court, they can hire a judge and get an immediate trial that will be accorded the same weight as a trial court decision under a "normal" schedule. When two businesses agree to hire a judge (who is usually a retired judge) to hear their case, the parties also can agree to many of the procedural shortcuts that have been discussed above. As with other ADR techniques, the parties also can agree that the proceedings are confidential and not open to the public.

Concluding Thoughts on Negotiations, Structured Negotiations, and Minitrials

Although negotiations are frequently superior to court litigation, they certainly are not always successful, as evidenced by the volume of civil trials. The fact that failed negotiations can lead to a trip to court can be viewed as a failure in planning, at least in contract disputes. Informal negotiations, structured negotiations, and minitrials are only *necessary* when the parties to a contract *failed to include an effective arbitration agreement in the contract.*

With an arbitration agreement, if negotiations break down, the alternative is not court litigation with all its attendant delays and costs, but rather a relatively quick and confidential trip to an arbitrator whose verdict is usually not appealable. The growth of all forms of ADR reveals the attractions of this alternative.

MEDIATION

mediator
A neutral third party used by parties seeking an out-of-court resolution of a dispute. The mediator's role is that of facilitating settlement and fashioning an agreement that the parties to the conflict are willing to accept.

A **mediator** is a neutral third party who is brought into a dispute by parties who are seeking alternatives to litigation or job actions in the workforce. The main difference between mediation and arbitration (discussed below) is that a mediator is a neutral third party *who does not have the power to render a binding decision.* Instead the mediator's job is one of negotiating with the parties and fashioning a resolution of the dispute that both parties can live with.

Mediation is prominent among the services offered by the *American Arbitration Association* (AAA). In comparison to arbitration or court litigation, mediation has the advantage that, in a mediated settlement, the participating parties *agree* to the outcome, so the leftover feelings of resentment may well be less than when one party, who passionately believes in its position, loses in arbitration or court litigation. Of course, it has the distinct disadvantage that all of the efforts expended may fail to produce a settlement, as the mediation process cannot dictate an outcome. The AAA recommends that contracts incorporate both mediation and arbitration agreements. The implication is that having the parties agree to a resolution is superior to a decision by an outside party such as an arbitrator, but that binding arbitration as the sequel to an unsuccessful mediation effort is still better than a court battle.

Mediation Mechanics

Mediators must be accepted by both parties. In most states, there is training required to serve as a mediator and there is some judicial supervision of mediators, but, unlike doctors or attorneys, mediators are not licensed in most states. Many mediators are attorneys, though that is not required. While selecting a mediator, disputants generally also agree on a number of other terms and conditions for the proposed mediation. Agreements nearly always include confidentiality requirements. Since mediation is a form of settlement negotiation, positions taken in mediation discussions cannot be used against either party in court if mediation fails. The role of mediators can mimic that of the presiding judicial officer at a minitrial because neither can impose a solution, but the opinion of an experienced third party is widely respected. Sometimes mediators will draft a settlement agreement and seek to get each side to agree to it, a process that is very similar to that which provides a nonbinding decision of a neutral party in a minitrial. The disputants are free to adopt or reject the proposal, modifying it if that will lead to resolution.

Historic Roles for Mediators

Historically, mediators have been used most frequently in labor disputes when strikes are threatened. Often, emotions on both sides of labor disputes prevent the involved parties from realistically bargaining. For decades, federal mediators have been called in to resolve labor disputes, most notably in recent years in the strike and lockout in Major League Baseball near the end of the 1994 season.

To facilitate settling labor disputes, the Federal Mediation and Conciliation Service (FMCS) was created by Congress in 1947 as an independent agency to promote sound and stable labor–management relations. The FMCS (http://www.fmcs.gov) offers a wide range of services including mediation in the event of a labor dispute, preventive mediation, and arbitration.

At the local level, mediation is being relied on with increasing frequency in matters ranging from marital breakups to petty crimes often involving fights in bars. Both federal and state courts are making use of mediation services and attorneys are said to prefer it because it gives them more control over outcomes than does arbitration. Most importantly, mediation offers the full array of advantages sought through ADR in the forms of cost reduction, confidentiality, speedy efforts at conflict resolution, and settlements that can be agreed to by both parties. The main shortcoming of mediation is that it does not guarantee that there will be a solution that both parties to the dispute will agree upon.

ARBITRATION

Promoting the use of this form of ADR, there is federal legislation in the form of the Federal Arbitration Act (FAA) and state legislation that generally follows the form of the federal act, under guidance provided by the Uniform Arbitration Act (UAA) and similar statutes. This assemblage of statutes is notable, primarily, because it provides support for the enforcement of arbitration agreements. The focus is clear: if the parties to a dispute executed a prior agreement to arbitrate any disagreement like the one at issue, courts are to refuse to accept a suit on the issue unless unusual events (such as an act of fraud) justify an exception, or unless there is a legitimate issue over whether the parties actually agreed to arbitrate the dispute.

arbitration
A process through which generally binding resolutions of disputes are imposed by disinterested third parties (not courts).

Arbitration requirements are most commonly part of a contract. Suppose Jim is hired to work for the Contrex Corporation. A condition of employment with Contrex is that Jim agrees that any legal claims Jim lodges against Contrex in connection with his employment will be taken to an arbitrator for resolution. The contract will specify the process for selecting an arbitrator or the pool of arbitrators from which one is to be selected. If Jim believes that he is a victim of racial discrimination, or that his benefit package has been changed in a way that is illegal, he cannot go to court with the claim. Should Jim file a suit in court, Contrex would move for a dismissal based on the arbitration agreement and, absent very unusual circumstances, the motion would be granted.

Prevalence of Arbitration Agreements

Many forms of business contracts include arbitration agreements. In addition to employment, arbitration agreements are common in brokerage agreements between stockbrokers and clients, in franchise agreements, in software development contracts, in construction contracts, and, increasingly, in virtually every form of contract. There are a number of federal statutes that give various parties rights, such as the Civil Rights Acts (especially Title 7, which deals with employment), the securities laws that protect investors from fraud and account mismanagement, and a host of other statutes, but the rights provided by these statutes can be subordinated to arbitration agreements. In other words, if a citizen believes that he or she has been harmed in way protected by one of the statutes, such as by securities fraud, the citizen cannot sue in court if the citizen agreed to arbitrate. In fact, unless a federal statute specifically indicates that Congress has exempted the statute from arbitration agreements, rights granted under the statute are subject to arbitration agreements. Many collective bargaining agreements between unions and management call for binding arbitration to resolve disputes or grievances.

In the following case, the plaintiff tried to avoid arbitration by claiming that civil rights claims were not amenable to arbitration. The Supreme Court had an emphatic response for the plaintiff.

Case 4-1

Robert D. Gilmer, Petitioner v. Interstate/Johnson Lane Corporation

United State Supreme Court
500 U.S. 20 (1991)

BACKGROUND AND FACTS

Interstate hired Gilmer to act as a securities representative. As a condition of employment, Gilmer was required to register with the New York Stock Exchange (NYSE), which required all securities representatives to agree to arbitrate any employment dispute rather than go to courts. Gilmer was fired at age 62 and he filed suit in federal district court based on the Age Discrimination in Employment Act (ADEA). Interstate moved to dismiss based on the arbitration agreement and the language of the Federal Arbitration Act, but the district court ruled for Gilmer. Interstate appealed to the court of appeals, which reversed the decision of the trial court to hear the case.

Opinion by White, Justice

The FAA was originally enacted in 1925, 43 Stat. 883, and then reenacted and codified in 1947 as Title 9 of the United States Code. Its purpose was to reverse the longstanding judicial hostility to arbitration agreements that had existed at English common law and had been adopted by American courts, and to place arbitration agreements upon the same footing as other contracts.

* * *

Its [FAA] primary substantive provision states that "[a] written provision in any maritime transaction or a contract evidencing a transaction involving commerce to settle by arbitration a controversy thereafter arising out of such contract or transaction . . . shall be valid, irrevocable, and enforceable, save upon such grounds as exist at law or in equity for the revocation of any contract." 9 U.S.C. § 2. The FAA also provides for stays of proceedings in federal district courts when an issue in the proceeding is referable to arbitration, § 3, and for orders compelling arbitration when one party has failed, neglected, or refused to comply with an arbitration agreement, § 4. These provisions manifest a "liberal federal policy favoring arbitration agreements."

* * *

Although all statutory claims may not be appropriate for arbitration, "[h]aving made the bargain to arbitrate, the party should be held to it unless Congress itself has evinced an intention to preclude a waiver of judicial remedies for the statutory rights at issue." Ibid. In this regard, we note that the burden is on Gilmer to show that Congress intended to preclude a waiver of a judicial forum for ADEA claims. [Some references deleted] If such an intention exists, it will be discoverable in the text of the ADEA, its legislative history, or an "inherent conflict" between arbitration and the ADEA's underlying purposes. Throughout such an inquiry, it should be kept in mind that "questions of arbitrability must be addressed with a healthy regard for the federal policy favoring arbitration."

* * *

Gilmer first speculates that arbitration panels will be biased. However, "[w]e decline to indulge the presumption that the parties and arbitral body conducting a proceeding will be unable or unwilling to retain competent, conscientious and impartial arbitrators." In any event, we note that the NYSE arbitration rules, which are applicable to the dispute in this case, provide protections against biased panels. The rules require, for example, that the parties be informed of the employment histories of the arbitrators, and that they be allowed to make further inquiries into the arbitrators' backgrounds. In addition, each party is allowed one peremptory challenge and unlimited challenges for cause. Moreover, the arbitrators are required to disclose "any circumstances which might preclude [them] from rendering an objective and impartial determination." The FAA also protects against bias, by providing that courts may overturn arbitration decisions "[w]here there was evident partiality or corruption in the arbitrators." There has been no showing in this case that those provisions are inadequate to guard against potential bias.

Gilmer also complains that the discovery allowed in arbitration is more limited than in the federal courts, which he contends will make it difficult to prove discrimination. It is unlikely, however, that age discrimination claims require more extensive discovery than other claims that we have found to be arbitrable, such as RICO and antitrust claims. Moreover, there has been no showing in this case that the NYSE discovery provisions, which allow for document production, information requests, depositions, and subpoenas, see 2 N.Y.S.E. Guide ¶ 2619, pp. 4318–4320 (Rule 619); . . . will prove insufficient to allow ADEA claimants such as Gilmer a fair opportunity to present their claims.

* * *

Decision and Outcome

The U.S. Supreme Court concluded that Gilmer had not met his burden of showing that Congress, in enacting the ADEA, intended to preclude arbitration of claims under that Act. Accordingly, the judgment of the Court of Appeals was affirmed. Because of the arbitration agreement, Mr. Gilmer could not go to federal court with the claim that he was a victim of age discrimination under the Age Discrimination in Employment Act. Instead, it was decreed that Mr. Gilmer would have to pursue his age discrimination claims in front of an arbitrator.

Questions for Analysis

1. Once an employee signs an employment contract that includes an arbitration agreement, who has the burden of proof with regard to the enforceability of the arbitration agreement?
2. In order for an arbitration agreement to be enforceable, do the parties have to be equal in bargaining power, according to Justice White?

Procedure under Arbitration Agreements

In most instances, cases go to arbitration because the parties agree in advance that disputes arising out of the contract are subject to arbitration. The following is an arbitration agreement between a software development company and its clients:

> 12.3   Any controversy or claim arising out of or relating to this Agreement, the breach, termination or validity hereof, or the transactions contemplated herein, if not settled by negotiation or mediation as provided in paragraphs 12.1 and 12.2 above, shall be settled by arbitration in Raleigh, N.C., in accordance with the CPR rules for Non-Administered Arbitration of Business Disputes, by three arbitrators. . . . The arbitration shall be governed by the United States Arbitration Act, 9 U.S.C. Sect. 1–18, and the award rendered by the arbitrators shall be final and binding on the parties and may be entered by any court having jurisdiction thereof and may include equitable relief.

Once the parties agree to arbitrate, the dispute remains outside the jurisdiction of the courts until a final "verdict" is rendered. In arbitration, a verdict is called an *award*. Arbitrator awards are enforced by the courts, which means that they are treated like a judgment from another court. An award enables a successful party in arbitration to obtain a writ of execution and seize assets of the losing party. Most of the time, writs of execution are not necessary as the losing party will simply write a check for the award to the award winner.

Submission

In courts, litigation begins when a plaintiff files a complaint, which is generally followed by an answer. In arbitration the process begins with a *submission* from the complaining party, to which the defendant is entitled to file a written response. It is common for arbitration agreements to contain short statute-of-limitations periods running, say, for periods of three weeks to two months. If the submission is based on an event that occurred at a point in time more distant than what is allotted by contract agreement, the alleged victim loses the right to complain. The time needed to get a hearing before an arbitrator is also typically short, often as little as one month. In the event of arbitration involving two businesses, both businesses usually are required to equally share the expenses of the arbitration process.

An arbitration agreement will contain the name of the arbitrator in the event of a dispute or, more commonly, an agreement on the method for selecting the arbitrator(s). In most cases, a single arbitrator is selected or named, but it is not unusual for the agreement to call for the selection of three arbitrators (as in the sample arbitration agreement provided above). As with mediators, arbitrators are often attorneys, though having a license to practice law is not a requirement to be an arbitrator. It is common for arbitrators to specialize in certain fields. Among the "focus areas" listed by the American Arbitration Association are commercial, construction, employment, insurance, labor, mass claims, and securities.

Hearing

In arbitration, the equivalent of a trial is called a *hearing*. The hearing takes place before an arbitrator and, although the presentation of arguments and evidence is adversarial, less formal rules apply than those used in courtroom litigation. The parties also can have a say in the procedural rules used, allowing the parties to truncate certain evidentiary procedures if the parties agree. As in court litigation, attorneys generally represent adversaries in arbitration.

Arbitration proceedings are not open to the public, compatible with confidentiality interests. Arbitrators bring a great deal of expertise to the issues being confronted, which makes theatrical presentations of evidence, which may have dramatic effects on juries, far less likely to influence outcomes. It is generally thought that this expertise also has the effect of dampening extreme variations in damage awards, though there certainly have been cases in which one party in arbitration has been awarded a very large sum.

Award

In arbitration, the *award* is the equivalent of a verdict in courtroom litigation. In most cases, the arbitrator is required to announce an award in writing within 30 days of an arbitration hearing. Unlike a verdict that is announced by a judge, the award is not justified by reference to existing law and precedent, unless the parties are willing to pay for the extra time needed to compose such a justification. Since arbitration is generally confidential, the verdict of an arbitrator does not have precedential value, either for other arbitrators or for courts. Unless the unusual conditions of fraud or lack of consent to the arbitration agreement are alleged, the award of an arbitrator cannot be appealed. As discussed above, if a party does not comply with the terms of the award, it can be enforced through the courts.

Appeals to the Courts

As first addressed in Chapter 3, there certainly is substantial value in the *final closure* of a dispute. Honoring this dictum, it is a goal of arbitration to not only have a hearing on a conflict within a short time span, but also to have the arbitrator assigned deliver any award quickly. In practice, arbitration succeeds in providing a relatively rapid end to conflicts in most cases, since in most cases there is no fraud, gross malfeasance, or lack of agreement to arbitrate that could serve as the basis for an appeal. An arbitrator must make both factual and legal decisions during and before the hearing, but neither can serve as grounds for appeal.

There are, however, limited grounds for court appeal of (a) the enforceability of an arbitration agreement or (b) the results of a decision by an arbitrator. Listed below are grounds for challenging enforcement of arbitration agreements or decisions of arbitrators. Managers should be mindful of exceptions that can keep arbitration agreements from being binding.

Scope of Authority of the Arbitrator

The next case illustrates the fact that the arbitrability of a dispute is a *judicial* decision. In some situations, where parties have entered a contract that contains an agreement that requires arbitration for some, but not all, of the possible sources of disagreement, it is not clear whether a particular dispute should be decided by courts or arbitrators. In general, it is for the courts, not arbitrators, to decide whether a dispute is arbitrable or must be taken to court.

Case 4-2

Gregory Carson et al., Plaintiffs-Appellees v. Giant Food, Inc., et al., Defendants-Appellants

United States Court of Appeals for the Fourth Circuit
175 F.3d 325 (4th Cir. 1999)

BACKGROUND AND FACTS

Plaintiffs are current and former African American employees of the supermarket food chain Giant Food. Claiming that Giant and its officers and managers discriminated against employees on the basis of race, age, and disability, plaintiffs brought suit in September 1996. They alleged numerous individual and class claims, including claims under the 1964 Civil Rights Act, the Age Discrimination in Employment Act (ADEA), and the Americans with Disabilities Act (ADA). The employees sought compensatory and punitive damages totaling $300 million, injunctive and declaratory relief, reinstatement of discharged employees, and attorneys' fees. After examining four collective bargaining agreements (CBAs) between the employees' unions and Giant, the district court refused to compel arbitration.

Opinion by Wilkinson, Chief Judge

The nondiscrimination provisions in the four CBAs [*Collective Bargaining Agreements* between Giant Foods and the United Food and Commercial Workers Union] are similar. The CBA negotiated by the United Food and Commercial Workers Union, Local 400, includes a clause in the preamble:

> WHEREAS, the Employer and the Union in the performance of this Agreement agree not to discriminate against any employee or applicant for employment because of race, color, religious creed, origin, age or sex.

* * *

In addition to the nondiscrimination provisions, the four CBAs also contain arbitration clauses defining the scope of arbitrable matters. The CBAs for Locals 639, 730, and 922 each state that

> Should any grievance or dispute arise between the parties regarding the terms of this Agreement, [the parties will try to resolve the matter]. . . . If agreement cannot be reached, the parties agree that within five (5) days they shall select a neutral and impartial arbitrator.

* * *

Defendants argue that the CBAs here clearly and unmistakably committed arbitrability to arbitration. They note that the CBAs provided for the arbitration of "any grievance or dispute arising between the parties regarding the terms of this Agreement" and any "controversy, dispute or disagreement . . . concerning the interpretation of the provisions of this Agreement." Because the dispute over whether statutory discrimination claims are arbitrable requires an interpretation of the terms of the CBAs, defendants assert that the parties agreed to resolve this threshold dispute by arbitration. Thus, defendants claim that the parties agreed to arbitrate arbitrability.

We disagree. The "clear and unmistakable" test set forth by the Supreme Court requires more than simply saying that the arbitrator determines the meaning of any disputed contractual terms. The courts have repeatedly rejected the assertion that general arbitration clauses, like the ones at issue here, commit to arbitration disputes over an arbitrator's jurisdiction.

For example, in *AT&T Technologies, Inc. v. Communications Workers of America,* the collective-bargaining contract committed to arbitration all "differences arising with respect to the interpretation of this contract or the performance of any obligation hereunder." Still, the Supreme Court held that "It was for the court, not the arbitrator, to decide in the first instance whether the dispute was to be resolved through arbitration."

* * *

The lesson from these cases is that if contracting parties wish to let an arbitrator determine the scope of his own jurisdiction, they must indicate that intent in a clear and specific manner. Expansive general arbitration clauses will not suffice to force the arbitration of arbitrability disputes.

* * *

Defendants argue that the CBAs in this case clearly and unmistakably require arbitration of employee federal discrimination claims. Each of those CBAs contains a specific provision banning discrimination on the basis of race and age. Further, the agreements provide for the arbitration of all disputes "regarding the terms" and "concerning the interpretation of the provisions" of the agreements. Taken together, defendants argue this language clearly and unmistakably provides for the arbitration of statutory discrimination claims.

We disagree. Broad, general language is not sufficient to meet the level of clarity required to effect a waiver in a CBA. In the collective bargaining context, the parties "must be particularly clear" about their intent to arbitrate statutory discrimination claims.

* * *

Decision and Outcome

The decision of the district court in this case was affirmed. The affirmation of the decision of the district court means that the plaintiffs can proceed with their case in federal court and do not have to submit their claims to an arbitrator.

Questions for Analysis

1. According to the Court of Appeals for the Fourth Circuit, who decides whether a dispute is subject to arbitration: the courts or arbitrators? Under what circumstances could arbitrators make that determination?

2. In spite of the language in the collective bargaining agreement (CBA), why did this court and the district court decide that the employees could take their claims to federal court rather than to an arbitrator?

3. See if you can write an agreement between a union and management that would preclude employees from being allowed to go to federal court to litigate civil rights claims.

Lack of Consent to Arbitration

The Federal Arbitration Act (FAA) does not require that an arbitration agreement be conspicuous in the way that the UCC requires warranty disclaimers to be prominent. As we have noted, however, business managers should be aware that courts have recognized a number of situations in which consent to arbitration can be challenged. Interestingly, if an arbitration agreement is buried in fine print and a patient or client did not have adequate opportunity to review the document containing the arbitration agreement, consent can be an issue. In some cases, the fact that the person asked to sign a document with an arbitration agreement was foreign or could not read has negated consent to an arbitration that has been questioned.

In the next case, the circumstances under which an arbitration agreement was accepted (signed) made "consent" an issue.

Case 4-3

Doncene Sosa, Plaintiff and Appellee v. Lonnie E. Paulos, M.D., Defendant and Appellant

Supreme Court of Utah
924 P.2d 357 (Utah 1996)

BACKGROUND AND FACTS

Plaintiff Doncene Sosa signed a document entitled "Physician-Patient Arbitration Agreement" shortly before undergoing knee surgery performed by defendant Lonnie Paulos, an orthopedic surgeon. After she filed a civil suit for medical malpractice related to the surgery, Dr. Paulos moved to stay the proceedings and compel arbitration under the agreement. The trial court denied the motion on the ground that the agreement was procedurally and substantively unconscionable. Dr. Paulos appeals.

Durham, Justice

The relevant facts are as follows: On November 6, 1991, Dr. Paulos performed a posterior cruciate ligament reconstruction on Ms. Sosa's left knee. According to the record, less than one hour prior to the surgery, after Ms. Sosa was undressed and in her surgical clothing, "someone from Dr. Paulos' office" gave her three documents and asked her to sign them. They were a "Patient Informed Consent and Release of Claims," a "Consent for Use of Freeze Dried or Flesh Donor Tissue," and the arbitration agreement in question here. Ms. Sosa stated in her affidavit that she signed all three documents without reading them. She specifically recalled that neither Dr. Paulos nor any member of his staff discussed the arbitration agreement with her at any time, either when she signed it or during any of her prior office visits. Immediately upon awaking from the anesthesia, Ms. Sosa became aware of a surgical complication. On July 15, 1994, Ms. Sosa filed a complaint for medical malpractice.

The arbitration agreement that Ms. Sosa signed discusses the following subjects:

1. Article 1, entitled "Agreement to Arbitrate," provides that disputes "as to medical malpractice . . . will be determined by submission to arbitration." Article 1 also states that both parties waive their constitutional right to a jury trial.

2. Article 2, entitled "All Claims Must Be Arbitrated," provides that all conceivable claims between the parties are subject to arbitration. . . .

Ms. Sosa argues that the facts surrounding her signing of the agreement, together with the substance of the agreement itself, demonstrate that it was procedurally and substantively unconscionable, as the trial court determined, and therefore unenforceable. Dr. Paulos, on the other hand, argues that the agreement is fair and even-handed and that Ms. Sosa had plenty of time to read the agreement and ask questions concerning its content. Because arbitration agreements are favored in Utah, Dr. Paulos argues, the trial court improperly failed to compel arbitration pursuant to the parties' agreement.

* * *

Procedural unconscionability focuses on the manner in which the contract was negotiated and the circumstances of the parties. Factors bearing on procedural unconscionability include (1) whether each party had a reasonable opportunity to understand the terms and conditions of the agreement, (2) whether there was a lack of opportunity for meaningful negotiation, (3) whether the agreement was printed on a duplicate or boilerplate form drafted solely by the party in the strongest bargaining position, id., (4) whether the terms of the agreement were explained to the weaker party, (5) whether the aggrieved party had a meaningful choice or instead felt compelled to accept the terms of the agreement, and (6) whether the stronger party employed deceptive practices to obscure key contractual provisions. Id.

Upon reviewing the record in this case, we agree with the trial court's conclusion that elements of procedural unconscionability surrounded the negotiation of this agreement. According to her uncontradicted affidavit, Ms. Sosa was not given a copy of the arbitration agreement until "minutes away" from surgery when she was already in her surgical clothing and in a state of fear and anxiety. She stated that she felt "rushed and hurried" to sign the documents and thus did not read them. The agreement was on a printed form and was drafted by Dr. Paulos, who was in a much stronger bargaining position considering the timing of the delivery of the agreement to Ms. Sosa. Neither Dr. Paulos nor any member of his staff discussed the arbitration agreement with Ms. Sosa at that time or at any other time prior to surgery. No one explained to her the options of not signing and discussing the matter further with Dr. Paulos.

* * *

Under these circumstances, we cannot conclude that the arbitration agreement was negotiated in a fair manner and that the parties had a real and voluntary meeting of the minds. Nor can we conclude that Ms. Sosa had a meaningful choice with respect to signing the agreement.

Decision and Outcome

So, the court refused to enforce the arbitration agreement. Mrs. Sosa was able to go to court to pursue her claim of medical malpractice against Dr. Paulos.

Questions for Analysis

1. What is procedural unconscionability? Try to think of another situation in which procedural unconscionability may surface involving arbitration agreements. Suppose a valet parks your car and gives you a ticket that says on the backside that any legal disputes you have against the valet or the parking lot must be conducted before an arbitrator. Suppose you were given the ticket at night and could not read the back of the ticket in the available light. Would you be a party to an enforceable arbitration agreement?

2. When you are a patient in a surgical gown, just before surgery, do you think that you are in a strong position to bargain? How could Dr. Paulos have avoided a charge of procedural unconscionability?

Other Bases for Not Enforcing Arbitration Agreements or for Court Appeals of Decisions of Arbitrators

Statutes That Do Not Allow Arbitration   There are some statutes that specifically disallow arbitration of claims brought under the statute. As an example, the worker-safety protections provided by the Occupational Safety and Health Administration (OSHA) are not subject to arbitration.

Statutory Challenges Based on the FAA   The FAA lists four grounds for overturning an award, including the claim that an arbitrator exceeded his or her authority. As is evident from the Carson case above (Case 4-2), it is for judges, and not arbitrators, to determine the authority of the arbitrator when there is a challenge to presumed authority of the arbitrator. In addition, under the FAA, if there is evidence that

1. the award was obtained as a result of fraud or corruption,
2. there is evidence of partiality of the arbitrator, or
3. there is evidence that the arbitrator is guilty of serious procedural error, such as refusing to hear relevant evidence,

an award can be challenged in a court of law.

Most of these "exceptions" are quite rare. Most arbitrators are honest, fair, and knowledgeable about both the subject matter of the dispute and the procedures utilized in arbitration. Therefore, most matters litigated before arbitrators cannot be successfully appealed.

Awards That Are Contrary to Public Policy Occasionally, there have been arbitration awards that have been successfully challenged as being contrary to public policy. In one memorable case involving a civil service employee in New York, the issue was whether stealing on the job was grounds for dismissal. The arbitrator in New York ruled that the employee was a kleptomaniac and, therefore, not responsible for his actions. A New York court ruled that the decision of the arbitrator was against public policy, which the court determined included allowance of employers to remove employees guilty of theft, no matter what the psychological basis for their stealing might be.

Mandatory Arbitration

Most arbitration agreements are entered voluntarily by individuals and/or companies. In most instances, the agreement to arbitrate disputes predates any arbitrable dispute, because the parties have an arbitration agreement in a contract, voluntarily agreed to by both parties.

There are also a number of situations in which arbitration is mandatory:

mandatory arbitration
Mandatory arbitration is the acceptable route for dispute resolution (at least initially) when public policy prohibits specific parties from taking their disputes directly to courts.

Public unions. In general, public unions that represent employees who work for various branches of government are denied the right to legally strike. When a dispute arises between such a union and management, **mandatory arbitration** is called for, as strikes are not a legal option. Some such disputes concern individual grievances, but, in others, the dispute is more broad-based, involving complaints over wages, hours, and working conditions for groups of workers.

Medical malpractice claims in some states. In some states, medical malpractice claims have been assigned to arbitration. No doubt in response to protests from doctors over what they regard as exorbitant costs of insurance against medical malpractice claims, some states require that malpractice claims by allegedly harmed patients first go to arbitration, which generally has the effect of enhancing the number of settlements and reducing the variability of awards.

court-annexed arbitration
Court-ordered arbitration that, while not binding, results in the settlement of a large proportion of cases.

Court-annexed arbitration. In some cases, at both the federal and state levels, courts have the power to order arbitration. Generally, **court-annexed arbitration** is applied when the amount in dispute is relatively small. Court-annexed arbitration is conducted much like a private arbitration proceeding: there is a neutral party to serve as the arbitrator, usually a retired judge or attorney, and both sides present their arguments and evidence without the formality and technical requirements of civil procedure. The decisions of court-annexed arbitrators, however, are not binding and either party can appeal. Generally, though, court-annexed arbitration motivates settlements. Not surprisingly, an additional advantage of court-annexed arbitration is that the parties get a verdict on their dispute much sooner than if they waited for space on a court docket. If a party appeals the judgment of a court-annexed arbitrator, and does not enjoy an improved outcome when a full-blown trial takes place, that party may be held responsible for the court costs and attorney fees of the other party to the dispute.

INTERNATIONAL ARBITRATION

Overview

The advantages of ADR relative to litigation are magnified when engaging in international business transactions. No U.S. firm wants to be resolving disputes in a Colombian court. In addition to language problems and the differences between U.S. and Colombian law, a U.S. firm likely would have doubts about the integrity of the courts in Colombia. Suspicions about the integrity of foreign courts generally, along with the expense and delays that accompany litigation in foreign courts, provide strong incentives for firms doing business internationally to place heavy reliance on the use of arbitration agreements in their contracts. Of course, it is not only U.S. firms that are suspicious of foreign courts, but foreign firms as well would be leery of the seemingly biased decisions they might face in a U.S. court. They, too, would be concerned with the expense and delays of litigating in any foreign venue. Hence, foreign firms can be equally determined to avoid U.S. courts (or other foreign courts), making them just as willing as U.S. firms to incorporate arbitration agreements in their international contracts.

Standard Clauses in International Contracts

In addition to basic clauses that require arbitration of contract issues, international contracts should include a number of specific requirements, such as

forum selection
The choice of the location in which actions to resolve disputes, including arbitration, will take place.

choice of law
Identification of what specific law will be applied in the event of a need for dispute resolution.

- **Forum selection.** In the event of a dispute, the parties to an international contract should specify the forum (court or arbitration organization or firm) for resolving the dispute. For example, the parties may specify that disputes will be resolved before the International Court of Arbitration, which is a branch of the International Chamber of Commerce (ICC).
- **Choice of law.** The parties to an international contract should agree on the contract law that will govern the contract in the event of a dispute. Just because a contract is with a foreign firm doesn't mean that specific law cannot be agreed to. Illustratively, there is no barrier to using, say, the state contract law of Illinois, which would be the Uniform Commercial Code in the sale of goods, in a dispute that is submitted to the International Court of Arbitration.
- *Payment.* The parties should specify the currency used to make payments under the contract. The relative values of currencies change and there is no need to add exchange rate risk to the risks borne by parties to a sale-of-goods contract.
- *Language.* When dealing with businesses whose native language is not English, U.S. firms would be well advised to insert a language clause that specifies the official language to be used in the contract. Translations are not exact and, therefore, a language clause is appropriate even though the contract may be translated into another language.
- *Force majeure.* It is common in international contracts to excuse performance when events take place that make performance as called for in the contract impossible. Force majeure clauses typically excuse performance when war, natural disasters, and political upheaval occur.

Resolving Disputes with Foreign Businesses

More than 120 nations are signatories to the 1958 United Nations Convention on the Recognition and Enforcement of Foreign Arbitral Awards, including all of the major commercial nations.[5] The basic premise of this treaty is that signatory nations have agreed that their courts will enforce awards of arbitrators. In general, a country isolates itself commercially if its courts do not recognize arbitration awards.

There are a number of organizations that provide arbitration services including the American Arbitration Association, the International Chamber of Commerce, and the London Court of Arbitration (LCA). According to the International Court of Arbitration, which

---

[5] See, http://www.epms.nl/arbit/nycmain.htm.

International Perspective   A Failure to Communicate

LAWSUIT HINGES ON A WORD—AND WHAT A WORD!

Understanding Ubernahmegesprache

What is the meaning of the German word Ubernahmegesprache? The answer to that question, and what was in the mind of a German executive when he said it, is a key to determining the outcome of a lawsuit alleging that thousands of investors were misled about Deutche Bank AG's $9.7 billion takeover of Bankers Trust Corp. in 1998, a federal judge said in a ruling made public Feb. 7.

In a magazine article in October 1998 (*DerSpiegel*), Deutche Bank's CEO denied that his company was engaged in "Ubernahmegesprache," a term generally used in reference to takeover talks. Lawyers for the company argue that the word actually has a more specific meaning, referring to *formal and structured talks where confidential documents have been exchanged*. Because Deutsche Bank's talks with Bankers Trust hadn't yet reached that level, the Bank contends that its CEO's comments in his magazine interview were true and not misleading. Investors who have sued the Bank and its CEO disagree. They are seeking damages of as much as $250 million.

U.S. securities law requires any comments by executives about material events that could affect stock prices to be truthful. In 1988, the Supreme Court concluded that a company could be sued after it falsely denied engaging in merger negotiations. That's why lawyers typically advise their clients to say "No comment." Stanford Professor of Law Joseph Grundfest, a former commissioner at the Securities and Exchange Commission, affirms this, indicating that "You can say 'No comment,' but if you speak to the matter you must do so truthfully."

Judgments rendered in past cases involving takeover issues have hinged on the difference between preliminary talks and advanced negotiations, but several legal specialists say this is the first such case they could recall involving a translation as well.

The stakes are high. Amid takeover speculation, Bankers Trust stock had risen 30 percent in a week. After the interview, many investors sold that stock based on the interview. Bankers Trust stock promptly fell in value by 6 percent. Shortly thereafter, Deutsche Bank announced a takeover of Bankers Trust. The ensuing suit, which has class action status, alleges that Deutsche Bank's CEO misled investors in an effort to drive Bankers Trust's stock price down and make it a less-expensive takeover target.

Lawyers for Deutsche Bank have submitted to the federal court an affidavit of Hans Herdt, former editor in chief of a German financial newspaper, who affirms the strict meaning of the $250 million word in question. Plaintiff's translator, a German citizen who translates documents for corporate clients, says the word means something far broader and "encompasses a spectrum of talks about a takeover ranging from preliminary, exploratory talks up through and including the formal structured talks understood by [Deutsche Bank's translator]." A jury will have to decide which translation is correct, at a high cost to one side or the other!

Source: *Wall Street Journal*. Eastern Edition by Jerry Markon. Copyright 2002 by Dow Jones & Co., Inc. Reproduced with permission of Dow Jones & Co., Inc., via Copyright Clearance Center.

is a branch of the ICC, "Among the available dispute resolution alternatives to the courts, arbitration is by far the most commonly used internationally. The reasons for this are clear:"

- *Final, binding decisions*—The ICC states that "arbitral awards are not subject to appeal."
- *International recognition of arbitral awards*—120 nations have signed the 1958 U.N. Treaty discussed above.
- *Neutrality*—Of course, one of the major reasons for arbitration is fear of partiality on the part of foreign courts.
- *Specialized competence of arbitrators*—Since the parties can designate their arbitrators, the parties select arbitrators known for their expertise in specialized areas.
- *Speed and economy*—The ICC claims that in one of its cases, "a multi-million dollar ICC arbitration was once completed in just over two months."
- *Confidentiality*—Only the parties themselves receive copies of the awards.

Arbitration International Style

As discussed above, the International Court of Arbitration is a branch of the International Chamber of Commerce. The ICA is not really a "court" in the traditional sense of the word but, rather, a supervising body that provides for arbitration. According to the ICC, the ICA "ensures the application of the Rules of Arbitration of the International Chamber of Commerce." The ICA does not decide cases on the merits; that is the job of individual arbitrators. The ICA is responsible for overseeing appointment of arbitrators, deciding upon challenges to arbitrators, scrutinizing and approving arbitral awards, and fixing arbitrator fees.

The increased formality of arbitration procedures at the international level reflects the added safeguards that are needed to convince businesses that they will be treated fairly in disputes with foreign companies. As with U.S. forms of arbitration, the sanctioning body for arbitration of international commercial disputes, in this case the ICC, seeks to get stipulations of facts from the parties in conflict, and then to promote settlements. According to the ICC, a "significant proportion" of cases submitted to the ICC are amicably settled.

Scrutiny of Awards

In contrast to the way domestic U.S. arbitration is handled, the ICA *scrutinizes* awards. According to the rules of the ICC, however, the ICA must approve all awards. In its scrutiny of arbitral awards, the ICA is allowed to call the arbitrator's attention to points of substance. According to the ICC, ICA "scrutiny of arbitral awards is a key element ensuring that arbitral awards are of the highest possible standards and thus less susceptible to annulment in national courts than they might otherwise be. The scrutiny process provides the parties with an additional layer of protection that would not otherwise be available, since arbitral awards are generally not subject to appeal."

Most U.S. business contracts with foreign businesses contain arbitration agreements, obviously for good reasons. According to statistics supplied by ICC, in 1999 there were 529 requests for awards from 1,354 parties who resided in 107 different countries. Arbitrators of 57 different nationalities were appointed under ICC rules and the amount in dispute exceeded over one million U.S. dollars in 58 percent of the disputes. Two hundred and sixty-nine awards (legal disputes in which the plaintiff won some money or satisfaction in the form of an injunction) were submitted to the International Court of Arbitration in the same year.

ONLINE DISPUTE RESOLUTION

online dispute resolution (ODR)
Resolution of dispute in cyberspace that does not involve court litigation, but instead relies upon settlement, mediation, and arbitration services.

Online dispute resolution (ODR) is a form of ADR that is used to resolve disputes that occur in cyberspace. Unlike traditional ADR, ODR can be accomplished electronically, which means that the disputants may not ever come in physical contact with each other. An advantage of ODR is that the infrastructure for dispute resolution is always available so that a proceeding can take place without the need for ensuring that it fits the schedules of the parties, of judges, or of government holidays.

The Most Common ODR Dispute—Domain Name Ownership

Many of the disputes that take place in cyberspace involve domain names. Domain names are the part of an Internet address that is to the left of the period of the top-level domain (TLD)—that is, just before ".com," ".org," or ".gov."[6] For example, AOL is the part of the

---

[6] ICANN has approved seven new TLDs, but the launching of the new TLDs has been mired in litigation. According to the ICANN website in May 2003, six new TLDs are accepting applications: info, biz, name, aero, coop, and museum. ICANN has approved pro as another TLD, but the registry agreement is still being negotiated. See http://www.icann.org/tlds/.

domain name of America Online in the domain name AOL.com that is *registered*. Domain names are administered by ICANN, the Internet Corporation for Assigned Names and Numbers. According to ICANN, "The Internet Corporation for Assigned Names and Numbers is the non-profit corporation that was formed to assume responsibility for the IP (Internet Protocol) address space allocation, protocol parameter assignment, domain name system management, and root server system management functions previously performed under U.S. Government contract by IANA [Internet Assigned Names Authority] and other entities."[7]

In a very real sense, the Internet has created new intellectual property in the form of domain names. Domain names, of course, are potentially a powerful advertising tool, but domain names also create clashes with trademark law (to be discussed in detail in Chapter 13). If a firm applies for and receives a domain name that is "identical to" or "confusingly similar to" a registered trademark, consumers may be misled as to whether the website is the Web address of the "same name" business or entity that is the trademark owner. For a period of time, opportunists applied for and received domain names for many of the largest corporations and celebrities, then offered to sell these domain names for fees, often at fees just under the cost of suing them in court. By the late 1990s, it was clear that an abuse was taking place and Congress passed the Anticybersquatting Consumer Protection Act (ACPA) of 1998. As a result of this act, cybersquatters, those who register domain names identical to or confusingly similar to registered trademarks, are liable for severe financial penalties up to $300,000 if they continue to use domain names of registered trademark owners.

ICANN's Uniform Domain Name Dispute Resolution Policy (UDRP)

Uniform Domain Name Dispute Resolution Policy
A policy devised by ICANN to reassign domain names when it is clear that the domain name owner does not have a legal right to use that domain name.

Although the ACPA has resolved some cybersquatting problems, it falls well short of resolving all of them, in large part because many of the registrants of domain names are not subject to the jurisdiction of the U.S. government. Recognizing this problem, ICANN has developed a **Uniform Domain Name Dispute Resolution Policy** (UDRP), which can be accessed at http://www.icann.org/dndr/udrp/policy.htm. Virtually all domain name disputes can be resolved using ICANN's UDRP quickly and without requiring court litigation.

Assume that MultiNationalCorporation has created and registered a trademark for which it is well known, say, MNC®. Let us suppose, further, that a Thai national, Johnny Wong, has a registered domain name, MNC.com, but does no business under that name and has offered to sell the domain name to MNC for $100,000. Wong is a cybersquatter, but he is not subject to the Anticybersquatter Consumer Protection Act because he not a U.S. citizen.[8] ICANN, however, has been under increasing pressure to facilitate transfers of domain names from cybersquatters to legitimate trademark owners and, so, it developed its Uniform Domain Name Dispute Resolution Policy, which took effect on January 1, 2000. Under this policy, ICANN applies a three-part test that enables trademark owners to get infringing domain names transferred to them through administrative proceedings supervised by ICANN.

According to ICANN, a domain name will be transferred to the trademark owner if

1. That domain name is identical to or confusingly similar to a trademark or service mark in which the complainant has rights.

2. The possessor of the domain name has no rights or legitimate interests in respect of the domain name.

3. The domain name has been registered and is being used in bad faith.

---

[7] http://www.icann.org/general/abouticann.htm.

[8] The Anticybersquatter Consumer Protection Act is discussed in some detail in Chapter 14.

In ICANN's administrative proceeding, the complainant must prove that each of these three elements is present.

For further guidance, ICANN lists examples of ownership in bad faith, which are

1. circumstances indicating that you have registered or you have acquired the domain name primarily for the purpose of selling, renting, or otherwise transferring the domain name registration to the complainant who is the owner of the trademark or service mark or to a competitor of that complainant, for valuable consideration in excess of your documented out-of-pocket costs directly related to the domain name; or

2. you have registered the domain name in order to prevent the owner of the trademark or service mark from reflecting the mark in a corresponding domain name, provided that you have engaged in a pattern of such conduct; or

3. you have registered the domain name primarily for the purpose of disrupting the business of a competitor; or

4. by using the domain name, you have intentionally attempted to attract, for commercial gain, Internet users to your website or other on-line location, by creating a likelihood of confusion with the complainant's mark as to the source, sponsorship, affiliation, or endorsement of your website or location or of a product or service on your website or location.

In the Johnny Wong versus MNC example, discussed above, Wong would lose on all three criteria and thus Wong's domain name would be transferred to MNC. In their domain name proceedings, ICANN makes use of three arbitration services: the National Arbitration Forum, the World Intellectual Property Organization (WIPO), and the CPR Institute for Dispute Resolution.[9]

The following is typical of many of the cases encountered by ICANN and, through ICANN, the three arbitration services mentioned above. This case involves Walkman radios manufactured by the Sony Corporation, which also has a registered trademark of that name, and Walkman.com, registered by RK Enterprises, a firm located in Visakhapatnam, India.

---

[9] Each of these organizations has its own website. See: http://www.arbitration-forum.com/, http://www.wipo.org, and http://www.cpradr.org/. In particular, the WIPO as an organizations has many more functions than just resolving domain name disputes, which are apparent from its website.

Case 4-4

Sony Corporation v. RK Enterprises

National Arbitration Forum
Claim Number FA0011000096109

Parties

The Complainant is Sony Corporation, Tokyo, Japan ("Complainant") represented by Robert B.G. Horowitz, Cooper & Hunham LLP. The Respondent is RK Enterprises, Visakhapatnam, India ("Respondent").

Registrar and Disputed Domain Name

The domain name at issue is "walkman.com" registered with Network Solutions, Inc.

Panel

The undersigned certifies that he has acted independently and impartially and to the best of his knowledge, has no known conflict in serving as a panelist in this proceeding.
Hon. James A. Carmody, as Panelist.

Procedural History

Complainant submitted a Complaint to the National Arbitration Forum (the "Forum") electronically on November 21, 2000; the Forum received a hard copy of the Complaint on November 27, 2000.

BACKGROUND AND FACTS

On November 30, 2000, Network Solutions, Inc. confirmed by e-mail to the Forum that the domain name **"walkman.com"** *is registered with Network Solutions, Inc. and that the Respondent (RK Enterprises) is the current registrant of the name. Network Solutions is a firm that facilitates domain name registrations. Network Solutions, Inc. has verified that Respondent is bound by the Network Solutions, Inc. 5.0 registration agreement and has thereby agreed to resolve domain-name disputes brought by third parties in accordance with ICANN's Uniform Domain Name Dispute Resolution Policy (the "Policy"). In other words, the registrant has agreed to arbitrate rather than litigate domain name disputes in accordance with ICANN's Uniform Domain Name Resolution Policy (UDRP). The Complainant (Sony) requests that the domain name be transferred from the Respondent to the Complainant. Complainant also contends Respondent has no rights or legitimate interests in the domain name in question. Likewise, Respondent has acted in bad faith by registering the domain name to intentionally attract Internet users to its website for commercial gain via a likelihood of confusion with the Complainant's mark.*

Hon. James A. Carmody, as Panelist

DISCUSSION

Paragraph 15(a) of the Rules instructs this Panel to "decide a complaint on the basis of the statements and documents submitted in accordance with the Policy, these Rules and any rules and principles of law that it deems applicable."

In view of Respondent's failure to submit a response, the Panel shall decide this administrative proceeding on the basis of the Complainant's undisputed representations pursuant to paragraphs 5(e), 14(a) and 15(a) of the Rules.

Paragraph 4(a) of the Policy requires that the Complainant must prove each of the following three elements to obtain an order that a domain name should be cancelled or transferred:

1. the domain name registered by the Respondent is identical or confusingly similar to a trademark or service mark in which the Complainant has rights;
2. the Respondent has no rights or legitimate interests in respect of the domain name; and
3. the domain name has been registered and is being used in bad faith.

Identical and/or Confusingly Similar

The Complainant has rights in the mark **WALKMAN.** Respondent's domain name, **walkman.com,** is identical to the Complainant's registered mark. [Citations omitted]. Also, the domain name in question is found to be confusingly similar because a reasonable Internet user would assume the domain name is somehow related to the Complainant's mark.

Rights or Legitimate Interests

Respondent has asserted no rights or legitimate interests in relation to the domain name at issue. Respondent is not commonly known by the domain name, nor is Respondent using the domain name in connection with a bona fide offering of goods or services. Consequently, Respondent's failure to show evidence sufficient to refute Complainant's assertions, entitles the Panel to conclude that Respondent has no such rights or legitimate interests in regard to the domain name at issue.

Registration and Use in Bad Faith

The Panel finds the Respondent has acted in bad faith by intentionally attempting to attract Internet users to its web site, primarily for the purpose of commercial gain, via a likelihood of confusion with the Complainant's famous mark.

Moreover, circumstances indicate Respondent was aware of the Complainant's famous mark prior to registration, which also allows the Panel to conclude Respondent acted in bad faith.

DECISION

Having established all three elements required under the ICANN Policy, the Panel concludes that the requested relief shall be granted.

Accordingly, it is ordered that the domain name **walkman.com** be transferred from Respondent to the Complainant.

Questions for Analysis

1. Do you think that the fame of Sony's Walkman stereo had something to do with the outcome of this case?
2. The Panelist found that the Respondent, RK Enterprises, acted in bad faith because it attempted to divert Internet traffic to its website. What are some other acts that RK Enterprises could have taken that would indicate bad faith?

Other Examples of Online Dispute Resolution Providers

As with other aspects of the Internet, innovation in ODR has been rapid. The Cyberlaw Developments box discusses CyberSettle.com, which is an online mechanism for settling disputes, particularly those that involve insurance companies. Not surprisingly, there are other online vendors offering both mediation and arbitration services. For mediation, there is Online Mediation (http://www.onlineresolution.com/om-how.cfm) and MediationNow (http://www.mediationnow.com/online). Online arbitration services include Online Resolution—Arbitration (http://www.onlineresolution.com/index-oa.cfm). According to its website, "Online Arbitration is similar to traditional arbitration, except that all communications take place online. The Online Arbitrator appointed for your case will be an experienced professional, who knows the subject area of your dispute." As the volume of e-commerce expands, ODR will become more significant.

Advantages and Disadvantages of Using ODR

Certainly, an advantage of ODR relative to traditional ADR is that through use of the computer, rather than personal appearances, the costs of "attending" negotiations, mediation, and arbitration proceedings are less. With computers, such services are available anytime and all the time on the Internet. Also, the out-of-pocket expenses associated with ODR are low, and sometimes zero, in contrast to the very high costs of court litigation and even traditional ADR. For disputes involving moderate amounts of money, ODR certainly can be the superior choice.

To date, however, most mechanisms for resolving disputes online, even those involving e-commerce, are unfamiliar to many businesses. For ODR to serve as an effective mechanism, both parties must agree to use ODR, even though parties unfamiliar with the process will be cautious in trying such a "new" procedure. In order for them to be enforceable, courts must accept ODR dispute resolutions. There are also jurisdiction issues that must be resolved. In at least one case, a federal district court refused to be bound by the results of a proceeding before WIPO involving domain names.[10] So, at this point, there remain questions over whether courts will accept decisions of online dispute resolution services and issue court orders enforcing their results. In the future, however, such transactions will

---

[10] *Webber-Stephen Products Co. v. Armitage Hardware and Building Supply, Inc.,* 2000 U.S. Dist. LEXIS 6335 (2000).

take place and there doubtless will be litigation needed to resolve issues over the enforceability of ODR rulings.

Summary

Good Reasons to Seek Alternatives to Litigation

- Disagreements that end up in courtrooms, especially those that involve two businesses, impose high costs and high risks on the parties involved. Costs include both direct monetary costs and hefty opportunity costs imposed on key company personnel.
- Risks are accentuated by the nature of the jury trial process, which results in a high degree of variability in awards (won or lost). There also can be extended delays in resolving conflicts in court, with this problem exacerbated by the fact that criminal cases take precedence over civil cases in court schedules. All of these factors favor reliance on *ADR (alternative dispute resolution)* mechanisms, the use of which has grown rapidly in recent decades.

The Various Forms of ADR Structure, Processes, and Outcomes

- Negotiation is the most common and least formal form of ADR. The parties to a dispute can deal (negotiate) directly with one another, or can have that task handled for them by attorneys or other agents who represent each party's interests.
- A negotiated settlement does need to be formalized in a written agreement (contract) that can be enforceable in court.
- Negotiations can be structured to include third parties.
- In a minitrial, evidence is presented before a third party who renders a nonbinding decision.
- In a summary jury trial, evidence is presented before a jury that is unaware that their decision is not binding.
- Parties reduce their waiting time for a judge by renting judges and presenting evidence in front of them.
- *Mediation* is a form of ADR that is somewhat more structured than negotiation and that always involves another party in addition to the disputants. The third-party mediator is involved as a neutral participant, agreed to by the parties in conflict.
- A mediator cannot impose a resolution on the parties, but attempts to facilitate a process that will lead to a mutually satisfactory settlement. A skilled mediator can often (but not always) defuse tempers, create an awareness of options for settlement that the conflicted parties were not aware of, encourage workable compromises, and help draft an enforceable settlement.
- Mediation is confidential and less expensive than litigation.
- Parties to mediation report the highest level of satisfaction among all forms of ADR.
- Historically, mediation has been used to resolve labor disputes, but increasingly it is being used in petty crime cases, such as bar fights, and in domestic divorce agreements.
- The most formal and "court-like" version of ADR is *arbitration*. Parties to arbitration enter into a contract, which requires them to accept, without appeal, the conclusions of the arbitrator(s).
- Clauses requiring *binding arbitration* of any disagreement are commonplace in contracts for employment, commercial sales including stock brokerage account agreements, insurance policies, and many other transactions.
- Parties who agree to have their dispute resolved by arbitration jointly choose an arbitrator (or sometimes a set of arbitrators).
- The arbitrator(s) conduct a hearing and render a decision, called an award if the plaintiff is entitled to compensation.
- Arbitration hearings are conducted with much less formality than is typical of court litigation and the proceedings are confidential.
- In the absence of fraud or some other form of serious misconduct, the decisions rendered in arbitration are unlikely to be modified by a court unless there is evidence that one of the parties did not agree to have legal disputes arbitrated.

- While arbitration of disputes occurs frequently because of the voluntary decisions of parties with a disagreement, it is also the mandatory form of dispute resolution in some settings.

Arbitration Can Be Voluntary or Mandatory	• Since they do not have the right to strike, employees (and unions representing employees) who work for public employers must arbitrate disputes.
	• In some states, plaintiffs with a claim based on medical malpractice must go before an arbitrator rather than a court.
	• In some legal disputes for relatively small amounts of money, courts have the power to order the parties to go through nonbinding arbitration.
International Issues in ADR	• Arbitration agreements are a common element in global business contracts.
	• Contracts between companies located in different countries should not only require arbitration of disagreements, but should also address the *place of arbitration,* the *applicable law,* and the *currency* in which any award will be paid.
ADR Has Been Used to Resolve Disputes in Cyberspace and Increasingly ADR Is Taking Place Online	• ADR is being applied to disputes in cyberspace. Efforts to resolve disputes involving domain names have occurred most frequently in cyberspace.
	• ICANN supervises assignments of *domain names* and numbers and provides recommendations when disputes arise as to dispute resolution entities.
	• ICANN will reassign a domain name if the complainant can show that the domain name owner has a domain name that is *confusingly similar to its trademark, does not have a legitimate claim to the domain name,* and is *using the domain name in bad faith.*
	• ADR is alive and well in cyberspace in the form of *online dispute resolution (ODR).* Although there are some issues still to be resolved, ODR appears to be growing rapidly in terms of both acceptability and enforceability.

Key Terms

arbitration, *100*	mandatory arbitration, *108*	summary jury trial, *98*
choice of law, *109*	mediator, *99*	Uniform Domain Name
court-annexed arbitration, *108*	minitrial, *97*	Dispute Resolution
forum selection, *109*	online dispute resolution, *111*	Policy, *112*

Questions for Review and Analysis

1. Discuss the economic factors that increasingly cause firms to make use of ADR relative to court litigation.
2. Why does the act of structuring negotiations often create a climate conducive to achieving a settlement?
3. Explain how the line can get blurred between assisted settlement negotiations and outright mediation?
4. Explain why it is both good and bad that (a) arbitrators are not bound by precedent and (b) their decisions are not appealable in many situations.
5. Discuss three differences between international arbitration and domestic arbitration.

If You Really Understood This Chapter, You Should Be Able to Provide Informed Commentary on the Following:

1. **Litigation Uncertainty.** According to one article, "Nationwide, the tort system may be in trouble and in need of reform. But in Alabama, jury awards to plaintiffs in damage cases are colossal and close to being out of control, according to judicial experts." Critics cite this case: a driver who had been drinking, was not using his seatbelt, and fell asleep at the wheel was recently awarded $50 million in actual damages and $100 million in punitive damages from General Motors by an Alabama jury. With jury awards such as this, is it any wonder that businesses shy away from personal injury and wrongful death cases that may go to trial? The case between Alex Hardy and General Motors is discussed at http://media.gm.com/corpcom/releases/g960604a.htm.

2. **Suppose an Arbitrator Makes a Mistake of Law.** Suppose it is clear that an arbitrator made a mistake of law. Does this justify an appeals court hearing the case and righting the wrong? The defendant, Broadway Realty, sold the plaintiff, Hembree, a house in a contract that contained an agreement that an arbitrator would resolve any disputes. A dispute did arise about the quality of the

roof and Hembree's claim was arbitrated. In making his decision, the arbitrator made a legal error by assuming that Broadway Realty was a builder when in fact it was a Realtor. The arbitrator found for Hembree based on a theory of implied warranty, which does apply to contracts builders have with homeowners, but does not apply in contracts with Realtors. Broadway Realty appealed to the courts to Redress the obvious legal error made by the arbitrator. Can the losing party in an arbitration get a second opportunity when the arbitrator makes a substantive legal error? Before you answer, consider that it was Broadway Realty that includes the arbitration agreement in all of its contracts with buyers. [*Hembree* v. *Broadway Realty and Trust Co.,* 728 P.2d 288 (1986).]

3. **Sanctions Associated with Violating Confidentiality Requirements.** Paranzino claimed that a mistake by Barnett Bank of South Florida cost her $100,000. Paranzino filed suit against Barnett Bank for breach of contract following her allegation that she went to the bank with $200,000 in cash, bought two certificates of deposit for $100,000 each, but was issued only one certificate. Paranzino received bank statements reflecting the $100,000 certificate of deposit for several months but did not protest before she filed her suit. With the litigation pending, Paranzino and Barnett Bank attended court-ordered mediation, at which time Paranzino was offered $25,000 as a settlement. Paranzino was apparently incensed by the offer and went to a local newspaper with her story, which was later reprinted by the newspaper. Barnett moved to have Paranzino's claim dismissed and to be fined for attorney fees because a clause in the court-ordered mediation required the parties to keep the mediation proceedings confidential. The trial court granted the motion to dismiss by Barnett Bank. What do you think? [*Paranzino v. Barnett Bank of South Florida, N.A.,* 690 So. 2d 725 (Fla. 4th DCA 1997).]

4. **Domain Names and World Intellectual Property Organization (WIPO).** The "21" Club is the name of a well-known restaurant in New York City. The complainant registered "21" Club as a trademark in the United States with the Patent and Trademark Office. On April 2000, a Chinese business, the 21 Club of Nanchang City, Jiangxi Province, Nanchang, JX 33046, received a domain name of "21club.net," after having applied for that domain name from NSI (Network Solutions, Inc., which does the actual registration of domain names). In answer to the charge that it was using "21 Club" in bad faith, the Chinese respondent claimed (a) it had never heard of the U.S. restaurant and (b) it had been using "21 Club" in China for a long period of time and had many Chinese visitors to its website. Does the complainant, "21" Club of New York, satisfy the criteria that ICANN has established for transfer of domain names? [Case No. D2000-1159 at http://arbiter.wipo.int/domains/decisions/html/2000/d2000-1159.html.]

Social Responsibility and Ethics in a High-Tech World

5. **Arbitration and Civil Rights Claims.** In the world of human resource management (HRM), arbitration of civil rights claims is among the hottest issues. The seminal case in the area is *Gilmer* (excepts appear in the chapter), which held that age discrimination claims under the Age Discrimination in Employment Act were subject to arbitration agreements in employment contracts. Since courtroom verdicts are perceived as more unpredictable than those of arbitrators, employers have massively moved for arbitration agreements in employment contracts, so much so that the EEOC complains that the antidiscrimination laws have effectively become privatized (see http://www.lalabor.com/material/arb_adr/eeoc_97_position_on_mandatory_arbitration.html#II). In 2002, the EEOC did achieve a victory in the U.S. Supreme Court when it recognized the right of the EEOC to file suit on behalf of an employee, even though the employee was subject to an employment contract that had an arbitration agreement, for civil rights claims against the employer(s). What do you think? Is it ethical for companies to almost completely limit employee access to court for civil rights claims through a pervasive use of arbitration agreements? Take a look at *Equal Employment Opportunity Commission v. Waffle House, Inc.,* 122 S. Ct. 754 (2002).

Using the Internet to Your Advantage

1. The ICANN website (http://www.icann.org/) has a wealth of information about domain names, online dispute resolution, and its Uniform Dispute Resolution Policy (see http://www.icann.org/udrp/udrp-schedule.htm). The ICANN website also provides links to domain name dispute resolution providers such as WIPO (http://arbiter.wipo.int/domains/), the National Arbitration Forum (http://www.arbforum.com/domains/), and the CPR Institute for Dispute Resolution

(http://www.cpradr.org/ICANN_Menu.htm). Each of these websites publishes its decisions about domain name disputes and adds to the growing body of law on this topic even though none of the aforementioned websites are courts of law.

2. There are many websites that are devoted to arbitration services. As mentioned in the chapter, the American Arbitration Association is located at http://www.adr.org. There are some firms that advertise expertise in arbitrating technical issues, as does Hill & Associates (http://www.batnet.com/oikoumene/tacr.html), which is a Swiss firm. Hill & Associates, who call their firm TACR (Technical Arbitration and Conflict Resolution), provide a hyperlink to a virtual library dealing with international issues in arbitration (http://www.mchapman.com/vl/pages/). The National Arbitration Forum (http://www.arb-forum.com/) not only offers arbitration but also advertises its mediation and domain name dispute resolution capabilities.

3. Many websites that advertise their mediation capabilities are labor-based organizations. For example, the Federal Mediation and Conciliation Service (http://www.fmcs.gov/), a branch of the U.S. government, was created by Congress in 1947 as an independent agency to promote sound and stable labor–management relations. The Coast to Coast Mediation Center (http://www.ctcmediation.com/) offers ". . . *workplace dispute resolution* training and system design. We provide customized solutions for corporations, professionals, and non-profits."

4. In addition to Cybersettle (http://www.cybersettle.com), there are a number of other companies that offer such services, such as SmartSettle (http://www.smartsettle.com/) and ClicknSettle (http://www.clicknsettle.com/index3.cfm?CFID=96000&CFTOKEN=81403321). Also, the Better Business Bureau (http://www.bbb.org/complaints/) offers its services to resolve disputes between businesses and customers.

Chapter **Five**

Application of Constitutional Law to Business

Learning Objectives

On completing this chapter, you should

1. Have an appreciation for the challenges faced by the framers of the Constitution as they sought to construct a durable balance between providing the federal government with sufficient power to govern the fledgling nation, while preventing uncontrollable concentrations of power and protecting individual rights.

2. Appreciate the importance of the Commerce Clause, both as a power source for the federal government and as a limitation on actions of state governments that interfere with interstate commerce.

3. Understand the basic powers of governments in terms of spending, taxing, and taking property of citizens for public purposes.

4. Understand the importance of the Bill of Rights as guarantor of individual rights vis-à-vis both federal and state governments.

5. Understand the importance of the Due Process and Equal Protection clauses in the Fourteenth Amendment.

OVERVIEW

Beating the British was the easy part. Establishing a government that the colonists would accept and that also would work to provide needed governance for the colonies required much more finesse than rallying resentment against the king of England. The British were defeated in 1781, though the colonists signed a peace treaty with England formally ending the Revolutionary War in 1783. The Articles of Confederation, which had been passed in 1777, went into effect on March 1, 1781. Article I of the Articles of Confederation states that "The title of this confederacy shall be, 'United States of America.'" Article II states that "Each State retains its sovereignty, freedom, and independence, and every power, jurisdiction, and right, which is not by this confederation expressly delegated to the United States."

Leading political figures in the ex-colonies, soon to be "states," were of the opinion that governments performed badly when too much power was centrally concentrated, as they believed it was in European monarchies. According to these thinkers, the king of England, who claimed to rule by "divine right," was typical of unconstrained governmental leaders who abused their power. The Articles of Confederation was the original document that was used by the ex-colonists to govern and it reflected the fear of centralized authority felt by many of the leaders of the U.S. revolution. The newly formed states created such a weak national government that the states, not surprisingly in retrospect, began to act like independent countries. State politicians quickly perceived that if inflows of goods from out-of-state businesses were taxed, or otherwise impeded with trade barriers, in-state businesses would benefit—and their owners would then likely vote for the obliging politicians who were protecting their business interests.

The unworkability of the Articles of Confederation quickly became apparent. The weakness of the federal or national (central) government allowed the separate states to make their decisions based solely on what was judged best for the state, rather than for the nation. The failures of the Articles of Confederation led to the *Federalist Papers* and the eventual adoption of the U.S. Constitution in 1789. Among the powers *delegated* to the newly formed federal government under the constitution was the power "To regulate Commerce with foreign Nations, and among the several States, and with the Indian Tribes."

DILUTING AND CONTROLLING CENTRAL GOVERNMENT POWER— CHECKS AND BALANCES

legislative
The branch of government that is composed of elected representatives: senators and members of the House of Representatives.

executive
The branch of government that is headed by the president or governor and enforces laws.

judicial
The branch of government charged with presiding over trials and interpreting and applying laws to particular cases.

veto
A veto is a vote by the president or chief executive officer that overturns a decision of both houses of the legislature with respect to a bill or proposed law.

Separation of Powers

Fear of concentrated political power caused the framers of the Constitution to set up a system of checks and balances—that is, a system of separating and dividing political power—by which, it was intended, that the concentration of excessive power in any element of the central government could be avoided. Federal political power was divided among three branches of government: **legislative, executive,** and **judicial.** The legislative branch was further divided into two bodies of Congress, the Senate and the House of Representatives.

Legislative Powers

Under the Constitution, majorities in both branches of Congress had to agree on a "bill" designed to create a new law before the bill could be submitted to the president for his approval or rejection. So the power of Congress to pass new laws was limited by the power of the president to veto new legislation. A **veto,** however, could be overridden by two-thirds majority votes in both houses of Congress, limiting the president's (executive branch's) power. Congress has the power to determine the jurisdiction of the federal judiciary and must approve presidential nominations to the federal bench.

Executive Powers

Ultimately, then, Congress has the power to make new laws, but the executive branch, headed by the president, has the task (and power) to *enforce* laws. The president appoints heads of the cabinet departments (Departments of State, of Commerce, of Defense, etc.) and other top officials in the federal government, such as chair of the Federal Reserve Bank, commissioners of the Federal Trade Commission, and so on, but does so subject to the advice and consent of the Senate. The executive branch is also responsible for conducting foreign policy and can make treaties with foreign governments with the advice and consent of the Senate.

Judicial Powers

Congress can pass new laws, approved by the president, but the Supreme Court is empowered to decide whether new laws are consistent with the U.S. Constitution if those laws are challenged in court. If the Supreme Court decides that a law is not consistent with the Constitution, which provides multiple protections for the rights of citizens, the Supreme Court has the power to declare that the law is *unconstitutional*. The Constitution includes the **Supremacy Clause,** which declares that federal law shall be the *supreme* law in the United States. Under this standard, the Supreme Court also can strike down, as unconstitutional, state laws that *conflict* with federal laws. The practical effect of the Supremacy Clause of the U.S. Constitution is to make any state law that is in conflict with any federal law unconstitutional. Of course, the U.S. Supreme Court does not have power to declare a law unconstitutional on its own. The Supreme Court can only declare a law (federal or state statute) unconstitutional if the law is challenged in court by a party who has standing by virtue of the law.

Supremacy Clause
The language in the U.S. Constitution that states that federal law is the supreme law of the land, superior to state law.

Federalism

Appended to the Constitution, as demanded by the original "states" to win their acceptance, is the lengthy "Bill of Rights" designating very specific protections to be guaranteed to U.S. citizens. The Bill of Rights includes the Tenth Amendment, which reserves to states and "the people" "[t]he powers not delegated to the United States by the Constitution." Note that, as was the case under the Articles of Confederation, the U.S. Constitution refers to "sovereign" states. Under the Constitution, the states are referred to as sovereign, but only to the extent that their laws do not conflict with the U.S. Constitution, treaties, or other federal laws. In other words, federal law prevails over state laws under the Constitution. This system of shared government is referred to as **federalism.**

The power of the federal government is limited to those powers *delegated* to it by Article 3 of the Constitution, which include powers to make treaties, to coin money, to promote science and the arts by passing patent and copyright legislation, and to regulate interstate commerce. Also, the U.S. Constitution provides that Congress is empowered to enact "all Laws which shall be necessary and proper for carrying into Execution the foregoing [delegated or enumerated] Powers."[1]

federalism
Our system of shared government between the federal government and the states. Powers not delegated to the federal government are reserved to the states and citizens.

Bill of Rights

As indicated above, the powers of the federal government are limited in a number of very specific ways by the **Bill of Rights,** which is composed of the first ten amendments to the U.S. Constitution. At the time when the then-free (from England) colonies were considering adoption of the Constitution, several states indicated that they would not sign the U.S. Constitution unless the Bill of Rights was part of the package. According to many state leaders at that time, the Bill of Rights was considered to provide essential protections of individual rights of citizens from the power of the *federal* government. During the twentieth century, various rulings of the U.S. Supreme Court carried the protections of the Bill of Rights to citizens vis-à-vis actions of *state* governments. A number of the specific protections provided by the Bill of Rights are discussed in some detail in this chapter, including the rights of freedom of expression, of freedom from unreasonable searches and seizures, and to due process. A later add-on, the Fourteenth Amendment, which provides for equal protection under state law, also gets some detailed attention.

Bill of Rights
Citizen protections that are contained in the first ten amendments to the U.S. Constitution.

---

[1] Although the Constitution refers to powers "delegated" to the federal government, those powers are often referred to as "enumerated" powers in subsequent court cases.

Nutz and Boltz   Challenges Faced by the Framers of the Constitution: What Is the Proper Role of the Judiciary?

The following is an article that appears at the official website of the U.S. court system (www.uscourts.gov). Some would contend that through their rulings, U.S. courts do "make" law, but the article below illustrates separation of powers between the three branches of government. It is probably more accurate to say that judges primarily interpret and apply the law, while Congress makes laws and the executive branch enforces them.

THE CONSTITUTION AND THE FEDERAL JUDICIARY

Article III of the United States Constitution establishes the judicial branch as one of the three separate and distinct branches of the federal government. The other two are the legislative and executive branches.

The federal courts often are called the guardians of the Constitution because their rulings protect rights and liberties guaranteed by the Constitution. Through fair and impartial judgments, the federal courts interpret and apply the law to resolve disputes. The courts do not make the laws. That is the responsibility of Congress. Nor do the courts have the power to enforce the laws. That is the role of the President and the many executive branch departments and agencies.

The Founding Fathers of the nation considered an independent federal judiciary essential to ensure fairness and equal justice for all citizens of the United States. The Constitution they drafted promotes judicial independence in two major ways. First, federal judges are appointed for life, and they can be removed from office only through impeachment and conviction by Congress of "Treason, Bribery, or other high Crimes and Misdemeanors." Second, the Constitution provides that the compensation of federal judges "shall not be diminished during their Continuance in Office," which means that neither the President nor Congress can reduce the salary of a federal judge. These two protections help an independent judiciary to decide cases free from popular passion and political influence.

Source: See http://www.uscourts.gov/outreach/structure.jpg and www.uscourts.gov/about.html.

U.S. Constitution, Article III:

The judicial Power of the United States, shall be vested in one supreme Court, and in such inferior Courts as the Congress may from time to time ordain and establish. The Judges, both of the supreme and inferior Courts, shall hold their Offices during good Behaviour, and shall, at stated Times, receive for their Services, a Compensation, which shall not be diminished during their Continuance in Office.

THE COMMERCE CLAUSE

Commerce Clause
Article I, Section 8 of the U.S. Constitution gives Congress and the federal government the power to regulate interstate and foreign commerce between the states and among the Indian tribes.

The power to regulate commerce among states was not delegated to the federal government without careful consideration, but that power has nonetheless led to unforeseen consequences. Sometimes called the Interstate Commerce Clause, the **Commerce Clause** in the U.S. Constitution has two thrusts. First, it is a *power source* for action of the federal government and, second, it is *restraint* on state law.

Power Source for the Federal Government

Experience under the Articles of Confederation quickly taught that states were apt to act in the interest of "home-grown" business activities, to the detriment of "national" interests. That's why the power to regulate interstate commerce was allocated to the federal government under the Constitution. Even the Constitution, however, did not prevent states from attempting self-serving actions, requiring litigation to firmly establish what is and isn't allowable. As early as 1824, in *Gibbons v. Ogden,* the Supreme Court ruled that the federal government's power to regulate interstate commerce meant that state laws that interfered with interstate commerce were unconstitutional.[2] In *Gibbons,* the State of New York issued an exclusive license to transport passengers into New York harbor to Robert Livingston and Robert Fulton. Ogden, who was transporting passengers to New York from New Jersey and from New York back to New Jersey, was fined by New York authorities and prohibited from continuing his trade. Ogden appealed his conviction to the U.S. Supreme Court, which ruled that the federal government's power to regulate interstate commerce preempted New York from blocking interstate commerce.

As a result of the Supreme Court's ruling in *Gibbons,* the authority of the federal government to regulate interstate commerce was clearly established. If interstate commerce was involved, as it was in the ferrying of passengers between New Jersey and New York, the federal government could regulate the activity. As a result of the Commerce Clause, the federal government could regulate all navigable waters, trains, canals, telegraphs and other interstate transmissions. This was so, even though the **Tenth Amendment** to the Constitution limited the power of the federal government to its enumerated powers.

Tenth Amendment
Reserves all powers not delegated to the federal government for the states and citizens. It is the amendment that most explicitly defines what is meant by "federalism."

The Tenth Amendment and Attempts to Expand Power of the Federal Government

As is discussed above, the Tenth Amendment reserves all powers not delegated to the federal government by the U.S. Constitution to the states and citizens. Article 3 of the U.S. Constitution does delegate to the federal government responsibility for regulating interstate commerce (and commerce with other countries and Indian tribes).

From the earliest days of the republic, the power of the federal government to regulate interstate commerce was unquestioned. In 1887, for example, Congress established the Interstate Commerce Commission, one of the first regulatory agencies. Beginning in 1916, however, based on its power to regulate interstate commerce, Congress passed a number of statutes that arguably went beyond the needs of regulating interstate commerce.

For example, responding to widespread stories of abuse and thwarted opportunities, Congress passed a child labor law prohibiting the interstate transportation of goods manufactured using children under 14 in factories, or using labor provided by children under 16 who worked more than eight hours a day, six days a week. Factory owners challenged, contesting the authority of the federal government to regulate what they regarded as purely *intrastate* activity, namely production. Congress claimed it had the authority to impose this law because it was only regulating goods that traveled in interstate commerce, but the Supreme Court rejected Congress's arguments based on the Tenth Amendment restriction on the power of the central government. The Supreme Court stated that the purpose of the legislation was to regulate production within a state, not the interstate transport of goods.[3]

When Franklin Roosevelt was elected president in 1932, the country was deep in an economic depression. Roosevelt's prescription for lifting the country out of the economic doldrums relied heavily on ambitious legislation that made use of production quotas (supply restrictions) to lift prices. Both the Agricultural Adjustment Act (AAA) and the National Industrial Recovery Act (NIRA) called for substantial involvement of the federal government in production controls and price-setting, activities that were normally considered *intrastate* matters. The AAA and the NIRA were both challenged by industry leaders and the Supreme Court in 1935 declared this legislation, the centerpieces of Roosevelt's recovery efforts, unconstitutional, citing the Tenth Amendment.[4]

---

[2] *Gibbons v. Ogden,* 22 U.S. 1 (1824).

[3] *Hammer v. Dagenhart,* 247 U.S. 251 (1916).

[4] *Panama Refining et al., v. Ryan et al.,* 29 U.S. 388 (1935).

"In" or "Affects" Interstate Commerce

Roosevelt was sufficiently dismayed by what he regarded as a backward Supreme Court that he threatened to "pack" the Supreme Court with new members and raise its number from 9 to 15. However, because of the deaths and resignations of several Supreme Court justices during the 1930s, Roosevelt was able to replace these justices with appointees who believed, as Roosevelt did, in expanding the power of the federal government. In 1942, the Supreme Court issued a federal government power–expanding opinion in *Wichard v. Filburn*.[5] Wichard was a wheat farmer in Ohio who grew more wheat than was allowed under a government quota plan, resulting in a challenge by a representative from the U.S. Department of Agriculture. According to the Supreme Court:

> The commerce power is not confined in its exercise to the regulation of commerce among the states. It extends to those activities intrastate which so **affect** interstate commerce, or the exertion of the power of Congress over it, as to make regulation of them appropriate means to the attainment of a legitimate end, the effective execution of the granted power to regulate interstate commerce . . . The power of Congress over interstate commerce is plenary and complete in itself, may be exercised to its utmost extent, and acknowledges no limitations other than are prescribed in the Constitution . . . It follows that no form of state activity can constitutionally thwart the regulatory power granted by the commerce clause to Congress. Hence the reach of that power extends to those intrastate activities which in a substantial way interfere with or obstruct the exercise of the granted power.[6]

In *Wichard,* the Supreme Court said that in aggregate, if Wichard, and others like him, did not limit their production to that allowed by a quota from the U.S. Department of Agriculture, interstate prices of wheat would be *affected* even though his production of wheat was not *in* interstate commerce. **The standard that emerged from *Wichard* and other parallel cases was that Congress had the power to regulate everything *in* interstate commerce and everything that *affects* interstate commerce.**

Further Expansions of Federal Power Using the Commerce Clause

Following the ruling in *Wichard,* the Supreme Court upheld the power of the federal government to regulate all sorts of activities that were only tangentially related to interstate commerce. In 1964 Ollie's Barbecue was a restaurant in Alabama that restricted its seating to whites only, even though it sold take-out food to blacks. Such practices were made illegal under the 1964 Civil Rights Act. In *Katzenbach v. McClung,* the Supreme Court upheld the power of Congress to regulate seating in the small Ollie's restaurant in Alabama.[7]

In Raleigh, North Carolina, Rex Hospital (the defendant), charged with monopolizing the local market for hospitals, tried to defend itself by claiming that the federal government could not regulate a purely local medical market.[8] The Supreme Court rejected the intrastate-only defense of Rex Hospital by stating that Rex Hospital ordered medical supplies and medicines from across state lines and served patients who came from other states and that its financing for planned expansions was also from out of state. Other decisions similarly upheld the authority of the federal government to regulate minimum wages paid to state employees, pensions administered by county authorities, and other seemingly local activities including the regulation of working conditions in small factories and local loan sharking. The *Rex Hospital* case (reviewed below) is illustrative of these cases.

---

[5] *Wichard v. Filburn*, 311 U.S. 111 (1942).

[6] *Id.* at 124 (emphasis added).

[7] *Katzenbach v. McClung*, 379 U.S. 294 (1964).

[8] *Hospital Building Co. v. Trustees of Rex Hospital et al.*, 425 U.S. 738 (1976).

Case 5-1

Hospital Building Co. v. Trustees of Rex Hospital et al.

Supreme Court of the United States
425 U.S. 738 (1976)

BACKGROUND AND FACTS

A suit under sections 1 and 2 of the Sherman Act (15 U.S.C. §§ 1, 2) was instituted in the United States District Court for the Eastern District of North Carolina by a corporation operating a proprietary hospital in Raleigh, North Carolina, against another corporation operating a private tax-exempt hospital in the same city. The plaintiff [Mary Elizabeth Hospital] contended that the defendants had conspired with others to restrain trade and commerce in the furnishing of hospital services in the city by blocking the relocation and expansion of the plaintiff's hospital. The District Court dismissed the amended complaint, holding that the plaintiff had not alleged a sufficient nexus between the alleged violations of the Sherman Act and interstate commerce, and the United States Court of Appeals for the Fourth Circuit affirmed.

Opinion by Mr. Justice Marshall, Delivered for a Unanimous Court

Petitioner identifies several areas of interstate commerce in which it is involved. According to the amended complaint, petitioner purchases a substantial proportion—up to 80%—of its medicines and supplies from out-of-state sellers. In 1972, it spent $112,000 on these items. A substantial number of the patients at Mary Elizabeth Hospital [the plaintiff], it is alleged, come from out of State. Moreover, petitioner claims that a large proportion of its revenue comes from insurance companies outside of North Carolina or from the Federal Government through the Medicaid and Medicare programs. Petitioner also pays a management service fee based on its gross receipts to its parent company, a Delaware corporation based in Georgia. Finally, petitioner has developed plans to finance a large part of the planned $4 million expansion through out-of-state lenders. All these involvements with interstate commerce, the amended complaint claims, have been and are continuing to be adversely affected by respondents' anticompetitive conduct.

* * *

In this case, the Court of Appeals, while recognizing that Sherman Act coverage requires only that the conduct complained of have a substantial effect on interstate commerce, concluded that the conduct at issue did not meet that standard. We disagree. The complaint, fairly read, alleges that if respondents and their co-conspirators were to succeed in blocking petitioner's planned expansion, petitioner's purchases of out-of-state medicines and supplies as well as its revenues from out-of-state insurance companies would be thousands and perhaps hundreds of thousands of dollars less than they would otherwise be. Similarly, the management fees that petitioner pays to its out-of-state parent corporation would be less if the expansion were blocked. Moreover, the multimillion-dollar financing for the expansion, a large portion of which would be from out of State, would simply not take place if the respondents succeeded in their alleged scheme. This combination of factors is certainly sufficient to establish a "substantial effect" on interstate commerce under the Act.

* * *

Accordingly, the judgment of the Court of Appeals is reversed, and the case is remanded for further proceedings consistent with this opinion.

Decision and Outcome

The Supreme Court reinstated the plaintiff's antitrust claim against the defendant Rex Hospital, ruling that, because their actions affected interstate commerce, they were subject to the Sherman Act, which is a federal statute.

Questions for Analysis

1. The defendant in this case was a hospital and was being sued for monopolizing the market for hospital patients in the Raleigh, North Carolina, area. What is the relevance of the plaintiff's impact on insurance and medical supplies?

2. According to Justice Marshall, what is the criterion for determining whether the federal antitrust laws reach the conduct of the defendant?

Limits to the Power of the Federal Government

Many of the efforts that the federal government has expended to intervene in matters previously considered purely local have stemmed from the desire to remedy local conditions that many regard as unjust, wasteful, or inefficient. Interventions in civil rights cases and in efforts to protect the environment generally are held in high regard. There is a fairly widespread concern, however, regarding the aggregate effect of an accumulation of "liberal" interpretations of the Commerce Clause. The focus of that concern has been that the power of the federal government to intervene in and regulate local matters has become nearly unlimited, as virtually every commercial activity, from growing wheat to arranging seating in small restaurants, *affects* interstate commerce in some way. In order to reduce the volume of court challenges to the authority of the federal government, many statutes, such as the civil rights acts and workers' safety statutes, limit their application to companies with 15 or more employees. Given the breadth of federal interventions in business activities, many have claimed (as did Bob Dole in the 1996 presidential election) that the Tenth Amendment has been effectively repealed. The alleged "powers not delegated to the United States by the Constitution, nor prohibited by it to the States," as described in the Tenth Amendment, appear to be virtually nonexistent.

Of course, any generalization is apt to have an exception, and there certainly have been federal statutes that have been declared unconstitutional because they violated the Tenth Amendment. Recently, a federal statute was enacted that made possession of an illegal firearm within a certain distance of a public school a federal crime. Justices on the Supreme Court struck down this legislation as outside the powers of the federal government and, by implication, applicable to activity that does not *affect* interstate commerce.[9]

LIMITATION ON THE POWERS OF STATE GOVERNMENTS

Court interpretations of the Commerce Clause have had two effects: (1) enhancing the power of the federal government to regulate anything that affects interstate commerce and (2) preventing states from erecting trade barriers that threatened to erode nationhood among all the states. As indicated earlier, the fact that the Constitution allocated responsibility for regulating interstate commerce to the federal government did not prevent state authorities from passing laws and regulations that favor in-state businesses at the expense of out-of-state businesses. So, during the course of our history, the U.S. Supreme Court has been quite active in preventing states from erecting interstate trade barriers. Of course, self-interest hasn't gone away, so there continue to be both economic and political reasons why elected and appointed state officials seek to enact protectionist laws that favor in-state interests.

[9] *United States v. Alfonzo Lopez Jr.,* 514 U.S. 549 (1995).

Unconstitutional State Laws

Since adoption of the Constitution, there have been literally hundreds of state laws declared unconstitutional by the U.S. Supreme Court and other federal courts. Given the large numbers of these rulings, it is useful to categorize the grounds for the adverse rulings in the following fashion:

discriminates against interstate commerce

An unconstitutional state law that taxes, erects a barrier, or otherwise disadvantages out-of-state businesses and goods relative to in-state businesses and goods.

- *A state law* **discriminates against interstate commerce.** State laws that impose additional costs on goods or commerce that crosses state lines are unconstitutional on their face. Numerous states established state milk commissions that created regulations that made milk produced out of state more expensive than milk produced in state. In case after case, protectionist regulations imposed by state milk commissions have been struck down.[10] In a number of other industries, similar types of discriminatory state statutes have been struck down (as illustrated in Case 5-2).

excessive burden on interstate commerce

An unconstitutional state law that treats in-state and out-of-state businesses equally, but places an excessive burden on interstate commerce.

- *A state law imposes an* **excessive burden on interstate commerce.** Some state laws that do not discriminate against out-of-state businesses are still struck down because they impose too great a burden on interstate commerce. In the state of Wisconsin, the legislature passed a statute outlawing tandem tractor-trailers on Wisconsin highways and freeways. Tandem tractor-trailers are trucks that have one tractor and more than one trailer. The Wisconsin state statute did not discriminate against out-of-state trucking firms; it applied its restrictions equally to in-state and out-of-state trucking firms. The statute did, however, substantially burden interstate commerce because tandem tractor trailers were common in the upper Midwest and trucking firms had to stop outside Wisconsin and hook up an additional tractor to haul a trailer across the state of Wisconsin. The U.S. Supreme Court declared the Wisconsin law to be one that imposed an undue burden on interstate commerce.[11]

roughly apportioned

State taxes must be apportioned to activities of a multistate business within the state.

- *State business taxes must be* **roughly apportioned** *to the activities of that business in the state.* A state can levy a nondiscriminatory business tax on gross receipts of a business, but that gross receipts tax must correspond to sales of that company within that state. The state of Rhode Island, which is the site of several Exxon gas stations, can impose a gross sales tax on Exxon, but only for its sales within the state. Rhode Island can impose a property tax on Exxon, but again only for the property it owns within the state.

act of interstate commerce

Goods that are moving from one state to another cannot be taxed by a state based on the act of transporting the goods from one state to another.

- *A state taxes the* **act of interstate commerce.** If a company is transporting cattle across a state, that state cannot levy a property tax on those cattle. A state can exact a toll for using a state highway. However, a state cannot tax *only* those goods that are traveling in interstate commerce (e.g., impose such a tax while not taxing the intrastate transport and sale of goods).

When Can a State Regulate?

Most state laws (statutes and regulations) do impact interstate commerce. If a state law is discriminatory toward interstate commerce, it is unconstitutional. When a state statute purports to prohibit the transmission of trash into a landfill from out-of-state sources, such legislation is discriminatory on its face and thus unconstitutional. Some state laws, however, affect interstate commerce but are not discriminatory. If a state statute is (1) rationally related to the achievement of a legitimate state objective and (2) does not create

---

[10] David L. Baumer, Richard F. Fallert, and Lynn H. Sleight, "State Milk Regulation: Extent, Economic Effects, and Legal Status," U.S. Dept. of Agr., Econ. Res. Serv. Staff Report No. AGES860404, April 1986.

[11] *Raymond Motor Transportation, Inc., et al. v. Rice, Secretary of Department of Transportation of Wisconsin et al.*, 434 U.S. 429 (1977).

an undue burden on interstate commerce, then it is constitutional. States regulate all sorts of things, such as pollution within state borders, standards for motor vehicles, and the internal governance of corporations incorporated within the state. Most of these laws are constitutional.

In Case 5-2, the standards for constitutional acceptability clearly were not met.

Case 5-2

Chemical Waste Management, Inc., Petitioner v. Guy Hunt, Governor of Alabama et al.

Supreme Court of the United States
504 U.S. 334 (1992)

BACKGROUND AND FACTS

The State of Alabama enacted a statute that required the operator of an in-state facility for the disposal of hazardous waste to charge a base fee of $26.50 for all generators of hazardous waste and an additional $72.00 fee per ton for hazardous waste that was generated out of state. The operator of an Alabama commercial landfill facility for hazardous waste disposal, alleging that the additional fee violated various provisions including the federal Constitution's commerce clause (Art. I, sec. 8, cl. 3), filed against defendants including the Governor of Alabama a state-court suit seeking declaratory relief and an injunction against enforcement of the state statute. The trial court, finding the only basis for the additional fee to be the origin of the waste, held that the additional fee violated the Commerce Clause. On appeal, the Alabama Supreme Court, reversing in pertinent part, held that the additional fee advanced legitimate local purposes that could not be adequately served by reasonable nondiscriminatory alternatives. This decision of the Alabama Supreme Court resulted in an appeal to the U.S. Supreme Court by Chemical Waste Management, Inc.

Opinion: Justice White Delivered the Opinion of the Court

No State may attempt to isolate itself from a problem common to the several States by raising barriers to the free flow of interstate trade. Today, in *Fort Gratiot Sanitary Landfill, Inc. v. Michigan Dept. of Natural Resources, post,* p. 353, we have also considered a Commerce Clause challenge to a Michigan law prohibiting private landfill operators from accepting solid waste originating outside the county in which their facilities operate. In striking down that law, we adhered to our decision in *Philadelphia v. New Jersey,* 437 U.S. 617 (1978), where we found New Jersey's prohibition of solid waste from outside that State to amount to economic protectionism barred by the Commerce Clause:

> [T]he evil of protectionism can reside in legislative means as well as legislative ends. Thus, it does not matter whether the ultimate aim of ch. 363 is to reduce the waste disposal costs of New Jersey residents or to save remaining open lands from pollution, for we assume New Jersey has every right to protect its residents' pocketbooks as well as their environment. And it may be assumed as well that New Jersey may pursue those ends by slowing the flow of *all* waste into the State's remaining landfills, even though interstate commerce may incidentally be affected. But whatever New Jersey's ultimate purpose, it may not be accompanied by discriminating against articles of commerce coming from outside the State unless there is some reason, apart from their origin, to treat them differently. Both on its face and in its plain effect, ch. 363 violates this principle of nondiscrimination.

* * *

These may all be legitimate local interests, and petitioner has not attacked them. But only rhetoric, and not explanation, emerges as to why Alabama targets only interstate hazardous waste to meet these goals. As found by the trial court, "[a]lthough the Legislature imposed an additional fee of $72.00 per ton on waste generated outside Alabama, there is absolutely no evidence before this Court that waste generated outside Alabama is more dangerous than waste generated in Alabama. The Court finds under the facts of this case that the only basis for the additional fee is the origin of the waste." . . . In the face of such findings, invalidity under the Commerce Clause necessarily follows, for "whatever [Alabama's] ultimate purpose, it may not be accomplished by discriminating against articles of commerce coming from outside the State unless there is some reason, apart from their origin, to treat them differently."

* * *

Decision and Outcome

The U.S. Supreme Court declared the fee charged by Alabama state authorities for out-of-state hazardous waste unconstitutional because it violated the Commerce Clause.

Questions for Analysis

1. Was this a case in which the Alabama statute was unconstitutional because the statute discriminated against out-of-state interests or did the statute impose an undue burden on interstate commerce?
2. Do you think that this case would have been differently decided if there was some showing that out-of-state waste was more hazardous than in-state hazardous waste?
3. By this ruling, what was the competitive evil that the Supreme Court was trying to avoid?

Preemption of State Powers to Regulate: Supremacy Clause

An issue that has enjoyed a long, prominent, and continuing life is whether federal regulation of subject matter precludes states from regulating the same subject. The Supremacy Clause of the U.S. Constitution makes federal law supreme over state laws so that, if there is a *conflict* between state and federal law, federal law prevails. There are federal laws against the possession and sale of marijuana. Some states, responding to pleas mostly from AIDS activists, have "legalized" the sale of marijuana for medical use. These laws are in conflict with federal laws and, thus, are unconstitutional.

An apparently conflicting standard is applicable to environmental protection laws. Many states regulate pollution, as does the federal government through the Environmental Protection Agency (EPA). Suppose a state regulates more stringently with respect to water pollution than is called for in the federal Clean Water Act? Is a state statute that sets a more stringent standard than is set by federal law legal? The answer is yes, provided that two conditions are met:

1. The state law does not unduly burden interstate commerce.
2. The state restrictions are not in an area of law that is exclusively reserved for the federal government. In other words, if **preemption** applies, all state laws are unconstitutional.

preemption
Takes place when a whole area of law is occupied by federal law and any state laws in the area are unconstitutional.

We have already discussed the undue burden test for state laws that affect interstate commerce. If the state law passes the undue burden test, it could still be declared unconstitutional if the U.S. Supreme Court rules that all state laws in the area are *preempted* by federal regulation.

Preemption occurs when any state laws in this area are considered a nuisance. Congress can preempt all state legislation by simply declaring in a statute it enacts that *only federal law applies.* In other areas, precedents from Supreme Court decisions have created preemption. All state laws regarding immigration, foreign policy, and airline safety are preempted by prior Supreme Court rulings. There are, additionally, numerous more narrowly circumscribed areas of law that are regulated federally and, hence, preempted from controls imposed by any state laws. In the *Cippoline* case (Case 5-3), the primary issue was whether required federal warnings on cigarettes preempted tort claims made in state courts based on the contention that the warnings were not reasonably adequate.

Case 5-3

Thomas Cipollone, Individually and as Executor of the Estate of Rose D. Cipollone, Petitioner v. Liggett Group, Inc., et al.

Supreme Court of the United States
505 U.S. 504 (1992)

BACKGROUND AND FACTS

This is a massive case with a lot of legal issues. Part of this case involved warnings on cigarettes. Rose Cipollone died after contracting lung cancer. She was a smoker for 42 years. She claims that based on the advertising of the defendant, she was attracted to cigarettes because it made her look and feel attractive and with it. Congress passed two statutes, one in 1965 and one in 1969, that required the sale of cigarettes to be accompanied by warnings about the health dangers of smoking tobacco products.

The Federal Cigarette Labeling and Advertising Act of 1965 (the 1965 Act) (1) recited statutory purposes of (a) adequately informing the public that cigarette smoking may be hazardous to health and (b) protecting the national economy from the burden imposed by diverse, nonuniform, and confusing cigarette labeling and advertising regulations; (2) required a specific warning to appear on cigarette packages; and (3) in section 5 (15 U.S.C. § 1334), which was captioned "Preemption," provided that (a) no statement relating to smoking and health, other than the statement required by section 4, would be required on any cigarette package and (b) no statement relating to smoking and health would be required in the advertising of any cigarettes the packages of which were labeled in conformity with the provisions of the 1965 Act.

Opinion: Justice Stevens Delivered the Opinion of the Court, Except as to Parts V and VI

Petitioner is the son of Rose Cipollone, who began smoking in 1942 and who died of lung cancer in 1984. He claims that respondents are responsible for Rose Cipollone's death because they breached express warranties contained in their advertising, because they failed to warn consumers about the hazards of smoking, because they fraudulently misrepresented those hazards to consumers, and because they conspired to deprive the public of medical and scientific information about smoking. The Court of Appeals held that petitioner's state law claims were pre-empted by federal statutes, 893 F.2d 541 (CA3 1990), and other courts have agreed with that analysis. [Footnotes deleted] The highest courts of the States of Minnesota and New Jersey, however, have held that the federal statutes did not pre-empt similar common law claims. Because of the manifest importance of the issue, we granted certiorari to resolve the conflict, 500 U.S. 499, 935 (1991).

* * *

Article VI of the Constitution provides that the laws of the United States "shall be the supreme Law of the Land; . . . any Thing in the Constitution or Laws of any state to the Contrary notwithstanding." Art. VI, cl. 2. Thus, since our decision in *McCulloch v. Maryland,* 4 Wheat. 316, 427, 4 L. Ed.579 (1819), it has been settled that state law that conflicts with federal law is "without effect." [References deleted] Consideration of issues arising under the Supremacy Clause "start[s] with the assumption that the historic police powers of the States [are] not to be superseded by . . . Federal Act unless that [is] the clear and manifest purpose of Congress." Accordingly, " '[t]he purpose of Congress is the ultimate touchstone' " of pre-emption analysis.

Congress' intent may be "explicitly stated in the statute's language or implicitly contained in its structure and purpose." In the absence of an express congressional command, state law is pre-empted if that law actually conflicts with federal law, or if federal law so thoroughly occupies a legislative field "'as to make reasonable the inference that Congress left no room for the States to supplement it.'"

* * *

In our opinion, the pre-emptive scope of the 1965 Act and the 1969 Act is governed entirely by the express language in § 5 of each Act. When Congress has considered the issue of pre-emption and has included in the enacted legislation a provision explicitly addressing that issue, and when that provision provides a "reliable indicium of congressional intent with respect to state authority," *Malone v. White Motor Corp.,* 435 U.S., at 505, "there is no need to infer congressional intent to pre-empt state laws from the substantive provisions" of the legislation. Such reasoning is a variant of the familiar principle of *expressio unius est exclusio alterius:* Congress' enactment of a provision defining the pre-emptive reach of a statute implies that matters beyond that reach are not pre-empted. In this case, the other provisions of the 1965 and 1969 Acts offer no cause to look beyond § 5 of each Act. Therefore, we need only identify the domain expressly pre-empted by each of those sections. As the 1965 and 1969 provisions differ substantially, we consider each in turn.

* * *

Petitioner's claims are pre-empted to the extent that they rely on a state law "requirement or prohibition . . . with respect to . . . advertising or promotion." Thus, insofar as claims under either failure to warn theory require a showing that respondents' post-1969 advertising or promotions should have included additional, or more clearly stated, warnings, those claims are pre-empted. The Act does not, however, pre-empt petitioner's claims that rely solely on respondents' testing or research practices or other actions unrelated to advertising or promotion.

Decision and Outcome

The claims of the family of the decedent, Rose Cipollone, are dismissed with regard to their claim based on state law that the warnings that accompanied the sale of cigarettes were inadequate. The plaintiff's claims on other grounds such as fraud in testing and research were not dismissed.

Questions for Analysis

1. What part of state law was preempted by the 1965 and 1969 legislation passed by Congress?
2. What claim of the plaintiff's still remains as a result of this case?
3. Explain the distinction drawn by the Supreme Court.

THE TAX AND SPENDING POWERS OF GOVERNMENTS

Tax and Spending Powers of the Federal Government

The federal government has very broad powers to tax and spend. Technically, tax bills must originate from the House of Representatives, but, in fact, legislators are generally inspired to submit a tax bill by the president, who presents a proposed budget to Congress each year.

The Constitution allows Congress to spend tax revenues to "provide for the common Defence and general Welfare of the United States." As with its ability to tax, the power of Congress to spend is virtually unlimited, except when that spending is held to violate one of the rights contained in the Bill of Rights or some other prohibition contained in the Constitution. Of course, the federal government spends money on a wide array of activities, ranging from national defense, to education, to medical research, and so forth.

Limitations on Taxing and Spending by State Governments

There are well-recognized limitations on a state's tax authority when it comes to dealing with federal government activities within the state. In the famous *McCulloch v. Maryland* case, the U.S. Supreme Court established the precedent that a state does not have the power to tax a federal instrumentality or to discriminatorily tax entities authorized by federal law.[12] In *McCulloch,* the state of Maryland had imposed a property tax on all banks not chartered by the state ("National" banks, identifiable by the presence of the word "National" in their name, are federally chartered). The historic ruling in this case, written for the Court by the fourth Chief Justice of the Supreme Court, Justice Marshall, stated that "the power to tax is the power to destroy." Thus, it was concluded, states cannot levy a property tax on federal buildings located within the state or discriminatorily tax federally chartered banks.

GOVERNMENTAL TAKINGS, PUBLIC USE, AND COMPENSATION

Power of Eminent Domain

government takings
An action of the government in which private property is taken from a citizen.

eminent domain
The power of government to take private land for public use upon paying fair compensation.

Both state and federal governments have the power to take property from citizens, but only if the **government taking** is for public use with just compensation provided to the property owner. At the federal level, the Fifth Amendment states, ". . . nor shall private property be taken for public use without just compensation." A state or the federal government can force property owners to part with their property in a condemnation, or **eminent domain**, proceeding, but there are constitutional constraints to ensure that

1. The acquisition of property is for the public good.
2. The property owner is not individually oppressed by, in effect, having to pay for public improvements.

So, if a government decides to build a public road or highway and someone's property is in the way, the government can condemn the property and build the road over the property. Landowners can challenge condemnation proceedings on either of two grounds: first, that the taking was not for *public purposes* and, second, that the compensation was not just, or equal to *fair market value*.

Regulatory Takings

Eminent domain actions by governments have been a frequent source of litigation. With far less frequency, citizens also have sued governments in *inverse condemnation* suits in which citizen plaintiffs claim that a regulatory action by government has rendered their property worthless or nearly so. If the plaintiff is successful in such a suit (s)he is entitled to recover the fair market value of the lost property. When governments expand airports, homeowners who are near the airport may find that their homes are uninhabitable because of the noise and vibrations from large jets. Of course, an uninhabitable home has little market value, so homeowners impacted in this fashion can claim that the value of their house has been confiscated by government activity. In a number of cases, property owners have been successful in inverse condemnation proceedings based on the claim that government regulations/activities, in effect, took their property. It is important to note that there is a wide range of government regulation that can have some effect on the value of privately owned property. Inverse condemnation suits have been successful only when a governmental action has had the effect of destroying all, or nearly all, of the value of the property, a situation that many find unfair.

---

[12] *McCulloch v. Maryland*, 4 Wheat. 316 (1819).

Case 5-4

First English Evangelical Lutheran Church of Glendale v. County of Los Angeles, California

Supreme Court of the United States
482 U.S. 304 (1987)

BACKGROUND AND FACTS

In 1957, appellant church purchased land on which it operated a campground, known as "Lutherglen," as a retreat center and a recreational area for handicapped children. The land is located in a canyon along the banks of a creek that is the natural drainage channel for a watershed area. In 1978, a flood destroyed Lutherglen's buildings. In response to the flood, appellee Los Angeles County, in 1979, adopted an interim ordinance prohibiting the construction or reconstruction of any building or structure in an interim flood protection area that included the land on which Lutherglen had stood. Shortly after the ordinance was adopted, appellant (Church) filed suit in a California court, alleging, inter alia, that the ordinance denied appellant all use of Lutherglen, and seeking to recover damages in inverse condemnation for such loss of use . . . Because appellant [the Lutheran church] alleged a regulatory taking and sought only damages, the trial court deemed the allegation that the ordinance denied all use of Lutherglen to be irrelevant. The California Court of Appeal affirmed. Appellant appealed to the U.S. Supreme Court, which agreed to hear the case.

Opinion: Chief Justice Rehnquist Delivered the Opinion of the Court

Consideration of the compensation question must begin with direct reference to the language of the Fifth Amendment, which provides in relevant part that "private property [shall not] be taken for public use, without just compensation." As its language indicates, and as the Court has frequently noted, this provision does not prohibit the taking of private property, but instead places a condition on the exercise of that power. [References deleted] This basic understanding of the Amendment makes clear that it is designed not to limit the governmental interference with property rights *per se,* but rather to secure *compensation* in the event of otherwise proper interference amounting to a taking. Thus, government action that works a taking of property rights necessarily implicates the "constitutional obligation to pay just compensation."

We have recognized that a landowner is entitled to bring an action in inverse condemnation as a result of "'the self-executing character of the constitutional provision with respect to compensation. . . .'" *United States v. Clarke,* 445 U.S. 253, 257 (1980), quoting 6 P. Nichols, Eminent Domain § 25.41 (3d rev. ed. 1972). As noted in JUSTICE BRENNAN's dissent in *San Diego Gas & Electric Co.,* 450 U.S. at 654–655, it has been established at least since *Jacobs v. United States,* 290 U.S. 13 (1933), that claims for just compensation are grounded in the Constitution itself:

> The suits were based on the right to recover just compensation for property taken by the United States for public use in the exercise of its power of eminent domain. *That right was guaranteed by the Constitution.* The fact that condemnation proceedings were not instituted and that the right was asserted in suits by the owners did not change the essential nature of the claim. The form of the remedy did not qualify the right. It rested upon the Fifth Amendment. Statutory recognition was not necessary. A promise to pay was not necessary. Such a promise was implied because of the duty to pay imposed by the Amendment. *The suits were thus founded upon the Constitution of the United States.*

Id. at 16. (Emphasis added.)

* * *

It has also been established doctrine at least since Justice Holmes' opinion for the Court in *Pennsylvania Coal Co. v. Mahon,* 260 U.S. 393 (1922), that "the general rule at least is that, while property may be regulated to a certain extent, if regulation goes too far, it will be recognized as a taking." *Id*. at 415. While the typical taking occurs when the government acts to condemn property in the exercise of its power of eminent domain, the entire doctrine of inverse condemnation is predicated on the proposition that a taking may occur without such formal proceedings.

* * *

Here we must assume that the Los Angeles County ordinance has denied appellant all use of its property for a considerable period of years, and we hold that invalidation of the ordinance without payment of fair value for the use of the property during this period of time would be a constitutionally insufficient remedy. The judgment of the California Court of Appeal is therefore reversed, and the case is remanded for further proceedings not inconsistent with this opinion.

Decision and Outcome

The court held that Los Angeles County was required to compensate the Lutheran Church for the regulatory taking of its property.

Questions for Analysis

1. The Fifth Amendment states that private property cannot be taken for public purposes without just compensation. What was the public purpose in this case?
2. At the end of the opinion, Justice Rehnquist states that merely declaring the ordinance unconstitutional is inadequate. As a result of this trial will the plaintiff recover (a) the fair market value of the property or (b) repeal of the ordinance and fair market value for the rental of the land during the time it was not available to the Church?

PROCEDURAL DUE PROCESS: THE FIFTH AND FOURTEENTH AMENDMENTS

procedural due process
If government takes a protected interest, they must provide notice before anything is taken and a hearing so that the defendant can respond to the claims made against him or her.

Both the Fifth and Fourteenth Amendments to the Constitution contain due process clauses that provide *procedural* safeguards against capricious actions by governments. The protective formula of **procedural due process** is the following: if a governmental action *takes* a protected interest, then the citizen affected is entitled to due process, which means notice and a hearing. Governmental action includes actions of the legislative as well as executive branches of government. Passing a law is a legislative action. The executive branch of government often acts through the police. Putting you in jail is an executive action.

Protected Interest

Protected interests includes *life, liberty,* and *property.* A government unit (local, state, or federal) that condemns your property in order to build a public highway is taking a protected interest, which you can contest in court. To a government that may throw you in jail, your liberty is a protected interest and you are entitled to a trial of your peers before facing any incarceration (some defendants in criminal cases waive their rights to a jury trial).

In actuality, protected interests are broader than just the Webster's Dictionary definition of life, liberty, and property. Various courts have held that when a government fires you from a government job, cuts off government benefits, or ejects you from a public school, it is engaged in a *taking* of a protected interest that entitles you to notice before the taking occurs and a follow-up hearing where you can face your "accusers" and contest the taking.

Notice and a Hearing

Notice and a hearing are essential elements of due process. In general, you are entitled to be notified *before* the government takes a protected interest and you are entitled to a hearing to present your side of the case. In a *criminal* trial, there are elaborate safeguards taken to ensure that the liberty (or life) of an individual not be taken without proof beyond a reasonable doubt. The formality of the hearing is often dictated by the severity of the governmental sanction. In cases where a high school student is ejected for class disruption, the hearing requirement may be satisfied by a conference with parents and teachers in the principal's office. When a person's liberty is at stake, the defendant is entitled to be represented by an attorney paid for by the state, a jury of one's peers, the right to face accusers, and a number of other procedural safeguards.

FOURTEENTH AMENDMENT—EQUAL PROTECTION

equal protection
The Fourteenth Amendment guarantees that citizens will be treated equally under the law. Governments must have strong justifications for actions that treat people differently based on race or gender.

The Fourteenth Amendment to the Constitution provides an **equal protection** standard, which decrees that a state cannot ". . . deny to any person within its jurisdiction the equal protection of the laws." The simple meaning of this phrase is that a state government is required to treat similarly situated citizens in a similar way. While addressed to state governments, the equal protection mandate of the Fourteenth Amendment has been made applicable to federal government actions as well through Supreme Court decision.

When Does the Equal Protection Clause of the Fourteenth Amendment Come into Play?

A court will be called upon to determine whether a law or action violates equal protection standards of the Fourteenth Amendment when that law or action distinguishes between citizens on some basis (such as race, gender, occupation, etc.). For example, licensed attorneys can charge money to compose a will for a client, but the same act is illegal if performed by someone who is not licensed by the state to practice law.

Depending on the classification applied to citizens by the law or action, courts in turn apply three different levels of scrutiny in determining whether the law or action violates citizens' rights to equal protection. If a state law distinguishes between people based on race, then the distinction must pass the **strict scrutiny** test, discussed immediately below. If the state law involves gender, then courts apply **intermediate scrutiny** to analyze different treatment under the law to see if it is constitutional. For distinctions that do not involve race (and citizenship and illegitimacy) or gender, such as requiring lawyers to have a license to practice law, the **rational basis test** applies. Courts have held that state governments have *police powers,* which are inherent to governments, to protect public safety and provide for the general welfare.[13]

In general, very few governmental distinctions based on race survive a challenge under the Equal Protection Clause of the Fourteenth Amendment, but most other governmental distinctions based on some other factor are legal.

Strict Scrutiny: Governmental Distinctions Based on Race, Citizenship, or Illegitimacy

strict scrutiny
Government distinctions based on race can only be justified if they are to achieve a compelling state objective and the objective can only be achieved by treating people differently based on race.

The most famous application of the Equal Protection Clause of the Fourteenth Amendment occurred in *Brown v. Board of Education,* when the U.S. Supreme Court struck down state legislation in Virginia that required the races to attend separate public schools.[14] *Race, citizenship,* and *illegitimacy* are considered by the courts to be *suspect factors* if they are critical elements of laws or government actions. In general, treating someone differently in law because of race, citizenship, or illegitimacy status is illegal under the Equal Protection Clause of the Fourteenth Amendment unless the different treatment can be justified under

---

[13] Note that "police powers," as applied to state government, is broader than simply apprehending criminals.

[14] *Brown v. Board of Education*, 349 U.S. 294 (1955).

the strict scrutiny test. A governmental action (law or police action) that distinguishes between citizens on the basis of suspect factors will be approved only if

- It is necessary to promote a compelling government interest.
- The different treatment actually advances the compelling governmental interest.
- There are no less discriminatory ways of accomplishing this compelling state objective.

In several subsequent cases, courts applied the strict scrutiny test to segregationist legislation that required separation of the races under laws enacted by state governments. All such laws were declared unconstitutional under the Fourteenth Amendment in this line of cases.

Reformers were not content, however, to rid our nation of racist legislation that placed legal obstacle in the way of African Americans, but instead conceived of "affirmative action" as a remedy for past injustice toward African Americans. Under affirmative action plans, it is commonly claimed, state government hiring standards were relaxed for African Americans, admissions to state universities were made easier for African Americans than for whites, and percentages of government contracts were "set aside" for minority contractors.

Somewhat ironically, one frequent application of equal protection litigation recently has focused on affirmative action programs adopted by state government units. In a series of cases, the U.S. Supreme Court has held that (1) the strict scrutiny test, listed above, applies to any governmental distinction based on race, (2) the strict scrutiny test applies with equal force regardless of whether the governmental distinction was intended to help or hurt blacks or whites, and (3) the Equal Protection Clause applies to actions of the federal government as well as to other government units.[15]

There are courts that have agreed that states and localities may have a compelling interest in redressing past discriminatory practices based on race. The Supreme Court has held, however, that any such government action that carries out affirmative action must

- Be narrowly focused and must be a response to clearly identified past episode(s) of unconstitutional or illegal discrimination against minorities that its policy/actions are intended to address.
- Have a goal and be limited to achieving that goal.
- Not trammel excessively on the rights of nonminorities.
- Put an end to the (affirmative) policy or actions once redress has been delivered.

Even if the action by the government that discriminates based on race is necessary to promote a compelling governmental interest, it will still be declared unconstitutional if there are *less discriminatory methods* available to achieve the same objectives. During the past 15 or so years, equal protection cases involving affirmative action have resulted in a number of court decisions concluding that government affirmative action plans based on race are unconstitutional. On the other hand, some governmental affirmative action plans based on race and gender have been upheld in legal challenges, particularly when the affirmative action plan was designed to redress past discrimination against minorities and women. Most recently the admissions policies at both the undergraduate and law school level at the University of Michigan have been challenged by white students under the 14th amendment. The University of Michigan has been using race as one of several factors in its admissions standards. The cases have been appealed to the U.S. Supreme Court and represent a major challenge to state affirmative action plans.[16]

---

[15] *Adarand Constructors, Inc. v. Pena*, 515 U.S. 200 (1995).
[16] *Guntter v. Bollinger,* 123 & Ct. 617 (2002); *Htaly v. Bollinger,* 155 L. ed. 2d 223 (2003).

Intermediate Scrutiny

A step down from suspect traits or factors, there exist classifications applied to what are often described as *protected classes,* which include sex or gender. The legality of classifications involving sex or gender is examined based on an intermediate scrutiny standard. Laws applying distinctions based on gender must be *substantially related* to important government objectives. In most states, schools require that sports teams be segregated by gender, in part to make sure that girls have an opportunity to participate, and in part to prevent larger and stronger boys from injuring girls. Segregating sports teams at public schools can be justified as being substantially related to the achievement of important governmental objectives, which are to provide for physical education and exercise for members of both sexes. Other examples of gender-based laws include laws regulating when women can work. In the past there were a number state laws that prohibited women from working night shifts, allegedly out of concern for the preservation of families. On the other hand, night shifts typically paid more, so that such legislation had the effect of holding down wages for women. Most of these laws have been repealed or struck down as violating the Equal Protection Clause.

Minimum Scrutiny—The Rational Basis Test

State government regulations, policies, and actions can make distinctions among citizens on various additional traits that are not in the "suspect" or "protected" classes. State laws have created legal distinctions that treat farmers differently from other classes of workers, affect poor and rich in different ways, and rest on various other classifications of citizens. The legal distinctions made by state laws generally involve the regulation of economic and social matters, such as who's entitled to drive a taxi in New York City, whether there can be a city-required dress code for taxi drivers, the basis for unemployment compensation benefits, and which kinds of farm crops are entitled to crop support payments. The legality of all classifications that do not involve *suspect* or *protected* classes (race, gender, national origin, illegitimacy) is examined by courts with decidedly less scrutiny, through application of a rational basis test. Under this liberal standard, courts uphold government regulations, policies, and actions as long as the government entity can provide any rational basis for its choices. Providing subsidies to farmers while not making matching payments to other occupations is legal if there is a rational basis, such as a goal of stabilizing prices and production of agricultural products. Limiting who gets the medallion required for driving a New York City taxi is legal, so long as there is a rational basis for the limitation, such as reducing congestion on city streets. Requiring taxi drivers to meet a dress code requirement can be justified if it is linked to making a city attractive for business travelers or tourists. It is difficult for a law or action to fail the minimal scrutiny–rational basis test, though some have.[17]

BILL OF RIGHTS

Overview

As briefly noted earlier, when the U.S. Constitution was written, several states balked at its ratification unless there were guarantees of individual rights incorporated. The first 10 amendments to the Constitution, regularly referred to as the Bill of Rights, provided the wanted guarantees. Assurance of the enactment of this set of protective amendments led to ratification of the U.S. Constitution. The table in the "Nutz and Boltz" box provides a handy reference source for the Bill of Rights protections incorporated in the Constitution.

The Declaration of Independence declares that all men are "endowed by their Creator with certain inalienable Rights" including "Life, Liberty and the pursuit of Happiness."

---

[17] *American Can Co. v. Oregon Liquor Control Comm'n*, 517 P.2d 691 (1973).

Nutz and Boltz Rights Protected by Bill of Rights

The texts of some of the amendments are edited and the table below is edited for pertinence to business.

Amendment	Shorthand Right	Comment
First: Congress shall make no law respecting an establishment of religion,	Establishment Clause	No official state religion.
or prohibiting the free exercise thereof;	Free Exercise Clause	Freedom to worship in any way that does not violate criminal law.
or abridging the freedom of speech, or of the press,	Freedom of speech Freedom of the press	No governmental interference with content of legal speech or of the press.
or the right of the people peaceably to assemble, and to petition the Government for a redress of grievances.	Freedom to assemble and petition the government	Freedom to hold peaceful political rallies and demonstrations.
Second: . . . the right of the people to keep and bear Arms, shall not be infringed.	Right to keep and bear arms	The right to keep and bear arms can be constitutionally limited by statutes such as the Brady Bill, which requires background checks before a gun can be purchased.
Third: No Soldier shall, in time of peace be quartered in any house, . . .	Restrictions on quartering soldiers	This amendment has limited relevance today.
Fourth: The right of the people to be secure in their persons, houses, papers, and effects, against un-reasonable searches and seizures,	Right to be free from unreasonable searches and seizures	In general, the police and governmental officials must obtain a search or arrest warrant to accost a person or enter their house. There are exceptions.
shall not be violated, and no Warrants shall issue, but upon probable cause, . . .	Search and arrest warrants must be supported by demonstrations of probable cause to a judge	Evidence obtained without valid search or arrest warrants cannot be used against defendants at trial.
Fifth: No person shall be held to answer for a capital, or otherwise infamous crime, unless on a presentment or indictment of a Grand Jury . . . ;	Right to be free from trials for serious crimes unless there has been an indictment	The requirement to gain an indictment before subjecting a defendant to a criminal trial screens out frivolous cases.
nor shall any person be subject for the same offence to be twice put in jeopardy of life or limb,	Prohibition against double jeopardy	Note that the same acts may be violations of state and federal law.
nor shall be compelled in any criminal case to be a witness against himself, nor be deprived	Prohibition against self-incrimination	Applies to persons but not to businesses whose internal records can be subpoenaed.
of life, liberty, or property, without due process of law; nor	Due Process Clause	Before a protected interest can be taken by the state, the person must be given notice and a hearing.

shall private property be taken for public use without just compensation.	Eminent domain	If property is taken by the state, the owner is entitled to Fair Market Value as compensation.
Sixth: In all criminal prosecutions, the accused shall enjoy the right to a speedy and public trial, by an impartial jury . . . to be confronted with the witnesses against him; . . .	Right to a speedy trial Right to a jury trial Right to confront witnesses	In some contexts, a criminal defendant has the right to be either charged with crime or released within 24 hours. Has this right even if those testifying against him are undercover agents.
and to have the assistance of counsel for his defence.	Right to counsel	Has the right to counsel before being questioned by police as a suspect. If unable to afford an attorney, has the right to one paid for by the state.
Seventh: In Suits at common law, where the value in controversy shall exceed twenty dollars, the right of trial by jury shall be preserved, . . .	Right to a jury trial in civil cases	There are some cases conducted by administrative agencies against business that do not entitle the business to a jury trial.
Eight: Excessive bail shall not be required, nor excessive fines imposed, nor cruel and unusual punishments inflicted.	No excessive bail No excessive fines No cruel and unusual punishments	Bail is supposed to be set at a level that will ensure the accused will show up for trial. The meaning of the Eighth Amendment is often at the center of the debate about capital punishment.
Ninth: The enumeration in the Constitution of certain rights shall not be construed to deny or disparage others retained by the people.	Rights of citizens not limited to those elucidated in the Bill of Rights	The idea was that at common law people had rights against other government intrusions and those rights continued after adoption of the Bill of Rights.
Tenth: The powers not delegated to the United States by the Constitution, nor prohibited by it to the States, are reserved to the States respectively, or to the people.	Powers not delegated to the federal government are reserved to the states and people	This amendment has been eroded by expansive interpretations of the Commerce Clause, which allows the U.S. government to regulate anything that affects interstate commerce.

The Framers of the Constitution clearly agreed that individuals had certain rights that should not be taken from them by any Act of Congress. Among those rights are the rights to freedom of expression and of religion, along with the right to bear arms, freedom from unreasonable searches and seizures, the right to due process, the right to a trial of one's peers, the right to counsel, and so on (see the table in the "Nutz and Boltz" box). Many of these guarantees, of course, reflect the experiences colonists had suffered under what they regarded as an unjust government imposed on the colonies by England. Not surprisingly, a sizeable portion of the rights guaranteed in the Bill of Rights has the most direct relevance to criminal defendants. The focus of our discussion, however, is on those rights, guaranteed by the Bill of Rights, that are more likely to affect businesses.

First Amendment

The **First Amendment** provides protection for many of our most basic rights as U.S. citizens by assuring our freedom to communicate freely. According to the First Amendment, "Congress shall make no law . . . abridging the freedom of speech, or of the press . . ." In spite of that seemingly blanket statement, both Congress and state governments have made laws that abridge freedom of expression. Among the laws that limit freedom of speech are:

Laws That Prohibit Criminal Speech   If a member of organized crime tells an associate to kill a rival mobster, such speech is not protected by the First Amendment. Similarly, speech that facilitates treason or that advocates the bombing of government buildings is not protected. "Fighting" words or words that are intended to incite a riot are also excluded from First Amendment protection.

Obscenity Laws and Laws That Protect Children   The Supreme Court has grappled with obscenity laws, in part because societal mores have changed so dramatically that much of what was obscene 50 years ago is no longer considered obscene. Congress and states continue to pass such laws, many of which are stricken as unconstitutional. Quite clearly, there are forms of expression that are considered constitutionally and legally obscene, particularly when sex acts involving children are depicted. In addition, there is a wide range of other statutory protections for children that involve laws that limit freedom of expression.

First Amendment
Guarantees, with some exceptions, nongovernmental interference with freedom of expression and religion.

Fraud and Defamation   Fraudulent speech may or may not be criminal, but it can be the foundation for a claim by the defrauded party against the fraudulent party. Fraud claims in connection with contracts are common and courts routinely impose judgments against parties who knowingly defraud innocent contracting partners. The federal securities laws provide for civil and, in some cases, criminal sanctions against those who use fraud in connection with the purchase or sale of securities. Defamation takes place when one person makes false statements about another, those statements are heard or seen by others, and those statements harm the victim's reputation. So, freedom of expression of fraudulent and/or defaming statements is not protected by the First Amendment.

Source: Copyright M. Wuerker. Reprinted with permission.

Ethical Challenges   Freedom of Speech vs. Workplace Harassment Law—A Growing Conflict

Thus reads the banner on a website provided by Professor Eugene Volokh, who teaches constitutional law at the UCLA Law School (http:www.law.ucla.edu/faculty/volokh/harass/).

> Religious articles in newsletter and Bible verses on paychecks—ILLEGAL "religious harassment," says a court.
>
> Anti-veteran posters at Ohio State University—ILLEGAL "veteran status harassment," says the federal government.
>
> Goya's "Naked Maja" painting displayed in a classroom—ILLEGAL sexual harassment, claims a professor; university takes the painting down for fear of liability.

Professor Volokh describes these and other conflicts on his website. Citing Circuit Court Judge Edith Jones in an opinion by the Fifth Circuit (*DeAngelis v. El Paso Mun. Police Officers' Association,* 51 F.3d 591 (5th Cir. 1995),

> "Where pure expression is involved, Title VII [of the 1964 Civil Rights Act] steers into the territory of the First Amendment. It is no use to deny or minimize this problem because, when Title VII is applied to sexual harassment claims founded solely on verbal insults, pictorial, or literary matter, the statute imposes content-based, viewpoint-discriminatory restrictions on speech."

Professor Volokh observes that

> Telling "ebonics" jokes, the federal government says, is unlawful. You may burn the American flag, advocate violent revolution, post indecent material on the Internet, but "disseminating derogatory electronic messages regarding 'ebonics'" to your co-workers is against the law. So said the Equal Employment Opportunity Commission, in a lawsuit filed in federal court, which was trying to force the Federal Home Loan Mortgage Corp. to "take prompt and effective remedial action to eradicate" such speech by its workers. Remarkably, the EEOC, aided by some courts and by state civil rights agencies, thinks it can get away with this, and so far it has. Without much fanfare, the law of "workplace harassment" has turned into a nationwide speech code. Under this speech code, it's illegal to say things that are "severe or pervasive" enough to create a "hostile or offensive work environment"—whatever that is—based on race, religion, sex, national origin, veteran status and an ever-widening list of other attributes. Here is a brief catalogue of some of what's been described

by various agencies and courts as "harassment": Coworkers' use of "draftsman" and "foreman" (instead of "draftsperson" and "foreperson"). "Men Working" signs. Sexually suggestive jokes, even ones that aren't misogynistic. Derogatory pictures of the Ayatollah Khomeini and American flags burning in Iran. In the words of one court's injunction: remarks "contrary to your fellow employees' religious beliefs." "Offensive speech implicating considerations of race." But the Supreme Court has never suggested that the workplace is somehow a First Amendment-free zone. Many of us talk to more people at work than we do anywhere else. The workplace is where we often discuss the questions of the day, whether they be the Oakland School Board's ebonics policy or affirmative action or religion. Private employers, like private newspaper publishers or private homeowners, are not bound by the First Amendment and may thus restrict what is said on their property. But the United States government, which is under a constitutional obligation not to abridge "the freedom of speech," can't go to court to insist on the "eradication" of political speech that it thinks is reprehensible. Of course, many harassment cases involve more than just impolitic jokes. The ebonics case, for instance, also involved some threats, which are constitutionally unprotected, and some one-to-one insults, which might also be properly punishable. If the EEOC had just sued over this conduct, there would be little constitutional difficulty. But the EEOC has no business claiming that toleration of e-mailed political opinion is "an unlawful employment practice." Harassment law has become both unconstitutionally overbroad and unconstitutionally vague. The federal government seems to think it's entitled to control what we say in our workplaces so long as a "reasonable person" would find that our speech makes the environment "hostile or offensive." The First Amendment, though, says otherwise.

Professor Volokh's website contains a great deal of carefully organized information for lawyers, students, and others about the conflict between freedom of speech and workplace harassment law.

Instructions on cites and getting permissions from Professor Volokh are available on this website.

Source: Excerpt from "A National Speech Code from the EEOC," *Washington Post,* August 22, 1997, by Eugene Volokh. Reprinted with permission of the author.

Intellectual Property Proscriptions   Copyright and trademark law have the effect of allowing the government to fine or even imprison individuals who infringe on the rights of owners of copyrights and trademarks. To express yourself by copying or singing a copyrighted material is illegal, as is placing a trademark on products for which the trademark owner has not authorized the use of his or her trademark.

Reasonable Restrictions on Time, Place, or Manner   Speech that is not illegal, fraudulent, or defamatory can nevertheless be censored by the government based on reasonable restrictions on time, place, or manner. An apt maxim is that "there is a time and place for everything." On radio and television, the Federal Communications Commission has regulated freedom of expression for years. George Carlin noted that there were seven dirty words that could not be uttered on television or radio. George, however, uttered these words, and others equally prurient, many times in his nightclub act. If you are willing to pay for cable TV or go to a nightclub that features raunchy entertainment, the First Amendment protects your right to do so. Precedents established by the Supreme Court have allowed government authorities, however, to censor freedom of expression when there is no way to avoid it or when it disrupts other lawful activities. Thus, people with a cause who want to demonstrate must obtain a parade permit; they cannot just stage a rally on public streets and disrupt traffic. Itinerant preachers are allowed to go on college grounds and exhort students to follow Jesus or Hari Krishna, but they cannot bring a bullhorn and disrupt classes.

Content of Freedom of Expression   If speech that a government wishes to censor is not criminal, fraudulent, or defamatory, or does not infringe intellectual property and is not in violation of reasonable restrictions on time, place, or manner, the First Amendment protections are very strong. Most restrictions on the content of free speech, commercial or political, are struck down as unconstitutional. In order for a government to censor content, it must show

1. The censorship is necessary to promote a compelling governmental interest.
2. The censorship actually advances the compelling governmental interest.
3. The censorship is not overly broad.

The same rigorous test applies whether the government is trying to restrict commercial or political freedom of expression, although some would argue that there is more protection for political speech. Commercial free speech restrictions have been successfully justified if the censorship is necessary to promote a substantial governmental interest. The government has acted in ways that limit product advertisements, as in the case of tobacco and alcohol, whereas governmental restrictions on the content of political speech are much less prevalent. All kinds of extreme political points of view are tolerated due to the First Amendment, but a relatively greater leeway is granted to government prohibitions on certain types of advertisements that feature "objectionable" products. For example, laws have been passed against both liquor and tobacco products.

Overly Broad   There are few governmental interests that justify restrictions on the *content* of freedom of expression. During the energy crises of the 1970s, several governmental regulatory bodies tried to prohibit advertising by utilities that sold electricity, reasoning that such restrictions would promote energy conservation. These restrictions were declared unconstitutional because they were viewed as overly broad. Many of the same kinds of objections have been lodged when the federal government has tried to censor content on the Internet, as reflected in Case 5-5.

Case 5-5

Janet Reno, Attorney General of the United States, et al., Appellants v. American Civil Liberties Union et al.

Supreme Court of the United States
521 U.S. 844 (1997)

BACKGROUND AND FACTS

Congress passed the Communications Decency Act of 1996 (CDA or Act) to protect minors from harmful material on the Internet. The CDA criminalizes the "knowing" transmission of "obscene or indecent" messages to any recipient under 18 years of age. Section 223(d) of the CDA prohibits the "knowing" sending or displaying to a person under 18 of any message "that, in context, depicts or describes, in terms patently offensive as measured by contemporary community standards, sexual or excretory activities or organs." Affirmative defenses are provided for those who take "good faith, . . . effective . . . actions" to restrict access by minors to the prohibited communications, § 223(e)(5)(A), and those who restrict such access by requiring certain designated forms of age proof, such as a verified credit card or an adult identification number, § 223(e)(5)(B). A number of plaintiffs filed suit challenging the constitutionality of §§ 223(a)(1) and 223(d).[18] After making extensive findings of fact, a three judge District Court convened pursuant to the Act entered a preliminary injunction against enforcement of both challenged provisions. The court's judgment enjoins the Government from enforcing § 223(a)(1)(B)'s prohibitions insofar as they relate to "indecent" communications, but expressly preserves the Government's right to investigate and prosecute the obscenity or child pornography activities prohibited therein.

Opinion: Justice Stevens Delivered the Opinion of the Court

The Internet is an international network of interconnected computers. It is the outgrowth of what began in 1969 as a military program called "ARPANET," [footnotes deleted] which was designed to enable computers operated by the military, defense contractors, and universities conducting defense-related research to communicate with one another by redundant channels even if some portions of the network were damaged in a war. While the ARPANET no longer exists, it provided an example for the development of a number of civilian networks that, eventually linking with each other, now enable tens of millions of people to communicate with one another and to access vast amounts of information from around the world. The Internet is "a unique and wholly new medium of worldwide human communication."

* * *

Sexually explicit material on the Internet includes text, pictures, and chat and "extends from the modestly titillating to the hardest-core." These files are created, named, and posted in the same manner as material that is not sexually explicit, and may be accessed either deliberately or unintentionally during the course of an imprecise search. "Once a provider posts its content on the Internet, it cannot prevent that content from entering any community." Thus, for example,

> when the UCR/California Museum of Photography posts to its Web site nudes by Edward
> Weston and Robert Mapplethorpe to announce that its new exhibit will travel to Baltimore and

[18] An extensive list of plaintiffs challenged the CDA, including American Civil Liberties Union; Human Rights Watch; Electronic Privacy Information Center; Electronic Frontier Foundation; Journalism Education Association; Computer Professionals for Social Responsibility; National Writers Union; Clarinet Communications Corp.; Institute for Global Communications; Stop Prisoner Rape; AIDS Education Global Information System; Bibliobytes; Queer Resources Directory; Critical Path AIDS Project, Inc.; Wildcat Press, Inc.; Declan McCullagh dba Justice on Campus; Brock Meeks dba Cyberwire Dispatch; John Troyer dba The Safer Sex Page; Jonathan Wallace dba The Ethical Spectacle; and Planned Parenthood Federation of America, Inc.

New York City, those images are available not only in Los Angeles, Baltimore, and New York City, but also in Cincinnati, Mobile, or Beijing—wherever Internet users live. Similarly, the safer sex instructions that Critical Path posts to its Web site, written in street language so that the teenage receiver can understand them, are available not just in Philadelphia, but also in Provo and Prague.

* * *

. . . Neither before nor after the enactment of the CDA have the vast democratic fora of the Internet been subject to the type of government supervision and regulation that has attended the broadcast industry. Moreover, the Internet is not as "invasive" as radio or television. The District Court specifically found that "[c]ommunications over the Internet do not 'invade' an individual's home or appear on one's computer screen unbidden. Users seldom encounter content 'by accident.'" It also found that "[a]lmost all sexually explicit images are preceded by warnings as to the content," and cited testimony that "'odds are slim' that a user would come across a sexually explicit sight by accident."

* * *

Regardless of whether the CDA is so vague that it violates the Fifth Amendment, the many ambiguities concerning the scope of its coverage render it problematic for purposes of the First Amendment. For instance, each of the two parts of the CDA uses a different linguistic form. The first uses the word "indecent," 47 U.S.C. A. § 223(a) (Supp. 1997), while the second speaks of material that "in context, depicts or describes, in terms patently offensive as measured by contemporary community standards, sexual or excretory activities or organs," § 223(d). Given the absence of a definition of either term, this difference in language will provoke uncertainty among speakers about how the two standards relate to each other and just what they mean. Could a speaker confidently assume that a serious discussion about birth control practices, homosexuality, the First Amendment issues raised by the Appendix to our *Pacifica* opinion, or the consequences of prison rape would not violate the CDA? This uncertainty undermines the likelihood that the CDA has been carefully tailored to the congressional goal of protecting minors from potentially harmful materials.

* * *

We are persuaded that the CDA lacks the precision that the First Amendment requires when a statute regulates the content of speech. In order to deny minors access to potentially harmful speech, the CDA effectively suppresses a large amount of speech that adults have a constitutional right to receive and to address to one another. That burden on adult speech is unacceptable if less restrictive alternatives would be at least as effective in achieving the legitimate purpose that the statute was enacted to serve.

* * *

We agree with the District Court's conclusion that the CDA places an unacceptably heavy burden on protected speech, and that the defenses do not constitute the sort of "narrow tailoring" that will save an otherwise patently invalid unconstitutional provision. In *Sable*, 492 U.S., at 127, we remarked that the speech restriction at issue there amounted to "'burn[ing] the house to roast the pig.'" The CDA, casting a far darker shadow over free speech, threatens to torch a large segment of the Internet community.

Decision and Outcome

The U.S. Supreme Court held that the Communications Decency Act was unconstitutional under the First Amendment because its prohibitions of exposing minors to indecent material were too broad and the language in the statute was too vague.

Questions for Analysis

1. Explain with precision why the Communications Decency Act was declared unconstitutional. What were the main problems with the CDA according to the U.S. Supreme Court?
2. Sexually explicit material is prohibited from broadcast TV but, according to this decision, such material cannot be excluded from the Internet. What is the basis for distinguishing between these two media as a means of censoring inappropriate material for minors?

Bill of Rights and State Governments

The First Amendment and the other nine amendments in the Bill of Rights mention only what the federal government cannot do. There is nothing in the Bill of Rights that prohibits state governments from banning, restricting, or censoring freedom of expression. However, the U.S. Supreme Court has ruled in a number of cases that the limitations the First Amendment imposes on censorship of freedom of expression apply with equal force to state governments. The Fourteenth Amendment, passed following the Civil War, was designed to ensure that state governments did not oppress newly freed slaves in the southern states. As discussed above, this amendment includes a Due Process Clause.

The U.S. Supreme Court has ruled that part of *due process* is freedom of expression and, therefore, that all the constraints on the actions of the federal government with respect to freedom of expression also apply to state governments. In a series of cases, the U.S. Supreme Court has ruled that the Due Process Clause of the Fourteenth Amendment also carries over virtually all the governmental constraints of the Bill of Rights to the actions of state governments, including those contained in the Fourth and Fifth Amendments (discussed below). Thus, state governments have been prohibited from engaging in unreasonable searches and seizures, must accord criminal defendants the right to a speedy trial, and generally must not violate the other protections guaranteed by the Bill of Rights.

Freedom of Religion

The First Amendment begins with an admonition, "Congress shall make no law respecting an establishment of religion, or prohibiting the free exercise thereof . . ." Although there are many implications of the alleged separation between "church and state," our concern is with the business implications of the Establishment Clause of the First Amendment. Sunday Blue Laws have been attacked under the Establishment Clause, but courts have held that establishing a universal day of rest is in the interest of society. Numerous religious displays in public buildings and parks have been attacked in court, with many of those attacks successful. If a religious display is balanced ecumenically, then it has a better change of withstanding a challenge based on the Establishment Clause.

If a law or action of government, federal or state, is attacked as being unconstitutional under the First Amendment, the U.S. Supreme Court has held that the law, to be valid

1. Must have a secular purpose.
2. Must not advance or inhibit a particular religion.
3. Must not cause the government to become excessively entangled with religion.

Modern Constitutional Religious Issues

Public School Vouchers Some public school systems, at both the high school and elementary levels, have been producing unsatisfactory results for a long time. It has been proposed that parents of students in failing schools be given taxpayer-supported *vouchers* that they could use to send their children to private (typically religious-affiliated) schools. A number of people have contended that voucher use in support of private religious schools is unconstitutional. A major test question for the legality of school vouchers is whether vouchers will cause state and local governments to become "excessively entangled" in religion (see the "Ethical Challenges" box). In June of 2002, the Supreme Court ruled that a voucher program in Cleveland, Ohio, that resulted in governmental payments to private schools that had religious affiliations did not offend the First Amendment and thus was constitutional because voucher programs have a secular purpose and do not necessarily cause excessive entanglement with a particular religion.[19]

[19] *Zelman, Superintendent of Public Instruction of Ohio, et al. v. Simmons-Harris, et al.*, 122 S. Ct. 2460 (2002).

Religious Practices   If a practice is illegal, calling it a religious service will not immunize the practice from criminal prosecution. Some practitioners of religious cults from Jamaica contend that smoking marijuana is a part of their religion, but that contention has not stopped authorities from arresting those participating in such "religious services."

Government Benefits   Courts have held that government employers have only a minimal obligation to make reasonable accommodations for the religious beliefs of their employees. In one case, an employee working retail claimed that he was entitled to unemployment compensation because he was fired from his job for refusing to work on the Sabbath.[20] The employee was newly hired and the most undesirable shifts were typically allocated to new hires. The U.S. Supreme Court did allow the employee to recover unemployment benefits after his firing for refusing to work on nights that he considered reserved by his religious beliefs.

Fourth Amendment: Protection against Unreasonable Searches and Seizures

The **Fourth Amendment** speaks for itself:

> *The right of the people to be secure in their persons, houses, papers, and effects, against unreasonable searches and seizures, shall not be violated, and no Warrants shall issue, but upon probable cause, supported by Oath or affirmation, and particularly describing the place to be searched, and the persons or things to be seized.*

Under this stricture, for the police or other governmental authorities to legally search your house or arrest you, they must have a search warrant in which probable cause has been demonstrated before a judge or magistrate. In criminal cases, probable cause is often established when police state before a judge or magistrate that a source of previously reliable information (in other words, a police informer) attests that a crime has taken place or evidence is located at a building or dwelling.

Fourth Amendment
Guarantees protection from searches and seizures by the government that are not accompanied by a search warrant based on a showing of probable cause.

Criminal Law Implications

For criminal defendants, the Fourth Amendment is a shield that prevents evidence that is illegally gathered from being used against them at a trial. If police, without a warrant, place a tap on the telephone of a suspected criminal and overhear conversations that indicate illegal drugs are being stored and distributed at the home of the suspect, that information cannot be used against the suspect at trial. Also, if police were to search the premises based on the wiretap, the illegal drugs seized from the site (by an illegal search) would not be admissible as evidence at trial. The proceeds of the subsequent search would be called "fruit" of the poisonous tree, which means that no evidence can be presented if the evidence was obtained only as a result of an unconstitutional search by the police.

Relevance to Business

Most businesses are not places where illegal drugs are stored, nor are they locations for other crimes. The Fourth Amendment, however, still has relevance to businesses. Businesses can invoke Fourth Amendment protection when government inspectors arrive without a search warrant. In a famous case involving officials from the Occupation Safety and Health Administration (OSHA), an inspector was turned away at the door by a factory owner when it was determined that the inspector did not have a search warrant.[21] Since that

---

[20] *Frazee v. Illinois Dep't of Employment Sec.*, 489 U.S. 829 (1989).

[21] See *Marshall v. Barlow's, Inc.*, 436 U.S. 307 (1978).

event, the general rule that has emerged is that businesses do have Fourth Amendment rights, but there are a number of significant exceptions. The fact that a business has Fourth Amendment rights means that police or government officials must have a search warrant to search the business, albeit with the following exceptions:

consent is given
Fourth Amendment protections do not prevent police searches or seizures if those searches are consented to by the owner or lawful possessor of the property.

reasonable expectation of privacy
The Fourth Amendment protects areas that citizens expect will not be open to public inspection.

random searches
A search in which there is no particularized showing of probable cause.

- *Government officials do not need a search warrant if* **consent is given.** In many cases it is not good business practice to play hardball with government officials and insist on search warrants every time the officials want to look at something on the premises. It is often much more effective to work with government officials rather than resist them at every turn. Most businesspeople allow government officials to inspect without a search warrant.

- *Plain view and* **reasonable expectation of privacy.** If the police or government officials can observe violations of law in plain view, then it is not illegal to act on what they saw, heard, or experienced. The Fourth Amendment only protects areas where the person has a reasonable expectation of privacy. A person cannot have a reasonable expectation of privacy about something that is in plain view to the police or a member of the public when they are not trespassing or using high-powered equipment to observe. A rule of thumb to consider is that if the evidence can be seen by a member of the public, then it can viewed by the police without a search warrant.

- *Enforcement of the statute is impossible without* **random searches.** Experience has shown that enforcement of some statutes, such as local sanitation laws for restaurants or fire codes, require warrantless searches, even though there is no showing of particularized probable cause. In other words, random searches of businesses without a showing of probable cause have been allowed in some industries. Also, when the industry is highly regulated, as is the case in transportation, random searches have been allowed because the interest in public safety has been held more weighty than the rights of a common carrier to privacy. In some warrantless search cases involving businesses, courts look favorably on administrative agencies that have engaged in such searches, if they have an overall plan for inspecting and enforcing a statute. In other words, the fact that the agency has some form of plan for inspections assuages court concerns that the searches are capricious and thus unreasonable.

Reasonable Expectation of Privacy on the Internet?

Suppose you communicate to your Internet Service Provider information about yourself including your email pseudonym. Do you have a reasonable expectation of privacy with respect to information that is communicated to a contracting partner such as your ISP? There have been few cases on point but in one recent case, a federal district court ruled that when a customer creates an email pseudonym through his or her ISP, it is not reasonable to expect that such information will remain private.[22]

Fifth Amendment Protection against Self-Incrimination

Self-Incrimination

self-incrimination
Testifying against oneself, which may occur under some coercion, such as prosecution for perjury or police intimidation.

The Fifth Amendment contains protections against having to testify against yourself or being tried for the same crime more than once. The Self-Incrimination Clause allows defendants in *criminal* cases to refuse to testify regarding the crime that they are being charged with. Furthermore, prior to the trial, there are elaborate constitutional safeguards

---

[22] *United States of America v. Hambrick*, 55 F. Supp. 2d 504 (WD Va. 1999).

Cyberlaw **Developments** Carnivore: Is the Government Eating Up Our Fourth Amendment Rights in Cyberspace?

The following is an excerpt of a statement made by an official from the U.S. Department of Justice about Carnivore, which is software developed for the FBI. Carnivore literally allows the FBI to examine millions of e-mails in a short period of time and allegedly discards the e-mails that are not of interest. In the past the government had to obtain a search warrant before examining private communications.

STATEMENT OF KEVIN V. DI GREGORY, DEPUTY ASSISTANT ATTORNEY GENERAL, UNITED STATES DEPARTMENT OF JUSTICE, BEFORE THE SUBCOMMITTEE ON THE CONSTITUTION OF THE HOUSE COMMITTEE ON THE JUDICIARY ON "CARNIVORE" AND THE FOURTH AMENDMENT, JULY 24, 2000

Mr. Chairman and Members of the Subcommittee, thank you for allowing me this opportunity to testify about the law enforcement tool "Carnivore" and the Fourth Amendment. On April 6, 2000, I had the privilege of testifying before you during a hearing on Internet privacy and the Fourth Amendment; I am pleased to continue to participate in the discussion today about "Carnivore" and its role in protecting individual privacy on the Internet from unwarranted governmental intrusion, and about the critical role the Department plays to ensure that the Internet is a safe and secure place.

Privacy and Public Safety

It is beyond dispute that the Fourth Amendment protects the rights of Americans while they work and play on the Internet just as it does in the physical world. The goal is a long-honored and noble one: to preserve our privacy while protecting the safety of our citizens. Our founding fathers recognized that in order for our democratic society to remain safe and our liberty intact, law enforcement must have the ability to investigate, apprehend and prosecute people for criminal conduct. At the same time, however, our founding fathers held in disdain the government's disregard and abuse of privacy in England. The founders of this nation adopted the Fourth Amendment to address the tension that can at times arise between privacy and public safety. Under the Fourth Amendment, the government must demonstrate probable cause before obtaining a warrant for a search, arrest, or other significant intrusion on privacy.

Congress and the courts have also recognized that lesser intrusions on privacy should be permitted under a less exacting threshold. The Electronic Communications Privacy Act ("ECPA") establishes a three-tier system by which the government can obtain stored information from electronic communication service providers. In general, the government needs a search warrant to obtain the content of unretrieved communications (like e-mail), a court order to obtain transactional records, and a subpoena to obtain information identifying the subscriber. See 18 U.S.C. §§ 2701–11.

* * *

To satisfy our obligations to the public to enforce the laws and preserve the safety, we use the same sorts of investigative techniques and methods online as we do in the physical world, with the same careful attention to the strict constitutional, statutory, internal and court-ordered boundaries. Carnivore is simply an investigative tool that is used online only under narrowly defined circumstances, and only when authorized by law, to meet our responsibilities to the public.

To illustrate, law enforcement often needs to find out from whom a drug dealer, for instance, is buying his illegal products, or to whom the drug dealer is selling. To investigate this, it is helpful to determine who is communicating with the drug dealer. In the "olden days" of perhaps 10 years ago, the drug dealer would have communicated with his supplier and customers exclusively through use of telephones and pagers. Law enforcement would obtain an order from a court authorizing the installation of a "trap and trace" and a "pen register" device on the drug dealer's phone or pager, and either the telephone company or law enforcement would have installed these devices to comply with the court's order. Thereafter, the source and destination of his phone calls would have been recorded. This is information that courts have held is not protected by any reasonable expectation of privacy. Given the personal nature of this information, however, the law requires government to obtain an order under these circumstances. In this way, privacy is protected and law enforcement is able to investigate to protect the public.

Now, that same drug dealer may be just as likely to send an e-mail as call his confederates. When law enforcement uses a "trap and trace" or "pen register" in the online context, however, we have found that, at times, the Internet service provider has been unable or even unwilling to supply this information. Law enforcement cannot abdicate its responsibility to protect public safety simply because technology has changed. Rather, the public rightfully expects that law enforcement will continue to be effective as criminal activity migrates to the Internet. We cannot do this without tools like Carnivore.

When a criminal uses e-mail to send a kidnaping demand, to buy and sell illegal drugs or to distribute child pornography, law enforcement needs to know to whom he is sending messages and from whom he receives them. To get this information, we obtain a court order, which we serve on the appropriate service provider. Because of the nature of Internet communications, the addressing information (which does not include the content of the message) is often mixed in with a lot of other non-content data that we have no desire to gather. If the service provider can comply with the order and provide us with only the addressing information required by court order, it will do so and we will not employ Carnivore. If, however, the service provider is unwilling or unable to comply with the order, we simply cannot give a criminal a free pass. It is for that narrow set of circumstances that the FBI designed "Carnivore."

Carnivore is, in essence, a special filtering tool that can gather the information authorized by court order, and only that information. It permits law enforcement, for example, to gather only the e-mail addresses of those persons with whom the drug dealer is communicating, without allowing any human being, either from law enforcement or the service provider, to view private information outside of the scope of the court's order. In other words, Carnivore is a minimization tool that permits law enforcement strictly to comply with court orders, strongly to protect privacy, and effectively to enforce the law to protect the public interest. In addition, Carnivore creates an audit trail that demonstrates exactly what it is capturing.

Source: http://www.usdoj.gov/criminal/cybercrime/carnivore.htm.

that are often labeled *Miranda* warnings. When an arrest is made the police must inform criminal suspects that:

a. You have the right to remain silent.

b. If you speak your statements could be used against you.

c. You have a right to an attorney.

d. If you cannot afford an attorney, the state will pay for a court-appointed attorney.

There are several things to remember about the Fifth Amendment. First, it applies equally to federal and state governments. Second, it is only a shield to possible criminal liability; it does not protect defendants in civil cases. For example, in the criminal prosecution of O.J. Simpson for the murder of two people, he did not take the witness stand, but in the civil case for wrongful death, Simpson, having been acquitted in the criminal case, was forced to take the witness stand. Third, the protections of the Fifth Amendment apply to actions of the police even before an actual trial takes place.

Application to Business

As is discussed above, businesses can take advantage of the Fourth Amendment, but they cannot take advantage of the Fifth Amendment for purposes of refusing to produce papers that may create criminal liability for a business or, more specifically, its management. In a criminal case, the diaries of a defendant cannot be subpoenaed, but internal memoranda circulated among executives that would incriminate the corporation and its managers are subject to subpoena, which the company cannot circumvent by reliance on the Fifth Amendment.

Summary

Formation of the U.S. Government and Separation of Powers

- Immediately after defeating the British, the Americans were compelled to form a government. The first government organization under the *Articles of Confederation* failed because of the weakness of the federal government.
- When the U.S. Constitution was composed in 1787, the power to regulate interstate commerce was allocated to the federal government.
- Framers of the Constitution separated power in a number of ways. Power was divided between the federal and state governments and among the three branches of government and certain inalienable rights were guaranteed to all citizens.
- Legislatures have the power to pass a *bill,* which becomes a law if the president does not veto the bill. The *executive branch* enforces the law and the *judicial branch* interprets the law, though, in practice, the distinctions are not always so clear.

Impact of the Commerce Clause as a Power Source for the Federal Government and a Limitation on the Actions of State Governments

- The *Commerce Clause* allocates to the federal government the power to regulate interstate commerce.
- Expansive Supreme Court interpretations of the meaning of interstate commerce have enabled the federal government to regulate *everything "in" interstate commerce* and everything that *"affects" interstate commerce.*
- The Commerce Clause also limits the power of state governments to enact legislation that affects interstate commerce. If state legislation *discriminates against* or places an *undue burden* on interstate commerce, it can be declared unconstitutional. Also state taxes must be apportioned to the activities of the taxpayer (such as a business) in the state in order to be constitutional.
- States cannot tax goods moving in interstate commerce through the state, nor can they tax out-of-state mail order catalogs or websites.

Preemption of State Laws, Powers of the Federal Government to Tax and Spend, and More Limitations on the Power of State Governments

- If there is a conflict between federal and state law, the *Supremacy Clause* of the U.S. Constitution makes federal law prevail over state law.
- There are areas of law for which all state laws are unconstitutional because the area of law has been *preempted* by the presence of extensive federal legislation. In general, state regulatory statutes that are more strict than federal laws are not unconstitutional unless the area is considered preempted from state law.
- The federal government has very broad powers to tax and spend. The federal government is prohibited from taxing exports from any state.
- The Constitution authorizes Congress to spend tax revenues to provide for the common defense and general welfare, which is a very broad set of powers.
- State governments are prohibited from taxing a federal instrumentality and both the federal and state governments have *due process* protections for citizens.

Governmental Takings of

- There are various ways in which governments *take* the property of citizens. Probably the most obvious is through *eminent domain*. In order to satisfy constitutional requirements, when private property is taken, it must be for the *public good* and *just compensation* must be paid.

Private Property through Eminent Domain, Regulation, and Due Process Limitations of the Fifth and Fourteenth Amendments	• In situations in which changes in regulations effectively *"take"* property from private citizens, the victims can file *inverse condemnation* suits to force the government to pay them the fair market value for their property. • Both the Fifth and Fourteenth amendments have due process clauses that require governments (federal and state) to *give notice* and *provide a hearing* before they take a *protected interest.* • Protected interests include life, liberty, property, and more, such as a job working for the state, social security benefits, and attendance at a public high school. • In any case in which a citizen may be incarcerated, he or she is entitled to trial by a jury of his or her peers.
Equal Protection Clause of the Fourteenth Amendment as It Applies to Race, Gender, and Other Distinctions	• The *Equal Protection Clause* is applied in different ways depending on the subject of discrimination. For discrimination based on race, courts apply the *strict scrutiny test* and do not allow a discriminatory practice by government units unless it promotes a compelling governmental objective and is *not overly broad.* • For distinctions made by governments based on gender, an *intermediate level of scrutiny* is applied. If such a distinction is made, the distinction must promote an important governmental objective to be legal. • For most other distinctions made among people, courts apply the *rational basis test.* For this test, the legislation must rest on some rational basis. As long as the claimed basis makes sense, the legislation is legal.
First Amendment Protection for Freedom of Speech and Religion	• The First Amendment guarantees that Congress will pass no laws that abridge freedom of speech or the press. In spite of that admonition, Congress and the states have passed laws that limit free speech when that speech is *criminal; obscene; fraudulent; defamatory; or not reasonably restricted by time, place, or manner.* • Virtually all government censorship of the content of free speech that is not any of the above is unconstitutional. Increasingly, courts are according the same protections to commercial speech as they do to political speech. • All of the protections of the Bill or Rights have been imposed on the states by virtue of interpretations of the U.S. Supreme Court of the Fourteenth Amendment, which guarantees due process protection. • The First Amendment also prohibits Congress from establishing a religion or preventing the free exercise of religious practices. Sunday Blue Laws and religious displays at holidays have been the focus of litigation, but most are legal as long as there is another purpose, such as a universal day of rest, or the religious displays are ecumenical or nonsectarian.
Fourth Amendment Protection from Unreasonable Searches and Seizures and Application to drug testing; Fifth Amendment Protection against Self-Incrimination	• The Fourth Amendment protects against *unreasonable searches and seizures.* In order for the police to obtain a search warrant, they must show *probable cause* to a neutral magistrate that a crime has taken place. • There are many exceptions to the requirement that police must have search warrants before they can search a home or a business. • If evidence of a violation of law is in plain view, the police do not need a search warrant to investigate. • Police or government officials do not need a search warrant if they have consent from the owner to inspect the premises. • For some statutes, courts have held that enforcement is impossible without random searches conducted without search warrants. In place of a search warrant, the courts have ruled that, if the agency conducting the search has some kind of administrative plan, they are entitled to search without getting a warrant. • The Fifth Amendment provides protection against being required to testify against yourself in a criminal case.

- The Fifth Amendment is not usable by corporations or corporate executives to keep corporate records from being used by the government to prosecute the corporation or management for violations of criminal law.
- The Fifth Amendment protections against self-incrimination do not apply to civil liability.

Key Terms

act of interstate commerce, *128*	executive, *121*	rational basis test, *138*
Bill of Rights, *122*	federalism, *122*	reasonable expectation of privacy, *148*
Commerce Clause, *123*	First Amendment, *141*	roughly apportioned, *128*
consent is given, *148*	Fourth Amendment, *147*	self-incrimination, *148*
discriminates against interstate commerce, *128*	government takings, *133*	strict scrutiny, *136*
eminent domain, *133*	intermediate scrutiny, *138*	Supremacy Clause, *122*
equal protection, *136*	judicial, *121*	Tenth Amendment, *124*
excessive burden on interstate commerce, *128*	legislative, *121*	veto, *121*
	preemption, *130*	
	procedural due process, *135*	
	random searches, *148*	

Questions for Review and Analysis

1. Discuss the way the U.S. government is structured so as to prevent unacceptable concentrations of power.
2. Discuss the importance of the Tenth Amendment to federalism and the sharing of power between the federal and state governments. What has been the impact of expansive interpretations of the Commerce Clause on federalism?
3. How are state governments restricted by the Commerce Clause?
4. Explain three different ways that freedom of expression is limited in spite of the unequivocal language of the First Amendment.
5. Explain what three different standards courts use in applying the Equal Protection Clause of the Fourteenth Amendment. Why is this done?

If You Really Understood This Chapter, You Should Be Able to Provide Informed Commentary on the Following:

1. **Separation of Powers.** The principle of separation of powers under the U.S. Constitution is not simply a historical doctrine that is irrelevant in today's politics. For years there have been proposals to give presidents more discretion in spending. The so-called line item veto was passed in 1996 by Congress, which enabled the president to selectively decide whether to spend money appropriated by Congress. Critics of the line item veto contended that it violated separation of powers by giving the president the power to rewrite acts of Congress by deciding whether to spend money that was already authorized and appropriated by Congress. According to the U.S. Supreme Court, "The Act empowers the President to cancel an 'item of new direct spending' such as § 4722(c) of the Balanced Budget Act and a 'limited tax benefit' such as § 968 of the Taxpayer Relief Act, § 691(a), specifying that such cancellation prevents a provision 'from having legal force or effect,' §§ 691e(4)(B)–(C)." In the case cited below, the U.S. Supreme Court debates the issue of separation of powers under the U.S. Constitution. The City of New York is the other party in the suit because they lost funds when President Clinton decided to exercise his powers under the Line Item Veto Act. [*William J. Clinton, President of the United States, et al. v. City of New York, et al.,* 524 U.S. 417 (1998).]

2. **Equal Protection and Affirmative Action.** As is well known, state statutes that require different treatment of people based on race are strictly scrutinized under the Equal Protection Clause of the Fourteenth Amendment. In the famous *Brown v. Board of Education* case, the U.S. Supreme Court struck down a number of state statutes that required segregation of students by race in the public schools. More recently, however, much of the litigation involving the Equal Protection Clause of the Fourteenth Amendment has been initiated by white plaintiffs alleging that affirmative actions

by state institutions have violated their rights. In these suits, the state is the defendant and generally defends affirmative action by claiming that such policies are necessary to ensure that various educational institutions are "diverse." Is diversity a valid basis for treating applicants to selective law schools, such as the law school at the University of Texas, differently based on race? Consider the lawsuit by Cheryl Hopwood, a white student denied admission to the law school at the University of Texas. [*Hopwood v. State of Texas,* 78 F.3d 932 (5th Cir. 1996).]

3. **Screen Scrapers and the First Amendment.** Screen scrapers are software programs that do what is implied by their name: they glean information from websites. Indeed, screen scrapers are commonly used by some firms to gather information available on Internet websites. An advantage of screen scrapers is that websites do the research, but screen scrapers reap the benefits by aggregating information available on these websites. Of course, websites that collect the information, often financial information, view screen scrapers negatively and claim that they misappropriate their information. Also, websites claim that screen scrapers violate copyrights, because they take arrangements of information developed by websites. Suppose a tour company directed its screen scraper at the website of a rival and, using the screen scraper, obtained all the prices offered by the rival tour company, then advertised prices slightly lower for each tour. Suppose the rival tour company applied for an injunction against the tour company with the screen scraper and the injunction was granted by federal district court. Is preventing a company that acquires information that is publicly available from advertising on websites using screen scrapers a violation of its First Amendment Rights? [*EF Cultural Travel BV, el al.v. Explorica, Inc., et al.,* 274 F.3d 577 (1st Cir. 2001).]

4. **Taxation of State Resources.** It is clear from a number of constitutional rulings by the U.S. Supreme Court that states cannot interfere with interstate commerce by taxing goods being transferred across state lines. What about state resources, such as coal, that a state such as Montana cannot possibly use more than a fraction of, for which the state knows that most will be transported across state lines and used in other states? Can Montana enact a 30 percent severance tax on coal mined within its borders knowing that out-of-state utilities will be footing the bill for most of the tax revenues? Does such a tax violate the Commerce Clause? [*Commonwealth Edison Co. et al. v. Montana et al.,* 453 U.S. 609 (1981).]

Social Responsibility and Ethics in a High-Tech World

5. **USA Patriot Act and the Fourth Amendment.** As a result of the terrorists' attacks of September 11, 2001, Congress passed and President Bush signed the USA Patriot Act (USAPA). Although there was a widespread perception that law enforcement needed to be strengthened to assist in preventing such attacks in the future, the new powers given to law enforcement by this legislation have caused many to be quite concerned. In particular, there is concern that under the USAPA our Fourth Amendment rights to be free of unreasonable searches and seizures have been undermined. The Electronic Frontier Foundation has been in the forefront of those who have warned that the USAPA allows the government to engage in unprecedented surveillance of online activities. According to the EFF,

- "The government may now spy on web surfing of innocent Americans, including terms entered into search engines, by merely telling a judge anywhere in the U.S. that the spying could lead to information that is 'relevant' to an ongoing criminal investigation."

- "The law makes two changes to increase how much information the government may obtain about users from their ISPs or others who handle or store their online communications."

- "One new definition of terrorism and three expansions of previous terms also expand the scope of surveillance. They are 1) § 802 definition of 'domestic terrorism' (amending 18 USC § 2331), which raises concerns about legitimate protest activity resulting in conviction on terrorism charges . . ."

The EFF has additional examples of situations in which the USAPA could lead to abuse by the government and to shrinkage of the freedoms given to U.S. citizens by the Bill of Rights, especially the Fourth Amendment. President Bush has said these are not "ordinary" times. Do you think that Congress and the president have overreacted to the threats posed by our enemies? For additional reading on the topic, see http://www.eff.org/Privacy/Surveillance/Terrorism_militias/20011031_eff_usa_patriot_analysis.html.

Using the Internet to Your Advantage

1. You should be able to find the U.S. Constitution using any search engine and simply inserting those words. An article-by-article look at the U.S. Constitution is available at http://www.law.cornell.edu/constitution/constitution.overview.html. The advantage of using the Cornell University website (technically, the website above was created by the Legal Information Institute, which is part of the law school) is that it gives article-by-article and section-by-section overviews. Constitution Facts (http://www.constitutionfacts.com/) not only has the U.S. Constitution, but also has famous quotes, crossword puzzles, a glossary of terms, and the Articles of Confederation. An ambitious project would be to compare and contrast the U.S. Constitution and the Articles of Confederation.

2. Protection of freedom of expression is a constitutional issue as well as a controversial political issue. The ACLU (http://www.aclu.org) frequently champions unpopular causes in an effort to strengthen protections provided by the Bill of Rights (at this writing the ACLU is fighting attempts to make burning the U.S. flag a crime). Also on the forefront of those concerned about freedom of expression on the Internet is the Electronic Frontier Foundation (http://www.eff.org). College campuses have been a major area of conflict in freedom of expression debates because of "speech codes" that make racist, sexist, and homophobic speech illegal and grounds for expulsion. There are a number of websites that feature articles on the topic, such as http://home.earthlink.net/~gotimgo/essays/freespch.htm, http://www.compleatheretic.com/pubs/essays/pccodes.html, and http://www.eff.org/CAF/academic/speech-codes.aaup.

3. As discussed in the chapter, elastic interpretations of the Commerce Clause have dramatically changed the balance between what the federal government and state governments can do and, also, the meaning of the tenth Amendment. A number of websites have looked at the growing power of the federal government resulting from court interpretations of the Commerce Clause: http://www.cato.org/pubs/policy_report/pr-so-cl.html and http://old.claremont.org/publications/lopez.cfm.

Chapter Six

Government Regulation of Business and Ethics

Learning Objectives

On completing this chapter, you should

1. Have a firm understanding of the process used by administrative agencies to promulgate rules and regulations.
2. Be able to discuss the main activities of administrative agencies.
3. Be familiar with the bases for court challenges to actions of administrative agencies.
4. Understand the basic features of Kantian ethics, and its application to business, as well as Utilitarianism.
5. Be able to discuss situations and markets where some form of self-regulation based on adherence to ethical codes is likely to be successful and when government regulation is required because ethical codes are not likely to be successful.

OVERVIEW

administrative agencies
An inclusive term for government agencies, bureaus, commissions, and boards, created by the legislative or executive branches of government, that administer and enforce the statutes that regulate society and the economy.

The title of this textbook is the *Legal Environment of Business in the Information Age.* It is noteworthy that most of that legal environment is the creation of administrative agencies of the federal and, to a lesser extent, state governments. **Administrative agencies** regulate virtually every facet of businesses including work safety within the work environment, hiring and firing and a host of other human resource management issues, product safety, pollution releases, advertisements, and on and on. Of course, businesspeople do not have to consult with government authorities before making every decision, but, in the modern business environment, failure to be cognizant of government regulations imposed by administrative agencies is a recipe for disaster. As the electronic environment becomes more important, regulations from administrative agencies are also having a major impact on the way e-commerce is conducted.

Federal agencies have expanded in both number and size, in large part because of elastic court definitions of the power of the federal government to regulate interstate commerce

Necessary and Proper Clause
Provision in the U.S. Constitution that grants to Congress the broad-based authority to use all means that are "necessary and proper" to perform its prescribed functions.

and broad application of the Necessary and Proper Clause within the Constitution. In many cases, the Necessary and Proper Clause has been the justification for creating administrative agencies that carry out the specific details of legislation that Congress has adopted but is not equipped to apply.

Ethical Impulses

In many contexts, American firms and professionals have been told, in effect, "clean up your act or else the government will have to intervene." Such a threat is potent as government regulation is often viewed as being a distinct negative. Compared with self-regulation, government regulation is viewed (probably correctly in most instances) as being more laden with inflexible rules, more public, and more likely to involve severe sanctions. In many industries self-regulation has been viewed as effective. For many years, professionals such as lawyers, doctors, dentists, and a host of others have been largely self-regulated with little help or interference from state licensing authority. In the typical form of self-regulation, states pass legislation that requires a professional to have a license to practice and then allow professionals themselves to decide who gets, keeps, and loses a professional license to practice.

government regulation
Government establishes laws in the form of statutes or regulations from administrative agencies that define legal and illegal conduct for the entities being regulated, generally businesses.

There are a host of other examples of self-regulation. The motion picture industry has established a rating system that informs potential viewers of what to expect in terms of sex and violence. As with many industries and professions, self-regulation is married with legal teeth. If a film is rated "X," then children under 18 are not allowed to enter. It is fair to say that, although some of the efforts of businesses to benefit the public through ethical practices are no doubt prompted by sincere motives, the threat of government regulation is also present in the background. Professional sports and academic institutions are additional prominent industries that largely self regulate.

self-regulation
Regulatory arrangement under which cohesive groups, such as doctors, lawyers, and the like, police the professional activities of members of the group, generally through ethical codes, licensure requirements, certification of quality by third parties or associations, and other means.

Ethics and Government Regulation in Cyberspace

With the growth of e-commerce, Internet fraud is a growing problem, prompting many to advocate additional regulation. In fact, there have been several statutes enacted at both the federal and state levels dealing with privacy, children, and pornography. Not surprisingly, most firms with a substantial Internet presence view government regulation of the Internet and e-commerce with suspicion and would prefer a means to avoid escalating government regulation. At present some aspects of fraud, security, and privacy protection are being self-regulated on the Internet by third-party monitors such as TRUSTe and the Better Business Bureau (BBBOnline). Whether ethical codes can forestall much more extensive government regulation of the Internet is an important issue with a highly uncertain outcome. Later in this chapter, attention will be focused on the interplay between ethics, technological changes, and government regulation.

ethics
The study and philosophy of human conduct with an emphasis on right and wrong.

ADMINISTRATIVE LAW

A Typical Case of Government Regulation

In many situations there has been a widespread perception held by both the public and policy experts that the workings of some free, unregulated markets are decidedly suboptimal. As a result, in many settings Congress passes a law (statute) that attempts to correct an identified suboptimal situation. Quite typically, the simple passage of a law does not resolve the problem being addressed, as there is an accompanying need for a government agency to enforce the statute and to issue additional regulations that clarify the effect(s) of the statute.

Nutz and Boltz   Key Regulatory Facts & Figures

THE FACTS

Although President Ronald Reagan succeeded in reversing the growing federal regulatory burden for a time, regulatory growth accelerated under President George Bush and exploded during President Bill Clinton's first term. Initially, the Republican-led 104th Congress made the reduction of spending by federal regulatory agencies a priority, and this focus led to a slower rate of growth in new regulations. Unfortunately, those efforts were short-lived.

THE NUMBER OF FEDERAL REGULATIONS*

FACT: Since 1997, the size, scope, and cost of the federal regulatory system has returned to pre-1994 levels and once again is increasing at record rates.

According to the U.S. General Accounting Office (GAO), between April 1, 1996, and September 30, 1999, federal regulatory agencies issued 15,280 final rules and sent them to Congress for review. Of this startling number, 222 were defined as "major" rules—rules that will have an annual effect on the economy of more than $100 million.

- By the end of 1998, the *Federal Register,* the daily government publication in which all proposed and final regulations are announced, was 68,571 pages long, 4,000 pages longer than in 1997.

- The massive Code of Federal Regulations (CFR), an annual listing of executive agency regulations published in the *Federal Register,* includes all regulations now in effect. In 1998, the CFR filled 201 volumes with a total of 134,723 pages; it occupies 19 feet of shelf space. In 1970, the CFR filled 114 volumes with a total of 54,834 pages.

- Between 1980 and 1998, the CFR grew by more than 32,000 pages—about 80 volumes. Between the end of 1976 and the end of 1980, it grew by 28,000 pages.

- During the eight-year presidency of Ronald Reagan, the number of pages in the *Federal Register* declined—by more than 22,642—from an all-time high of 73,258 pages in 1980 (President Jimmy Carter's last year in office) to 50,616 pages in 1988.

Source: http://www.regulation.org/keyfacts.html.

* Regulatory studies, statistics, and information from the conservative perspective of the Heritage Foundation (www.heritage.org).

Federal Register
Federal publication in which all changes in administrative agency regulations must be published.

enabling statute
A statute that authorizes the creation of and, hence, gives power to an administrative agency.

Since there is now a multitude of government agencies, largely acting independently of one another, the combined effect of government agencies frequently issuing new regulations is a complex and constantly changing legal environment. All federal agencies issuing new regulations are required to announce those changes in the **Federal Register** (http://www.access.gpo.gov/su_docs/aces/aces140.html). The volume of regulatory change announcements that appear in this document is enormous, as discussed below.

Enabling Statutes

An **enabling statute** is a statute that authorizes the creation of and, in the process gives power to, an administrative agency. Examples of enabling statutes include

- The Clean Air Act of 1971, which created the Environmental Protection Agency.
- The Occupation Safety and Health Act of 1970, which created the Occupational Safety and Health Administration.
- The Securities Exchange Act of 1934, which created the Securities and Exchange Commission.

This list could be extended for several pages if all federal administrative agencies were listed. In addition, of course, there are numerous additional agencies in every state. Some measure of the volume of regulatory law generated by administrative agencies can be gleaned from the "Nutz and Boltz" box from Heritage.org. Note that, as a footnote to the box indicates, this site has a transparent conservative leaning. Even with its political agenda clear, however, the indicators of the breadth of agency involvement in American life and the volume of regulations are instructive.

Nutz and Boltz OSHA 30-Year Milestones

OSHA's mission is to send every worker home whole and healthy every day. Since the agency was created in 1971, workplace fatalities have been cut in half and occupational injury and illness rates have declined 40 percent. At the same time, U.S. employment has nearly doubled from 56 million workers at 3.5 million worksites to 105 million workers at nearly 6.9 million sites. The following milestones mark the agency's progress over the past 30 years in improving working environments for America's workforce.

May 29, 1971 First standards adopted to provide baseline for safety and health protection in American workplaces.

June 23, 1978 Cotton dust standard promulgated to protect 600,000 workers from byssinosis; cases of "brown lung" have declined from 12,000 to 700 in last 22 years.

November 14, 1978 Lead standard published to reduce permissible exposures by three-quarters to protect 835,000 workers from damage to nervous, urinary and reproductive systems. (Construction standard adopted in 1995.)

January 16, 1981 Electrical standards updated to simplify compliance and adopt a performance approach.

November 25, 1983 Hazard communication standard promulgated to provide information and training and labeling of toxic materials for manufacturing employers and employees (other industries added August 24, 1987).

December 31, 1987 Grain handling facilities standard adopted to protect 155,000 workers at nearly 24,000 grain elevators from the risk of fire and explosion from highly combustible grain dust.

March 6, 1989 Hazardous waste operations and emergency response standard promulgated to protect 1.75 million public and private sector workers exposed to toxic wastes from spills or at hazardous waste sites.

December 6, 1991 Occupational exposure to bloodborne pathogens standard published to prevent more than 9,000 infections and 200 deaths per year, protecting 5.6 million workers against AIDS, hepatitis B, and other diseases.

January 14, 1993 Permit-required confined spaces standard promulgated to prevent more than 50 deaths and more than 5,000 serious injuries annually for 1.6 million workers who enter confined spaces at 240,000 workplaces each year.

June 27, 1994 First expert advisor software—GoCad—issued to assist employers in complying with OSHA's cadmium standard.

August 9, 1994 Fall protection in construction standard revised to save 79 lives and prevent 56,400 injuries each year.

August 10, 1994 Asbestos standard updated to cut permissible exposures in half for nearly 4 million workers, preventing 42 cancer deaths annually.

August 30, 1996 Scaffold standard published to protect 2.3 million construction workers and prevent 50 deaths and 4,500 injuries annually.

November 14, 2000 Ergonomics program standard promulgated to prevent 460,000 musculoskeletal disorders among more than 102 million workers at 6.1 million general industry worksites.

Source: http://www.osha.gov/as/opa/osha30yearmilestones. html. OSHA "milestones" edited by authors.

Code of Federal Regulations
A codification of the general and permanent rules published in the *Federal Register* by the executive departments and agencies of the federal government.

As stated in the second bullet in the "Nutz and Boltz" box on page 158, the **Code of Federal Regulations,** the total of all federal regulations issued by federal agencies, currently in force, comprises 201 volumes and 134,723 pages, occupying 19 feet of bookshelf space! Courts have made it clear to businesses many times that ignorance of the law is no excuse for not complying with the requirements of the many volumes of government regulation.

Typical Regulatory Agency: Occupational Safety and Health Administration

As an illustration of the nature of federal agency regulation, consider the following glimpses of activities of the Occupation Safety and Health Administration. Prior to 1970, unions and other worker groups claimed that worker safety was inadequately protected by existing laws and that federal regulation was needed. In 1970 Congress responded with the Occupational Safety and Health (OSH) Act, which was signed into law by President Nixon in December of that year. The OSH Act created the Occupational Safety and Health Administration (OSHA), a federal administrative agency empowered by the OSH Act to enact detailed regulations regarding workplace safety. OSHA has in fact enacted thousands of workplace regulations, so many that it has been estimated that no factory in the United States is fully in compliance with all of OSHA's regulations.

The "Nutz and Boltz" box on page 159, provided by OSHA itself, touts OSHA's accomplishments. Of course, you wouldn't expect the agency's promotional literature to try to balance the "good" it has done against the burdens it brings to companies and the economy. A full accounting, of course, would require measures of the costs of compliance, including losses in labor productivity, netted against the benefits OSHA claims. Generally, however, the costs borne by businesses of compliance with OSHA regulations must be measured against the lives saved and injuries prevented by safety regulations. Few would contend that workplaces in the United States are not much safer than they were before the OSH Act was passed.

Administrative Procedures Act

Administrative Procedures Act
The part of administrative law that defines the procedure(s) an administrative agency must follow to enact new regulations.

For OSHA, and other administrative agencies, to issue a work safety regulation, it must (as all agencies must) comply with the **Administrative Procedures Act** (APA) of 1946, which requires notice and a hearing, the basic elements of due process. Under the APA, *notice* is provided when a proposed regulation is announced in the *Federal Register*. The *Federal Register* is published on a daily basis and attorneys representing businesses must routinely scrutinize the *Federal Register* to make sure that their clients are not surprised by new federal regulations that impact their businesses. When a proposed regulation is announced in the *Federal Register,* the notice also must announce the date of a hearing so that members of the public, including affected businesses, worker groups, and other interested parties such as advocacy groups, can make their views known about the proposed regulation.

Not All Regulations Are Treated Equally

Substantive Regulations

substantive regulation
New laws or regulations created by agencies and authorized by congressional delegations of power, which have the same force as statutes enacted by Congress.

Regulations from administrative agencies are classified as either *substantive, interpretative,* or *procedural.* Substantive rules are the most significant and, before an agency can enact a substantive regulation into law, it is required to fully comply with the due process requirements (discussed above) of the APA in terms of notice in the *Federal Register* and the scheduling of a hearing to receive comments from interested parties. **Substantive regulations** represent new law, enacted under the authority granted to the issuing agency by the enabling statute that created the agency.

Interpretative Regulations

interpretative regulation
Rulings or published discussions from agencies that indicate how the issuing administrative agency interprets the statutes and substantive regulations it oversees.

Contrasting with the requirements for substantive regulations, an **interpretative regulation** can be issued by a federal agency without meeting due process requirements of the APA, though the APA still governs procedures for issuance of such regulations. Interpretative regulations are just that: they represent how the agency interprets the statute it is supposed to enforce. Illustratively, the Securities and Exchange Commission (SEC) often issues interpretative regulations through publication of letters of inquiry that they receive and their responses to such inquires. As an illustration of this process, the SEC regularly receives letters from attorneys representing firms asking whether a firm can qualify for relatively inexpensive "private placement offerings" (sales of securities, for example, to an insurance company rather than to the general public) if they do the specific things that the attorney discusses in his or her letter of inquiry. As the requirements for a "public" offering

Nutz and Boltz   Department of Labor

OCCUPATIONAL SAFETY AND HEALTH ADMINISTRATION

29 CFR Part 1910

[Docket No. S–777]

RIN 1218–AB36

Ergonomics Program

AGENCY: Occupational Safety and Health Administration (OSHA), Department of Labor.

ACTION: Final rule.

SUMMARY: The Occupational Safety and Health Administration is issuing a final Ergonomics Program standard (29 CFR 1910.900) to address the significant risk of employee exposure to ergonomic risk factors in jobs in general industry workplaces. Exposure to ergonomic risk factors on the job leads to musculoskeletal disorders (MSDs) of the upper extremities, back, and lower extremities. Every year, nearly 600,000 MSDs that are serious enough to cause time off work are reported to the Bureau of Labor Statistics by general industry employers, and evidence suggests that an even larger number of non-lost worktime MSDs occur in these workplaces every year.

The standard contains an "action trigger," which identifies jobs with risk factors of sufficient magnitude, duration, or intensity to warrant further examination by the employer. This action trigger acts as a screen. When an employee reports an MSD, the employer must first determine whether the MSD is an MSD incident, defined by the standard as an MSD that results in days away from work, restricted work, medical treatment beyond first aid, or MSD symptoms or signs that persist for 7 or more days. Once this determination is made, the employer must determine whether the employee's job has risk factors that meet the standard's action trigger. The risk factors addressed by this standard include repetition, awkward posture, force, vibration, and contact stress. If the risk factors in the employee's job do not exceed the action trigger, the employer does not need to implement an ergonomics program for that job.

If an employee reports an MSD incident and the risk factors of that employee's job meet the action trigger, the employer must establish an ergonomics program for that job. The program must contain the following elements: hazard information and reporting, management leadership and employee participation, job hazard analysis and control, training, MSD management, and program evaluation. The standard provides the employer with several options for evaluating and controlling risk factors for jobs covered by the ergonomics program, and provides objective criteria for identifying MSD hazards in those jobs and determining when the controls implemented have achieved the required level of control.

The final standard would affect approximately 6.1 million employers and 102 million employees in general industry workplaces, and employers in these workplaces would be required over the ten years following the promulgation of the standard to control approximately 18 million jobs with the potential to cause or contribute to covered MSDs. OSHA estimates that the final standard would prevent about 4.6 million work-related MSDs over the next 10 years, have annual benefits of approximately $9.1 billion, and impose annual compliance costs of $4.5 billion on employers. On a per-establishment basis, this equals approximately $700; annual costs per problem job fixed are estimated at $250.

DATES: This final rule becomes effective on January 16, 2001.

Compliance. Start-up dates for specific provisions are set in paragraph (w) of § 1910.900. However, affected parties do not have to comply with the information collection requirements in the final rule until the Department of Labor publishes in the **Federal Register** the control numbers assigned by the Office of Management and Budget (OMB). Publication of the control numbers notifies the public that OMB has approved these information collection requirements under the Paperwork Reduction Act of 1995.

ADDRESSES: In compliance with 28 U.S.C. 2112(a), the Agency designates the Associate Solicitor for Occupational Safety and Health, Office of the Solicitor, Room S–4004, U.S. Department of Labor, 200 Constitution Avenue, NW., Washington, DC 20210, as the recipient of petitions for review of the standard.

FOR FURTHER INFORMATION CONTACT: OSHA's Ergonomics Team at (202) 693–2116, or visit the OSHA Homepage at www.osha.gov.

SUPPLEMENTARY INFORMATION:

Table of Contents

The preamble and standard are organized as follows:

I.   Introduction

II.   Events Leading to the Standard

III.   Pertinent Legal Authority

procedural regulation
Rules created by administrative agencies that detail the procedures to be used in the application of regulations, complaints against regulatory actions, and so forth.

administrative law
Rules and regulations created by administrative agencies that (1) enable the agencies to regulate business and society in accordance with statutes the legislative body adopts and policies of the chief executive and (2) provide for regulation of their own behavior.

of securities are far more arduous (and expensive) than are private placements, a firm pursuing a private placement cannot afford to take a course of action that the SEC will later rule disqualifies it from the private sale of securities. The SEC will respond to the request described above with a formal opinion letter. If the SEC thinks the question raised is sufficiently general, it may publish the opinion (without disclosing the identity of the firm in question). Such published opinions serve as interpretative regulations, revealing how the SEC interprets a portion of the securities laws that deal with qualifying for private placements of securities.

Most of the focus of this chapter is on substantive regulations. Occasionally, there are disputes over whether a regulation is interpretative or substantive. A business or other interested party can challenge the issuance of what the issuing agency presents as an interpretative regulation if the agency did not go through the requirements of the APA and the regulation is, in fact, a substantive regulation.

Procedural Regulations

Procedural regulations are the rules for procedure that agencies create to supervise **administrative law.** When a company files a complaint against an agency action, it must use the forms and other procedural minutiae required by the agency to move its complaint forward. Procedural regulations are akin to the Federal Rules of Civil Procedure applied in civil litigation. Procedural regulations can become an issue in court when an agency does not follow its own procedural rules, when it is challenged either internally by an employee or externally by a business or advocacy group.

ADMINISTRATIVE AGENCIES

Federal and state administrative agencies do more than just issue regulations. In virtually all cases, agencies also are charged with some enforcement responsibilities. Typically, administrative agencies also collect and compile information, publish reports, and perform investigations.

Political Aspects

Administrative agencies are part of the executive branch of government and, as such, answer to the president as chief executive in the case of federal agencies, and to a governor at the state level.[1] When a new administration is elected, the president (or governor) will have

---

[1] Technically, independent administrative agencies, often called commissions or boards, are not part of the executive branch of government in the sense that these independent agencies set their own agenda and do not answer directly to the president.

Nutz and Boltz   Independent Administrative Agencies

There are about 115 "independent" federal administrative agencies. Here is just a small sample, with each agency's website:

Architectural and Transportation Barriers Compliance Board, www.access-board.gov

Bureau of Alcohol, Tobacco, Firearms, and Explosives, www.atf.treas.gov

Consumer Product Safety Commission (CPSC), www.cpsc.gov

Federal Reserve System, www.federalreserve.gov

Federal Trade Commission (FTC), www.ftc.gov

Food and Drug Administration, www.fda.gov

National Highway Traffic Safety Administration, www.nhtsa.dot.gov

Occupational Safety and Health Review Commission, www.oshrc.gov

Social Security Administration (SSA), www.ssa.gov

authority to appoint the heads of most administrative agencies and cabinet officers. At the federal level, many of these appointments require a majority vote of approval from the Senate. Even so, in most cases the president is able to select his own people to head administrative agencies. When President Bush took office in 2001, he had authority to make over 6,000 political appointments to head up his government. Most of these political appointees serve at the pleasure of the president, which means that they can be fired whenever the president is displeased with their performance.

Independent Administrative Agencies

independent administrative agencies
These agencies are independent in the sense that they are headed by commissioners who have fixed terms and do not serve at the pleasure of the president. Technically, these agencies are not part of the executive branch of government but, rather, set policy independently based on their interpretation of the enabling statute that created the agency.

In contrast to the picture presented above, there are numerous **independent administrative agencies** that are governed by appointed commissioners with fixed terms. The Federal Reserve Board, currently headed by Chairman Allen Greenspan, has seven appointed governors who serve for 14-year terms, while the chair and vice chair serve four-year terms. When a new president is elected, the president can appoint a new governor (or a new chair or vice chair) only when an existing term expires. Only one 14-year term expires in each two-year period, limiting a sitting president's ability to "stack" the Federal Reserve Board with hand-picked members. For most administrative agencies there are prohibitions against selecting all the commissioners from a single political party.

The existence of *independent agencies* reflects the view that some functions, such as control of the nation's money supply, are so important that they should be shielded from political pressure from a current administration, with their course of action chosen by experts within the agency. Needless to say, there is wide agreement that Chairman Greenspan and other members of the Federal Reserve System should make monetary policy decisions based on economic conditions, without possible political pressure from a sitting president. Listed in the "Nutz and Boltz" box are some of the prominent independent administrative agencies.

Actions of Administrative Agencies

Investigations

In order to intelligently enforce regulations that carry out the goals of statutes passed by Congress, employees of administrative agencies must investigate. In most cases, agencies require companies to report to the agency, even if it means that a company must report its own violations of law. For example, OSHA requires companies to report all work-related deaths that occur, which can subsequently lead to sanctions against the reporting employer.

Similarly, the Equal Employment Opportunity Commission (EEOC) requires companies to report demographic data that, likewise, could form the basis of a subsequent lawsuit. As discussed in the previous chapter, under the Constitution, companies cannot claim Fifth Amendment privilege against revealing damaging information.

In addition to requiring self-reporting, administrative agencies also employ their own investigators and inspectors. The Environmental Protection Agency (EPA) uses investigators to determine whether companies are violating the Wetland Preservation Act when they drain pools of water on their own land. EPA investigators also monitor company discharges into bodies of water in order to determine whether there are violations of the Clean Water Act. The Securities and Exchange Commission, relying on its own staff of accountants and lawyers, investigates allegations of fraud in connection with the sale of securities.

Subpoena Power

subpoena power
A subpoena is a written court order requiring the attendance of the person named in the subpoena at a specified time and place for the purpose of being questioned under oath concerning a particular matter that is the subject of an investigation, proceeding, or lawsuit. A subpoena also may require the production of a paper, document, or other object relevant to the particular investigation.

The power of an administrative agency to investigate is augmented by the power to subpoena relevant information. Agency subpoenas can be wide-ranging, but must be tied to the agency's scope of authority as granted by Congress. Administrative agencies have the power to issue subpoenas to any party or company, not just to the group of companies that they directly regulate. For example, an agency that regulates practices of banks could subpoena information from companies that borrow money from the bank. The right of an agency to freely use broad subpoena powers is the focus of the following case.

Case 6-1

Donovan, Secretary of Labor, et al. v. Lone Steer, Inc.

Supreme Court of the United States
464 U.S. 408 (1984)

BACKGROUND AND FACTS

A Department of Labor official served an administrative subpoena duces tecum *[a requirement to produce records] on a motel/restaurant operator's employee in the motel lobby, pursuant to 9 and 11(a) of the Fair Labor Standards Act. The subpoena directed an officer or agent of the motel operator with personal knowledge of the operator's records to appear at the Department of Labor Wage and Hour Division in Bismarck, North Dakota, and to produce certain payroll and sales records. In the subpoena, the government was requesting payroll data to determine whether workers were being paid in accordance with the requirements of the Fair Labor Standards Act. In an action filed by the operator, the United States District Court for the District of North Dakota held that enforcement of the subpoena would violate the Fourth Amendment because the Secretary of Labor had not previously obtained a judicial warrant.*

Opinion: Justice Rehnquist Delivered the Opinion of the Court

Pursuant to those provisions [of the Fair Labor Standards Act], an official of the Department of Labor served an administrative subpoena duces tecum on an employee of appellee Lone Steer, Inc., a motel and restaurant located in Steele, N.D. The subpoena directed an officer or agent of appellee with personal knowledge of appellee's records to appear at the Wage and Hour Division of the United States Department of Labor in Bismarck, N.D., and to produce certain payroll and sales records. In an action filed by appellee [Lone Steer, Inc.] to challenge the validity of the subpoena, the District Court for the District of North Dakota held that, although the Secretary of Labor had complied with the applicable provisions of the FLSA in issuing the subpoena, enforcement of the subpoena would violate the Fourth Amendment of the United States Constitution because the Secretary had not previously obtained a judicial warrant.

* * *

We think that the District Court undertook to decide a case not before it when it held that appellants may not "enter upon the premises" of appellee to inspect its records without first having obtained a warrant. The only "entry" upon appellee's premises by appellants, so far as the record discloses, is that of Godes on February 2, 1982, when he and Gerald Hill entered the motel and restaurant to attempt to conduct an investigation. The stipulation of facts entered into by the parties, App. 11–17, and incorporated into the opinion of the District Court, App. A to Juris. Statement 2a-8a, describe what happened next:

> They asked for Ms. White and were told she was not available but expected shortly. They were offered some coffee, and waited in the lobby area. After 20–30 minutes, when Ms. White had not appeared, Mr. Godes served an Administrative Subpoena Duces Tecum on employee Karen Arnold. [Citations omitted]

An entry into the public lobby of a motel and restaurant for the purpose of serving an administrative subpoena is scarcely the sort of governmental act which is forbidden by the Fourth Amendment. The administrative subpoena itself did not authorize either entry or inspection of appellee's premises; it merely directed appellee to produce relevant wage and hour records at appellants' regional office some 25 miles away.

* * *

> The short answer to the Fourth Amendment objections is that the records in these cases present no question of actual search and seizure, but raise only the question whether orders of court for the production of specified records have been validly made; and no sufficient showing appears to justify setting them aside. No officer or other person has sought to enter petitioners' premises against their will, to search them, or to seize or examine their books, records or papers without their assent, otherwise than pursuant to orders of court authorized by law and made after adequate opportunity to present objections. . . .

Id., at 195 (footnotes omitted).

* * *

Our holding here, which simply reaffirms our holding in *Oklahoma Press,* in no way leaves an employer defenseless against an unreasonably burdensome administrative subpoena requiring the production of documents. We hold only that the defenses available to an employer do not include the right to insist upon a judicial warrant as a condition precedent to a valid administrative subpoena.

Decision and Outcome

The subpoena issued by the U.S. Department of Labor was valid and did not have to be approved by a judge. This decision significantly frees up administrative agencies from the burdens of going before a judge every time they want to obtain records from a business or individual suspected of a crime or violation of civil law.

Questions for Analysis

1. Did the Supreme Court hold that a subpoena of company records is the same as a search of the workplace premises? What is the difference according to the Court?
2. What limitations does the Supreme Court say in this case are imposed on the power of federal agencies to seek information through subpoenas? Does it appear to you that the Department of Labor, which enforces the Fair Labor Standards Act, should be able to subpoena the records of an employer for possible violations?

Discretionary and Maintenance Powers of Administrative Agencies

Administrative agencies are charged with regulating broad arenas of economic activity or economic activity impact. The EPA, for example, is charged with protecting the environment. In connection with those activities and pursuant to the Clean Water Act, the EPA has the power to issue permits to companies for the discharge of pollutants into navigable waters. Other agencies are charged with administering various entitlement programs and, therefore, must decide whether a recipient qualifies for continued aid. The Social Security Administration, for example, makes decisions about coverage provided by various components of the Social Security system including those focused on disability, retiree pensions, and death benefits. For federal lands, the Bureau of Land Management must make decisions on a broad array of requests dealing with grazing and water rights, mining and drilling rights, and hunting and wildlife preservation controls. The Department of Interior operates national parks and must make wildlife management decisions.

Dealing with Government Officials

Administrative agencies are staffed by people (often pejoratively called *bureaucrats*) required to make decisions that have significant impacts on the businesses they regulate. Many such decisions are made with wide latitude for discretion. In general, courts defer to the discretion of agency decision makers, so long as there is no evidence of fraud, corruption, or capriciousness in a decision. In working with government officials, businesspeople should be aware that government officials have significant power and that antagonistic relationships are not likely to benefit the businesses they work for. In general, agency employees want their forms carefully and fully filled out, so that if their decisions are subsequently challenged, they will have something to fall back upon. Cooperation from the businesspeople with whom agency staff members come in contact goes a long way toward allowing both parties to do their jobs, without the distraction of conflict resolution.

Sanctions from Administrative Agencies

sanction
Enforcement and/or punishment power possessed by an administrative agency. May include, but not be limited to, fines, revocation or denial of license, seizure of property, and the withholding of benefits.

The power of administrative agencies is considerable. Indeed, federal and state agencies have the power to shut down businesses, large and small. The list below shows the range of **sanctions** available to agencies, though no single agency has the power to impose each and every sanction listed. Among the sanctions available to agencies are

- Imposition of a fine or civil penalty.
- Denial, revocation, or suspension of a license, such as a license to pollute or to transport hazardous waste.
- Seizure of property.
- Withholding of benefits or relief.
- Petitioning the federal courts for criminal and civil sanctions, particularly injunctions or cease and desist orders.

Adjudication

administrative law judge (ALJ)
An agency employee who serves as a judge in suits brought by the employing agency against a business.

Administrative Law Judges

Administrative agencies typically have their own judges, called **administrative law judges (ALJs)**. ALJs hear cases that an administrative agency pursues against businesses subject to the agency's jurisdiction. ALJs operate like judges, but also have the *power to*

Nutz and Boltz Creation of Government Agencies and Adjudication

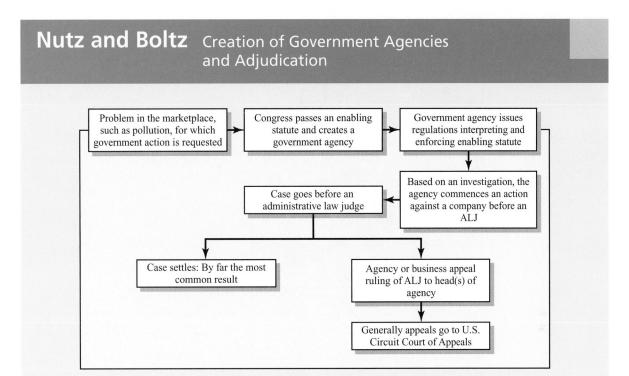

find facts, which is extremely important if an agency case is appealed to the courts. In a typical case, an administrative agency investigates a possible violation of its enabling statute or its amendments, other statutes that the agency has been charged with enforcing, or regulations promulgated by the agency. If investigators believe that a violation has taken place, the first step will likely be a meeting with the accused defendant business. In most cases a settlement is worked out. In some cases, however, the parties can't agree and litigation may be initiated before an agency ALJ.

Although ALJs are not part of the federal judiciary, and are in fact actually employees of the agency, they have a good reputation for impartiality and integrity. When a case comes before an ALJ, the plaintiff is the agency itself and the defendant is the business or individual(s) charged with a violation of law. This phase of an administrative law hearing parallels a civil trial before a federal judge without a jury. After the evidence is presented, the ALJ can find either for the agency or for the defendant business.

Decisions of ALJs and Courses of Actions by the Parties

If the ALJ finds for the business, the case is dismissed, but the investigative wing of the agency that brought the suit can appeal to agency heads (commissioners, governors—there are a plethora of names for the heads of agencies) to have the case reinstated. In most cases, however, when the ALJ finds that the case does not have merit, investigators let the case drop.

In cases in which the ALJ finds that the charges against the business have merit, (s)he may impose sanctions, either fines or civil penalties, against the business. If the business does not accept the verdict of the ALJ, it too can appeal to the head of the agency and seek a reversal.

Source: From *Herblock: A Cartoonist's Life* (Times Books, 1998).
Reprinted with permission of The Herb Block Foundation.

Judicial Review

judicial review
Occurs when judges, typically at the federal court of appeals level, assess appeals from final decisions of administrative agencies as to the constitutionality or legality of agency actions.

arbitrary and capricious
Actions of administrative agencies, including promulgation of rules and regulations, can be challenged if these regulations are without technical or scientific foundation.

If an agency (1) initiates an action against a business, (2) obtains a favorable verdict before an agency ALJ, and (3) the heads of the agency affirm the ALJ verdict, the affected business can appeal to the federal courts for **judicial review.** In most cases, such an appeal goes to a federal appeals court rather than to a federal district court. In this sequence, the federal court of appeals will generally accept the *factual findings* of the ALJ. If the appeal of the business is going to be successful before a federal court of appeals, it will have to be successful based on an *error of law* committed by the agency or the ALJ. Among the possible errors of law that could justify overturning an agency decision are

- *The action of the agency was arbitrary and capricious.* If there was no scientific or technical foundation for the issuance of a regulation by the agency, the regulation, and thus the legal action against the business by the agency before the ALJ, can be overturned based on the **arbitrary and capricious** standard. *If an agency has a solid technical foundation for its decision to issue a regulation, courts will generally defer to the judgment of the agency.*

- *The action of the agency exceeded its authority under the enabling statute.* In many situations, the boundary lines for an administrative agency's authority are not well defined, or a change in technology or societal conventions can introduce new variables into setting that boundary. Administrative regulations and other agency actions can be challenged in federal court if the defendant claims that the agency **exceeded its authority** under its enabling statute. A famous case involving the boundary lines of agency authority was brought to court when the Securities and Exchange Commission (SEC) sought to take control of the Teamsters' pension plan, which was largely funded with securities (stocks and bonds). The Teamsters successfully challenged the attempted

exceeded its authority
An administrative agency exceeds its authority when a court determines, after examining the enabling statute, that the agency is not empowered by the enabling statute to perform the challenged action, including enacting regulations outside the authority given to the agency.

expansion of SEC authority, arguing that the SEC exceeded its authority by attempting to take over management of the Teamsters' pension.[2]

- *Actions of the agency violate constitutional protections, particularly Bill of Rights provisions.* An action by an administrative agency is a governmental action and, thus, is subject to constitutional challenge. When an administrative agency such as the Federal Communications Commission fashions regulations that effectively censor content on broadcast television, there are potential First Amendment issues that defendants can use as defenses in an action brought against them by the FCC. Warrantless searches by government inspectors for various agencies also have been challenged under the Fourth Amendment. Other administrative agency actions affect individuals and may deprive them of constitutional rights. Some cutoffs of government benefits imposed by administrative agencies, without due process, notice, and a hearing, have been successfully challenged as violating constitutional rights of due process. In addition, some government regulations have been struck down as being unconstitutionally vague.

Appropriateness of Judicial Review—Standing

There are several timing-related issues for parties who wish to challenge an administrative agency action or regulation. First, a party challenging an agency action must have *standing to sue.* As is discussed in Chapter 3, a party has standing to sue when that party has a real, current interest at stake. A real current interest includes being subject to any action of the targeted administrative agency that could result in a fine or civil sanction. Thus, any business that is the target of agency adjudication before an ALJ has standing to challenge the appropriateness of the agency's regulations on the grounds that those regulations are not constitutional, are not within the authority of the agency, or are arbitrary and capricious.

Exhaustion of All Internal Remedies

Courts will not take a case appeal that can be resolved in the favor of the appealing party through internal actions of the agency. If a federal employee alleges that she has been the victim of sexual harassment and the agency has an internal grievance policy, a court will not hear the case unless the employee has made use of the agency internal grievance policy. If an ALJ rules adversely to a company in an environmental case, the company must first appeal the decision of the ALJ to the administrator (head) of the EPA before the company is entitled to challenge the EPA action in federal court. If a party challenging an action of an administrative agency does not exhaust internal remedies and goes to court prematurely, the consequences are most likely that the party's case will be dismissed in court.

ripeness
A dispute is not ripe for judicial resolution if the party appealing to the court has not exhausted all internal remedies available to that party offered by the government agency.

In general, courts will not hear cases that may have mere *hypothetical* adverse consequences for the party filing suit. Thus, if an agency passes a regulation that a company is convinced will adversely affect it, that company cannot sue to get the regulation overturned unless and until the agency actually hauls the company before an ALJ. As with most legal principles, there are exceptions under which a company can file a claim in court before the agency has actually filed suit against the company. According to precedents in this area, a dispute is **ripe** when the action of the agency has a *sufficiently direct and immediate impact* as to make judicial review appropriate. Application of this standard is illustrated in Case 6-2.

[2] *John Daniel v. International Brotherhood of Teamsters, et al.,* 561 F.2d 1223 (7th Cir. 1977).

Case 6-2

Ohio Forestry Association, Inc., Petitioner v. Sierra Club, et al.

Supreme Court of the United States
523 U.S. 726 (1998)

BACKGROUND AND FACTS

Pursuant to the National Forest Management Act of 1976 (NFMA), the United States Forest Service developed a Land and Resource Management Plan (Plan) for Ohio's Wayne National Forest. Although the Plan makes logging in the forest more likely—it sets logging goals, selects the areas suited to timber production, and determines which probable methods of timber harvest are appropriate—it does not itself authorize the cutting of any trees. When the Plan was first proposed, the Sierra Club and another environmental organization (collectively Sierra Club) pursued various administrative remedies to bring about the Plan's modification, and then brought this suit challenging the Plan's lawfulness on the ground that it permits too much logging and too much clear-cutting. The District Court granted the Forest Service summary judgment, but the Sixth Circuit reversed. The latter court found the dispute justiciable because, inter alia, *it was "ripe for review" and held that the Plan violated the NFMA.*

Opinion: Justice Breyer Delivered the Opinion of the Court

This case focuses upon a plan that the Forest Service has developed for the Wayne National Forest located in southern Ohio. When the Service wrote the plan, the forest consisted of 178,000 federally owned acres (278 sq. mi.) in three forest units that are interspersed among privately owned lands, some of which the Forest Service plans to acquire over time. The Plan permits logging to take place on 126,000 (197 sq. mi.) of the federally owned acres. At the same time, it sets a ceiling on the total amount of wood that can be cut—a ceiling that amounts to about 75 million board feet over 10 years, and which, the Plan projects, would lead to logging on about 8,000 acres (12.5 sq. mi.) during that decade. According to the Plan, logging on about 5,000 (7.8 sq. mi.) of those 8,000 acres would involve clearcutting, or other forms of what the Forest Service calls "even-aged" tree harvesting.

* * *

As this Court has previously pointed out, the ripeness requirement is designed

> "to prevent the courts, through avoidance of premature adjudication, from entangling themselves in abstract disagreements over administrative policies, and also to protect the agencies from judicial interference until an administrative decision has been formalized and its effects felt in a concrete way by the challenging parties." *Abbott Laboratories v. Gardner,* 387 U.S. 136, 148–149 (1967).

In deciding whether an agency's decision is, or is not, ripe for judicial review, the Court has examined both the "fitness of the issues for judicial decision" and the "hardship to the parties of withholding court consideration." To do so in this case, we must consider: (1) whether delayed review would cause hardship to the plaintiffs; (2) whether judicial intervention would inappropriately interfere with further administrative action; and (3) whether the courts would benefit from further factual development of the issues presented. These considerations, taken together, foreclose review in the present case.

* * *

Third, from the courts' perspective, review of the Sierra Club's claims regarding logging and clearcutting now would require time-consuming judicial consideration of the details of an elaborate, technically based plan, which predicts consequences that may affect many different parcels of land in a variety of ways, and which effects themselves may change over time. That review would have to take place without benefit of the focus that a particular logging proposal could provide. Thus, for example, the court below in evaluating the Sierra Club's claims had to focus upon whether the Plan as a whole was "improperly skewed," rather than focus upon whether the decision to allow clearcutting on a particular site was improper, say, because the site was better suited to another use or logging there would cumulatively result in too many trees' being cut. And, of course, depending upon the agency's future actions to revise the Plan or modify the expected methods of implementation, review now may turn out to have been unnecessary.

This type of review threatens the kind of "abstract disagreements over administrative policies," ***, that the ripeness doctrine seeks to avoid. In this case, for example, the Court of Appeals panel disagreed about whether or not the Forest Service suffered from a kind of general "bias" in favor of timber production and clear-cutting. Review where the consequences had been "reduced to more manageable proportions," and where the "factual components [were] fleshed out, by some concrete action" might have led the panel majority either to demonstrate that bias and its consequences through record citation (which it did not do) or to abandon the claim. All this is to say that further factual development would "significantly advance our ability to deal with the legal issues presented" and would "aid us in their resolution."

* * *

For these reasons, we find the respondents' suit not ripe for review. We vacate the decision of the Court of Appeals, and we remand this case with instructions to dismiss.

Decision and Outcome

The U.S. Supreme Court reversed the decision of the Sixth Circuit Court of Appeals and ruled that the dispute over possible logging at Wayne National Forest was premature and therefore not ripe for dispute. The Supreme Court did not let a trial take place where the plaintiffs were arguing that the defendant had a bias toward logging before the first tree had been cut at Wayne National Forest.

Questions for Analysis

1. What is the Supreme Court talking about when it says that "further factual development" is necessary to make clear the legal issues in dispute? Does this ruling mean that trees have to be cut down before the Sierra Club can challenge the cutting plan developed by the National Forest Service?

2. The Supreme Court quotes from the *Abbott Laboratory* case that the ripeness requirement is designed to prevent what types of delays? Do you think that the real purpose of the suit by the Sierra Club was delay until the National Forest Service devised a more tree-friendly plan?

The Power of Information

In today's information age, the party that controls relevant information is likely to have enormous leverage in disputes with those who are informationally disadvantaged. Federal agencies have tremendous informational advantages, not only because they have the resources to store huge paper and computer files, but also because federal agencies can compel the firms they regulate to produce information and submit the information to them, providing agencies with a great deal of company information that would not be voluntarily offered. Indeed, much of the information obtained from firms is sensitive and proprietary, containing trade secrets and valuable marketing research data. In the past, the tendency of agency decision makers has been to "classify" information and not allow it to be available to the public.

Freedom of Information Act (FOIA)

The act that, with some significant exceptions, allows citizens to examine the work of government agencies.

Freedom of Information Act, 1966

Responding to claims of abusive actions by federal agencies, Congress passed the **Freedom of Information Act (FOIA)** in 1966. State legislatures followed suit, passing their own versions of the FOIA. The federal version allows citizens to obtain government records without a justifying reason for making the request. In theory, government agencies must respond within 10 days to a request for information, but the citizen bears the burden of paying for making the records available. Certain groups, such as public interest groups and newspapers, have their costs of reproducing requested records waived.

Not all government records are obtainable through the FOIA. Among the types of records that cannot be obtained through FOIA requests are

- Records that relate to national defense or foreign policy.
- Records that relate to personnel files.
- Records that are required by statute to be kept secret, such as adoption records and arrest records of juveniles.
- Trade secrets and confidential information given to government agencies. It is important to note that many trade secrets are discovered through FOIA. It is incumbent upon a business supplying sensitive information to the government to designate it as such to avoid inadvertent disclosure.
- Information compiled by law enforcement officials.
- Internal memoranda that reflect decision making.

Although government agencies must respond within 10 days to a FOIA request, actual compliance with the request can take much longer or be denied if the agency believes that the request falls into one of the categories listed above.

Government in Sunshine Acts

Government in Sunshine Acts
A right, with some significant exceptions, that citizens have to be informed in advance of the time, place, and agenda of meetings held by government officials.

At the federal and state levels of government, and sometimes at the local level, governmental business must be conducted in a way that makes it accessible to the public. Of course, there are numerous exceptions to the requirement that all government meetings be open to the public, but the general rule is that the public is entitled to *notice* before governing units, including agencies, hold a meeting. The notice must specify if the meeting is open to the public and, if not, the reason why the meeting is closed. It is legitimate under **Government in Sunshine Acts** to close meetings that will reveal trade secrets, targets of law enforcement investigations, issues related to national defense, and crop projections of the U.S. Department of Agriculture, which would give commodity traders financial advantages. A host of other detailed exceptions exist. For example, when the policy-making body for the Federal Reserve System makes its decisions about monetary policy, that meeting is closed to the public.

Federal Privacy Act of 1974

Federal Privacy Act
Act affirming a right, with some significant exceptions, that citizens have against government disclosures of information collected about them by government agencies unless the citizen has given permission for the disclosure.

The **Federal Privacy Act** of 1974 does provide citizens some protection for information about them collected and stored in government files. The scope of the Federal Privacy Act, however, is limited to information collected by federal agencies and does not protect against invasions of privacy that occur when private medical or financial records are uncovered by private sources. The essence of the act states that, "No agency shall disclose any record which is contained in a system of records by any means of communication to any person, or to another agency, except pursuant to a written request by, or with the prior written consent of, the individual to whom the record pertains, unless disclosure of the record would be— . . ." The foregoing quote is followed by 13 separate exceptions, so the protection offered by the Privacy Act is leaky at best.

Congressional Controls of Administrative Agencies

Budgetary Powers

Although the president may send budgetary recommendations to Congress, ultimately it is Congress that must agree to approve bills that provide funding for administrative agencies.

There are times when agencies act in ways that displease majorities in Congress, who can respond by cutting agency budgets. More commonly, actions that displease Congress are policy decisions of the president and so, without any culpability on their part, an agency may be caught in a political crossfire between Congress and the president. In any event, Congress can cut the budget of an agency for any reason it wishes, including a pattern of acts contrary to its wishes. As a result, agency employees are generally very anxious to respond positively to requests from members of Congress.

Sunset Legislation

sunset legislation
Legislation that requires the termination of a government agency or program at a date certain unless the legislature decides to reinstate the program or agency.

The late Senator Barry Goldwater, who ran unsuccessfully for president in 1964, once commented that the closest thing to eternity here on earth was the duration of a federal agency. Congress, however, has the power to include a "sunset" provision in the enabling statute that creates an agency. The effect of a sunset provision is that, at the expiration time set in the sunset clause, the agency automatically goes out of existence, unless Congress decides to reauthorize the agency. Congress has used this provision sparingly, but sunset legislation has been used more frequently at the state level.

Cost–Benefit and Other Quantitative Analysis

cost–benefit analysis
Analysis of the overall values of costs and benefits associated with a proposed course of action. For some federal agencies, favorable conclusions from a cost–benefit analysis are required to justify the implementation of new regulations.

For some agencies, Congress has required that cost–benefit analyses be employed to justify additional regulations. Cost–benefit analysis requires quantification of both the costs imposed by a proposed regulation and its benefits. A proposed regulation is justified by cost–benefit analysis when the benefits of the regulation are estimated to be greater than the costs. Costs of a regulation include, but are not limited to, compliance costs, possible price changes, budgetary outlays, and distortion of consumer choices. The benefits of government regulations include the value of public goods provided, such as public schools, or the avoidance of market failures, such as a reduction in pollution. The precision of cost–benefit analysis is open to question, as the results often depend on a lengthy list of economic assumptions that are not apparent to decision makers and others interested in the action unless they are skilled in economics. Still, cost–benefit analyses probably prevent some economically inefficient regulations from being advanced, though such analysis does not provide a precise instrument for estimating the net worth of a new government regulation or program.

Concluding Thoughts about Federal and State Administrative Agencies

Administrative agencies, which are a fact of life, have created and control much of the legal environment of business. Regardless of the political views of managers regarding the efficacy of government regulation, it is good business to work with government regulators. In most cases, a business and an agency can settle differences with or without consent decrees. In cases in which a business rejects findings of agency investigators that it has violated a regulation or the statute that the agency enforces, adjudication before an ALJ is a virtual certainty. In some such cases, the business will prevail. In the event the firm loses, once all internal appeals within the agency have been completed, the company can still appeal to federal courts, which can rule that the agency failed to prove its case (very rare), that the agency exceeded its authority under the enabling statute, that the regulations promulgated by the agency are arbitrary and capricious (lacking in a technical foundation), or that the regulation violates the U.S. Constitution, usually some element of the Bill of Rights.

More often, agency findings and decisions will be upheld in the courts. Federal and state agencies have become increasingly powerful and increasingly involved in commercial and personal lives. Congress has responded to these developments by passing legislation that limits the authority of agencies and allows citizens access to agency information. Keep in

International Perspective

Most of the countries of Europe are members of the European Union and are embarked in an experiment in government in which much national sovereignty has been ceded to international rule through the EU. Complaints about loss of sovereignty and too much bureaucracy are perhaps inevitable. Witness the comments below from a very partisan group that wants Britain to secede from the EU.

THE TRUTH ABOUT EUROPE

EU Law: What Is It? And What Happened to UK Law?

There is no more an alarming sign of a society taking leave of its senses than when its officials, with full support of the law, can do something that defies all humanity and commonsense—*and no one takes any notice!*[1]

1. EU law is certainly not made by elected MEPs in the European Parliament. It is made through Directives (*which need legislation by national Governments*) and Regulations (*which become law immediately as they stand*) that come from the European Commission and the Council of Ministers. There are also Council Decisions, Recommendations, Opinions and Resolutions. Similar categories are produced by the Commission. Commission regulations are produced by committees of officials and need not require political approval at all—***Rule by pure Bureaucratic Decree! Commission regulations now account for 88% of all EU law!***

2. In 1973 there were 343 Regulations, 143 Directives and 194 "Other" EU laws. By 1996 these figures were 3070 Regulations, 2964 Directives and 8037 "Others". They bypass UK Parliamentary control using Statutory Instruments and Ministerial Orders. UK Civil Servants, "translating" EU law, always make things far worse.

3. EU law is law through International Treaty (*mainly The Treaty of Rome, Single European Act, The Maastricht Treaty and the Amsterdam Treaty*). A European Court of Justice (ECJ) decides disputes. Because of the way the Treaties were written the ECJ always decides in a manner that furthers "ever closer European integration and harmonisation". That means the ECJ can and does develop law beyond the strict wording of the original treaties. It has developed law to such an extent that it is no longer distinguishable from ordinary UK law; it overrides UK law; ***it is law beyond any democratic political control*** (*see TEC leaflet 8*).

[1] Christopher Booker and Richard North, *The Mad Officials: How the Bureaucrats Are Strangling Britain* (London: Constable, 1994).

Source: http://members.tripod.com/eurotruth/09.htm.

---

mind that most agency activities that affect the legal environment of business have evolved out of what are considered failures of businesses to perform in ways that are fully satisfactory. The EPA was created when it became apparent that businesses were not going to voluntarily limit the amount of pollution they emitted to reasonable amounts. The SEC was created in the aftermath of the Stock Market Crash of 1929, when it was widely perceived that fraud pervaded securities markets. It can be claimed that far less administrative regulation of business activities would be required if businesses acted more ethically.

ETHICS IN BUSINESS

Just for show or authentic? There are several ways of thinking about the role of ethics in business. One way is to cynically view all actions of businesses that are aimed at creating goodwill from their positive reputation for ethical action as nothing more than marketing ploys and attempts to ward off increased government regulation. Another view of company actions that appear to set new standards for ethical conduct concludes that, perhaps, exposure to ethics in business management programs plus the threat of adverse publicity have created increased sensitivity to the value of ethical actions in business managers.

Certainly, if you ask the typical business manager about profits and the role of ethics, most would say that they are *not* in the business of maximizing profits and that, as business leaders, they have responsibilities to customers, employees, and their community that occasionally mean that they have to sacrifice some profits in order to respond to these other responsibilities.

Ethics is a subject that, for hundreds of years, has attracted some of the world's best minds including John Rawls, Immanuel Kant, John Stuart Mill, and many others. It is our observation that most business managers do not rely on formal ethical theories or structures (such as the Kantian *categorical imperative*) in their management activities. Instead, it is more accurate to say that most business leaders are in business to make money, but that they also have a desire to be honest and ethical. In any form of commerce—bricks and mortar or bricks and clicks—there certainly are limitless decisions that managers must make that have ethical components and for which managers need an ethical compass.

Kantian Ethics: The Categorical Imperative

categorical imperative
Immanuel Kant insisted that any proposed ethical rule be (1) universalizable and (2) reversible in the sense that it applies equally to the person proposing the rule. Widespread adherence would dramatically reduce the need for administrative agencies.

While a claim of relevance in modern business management for Immanuel Kant, an eighteenth-century German scholar and philosopher, may seem to be a stretch for many, he is widely viewed as having developed a criterion for examining actions of businesspeople (and others) that continues to provide an effective framework for ethical management decision making. According to Kant, ethical people should be guided by what he labeled the **categorical imperative,** as referenced above. As is the case with essays from most philosophers, Kant's work is full of big words for relatively simple concepts. Kant believed that ethical conduct involved behavior that was *universalizable* and *reversible.* If an actor could say, "what I am doing could be done by others and the world would not be a worse place," then the action passes the first part of the Kantian ethical test. If the actor can answer "no" to the query "If someone in my position did to me what I doing to others, would I object?" then the behavior passes the second part of the categorical imperative test for ethical behavior.

Application of Kant to the Modern Business Environment

If *one* company pollutes, the world will not be a much worse place to live, but, certainly, if all businesses were to pollute without restraint, the world would be unlivable. Thus, an individual firm's decision not to control its pollution output fails the Kantian ethical test. According to Kant, people should never be used as means to an end, but should always be the end in themselves. So, it would be unethical, according to Kantian ethics, to test the safety of drugs on residents of Third World countries. Quite simply, such testing is "using" people and could not be justified using Kant as a guide for business ethics.

Importance and Attractiveness of Kantian Ethics

The ethical principles elucidated by Immanuel Kant remain attractive in the United States because of their emphasis on individual rights and the avoidance of "using" people. Americans have always resisted fixed class lines, so codes of conduct that are universalizable appeal to the populism that pervades the American ethos. Most Americans react negatively to rules that do not apply to all in society. Not surprisingly, many modern-day ethicists continue to draw heavily on the work of Kant.

Utilitarianism

The business ethical system most competitive with the Kantian system is often called *utilitarianism,* which in essence justifies actions that produce the greatest good for the greatest number of people. A problem with utilitarianism is that it can be used to justify all kinds of sacrifices of individuals that may in the long run benefit society as a whole. Thus, utilitarians can ethically justify testing AIDS drugs by giving some AIDS victims experimental treatments while giving others placeboes, knowing full well that those receiving the placeboes will most likely die at much higher rates than those receiving the new drugs.[3] Without conducting double-blind tests (both those administering and those taking the treatments do not know which treatment is being received), there is really no way of measuring the effectiveness of new and promising drugs.

Utilitarianism is a rationale for economists' use of cost–benefit analysis, which is the most common method of evaluating the economic effectiveness of government programs. Announcements of changes in the gross domestic product (GDP) in some sense measure changes in the average economic well-being in society, which is close to what utilitarians focus on—namely, the greatest good for the greatest number of people. Quarterly changes in GDP, however, do not measure the number of those living in poverty and despair or the distribution of wealth and income. It is quite possible for GDP to grow while the number of Americans living in poverty also increases. If overall economic growth occurs at the expense of those lowest on the economic totem pole, it is certainly conceivable, from a Kantian perspective, that there would be numerous claims that society is worse off.

There is a right and wrong, in most cases. In general, the prescriptions of both Kantian ethics and utilitarianism are not in opposition. Consider fraud, which occurs when one person uses another by lying to the other person in order to increase his or her own wealth at the expense of the other person. Fraud is clearly unethical under the Kantian system because it violates the categorical imperative. Fraud is also unethical under utilitarianism because, if fraud is prevalent in the economic system, as it is in many less developed countries, overall economic growth will be less. Contracting parties will have to devote significantly more resources to checking out the veracity of claims made by their contracting partners. As a useful exercise in the application of ethical decision making, try to imagine other business situations, in such areas as hiring, advertising, and product design, in which ethics are important, and try to determine whether various courses of action are ethical if a person subscribes to Kant or adheres to utilitarianism.

Determining Reasonable Standards of Ethical Behavior for Businesses

It would be helpful for business managers to have guidelines for ethical business conduct that are easy to keep in mind and practical. To that end, it is appropriate to keep in mind that ethics and law are certainly not the same thing, though the two are intertwined for reasons that should be clear by now. In general, it is unethical to engage in business conduct that violates the law, especially if the legal transgressions allow the violating company to make more profits. Merely complying with the law, however, is likely to be a necessary but not sufficient condition for being an "ethical company." Most people would define ethical business behavior as lawful behavior that advances the *greater good of society,* even if company profits are not increased or, in fact, are decreased by the behavior.[4] So, an ethical company might choose to purchase paper from firms that sell recycled paper, even if such paper costs more and is less effective for some uses. Purchasing recycled paper arguably reduces demand for trees and, thus, preserves the environment. Of course, when businesses do rely exclusively on recycled paper, they make that fact known.

---

[3] A placebo is a "fake" pill. It is a pill that has no medical benefits.

[4] "Greater good of society" is consistent with the utilitarian goal of the greatest good for the greatest number of people.

Societal Greater Good

What advances the greater good in society is, of course, not always obvious, but there are a number of goals, sensitive to business decisions, with which virtually all in U.S. society agree. These include

- *Protection of the environment.* Virtually everyone agrees that the earth's ecology is fragile and that human actions, especially in production and consumption, can adversely affect the natural environment.

- *Antifraud measures.* Most people, including businesses managers, think that fraud is a negative and that measures to reduce fraud or deceptive business practices are a benefit. In general, fraud is unethical, even in instances when it is not illegal. In business, if one firm can get away with fraud, others also will be encouraged to engage in like actions. An unavoidable result is lost business productivity as sizeable amounts of resources must be devoted to fraud and antifraud measures.

- *Tolerance.* People do not choose their color, race, gender, and, some would add, sexual orientation. In addition, there are choices that most people make about religion, hobbies, and political parties that are largely personal and do not significantly affect others. Most consider it unethical for a business to discriminate about things that do not affect the business. Of course, many of the characteristics listed above are protected by law from explicit discrimination. Beyond that, many would argue that ethical companies should reach out and encourage diversity.

- *Provision of a social safety net.* There are always people who fall through the cracks of the economic platform that provides for society's needs. Rules are established by businesses to provide for pensions, health care, and other benefits. Occasionally, there are hardship cases in which some individuals, perhaps for technical reasons, do not qualify for benefits. It can be argued that ethical companies may bend the rules to make sure that employee hardship is not compounded by a loss of benefits. Similar choice situations may crop up in connection with plant locations, sales of products that are discovered to be harmful, and political issues.

- *Customer interests.* There are many ethical challenges that must be dealt with when businesses make decisions affecting customers. Is it ethical for a business to sell products that it knows are being misused in ways that can harm customers? As an example, suppose market research indicated that your firm could increase its sales of model airplanes if it increased the amount of glue sold with each unit. It is well known that some users of these products sniff glue to get high.

  Ethics also come into play when companies are deciding how to invest their resources. There are legal as well as ethical reasons for firms to test their products for long-term side effects even though, in the short term, such research is costly.

- *Shareholder interests.* The Enron scandal reminds us that shareholders are people, many of whom are also employees. It has been said that the short-term focus of many managers on their companies' stock prices has driven them to act in ways that may harm the long-term interests of the company, its employees, and shareholders. In the extreme, in the Enron case, financial records were falsified to sustain elevated stock prices when, in reality, the company was on the verge of collapse. All the while, top executives were selling their holdings of Enron stock. Clearly fraud is unethical, but it is sometimes not clear when being optimistic about a company's future crosses the line into blatant misrepresentation of the company's true future prospects.

- *Community interests.* Companies occupy physical space and are members of geographical communities whether they want to be or not. Often, a local community depends on companies for employment and, to a lesser extent, for support in broader, even charitable forms. Some labor groups have tried to insinuate that a company that relocates production from the United States to often much-lower-cost, foreign locations is unethical.

In the Alternative, Government Regulation

It can be argued with great conviction that a company that causes significant pollution is acting unethically. This certainly would be the case under the Kantian categorical imperative that calls for universality and reversibility. Clearly, if all companies polluted, the result would be untenable and unsustainable. Companies that pollute could be exhorted to voluntarily clean up their acts and not pollute, but such a program is not likely to be successful because the companies that continued to pollute would make considerably more profits than those that did not.

The Forces of Economics Cannot Be Ignored

free rider
An economic agent (e.g., a company) that benefits from the socially desirable actions of others while not being a participant in those actions and, hence, avoiding the accompanying costs.

In economics, a **free rider** is a party that can derive benefits without paying for the associated costs. If a community that periodically suffered from floods built a dam based on voluntary contributions, those who did not contribute would still benefit from construction of the dam, weakening the motivation to contribute. The same problem plagues voluntary efforts to clean up the environment; free riders benefit from pollution abatement efforts of other firms without incurring the significant costs associated with installing pollution control technology themselves. When the free rider problem is present, government regulation is often the result. Since government regulation, such as the Environmental Protection Agency, is funded by taxes, everyone must contribute.

This same phenomenon is important where property rights are not well established, such as is the case in ocean fishing. In the aggregate, it makes sense for all fishermen to join together and restrain fish hauls so that certain parts of the ocean, or the entire ocean, will not be overfished. However, an individual fisherman can reasonably believe that (s)he is much better off trying to catch all the fish possible, while others conserve.

From these examples and others that could be added, one principle on the interface between ethics and government regulation is apparent:

> When the *free rider* problem is severe, and there are significantly larger profits to be made by disregarding social costs borne by society in terms of more pollution, depletion of fish stocks, etc., appeals to ethics are not likely to be successful and government regulation is likely.

The free rider problem *is severe* when there are thousands of actors (e.g., polluters) and the effect of one actor (polluter) on the environment is inconsequential. In other situations, the effect of the actions of a single individual is more evident and appeals to ethics are likely to be more effective. Churches are created by relatively small communities of individuals joining together and voluntarily contributing to the construction of a church. Once the church is built, it is not common that noncontributors are barred from attending and benefiting from the services that churchgoers receive. Public radio is largely funded by contributions from listeners, even though noncontributors can tune in and benefit from broadcasts.

Antifraud and Pro-Customer Measures

Since business fraud is potentially contagious and is injurious to business productivity, effective industrywide antifraud mechanisms are in the collective interest of businesses (as well as customers). It appears that, for a wide range of industries, a number of alternative fraud prevention systems are possible, ranging from industry self-regulation to government regulation. Often, effective protection is provided by a hybrid of government regulation and self-regulation.

Self-Regulation by Individual Firms

There are numerous mechanisms used both by individual firms and by industries to assure customers of honest dealings. Department stores have found that a no-questions-asked policy on most returns is good business. Many companies establish customer complaint departments and make extensive use of surveys to investigate and monitor customer satisfaction. Employees found guilty of cheating customers, or even of rude behavior, are subject to reprimand or discharge. Economic studies have concluded that adverse publicity is very effective at scaring away repeat customers. Companies that deliver actual performance that diverges markedly from what they advertise will forfeit the benefits of that advertising as word of mouth undermines company claims.

Certification and Collective Trademarks

Various associations and industry groups have recognized the collective harm associated with lack of customer confidence and have developed innovative ways of combating both perceptions of fraud and fraud itself. The Better Business Bureau (BBB) has operated for years signaling customers that a company is or is not a member. Members of the BBB have a reputation for honesty and, when a customer threatens to report the company to the BBB, that threat carries weight with most companies.

certification and collective marks
Trademarks licensed by third-party certifiers of quality such as Underwriters Laboratories or marks that members of associations license to members to display.

A naturally skeptical consuming public may pay limited attention to company claims that their products enjoy high levels of quality. Recognizing this problem, many companies make use of third-party **certification marks.** One of the most recognized certifications is the UL® mark, indicating that the products so marked conform to safety standards established by *Underwriters' Laboratories,* a well-regarded product-testing institution. Similar roles are played by the *Good Housekeeping Seal of Approval* and by TRUSTe, which certifies that a website conforms to certain privacy standards.

The use of **collective marks** generally signifies that a company is a member of an association that is known for "high standards." Companies displaying a collective mark can assert that their group is known for certain standards and that, as a member of the group, they live up to those standards. Presumably, if the group determines an individual company does not live up to those standards, that company can be ejected from the group, losing the right to display the collective mark. The Chamber of Commerce has a well-regarded collective mark that is used by members. Certification and collective marks can be registered with the Patent and Trademark Office in Washington, D.C.

Licensure and Self-Regulation of Professionals

For many professions such as law, accounting, medicine, real estate, and securities trading, state law requires a license to practice. Issuance of the license, however, is controlled by each of the individual groups of professionals themselves. Obtaining a license to practice in the profession generally requires passing a test to show required levels of competency, but retention of the license is contingent upon good behavior. Complaints to the state bar association that an attorney is cheating clients is followed with an investigation by representatives of the bar association. Stock brokers (and dealers and advisors) are required to be registered with the Securities and Exchange Commission in order to practice their profession and can lose their right to practice if they violate antifraud rules. Medical doctors who repeatedly make mistakes (a surgeon who removes the wrong limb from an amputation patient would be a candidate) are apt to lose their licenses to practice medicine.

Direct Government Regulation: Full Disclosure

Fraud and related illegal activities are combated in many industries by full disclosure requirements imposed by government. If a firm does not comply with governmental *full disclosure* requirements, it is presumed that fraud has taken place, in which case customers,

Ethical Challenges   Conflicts of Interest and Full Disclosure: Enron, Arthur Andersen, and the SEC

In 1934 Congress passed an enabling statute that created the Securities and Exchange Commission (SEC) and it was given responsibility for regulating the stock market. A cornerstone of stock market regulation under the SEC has been full disclosure, the idea being that if companies fully disclose their financial worth, investors can make rational choices in investing. Since there is a conflict of interest when a company is asked to value itself, the SEC has required large companies, such as Enron, to pay for audited annual reports by accounting firms such as Arthur Andersen, a firm that employs many certified public accountants (CPAs).

Of course, accounting firms such as Arthur Andersen do more than simply value firms. Andersen derives much of its income by offering advice (consulting) to client firms, including the firms that they audit. Accountants who have examined many firms are able to spot potential firm vulnerabilities in terms of excessive inventory, inadequate liquid reserves, and so on. To many, the collapse of Enron was most devastating because it was so unexpected. Enron's collapse was unexpected because its latest annual report, prepared by Arthur Andersen, gave no indication that the company was on the edge of bankruptcy. The regulatory system developed and maintained by SEC broke down because investors were not accurately informed as to the true financial condition of Enron. Some have suggested that Andersen did not accurately report Enron's financial condition because it did not want to jeopardize its consulting income from Enron, which was in the millions.

The SEC was well aware of the potential conflict created by allowing accounting firms to prepare annual reports. In 1997 the SEC considered, but ultimately rejected, a regulation that would have prevented accounting firms that received substantial consulting income from client-firms from also performing audits for those firms that are used as annual reports. Although preventing accounting firms from performing a dual function of accepting consulting fees and performing audits seems reasonable, the practical effect of preventing this conflict of interest is that small and medium-sized firms would have to hire two accounting firms whereas previously they only had to hire one if they wanted advice from accountants. It is clear, however, that Andersen did not do its duty to the public to fairly report the financial condition of Enron. Fallout from the Enron bankruptcy and scandal has caused a much-needed reevaluation of some of the generally accepted accounting standards (GAAS). In addition, the SEC is under intense pressure to provide some hard and fast rules that will produce more accurate annual reports so that investors, stockholders, and others can "look at the books" and make rational investment decisions.

A likely outcome of the Enron debacle is that there will be increased reliance on government regulations and decreased reliance on the ethical standards adhered to by most accountants. Is this a good outcome? Should more government regulation be the outcome of each financial scandal? Under existing rules, how many companies accurately report their financial condition year after year because most accountants can be relied upon to adhere to ethical codes required of CPAs?

as well as the government, can file a claim. In the consumer loan industry, lenders are required to disclose to borrowers standardized measures of the cost of obtaining money including interest rates charged (the *annual percentage rate of interest*) computed uniformly along with all other fees to be charged for granting a loan. The SEC requires issuers of new securities for sale to the public to provide a prospectus that fully discloses all material facts that would be of concern to a reasonably prudent investor considering purchasing those securities.

Direct Government Regulation: Seek and Destroy

In some industries, administrative agencies have staffs assigned to the task of seeking out and prosecuting fraud. Both the SEC and the FTC have field investigators whose tasks are, in turn, the uncovering of securities fraud and the identification of unfair and deceptive trade practices. Unfortunately, the existence of teams of investigators in the SEC, the FTC, and other agencies reflects a determination that the problems of fraud, deception and so forth are so prevalent that active investigations are necessary to effectively counter abuses.

Areas in Which Self-Regulation Has Been Ruled Out

Based on past experiences, there now are broad areas of business activity in which self-regulation has been replaced by government regulation. Among such areas of business are

- *Worker safety*—Regulated federally by the Occupational Safety and Health Agency (OSHA), with additional state-level agencies also involved.
- *Protection of the environment*—Regulated (federally) by the Environmental Protection Agency, with additional state-level agencies also involved.
- *Antidiscrimination protection*—Equal Employment Opportunity Commission.

This list easily could be extended with other, less-broad categories. In each of the listed areas, there was a widespread perception that free market outcomes were unsatisfactory and that government regulation was appropriate. Of course, a factory owner in the late nineteenth century could have cleaned up his factory, paid for injuries incurred by workers on the job, avoided discrimination based on race or gender, and treated its waste before dumping it into the ground or groundwater. However, a factory owner unilaterally instituting such "ethical" standards for conducting business would have had difficulty competing with other factory owners who did not incur the added expenses for worker and environmental protection. The free rider phenomenon prevents ethical behavior from surfacing.

Third World Ethical Challenges

The hard-fought victories for worker safety and improved workplace conditions U.S. labor has won are vulnerable to being competed away by workers in Third World countries. Of course, Third World workers do not initiate this competition, but simply respond to offers of work from multinational corporations that seek to improve profit margins by cutting labor costs. Some regard the decision of a U.S. company to locate production facilities abroad (instead of in the "domestic" United States) as unethical. The presumption is often that the "ethical" decision would be to hire domestic workers rather than going abroad. Serious "ethicists," however, hold that this view implicitly accepts a normative judgment that U.S. companies should value the interests of U.S. workers (humans) above those of foreign workers (humans). Wary of the public view on this issue, when a U.S. firm decides to locate production within the United States, that choice usually is well advertised, while a decision to open a plant in Mexico may not be advertised.

When in Rome, Do as the United States Does

For firms that decide to use cheap foreign labor—Nike is a notable example—the conventional "ethical" opinion is that the U.S. firm has an obligation to change the standard terms of trade in foreign labor markets. Even though a U.S. firm is attracted to the foreign location because of cheaper labor, the "ethical" thing to do (according to this reasoning) is to make foreign labor more expensive by unilaterally adopting worker safety measures that are higher than called for under the laws of the foreign country. Also "ethicists" often suggest that paying the low wages prevalent in the foreign country for workers of higher-than-average skill (for that country) is also immoral. In like fashion, these ethicists contend that U.S. companies should not take advantage of lax environmental standards but, instead, should unilaterally apply standards similar to the ones that are prevalent in the United States.

It should be noted that what is "ethical" with regard to the use of foreign labor is not at all clear. U.S. companies that produce products in a process that requires repetitive, unskilled labor have a tough time competing with foreign manufacturers, especially in textiles. Both Kathy Lee Gifford and Nike have been targets of pro-labor groups in the United States for their reliance on foreign labor in countries that have minimum wages that are less than 50 cents per hour. Less well-known manufacturers routinely rely on foreign labor for textile products with less notoriety. The alternative for Kathy Lee and Nike is to raise prices (imposing the costs of their "more ethical behavior" on consumers, who are mostly U.S. citizens) or to accept lower profits (which may result in bankruptcy and involves having the costs of its choices imposed on stockholders, who are mostly U.S. citizens).

Product Liability Issues

In many high-profile product liability cases, it has been revealed that manufacturers have engaged in cost–benefit analysis, weighing the incremental harm of a particular product design against the cost of alternative (generally "improved") designs. In some cases, manufacturers have concluded that switching to safer designs is not cost justified because the savings in lives and injuries do not outweigh the costs of a safer design. Are manufacturers always "ethically" required to pick the safest design for a product, regardless of cost? If the cost of a safer design prices the product out of its market, is a company still required to disregard cost when designing a product?

In Case 6-3, warnings on the product package were very explicit and, yet, were disregarded by the plaintiff, who suffered horrible injuries. Are manufacturers required to make products so safe that no one, not even the least competent and most reckless user, gets injured using the product? If a large corporation puts a product into the stream of commerce, is it always obligated to pay for injuries associated with use of its product(s), regardless of the fault of the user/victim? When confronted with a choice between a horribly injured or deceased victim and a large corporation, how often do you think juries find in favor of the corporation? Should the courts take some choices away from juries?

Case 6-3

Alison Nowak, et al. v. Faberge USA Inc., t/d/b/a/ Aqua Net

United States Court of Appeals for the Third Circuit
32 F.3d 755 (3rd Cir. 1994)

BACKGROUND AND FACTS

Faberge manufactures Aqua Net hairspray worldwide in both aerosol and nonaerosol pump spray containers. Aqua Net contains a mixture of butane or propane, as the aerosol propellant, and alcohol, as a solvent for the propellant and the hair-holding agent. Alcohol is flammable and both propane and butane are extremely flammable. Aerosol cans of Aqua Net carry a warning on the back stating, among other things, "Do not puncture" and "Do not use near fire or flame."

On April 3, 1989, Alison Nowak, a 14-year-old girl, tried to spray her hair with a newly purchased aerosol can of Aqua Net. The spray valve would not work properly. Alison decided to cut open the can with a can opener. She thought she could then pour the contents into an empty pump bottle of Aqua Net that had a working spray mechanism. Alison was standing in the kitchen near a gas stove when she punctured the can. A cloud of hair spray gushed from the can and the stove's pilot light ignited the spray into a ball of flame. Alison suffered severe, permanently disfiguring burns over 20 percent of her body. The district court (the trial court) made an implicit determination that the product was defective in its warning and sent the case to a jury, which returned a verdict for the plaintiff, Allison Nowak.

Opinion by Roth

Under Pennsylvania strict liability law, a defect may be in the warnings given for the use of the product as well as in the design of that product. A product can be held to be defective "if it is distributed without sufficient warnings to notify the ultimate user of the dangers inherent in the product." [References deleted] In *Mackowick* [a previous product liability case], the Pennsylvania Supreme Court reaffirmed *Azzarello* [another product liability case], explicitly holding that the determination that a product is defective because of inadequate warnings is initially a question of law to be answered by the trial judge.

Our review of the record in this case demonstrates that the trial judge did not make an *explicit* determination, prior to sending the case to the jury, that Faberge's product was defective, either as to the spray mechanism or as to the warnings on the can. The Nowaks argue that the judge *implicitly* made the necessary threshold legal finding in three ways: by sending the case to the jury, by denying Faberge's motion for a directed verdict, and by ruling against one of Faberge's motions in limine that challenged the Nowaks' ability to present evidence on the inadequacy of the warning. The Nowaks also argue that Faberge failed to request a specific ruling by the judge that its product was defective. Based on our reading of Pennsylvania law and our review of the record, these arguments are valid.

* * *

For the reasons stated above, however, we find that the district court implicitly made the threshold risk-utility determination that appellant's product was defective under the facts, as alleged, by sending this case to the jury. We conclude that this is a sufficient determination under Pennsylvania law. We will, therefore, affirm the verdict and judgment of the district court.

Decision and Outcome

The U.S. Court of Appeals for the Third Circuit held that there was enough evidence to send this case to a jury on the issue of whether the warning was adequate, even though there were warnings against puncturing and using near fires or open flames.

Questions for Analysis

1. We can conclude from the nature of the injuries that Allison Nowak, the plaintiff, was probably horribly disfigured as a result of this accident. Since Faberge is a large company, is the "ethical" verdict the one that was reached by the court—that Allison should recover? After all, Faberge undoubtedly has the money to pay for her medical bills and for pain and suffering, now and in the future. So, in fairness, isn't it clear that, ethically, Faberge should have to pay? What about individual responsibility? Don't we all pay higher prices if we compensate victims who are irresponsible?

2. The Aqua Net product has two warnings on it: Do not puncture and do not use near fire or flame. The plaintiff did both of the prohibited acts in this case. If these warnings are inadequate, as they apparently were judged to be by the district court, what warning would have been adequate?

Internet Ethics

A poll taken in 2000 revealed that 25 percent of Americans believed that they could become physically ill from computer viruses. Their awareness of other side effects of cruising on the Internet is even less informed. Most computer users do not know what a cookie is or how they are used. Cookies have many uses, but one of the most important is to record the clickstream history of website visitors between visits. This information can used by a website to plan marketing campaigns or can be sold to third parties for the same or other purposes.

Is the Information Being Gathered Voluntarily Provided?

There are virtually no legal prohibitions against voluntary exchanges of information on the Internet unless one of the parties to an exchange is under age 13. For those unaware of the

Cyberlaw Developments

Adverse Publicity and Lawsuits Force DoubleClick to Back Down on Its Plan to Link Clicksteam Data to Personal Information

STATEMENT FROM KEVIN O'CONNOR, CEO OF DOUBLECLICK

NEW YORK—(BUSINESS WIRE)—March 2, 2000—The following is a statement from Kevin O'Connor, CEO of Doubleclick:

"Over the past few weeks, DoubleClick has been at the center of the Internet privacy controversy. During this time, we have met and listened to hundreds of consumers, privacy advocates, customers, government officials and industry leaders about these issues. The overwhelming point of contention has been under what circumstances names can be associated with anonymous user activity across Web sites."

"It is clear from these discussions that I made a mistake by planning to merge names with anonymous user activity across Web sites in the absence of government and industry privacy standards."

"Let me be clear: DoubleClick has not implemented this plan, and has never associated names, or any other personally identifiable information, with anonymous user activity across Web sites."

"We commit today, that until there is agreement between government and industry on privacy standards, we will not link personally identifiable information to anonymous user activity across Web sites."

Source: Center for Democracy & Technology, Press Release, March 2, 2000, *available at* http://www.cdt.org/privacy/000302doubleclick.shtml.

It is clear from the statement that claims of unethical behavior by privacy groups can have an impact. Further, this episode suggests that more government regulation dealing with privacy in cyberspace is on the horizon.

power of cookies, those who visit websites that do not spell out their privacy policies, or those who visit websites that don't adhere to their stated privacy policies, cookies accomplish an involuntary extraction of information. At present, most websites can only link clickstreams with browsers and e-mail addresses, but all that could change quickly. There are plans to link information gathered from cookies with credit card information and with information obtained from grocery VIP cards that are swiped at cash registers. With the envisioned combination of data sources, it is possible that, within a short period of time, cookie information will be linked with personal identifying information including names, addresses, phone numbers, credit histories, purchase histories, and so forth.

At this point, it remains possible that website owners and Internet service providers will get together and agree on a code of conduct for the use of cookies, for privacy policies, and for other matters affecting the involuntary extractions of information. As a possible candidate for self-regulation of privacy policies in cyberspace, consider the P3P movement described in the "Cyberlaw Developments" box on page 185. In spite of this movement, remember that there are reasons to believe that self-regulation by websites and other cyberspace entities will not be effective so that, eventually, comprehensive government regulation will be imposed. If commercial websites and ISPs are not able to gain general acceptance for a code of conduct that respects the privacy of Internet users, more government regulation of websites seems inevitable. Cyberspace is providing another test of the viability of ethical self-regulation.

The P3P movement describes itself below. Essentially, it is a way of telling your browser your privacy preferences and having that browser communicate with websites it is directed to visit by the user. When a browser encounters a website that doesn't conform with the user's privacy preferences, because, for example, the website sells information gathered about users or customers to third parties, the user is alerted and can decide to stop browsing that website. User preferences are gleaned from a survey that the user completes and the results of that survey are then matched with privacy policies of websites visited through the user's browser. In order to be effective, mass participation of users is required. Whether users will complete privacy surveys and understand what they are being asked to answer is open to question. Again, the results of the 2000 survey that revealed that one-fourth of computer users believed that they could get physically sick from a computer virus strongly indicate that many users are woefully uninformed about basic computer issues.

PLATFORM FOR PRIVACY PREFERENCES (P3P) PROJECT

What Is P3P?

The Platform for Privacy Preferences Project (P3P), developed by the World Wide Web Consortium, is emerging as an industry standard providing a simple, automated way for users to gain more control over the use of personal information on Web sites they visit. At its most basic level, P3P is a standardized set of multiple-choice questions, covering all the major aspects of a Web site's privacy policies. Taken together, they present a clear snapshot of how a site handles personal information about its users. P3P-enabled Web sites make this information available in a standard, machine-readable format. P3P enabled browsers can "read" this snapshot automatically and compare it to the consumer's own set of privacy preferences. P3P enhances user control by putting privacy policies where users can find them, in a form users can understand, and, most importantly, enables users to act on what they see.

Source: www.w3.org/p3p.

Concluding Thoughts

It's clear that the single-minded pursuit of business financial success is often at odds with ethical ideals. Were business managers more universally determined to place ethical conduct first and profitability second, there would be far less need for government intervention (and the accompanying accumulation of administrative law). However, economic forces are powerful and free rider problems are widespread. So, it seems, we have little alternative but to accept the presence of a wide array of administrative agencies that involve themselves in virtually all facets of business activity. As a consequence, business managers need to be as conversant in the legal requirements they face as they are in other management skills.

There likely will remain areas of business activity where self-regulation can be very effective, especially for licensed professionals. It also may be possible for businesses themselves to play a larger role in self-regulating against fraud, as it is in the interests of both industries and the individual firms that populate industries to avoid fraud. With evolutionary changes in the availability of information, adverse publicity for "bad" business behavior also may become a more effective deterrent to unethical conduct. Even conceding these kinds of conduct-policing prospects, since the laws of economics cannot be repealed and profit incentives are powerful, there will remain broad areas of business activity that will require regulatory control. Regulations generally make a socially undesirable activity (like polluting) illegal or subject to suit. This radically changes the profitability of that activity, altering the economic incentives firms face.

Summary

Interplay between Government Regulation and Ethics: If Businesses Are More Ethical, They may Face Less Government Regulation

- Most of the legal environment of business originates from and is enforced by *administrative agencies,* especially those headquartered in Washington, D.C.
- In combination, the *Commerce Clause* and the *Necessary and Proper Clause* in the U.S. Constitution have enabled Congress to create numerous administrative agencies that can regulate virtually everything that affects interstate commerce.
- Compared with government regulation, adherence to industry ethical codes is often viewed more favorably by businesses. Business is often partially regulated by government and does part of the job itself (i.e., *self-regulates*).
- Ethical conduct on the Internet is increasingly becoming an important issue. Threats of government regulation have sent websites scrambling to devise *self-regulation* plans.
- Most government regulation can be traced to a perception that outcomes from unregulated markets are unsatisfactory.

Creation Structure and Powers of Administrative Agencies.

- Congress has passed many statutes that affect business, but it also has created government agencies by passing *enabling statutes* through which Congress delegates to a created agency the power to issue regulations and enforce laws within its authority.
- The combined volume of regulations originating from administrative agencies far exceeds that from any other source of law in the United States.
- When enacting new *substantive* regulations, administrative agencies must comply with the Administrative Procedures Act (APA). Proposed regulations appear in the *Federal Register* and enacted regulations become part of the Code of Federal Regulations.
- When administrative agencies enact *interpretative* or *procedural* regulations, they do not have to comply with APA due process requirements.
- Many administrative agencies are headed by political appointees who serve at the pleasure of the president or the governor of the state. For *independent agencies,* the chief executive can only appoint or reappoint (new) heads or commissioners when their terms of office expire unless there is evidence of malfeasance in office, such as taking bribes.
- Administrative agencies perform many functions including investigations. Often agencies require the businesses they regulate to provide self-reported data.
- Agencies are entitled to issue subpoenas for relevant information to any "person," including businesses outside their scope of authority.
- The people who staff administrative agencies have wide discretion to decide many matters that can have substantial effects on the profits of businesses. In general, it is a good management practice to cooperate with governmental officials.

Adjudication before Administrative Law Judges

- If an agency and a business cannot agree, the agency has the power to begin adjudication against the company before an *administrative law judge (ALJ).*
- Decisions of administrative law judges can be appealed by either the agency or the business. Ultimately, final decisions of administrative agencies are subject to review in federal courts.
- Agencies frequently have a choice in how to enforce an enabling statute. They either can legally pursue individual firms and create a trail of precedents or can issue a regulation that establishes a general rule.

Judicial Review, Standards of Judicial Review, and Standing to Sue

- Judges, generally at the court of appeals level and higher, can and do review regulations issued by and enforcement actions taken by administrative agencies.
- Federal judges can reverse the actions of a federal agency if the actions are deemed arbitrary and capricious, judged to exceed the agency's authority under the enabling statute, or deemed to violate the constitutional rights of a citizen or business.
- To challenge an administrative agency action, a plaintiff must have *standing* to sue, meaning that he or she must have a real, current interest at stake. Also, plaintiffs in federal court to challenge an

action of an administrative agency must have exhausted all internal remedies and the challenge must be *ripe,* in the sense that it is not a challenge of a hypothetical event.

Statutory Reforms and Congressional Oversight Designed to Prevent Administrative Agency Abuses	• In an effort to curb abuses, Congress passed the *Freedom of Information Act,* which allows citizens to request information stored by administrative agencies. Agencies must produce this information at the citizen's expense unless the information is classified because of various security or privacy issues. • *Sunshine Acts* at the federal and state level require agencies to announce the agendas for meetings and to indicate whether the meetings are open to the public. There are, however, numerous bases for excluding the public from meetings where official government business is taking place. • Congress does have the power of the purse strings to rein in a federal agency that strays from what Congress believes is the agency's mission. Congress also can change the enabling statute that defines the powers of any agency. • *Sunset legislation* causes an agency to cease its existence at a prescribed time unless Congress or a state legislature decides to reauthorize the agency. • The *Federal Privacy Act of 1974* protects against unauthorized secondary use of personal information stored by federal agencies unless consent is provided or unless the information falls into one of numerous exception categories. • Congress can require administrative agencies to perform *cost–benefit analyses* or *risk–benefit analyses* to justify new regulations. These economic tests of regulation likely prevent very bad regulations from getting enacted.
Ethics Is Important in Business Today. Ethical Action Is Reinforced by the Prospect of Government Regulation and Adverse Publicity; Still, Basic Economics Cannot Be Ignored	• Ethics in business is partly motivated by defense, forestalling more severe government regulation, and is partly motivated by a sincere desire to make the world a better place to live. Most business managers reject the notion that their sole functions are to maximize profits or shareholder wealth. • Immanuel Kant devised a system of ethics in business that is universalizable and reversible. Many of the goals for a better society, such as a healthier environment, tolerance, absence of fraud, and maintenance of a safety net for the disadvantaged, are not sources of a great deal of controversy. • Utilitarianism is an ethical philosophy that supports actions that produce the greatest good for the greatest number of people. • For companies that appear to behave unethically, the consequence of adverse publicity can be very severe. Some companies have gone out of business as a result of adverse publicity. • Ethics in business is often seen as an alternative to government regulation, which is more public and less flexible than various forms of self-regulation. • The forces of economics cannot be ignored. When *free riders* can make significantly more money than those that adhere to ethical business practices, it is time to consider government regulation. Also, businesses will act more ethically if they get favorable publicity as a result.
Ethics Play a Prominent Role in Self-Regulation That Can Take the Form of Codes of Conduct, Association Rules and Other Devices, and Enlightened Decisions; Cyberspace Creates New Ethical Challenges	• Attempts to reduce the incidence of fraud in business can take the form of self-regulation, industry–government partnerships, and active government investigations of industry fraud. • Antifraud measures self-applied by industry often are implemented through associations that have codes of behavior, collective trademarks, and other devices that contribute to antifraud protections. • In government regulation, compliance costs averaged over all output are often significantly less for larger firms. • Many ethical challenges arise when a firm must make a decision on whether to locate production domestically or in a foreign country. In many instances, ethical experts recommend that businesses try to improve labor markets for Third World workers. • Cyberspace is a commercial frontier where business ethics are challenged in new ways. Probably the biggest challenge involves involuntary extractions of information.

Key Terms

administrative agencies, *156*
administrative law, *162*
administrative law judge
  (ALJ), *166*
Administrative Procedures
  Act, *160*
arbitrary and capricious, *168*
categorical imperative, *175*
certification and collective
  marks, *179*
Code of Federal
  Regulations, *159*
cost–benefit analysis, *173*

enabling statute, *158*
ethics, *157*
exceeded its authority, *168*
Federal Privacy Act, *172*
Federal Register, 158
free rider, *178*
Freedom of Information
  Act (FOIA), *171*
Government in Sunshine
  Acts, *172*
government regulation, *157*
independent administrative
  agencies, *163*

interpretative regulation, *160*
judicial review, *168*
necessary and proper
  clause, *157*
procedural regulation, *162*
ripeness, *169*
sanction, *166*
self-regulation, *157*
subpoena power, *164*
substantive regulation, *160*
sunset legislation, *173*

Questions for Review and Analysis

1. State the three or four steps that must be completed in the creation of a federal administrative agency.

2. What steps must an administrative agency go through in order to create a new, substantive regulation?

3. When a party appeals a decision of an administrative agency to a federal court, under what circumstances is the appealing party likely to be successful?

4. Discuss the legislation and actions taken by Congress to curb abuse by federal agencies.

5. What are some advantages and disadvantages of regulating conduct of members of a professional through codes of ethics as opposed to having an administrative agency regulate the profession?

If You Really Understood This Chapter, You Should Be Able to Provide Informed Commentary on the Following:

1. **Powers That Can Be Delegated to Administrative Agencies.** Are there limits on the powers that Congress can delegate to an administrative agency such as the Environmental Protection Agency? The Clean Air Act requires the EPA to promulgate and periodically revise national ambient air quality standards (NAAQS) for each air pollutant identified by the agency as meeting certain statutory criteria. For each pollutant, EPA sets a primary standard at a concentration level "requisite to protect the public health" with an "adequate margin of safety" and a "secondary standard" at a level "requisite to protect the public welfare." Are the foregoing terms adequately specific or does such as statute as the Clean Air Act unconstitutionally delegate power to the EPA because of the vagueness of terms such as public health and adequate margin of safety? [*American Trucking Associations, Inc., et al. v. Environmental Protection Agency,* 175 F.3d 1027 (DC Cir. 1999).]

2. **Challenging Actions of Agencies Because They Are Arbitrary and Capricious.** It has long been held that nonaction by an administrative agency is not grounds for a suit by interested parties. For example, if there were a series of on-the-job accidents and the Occupational Safety and Health Administration (OSHA) did not act, OSHA would not be compelled to justify not enacting new, tougher worker safety regulations. On the other hand, when an agency does act, it generally must have a scientific basis for its actions. Otherwise, it is vulnerable to the charge that its actions were arbitrary and capricious and, thus, challengeable by interested parties that have standing to sue. What about when an agency proposes a regulation, a new administration is elected, and the agency, which has new leadership, proposes to rescind its proposal? Does an agency need to have a technical foundation for rescinding a regulation it proposed earlier? [*Motor Vehicle Manufacturers Association v. State Farm Mutual Automobile Insurance Co.,* 463 U.S. 29 (1983).]

3. **Court Deference Accorded to Administrative Agencies in Interpretations of the Statute They Administer.** The National Labor Relations Act allows all covered employees to organize and form unions but exempts agricultural laborers. What is the meaning of "agricultural laborer"? Suppose the employees in question performed "live-haul" operations. This would involve chicken catchers, forklift operators, and truck drivers working in an agricultural setting. Suppose that the National

Labor Relations Board, which initially decides whether employees are covered by the National Labor Relations Act (NLRA), decides that employees engaged in "live-haul" operations are covered employees under the NLRA and thus entitled to hold union elections. Are the courts required to accord deference to an administrative agency's interpretation of the statute that creates the agency and thus defines its scope of authority? [*Holly Farms Corporation v. National Labor Relations Board,* 517 U.S. 392 (1996).]

4. **Scope of Authority of Administrative Agencies.** Most pension plans invest contributions collected by a company and its employees in the securities market, chiefly in stocks and bonds. Although most pension plans are honestly operated, there was a good deal of evidence that the Teamsters pension plan was not, at least during the 1950s and 1960s. The Securities and Exchange Commission (SEC) was charged by Congress in 1934 with regulating securities markets and punishing fraud. Since the Teamsters pension plan was apparently riddled with fraud and most of its assets were held as securities, it would seem a natural fit for the SEC to exercise authority over securities fraud. When members of the Teamsters Union filed a class action suit alleging fraud in administration of their pension plan, the SEC filed an amicus brief supporting the plaintiffs' claims that, not only was there common law fraud, but the Teamsters' operation of the pension plan also amounted to violations of the Securities Exchange Act of 1934. This interpretation of the Securities Act could have dramatically expanded the authority of the SEC because it would recognize SEC authority to intervene in cases involving alleged mismanagement of pension plans, which are a huge source of funds for securities markets. How do you think this case was decided? [*International Brotherhood of Teamsters, Chauffeurs, Warehousemen & Helpers of America v. United States,* 439 U.S. 551 (1978).]

5. **Warrantless Searches by Administrative Agencies.** As noted in the chapter, businesses are entitled to the protection of the Fourth Amendment when representatives of administrative agencies visit and want to inspect their work site(s). There are, however, numerous exceptions to this rule, especially if the business is in an industry that has historically been subject to close supervision and if enforcement of the enabling statute is difficult without warrantless searches. Also, if the administrative agency has a plan for its searches, courts are more sympathetic than if the searches appear to be based on arbitrary whims of officials at agencies. Suppose Congress short-circuits the process by declaring in the enabling statute that federal officials enforcing the statute have the power to search without a search warrant. In 1978, a federal mine inspector attempted to inspect the premises of a stone quarry operator under authority granted by 103(a) of the Federal Mine Safety and Health Act of 1977 (30 U.S.C.S.§ 813(a)), which provides that federal mine inspectors are to inspect all mines at set intervals to ensure compliance with health and safety standards and to make follow-up inspections to determine whether previously discovered violations have been corrected, and which also authorizes mine inspectors to inspect any coal or other mine without having first obtained a warrant. In this case the mine operator was previously cited for a violation of the Federal Mine Safety and Health Act and the purpose of the inspection was to make sure that the violation has been remedied. [*Donovon v. Dewey,* 452 U.S. 594 (1981).]

Social Responsibility and Ethics in a High-Tech World

6. **Art, Decency, and Government Agencies.** Art, decency, and government are not often found together in the same sentence and, yet, there has been a lot of litigation about these three words during the last 10 years. Of course, artists have traditionally placed high values on unrestrained freedom of expression even when this freedom shocks or offends large segments of the population. Some would add that artists go out of their way to shock and offend. Indeed, artists themselves often make the statement that they intend their work to be "provocative." Understandably, what upsets some people the most is situations in which the government funds art that shocks and offends. This was the case with Andres Serrano's work *Piss Christ,* which featured a crucifix in a urinal. In 1989 Serrano was awarded $15,000 by the Southeast Center for Contemporary Art, an organization that received support from the National Endowment for the Arts (NEA), an agency of the federal government. Following the revelation of public funding for *Piss Christ* and other provocative works of "art," Congress amended the National Foundation on the Arts and Humanities Act that vests the NEA with authority to fund works of art.[5] The amendment requires

the chairperson of the NEA to take into consideration "general standards of decency and respect for diverse beliefs and values of the American public." Under the First Amendment, can agencies of the federal government take into account standards of decency and respect for religious beliefs or is this government censorship of content prohibited by the First Amendment? Notice that the plaintiff in the case cited below is Karen Finley, a "performance" artist whose livelihood would most certainly be affected by a requirement that the NEA take "decency" into account in awarding its grants to artists. [*National Endowment for the Arts v. Karen Finley,* 524 U.S. 569 (1998).]

Using the Internet to Your Advantage

1. There is a wealth of websites that enable a person to quickly access government. In fact, virtually every government agency, bureau, program, and any other entity has a website. A website to start with is First Government at http://www.firstgov.gov/, which has a large number of useful hyperlinks. For example, by clicking Laws and Regulations, you can access an electronic Code of Federal Regulations (CFR): http://www.access.gpo.gov/ecfr/. The CFR has all the substantive regulations enacted by federal administrative agencies. Another click takes you to PACER (Public Access to Court Electronic Records), discussed in the previous chapter: http://pacer.psc.uscourts.gov/.

2. There are also private nonprofit guides to the U.S. Government. The Uncle Sam website at http://www.uncle-sam.com/home.html#siteguide provides access to all independent agencies such as the Federal Trade Commission, the Securities and Exchange Commission (http://www.uncle-sam.com/executivedepts.html), and so on, as well as to executive departments such as cabinet offices (http://www.uncle-sam.com/executivedepts.html).

3. The National Archives and Records Administration provides access to the *Federal Register,* where proposed and enacted regulations of administrative agencies are available to the public (http://www.archives.gov/federal_register/index.html). Many of the bureaus, commissions, and cabinet offices are increasingly relying on what is described as e-rulemaking and the results of this work are available at http://www.archives.gov/federal_register/public_participation/rulemaking_sites.html.

4. At a certain point, redundancy becomes apparent. Many of the sites listed above also can be accessed at the website of the U.S. Government Printing Office (GPO): http://www.gpo.gov/. The Louisiana State University Library offers a complete list of government agencies, government boards and committees, and a great deal of other useful information about government: http://www.lib.lsu.edu/gov/fedgov.html. According to this website there are 114 independent government agencies, 858 executive bureaus, and 73 government boards and commissions. The Directory at LSU is a partnership with the Federal Depository Library Program.

[5] Also funded in 1989 was the homoerotic art of Robert Maplethorpe.

Part Two

The Common Law and Interfaces with the Internet

Chapter Seven

Basic Contract Law

Learning Objectives

On completing this chapter, you should:

1. Know the results of agreeing to be bound in a contract.
2. Be conversant in the language of contract law.
3. Know the building blocks of contracts: offer, acceptance, consideration, capacity, and legality.
4. Be aware of the major forms of taints on contractual agreements, including fraud, duress, and mistake, that can make a contract voidable.
5. Know the types of contracts that must be in writing to be enforceable.
6. Be able to discuss how contractual obligations are discharged.
7. Be able to competently discuss damages in the event of a contractual breach.

OVERVIEW

Importance of Contract Law

contract
An agreement that can be enforced by law. Not all agreements are contracts.

Among branches of law, **contract** law is uniquely linked with business. It is because of the demands of business that law in this area evolved and continues to evolve to facilitate, rather than impede, commercial practices of business. Business is an inherently risky endeavor and people in business generally seek to avoid or reduce risk when possible. Contracts are instrumental in reducing risk and also serve to increase business efficiency.

Adam Smith pointed out in the *Wealth of Nations,* published in 1776, that as the size of a market expands, increased specialization takes place, permitting production efficiency gains. In order to meet expanding market demands, one-person operations gave way to combinations of workers, capital, and the other basic factors of production. Within a business, the services of all factor inputs—land, labor, and capital—are linked by contracts. Indeed, freedom to contract was and is regarded as a foundation for our capitalist economic system.

Preview of Coming Chapters: Regulatory Constraints on Freedom to Contract

Although contracts generally have beneficial effects for business, there are situations in which *agreements* cannot serve as legally enforceable contracts. In fact, a good deal of the regulatory law that is broadly approved by most Americans, including labor, environmental, securities, and equal opportunity employment laws, imposes limitations on freedom to voluntarily enter into contracts. For example, contracts that condition employment on an employee's refusal to become a member of a union, often called "yellow dog" contracts, were outlawed by the Norris LaGuardia Act in 1933. Another example is provided by securities law, which regulates exchanges of stocks and bonds and requires that purchasers be given accurate information before a business owner can "contract" for the sale of shares of ownership in his business. The focus of later chapters in this textbook is on various regulatory constraints on freedom of contract.

In this chapter, however, we focus on contracts themselves, and not on regulatory limitations on freedom to contract. We discuss, among other topics, how a contract is created, its legal consequences, and court remedies for breach of contract.

WHAT IS A CONTRACT?

A contract is an agreement that creates legally enforceable obligations to perform. The *Restatement of Contracts* defines a contract as a "promise or set of promises for the breach of which the law gives a remedy, or the performance of which the law in some way recognizes as a duty."[1] In ordinary English, if you enter into a contract, but then do not perform, the other party to the contract can take you to court for some kind of remedy, usually in the form of money damages, which are theoretically set equal to the court estimation of your damages.

Valid contracts require that

1. There is an *agreement,* which normally includes an *offer* and *acceptance* of that offer.
2. There is *consideration,* that is, each side to the contract agrees to do something such as perform services or pay money that they were not previously obligated to do.
3. *Both parties to the contract have capacity to contract,* that is, both parties are over 18 and know what they are doing.
4. *Performance under the contract is legal,* so that each party to the contract can perform under the terms of the contract without violating a law or public policy.

Distinguishing between Agreements and Contracts

Clearly, contracts must meet strict requirements. It is not surprising, then, that there can be many *agreements* that are not *contracts*. An agreement that is not a contract cannot entitle an aggrieved party (who has not breached the agreement) to go to court for redress. As an illustration, a promise to make a gift is not enforceable in court because the promise is not supported by *consideration* (discussed below). As recognized above, some agreements are illegal by government regulation or statute. In addition, some are void because they are contrary to public policy. A public official could agree to change her mind on an issue in return for a bribe offered by an interested party. If the public official rendered a desired "favorable" ruling, the "contract" calling for a bribe payment would not be enforceable, even though both parties agreed to the contract.

---

[1] The *Restatements* are just that—restatements of what top scholars in a particular branch of law think the law is, based on court precedents. The *Restatements* are the product of the American Law Institute, which is composed of learned lawyers and judges. There are many *Restatements* of various branches of law including contracts and torts. Although the *Restatements* do not have the force of law like state statutes do, they are very influential with judges, who rely heavily on common law precedents, particularly in areas of law such as contracts.

The Common Law of Contracts and the Uniform Commercial Code

This chapter focuses a good bit of attention on the *common law of contracts*. Since each state has its own common law tradition, each state has its own common law of contracts. Contracts are intended to reduce uncertainty by enabling business managers to plan, invest, and conduct business based on agreements they have with others. When the basic law of contracts varies from state to state, it adds to uncertainty. As the geographic scope of businesses in the United States increased through our history, there was growing dissatisfaction with a "common law" of contracts that varied from state to state. In the next chapter (Chapter 8), we examine the Uniform Commercial Code (UCC), which was developed because of dissatisfaction with the common law of contracts. The UCC has been adopted by all 50 states. The impact of the UCC has been to *regularize* (make uniform) the legal treatment of contracts in all 50 states for the sale of tangible physical goods and other transactions governed by the UCC. For most contracts, such as employment, rental, and service agreements, the common law of contracts in each of the 50 states continues to supply the substantive law.

THE TERMINOLOGY OF CONTRACT LAW

Issues in contract law are easier to discuss and understand when proper terminology ("legalese") is used. Once a contract issue is properly classified, the rules of law that apply to that classification are relatively straightforward and understandable. So, readers are encouraged to (1) try to classify any particular contract issue in terms as narrow as possible and (2) begin thinking in and using the language of contract law. Using the "legalese" associated with contract law will enhance issue recognition and, hence, the capacity for avoidance and resolution of contract problems.

Valid, Void, Voidable, and Unenforceable

Valid   A *valid* contract is a contract that is enforceable. A valid contract has the characteristics discussed above, which include the option to go to court to seek redress if the other party to the contract does not perform.

Voidable   A *voidable* contract is a contract that can be voided by one of the contracting parties. A contract is voidable if there is a victim whose participation in the contract was induced by an unfair means. If a person was induced to sign a contract based on **fraudulent misrepresentation,** then the defrauded party can refuse to perform and avoid damages for breach of contract. In fact, the defrauded party can sue the fraudulent party to *rescind* the contract and get back any money or other consideration (things of value) exchanged. Other considerations that entitle a victim to get out of a contract without liability include the formation of contracts with minors, formation of contracts that are the result of force or threat of force, and contracts with other defects that are discussed later in the chapter. It should be noted that, even if a party to a contract is a victim of fraud, that party may choose to honor the contract entered, so a voidable contract has the potential of being a valid contract.

fraudulent misrepresentation
A misrepresentation of material facts, knowingly provided with the intent of deceiving another and in a form that a reasonable person could rely on to his or her detriment.

Void   A *void* contract is a contract that courts will refuse to consider because the contract violates a statute or regulation or conflicts with public policy. Gambling contracts, contracts between unlicensed professionals and clients, and contracts that call for performance that would undermine a goal of public policy are examples of void contracts. A difference between void and voidable contracts is that a voidable contract is enforceable at the option of the victim, whereas a void contract is not enforceable at all. It is notable that courts generally will not allow a party to a void contract to recover money or other consideration that may have been lost while participating in the void contract.

Unenforceable   If a contract is *unenforceable,* either party to the contract can decide not to go through with the contract. Although not all contracts have to be in writing to be enforceable, there are certain contracts that courts do require to be in writing. Contracts for purchases and sales of real estate are prominent examples. Either the buyer or the seller in an "oral" real estate agreement can decide not to perform without liability because contracts for the sale of real estate must be in writing to be enforceable. As compared to a voidable contract, if a contract is unenforceable, there is no "victim" who has the option to decide whether to go ahead with the contract or bail out. Either party to an unenforceable contract can decide not to perform.

Bilateral and Unilateral

bilateral contract
A contract formed when a promise is given in exchange for a promise.

Most contracts are *bilateral* in the sense that a promise is *exchanged* for a promise. In a typical service contract, a seller promises to perform certain tasks, such as repairing a faulty electrical system, by a certain date and the employer (buyer of the services) promises to pay for the services in the way called for in the contract. When two promises are exchanged, both parties are *promisors* with respect to the promises they make and *promisees* as to the promises made by the other party. In a breach of contract suit, one promisee sues for the failure of the other party to live up to the promise(s) made in creating the contract. The core requirement of a **bilateral contract** is that both parties are legally bound to adhere to their promises.

unilateral contract
A contract formed when one promisor offers terms that can be accepted only by an offeree's performance.

There are some contracts that are properly termed *unilateral* because there is only one promisor. Reward contracts are typical of **unilateral contracts.** If Jeff posts a reward *offer* indicating that he will pay $50 for the return of his dog, Fifi, the only way to *accept* that offer is to perform by finding and returning Fifi. Promisees in such a unilateral reward contract are not bound to the promisor, and even if they say they are going to look for the dog, no enforceable performance can be expected. Unilateral contracts are different from bilateral contracts in that the party making the promise (the promisor) is bound if the other party performs what is called for in the promise, but not vice versa. As we will see shortly, unilateral contracts often are a poor way of doing business, in part because a promisor can withdraw his promise (or offer) at any time before performance has been completed, leaving the promisee without a remedy even if performance is partially completed.

Executory and Executed

executory contract
A contract that calls for future performance, not yet completed.

In contract law, a promise of performance to be completed in the future is an *executory* promise. A promise that has already been performed is a promise that has been *executed*. Thus, the two terms, *executory* and *executed,* refer to timing issues as related to promises. In a typical sales contract, at the conception of the contract (which can take place when the parties sign), both parties are promising to perform certain actions in the future. At the beginning of a contract, the contract created is classified as an *executory bilateral* contract in which each party is liable to the other for failure to perform as called for in the contract. Executory bilateral contracts are the norm in business transactions. When the duties called for in an **executory contract** have been fully performed, the contract is an **executed contract.**

executed contract
A contract under which the duties called for from the contracting parties have been fully performed.

Express and Implied

express contract
A contract based on an explicit agreement, written or oral, between contracting parties.

An **express contract** contains an explicit agreement between parties that there is a contract. An employment contract is an express contract because the wage or salary agreed upon is explicitly in return for work to be performed by the employee. A bid made at an auction creates an explicit contract if the auctioneer hammers down the gavel indicating that the bid has been accepted. Express contracts should not be confused with written contracts. Thousands of contracts are made everyday on stock exchanges for the purchase and sale of stock, which represents ownership in corporations, and virtually all of these contracts are express, but not written.

Some contracts are *implied,* based on conduct. A contract is implied because the conduct of the parties indicates consent to be bound in a contract. If Jane feels ill and goes to see a doctor, after treatment she is likely to pass by a worker who will inquire about how Jane wants to pay for the services rendered. In this setting, the conduct of both parties created an **implied contract.** When Jane checks in with the doctor, it is implied that she will pay for medical services rendered. Such implied contracts arise from routine situations that occur millions of times each day in the United States, generally without controversy. Now, if Jane were told that the doctor's services were of extraordinary value and she owed him $10,000 for just one visit, Jane would not be legally obligated to pay a sum approaching that amount. Jane's visit to the doctor implied a willingness to contract, but only under *reasonable* terms.

implied contract
A contract formed in part or in whole based on the conduct of the parties.

Quasi-Contract

Even in the absence of a valid explicit agreement between parties, one party may, nevertheless, be able to recover from another party based on a claim of *unjust enrichment* (sometimes called *quantum meruit*). Unjust enrichment provides a basis for a damage award given to someone who has been economically injured as a result of a **quasi-contract** with another. Technically a quasi-contract exists when

quasi-contract
An assumed contract, imposed by courts in the interest of fairness, generally to prevent the unjust enrichment of one party at the expense of another.

1. The plaintiff conveys benefits to the defendant,
2. In the expectation of receiving compensation,
3. The defendant knowingly receives the benefits, and
4. The transfer results in *unjust enrichment* for the defendant if the defendant has failed to pay reasonable compensation for the benefits received.

The key factor in this conceptualization of damages is the *knowing receipt* of benefits by the defendant. If a neighbor boy comes to your house with a lawn mower, you raise your hand to greet him, and he starts cutting your backyard, you may not have formally executed a (valid) contract with the boy. Yet, he would be entitled to collect for the fair market value of the services rendered based on quasi-contract. On the other hand, if you took a vacation and, upon your return, discovered that your lawn had been cut during your absence by the same neighborhood boy, he would not be entitled to recovery because you did not knowingly receive the benefits.

Knowledge Transfers between Firms

It is important for business students to recognize that, in the near future, they could be on either side of a quasi-contract dispute. Quite frequently, small firms develop ideas that have substantial market value but lack the resources to commercialize their creations. Large and medium-sized firms are often on the lookout for partnerships with small firms who develop innovative technology or other "ideas" but need commercial development support from the more established firm(s). Of course, the small firm generally is properly reluctant to reveal its idea or new technology without some guarantee of payment, while the large firm does not want to get sued if it develops a product in the same general area but does not use the idea of the smaller firm.

With this situation having become quite common, large firms (typically) have developed contract forms that incorporate language that calls for payments to the small firm if

Ethical Challenges   Ethical Challenges Associated with Knowledge Transfers I

Consider the following tall tale, carefully constructed to avoid a direct representation of any actual company.

A leading global household product manufacturer enjoys the dominant market share of sales of toothpaste that fights plaque, helping to prevent tooth decay. A small local startup bioengineering company develops a toothpaste ingredient that its tests show is significantly more effective (than the leading brand's active ingredient) at eliminating plaque and preventing decay. While the local firm lacks the capacity to produce and market toothpaste on a broad-based national scale, it is able to provide limited production, which it sells through health product chains. In a matter of a few months, it displaces the global brand as the top seller in these outlets, getting the attention of the global "competitor."

The large company approaches the startup and, after a period of discussion and negotiation, offers to acquire exclusive rights to the startup firm's formulation (IP), predicting a great future for the partnering arrangement with a predicted volume of sales and earnings that the smaller firm could never enjoy without a global scope partner. The deal (contract) is consummated with a limited up-front payment (say, $1.5 million) and a schedule of future royalty payments to begin in the near term, based on the volume of actual future toothpaste sales that incorporate the startup's technology.

The rest of this tale doesn't necessarily go as the startup hoped. In a few months, it becomes evident that the large company has continued to maintain its dominant market share selling its old formulation toothpaste, with no sales of the new formulation on the horizon. When the small company complains, it is told that additional studies have shown the new formulation not to be effective, after all, and that additional research will be needed before it can be put to work. In the interim, of course, the global company will have to continue marketing its successful product and the small company will have lost even the sales it had enjoyed in health product stores!

While not in the market described in our tall tale, the authors of this text have, on more than one occasion, been involved in litigation that exactly parallels the situation described. Clearly, the construction of agreements between IP creators and their partners needs to be carefully planned and constructed to avoid this outcome.

MARKET ALTERNATIVES FOR PRESENTING IDEAS

Potentially large profits are available to both contracting parties with a productive transfer of knowledge between firms. Not surprisingly, in light of both the commercial desirability of such transfers and the difficulties of identifying suitable partner firms, firms that specialize in combining idea people and technology with more established firms that could make use of such ideas have appeared in sizeable numbers in recent years. Knowledge Express (http://www.knowledgeexpress.com/) represents itself as a company that provides knowledge transfer services including searching "licensable technologies from corporate, government and university sources." A search of the World Wide Web using "knowledge transfer" as a search term will reveal a number of competing firms.

its idea is used (generally if the idea is patentable), but requires the small firm to waive its right to sue if the idea is not patentable or if the idea is not used. Small firms generally are able to require that the large firm sign a nondisclosure agreement (NDA), which means that, even if the large firm does not use the idea, it will not disclose the idea to others. When meetings, information exchanges, and contract terms are not carefully planned and constructed, the results can be messy, costly, and often unproductive quasi-contract suits.

Consider whether Case 7-1 illustrates some of the issues brought up in the Ethical Challenges box. If you are tying to keep score, Kennametal is a quite large, high-tech company.

Case 7-1

Permanence Corporation, Plaintiff-Appellant[2] v. Kennametal, Inc., Defendant-Appellee

United States Court of Appeals for the Sixth Circuit 908 F.2d 98 (6th Cir. 1990)

BACKGROUND AND FACTS

Permanence was formed by its president and majority shareholder Charles S. Baum in 1969 for the purpose of developing and exploiting certain processes developed by Baum. In the 1970s Permanence conducted research and manufactured products in the tungsten carbide field. On May 24, 1977, Permanence obtained U.S. Patent No. 4,024,902 (hereinafter Patent 902) for a process to form an alloy by incorporating tungsten carbide into a steel matrix. The patent was entitled "metal sintered tungsten carbide composites and method of forming the same."

On February 8, 1979, Permanence executed a written agreement with defendant Kennametal, a publicly traded corporation specializing in the manufacture of tools, tooling systems, and supplies for the metal working industry.

In the contract between the parties, Permanence granted Kennametal the nonexclusive right to the licensed patents (existing Patent 902 and patents that would issue from applications owned by Permanence) for a period of 24 months subject to the nonexclusive license previously granted to Masco Corp. for Patent 902. For the nonexclusive license, Kennametal agreed to pay Permanence a consideration of a $150,000 fee and a royalty rate of 2 3/4 percent on the net sales price of products made by Kennametal using processes that fell under valid claims of the licensed patents. Advance royalties of $100,000 were to be paid upon the signing of the agreement for the nonexclusive license.

The agreement also provided that Kennametal would have the option to obtain the exclusive license to the patents. On February 5, 1981, Kennametal exercised its option and paid an additional $250,000 for the grant of the exclusive agency—$150,000 for the exercise of the option and a second $100,000 in advance royalties.

Seven years later on April 18, 1988, Permanence filed a one-count complaint alleging that Kennametal had breached the contract by not fulfilling an obligation to use best efforts to exploit the patents. As there was no express "best efforts" provision in the contract, plaintiff argued that the grant of an exclusive agency imposes on the licensee (Kennametal) an implied duty to use best efforts to exploit. On February 1, 1989, Kennametal moved for summary judgment, arguing that it had spent $500,000 for the use of the patented technology of Permanence and that a best efforts obligation had specifically been negotiated out of the agreement.

Opinion Contie, Senior Circuit Judge

The sole issue before this court on appeal is whether the district court erred in its order granting summary judgment that as a matter of law an implied best efforts obligation did not arise in the contract between the parties.

* * *

Plaintiff concedes that there was no best efforts obligation to exploit the non-exclusive license initially granted to Kennametal for a $150,000 fee and $100,000 in advance royalties. Yet royalties (2 3/4 %) were also to be paid on products manufactured under the non-exclusive license. Moreover, the royalty rate for both the exclusive license and the non-exclusive license after 24 months was contingent on whether the products manufactured by Kennametal under the patents were ones which

---

[2] The appellant is the party (or parties) appealing the verdict of the lower court. The appellee is the party that is contesting the appeal. Sometimes both parties appeal the decision of the trial court; the defendant may appeal an adverse decision on the issue of liability, while the plaintiff may appeal the amount of damages awarded by the trial court.

directly competed with products sold by Masco that had been produced under the non-exclusive license previously granted to it. The fact that the relationship with Masco subsequently proved to be unproductive and did not generate royalties for Permanence does not justify imposing an implied covenant to exploit on Kennametal.

The key provisions of the contract between Permanence and Kennametal which militate against implying a covenant to use best efforts are Kennametal's obligation to pay $150,000 in order to exercise the option for the exclusive license and the $100,000 in additional advance royalties paid under the exclusive license. Courts have held that by imposing a substantial minimum or advance royalty payment, the licensor, in lieu of obtaining an express agreement to use best efforts, has protected himself against the possibility that the licensee will do nothing. Rather than leaving the licensor at the mercy of the licensee, the demand for a substantial up-front or advance royalty payment creates an incentive for the licensee to exploit the invention or patent. In the present case, Permanence received a substantial total advance payment of $250,000 for its right to the exclusive license and, unlike the licensor in the majority of cases where a duty to exploit has been implied, did not depend for its consideration solely on Kennametal's sale of products developed under the patents.

* * *

Decision and Outcome

The court affirmed the decision of the trial court to grant a motion for a summary judgment, thus dismissing the case that Permanence filed against Kennametal.

Questions for Analysis

1. According to the court in this case, under what circumstances would the licensee, the defendant, Kennametal have an obligation to use "best efforts" to sell the patent that was licensed to it by the plaintiff, Permanence?

2. Does the plaintiff have any recourse in this case? Can the plaintiff go to another potential licensee? Why not?

3. Is this a case in which the inventor's creation will stay on the shelf unless the established company, Kennametal, decides it wants to exploit the patent more fully?

CONTRACT FORMATION

There are five elements to contract formation: *offer, acceptance, consideration, capacity of the parties to the contract,* and *legality.* Unless all of these five elements are present, an "agreement" is not a valid contract. Each of these elements, in turn, has subelements. This requires us to focus narrowly on possible flaws to the validity of a contract. What is discussed next is the theory of contract formation under the common law, taking account of the required elements of contract formation. In practice, courts are focusing increasingly on the *conduct* of the parties to a contract and on commercial practices within the relevant industry.

Offer

The contracting process begins with an *offer,* which is made by the *offeror.* When the offeror makes an offer, (s)he creates an opportunity for the offeree (the person to whom the offer is made) to form a contract by agreeing to the offer with an acceptance. Under the common law of contracts, an offer has three elements. An offer must embody *intent,* it must provide *certainty and definiteness of terms,* and it must be *communicated* to the offeree.

Intent

Intent to make an offer is judged by an *objective* standard. It is immaterial whether, subjectively, the offeror really intended to make an offer or not. Under the law, intent is judged from the perspective of a hypothetical "reasonable person." The criterion courts use, and

INTERNET ADVERTISEMENTS ARE ALSO OFFERS

One impact of the Internet is that the line between advertisements and legal offers has been blurred if not obliterated. On the Internet, thousands of websites advertise their products, but they also make offers that are legally binding if a customer clicks the "yes" button, signifying assent to the offer. As discussed below, the traditional view of most advertisements is that they are invitations to bargain, not legally binding offers. On the Internet, however, advertisements are also offers capable of creating a binding contract if a customer assents to the offer/advertisement. Unlike ads in newspapers or TV commercials, Internet customers have the power to create a contract at the time they see a website advertisement of goods or services available.

what they ask juries to consider, is "What would a reasonable person (reasonable offeree) have thought under the circumstances?" If a reasonable person would have thought that the offeror *intended* to make an offer, then the intent element is satisfied. By using the reasonable person standard, courts can consider the circumstances under which the offer was made. If the offeror was in his office during regular business hours, meeting with a possible business partner, it is more likely that an offer has been made than if the offeror was at a bar with a drink in hand, even though many contracts have been formed in bars.

Advertisements That Are Not Offers and Those That Are It is important to distinguish between *intent to make an offer* and an *invitation to bargain*. Most advertisements are interpreted by courts as invitations to bargain unless the advertisement is very specific (which many are). Merely stating in a catalog or an advertisement in a newspaper that a particular brand of clothing is available for sale at 20 percent off the normal price is considered a solicitation of offers. When customers arrive and offer to buy clothes at a discounted price, the store can accept or refuse the offer. The more specific the offer, however, the more likely it is that courts will interpret an advertisement as an offer. Show a particular piece of business equipment with a particular price in an ad, and the advertisement will be considered to be an offer.

Prior Conduct between the Parties In many contract dispute cases, courts infer intent from prior conduct or from what is common in the industry involved. If Jim is in the habit of hiring Jerry to accompany him to auctions to buy livestock and has regularly paid Jerry $500 per trip, an offer takes place if Jim tells Jerry to "get suited up; we are going to Kansas City for an auction." Under the circumstances, it is reasonable for Jerry to believe that Jim has made an offer to employ him for the auction in Kansas City.

Alternatively, consider the following statement by Bill, "I am considering selling my house. Would you think that $150,000 is an excessive price?" Such a statement would be considered an invitation to bargain, rather than an offer in which Bill was inviting an acceptance. In order for Bill to be deemed to have the requisite intent, there has to be a showing that the offeror was doing more than just speculating aloud.

Certainty and Definiteness of Terms

At common law, an offer to contract has to contain the essential terms of the contract so that the contract offer is reasonably *certain*. At a minimum, the offer has to contain the *identities of the parties* to the contract, the *subject matter* of the contract, the *price,* and the *quantity.* In most contracts, the offer actually has to contain more than these four elements. If a material term in a contract offer is missing, then the offer is *incomplete.* Under such circumstances, a response by the offeree that fills in the missing material terms would transform the original offeror into the offeree and the original offeree into the offeror. In analyzing contract formation, it is common for the parties to change hats from offeror to offeree.

In Case 7-2, as you'll see, plaintiffs and defendants have far different perceptions of whether a contract existed. Think about any defects in contract formation that come to mind as you read this case.

Case 7-2

Ben Hunt Jr. and Jeanne B. Hunt, Husband and Wife; George W. Brown and Coweta Jean Brown, Husband and Wife v. McIlroy Bank and Trust

Court of Appeals of Arkansas
Ark. App. 87, 616 S.W.2d 759 (1981)

BACKGROUND AND FACTS

McIlroy Bank and Trust filed a foreclosure suit against the Hunts and Browns (the defendants), alleging that appellants (the defendants) were in default on six separate promissory notes due and payable to the appellee (McIlroy Bank and Trust). The appellants are Ben Hunt, Jeanne Hunt, George Brown, and Coweta Brown, all of whom were doing business at S.B.H. Farms. Appellants filed a general denial, alleged a number of affirmative defenses, and counterclaimed against appellee for $750,000, contending appellants were damaged as a result of certain misrepresentations and a breach of an oral contract by the appellee to loan appellants monies. The trial court found that appellants failed to produce evidence of fraud or misrepresentation, nor was there proof of an oral agreement or contract requiring appellee to loan monies to appellants. The court dismissed appellants' counterclaim and entered judgment in favor of appellee on its complaint.

Opinion by Glaze

In reviewing the record before us, we keep foremost in mind two legal principles when deciding whether a valid contract was entered into by appellants and appellee in October, 1976: (1) A court cannot make a contract for the parties but can only construe and enforce the contract which they have made; and if there is no meeting of the minds, there is no contract, and (2) It is well settled that in order to make a contract there must be a meeting of the minds as to *all* terms.

* * *

After a study of the evidence presented at trial, we have no hesitancy in agreeing with the chancellor that the appellants failed to prove a contract existed between themselves and the appellee. Appellee's officer, Larkin, and appellant Ben Hunt initially discussed the financing of the expansion of the S.B.H. Farm operation, but the total amount of loan proceeds was never decided. Hunt said that at one time Larkin told him he could have up to $750,000. Larkin testified that the appellee was willing to loan in excess of $500,000, and it could have been $700,000. Both Larkin and Hunt agreed that no interest rate or repayment terms were ever agreed upon. There apparently was some discussion that long term permanent financing would be necessary, but the terms of such financing were left to future determination. Meanwhile, short term notes were signed by appellants for loan proceeds so the farm expansion could commence. Although Larkin and Hunt may have generally agreed on a course of action as to the need for financing the farm project, they never agreed on the essential, much less all of, the terms of a contract to loan monies. There is no way that a court could take the general terms discussed between Larkin and Hunt regarding an open-ended loan with no repayment provisions and be asked to enforce an agreement without filling in necessary terms essential to the formation of a contract. The subject matter of the proposed agreement was indefinite and the mutual assent and obligations were so vague as to be unenforceable.

* * *

In accordance with the foregoing, we affirm the trial court's findings and decision.
Affirmed.

Decision and Outcome

The Court of Appeals ruled that the trial court did not make a mistake by dismissing the defendants' claims that they had a contract with McIlroy Bank and Trust because the negotiations between the parties were not sufficiently certain to constitute a contract.

Questions for Analysis

1. The court in this case indicated that there was not a contract because the essential terms of the loan contract were not agreed upon. To what specific terms is the court referring?

2. In addition to lacking a meeting of the minds on the essential terms of the contract, the "agreement" was oral. Does this case suggest that the maxim "Get it in writing" is apt for this case? Exactly what would have to be in writing for the court's conclusion to have been reversed?

Communication

A direct offer by party A to sell to B does not mean that yet another party I can "accept" the offer. A party cannot accept an offer unless the offer has been *directed toward* him or her. Of course, offers do not have to be personal to particular offerees, as an offeror can make offers to a class of offerees, such as potential customers. Nevertheless, if the offeree is unaware of the offer at the time the offeree renders performance (e.g., a party using tag information to return a lost pet to its owner, while not knowing of a reward offer), the offeree is not entitled to whatever compensation was promised in the offer (i.e., in the reward offered for the pet's return).

Acceptance

Under the common law of contracts, an *acceptance* possesses three elements: (1) the offeree must possess *intent* to be bound by the offer, (2) the acceptance must be *complete and unqualified,* and (3) the acceptance must be *communicated* to the offeror.

Intent

Intent on the part of an offeree is evaluated by the same standard that is applied to an offeror. The question that is asked is, "What would a reasonable offeror think under the circumstances?" If the words or actions of the offeree would lead a reasonable offeror to believe that the offeree intended to accept the offer, then the intent element of the acceptance is satisfied. Again the "reasonable person" standard enables juries to consider all the surrounding facts in determining whether the offeror was justified in believing that the offeree intended to accept the offer provided.

Complete and Unqualified

Under the common law of contracts, an acceptance must be *complete* and *unqualified.* The complete and unqualified requirement often has been referred to as the *mirror image rule.* At common law, the offeree must agree to accept *each and every term* in the offer without qualifications. If the offeree does not accept each term in the offer, it is considered a *rejection* of the offer. If the offeree adds additional terms to the offer in his or her acceptance, it is considered a *counteroffer* and, thus, also a rejection of the original offer. When an offeree makes a counteroffer, the offeree immediately becomes the offeror with respect to the counteroffer and the offeror becomes the offeree with all roles of the parties reversed.

Communicated to the Offeror

In order to complete an acceptance, an offeree must communicate acceptance to the offeror. Of course, an acceptance can be mistransmitted. As a result, on occasion there is litigation related to the communication requirement. Under the common law of contracts, risk of loss due to mistransmission is borne by the offeror if the offeree uses the *authorized* means of communication, which is

1. The same means of transmission used to make the offer (if the offer does not authorize a specific means of acceptance) or
2. The means of transmission authorized in the offer.

If an offer is made to the general public through a magazine, but the offer requires acceptance by first-class mail, then a faxed acceptance sent instead would not bind the offeror, as the offeree did not use the *authorized* means of acceptance.

Termination of an Offer

A live offer is akin to a loaded gun; it may be activated or triggered by events beyond control of the offeror and, thus, it is a significant legal issue to determine when an offer expires or is terminated. Traditionally, there are two types of events that terminate offers: actions of the parties and operation of law.

Actions of the Parties

Under common law, an offeror can *revoke* an offer at any time, even if the offeror states in the original offer that it will remain open for a longer specified time span. There are, of course, exceptions to this rule, but, in general, an offeror can withdraw an offer at any time. If the offeror revokes an offer, the revocation is effective when it is received by the offeree(s), which brings the mailbox rule back into play if the parties rely exclusively on surface mail. If an offeror attempts to revoke an offer, but an offeree has already dispatched an acceptance, a contract is formed if the dispatch of the acceptance occurs before the communication of the revocation to the offeree.

Exceptions: Irrevocable Offers

There are a few narrow exceptions to the rule that an offer can be revoked at any time. When an offeree relies *to his detriment* on an offer made by an offeror, then the doctrine of **promissory estoppel** makes the offer irrevocable.

Promissory estoppel is applicable when

promissory estoppel
This is the doctrine that assures that a promise (offer) will be binding as, otherwise, an offeree would be harmed by relying on a promise made.

1. The offeror makes an offer that the offeror knows, or should know, will be relied upon by the offeree.
2. The offer is relied upon by the offeree.
3. The reliance is detrimental to the offeree in the absence of contract performance by the offeror.
4. Injustice can only be prevented by enforcing the promise.

If a rich person makes a promise to a church to donate $10,000,000 towards the construction of a hospital and the church then spends $1,000,000 acquiring real estate for construction of the hospital, the church can sue to enforce the promise under promissory estoppel.[3]

---

[3] Damages under promissory estoppel would be the reliance costs of $1,000,000 rather than the $10,000,000 promised.

Other Terminations of Offers

Lapse of Time   If nothing is said in an offer regarding offer expiration, the offer lapses after a *reasonable* period of time. Reasonableness in this context depends on the industry. The more volatile the price movements in the industry, the more quickly offers lapse. In the stock market, an offer without a defined time period may be deemed lapsed after 30 minutes, while an offer to buy a house may last for a week or longer, if there is no statement in the offer on when the offer expires. For most transactions, it is prudent to put an expiration date in the offer because of the large possible consequences that result, depending on whether or not the offer is accepted.

Rejection of an Offer   An offer terminates if the offeree rejects the offer. Counteroffers are considered rejections under the common law of contracts. If an offer states that it will remain open for 10 days and the offeree rejects the offer on day three, the offeree cannot "accept" the offer on day eight. However, the offer can be revived if the offeror makes the same offer again.

Operation of Law   There are certain events that terminate offers by operation of law. These events also operate after a contract has been formed. If a legal change occurs that makes performance of a contract illegal—that is, there is a *supervening illegality*—the offer is terminated. Also, if the subject matter of the contract is destroyed or some other event makes offered performance impracticable, the offer is terminated. Suppose Rocco, a promoter of rock concerts, makes an offer to bring in the band Creed for a concert, but, subsequent to the offer, the concert facilities are destroyed in a fire. The offer to engage Creed is terminated by operation of law. Similarly, *death or incapacity* of the offeror or offeree terminates the offer. The incapacity of either party could be physical or mental.

Consideration

consideration
This is the thing or act of value provided in exchange for a promise, which is required for a valid contract to be formed.

legal detriment
Legal detriment is a *real* burden that qualifies as consideration provided by a party to a contract. A legal detriment may involve a promise to pay money, to deliver services or products, or to refrain from certain actions (such as suing another designated party).

In brief, **consideration** is the exchange element in a contract. In order to be enforceable, a promise must be supported by consideration. In contract law, a *promisor* makes a promise and the *promisee* is the recipient of the promise. If a promisor promises to pay the promisee $500 in two weeks, and nothing more occurs other than the promisee agreeing to accept the gift, the promisor has promised to perform an unenforceable agreement. In order for the promisee to legally enforce the promise (to be paid money or other things of value), the promisee must incur a **legal detriment** in return. Also, in order to be valid, consideration must be bargained for.

The Legal Detriment Theory of Consideration

There are three categories of legal detriment that qualify as consideration. First, note that the *promise* of a promisor to pay $500 *is* consideration. That is, a promise to pay money is consideration. If the promisee promised to "pay back" in a year $500 borrowed today, that promise would be a *loan agreement.* If the promisee promised to perform services in return for the $500, the agreement would be an *employment or service contract.* If the promisee agreed not to sue the promisor in return for $500, the agreement or contract would be called a *settlement.* If a promisee agrees to pay money, perform services, or refrain from pursuing a legal claim, the promisee has incurred a legal detriment that is capable of supporting a promise by the promisor to, in turn, pay money (or perform services, or settle a lawsuit).

Benefits of a Contract Can Accrue to Third Parties   The benefits of consideration do not have to be directed toward the promisor. If a promisor agreed to pay $500 to the promisee, there would be a valid contract if the promisee agreed in return to tutor the children of the promisor. The benefits of a contract need not accrue to the party agreeing to pay money; instead, the benefits of the contract can be directed toward a third party, in our example, the tutored children. In examining the consideration element in contracts, students are advised to determine whether the party receiving the benefits of a promise has incurred a legal detriment. If the answer is yes, then the consideration element in contracts has been satisfied.

Adequacy of Consideration

In general, courts will not consider the *adequacy* of consideration. Courts are not in the business of setting "fair" prices and so, if a party to a contract strikes a poor deal, the party cannot go to the courts and claim the contract is unfair. Having said that, however, we must recognize that in egregious situations, particularly when one side is relatively uneducated, poor, and without alternatives, contracts are sometimes voided (not enforced) by courts due to *unconscionability*. Unconscionability, which may be defined as involving terms that are so out of line with common standards of fairness as to shock the conscience, provides a defense against the enforcement of any contract regulated by the UCC as well as contracts regulated by the common law.

Past Consideration

Jim rescues Mary from a burning building at considerable peril to his own safety. Three weeks later, in gratitude for Jim's selfless gesture, Mary promises to pay Jim $10,000 for his own medical bills as well as the danger he endured to save her. Three months later, Mary still has not paid Jim and his patience is wearing thin. Can Jim sue Mary for the promise she made to pay him $10,000? The answer is a definite no. Gratitude for past actions does not qualify as consideration.

It should be clear by now that courts have a lengthy laundry list of requirements to consider in determining the validity and enforceability of contracts. That list is of critical importance in Case 7-3.

Case 7-3

O'Neal v. Home Town Bank of Villa Rica et al.

Court of Appeals of Georgia
237 Ga. App. 325, 514 S.E.2d 669 (Ga. Ct. App. 1999)

FACTS AND CASE BACKGROUND

"Banker Fred L. O'Neal originated the idea of a new community bank in Villa Rica and expended significant effort to organize it. In the course of his work he recruited organizers for the bank who allegedly promised and assured him repeatedly that he would be compensated with employment by the bank for at least three years. Near the time it was organized the bank hired O'Neal, without written agreement or formal board approval of a multi-year contract. Four months later and after Home Town Bank of Villa Rica was formed, the board voted to terminate O'Neal, as an employee at will. O'Neal sued the bank and the organizers (collective 'bank') in multiple counts: breach of contract, quantum meruit, fraud, conspiracy, breach of fiduciary duty, intentional and negligent infliction of emotional distress, attorney fees and costs, securities fraud, and defamation, both slander and libel."

"O'Neal challenges the grant of summary judgment on each count. Summary judgment is authorized only when all undisputed facts and their reasonable inferences, viewed most favorably to the non-moving party, preclude a triable issue as to at least one essential element of the case."

Case Decision: Beasley, Presiding Judge

At best O'Neal's evidence supports a finding that leading up to the formation of the bank, O'Neal and the organizers repeatedly discussed that once it was formed the bank would hire O'Neal and give him a contract similar to that of the CFO. "Unless an agreement is reached as to all terms and conditions and nothing is left to future negotiations, a contract to enter into a contract in the future is of no effect." Because the terms of the alleged three-year agreement were not nailed down, it is not enforceable.

Second, O'Neal testified that the consideration he gave in exchange for the three-year employment agreement was his past effort to organize the bank . . . The Court reasoned that past consideration generally will not support a subsequent promise, and the situation presented was no exception. This is so in part because the purported consideration was not rendered to the bank which had yet to be established when the promotion and organization took place. These services perhaps were rendered to benefit the organizers, but as shown above the agreement with the organizers is not enforceable.

Third, "a verbal contract for services to begin in the future and continue for a year [or more] is void under the Statute of Frauds."

* * *

In sum, what remains for trial are the claims of libel and corresponding costs and fees.

Judgment affirmed in part and reversed in part.

Decision and Outcome

The Court of Appeals of Georgia ruled that past consideration is not a basis for a contract. The contract claim of the plaintiff was dismissed.

Questions for Analysis

1. The court lists three reasons for not finding that there was a contract between the plaintiff and the defendant bank. In view of how unambiguous the court found the evidence, should the plaintiff consider a malpractice suit against his attorney for bringing a suit that was a loser from the beginning?
2. Should the plaintiff be allowed to recover for services rendered during the four-month period when he was working?
3. What does this case suggest with regard to the downside (risks) of getting too personally involved with a project, willing to work without a contract?

Preexisting Duty

If a person is already obligated to do something by law, or to refrain from some action because of a legal prohibition, then for that person to agree not to violate the law is not legal consideration. Allegedly, organized crime used to approach store owners and offer "protection" contracts under which, if the store owner paid the protection money, the thugs in the criminal ring would refrain from burning down the store. A promise to refrain from violating a criminal statute, however, is not valid consideration because all citizens have a *preexisting duty to obey the law*. Of course, organized crime did not and does not generally look to the courts for enforcement of agreements.

Preexisting Contractual Duty

Assume that Carol has a contract to build a house for Craig and that the contract price is $100,000. If Carol claims that a strike by bricklayers makes performance at $100,000 impossible, but agrees to complete construction for a total price of $110,000, the agreement to add an additional $10,000 to the contract price lacks consideration. In order for the $110,000 contract price to be enforceable under common law standards, Carol must perform an additional assignment. Building a $50 sandbox in the rear of the house, however, could enable Carol to collect the additional $10,000. Since this is a trivial subterfuge to get around a common law contract rule that is long on formalism but requires divergences from commercial practices, this rule has been abolished under the UCC, which allows for modifications of existing contracts without new consideration (see the next chapter).

Illusory Promises

illusory promise
Agreements that appear to contain consideration but that, in fact, do not because the promises do not impose legal detriments on the promissors.

Some promises (offers) appear to contain consideration but do not. Such promises are often called **illusory promises.** Recall that the foundation for consideration is that each promisor actually incurs a legal detriment. If the promisor does not incur a legal detriment, meaning that the promisor has made a promise that does not bind him or her in any specific way, the resulting agreement lacks consideration and thus is not a contract. A promise by Keith to purchase as much grain as he wants to from Jerry does not bind Keith to any particular quantity and, thus, the promise lacks consideration. Even if Jerry had worked out price, quality, and delivery terms, a promise by Keith to purchase as much as he wants to fails to bind Keith in any way.

Similarly, a promise by an offerer to perform in a certain way, coupled with the retention of the right to cancel at any time for any reason without notice, does *not* bind the offerer. There is no consideration if the promisor does not incur a legal detriment. Retention of the right to cancel at any time curtails any legal detriment.

It is important to note, however, that small changes in illusory promises can result in the necessary consideration for a binding contract. If the promisor promises to purchase a quantity of widgets from the promisee, while retaining the right to cancel, but the promisor also promises to provide *notice* before canceling, there is consideration. Also, if the promisor agrees not to cancel unless some valid reason occurs, consideration is present even if the valid reasons are not specified.

Effect of Lack of Consideration

The effect of lack of consideration is that the supposed agreement is left unenforceable. Either party to an agreement that does not have consideration can rescind or cancel. The promisor may have made a binding promise but, if the other party to the agreement did not make a promise that involved consideration, the promisor who agreed to be bound can cancel his obligations under the agreement, which is not a contract.

Promises That Are Enforceable without Consideration

While consideration is generally a required element in a contract, some promises are enforceable without consideration, but only if the conditions for promissory estoppel are satisfied. The conditions necessary to invoke promissory estoppel were discussed above in connection with irrevocable offers.

Capacity

**capacity
(to contract)**
Capacity is required to have legal standing to enter into a valid contract. Capacity requires competency and adult age.

Unrestricted freedom to contract assumes that both parties to a contract are *capable* of looking out for their own self-interest. For some people, that assumption is questionable, either because they are too young or because they are otherwise disabled mentally. In general, both parties to a contract must have legal **capacity to contract** or else the resulting contract is voidable based on incompetence (lack of capacity). When a minor or a mental incompetent uses lack of capacity to escape contractual obligations, he or she is said to *disaffirm* the contract—an action that, quite simply, is the same as voiding the contract.

Minors

The contractual age of capacity is 18 in 49 states (it is age 19 in Nebraska). A contract between a minor and an adult can be voided or disaffirmed at the option of the minor. So, a minor can sign a contract; receive the consideration, such as a new CD player; and then later decide to disaffirm the contract and get his or her money back. If the minor has the consideration (such as a CD player), he must return it, but, in most states, the minor's right to disaffirm is not contingent upon return of consideration. If the minor loses the consideration or the consideration is damaged or wrecked, the minor can still disaffirm and claim a refund. In contrast, the adult party to a contract with a minor cannot use the minor's lack of capacity and cancel or disaffirm the contract due to lack of capacity on the part of the minor.

Ratification

Upon turning 18, a minor still has the power to disaffirm a contract entered prior to becoming 18. That option, however, is limited to a short period of time. If the minor makes a payment on a contract after turning 18, the minor will be deemed to have *ratified* the contract. For contracts that straddle minority and majority status, once a contract is ratified, it becomes a valid contract. If a minor simply does nothing after turning 18, makes a payment as called for in the contract, or continues using the consideration received under the contract, the minor loses the right to disaffirm and the contract is deemed ratified.

Exceptions

While the law of contracts is structured with the socially desirable goal of protecting minors from foolish decisions, the resulting right of minors to disaffirm can make engaging in business with minor customers very risky. If contracts with minors are casually disaffirmable at the option of the minor, then banks (which can make student loans), sports agents, and a host of others who sometimes deal with minors will be reluctant to do so. So, complicating this situation, the right of minors to escape contract obligations is filled with state-by-state exceptions regarding the disaffirmability of educational loans, insurance contracts, agreements with banks, and agency agreements, and the exceptions allowed differ from state to state.

Most states have an exception in the case of *necessaries*. An adult party who contracts to supply a minor with necessary goods and services (food, clothing, shelter, and job-related products such as employment placement services and even automobiles) can recover the *fair market value* of the necessary from the minor or his or her parents. Even with numerous exceptions to the right to disaffirm, engaging in business transactions that require formal contracts with a minor brings considerable risk as courts are very intolerant of sharp dealings that harm a minor, even if the consideration is a necessary.

Adults Who Are Incompetents

Adults can become incompetent to participate in contracts due to a number of causes. Illustratively, an adult who becomes so intoxicated with alcohol or drugs that she does not know the consequences of the contract she signs is an incompetent and, thus, can later disaffirm the contract. The test of incapacity due to alcohol or drugs is different than those used by the police to determine if a person is driving under the influence (DUI). A person could be legally drunk (legally incompetent) for purposes of operating a motor vehicle while still having contractual capacity. To disaffirm a contract due to intoxication, the adult must have been "totally bombed" at the time and the disaffirmation must occur within a short time of regaining sobriety.

A contract with someone who has been judged incompetent by the state is void and is no contract at all. People who live at mental institutions or have guardians appointed by the state to act on their behalf are incompetents and have no capacity to contract. In some contracts, an adult can claim incompetence to contract based on temporary incapacity accompanying a mental disorder, such as extreme depression or schizophrenia. The temporarily incompetent adult can disaffirm upon regaining his or her mental faculties. Alternatively, if a guardian is appointed, the guardian can use incapacity at the time the contract was executed to disaffirm. Generally, in order to disaffirm, an incompetent adult must return any contract consideration received. Be aware, however, that the rules regarding contracts with incompetents vary from state to state.

Legality

Contracts must be *legal* to be valid. Such a statement may seem tautological, but, in contract law, legality has a specific meaning that is not immediately obvious. Quite certainly, if performance of a contract entails a violation of a statute, state or federal, the contract is void due to illegality. Among such illegal contracts that sometimes affect businesses are agreements that involve gambling, contracts between unlicensed professionals and clients, and loans with interest charges that exceed legal limits (**usury law** limits).

usury laws
Laws that set ceilings on the interest rates that can be charged on loan contracts.

Contracts Contrary to Statutes

Gambling   A state can outlaw gambling, even though it is sometimes unclear what the difference is between illegal gambling and involvement in stock market speculation and other risky ventures. Gambling, in law, involves the *creation of risk that had no prior existence* whereas speculation, hedging, and participation in other risky ventures essentially involve transference of risk from one party to another rather than creation of risk.

Usury Laws   Many states have usury statutes that limit the amount of interest that can be charged on various types of loans. The usury limits on interest vary from state to state and vary within states, depending on the type of loan: personal, mortgage, or business. In some states, the penalty for usurious loans is forfeiture of all interest and, in other states, the creditor forfeits both principal and interest for loans with interest rates that exceed legal limits.

Licensing Requirements   In all states, practitioners of various professions and occupations must be licensed. Among the professions and occupation groups for which licenses are required are law, medicine, plumbers, beauticians, and morticians, just to name a few. For the foregoing professionals and others who are required to obtain licenses to practice, a competency exam is generally required along with educational attainments and/or sometimes apprenticeships. Contracts with unlicensed professionals (for the delivery of professional services) are illegal and void at law. A client contracting with an unlicensed professional can receive the services called for and then refuse to pay the service provider. Courts will not protect unlicensed professionals, as is illustrated by Case 7-4.

Case 7-4

Cevern, Inc. v. Ferbish

District of Columbia Court of Appeals
666 A.2d 17 (DC 1995)

FACTS AND CASE BACKGROUND

"Cevern, Inc., the appellant, brought an action to establish a mechanic's lien on the home of appellees Robert Ferbish and Viola Stanton. Cevern sought to recoup a balance of $10,295.61 it said was owed to it for work performed under a home improvement contract with Thelma Ferbish, also an appellee, who allegedly acted as the owners' agent. Appellees counterclaimed, alleging that they had expended $43,600 to correct Cevern's work."

"On August 24, 1992, the scheduled date of trial, counsel for appellees orally moved for summary judgment, asserting that Cevern was not licensed at the time it entered into the home improvement contract. The trial judge granted the motion the next day on the ground that '[Cevern] was not a licensed contractor at the time it received payment on the home improvement contract . . . notwithstanding the fact that [Cevern] subsequently received a valid license before the work was completed.' The judge also rejected Cevern's claim for recovery in quasi-contract. At appellees' request, he

dismissed without prejudice their counterclaim. On September 3, 1992, Cevern moved for reconsideration of the judgment, which the trial judge denied. Also, pursuant to a request in appellees' opposition, the judge entered judgment in their favor for $14,000, the amount counsel for appellees stated they had paid to Cevern."

Case Decision: Farrell, Associate Judge

In entering judgment for appellees for $14,000 in restitution, the trial judge declared that, under this court's decisions, "a contract made in violation of a licensing statute that is designed to protect the public will usually be considered void and unenforceable, and the party violating the statute cannot collect monies due on a quasi-contractual basis." Therefore, since Cevern accepted an advance payment from appellees on August 31, 1990 it could recover neither in contract nor in quantum meruit. The fact that Cevern acquired a license before completing the contracted-for work, and before receiving the balance of payment therefor, did not avail it. The judge explained:

> The purpose of licensing statutes would be frustrated if recovery were permitted for work performed without a license. . . . This rationale equally applies to situations where the contract is entered before the issuance of a license, or where some of the preliminary work is done before a license is issued, and a balance of the work is completed after the license has issued. . . . Such a "straddle" arrangement would also run afoul of the underlying rationale for the statutory and regulatory scheme in this area of the law.

In the District of Columbia it is a principle of long standing that an illegal contract, made in violation of a statutory prohibition designed for police or regulatory purposes, is void and confers no right upon the wrongdoer.

* * *

The judgment of the Superior Court is *Affirmed.*

Decision and Outcome

The District of Columbia Court of Appeals ruled that because the plaintiff did not have a license at the time the contract was formed, he was not entitled to collect any money on the contract because it was illegal.

Questions for Analysis

1. Is the court saying that the plaintiff cannot recover because he is not licensed or because he was not licensed at the time the contract was signed?
2. At the time of the contract, did it matter that the defendant, who had paid Cevern $14,000, was also participating in an illegal contract? Are licensing statutes tilted toward the unlicensed party in contract law? Why do you think that this tilt may exist? What would you expect professional groups to claim as the purpose of licensing statutes? Could there be other explanations?

---

unconscionable contract
An agreement that is void at law because it requires one party, generally with limited bargaining power, to accept terms that are unfair and that, symmetrically, unfairly benefit the party with superior bargaining power.

Contracts Contrary to Public Policy

Courts consider contracts contrary to public policy void. Prominent among the contracts that courts consider contrary to public policy are **unconscionable contracts.** Among the examples of unconscionable contracts are

Contracts excusing intentional actions: It is common in high-risk sports activities, such as hang-gliding and bungee-jumping, for operators to secure contractual waivers of liability from participants for any negligence on the part of operators or employees of the business. The operator of facilities offering such activities is concerned that if someone is injured, there will be a costly and uncertain lawsuit—one that could cost millions if the business loses. By signing waivers of liability, customers acknowledge the risks of the activity engaged in and voluntarily *assume these risks.* However, if

ONLINE DISTRIBUTION OF ILLEGAL PRODUCTS

The Internet facilitates sales of illegal and quasi-legal products. The website Buy Steroids Online (http://www.buy-steroids-online.nu/) offers to sell anabolic steroids online in advertisements that feature bodybuilders. Other websites sell Viagra, which is a prescription medicine, online after a doctor "examines" the purchaser online and then writes a prescription. Online gambling is readily available through hundreds of Internet sites, most of which are located in other countries. The anonymity of the Internet has made heretofore risky and illegal transactions a lot less risky for vendors and purchasers. Customers of illegal and quasi-legal websites should be aware that, since the contracts offered are illegal, they are void and courts will not allow themselves to be used to obtain a return of money or other consideration provided under the terms of such contracts. Dealing with the quasi-legal websites that peddle drugs or offer opportunities to gamble is strictly a *caveat emptor* (buyer beware) situation. Buyers in these illegal and quasi-illegal contracts have none of the protections that have been built into U.S contract law.

operators of these establishments try to obtain complete waivers of liability for all actions of employees, including intentionally harmful actions, courts will declare the contracts unconscionable.

Entities that owe duties to the public: Airlines, inn-keepers, banks, and utilities are all restricted by unconscionability constraints from requiring customers to sign contracts that absolve the service provider of liability for various acts of negligence. If a business has a duty to the public and reliance on that business is, in some reasonable sense, unavoidable (as would be the case with a common carrier such as an airline), then contracts that negate liability for negligence are unconscionable. So, airlines are prohibited from absolving themselves of liability for lost luggage, though there are statutory caps on the amount of liability per piece of luggage. If the contents of a passenger's luggage are especially valuable, that customer is encouraged to pay more for insurance and to alert the airlines that his or her luggage is especially valuable, requiring extra precaution in its handling.

Contracts in restraint of trade: A legacy from English common law is court determination to closely scrutinize trade restraints. A *covenant not to compete* is sometimes contained in employment contracts. Employment contracts that prohibit ex-employees from ever working in an industry upon terminating employment are considered unreasonable trade restraints and therefore unconscionable and thus void. Employers and others can enforce contracts that include covenants not to compete, *but these clauses must be reasonably limited in time and space.* For highly skilled programmers, a computer company may be able to enforce a prohibition on the programmer working for a rival within two years of separation of employment. Covenants not to compete also often accompany the sale of a company through which the seller(s) of the company being purchased agree not to set up a rival firm for a period of time in a certain area.

Nutz and Boltz   Noncompetes in the Absence of Uniformity

Contracts restricting future employment with a competitor are very popular throughout the United States, especially in information-based occupations. Interestingly, there are marked differences in state laws controlling the applicability of such contracts. California courts have consistently held that such contracts violate the state's public policy interest in promoting individual's freedom to choose where to work as codified in an 1872 state law. This, in the eyes of many, makes California an escape hatch for people who have signed noncompete contracts in the 47 states where they are permitted.

On his first day of employment with Medtronic Inc. in Minnesota in 1995, Mark Stultz signed a post-employment restrictive agreement intended, presumably, to prevent Medtronic *trade secrets* from being shared with a competitor. Stultz later left Medtronic and went to work in California for Advanced Bionics Corporation in a position paralleling the one he held at Medtronic, involving the marketing of spinal cord stimulator devices. According to Medtronic, as quoted in the June 3, 2001, *LA Times,* "The object of this [suit] is not to hurt employees. The object is to protect the single most important resource Medtronic has, and that is its ideas . . . Mark Stultz knows where we're going with our product and where we're not going . . . He knows what blind alleys we've gone down. If a competitor knows that, it's a huge advantage because then they don't have to go down those blind alleys." Advanced Bionics' president claims that his company wanted Stultz for his expertise in marketing spinal cord stimulators and his relationships with widely known leaders in that arena, not for any trade secrets.

Not surprisingly, this situation has led to a court battle between the two companies, as Stultz attempts to work in his chosen profession in a state that is highly supportive of the freedom to do so, though even California prohibits the sharing of trade secrets with new employers. As the combatants have squared off, this matter has pitted courts in Minnesota and California against each other as the involved courts in each state have acted, in separate actions, to apply their own state law to this matter. A hearing in June of 2001 in the California court was expected to address the question of whether the Minnesota contract is enforceable under California law. Depending on the outcome of this case, California can enhance or injure its reputation as an escape valve for high-value workers in technology-dominated industries.

Needless to say, legal battles over noncompete contracts are costly and are a potent disincentive to hiring workers with high-tech skills away from a competitor (by mid-year 2001, Advanced Bionics was reported to have spent more than a million dollars in its battle over Stultz). Critics of noncompetes characterize the employment terms they impose as akin to indentured servitude and a cottage industry exists to assist employees in escaping employment restrictions. YourNonCompete.com, which offers legal strategies for breaking noncompete contracts, reports an average of 5,000 hits per month and 50 purchases per month of its information package.

Note: In March 2003, the California Supreme Court upheld a ruling of a Minnesota court that enjoined Stultz from working for Advanced Bionics. Although the convenant not to compete would be enforceable in California, the California Supreme Court deferred to the Minnesota courts because of a choice of law clause in Stultz's contract with Medtronic, Inc. Advanced Bionics Corp. v. Medtronic, Inc., 59.P.3d231(2003).

GENUINENESS OF ASSENT

The freedom to bargain and contract is negated when an agreement is tainted by proof that it was obtained as a result of mistake, fraud, misrepresentation, undue influence, or **duress.** The effect of showing that an agreement is tainted is that the contract becomes voidable at the option of the injured party. Thus, evidence of fraud can be used as a *defense* in a breach of contract suit. On this basis, a defendant can claim that he refuses to perform because he was induced to sign the contract at issue through the lies and misrepresentations of the plaintiff. Often, victims of fraud sue to *rescind* a contract so that they can get back their money or

GEOGRAPHIC DIMENSIONS OF CYBERSPACE

Covenants not to compete were traditionally enforceable only if limited in time and geographic space. A measuring stick for the geographic limits of the covenant was the area where the ex-employer actually makes sales. With the World Wide Web, all firms with a website literally (1) are advertising to the world and (2) can make sales throughout the world. Moreover, since so much work is electronic, the need for employees to come to a central location is attenuated. An ex-employee with valuable trade secrets could work for a nearby rival of his former employer while being physically located out of state and, quite possibly, out of the jurisdiction of courts in the former employer's state.

other consideration transferred. On the other hand, if the victim of fraud decides to go ahead with contract performance, the defrauding party also must perform or risk a lawsuit.

Mistake

If both parties to a contract are mistaken as to a material fact, either party can void the contract. In order for a mistake to be voidable, the mistake must be mutual *or* must be an error about which one party knows or should have known that the other party is mistaken. In one famous "classic" case from history, both parties to a sales contract involving cotton believed that a cotton shipment would arrive in England from Bombay, India, on board a ship called the *Peerless*.[4] Unknown to each party, there were two ships named *Peerless* that left Bombay within a few months of each other. When the first *Peerless* arrived, the buyer paid for and took delivery of what he believed to be his cotton. When the second *Peerless* arrived, the seller sued because the buyer refused to purchase the cotton shipment that had been contracted for. The buyer was able to escape contractual liability by showing that the parties to the contract had made a mutual mistake about two *Peerless* ships.

Construction contracts on major projects are often formed after general contractors have been asked to submit bids. If six contractors submitted project bids on a project, five of which were between $900,000 and $1.1 million with the other at $100,000, it is fairly obvious that the last bid amount was the result of a typing mistake. The owner of the construction site could not snap up the $100,000 bid because he would know, or should know, that the contractor had made a mistake.

Fraud and Misrepresentation

Fraud occurs when one party to a contract knowingly lies about an important fact to the other party, who reasonably relies on those lies and suffers damages as a result. Although there are various definitions of contractual fraud, most would agree that if the plaintiff showed the following, he would have proved fraud[5]:

1. There is *misrepresentation of an important fact.* Fraud occurs when the fraudulent party says something that relates to the contract that is not true. Students should distinguish false statements of fact from *opinions* about a future event. In general, opinions are not the basis for fraud. *Professional opinions,* however, can be a foundation for fraud. If an

---

[4] *Raffles v. Wichelhaus,* 159 Eng. Rep. 375 (Exch. 1864).

[5] Note that the elements of contractual fraud are the same as for tortious fraud or deceit.

attorney offers an opinion about the legal impact of a document and that opinion is false, fraud can exist if the other elements of fraud are present.

2. *Scienter exists.* This is knowledge that the statements made are false.

3. There is an *intent to defraud.* The purpose of the lies (knowing misrepresentations of material facts) was to induce the other party to enter into a contract.

4. The nonfraudulent party *reasonably relied* on the fraudulent statements. If the alleged victim of fraud does not take the ordinary precautions applied by businesspeople, then courts will not bail out an allegedly defrauded party to a contract.

5. The fraud is the *proximate cause* of the victim's *damages.* As discussed earlier, proximate cause is legal causation, which exists when damages are reasonably foreseeable and there is a direct link between the fraud and the victim's damages.

If fraud is shown, the contract involving such fraud is voidable at the option of the victim and the victim can sue for damages. If misrepresentation is shown (fraud without the intent elements 2 and 3 above), the contract is voidable, but a suit for damages is not allowed. If Nancy, the owner and seller of a house, asserts that the foundation of the house is sound, while knowing that the foundation is sinking, she has committed fraud. If Nancy is unaware of the subsidence and states that the foundation of her house is intact, she has made an "innocent" misrepresentation. If a buyer relied on her sincere belief that the foundation was sound, the buyer could get his money back when the subsidence was detected. If the misrepresentation by Nancy was not innocent, the buyer may be able to recover for other expenses associated with the purchase of the house and lost opportunities elsewhere.

Source: Copyright © *The Toledo Blade.* Reprinted with permission.

Undue Influence

There are certain relationships that require one party to carefully avoid taking advantage of the other party. For example, attorneys are supposed to put the interests of their clients above their own in business transactions. In many family situations, a stronger party has a duty to not take advantage of a weaker party, particularly if the weaker party is ill or is much less educated or sophisticated. Undue influence makes a contract voidable at the option of the weaker party if (1) the bargain is objectively unfair, (2) the stronger party owed a fiduciary duty to the weaker party or the weaker party was in a weakened mental state, and (3) the weaker party had no access to outside counsel. In order to negate charges of undue influence, particularly when dealing with family members, a person should insist that the family member see an outside attorney or accountant. Professionals who have business dealings with clients similarly should insist that the client consult a nonaffiliated financial advisor before contracting with a client.

Duress

duress
Force, the threat of force, or use of some other form of pressure to induce a person to act in a way that he or she would not choose in the absence of the duress.

A contract that is the result of force, threat of force, threat of criminal prosecution, or blackmail is voidable at the option of the victim. Note, however, that a contract that is the result of the threat of civil litigation is a valid *settlement*. In some cases, an agreement between parties is tainted by economic blackmail. Economic blackmail can occur when a large corporation has more than one contract with another, smaller firm that has cash flow problems. Courts have allowed duress as a defense in economic blackmail cases when the large firm extracted a harsh bargain in subsequent contracts by threatening to withhold valid cash payments in the prior contract.

WRITING REQUIREMENTS AND THE STATUTE OF FRAUDS

Most contracts are enforceable even though they are not in writing. There are six types of contracts, which can be categorized as "important" contracts, that must be in writing to be enforceable. These six types of contracts should be thought of as exceptions to the general rule that oral agreements stand as valid contracts, provided the claimed agreement can be proved by a preponderance of the evidence in court. The following important contracts generally are not enforceable unless they are in writing:

1. *Surety (or guarantor) contracts* in which a surety (guarantor) promises a creditor that if a covered debtor does not pay the amount owed on a loan, he, the surety, will make the payment. Bonding companies, which are often required in government construction contracts, are sureties or guarantors of performance.
2. Contracts in which an *executor to a will agrees to be personally liable* for the debts of the deceased.
3. Contracts that, by their terms, *cannot be performed within one year.* For example, a two-year employment contract cannot be performed within one year.
4. *Marriage contracts,* including prenuptial agreements, must be in writing. Marriage contracts are not so significant nowadays with the demise of dowries, but prenuptial agreements are increasingly common.
5. Any contract significantly involving *real estate,* including sales, mortgages (real property is collateral for a loan), easements, drilling rights, and insurance contracts.
6. Contracts involving the *sale of goods* when the selling price *exceeds $500.* This is a UCC rule. Under proposed revisions to the UCC, the new limit will be $5,000.

Exceptions to the Exceptions

As a general rule, oral contracts are enforceable as long as the terms of an oral agreement can be proved. While the six types of exceptional (important) contracts listed above generally must be in writing, there are exceptions applicable to these categories. If the elements of *promissory estoppel* are present, promises made with respect to one of these six categories are still enforceable. Notable among other exceptions that apply to the six important contracts are

1. In a surety contract, if the surety orally promises the debtor that he (the surety) will pay the debtor's debt to the creditor, the *creditor* can enforce this oral promise made by the surety (or guarantor) (as a third-party beneficiary of the contract, as discussed below).

2. In some states, there is a part performance exception to oral contracts for the sale of real estate. If the buyer takes possession of the real estate, makes significant improvements to the land and buildings, and/or pays some or all of the purchase price agreed to, then an oral sale of real estate is an enforceable contract.

3. Under the UCC, there are three exceptions to the rule that contracts for the sale of goods whose price in total exceeds $500 must be in writing. These exceptions are discussed in the next chapter.

Sufficiency of the Writings

If writing is required for a contract to be legally enforceable, the writing does not have to be on one piece of paper. Courts have "pieced together" contracts that consisted of letters, internal memoranda, invoices, and purchase orders, the combination of which included all of the elements required of a contract. Increasingly, electronic records in the form of e-mails also have become parts of contracts when contracts are composed of several components. At a minimum, writings must identify the parties to the contract, the subject matter of the contract, the price, the quantity, and other material terms.

Parol Evidence Rule[6]

parol evidence rule
Court rule that excludes evidence on parties' prior or current discussions, negotiations, statements, or oral arguments if that evidence is at odds with the express terms of the particular contested contract.

Whether a writing is required or not, if there is a written contract, the **parol evidence rule** operates to exclude *outside* or *extrinsic* evidence of words spoken at the time of contract formation. If, for example, in a contract suit one party claims that the other party orally assured him that "the company never enforces the warranty disclaimers in boldface print near the signature line," evidence of such an oral statement would be excluded under the parol evidence rule. The parol evidence rule also excludes outside writings that are in conflict with a written contract or that represent prior negotiations. If the parties want to exclude all outside evidence, it is common for a contract to include an *integration* clause that states that the *complete agreement* between the parties *is contained* within the four corners of the written agreement.

Even with integration clauses, outside or parol evidence is not excluded if such evidence is submitted to clear up incomplete or ambiguous agreements, or if the parol evidence is submitted to prove fraud or other taints on an agreement. Without an integration clause, evidence of a trade usage or prior course of dealing is admissible to courts and juries in understanding what the parties agreed to in the written contract. To avoid having to deal with such additional and possibly extraneous evidence in the event of a dispute, integration clauses are used in many contracts.

PERFORMANCE AND DISCHARGE OF CONTRACTUAL OBLIGATIONS

In most cases, the contractual obligations of both parties to a contract are discharged without liability by the performance called for in the contract. For contracts involving the sale of goods, the required performance is governed by the UCC perfect tender rule (discussed in the next chapter). For all other contracts, a less than perfect performance, often labeled *substantial performance,* entitles the promisor to the contracted for consideration (generally money) *minus* the cost of repair (cost of cure). In a construction contract, if there are minor discrepancies between performance called for in the contract and that which is provided, the builder is entitled to the contract price minus the costs incurred by the owner to make the house, or other structure, conform to what was called for in the contract.

---

[6] The word "parol" in law refers to something spoken or said.

Nutz and Boltz   Delegations of Contractual Duties

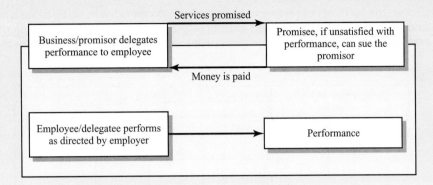

Material Breach

material breach
Failure of a party to a contract, when there is no legal excuse for that failure, to perform his or her duties under the contract so that the essential purpose of the contract is unfulfilled.

If the performance offered by a party fails in the *essential purpose* of the contract, then such performance amounts to a **material breach.** In a house construction contract, if the house is so poorly constructed that the building inspector will not issue a certificate of occupancy certifying that the dwelling is fit for human inhabitation, then the builder has failed in the essential purpose of the contract. In a service contract involving installation of software, if the software does not work after installation, the contract has been breached.

In some cases, late performance is considered a material breach. If the promisee wants to make clear beforehand that late performance is a material breach, the promisee should insist on a *time is of the essence clause.* Whether performance offered by the promisor constitutes *substantial perfomance,* which fulfills the essential purpose of the contract, or whether a material breach has occurred, is a decision for juries to decide. If the promisor materially breaches a contract, the obligation of the promisee to pay money to the promisor is eliminated.

Delegation of Duties

For the vast bulk of contracts, the promisor is a business and responsibility for performing is *delegated* to employees. In general, all contractual duties can be delegated to employees or others who are willing to perform the duties called for in the contract. In some contracts, the special skills of the promisor are the reason the contract was formed, in which case the duties of the promisor cannot be delegated. Again, a promisee who does not want ambiguity on this issue can simply insert a clause in the contract that prohibits delegations because of the special skills of the promisor. Star athletes and featured entertainers possess unique skills that cannot be delegated. If a promoter contracted with Eminem to perform at an outdoor stadium, Marshall Mathers (Eminem's "real" name) could not delegate to a local "garage" band his promise to perform.

The party to whom the duties of the contract are delegated is the *delegatee.* If performance is unsatisfactory, the promisee cannot sue the delegatee for breaching the contract because there is no *privity of contract* between the parties. The promisee can only look to and sue the delegator, who is generally the employer of the delegatee.

Nutz and Boltz

If the car is defective, the purchaser can refuse to pay the bank because the assignee takes the contract subject to the defenses the obligor had against the obligee. On the other hand, if the car is not defective, but the purchaser defaults on paying the bank, the bank can take legal action against the purchaser.

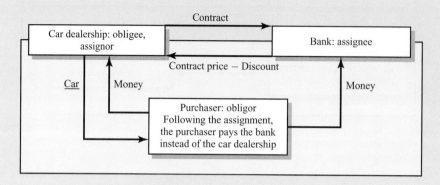

Assignment of the Benefits of a Contract

If Jack buys a car from Smith Automobiles, he probably would want to "finance" the purchase, paying for the car in installments. Smith Automobiles may have expertise in selling cars, but they may be reluctant to evaluate the creditworthiness of Jack, service the loan, incur collection expenses, and so forth. It is common for automobile dealerships to assign their installment sales contracts to banks or other financial institutions. The recipient bank or other financing institution will pay a discounted cash amount to the car dealership and then assume responsibility for collecting the loan.

Effect of an Assignment

In a typical installment sales contract, the seller becomes an assignor when he accepts money from a financial institution in return for assignment of the contract. As assignee, the bank is responsible for *notifying* the purchaser that payments are to be made to it, not to the car dealership. Suppose the car malfunctions and the purchaser claims that it wants the car repaired first before continuing to make payments on the car. In general, assignees (banks) take the benefit of the contract subject to defenses that the purchaser had against the seller (assignor). In other words, if the purchaser had a defense against the seller, that defense is good against the assignee.

Assignability of a Contract

In general, the benefits of any contract can be assigned as long as the obligations of the promisor/obligor (often a purchaser) are not increased by the assignment. Assignments are prohibited when the promisor/obligor is required to perform personal services for the promisee. A manservant may be willing to serve an English aristocrat, but that same servant may object to serving a rock star whose lifestyle is much different. An assignee steps into the shoes of the assignor, which means that if the purchaser/obligor does not live up to his obligations, the assignee can sue for breach of contract.

Nutz and Boltz Third Party Beneficiary Contract

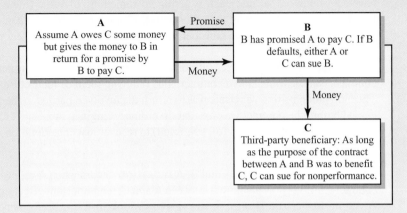

Third-Party Beneficiaries

If the purpose of a contract is to benefit a third party, the promisor who fails to perform can be sued by either the promisee or the third-party beneficiary. If Jim divorces Mary and, as part of the divorce settlement, promises to pay for his daughter Jenny's college education, then when Jenny graduates from high school, she is the intended beneficiary of the contract between Jim and Mary. If Jim does not pay for Jenny's college education, either Mary, Jenny, or both could sue Jim. In the divorce settlement, Jenny was a *donee* beneficiary, as Jim was intending to make a gift to Jenny. In other cases, the third-party beneficiary is owed money by the promisee and the promisor has promised to pay or perform services for the *creditor* beneficiary (see "Nutz and Boltz" box).

In many contracts, a third party is *incidentally* benefited by performance delivered by the promisor. For example, if a fertilizer company makes timely deliveries to a plant nursery, a beekeeper located up the road may benefit because his bees will expend less energy obtaining nectar for honey making. However, since the purpose of the contract between the fertilizer company and the plant nursery was not to benefit the beekeeper, the beekeeper as an *incidental* beneficiary would have no standing to sue if the fertilizer company did not deliver as promised.

Discharge of Contractual Obligations

Material Breach

As mentioned above, if one party to a contract materially breaches the contract, the contractual obligations of the other party are discharged. If an employee fails to show up for work, she has breached the employment contract and the employer does not have to pay the employee. In some cases, a promisor knows in advance that he is not going to perform on a contract and announces to the other party that performance is unlikely. Such behavior is characterized as an *anticipatory breach* and it, too, discharges the other party from contractual obligations. The victim of an anticipatory breach can sue immediately (for breach of contract) while terminating any performance called for under the contract. Alternatively, the nonbreaching party could encourage the other party to reconsider and perform as promised.

Rescission

Sometimes both parties to a contract decide that they want to end the contract. If both sides still have promises to fulfill, then they can agree to cancel the contract and each side will have consideration because each is giving up something of value (the right to receive the benefit of performance from the other party). If only one party to a contract has promises to fulfill, then there must be consideration for the agreement to cancel that performance, even if it is only trivial.

Note further that "victims" (minors, defrauded parties, mistaken parties) in voidable contracts can sue to rescind a contract, thus relieving them of their obligations to perform. The motivation behind **rescission** is to return the involved parties to the positions they occupied before the contract was formed. In ordinary English, most suits to rescind voidable contracts are suits by victims (of, say, fraud) to recover lost consideration, generally money.

rescission
Cancellation of a contract, generally with the contracting parties returned to their pre-contract status.

Novation

Imagine a contract between A and B. A **novation** occurs when A agrees that the previous contract with B is now a contract between A and C. An important effect of a novation is that A can no longer sue B once A has agreed to look to C for performance. Novations are common when businesses are formed. Suppliers and creditors initially require *personal signatures* of the lead shareholders in a newly formed business. As the business establishes itself and its creditworthiness, creditors and suppliers will accept a substitution of the obligations of the established business (entity C) for those of the original shareholders (the Bs in the original contract arrangement).

novation
Substitution, by agreement, of a new contract for a previous contract, generally with the substitution of a new party to the contract in place of a previous contracting party.

Accord and Satisfaction

It is common in business that contractual expectations may not be realized while a contract is in existence. Rather than suing or walking away from the contract, the parties may negotiate a new *accord.* When the terms of that new accord are performed, a *satisfaction* takes place. Contract modifications are common and the only legal pitfall that occasionally accompanies the recontracting is that there must be consideration for contract modifications.[7] With an accord and satisfaction, the *same* (original contracting) *parties* make a new agreement, whereas with a novation, *new parties* agree to abide by the same (old) contract.

Discharge by Operation of Law

A promisor's obligations under a contract are discharged without liability if, subsequent to formation, the promisor dies, becomes incapacitated, or declares bankruptcy or if performance is declared illegal due to a change in the law. Many of these events are the same as those that operate by law to terminate an offer.

Discharge Due to Impossibility

Closely related to discharge by operation of law is discharge due to **impossibility.** In fact, there are several legal excuses under impossibility that overlap with operation of law. According to some sources, a legal change subsequent to formation of a contract that makes performance illegal creates a discharge due to impossibility. Other legal excuses due to impossibility include war, acts of God, incapacity, or death of the promisor.

Under either standard, it is important to distinguish the comment "I cannot perform" from "It cannot be accomplished." Only the latter statement can be the foundation for the legal excuse of impossibility. Under both concepts, it is assumed that the promisor has made a good-faith attempt to perform, but circumstances beyond his control have made performance impossible, or at least extremely difficult. These circumstances are to be distinguished from ordinary price changes or weather changes that are normal risks of doing business.

impossibility
Condition or situation that relieves a party to a contract from performance of the duties called for in the contract when, through no fault of the contracting parties, performance would be objectively impossible or highly impracticable.

---

[7] Under the UCC, contracts can be modified without consideration.

Case 7-5

The Opera Company of Boston, Inc., Appellee v. The Wolf Trap Foundation for the Performing Arts, Appellant

United States Court of Appeals for the Fourth Circuit
817 F.2d 1094 (4th Cir. 1987)

BACKGROUND AND FACTS

This suit between the parties arises under a contract between the plaintiff, The Opera Company of Boston, Inc. (Opera Company), and the defendant, The Wolf Trap Foundation for the Performing Arts (Wolf Trap), by which the Opera Company for its part agreed to give four "fully staged orchestrally accompanied [operatic] performances to the normally recognized standards" of the Opera Company. Wolf Trap, in turn, for its part under the contract, was obliged to make the payments and also to furnish the place of performance including an undertaking "to provide lighting equipment as shall be specified by the Opera Company of Boston's lighting designer."

Both parties to the contract performed apparently all their obligations under the contract through the operatic performance on June 14. These performances had been fully sold as well as had the remaining performance on June 15. During this final day, the weather was described as hot and humid, with rain throughout the day. Sometime between 6:00 and 6:30 P.M., a severe thunderstorm arose causing an electrical power outage. As a result, all electrical service in the park—in its roadways, parking area, pathways, and auditorium—were out. Conferences were had among representatives of the Park Service and that of Wolf Trap.

The Park Service recommended the immediate cancellation of the performance and advised Wolf Trap if the performance were not cancelled, it disclaimed any responsibility for the safety of the people who were to attend as well as those who were to perform. It was the Park Service's view that a prompt cancellation was necessary to enable the parties to leave the park safely and to prevent others from coming. Wolf Trap agreed and the performance was cancelled.

While some of these discussions were being carried on, a representative of the Opera Company was present, but she took no part in the decision to cancel, though she voiced no objection. Since the performance was cancelled, Wolf Trap failed to make the final payment under the contract to the Opera Company. Five years after the cancellation, the Opera Company filed this suit to recover the balance due under the contract.

Opinion: Russell, Circuit Judge

The single question on appeal is whether this dismissal of Wolf Trap's defense of impossibility of performance was proper. The resolution of this issue requires a review of the doctrine of impossibility. We proceed first to that review.

III.

It is now recognized that "A thing is impossible in legal contemplation when it is not practicable; and a thing is impracticable when it can only be done at an excessive and unreasonable cost." (citing authorities) The doctrine ultimately represents the ever-shifting line, drawn by courts hopefully responsive to commercial practices and mores, at which the community's interest in having contracts enforced according to their terms is outweighed by the commercial senselessness of requiring performance. When the issue is raised, the court is asked to construct a condition of performance based on the changed circumstances, a process which involves at least three reasonably definable steps.

* * *

IV.

Applying the law as above stated to the facts of this case, we conclude, as did the district judge, that the existence of electric power was necessary for the satisfactory performance by the Opera Company on the night of June 15 . . . The district judge, however, refused to sustain the defense because he held that if the contingency that occurred was one that could have been foreseen reliance on the doctrine of impossibility as a defense to a breach of contract suit is absolutely barred. As we have said, this is not the modern rule and he found that the power outage was foreseeable. In this the district judge erred. Foreseeability, as we have said, is at best but one fact to be considered in resolving first how likely the occurrence of the event in question was and, second whether its occurrence, based on past experience, was of such reasonable likelihood that the obligor should not merely foresee the risk but, because of the degree of its likelihood, the obligor should have guarded against it or provided for non-liability against the risk. This is a question to be resolved by the trial judge after a careful scrutiny of all the facts in the case. The trial judge in this case made no such findings. The cause must be remanded for such findings. In connection with that remand, the parties may be permitted to offer additional evidence on the matters in issue.

* * *

The judgment herein must, therefore, be vacated and the action remanded to the district court to make findings, based on a statement of reasons, whether the possible foreseeability of the power failure in this case was of that degree of reasonable likelihood as to make improper the assertion by Wolf Trap of the defense of impossibility of performance.

Decision and Outcome

The U.S. Court of Appeals of the Fourth Circuit ruled that the case should be remanded back to the trial court for it to determine whether the foreseeability of a power failure was sufficiently likely so as to make improper the assertion of the defense of impossibility.

Questions for Analysis

1. According to the court of appeals in this case, if an event was foreseeable, could that event, even so, provide the grounds for the impossibility defense?
2. If an event is foreseeable and there is no allocation of risk, and then the event occurs, the promisor must have implicitly assumed that risk. Is that logic consistent with the case logic as explained by the U.S. Court of Appeals?

Discharge Due to the Occurrence or Nonoccurrence of a Condition

Parties to a contract can condition performance on events that are within or outside the control of the parties to the contract. If Mary makes an offer to Peter, "You will have a job working for me if you graduate from college this spring," a *condition precedent* for hiring Peter has been established—namely, that he graduate from college during the spring. If Peter should fail to graduate from college during the spring, Mary's obligation to hire Peter is eliminated.

Reflecting a condition precedent that is outside of the control of the parties, Henry may tell George that he will have a job working in the White House if presidential candidate B beats candidate G. Obviously, Henry's obligation to hire George is based on a condition that is outside the control of either party to the contract.

When a *condition subsequent* occurs, the promisor's obligation to perform also ceases. If Henry tells Sam, "You have a job at my store as long as you always show up to work sober," Henry's obligation to employ Sam ceases if Sam shows up to work drunk.

CONTRACTUAL REMEDIES

Most contract law remedies involve an award of money to compensate for breaches. In rare instances, there are other remedies that involve injunctions or specific performance requirements. In contrast to tort remedies, intent is not a factor in determining damages. In other words, the amount of damages awarded does not depend on whether the breaching party attempted to perform and failed, or deliberately defaulted on a contract.

Monetary Damages

Compensatory Damages

The legal underpinning for *damages* (money awards) in contract cases generally is the intent to compensate the nonbreaching party for the losses incurred as a result of the breach of contract. Typically, damages awarded are inadequate to fully compensate the nonbreaching party because attorney fees and other "costs" are not added for a successful plaintiff unless there is a clause in the contract at issue awarding the winning party in contract litigation attorney fees and court costs. Of course, damages must be proved with reasonable certainty and courts are notably conservative in the requirements of proof. So, lost profits generally are not recoverable for new businesses that do not have a track record upon which to base damages.

Reliance and Restitution Damages

In some contracts, the nonbreaching party also incurs costs due to reliance upon the breaching party's promised performance of its contract obligations. When there is adequate proof, reliance costs can be recovered. Reliance costs are more often recovered by a plaintiff in a promissory estoppel case, which is explicitly based on the detrimental reliance costs incurred by the promisee.

When the nonbreaching party sues as a result of a breach, that party can recover *restitution* expenses, which typically are composed of the consideration given to the breaching party before the breach takes place. Also, in voidable contracts, if the victim sues to rescind the contract, the victim is basically suing for restitution expenses to recover consideration given to the other party. Finally, in quasi-contract suits, the plaintiff is suing for restitution to prevent the *unjust enrichment* of the breaching party.

Consequential Damages

In some contracts, breach will entail unusual expenses that are not "typical." Consider again, for our example, a common carrier contract. It is a breach of contract for the carrier, say an airline, to lose a passenger's luggage. Damages for lost luggage are fixed to an amount ($750) as set by statute. In some cases, however, the value of a customer's luggage and/or goods in the luggage exceed $750. In such cases, to avoid the $750 limitation on possible recovery, it is incumbent upon the customer to inform the airline that his or her luggage or its contents are especially valuable. As noted previously, such a concerned passenger would likely face an increased insurance charge on his or her luggage, which would further put the carrier on notice to handle that luggage with particular care. **Consequential damages** are recoverable in contract cases of this sort so long as the breaching party was reasonably aware of the extra expenses (consequential damages) associated with a breach. However, the burden is upon the nonbreaching party to *notify* the breaching party if the expenses of loss are not reasonably foreseeable.

consequential damages
Damages that do not occur immediately or directly from a contract breach but may be reasonably foreseeable as occurring subsequently "as a consequence" of the breach. Lost profits are a frequently claimed form of consequential damages.

Liquidated Damages

Proving damages is inherently uncertain and juries and judges can become confused when accountants and economists argue about variable costs, fixed costs, and other minutiae that affect damage calculations. If damages are difficult to estimate, as they are, for example,

liquidated damages
A damage amount, agreed to within a contract by the contracting parties, that represents a reasonable value for a damage award in the event of a contract breach.

with late performance in a road construction contract, the parties can agree in advance on a formula for calculating damages. With liquidated damages clauses, the parties stipulate (agree) in advance to a formula for calculating damages. Such clauses are enforceable as long as they are reasonable. If the damage formula in a liquidated damages clause is excessive, courts will label it a *penalty* and refuse to enforce it.

Mitigation of Damages

mitigation of damages
Actions taken, which are reasonable, to offset or minimize damages incurred due to a contract breach.

The nonbreaching party in a contract case has an obligation to mitigate damages as much as is reasonable. If the nonbreaching party is a landlord, the landlord has an obligation to rent out the premises (assuming a willing tenant can be located easily), even though the previous tenant breached the lease. If an employee has been wrongfully discharged in contravention of an employment contract, the employee nevertheless would have an obligation to take a comparable job offer from another employer. For both the landlord and the ex-employee, there are reasonableness constraints on the obligation to mitigate damages. An executive who is wrongfully fired from her job does not have to respond to a help wanted placed in the front window of the local McDonald's outlet to have a claim for lost compensation. A landlord who is willing to rent out his basement apartment to college coeds does not have to rent to a member of the Hell's Angels to have a claim for lost rents.

Other Remedies

The remedies discussed below are *equitable* remedies, which means they are issued at the discretion of the presiding judge. These remedies were discussed in Chapter 1. In order to obtain an equitable remedy, the petitioning party must not be engaging in sharp dealing. Since equitable remedies are discretionary with the judge, "in order to obtain equity, the party must act equitably." Both the equitable remedies of injunctions and *specific performance* are appropriate when monetary damages are inadequate to compensate the plaintiff for the total costs of the breaching party's behavior.

Injunctions

injunction
Court order to a party to do some specific thing or to refrain from doing some specific thing.

As discussed earlier, to merit injunctive relief, a plaintiff must show that (1) (s)he is likely to succeed on the merits when the case comes to trial and (2) irreparable harm is taking place so that the defendant must be stopped from further breaches of contract. A plaintiff is likely to win on the merits when it is obvious that a breach of contract has occurred.

Specific Performance

In some cases, the consideration in a contract is unique and there are no market alternatives that are available at reasonable prices. Real estate, works of art, and family heirlooms are all examples of consideration that cannot be reproduced on the market. In these cases, the nonbreaching party does not want a monetary award so much as it wants the actual consideration that was the subject matter of the contract. If the court grants specific performance to the plaintiff, it is ordering the defendant to perform as promised in the contract. In a sale of real estate, a court could order the defendant to transfer the deed for the real estate to the plaintiff/buyer.

Summary

Legal Impact of Signing a Contract, the Common Law of Contracts, and the Uniform Movement

- A contract creates legally enforceable obligations to perform.
- Since each state has its own common law tradition, each state has its own common law of contracts. Contracts are supposed to reduce uncertainty by enabling business managers to plan, invest, and conduct business based on agreements they have with others. When the basic law of contracts varies from state to state, it adds to uncertainty.
- The impact of the UCC has been to *regularize* the legal treatment of contracts in all 50 states.

Contractual Language: It Is Important to Understand the Contractual Law Meaning of Valid, Void, Voidable, Unenforceable, Bilateral, Unilateral, Executory, Executed, and Quasi-contract

- A *valid* contract is a contract that is enforceable.
- A *voidable* contract is a contract that can be voided by one of the parties.
- A *void* contract is a contract that courts will refuse to consider and enforce because the contract violates a statute or is against public policy.
- If a contract is *unenforceable,* either party to the contract can decide not to honor the contract.
- Most contracts are *bilateral* in the sense that a promise is *exchanged* for a promise.
- A promise that has been performed is a promise that has been *executed.*
- An *express* contract contains an explicit agreement between the parties that there is a contract.
- A contract is *implied* when the conduct of the parties indicates consent to be bound in a contract.
- If there is no agreement between the parties, one party may, nevertheless, be able to recover from another party based on *quasi-contract* (sometimes called *quantum meruit*).
- Large firms, in particular, have developed contract language that pledges payments to small firms if their ideas are used (generally if their ideas are patentable) but requires the small firms to waive their rights to sue if their ideas are not patentable or not used.

There Are Five Elements to Every Contract: Offer, Acceptance, Consideration, Capacity, and Legality; It Is Important to Know When a Contract Is Not Valid because One of the Essential Elements of the Contract Is Missing

- There are five required elements in contract formation: *offer, acceptance, consideration, capacity of the parties of contract,* and *legality*.
- There are three categories of legal detriments that qualify as consideration. If a promisee agrees to pay money, perform services, or refrain from pursuing a legal claim, the promisee has incurred a legal detriment that is capable of supporting a promise by the promisor to pay money (or perform services, or settle a lawsuit).
- Gratitude for past actions does not qualify as consideration.
- Some promises appear to contain consideration, but actually do not. Such promises are often called *illusory* promises.
- The contractual age of capacity is 18 in 49 states. In Nebraska it is 19.
- Many contracts between a minor and an adult can be voided or *disaffirmed* at the option of the minor but not at the option of the adult.
- Adults can become incompetent to form contracts due to a number of causes, typically intoxication or mental illness. However, a person could be legally drunk (legally incompetent) for purposes of operating a motor vehicle while still having contractual capacity.
- Contracts must be *legal* to be valid.
- Certain contracts have been held unconscionable and thus void at law. Some unconscionable contracts attempt to excuse liability for intentional actions of one party.

Certain Events, Such as Fraud, Undue Influence, Duress, and Mistake Make a Contract Voidable as, When They Are Present, There Is No Assurance the Parties Truly Agreed to the Contract

- Fraud occurs when one party to a contract knowingly lies about an important fact to the other party, who reasonably relies on those lies and suffers damages as a result.
- Fraud can be used as a *defense* in a breach of contract suit by a defendant, claiming that he is not going to perform because he was induced into executing the contested contract only because the plaintiff lied to him.
- If both parties to a contract are mistaken as to a material fact, either party can void the contract.
- A contract that is the result of force, threat of force, threat of criminal prosecution, or blackmail is voidable at the option of the victim.
- There are six types of important contracts that must be in writing to be enforceable: surety contracts, agreements for the executor to a will to be personally liable, those that cannot be performed within one year, marriage contracts, real estate contracts, and agreements for the sale of goods for more than $500.
- There are several important exceptions to mandatory written contracts.
- Whether a writing is required or not, if there is a written contract, the *parol evidence rule* operates to exclude outside or extrinsic evidence.

A Party to a Contract Normally Discharges His or Her Contract Obligation by, in Fact, Performing, but There Are a Number of Ways in Which Contractual Obligations Can Be Discharged

- If the performance offered by a party fails in the *essential purpose* of the contract, then such performance amounts to a *material* breach.
- Discharge of contractual obligations can be due to material breach, rescission, novation, accord, and satisfaction; by operation of law; and through discharge due to impossibility.
- Most contract remedies award money to compensate for the breach of a valid contract.
- In rare instances, there are other remedies that involve injunctions or specific performance requirements.
- Monetary damages can be compensatory, restitution, consequential, and liquidated.
- Plaintiffs in breach of contract suits have an obligation to mitigate damages.

Key Terms

bilateral contract, *195*
capacity (to contract), *207*
consequential damages, *223*
consideration, *204*
contract, *192*
duress, *212*
executed contract, *195*
executory contract, *195*
express contract, *195*
fraudulent
    misrepresentation, *194*

illusory promise, *207*
implied contract, *196*
impossibility, *220*
injunction, *224*
legal detriment, *204*
liquidated damages, *224*
material breach, *217*
mitigation of damages, *224*
novation, *220*
parol evidence rule, *216*
promissory estoppel, *203*

quasi-contract, *196*
rescission, *220*
unconscionable contract, *210*
unilateral contract, *195*
usury laws, *209*

Questions for Review and Analysis

1. What are the legal consequences of a valid contract? What are the legal consequences of a void contract, a voidable contract, and an unenforceable contract? Provide one example of a void, a voidable, and an unenforceable contract.

2. Quasi-contracts and promissory estoppel provide remedies when the discussions and actions between two parties do not result in a contract. What are the elements of a quasi-contract and promissory estoppel, how do such legal events typically occur, and what are the remedies provided?

3. Why, in general, do courts not consider the adequacy of consideration? Under what circumstances do the courts remedy gross imbalances of consideration?

4. Discuss three legal circumstances in which the promisor to a valid contract can be excused from performing without being liable to the promisee?

5. Liquidated damages clauses are being relied on increasingly in commercial contracts. Why do you suppose that experienced businesses want such clauses in their contracts?

If You Really Understood This Chapter, You Should Be Able to Provide Informed Commentary on the Following:

1. **Express versus Implied Contracts.** Engelcke planned to design and manufacture "Whizball," an electronic game. Engelcke asked Eaton, an employee, if he could design the electronic schematic for the game and also asked Eaton how much he would charge if he did the work during his off-duty hours. Eaton responded that he estimated he could design the schematic in three months at a cost of $1,200 to $1,500. Engelcke asked him to proceed, telling him that compensation would be figured when the project was completed. After Eaton began work on the project, Engelcke made several design changes that necessitated changing the electronics and circuitry. Eaton and Engelcke had numerous conversations regarding additional compensation for Eaton because of the increased length and complexity of the design project. Engelcke repeatedly assured Eaton he would be paid for the work, but the parties never reached an agreement as to the amount Eaton was to be compensated. Eaton worked on the project during his off-duty hours for 11 months and

produced a schematic that was 90 percent complete. His job with Engelcke was then terminated. Eaton filed suit and the court had to decide (1) whether there was a contract between the two and (2) what the damages were. Are these "loose" types of agreements an appropriate way to do business? Doesn't this kind of breakdown in communications frequently occur? See *Eaton v. Engelke Manufacturing, Inc.,* 681 P.2d 1312 (Wash. App. 1984).

2. **Capacity and Fraud.** It is well known that an adult who contracts with a minor does so at his peril because the minor is entitled to disaffirm any contract that does not involve necessaries and recover all monies paid by the minor to the adult in connection with the contract. However, we might wonder how these principles are affected if the minor tricked the adult party into believing that the minor was of the age of majority? Does the fact that the minor engaged in fraud that led to a contract with an adult change the legal options available to a minor? Compare *Hartman Auto Sales, Inc. v. Jaye,* 214 So. 2d 97 (1968) with *Rose v. Sheehan Buick, Inc.,* 204 So. 2d 903 (1967).

3. **Employment at Will and Promissory Estoppel.** Employment-at-will contracts are common. In this type of contract, the employer is free to hire and fire an employee *at will,* for any cause or with no cause. Similarly, the employee is free to quit for any or no reason. Most employees work on an at-will basis; they do not have the job security of an employment contract and can be discharged at any time, but with a growing number of exceptions, such as discrimination based on race, and so forth. An interesting legal issue has arisen concerning whether there are any damages when an employer induces an employee, who is currently working on an employment-at-will basis, to switch jobs, and then fires the employee shortly after beginning the new job, or even before the new job has begun. Since there are no guarantees at either location, how can an employee claim to be damaged when induced to leave his or her "old" job? Quite certainly, losing one's job, even for a person working at will, is a significant loss. Some courts have applied the principles of promissory estoppel to find that the promissee, the party to whom the new job was dangled, or promised, can pursue a remedy. If promissory estoppel were determined to be a viable cause of action, how would damages be computed? [*Julie Goff-Hamel v. Obstetricians & Gynecologists, P.C.,* 256 Neb. 19, 588 N.W. 2d 798 (1999).]

4. **Duress and Drug Testing.** The National Collegiate Athletic Association (NCAA) sets rules that determine the eligibility of college athletes. Although, for some, stardom in college sports is a springboard for a career in professional athletics, for the vast majority of college athletes, college sports are an extra-curricular activity. Because of concerns about the integrity of athletic contests in high-profile sports, drug testing has become commonplace and is required by NCAA rules. In order to administer such tests, college athletes must sign forms "consenting" to drug tests. The term *consent* is really a misnomer because, if a student wants to compete in college sports controlled by the NCAA, they must consent to drug tests or be denied eligibility. In relation to student athletes, the NCAA is a monopoly; there is no student participation in establishing rules, and all participants are potentially subject to drug tests. When student athletes sign "consent" forms, are those signatures tainted by duress, given the huge imbalance in bargaining power? See the arguments of dissenting judges on the California Supreme Court in *Jennifer Hill et al. v. National Collegiate Athletic Association,* 7 Cal. 4th 1 (1994).

5. **Exculpatory Clauses.** Exculpatory clauses are commonplace in many endeavors. For many activities such as participation in sports, players and often their parents must sign exculpatory clauses agreeing not to sue the promoters or league officials for negligence. Suppose you want to obtain a driver's license to operate a motorcycle and, in order to obtain the license, you have to complete a course operated by a facility that trains people to safely ride a motorcycle. Suppose, further, that in order to get the training to operate a motorcycle, the facility requires you to sign a contract in which you agree to completely release the facility from liability for negligence. In general, properly composed exculpatory clauses are enforceable so long as the entity trying to enforce the clause is not an essential public facility such as a common carrier or utility. If the state mandates that all motorcycle operators must receive safety training, can a motorcycle school claim that its training is voluntary? See *Anne M. Fortson v. Ross McClellan,* 508 S.E.2d 549 (N.C. Ct. App. 1998). Ms. Fortson was a student who was injured while receiving motorcycle training after signing an agreement not to sue the training school or the instructors. Can she avoid a motion for a summary judgment?

6. **When Does Acceptance Take Place?** Timing issues continue to be decisive in contract cases. A valid offer is like a live gun: if it is accepted, both the offeror and the offeree are bound to contractual performance in the typical executory, bilateral agreement. On May 16, 1985, Embree executed an "Agreement for Directory Advertising" so that its advertisements would appear in Bell's phone book. According to the contract, "This agreement shall become enforceable when signed by the Advertiser and accepted by the Publisher. The Advertising specified on the face of this agreement shall be considered to have been accepted by the Publisher on the scheduled customer close date . . ." and "Cancellation may be made if either party sends notice in writing not less than five (5) days before the scheduled customer close date of the director issue . . ." The agreement itself listed the close date as May 13, 1985. On July 22, 1985, Embree attempted to cancel the agreement by giving written notice to Bell, but Bell did not respond and Embree's advertisement was published in October of 1985. The court in this case viewed Embree as the offeree and Bell as the offeror, even though Embree made use of an agreement written by Bell. The issue in this case is "When did the acceptance occur?" Clearly, Embree had tendered the agreement after the close date so the close date has no legal significance in the case. [*Embree, Inc. v. Southwestern Bell Media, Inc.*, 772 S.W.2d 209 (TEX. App. 1989).]

Social Responsibility and Ethics in a High-Tech World

7. **Contractual Purposes.** Assuming the parties to a contract possess full information, in theory a contract should benefit all because each party always has the option of not agreeing to the contract. Of course, we know some contracts have disastrous consequences, mainly because things don't always go as planned. An issue that has become more and more prominent involves warnings, indemnity clauses, and exculpatory clauses (clauses that eliminate liability for a firm). The idea is that businesses are seeking to limit their downside risk, which in theory seems achievable by creating conspicuous paper trails. If, for example, you operate a roller skating rink, it is important to get all skaters to sign statements that they will not hold the facility liable for negligence that takes place either through the actions of other skaters or by the facility itself. Many drugs are now sold with a small booklet that lists the possible side effects of such drugs, when interactions with other drugs can be harmful, and what kind of persons should be especially careful about taking this drug. In online transactions, purchasers are often confronted with lengthy sets of terms that have nothing to do with the items being purchased but instead shift jurisdiction from the purchaser's home state to the seller's state, make the applicable laws an option of the seller, and so on. Most of the firms writing and relying on exculpatory clauses know full well that customers are not going to read these clauses and, yet, they are part of seemingly routine agreements. Is it ethical for a firm to

   a. Make every transaction subject to a written agreement loaded with exculpatory language?

   b. Incorporate exculpatory language even though they know it is unenforceable?

   Clearly, getting children to "agree" not to sue for negligence of staff at a roller rink is of questionable legal value since children, lacking the ability to consent, cannot sign away their rights. For less-educated people, however, even though such clauses are not enforceable, they may dissuade some from pursuing available legal remedies. Is this ethical? If a mother came up to you crying because her son had just broken his arm, would you tell her that she cannot recover because her son signed away his right to sue? Are we doomed to a future in which each of us signs away our rights, time and time again, because we are too busy to read the legalese in consent forms?

Using the Internet to Your Advantage

1. The Cornell University Legal Information Institute (LII) has assembled an online overview of basic contract law at http://www.law.cornell.edu/topics/contracts.html. A user-friendly online copy of the Uniform Commercial Code is accessible at http://www.law.cornell.edu/ucc/ucc.table.html and there is also a hyperlink to the United Nations Convention for the International Sale of Goods located at the Legal Information Institute website. Hyperlinks are also provided at the LII Web page to recent U.S. Supreme Court and U.S. Courts of Appeals decisions involving contract law.

2. For those who want to mix law, humor (not all of which is tasteful), and a healthy disrespect for authority, the 'Lectric Law Library (http://www.lectlaw.com/) is an area that provides some of each. The Laypeople's Law Lounge (http://www.lectlaw.com/lay.html) has some information

dealing with contract law and many other topics, again for those with an iconographic sense of humor. Other interesting topics in business law generally can be accessed at http://www.lectlaw. com/bus.html.

3. For the common law of contracts, probably the best sources are found in Restatements composed by the American Law Institute (ALI) (http://www.ali.org/). Discussion about the ALI and Restatements can be found at http://www.ali.org/ali/thisali.htm. An even broader discussion of the Restatements and their linkage with Lexis-Nexis is available at http://www.law.harvard.edu/ library/research_guides/restatements.htm#RestatementsLexisNexis.

4. The private sector is offering contract assistance online. For example, Contracts Online (http://www.contractsonline.net/index.html) offers contracts online that are downloadable. Other organizations appear to gratuitously offer contract law notes online at http://www.bigwig. net/sljohn/Contract.html. Law Links (http://resource.lawlinks.com/Content/Legal_Subject_Index/ Contract%20Law/contract_law.htm) appears to be just that; it links together legal discussions of various points of contract law from many sources, including some of those cited above.

Chapter **Eight**

Commercial Law: The Uniform Commercial Code (UCC)

Learning Objectives

On completing this chapter, you should

1. Know the origin and rationale for the creation of the UCC.
2. Be aware of how the UCC differs from the common law re contracts.
3. Be aware of how and when additional terms in an acceptance can become part of a contract under the UCC.
4. Be able to discuss how the UCC deals with express and implied warranties, disclaimers, and limitations of liability.
5. Be able to discuss the perfect tender rule, breach of contract, and damages under the UCC.

OVERVIEW

This chapter extends what was discussed in Chapter 7 by focusing on the Uniform Commercial Code (UCC) and, in the process, provides the foundation for Chapter 9, which deals with contract law for e-commerce. There were two persistent forces that led to the creation of the Uniform Commercial Code. The first was the near universal desire to have *uniform* commercial contract law in place of the hodgepodge of common law standards that varied from state to state. The second was the parallel desire to get the law "out of the way" when two or more parties were attempting to make business deals. Drafters of the UCC viewed commercial law as something that should be shaped by commercial practices of businesses and consumers rather than the other way around. At the same time, a strong theme that permeates the UCC is a prohibition of *unconscionable* bargains that unreasonably take advantage of the superior bargaining power of one contracting party to the detriment of another.

Article 2 (of the UCC)
Deals with the sale of tangible goods that are movable.

Reforms Are Part of the Story

The UCC contains nine articles (see "Nutz and Boltz" box), but the exclusive focus in this chapter is on **Article 2,** dealing with sales. As this chapter is being written, Article 2 of the UCC is being rewritten by the National Conference of Commissioners on Uniform State

Nutz and Boltz   Transactions Governed by the UCC

Article 1: General Provisions	Purpose of the UCC; general guidance and definitions
Article 2: Sales	Applies to sales and leases of goods
Article 3: Negotiable Instruments	Use of checks, promissory notes, and other financial instruments
Article 4: Bank Deposits	Rights and duties of banks and their clients
Article 4A: Funds Transfers	
Article 5: Letters of Credit	Guaranteed payment by a bank that extends credit on behalf of a client
Article 6: Bulk Transfers and Bulk Sales	Sale of a large part of a company's material
Article 7: Warehouse Receipts, Bills of Lading, and Other Documents of Title	Papers proving ownership of goods being shipped
Article 8: Investment Securities	Rights and duties related to stock or other ownership interests
Article 9: Secured Transactions	Sales in which seller holds a financial interest in goods sold

Laws (NCCUSL, see www.nccusl.org). The rewriting project began in 1996, with a number of tentative drafts circulated since then. Increasingly, contract law is becoming politicized as consumer advocates and business groups are delving into the details of proposed changes to Article 2 of the UCC. A good bit of the attention of advocacy groups attempting to influence the evolution of contract law has been focused on proposals for a uniform law of e-commerce. When relevant, this chapter reviews proposed changes in Article 2, though there is no assurance that the most recent draft of the revisions of Article 2 of the UCC will be final.

Focusing on How the UCC Differs from the Common Law of Contracts   A clear understanding of contract law is aided by reviewing the differences between the common law of contracts (Chapter 7) and the UCC. Historically, a number of the principles of the established common law of contracts were at odds with actual commercial practices that were favored by contracting parties for the flexibility and efficiency they offered. Most of these mischievous common law obstacles to voluntary contracting mechanisms were either modified or eliminated in the UCC (an example is provided in the "Nutz and Boltz" box above).

The UCC Is Relevant—Only When the Parties to a Contract Do Not Specify the Terms Themselves   As we proceed, it is important to be mindful that the UCC is not actually "the law" of commercial contracts! For the most part, the UCC is a **gap-filler** and is only pertinent if the parties themselves do not supply a contract term. For example, if nothing is said in a sales contract about delivery, then under the UCC, the goods are considered delivered to the buyer when they are given to the buyer at the seller's establishment. In like fashion, under the UCC, if nothing different is said in a sales contract, payment is due at the time of delivery of goods. We all know that in many sales contracts the seller will deliver goods to the buyer's place of business and payment need not be immediate. However, the "standard terms" as dictated by the UCC are applicable unless the parties agree to something else, which they generally do.

gap-filler
Terms in the UCC that are part of a contract if there is no written term in the contract, or the term is left "open."

International Perspective Convention for the International Sale of Goods

The United Nations Convention on Contracts for the International Sale of Goods (CISG) is the uniform international sales law of countries that account for two-thirds of all world trade. As a service to the world trade community, the Pace University School of Law offers an annotated electronic library on the CISG on the World Wide Web (http://www.cisg.law.pace.edu/cisg/text/cisg-toc.html).

As we will see, most of the provisions of the CISG are very similar to those of the UCC. The Preamble of the CISG reads as follows:

PREAMBLE

THE STATES PARTIES TO THIS CONVENTION,

BEARING IN MIND the broad objectives in the resolutions adopted by the sixth special session of the General Assembly of the United Nations on the establishment of a New International Economic Order,

CONSIDERING that the development of international trade on the basis of equality and mutual benefit is an important element in promoting friendly relations among States,

BEING OF THE OPINION that the adoption of uniform rules which govern contracts for the international sale of goods and take into account the different social, economic and legal systems would contribute to the removal of legal barriers in international trade and promote the development of international trade[.]

It seems clear that the same forces that compelled development of the UCC in the United States have been at work in the development of the CISG internationally. It is also important to note that the UCC applies to all (business and consumer) sales of goods, whereas the CISG applies only to business-to-business sales of goods.

ARTICLE 2 OF THE UCC

Scope

As mentioned above, Article 2 of the UCC applies when a contract involves the sale of goods. According to UCC "legalese" in Article 2-105, *goods* are "all things (including specially manufactured goods) which are movable at the time of identification to the contract for sale." A UCC **good** cannot be *real property* (such as land), which is not moveable, nor can it be *intangible,* which has no physical existence, as would be the case with patent rights. **Identification** of a good takes place when the good is in existence (the item has been made) and has a specific, recognizable identity, denoted by a unique marking or by some other means of distinguishing the good (or goods) that is (are) the subject of a contract.

good
Under the UCC, a good is all things that are tangible and moveable.

identification
Takes place under the UCC when a good is in existence and can be distinguished from other goods.

There are many sales contracts that involve a combination of both goods and services. The UCC is the contract law that governs the transaction if the *goods* portion of the contract dominates relative to the *services* part. If there are monetary values separately assigned with the goods and with the services, the larger one controls whether the contract is governed under UCC rules or by the common law of contracts.

Merchants and Good Faith

In general, the UCC holds sellers to high standards if they are considered *merchants*. Under Section 2-104, a merchant is an entity that

> deals in goods of the kind or otherwise by his occupation holds himself out as having knowledge or skill peculiar to the practices or goods involved in the transaction or to whom such knowledge or skill may be attributed by his employment of an agent or broker or other intermediary who by his occupation holds himself out as having such knowledge or skill.

Ethical Challenges   Commercial Morality and Ethics under the UCC

Popular myths have often likened commercial morality to the law of the jungle and yet the facts would suggest otherwise. In the UCC, two ethical terms, or concepts, are used extensively to take away advantages that may be appropriated by stronger, more aggressive parties in a contract. The term "good faith" is used 16 times in Article 2 of the UCC, which deals with the sale of goods, while "unconscionable" is appears 4 times. Under the UCC, only merchants are held to the standard of "good faith," which is a higher standard than is imposed on nonmerchants. The consequence for a merchant found to be not acting in good faith is that the courts can decide not to enforce a contract between the merchant and another party, generally a consumer.

There are two types of events that many regard as unconscionable:

1. Selling a defective consumer good with a warranty that limits damage recoveries on the part of the consumer to replacement of the defective product.
2. Allowing one side in a contract to cancel without providing notice to the other side.

Under the UCC, the first event is deemed unconscionable by Section 2-719(c) and the second can be unconscionable under Section 2-309. Section 2-302 warns the parties generally that "If the court as a matter of law finds the contract or any clause of the contract to have been unconscionable at the time it was made the court may refuse to enforce the contract . . ." Claims of lack of "good faith" or "unconscionability" frequently appear in UCC litigation, indicating the importance these concepts occupy in commercial law. Undoubtedly, actual commercial practice often falls significantly short of what is theoretically called for by the UCC, but at least the UCC shoots high, rather than low, on commercial morality.

---

good faith
Merchants are required under the UCC to be honest in fact in their conduct and transactions.

The UCC calls for all contracts to be constructed and executed in **good faith**, which it defines as "honesty in fact in the conduct or transaction concerned." In general, recognizing that merchants have more knowledge about the goods they are selling than do purchasers, merchants are held to higher standards of conduct. For example, unless something is stated to the contrary in the applicable contract, all goods sold by a merchant are required to be *fit for the ordinary purposes to which such goods are used*. For second-hand sales, no such requirements are imposed—for example, on consumers who resell their used cars.

What Is a Sale?

sale
Occurs when title to a good is transferred from seller to buyer for a price.

A **sale** takes place when *title to goods transfers from seller to buyer for a price*. There are a number of transactions, however, that transfer title or possession of goods from one party to another but are not *sales*. For example, a gift takes place when title to goods is transferred, but the transfer does not involve a price. A lease occurs when physical possession of the good is transferred but the lessor (a bailor in UCC language) retains title. Of course, many leases with options to buy at the expiration of the lease closely resemble installment sales contracts. To address this, the UCC has added Article 2A, governing leases, which many states have adopted.

The Legal Rights of Thieves and Those Who Deal with Them

bona fide purchaser for value
A person who pays money or property for a good in good faith believing the seller is the owner of the goods.

Unlike gifts and leases, thefts of goods and subsequent sales do not transfer title from the rightful owner to a **bona fide purchaser for value.** A bona fide purchaser for value is someone who innocently pays money to a thief for goods and later discovers that the goods were stolen. In a contest between an innocent buyer (from the thief) for value and the original owner, the original owner prevails even if the thief presented the innocent buyer with documents of title that looked authentic.

For example, Adolph is a member of organized crime and hijacks a shipment of computers destined for an Office Depot® outlet. Adolph erases the serial numbers on the computers and sells them instead to Circuit City® with counterfeit serial numbers on them. Each computer, however, is uniquely identifiable not only by serial numbers but also by its computer chips, which incorporate a type of cyber address. Through its investigations, Office Depot traces several of its stolen computers and determines that each was purchased from a Circuit City outlet. Assume that police arrest Adolph but are unable to recover any monetary assets from him. Since Circuit City paid full value to Adolph, it resists returning the computers to their rightful owner, Office Depot. Unfortunately for Circuit City, under the UCC, since a thief cannot pass good title, Office Depot will be awarded the computers in the event of litigation.

Transfer of Title

Under the UCC (Section 2-401), the parties to a contract have almost complete discretion among themselves as to when title transfers, again so long as the goods are identified. If the parties say nothing about transfer of title, then UCC gap-fillers apply. Under the UCC, title transfers to the buyer

- When the seller completes all obligations necessary to deliver the goods or
- If the goods do not have to be moved because they are located at a warehouse managed by a third party, when the seller delivers documents of title such as a bill of lading.

Passing of Title: Shipment and Destination Contracts   If the place of delivery is not specified, then title passes when a seller delivers the goods to a common carrier (Section 2-509). Such a contract is called a **shipment contract.** In a **destination contract,** title passes when the seller delivers the goods to the destination specified in the contract, in most cases, the buyer's business or home. For a concrete example, title to goods sold by a manufacturer to a retailer transfers to the buyer when the goods are picked up by UPS, if nothing different is indicated in the contract. If the contract specifies that the seller is to deliver the goods to the buyer's dock, then title to the goods does not transfer until the UPS truck off-loads the goods at the buyer's dock.

Risk of Loss and Insurance   Title to goods is important because, in general, the party who owns the goods bears any **risk of loss.** There are, however, important exceptions to this principle. The UCC allows a purchaser to insure goods against loss, even before title to goods is transferred, as long as the goods are identified by contract (Section 2-501). Conversely, after title to goods is transferred to a buyer, the UCC allows the seller to insure the goods sold against loss if the seller retains a security interest in the goods. A seller retains a security interest when the buyer is paying for the goods through installment payments.

In general, sellers bear the risk of loss in shipment contracts until the goods are transferred to a common carrier, at which time risk of loss is transferred to the buyer (Section 2-509). Of course, this risk could be altered by contract terms that reserve risk of loss to the seller. In destination contracts, the seller retains risk of loss until the goods are transferred to the destination specified in the contract, again with the proviso that this result could be changed by a term in the contract. Consider Case 8-1 involving risk of loss.

Third-Party Possession of the Goods   If goods under contract are in the physical possession of a third party, such as a warehouseman, then risk of loss passes to the buyer when documents of title are transferred to the buyer by the seller.

shipment contract
A contract that does not specify a location where the goods are to be shipped.

destination contract
A contract that does specify the location where goods are to be shipped.

risk of loss
A risk that goods will be damaged or destroyed after the contract is executed.

Case 8-1

Lynch Imports, Ltd., Plaintiff-Appellee v. Joseph B. Frey et al., Defendants-Appellants

Appellate Court of Illinois, First District, Fifth Division
558 N.E.2d 484 (1990)

BACKGROUND AND FACTS

Defendants, Joseph and Stephanie Frey (buyers), appeal from an order of the circuit court of Cook County, granting summary judgment on the complaint of plaintiff, Lynch Imports, Ltd. (seller). Count I of the complaint sought damages in the sum of $8,706 for the breach of an automobile sales contract, while count II sought damages of $4,706 for wrongful stoppage of a check.

On October 22, 1987, buyers agreed to purchase a 1987 Volkswagen automobile from the seller for the price of $8,706. The agreement was set forth in a "CAR PURCHASE ORDER" form (here-inafter referred to as purchase contract). The following words were handwritten on the purchase contract: "car to be in totally acceptable condition or money will be refunded to the customer" and "acceptable subject to inspection."

On October 24, buyers took possession of the vehicle and paid seller $4,706, in the form of a check, as part payment on the purchase price. The balance of the purchase price was to be financed. Two riders that were attached to and made part of the purchase contract were also signed. Of the two, rider 2 is significant for purposes of this appeal and provided in pertinent part:

> *(1) Buyer, at buyer's cost will have the vehicle fully covered under liability and collision auto-mobile insurance from the instant that buyer takes possession. . . .*
>
> *It is expressly understood that this rider does not authorize buyer to return said vehicle to the seller without seller's prior authorization. Automobiles are not sold on approval; no sales person or other employee of seller is ever authorized to sell a vehicle with a condition that the buyer may later return it.*

About two to three days thereafter, the buyers brought the vehicle to the seller so that the air conditioner could be installed. When they returned in the evening to pick up the vehicle, they were informed that the air conditioner had been installed, but that the vehicle sustained body damage in an accident. The buy-ers refused to take delivery of the automobile vehicle because of the damage and demanded that a new and undamaged vehicle be substituted. When the seller refused, buyers stopped payment on the check and cancelled their application for financing the balance of the purchase price. The seller then filed its complaint in the circuit court of Cook County.

Opinion: Justice Gordon Delivered the Opinion of the Court

Buyers contend that it was an error for the trial court to grant summary judgment in favor of seller because there still remained issues of material fact precluding summary judgment. Summary judg-ment is appropriate where pleadings, depositions and admissions on file together with affidavits, if any, show that there is no genuine issue of material fact and that the movant is entitled to judgment as a matter of law. [References deleted] Where the facts are undisputed and can lead to but a single conclusion, a trial court may properly enter a summary judgment.

The buyers contend that there is an issue of material fact as to whether they "accepted" the vehi-cle on October 24. Buyers argue that they did not "accept" the vehicle and therefore had the right to reject it, which they properly did, when it was damaged upon its return to the seller to install the air conditioner. The seller maintains that no fact issues exist to negate the conclusion that buyers ac-cepted the car when they took possession on October 24. We agree with the buyers.

Under the provisions of section 2–606 of the Uniform Commercial Code (Ill. Rev. Stat. 1987, ch. 26, par. 2–606), acceptance is deemed to have occurred when the buyer either signifies that the vehicle was conforming or "takes or retains" the vehicle in spite of its nonconformity. Section 2–606 provides in pertinent part:

(1) Acceptance of goods occurs when the buyer

(a) after a reasonable opportunity to inspect the goods signifies . . . that the goods are conforming or that he will take or retain them in spite of their non-conformity." Ill. Rev. Stat. 1987, ch. 26, par. 2–606(1)(a).

* * *

Contrary to the seller's contention, this question of fact as to whether the buyers waived their right to defer acceptance is not resolved by the execution of rider 2. As previously noted, rider 2 provides for the buyers to obtain insurance upon taking possession and further states:

"It is expressly understood that this rider does not authorize buyer to return said vehicle to seller without seller's prior authorization. Automobiles are not sold 'on approval'; no salesperson or other employee of seller is ever authorized to sell a vehicle with the condition that the buyer may later return it."

* * *

Under section 2–509 of the Uniform Commercial Code (Ill. Rev. Stat. 1987, ch. 26, par. 2–509), the risk of loss does not pass to the buyer until the buyer accepts the goods, even though the buyer obtains an insurable interest under section 2–501 (Ill. Rev. Stat. 1987, ch. 26, par. 2–501) after the goods are identified to the purchase contract. Thus rider 2, which provides for the buyer to obtain insurance, is not conclusive on its face to pass the risk of loss to the buyer. Here the only evidence concerning the execution of rider 2 and of any conversations surrounding the removal of the vehicle by the buyers is in the contested portion of the Lynch affidavit and therefore inappropriate for summary judgment consideration.

* * *

Decision and Outcome

The court remanded this case back to the trial court to decide the issue of whether the buyers actually accepted the car. If buyers had not accepted the car, then sellers still bore risk of loss.

Questions for Analysis

1. How does Section 2-509 of the UCC define "acceptance" and risk of loss? Is the fact that the buyer arranged to insure the car sufficient to prove that the buyer accepted the car?

2. The trial court granted the seller's motion for a summary judgment. What issue of fact does the defendant buyer contend is in dispute? Why doesn't rider 2 resolve the issue?

Agreements under the UCC

The UCC differs significantly from the common law in the *formation* of a contract and in the *terms that are part of the contract*. The common law uses a mechanistic formula that requires all offers to be *clear* and *definite* in their terms and to *contain all material terms*. Under the common law of contracts, any additional terms put forward by offerees are viewed as creating *counteroffers,* and thus are deemed to be *rejections* of the original offer.

In contrast, the UCC places much more emphasis on intent. The question asked by the UCC is whether the parties *intended* to make a contract. If the answer is yes, then the specific terms of the contract can be supplied by a variety of sources, including

- Prior conduct between the parties.
- Custom and usage within the industry.
- Terms added by either party in communications regarding the contract.

International Perspective — Termination of Offers under the CISG

The rules regarding termination of an offer under the CISG are virtually identical to those of the UCC (see Article 16).

ARTICLE 16

1. Until a contract is concluded an offer may be revoked if the revocation reaches the offeree before he has dispatched an acceptance.

2. However, an offer cannot be revoked:

    a. if it indicates, whether by stating a fixed time for acceptance or otherwise, that it is irrevocable; or

    b. if it was reasonable for the offeree to rely on the offer as being irrevocable and the offeree has acted in reliance on the offer.

- Gap-fillers from the UCC.
- Reasonable terms, including price.

Terms Required in the Offer

Businesspeople are heard to claim that they reach agreements based on handshakes and then they "turn them over to the lawyers to make the agreements legal." In accordance with this claim of business "practice," the UCC places great emphasis on "intent" in determining whether a contract exists. Not all material terms need be in the offer. If a term is left *open*— that is, not mentioned in the contract—then, at a minimum, applicable UCC gap-fillers are available to be used. For example, as indicated earlier, if nothing is said about payment, the UCC requires that the buyer pay the seller in full at the time of delivery of the goods. On the other hand, if the parties have had a continuing series of contracts in which the buyer orders goods and the seller accepts payment within 30 days of delivery, that *prior conduct* between the parties will be relied on to determine the payments term in the contract.

Output and Requirements Contracts

output contract
Contract in which the buyer agrees to purchase all the output of the seller during a period of time.

requirements contract
Contract in which the buyer agrees to purchase all of its requirements for a particular good from a single seller during a period of time.

At a minimum, a contract governed by the UCC requires that the parties be identified, the subject matter be clear, and the quantity be determinable, subject to two major exceptions. In output and requirements contracts, even quantity can be left unspecified. In an **output contract,** the buyer agrees to buy all of the output of the seller. Such contracts are common in agriculture where the buyer, typically a food processor, agrees to purchase all of the output of the seller, a farmer or cooperative, even though the exact quantities cannot be determined because they are dependent upon weather and other factors. In a **requirements contract,** the seller agrees to sell all of its goods that the buyer wants even though the buyer does not know its needs beforehand. A tire maker may have a requirements contract with an automobile manufacturer, who obviously does not know its needs for tires ahead of time because they depend on the number of cars its customers choose to order and buy.

Termination of the Offer

irrevocable (offers)
Written offers by merchants that cannot be withdrawn during the period of time the offer states it will remain open.

Under the common law of contracts, an offeror can revoke an offer at any time, even if the offeror had guaranteed that the offer would remain open for a period of time. In contrast, under the UCC, when a *merchant* makes an offer in the form of a signed writing, that offer is **irrevocable** during the time span stated in the offer. This rule, the irrevocability of offers during the period stated in the offer, reflects commercial practice and, thus, is part of the UCC. As with most related UCC rules, this requirement applies only to merchants and not to all sellers.

UCC Acceptances: Problems with the Last Shot Rule

Conflicts between the common law of contracts and commercial practice are most evident in the way *acceptances* are treated. Under the common law, acceptances must be *complete* and *unqualified;* the common law "mirror image" rule requires the offeree to accept each and every term in the offer and prohibits the inclusion of any additional terms. In commercial practice, offers are generally placed through buyer purchase orders, which are responded to by sellers with deliveries of goods and invoices. Typically, the language in sellers' invoices (or in their bills) does not match the language in the buyers' purchase orders. Under the common law, a seller's invoice thus becomes a counteroffer and dictates the terms of the contract if the buyer accepts the goods at his or her dock and makes payment. The fact that language in an invoice requires the buyer to bear risk of loss during shipment and prior to delivery would generally only become evident if the goods being shipped were destroyed en route to the buyer.

The transaction pattern described above also can be reversed. A buyer can order goods over the phone and the seller can respond with delivery of requested goods and an invoice. When the buyer receives the invoice, he or she can send a check, along with buyer company language that adds a number of terms to the "contract," including delivery terms that make the agreement a "destination" contract, under which the seller bears risk of loss. *In either scenario, the firm that sends the last piece of paper (either a purchase order or invoice) is able to control the contract.*

Additional Terms in the Acceptance

Under UCC Section 2-207,

> (1) A definite and reasonable expression of acceptance or a written confirmation which is sent within a reasonable time operates as an acceptance *even though it states terms additional to or different from those offered or agreed upon,* unless acceptance is expressly made conditional on assent to the additional or different terms. [Emphasis added]

additional terms
Terms in the acceptance that are not in the offer and add to the terms in the offer.

different terms
Terms in the acceptance that differ from terms in the offer.

A UCC acceptance can contain **additional terms** and even **different terms** from those in the offer and still be an acceptance, so long as the acceptance *does not require* inclusion of these additional terms. If the acceptance does require inclusion of the additional terms that appear in the acceptance, then the acceptance is a counteroffer.

Section 2-207(2) treats additional terms in the acceptance as proposals that become part of the contract unless

a. the offer expressly limits acceptance to the terms of the offer;

b. they materially alter it; or

c. notification of objection to them has already been given or is given within a reasonable time after notice of them is received.

These rules regarding additional terms in the acceptance only apply to contracts between merchants. The offeror can dictate the actions that constitute an acceptance and, if the offeror indicates in the offer that no additional terms in the acceptance will be part of the contract (Section 2-207(2)(a)), additional terms in the acceptance are not part of the contract, but rather a counteroffer.

Material Alteration?

Section 2-207(2)(b) prohibits additional terms in the acceptance from being part of the contract if these terms "materially alter it." In cases that have gone before various state courts, warranty disclaimers (discussed later in the chapter) have been held to materially alter a contract. It is worth noting that in the proposed new Section 2-207 of the latest revision of Article 2, Sales, there is no such limitation on the inclusion of additional terms.

In other words, if Revised Article 2 of the UCC is adopted by the states, and it seems likely that this will occur, it will be permissible *to insert additional terms in the acceptance that can materially alter the contract* and those terms will become part of the contract unless promptly objected to by the other party.

Burden on Offeror to Object   Additional terms in the acceptance become part of the contract provided they pass the tests given above regarding material alterations, counteroffers, and offers that prohibit additional terms, unless under Section 2-507(2)(c) the *offeror* objects within a reasonable time after notice of these terms has been received. Let us assume that you are a buyer, you have sent your purchase order to a seller, and the seller informs you over the phone that the goods you ordered will arrive tomorrow via UPS 24-hour option. At this point the buyer is the offeror. The goods arrive along with an envelope that contains an invoice with additional terms or terms that differ from those in the purchase offer. Are the additional terms in the invoice part of the contract? The answer is yes, unless you object within a reasonable time, probably 10 days or less.

Additional or Different Terms

Conceptually, there is less difficulty dealing with an acceptance that contains *additional terms* than with one that contains *different terms*. If an important term is missing in a contract at issue, then UCC gap-fillers would provide the term. But, with an additional term in the acceptance that is on point, that added term controls. For example, if the term concerned timing of payment, that term is discussed by UCC Section 2-310, Open Time for Payment or Running of Credit; Authority to Ship under Reservation.

On the other hand, if a term in an acceptance *differs* from a term in an offer, there are a variety of ways in which the conflicting term may be reconciled. Often, the most logical application of the UCC to this situation is a simple cancellation of the conflicting term with a UCC gap-filler replacing the cancelled term.[1] Alternatively, a court could revert back to the "last shot" rule, with the terms in the acceptance determining the terms of the contract unless the additional or different terms were objected to by the offeror in a reasonable amount of time. There is a general preference for the UCC gap-filler solution because the last shot rule results in case outcomes decided by trivial timing issues.

What if the Writings Just Don't Agree but the Parties Proceed as Though They Do?

For most commercial sales contracts, parties do not read the fine print in either the invoice or purchase order. The contents of these documents only become an issue when something goes wrong, typically either by the goods not conforming (not being what the buyer ordered) or due to an issue regarding delivery or payment. When attorneys for the buyer and seller examine documents from the other side, there are often sizeable conflicts between the terms in each document. According Section 2-207(3):

> Conduct by both parties which recognizes the existence of a contract is sufficient to establish a contract for sale although the writings of the parties do not otherwise establish a contract. In such a case the terms of the particular contract consist of those terms on which the writings of the parties agree, together with any supplementary terms incorporated under any other provisions of this Act.

Again, the importance of the gap-filler role of the UCC is evident. The "supplementary terms incorporated under any other provisions of this Act" bring in Section 1-205, which indicates that, for firms that have had prior dealings, courts will examine prior conduct to

---

[1] *Ionics, Inc. v. Elmwood Sensors, Inc.,* 110 F.3d 184 (1st Cir. 1997).

course of dealing
Prior conduct between the parties in previous contracts that can be used to define open terms in a contract.

usage of trade (trade usage)
The ways similar transactions are usually handled within the industry.

determine the terms of the contract when the writings are unclear or in conflict. According to Section 1-205(3):

> A **course of dealing** [prior conduct] between parties and any **usage of trade** in the vocation or trade in which they are engaged or of which they are or should be aware give particular meaning to and supplement or qualify terms of an agreement.

Confused? Consider Case 8-2.

Case 8-2

Ionics, Inc., Plaintiff-Appellee v. Elmwood Sensors, Inc., Defendant-Appellant

United States Court of Appeals for the First Circuit
110 F.3d 184 (1st Cir. 1997)

BACKGROUND AND FACTS

The plaintiff, Ionics, Inc. (Ionics), purchased thermostats from Elmwood Sensors, Inc. (Elmwood), defendant, for installation in water dispensers manufactured by the former. Several of the dispensers subsequently caused fires, which allegedly resulted from defects in the sensors. Ionics filed suit against Elmwood in order to recover costs incurred in the wake of the fires.

The following exchanges of communications occurred between the parties: First, Ionics sent a purchase order to Elmwood that contained the following terms:

> *18. REMEDIES—The remedies provided Buyer herein shall be cumulative, and in addition to any other remedies provided by law or equity. A waiver of a breach of any provision hereof shall not constitute a waiver of any other breach. The laws of the state shown in Buyer's address printed on the masthead of this order shall apply in the construction hereof.*

> *19. ACCEPTANCE—Acceptance by the Seller of this order shall be upon the terms and conditions set forth in items 1 to 17 inclusive, and elsewhere in this order. Said order can be so accepted only on the exact terms herein and set forth. No terms which are in any manner additional to or different from those herein set forth shall become a part of, alter or in any way control the terms and conditions herein set forth.*

Near the time when Ionics placed its first order, it sent Elmwood a letter that it sends to all of its new suppliers. The letter states, in part:

> *The information preprinted, written and/or typed on our purchase order is especially important to us. Should you take exception to this information, please clearly express any reservations to us in writing. If you do not, we will assume that you have agreed to the specified terms and that you will fulfill your obligations according to our purchase order. If necessary, we will change your invoice and pay your invoice according to our purchase order.*

Following receipt of each order, Elmwood prepared and sent an "Acknowledgment" form containing the following language in small type:

> *THIS WILL ACKNOWLEDGE RECEIPT OF BUYER'S ORDER AND STATE SELLER'S WILLINGNESS TO SELL THE GOODS ORDERED BUT ONLY UPON THE TERMS AND*

CONDITIONS SET FORTH HEREIN AND ON THE REVERSE SIDE HEREOF AS A **COUNTEROFFER.** *BUYER SHALL BE DEEMED TO HAVE ACCEPTED SUCH COUNTEROFFER UNLESS IT IS REJECTED IN WRITING WITHIN TEN (10) DAYS OF THE RECEIPT HEREOF, AND ALL SUBSEQUENT ACTION SHALL BE PURSUANT TO THE TERMS AND CONDITIONS OF THIS COUNTEROFFER ONLY; ANY ADDITIONAL OR DIFFERENT TERMS ARE HEREBY OBJECTED TO AND SHALL NOT BE BINDING UPON THE PARTIES UNLESS SPECIFICALLY AGREED TO IN WRITING BY SELLER* [emphasis added].

It is undisputed that the Acknowledgment was received prior to the arrival of the shipment of goods. Although the district court, in its ruling on the summary judgment motion, states that "with each shipment of thermostats, Elmwood included an Acknowledgment Form," Order of the District Court, August 23, 1995, this statement cannot reasonably be taken as a finding in support of the claim that the Acknowledgment and the shipment arrived together.

Before trial, the district court denied Elmwood's motion for partial summary judgment. The District Court of Massachusetts subsequently certified to this court "the question whether, in the circumstances of this case, § 2-207 of M.G.L. [Massachusetts General Laws] c. 106 has been properly applied." Order of the district court, November 6, 1995.

Opinion by Torruella

As we have noted, the Acknowledgment Form expressed Elmwood's willingness to sell thermostats on "terms and conditions" that the Form indicated were listed on the reverse side. Among the terms and conditions listed on the back was the following:

9. WARRANTY

All goods manufactured by Elmwood Sensors, Inc. are guaranteed to be free of defects in material and workmanship for a period of ninety (90) days after receipt of such goods by Buyer or eighteen months from the date of manufacturer [sic] (as evidenced by the manufacturer's date code), whichever shall be longer. THERE IS NO IMPLIED WARRANTY OF MERCHANTABILITY AND NO OTHER WARRANTY, EXPRESSED OR IMPLIED, EXCEPT SUCH AS IS EXPRESSLY SET FORTH HEREIN. SELLER WILL NOT BE LIABLE FOR ANY GENERAL, CONSEQUENTIAL OR INCIDENTAL DAMAGES, INCLUDING WITHOUT LIMITATION ANY DAMAGES FROM LOSS OF PROFITS, FROM ANY BREACH OF WARRANTY OR FOR NEGLIGENCE, SELLER'S LIABILITY AND BUYER'S EXCLUSIVE REMEDY BEING EXPRESSLY LIMITED TO THE REPAIR OF DEFECTIVE GOODS F.O.B. THE SHIPPING POINT INDICATED ON THE FACE HEREOF OR THE REPAYMENT OF THE PURCHASE PRICE UPON THE RETURN OF THE GOODS OR THE GRANTING OF A REASONABLE ALLOWANCE ON ACCOUNT OF ANY DEFECTS, AS SELLER MAY ELECT.

Neither party disputes that they entered into a valid contract and neither disputes the quantity of thermostats purchased, the price paid, or the manner and time of delivery. The only issue in dispute is the extent of Elmwood's liability.

In summary, Ionics' order included language stating that the contract would be governed exclusively by the terms included on the purchase order and that all remedies available under state law would be available to Ionics. In a subsequent letter, Ionics added that Elmwood must indicate any objections to these conditions in writing. Elmwood, in turn, sent Ionics an Acknowledgment stating that the contract was governed exclusively by the terms in the Acknowledgment, and Ionics was given ten days to reject this "counteroffer." Among the terms included in the Acknowledgment is a limitation on Elmwood's liability. As the district court stated, "the terms are diametrically opposed to each other on the issue of whether all warranties implied by law were reserved or waived." Order of the District Court, August 23, 1995.

We face, therefore, a battle of the forms. This is purely a question of law. The dispute turns on whether the contract is governed by the language after the comma in § 2-207(1) of the Uniform Commercial Code, according to the rule laid down by this court in *Roto-Lith, Ltd. v. F.P. Bartlett & Co.,* 297 F.2d 497 (1st Cir. 1962), or whether it is governed by subsection (3) of the Code provision, as enacted by both Massachusetts, Mass. Gen. L. ch. 106, § 2-207 (1990 and 1996 Supp.), and Rhode Island, R.I. Gen. Laws § 6A-2-207 (1992).

* * *

There is some uncertainty on the question of whether Massachusetts or Rhode Island law governs. We need not address this issue, however, because the two states have adopted versions of section 2-207 of the Uniform Commercial Code that are virtually equivalent.

* * *

III. LEGAL ANALYSIS

Our analysis begins with the statute. Section 2-207 reads as follows:

§ 2-207. Additional Terms in Acceptance or Confirmation

1. A definite and seasonable expression of acceptance or a written confirmation which is sent within a reasonable time operates as an acceptance even though it states terms additional to or different from those offered or agreed upon, unless acceptance is expressly made conditional on assent to the additional or different terms.

2. The additional or different terms are to be construed as proposals for addition to the contract. Between merchants such terms become part of the contract unless:
   a. the offer expressly limits acceptance to the terms of the offer;
   b. they materially alter it; or
   c. notification of objection to them has already been given or is given within a reasonable time after notice of them is received.

3. Conduct by both parties which recognizes the existence of a contract is sufficient to establish a contract for sale although the writings of the parties do not otherwise establish a contract. In such case the terms of the particular contract consist of those terms on which the writings of the parties agree, together with any supplementary terms incorporated under any other provisions of this chapter.

* * *

A plain language reading of section 2-207 suggests that subsection (3) governs the instant case. Ionics sent an initial offer to which Elmwood responded with its "Acknowledgment." Thereafter, the conduct of the parties established the existence of a contract as required by section 2-207(3).

Furthermore, the case before us is squarely addressed in comment 6, which states:

6. If no answer is received within a reasonable time after additional terms are proposed, it is both fair and commercially sound to assume that their inclusion has been assented to. Where clauses on confirming forms sent by both parties conflict [,] each party must be assumed to object to a clause of the other conflicting with one on the confirmation sent by himself. As a result[,] the requirement that there be notice of objection which is found in subsection (2) [of § 2-207] is satisfied and the conflicting terms do not become part of the contract. The contract then consists of the terms originally expressly agreed to, terms on which the confirmations agree, and terms supplied by this Act.

* * *

We hold, consistent with section 2-207 and Official Comment 6, that where the terms in two forms are contradictory, each party is assumed to object to the other party's conflicting clause. As a result, mere acceptance of the goods by the buyer is insufficient to infer consent to the seller's terms under the language of subsection (1). Nor do such terms become part of the contract under subsection (2) because notification of objection has been given by the conflicting forms. See § 2-207(2)(c).

* * *

Decision and Outcome

The court held that the defendant's motion for a summary judgment was denied and the case will go to trial on the issue of damages. Since there was a conflict between Ionics' purchase order and

Elmwood's acknowledgement letter with respect to damages, both terms are discarded and the UCC gap-filler is used, which does allow a buyer to sue for consequential damages caused by the fires.

Questions for Analysis

1. As a result of the court ruling, what does the contract consist of? If the terms of communications from the parties conflict, how does that affect the contract?
2. If the terms of the communications between the parties conflict, what is the role of the UCC gap-fillers?
3. Can the defendant be sued for a breach of the implied warranty of merchantability?
4. Are the plaintiff's recoverable damages limited to repair of defective parts as indicated in the limitation of liability stated above?

Open Terms

open term
Term in a contract about which nothing is stated. If the term is open, a UCC gap-filler will be supplied.

In UCC parlance, an **open term** is a term that is not specified in a contract. As has been suggested above, most open terms can be filled in by courts, using *prior conduct* or *trade usage* provisions in accord with Section 1-205 of the UCC. For some open terms, such as price, the UCC has special gap-filling procedures as provided in Section 2-305:

Open Price Term.

1. The parties if they so intend can conclude a contract for sale even though the sales price to be paid is not settled. In such a case the price is a reasonable price at the time for delivery if
   a. nothing is said as to price; or
   b. the price is left to be agreed by the parties and they fail to agree; or
   c. the price is to be fixed in terms of some agreed market or other standard as set or recorded by a third person or agency and it is not so set or recorded.

About the only term for which UCC gap-fillers cannot be used is quantity. Section 2-204(3) states that

> Even though one or more terms are left open a contract for sale does not fail for indefiniteness if the parties have intended to make a contract and there is a reasonably certain basis for giving an appropriate remedy.

Courts have interpreted this subsection to mean that an appropriate remedy *cannot* be reasonably certain if quantity is not determined. As noted above, however, requirements and output contracts do not fail on the indefiniteness basis even though, at the time the contract is formed, exact quantities cannot be determined. In requirement and output contracts, the good faith provisions of the UCC prevent the contracting parties from exploiting temporary advantage when price changes unexpectedly. If, for example, the market price were to double in a requirements contract involving natural gas, while the contract price remained the same, the buyer could not double his "requirements," taking advantage of the temporarily higher market price and reselling what he cannot use on the open market.

Writing Requirements: Statute of Frauds

Statute of Frauds
Under the UCC, the Statute of Frauds requires contracts that exceed $500 to be in writing.

The **Statute of Frauds** section of the UCC indicates that "*a contract for the sale of goods for the price of $500 or more is not enforceable by way of action or defense unless there is some writing sufficient to indicate that a contract for sale has been made between the parties and signed by the party against whom enforcement is sought or by his authorized agent or broker.*"[2] Not all material terms must be in writing under the UCC, but the party being sued must have signed something indicating assent to the contract.

[2] Section 2-201(1). The most recent revision of Article 2 has not been passed by the NCCUSL, but it requires contracts over $5,000 to be in writing.

Nutz and Boltz   Summary of UCC Treatment of Additional Terms in the Acceptance

Action	Response	Legal Consequence
Offeror makes an offer to the offeree	Offeree responds with additional terms in the acceptance	The additional terms are part of the contract, unless (1) the additional terms materially alter the contact, (2) the acceptance is conditioned upon acceptance of the additional terms, or (3) the offeror objects within a reasonable period of time
Offeror makes an offer that is expressly limited to the terms in the offer	Offeree responds with additional terms in the acceptance	The offeree has made a counteroffer
Offeror makes an offer to the offeree	Offeree responds with additional terms in the acceptance and conditions acceptance to acceptance of the additional terms	The offeree has made a counteroffer
Offeror makes an offer to the offeree	Offeree responds with an acceptance that contains different terms	A contract is formed but the conflicting terms are discarded and supplanted by terms based on prior conduct, trade usage, or UCC gap-fillers

UCC Exceptions to the Statute of Frauds

There are, however, notable UCC exceptions to the $500 writing requirement as reliance on oral contracts is common in commercial practice. Indeed, the UCC calls for enforcement of oral contracts that involve the sale of goods for more than $500.

specially manufactured
Goods that are customized for the buyer and that the seller does not normally sell.

   a. if the goods are to be **specially manufactured** for the buyer and are not suitable for sale to others in the ordinary course of the seller's business . . . ; or

   b. if the party against whom enforcement is sought admits in his pleading, testimony, or otherwise in court that a contract for sale was made . . . ; or

   c. with respect to goods for which payment has been made and accepted or which have been received and accepted.

For each of these exceptions to the Statute of Frauds writing requirements, it generally can be argued that there is good evidence of a contract. Goods that are specially manufactured for a buyer, and which have no other market, were most probably manufactured by the seller as a result of an agreement with the buyer. In parallel fashion, if the defendant in a case in which there is not a written contract admits, in a legal proceeding, that there was in fact an agreement between the parties for the sale of goods involving more than $500, courts will treat this as good evidence that a contract existed. Similarly, if a buyer pays for and accepts goods from a seller, those acts are generally viewed as confirming the existence of a contract between the two parties.

Written Confirmation of a Prior Oral Agreement

The UCC requires that the party against whom enforcement is sought (a defendant in a breach of contract case) must have signed something, even though what was signed need

Nutz and Boltz   The Common Law, the UCC, and Contract Modifications

As an illustration of the way the common law of contracts got in the way of commercial practice, consider the common law requirement that modification of existing contracts must be supported by new consideration. Suppose that, subsequent to the formation of a valid contract that is governed by the common law of contracts, conditions change and both parties to a contract recognize that the original terms of the contract are no longer realistic. It is typical in many industries for one side (the side that is hurt by the change subsequent to contract formation) to propose a change in the contract price term. Under the common law, if two businesspeople decide to change just the price term in the contract, that change is unenforceable because the change is not supported by new consideration. Suppose that Jim agreed to build a garage for Sam for $10,000 but, subsequent to the contract, the price of concrete dramatically increased and Jim would not make a profit. If Sam agreed, in light of the unexpected change, to increase the price paid for the garage to $11,000, that increase would be unenforceable unless Jim agreed to perform some additional task, even if the additional task was trivial, like sweeping the driveway.

In contrast, the UCC allows existing contracts to be modified by joint agreement of the contracting *parties without consideration*, which is consistent with commercial practice. The common law rule is contrary to commercial practice, but the UCC rule is consistent with it. The preexisting contractual duty rule was the source of a lot of mischief, so under the UCC it was eliminated.

not contain all material terms. There is, however, an exception to this rule, when one party sends a written confirmation of a prior oral agreement and the other party does not respond within 10 days. If there is no response from the receiver of the written confirmation, *the contract is enforceable against the receiving party*. The party sending the letter to the other party must sign that written confirmation for it to be enforceable. This provision of the UCC only applies to contracts between merchants, but it illustrates the importance of examining and responding to mail. For the sending party, it makes sense to send any written confirmation as *registered mail* to provide a paper trail of proof that the letter was received.

WARRANTIES

Overview

express warranties
Promises made about the quality of goods.

There are two types of warranties in UCC contracts: *express* and *implied*. **Express warranties** involve promises made about the quality of goods that are being sold. Such warranties are reviewed in some detail below.

implied warranties
Under the UCC, goods sold are subject to implied warranties unless those warranties are expressly disclaimed.

Implied warranties are part of every UCC contract, unless they are *disclaimed* in the contract. A good bit of the litigation associated with the sale of goods is related to disclaimers of implied warranties. A warranty disclaimer exists when the seller in a sales contract states that he or she disclaims or repudiates (**in boldface print so that the disclaimer is apparent to the average buyer**) an implied warranty. As an alternative to simply disclaiming implied warranties, sellers often try to *limit* their liability for breach of warranty, express or implied. **Limitations of liability**—that is, limits on the damages that can be collected in a breach of contract claim—are also a source of controversy and litigation.

limitations of liability
Clauses that limit the amount of damages a buyer can be awarded for breach of a warranty.

Contract law and tort law come together in connection with product liability. If a product is defective and its defect is the proximate cause of a user's injuries, there likely is both a breach of warranty and a tort-based strict liability (discussed in Chapter 10). This chapter deals with product liability cases that are also breaches of warranties, express or implied, but be aware that, in most product liability cases, the plaintiff also claims that sellers of defective products are simultaneously committing torts.

Express Warranties

With regard to the "creation" of express warranties, according to UCC Section 2-313(1):

> (a) Any affirmation of fact or promise made by the seller to the buyer which relates to the goods and becomes part of the basis of the bargain creates an express warranty that the goods shall conform to the affirmation or promise.

Section 2-313 also indicates that an express warranty is created when the seller describes the goods or furnishes a sample or demonstration and the other conditions are present, namely, that the promises relate to the goods and become part of the basis of the bargain.

Factual Statements versus Salesmanship

Factual statements about the quality of a good for sale can create an express warranty. *Warranty* is a synonym for *guarantee* and, if goods sold do not live up to their guarantee, the seller has breached a warranty. Warranties are not based on best efforts or any absence of negligence but, rather, on an agreement: when a seller makes a promise about the quality of a good, it creates strict liability for the seller.[3] If the qualities described in the warranty are not present in the good sold to the buyer, the seller is liable for breach of the warranty even if the seller used best efforts to make or sell the product and was not at all negligent in production or distribution.

In general, *factual statements* form warranties while *opinions* about a product do not. If the sales brochure for a car says that the car's engine has 220 horsepower, that statement creates a warranty. If the car salesman contends that the car "is just right for your personality," no warranty has been created. In general, factual statements refer to *prior* events, while opinions refer to *future* events that may or may not occur. The dividing line between factual statements and opinions is not always clear, but the more precise the statement, the more likely the statement will be deemed factual, thus possibly creating a warranty. Other factors used by courts to make decisions about whether a warranty has been formed include the determination of whether the buyer is ignorant about the factual claim and whether the buyer has an informed opinion about the fact. A warranty would be formed if a professional mechanic indicates that a used car is mechanically sound, particularly if the buyer is not sophisticated about cars. Opinions by experts can form warranties if the buyer is not equally knowledgeable.

Case 8-3 involves the creation of an express warranty. Notice that pieces of paper can be part of a contract under the UCC and that these pieces of paper can create warranties.

---

[3] Strict liability is discussed in some detail in Chapter 10, "Torts: Wrongs and Their Remedies." When a party is strictly liable, it means liability without fault. To recover, the other party does not have to show that the seller making the promise was somehow less than commercially careful about making or distributing the product.

Case 8-3

W. Hayes Daughtrey, et al. v. Sidney Ashe, et al.

Supreme Court of Virginia
413 S.E.2d 336 (1992)

BACKGROUND AND FACTS

Plaintiff, Daughtrey, purchased a diamond bracelet from Ashe, defendant jeweler, who described the diamonds as merely "nice," but signed an appraisal form that described them as "H color and v.v.s. quality." The form stated that it was for insurance purposes only. Several years later, plaintiff had several other jewelers look at the bracelet. They told him that the diamonds were not of v.v.s. quality. The defendant offered to refund the purchase price upon the return of the bracelet but declined to replace the diamonds with others of v.v.s. quality. Plaintiff filed a suit for specific performance. The trial court found that the diamonds were of a substantially lesser grade than v.v.s. but concluded that the plaintiff had not proven that the appraisal form was a term or condition of the sale nor a warranty upon which he relied in the purchase of the bracelet and denied relief for breach of warranty. The plaintiff appeals.

Opinion by Whiting

In this dispute between the buyers and the sellers of a diamond bracelet, the principal issues arise under the Uniform Commercial Code—Sales. Code §§ 8.2-101 through -725. Specifically, they are: (1) whether the sellers' appraisal statement of the grade of diamonds on the bracelet is a description of the goods under Code § 8.2-313(1)(b), and therefore an express warranty; and (2) whether such a statement made the description "a part of the bargain" under Code § 8.2-313(1)(b), and therefore an express warranty, when the buyers did not know of the warranty until some time after the purchase price was paid and the bracelet was delivered.

* * *

First, we consider whether Ashe's statement of the grade of the diamonds was an express warranty. Code § 8.2-313 provides in pertinent part:

1. Express warranties by the seller are created as follows:

   . . .

   b. any description of the goods which is made part of the basis of the bargain creates an express warranty that the goods shall conform to the description.

The Ashes argue that the statement in the appraisal form is not an express warranty for two reasons.
   First, they say the "appraisal on its face stated that it was 'for insurance purposes only.'" However, we think that the balance of the emphasized language in the appraisal form demonstrates that the limiting language relates *only* to the statement of the *appraised value*. Therefore, Ashe's description of the grade of the diamonds should be treated as any other statement he may have made about them.
   Second, the Ashes contend that Ashe's statement of the grade of the diamonds is a mere opinion and, thus, cannot qualify as an express warranty under Code § 8.2-313(2). Code § 8.2-313(2) provides:

   It is not necessary to the creation of an express warranty that the seller use formal words such as "warrant" or "guarantee" or that he have a specific intention to make a warranty, but an affirmation merely of the value of the goods or a statement purporting to be merely the seller's opinion or commendation of the goods does not create a warranty.

* * *

Next, the Ashes maintain that because the description of the diamonds as v.v.s. quality was not discussed, Daughtrey could not have relied upon Ashe's warranty and, thus, it cannot be treated as "a part of the basis of the bargain."

* * *

Our construction of Code § 8.2-313, containing language identical to § 2-313 of the Uniform Commercial Code, is supported by a consideration of the following pertinent portions of the Official Comment to the Uniform Commercial Code section:

   The present section deals with affirmations of fact by the seller, descriptions of the goods . . . exactly as any other part of a negotiation which ends in a contract is dealt with. No specific intention to make a warranty is necessary if any of these factors is made part of the basis of the bargain. In actual practice affirmations of fact made by the seller about the goods during a bargain are regarded as a part of the description of those goods; hence *no particular reliance* on such statements need be shown in order to weave them into the fabric of the agreement. Rather, any fact which is to take such affirmations, once made, out of the agreement requires clear affirmative proof. The issue normally is one of fact.

* * *

Ashe introduced no evidence of any factor that would take his affirmation of the quality of the diamonds out of the agreement. Therefore, his affirmation was "a part of the basis of the bargain." Accordingly, we hold that the Daughtreys are entitled to recover for their loss of bargain, and that the court erred in ruling to the contrary.

Therefore, we will reverse the judgment of the trial court and remand the case for further proceedings to ascertain the Daughtreys' damages.

Decision and Outcome

The court held that there was sufficient evidence that the appraisal form signed by the seller created an express warranty and thus the case is remanded on the issue of damages.

Questions for Analysis

1. According to the court in this case, who bears responsibility for demonstrating that an affirmation of fact about a good is or is not part of the basis of the bargain? Why is it important to determine whether an affirmation of fact is part of the basis of the bargain?
2. According to this court, can a warranty be created without knowledge of the purchaser? If a seller utters an opinion about a product but then supplies written documentation, is the documentation part of the contract? Isn't it common to find all kinds of terms in the bottom of the box when goods are unboxed?

Warranties Relate to the Goods and Are Part of the Basis of the Bargain

If a seller makes promises that do not relate to the goods sold, those statements do not create warranties. Furthermore, if a buyer does not rely on statements made about the goods by the seller, those statements do not create a warranty. In general, however, factual statements about goods do create warranties and little proof is required to show that the buyer relied on the statements. Advertisements in brochures that are given to buyers form warranties about the product even if there is no evidence that the buyer read the brochures.

Sellers Cannot Exclude Express Warranties

Courts are not enthusiastic about enforcing terms in a contract that are in conflict with what the firm advertises on television or in other media outlets. In general, a seller cannot disclaim promises made in selling materials. The old saying that "the broad print giveth and the fine print taketh away" does not apply. According to Section 2-316, Exclusion or Modification of Warranties, "negation or limitation [of express warranties] is inoperative to the extent that such construction is unreasonable." In other words, courts are not going to allow an automobile manufacturer to advertise that its windshields are shatterproof but sell their cars with a contract that negates all express warranties of the toughness of their windshields. To the extent that language in the contract negates a warranty, that language is inoperable.

Implied Warranty of Merchantability

implied warranty of merchantability
Unless disclaimed, it is an implied term in the contract that the goods sold are fit for the ordinary uses for which such goods are used.

An implied warranty is part of every contract unless it is *disclaimed* (as discussed below). The **implied warranty of merchantability** applies to the sale of all goods and guarantees, among other things, that the goods "are fit for the ordinary purposes for which such goods are used." If a bicycle shop sells a bicycle and the buyer takes the bike out for a spin in the neighborhood, applies the brakes, and finds that the brakes don't work, the implied warranty of merchantability would be breached. It is reasonable to believe that a bicycle will have brakes that stop the bicycle. The bike's faulty brakes surely fail to conform to reasonable expectations of most bicycle users.

Nutz and Boltz   Warranties at a Glance

Type of Warranty	How Created	Description
Express warranty	Made by the seller	Affirmation of fact that the goods meet certain standards of quality, description, performance, or condition.
Implied warranty of merchantability	Implied by law and part of the contract unless specifically disclaimed by the seller	Implied that the goods • Are fit for the ordinary purposes for which they are used. • Are adequately contained, packaged, and labeled. • Are of an even kind, quality, and quantity within each unit. • Conform to any promise of affirmation of fact made on the container or label. • Pass without objection in the trade. • Meet a fair average or middle range of quality for fungible goods.
Implied warranty of fitness for a particular purpose	Implied by law and part of the contract unless disclaimed by the seller	Implied that the goods are fit for the purpose for which the buyer or lessee acquired the goods if the seller or lessor (1) has reason to know the particular purpose for which the goods will be used and (2) makes a statement that the goods will serve that purpose, and (3) the buyer relies on the statement and buys or leases the goods.

Benchmarks are used to evaluate whether the implied warranty of merchantability has been breached. The implied warranty of merchantability is largely based on a *consumer expectations test.* If a buyer sues a seller for breach of the implied warranty of merchantability, when the case goes to trial, the jury will be asked to determine if the product performed as it was described in the sales contract. Benchmarks listed in Section 2-314 for the jury to consider are

- Would the good pass without objection in the trade under the contract description of the good?
- Is the good within customary variations permitted by the agreement?
- Is the good adequately packaged, labeled, and contained?
- Does the good conform to the promises made in the label?

Although the implied warranty of merchantability provides a strong pro-consumer guarantee of the quality of products purchased, sellers often disclaim the implied warranty of merchantability, or try to limit their liability for breaching this implied warranty.

Implied Warranty of Fitness for a Particular Use

If a seller *knows or should know* the use the buyer intends to make of a good purchased from the seller, and the buyer relies on the seller's recommendations, Section 2-315 of the UCC creates another implied warranty called the *implied warranty of fitness for a particular use*. The implied warranty of fitness for a particular use is not part of every sales contract like the implied warranty of merchantability is. This implied warranty takes effect if, at the time of contracting,

1. The seller has reason to know any particular purpose for which the goods are required and
2. The buyer relies on the seller's skill or judgment to select or furnish suitable goods.

As with the implied warranty of merchantability, the implied warranty of fitness for a particular use rests on the assumption that the seller is more knowledgeable about the goods sold than the buyer is, and that the buyer relies on the seller's judgment. If there is evidence to the contrary, such as

1. The fact that the buyer's knowledge of the goods is equal to or superior to the seller's, or
2. The buyer hired someone to assist in the purchase of the goods and relied on the person who was hired, or
3. The buyer supplies specifications of the goods to the seller,

then there is no implied warranty of fitness for use.

Warranty Disclaimers

The UCC does not always require a seller to stand behind goods sold. As discussed above, a seller cannot disclaim an express warranty. However, a seller is not required to make express warranties and can sell its products without UCC implied warranties. To do this, a seller can label the goods "**as is**" or "with all faults," which negates all implied warranties and provides notice to buyers that the sale is made under conditions of *caveat emptor,* or *buyer beware*. The effect of **caveat emptor** is to require the buyer to assume the entire risk for the quality of the good purchased. The buyer has the right to inspect any item before purchase but, once the purchase is made, the buyer does not have a legal right to complain.

Although the UCC does not require that a sales contract contain any express or implied warranties, Section 2-316 requires warranty exclusions or limitations of liability to be *conspicuous* and to *name* the implied warranties that are excluded or limited. The conspicuousness requirement of **warranty disclaimers** or exclusions is intended to cut down on the element of surprise; warranty disclaimers cannot be buried in the fine print of a sales contract. In order to satisfy the conspicuousness requirement, attorneys recommend that disclaimers or *limitations of liability* (discussed below) (1) be located near the contract signature line and (2) be in boldface print with at least 12-point type. If you take a look at the sales contract for your last purchase of a consumer electronic product, you will see either (or both) warranty disclaimers and/or limitations of liability. In Case 8-4, consider whether there was a breakdown in communications between the firm's attorneys and management.

as is
Refers to the sale of a good in which the seller is not making any guarantees about the quality of the good. Caveat emptor (buyer beware) is the rule of law that applies.

caveat emptor
The Latin for "buyer beware," it means the seller is not guaranteeing the quality of the goods. If there is a defect in the good, the buyer bears all liability for not inspecting the good and recognizing the defect.

warranty disclaimers
Conspicuous clauses informing buyers that the seller is not guaranteeing the express or implied quality of goods sold under contract.

Case 8-4

Ressallat et al., Appellants and Cross-Appellees v. Burglar & Fire Alarms, Inc., Appellee and Cross-Appellant; Physicians Insurance Company of Ohio, Appellant and Cross-Appellee; General Telephone Company of Ohio

*Court of Appeals of Ohio, Third Appellate District,
Crawford County
79 Ohio App. 3d 43 (1992)*

BACKGROUND AND FACTS

This is an appeal by the plaintiffs, Medhi M. and Judith Ressallat, and a cross-appeal by defendant Burglar & Fire Alarms, Inc. (BFA or appellee), from judgments rendered by the Crawford County Court of Common Pleas on the parties' motions for summary judgment.

On October 7, 1974, the Ressallats (appellants) entered into an agreement with BFA for the purchase of a burglar alarm system for their home. The system was designed to alert the Ressallats, both via warning lights and the sounding of a horn, when an unauthorized person had entered the house. The burglar alarm system was linked with the telephone system so that, simultaneous with the sounding of the alarm, a call was placed through the telephone lines to BFA's "central monitoring station." The Ressallats paid a monthly fee for these services.

In September 1986, the Ressallats' home was burglarized. The burglar apparently obtained unimpeded access to the house by cutting the exposed telephone wires so as to prevent transmission of the alarm. Inside the house, wires to the burglar alarm horn were severed at the electric service box. Jewelry and coins worth over $100,000 were stolen from the house. The Ressallats' insurance company, Physicians' Insurance Company of Ohio (PICO), reimbursed the Ressallats in the amount of $17,125.37, the maximum payable on their homeowners' policy.

Opinion by Evans

In September 1988, the Ressallats filed suit against BFA and others. However, on November 17, 1988, that suit was voluntarily dismissed, pursuant to Civ.R. 41(A). This suit was timely refiled on November 13, 1989. . . . The complaint sounded in contract and tort, alleging that BFA had breached its express warranty on the burglar alarm system, had negligently sold, installed, and maintained the system, and had breached the implied warranties of merchantability and fitness.

* * *

On November 7, 1990, appellee BFA filed a motion for summary judgment on the following bases: . . . (2) that BFA had effectively disclaimed all warranties under its contract with appellants, thus barring them from any related causes of action; and . . . Along with their response to appellee's motion, the Ressallats filed a motion for "partial summary judgment," requesting a declaration from the trial court that the disclaimers of warranty relied on by BFA were "inconspicuous as a matter of law," and thus invalid.

The trial court denied the Ressallats' motion, ruling that BFA's warranty disclaimer was, as a matter of law, *conspicuous.* The court sustained BFA's motion in part, and denied it in part, finding that the action had been timely filed, and that there were no issues of fact to be resolved, in that no action on the part of BFA could be found to be the proximate cause of the Ressallats' loss.

* * *

The code itself defines "conspicuous," and provides that a determination of conspicuousness is a matter of law for the court to decide. R.C. 1301.01(J) provides:

> "(J) 'Conspicuous.' A term or clause is conspicuous when it is so written that a reasonable person against whom it is to operate ought to have noticed it. A printed heading in capitals (as: NONNEGOTIABLE BILL OF LADING) is conspicuous. Language in the body of a form is 'conspicuous' if it is in larger or other contrasting type or color. . . . Whether a term is 'conspicuous' or not is for decision by the court."

The disclaimer of warranties at issue herein appears on the back page of the sales contract, which was signed on the front by both parties. The disclaimer is buried in the middle of a full page of small type, in a style identical to the rest of the text on the page. There are no outstanding headings alerting a purchaser to the disclaimer, and there is no mention of "merchantability" as required by R.C. 1302.29. Furthermore, Dr. Ressallat testified in his deposition that the disclaimer was not mentioned by the salesman at the time of the sale of the burglar alarm system, nor was it brought to his attention that anything was printed on the back page of the contract.

We believe the court erred in concluding that the disclaimer of warranties in these parties' contract was conspicuous. First, the disclaimer fails to mention "merchantability," a requirement of the code which must be fulfilled if a disclaimer of the implied warranty of merchantability is to be found valid. Additionally, we find that the trial court ignored the statutory language and applied an improper standard in determining that the disclaimer was conspicuous. In making that determination, the court stated:

> "These warranties and conditions are not hidden, but clearly spelled out in common understandable language which leaves no doubt as to what is and what is not covered, and when."

While we agree that the common, ordinary definition of "conspicuous" can be "not hidden," or "clearly spelled out," the code explicitly sets forth what the term means under the circumstances of this case. One's understanding of the terminology bears no relation to conspicuousness under the code. In the disclaimer at issue, there are no prominent headings, and there is no print of a different style or color that would draw one's attention. The disclaimer wording blends in with the surrounding "terms" and "conditions" and is in no way more noticeable. We find that the disclaimer in the contract is, as a matter of law, inconspicuous.

* * *

Decision and Outcome

The Ohio Court of Appeals overruled the trial court in its finding that the warranty disclaimer of the implied warranty of merchantability was conspicuous. Since the trial court was overruled, the case was remanded back to the trial court on the issue of whether the defendant's products breached the implied warranty of merchantability. The ruling of the Ohio Court of Appeals that the warranty disclaimer was inconspicuous meant that it is unenforceable.

Questions for Analysis

1. What could BFA have done to make the warranty disclaimer clearly conspicuous? Is it enough to make the warranty disclaimer in boldface type in order to satisfy the court's criteria for conspicuousness?

2. According to the court's opinion, is it a court decision or a jury decision as to whether a warranty disclaimer is conspicuous or not?

Limitations of Liability

Most vendors would seriously impair their success at selling goods if they excluded all express and implied warranties. Buyers would have serious questions in their minds about the quality of goods being offered for sale if the seller would not even guarantee that they were fit for the ordinary uses for which such goods are employed. In most cases, sellers sell goods with some warranty as to quality, but attempt to *limit liability to replacement of defective parts*. In general, courts enforce limitations of liability for breach of warranty so long as the limitations are *conspicuous* and *not unconscionable*.

Potential Liability Due to Warranties

If a buyer claims breach of warranty, that buyer as plaintiff must show

1. The existence of the warranty, express or implied.
2. The goods were not in the condition warranted when sold.
3. There was proximate causation between the breach of warranty and the plaintiff's damages.

consequential damages
Damages recoverable in court as a result of a breach of contract that the seller should have known about and that could not be avoided by the buyer through cover.

With no limitations of liability, the plaintiff can sue for compensatory damages, which may include **consequential damages,** if the seller had reason to know of these damages. If the buyer is a business, it may be able to recover for lost profits as a consequence of the breach of warranty. For example, if a seller of components knows that the components it sells to a buyer enable the buyer to make a profit on goods the buyer manufactures, and knows that failure to deliver conforming goods will cause the buyer to be unable to properly produce those goods, the buyer may be able to recover lost profits if the seller defaults and does not deliver the conforming goods.

Consequential Damages According to the UCC (Section 2-715(2)), consequential damages resulting from the seller's breach include

> (a) any loss resulting from general or particular requirements and needs of which the seller at the time of contracting had reason to know and which could not reasonably be prevented by **cover** or otherwise; and
>
> (b) injury to person or property proximately resulting from any breach of warranty.

cover
A buyer who has received notice from breach of contract from the seller can go in good faith out on the market and secure substitute goods.

In the example above involving a seller of components to a manufacturer, the seller could be liable to the buyer for lost profits if the seller had reason to know that the buyer would lose profits as a result of the seller's failure to properly deliver the goods and its knowledge that there was not sufficient time to go to the market and secure alternative cover. According to the UCC, cover occurs when a buyer who is a victim of breach of contract is able to get suitable alternative goods from another seller. Between businesses, it is very common for the seller to limit its liability by disclaiming responsibility for consequential damages (see Clause 9 in Case 8-2).

Consumer Goods and Personal Injury Another kind of consequential damage is personal injury. According to Section 2-719(3): "Consequential damages may be limited or excluded unless the limitation or exclusion is unconscionable. Limitation of consequential damages for injury to the person in the case of consumer goods is prima facie unconscionable, but limitation of damages where the loss is commercial is not." Since the UCC calls for nonenforcement of **unconscionable** terms in a contract, the latter sentence from Section 2-719(3) means that limitations of liability for *consumer goods* will not be enforced if personal injury is involved.

unconscionable
Terms in a contract that are so one-sided as to shock the conscience of the court. Normally occurs when one side is economically powerful and the other side does not have realistic alternatives.

Who Is Liable When a Warranty Is Breached and How Far Does Liability Extend?

Under the UCC, liability extends all the way up and down the marketing chain. For a typical good, raw materials suppliers and component makers sell to a manufacturer, which then makes the finished product, boxes it up, and ships to a distributor. The distributor then sells the product to a retailer, which sells it to a consumer. The consumer may well give the product

Nutz and Boltz   Warranty Disclaimers and Limitations of Liability

When it comes to warranty disclaimers, there has been much litigation surrounding them and so sellers typically err on the side of too much. It is not enough to simply state that "there are no expressed or implied warranties that apply to this sale," according to the courts. Courts have held that to disclaim an implied warranty, the warranty must be named specifically. Consider the following:

DEALER WARRANTY DISCLAIMER

PURCHASER (BUYER)

NAME _____
ADDRESS _____
CITY _____
STATE _____ ZIP _____
PHONE _____

SELLER (DEALER)

NAME _____
ADDRESS _____
CITY _____
STATE _____ ZIP _____
PHONE _____

VEHICLE IDENTIFICATION

YEAR _____ MAKE _____ MODEL _____ ID # _____

DATE OF SALE _____

ODOMETER READING _____
ODOMETER STATEMENT ATTACHED
☐ YES   ☐ NO

☐ **USED VEHICLE — DEALER'S WARRANTY DISCLAIMER**

The above described used motor vehicle is being sold "as is" and "with all faults" without any warranty, either expressed or implied. The purchaser will bear the entire expense of repairing or correcting any defects that may presently exist or that may occur in the vehicle. The dealer shall not have any responsibility for consequential damages, damages to property, damages for loss of use, loss of time, loss of profits, or income, or any other incidental damages with respect to any defect or malfunction or unfitness or other deficiency of this vehicle.

☐ **NEW VEHICLE — DEALER'S WARRANTY DISCLAIMER**

The only warranties applying to this vehicle are those offered by the manufacturer. The selling dealer disclaims all warranties, either expressed or implied, including any implied warranties of merchantability or fitness for a particular purpose, and neither assumes nor authorizes any person to assume for it any liability in connection with the sale of this vehicle. Purchaser shall not be entitled to recover from the dealer any consequential damages, damages to property, damages for loss of use, loss of time, loss of profits, or income, or any other incidental damages.

DATE _____

Purchaser acknowledges that he has read, understands and accepts all of the provisions of this dealer warranty disclaimer covering the vehicle identified above.

BUYER'S(S) SIGNATURE(S) _____   _____
                                                                          CO-BUYER

WITNESS: _____

DEALER'S SIGNATURE OR
AUTHORIZED REPRESENTATIVE _____

WITNESS: _____

Notice that this warranty disclaimer for new vehicles specifically names and disclaims the implied warranty of merchantability and fitness for a particular purpose.

Source: Copyright © 1978 Keary Advertising Co., Inc. Reprinted with permission.

to a member of his or her family and, if the product is defective by virtue of a breach of warranty, the party injured could be the consumer, a family member, or even a third party.

privity of contract
Contracting partners are in privity of contract; all others are not.

Under the UCC, liability for breach of warranty is based on *seller status,* not on **privity of contract** or whether a party manufactured the goods or had an opportunity to inspect the goods before sale to the consumer. Thus, in the example above, the manufacturer, distributor, and retailer are most certainly liable if the good breaches an express or implied warranty that has not been disclaimed. For most states, liability for breach of warranty under the UCC extends to consumer, users, and even third parties who it is reasonable to expect will be harmed by defective goods. Where it is anticipated that a component to a larger product, such as a tire in an automobile, will reach a consumer in the same condition in which it left the component supplier's dock, component suppliers can be liable, even though they have no contractual relationship with the consumer.

BREACH OF CONTRACT UNDER THE UCC

breach of contract
Under the UCC, if the goods delivered deviate in any way from what is called for in the contract, it is a breach of contract.

perfect tender rule
Sellers are required to deliver goods that conform perfectly to what is called for in the contract for sale.

There is no such thing as a *material* **breach of contract** under the UCC. If the goods offered by the seller do not conform perfectly to those called for by the contract, the buyer has the right to reject the goods. This is called the **perfect tender rule.** When purchasing a car, a buyer has numerous choices as to make: model, engine, and other features including color. If a car is ordered and every feature of the car conforms to those called for in the contract except for color, the buyer has the right to reject the car. There is no requirement that the buyer justify the rejection by showing that the car offered does not fulfill the essential purposes of the contract.

Exceptions

However, the fact that the buyer has the right to reject nonconforming goods under the perfect tender rule does not mean that the right to reject is unlimited. Typical exceptions include

- If there is time within the contract duration for performance, the seller must be given a reasonable opportunity to cure (offer a good that perfectly conforms to that called for in the contract).
- If the buyer does reject the goods, it must occur within a reasonable time or else the buyer will be deemed to have accepted the goods. No acceptance can take place until the buyer has had an opportunity to inspect the goods.
- The buyer does not have to reject all nonconforming goods if just some of the goods in a sale do not conform.
- In an installment contract under which the seller has been shipping goods over a period of time, the buyer does not have the right to terminate an entire contract just because some of the goods or one shipment (among many) does not conform to what is called for in the contract, unless the nonconformity undermines the entire contract.

commercial impracticability
A contingency takes place, the non-occurrence of which was a basic assumption of the parties to the contract, or the promisor is, in good faith, complying with a changed law.

Excuses for Nonperformance: Commercial Impracticability

The common law of contracts allows a promisor to escape liability for contract performance when a change in conditions that is unanticipated makes performance impossible. The common law theory is that, had the parties considered this change, they would have allocated risk of nonperformance to the promisee. The UCC version of impossibility is **commercial impracticability.** The UCC standard for excusing performance due to an event that was not anticipated when the contract was formed is more *liberal* than the common law standard, as far more events would be allowed to excuse performance of a

Nutz and Boltz   Rights and Remedies of Sellers and Buyers in the Event of Breach of Contract

Buyer breaches before receiving the goods	The seller may 1. Cancel the contract. 2. Identify the goods; minimize losses if necessary by completing manufacture or stopping production and salvaging the goods. 3. Withhold delivery or, if needed, stop delivery. 4. Resell the goods in a commercially reasonable manner. 5. Sue the buyer to recover the price loss suffered by having to resell the goods and any resulting damage.
Buyer breaches after receiving the goods	The seller may 1. If the buyer does not pay, sue to recover the purchase price and resulting incidental damages. 2. If the buyer wrongfully rejects the goods or revokes an acceptance, the remedies depend on the following: • If the seller reclaims the goods, the remedies are the same as if the buyer had breached before receiving the goods. • If the seller does not reclaim the goods, the seller can sue to recover the purchase price and any resulting damages.
Seller repudiates contract by announcing he will not deliver goods	The buyer may 1. Do nothing and await performance of the repudiating party for a commercially reasonable time. 2. Resort to any remedy for breach (Section 2-703 or 2-711), even though he has notified the repudiating party that he would await the latter's performance and has urged retraction. 3. In either case, suspend his own performance and take commercially reasonable steps to minimize damages including going out on the market and purchasing substitute goods.
Seller delivers nonconforming goods	The buyer may 1. Reject nonconforming goods. 2. When the goods are unique, request specific performance or delivery of the goods if unable to obtain cover from the market.

promisor without liability under the UCC than is the case under the common law of contracts. For example, a strike by workers supplying some essential components to a product that the seller was contracted to deliver probably would be allowed as a commercial impracticability, but likely would not qualify as an impossibility under the more strict common law standard.

In the UCC's terms that are descriptive of commercial impracticability, contract performance can be excused when such performance is made impracticable "by the occurrence of a contingency, the non-occurrence of which was a basic assumption on which the contract was made." So, if something unexpected occurs that makes contract performance far more difficult, the UCC standard is met. A burden is imposed on the seller seeking to escape an obligation to perform to prove that something took place that was both unforeseen and not reasonably foreseeable. Wars and embargoes generally qualify as unforeseeable, but price fluctuations are normally not unusual enough to allow a seller to get out of a contract, unless the price change was greater than 100 percent of the price and truly unprecedented in magnitude.

REMEDIES, DAMAGES, RIGHTS, AND OBLIGATIONS

As with the common law, the UCC theory of damages embraces the objective of restoring the nonbreaching party to the position that (s)he would have occupied had the contract not been breached. The UCC, however, goes farther than just providing guidance for computing damages; the UCC also provides contract participants with encouragement for commercial reasonableness, even if that party has just breached its contract by sending nonconforming goods. By providing incentives to behave reasonably, the UCC has the effect of reducing joint costs associated with contract breaches.

Damage Categories

Market Damages

Under the UCC, there are three types of damage categories: *market, incidental,* and *consequential.* Market damages are simply the difference between the market price and the contract price times the contract quantity. Mathematically, damages (D) may be expressed as $D = (P_m - P_k)Q_k$.[4] As discussed earlier in this chapter, at a minimum, the UCC requires quantity to be specified; otherwise there is no reasonable way of determining damages. Generally, under the UCC, the seller is required to resell goods if a sale can be effected and the breach of contract award to the seller would be the difference between the market and contract values resulting from the multiplication of price times quantity. If the seller cannot resell the goods at issue, then the seller is entitled to collect the entire contract price.

Incidental Damages

incidental damages
The costs incurred by the nonbreaching party in dealing with costs attributable to the breach of contract and the costs of the nonbreaching party having to go to the market an extra time.

Incidental damages are the costs of going back on the market. If a buyer defaults and refuses to accept delivery of the goods that (s)he contracted for, then the seller is required under the UCC to resell the rejected goods, if possible, on the market. The seller is entitled to collect the difference between the market and contract price. The additional costs of going back to the market to line up another buyer are called incidental damages and are recoverable under the UCC (Section 2-710). The UCC authorizes a buyer who has been the victim of a default by the seller to go to the market and cover by purchasing substitute goods. According to Section 2-712(2), "The buyer may recover from the seller as damages the difference between the cost of cover and the contract price together with any incidental or consequential damages as hereinafter defined (Section 2-715), but less expenses saved in consequence of the seller's breach."

---

[4] In the expression above, P and Q stand for price and quantity, respectively, and m and k designate market and contract, respectively. The expression above is appropriate to compute the market damages associated with a default (or failure to send the goods promised) by the seller. Sellers tend to default when the market price rises above the contract price. To compute the market damages when buyers default, $D = (P_k - P_m)Q_k$. Buyers default when the market price is lower than the contract price.

Qualifying to Collect Consequential Damages

There are two requirements that must be met for a buyer to collect for consequential damages: (1) the seller had reason to know of these damages and (2) the damages are the result of the seller's breach. It is clear that the value of damages attributable to consequential damages could substantially exceed the contract price. In other words, a seller that provides nonconforming goods could be liable to the buyer for far more than the contract price. As an example, when a breach of warranty results in personal injury, the seller's losses typically far exceed the contract price.

A breach of contract by a buyer generally does not involve consequential damage recoveries. This is because the losses to sellers are adequately compensated by recovery of specified contract prices and the incidental costs of going back to the market to sell the goods, less amounts recovered by reselling the goods on the market. The UCC does allow the seller to recover lost profit.

Repudiation of the Contract

Although either party, buyer or seller, can repudiate a contractual obligation in advance of the time of performance, it is more common for the seller to announce to the buyer that, for whatever reason, he (the seller) will not be delivering the goods that the contract called for. Under the common law of contracts, such behavior would be called *anticipatory breach*. The UCC uses new language to cleanse itself of any confusion with the standards applied by the common law term. Under UCC Section 2-610, anticipatory repudiation occurs "[w]hen either party repudiates the contract with respect to a performance not yet due the loss of which will substantially impair the value of the contract to the other . . ."

The UCC allows an "aggrieved party," the victim of an anticipatory breach,

a. for a commercially reasonable time [to] await performance by the repudiating party; or

b. [to] resort to any remedy for breach (Section 2-703 or Section 2-711), even though he has notified the repudiating party that he would await the latter's performance and has urged retraction; and

c. in either case [to] suspend his own performance or proceed in accordance with the provisions of this Article on the seller's right to identify goods to the contract notwithstanding breach or to salvage unfinished goods (Section 2-704).

In effect, the UCC grants all the options to the aggrieved party. The aggrieved party can do nothing and urge the other party to amend his or her intention to default on agreed-to performance, or the aggrieved party can sue immediately or sue anytime within four years, which is the statute of limitations under the UCC for filing a claim. In any case, the aggrieved party can stop its own performance without legal liability.

Cover, Consequential Damages, and Contract Breaches

When the aggrieved party is the buyer, the options available lead back to a discussion of "cover." If the seller announces in advance that the promised deliveries of goods will not be made, the buyer is entitled to go out onto the market and cover by purchasing substitute goods and to sue for the difference between the market and contract price plus incidental costs. If the buyer is not able to cover by purchasing substitute goods, then the buyer may be able to recover for consequential damages in the form of lost profits.

This process also can work in reverse. If the buyer announces that he or she will not accept or pay for goods as promised in a sales contract, the seller can sell the goods in the market and sue for the difference in price plus incidental costs. If the goods are customized and cannot be sold in the market, the seller can possibly get the contract price as damages, less whatever is earned in salvage sales and in selling costs avoided.

International Perspective   International Business-To-Business Sales and the CISG

In business-to-business (commercial) sales, the marketplace is truly global, with enormous volumes of transactions between firms domiciled in different countries. The UCC is not applicable to such transactions. While the main harmonizer of international transactions continues to be arbitration, the United Nations has provided legal structure that parallels the UCC and serves the same role(s) for many international commercial contracts that the UCC serves within the United States. The U.N. provided apparatus is known as the CISG (Contracts for the International Sale of Goods).

Firms engaged in international product transactions can (and should) incorporate choice-of-law clauses in their contracts. In the absence of such clauses, the CISG serves (like the UCC) as a gap-filler for terms the transacting parties failed to include or pin down with precision in their disputed contract(s). Both in procedure and in the forms of the gap-fillers provided, the CISG parallels the UCC. Under the CISG, if a contract doesn't set prices with required precision, then prices are set at levels that are "reasonable" for the items sold at the time of contract formation, just as under the UCC. In like fashion, the CISG parallels the UCC in terms dealing with delivery, obligation to pay, risk of loss, warranty disclaimer, and so forth. As with the UCC, in the event of a contract breach, damages are typically based on differences between contract and market replacement prices at the time of breach, while the non-breaching party has an obligation to act to mitigate damages.

CONCLUDING COMMENTS ON THE UCC

Development of the UCC was motivated in part by a desire to get the law out of the way when businesspersons want to do business. To a large extent, this goal has been achieved with flexible rules based on intent of the parties, replacing the formalistic rules that characterize the common law's handling of contracts. The other motivating goal for development of the UCC was creation of uniform treatment for businesses that operated throughout the United States. Composers (NCCUSL) of the UCC have been very successful in ironing out legal anomalies among the states in contract law involving the sale of goods. In spite of these laudable efforts, businesses still regard court litigation based on the UCC as inefficient and too slow. Most litigation between businesses takes place before arbitrators rather than in the courts, though substantive contract law is based on the UCC. International contracts rely even more heavily on arbitration, with the CISG enjoying a role in international transactions that parallels the role of the UCC in domestic sales transactions.

Summary

The UCC Has Made Commercial Contract Law Uniform or Nearly So across the States; under the UCC Merchants Are Held to Higher Standards

- The Uniform Commercial Code (UCC) is precisely that—a uniform contract law for commercial transactions.

- This chapter showed how the UCC differs from the common law of contracts. For many rules of contract law, the UCC and the common law rules are the same, but in critical ways they are quite different.

- The UCC allows parties to a sales contract great latitude in determining the terms of the contract. A primary role of the UCC is to serve as a *gap-filler* when the parties to a contract neglect to specify any needed term(s).

- Article 2 of the UCC provides contract law for the sale of goods.

- Internationally, the *Convention on Contracts for the International Sale of Goods (CISG)* is the contract law for two-thirds of world's international trade. The CISG is very similar to the UCC.

- Under the UCC, merchants are expected to conduct themselves in good faith, which requires honesty in fact in the transaction they are engaged in.

- Merchants are held to higher standards than customers under the UCC. They are expected to be knowledgeable about the goods that they buy and sell.

The UCC Defines Sales of Goods, Risks of Loss, and the Time When Title Transfers	• A sale occurs when title to a good transfers from seller to buyer for a price. A thief cannot pass title to a good, but a gift does pass title, though not for money or other compensation. • If nothing is said in a contract, title to goods transfers when the seller delivers the goods to the buyer. In *shipment contracts,* title transfers when the goods are given to a third-party shipper, but in *destination contracts,* title does not transfer until the goods are delivered to the buyer. When documents of title are held by a third party, title transfers when the documents are transferred to the purchaser. • In general, risk of loss is borne by the title holder, though the parties can modify this result in the contract. Buyers can insure goods, the title to which is held by sellers, and sellers can insure goods with title held by purchasers.
An Important Feature of the UCC Is That It Imitates Commercial Practices: Written Offers Are Irrevocable, There Can Be Additional Terms in the Acceptance, and Gap-Fillers and Prior Conduct Can Be Used to Supplement Written Contracts	• Agreements under the UCC are not defined mechanistically as they are under the common law of contracts. Acceptances can contain additional terms and courts will take into account *prior conduct* of the parties and *custom and usage* within an industry to define the terms of a contract. In addition, UCC gap-fillers are used when none of the above is usable. • At a minimum, the UCC requires that the parties and subject matter of a contract be identified and that quantity be determined, except where *output and requirements contracts* are involved. • Under the UCC, a signed written offer by a merchant is irrevocable during the time span stated in the offer, up to a period of three months. • Additional terms in the acceptance can be part of the contract unless the offer states that no additional terms in the acceptance are allowed, the offeror objects within a reasonable period of time, the acceptance is conditioned upon acceptance of the additional terms, or the additional terms materially alter the contract. • When additional terms in an acceptance are different from those in the offer, it is assumed that each party to the contract objects to that term in the other party's contract proposal and UCC gap-fillers are used. • When the contracting parties have a course of dealing, prior conduct can supply content for the additional terms. • Under the UCC, a contract can be modified without additional consideration as long as the change is bargained for.
The UCC Has Its Own Requirements for When a Contract Must Be in Writing	• The UCC requires contracts for the sale of goods in excess of $500 to be in writing, but it allows exceptions if the goods are specifically manufactured for the buyer, admitted in a court proceeding, or accepted or paid for by the buyer. • If a merchant sends a written confirmation of a prior oral agreement and it is signed, a contract is formed unless the receiver objects within 10 days. • Promissory estoppel is usable in contracts involving the sale of goods.
The UCC Defines How Express Warranties Are Created, but Implied Warranties Are Assumed to Be Part of Every Contract Unless Disclaimed; Allows for Warranty	• The UCC defines express warranties as any affirmation of fact about the quality of a good that is part of the basis of the bargain. Express warranties can be created by advertising, descriptions of the goods, samples, and opinions of experts. • Under the UCC, there are implied warranties that are part of every sales contract unless disclaimed. These warranties are the *implied warranties of merchantability and fitness for a particular use.* • A seller can disclaim implied warranties by selling goods "as is" and "with all faults" except where other laws prohibit the disclaimers, but the disclaimers must be conspicuous. • Sellers are entitled to limit liability for the breach of an express or implied warranty unless the limitation of liability is unconscionable. • The UCC considers limiting liability for personal injury in the sale of consumer goods to be unconscionable.

| *Disclaimers and Limitations of Liability Subject to Federal Legislation and Conscionability Constraints; and, for Goods That Do Not Conform to the Contract, Employs the Perfect Tender Rule* | • The implied warranty of merchantability requires that the goods sold be fit for the ordinary uses for which such goods are intended.
• The implied warranty of fitness for a particular use applies when the seller knows, or should know, the use the buyer intends to make of goods sold and when the buyer relies on the seller's judgment.
• Liability for breach of warranty under the UCC extends both up and down the marketing chain and is not limited to manufacturers. All sellers are liable unless they disclaim liability with conspicuous language in the contract. *Privity* of contract is not required to sue a seller for breach of warranty.
• The *perfect tender rule* under the UCC allows buyers to reject goods that do not conform to those specified in the contract in every respect. Sellers do have the right to cure defects in the goods if time for performance has not expired, and buyers have only a reasonable time to reject tendered goods.
• In installment contracts, sending some nonconforming goods does not entitle buyers to terminate the contract unless the nonconformities undermine the entire contract. |
| *The UCC Allows Sellers to Escape Liability Based on Commercial Impracticability; Damages under the UCC Allow for Recovery of Compensatory, Consequential, and Incidental Cost Damages* | • When an unforeseeable event occurs, promisors may be excused the obligation to perform under the doctrine of *commercial impracticability*. The UCC standard of commercial *impracticability* is more liberal than the common law standard of *impossibility*.
• The typical remedy for contract breach under the UCC is award of the difference between market price and contract price, plus incidental costs and consequential damages.
• In order to recover for consequential damages, the nonbreaching party must be able to show that the breaching party had reason to know of these damages.
• If a contract is repudiated, the other party to the contract can sue immediately, can wait until the time of performance, and can pursue any commercially reasonable means of mitigating damages such as going out on the market and procuring substitute goods.
• Most of the provisions of the CISG are similar or identical to those of the UCC. |

Key Terms

Questions for Review and Analysis

1. Legal uncertainty is a risk borne by businesspeople, in addition to other business risks. Explain how the UCC reduces this particular form of risk.
2. Most business purchases involve orders for goods from other businesses using purchase orders. Typically, those purchase orders are answered with invoices from the seller. Why are the differences in the UCC relative to the common law ideally suited for dealing with this set of business practices?
3. Under the UCC, what is the difference between express and implied warranties? What is the difference between a warranty disclaimer and a limitation of liability?

4. Discuss the remedies available to buyers when the seller (1) announces that it will default on promised deliveries or (2) delivers goods that do not conform to those called for in the contract.

If You Really Understood This Chapter, You Should Be Able to Provide Informed Commentary on the Following:

1. **Implied Warranty of Fitness for a Particular Use.** Suppose the plaintiff/user of a product, using the product as it was intended to be used, is injured. The plaintiff, Daniel Freeman, purchased a Case International 1130 tractor with a mower attachment (1130, mower, or tractor) to care for his lawn. On May 22, 1992, the second time he used the 1130, Freeman suffered a serious accident. While Freeman was mowing his lawn near a rocky slope, the mower blades glanced off of a partially buried boulder. Freeman lifted his foot off the speed ratio control pedal, bringing the tractor to a stop; he then pushed in the clutch and brake pedals and raised the mower attachment, intending to see if the rock had damaged the blades. Suddenly, the mower lunged forward, toward, and then over the rocky embankment. Freeman leapt away from the machine, rolling 40 feet down the hill. He came to rest on his stomach, safely, but the 1130 tumbled down on top of him, with the mower blades still activated. The blades severely and permanently injured him. Can Freeman claim that the manufacturer breached the implied warranty of fitness for a particular use when he was using the mower for its intended purpose? [*Daniel Freeman v. Case Corporation*, 118 F.3d 1011 (4th Cir. 1997)].

2. **Good Faith.** Suppose that two businesspeople have an agreement that the seller will supply all the cement that the buyer wants for the next two years, but price for the third year is not specified. As to price for the third year, it was limited by the term "not to exceed $38.00 per short ton." Suppose, further, that when the third year, comes, the seller states that the price is $38.00, the maximum allowed under the agreement. If the buyer refuses to continue with purchases and the seller sues, can the buyer defend by saying that the seller's setting of the price at the maximum contemplated in the original agreement constitutes lack of good faith? This issue arose in *Marquette Co. v. Norcem, Inc.,* 494 N.Y.S.2d 511 (Sup. Ct., App. Div., NY 1985).

3. **Creation of Express Warranty.** Suppose you've shopped for a used car and buy one from a seller, not a dealership, who tells you that the car is in "good mechanical condition." Then, you begin to have problems the day after you buy the car. The plaintiff in such a case, Brian Felley, paid $5,800 for a car he bought from the Singletons (defendants) after test-driving the car and discussing its condition with defendants. The car was a 1991 Taurus with 126,000 miles on the odometer. At trial, plaintiff testified that he soon began experiencing problems with the car. On the second day after his purchase, plaintiff noticed a problem with the clutch. Over the next few days, the clutch problem worsened to the point where plaintiff was unable to shift gears no matter how far he pushed in the clutch pedal. Plaintiff presented an invoice dated June 18, 1997, showing that he paid $942.76 on that date for the removal and repair of the car's clutch. Plaintiff further testified that the car developed serious brake problems within the first month that he owned it. Later the plaintiff had the car examined by an expert mechanic, who testified that the brake system of the car was basically shot and that the damaged condition of the brakes would have been apparent to the defendants who had driven the car for the last three years. Does a statement by a seller that a used car with 126,000 miles on it is in "good mechanical condition" create an express warranty? [*Brian D. Felley v. Thomas Singleton and Cheryl Singleton,* 302 Ill. App. 3d 248, 705 N.E. 2d 930 (Ill. App. Ct. 1999).]

4. **Implied Warranty of Merchantability.** The plaintiff, patronizing an outlet of the Wendy's Hamburger chain, ordered a double hamburger with "everything" on it. Halfway through eating the burger, the plaintiff, Fred Goodman, crunched down on a bone the size of his little fingernail. As a result, Goodman had to have two teeth pulled and a root canal in a third tooth. Quite obviously, the sale of a hamburger was not accompanied by written contract. Goodman sued for breach of the implied warranty of merchantability as well as negligence in inspection on the part of Wendy's. Goodman also sued the supplier of meat to Wendy's, alleging that the meat supplier also breached the implied warranty of merchantability and was negligent. Wendy's claimed that bone is a natural part of meat and is a risk that consumers bear when eating their products, while Goodman claimed the hamburger failed the reasonable consumer expectations test. Wendy's claimed that bones are part of fish and steak and that consumers know about these risks. What do you think? [*Goodman v. Wenco Management,* 394 S.E.2d 832 (N.C. App. 1990).]

5. **Damages under the UCC.** In many markets, there are food brokers who purchase from growers and resell to restaurants. Fresh Network was a food broker that contracted with KMG Harvesting for delivery of 14 loads of lettuce for resale. Fresh Network had contracts on a cost-plus basis for resale to fast-food restaurants in Ohio. The cost-plus contracts called for the restaurants buying from Fresh Market to pay Fresh Market's cost of acquiring the lettuce plus a percentage. KMG Harvesting was aware of the cost-plus contracts Fresh Network had with the fast-food restaurants. The price of lettuce rose sharply after the contract between Fresh Network and KMG was agreed to, and KMG refused to deliver the lettuce. Fresh Network went out on the market and purchased 14 loads of lettuce at nine cents a pound more than the contract price. Fresh Network sued for the difference in contract price plus the incidental costs of going out on the market. The jury found for Fresh Network and KMG appealed, claiming that Fresh Network did not realize a loss because of the breach of contract. KMG claimed that since Fresh Network had a cost-plus contract, it actually made more money from its buyers because the price of lettuce rose and it had to pay the higher price. KMG claimed that if Fresh Network is able to recover the difference between the contract price and the market price, it will realize a windfall. What do you think should be the proper measure of damages? [*KMG Harvesting v. Fresh Market,* 36 Cal. App. 4th 376 (1995).]

Social Responsibility and Ethics in a High-Tech World

6. **Manufacturers and Distributors.** Many times, manufacturers establish long-term relationships with distributors. Often, manufacturers are much larger firms than their distributors and these distributors sometimes become dependent on their manufacturer. Many times independent distributors are actually small "mom and pop" operators who have been loyal to the manufacturer for years. If the manufacturer decides to vertically integrate (establish a distribution capability also), then the manufacturer becomes a competitor as well as a supplier, which can create conflicts of interest. If the manufacturer decides to change its method of distribution, away from relying on independent distributors, the distributors are typically very vulnerable to such shifts. Recognizing this problem, some manufacturers have policies that prohibit distributors from purchasing from them more than a certain percentage of the products they handle, so that the dependency problem is not so acute if and when the manufacturer experiments with new methods of distribution. It would appear that an ethical issue arises when a manufacturer secretly makes plans to change its methods of distribution, knowing that such changes will harm its independent distributors. Shouldn't manufacturers at least inform their distributors well before making such changes so that the distributors can adjust their business practices and minimize dislocations? Is it ethical under the Kantian categorical imperative to "use" other people in the fashion that results if early notice is not given?

   Of course, one may ask, isn't the risk that a manufacturer will change its methods of distribution a normal business risk that firms, such as distributors, simply have to bear? You might note that suits between manufacturers and their distributors are common, particularly when changes in distribution methods are made by manufacturers, but distributors are not informed of the changes until after they occur.

Using the Internet to Your Advantage

1. Online versions of the UCC are available in a variety of formats. As mentioned previously, the Cornell University School of Law supports the Legal Information Institute, which has a very accessible copy of the UCC, complete with a user-friendly search capability, at http://www.law.cornell.edu/ucc/ucc.table.html. In addition, the state of Arizona provides online access to the UCC and to the filings required by the UCC under other articles that were not the focus of this chapter at http://www.sosaz.com/business_services/ucc/2001/Uniform_Commercial_Code.htm. The organization that was responsible for composing and promoting the UCC is the National Conference of Commissioners on Uniform State Laws (NCCUSL), which maintains online versions of the UCC as well as proposals for changes to the nine articles of the UCC (http://www.nccusl.org/).

2. The Pace University School of Law maintains an Institute of International Commercial Law and has an online version of the CISG at http://cisgw3.law.pace.edu/. According to the Institute, it is a myth that "there are hardly any cases under the CISG"; they have compiled over 850 cases that can be accessed at http://cisgw3.law.pace.edu/cisg/text/caseschedule.html. Another website

that contains a wealth of information about international contracts is called Heiros Gamos (http://www.hg.org/commerc.html).

3. Need a lawyer for aviation or business law? Just go to FreeAdvice.com (http://freeadvice.com/index.htm). According to its website, "FreeAdvice.com® is the leading legal site for consumers and small businesses. It provides general legal information to help people understand their legal rights in 125+ legal topics, but is not a substitute for personal legal advice from an attorney." The FreeAdvice.com website offers some very readable discussion about basic contract law, such as an article entitled "What Is a Contract?" (http://www.freeadvice.com/law/518us.htm). Discussion of contract law at a higher (law school) level can be found at FindLaw (http://www.findlaw.com/). Sophisticated discussion of contract law can be found at http://stu.findlaw.com/outlines/contracts.html.

Chapter Nine

Current and Future Contract Law for E-Commerce

Learning Objectives

On completing this chapter, you should

1. Be familiar with the parallels between the historical evolution of contract law and the evolution, both in the recent past and prospective, of e-commerce law.
2. Be able to discuss the areas of coverage and the intended effects of UCITA, UETA, E-SIGN, and revised Article 2 of the UCC.
3. Be familiar with the forms of and implications of clickwrap, boxtop, shrinkwrap, and like agreements.
4. Be able to meaningfully discuss the concepts and/or roles of electronic parity, authentication, encryption, biometrics, digital signatures, Certification Authority, and the E-Sign Act.

INTRODUCTION: POTENTIAL FOR CHAOS OR UNIFORM TREATMENT

The Internet is a wonderland enjoyed by the young, old, and those in-between. It is also, however, a vast commercial marketplace where many thousands of contracts are formed every second. The Internet and e-commerce have created new situations that have generated sweeping proposals for fundamental changes in contract law.

In many ways, however, e-commerce has created what Yogi Berra might have described as "deja vu all over again" for commercial contract law. During the first half of the twentieth century, when many U.S. businesses expanded their geographic scope, there was a tremendous desire for *uniform* treatment of contracts for the sale of goods throughout the United States. Those pressures resulted in creation and adoption of the UCC. That same dynamic is now at work in the e-commerce arena. There is broad recognition of the desirability of uniform contract law to govern e-commerce. To date, however, though some progress has been made, a uniform set of laws governing contract law in cyberspace does not exist.

U.S. Law Is Only Part of the Story

In this chapter, proposals for providing uniform e-commerce contract law *in the United States* are reviewed. There is, of course, a wide world outside the United States, all of which has access to U.S. websites (and vice versa). Our review of federal and state legislation to reform and make uniform e-commerce contract law is necessarily incomplete because it does not include extensive analysis of international e-commerce contract laws. Some aspects of the interface between cyberspace and international law are discussed in Chapter 23.

E-COMMERCE CONTRACT LAW LEGISLATION

Throughout this chapter, there are references to the UCC, UETA, UCITA, and E-SIGN. As you know, *UCC* stands for Uniform Commercial Code, a uniform body of contract law adopted by all 50 states. The UCC was championed by the National Conference of Commissioners on Uniform State Laws (NCCUSL; see the "Nutz and Boltz" box) and remains the organization's most significant accomplishment. The NCCUSL is in the process of revising Article 2 of the UCC, which governs the sale of goods, and this chapter provides some reference to the proposed revisions that apply to e-commerce contracts. The UCC remains the law that governs e-commerce transactions involving physical goods.

The NCCUSL also has drafted and put forward the *Uniform Electronic Transactions Act (UETA),* which has been adopted by the legislatures in 41 states. Although there have been some objections by consumer advocacy groups, UETA seems destined to be adopted by all 50 states. With some significant exceptions for certain types of contracts, UETA creates parity between paper and electronic records. The basic thrust of UETA was reinforced by Congress with the passage of the *Electronic Signature in Global and National Commerce Act (E-SIGN)*, which also serves to create parity between electronic and paper records as well as facilitating digital signatures. Both UETA and E-SIGN apply to the sale of goods.

The most controversial and unsuccessful of the NCCUSL proposals for dealing with the novel legal issues created by e-commerce is the *Uniform Computer Information Transactions Act (UCITA)*. As with the UCC and UETA, UCITA was composed and propounded by the NCCUSL, but unlike the UCC and UETA, only two states (Virginia and Maryland) have adopted UCITA. When proposed by the NCCUSL, UCITA was envisioned to be to transfers of *computer information* what the UCC was to the sale of goods. Concerns of consumer advocates and states' attorneys general that UCITA gives too many options to Internet vendors and websites have caused most states to choose not to adopt UCITA. Still, UCITA addresses many of the important and unique legal issues that are created by online transfers of information. In spite of UCITA's lack of widespread legislative adoption, the authors believe that UCITA is influencing court decisions that are providing common law rulings on some of the novel issues created by e-commerce.

So, some progress has been made on creating a uniform e-commerce contract law, but much remains to be done. This chapter discusses four important legal issues that have emerged with the growth of e-commerce. The "Nutz and Boltz" box provides a self-description of the NCCUSL, which has become a major player in legal debates about electronic records and uniform laws for e-commerce.

Four Basic E-Commerce Contract Issues

parity with paper
With "parity," electronic records will be treated the same, and be just as legally binding, as paper records.

There are other e-commerce contract law issues now and surely there will be new ones in the future. Up to now, however, the four focused on in this chapter have been the sources of the lion's share of controversy, with legal resolution of these issues not completely clear at this point. The four basic issues are

1. *Parity between electronic and paper records.* In order for e-commerce to flourish, **parity between electronic and paper records** is required. In other words, unless

Nutz and Boltz   National Conference of Commissioners on Uniform State Laws

The National Conference of Commissioners on Uniform State Laws has worked for the uniformity of state laws since 1892. It is a non-profit unincorporated association, comprised of state commissions on uniform laws from each state, the District of Columbia, the Commonwealth of Puerto Rico, and the U.S. Virgin Islands. Each jurisdiction determines the method of appointment and the number of commissioners actually appointed. Most jurisdictions provide for their commission by statute.

There is only one fundamental requirement for the more than 300 uniform law commissioners: that they be members of the bar. While some commissioners serve as state legislators, most are practitioners, judges, and law professors. They serve for specific terms, and receive no salaries or fees for their work with the Conference.

The state uniform law commissioners come together as the National Conference for one purpose—to study and review the law of the states to determine which areas of law should be uniform. The commissioners promote the principle of uniformity by drafting and proposing specific statutes in areas of the law where uniformity between the states is desirable. It must be emphasized that the Conference can only propose—no uniform law is effective until a state legislature adopts it.

The Conference is a working organization. The uniform law commissioners participate in drafting specific acts; they discuss, consider, and amend drafts of other commissioners; they decide whether to recommend an act as a uniform or a model act; and they work toward enactment of Conference acts in their home jurisdictions.

The uniform law movement began in the latter half of the 19th century. The Alabama State Bar Association recognized as early as 1881 the legal tangles created by wide variations in state laws. But it was not until 1889 that the American Bar Association decided, at its 12th Annual Meeting, to work for "uniformity of the laws" in the then 44 states.

Within a year, the New York Legislature authorized the governor to appoint three commissioners to explore the best way to effect uniformity of law between increasingly inter-dependent states. The ABA endorsed New York's action. The result was the first meeting of the Conference of State Boards of Commissioners on Promoting Uniformity of Law in the U.S.

Seven states sent commissioners to that first meeting of the Conference in Saratoga Springs, New York, in 1892. By 1912, every state had appointed uniform law commissioners. The U.S. Virgin Islands is the last jurisdiction to join, appointing its first commission in 1988.

Since its organization, the Conference has drafted more than 200 uniform laws on numerous subjects and in various fields of law, setting patterns for uniformity across the nation. Uniform acts include the Uniform Probate Code, the Uniform Child Custody Jurisdiction Act, the Uniform Partnership Act, the Uniform Anatomical Gift Act, the Uniform Limited Partnership Act, and the Uniform Interstate Family Support Act.

Most significant was the 1940 Conference decision to attack major commercial problems with comprehensive legal solutions—a decision that set in motion the project to produce the *Uniform Commercial Code.* [Emphasis added] The Code took ten years to complete and another 14 years before it was enacted across the country. It remains the signature product of the Conference.

Today the Conference is recognized primarily for its work in commercial law, family law, the law of probate and estates, the law of business organizations, health law, and conflicts of law. It rarely drafts law that is regulatory in nature.

Source: Reprinted with permission of the National Conference of Commissioners on Uniform State Laws.

online agreements are enforced, little e-commerce will take place. The prospect of treating *electronic records* the same as *paper records* is opposed by many groups who are advocates of consumer interests. "Record" is the legal term now used to replace "document" or "writing."

2. *Enforceability of shrinkwrap, clickwrap, and boxtop agreements and licenses.* There are significant contract formation and enforceability issues associated with shrinkwrap, clickwrap, and boxtop agreements and licenses. In many situations, buyers are bound by

Nutz and Boltz   Getting Acquainted With the Law of Online Contracts

UCC	Universal Commercial Code—applies to the transactions listed in the Nutz and Boltz box on page 244 in Chapter 8
Article 2	The sale of goods
Section 2-207	Additional terms in the acceptance
Revised Article 2	
Section 2-211	Legal recognition of electronic records and authentications
Section 2-212	Legal attribution
UCITA	Uniform Computer Information Transactions Act
Section 212	Efficacy and Commercial Reasonableness of the
Section 213	Attribution Procedure
Section 214	Electronic Error: Consumer Defenses
UETA	Uniform Electronic Transactions Act
Section 103	Applies to electronic records and signatures for commerce purposes
Section 104	Excludes transactions covered by other laws
Section 106	Electronic signatures are valid
Section 204	Legal recognition of electronic records
E-SIGN	Electronic Signature in Global and National Commerce Act
Section 101	Legal recognition of electronic records if the records can be stored and reproduced; digital signatures are valid if consented to by the parties

agreements that are appended to the basic transaction (purchases of goods or transfers of computer information, i.e., software) that have significant legal effects that are not apparent to purchasers at the time of purchase.[1]

3. *Attribution procedures.* With electronic (mouse-click) purchases, a vendor needs secure mechanisms to be assured that an order received is legitimate. The vendor is also desirous of having a procedure that legally points to an individual so that individual's credit card can be debited by the vendor. Accompanying concerns revolve around the conditions under which a vendor can sue a person for an order received online from a website visitor.

4. *Digital signatures.* With standard paper contracts, signatures have operated to uniquely identify parties to a contract. Obviously, that is a problem in e-commerce transactions. Recent legislation by Congress attempts to provide several acceptable substitutes to traditional signatures in electronic commerce, but not without some remaining concerns.

scope of UETA
UETA deals comprehensively with e-commerce and contract law, addressing the sale of goods, including e-commerce sales of tangible products.

Parity between Paper and Electronic Records: Combined Effect of UETA and E-SIGN

The UETA has been enacted in 41 states and more recently, in 2000, Congress passed the E-SIGN Act. The **scope of the UETA** is contained in Section 201, Legal Recognition of Electronic Records. According to subsection (a), "a record may not be denied legal effect, validity or enforceability solely because it is in the form of an electronic record." Subsection (b) indicates that, "[I]f a rule of law requires a record to be in writing, or provides

---

[1] Clickwrap, shrinkwrap, and boxtop licenses are explained in detail later in the chapter.

consequences if it is not, an electronic record satisfies that rule." Thus, e-mails, as an example, could supply evidence of a written agreement that is required by the statute of frauds. The bottom line is that UETA grants electronic records parity with paper records, but there are a significant number of kinds of contracts for which UETA does not apply.

The language used in E-SIGN is similar: Section 101 states that no contract, agreement, or record entered into online shall be denied legal effect solely because it is in electronic form, so long as the electronic records can be stored and reproduced. Both UETA and E-SIGN have exclusions for certain significant types of contracts. In the case of UETA, the most significant exclusion is that it does not apply to contravene any state law that prohibits use of electronic records or requires a type of contract to be in writing. E-SIGN does not apply to court papers, wills, prenuptial agreements, divorce decrees, evictions, and health insurance terminations among others. Both UETA and E-SIGN allow for the sale of goods to be conducted entirely with electronic records.

Possible Changes in E-Commerce Contract Law

scope of revised Article 2 of the UCC
Deals with sales of goods in the real world or through e-commerce.

UCC Revisions of Article 2   Article 2 of the UCC, which governs the sale of goods, is being revised to accommodate e-commerce. Proposed Section 2-211, Legal Recognition of Electronic Contracts, Records, and Signatures, states with now-familiar language that "(1) A record or signature may not be denied legal effect or enforceability solely because it is in electronic form." Revisions of Article 2 by the NCCUSL began in 1996 and have consistently included provisions that grant parity to electronic records. Currently, UETA is applicable to Article 2 transactions involving the sale of goods, which means that electronic records have the same effect as written records in the sale of goods.

scope of UCITA
UCITA deals with contracts involving computer software, multimedia interactive products, computer data and databases, and Internet and online information. It does not deal with Internet sales of tangible goods.

The Uniform Computer Information Transactions Act   In trying to address the many challenges to the UCC posed by e-commerce, the commissioners at the NCCUSL decided not to revise the UCC with respect to the *licensing* of computer information as had originally been proposed.[2] Instead of completing a new section of the Uniform Commercial Code, the authors have renamed the proposed uniform statute, the *Uniform Computer Information Transactions Act (UCITA)*. The **scope of UCITA** includes *computer software, multimedia interactive products, computer data and databases, and Internet and online information.*

UCITA Grants Parity to Electronic Records Also   Section 107(a) of UCITA makes it clear that "A record or authentication [signature] may not be denied legal effect or enforceability solely because it is in electronic form." So both the proposed changes to the UCC and UCITA are in agreement with UETA and E-SIGN that parity is to be accorded to paper and electronic records.

The Electronic Records Parity Debate

The first "Cyberlaw Developments" box (page 270) provides a statement of John M. McCabe, Legislative Director of the NCCUSL. As is apparent, Mr. McCabe is strongly in favor of UETA and of establishing legal parity between paper and electronic records. For some perspective and balance, we provide exposure to the other side of the argument. Gail Hillebrand of the Consumers Union, a consumer advocacy group, writes in the second "Cyberlaw Developments" box (page 272) about the dangers of allowing electronic records to substitute for paper records.

---

[2] When the need for e-commerce revisions of the UCC first became apparent, the commissioners of the NCCUSL originally sought to modify Article 2 of the UCC, but they abandoned such efforts when the enormity of the task became apparent, and thus the Uniform Computer Information Transactions Act (UCITA) was born.

John M. McCabe
Legislative Director/Legal Counsel
jmmccabe@nccusl.org

Memo to: Interested Parties

Subject: The Uniform Electronic Transactions Act and Consumers

The Internet is the marketplace for the 21st Century, but it is a marketplace where the principal advantage belongs to the buyer and the borrower, not the seller or the lender. It is a marketplace without borders. Every seller and every lender must compete with their counterparts in every part of the world. It is capitalism and price competition in its most merciless form. Consumers receive understandable comparative information on price and other terms of deals in nanoseconds. Do you want to buy a car? On the "Net" the best price and best financing deal are a keystroke away. You may also ask other consumers about their experiences with the model that you may want to buy in the nearest chat room or bulletin board. There is no place for sellers and lenders to hide on the Internet, and the power it gives to consumers is extraordinary and unprecedented.

80 million people in the United States are on-line. They have reached into their wallets to do their business there. On-line retail sales, alone, rose to an estimated $20 billion from almost zero in 1999. Businesses spent an additional $109 billion buying from each other in the same year. By 2003, estimates suggest on-line retail sales of $144 billion and business sales of $1.3 trillion. Consumers like electronic transactions for their convenience and speed, and because they can comparison shop as never before. They are voting with their modems and buying with a click. It is an unstoppable tide.

The Uniform Electronic Transactions Act (UETA), approved by the National Conference of Commissioners on Uniform State Laws in 1999, was drafted to eliminate any doubt concerning the enforceability of electronic transactions, whether in the form of retail Internet transactions, electronic credit transactions, electronic data interchange or e-mail usage. UETA is designed to put electronic transactions on a par with paper transactions.

Concerns have been raised in consumer circles about electronic consumer transactions; fears about the unknown impact upon consumers engaged in this new marketplace. The arguments are as follows: electronic transactions are unfamiliar; they take place too quickly; consumers won't find all the terms of a deal before signing on to it; there may be new opportunities for fraud.

UETA responds to these concerns, but not by confining consumer transactions to the paper world. The paper world prevents consumers from obtaining the best information for making good choices. That is why much consumer law is concerned with disclosure of information-disclosure that often defeats itself because the consumer does not get information in understandable forms. The Internet is disclosure with a vengeance. There is also fraud in the paper world, made easier by consumer inability to obtain and process information about cost-effective choices. UETA does not confine consumer transactions to the paper world because that does not benefit consumers.

It is important to make sure that the rules which validate electronic transactions do not burden those who are unprepared for electronic transactions. UETA applies only to transactions in which the parties have agreed to do business with each other, electronically. For an electronic record to be effective, it must be capable of being retained by the recipient. The sender of a record cannot inhibit the ability of the recipient to print or store the electronic record. Simply put, electronic records and signatures may not be imposed on anybody, but particularly those who do not have computers or access to them.

* * *

"Under no circumstances should electronic commerce operate independently from existing legal systems," says Patricia Brumfield Fry, chair of the UETA drafting committee. "While every estimate of growth of electronic commerce has been exceeded in a matter of months, the power of the consumer in dealings with merchants has kept pace. Until it is shown that specific needs have arisen online, the electronic market should be dealt with on a par with existing markets. UETA assures consumers the protections and safeguards which have been developed through the decades, and lets them take full advantage of the benefits of electronic commerce."

Source: Reprinted with permission of the National Conference of Commissioners on Uniform State Laws.

The passage of E-SIGN at the federal level seems to have resolved the electronic parity debate in favor of granting parity to electronic records, but there are many contracts excluded from E-SIGN or UETA coverage. For basic e-commerce, however, it seems clear that electronic records can be used to create legally enforceable contracts. In the future, much of the debate will center on what types of contracts can be in electronic form, as both E-SIGN and UETA cordon off from their reach broad categories of contracts.

ENFORCEABILITY OF SHRINKWRAP, CLICKWRAP, AND BOXTOP AGREEMENTS

Electronic Commerce

The basic principles of contract law must be substantially modified to deal with the commercial realities of Internet transactions. In such transactions, intent often must be gleaned from electronic agents that operate based on artificial intelligence. Needless to say, intent is just one of the issues that has had to be dealt with in attempting to meld traditional contract law with e-commerce. Of course, new technologies always present new challenges to traditions. With regard to contracting, you may note that Internet e-commerce transactions are not as revolutionary as they might seem. Electronic commerce has been around since the telegraph; the Internet is only the latest "improvement." However, the penultimate technology before the Internet was EDI (electronic data interchange).

Electronic Data Interchange

electronic data interchange (EDI)
Electronic data interchange, as the label indicates, is the electronic exchange of business information in a structured format. Commonly, EDI is used to coordinate activities involving two businesses.

Electronic data interchange (EDI) is a closed system in which one company's computer communicates with another computer at a different company and, through this process, creates new, legal contracts with no direct human intervention. EDI has proved to be a very efficient means of coordinating transactions between two large companies with business linkages that are expected to continue for an indefinite duration. Consider an apparel manufacturer such as one of the famous clothing brand names—maybe Calvin Klein. Suppose the Calvin Klein Company has a contract with the department store J.C.Penney. When its inventories of Calvin Klein products become low, J.C.Penney's computers contact Calvin Klein's computers and request shipments of the appropriate replacements. The EDI between these two computers creates legally binding contracts even though there is no individualized attention from human agents on either side of agreement. There is, however, an overall EDI agreement that deals with terms of the contracts, essentially agreements to

Cyberlaw **Developments** Uniform Electronic Transactions Act: Consumer Nightmare or Opportunity?

[Author's note: This article was written while the California proposal was still in bill form. It has since been enacted. All of the protections described here as found in the California bill are now part of the California UETA.]

Consumers Union West Coast Regional Office. Prepared 8/23/99.

1. Should a lender be allowed to send a foreclosure notice only to an email address that is five years old?
2. If a consumer needs a paper copy of a disclosure or contract notice sent by email, should the consumer have to pay a fee to get a copy of that notice?
3. Should a salesperson be able to sign a consumer up to receive all future notices by email when the consumer does not own a computer?
4. If a law requires that a certain type of contract be in writing, should a record of a phone call satisfy that requirement?
5. Should utility shutoff warnings go only to an email address that might be shared within a family and checked primarily by the children?

Are the consumer warning bells going off in your head? Well, all of these scenarios and more will be permitted by the new Uniform Electronic Transactions Act (UETA). UETA is coming soon to your state legislature.

WHAT IS UETA?

UETA is a uniform law approved July 1999 by the National Conference of Commissioners on Uniform State Laws (NCCUSL). If adopted by state legislatures, UETA will elevate electronic records and signatures to the same legal status accorded paper records and handwritten signatures. UETA is grounded on three premises:

- That most state law requirements for a writing can be satisfied by an electronic record, including an email.
- That most state law requirements for a signature can be satisfied by an electronic signature.
- That, in most cases, the parties to a contract can agree to any form of electronic communication.

UETA'S UNDERLYING PREMISES ARE PROBLEMATIC

Often, however, these premises do not apply in consumer contracts. The first premise will be true in only some consumer situations. An electronic record may be just as good as a written record for an inexpensive transaction that is completed in a short time. On the other hand, a consumer entering into a five-year car loan or a 30-year mortgage needs the note and contract in a form that he or she can keep. Home computers are replaced every few years, and previously downloaded contracts are unlikely to be copied over to a new system. Change-of-terms notices for a service provider operating only on the Internet probably can be delivered by email, but a notice that your car is being recalled for a safety problem should arrive in the mail.

The first premise also assumes that email arrives at least as reliably as regular mail, which is contrary to the experience of many consumers. Consumers currently may change email addresses more frequently than they move. Those with email addresses seem to check them either far more frequently or far less frequently than their daily check of the regular mail. In addition, an Internet email provider may go out of business, leaving a consumer with no choice but to obtain a new email address.

As to the second premise, an electronic signature does not always fully serve the purposes of a written signature. Where there is a risk of forgery, a written signature may provide additional safeguards because it may be harder to forge than a purported electronic signature. An electronic click made at home may not serve the purpose of emphasizing the seriousness or the particular risks of a transaction as well as a written signature.

The third premise of UETA is reflected in the broad deference it gives to the autonomy of contracting parties. It defers to the agreement without distinguishing between negotiated agreements and standard form contracts or contracts of adhesion. This approach could give wide latitude to drafters of standard form contracts to define and impose the conditions of electronic communication.

For example, UETA adopts the principle that each party should be able to determine when it will receive information electronically, and when it wishes to insist on receiving a paper communication. This sounds good in theory, but in practice it allows one-sided contracts. UETA also allows an on-line seller to insist on sending all information to the consumer electronically. The seller, however, can require that the consumer communicate any complaints, refund requests, billing disputes or other communications to the same company only by regular mail.

Here is another example of a perverse effect created by UETA's rule of autonomy to contracting parties. UETA contains definitions of both "sent" and "received." According to these provisions, material is "sent" when it enters a computer system or a server that is outside the control of the sender. Further, that information is "received" when it enters the recipient's computer. These definitions contain loopholes. A message is received even when the recipient cannot open or read it; or when the message was automatically discarded by a junk mail filter. The definitions nevertheless do capture the basic idea that something is received when it gets to you or to a place where you can retrieve it.

UETA permits the parties to the contract to vary these definitions so that "sent" and "received" can be redefined to be anything. Under UETA, a web seller could define information to have been received by the buyer at the moment that the seller posts that information to its own website—even if the customer is not aware of its posting.

Source: Excerpt from July/August 1998 issue of *NCLC Reports, Credit & Usury Edition*. Prepared by Gail Hillebrand, Consumers Union of U.S., West Coast Regional Office. Reprinted with permission.

agree in the future. EDI orders (contracts) for the replacement inventory items described are formed electronically, without human intervention, are legally enforceable based on the current UCC, and will apply when Revised Article 2 is enacted by the states.

CONTRACT FORMATION ISSUES INVOLVING THE INTERNET

It is virtually impossible to browse the Internet without encountering offers. Indeed, the opening frames shown by Internet service providers (ISPs), such as America Online (AOL), are accompanied by legally binding offers to contract. The offeror in this case is a company whose offer is "online" for all who browse the site to see. If the member uses search engines, (s)he will be exposed to banners that include additional offers to sell various products. The offers are electronic, though prospective customers can print them. There is a question as to what such offers actually are, however. Assume that an offeror is trying to sell a digital camera. Generally, the online ad will provide both narrative and visual depictions of the product(s), and a prospective customer is invited to purchase the product online. Often the seller will request credit card information to complete the sale, but generally other methods of payment are also accepted.

Electronic Fine Print: Clickwrap "Agreements"

The focus now turns to the question of what additional terms can become part of the contract once the purchaser has indicated assent to the basic transaction, which is generally a purchase of a tangible product or a license to use software. Generally there is nothing legally objectionable to online purchases, but significant legal controversies have arisen with respect to additional terms that sellers tack onto, say, the commodity purchase or software licensing agreement. Typically, before the transaction is completed, the purchaser is informed that the sale is accompanied by additional terms to which the purchaser is asked to click (with a mouse) either "I agree" or "I don't agree" buttons. If the purchaser does not click "I agree," the transaction does not take place. These additional terms that accompany online transactions are called **clickwrap agreements.** It is the enforceability of these additional terms that are clickwrapped into the basic transaction that is the subject of much litigation.

In the pages below, there are references to *clickwrap, shrinkwrap,* and *boxtop* licenses or agreements.[3] If a purchase of goods or a license of software takes place in an online transaction, the language or terms that are contained in the "I agree" statement is what is referred to as a *clickwrap* license (or agreement). The Caspi case, Case 9-1, is based on a dispute about a clickwrap agreement. In over-the-counter sales of software, the purchaser is generally given a CD that is wrapped in cellophane with a warning that if you open the cellophane, which is *shrinkwrapped,* you are bound by the terms of the license, the **shrinkwrap agreement.** In many transactions, the goods a consumer purchases are packaged in a box that has a statement of the terms and conditions of sale. That statement is a **boxtop license or agreement.** When you purchase a computer or most any consumer electronic appliance, you will see a boxtop agreement among the papers or goods in the box. Among the terms found in some boxtop agreements is a statement that if you retain the goods for more than, say, 30 days, you are bound by all the terms in the boxtop agreement.

Case 9-1 shows consequences of online contracting that might not have been anticipated. The plaintiffs in this case effectively had to travel to the state of Washington because of a forum selection clause buried deep in the clickwrap agreement they had with the Microsoft Corporation. Important legal rights are contained in clickwrap agreements, often called End User License Agreements.

---

[3] When consumers or businesses "purchase" software, they are really paying money for the right to use the software purchased, subject to conditions and restrictions such as a prohibition against copying the software for friends and reselling it. The terms and conditions that accompany a "sale" of software, or, more technically, the right to use such software, are known as a *license.*

Case 9-1

Steven J. Caspi et al. v. The Microsoft Network, L.L.C.

Superior Court of New Jersey, Appellate Division
323 N.J. Super. 118, 732 A.2d 528 (N.J. Super. Ct. App. Div. 1999)

FACTS AND CASE BACKGROUND

Plaintiffs are subscribers of Microsoft Network (MSN), an online computer service. Two of the plaintiffs reside in the state of New Jersey. The plaintiffs allege fraud and breach of contract on the part of

MSN, claiming that they were victimized by negative option billing, which means that the plaintiffs were charged with paying for software unless they took action to say they did not want the software. Plaintiffs sue in state court in New Jersey and defendants (MSN) cite a forum selection clause, which is part of the subscribers' contracts with MSN. The forum selection clause requires that lawsuits against MSN must be litigated in the state of Washington.

Opinion: Kestin, J.A.D.

We are here called upon to determine the validity and enforceability of a forum selection clause contained in an on-line subscriber agreement of the Microsoft Network (MSN), an on-line computer service. The trial court granted defendants' motion to dismiss the complaint on the ground that the forum selection clause in the parties' contracts called for plaintiffs' claims to be litigated in the State of Washington. Plaintiffs appeal. We affirm.

The four named plaintiffs are members of MSN. Two reside in New Jersey; the others in Ohio and New York. Purporting to represent a nationwide class of 1.5 million similarly aggrieved MSN members, plaintiffs, in May 1997, moved for multi-state class action certification. [Citations omitted]

Shortly thereafter, defendants moved to dismiss the amended complaint for lack of jurisdiction and improper venue by reason of the forum selection clause which, defendants contended, was in every MSN membership agreement and bound all the named plaintiffs and all members of the class they purported to represent. That clause, paragraph 15.1 of the MSN membership agreement, provided:

> This agreement is governed by the laws of the State of Washington, USA, and you consent to the exclusive jurisdiction and venue of courts in King County, Washington in all disputes arising out of or relating to your use of MSN or your MSN membership.

Plaintiffs cross-moved, *inter alia,* to strike a certification submitted in support of defendants' motion to dismiss and to compel the deposition of the certificant.

* * *

Before becoming an MSN member, a prospective subscriber is prompted by MSN software to view multiple computer screens of information, including a membership agreement which contains the above clause. MSN's membership agreement appears on the computer screen in a scrollable window next to blocks providing the choices "I Agree" and "I Don't Agree." Prospective members assent to the terms of the agreement by clicking on "I Agree" using a computer mouse. Prospective members have the option to click "I Agree" or "I Don't Agree" at any point while scrolling through the agreement. Registration may proceed only after the potential subscriber has had the opportunity to view and has assented to the membership agreement, including MSN's forum selection clause. No charges are incurred until after the membership agreement review is completed and a subscriber has clicked on "I Agree."

The trial court observed:

> Generally, forum selection clauses are prima facie valid and enforceable in New Jersey. New Jersey courts will decline to enforce a clause only if it fits into one of three exceptions to the general rule: (1) the clause is a result of fraud or "overweening" bargaining power; (2) enforcement would violate the strong public policy of New Jersey; or (3) enforcement would seriously inconvenience trial. The burden falls on the party objecting to enforcement to show that the clause in question fits within one of these exceptions. Plaintiffs have failed to meet that burden here.

Judge Fitzpatrick correctly discerned that:

> New Jersey follows the logic of the United States Supreme Court decision in *Carnival Cruise Lines v. Shute,* 499 U.S. 585, 111 S. Ct. 1522, 113 L. Ed.2d 622 (1991). . . . In *Carnival,* cruise ship passengers were held to a forum selection clause which appeared in their travel contract. The clause enforced in *Carnival* was very similar in nature to the clause in question here, the primary difference being that the *Carnival* clause was placed in small print in a travel contract while the clause in the case *sub judice* was placed on-line on scrolled computer screens.

* * *

Further, plaintiffs were not subjected to overweening bargaining power in dealing with Microsoft and MSN. The Supreme Court has held that a corporate vendor's inclusion of a forum selection clause in a consumer contract does not in itself constitute overweening bargaining power. In order to invalidate a forum selection clause, something more than merely size difference must be shown. A court's focus must be whether such an imbalance in size resulted in an inequality of bargaining power that was unfairly exploited by the more powerful party.

* * *

After reviewing the record in the light of the arguments advanced by the parties, we are in substantial agreement with the reasons for decision articulated by Judge Fitzpatrick. . . . Moreover, as a matter of policy interest and apart from considerations bearing upon the choice-of-law provision in the forum selection clause, plaintiffs have given us no reason to apprehend that the nature and scope of consumer fraud protections afforded by the State of Washington are materially different or less broad in scope than those available in this State.

Decision and Outcome

In this case, the court ruled that the forum selection clause was enforceable, which meant that the plaintiffs had to go to the state of Washington to pursue their claims against Microsoft based on fraud and breach of contract. The court rejected the contention that MSN had overwhelming bargaining power relative to the plaintiffs because of the availability of other such services.

Questions for Analysis

1. How many students who are members of various online services carefully read their membership agreements?

2. Note that, even though MSN is provided by a very large corporation, the court did not agree that this resulted in unfair bargaining power. What additional fact may have tipped the scale in favor of the defendants? *Hint:* Suppose there was no other online service.

Additional Terms and Acceptances with a Click

Common Law Contract Rules

Under the common law of contracts, an acceptance must be *complete* and *unqualified,* meaning that the offeree agrees to each and every term in the offer and does not add additional terms. If an offeree adds additional terms in an acceptance, or requests a change in the offer, the offeree has made a counteroffer and becomes the offeror. In the past, the absolutist approach of the common law of contracts clashed with commercial practice that often involved company forms, such as invoices (from the seller) and purchase orders (from the buyer), that each contain contract terms.

UCC Modifications of the Acceptance Rule

When the UCC was enacted, it specifically allowed for additional terms in acceptances (see discussion in Chapter 8 about Section 2-207 of the UCC). Under the UCC, an offeree could accept the offer of an offeror but add additional terms without having the acceptance be termed a rejection of the offer and a counteroffer. Of course, the offeror had the opportunity to reject the additional terms proposed for the contract by the offeree.

Online Contracting

The practice of adding additional terms to basic transactions is accentuated in online contracting. Before even the most basic purchase of a T-shirt takes place, often the purchaser has to agree to a whole raft of terms by clicking an "I agree" button. In virtually all cases, significant legal issues have been decided in favor of the online vendor, who has written the terms contained in the clickwrap agreement.

Section 2-207 of the Proposed UCC

The trend toward allowing additional terms in the acceptance is accentuated in proposed Section 2-207 of the UCC, which makes it easier than in the current Article 2 of the UCC to include additional terms in a contract that were not in the original offer. Proposed new Section 2-207 of the UCC states that

> If (i) conduct by both parties recognizes the existence of a contract although their records do not otherwise establish a contract, (ii) a contract is formed by an offer and acceptance, or (iii) a contract formed in any manner is confirmed by a record that contains terms additional to or different from those in the contract being confirmed, the terms of the contract, subject to Section 2-202, are:
>
> a. terms that appear in the records of both parties;
>
> b. terms, whether in a record or not, to which both parties agree; and
>
> c. terms supplied or incorporated under any provision of this Act.

Under the current Article 2, *additional terms* in an acceptance were not part of the contract if these terms *materially altered* the contract.[4]

Case 9-2 illustrates the difficulties of applying "old" UCC law to e-commerce transactions. The focus of this case is on a boxtop license—additional terms of the license agreement between the licensor and licensee in the box that contains the software. Following the adverse ruling in this case, sellers learned what to do and what not to do so that boxtop, as well as clickwrap and shrinkwrap, licenses would be enforced by the courts.

---

[4] Section 2-207(2): "Between merchants such terms become part of the contract unless: . . . (b) they materially alter it. . . ."

Case 9-2

Step-Saver Data Systems, Inc. v. Wyse Technology

U.S. Court of Appeals for the Third Circuit
939 F.2d 91 (3rd Cir. 1991)

FACTS AND CASE BACKGROUND

Step-Saver was among the leaders in value-added retailing for International Business Machines (IBM). Step-Saver developed multi-user capabilities within microcomputer technology, which meant that purchasers could buy fewer computers because all the computers are linked together. After evaluating its needs, Step-Saver selected a multi-user operating system from TSL called Multilink Advanced. The software Step-Saver was selling was supposed to operate with an operating system by Microsoft (MS-DOS) or software developed by Step-Saver. The target audience was law and medical offices. Almost from the start, dissatisfied customers complained that Multilink Advanced did not operate as warranted.

In TSL's software there was a boxtop license that purported to be the complete understanding between the parties (TSL and licensees of its software) and a disclaimer of all express and implied warranties. The boxtop license gave purchasers 15 days to return the software; otherwise they were bound by the terms in the boxtop license. Based on the language in the boxtop, TSL moved for, and was granted, a motion for a directed verdict.

Opinion: Wisdom, Judge

Ii. THE EFFECT OF THE BOX-TOP LICENSE

The relationship between Step-Saver and TSL began in the fall of 1984 when Step-Saver asked TSL for information on an early version of the Multilink program. TSL provided Step-Saver with a copy of the early program, known simply as Multilink, without charge to permit Step-Saver to test the program to see what it could accomplish. Step-Saver performed some tests with the early program, but did not market a system based on it.

In the summer of 1985, Step-Saver noticed some advertisements in *Byte* magazine for a more powerful version of the Multilink program, known as Multilink Advanced. Step-Saver requested information from TSL concerning this new version of the program, and allegedly was assured by sales representatives that the new version was compatible with ninety percent of the programs available "off-the-shelf" for computers using MS-DOS. The sales representatives allegedly made a number of additional specific representations of fact concerning the capabilities of the Multilink Advanced program.

* * *

From August of 1986 through March of 1987, Step-Saver purchased and resold 142 copies of the Multilink Advanced program. Step-Saver would typically purchase copies of the program in the following manner. First, Step-Saver would telephone TSL and place an order. (Step-Saver would typically order twenty copies of the program at a time.) TSL would accept the order and promise, while on the telephone, to ship the goods promptly. After the telephone order, Step-Saver would send a purchase order, detailing the items to be purchased, their price, and shipping and payment terms. TSL would ship the order promptly, along with an invoice. The invoice would contain terms essentially identical with those on Step-Saver's purchase order: price, quantity, and shipping and payment terms. No reference was made during the telephone calls, or on either the purchase orders or the invoices with regard to a disclaimer of any warranties.

Printed on the package of each copy of the program however, would be a copy of the box-top license. The box-top license contains five terms relevant to this action:

1. The box-top license provides that the customer has not purchased the software itself, but has merely obtained a personal, non-transferable license to use the program.
2. The box-top license, in detail and at some length, disclaims all express and implied warranties except for a warranty that the disks contained in the box are free from defects.

* * *

The district court held, as a matter of law, that the box-top license was the final and complete expression of the terms of the parties' agreement. Because the district court decided the questions of contract formation and interpretation as issues of law, we review the district court's resolution of these questions de novo.

Step-Saver contends that the contract for each copy of the program was formed when TSL agreed, on the telephone, to ship the copy at the agreed price. The box-top license, argues Step-Saver, was a material alteration to the parties' contract, which did not become a part of the contract under UCC § 2-207.

* * *

To understand why the terms of the license should be considered under § 2-207 in this case, we review briefly the reasons behind § 2-207. Under the common law of sales, and to some extent still for contracts outside the UCC, an acceptance that varied any term of the offer operated as a rejection of the offer, and simultaneously made a counteroffer. This common law formality was known as the mirror image rule, because the terms of the acceptance had to mirror the terms of the offer to be effective. If the offeror proceeded with the contract despite the differing terms of the supposed acceptance, he would, by his performance, constructively accept the terms of the "counteroffer", and be bound by its terms. As a result of these rules, the terms of the party who sent the last form, typically the seller, would become the terms of the parties' contract. This result was known as the "last shot rule."

* * *

The reasons that led to the rejection of the last shot rule, and the adoption of section 2-207, apply fully in this case. TSL never mentioned during the parties' negotiations leading to the purchase of the programs, nor did it, at any time, obtain Step-Saver's express assent to the terms of the box-top license. Instead, TSL contented itself with attaching the terms to the packaging of the software, even though those terms differed substantially from those previously discussed by the parties. Thus, the box-top license, in this case, is best seen as one more form in a battle of forms, and the question of whether Step-Saver has agreed to be bound by the terms of the box-top license is best resolved by applying the legal principles detailed in section 2-207.

* * *

Decision and Outcome

The court decided that since Section 2-207 applied, the additional terms in the boxtop license were part of the contract only if the parties agreed to the additional terms or if those terms did not materially alter the contract. The court ruled that the warranty disclaimers did, in fact, *materially alter* the contract and, thus, that they did not become part of the contract.

Questions for Analysis

1. If TSL was only willing to sell the software with the warranty disclaimers, how, realistically, could it have communicated this information to its purchasers? If most of its contracts were agreed to over the phone, how many customers would be willing to listen to long-winded discussions of warranty disclaimers?

2. Would the result have been different in this case if TSL sought to limit liability to replacement of defective copies, rather than disclaiming all warranties? Is a limitation of liability a material alteration of the contract?

Buy Now; Find Out What You Agreed to Later

In many transactions, the offer to sell is accompanied by terms that are not apparent to the purchaser before the decision to purchase is made. In a shrinkwrap agreement, the customer is bound by the terms of the contract even though the customer cannot know what many of the terms are until (s)he has paid her money and breaks open the (shrink) wrapping around the CDs or diskettes that contain the wanted software program. A "boxwrap" (or boxtop) agreement has similar characteristics in that often the consumer can only discover the terms of the contract by opening the box and reading the terms of the contract.

The Hill case, Case 9-3, illustrates the need for customers to read boxtop agreements and respond promptly. Note that there is no requirement for an arbitration clause to be highlighted among the clauses in the boxtop agreement.

Case 9-3

Rich and Enza Hill v. Gateway 2000, Inc.

U.S. Court of Appeals for the Seventh Circuit
105 F.3d 1147 (7th Cir. 1997)

FACTS AND CASE BACKGROUND

Rich and Enza Hill purchased a Gateway 2000 computer based on a phone conversation from a representative of Gateway. When the box containing the computer arrived, there were additional terms in the box that Gateway claimed were part of the contract. The Hills were given 30 days to decide whether they would be bound by the terms or whether they wanted to return the computer.

Among the additional terms in the box was an arbitration clause. The arbitration clause required that all disputes regarding performance of the Gateway 2000 computer were subject to being arbitrated and that the customer did not have the right to pursue a remedy in court. The Hill's complained that the arbitration clause was not prominent and that they should not be bound by terms of a contract that they did not know about when they agreed to the contract.

Opinion: Easterbrook

One of the terms in the box containing a Gateway 2000 system was an arbitration clause. Rich and Enza Hill, the customers, kept the computer more than 30 days before complaining about its components and performance. They filed suit in federal court arguing, among other things, that the product's shortcomings make Gateway a racketeer (mail and wire fraud are said to be the predicate offenses), leading to treble damages under RICO for the Hills and a class of all other purchasers. Gateway asked the district court to enforce the arbitration clause; the judge refused, writing that "the present record is insufficient to support a finding of a valid arbitration agreement between the parties or that the plaintiffs were given adequate notice of the arbitration clause." Gateway took an immediate appeal, as is its right. [Citations omitted]

The Hills say that the arbitration clause did not stand out: they concede noticing the statement of terms but deny reading it closely enough to discover the agreement to arbitrate, and they ask us to conclude that they therefore may go to court. Yet an agreement to arbitrate must be enforced "save upon such grounds as exist at law or in equity for the revocation of any contract." A contract need not be read to be effective; people who accept take the risk that the unread terms may in retrospect prove unwelcome. Terms inside Gateway's box stand or fall together. If they constitute the parties' contract because the Hills had an opportunity to return the computer after reading them, then all must be enforced.

ProCD, Inc. v. Zeidenberg holds that terms inside a box of software bind consumers who use the software after an opportunity to read the terms and to reject them by returning the product. Likewise, *Carnival Cruise Lines, Inc. v. Shute* enforces a forum-selection clause that was included among three pages of terms attached to a cruise ship ticket. *ProCD* and *Carnival Cruise Lines* exemplify the many commercial transactions in which people pay for products with terms to follow; *ProCD* discusses others. The district court concluded in *ProCD* that the contract is formed when the consumer pays for the software; as a result, the court held, only terms known to the consumer at that moment are part of the contract, and provisos inside the box do not count. Although this is one way a contract could be formed, it is not the only way: "A vendor, as master of the offer, may invite acceptance by conduct, and may propose limitations on the kind of conduct that constitutes acceptance. A buyer may accept by performing the acts the vendor proposes to treat as acceptance." Gateway shipped computers with the same sort of accept-or-return offer *ProCD* made to users of its software. *ProCD* relied on the Uniform Commercial Code rather than any peculiarities of Wisconsin law; both Illinois and South Dakota, the two states whose law might govern relations between Gateway and the Hills, have adopted the UCC; neither side has pointed us to any atypical doctrines in those states that might be pertinent; *ProCD* therefore applies to this dispute.

* * *

The decision of the district court is vacated, and this case is remanded with instructions to compel the Hills to submit their dispute to arbitration.

Decision and Outcome

The decision of the District Court that the Hills could proceed in the federal courts was reversed because the Seventh Circuit Court of Appeals held that the arbitration clause was enforceable.

Questions for Analysis

1. When, according to the court of appeals, did the customer accept the offer of the seller?
2. Is it commercially feasible for a sales representative to read (and be prepared to explain) the fine print over the phone?
3. Are this case and the previous case consistent?

The enforceability of clickwrap agreements raises two fundamental issues of contract law—formation and assent.

The formation of a contract between buyer and seller typically occurs before the buyer takes possession of the goods. The buyer and seller negotiate the terms of the sale, often memorializing their understanding in a written agreement, and then the goods are tendered. By contrast, when a consumer purchases software that displays a clickwrap agreement at the time of installation, the consumer has already purchased the product and is being asked to consent to the contract that purportedly memorializes their agreement. In this case, the question becomes "is the contract formed at the moment of purchase or later when the buyer assents to the terms of the clickwrap agreement?" Consumers have argued that such agreements are unconscionable because the parties lack the opportunity to bargain over or modify the terms of the agreement.

Clickwrap agreements also challenge our understanding of the manifestation of the buyer's assent. A contract is traditionally enforceable when the parties sign an agreement. In a clickwrap scenario, however, the buyer consents not with a written signature but with the click of a mouse. Is this sufficient to bind the buyer to the terms of the clickwrap agreement?

Source: This article is reprinted with permission from the August 11, 1998 edition of *New York Law Journal.* Copyright © 1998 NLP IP Company. All rights reserved. Further duplication without permission is prohibited.

Modern Contract Law: Layers of Terms

Enforceability of X-Wrap Agreements

The distinctions between the specifics of many e-contracts and traditional requirements for valid contracts should be clear. In e-commerce, *intent* is presumed by the electronic offer made by the vendor. The offeree's intent to assent to the terms of the contract provided by the offeree is manifested by a *click* from the customer or even by the operation of an electronic purchasing agent. As we have seen, the offeree of an offer made from a website often cannot know the full terms of contract until after physical or electronic transfer of the product has occurred. In effect, the buyer learns the terms of what he or she has assented to after paying money and receiving the product. After transacting, the legal question becomes, "Is the customer bound by terms of an agreement that he or she learns about after purchase?" The answer is yes, provided several conditions are met, including:

1. The customer must be given *clear notice* of the additional terms, which must be written in understandable English.
2. The customer must be given *clear notice as to what constitutes acceptance.* Acceptance could be manifested by a click at the appropriate button, by breaking the wrapping around software, or by choosing not to return a product in a specified time interval.
3. The customer must have an *opportunity to inspect the terms* in the wrap agreement.
4. The customer has an *unqualified right to return the merchandise* for a full refund if the customer does not agree to the terms contained in the clickwrap, shrinkwrap, or boxwrap.
5. The customer cannot be bound by *terms that are unconscionable* in light of ordinary commercial standards.

After some initial reluctance on the parts of the courts to enforce X-wrap (clickwrap, shrinkwrap, and boxtop) agreements and some egregious examples of overreaching (or unfairness) on the part of websites and vendors, it is clear that these agreements are now considered enforceable as long as the five conditions listed above are satisfied. X-wrap agreements continue to be a source of controversy and litigation. In Chapter 23 we discuss the EU approach to X-wraps, which is much more consumer friendly.

ATTRIBUTION

Who Is Accepting?

With click-on acceptances, the advantage of unique signatures is lost. Clearly, a vendor has a difficult time determining whether the clicker (the person clicking the acceptance dot) is the offeree to whom the offer was made. When fraud or mistake is present in interactions between computers, and between computers and individuals, the crucial issue is: How can the website really know whom it is dealing with? Attribution, in its legal application, corresponds to vendors ascribing actions to the "other party" in forming a contract. In some discussions of this issue, attribution is called *nonrepudiation;* if a website or vendor follows a reasonable **attribution procedure,** it precludes the purchaser from repudiating transactions in most cases. In other words, if a website can establish attribution, it can debit your credit card.

The risk of e-commerce fraud or mistake can be reduced if the parties have a prior relationship, which makes identification of purchasers far more reliable. Use of passwords is a common way of identifying purchasers. In spite of precautions taken by vendors, however, there are instances in which it is the vendor who must assume the losses associated with fraudulent clicks. If the clicker is a minor, for example, the vendor is subject to having any contract tentatively formed disaffirmed.

attribution procedure
Means of identifying and attributing to a specific party a specific electronic event, such as an online purchase.

Gathering Information about Visitors to a Website

In its efforts to avoid fraud and mistake(s), often vendors seek to establish a "relationship" by making customers and other visitors to their websites "members." Generally, to become a website member, one must provide a good bit of personal information. For site members, a password can be used as a substitute for signatures. As will be addressed in a bit more detail below, if a website uses commercially reasonable procedures for identifying a customer, the risk of unauthorized use of a password can be shifted from the website vendor to the customer.

Attribution Procedures and Consumer Defenses

According to Section 102(5) of UCITA " 'Attribution Procedure' means a procedure established by law, administrative rule, or agreement, or a procedure otherwise adopted by the parties, to verify that an electronic event is that of a specific person or to detect changes or errors in the information. The term includes a procedure that requires the use of algorithms or other codes, identifying words or numbers (passwords), encryption, callback or other acknowledgment, or any other procedures that are reasonable under the circumstances." Translated into English, *attribution procedure* means a procedure for *attributing* to a specific individual a specific electronic event such as an order for software placed over the Internet.

Case I: Attribution in the Absence of Special Arrangements

We can view attribution in two cases, with the second being by far the preferred situation for legitimate vendors. In Case I, attribution, in the absence of any special arrangement, requires the person relying on attribution to prove it.[5] In other words, if a vendor receives an order for an item from a customer and bills the customer, the vendor has the burden of showing that the customer placed the order if the customer denies responsibility. Section 213(a) of UCITA states that "[An electronic event] is attributed to a person if it was the act of that person or its electronic agent, or the person is otherwise bound by it under the law of agency or other law. The party relying on attribution . . . has the burden of establishing attribution."

As pointed out by Professor Nimmer, just because the vendor has the burden of establishing attribution does not mean all is lost. If the vendor has evidence that the goods ordered were shipped to the website visitor's address and goods are found on the premises of the visitor, the burden of proof is probably met. Professor Nimmer contends that vendors have a much more difficult time demonstrating fraud when the items ordered are computer information or services.

Case II: Attribution When a Reasonable Procedure Is Used

If an attribution procedure relied on is *reasonable,* then the person pointed to by the attribution procedure must pay for the products ordered, unless that person can show that he or she did not order the products. In other words, the burden of proof is upon the person pointed to by the attribution procedure. Section 214 of UCITA requires that an attribution procedure be commercially reasonable and defines commercial reasonableness "in light of the purposes of the procedure." *Also, UCITA requires that both parties agree to use the attribution procedure.* In virtually all cases, this means that a website asks the consumer to click "I Accept" in a clickwrap agreement involving a licensing of information by the consumer.

Under UCITA, a vendor must have a procedure for determining who the purchaser is and that procedure must be reasonable in light of the importance of the transaction. Similar provisions exist in both UETA and the UCC. According to the reporter's notes for UCITA, "[t]he general requirement of commercial reasonableness is that the procedure be a commercially reasonable method of identifying the party as compared to other persons." The reporter goes on to note that vendors are not required to use "state of the art procedures."

Attribution under UETA and UCITA

Under Section 1-108(a) of UETA, "[a]n electronic record or electronic signature is attributable to a person if it was the act of the person. The act of the person may be proved in any manner, including a showing of the efficacy of any security procedure applied to determine the person to which the electronic record or electronic signature was attributable." Section 1-108(b) indicates that "[T]he effect of an electronic record or electronic signature attributed to a person under subsection (a) is determined from the context and surrounding circumstances at the time of its creation, execution, or adoption, including the parties' agreement, if any, and otherwise as provided by law." If a purchaser gives her name and credit card number to execute a purchase, and clicks "I Accept" to the attribution procedure, that combination of acts is likely to be adequate attribution by that person.

In simple terms, both UETA and UCITA require a showing that

1. The attribution procedure being used is *commercially reasonable.*
2. The *parties agreed to use* the attribution procedure.

---

[5] See Professor Raymond Nimmer, "Contract Law in Electronic Commerce," paper presented at The New Media Conference, sponsored by the Practicing Law Institute, New York, January 2000.

3. The party (generally a website) *accepted or relied* on the electronic event in good faith and complied with other aspects of the attribution procedure.

4. The *attribution procedure indicated* that the electronic event was that of the person to whom attribution is sought.

So, unless there is a law established by a governmental body that provides otherwise for attribution, a vendor can rely on *commercially reasonable* attribution procedures as long as the other qualifications are present, which include *assent of both parties* to the attribution procedure. Of course, it is the vendor who normally sets up an attribution procedure and is the party in charge of securing assent from the other party (generally a customer), with assent generally provided by the clicking of a radio button on a website.

For example, Sally is interested in purchasing a book from Amazon.com. Sally participates in supplying Amazon with information about herself, along with a credit card number. Sally orders the book and her credit card account is debited for the purchase price of the book. Sally is liable for the value of the book even if she claims that she did not order the book, and she would have the burden of proof to show she did not order the book.

Electronic Errors and Consumer Defenses

Under UCITA, if a consumer makes an error by clicking on the wrong button, and if there is no reasonable method for immediate detection and/or correction of this error, "a consumer is not bound by an electronic message that the consumer did not intend and which was caused by an electronic error, if the consumer . . ."[6] does several appropriate things upon learning of the error or the reliance on the error by the other party (the vendor), whichever occurs first. The buyer must

1. *Notify* the other party of the error.

2. *Cause delivery to the other party* of all copies of the information (generally software) or, pursuant to reasonable instructions from the other party, deliver to another person or destroys all copies.

3. *Not use or receive any benefit* from the information or cause the information or benefit to be made available to a third party.

In ordinary English, the consumer is required to act promptly when (s)he discovers an error to counteract the error. Suppose a consumer was ordering 10 video games from a website that featured such games but, inadvertently, the consumer typed in 110 for quantity. Upon discovering this error, this consumer must promptly notify the vendor, return the unwanted merchandise, and not use it or gain advantage nor allow others to do so. The same consumer defenses apply under UETA, which is the overlay for Article 2 of the UCC.

DIGITAL SIGNATURES

The Importance of Signatures

It is difficult to overemphasize the importance of signatures in contract law. A signature uniquely identifies an individual and makes it very difficult for a signatory to disclaim responsibility for a signed agreement. Additional security can be garnered when notaries are used to affirm identities of those signing a contract, because notaries require a document

---

[6] UCITA Section 213(b).

signer to produce other identification that has the signatory's signature as additional verification of authenticity.

Finding a substitute for signatures in cyberspace has presented a number of challenges, but the market and changes in laws are providing responses to this problem. Note that current contract law terminology does not use the word *signature,* but rather the term **authenticate,** to signify assent to a contract.

authenticate
Verify the identity of a party authorizing an electronic agreement and then authorize the electronic event.

At common law, signatures are made valid in a number of ways. They can occur through agents, stamps, printed signatures, or engraved signatures. With EDI, an overall agreement between partnering companies effectively substitutes for signatures. The UCC is even more liberal in accepting as a signature "any symbol executed or adopted by a party with present intention to authenticate a writing."

According to Section 102(6) of UCITA,

6. "Authenticate" means:

a. to sign; or

b. with the intent to sign a record, otherwise to execute or adopt an electronic symbol, sound, message, or process referring to, attached to, included in, or logically associated or linked with, that record.

UCITA addresses the use of technology to substitute for signatures. Signing a document is one method to authenticate intent to contract, but other ways such as encryption (discussed below) are being used as substitutes for signatures. In addition, biometrics is increasingly being used to authenticate contracts. One example of **biometrics identification** relies on comparing signatures using electronic digitizer pads. Other examples of biometrics include making use of unique biometric records (such as retina images, fingerprints, and voices) to verify that the person who is purporting to authenticate a contract is in fact that person. At present, however, the most widely used method of authenticating an agreement in e-commerce transactions (as a substitute for a signature) makes use of encryption.

biometric identification
Scientific means of identifying an individual by unalterable characteristics such as fingerprints, voice patterns, retina images, and so forth.

Encryption and Cryptography

cryptography
Mechanisms for translating messages into coded form, to prevent their use by unauthorized recipients, then allowing authorized recipients to decode and read the original messages.

For centuries, **cryptography** has been used to disguise communications that may be intercepted, particularly in military contexts. Cryptography has been applied to various means of electronic communications including telex, fax, electronic funds transfers, and EDI. Indeed, banks were unwilling to operate ATM machines until there was a safe way of encrypting (scrambling) the data sent from the banks' computers to ATM machines. Each of the communication mechanisms listed above is a closed system, intended to provide (generally) two-way communication. However, such communications can be subject to interception by a saboteur or spy who has detailed knowledge of the underlying technology. During World War II, U.S. intelligence spent considerable resources trying, ultimately successfully, to crack (unscramble) codes used by the Japanese and Germans to encrypt transmissions of orders that directed their military operations.

What Does Cryptography Do?

With the advent of the Internet, communications are open and much more susceptible to interception. Those intercepting communications can obtain credit card numbers and make unauthorized purchases. This activity, commonly called "identity theft," is becoming more common. Cryptography is the science of transforming data to hide its content and prevent its unauthorized modification or use. The "key" to encrypted communications is a decoding mechanism, or key, that should be kept secret. The sender of sensitive data encrypts (scrambles) those data using a key to make the message unintelligible to interceptors. The intended recipient has a key that enables him or her to decrypt (unscramble) the message

VeriSign® Authentic Document IDs

CREATE VERIFIABLE PROOF OF YOUR ONLINE TRANSACTIONS

Authentic Document IDs allow you to "digitally notarize" the documents you transmit online by creating proof of an electronic document's state at a particular point in time.

With an Authentic Document ID installed on your computer, you can access VeriSign's Authentic Document Service: by simply right-clicking your document, you create a digital receipt containing a fingerprint of the electronic file, the date and time the file was digitally signed, the identity of the person that signed the document, and VeriSign's independent verification.

To help create a trusted environment for e-commerce and the exchange of documents over the Internet, the U.S. Congress recently approved the E-Sign act [discussed below]. Under the act, documents signed online with an electronic signature will have the same legal force as a paper contract.

VeriSign's Authentic Document ID lets you build trust for the documents you exchange online by providing VeriSign's witness to the files submitted to VeriSign's Authentic Document Service for digital notarization.

With the Authentic Document Service, you can digitally notarize electronic files of any type or size that your business needs to preserve or control:

- Business plans
- Contracts
- Accounting records
- Architectural designs and CAD drawings
- Credit reports
- Digital images

and make it intelligible again. In some cases, the keys of the sender and recipient are the same, but, increasingly, encryption is accomplished with asymmetric keys, some "public" and some "private."

certification authorities
Agents that serve as electronic notaries, providing identifications of parties engaged in electronic agreements.

Encryption requires a third party, often labeled a **certification authority** (CA). A CA is really just a notary in cyberspace. Making use of the CA, a sender looks up the recipient's public key and uses it to encrypt the message to be sent. The recipient uses its private key to decrypt the message. Owners never have a need to transmit their private keys to anyone in order to have their messages decrypted; thus, the private keys are not in transit and are not vulnerable.

Consider the offerings by Verisign.com, which provides CA services.

The Electronic Signatures in Global and National Commerce Act (E-SIGN)

E-SIGN Act
A federal statute that seeks to provide uniform legal treatment of contracts formed electronically, using specified electronic methods of authentication.

At the time that Congress passed and the president signed the **Electronic Signatures in Global and National Commerce Act (E-SIGN) Act,** most states had passed their own electronic signatures acts. Needless to say, the statutes enacted were not uniform from state to state. To date, UETA has been adopted by 41 states, but much of state law is not subject to UETA. The E-SIGN Act is federal legislation that will apply to all states. The core provision of the E-SIGN Act decrees that no contract, record, or signature shall be denied legal effect because it is in electronic form. E-SIGN requires that an electronic record must be *printable* and *storable* and *the parties must agree separately* if they use digital signatures.

The E-SIGN Act went into effect October 1, 2000. The net result of the E-SIGN Act is to make it much easier for businesses and consumers to agree to binding contracts electronically. More legislation and technological developments are likely in this area as e-commerce continues to expand.

Cyberlaw **Developments** What Is the Role of the U.S. Government in Cryptography?

The U.S. government plays many roles in cryptography, ranging from use to export control to standardization efforts to the development of new cryptosystems. Recently the government has taken an even bigger interest in cryptography due to its ever-increasing use outside of the military. [The U.S. government plays a much larger role in cryptography than any other government in the world.]

* * *

In the past, the government has not only used cryptography itself, but has cracked other country's codes as well. A notable example of this occurred in 1940 when a group of Navy cryptanalysts, led by William F. Friedman, succeeded in breaking the Japanese diplomatic cipher known as Purple.

In 1952, the U.S. government established the National Security Agency (NSA), whose job is to handle military and government data security as well as gather information about other countries' communications. Also established was the National Institute of Standards and Technology (NIST), which plays a major role in developing cryptography standards.

During the 1970's, IBM and the U.S. Department of Commerce—more precisely NIST (then known as NBS, The National Bureau of Standards)—developed along with NSA the Data Encryption Standard (DES). This algorithm has been a standard since 1977, with reviews leading to renewals every few years. The general consensus is that DES will not be strong enough for the future's encryption needs. Therefore, NIST is currently working on a new standard, the Advanced Encryption Standard (AES), to replace DES. In the intermediate stage, triple-DES is the encryption standard. It is expected that AES will remain a standard well into the 21st century.

Currently there are no restrictions on the use or strength of domestic encryption (encryption where the sender and recipient are in the U.S.). However, the government regulates the export of cryptography from the U.S. by setting restrictions on how strong such encryption may be. Cryptographic exports are controlled under the Export Administration Regulations (EAR), and their treatment varies according to several factors including destinations, customers, and the strength and usage of the cryptography involved. In January 2000, the restrictions were significantly relaxed; today, any cryptographic product can be exported to non-governmental end-users outside embargoed destinations (states supporting terrorism) without a license.

Source: From RSA Laboratories' Frequently Asked Questions About Today's Cryptography, Version 4.1. Copyright © 2000 RSA Security, Inc. Reprinted with permission.

Summary

E-Commerce Has Created New Forms of Transactions That Have Created New Challenges for Commercial Contract Law; to Date, There

- E-commerce is now plagued by some of the same problems that led to the passage of the UCC. In the absence of uniform legislation, state-by-state differences are inevitable with respect to e-commerce. State-by-state differences in e-commerce contract law are widely viewed as undesirable.

- A number of uniform bills have been proposed and partially enacted, including UETA, UCITA, and revisions to Article 2 of the UCC.

- At the federal level, E-SIGN was passed to legalize electronic records and digital signatures.

- A major focus of the *uniform acts* is creating legal parity between paper records and electronic records.

- The UCITA covers licenses of computer software but does not cover the sale of goods on the Internet. The scope of the UCITA includes computer software, multimedia interactive products, computer data and databases, and Internet and online information.

Have Been a Number of Proposals for Uniform Laws, but No Proposal Has, as Yet, Met with Complete Success in Being Adopted by a Large Number of States	• The UETA deals comprehensively with e-commerce and contract law, except when other state laws indicate that electronic records are not legally enforceable. • The UCC covers the sale of goods, including e-commerce sales. • E-SIGN applies to all contracts affecting interstate commerce, except those specifically excluded such as mortgage foreclosures and divorce decrees. • To have parity with paper records, E-SIGN requires electronic records be storable and printable.
Increasingly, Contracts Are Being Created Electronically, Often without Human Intervention	• The basic principles of contract law are modified to deal with Internet transactions. • *Intent* often is inferred from the operations of electronic agents and "signatures" can occur with a response to an invitation to click to accept. • *EDI contracts* can be formed electronically without human intervention. • Surfing the Internet most likely means that you will encounter opportunities for binding offers to contract.
Traditional Contract Rules Are Increasingly Being Stretched to Accommodate Commercial Practices That Make Use of X-Wrap Terms That Appear on Computer Screens, in Boxes, and under Cellophane	• The revised Section 2-207 of the UCC makes it easier to include additional terms in contracts that are not in the offers. • *Clickwrap agreements* can add additional terms to an agreement that may involve agreements to arbitrate, forum selection clauses, warranties, return policies, reproductions, and other "fine print." • *Shrinkwrap agreements* bind a customer to the terms in a contract even though the customer cannot know what many of the terms are until the software, CD, or diskette is purchased. • *Boxtop agreements* are papers often found in the bottom of boxes containing tangible goods. Such agreements have the same legal effect as do clickwrap and shrinkwrap agreements. • The customer is bound by the terms of an agreement that he or she learns about after purchase when the customer has been given *clear notice of the additional terms, clear notice as to what constitutes acceptance, an opportunity to inspect the terms in the wrap agreement,* and *an opportunity to return the goods* if the customer objects to the additional terms. • With *click-on acceptances,* if the clicker is a minor, the vendor is subject to having the contract disaffirmed.
Attribution Is Established if the Parties Agree on a Commercially Reasonable Procedure; Mistakes Are Correctable if the Mistaken Party Acts Promptly	• If a person, or his or her agent, commits an electronic act, then the event is attributed to that person. • The burden of establishing attribution falls on the party relying on attribution through an electronic event unless a commercially reasonable attribution procedure is agreed to by both parties and is used. • A consumer is not bound to an agreement made in error by clicking the wrong button if the consumer notifies the other party of the error, returns the misordered merchandise, and does not use it to gain advantage.
Congress Has Passed the E-SIGN Act to	• In cyberspace, the most often used substitute for signatures is encryption and digital signatures. • Certification authorities verify the identity of an online signatory and perform the same functions as notaries.

Accommodate Digital Signatures, Which Make Use of Encryption and Certification Authorities	• Other means of uniquely identifying individuals in cyberspace include passwords, user IDs, and biometrics. • Congress passed the E-SIGN Act, which states that for most contracts, signatures will not be denied legal effect merely because they are electronic as long as the parties have agreed to the electronic format. • E-SIGN allows for digital signatures that make use of passwords, biometrics, and encryption.

Key Terms

attribution procedure, *282*
authenticate, *285*
biometric identification, *285*
boxtop licenses or
    agreements, *274*
certification authorities, *286*

clickwrap agreements, *274*
cryptography, *285*
electronic data
    interchange (EDI), *271*
E-SIGN Act, *286*
parity with paper, *266*

scope of revised Article 2 of
    the UCC, *269*
scope of UCITA, *269*
scope of UETA, *268*
shrinkwrap agreements, *274*

Questions for Review and Analysis

1. What steps should you take to ensure that an electronic contract is legal and enforceable? What requirements are necessary under E-SIGN or UETA to ensure that an electronic contract is valid?

2. Under what circumstances could you agree to a contract and later find out what you agreed to? What safeguards exist in contract law when clickwrap, shrinkwrap, or boxtop terms appear that you do not agree with?

3. What online transactions are governed by the UCC, UETA, UCITA, and E-SIGN?

4. What is the basic goal of attribution procedures from the point of view of online vendors? What is the legal result if you agree to an attribution procedure put forward by an online vendor and the vendor relies on your clicks?

5. What is the point of a digital signature? How reliable are digital signatures relative to paper signatures? What other procedures are available to uniquely identify the parties to an online contract?

If You Really Understood This Chapter, You Should Be Able to Provide Informed Commentary on the Following:

1. **Click-On Agreements.** Netscape offers "free" software called SmartDownload but claims that its software is subject to an end user license agreement (EULA). SmartDownload is a program that makes it easier for its users to download files from the Internet without losing their interim progress when they pause to engage in some other task, or if their Internet connection is severed. The plaintiffs in this case clicked the box indicating that they wanted to download the software, which Netscape clearly indicated was subject to the EULA. There was not, however, any separate requirement by Netscape that users agree to Netscape's EULA, which contained an arbitration clause. Those taking advantage of the free software are invited to "Please review" the terms of the EULA. Are licensees of free software bound by an EULA that does not require a separate expression of assent in the form of requiring the licensee to indicate assent before allowing downloading? A preliminary question that the court dealt with was whether the parties had a contract. What do you think? Does an offer to allow visitors to download software create a contract? [*Christopher Specht, et al., v. Netscape Communications and America Online, Inc.,* 150 F. Supp. 2d 585 (S.D.N.4. 2001).]

2. **Browse-Wrap Agreements.** Suppose that a website states that the information made available on its website about the timing and availability of concerts is subject to a license agreement and the license agreement is made available to visitors via a hyperlink. Visitors are informed in the license agreement that commercial use of the information on the plaintiff's website is prohibited. Defendant is another website that gained access to plaintiff's website, copied the information, and made that information available on its website. On the plaintiff's website, access to concert information requires clicks that refer to a license agreement that supposedly binds visitors to the terms of the

license. Defendant claims that it is not in a contract with the plaintiff merely because it visits the plaintiff's website. Plaintiff claims that browsing through its website makes visitors subject to the terms of a license agreement that are available through a hyberlink. What do you think? Does visiting a website make you a contracting partner with the website? [*Pollstar v. Gigmania Ltd.,* 170 F. Supp. 2d 974 (E.D. Cal. 2000).]

3. **UCC Jurisdiction over Software Contracts?** Since UCITA has been adopted in only two states, an issue arises as to how the courts should treat software transactions. In *Architectronics, Inc. v. Control Systems Inc.* (CSI), the issue was the length of the statute of limitations period. In New York there is a six-year statute for common law contracts, but the UCC statute of limitations is four years. In the transaction, Architectronics developed drivers that enhanced the value of CAD-Source, which was a very popular computer-aided design software program owned by CSI. The court had to determine if the transaction was primarily the "sale" of software or a transfer of intellectual property rights. If the transaction was primarily a sale of software, then the UCC applied and the plaintiff's case would be dismissed because the alleged breach of contract took place more than four years previously. If the transaction was a transfer of intellectual property, the common law of contracts would apply and the plaintiff could go to trial and try to prove his case. The case was decided based on court interpretations of whether the transaction was primarily a sale or a transfer of intellectual property. Is this kind of case likely to be repeated in the future? [*Architectronics, Inc. v. Control Systems, Inc.,* 935 F. Supp. 425 (S.D.N.4. 1996).]

4. **Electronic Contracts and Notice.** In many agreements between websites and their subscribers, the terms of the contract call for notices to be sent to the subscriber's e-mail address. The agreement between the website and the subscriber may call for notification before rate increases, but that notification may be electronic. In nonelectronic contracts, such notices are common and, if the subscriber changes addresses, the U.S. Postal Service has procedures for changing mailing addresses. Although there are some services that can be used, to date most e-mail addresses are tied to ISPs and, when a member leaves, there is no provision for forwarding e-mail to the new e-mail address of the contracting partner. Should a subscriber to an electronic service forfeit valuable rights because there is no generally recognized service for forwarding e-mail from old to active e-mail addresses? The issue may not be a great problem because there are no cases in which this issue has arisen in litigation, but potentially the problem looms unless the subscriber takes the initiative and contacts that website contracting partner from its new e-mail address.

5. **Are Donees Bound by License Restrictions Imposed on Donors?** The plaintiff, Melissa Westendorf, received a computer from a friend. The computer was purchased from Gateway 2000, the defendant, and accompanying the computer was software that had a shrinkwrap license, which indicated that the purchaser agreed to all the terms of the shrinkwrap license if he or she retained the computer for more than 30 days. The software, *gateway.net,* was for the defendant's Internet access agreement, but it never performed properly. Plaintiff seeks to sue for the lack of service from the software, but defendant claims that the plaintiff is bound by the terms of a shrinkwrap license that requires arbitration for any dispute. Are beneficiaries of gifts bound by the restrictions that Gateway imposes on its purchasers? The plaintiff in this case sought to create a class of plaintiffs based on other users of *gateway.net.* [*Westendorf v. Gateway 2000 Inc.,* 2000 Del. Ch. LEXIS 54 (2000).]

Social Responsibility and Ethics in a High-Tech World

6. **Promises, Promises.** Much has been said about e-commerce, and a lot of the discussion has been negative. Increasingly, websites are claiming that if you do business with them, you are bound by the terms of various licensing agreements. The license agreement could give you the right to browse the website; it may make you a member of a club sponsored by a website; or it may accompany purchase or downloading of software. Typically, the license agreements are three and four pages long and make use of cumbersome legalese that is barely decipherable even if the reader has a law degree. In addition, websites maintain the right to change license agreements upon giving notice to subscribers. Most e-mail addresses are the target of spam, so you have to be careful to read every e-mail to make sure you are not being notified of something important. Typically, if you have a problem with a website, you have to go to another state to file a claim before an arbitrator as the choice of law has already been made (you probably do not remember that, in

the license agreement, you "agreed" to arbitrate disputes in a state selected by the website and under laws picked by the website). Buried in some license agreements have been prohibitions against users of software criticizing the software in print or in response to questions from the media. It would seem that free speech is a right that can be legally signed away and the courts may be called upon to enforce such agreements.

As a possible, future owner of a website, would you hire an attorney to write privacy statements, licenses, and terms of service agreements that (a) are loaded with legalese and (b) make sure that consumers that visit your website or buy some of your products can never get to court to complain because they have already signed their rights away? As a future voter, would you want the government to intervene and set limits on some of the most egregious terms in license agreements? Note that the EU has gone this route and that, within the EU, courts are empowered to choose not to enforce "choice of law" or "forum" clauses. Such a court choice would mean that, if you received defective goods or software from a website, you could sue for redress in your own country under your own laws. Is this kind of government regulation what we want in the United States?

Using the Internet to Your Advantage

1. The organization that was responsible for composing and promoting the UCC is the National Conference of Commissioners on Uniform State Laws (NCCUSL), which maintains online versions of the UCC as well as proposals for changes to the nine articles of the UCC (http://www.nccusl.org/). At the NCCUSL website, the complete text of the Uniform Computer Information Transactions Act (UCITA) can be found (at http://www.nccusl.org/nccusl/ ActSearchResults.aspx) as well as the Uniform Electronic Transactions Act (UETA) and the proposed changes to Article 2 of the UCC. The Electronic Signatures in Global and National Commerce Act (E-SIGN) is available at the Thomas Locator (http://thomas.loc.gov/) at http://thomas.loc.gov/cgi-bin/query/D?c106:1:./temp/~c1068nbfm4::.

2. The Federal Trade Commission has assembled at http://www.ftc.gov/bcp/menu-internet.htm. over 50 articles that are accessible online dealing with what it regards as Internet or online scams. Many of these articles deal with illegal or dubious offers made online to unsuspecting Internet browsers. In a similar vein, the Securities and Exchange Commission has assembled at http://www.sec.gov/investor/online.shtml. nine articles about what it terms "online fraud." The Food and Drug Administration is concerned about possible fraud committed by online pharmacies and has assembled at http://www.fda.gov/oc/buyonline/prfags.htm. a number of articles that discuss the dangers associated with ordering and buying drugs online.

3. The BNA (Bureau of National Affairs) publishes online a number of very informative articles about e-commerce (http://www.bna.com/products/ip/eplr.htm). Using the Google™ search engine to find for websites offering guidance on e-commerce law yielded the following websites that appear interesting and informative for students: http://www.denniskennedy.com/ecomlaw.htm; the Internet Law and Policy Forum (http://www.ilpf.org/), which offers lively discussion about important e-commerce policy issues such as jurisdiction, electronic authentication, content liability, and self-regulation; and the *Internet Law Journal* (http://www.tilj.com/), which also has a number of e-commerce law articles that are accessible online.

Chapter Ten

Torts: Wrongs and Their Remedies

Learning Objectives

On completing this chapter, you should

1. Be familiar with the three types of torts: intentional, negligence, and strict liability.
2. Be able to distinguish between defamation, invasion of privacy, and intentional infliction of emotional distress.
3. Be able to apply the criteria for liability using the reasonable person test in negligence cases.
4. Understand how both negligence and strict liability are used in product liability cases.
5. Be aware of the three types of product defects: manufacturing, design, and inadequate warnings.

OVERVIEW

This chapter reviews the principles of tort law, which are applied in the next chapter to cyberspace and to other settings in which new technology has created pressure for or resulted in recent legal changes in tort law.

tort
A noncontractual wrong that causes injury.

A **tort** is a noncontractual, civil *wrong*. It can be an act or a spoken wrong, or a nonaction (carelessness) that is wrong, resulting in *injury* being inflicted on a person or property. When such a legal wrong (tort) is committed, the victim(s) often will ask for a court remedy. The typical remedy for a tort is compensatory monetary *damages* (the defendant pays the plaintiff compensation for the injuries inflicted due to the tort), though other court remedies in the form of punitive damages (designed to punish the defendant and dissuade other similarly situated possible defendants) also may be possible.

A *tort* is a violation of duties required by society of all parties as a matter of law. These required duties are separate from the duties required by contract, which are voluntarily assumed by the contracting parties. So a tort is a noncontractual interaction in which one party (who may become a defendant) wrongfully harms another party (who may be a plaintiff in a resulting lawsuit). As is likely quite apparent to you, there are many ways in which one party can do wrongful harm to another by act or the failure to act. Consequently, there are many forms of torts that are readily recognizable as grounds for legal action. This chapter provides the basics of tort law, which must be understood to grapple with modern day torts of all forms.

Elements of a Tort Claim

A typical tort case involves two parts: *liability* and *damages.* First, *a plaintiff must show that the defendant is liable to the plaintiff.* In other words, the plaintiff must be able to show that he or she has been the victim of a civil wrong, such as being harmed because of the defendant's failure to take proper precautions (i.e., the defendant is not paying attention to the road while driving). Second, *the plaintiff has the requirement to show what his or her damages are.* Tort law provides compensation for a variety of harms including pain and suffering, loss of income, damage to property, and mental anguish.

Classification of Torts

Torts are classified into categories that have relevance to the damages phase of tort litigation:

- A tort is classified as *intentional* if the plaintiff is able to prove the defendant committed an intentional act that he *knew or should have known* would harm the plaintiff. Assault, battery, defamation, and trespass are all intentional torts and are discussed below.

- A second category of torts is composed of those based on *negligence* of the defendant. In a tort based on negligence, the defendant is being sued, not because (s)he intended to harm the plaintiff, but because (s)he was *insufficiently careful* in view of the surrounding circumstances and, so, *violated a duty expected by society.*

- The last category of torts contains *strict liability* torts, which involve liability *without* a showing of *fault.* If a defendant engages in high-risk activities, such as using dynamite in construction, the defendant is liable for all resulting damages even if there is no showing that the defendant was negligent or careless in any way. Also, if the defendant sells a product that has a defect, the defendant is liable for the harm incurred by the plaintiff regardless of whether the defendant was reasonably careful in the manufacture or design of the product.

Understanding tort law is much easier if torts are classified into one of the three categories above, as the standards of proof and damages vary depending on the category of tort.

Damages

Compensatory Damages

compensatory damages
A damage award intended to compensate for the value of injury incurred from a tort.

Damage awards in tort cases can take several forms. Generally, the legal rationale for an award of damages in tort is based on the standard that a defendant should compensate a plaintiff for the wrongful harm caused by his or her actions (or inactions). **Compensatory damages** can be straightforward when property is damaged, as the plaintiff is generally entitled to the fair market value of the property damaged. Damage computations are more difficult to estimate when the damages involve **personal injury** to or the **wrongful death** of another person or persons. Juries can render quite variable awards when plaintiffs' injuries involve losses of limbs or of life. Also, plaintiffs in tort cases are allowed to recover compensation for pain and suffering, which is another factor that adds significantly to the variability of damage awards. Damage awards aimed at compensating for these tort injuries (*compensatory damages*) can be very sizeable, confronting businesses of all types with significant risk management challenges.

personal injury
Loss of an eye, a limb, or some other serious and even debilitating injury due to the wrongful act of another.

wrongful death
A death resulting from the wrongful act of another.

Punitive Damages

punitive or exemplary damages
Damage awards, in addition to compensatory awards, intended to punish and make an example of the defendant's tortious actions.

In the event of injury due to *intentional* wrongdoing, additional monetary awards described as **punitive or exemplary damages** may be imposed by a court. The legal rationale for such awards is to impose financial punishment on the defendant, providing incentives for avoidance of like future wrongs both by the defendant and by others whose actions could result in similar tort liability exposure. Although intent of some form is necessary when a jury awards punitive damages, this term is sometimes elastically viewed as meaning that the defendant exhibited *a reckless disregard for public safety* as when, for example, a corporation weighs profits against human life in designing products (see the Ford Pinto case, Case 10-5, later in this chapter). In some cases, there are punitive damage awards that are multiples of compensatory damage awards.

Other Remedies

In addition to damage awards for civil torts, courts may issue *injunctions* to prohibit acts that are viewed as wrongful. Sometimes damages awarded in a tort case are *nominal*—they are modest in amount (e.g., $1) and are intended as symbolic recognition of the wrong done, though substantial harm may not have been done.

INTENTIONAL TORTS

intentional tort
An injurious wrongful action in which the perpetrator of the injury engaged in the act with intent, even though the injury was not intended.

An **intentional tort** occurs if there is *intent* by the defendant *to engage in the act* that results in injury, even if the injury suffered is not intended. There are many torts that involve physical trespass on another. These include assault, battery, and false imprisonment. These torts are not the main focus of the tort discussions in this textbook, but business students should be aware of what constitutes civil assault, battery, and false imprisonment.

When Is a Company Liable for Assaults, Batteries, or Other Intentional Torts of Employees?

In most cases, businesses are not liable for actions of employees who commit assaults, batteries, and false imprisonment because the businesses can claim that the employees are acting outside their scope of employment.[1] However, companies have been liable for employee-committed assaults and batteries if, at the time of the tort, the employee (1) was working at his or her job and (2) was advancing the interests of the company. An additional factor the courts consider in determining the liability of a company for an intentional tort of an employee is whether the company had prior notice of aggressive actions by that employee.

Alternatively, the employer is likely to be liable if there is evidence that management aided and abetted or was cognizant of tortious behavior by employee(s). If a security guard incarcerates several minority youth based on a racial profile of likely shoplifters provided by the employer, the employer is liable for false imprisonment. On the other hand, if an employee suddenly becomes delusional without prior warning signs and shoots people walking next to the employer's factory, the employer is not liable unless, perhaps, it was negligent in its security precautions.

Defenses to Assault, Battery, and False Imprisonment

For assault and battery, there are four defenses: *consent, defense of self, defense of property,* and *defense of others*. If a defendant qualifies for one of these defenses, (s)he will escape liability even though (s)he assaulted or battered the plaintiff. In sporting contests, participants generally cannot sue if they are injured by a battery from someone on the other team

---

[1] Scope of employment is discussed in Chapter 15.

Nutz and Boltz   Traditional Intentional Torts

Tort	Elements	Examples
Assault	Defendant intentionally places plaintiff in fear of immediate harmful or offensive contact	Swinging a fist, waving a knife, pointing a gun, a male stalking a female
Battery	Defendant intentionally contacts plaintiff in a harmful or offensive manner	Striking with a hand, cutting with a knife, shooting, sexual battery such a molestation or rape
False imprisonment	Defendant intentionally detains without justification plaintiff in boundaries set by the defendant	Criminal kidnapping, unjustified detention by store owner, locking the door on someone

because, by playing in the sport, they have consented to the risks inherent in the activity, including batteries.

You can use reasonable force under the circumstances confronted to defend yourself, your property, or someone else. It is reasonable to block a punch thrown by someone who is swinging a fist at you, but it is not reasonable to stab someone who is about your size and has pushed you. Using a spring gun to defend an unoccupied building is using excessive force and the defense is lost.

False Imprisonment Statutes

Businesses have been held liable for false imprisonment when they have falsely accused and detained customers for shoplifting. On the other hand, businesses have a legitimate right to protect their inventory and to detain shoplifters. It is inevitable, however, that mistakes will be made; someone will be wrongly accused of shoplifting by store staff. In virtually all states there are store owner statutes that provide defenses for a storeowner against charges of false imprisonment if

1. The store owner had a *reasonable basis* for detaining the customer (there were some suspicious actions).
2. The store owner *behaves reasonably* and attempts to minimize possible embarrassment in the event that a mistake is made.

Business Torts

Although many businesses have been sued for assaults, batteries, and false imprisonments committed by their employees, these torts more commonly occur in a nonbusiness context and employers are not liable for such torts. The next set of torts we discuss mainly occurs in a business setting.

Intentional Infliction of Emotional Distress

It is a civil wrong to intentionally inflict emotional distress on another person. Intentional infliction of emotional distress is a tort claim that is making its way to court with increasing frequency, often being applied in somewhat novel situations, which may include sexual harassment and cyberstalking.

The tort of intentional infliction of emotional distress involves *conduct so extreme and outrageous that it results in severe emotional distress* to another person. To be actionable, the conduct must be outrageous to a *reasonable person,* beyond the bounds of decency in a civilized society, and must result in far more than mere indignation and annoyance. Courts have held that embarrassment, humiliation, anger, fear, and worry can be indicators of severe mental distress. Certainly, if the victim of this tort injury sought medical help following the defendant's actions, it would be evidence of severe emotional distress.

A business that has an agent making harassing after-midnight phone calls to a delinquent customer on a regular basis may be found liable for the emotional distress caused, while the same phone calls during normal waking hours may be liability-free. Collection agencies are often defendants in intentional infliction of emotional distress cases and high-pressure sales operations also are targets for such cases. Another group of typical defendants for this tort is practical jokers, whose "jokes" cross the line and cause severe emotional distress because of outrageous behavior. Putting a live snake in a woman's purse might qualify. In addition, victims of sexual harassment are frequently plaintiffs in intentional infliction of emotional distress cases, in part because the statute of limitations (time for filing the suit) under the Civil Rights Act is short (six months).

Case 10-1 illustrates business exposure to liability for in-the-workplace harassment and related misbehavior.

Case 10-1

Leta Fay Ford v. Revlon, Inc.

Supreme Court of Arizona
153 Ariz. 38, 734 P.2d 580 (1987)

FACTS AND CASE BACKGROUND

Leta Fay Ford had worked for Revlon, Inc., for 10 years, working her way up from a clerical position to a buyer position. In October 1979, Revlon hired Karl Braun as the new manager for the purchasing department, making him Ford's supervisor. On April 3 of 1980, Braun invited Ford to dinner "to discuss business." At dinner, business soon turned to Braun's personal interest in Ford. At the end of dinner, as Ford started to leave, she was ordered by Braun to sit down, that she was not going anywhere, and that he planned to spend the night with her. Ford rejected these advances and was told by Braun that "you will regret this . . ."

A month later, on May 3, Revlon held its annual service awards picnic. At the picnic, Braun followed Ford around most of the day and, at one point, pressed close to her and graphically described his intent to have sex with her. Later in the day, Braun grabbed Ford in a chokehold as she came out of the restroom, fondled her with his other hand as he continued holding her, and repeated his intentions. A friend of Ford's jerked Braun's arm loose and Ford wrenched herself free and ran away from Braun. This day's event prompted Ford to initiate a series of meetings with numerous members of Revlon management to report her complaints and ask for relief. The recipients of her presentations, protests, and requests for help included the Phoenix Revlon controller, the personnel manager for the clerical and technical group in the Phoenix plant, the personnel manager for executives, the director of personnel at the Phoenix plant, a human resources manager "trouble shooter" in Revlon headquarters, the vice president of industrial relations and operations, and others.

This series of interactions continued from May until December and into the next year. In various meetings, Ford was visibly shaken and very emotional. On February 23, 1981, Ford submitted a written request for a transfer out of the purchasing department. On February 24, Braun placed Ford on a 60-day probation because of her allegedly poor work performance.

On February 25, Ford had another meeting with Revlon management personnel regarding her harassment. At this meeting, she submitted a handwritten complaint that read, in part:

> *"I want to officially register a charge of sexual harassment and discrimination against K. Braun. I am asking for protection from Karl Braun. I have a right to be protected. I am collapsing emotionally and physically and I can't go on."*

After this meeting, Ford was told that Braun's actions would be investigated and that he would be closely watched. Not until three months later, on May 8, was a report on Ford's charges written—a report that corroborated Ford's charge of sexual assault and that recommended that Braun be censured. On May 28, nearly 14 months after Ford's initial complaint, Braun was issued a letter of censure from Revlon. In October of 1981, Ford attempted suicide. On October 5, Revlon terminated Braun. In April of 1982, Ford sued Braun and Revlon for assault and battery, and for intentional infliction of emotional distress. At trial, two written personnel policies were admitted as evidence. One policy, dealing with employee complaints, indicated that "Any employee who has a complaint about any aspect of . . . employment is entitled to have the complaint heard, investigated and, if possible, resolved." Legitimate complaints were to be dealt with as quickly and fully as possible according to this policy. A second written policy defined sexual harassment in accordance with the Equal Employment Opportunity Commission (EEOC) guidelines and provided that personnel executives who were made aware of allegations of sexual harassment are responsible for investigating promptly, fully, and with the highest degree of confidentiality, and for taking . . . actions to deal with alleged violations or for referring them to higher authority for disposition.

At trial, the jury found Braun liable for assault and battery, but not for intentional infliction of emotional distress. The jury found Revlon liable for intentional infliction of emotional distress but not liable for assault and battery. The jury assessed damages of $100 in compensatory damages and $1,000 in punitive damages against Braun. The jury assessed damages of $10,000 in compensatory damages and $100,000 in punitive damages against Revlon.

Revlon appealed this decision and the court of appeals reversed the judgment of the trial court against Revlon. The Appeals Court indicated that since Braun (as agent) was found not guilty of intentional infliction of emotional distress, then Revlon (as principal) could not be found guilty. The Supreme Court granted review because its members disagreed with this limitation on the liability of Revlon.

Opinion of the Court: En Banc

The court of appeals held that Revlon could not be liable for intentional infliction of emotional distress if Braun was not liable. Per the appeals court, Revlon's liability is inextricably tied to the acts of Braun. Since Braun's acts did not constitute intentional or reckless infliction of emotional distress, then the inaction of Revlon on Ford's complaint certainly could not reach that level.

We disagree. Admittedly, when the master's liability is based solely on the negligence of his servant, a judgment in favor of the servant is a judgment in favor of the master. When the negligence of the master is independent of the negligence of the servant, the result may be different.

* * *

In a case factually similar to this one, the U.S. Court of Appeals for the Fourth Circuit recognized that a corporation could be liable for intentional infliction of emotional distress because its supervisor was aware of the sexual harassment of an employee by a manager and failed to stop it even though the underlying harassment might not rise to the level of either assault and battery or intentional infliction of emotional distress. We believe Revlon's failure to investigate Ford's complaint was independent of Braun's abusive treatment of Ford.

* * *

The three required elements for the tort of intentional infliction of emotional distress are: first, the conduct of the defendant must be "extreme" and "outrageous"; second, the defendant must either intend to cause emotional distress or recklessly disregard the near certainty that such distress will result from his conduct; and third, severe emotional distress must indeed occur as a result of defendant's conduct. We believe that the conduct of Revlon met these requirements. First, Ford made numerous Revlon managers aware of Braun's activities at company functions. Ford did everything that could be done, both within the announced policies of Revlon and without, to bring this matter to Revlon's attention. Revlon ignored her and the situation she faced, dragging the matter out for months and leaving Ford without redress. Here is sufficient evidence that Revlon acted outrageously.

Second, even if Revlon did not intend to cause emotional distress, Revlon's reckless disregard of Braun's conduct made it nearly certain that such emotional distress would in fact occur. Revlon knew that Braun had subjected Ford to physical assaults, vulgar remarks, that Ford continued to feel threatened by Braun, and that Ford was emotionally distraught. . .

Third, it is obvious that emotional distress did occur. Ample evidence, both medical and otherwise, was presented describing Ford's emotional distress. . .

We also note that Revlon had set forth a specific policy and several guidelines for the handling of sexual harassment claims and other employee complaints, yet Revlon recklessly disregarded these policies and guidelines. Ford was entitled to rely on the policy statements made by Revlon . . .

* * *

Decision and Outcome

The court held that Revlon's failure to take appropriate action in response to Ford's complaint of sexual harassment by Braun constituted the tort of intentional infliction of emotional distress. The judgment of the trial court was reinstated.

Questions for Review

1. Explain the Supreme Court's rationale in holding that Revlon (the principal) was liable for the tort of intentional infliction of emotional distress when Braun (the agent) was not.

2. Suppose the jury had held Braun liable for intentional infliction of emotional distress. Do you think it would be possible in that case for the Supreme Court to conclude that Revlon was not also liable?

3. Explain and illustrate three elements that must be present for the tort of intentional infliction of emotional distress to occur.

Invasion of Privacy

Tort law protects against the following:

1. *Intrusion into a person's solitude* by illegally searching their premises or belongings, by bugging or wire-tapping their residence, by the unauthorized intrusion into their financial records, and so forth.

2. By the *public revelation of information that places a person in a false light,* such as by attributing to a person ideas not held or actions not taken by that person.

3. By the *public revelation of facts* about a person that *a reasonable person would find repugnant.* The revelation of abuse of alcohol or drugs or the revelation of information regarding a private citizen's sex life or financial affairs could result in court action.

4. *Commercial use of someone's name or likeness without permission.*

Each of these four items is considered an invasion of privacy.

Reasonable Expectations of Privacy   Courts use the concept of a reasonable expectation of privacy to determine if a possible invasion of privacy tort (or a violation of the Fourth Amendment) occurs. If it is reasonable for people to expect privacy, as with what they do behind closed doors in a bathroom or a bedroom, then the courts will protect that interest. Most people are reasonable when they expect a phone conversation to be private. People believe that their academic records should be kept private unless they choose to disclose them as well as psychological counseling reports. Even trash is considered private.

Public Figures   Unlike ordinary citizens, public figures such as a president, a senator, a police chief, or a movie star make their livings in the public eye and, in many cases, by attracting attention to themselves. Accompanying this status is a strict limitation on protection from invasions of privacy. For public figures, courts have concluded that the public's right to information generally takes primacy over bruised egos. Facts that are part of the public record also may be repeated without fear of liability. Note that, both for

The tort of intentional infliction of emotional distress requires a showing by the plaintiff that the defendant has engaged in extreme and outrageous behavior that causes severe emotional distress. See if you think that the following fits that definition. Also note that cyberstalking has been made a crime in a number of states.

CYBERSTALKING

Four years ago, the word cyberstalking hadn't been coined yet. No one knew what to call it; some called it online harassment, online abuse, or cyber-harassment. And we're not talking two people arguing with each other or calling each other bad names. There were incidents where it had gone beyond an annoyance and had become frightening. As more and more incidents became known and victims reached out to law enforcement for help, all they received were either blank stares or were told to turn off their computer. States didn't have laws in place to protect victims, and their harassers kept up the harassment, which escalated sometimes to real-life stalking situations.

What is cyberstalking? It's when an online incident spirals so out of control it gets to a point where a victim fears for his or her life.

Case Example 1

In 1999, "Nanci" went into a Worcester, Massachusetts, romance chat room. Another chatter commented that he did not like her username. She defended herself and soon the two began arguing with each other in the chat room. But the argument didn't end. Each time Nanci tried to log onto the chat room, her harasser was there, waiting for her, and became more aggressive. At one point, he told her he'd hired someone else in the chat room to beat her up; another time he posted information he'd found out about her online—who her father was and where she lived—then said he wouldn't be happy until she was "6 feet under the ground."

Justifiably horrified, Nanci went to her local police, who basically laughed at her and told her there was nothing to be done. Yes, even with the implied death threat.

The harasser became more aggressive and began e-mailing or Instant Messaging Nanci, telling her what kind of car she was driving, where she'd been earlier that day, and the name of her daughter. Nanci went to the State Police, the county District Attorney, then the State Attorney General. Each one pointed fingers at the other, claiming they couldn't help her, but that the other department should.

Nanci finally hired a lawyer, filed a civil suit, then contacted local media. When she appeared in court with TV journalists following her, the DA backed down and began helping her. Charges were finally filed against her cyberstalker, and a trial date [was] set.

"Cyberstalking often receives a low priority in computer crime cases," says Greg Larson, vice president of Internet Crimes, Inc. "Police departments usually have limited manpower for computer crimes, so in importance, these cases seem to be put on the back burner until a serious incident occurs."

Source: From Jayne A. Hitchcock, "Cyberstalking," *Link-Up,* July/August 2000, Vol. 17. Reprinted with permission of the author.

invasions of privacy and for defamation (discussed below), public figures and public officials have dramatically diminished rights to privacy and are much more exposed to criticism that would be defamatory to nonpublic figures or officials. Case 10-2 illustrates these principles.

Case 10-2

Richard G. Godbehere et al. v. Phoenix Newspapers, Inc. et al.

Supreme Court of Arizona
162 Ariz. 335, 783 P.2d 781 (1989)

FACTS AND CASE BACKGROUND

In the spring and summer of 1985, newspaper publishers in the Phoenix, Arizona, area printed over 50 articles, editorials, and columns about local law enforcement. The publications stated that the plaintiff law enforcement officers and employees engaged in illegal activities, staged narcotics arrests to generate publicity, illegally arrested citizens, misused public funds and resources, committed police brutality, and generally were incompetent at law enforcement. Sheriffs, deputies, and civilian employees of the sheriff's office brought libel and invasion of privacy action against the newspapers. Plaintiffs alleged that the publications were false, damaged their reputations, harmed them in their profession, and caused them emotional distress.

In the Maricopa County Superior Court, all invasion of privacy claims were dismissed. Plaintiffs appealed and the court of appeals affirmed the trial court's verdict. Plaintiffs then appealed to the Arizona Supreme Court.

Opinion of the Court: Feldman, Supreme Court Vice Chief Justice

We granted this review to determine whether Arizona should recognize a cause of action for false light invasion of privacy, and if so, what the proper standard should be.

* * *

In 1890, Samuel Warren and Louis Brandeis published an article advocating the recognition of a right to privacy as an independent legal concept [citations omitted]. [T]hey also described how courts used contract and property law to protect thoughts, ideas, or expressions from wrongful appropriation. Warren and Brandeis contended these were nothing more than "instances and applications of a general right to privacy." Hence, they supported recognition of the right "to be let alone."

* * *

In 1960, Dean Prosser concluded that four separate torts had developed under the right of privacy rubric: (1) intrusion on the plaintiff's seclusion or private affairs; (2) public disclosure of embarrassing private facts; (3) publicity placing the plaintiff in a false light in the public eye; and (4) appropriation of the plaintiff's name or likeness for the defendant's advantage . . . In 1977, the *Restatement* [*of Torts*] adopted Prosser's classification. Although each tort is classified under invasion of privacy, they "otherwise have almost nothing in common except that each represents an interference with the right of the plaintiff 'to be let alone.'"

* * *

False light invasion of privacy . . . protects against the conduct of knowingly or recklessly publishing false information or innuendo that a "reasonable person" would find "highly offensive." . . . Thus, we believe the tort action for false light invasion of privacy provides protection against a narrow class of wrongful conduct that falls short of "outrage," but nevertheless should be deterred. . . . Unless the interest in protecting privacy rights is outweighed by the interest in protecting speech, . . . we see no reason not to recognize an action for false light invasion of privacy.

* * *

IS FALSE LIGHT AVAILABLE IN THIS CASE?

Finally, publishers contended that even if we recognize false light actions, the action does not lie in this case. They argue that not only do the publications discuss matters of public interest, but plaintiffs have no right of privacy with respect to the manner in which they perform their official duties. We agree.

We have specifically held that the right of privacy does not exist "where the plaintiff has become a public character . . ." In addition, privacy rights are absent or limited "in connection with the life of a person in whom the public has a rightful interest, [or] where the information would be of public benefit." . . . It is difficult to conceive of an area of greater public interest than law enforcement. . . . Therefore, we hold that there can be no false light invasion of privacy action for matters involving official acts or duties of public officers.

Consequently, we adopt the following legal standard: a plaintiff cannot sue for false light invasion of privacy if he or she is a public official and the publication relates to performance of his or her public life or duties.

* * *

The Supreme Court has held that "the public official designation applies at the very least to those among the hierarchy of government employees who have, or appear to the public to have, substantial responsibility for or control over the conduct of government affairs." . . . The sheriff and the deputies here are public officials. The publications at issue concern the discharge of their public duties and do not relate to private affairs. Therefore, plaintiffs have no claim for false light invasion of privacy.

Decision and Outcome

The court held that public officials have no right of privacy from publications that write about the way these officials carry out their official duties.

Questions for Review

1. Newspapers in Phoenix obviously published materials that were highly critical of local law enforcement. Arizona courts appear to be endorsing this activity. Compose a short essay describing the benefits for a democratic society of having a press that is free to engage in such activities.

2. If the newspapers had written equally critical articles about a local owner of a chain of fast-food restaurants who then sued for false light invasion of privacy, would the court outcome have been different? Why?

3. What would have been different if the published materials delved into the private lives of the sheriff, deputies, and so forth?

4. Are the police public figures or public officials? Is it fair to say that the court contends that, within their area of official responsibilities, public officials are to be treated like public figures?

Commercial Use of Someone's Name or Likeness without Permission: Misappropriation

Commercial use of someone's name or likeness is traditionally lumped in with other invasions of privacy. However, this invasion of privacy is really a *misappropriation:* a wrongful taking of a property right owned by another without compensation or permission. Some years back, a Port-a-John company sold its products with the slogan, "Heeere's Johnny," the classic introduction for a late night talk show host, Johnny Carson, who was popular with your parents. Carson successfully sued the company for using a phrase associated with his show. Increasingly, courts have ruled that celebrities have property rights in their names or likenesses. Indeed, it is increasingly common for those rights to persist even after death. The Elvis Presley estate has been able to successfully sue "Elvis" impersonators and others who have used the "King's" name or likeness without authorization and have been paid for their activities. The Presley estate is able to sue impersonators and others who use the Presley persona to entertain or sell products, because, while he was still alive, Elvis Presley willed his right of publicity to his estate. Following successful litigation by the Presley estate against impersonators, other celebrities have followed Presley's example.

More discussion of misappropriations will be provided below when the tort of *trespass to personal property* is examined. Extensive discussion of invasions of privacy that occur with the aid of new technology is provided in the next chapter.

Defamation

The legal definition of defamation is making (1) *untrue statements* to (2) *third parties,* spoken or written, that are (3) *harmful* to an individual's *reputation.* Defamation is a common law tort and applicable legal standards vary somewhat from state to state. Violating this required standard of conduct orally is the tort of *slander* while breaching this duty in writing is *libel.* Libel also occurs if the defamatory statements are captured on audio or videotape. In a business setting, making false statements about a company's products, its business practices, or other business matters is equally wrongful (this tort is sometimes called *product disparagement*).

Must Be Seen or Heard by Third Parties

An essential element of a defamation claim is the *publication* of the false statement(s) to a *third party.* Accusing your partner of stealing company assets in a private conversation is not defamation, while telling your accountant that your partner has been stealing is, if the charge is not factual. Making false statements to a third party, having such statements overheard by a third party even if they are addressed to the alleged offender, having your secretary type notes or a letter containing your charges, or airing such claims in an Internet communication can make you a defendant in a defamation suit. Whatever the medium, anyone who repeats (replicates) a defamatory statement is also liable for defamation damages even if the source of the statement is cited.

Slander versus Libel

At common law, certain kinds of spoken statements are considered slanderous per se (i.e., as a matter of law). These include statements that a person has a socially unacceptable communicable disease, that a person has committed improprieties while engaging in a profession or trade, that a person has committed a serious crime or been imprisoned for such a crime, or that an unmarried woman is unchaste. For such statements, a finding that these statements were made and published to third parties is sufficient to result in a judgment for damages because these statements are *presumed* harmful to one's reputation.

In the absence of such per se slander violations, a victim of slander is not entitled to monetary damages unless there is proof of "special damages." In other words, the plaintiff in a slander case must prove actual economic or monetary losses to be entitled to collect any damages. In contrast to slanderous statements, libelous (written) statements are viewed by the court system as having more enduring and broad circulation, and are assumed to more likely reflect deliberation on the part of the defendant. As such, a defendant who libels another is liable for damages without the plaintiff having to prove any specific injury. In a libel case, the damage could simply be the humiliation associated with the libelous writings.

Defenses to Defamation

Truth   In the United States, *truth* is the fail-safe antidote to defamation claims. So, if a defendant in a defamation suit can prove that the allegedly defamatory statements were actually true, no tort has been committed. Note that truth is an affirmative defense, which means that the defendant in a defamation case would have the burden of proof in establishing that the plaintiff was, in fact, guilty of the things attributed to him or her by the defendant.

Absolute Privilege   Another defense to defamation claims is based on *privilege*. In certain settings, such as legislatures and courtrooms, there is *absolute privilege:* statements made by attorneys and judges during a trial are exempt from defamation claims as are statements made by legislators during legislative debates (even if statements are made maliciously with full knowledge that they are untrue)! This **privileged speech** standard views court and legislative personnel as dealing with public interest matters in which there should be no limitation or restriction on full and free expressions and statements. Of course, there are sanctions for lying in court, which range from censure of judges and lawyers to criminal liability for witnesses who lie (commit perjury) under oath.

Qualified Privilege   There also are circumstances in which there is more restricted **qualified privilege.** If statements are made in good faith, with absence of malice, and communicated only to those who have a legitimate reason for receiving the information provided, the source of such statements is exempt from defamation claims. In defamation law, malice means that the speaker or writer knows the statements are false or has a reckless disregard for the truth. It does not mean the speaker or writer bears ill will towards the target of his or her falsehoods. So providers of letters of recommendation for jobs or for college admissions, managers who provide work performance evaluations, and other sources of like documents enjoy protection from defamation claims, conditional upon their privilege not being abused.

> *Job recommendations.* Not surprisingly, many defamation suits arise from workplace statements, most often stemming from unfavorable job evaluations and unfavorable references for new jobs. In many states there is legislation that protects employers from suits by ex-employees for mistakes made in job references, so long as there is a showing by the defendant/employer that there was a basis for making the statement.
>
> Suppose Sally was discharged from Acme based on suspicion that she falsified expense reports when she was traveling on behalf of Acme. Suppose, further, that Sally did not falsify expense reports, but when the issue came up, Sally resigned rather than undergo the hassle. If Sam in the Acme HRM office truthfully fills out a job recommendation form from Balzak, a prospective future employer of Sally, saying that Sally would not be rehired at Acme because of suspicions of fraud, Sam and Acme would not be liable to Sally for defamation. On the other hand, if Sam indicated that Sally was uncooperative and used profane language on the job, even though there was no evidence of that in her work record, Sam and Acme would be liable for defamation. Many companies, however, still adhere to the following rules, which have eliminated liability for defamation from ex-employees:
>
> * The ex-employer will verify dates of employment and job title.
> * The ex-employer will answer whether they would consider rehiring this employee again.
>
> Such employers refuse to answer any other inquiries about the job experience they had with the ex-employee. Courts have universally absolved employers of liability for defamation if they do nothing more than verify employment dates and job titles and answer whether they would rehire the person.
>
> *Mistakes by credit bureaus.* Also there is federal legislation protecting credit bureaus if they make a mistake in reporting someone's credit record, so long as corrective action

privileged speech
Speech that is immune to defamation claims, such as statements made by lawyers, judges, and legislators in the course of their work in courts and in legislative debates.

qualified privilege
Protection against defamation claims accorded to statements made in good faith, with an absence of malice, and communicated only to those with a legitimate need for the kind of information provided.

is taken promptly once the mistake is pointed out. Under the Fair Credit Reporting Act, credit bureaus are required to investigate errors that are pointed out to them by people who claim their credit histories are being misreported. If the credit bureau reinvestigates and decides not to change its data on the person, that person's version of events must be included in the credit report also. A credit bureau could be liable to someone whose data they have misrepresented if they take an inordinately long time to reinvestigate or make changes on the person's credit report.

Public figures and public officials when the media are the defendants. As was the case with invasion of privacy issues, public figures and public officials are less shielded than private citizens from defamatory statements, mainly because of the U.S. Supreme Court's view of the First Amendment.[2] To expect recovery in a defamation suit, a public figure must be able to prove that the defendant knew a published statement was false or exhibited a reckless disregard for the truth. This additional proof requirement is often called *legal malice.* Publishers (of newspapers, magazines, etc.), who are often targets of defamation suits, attempt to protect themselves by having two or more independent sources for information in potentially troublesome articles.

Fraudulent Misrepresentation, Conversion, and Trespass to Land

Remembering that torts are acts and forms of conduct that can also be criminal, a focus on misrepresentation, conversion, and trespass will complete our journey through intentional torts. This section also involves a shift from a focus largely on intentional torts against people to intentional torts against property.

Fraudulent Misrepresentation (Deceit)

fraudulent misrepresentation (fraud)
The deliberate misrepresentation of facts in order to gain an advantage.

There is a difference between statements that innocently misrepresent reality and those that are termed *fraud.* **Fraudulent misrepresentation** (or just **fraud**), however, involves intent, as it is the deliberate misrepresentation of *facts* in order to gain an advantage. More than salesmanship or business "puffery" is required to establish fraudulent misrepresentation. So a salesman's claim that his company's used cars are the absolute best available is not fraud, because it is merely an *opinion,* not a statement of facts. It is fraud, however, to sell used cars with rolled-back odometers while misrepresenting the true mileage on the cars sold. It is fraud to knowingly sell a warehouse with a leaking roof while representing the roof as leak-free. It also would be fraud for an attorney to attempt to involve you in a tax evasion that the attorney knows or has reason to know is illegal.

Generally, to establish damages for fraudulent misrepresentation, the following elements are required:

1. A misrepresentation of facts material to the issue at hand.
2. Knowledge that the "facts" presented are false or there is "reckless disregard for the truth."
3. Intent to induce reliance on the misrepresented facts.
4. A reasonable reliance on the misrepresented facts on the part of the injured party.
5. Actual damages that occur as a result of reliance on the misrepresentation.

Students should be mindful that the elements of the tort of deceit or fraud are the same as those for contractual fraud. It is a tort to deceive someone in a noncontractual situation, such as obtaining entrance to a bar using a fake ID, and it is also a crime. To round out this

---

[2] In the landmark case *New York Times Co. v. Sullivan,* 376 U.S. 254 (1964), the U.S. Supreme Court held that if the media published defamatory material about a public official, the public official also had to show that the defendant media knew the statements were false or had a reckless disregard for the truth.

discussion, we note that it is a crime to obtain property under false pretenses such as by offering goods for sale, collecting the money, and absconding with the money without delivering the product or by writing a bad check, knowing the check will bounce. Defenses against damage awards in fraudulent misrepresentation cases involve a showing by the defendant that one of the five elements of fraud is not present.

Wrongful Takings and Intermeddling: Conversion

Conversion is the taking and/or using of someone else's personal property without permission and without justification. Cars, boats, planes, stereos, art, jewelry, and countless other items can be converted. If Jim goes into another student's dorm room and, without permission, takes his stereo to set up and enjoy in his own room, Jim has committed the tort of conversion and can be liable to the victim for the full (fair market) value of the stereo. Of course, under criminal law, Jim has committed larceny by stealing the stereo and is subject to criminal prosecution. With civil tort law, the victim doesn't have to wait for criminal prosecution but can pursue damage recovery on his own. So conversion is the civil side of theft.

Intent is not necessarily an element in conversion. If an individual *mistakenly* believes that he or she is entitled to personal property items taken, there is still conversion. If an individual unknowingly buys stolen goods, that buyer if guilty of conversion in spite of absence of knowledge that the goods were stolen. Damages in conversion cases are equal to the value of the converted property, but the defendant is entitled to that property. It is also important to recognize that acts far less serious than criminal theft can constitute conversion. Even temporary exercises of dominion or control over the personal property of another can be conversions. This could even include such acts as being clumsy in a store, knocking over and breaking a lamp.

Defenses against conversion claims would include efforts to show that the personal property in possession of the defendant is not the missing property, that the plaintiff has no ownership right in the property superior to that of the defendant, or that the property was taken out of necessity—*I took the horse to care for it as the owner was abusing the animal and letting it starve to death.* It is also a defense to claim the exercise of control over the personal property was so slight that a conversion did not take place.

Trespass

Trespass occurs when, without consent, an individual goes onto another's property (land) or interferes with the rights of the owner of personal property to the exclusive possession, use, and enjoyment of that property. In the eyes of the law, land and improvements to land (such as buildings) are *real property* while all other items owned (money, cars, furniture, etc.) are *personal property*.

Trespass to Real Property   A trespass to land occurs when a person, without permission, goes on, over, or under another's land; causes something else to intrude into another's land; remains on the land when asked to leave; or permits anything to remain on the land. So it is a tort to walk on your neighbor's land without permission. You may not lawfully dam the creek that runs through your pasture and cause a lake to form on your upstream neighbor's cornfield. You can't legally drive your SUV through the neighbor's tulip bed, spray his house with a hose, or build a barn partly on his property. It is permissible to fly over property you don't own so long as you maintain minimum altitudes as required by aviation regulations.

Defenses against a trespass charge include a showing that the supposed property owner did not, in fact, own and/or have the right to possess the property. Also, it is a defense to show that there was good and just cause for the trespass—for example, it was necessary to relieve a situation that was dangerous to someone else or to the public at large. It is legal to retrieve personal property owned by the trespasser, as in repossessions of cars, so long as violence does not occur.

TRESPASS IN CYBERSPACE

Cyberspace has allowed for dramatic expansions of second-hand sales. Shrewd shoppers, who heretofore had to scour garage sales and flea markets to obtain bargains, now regularly use Internet auction sites such as eBay.com. eBay, however, is not the only auction site, though it is a leading site with the advantages offered by large volume. Indeed, the value of an auction site is directly related to its size, as the more buyers and sellers come to a website, the greater are the numbers of purchase and sale options available.

Aggregators are websites that electronically assimilate and organize the offerings and bids from several auction sites simultaneously. Aggregators make use of software robots that perform searching, copying, and retrieving functions that consume large amounts of the processing and storage capacity of the auction sites and can cause the auction website to "crash." Auction websites such as eBay often specifically prohibit many of the functions that aggregators use to collect information at their sites to make their sites more usable and attractive to their own subscribers. Is an aggregator's electronic foray into a public website (such as eBay's) a trespass? Although Case 10-3 gave a definitive answer to eBay and Bidder's Edge, the law in this area is not well established.

Trespass to Personal Property   Trespass to personal property involves intentional and wrongful interference with the owner's possession or use of personal property. Personal property, as opposed to real property, is property that can be moved. Hiding your roommate's sleeping bag, preventing him from camping out to be in line for a basketball ticket allocation, is a trespass to personal property. Proof that a trespass is *justified* serves as a defense. This is the legal basis for an auto repair shop holding a customer's car after repairs are completed if the customer hasn't paid for the repairs made.

Court awards for trespass to personal property are often zero because they are based on any difference in the fair market value of the personal property before and after the trespass. Trespass to personal property is often also a conversion and, since damages are higher (equal to fair market value of the thing converted) under a conversion claim, it is preferred by most plaintiffs. Even though damages for trespass to personal property are generally less than those for conversion, trespass to personal property is a tort and victims of torts are entitled to obtain court injunctions for continuing violations. The ability to petition the courts for an injunction is particularly relevant in cyberspace.

Case 10-3

eBay, Inc., v. Bidder's Edge, Inc.

United States District Court for the Northern District of California

100 F. Supp. 2d 1058 (N.D. Calif. 2000)

BACKGROUND AND FACTS

eBay is an Internet-based, person-to-person trading site. [Citations omitted] eBay offers sellers the ability to list items for sale and prospective buyers the ability to search those listings and bid on items. The seller can set the terms and conditions of the auction. The item is sold to the highest bidder. The transaction is consummated directly between the buyer and seller without eBay's involvement.

Users of the eBay site must register and agree to the eBay User Agreement. Users agree to the seven page User Agreement by clicking on an "I Accept" button located at the end of the User Agreement. The current version of the User Agreement prohibits the use of "any robot, spider, other automatic device, or manual process to monitor or copy our web pages or the content contained herein without our prior expressed written permission."

eBay currently has over 7 million registered users. Over 400,000 new items are added to the site every day. Every minute, 600 bids are placed on almost 3 million items. Users currently perform, on average, 10 million searches per day on eBay's database. Bidding for and sales of items are continuously ongoing in millions of separate auctions.

A software robot is a computer program which operates across the Internet to perform searching, copying and retrieving functions on the web sites of others. A software robot is capable of executing thousands of instructions per minute, far in excess of what a human can accomplish. Robots consume the processing and storage resources of a system, such as that maintained by eBay, making that portion of the system's capacity unavailable to the system owner or other users. Consumption of sufficient system resources will slow the processing of the overall system and can overload the system such that it will malfunction or "crash." A severe malfunction can cause a loss of data and an interruption in services.

BE [Bidder's Edge] is a company with 22 employees that was founded in 1997. The BE web site debuted in November 1998. BE does not host auctions. BE is an auction aggregation site designed to offer on-line auction buyers the ability to search for items across numerous on-line auctions without having to search each host site individually. As of March 2000, the BE web site contained information on more that five million items being auctioned on more than one hundred auction sites. BE also provides its users with additional auction-related services and information. The information available on the BE site is contained in a database of information that BE compiles through access to various auction sites such as eBay. When a user enters a search for a particular item at BE, BE searches its database and generates a list of every item in the database responsive to the search, organized by auction closing date and time. Rather than going to each host auction site one at a time, a user who goes to BE may conduct a single search to obtain information about that item on every auction site tracked by BE. It is important to include information regarding eBay auctions on the BE site because eBay is by far the biggest consumer to consumer on-line auction site.

On November 9, 1999, eBay sent BE a letter reasserting that BE's activities were unauthorized, insisting that BE cease accessing the eBay site, alleging that BE's activities constituted a civil trespass and offering to license BE's activities. eBay and BE were again unable to agree on licensing terms. As a result, eBay attempted to block BE from accessing the eBay site with its software robots; by the end of November, 1999, eBay had blocked a total of 169 IP addresses it believed BE was using to query eBay's system. BE elected to continue crawling eBay's site by using proxy servers to evade eBay's IP blocks.

The parties agree that BE accessed the eBay site approximate 100,000 times a day. eBay alleges that BE activity constituted up to 1.53% of the number of requests received by eBay, and up to 1.10% of the total data transferred by eBay during certain periods in October and November of 1999 and alleges damages between $40,000 and $70,000 due to the demands made on their system by BE's software robots.

eBay now moves for preliminary injunctive relief preventing BE from accessing the eBay computer system based on nine causes of action: trespass, false advertising, federal and state trademark dilution, computer fraud and abuse, unfair competition, misappropriation, interference with prospective economic advantage and unjust enrichment.

Opinion by Ronald M. Whyte, U.S. District Court Judge

According to eBay, the load on its servers resulting from BE's web crawlers represents between 1.11% and 1.53% of the total load on eBay's listing servers. eBay alleges both economic loss from BE's current activities and potential harm resulting from the total crawling of BE and others. In alleging economic harm, eBay's argument is that eBay has expended considerable time, effort and money to create its computer system, and that BE should have to pay for the portion of eBay's system BE uses.

* * *

If BE's activity is allowed to continue unchecked, it would encourage other auction aggregators to engage in similar recursive searching of the eBay system such that eBay would suffer irreparable harm from reduced system performance, system unavailability, or data losses. [Citations omitted.] BE does not appear to seriously contest that reduced system performance, system unavailability or data loss would inflict irreparable harm on eBay consisting of lost profits and lost customer goodwill. Harm resulting from lost profits and lost customer goodwill is irreparable because it is neither easily calculable, nor easily compensable and is therefore an appropriate basis for injunctive relief. Where, as here, the denial of preliminary injunctive relief would encourage an increase in the complained of activity, and such an increase would present a strong likelihood of irreparable harm, the plaintiff has at least established a possibility of irreparable harm.

* * *

BE correctly observes that there is a dearth of authority supporting a preliminary injunction based on an ongoing trespass to chattels. In contrast, it is black letter law in California that an injunction is an appropriate remedy for a continuing trespass to real property. If eBay were a brick and mortar auction house with limited seating capacity, eBay would appear to be entitled to reserve those seats for potential bidders, to refuse entrance to individuals (or robots) with no intention of bidding on any of the items, and to seek preliminary injunctive relief against non-customer trespassers eBay was physically unable to exclude . . . The court concludes that under the circumstances present here, BE's ongoing violation of eBay's fundamental property right to exclude others from its computer system potentially causes sufficient irreparable harm to support a preliminary injunction.

* * *

I. TRESPASS

Trespass to chattels "lies where an intentional interference with the possession of personal property has proximately cause[d] injury." Trespass to chattels "although seldom employed as a tort theory in California" was recently applied to cover the unauthorized use of long distance telephone lines. Specifically, the court noted "the electronic signals generated by the [defendants'] activities were sufficiently tangible to support a trespass cause of action." Thus, it appears likely that the electronic signals sent by BE to retrieve information from eBay's computer system are also sufficiently tangible to support a trespass cause of action.

In order to prevail on a claim for trespass based on accessing a computer system, the plaintiff must establish: (1) defendant intentionally and without authorization interfered with plaintiff's possessory interest in the computer system; and (2) defendant's unauthorized use proximately resulted in damage to plaintiff . . .

a. BE's Unauthorized Interference

eBay argues that BE's use was unauthorized and intentional. eBay is correct. BE does not dispute that it employed an automated computer program to connect with and search eBay's electronic database. BE admits that, because other auction aggregators were including eBay's auctions in their listing, it continued to "crawl" eBay's web site even after eBay demanded BE terminate such activity.

BE argues that it cannot trespass eBay's web site because the site is publicly accessible. BE's argument is unconvincing. eBay's servers are private property, conditional access to which eBay grants the public. eBay does not generally permit the type of automated access made by BE. In fact, eBay explicitly notifies automated visitors that their access is not permitted. "In general, California does recognize a trespass claim where the defendant exceeds the scope of the consent." *Baugh v. CBS, Inc.,* 828 F. Supp. 745, 756 (N.D. Cal. 1993).

* * *

b. Damage to eBay's Computer System

* * *

eBay is likely to be able to demonstrate that BE's activities have diminished the quality or value of eBay's computer systems. BE's activities consume at least a portion of plaintiff's bandwidth and server capacity. Although there is some dispute as to the percentage of queries on eBay's site for which BE is responsible, BE admits that it sends some 80,000 to 100,000 requests to plaintiff's computer systems per day. Although eBay does not claim that this consumption has led to any physical damage to eBay's computer system, nor does eBay provide any evidence to support the claim that it may have lost revenues or customers based on this use, eBay's claim is that BE's use is appropriating eBay's personal property by using valuable bandwidth and capacity, and necessarily compromising eBay's ability to use that capacity for its own purposes.

* * *

Decision and Outcome

The court granted eBay's request for an injunction preventing BE from using its software robots, web crawlers, or any automated query program to trespass on eBay's bidding software. eBay, however, was required to post a $2,000,000 bond if the defendant was found at trial to be wrongly enjoined.

Questions for Analysis

1. Explain precisely the nature of the trespass to personal property that eBay alleged was occurring as a result of BE's activities?
2. Why was the court not convinced by BE's argument that, because eBay's website is publicly accessible, BE could not be trespassing when it accessed eBay's site?

NEGLIGENCE

Torts (wrongs) involving *negligence* are not the result of intent on the part of the defendant to harm the plaintiff, but rather are harms that can be viewed as occurring by accident or by mistake. With negligence, an individual or business engages in actions or conduct not intended to harm another but that, unfortunately, does. Quite often, the lack of intent does not free the negligent party of responsibility (liability) for the harm caused. An "It was an accident" plea can be expected to prompt the familiar refrain, "Tell it to the judge."

Liability for injury/damage suffered through negligence arises when the following four elements exist:

1. The defendant owes a *duty of care* to the plaintiff.
2. The defendant *breaches* that duty of care by negligence.
3. The plaintiff suffers *measurable damage.*
4. The defendant's negligence is the *proximate cause* of the injury.

Duty of Care

Tort law applies the *reasonable person standard* in determining what the duty of care is. The court system, as agent for "society," views a reasonable person as someone who is prudent, careful, honest, and skilled at avoiding causing injury to others. It is presumed that individuals have a *duty of care* for others and that a reasonable person would live up to a reasonable *standard of care* when interacting with others. Reasonable persons do not engage in reckless behavior. They obey speed limits, make sure that floors in stores they invite people into are not slippery, and screen employees who work with minors to make sure they are not child molesters. In other words, tort law requires reasonable persons to take reasonable precautions against reasonably foreseeable risks. Actions (or inactions) that fall short of this standard are sources of tort liability risk based on negligence.

Causation or Proximate Cause

For a defendant to be liable in a negligence case, causation must be established. The standard test for causation is the "but for" test—"but for Mr. Smith running a red light and hitting plaintiff's car, the plaintiff would not have suffered the (work) disability that has reduced his earning capacity by $1 million." A problem exists with this causation test, however, in its potential for extending the links of causality (hence, liability) to relatively remote actions. In addition to satisfying the "but for" test, the plaintiff in a negligence case also must be able to show that the harm he or she endured was *reasonably foreseeable* to the defendant.

It could be argued that "But for Mr. Smith's Rolex losing time, getting him off to a late start for an important meeting, he would not have been speeding, would not have lost control of his car, and would not have injured the plaintiff." So can Mr. Smith (and/or his lawyer) conclude that the Rolex Company is responsible for Mr. Smith's injury? Not likely. A court would ask if the faulty watch was the proximate cause (the legal cause) of Mr. Smith's injury (instead of his own choice to speed, remote from the control of the Rolex Company), doubtless concluding that it was Smith's choice to speed (Mr. Smith's own negligence) that resulted in the plaintiff's injuries. If Rolex was negligent in making its product, nevertheless, it is not reasonably foreseeable that the failure of the Rolex to work would cause a user to speed and harm the plaintiff.

proximate cause
For the purpose of establishing liability, the legal cause of a tort injury.

Foreseeability

In many cases, whether a defendant is living up to his or her duty of care responsibility depends upon whether or not the event of injury from the defendant's conduct would be *foreseeable* by a reasonable person. You shouldn't be surprised to find that a court, adhering to the reasonable person standard, would conclude that truck drivers have a duty of care for other users of roads, that running a red light might *reasonably* be expected to result in collisions with other vehicles, and that the collision of the cement truck with a car alluded to above was, indeed, the cause of plaintiff's costly injuries. In like fashion, courts are likely to find the necessary elements for damages in negligence cases whenever it is reasonably foreseeable that the defendant's careless or reckless actions could result in injuries. It is reasonably foreseeable that a restaurant that serves "undercooked" meat and has no system for checking to make sure such events do not occur is liable for the reasonably foreseeable consequences.

Case 10-4 illustrates the application of proximate cause and how it provides limits on liability when bizarre situations occur, even though the defendant was negligent in carrying out its duties.

Case 10-4

Karen R. Robblee et al. v. Budd Services, Sumitomo, et al.

Court of Appeals of North Carolina
136 N.C. App. 793 525 S.E.2d 847 (N.C. Ct. App. 2000)

FACTS AND CASE BACKGROUND

Sumitomo Electric Lightwave Corporation is a global technology company with facilities in numerous locations around the world. Its Research Triangle (North Carolina) facility relied on Budd Services to provide security and to limit facility access to employees and visitors with proper access cards. In April of 1994, a disgruntled former employee entered the Sumitomo facility using an old "temporary" access card that he still had from his initial employment and shot five people, including himself. He and two of the workers died. Workers and families of those killed filed a number of suits against Sumitomo and Budd Services, including the instant case.

After the settlement of numerous claims, Juliette Shipley sought damages from Budd, claiming that Budd was negligent and that Budd's negligence caused her to suffer severe emotional distress with an attendant loss of earning capacity and other injuries. According to the plaintiff's pleadings, while Budd Services had obtained the former employee's worker security badge, it had not gotten a temporary access card that the gunman used to get into the Sumitomo facility. According to the plaintiff's suit, the security company should have tracked temporary access cards and, with an accurate record of cards issued, should have required the return of the employee's access card when his employment terminated eight months prior to the shooting spree.

In the Durham County, North Carolina, Superior Court, summary judgment was entered in favor of the defendant, Budd Services, decreeing that Budd Services had no liability for any emotional distress injury suffered by the plaintiff.

Opinion of the Court: Martin, Appeals Court Judge

Juliette Shipley [plaintiff] seeks damages from Budd for emotional distress suffered by reason of Budd's negligence. Plaintiff Shipley alleges that Budd negligently performed its contractual duty to provide security at Sumitomo, and this negligence caused her to suffer severe emotional distress. The issue presented by her appeal is whether it was reasonably foreseeable that she would suffer emotional distress as a result of Budd's negligent failure to retrieve a temporary access card from [the gunman] and to otherwise prevent his entry into the Sumitomo plant. We hold that it was not and affirm the entry of summary judgment in favor of Budd.

* * *

An action for the negligent infliction of emotional distress has three elements: (1) defendant engaged in negligent conduct; (2) it was reasonably foreseeable that such conduct would cause the plaintiff severe emotional distress; and (3) defendant's conduct, in fact, caused plaintiff severe emotional distress. [Citations omitted] The plaintiff must show that the distress suffered was "a proximate and foreseeable result of the defendant's negligence." . . . In her complaint, plaintiff Shipley alleges that "[a]s a direct and proximate result of the negligence by Budd Services, Inc., resulting in the shootings . . . and *his attempt to kill Juliette Shipley,* Ms. Shipley suffered severe emotional distress."

* * *

Thus, the inquiry in the present case must focus on whether Shipley's emotional distress was a foreseeable and proximate result of Budd's negligence.

* * *

[I]n this case we hold that the emotional distress suffered by Shipley was not a reasonably foreseeable consequence of any negligent conduct on Budd's part. Viewed in the light most favorable to plaintiff Shipley . . . , the evidence shows that Budd . . . negligently failed to retrieve [the access] card from [the gunman] after his employment at Sumitomo terminated, allowing [him] to gain entry to the factory where he killed two people and injured several others. The evidence permits a reasonable inference that plaintiff Shipley was at least one of [his] targets.

* * *

These facts are sufficient to support a finding that Budd engaged in negligent conduct, and that plaintiff Shipley suffered severe emotional distress. However, these facts do not support an inference that Shipley's emotional distress was a reasonably foreseeable result of Budd's negligent acts; Budd's negligence in failing to retrieve the access card and Shipley's emotional distress are simply too attenuated to support a finding of reasonable foreseeability . . . The possibility that (1) defendant's negligence in failing to retrieve the temporary access card (2) would combine with [the ex-employee's] rage against his former employer (3) to result in a workplace shooting (4) which would cause Shipley to suffer emotional distress, was, like the situation in *Sorrells,* "too remote to permit a finding that it was reasonably foreseeable." Therefore, an essential element of plaintiff's claim is non-existent and summary judgment in favor of Budd must be affirmed.

Decision and Outcome

The court ruled in favor of the defendant because it held that the harm that plaintiff incurred was not reasonably foreseeable.

Questions for Analysis

1. Can you imagine facts that would make the security firm liable for negligent infliction of emotional distress? Aren't security firms hired precisely to deal with these freaky situations when an employee loses control of his or her actions?

2. Why is it important that there be reasonable limits to liability? Suppose a car mechanic did a negligent job and George's car would not start, prompting him to get a cab. Suppose, then, that the cab driver was drunk and George was killed in an accident. Is it not true that, "but for" the car mechanic's negligence, George would still be alive? Is it not true that applying the "but for" test, there would be a lot more litigation and people would have to be extraordinarily cautious?

Duties of Landowners/Property Owners

A few states, including California, expect owners of property to exercise *reasonable care* to protect *anyone* who comes onto the property owned from injury. Most jurisdictions, however, adhere to a common law tradition that has maintained different classes of liability exposure for different classes of property incursions.

Duties to Trespassers

Under common law, anyone who enters a landowner's property without consent is a *trespasser*. With occasional exceptions, in a common law jurisdiction, the property owner owes the trespasser no duty of care to warn of dangerous conditions, unless the doctrine of attractive nuisance applies. Hence, a street person who falls into the property owner's septic tank that had been left open for cleaning has no viable claim for ruined clothes or any other injury, unless the condition that resulted in injury is deemed to be the result of *gross misconduct* on the part of the property owner. However, a property owner is liable for intentionally injuring a trespasser, street person or not.

The protection from liability to trespassers generally is voided if the trespassers do not have an adult capacity for reason and if they are attracted to something on the property that results in foreseeable exposure to risk of injury. So, if a toddler who wanders into your yard to get to your unfenced swimming pool falls into that pool and drowns, you are liable. Likewise, you are liable if kids are attracted to the barn where a rope from a second floor loft provides thrilling rides to the ground. The traditional label for man-made structures that provide this liability exposure is **attractive nuisance**.

attractive nuisance
A man-made structure that attracts attention (as would a backyard swimming pool) and may cause injury.

Licensees and Business Invitees

Anyone who comes on your property with permission, including a social guest, is a *licensee* (and you, the property owner, are the *licensor* who licensed your guest to come onto your property). Licensees are entitled to warnings of *hidden* dangers (contamination in your swimming pool, inadequate supports for the upstairs deck where you are entertaining, etc.). A *business invitee* is entitled to even more protection from risks than licensees. A business invitee is anyone who is invited onto your place of business or to your home for business purposes. Landowners have an obligation to warn of dangerous conditions that they knew about, *or should have known about. Slip and fall* injury cases are frequent occurrences for retail businesses. If it can be argued that an injury occurred because the store was not diligent enough in discovering dangerous conditions (the slippery floors) and providing warnings, then the case will go to a jury. Historically, juries have often been sympathetic to customers and, so, if such a case is not dismissed before trial, a handsome settlement for the plaintiff is quite possible. Closely related are falling object injuries in stores, caused by TVs, computer monitors, and other heavy objects falling from shelves.

Duties of Professionals

A significant concern to professional service providers, including doctors, lawyers, engineers, and accountants, is the standard of care that they are expected to meet in their delivery of services to their customers. A member of a learned profession is held responsible for meeting the standards of the profession. Malpractice cases are generally based on negligence in which it is contended that professional standards have not been met, breaching the practitioner's duty of care to an injured party. If a professional holds herself out as a specialist within a profession, then she will be held to the standards of specialists within the field. Not surprisingly, a brain surgeon is held to a higher standard of care and treatment for head injuries than is a general practitioner in medicine.

Negligence Per Se

In some classes of negligence torts, statutes serve to establish standards of conduct/action so that no court determination of what a reasonable person would do is required to establish liability. When the state or federal government sets a safety rule (statutory or regulatory), and a defendant violates the rule, there is no issue as to whether the defendant acted reasonably—clearly (legally) she or he did not. If Mary is driving 65 in a 45 MPH zone and an accident occurs, Mary is liable *per se* because she broke a safety law that is the proximate cause of the plaintiff's injuries.

Res Ipsa Loquitur

In the lengthy list of torts discussed above, there is not a presumption of liability imposed on the defendant and a plaintiff must prove (by a preponderance of the evidence) the elements of liability. However, some injurious wrongs may be viewed as so obvious that it becomes the duty of a defendant to disprove what appears to be obvious. The Latin phrase *res ipsa loquitur* is literally translated as "the thing speaks for itself." Res ipsa loquitur is applicable when (1) the instrumentality causing the injuries was totally in control of the defendant and (2) those injuries would not normally have taken place but for negligence on the part of the defendant. If the doctrine of res ipsa loquitur applies, the case will normally go to a jury because a motion for a directed verdict by the defendant will be denied.

In some cases, mistakes by professionals are obvious, as when doctors amputate the wrong limbs or attorneys miss important deadlines that prejudice their clients' cases. If Sally, with serious circulatory problems in her left leg, goes into a hospital to have that leg amputated, only to wake up post-operatively to discover that the surgeon has removed her right leg, it can be presumed that there was negligence on the part of the surgeon (and perhaps other members of the "service" provider team). Clearly, with Sally asleep from anesthesia, the surgeon and his assistants *had control* of the situation that resulted in injury and it is apparent that the injury would not normally have occurred *but for negligence*. Torts that reflect this combination of elements require defendants to disprove their negligence—defendants are presumed liable unless they can prove otherwise.

Defending Liability in Negligence Suits

As plaintiffs seek to establish liability in tort cases by proving that the elements of their tort claims are facts, defendants just as vigorously defend themselves against the determination that they are liable. There are a number of specific defenses that are important in tort claims. Included in our discussion below are a number of standard defenses including superseding or intervening cause, assumption of risk, contributory negligence, comparative negligence, and Good Samaritan protections.

Superseding or Intervening Cause

Even when a wrongful action with potential to harm another has occurred, the chain of causation between wrongful act and liability for injury can be broken by an *intervening* event or condition. Derrick, driving without keeping a close lookout, hits a pedestrian in a crosswalk, knocking the pedestrian against a guardrail at the edge of the road. Unfortunately, a storm has just downed a power line a short distance away, charging the guardrail with current. The pedestrian is killed by the electric charge.

In this situation, Derrick would be liable for any injuries suffered as the direct result of his car's impact with the pedestrian but would not be responsible for the death from electrocution. The deadly electrical charge was an unforeseeable *intervening* event that *superseded* the car's impact as the cause of the *wrongful death*. When the defendant claims that a superceding event occurred, the defendant is contesting whether his or her negligence is the proximate cause of the plaintiff's damages, or at least that the defendant's behavior is only partially to blame for those damages.

Assumption of Risk

Anyone who *voluntarily* enters into an activity or situation that is foreseeably risky, then suffers injury of the type that might be anticipated, can be banned from any recovery for injury by an *assumption of risk* defense. So a plaintiff who sues a downhill skiing facility for her broken leg is likely to run into an assumption of risk defense. Skiing is known to be risky and skiers voluntarily assume this risk by paying money and ascending the slopes. It should be noted that this defense does not apply if artificial conditions, such as man-made structures on a slope, create conditions that are unusually hazardous—conditions that the skier (customer) could not reasonably foresee, but that the facility operator knew or should have known existed.

In high-risk sports and other sportslike activities, it is prudent for the operator of the vending facility to have customers sign forms that acknowledge awareness of the risk and that these risks are voluntarily assumed by the customers. Be wary, though, that a signature acknowledging risk assumption does not prevent liability for a hazardous condition that the customer would not have reason to know about! In addition, minors do not have the capacity to sign their rights away.

Contributory Negligence

contributory negligence
Doctrine under which a defendant is immune from liability if a plaintiff contributed to any degree to his or her own injury.

Under traditional common law, **contributory negligence** by the plaintiff is an affirmative defense against a claim of negligence by the defendant, with certain specific exceptions. Under a contributory negligence standard, if a plaintiff's own negligence *contributed* to his or her injury, that plaintiff is barred from establishing liability on the part of the defendant. The standard used regarding whether the plaintiff was contributorily negligent is the same as that applied to evaluate whether the defendant was negligent: the reasonable person standard.

The harshness of the contributory negligence defense exists because of the lack of a mechanism for allocating blame on a percentage basis. As long as the defendant can show that the plaintiff's negligence contributed in any way to his or her injuries, the plaintiff is barred from any recovery even though *most* of the fault for the accident lay with the defendant. The harshness of the contributory negligence doctrine has caused all but five states to abandon it in favor of a *comparative negligence* standard.

comparative negligence
Doctrine under which liability (responsibility for damages) is allocated between plaintiff and defendant in accordance with their relative responsibilities for the injury suffered.

Comparative Negligence

With most states having switched from a contributory negligence to a comparative negligence standard, it is useful to know the basic mechanics of typical **comparative negligence** systems. In such systems, damages in the simplest case are allocated in proportion to the responsibility (fault) of the parties for the injuries sustained. Hence, in the situation above where a court had determined that a fair value for compensation of an injured pedestrian's injuries was $300,000, if the plaintiff pedestrian was found to be $\frac{1}{3}$ (33 percent) responsible for the accident and injury, and the defendant $\frac{2}{3}$ (67 percent) responsible, the court would award $200,000 ($\frac{2}{3}$ of the $300,000) to the plaintiff with the defendant liable for that sum.

Often this standard is modified, with a partial comparative negligence scale imposed that is likely to include a fault threshold for establishing liability. The threshold might involve a *50 percent rule*. With a 50 percent rule, damages are awarded on a simple comparative negligence basis as long as the plaintiff is less than 50 percent at fault. However, if the plaintiff's "contributory" share of responsibility is 50 percent or more, the defendant is held free of liability for any injury suffered by the plaintiff.

Good Samaritan Statutes

Willard is at a baseball game when he has a heart attack. A doctor attending the game runs to his car for his medical bag and goes to Willard's aid before any rescue vehicle can arrive. In spite of the rescuing doctor's effort to resuscitate Willard, and those of the rescue squad, things go badly for Willard and he dies. Willard's wife sues the doctor, claiming mistakes in the emergency care he provided (i.e., negligence). The threat of lawsuit provides a strong incentive to choose to not provide such aid. Recognizing this problem, most states have adopted *Good Samaritan statutes*. Under these statutes, if someone aids another in need, the injured party or his survivors are barred from a claim of negligence (but not reckless behavior) against the rescuer.

STRICT LIABILITY

strict liability
Liability for injury that exists as a matter of law, even when there is no fault in an event that causes injury.

Intentional torts and torts attributable to negligence involve actions where the defendant is *at fault* for his or her conduct that caused injury. In the former case, the fault is motivated by a desire to cause harm, while in the latter case fault is attributable to carelessness. There is another category of torts, called **strict liability,** for which liability for injury is imposed for a reason or reasons other than fault—even when a high degree of care to avoid injuries is exerted.

Strict liability is associated with activities that are inherently risky to the public (others), even when reasonable care is taken. The law considers it fair and just that there be compensation when the defendant chooses to engage in such activities and injuries are suffered. Putting on fireworks displays, using explosives for earth excavation or demolition, crop-dusting, storing hazardous wastes, harboring wild animals, and other abnormally dangerous activities bring exposure to strict liability. In recent years, storage of hazardous wastes has generated many class action lawsuits based on contaminated water supplies, playgrounds, or landfills.

Product Liability in Contract and Tort

Product liability law consists of both contract and tort law. In Chapter 8, we discussed warranty law and the sale of goods under the UCC. When a manufacturer or seller makes an express warranty about a product, it creates strict liability for that manufacturer. If the product does not possess the qualities the seller warrants, or guarantees, the seller is liable to the buyer regardless of whether seller or manufacturer was careful in the production, design, and sale of the product in question. As to the implied warranty of merchantability, it is based on a consumer expectations test, that is, are the goods fit for the ordinary uses for which such goods are used? It is common for victims of malfunctioning products to sue in both contract and tort. In this chapter we are going to discuss the tort side of product liability law.

product liability
The liability borne by vendors for injuries caused by the sales of defective products.

The most prominent applications of strict liability occur in connection with **product liability**—the liability borne by sellers when they sell defective products to the public. In a series of cases that have been both widely applauded and criticized, courts have increasingly applied strict liability in tort to product liability cases. Product liability has evolved to the following standard:

If you sell a product that has a *defect* and that defect is the *proximate cause* of a user's *damages,* you are liable for the resulting damages.

Restatements of Torts: Second and Third

Restatements are simply that: restatements of what learned judges and attorneys in an area of law view as the common law at the time.[3] Every 20 years or so, the *Restatements* are restated. Section 402A of the *Restatement (Second),* composed in 1977, was one of the most widely cited and influential sections of the *Restatement (Second) of Torts* law.[4] Section 402A of the *Restatement (Second) of Torts* states that and places liability on

1. One who sells any product in a defective condition unreasonably dangerous to the user or consumer or to his property is subject to liability for physical harm thereby caused to the ultimate user or consumer, or to his property, if
   a. the seller is engaged in the business of selling such product, and
   b. it is expected to and does reach the consumer without substantial change in the condition in which it was sold.
2. The rule stated in Subsection 1 applies although
   a. the seller has exercised all possible care in the preparation and sale of his products, and
   b. the user or consumer has not bought the product from or entered into any contractual relation with the seller.

Even though the *Restatements* do not have the legal status of a state or federal statute, most judges freely quote from and adhere to the *Restatements*. They are a good prediction as to how the courts will resolve legal disputes involving torts as, since the *Restatement (Second)* was published in 1977, courts have extensively used it as the standard for liability in product liability cases. Publication of *Restatement (Third)* in 1998 has not undermined the vitality of Section 402A of the *Restatement (Second),* listed immediately above.

What Section 402A of the Restatement of Torts Covers: Sellers Are Liable, Not Just Manufacturers

Note at the onset that Section 402A places liability on *sellers,* not just the company that makes the products, in most cases, a manufacturer. A consumer electronic product that explodes in the face of a consumer would generate liability for the manufacturer, the distributor (assuming it was a different business), and the retailer. The fact that the product is sold in a box and the box specifically states **DO NOT OPEN** does not absolve distributors and retailers who had no opportunity to inspect the product prior to sale. Those companies farther down the marketing chain, such as retailers, can file a cross-claim or a third-party interpleader against the manufacturer saying, in effect, "While we may be technically liable, the manufacturer is primarily liable and the plaintiff should collect first from the manufacturer." In most states, retailers can direct that court-awarded damages be collected first from manufacturers, but if the assets of the manufacturer are insufficient, then retailers and distributors may have to pay damages. There also have been suits against suppliers of components to manufacturers that have been successful. The main point is that all

---

[3] Restatements are composed by the American Law Institute (http://www.ali.org/).

[4] The *Restatement (Second)* was published in 1977. Unless otherwise designated, we discuss the *Restatement (Second) of Torts* and then look at the changes brought about by the 1998 *Restatement (Third) of Torts.*

commercial *sellers* in the marketing chain are potentially liable to consumers if a product is sold in a defective condition.

Strict Liability and Product Defect

The essence of Section 402A is that sellers are liable without fault, but the plaintiff still has to show that the product was *defective*. The fact that a seller has exerted reasonable or even extraordinary care in the sale of the product is irrelevant. If the product is sold in a *defective condition that makes it unreasonably dangerous,* liability on the part of the seller is established. So, under Section 402A, it is no longer necessary for a consumer to establish that a seller or manufacturer was negligent. If a manufacturer produces a product that has a defect, or a seller sells a defective product, and the other conditions for tort liability are satisfied (such as proximate cause and damages), then the defendant(s) is (are) liable for the resulting damages.

The question then becomes, in most product liability cases, what is a product defect? The courts have defined three types of defects: *manufacturing, design*, and *inadequate warnings* defects.

Manufacturing Defects

manufacturing defect
A product defect that generally is the result of a mistake in the manufacturing process.

Manufacturing defects are the least controversial. In general, **manufacturing defects** are the result of mistakes made at a factory. For most companies, manufacturing defects are usually quite rare. Manufacturing defects typically are the cause when parts fall off a machine, making the machine unreasonably dangerous. Consider a chain saw, for example. A chain saw operator could be seriously injured if the saw's handgrip is loose, allowing the operator's hand to contact the moving chain.

The Consumer Expectations Test It is relatively easy to give examples of manufacturing defects, but it is more difficult to formulate a conceptual criterion for "defective." One definition can be formed based on a variant of the *consumer expectations test*—that is, on asking how an ordinary consumer would expect a product to perform. Ordinary consumers expect a bicycle to stop when the brakes are applied. If a consumer purchases a bicycle, gives it to one of her children, and an accident occurs because the brakes were not properly installed, the product will undoubtedly fail the consumer expectations test. Still, consumer expectations tests can be ambiguous and are capable of abuse, even though the *Restatement (Second) of Torts* indicates that a product is *unreasonably dangerous* (defective) if it is "dangerous to an extent beyond that which would be contemplated by the ordinary consumer who purchases it, with the ordinary knowledge common to the community as to its characteristics." Plaintiff's attorneys, whose clients are often dead or horribly maimed, can simply ask the jury whether "you expect to be in the condition of my client as a result of using the defendant's product."

Manufacturing Defect: Does the Product Conform to the Manufacturer's Product Design? A less ambiguous test of whether the product possesses a manufacturing defect is to ask, "does the product in question *depart* from the manufacturer's intended design?"[5] If the answer is yes, then a manufacturing defect has been established. In other words, if the design of the product calls for certain screws to be set in a particular location and, in fact, the screws are not there and the consumer is injured as a result of the screws not being in their intended position, a manufacturing defect is established. Using the *manufacturer's intended design test* requires a plaintiff to show the manufacturing defect with some precision.

Design Defects

design defect
A product defect that results from faulty design.

Design defects are likely to be a more serious problem for sellers than manufacturing defects. With a manufacturing defect, typically, only a very few products are affected—just the defectively manufactured products that somehow got through the company's quality

---

[5] Section 2(a) of the 1998 version of the *Restatement (Third) of Torts.*

control tests. When a product is judged to have a design defect, all of the same-design products are capable of generating liability. As a result, in design defect cases, very large class action suits are common. In such cases, the combination of attorney fees, damage awards, and bad publicity can bankrupt even large corporations.

Casualties of Product Liability Suits Based on Design Defects   There have been a number of products in high-profile cases that have been judged to have design defects. The drug DES, which was used as an anti-nausea drug for pregnant women, also resulted in higher rates of cancer for daughters of mothers who took the drug.[6] The IUD (interuterine device), a contraceptive device, was defectively designed according to the courts, because it caused women to become sterile as well as to suffer other medical problems.[7] Ford Pintos were judged to be defectively designed, resulting in their tendency to burst into flames when struck from the rear (discussed in Case 10-5). Silicon breast implants have been the subject of design defect lawsuits, though the scientific evidence of a link between the implants and the ailments the female plaintiffs have complained of is weak.[8] Similarly, allegations are being made about the links between cell phones and brain cancer, again, in spite of the fact that the evidence of a scientific link between the two is sparse.[9] Quite recently, Ford Explorers and the tires manufactured for those vehicles by the Bridgestone/Firestone Co. have both been accused of design defects: the Explorers for their tendencies to roll over and Bridgestone tires for their tendency to suffer tread separations from the tire casing.

Consumer Expectations Test, Again   Again, the consumer expectations test can be used to define a design defect by simply asking whether an ordinary consumer would expect to be in the condition of the plaintiff as a result of using the defendant's product. If the answer is no, then the product does not pass the consumer expectations test. Assume that you are driving a relatively cheap car, you are hit from the rear, and the gas tank explodes. The jury could be asked, "Would you expect the gas tank to blow up and burn over 80 percent of your body when struck in the rear by a vehicle going 25 MPH?" Since the question answers itself (in the negative), the consumer expectations test as applied to design defects is quite subject to elastic interpretations. The hypothetical facts assumed above were largely evident in the *Ford Pinto* case discussed as Case 10-5.

---

[6] *Collins v. Eli Lilly Co.*, 116 Wis.2d 166, 342 N.W.2d 37 (1984).

[7] *Coursen and Cook v. A.H. Robins Company*, 764 F.2d 1329 (9th Cir. 1985).

[8] *In re Silicone Gel Breast Implants Products Liability Litigation*, 837 F. Supp. 1128 (N.D. Ala. 1993).

[9] "Cell Phones and Brain Tumors: A Bad Connection?" *PR Newswire*, March 6, 2000. Source: National Brain Tumor Foundation, www.braintumor.org.

Case 10-5

Richard Grimshaw, Minor v. Ford Motor Company

Court of Appeal of California, Fourth District, Division 2
119 Cal. App. 3d 757, 174 Cal. Rptr. 348 (Cal. App. 1981)

FACTS AND CASE BACKGROUND

A 1972 Ford Pinto hatchback automobile unexpectedly stalled on a freeway, erupting into flames when it was rear ended by a car proceeding in the same direction. Mrs. Lilly Gray, the driver of the

*Pinto, suffered fatal burns and 13-year-old Richard Grimshaw, a passenger in the Pinto, suffered se-
vere and permanently disfiguring burns on his face and entire body. Grimshaw and the heirs of Mrs.
Gray (Grays) sued Ford Motor Company and others. Following a six-month jury trial, verdicts were
returned in favor of plaintiffs against Ford Motor Company. Grimshaw was awarded $2,516,000
compensatory damages and $125 million punitive damages; the Grays were awarded $559,680 in
compensatory damages. On Ford's motion for a new trial, Grimshaw was required to remit all but
$3 1/2 million of the punitive award as a condition of denial of the motion.*

Opinion by Tamura

In 1968, Ford began designing a new subcompact automobile which ultimately became the Pinto.
Mr. Iacocca, then a Ford vice president, conceived the project and was its moving force. Ford's objective was to build a car at or below 2,000 pounds to sell for no more than $2,000.

Ordinarily marketing surveys and preliminary engineering studies precede the styling of a new automobile line. Pinto, however, was a rush project, so that styling preceded engineering and dictated engineering design to a greater degree than usual. Among the engineering decisions dictated by styling was
the placement of the fuel tank. It was then the preferred practice in Europe and Japan to locate the gas
tank over the rear axle in subcompacts because a small vehicle has less "crush space" between the rear
axle and the bumper than larger cars. The Pinto's styling, however, required the tank to be placed behind
the rear axle leaving only 9 or 10 inches of "crush space"—far less than in any other American automobile or Ford overseas subcompact. In addition, the Pinto was designed so that its bumper was little more
than a chrome strip, less substantial than the bumper of any other American car produced then or later.

* * *

Crash Tests:

* * *

The crash tests revealed that the Pinto's fuel system as designed could not meet the 20-mile-per-hour
proposed standard. Mechanical prototypes struck from the rear with a moving barrier at 21 miles per
hour caused the fuel tank to be driven forward and to be punctured, causing fuel leakage in excess of
the standard prescribed by the proposed regulation. A production Pinto crash tested at 21 miles per
hour into a fixed barrier caused the fuel neck to be torn from the gas tank and the tank to be punctured
by a bolt head on the differential housing. In at least one test, spilled fuel entered the driver's com-
partment through gaps resulting from the separation of the seams joining the rear wheel wells to the
floor pan. The seam separation was occasioned by the lack of reinforcement in the rear structure and
insufficient welds of the wheel wells to the floor pan.

* * *

The Cost to Remedy Design Deficiencies:

When a prototype failed the fuel system integrity test, the standard of care for engineers in the industry was to redesign and retest it. The vulnerability of the production Pinto's fuel tank at speeds of
20 and 30-miles-per-hour fixed barrier tests could have been remedied by inexpensive "fixes," but
Ford produced and sold the Pinto to the public without doing anything to remedy the defects . . .
Equipping the car with a reinforced rear structure, smooth axle, improved bumper and additional
crush space at a total cost of $15.30 would have made the fuel tank safe in a 34 to 38-mile-per-hour
rear-end collision by a vehicle the size of the Ford Galaxie. If, in addition to the foregoing, a bladder
or tank within a tank were used or if the tank were protected with a shield, it would have been safe in
a 40 to 45-mile-per-hour rear impact. If the tank had been located over the rear axle, it would have
been safe in a rear impact at 50 miles per hour or more.

* * *

Some two weeks before this case went to the jury, the Supreme Court in *Barker v. Lull Engineering
Co*. (1978) 20 Cal.3d 413 [143 Cal.Rptr. 225, 573 P.2d 443, 96 A.L.R.3d 1], formulated the following "two-pronged" definition of design defect, embodying the "consumer expectation" standard and
"risk-benefit" test: "First, a product may be found defective in design if the plaintiff establishes that
the product failed to perform as safely as an ordinary consumer would expect when used in an intended or reasonably foreseeable manner. Second, a product may alternatively be found defective in

design if the plaintiff demonstrates that the product's design proximately caused his injury and the defendant fails to establish, in light of the relevant factors, that, on balance, the benefits of the challenged design outweigh the risk of danger inherent in such design." (*Id.,* at p. 432.)

* * *

PUNITIVE DAMAGES

Ford contends that it was entitled to a judgment notwithstanding the verdict on the issue of punitive damages on two grounds: First, punitive damages are statutorily and constitutionally impermissible in a design defect case; second, there was no evidentiary support for a finding of malice or of corporate responsibility for malice. In any event, Ford maintains that the punitive damage award must be reversed because of erroneous instructions and excessiveness of the award.

* * *

Ford argues that "malice" as used in section 3294 [of the California Code] and as interpreted by our Supreme Court in *Davis v. Hearst* (1911) 160 Cal. 143 [116 P. 530], requires *animus malus* or evil motive—an intention to injure the person harmed—and that the term is therefore conceptually incompatible with an unintentional tort such as the manufacture and marketing of a defectively designed product. This contention runs counter to our decisional law. As this court recently noted, numerous California cases after *Davis v. Hearst, supra,* have interpreted the term "malice" as used in section 3294 to include, not only a malicious intention to injure the specific person harmed, but conduct evincing "*a conscious disregard of the probability that the actor's conduct will result in injury to others.*" [Emphasis added]

* * *

Applying the above precepts to the instant case, Ford has failed to demonstrate prejudice from the claimed defect in the instructions on malice. When the instructions are read as a whole, the jury could not possibly have interpreted the words "conscious disregard of its possible results" to extend to the innocent conduct depicted by Ford. The term "motive and willingness . . . to injure" and the words "wilful," "intentional," and "conscious disregard" signify *animus malus* or evil motive.

* * *

Ford's final contention is that the amount of punitive damages awarded, even as reduced by the trial court, was so excessive that a new trial on that issue must be granted. Ford argues that its conduct was less reprehensible than those for which punitive damages have been awarded in California in the past; that the $3 1/2 million award is many times over the highest award for such damages ever upheld in California; and that the award exceeds maximum civil penalties that may be enforced under federal or state statutes against a manufacturer for marketing a defective automobile. We are unpersuaded.

Decision and Outcome

The California Court of Appeals upheld the finding of the jury that the design of the Ford Pinto was defective and that the jury instruction comported with California law. The same court also held that the plaintiff was entitled to punitive damages if the defendant's actions showed a conscious disregard for the safety of others.

Questions for Analysis

1. In California, as a result of this case, what are the criteria for determining whether the design of a product is defective?
2. What kind of defective designs give rise to punitive damages according to this case?
3. Why did Ford argue that the $3.5 million punitive damage award was excessive? What was the court's answer?

Restatement (Third) of Torts: *Definition of a Design Defect*

Per a definition used both by courts and by the 1998 version of the *Restatement of Torts,* a design is defective "when the foreseeable risks of harm posed by the product could have been reduced or avoided by the adoption of a reasonable alternative design, and failure to use the alternative design renders the product not reasonably safe." Implicitly, the 1998 version of the *Restatement of Torts* incorporates a trade-off between "foreseeable risks" and the costs of an "alternative design." Generally, foreseeable risks include loss of human life and personal injury. The costs of alternative designs refers to additional costs borne by the manufacturer. Although trade-offs between lives and profits, or costs, are repugnant to most people, such trade-offs are contemplated when courts and juries evaluate whether a product is defectively designed.

Foreseeable Use versus Intended Use   Notice that the 1998 *Restatement* definition of a design defect does not require that a product be used for its *intended* purpose in order for it to have a design defect. At one time, when faced by lawsuits based on crashworthiness, automobile manufacturers claimed that their designs were not defective just because they were not crashworthy. Even though customers, users, and bystanders were hurt or killed in crashes at relatively low speeds, automobile manufacturers claimed that automobiles *were not intended to be crashed* against other vehicles or immovable objects.

The 1998 *Restatement* definition of a design defect places emphasis on whether the use of a product is *foreseeable,* and not whether the use was the *intended* use. If the use is foreseeable, then the product must be designed to guard against such foreseeable harm, or there should be a warning that adequately apprises consumers of these risks. Warnings are required even if the harm comes from uses of the product that are far removed from what's intended by the manufacturer. Illustratively, airplane glue's intended use is in assembling model airplanes. It is known, however, that some children abuse airplane glue and get high sniffing it. It is common for sellers of model airplane glue to provide conspicuous warnings against sniffing their glue.

Industry Practice and Government Regulation   In some cases, design defects are relatively easy to recognize. If a design falls below *industry standards* with respect to safety features, it is relatively easy for a jury to conclude that the product was unreasonably dangerous by reason of a defective design. As with the damages phase of a product liability case, expert witnesses are often called in by each side to try to explain what safety features are common within the industry and whether the defendant's product did or did not meet those standards. In addition to the *Ford Pinto* case discussed above, there have been other vehicular product liability cases that involved placement of gas tanks, airbag deployment, inappropriate openings of hatchbacks, and, now, tires that separate without warning, as was alleged in the recent Bridgestone/Firestone tire cases.

Also, for many products the government requires safety features. The Consumer Product Safety Commission, the National Highway Transportation Safety Administration, and the Food and Drug Administration all issue regulations that apply to particular products and to classes of products. Products for which designs or performance do not conform to government mandated requirements are unreasonable *per se*. However, as noted above, products with designs that do comply with all government standards in the applicable area can, nevertheless, be deemed defective.

Inadequate Warnings

The third type of product defect is the lack of adequate warnings and/or instructions. According to the *Restatement (Third) of Torts,* "A product is defective because of inadequate instructions or warnings when the foreseeable risks of harm posed by the product could have been reduced or avoided by the provision of reasonable instructions or warnings by the seller and the omission of the instructions or warnings renders the product not reasonably safe."

The *Restatement* lists four factors that are guides in determining whether the warnings are adequate:

1. The gravity and risks posed by the product.
2. The content and comprehensibility of the warnings.
3. The intensity of the expression.
4. The characteristics of the user group.

If the risk of harm is great and the harm associated with the risk is serious, then it is imperative for the manufacturer to provide a warning that is comprehensible to the expected user group. The more serious the harm, the more intense the warning should be. Pictures may be effective in supplementing written warnings, particularly if the target group for a product is children or people who may not speak or read English fluently, such as immigrants. There have been many cases in which the language used in a warning or the location of a warning was judged inadequate.

Relationship to Product Design   The adequacy of warnings is conditionally related to product design. Prudence suggests that a manufacturer should make a product as safe as possible, while still retaining the functionality of the product. A manufacturer cannot simply design its products and provide a barrage of warnings. On the other hand, a comment to Section 402A of the *Restatement (Second)* indicates that, "Where warning is given, the seller may reasonably assume that it will be read and heeded; and a product bearing such a warning which is safe for use if it is followed, is not in defective condition nor is it unreasonably dangerous." Once a warning is given, then the *Restatement's* comment to Section 402A suggests that manufacturers are not liable to those who ignore the warnings.

Obligation to Warn about Foreseeable but Nonobvious Risks   If the risk of harm from a product is obvious, then there is no obligation to warn. Razors are commonly known to cut flesh and hammers are a well-known hazard to fingers. There is no need for manufacturers to warn about such obvious risks. Manufacturers, however, are obligated to warn about foreseeable risks of harm that could have been reduced by adequate warnings. The *Restatement* obligates sellers to warn about *foreseeable* risks and not necessarily about risks that may occur when the product is being used for its *intended* use. Gasoline is not intended to be swallowed, nor glue sniffed, and yet these misuses of these products are foreseeable, so warnings against such uses are required. In general, manufacturers have an obligation to warn about foreseeable risks even when those risks only occur when the product is being misused. A benefit, from the point of view of manufacturers, is that when warnings are ignored, users are less likely to recover if they are injured because *an adequate warning establishes the foundation for assumption-of-risk defense.*

Defenses Available to Manufacturers and Sellers in Product Liability Cases

Misuse of Product, Ignoring of Warnings, and Assumption of Risk

misuse
Use of a product for purposes for which it is not designed.

Most states allow *misuse* of a product as a defense in product liability cases. Often, misuse of a product occurs in connection with ignoring warnings, but ignoring warnings is not essential to the misuse defense. In the absence of any warnings, if a consumer drives a motor vehicle at an excessive rate of speed or in hazardous driving conditions

Ethical Challenges Recommendations for Marketers

When promoting and/or enhancing product design for additional consumption, the starting point for marketers is to look at the characteristics of the consumer segments being targeted. Commentators have suggested that target market decisions should include an ethical component regarding the potential vulnerability of segment members. Research has shown that consumers feel that targeting vulnerable segments is unethical, particularly if the products are dangerous or of questionable value. Inappropriate targeting strategies could result in negative publicity, including boycotts.

The pervasive theme of this analysis is that marketers must consider not only the intended uses of their products as stated by product designers, but also how people will overuse them, particularly in light of product advertising and labeling. This perspective is now discussed in terms of designing products and their warnings. While we agree that physical design issues, including the development of guards and safety devices, should precede the creation of warnings, we believe the overall product design should fully integrate warnings into the total offering.

For more than forty years safety experts have argued that the primary steps in developing safe products are to eliminate hazards from products or to provide safety devices. Only then should warnings and instructions become relevant. The three safety priorities established in 1955 by the National Safety Council are:

Principle 1: Hazard Elimination. If practical, design the hazard out of the product, workplace, job or facility via engineering means.

Principle 2: Safety Guards, Enclosures. If a hazard cannot be eliminated, guard against it or use safety design techniques to reduce risks.

Principle 3: Safety Warnings and Instructions. If the hazard cannot be guarded against, warn or instruct the user about the danger under reasonably foreseeable conditions of service and commerce.

Our analysis suggests adding a fourth principle:

Principle 4: Advertising and Labeling. In addition to proper warnings and instructions, advertising and labeling should not explicitly or implicitly encourage dangerous product overuse.

Source: From "Excessive Consumption: Marketing and Legal Perspectives," by Karl A. Boedecker, *American Business Law Journal*, Winter 1999, Vol. 36. Reprinted with permission from the *American Business Law Journal*.

---

and a crash results, the consumer is unlikely to recover. If a manufacturer of tires for automobiles places a warning on its products that they are not to be inflated beyond 35 pounds per square inch and a user inflates them to 60 pounds per square inch, then has a blowout, the manufacturer can claim that the user misused the product and assumed the risk by ignoring the warning.

For an obvious risk, there is no need for the manufacturer to place a warning. If a user is aware of an obvious risk and voluntarily *assumes that risk,* the user gives manufacturers an *assumption-of-risk defense* if the user is harmed by the product. The function of warnings on products is to make nonobvious risks obvious. If a user ignores a warning, and heeding the warning would have prevented the harm, then he or she has assumed the risk and cannot successfully sue. Because of fear of lawsuits, based on precedents that have occurred, most products are loaded with warnings, as manufacturers are motivated to err on the side of safety. Users of hairspray are warned not to use the product near an open flame even though the risk is obvious to most people. Consumers are warned not to swallow household cleaning products such as Drano and Comet. Purchasers of pharmaceutical drugs are warned about a plethora of possible side effects and of dangerous combinations with other drugs and alcohol.

Even though there is significant overlap between the defenses of (1) *misuse* of the product, (2) *ignoring of warnings,* and (3) *assumption of risk,* each defense is separate and does not rely on a combination of the other two.

- Even without warnings, a *misuse of a product* can absolve sellers of liability if harm occurs. There are no warnings on automobiles not to exceed speed limits, but a user cannot recover from the manufacturer if she drives at 100 miles per hour on a rainy day and crashes her car.
- As discussed above, a manufacturer is entitled to assume that users will not ignore warnings that are reasonably apparent. *Users who ignore warnings* and are hurt are not entitled to recover against manufacturers/sellers if the harm they incurred would have been avoided had they heeded the warning, regardless of whether users fully appreciated the risks of ignoring the warning.
- An assumption-of-risk defense requires that the user (1) was *aware of the risk* and (2) *voluntarily chose* to assume the risk. Experienced truck drivers who light up a cigarette while fueling have assumed the risk of the resulting consequences. At most gas stations, of course, there are prominent warnings not to smoke near gas pumps.

In many cases, when the facts are not in dispute, a defendant is able to show that it is entitled to avoid liability based on the undisputed facts that the plaintiff misused the product, ignored a warning, or assumed the risk. The result is that the case is dismissed before it ever gets to trial.

Tampering

tampering
Alteration of a product after it is out of the control of the manufacturer in a way that makes it potentially injurious.

Manufacturers can use **tampering** as a defense if they can show that a product was safe when it left their hands but was altered or tampered with by someone farther down the marketing chain, even by consumers. A famous case involving Tylenol occurred some years ago when a demented individual took Tylenol bottles from store shelves, laced them with cyanide, and later placed them back on the shelves. The poisoned pills caused the deaths of several unsuspecting customers. Since that time, virtually all manufacturers of over-the-counter drugs have packaged their products in tamper-resistant containers with warnings not to purchase or use the product if the seals have been broken. At this point, it would probably be a design defect if an over-the-counter drug was not packaged this way as the chance of tampering is foreseeable. The main point is that, with reasonable precautions taken by a manufacturer, establishing that a product was safe when it left the producer's control and was damaged by another company, a third party, or a consumer, when injuries take place, the manufacturer has an effective tampering defense available.

Government Contractor Defense

If a manufacturer designs a product that conforms to a government contract, such as a weapon or an aeronautical vehicle, and a defect in the design results in harm to a user or bystander, the manufacturer can defend by claiming that it is not responsible for the design of the product, as that was dictated by a government contract. To complete this story, in general, governments cannot be sued either, even though a product they requisition from a private firm turns out to be harmful or deadly.

State-of-the-Art Knowledge

Manufacturers have an obligation to test their products and to discover possible risks associated with them. In some cases, when hidden risks only become apparent long after a product was sold, a defense available to manufacturers is that they did not know and that there was no reasonable way of knowing of these risks because of the state of science at the time of production. This defense is generally effective, though there have been instances in which courts have held that companies had obligations to push back the bounds of ignorance on the subject. With contraceptive products that rendered women unable to bear children after use or caused birth defects, courts have indicated that the producers should have discovered these risks.[10] The precedents for contraceptive products have been sufficiently intimidating that American firms have virtually ceased new product development in that area. The recent "morning after" products, such as RU 486, have all been developed by European firms.

Future of Product Liability Law

It is likely that some form of product liability reform that prevents "excessive" damage awards is in our future. However, there will not be a retreat back to the time when plaintiffs had to prove that defendants (sellers or manufacturers) were negligent. Instead, the focus of product liability cases will continue to be upon determining whether the product in question contained a "defect." In cases where a manufacturing defect is alleged, the difficulties of determining whether there is a defect will continue to be less than when a design defect is alleged. Design defects potentially affect large numbers of people and, therefore, will be contested with more intensity. It seems clear to the authors that exclusive reliance on a subjective consumer expectations test is unwarranted and can sometimes lend itself to excessive damage awards. Of course, opinions can and do differ.

State-of-the-Art Defense

Manufacturers should be experts in the qualities of their products. They have a duty to test for possible hidden risks even though such testing is expensive. Manufacturers do not, however, possess God-like qualities to predict what science will turn up in the future. Unless there are extraordinary circumstances, manufacturers should be able to rely on existing science in designing their products. If, after their products are in the stream of commerce, scientists discover that this or that product can lead to increased risk of cancer or other chronic diseases after extensive exposure to the drug, charging manufacturers with liability for a design defect can be expected to lead to less innovation in the future.

Caps on Damages

punitive damages caps
Statutes that set upper limits on the amounts that juries can award for punitive damages.

A number of proposed tort reforms call for limitations on damages; that is, setting **punitive damages caps.** It seems clear that only the largest damage awards receive extensive publicity and empirical showings that damage awards are growing at an unreasonable rate have not been convincingly presented. The focus of reform efforts has been on limiting awards for pain and suffering in personal injury cases to between $250,000 and $500,000 and on limiting punitive damage awards to multiples of compensatory damages that are in the three to four range. With such limitations, if actual or compensatory damages in a case were set at, say, $1 million, then punitive damages would be limited to $3 million to $4 million. All the reforms listed above, but especially the damage award limitations, are vigorously opposed by most attorney organizations, especially those of trial lawyers, who often work for plaintiffs on a contingency fee basis, meaning that they receive a percentage of the damage award.

---

[10] In a case cited above, the A.H. Robins company is still being sued for the IUD, which has not been sold in the United States for more than a decade.

Nutz and Boltz   Torts

Intentional torts to person	Assault, battery, false imprisonment, infliction of emotional distress, invasion of privacy, and defamation.	Defenses for assault and battery include consent and defense of self, property, or others. Defenses for defamation include absolute privilege, qualified privilege, and public figure.
Intentional torts to property	Fraudulent misrepresentation, conversion, and trespass to land, trespass to personal property.	Defenses to fraud include lack of reasonable reliance by plaintiff and no proximate cause between the fraud and damages. Defenses for conversion include proving that the plaintiff has no superior property right or the property was taken out of necessity. Defenses against trespass include showing that the property owner did not have the right to possess the property or the trespass was in necessity.
Negligence	The following four elements must be present for liability: (1) duty of care, (2) breach of that duty, (3) measurable damage, and (4) proximate cause between breach and damages.	Defenses include assumption of risk, contributory negligence, intervening cause.
Strict liability	Defendant is engaged in an unusually dangerous activity or is selling a product that contains a defect.	Defenses include obvious danger, assumption of risk, ignoring warning, tampering with the product after it leaves the manufacturer, government contractor, state of the art.

Summary

Tort Are Civil Wrongs and Are Normally Classified as Intentional, Negligence, and Strict Liability

- A *tort* is a noncontractual, civil *wrong*.
- Torts are commonly classified as (1) *intentional*, (2) *unintentional* (*negligence*), or (3) *strict liability* torts, depending on the intentions of the defendant.
- Damages are awarded in the form of *nominal, compensatory,* or *punitive*.
- For an intentional tort claim to have merit before a court, it must be true that the defendant knew what he (she) was doing and the defendant knew, or should have known, the possible consequences of the action taken.

There Are a Number of Intentional Torts, Which Involve Harm to a Person's Mental Tranquility as Well as Personal Injury for Which Courts Will Give Remedies;

- The intentional torts of assault, battery, and false imprisonment are acts that cause physical harm or threat of harm to others or wrongfully detain them. These actions are often crimes as well as torts.
- Intentional infliction of emotional distress, the *tort of outrage,* is intentional conduct so extreme and outrageous that it results in severe emotional distress to another person.
- Tort law protects against a number of forms of invasion of privacy including (1) commercial use of someone's name or likeness without permission; (2) intrusion into a person's solitude by illegally searching his or her premises or belongings, by bugging or wire-tapping his or her residence, by the unauthorized intrusion into the person's financial records, and so on; (3) the public revelation of information that places a person in a false light, such as by attributing to a person ideas not held or actions not taken by that person; (4) the public revelation of facts about a person that a reasonable person would find repugnant.

Victims of Intentional Infliction of Emotional Distress, Invasions of the Right of Privacy, Defamation, and Fraud Are Entitled to Sue for Redress	• The essential elements of a defamation claim are *publication* of false statement(s) to a *third party that harm a person's reputation.* Violating the required standard of conduct orally is the tort of *slander* while breaching this duty in writing is *libel.* • Defenses to defamation suits are the *truth, absolute privilege, qualified privilege,* and some *public figure* claims. • Generally, to establish damages for fraudulent misrepresentation, the following elements are required: (1) a misrepresentation of material facts, (2) knowledge that the "facts" presented are false or show "reckless disregard for the truth," (3) intent to induce reliance on the misrepresented facts, (4) a reasonable reliance on the misrepresented facts on the part of the injured party, and (5) actual damages that occur as a result of reasonable reliance on the misrepresentation.
Among the Intentional Torts That Are Directed against Property Are Conversion and Trespass	• *Conversion* is the taking and/or using of someone else's personal property without permission and without justification. • *Trespass* occurs when, without consent, an individual goes onto another's property (land) or interferes with the rights of the owner of personal property to the exclusive possession, use, and enjoyment of that property. • In the eyes of the law, land and improvements to land (such as buildings) are *real property* while all other items owned (moveable items such as money, cars, furniture, etc.) are *personal property.* • Trespass to personal property involves serious interference with the personal property of another.
Negligence Is Based on the Breach of a Duty of Care When the Defendant Owes a Plaintiff Such Care and the Breach of That Duty Is the Proximate Cause of the Plaintiff's Damages; the Tort of Negligence Is Flexible and Can Be Applied to Professional Actions, to Accidents That Occur at Home, or to a Wide Array of Other Activities; There Are a Number of Defenses to Negligence Claims	• *Negligence* involves an individual or business engaging in actions or conduct that is not intended to harm another but that, unfortunately, does. The tort of negligence is based on *lack of reasonable care.* • Liability for injury/damage suffered through negligence arises when the following four elements exist: (1) the defendant owes a *duty of care* to the plaintiff, (2) the defendant *breaches* that duty of care by negligence, (3) the plaintiff suffers *cognizable damage,* and (4) the defendant's negligence is the *proximate cause* of the injury. • Anyone who comes on your property with permission, including a social guest, is a *licensee.* Licensees are entitled to warnings of *hidden* dangers. • A person invited onto your premises for business purposes is a business *invitee.* • Business invitees are entitled to be warned of all hidden dangers that the owner knows or should know about. • A member of a learned profession is held responsible for meeting the standards of the profession in the delivery of services. *Malpractice* cases are negligence cases in which it is contended that such standards have not been met, breaching the practitioner's duty of reasonable care to an injured party. • In some classes of negligence torts, statutes serve to establish standards of conduct/action so that no court determination of what a reasonable person would do is required to establish liability. This is called negligence *per se.* • *Res ipsa loquitur* is applicable when the instrumentality causing the injuries was totally in control of the defendant and those injuries would not normally have taken place, but for negligence on the part of the defendant. If this doctrine applies, the burden of proof shifts to the defendant and the case will normally go to a jury. • Defenses to negligence suits include *superseding or intervening cause, assumption of risk, contributory negligence, comparative negligence,* and *Good Samaritan protections.*
Strict Liability Is Imposed When the Actor Is Doing Actions That Are Unusually	• *Strict liability* is a category of torts. It exists when liability for injury is imposed for a reason or reasons other than fault—even when a high degree of care to avoid injuries is exerted. • Strict liability is applied to activities that are unusually dangerous, such as storing hazardous wastes or using dynamite. • Strict liability is also applied to sellers who sell defective products. • High-profile product liability cases are a fact of life in the U.S. economy.

Dangerous or Selling Products to the Public That Would Be Unreasonably Dangerous if Sold in Defective Condition; Manufacturers Are Also Liable if They Are Negligent in Inspecting Their Products or Do Not Comply with Government Regulations	• When a vendor sells a product, the ordinary rules of negligence apply. • If negligence of a vendor creates a *foreseeable risk* to third parties, the vendor is liable in tort. • Manufacturers are liable to customers and others when they are negligent in inspecting and testing their products for defects and hidden dangers. • Failure to comply with government performance and design regulations makes a manufacturer liable per se for its products. • Compliance with government regulations in performance and design, however, does not insulate manufacturers from liability for defective designs except when federal regulation is so extensive that state law is preempted. • In general, industry practices provide a benchmark for safety features for a product. Failure of a manufacturer to meet industry standards for safety is strong proof that the design of the product is defective. As with government regulations, however, adherence to industry standards does not ensure that a company will not be sued for a defective product design. • A manufacturer is liable to victims if it is negligent in manufacturing a product.
Strict Liability in Tort Has Been Imposed on Manufacturers and Sellers of Products; Damages for Defective Products Can Be Sizeable	• Because of the difficulty of proving negligence in manufacturing, product liability law only requires a showing that an injury-causing product was defective when sold. It is not necessary to show fault on the part of the seller as long as there is a showing of a connection between the product defect and the resulting harm to the plaintiff. *This is the strict liability standard.* • Section 402A of the *Restatement (Second) of Torts* is often used to define a product defect. • Section 402A applies to sellers as well as manufacturers. • Victims of defective products can sue for compensatory damages for wrongful death, including claims for pain and suffering, lost future income, fair market value of lost property, and punitive damages when there is a showing of intent or gross disregard for the safety of the public.
There Are Three Types of Product Defects: Manufacturing, Design, and Lack of Adequate Warnings; of the Three, Manufacturing Defects Are Potentially the Most Serious and Are the Subject of Many High-Profile Lawsuits Involving Class Actions	• There are three types of product defects: *manufacturing, design,* and *failure to warn.* • Manufacturing defects exist when a product does not conform to product specifications. • Design defects result if a manufacturer does not conform to government safety regulations or industry standards with regard to product design. Also, manufacturers are expected to design products so that there is a reasonable relationship between safety features and possible harm from use or misuse of products. • Courts make use of consumer expectations tests for both manufacturing and design defects. • Manufacturers have a duty to make products safe for foreseeable uses, even if the foreseeable use is not the use intended by the manufacturer. • Manufacturers have a duty to warn about hidden risks that they knew or should have known about on their products. Warnings must be reasonable and comprehensible to intended users. The reasonableness or adequacy of warnings depends on the severity of the risks, the intensity of the warnings, and the characteristics of intended users.
There Are a Number of Defenses Available to Sellers in Product Liability Cases Including	• Among the defenses available to manufacturers are *misuse* of the product, *ignoring of warnings,* and *assumption of risk.* These defenses frequently overlap one another other. When consumers misuse products they are frequently ignoring warnings, which means that they have assumed the risks of the possible resulting harm. • Other defenses available to manufacturers include *tampering, government contractor defense,* and *state-of-the-art* defense. • If a product is tampered with after it left the manufacturer, the manufacturer is not liable.

Product Misuse, Assumption of Risk, Tampering, Government Contractor, and State of the Art

- The same is true if the design of the product was dictated by the government.
- The state-of-the-art defense is not absolute, though in general manufacturers can successfully claim that they did not know of the risk because *no one* knew of the risk.

There Are Many Proposals for Reform of Product Liability Law; It Is Possible That Federal Law Will Be More Important in the Future of Product Liability Law

- Proposals for product liability reform focus on supplanting state law with federal law, eliminating joint and several liability, and placing caps on punitive damage awards.
- In the future, product liability law will be faced with a number of significant issues: will product liability continue to be governed by state law, or will it be supplanted by federal law, and what is the future of the state-of-the-art defense? If these issues were addressed, the uncertainty facing manufacturers would be significantly lessened.

Key Terms

attractive nuisance, *312*
comparative negligence, *314*
compensatory damages, *293*
contributory negligence, *314*
design defect, *317*
fraudulent misrepresentation (fraud), *304*
intentional tort, *294*

manufacturing defect, *317*
misuse, *322*
personal injury, *293*
privileged speech, *303*
product liability, *316*
proximate cause, *310*
punitive damages caps, *325*

punitive or exemplary damages, *294*
qualified privilege, *303*
strict liability, *315*
tampering, *324*
tort, *292*
wrongful death, *293*

Questions for Review and Analysis

1. Explain "intent" as used in tort law. Suppose the defendant in an intentional infliction of emotional distress case passed a lie detector test, answering no after being asked, "Did you intend to scare the plaintiff so badly that she had to quit her job?" after admitting that he put a snake in her desk. Why are the possibly sincere beliefs of the defendant not decisive on the issue of legal intent?

2. Explain how the *reasonable person test* is flexible and useable by juries in both "usual" and "unusual" factual situations.

3. Explain the difference between facts and opinions for purposes of demonstrating that a defendant is liable for fraud or defamation.

4. Explain why *industry practices* can be a defense in a claim based on negligence but not if the claim is based on strict liability. If everyone in the industry employs certain safeguards, is that always enough to satisfy a claim based on negligence? On strict liability?

5. Suppose you were representing a plaintiff in a product liability claim in which you claim that the design of the product was defective. In such cases, there are three benchmarks that are often used: (1) what other companies do, (2) compliance with applicable government regulations, and (3) the costs and benefits of alternative product designs. Would you tell your client, "Two out of three ain't bad," or that they had to win on all three factors or just one of the factors listed above?

If You Really Understood This Chapter, You Should Be Able to Provide Informed Commentary on the Following:

1. **Product Liability: Real and Perceived.** In 1992 Linda Hagen and her sister, Barbara Parker, drank from a can of Coke that both agreed tasted "flat." The ladies were drinking the Coke at night and held the bottle up to the light and both observed what they believed to be a used condom.

According to testimony, the ladies claimed that the condom they saw in the Coke had "oozy stringy stuff coming out of the top." Both ladies were extremely distress and nauseated, had to have tests for AIDS (which turned out negative), and sued the Coca-Cola Bottling Co. for negligence. Dr. Forrest Bayer, a beverage analyst hired by Coca-Cola, also said he first thought the object was a condom, but upon closer examination he concluded that the object was mold. Defendant contends that its investigation revealed that (1) there was not a condom in the Coke bottle and (2) there is no evidence that plaintiffs ingested anything unhealthy. The defendants filed a motion for a summary judgment to have the case dismissed. The plaintiffs are suing in part based on the emotional distress they suffered when they concluded the foreign object was in the bottle after each had taken a drink. If the evidence shows that there was a foreign object in the bottle, but not the one the plaintiffs perceived, should the plaintiffs be able to submit a case to a jury based on the emotional distress they incurred when they wrongly concluded that a used condom was in the bottle of Coca-Cola? [*Linda Hagen, et al. v. Coca-Cola Bottling Co., et al.,* 804 So. 2d 1234 (Fla. 2001).]

2. **Defamation: Factual Statement or Opinion.** Suppose that an attorney whose name was included in a directory was labeled an "ambulance chaser" and was interested only in "slam dunk cases." The directory, maintained by the American Association of University Women (AAUW), purported to be a directory of attorneys available to bring lawsuits based on gender discrimination. Of the 275 attorneys listings in the directory, only one, for Leonard Flamm was negative, quoting a client who attached the ambulance chaser label to Mr. Flamm. Flamm filed a defamation suit against the AAUW. The defendant AAUW filed a motion to dismiss claiming that the descriptions "ambulance chaser" and interested only in "slam dunk cases" are opinion statements and not a foundation for a defamation suit. If you were representing Mr. Flamm, how could you show that he was not an "ambulance chaser"? The court in this case ruled that for a plaintiff to maintain a defamation suit based on an issue of public concern, the plaintiff bore the burden of proving that that statements made about him were "provably false." Does "ambulance chaser" fall into that category? See *Leonard N. Flamm, Esq. v. American Association of University Women, et al.,* 201 F.3d 144 (2nd Cir. 2000).

3. **Seller's Liability for Ultrahazardous Activities.** It has been a rule of law for some time that disposal, storage, and treatment of hazardous waste is an ultrahazardous activity for which a strict liability standard is justified. The plaintiffs lived near a battery-recycling facility that handled battery acids and lead. Ultimately, the plaintiffs were harmed by lead contamination that was traced to the battery recycling facility. The plaintiffs settled with the battery recycling facility, but seek also to sue major suppliers of the battery recycling facility. The sellers contend that once they sold batteries to the recycling facility, they no longer had control over the batteries and therefore should not be liable. The sellers contend that gun manufacturers are not liable for the crimes committed with their products and therefore battery sellers should not be liable if a recycling center causes damage while processing their batteries. What do you think? [*Thompson v. Zero Bullet Co., Inc.,* 692 So. 2d 805 (Ala. 1997).]

4. **Design Defects and Federal Law.** Congress frequently passes statutes that affect safety, and a legal issue that often arises is whether a federal statute preempts common law product liability suits based on state law. In Pennsylvania, the plaintiff, Daniel Cellucci, suffered permanent brain injuries in an automobile accident. Through his attorney, plaintiff contends that the design of the 1986 Chevy Cavalier he was driving at the time of the accident was defective because it did not have an airbag. The plaintiff is proceeding with his lawsuit under the common law of the state of Pennsylvania, but the defendant, General Motors, files a motion for a summary judgment dismissal based on the National Traffic and Motor Vehicle Safety Act (Safety Act) of 1996. The Safety Act does not mandate air bags for all cars on the highway, but defendant claims that if this suit is allowed to proceed and it loses, state common law will be in conflict with the Safety Act. If Congress passes a Safety Act for motor vehicles and establishes a national regulatory agency (the National Highway Transportation Safety Administration (NHTSA)), is there any room for state common law product liability claims? [*Cellucci v. General Motors, Inc.,* 706 A.2d 806 (Pa. 1998).]

5. **Warnings, Warnings, Warnings.** An issue that could be raised is whether lawyers have been too successful, resulting in an excessive number of warnings, especially for pharmaceutical drugs.

The typical over-the-counter drug is loaded with fine-print labels that warn against taking various drugs if the user is old, young, or pregnant; has certain medical histories; or is taking various other drugs. For prescription drugs, often the warnings are even more voluminous and written in language that can be incomprehensible to those without medical training. If there are a few precautions that users of certain drugs should take, can the manufacturers of those drugs afford to focus on those dangers so that drug labels do not get cluttered with too many, largely irrelevant warnings? Do the real dangers associated with certain drugs get lost in a glut of warnings that only affect a very few people? Should Congress authorize the FDA to write labels for sellers of pharmaceutical drugs so that the warnings cannot be attacked as being inadequate?

6. **Defamation, Invasion of Privacy, and Intentional Infliction of Emotional Distress.** A tabloid newspaper, the *Sun,* owned by Globe International, Inc., admitted that it asked its "reporters" to use a *TOH* approach to writing its stories. TOH stands for "top of the head," which refers to a technique of "journalism" that involves showing a reporter a picture and asking him or her to make up a story about the picture. In this particular case, a reporter for the *Sun* was shown a picture of a 96-year-old woman carrying newspapers and the story that came into the reporter's head was that the woman quits her paper route because she becomes pregnant at 101. The article recounts an alleged incident with a "reclusive millionaire" that led to the pregnancy. Nellie Mitchell, the woman in the photograph, in fact delivered papers for a small newspaper located in Mountain Home, Arkansas, but, needless to say, she did not quit her paper route because she became pregnant at 101. On behalf of Ms. Mitchell, who had died in the interim, People's Bank sued Globe International and the *Sun* newspaper for defamation, invasion of privacy by placing Ms. Mitchell in a false light, and intentional infliction of emotional distress. The jury found for Ms. Mitchell in the amounts of $650,000 for compensatory damages and $850,000 for punitive damages. The Globe appeals each of these verdicts. Which of these claims do you think survived appeals? Explain why. [*People's Bank & Trust Co. v. Globe International, Inc.,* 786 F. Supp. 791 (W.D. Ark.1992).]

Social Responsibility and Ethics in a High-Tech World

7. **State-of-the-Art Defense.** As technology advances, many of the products introduced into the stream of commerce are very complicated and can have consequences that are discovered only long after the products are used. For medical products in particular, long-term effects cannot be known with perfect certainty. Pharmaceutical drugs must pass rigorous screening by the Food and Drug Administration before being sold and, yet, unforeseen injurious consequences still can occur. The results can be personally devastating, including such disasters as birth defects, infertility, and higher rates of cancer. When juries see the devastating impact of drug-caused injuries, damage awards are likely to be very significant. A long-term consequence is that, in areas where damages are likely to be great (as has been the case with fertility and contraception drugs), research by pharmaceutical firms will be aborted for fear of lawsuits. Does it make sense to insulate the design of pharmaceutical drugs from legal challenges if they have been approved by the FDA and there is no evidence that the company seeking approval for the drug has withheld adverse information from the FDA? Do high-tech companies have a duty to anticipate the future, even though scientific opinion at the time does not indicate unforeseen injurious side effects? It has been noted that RU 486, the newest birth control product introduced in U.S. markets, was developed by European companies and that no U.S. company has introduced new birth control products in over 20 years.

Using the Internet to Your Advantage

1. There are a number of Internet websites that investigate the costs of the U.S. tort system. Most of these websites are critical of the high costs of transferring assets (from defendants to plaintiffs) through tort law. A study of U.S. and Illinois tort claims was conducted by Northern Illinois University and is reported at http://www.icjl.org/data2/niu.htm. The America Tort Reform Association (http://www.atra.org/) maintains a website that lists state-by-state tort reform efforts. Of course, there are those who think that the U.S. tort system is working just fine. The Association of Trial Lawyers of America maintains a website (http://www.atlanet.org/homepage/trmp1028.htm) that is currently touting a "triumph" by U.S. consumers over recent attempts by the National Association of Manufacturers, insurers, and the tobacco companies to reform the tort system in ways that limit rights of victims to pursue legal remedies. The pro-business research group, the

Cato Institute (http://www.cato.org), begins its analysis of the tort system with the following contention: "By all reasonable measures, the American tort system is a disaster." Their recommendations for reform of the tort system are presented at http://www.cato.org/pubs/regulation/reg19n1e.html.

2. A number of government agencies deal with products that are the subject of product liability litigation. The Consumer Product Safety Commission (http://www.cpsc.gov) maintains a website that seeks reports of what consumers consider unsafe products. Of course, the Federal Trade Commission (http://www.ftc.gov) has a large stake in rooting out consumer fraud and unfair and deceptive trade practices that frequently become the subject of tort suits. Also, the Food and Drug Administration (http://www.fda.gov) has responsibility for the safety of food additives and pharmaceutical drugs that have been at issue in many lawsuits.

3. Views about individual torts create their own interest groups. FindLaw offers an excellent article about "Defamation Claims by Fired Employees" at http://articles.corporate.findlaw.com/articles/file/00088/001929/title/subject/topic/labor%20%20employment%20law_employment/filname/laboremploymentlaw_3_60. The state of Massachusetts maintains a website (http://www.lawlib.state.ma.us/aboutsexharass.htm) that provides information to victims of intentional infliction of emotional distress and harassment. Of course, there are numerous websites that provide useful information about abridgements of privacy. The Electronic Frontier Foundation (http://www.eff.org/) provides a scoreboard for recent legislative and legal actions concerning privacy.

Chapter Eleven

Cybertorts, Privacy, and Government Regulation

Learning Objectives

On completing this chapter, you should

1. Be familiar with how the concepts of torts of defamation and invasion of privacy are applied in cyberspace.
2. Understand the impact of the Communications Decency Act on defamation suits against ISPs.
3. Be familiar with the activities of the Federal Trade Commission in policing the Internet to guard against unfair and deceptive trade practices that compromise privacy in cyberspace.
4. Be able to discuss reasonable expectations of privacy on the Internet.
5. Know the statutory protection that has recently been enacted to safeguard privacy in cyberspace.

OVERVIEW

Chapter 10 provided coverage of basic tort law and an array of mostly "traditional" applications of tort law. The recent explosive growth of electronic interconnectedness and e-commerce creates a large volume of new potential tort exposures. With increasing dependence on electronic links for the conduct of communications and business transactions, the impact of many torts, especially defamation and invasions of privacy, is likely to be much more devastating. New technologies have created new and novel methods of storing and communicating important information, simultaneously creating opportunities for new ways of intruding on the privacy of such information—hence, on the rights of individuals—an invitation for tort claims.

From basic and traditional tort law, we know that businesses have broad concerns for tort liability for defamation, both written and oral. This chapter begins with an extension of our knowledge regarding defamation in a wired world, then continues with an array of new and novel applications of privacy law, necessitated by modern cyberworld developments. The chapter concludes with a discussion of the recent increases in government regulation of Internet communications affecting children, medical records, and financial records. More legislation is likely as complaints of electronic snooping continue to grow louder.

DEFAMATION AND THE INTERNET

defamation
A false statement, spoken or written, that causes harm.

By way of review, defamation requires a showing by the plaintiff that the defendant

1. Made untrue statements
2. That were published or reproduced in some way and
3. Harmed the reputation of the plaintiff.
4. If the plaintiff is a public figure and the defendant is the media, the plaintiff must *also* show that the defendant knew the statements made were false or else had a reckless disregard for the truth.

The fourth element, applicable when the defendant is the media and the plaintiff is a public figure or official, is called *malice*. Legal malice in defamation law does not mean that the plaintiff must show that the defendant hated the plaintiff or bore him ill will. The requirement to show malice in defamation cases is merely that the defendant had no basis for making the statements, because either he knew the statements were false or did not make customary checks as to the veracity of the statements.

Computer-based electronic communication (particularly e-mail) has become an integral component of communication and information transmission throughout the world. Also, websites and electronic bulletin boards are accessible throughout the planet. This form of communication allows the cheap, efficient, and nearly instantaneous transport of information to any website or computer in the world. Because of the computerization of information, communication torts such as defamation, invasions of privacy, and copyright violations (discussed in Chapter 14) have much more serious consequences.

Liability for Republication and Distribution of Defamatory Material

Publisher Liability

According to the *Restatement (Second) of Torts,* "one who repeats or otherwise republishes defamatory matter *is subject to liability as if he had originally published it*" [emphasis added]. Hence, when defamatory material is duplicated by the media, there is a potential for newspapers, journals, and magazines to face tort liability for printed information. The public policy view behind this allocation of liability is that publishers scrutinize the content of what they publish, choosing content with an eye to sales and profits so, therefore, it is entirely legitimate that they also bear responsibility for publishing defamatory materials. That is, since publishers have the opportunity to know and control the content of the material being published, they also have a duty to avoid the publication of defamatory information and are subject to the same liability for defamation as the original authors of that information.

Distributor Liability

On the other hand, liability for defamation has typically not been imposed on distributors of written documents such as newsstands, bookstores, and other sales outlets, or on libraries. Distributors are clearly distinct from publishers. If their duty to be liable for the content of what they are distributing were the same as that of publishers, it would severely reduce freedom of expression. Distributors of books, including newsstands and libraries, simply do not have the resources to examine the content of all of the materials they distribute and, furthermore, they do not have the legal right to control book content. So, imposing such a burden would curtail the distribution of written materials, resulting in a severe abridgement of First Amendment protection of freedom of expression and the press.

Liability of Bookstores versus Publishers

In *Smith v. California,* the U.S. Supreme Court considered the case of a bookstore that was convicted of violating a Los Angeles city ordinance that outlawed possession of obscene writings or books.[1] Note that this 1959 case does not deal with defamation but, instead, with the issue of whether a bookstore is subject to the same liabilities as a publisher for carrying obscene materials or whether a distinction between the two is made.

In the *Smith* case, the book at issue was one of many thousands for sale in the defendant bookstore and no evidence indicated that the bookstore owner or other personnel had reviewed the book. Upon consideration of the obscenity ordinance at issue, the Supreme Court reasoned that "by dispensing with any requirement of knowledge of the contents of the book on the part of the seller, the ordinance tends to impose a severe limitation on the public's access to constitutionally protected matter." Since it is unreasonable to expect a bookstore owner/operator to review and be familiar with everything a bookstore sells, the ordinance would impede the sales of all books, both obscene and not obscene.

Based on the First Amendment, the Supreme Court overturned the conviction of the bookstore and, through its opinion, endorsed the application of a clear distinction between publishers and distributors that extends to determining defamation liability. Based on this distinction, *distributors* of written works that contain *defamatory* content are shielded from liability unless they know or should have known (have reason to know) of the defamatory content of the work(s) they have sold. Courts have continued to rely on this distinction as they have been confronted with defamation claims stemming from Internet messaging, as Case 11-1 illustrates.

[1] *Smith v. State of California,* 361 U.S. 147 (1959).

Case 11-1

Cubby, Inc. v. Compuserve Inc.

United States District Court for the Southern District of New York 776 F. Supp. 135 (S.D.N.Y. 1991)

FACTS AND CASE BACKGROUND

CompuServe develops and provides computer-related products and services, including CompuServe Information Service ("CIS"), an on-line general information service or "electronic library" . . . Subscribers . . . have access to over 150 special interest "forums," which are comprised of electronic bulletin boards, interactive online conferences, and topical databases.

One forum available is the Journalism Forum . . . Cameron Communications, Inc. ("CCI"), which is independent of CompuServe, has contracted to "manage, review, create, delete, edit and otherwise control the contents" of the Journalism Forum "in accordance with editorial and technical standards and conventions of style as established by CompuServe." [Citations omitted]

One publication available as part of the Journalism Forum is Rumorville USA ("Rumorville"), a daily newsletter that provides reports about broadcast journalism and journalists. Rumorville is published by Don Fitzpatrick Associates of San Francisco ("DFA"), which is headed by defendant

Don Fitzpatrick. CompuServe has no employment, contractual, or other direct relationship with either DFA or Fitzpatrick; DFA provides Rumorville to the Journalism Forum under a contract with CCI. The contract between CCI and DFA provides that DFA "accepts total responsibility for the contents" of Rumorville. The contract also requires CCI to limit access to Rumorville to those CIS subscribers who have previously made membership arrangements directly with DFA.

CompuServe has no opportunity to review Rumorville's contents before DFA uploads it into CompuServe's computer banks, from which it is immediately available to approved CIS subscribers . . . Compuserve maintains that, before this action was filed, it had no notice of any complaints about the contents of the Rumorville publication or about DFA.

Opinion by Leisure, District Judge

A. THE APPLICABLE STANDARD OF LIABILITY

* * *

Ordinarily, "'one who repeats or otherwise republishes defamatory matter is subject to liability as if he had originally published it.'"[Citations omitted] With respect to entities such as news vendors, book stores, and libraries, however, "New York courts have long held that vendors and distributors of defamatory publications are not liable if they neither know nor have reason to know of the defamation."

The requirement that a distributor must have knowledge of the contents of a publication before liability can be imposed for distributing that publication is deeply rooted in the First Amendment, made applicable to the states through the Fourteenth Amendment. "The constitutional guarantees of the freedom of speech and of the press stand in the way of imposing" strict liability on distributors for the contents of the reading materials they carry. In *Smith,* the Court struck down an ordinance that imposed liability on a bookseller for possession of an obscene book, regardless of whether the bookseller had knowledge of the book's contents. The Court reasoned that

> "Every bookseller would be placed under an obligation to make himself aware of the contents of every book in his shop. It would be altogether unreasonable to demand so near an approach to omniscience." And the bookseller's burden would become the public's burden, for by restricting him the public's access to reading matter would be restricted. If the contents of bookshops and periodical stands were restricted to material of which their proprietors had made an inspection, they might be depleted indeed.

* * *

With respect to the Rumorville publication, the undisputed facts are that DFA uploads the text of Rumorville into CompuServe's data banks and makes it available to approved CIS subscribers instantaneously. [Footnotes deleted] CompuServe has no more editorial control over such a publication than does a public library, book store, or newsstand, and it would be no more feasible for CompuServe to examine every publication it carries for potentially defamatory statements than it would be for any other distributor to do so.

* * *

Technology is rapidly transforming the information industry. A computerized database is the functional equivalent of a more traditional news vendor, and the inconsistent application of a lower standard of liability to an electronic news distributor such as CompuServe than that which is applied to a public library, book store, or newsstand would impose an undue burden on the free flow of information. Given the relevant First Amendment considerations, the appropriate standard of liability to be applied to CompuServe is whether it knew or had reason to know of the allegedly defamatory Rumorville statements.

* * *

Decision and Outcome

The court granted CompuServe's motion for summary judgment because it ruled that an ISP was to be treated as a distributor and not as a publisher. Hence, the court ruled, CompuServe was not liable for defamation unless it knew, or should have known, that the material displayed in Rumorville was defamatory.

Questions for Analysis

1. What is the standard of liability for libel? What three things must the plaintiff show in order to recover?
2. What is the difference in liability for libel among authors, publishers, and distributors? In this case, is the court saying that it pays for an ISP to be deliberately ignorant of what is taking place in its chat rooms and forums?

ISPs
Internet service providers such as AOL, Yahoo!, a university web-server system, and so forth that are generally treated as *distributors* of publications rather than as *publishers*.

In marked contrast to the decision rendered in Case 11-1, in 1995 a New York Supreme Court held in *Stratton Oakmont, Inc. v. Prodigy Service* that an **ISP** *was* liable for defamatory materials that appeared on a bulletin board it sponsored.[2] In an effort to distinguish itself from other ISPs, Prodigy marketed itself as a family-oriented ISP. The court in the *Stratton* case ruled that, since Prodigy advertised that it reviewed content that it displayed on its server, it was thus lumped in with other publishers. As a result of the *Stratton* case, the apparent consequence of supervising the content of what appears on its server is that an ISP *would be liable* for defamatory material that appears on bulletin boards it purports to supervise.

In the aftermath of the *Stratton* decision, there appeared to be serious potential consequences for ISPs, associated with the supervision of content reproduced on their servers. Many organizations, including most universities, maintain their own servers and, so, are ISPs. For a time, in the aftermath of the *Stratton* decision, universities made it clear that they *did not supervise* the content of what appeared on web space they make available on their servers for faculty, staff, or members. Their fears were allayed by the passage of the Communications Decency Act and the defamation case decisions that have taken place since its passage.

The Communications Decency Act (CDA) of 1996

When powerful interests are exposed to unforeseen legal liability, Congress has been known to come to their rescue. In no small way, the chink in the armor of Internet service providers exposed by the 1995 *Stratton* decision sped enactment of the *Communications Decency Act (CDA) of 1996,* which was aimed at undoing the chilling effect on editorial control by ISPs.[3] As a result of the *Stratton* decision, ISPs that censored objectionable (generally pornographic but also racially offensive) material from their members exposed themselves to additional liability if some remaining materials were defamatory. The CDA trumped this court decision by exempting ISPs from state common law defamation claims, regardless of whether the ISP advertises that it reviews content.

Internet Service Providers

With a clear intent of protecting ISPs from defamation suits, Congress in Section 230(C) of the CDA, decreed that no "provider or user of an interactive computer service shall be treated as the publisher or speaker of any information provided by another information content provider." In the CDA, ISPs are referred to as "interactive computer service" providers. In this provision, Congress rejected the notion of classifying ISPs as *publishers* in the event of defamation claims. The CDA provides immunity from liability for defamation if an ISP has policies and practices directed toward restricting the Internet publication of materials the ISP viewed as obscene, lewd, lascivious, filthy, excessively violent, harassing, or otherwise objectionable, whether or not such material is constitutionally protected by the First Amendment.

[2] 1995 N.Y. Misc. LEXIS 712 (1995).
[3] Pub. L. No. 104-104, codified at 47 U.S.C. § 230.

State Defamation Laws Are Preempted

The CDA, which is a federal statute, also explicitly preempts inconsistent state laws that provide the foundation for defamation suits. As a result of the CDA, an ISP will not be punished by being subjected to possible defamation suits if the ISP tries to clean up content on its server. Case 11-2 is illustrative of that principle.

Case 11-2

Kenneth M. Zeran v. America Online, Inc.

United States Court of Appeals for the Fourth Circuit
129 F.3d 327 (4th Cir. 1997)

FACTS AND CASE BACKGROUND

In this case, an unidentified person posted a message on an AOL bulletin board advertising "Naughty Oklahoma T-Shirts." The posting described the sale of shirts featuring offensive and tasteless slogans related to the April 19, 1995, bombing of the Alfred P. Murrah Federal Building in Oklahoma City. Those interested in purchasing the shirts were instructed to call "Ken" at Zeran's home phone number in Seattle, Washington. As a result of this . . . prank, Zeran received a high volume of calls, comprised primarily of angry and derogatory messages, but also including death threats. Zeran could not change his phone number because he relied on its availability to the public in running his business out of his home . . . Zeran called AOL and informed a company representative of his predicament. The employee assured Zeran that the posting would be removed from AOL's bulletin board . . . The parties dispute the date that AOL removed this original posting from its bulletin board.

Over the next four days, an unidentified party continued to post messages on AOL's bulletin board, advertising additional items including bumper stickers and key chains with still more offensive slogans. During this time period, Zeran called AOL repeatedly and was told by company representatives that the individual account from which the messages were posted would soon be closed. Zeran also reported his case to Seattle FBI agents. By April 30, Zeran was receiving an abusive phone call approximately every two minutes.

Zeran first filed suit on January 4, 1996, against radio station KRXO in the United States District Court for the Western District of Oklahoma. On April 23, 1996, he filed this separate suit against AOL in the same court. Zeran did not bring any action against the party who posted the offensive messages. After Zeran's suit against AOL was transferred to the Eastern District of Virginia, AOL answered Zeran's complaint and interposed 47 U.S.C. § 230 as an affirmative defense. AOL then moved for judgment on the pleadings pursuant to Federal Rules of Civil Procedure. The district court granted AOL's motion, and Zeran filed this appeal.

Opinion by Wilkinson, Chief Judge

I. "The Internet is an international network of interconnected computers," currently used by approximately 40 million people worldwide. [Citations omitted] One of the many means by which individuals access the Internet is through an interactive computer service. These services offer not only a connection to the Internet as a whole, but also allow their subscribers to access information communicated and stored only on each computer service's individual proprietary network. AOL is just such an interactive computer service. Much of the information transmitted over its network originates with the company's millions of subscribers. They may transmit information privately via electronic mail, or they may communicate publicly by posting messages on AOL bulletin boards, where the messages may be read by any AOL subscriber.

* * *

II. A. Because § 230 was successfully advanced by AOL in the district court as a defense to Zeran's claims, we shall briefly examine its operation here. Zeran seeks to hold AOL liable for defamatory speech initiated by a third party. He argued to the district court that once he notified AOL of the unidentified third party's hoax, AOL had a duty to remove the defamatory posting promptly, to notify its subscribers of the message's false nature, and to effectively screen future defamatory material. Section 230 entered this litigation as an affirmative defense pled by AOL. The company claimed that Congress immunized interactive computer service providers from claims based on information posted by a third party. The relevant portion of § 230 states: "No provider or user of an interactive computer service shall be treated as the publisher or speaker of any information provided by another information content provider." By its plain language, § 230 creates a federal immunity to any cause of action that would make service providers liable for information originating with a third-party user of the service. Specifically, § 230 precludes courts from entertaining claims that would place a computer service provider in a publisher's role. Thus, lawsuits seeking to hold a service provider liable for its exercise of a publisher's traditional editorial functions—such as deciding whether to publish, withdraw, postpone or alter content—are barred.

The purpose of this statutory immunity is not difficult to discern. Congress recognized the threat that tort-based lawsuits pose to freedom of speech in the new and burgeoning Internet medium. The imposition of tort liability on service providers for the communications of others represented, for Congress, simply another form of intrusive government regulation of speech. Section 230 was enacted, in part, to maintain the robust nature of Internet communication and, accordingly, to keep government interference in the medium to a minimum. In specific statutory findings, Congress recognized the Internet and interactive computer services as offering "a forum for a true diversity of political discourse, unique opportunities for cultural development, and myriad avenues for intellectual activity." It also found that the Internet and interactive computer services "have flourished, to the benefit of all Americans, *with a minimum of government regulation*." Congress further stated that it is "the policy of the United States . . . to preserve the vibrant and competitive free market that presently exists for the Internet and other interactive computer services, *unfettered by Federal or State regulation*."

* * *

Section 230 . . . plainly immunizes computer service providers like AOL from liability for information that originates with third parties. Furthermore, Congress clearly expressed its intent that § 230 apply to lawsuits, like Zeran's, instituted after the CDA's enactment. Accordingly, we affirm the judgment of the district court.

Decision and Outcome

The court ruled that Section 230 of the CDA immunizes ISPs from liability for defamatory material that originates from third parties as long as the ISP did not contribute to the content of the material.

Questions for Analysis

1. Does it now appear that an ISP is a "publisher" or a "distributor"?
2. What impact does the *Zeran* case have on courts' reliance of a distinction between "publishers" and "distributors" in defamation liability cases?
3. Does an ISP have a strong incentive to police the content on its servers? Explain why or why not.
4. As an individual or business owner subject to Internet defamation, whom would you sue? What are your chances for recovery?

Who Qualifies as an Interactive Computer Service?

Current court interpretation of the CDA appears to free ISPs from liability in defamation suits, even if they have knowledge of the defamatory material, unless the ISP itself is the information content creator. In light of this standard, there are distinct advantages to firms that qualify as an "interactive computer service" within the meaning of the CDA. This is particularly true since employers are common targets for ex-employees who accuse them of defamation. By qualifying as an ISP, employers have been able to use the CDA as a defense when ex-employees have claimed that defamatory material was published on company servers.

International Perspective

The fact that U.S. law under the CDA exempts ISPs from most liability associated with republishing defamatory material does not resolve the issue of ISP liability for defamation. A businessman in Australia alleges he was defamed by the Dow Jones and Co. based on an article that appeared in the business periodical *Barron's* and on the Internet. The highest court in Australia refused to dismiss the case. The defendant, Dow Jones Co., claims that if this suit can go forward, it is possible that it will be liable for defamation [suits in locales spanning the globe] from Afghanistan to Zimbabwe. The fact that the Internet is a worldwide [communications vehicle] may make actions that were formerly local now carry worldwide legal liability throughout 190, and counting, nations.

LANDMARK RULING IN INTERNET CASE

SYDNEY, Australia, Dec. 10, 2002

The court dismissed Dow Jones' contention that it would have to consider the defamation laws from "Afghanistan to Zimbabwe" in every article published on the Internet.

In a landmark case, Australia's highest court on Tuesday gave a businessman the right to sue for defamation in Australia over an article published in the United States and posted on the Internet.

Analysts suggest the ruling against international news service Dow Jones & Co.—the first by a nation's top court to deal with cross-border Internet

defamation—could set a precedent and affect publishers and Web sites that post articles in the 190 nations that allow defamation cases.

"This is a significant ruling in that it could push publishers into having to consider every conceivable defamation law in the world before posting something online," said **CBSNews.com Legal Analyst Andrew Cohen.** "On the other hand, it still is enormously difficult to collect upon a foreign judgment even if these Internet plaintiffs win, so the news isn't all that dire for online sites."

The High Court of Australia unanimously dismissed an appeal by Dow Jones & Co. aimed at stopping a defamation suit in Australia by mining magnate Joseph Gutnick.

Gutnick claimed that a 7,000-word article that had appeared in *Barron's* in October 2000 portrayed him as a schemer given to stock scams, money laundering and fraud. The article was also published online.

The decision means Gutnick can sue New York–based Dow Jones & Co. in his home state of Victoria, in Australia.

Dow Jones & Co., which publishes *The Wall Street Journal, Barron's,* Dow Jones Newswires and several stock market indicators, said it was disappointed with the ruling and promised to continue its defense.

Source: "Landmark Ruling in Internet Case, Sydney, Australia," December 10, 2002, CBS News Archives. Copyright © 2002 CBS News. Reprinted with permission.

Application of the CDA to Those That Recommend Stocks

Suppose that an ISP hosts a stock recommendation service that it outsourced to third parties. Suppose further that the third parties made mistakes that defamed a publicly traded company and harmed its market value. Should an ISP be liable under Section 230 of the Communications Decency Act for misquotes from an investors' service firm that is provided space [published] by the ISP? Applying the same logic as was used in the *Zeran* case, the Tenth Circuit Federal court of Appeals answered "no" and exonerated America Online in a case focusing on this issue.[4]

Application to Online Reporters and ISPs

One of the intense disagreements that occurred during the Clinton-Lewinsky scandal was that between an online reporter, Matt Drudge, and members of Clinton's staff. The *Drudge Report* first broke the news that President Clinton was intimately involved with Monica Lewinsky, a White House intern. Members of Clinton's staff denigrated the accuracy of the *Drudge Report* and refused to answer questions about issues it raised. Sidney Blumenthal,

---

[4] *Ben Ezra, Weinstein and Co. v. America Online,* 206 F.3d 980 (10th Cir. 2000).

assistant to the president and a former reporter himself, became a target of the *Drudge Report* when Drudge alleged Blumenthal had beaten his wife. Blumenthal, a public figure, not only sued Matt Drudge but also sued America Online (AOL), an ISP that advertised the availability of the *Drudge Report* on its server and paid Drudge money for the online hits it generated. In *Blumenthal v. Drudge,* the trial court granted a motion for summary judgment filed by AOL contending that, as an ISP, it had no liability for what appeared in the *Drudge Report.*[5]

INVASIONS OF PRIVACY IN CYBERSPACE

Overview

Threats to personal privacy in cyberspace originate from two sources: the government and other private individuals, mainly businesses that operate websites and sell software. In the wake of the September 11, 2001, attacks, demands for greater government powers, especially over the Internet, are increasing. The federal government has been given greater authority to investigate criminal activity under the USA PATRIOT Act, which modified the Electronic Communications Privacy Act, as discussed below. Since this is a tort chapter, the main discussion of the USA PATRIOT Act is provided not here, but in Chapter 22, which deals with cybercrime issues.

Constitutional Protection of Privacy

Americans have always had a high regard for privacy. Arguably, one of the critical factors igniting the revolution against England was the lack of respect for privacy of the colonials shown by authorities answering to the king of England. Certainly, the Fourth Amendment to the Constitution reflects the pervasive fear that colonial Americans had of government—in the case of this Amendment, that they would be subjected to unreasonable searches and seizures.

The text of the Fourth Amendment reads as follows:

> The right of the people to be secure in their persons, houses, papers, and effects, against unreasonable searches and seizures, shall not be violated, and no Warrants shall issue, but upon probable cause, supported by Oath or affirmation, and particularly describing the place to be searched, and the persons or things to be seized.

State Common Law Protection of Privacy

As discussed in the previous chapter, tort common law provides protection from various types of invasions of privacy. Since it is common law, state protections of privacy vary from state to state. In many states there are four actions that constitute tortious invasions of privacy:

1. Intrusion upon the plaintiff's seclusion or solitude or into his private affairs.
2. Public disclosure of embarrassing private facts about the plaintiff.
3. Publicity that places the plaintiff in a false light in the public eye.
4. Appropriation, for the defendant's advantage, of the plaintiff's name or likeness.

The last is really a *taking* of the right of publicity, while the first three actions define what most of us think of as invasions of privacy.

Reasonable Expectation of Privacy (from Governmental Action)

On the government intrusions front, the Fourth Amendment indicates that people have *reasonable expectations of privacy* with respect to themselves, their houses, and their papers and effects. If the government is going to search or seize a person, paper, or a house in the

---

[5] 992 F. Supp. 44 (D.D.C.1998).

United States, the Fourth Amendment requires the governmental authority to obtain a search warrant. In order to get a search warrant, governmental authorities must show "probable cause" that a crime has been committed before a neutral magistrate or judge. **Probable cause** is shown when the police officer or other governmental official seeking a search warrant reveals evidence that makes it *more likely than not* that a crime has taken place. The Fourth Amendment also requires that search warrants be reasonably specific. Of course, there are a number of exceptions to the Fourth Amendment, such as when police officers are in hot pursuit of an alleged criminal and there is a substantial threat that the criminal will destroy evidence of a crime.

probable cause
Evidence that indicates that it is more likely than not that a crime has been committed.

Electronic Communications Privacy Act 1986[6]

The Electronic Communications Privacy Act (ECPA) amended Title III of the Omnibus Crime Control and Safe Streets Act of 1968 that was passed in the aftermath of a Supreme Court decision holding that electronic wiretaps of telephone conversations were, indeed, *searches* that were subject to the Fourth Amendment's protections.[7] So, when two people are having a telephone conversation, there is a reasonable expectation that the conversation is private. For the government to record such conversations, *it is required to obtain search warrants*. The ECPA was designed to add privacy protection to radio paging devices, e-mail, cellular telephones, private communication carriers, and computer transmissions. There are, however, a number of important employer-related exceptions to the ECPA that will be discussed in Chapter 16.

Coverage of the ECPA   The ECPA extends the protections (from governmental monitoring) of the Omnibus Crime Control and Safe Streets Act to

- E-mail, cellular telephones, radio paging devices, private communication carriers, and computer transmissions.
- Both storage and transmission of digitized textual information (email) and voice mail.
- Customer records of electronic service providers.

To intercept or view any of the above without permission of the other parties involved, federal law enforcement officials must obtain a search warrant. Obtaining a search warrant is no small feat, with courts unwilling to casually issue broad search warrants for the FBI to intercept a lot of electronic communications for *possible* violations of criminal law. The ECPA also prohibits providers of *electronic communication services,* including ISPs, from disclosing contents of communications that have been stored without lawful consent of the person who originated the communication. Although the ECPA was primarily designed to define boundaries for law enforcement, it also made private wiretaps and interception of electronic communication a federal crime. Because of the ECPA, it is a federal crime for someone to intercept your cell phone conversations.

The ECPA also restricts government access to subscriber and customer records belonging to electronic service providers, including ISPs. In order to obtain customer records, the government must obtain a search warrant, a court order, or an authorized administrative or grand jury subpoena to access service provider records without first notifying a subscriber or customer.

Criticism of the ECPA   Critics of the ECPA maintain that its provisions make it too easy for the FBI and other law enforcement agencies to obtain customer records from ISPs. A demand for such records can be issued, accompanied by a statement certifying that the

---

[6] Pub. L. No. 99-508, codified at 18 U.S.C. §§ 2510–2521.
[7] *Katz v. The United States*, 386 U.S. 954 (1967).

information sought pertains to an investigation of foreign counterintelligence operation and that the targeted ISP is authorized to hand over customer records without judicial review. The ECPA also increases the number of federal crimes for which wiretaps on telephones and other interceptions of electronic communications are authorized. The USA PATRIOT Act (discussed in Chapter 22), makes additional inroads into the protections supposedly provided by the ECPA from government intrusions on the Internet.

Carnivore

Carnivore
An FBI software program used to snoop into e-mail and other Internet communications.

The threats to personal privacy posed by governmental action are ongoing in cyberspace, especially in the wake of September 11, 2001. One of the most controversial tools used by the government is **Carnivore,** a software program developed by the Federal Bureau of Investigation (FBI). Carnivore makes use of "packet sniffing," which is a means of marking all packets of information that contain words such as "bomb," "biological agents," and other suspicious terms. Carnivore is normally directed toward all the email that originates or is received by an ISP, such as AOL or Mindspring. In effect, Carnivore "eats" every email transmission from an ISP and "spits" out all those that do not contain suspicious words such as "bomb." Targets of Carnivore include terrorists, child pornographers, and those engaged in fraud. Although there is a potential for abuse, the use of Carnivore is limited by the Electronic Communications Privacy Act. Critics are not satisfied with assurances that the inappropriate use of Carnivore has been and will be held in check.

In the aftermath of September 11, 2001, it is reasonable to expect additional governmental inroads into privacy, both in the real world and in cyberspace. Intelligence reports suggest that the September 11 terrorists made extensive use of the Internet in coordinating their plans. Government use of Carnivore and other snooping tools in cyberspace can likely be expected to increase in the future.

Reasonable Expectation of Privacy (from Intrusions by Private Parties)

In discussing objectionable invasions of privacy by private parties, courts again have relied on the constitutional law concept of *reasonable expectation of privacy* that has long been used to define the scope of the Fourth Amendment. Courts apply this standard when evaluating whether actions by private entities are tortious because they subject individuals to unreasonable intrusions into their solitude or private affairs.[8] Of course, actions that are deemed tortious can empower victims to sue for invasion of privacy.

In the physical world, people have a reasonable expectation of privacy when they go to the bathroom. A hidden camera in a bathroom would be regarded as an invasion of privacy. The same applies to conversations with doctors, psychiatrists, and financial counselors; people expect these conversations to remain confidential. On the other hand, if a person can be observed naked from a location in which the photographer is not trespassing or using a telescopic lens, that person cannot object when his or her bare derriere is displayed in a tabloid.

In the cyberworld, opportunities for intrusions into private affairs are magnified. Case 11-3 illustrates the perils of giving out information to ISPs. In general, unencrypted information distributed over the Internet is vulnerable to interception or unintended secondary use. The case makes it clear that the Internet is not a place where a person should have a reasonable expectation of privacy unless the recipient of information provided has promised not to disclose that information. Note, further, that the defendant in this case tried to make use of the Electronic Communications Privacy Act to block introduction into a criminal trial evidence obtained from the customer records of an ISP.

---

[8] Common law torts of invasion of privacy were discussed in some detail in Chapter 10.

Case 11-3

United States of America v. Scott M. Hambrick

U.S. District Court for the Western District of Virginia
55 F. Supp. 2d 504 (W. D. Va. 1999)

FACTS AND CASE BACKGROUND

Scott Hambrick sought to suppress information obtained by the government in a criminal prosecu-
tion. Mr. Hambrick claims his Fourth Amendment rights were violated because personal information
was obtained from his Internet service provider (ISP). Mr. Hambrick disclosed information to the ISP
(MindSpring) including his Internet surf name, Blowuinva. The implication of this case is that infor-
mation revealed to one party in connection with an Internet transaction can be obtained by the gov-
ernment as long as it has a search warrant.

Opinion by James H. Michael Jr., Judge

Although Congress is willing to recognize that individuals have some degree of privacy in the stored
data and transactional records that their ISPs retain, the ECPA is hardly a legislative determination
that this expectation of privacy is one that rises to the level of "reasonably objective" for Fourth
Amendment purposes. Despite its concern for privacy, Congress did not provide for suppression
where a party obtains stored data or transactional records in violation of the Act. Additionally, the
ECPA's concern for privacy extends only to government invasions of privacy. ISPs are free to turn
stored data and transactional records over to nongovernmental entities. [Citations omitted.] ("[A]
provider of electronic communication service or remote computing service may disclose a record or
other information pertaining to a subscriber to or customer of such service . . . to any person other
than a governmental entity."). For Fourth Amendment purposes, this court does not find that the
ECPA has legislatively determined that an individual has a reasonable expectation of privacy in his
name, address, social security number, credit card number, and proof of Internet connection. The fact
that the ECPA does not proscribe turning over such information to private entities buttresses the conclusion that the ECPA does not create a reasonable expectation of privacy in that information. This,
however, does not end the court's inquiry. This court must determine, within the constitutional framework that the Supreme Court has established, whether Mr. Hambrick's subjective expectation of privacy is one that society is willing to recognize.

* * *

When Scott Hambrick surfed the Internet using the screen name "Blowuinva," he was not a completely anonymous actor. It is true that an average member of the public could not easily determine
the true identity of "Blowuinva." Nevertheless, when Mr. Hambrick entered into an agreement to
obtain Internet access from MindSpring, he knowingly revealed his name, address, credit card number, and telephone number to MindSpring and its employees. Mr. Hambrick also selected the screen
name "Blowuinva." When the defendant selected his screen name, it became tied to his true identity in all MindSpring records. MindSpring employees had ready access to these records in the
normal course of MindSpring's business, for example, in the keeping of its records for billing purposes, and nothing prevented MindSpring from revealing this information to nongovernmental actors. Also, there is nothing in the record to suggest that there was a restrictive agreement between
the defendant and MindSpring that would limit the right of MindSpring to reveal the defendant's
personal information to nongovernmental entities. Where such dissemination of information to non-
government entities is not prohibited, there can be no reasonable expectation of privacy in that
information.

Although not dispositive to the outcome of this motion, it is important to note that the court's decision does not leave members of cybersociety without privacy protection. Under the ECPA, Internet
Service Providers are civilly liable when they reveal subscriber information or the contents of stored
communications to the government without first requiring a warrant, court order, or subpoena. Here,

nothing suggests that MindSpring had any knowledge that the facially valid subpoena submitted to it was in fact an invalid subpoena. Had MindSpring revealed the information at issue in this case to the government without first requiring a subpoena, apparently valid on its face, Mr. Hambrick could have sued MindSpring. This is a powerful deterrent protecting privacy in the online world and should not be taken lightly.

The defendant's motion to suppress also embraces evidence found in his home pursuant to a residence search warrant. The defendant contends that because the residence search warrant was supported by an affidavit reciting evidence allegedly protected as to the defendant by his right to privacy, the court likewise must suppress the materials seized from his home. As this court has found that the MindSpring materials are not so protected, the predicate for this motion to suppress the materials seized from the defendant's home fails, and therefore the court does not suppress such materials.

Decision and Outcome

The court denied the defendant, Hambrick's, motion to suppress evidence obtained by the government from Hambrick's ISP, MindSpring. Note that the government did have a subpoena that it issued to MindSpring, though the subpoena was defective in some way.

Questions for Analysis

1. Does this case stand for the proposition that what you tell one person or company on the Internet can be subpoenaed by federal and state authorities?
2. What protection does the Electronic Computer Protection Act provide?

Government Action against Invasions of Privacy

The Federal Trade Commission (FTC) was established in 1914 to combat "unfair and deceptive trade practices." The activities of the FTC are wide-ranging and oversight of many Internet activities comes within its purview. At this point, the FTC has identified as "deceptive" numerous practices that are prevalent among firms operating on the Internet. A number of these are discussed in the *GeoCities* case below (Case 11-4).

According to the FTC, there are five principles of *fair information practices:*

Notice/awareness—Consumers should be notified as to who is gathering data and the uses that will be made of those data.

Choice/consent—Consumers should consent to any secondary use for data provided. There should be opt-in and opt-out provisions.

Access/participation—Consumers should have the right to contest the accuracy of the data collected.

Integrity/security—There should be managerial mechanisms in place to guard against loss, unauthorized access, or disclosures of data.

Enforcement/redress—There should be remedies available to victims of information misuse. The FTC envisions self-regulation by industry groups, private rights of action based on invasion of privacy, and government enforcement as in the *GeoCities* case below.

Website Adherence to Fair Information Principles

As a background to the *GeoCities* case, consider the following statistics compiled by the FTC in its report to Congress entitled, "Privacy Online: Fair Information Practices in the Electronic Marketplace."[9] According to the FTC, based on a random sample of 324

[9] The FTC Privacy Report was issued May 2000.

websites on the Internet, 97 percent of the websites collect personal information and personal identifying information, but only 62 percent post a privacy policy. With regard to implementation of the FTC fair information principles, only 55 percent of the websites provide notice that qualifies according to FTC standards, which requires that a website post

- A privacy policy.
- A clear indication of what personal information is collected.
- Description of how the site uses that information.
- Whether the information is disclosed to third parties.

Fifty percent of the websites in the FTC survey provided consumer choice, allowing users to opt out of the data collection. Forty-three percent of the websites in the survey provided consumers access to information gathered about them and 55 percent had a statement about the security measures the website takes to ensure from interception by others the integrity of the information collected. Only 20 percent of the websites implemented all four (notice, choice, access, and security) of the FTC Fair Information Principles listed above.

It is the goal of the FTC that every website adhere to the fair information principles listed above. At a minimum, the FTC will consider litigation against any website that violates its own promises made at its website. To date, however, there is no legal liability for websites that do not have privacy policies, but only for sites that do not adhere to the claims made in their privacy statements. In the second term of the 107th Congress in 2002, Senator Fritz Hollings of South Carolina introduced a bill that would require websites to adhere to the FTC's fair information principles, but the bill did not get through the committee to which it was assigned.[10]

Data Collection and Computers

A hallmark of civilized society is the compilation of data about its citizenry. In developed countries, notably the United States, information is collected about people from the time of their birth to their death and beyond. For most people in the United States, medical records are routinely collected and stored, as are recordings of real estate transactions, tax records, school grades, license plates, and the list goes on and on. Until recently, the bulk of the personally identifying records that were collected were stored as *paper* records. Although there have always been embarrassing disclosures that threatened careers or proved a prominent person was a liar, the work of digging up records in paper form was by no means trivial. Computerization of records has changed all that. With appropriate software, a skilled operator can aggregate and parse enormous volumes of data so that comprehensive profiles of large numbers of individuals can be assembled.

Government Records   Ironically, a great deal of personal information is gathered and stored by government sources, then made available to private users whose intentions are not always benign. Car insurance companies have been able to tap into state Department of Motor Vehicle data, using the information obtained to justify rate increases to insured customers. Adopted children now make use of records that mothers were assured at the time of adoption would forever remain private. In some states there have been situations where predatory men, seeing an attractive woman in a car, have copied down the car license plate number, contacted the Department of Motor Vehicles, and obtained the woman's address.

Federal Legislation   At the federal level, the Privacy Act of 1974 essentially prohibits *federal agencies* that store records about citizens from disclosing that information, but there are numerous exceptions and most privacy advocates believe the Privacy Act needs

---

[10] S. 2201, 107th Congress (2002).

substantial revisions and updating.[11] In parallel fashion, the Buckley-Pell Amendment to the Family Educational Rights and Privacy Act denies federal funds to educational institutions that do not maintain confidentiality of student records.[12] There are a number of recent proposals for additional privacy protections and some new statutes at the federal level designed to protect the privacy of children and medical and financial records, particularly online disclosures. We'll take a look at a number of these developments.

State Privacy Statutes   In addition to state common law torts for generalized invasions of privacy, many states have individual privacy statutes that apply to state records, juvenile criminal files, medical records, and other data collected by government and private sources. There is considerable variance among the states as to what records are protected. One of the major complaints of large health care providers and insurance companies is the difficulty of complying with a multitude of state privacy laws, many of which are inconsistent or contradictory. For example, some states have laws that *deny* patients the right to access their medical records, while others *guarantee* patients access to their medical records.

Internet Data Collection and Cookies

There are websites and software that promise the ability to unearth all kinds of information about co-workers, relatives, and others, including criminal records, credit reports, health records, and other data.[13] Ordinary transactions between consumer and businesses online are threatened by "identity thieves," who intercept Internet transmissions and accompanying credit card numbers. As the *Hambrick* case above illustrates, there is no reasonable expectation of privacy for information that is given to Internet businesses without guarantees of confidentiality.

cookies

Small software programs, installed on browsers' hard drives by websites they visit, that allow data to be gathered by the website on the computer users' other web destinations.

In the minds of many, **cookies** pose the greatest threat to Internet privacy. According to one website, named "Cookie Central,"[14]

> Cookies are a very useful tool in maintaining state variables on the Web. Since HTTP is a "stateless" (non-persistent) protocol, it is impossible to differentiate between visits to a website, unless the server can somehow "mark" a visitor. This is done by storing a piece of information in the visitor's browser.
>
> This is accomplished with cookies. Cookies can store database information, custom page settings, or just about anything that would make a site individual and customizable. An analogy I like to use is that cookies are very much like a laundry "claim-check" of sorts. You drop something off, and get a ticket. When you return with the ticket, you get that same something back.

Cookies allow websites to track where you have traveled in cyberspace from the time you leave the cookie-placing website until your return to that website. While cookies have a number of uses, their primary function is the recording of clickstreams—that is, tracking what sites you have clicked on (visited) since you last visited the cookie-placer's site. Clickstreams are the information marketers want because they can then select targeted advertising for goods they think you may want based on your clickstreams.

To most Internet users, the most objectionable aspect of cookies is the involuntary nature of the information extraction. To date, however, the act of merely attaching a cookie to a browser by a website has not created, and has not been viewed as, an actionable invasion of privacy. A class action suit filed by plaintiffs in New York alleged that when DoubleClick, an Internet advertising company, placed cookies on their browsers it violated

---

[11] 5 U.S.C. § 552a (1994).

[12] 20 U.S.C. § 1232 et seq.

[13] http://www.sfxserve.co.uk/Homepage/ecomm2u/CyberSpy.html.

[14] This website is an AOL recommendation that answers frequently asked questions about cookies. See http://www.cookiecentral.com/faq/#1.1.

Ethical Challenges   Ethical Issues in Cyberspace

ETHICAL EXPECTATIONS

With the power of today's software, the potential for unscrupulous behavior by companies that have websites on the Internet is evident. Some would regard operating a website and engaging in the following practices as unethical:

- Collecting information without informing the customer.
- Secondary use of personally identifiable data.

- Not having a privacy statement.
- Not having a means for consumer users to correct inaccuracies.
- Not having a means to opt out of the system, if the consumer does not want to have personal data transmitted or sold to third parties.
- Soliciting entrants to a contest with the intent of gathering information from applicants.

various federal statutes, including the Electronic Communications Privacy Act as well as state law for invasion of privacy.[15] Although the federal district court in New York did not deal with the state claims, it dismissed all of the plaintiffs' claims based on federal law.

In another action against DoubleClick, a California plaintiff, Harriet Judnick, sued DoubleClick for (1) placing a cookie on her browser and (2) threatening to merge browser data with personal information obtained from other sources.[16] The State of California has constitutional protection for privacy that is not restricted to governmental intrusions. Prior to the trial in the California case, DoubleClick announced plans to abandon all efforts to merge personal data with data collected by cookies. At the time of the writing of this book, the *Judnick v. DoubleClick* litigation was unresolved. At present, then, the practice of websites placing cookies on browsers appears to be quite common and, apparently, legal.

In addition to being viewed as unethical, many of the practices listed in the "Ethical Challenges" box are being attacked as unfair and deceptive trade practices, which the FTC has authority to halt. In Case 11-4, the defendant was accused of many of the abuses listed above.

[15] *In re DoubleClick, Inc. Privacy Litigation*, 154 F. Supp. 2d 497 (S.D.N.Y. 2001).
[16] *Judnick v. DoubleClick*, CV-000421, Marin County, California (2000).

Case 11-4

Federal Trade Commission

[File No. 982-3015]
GeoCities; Analysis to Aid Public Comment
Proposed Consent Decree
Thursday, August 20, 1998
*63 Fed. Reg. 44624

FACTS AND CASE BACKGROUND

The Federal Trade Commission (FTC) is charged with responsibility for identifying and prohibiting unfair and deceptive trade practices. The GeoCities case gave the FTC an opportunity to address several issues dealing with the use of information gathered by an Internet website. Among the issues addressed in this case are the acquisition, use, and sale of identifying, personal information without the customer's consent. The FTC identified three deceptive trade practices, which GeoCities agreed in this consent decree to cease and desist: (1) that the defendant, GeoCities, gathered and sold information on members, which GeoCities promised would not be sold or distributed; (2) that the defendant collected optional information that it claimed would not be sold to third parties, but in fact was sold; and (3) that they collected personally identifiable information from children without their parents' knowledge or consent.

Case Decision by the Federal Trade Commission

Part I of the proposed order prohibits GeoCities from making any misrepresentation about its collection or use of personal identifying information from or about consumers, including what information will be disclosed to third parties and how the information will be used. The order defines "personal identifying information" as including but not limited to, "first and last name, home or other physical address (e.g. school), email address, telephone number, or any information that identifies a specific individual, or any information which when tied to the above becomes identifiable to a specific individual."

Part II of the proposed order prohibits GeoCities from misrepresenting either the identity of a party collecting any personal identifying information or the sponsorship of any activity on its Web site.

Part III prohibits GeoCities from collecting personal identifying information from any child if GeoCities has actual knowledge that the child does not have a parent's permission to provide the information. The order defines "child" as ages twelve and under.

Parts IV and V of the order are designed as fencing-in provisions to prevent violations of consumers' information privacy in the future. Part IV orders GeoCities to post a clear and prominent notice on its Web Site explaining GeoCities' practices with regard to its collection and use of personal identifying information. The notice must include the following:

a. What information is being collected;

b. Its intended use(s);

c. The third parties to whom it will be disclosed;

d. How the consumer can obtain access to the information; and

e. How the consumer can have the information removed from GeoCities' databases.

The notice must appear on the Web site's home page and at each location on the site at which such information is collected, although the collection of so-called "tracking" information need only be disclosed on the home page.

Part IV includes a "safe harbor" provision that deems a specified procedure to be in compliance with this Part. It would allow GeoCities to post a Privacy Notice on its home page along with a clear and prominent hyperlink to that notice at each location on the site at which personal identifying information is collected. The hyperlink would be accompanied by the following statement:

NOTICE: We collect personal information on this site. To learn more about how we use your information click here.

Decision and Outcome

The FTC action in the *GeoCities* case was later enacted into law as the Children's Online Privacy Protection Act (COPPA), discussed below. Before personally identifying information can be collected from children, defined as 12 and under, GeoCities had to obtain permission of the child's parent or guardian.

Questions for Analysis

1. The FTC has already issued a number of regulations regarding games and sweepstakes in non-Internet settings. Does it make sense for the FTC to apply general principles of prohibiting deceptive trade practices in both Internet and non-Internet locations.

2. Do you think that this type of consent decree is a way for the government to regulate the content of websites? Why aren't the common law remedies of contract fraud and the tort of deceit likely to be adequate protection?

Use of Private Information, Fraud, and Identity Theft

As discussed in Chapter 9, UCITA, UETA, and revised Article 2 of the UCC require vendors to develop commercially reasonable attribution procedures in order to make their click-on contracts enforceable. Commercially reasonable attribution procedures often entail the collection of personal information about the purchaser such as name, address, phone numbers, credit card numbers, e-mail addresses, and other information. The goal behind this collection of data is to identify who is responding to the offer made by a vendor at its website and, according to both UCITA and UETA, that identification process must be commercially reasonable. Once these data are collected, however, their subsequent use is a source of controversy. If personal information requested and stored by websites is intercepted or falls into the wrong hands, customers could be victims of identity theft. Additionally, customer information that is legitimately collected for attribution purposes is often resold by websites to other vendors and advertisers, sometimes without consent of its customers; sometimes notice of resales of customer information is buried in 10-page privacy policies that reserve the right to change unilaterally.

Identity Theft

identity theft
The appropriation of your personal information—name, address, credit card account number, and so forth—to commit theft or fraud.

A serious current problem on the Internet is **identity theft.** According to the FTC, your identity can be stolen by someone "co-opting your name, Social Security number, credit card number, or some other piece of your personal information for their own use. In short, identity theft occurs when someone appropriates your personal information without your knowledge to commit fraud or theft." The FTC lists several ways in which identity thieves work, including

- They open a new credit card account, using your name, date of birth, and Social Security number. When they use the credit card and don't pay the bills, the delinquent account is reported on your credit report.
- They call your credit card issuer and, pretending to be you, change the mailing address on your credit card account. Then, your imposter runs up charges on your account. Because the resulting bills are being sent to the new address, you may not immediately realize there is a problem.
- They establish cellular phone service in your name.
- They open a bank account in your name and write bad checks on that account.

The Identity Theft and Assumption Deterrence Act of 1998, which became effective October 30, 1998, makes identity theft a federal crime with penalties up to 15 years' imprisonment and a maximum fine of $250,000.[17] This act makes the person whose identity was stolen a *true* victim. Previously, only the credit card companies who suffered monetary losses were considered victims. This legislation enables the Secret Service, the Federal Bureau of Investigation, and other law enforcement agencies to combat this crime. It allows for the identity theft victim to seek restitution if there is a conviction. It also establishes the Federal Trade Commission as a central agency to act as a clearinghouse for complaints (against credit bureaus and credit grantors), referrals, and resources for assistance for victims of identity theft.

spyware
Software that allows sophisticated information retrieval and reporting.

Spyware

Spyware is somewhat akin to cookies. However, it is not centered on website visits but, rather, on the use of computers and software. The typical scenario involving spyware begins

---

[17] Pub. L. No. 105-318, codified at 18 U.S.C. § 1028.

WASHINGTON (October 5, 2000)—Senator John Edwards on Thursday proposed legislation to protect the privacy of people who use computer software programs that secretly track the shopping habits and other interests of Internet surfers.

The measure would uncloak so-called spyware programs that use encrypted codes to monitor the activities of unsuspecting computer users and share the personal information with advertisers, telemarketers or other businesses.

The Spyware Control and Privacy Protection Act is the latest in a series of proposals by Senator Edwards to protect the privacy of personal records amassed by Internet businesses, banks, health insurance providers, and telephone companies.

Under the spyware bill, software providers that use codes to track the activities of Internet users would have to notify consumers in plain language when the users buy or download programs. No information on Internet surfing habits could be collected without first obtaining each consumer's permission. Businesses that gather data would have to let individuals know what information has been assembled, provide a way to correct errors, and safeguard the data against unauthorized access by hackers.

with the sale (licensing) of software use. In the most prominent form of spyware, the software provided contains electronic agents that report the uses made of the software by the purchaser (or licensee) to the software copyright owner, who then either sells this information to third parties or uses the information for marketing purposes.

One form of spyware is software that enables the owner to monitor what other users of his or her computer are doing, where they are chatting, what is said, and/or what websites are visited. Consider the following advertisements:

Spector 2.1

Install Spector on your PC and it will record EVERYTHING your spouse, kids and employees do on the Internet.

Spector SECRETLY takes hundreds of screen snapshots every hour, very much like a surveillance camera. With Spector, you will be able to see EVERY chat conversation, EVERY instant message, EVERY e-mail, EVERY web site visited and EVERY keystroke typed.

>>> *Tell me more*
>>> *Purchase, Download & Install in 5 minutes*

eBlaster 2.0

Track Spouse, Children or Employee online activity by receiving email reports of everything they do online.

eBlaster delivers detailed activity reports, including all web sites visited, all applications run, and all keystrokes typed, right to your e-mail address, as frequently as every 30 minutes.[18]

It is likely that Congress will be called to address spyware invasions of privacy of various forms. Senator John Edwards of North Carolina in October of 2000 issued the press release shown in the "Cyberlaw Developments" box.

---

[18] http://www.spectorsoft.com/.

GOVERNMENT REGULATIONS

FTC Regulations Regarding Children's Sites

According to the Federal Trade Commission (in 1998), the application of fair information practice principles requires special adaptations when the target audience is children.[19] Noting that there are an extensive assemblage of federal and state laws that protect children from alcohol, tobacco, and pornography, as well as laws that require parental consent for activities involving children, the FTC has developed its own set of child-oriented regulations. The FTC states that the following practices appear contrary to the Federal Trade Commission Act, which prohibits unfair and deceptive trade practices. Per the FTC:

> It is a deceptive practice to represent that a site is collecting personal identifying information from a child for a particular purpose (e.g. to earn points to redeem a premium), when the information will also be used for another purpose that parents would find material, in the absence of a clear and prominent disclosure to that effect; and
>
> It is likely to be an unfair practice to collect personal identifying information, such as a name, email address, home address, or phone number, from children and to sell or otherwise disclose such identifying information to third parties, or to post it publicly online, without providing parents with adequate notice and an opportunity to control the collection and use of the information through prior parental consent.

The FTC's position is that it will prosecute sites that collect information from children without verifiable parental notice and consent. The FTC also indicates that to conform to suitable notice requirements, websites should explain in sufficient detail what is offered in the way of email, message boards, chat rooms, and other services such as web pages. These FTC stances make websites legally vulnerable if they do not provide adequate notices. One result of the FTC's actions is that pornographic websites typically display prominent notices warning those entering the website that they must be at least 18 years old.

The Children's Online Privacy Protection Act (COPPA) of 1998 applies to websites either that are directed to children or for which the operator knows that personal information is collected from children.[20] COPPA requires notices with regard to what information is collected, how the information is to be used, and the operator's disclosure practices to third parties. Besides the required notice, COPPA requires *verifiable parental consent* before information can be collected from children. For purposes of COPPA, children are defined as anyone under 13 years of age. In addition, a website cannot condition a child's participation in giveaways and games on the provision of information. Finally, COPPA requires websites to establish reasonable procedures to protect the confidentiality, security, and integrity of the personal information collected. Under COPPA, sites that serve children are expected to protect access to stored data of email addresses or other personal information about children from hackers who may be pedophiles.

Financial Records: The Gramm-Leach-Bliley Act, 1999

The Gramm-Leach-Bliley Act is largely directed towards deregulating some activities of the banking industry.[21] Title V of the act, however, deals with Privacy and Disclosure of Nonpublic Personal Information and declares that, "It is the policy of the Congress that

---

[19] www.ftc.gov/reports/privacy3/fairinfo.htm.

[20] Pub. L. No. 105-277, codified at 15 U.S.C. § 6501.

[21] Pub. L. No. 106-102, codified at 15 U.S.C. § 6801–6810.

each financial institution has an affirmative and continuing obligation to respect the privacy of its customers and to protect the security and confidentiality of those customers' nonpublic personal information." In furthering that policy, Title V requires each agency that has authority over financial institutions to fashion regulations that

- Ensure the security and confidentiality of customer records and information.
- Provide protection against any anticipated threats or hazards to the security or integrity of those records.
- Protect against unauthorized access to or use of such records or information.

Section 502 of the act prohibits a financial institution from disclosing to a third party any nonpublic personal information, "unless such financial institution provides or has provided to the consumer a notice that complies with section 503." The concern expressed in Section 502 is that customer nonpublic information will be given out to third parties for marketing purposes without customer consent. Section 502 requires that customers be clearly informed before their nonpublic information will be given to third parties and that customers have an opportunity to opt out of such disclosures. Finally, Title V prohibits a financial institution from disclosing account numbers or similar access numbers including credit card information to "unaffiliated third parties for use in telemarketing, direct mail marketing, or other marketing through electronic mail to the consumer." Title V does allow financial institutions to report and transmit customer financial data, such as giving out credit information of a customer to a credit bureau. The Federal Trade Commission has a detailed list of "Do's" and "Don'ts" at http://www.ftc.gov/privacy/glbact/index.html.

Medical Records: The Health Insurance Portability and Accountability Act (HIPAA) of 1996

When Congress passed the Health Insurance Portability and Accountability Act (HIPAA) of 1996, there had been a number of widely publicized situations that involved workers who could not afford to change jobs because health insurers at "new" employers would not pay for "pre-existing" medical conditions. HIPAA basically made it illegal for health insurers to deny coverage for preexisting medical conditions and that part of the statute has been a notable success.

The other part of HIPAA that has attracted increasing attention addresses protection of the privacy of medical records. At this point the scenario has become familiar. Computerization of medical records has made them increasingly easy to store and distribute. There have been a number of instances in which medical records have been sold to (or otherwise obtained by) third-party marketers (see insert below). Women who are prescribed antinausea drugs during pregnancy suddenly have been inundated with ads from companies selling maternity clothes. There also have been cases of disclosures of medical records that were clearly inappropriate and that have led to extreme embarrassment. Patients were given no assurance when they provided medical information that it would not end up in the hands of vendors or others who are not in any way involved in their treatment.

HIPAA called for Congress either to enact privacy legislation by August of 1999 or, failing that, to empower the Department of Health and Human Services (HHS) to fashion its own regulations. Congress did not act, so HHS issued regulations that, after some political maneuvering, became law during the spring of 2003. The basic principle behind HHS's HIPAA regulations is that *nonconsensual secondary use of personally identifying medical records is illegal,* though there are a number of exceptions to this rule. HIPAA regulates health care providers, insurance companies, and HMOs among others. Transfers of medical information between "covered" entities (health care providers, insurers, and HMOs) for the purposes of furthering treatment, handling payments, or maintaining health care operations are legal under HHS regulations. All other transfers of medical records require consent of patients, with a number of specific exceptions. The following list of such exceptions is not exhaustive. A nonconsensual transfer of medical records is allowed if it is used by

- Public health authorities for purposes of preventing the outbreak of communicable diseases.
- Medical researchers who have a panel that reviews the need for personally identifying medical information. The costs of obtaining consent from patients for medical records is often prohibitive to medical researchers.
- Law enforcement pursuant to an investigation. Although there is some language about probable cause, a search warrant is not required for law enforcement to examine medical records stored by a medical facility regulated by HIPAA.
- Officials performing oversight for purposes of determining whether medical services are being efficiently delivered and whether fraud and abuse are occurring.

There are eight other exceptions that are listed by HSS as to when nonconsensual secondary use of medical records is permitted. Although the protection of medical records under HIPAA may seem leaky, it represents a significant improvement over the prior situation where the rules regarding medical records were not at all clear.

THE EUROPEAN UNION AND PRIVACY

In 1996, the nations of the European Union (EU) banded together to enact legislation that maintains strict governmental protection for privacy. By and large, the United States relies on voluntary industry codes for the protection of privacy, whereas the EU regards voluntary industry codes as deficient. In addition to governmental codes on privacy, the EU Data Protection Directive forbids transmission of data between member nations and others where privacy protection is inadequate.[22] The EU Data Protection Directive went into effect in 1998 and, at that time, the EU view was that database protections in the United States were inadequate so that data sharing between U.S. entities and companies located in the EU should not be allowed.

There was concern that literal application of the EU Data Protection Directive could cause a significant interruption of vital data transmissions between the United States and the EU nations. The United States was given until the end of 1999 to remedy its privacy laws before the impact of the EU Directive was scheduled to become effective. In 1999 the U.S. Department of Commerce produced a "safe harbor" agreement, under which U.S. companies, if they agree to the safe harbor regulations, are permitted to share date with EU firms.[23] To date there has not been an interruption in trade between U.S. and EU companies, but the "safe harbor" agreements fashioned by the U.S. Department of Commerce and the EU appear to be fragile, with the EU pressuring the United States to provide more protection for the privacy of personal information.

[22] See http://europa.eu.int/geninfo/legal_notices_en.htm#personaldata, which contains information about and a link to the EU Data Protection Directive.

[23] See the website article "EU to U.S.: Privacy Rules Not Good Enough," http://www.thestandard.com/article/0,1902,4289,00.html.

International Perspective E.U. Privacy Directive Is Threat to Banks

When it comes to banks, the impact could be a disruption of data flow between Europe and the United States. For instance, a U.S. bank that offers credit cards in Germany may not be able to process the transactions in the United States. Similarly, a German customer buying goods in New York may not be able to use his German-issued credit card. Authorization for the purchase must come from a computer system in Europe, and the question arises whether it is permissible to transfer the personal information to the United States, said Swire, the author of a book on the European date protection directive—"None of Your Business: World Data Flows, Electronic Commerce and the E.U. Privacy Directive" with co-author Robert Litan—to be released later this month by the Washington-based Brookings Institution.

Business lending and loan syndication will also be affected. Banks taking part in a syndication will want to see the underlying documents, which may contain personally identifiable information. "Once again it is hard to see how transfers out of Europe of personal information would be permitted under the directive," said Swire. Although he adds that for some transactions it may be possible to get consent in advance from each person named in the documents transferred to the third country.

When it comes to investment banking, a wide range of transactions include personally identifiable information and many international transactions involve the sharing of information between American and European offices of one or more banks. "The discussion here shows major potential problems with respect to market analysis and especially hostile takeovers," said Swire. "The directive may also create obstacles to the ability of European firms to raise money for the United States."

Source: From "E.U. Privacy Directive Is Threat to Banks," by Claire Chapman, *Thomson's International Banking Regulator,* October 5, 1998, Vol. 10, Issue 38, p. 1.

Summary

Under State Common Law Rulings, ISPs That Merely Republished Defamatory Material That Appeared at Websites Were Not Liable for the Defamation unless They Supervised Content

- The significance of tort claims stemming from Internet activities may grow to dominate that of traditional torts as commercial as well as personal activities move to the Web.
- One important tort that involves Internet activities and that already has a significant litigation history is defamation.
- In a defamation suit, the plaintiff must show the defendant made false statements about him or her, that the false statements were heard by third parties, and that the false statements harmed his or her reputation.
- Not only are authors of defamatory comments liable, but also those who repeat or republish defamatory comments are liable.
- Internet service providers have been targets of defamation suits.
- Initially, ISPs were viewed like bookstores and, thus, not subject to liability as distributors of defamatory material that appeared on their servers.
- In one defamation decision (*Stratton*), however, an ISP was viewed by the court as a publisher because it claimed to *supervise* content and, thus, was responsible for and *liable for* defamatory material that appeared on its server.

Congress Passed the Communications Decency Act to Immunize ISPs from State Defamation Suits so Long as

- Section 230 of the Communications Decency Act (CDA) of 1996 bars suits that place ISPs in the same legal position as publishers, protecting them from liability for materials provided by third parties.
- The CDA preempts state law with respect to ISP liability for republication of defamatory statements.
- Employers are also increasingly being shielded from liability for defamation unless there is evidence that the employer knew the statements about its employee or former employee were false or reflect a reckless disregard for the truth.

the ISP Does Not Contribute to the Content of the Defamatory Material; the Protection the CDA Provides to ISPs Is Broad	• The CDA immunizes ISPs from liability for republishing stock tips from websites even if those tips may be viewed as fraudulent. • The CDA also immunizes ISPs that republish materials from websites that are accused of defamation. • If employers provide a server, they may be able to qualify for server (ISP) immunity under the CDA.
The Internet Has Created Many New Challenges to the Right of Privacy; Fourth Amendment and Common Law Invasion of Privacy Torts Are Being Tested in Courts and Abuses in the Area of Collection of Information from Children and Storage and Use of Financial and Health Data Have Caused Congress to Enact Protective Regulation	• There are legal remedies for invasions of privacy, whether committed by the government or by private entities. • The Fourth Amendment protects against governmental invasions of privacy. For most searches, search warrants are required, which requires that the government show probable cause before a neutral magistrate that it is likely that a crime has been committed. • It is an actionable tort for a defendant to invade an area where a plaintiff has a reasonable expectation of privacy. • Information communicated to ISPs is not protected by the reasonable expectation of privacy of the subscriber. • There are numerous actions that have been taken by websites to collect information from visitors without their knowledge or consent. Furthermore, much of that information is collected for resale to other firms. • Many websites do not have privacy policies and, yet, 97 percent of websites collect identifying information. • Many websites collect information from children or transmit sensitive medical and financial information. As a result, government regulation has been applied.
Among Government Agencies, the Federal Trade Commission Has Taken the Lead in Defining Unfair and Deceptive Trade Practices in Cyberspace and Has Initiated Litigation against Those Who Collect Information from Children, do Not Follow Their Own Privacy Statements, and Steal Identities Through Credit Card Fraud	• The Federal Trade Commission has elucidated five principles of fair information practices that include *notice, choice, access, integrity, and redress*. • A huge amount of personally identifying information is stored by public and private sources. • A particularly troublesome practice is the placement of *cookies* on Web browsers by websites. Using *cookies*, information is extracted without knowledge or consent of website visitors. • In some high-profile cases, websites have not followed guarantees made to visitors regarding their own practices with respect to the gathering of information and the use of that information. • Privacy policies at websites are increasingly common and detailed. The effect of a privacy policy is that companies that do use cookies can claim that visitors were informed of the cookies and of the use of the information extracted using cookies or other information-gathering instruments. • With growth of the Internet, the incidence and significance of identity theft have risen dramatically. Identity theft occurs when someone obtains personally identifiable information about you in order to impersonate you. • The threat of identity theft has inspired websites to make additional investments in security in order to guarantee that transmissions with customers are secure and are not intercepted.

Among Recent Acts Adopted by Congress Are the Children's Online Privacy Protection Act, the Gramm-Leach-Bliley Act, and HIPAA regulations; the EU Has Enacted Regulations That Also Impact U.S. Practices

- The FTC has special concerns about the collection of information from children as children can be manipulated into providing information that their parents would not want revealed.

- The Children's Online Privacy Protection Act of 1998 makes it illegal to gather information from children without prior approval from parents.

- The Gramm-Leach-Bliley Act of 1999 prohibits banks and other financial institutions from revealing nonpublic financial information to third parties unless they have informed their customers and given them an opportunity to opt out of such disclosures.

- The Health Insurance Portability and Accountability Act (HIPAA) of 1996 outlaws distribution of personally identifiable medical information unless it is for the purpose of treatment, payment, or operations, with some important exceptions for public health, medical research, and law enforcement, among others.

- The European Union has stronger protection for the privacy of personal records than the United States and their Data Protection Directive prohibits sharing of data with countries that do not subscribe to their standards. Negotiations between the EU and the Department of Commerce are ongoing.

Key Terms

Carnivore, *343*	identity theft, *350*	probable cause, *342*
cookies, *347*	ISPs, *337*	spyware, *350*
defamation, *334*		

Questions for Review and Analysis

1. Explain how common law state court rulings prompted Congress to pass the Communications Decency Act. What does the CDA do?

2. What constitutional and statutory protections of privacy existed before the Internet became prevalent?

3. What is meant by a "reasonable expectation of privacy"? How is this concept used by courts to define limits of what privacy rights are protectible under the law? What expectations of privacy are reasonable in cyberspace?

4. What have been the main thrusts of the Federal Trade Commission in regulating cyberspace? What statutory authority does the FTC have to combat fraud and unfair trade practices in cyberspace?

5. Describe the legislation, recently passed by Congress, that provides some protection against attacks on privacy that have occurred in cyberspace.

If You Really Understood This Chapter, You Should Be Able to Provide Informed Commentary on the Following:

1. **Defamation, ISPs, and Right to Edit.** It is clear that the Communications Decency Act absolves ISPs of liability for defamatory material as long as they have no say in the content of the defamatory material. The *Drudge Report* (www.drudgereport.com) is one of the most widely visited websites because it often carries political stories that later appear in the more established media. America Online (AOL), an ISP, signed a licensing agreement with Matt Drudge, originator of the *Drudge Report,* whereby the *Drudge Report* is made available to AOL members for one year in return for royalties from AOL. The Drudge-AOL agreement calls for Drudge to create, edit, update, and otherwise manage the *Drudge Report,* but AOL maintained the right to remove content that AOL reasonably determined violated its guidelines. On August 10, 1997, at the height of the Monicagate furor, the *Drudge Report* ran an article that alleged that Sidney Blumenthal, one of President Clinton's advisors, had a history of spousal abuse. Blumenthal sued both the *Drudge Report* and AOL. Based on the CDA, AOL moved for summary judgment. Does the agreement that AOL had with Drudge take it out of the protection of the CDA? [*Blumenthal v. Drudge,* 992 F. Supp. 44 (D.D.C. 1998).]

2. **Secret Collection of Customer Data.** In November of 1999, RealNetworks was sued in a class action for common law invasion of privacy and under the Consumer Fraud and Abuse Act. The claimants in the suit allege that RealNetworks' software, RealJukeBox, was engineered to collect

various details about the listening habits of those who used the software to listen to Internet music and send the information back to RealNetworks. The plaintiffs in this suit claim that the secret reports of RealJukeBox software to RealNetworks violated assurances in their privacy statement that guaranteed that consumers "can expect to be notified of what information this site tracks about you." Once the lawsuit was filed, RealNetworks (1) apologized, (2) distributed software that enabled customers to block further collection of data by RealJukeBox software, and (3) claimed that it did not store the information it secretly collected. Is that good enough or should the plaintiffs be able to sue RealNeworks for damages? [*Starrett v. RealNetworks,* 99-cv-5569 (E.D. PA Nov. 9, 1999).]

3. **Right of Privacy and Lack of Uniformity of State Laws.** In a messy divorce case, the soon-to-be ex-wife determined, with the help of her brother, that her husband's girl friend, later his new wife, had been using a screen name that insinuated that the ex-wife would welcome having phone sex or physical sex. The new girl friend, Terry Jessup-Morgan, adopted the screen name Barbeedol, because the ex-wife's name was Barbara Smith, and posted, on an electronic bulletin board, the phone number of Barbara Smith's parents, which was where Barbara Smith was residing. As can be expected, Barbara Smith and her parents received a huge number of unwanted phone messages. Through a subpoena to America Online (AOL) in connection with the divorce, Barbara was able to obtain Terry Jessup's AOL screen name. Jessup sued AOL for $47 million under eight separate counts including breach of contract and violation of the Electronic Communication Privacy Act. Jessup also sued AOL for breach of privacy, contending that by revealing her screen name, AOL intruded into Jessup's seclusion or revealed private facts about Jessup. Although the suit was filed in Michigan, the court determined that Virginia law applied. The federal district court granted AOL's motion to dismiss as to the privacy claims. Can you explain why? [*Terry Jessup-Morgan v. America Online, Inc.,* 20 F. Supp. 2d 1105 (E.D. Mich. 1998).]

4. **Browser Companies and Government Subpoenas.** The same judge that was asked to rule on the request by the record companies for an injunction against Napster was also asked to rule on the following issue. Can the Federal Trade Commission subpoena information from Netscape regarding two of its subscribers for whom Netscape supplied e-mail addresses? The FTC wanted account holders' names, addresses, telephone numbers, and billing records, and the length and type of service provided to them by Netscape. Netscape contends that supplying such information is barred by the Electronic Communications Privacy Act (ECPA), which was mentioned in the *Hambrick* case in the chapter. At issue in this case is whether there is a difference in the treatment called for by the ECPA as to how discovery subpoenas are dealt with relative to trial subpoenas. The ruling (http://legal.web.aol.com/decisions/dlpriv/ftcnetscape.html) by Judge Patel should provide some solace to those favoring greater protection from government attempts to snoop in cyberspace. How would you compare the court's decision in this case to the one reached in *Hambrick?*

5. **Down and Dirty with the Details of Privacy Regulation.** The Gramm-Leach-Bliley (GLB) Act has significantly augmented privacy protection for financial data stored by banks and other financial institutions. Perhaps the primary threat to privacy that prompted the passage of GLB was a concern that banks would be tempted to sell financial data to telemarketers and others who are widely perceived as nuisances. However, to contend that banks can never share financial data with third parties is unworkable; there are occasions when sharing data with third parties clearly assists customers and others such has health care insurers. After the passage of GLB, a question arose as to whether a bank could respond to a merchant as to whether a customer's checking account had sufficient funds to cover a purchase. If such a call is received, how can the bank know whether it is really a merchant making the call or some private investigator hired by an online gambling operation that is illegal in the United States? For those who have a high tolerance for details of government regulations, see the FTC Gramm-Leach-Bliley compliance requirements at http://www.ftc.gov/privacy/glbact/glb-faq.htm#I.

6. **Children's Privacy.** As discussed in the chapter, Congress passed the Children's Online Privacy Protection Act, which, basically, prohibits online collection of information from children (under 13) without written consent of parents. In a recent action, the FTC initiated action against the Ohio Art Company, manufacturer of the Etch-A-Sketch drawing toy, based on the following facts.

   The FTC alleges that The Ohio Art Company collected personal information from children registering for "Etchy's Birthday Club." The site collected names, mailing addresses, e-mail addresses, ages, and dates of birth from children who wanted to qualify to win an Etch-A-Sketch toy on their birthdays. The FTC charged that the company merely directed children to "get your parent or guardian's permission first," and then collected the information without first obtaining parental consent as required by the law. In addition, the FTC alleged that the company collected more information from children than was reasonably necessary for children to participate in the "birthday club" activity, and that the site's privacy policy statement did not clearly or completely disclose all of its information collection practices or make certain disclosures required by COPPA. The site also failed to provide parents the opportunity to review the personal information collected from their children and to inform them of their ability to prevent the further collection and use of this information, the FTC alleged.

The Ohio Art Company agreed to pay the FTC $35,000. Is this an example of too much government regulation? Other FTC actions against alleged violators of COPPA are discussed at http://www.ftc.gov/opa/2002/04/coppaanniv.htm.

Social Responsibility and Ethics in a High-Tech World

7. **Protection Provided by Privacy Policies.** Privacy concerns on the Internet have inspired a lot of debate, new laws, and continuing disagreements. One problem that has been identified by modern researchers is the increasing complexity of privacy policies that are generally listed at the bottom of websites. Typically, website privacy policies are loaded with legalese that includes waivers of the right to pursue legal claims in court because of arbitration clauses, choice of law clauses, warranty disclaimers, and other exclusions of liability. In addition, websites often reserve the right to change their policies so that a prudent visitor must check the privacy policy each time a visit is made. Certainly, most website visitors do not have the time to check website privacy policies for changes at every visit.

For all but the most skilled computer sleuths, it is impossible to determine whether a website actually adheres to its own privacy policies. Knowing that there is skepticism about adherence to website privacy policies, many websites display logos of third-party guarantors of adherence to the claims made in privacy policies, such as TRUSTe. These third-party guarantors, however, have their own complicated language that discusses what they (the third-party guarantors) guarantee and what they do not guarantee.

Exasperation with the complicated and sometimes misleading language used in website privacy statements has prompted calls for minimal government-required guarantees. As discussed in the chapter, already there are three types of websites that are now, or will be in the near future, subject to more intense government regulation: websites of financial institutions, websites that are directed toward children, and health care–related websites. Recognizing the threat of more government regulation, many websites are trying to self-regulate. Using third-party guarantors is an attempt at self-regulation. Other complicating factors include the presence of offshore websites that are not subject to the jurisdiction of U.S. authorities. Needless to say, additional legal changes in regulation of websites and their privacy policies are likely.

Using the Internet to Your Advantage

1. There are a number of government websites that discuss and address the regulation of various aspects of privacy. The Federal Trade Commission (FTC) (http://www.ftc.gov) has been given responsibility for enforcing the Gramm-Leach-Bliley Act as it relates to the protection of the privacy of financial data. The FTC has issued a number of widely quoted studies on privacy. The latest one is available at http://www.ftc.gov/reports/privacy2000/privacy2000.pdf. For those interested in international trade, assistance on privacy issues can be obtained from the U.S. Department of Commerce (http://www.commerce.gov). Note further that for those intending to share data with companies located in the EU, it is necessary to comply with the EU Data Privacy Directive. The U.S. Department of Commerce has negotiated with the EU and fashioned a "safe harbor" regulation that has been agreed to by the EU. If a U.S. firm is certified by the DOC, it is legal for companies located in EU countries to share data with the firm. The DOC safe harbor regulations are discussed at http://www.export.gov/safeharbor/SafeHarbor.htm.

2. The most credible attempts at self-regulation make use of third-party guarantors. Among the industry leaders are TRUSTe (http://www.truste.com), the Better Business Bureau (BBB Online) (http://www.bbbonline.org/), PricewaterhouseCoopers BetterWeb (http://www.pwcbetterweb.com/), and CPA WebTrust (http://www.cpawebtrust.org/). Another attempt at self-regulation is the

P3P project (http://www.w3.org/P3P/), which is an attempt to coordinate interactions between browsers and websites. If parties cooperate, the vision of the P3P project is that browsers would be programmed by operators to reflect their preferences with regard to privacy. When the programmed browser encounters a website, it would immediately be able to determine if the practices of the website are compatible with those of the browser operator.

3. There are a number of private watchdog organizations, some of which have a particular focus and some of which are general. The Electronic Frontier Foundation (http://www.eff.org) is probably the leading group that (1) promotes privacy measures for consumers and (2) has uncovered a number of seemingly innocuous measures used by corporations that were actually surreptitious mechanisms designed to gather consumer data without authorization. Another private privacy foundation, the Electronic Privacy Information Center (http://www.epic.org), provides comprehensive reporting of privacy-related legislation, both in the United States and worldwide. Similarly, the Center for Democracy and Technology (http://www.cdt.org) focuses on legislative actions that impact privacy. The Direct Marketing Association (DMA) (http://www.the-dma.org) is operating under the shadow of government regulation, as politicians have threatened punitive government regulation because of the annoyances caused by spammers, telemarketers, and junk mailers. The DMA website provides an opportunity to remove your name, address, and e-mail address from members' databases.

Chapter Twelve

Property: Real, Personal, and Intellectual

Learning Objectives

On completing this chapter, you should

1. Be familiar with the ways in which property is classified: tangible, intangible, real, personal, and intellectual.
2. Understand the basic characteristics of real and personal property and the methods of transferring property ownership.
3. Be familiar with the basic requirements of patentability including novelty, nonobviousness, and appropriate subject matter.
4. Understand patent infringements and how damages are determined by courts in patent infringement cases.
5. Know what a trade secret is and how trade secret misappropriation occurs.

OVERVIEW

For most people, mention of the word *property* conjures up images of a house, a car, or some other physical object. This chapter examines some of the salient legal features of tangible property, which may be in the form of *real property* (such as land) or in the form of personal property (such as houses, cars, stereos, etc.). In addition, this chapter deals with something called *intellectual property*. Such "property" exists largely in the form of *intangible* rights, so labeled because they have no palpable physical form or characteristics. As we will see, increasingly, the most important property owned by businesses is in the form of intellectual property (IP), particularly as reflected in patents and trade secrets. The remainder of the text's discussion of IP takes place in the next chapter, which focuses on copyright and trademark law.

This chapter explores the main forms of *property rights,* then focuses attention (mostly) on IP rights under patents and trade secrets. Quite obviously, property law is an extensive topic, so the best we can do in the next two chapters is skim the surface of this body of law.

REAL PROPERTY

real property
Land and anything firmly attached thereto, such as a house, office building, and so forth.

Real property is land and anything firmly attached thereto such as buildings, trees, and mineral reserves underneath the land's surface. Real property *rights* give owners the right to exclude others from trespassing on the surface, subsurface, or airspace to a "reasonable" level (generally, a few hundred feet). A basic characteristic of real property is that it is not moveable, even though a building could be destroyed or, in some cases, carted off. Personal property items such as plumbing fixtures become real property when they are firmly attached to a building or dwelling.

Aspects of Real Property

Air and Mineral Rights

At common law, in addition to the surface, a landowner owned a shaft of space above and below the land—conceptually, ownership extended to the heavens above and below the land surface to the center of the earth. With the advent of air travel, ownership of the shaft of airspace to the heavens was lowered to a "reasonable" level, generally several hundred feet. A landowner's rights to airspace enable him to prevent someone from stringing wire 50 feet over his land, but do not allow him to sue an airline company for "trespass" when a plane invades his airspace 1,500, 5,000, or 30,000 feet above the surface.

The depth of mineral rights continues to be to the center of the earth. Owners of a land tract can exploit their mineral reserves as deeply as such reserves can be extracted and they can prevent others from slant drilling under the surface of their land. Where a common pool of oil exists under the land of several adjacent landowners, such as is common in Texas, government authorities regulate the extraction of oil. Otherwise, resources would be wasted as each landowner could seek to pump out as much oil as possible. In areas where mineral reserves are known to be valuable, it is common for landowners to sell or lease their mineral reserves separately from surface use.

Fixtures

When personal property is firmly attached to real property, it *becomes* real property. Such property is often called a *fixture*. Quite obviously, all buildings are built from personal property items such as bricks, concrete, steel rods, and so forth. Once building materials are used, they become *annexed* to the real property and are part of the real property. When carpets or cupboards are firmly attached to a building, they too become fixtures and, thus, real property. For some personal property, such as pool tables and appliances, it is unclear whether such property is real or personal. In determining whether such property is personal or real, courts look at a number of factors, including

- *Intent of the party installing the property.* A question asked by courts is whether, at the time of installation of the property in question, it is reasonable to believe that the owner meant for the property to be a permanent addition to the real property. Often in transfers of real property, the contract between buyer and seller will specify whether curtains, for example, stay with the house, or whether the seller takes the curtains with her or him.

- *Degree of attachment to real property.* The more attached the property is, the more likely a court is to hold that the property is a fixture and thus real. There is an exception in the case of trade fixtures, which are fixtures installed by a commercial tenant operating a business. Normally, unless withdrawing such fixtures would damage the premises, a businessperson can take trade fixtures, such as shelving, when the tenancy ends.

- *Ownership of the property.* It is much less likely that tenants are making permanent improvements to real property when they make improvements than when owners do the same thing. Courts take into account whether landowners or tenants are adding something to the premises that may or may not be a permanent addition.

Transfers of Ownership of Real Property

deed
A document of title that describes real property and identifies its owner(s).

A transfer of ownership of real property typically begins when the prior owner *signs* a **deed,** which is a document that signifies ownership of real property and contains a legal description of the land. A transfer of ownership of real property also requires that the seller *deliver* the deed to the purchaser. Deeds are typically recorded at the county recording office or some other location where public documents are maintained for public inspection. By making deeds available for public inspection, the true ownership of real property can more easily be determined. Also, those who have claims on a parcel of real estate (such as liens or other encumbrances as discussed below) are required to file their claims in the same office, so that potential purchasers of real estate can determine what claims are being made against the landowner and the property.

Types of Deeds

General Warranty

There are several kinds of deeds, notably general warranty, special warranty, and quitclaim. In *general warranty* deeds, the seller (sometimes called grantor), *warrants,* or promises, that he or she is the true owner of the land and that there are no liens or encumbrances that are not described on the deed. If the purchaser were to buy the real estate and an oil company claimed that it owned rights to drill for oil on the land, the purchaser could sue the seller based on a breach of a general warranty deed. A general warranty deed offers buyers the greatest degree of title protection from the sellers.

Special Warranty

A *special warranty* deed is one in which the seller warrants that since the time when he or she occupied the land, no liens or encumbrances that would diminish the value of the land to the purchaser have been incurred. In this form of deed, however, the seller is not making any claims about events that occurred before he or she purchased the land. In addition to warranties provided by sellers, buyers usually buy *title insurance,* which obligates the title insurance company to pay out damages if there is cloud on the title, such as an easement (discussed below) that was not referred to in the deed to the insured property.

Quitclaim

In a *quitclaim* deed, the seller is not making any claim to ownership of the property but is promising to convey whatever interest he or she has in the premises to the buyer. Quitclaim deeds are not common in real estate sales, but they are useful to clear up clouds to title of real estate. If the person giving the quitclaim deed has a possible claim on property, they can give up that claim by signing over a quitclaim deed. Usually, in these transactions the current owner and occupier of the land is trying to clear up any possible claims to her property. The owner will pay settlement monies in return for quitclaims from those who might have an ownership claim on the property, such as an easement or lien, to remove the clouds on her title, often as a prelude to selling the land herself.

Liens or Encumbrances

Liens or encumbrances are claims that various (nonowner or nonpossessor) parties have on real property. For example, an easement is the right to trespass on another's real estate, which diminishes the value of the real estate to a potential buyer. It is possible that an owner of adjacent property had purchased or acquired the right to cut across his neighbor's property. More often, an electric power company or a gas pipeline company owns the right to run lines across a property. Liens or encumbrances are recorded in the same location as real estate deeds (most commonly, in a county courthouse), allowing buyers to easily "search" for any claims against property they are buying. In spite of the recording of liens and encumbrances, unpleasant surprises do occur in real estate transactions, justifying the costs of title insurance (see the *Miller* case, Case 12-1).

Among the prominent liens or encumbrances against real estate are the following:

- A *mortgage* is a pledge of specified property as security for loans.
- An *easement* is a right of passage over a neighbor's land or waterway. Easements are often held in connection with mineral rights, but an easement could simply be a right to trespass. As mentioned above, electric power companies are often granted easements to (1) hang wires across premises and (2) trespass to maintain those wires.
- Other *liens* or *encumbrances* may include claims that unsecured debtors have against the owners of real property. In many states, homestead laws prevent creditors from evicting debtors from their homes to satisfy debts. The filing of a lien against a debtor's property, however, allows the lien holder, in the event of sale, to claim the proceeds of the sale of the debtor's property above the priority of the seller.
- *Long-term leases* usually have a duration of more than three years.
- *Restrictive covenants* may prevent a landowner from doing certain things, such as establishing a business that would make the land much more valuable. A restrictive covenant is an example of an *encumbrance*.

This list is not exhaustive.

Recording Acts

Between seller and buyer, the transfer of a signed deed is all that is necessary to transfer title to a parcel of real estate. As discussed above, the *recording acts* make ownership of real property part of the public record. The recording acts make deeds and other liens or encumbrances on real property generally available to the public, serving to prevent an owner of real estate from selling the same real estate more than once. A basic feature of the recording acts is that a *subsequent* bona fide purchaser for value has priority over a prior purchaser that did not record the transfer of real estate. When a purchase of real estate occurs, the purchaser (generally through his attorney) will record the transfer of deed at the county recording office *before* the seller is paid for the real estate. If the transfer of real estate is not recorded, an unscrupulous seller could sell the same real estate to another purchaser, who would have a superior claim to that of the first purchaser if that purchaser did not promptly record the ownership change.

In Case 12-1, an easement not disclosed on a general warranty deed is the subject of a lawsuit.

Case 12-1

Fidelity National Title Insurance Company, Plaintiff and Appellant v. Clayton L. Miller, Defendant and Respondent

Court of Appeal of California,
Fourth Appellate District, Division One
215 Cal. App. 3d 1163 (1989)

BACKGROUND AND FACTS

In 1953 Miller encumbered the property with a restrictive covenant [an encumbrance] granting neighbor Whitby a "view easement." The Whitby restrictive covenant was recorded in the county recording office. Years later Miller wanted to convey the property to his daughter and son-in-law, Jean and Raymond Gazzo (together Gazzo). Miller told Gazzo he had given Whitby a view easement. Apparently Miller was unsure whether Whitby had recorded her restrictive covenant. In 1986 Gazzo and Miller opened escrow. Fidelity National Title Insurance Co. issued a preliminary report not mentioning the Whitby encumbrance. Gazzo asked Fidelity whether the property was encumbered by a restriction not appearing on the preliminary report. Fidelity found nothing. Fidelity issued a title insurance policy to Gazzo not mentioning the Whitby encumbrance. Miller conveyed the property to Gazzo by unrestricted grant deed without excepting or stating the Whitby restrictive covenant. After escrow closed, Gazzo discovered the Whitby encumbrance had been recorded.

Gazzo made a claim against Fidelity under the title insurance policy. Fidelity paid Gazzo $125,000 under the title insurance policy for the diminution in the property's value resulting from the Whitby encumbrance. Gazzo executed a release and assignment of rights favoring Fidelity. Fidelity then filed suit against Miller claiming that Miller issued a general warranty deed that did not mention the view easement. Miller claims that he orally disclosed the existence of the easement to Gazzo and that the improperly prepared deed was due to negligence by Fidelity. Miller filed a motion for a summary judgment that was granted by the trial court. Fidelity appeals the granting of the motion for a summary judgment by the trial court.

Opinion by Kremer

"[A] grant deed to encumbered property without words of restraint breaches this covenant. The seller may not defend on the ground that the buyer had notice from the preliminary title report or otherwise; the action is on breach of contract and does not require a showing of reliance or misrepresentation. [Citations omitted] The covenant is breached, if untrue, when the instrument is executed."

Section 1113 [of the California Code] implies the covenants against prior conveyances and encumbrances "from the use of the word 'grant' unless such covenants are restrained by express terms in the deed. Therefore, the grantor who does not want to imply the statutory warranties can specify that his grant is made without warranty of any kind or can specifically set forth in the deed the encumbrances to which the property is subject. The description of the encumbrances will negate any implication of warranty against those encumbrances."

* * *

By its terms section 1113 implies a covenant against encumbrances in a grant deed "unless restrained by *express terms* contained in such conveyance." [Italics added.] "There can be no implied covenant where the subject matter is *expressly agreed* upon by the parties to the contrary." (Italics added.) Miller presented no evidence compelling a finding as a matter of law that he and Gazzo expressly agreed to exclude from their contract section 1113's implied covenant against encumbrances. Indeed, in his points and authorities supporting his motion Miller admitted "none of the writings surrounding the transaction contain an exception from the conveyance of the Whitby Covenant." Further, Miller cites no authority suggesting the implied covenant can be deleted by implied agreement.

* * *

Further, on this record a fact finder could reasonably infer there was no agreement between Miller and Gazzo that the grant deed would not contain the statutorily implied covenant against encumbrances. Gazzo's surprise upon discovering the recorded Whitby covenant and his filing a claim against Fidelity suggest he had no such agreement with Miller. Also casting doubt on the existence of any such agreement is Miller's claim he executed the facially unrestricted grant deed because he in fact believed the property was unencumbered in justifiable reliance on Fidelity's representations.

Decision and Outcome

The decision of the trial court to grant a motion for a summary judgment in favor of Miller, the defendant, was reversed and the case was remanded to the trial court for a trial.

Questions for Analysis

1. On what basis can Fidelity, the title insurance company, sue Miller? Wasn't the root cause of this litigation the fact that Fidelity failed to do its job and discover the encumbrance that was apparently recorded?

2. A real estate sale is one type of transaction that must be in writing to be enforceable. Did Miller make a mistake by orally telling his son-in-law about the encumbrance but not recording it on his warranty deed?

Priority under the Recording Acts

As mentioned above, state recording acts provide notice to the world of ownership of real property. In general, if fraudulent party (A) sells real estate to B and B does not promptly record the transfer of the deed, A could sell the same property to C. If C recorded the transfer of deed before B, C would be the new property owner. There are, however, significant differences in the recording acts among the states. State recording act statutes are generally classified as *notice, race,* and *notice-race:*

- In *notice* states, C's ownership claim prevails over B's only if C had no notice of the prior transfer of the deed to B. C need not record first to be awarded priority.
- In *race* states, priority is established by the first recorded transfer, regardless of notice.
- In *notice-race* states, if B and C had no notice of each other's transactions, the first to record would be given ownership of the real estate.

Leases

Real property is often leased. Under a lease, the owner (or lessor/landlord) grants temporary possession to a lessee (or tenant). Because leasing of real property is so common, and because landlords generally have leverage over tenants, a sizeable branch of law, called landlord-tenant law, has developed. Landlord-tenant law evolved rapidly as the main form of leases changed during the twentieth century from those providing agricultural tenancy to those covering city-dweller apartments. Recalling that property ownership entails a bundle of rights, it should come as no surprise that such a bundle can be divided in various ways. The division of property rights between landlords and tenants has been significantly influenced by protective legislation that requires landlords to maintain leased premises in *habitable condition,* to give *notice* before eviction, and to *adhere to building codes.*

PERSONAL PROPERTY

As discussed above, real property is land and anything firmly attached thereto such as buildings, fixtures, and trees. All other property is personal property. Personal property is often divided into tangible and intangible categories, with intellectual property in the intangible personal property box.

Tangible Personal Property

Tangible personal property is personal property that you can touch and is moveable. Clothes, cars, and tables are all examples of tangible personal property. As with real property, a trespass against personal property is a tort, and victims are entitled to damages. As with real property, certain uses of personal property are legally restricted. Alcohol cannot be sold to minors, shooting guns inside a city is generally illegal, and so on.

Transfers of Tangible Personal Property

Most sales of personal property are not accompanied by documents of title, though some are. If you purchase a table or a soft drink, the seller does not give you a paper title to these forms of personal property that is functionally equivalent to a deed in real estate. Normally, the document that a buyer receives that most closely corresponds to a title for personal property is a sales receipt or bill of sale. For some forms of personal property, documents of title are used: motor vehicles, private airplanes, and some kinds of more exotic forms of personal property such as original works of art, pure breeds of animals, and other products whose pedigree constitutes a significant part of its value.

Leases and Bailments

As with real estate, possession and ownership of personal property can be separated, as occurs when U-Haul® rents its trailers and trucks to those who have something large to move. When an owner of personal property leases or rents that property to another, the owner is termed a *lessor* or *bailor* and the renter is a *lessee* or *bailee*. As with real property, there is a branch of law that deals with the rights and duties of the parties when a *lease* or *bailment* of personal property occurs. Longer-term rentals of business equipment are typically called leases, while shorter term rentals are bailments. Many leases of personal property used in business have a fixed term, but some are open-ended. It is quite common for the lessee to have an option to purchase personal property he or she has been leasing at the end of the lease.

bailment
A short-term rental of personal property.

A more temporary rental of personal property is called a **bailment.** In a bailment, the owner of the personal property becomes the bailor and transfers possession of the property with the understanding that the bailee will return the property in a short period of time. As mentioned above, the U-Haul® Company is a prominent bailor. Bailees are required to use reasonable care and are responsible for damage to the bailed property or for the entire value of the property if they fail to return the property. In practice, bailors often offer insurance policies so that bailees will not be liable for the entire value of the bailed property if they are momentarily careless.

Bailors owe duties to bailees to inspect and check to see that the equipment and vehicles they rent out are not in a condition that would make them dangerous to bailees. Failure to use reasonable care in renting out bailed equipment makes bailors liable to bailees. Of course, when a bailee is injured using rented equipment, there is generally an issue over whether the equipment or vehicle was defective or whether the bailee was negligent at the time the accident occurred. Many bailments involve chain saws, snowmobiles, and other equipment that can seriously harm users if (1) the equipment is not in good working order when rented out and (2) the operator is momentarily distracted, operates the equipment while intoxicated, or any of a multitude of other factors. For a business to defend itself in bailment suits involving the rental of allegedly defective equipment, it is imperative that the business has maintenance inspection records to rebut inferences that the equipment they rented out was defective. It is also prudent for a business to require bailees of sports equipment to sign a separate form that (1) warns them of the risks inherent in the sport or activity and (2) voluntarily waives their right to sue based on assumption of risk.

Lost, Mislaid, and Abandoned Property

Lost Property

Personal property can be acquired by means other than production, sale, or gift. The *finder* of lost property is the owner of the lost property against anyone in the world, *except for the original owner*. The issue in these situations often is what constitutes lost property? Property is considered *lost* when the owner negligently or inadvertently leaves the property somewhere, where it is subsequently found by a finder. The law makes a distinction between lost property and mislaid property. Property is considered *mislaid* if it is left by the owner with the intention of returning or where it is reasonable to assume that the owner will remember where the property was mislaid and return to reclaim it. If a person loses jewelry because of holes in her pockets, the jewels are lost property, not mislaid property. If a person forgets to pick up a credit card after paying for a meal in a restaurant, the credit card is mislaid as it is likely that the person will later realize the loss, call the restaurant, and reclaim the mislaid credit card.

Mislaid Property

In contrast to the situation with lost property, the owner of the premises where mislaid property is located becomes the rightful possessor of the mislaid property and has a superior claim to the mislaid property relative to another finder. If Carl owns a restaurant and Mary finds an expensive watch on the floor in a dark corner, the watch would probably qualify as mislaid property and Carl would have the superior claim to the watch relative to Mary. On the other hand, it is likely that the owner of the watch would retrace his steps and contact Carl's restaurant in an attempt to find his watch. Technically, since the watch would qualify as mislaid property, Carl would be a bailee of the watch and liable to the owner if an employee stole the watch or it was somehow lost from the "lost and found" box.

To remove ambiguity between lost versus mislaid property, many states have enacted *estray statutes* that allow finders of lost or mislaid items to advertise that they have found property. If the property is not claimed by the true owner within a period of time, often a year, the finder of the item in question becomes the owner, except for mislaid property, in which case the mislaid property becomes the property of the owner of the premises where the property was found.

Abandoned Property

Property is considered abandoned if the owner discards the property with intent to give up his or her rights in the property, such as occurs when a person puts property in a trash can. Property is also considered abandoned if it is lost or mislaid and the original owner has stopped searching for the property. The finder of abandoned property becomes the owner, even against the original owner.

Intangible Personal Property

All intellectual property is intangible, but intangible personal property encompasses more than just IP. Property is intangible if the rights associated with the property exist symbolically rather than physically. The following are examples of intangible property that is *not* IP:

- A stock certificate is intangible property that represents an ownership interest in a corporation.
- A bankbook is intangible property that represents a claim on a bank for the amount of money correctly indicated by the bankbook.
- Credit cards are symbols of intangible property that represent an ability to transfer money from a source that has a reputation for reliability, such as American Express®.

INTELLECTUAL PROPERTY

intellectual property (IP)
Property, often in the form of ideas or knowledge, that can be of great value.

All **intellectual property (IP)** is intangible (it cannot be touched). In other words, it is property defined by various legally enforceable rights. A patentee (owner of a patent) owns the right to prevent others from making, using, or selling the patented invention. The invention itself may be composed of a new pharmaceutical drug, the process for making that drug, or the machines that make the drugs. Each is patentable (the chemical composition of the drug, the process for making it, and the machine that makes it) and, yet, the patentee may have no physical facilities to produce the patented product. Instead, the patentee may decide to license the right to make its patented product to a more established pharmaceutical firm and collect its reward in the form of royalties from drug sales made by the licensee. When pills containing the patented drugs are made, the patentee does not own those pills but, rather, just owns the right to exclude others from making those pills except by agreement.

The most prominent forms of intellectual property are patent, trade secret, copyright, and trademark. We discuss the first two in this chapter and the latter two in the next chapter.

MANAGING INTELLECTUAL PROPERTY

Management of intellectual property is no longer "just a lawyer's thing." Today, managers in companies of all sizes must be cognizant of the basics of IP law in their daily decision making. Mistakes in the management of IP are legendary and are the frequent focus of articles in newspapers and other periodicals, of the courts, and increasingly in the training of future managers. Consider the following situations:

1. The company you work for is an aggressive leader in high-tech and has a large staff of scientists and engineers who have made important contributions in their disciplines. Many of these staff members regularly attend academic and trade expositions where scientific papers are presented.
2. You are considering an important product launch, but the market acceptance of the product is questionable. You hire an outside firm to conduct market research.
3. Many of your employees are young software engineers who are much in demand. Most of these employees expect to work for several employers during their careers and some also anticipate heading up their own firms in the not-too-distant future.

Each of the foregoing confronts "management" with the potential for significant IP protection problems, as each of these situations creates opportunities for specialized knowledge, techniques, product ideas, and so forth to escape from the control of the company. At the end of this chapter, you should be able to recognize the IP law issue inherent in each of the three management challenges listed above. Recognition of IP issues is essential for managers who want to manage effectively. Decisions to apply for patents, to rely on trade secrets, or to apply combination strategies to IP protection are *management* decisions. Lawyers can be useful for pointing out the costs and benefits of alternative choices, but, ultimately, IP decisions are management decisions. The success of managers is increasingly tied to their success at managing IP. Therefore, knowledge of the basics of IP law should be part of the skill set that modern managers possess.

LEGAL PROTECTION OF INVENTORS: PATENT LAW

In the late 1700s, influential citizens in the collection of colonies that was to become the United States were aware of the need to protect and encourage the creation of intellectual property. Article 1, Section 8 of the U.S. Constitution contains enumerated (or delegated) powers of the federal government. Among those powers are the power to "promote the Progress of Science and useful Arts, by securing for limited Times to Authors and Inventors the exclusive Right to their respective Writings and Discoveries." Among the first acts of the U.S. Congress after the Constitution was ratified in 1789 was adoption of the Patent Act of 1790. In 1790, three patents were issued; in 1998 over 147,000 patents were issued and the PTO received nearly 250,000 applications that year. Most economists and business analysts attribute much of the strength of the U.S. economy to its leadership in intellectual property. For the inventions that qualify, patents provide the most extensive legal protection.

Institutional Aspects of Applying for Patents

Patent and Trademark Office

Congress created the Patent and Trademark Office (PTO) to make decisions on patent applications. As the name implies, the PTO also makes decisions regarding trademarks under the Lanham Act (discussion of trademarks takes place in the next chapter). An inventor applying for a patent sends his or her application to the PTO, which makes a decision as to whether the invention qualifies for a patent based on the Patent Act, regulations of the PTO, and precedents created by federal courts.

Court of Appeals for the Federal Circuit

All decisions made by the PTO are subject to review by the federal courts. In 1982 Congress created the Federal Circuit in Washington, D.C., to specialize in patent cases (technically, the Court of Appeals of the Federal Circuit [CAFC]). All appeals from the PTO and from federal district courts go through the CAFC. Appeals from the CAFC are to the U.S. Supreme Court.

PTO Procedures

The PTO and Internet Assets

Patent applicants must fill out and file a patent application using forms supplied by the PTO.[1] Although an applicant is not required to obtain the services of an attorney in this endeavor, such services are strongly recommended.

The PTO has recently made increasing use of the Internet through its website at http://www.uspto.gov. At the PTO website, applicants can download the forms required for

---

[1] Actual patent applications involve more than just filling out some forms; there are requirements to supply data about the state of technology in the field, the best mode for making the invention, and what is being claimed as original.

patent applications and can access a range of helpful information, including listings of IP attorneys. In addition, the PTO provides search engines to assist applicants in determining whether what they are trying to patent has already been patented. Quite obviously, the PTO will not issue two patents for the same invention. There are also well-organized patent search engines furnished by the private sector. For a number of years, IBM maintained a widely used patent search engine. This practice ended in 2000 when IBM and the Internet Capital Group created Delphion, which is an independent, stand-alone entity that provides patent search services (http://www.delphion.com).

Patent Examiner

patent examiner
An employee of the Patent and Trademark Office (PTO) who reviews (examines) applications for patents.

Once a patent application has been completed, it is submitted to the PTO, at which time, generally, the PTO will assign a **patent examiner** to the application. Efforts are made to assign applications to examiners who are familiar with the discipline of the application. An applicant interested in patenting a new drug or life form would typically be assigned to an examiner with a background in the biological sciences. An applicant whose invention is a new machine for making a product would generally be assigned to an examiner with training in mechanical engineering or a related field. Recently, as the number of software-related patents has increased, so too has the number of PTO examiners with training in computer science.

Secrecy

In the past, when a patent applicant's submission was rejected, the application remained sealed, unavailable to the public and competitors of the patent applicant. The thinking was that if society is not awarding the applicant with a patent, then the applicant should not have to reveal what he had invented. Also, since patent applications describe the invention in some detail, they are a potential source of trade secrets that could give rival firms advantages.

Disclosure of Patent Applications under the American Inventors Protection Act

In 1999, Congress passed the American Inventors Protection Act, which adopts the *European rule* with respect to patent applications. Henceforth, if an applicant for a U.S. patent also files for a patent in a foreign country, the application before the PTO will be published 18 months after filing. Only applicants that do not file their applications with any foreign countries will be assured that their applications for patents will not be made publicly available if a patent is not issued. The American Inventors Protection Act also changed the U.S. Patent Act in other ways, which are discussed below.

Requirements for Patentability

Novelty

Section 101 of the Patent Act explains that "Whoever invents or discovers any new and useful process, machine, manufacture, or composition of matter, or any new and useful improvement thereof, may obtain a patent therefor, subject to the conditions and requirements of this title." A way of analyzing whether an invention is patentable is to decide whether the invention falls outside Section 101 and the sections of the Patent Act that are incorporated by reference in Section 101. From Section 101, to obtain a patent, an inventor must have invented something that is *new*. Reinventing the wheel will not earn the reinventor a patent.

Section 102(a): What Is in the Public Domain at the Time of Invention

Section 102 of the Patent Act defines newness or novelty according to various criteria, but if the invention is not new, a patent will not be issued. According to Section 102,

A person shall be entitled to a patent unless—

a. the invention was known or used by others in this country, or patented or described in a printed publication in this or a foreign country, before the invention thereof by the applicant for patent . . .

Nutz and Boltz   Patent Timing Issues

Time	§ 102(a) x	§ 102(g) y	§ 102(b) z	Line
	Date of invention (conception)	Reduction to practice	Filing date	

Prior to *x*, if the invention is known, used, or made in the United States, it cannot be patented. If the invention is described or patented anywhere before *x*, the patent will not be issued. (Section 102(a))

If the invention was patented or described in a publication more than one year prior to *z*, it cannot be patented. (Section 102(b))

If the invention was on sale or used in the United States more than one year prior to *z*, it cannot be patented. (Section 102(b))

If the inventor is not reasonably diligent between *x* and *y*, then a patent will not be issued if there is a second inventor who invented and reduced to practice between *x* and *y*. (Section 102(g))

Critical Date, Conception, Reduction to Practice   The critical date for Section 102(a) is the date of the *invention*. If the events described in Section 102(a), such as "the invention was known . . . ," occur *before* the critical date, the invention will not qualify as "new" and therefore it is ineligible to receive a patent. Under patent law, several steps in the inventive process are recognized. An invention is viewed as occurring *at the date* when the mental steps necessary to construct the invention are *conceived* as long as the inventor was reasonably diligent in completing the invention, called *reduction to practice*.[2] An invention is conceived when drawings and plans are laid out with sufficient detail that a person knowledgeable in the industry could reproduce the invention. When the actual invention is constructed, it is "reduced to practice." In the "Nutz and Boltz" box, *x* marks the critical date for purposes of Section 102(a) as long as the inventor is reasonably diligent in constructing the invention in the time interval between *x* and *y*.

Four Disqualifiers in Section 102(a)   Section 102(a) indicates that, if the invention is (1) *known* or (2) *used* by others in *this country*, there is no more room for a claim of invention of that item or process. Similarly, (3) if the product or process is *patented* in this or in a foreign country or (4) *described* in a printed publication in *this or another country*, that item or process cannot qualify for a patent. If any of these events have occurred before *x* on the time line in the "Nutz and Boltz" box, the "invention" is not "new."

It is also important to link geographic scope with the disqualifying condition(s). The first two disqualifiers are limited geographically to *this country*, while the last two pertain to events *anywhere in the world*.

Conception, Filing a Patent Application, and Keeping Adequate Records   Section 102 (a) grants priority, and thus eligibility for receiving a patent, to the inventor who first *conceives*

---

[2] For some inventions, reduction to practice is not necessary or feasible (consider a patent for a new type of atomic weapon). For those inventions, reduction to practice occurs when the patent application is filed.

of an invention. Priority in the United States (unlike most of the rest of the world) is based on *first to invent* and *not first to file* with the PTO. If there is a contest about which inventor has priority, it is vitally important for the inventor to keep adequate records to document when he or she actually figured out the invention with sufficient precision that he or she can be deemed *first to conceive*. It is the responsibility of management to made sure that technical staff (scientists, engineers, and others working in labs) are careful to keep detailed records for possible use later if there is a legal challenge over who was first to invent.

Section 102(b): One-Year Rule

Section 102(b) also contains four more disqualifying conditions. The text of Section 102(b) reads,

> [A person shall be entitled to a patent unless—]
>
> b. the invention was patented or described in a printed publication in this or a foreign country or in public use or on sale in this country, more than one year prior to the date of the application for patent in the United States . . .

One Year from Filing Date Again, it is important to keep the geographic scope linked with the various provisions that create loss of rights to patent a useful invention. The first two conditions in Section 102(b) apply to the entire world. If the invention has already been *patented* or *described* in a printed publication anywhere in the world, the applicant is not entitled to a U.S. patent for the invention if these events occurred more than one year prior to *filing* of the application with the PTO. The critical date for Section 102(b) is the *filing date* (z on the time line in the "Nutz and Boltz" box), not the date of conception.

Published or Patented Anywhere in the World Section 102(b) places a heavy burden on applicants to be aware of patenting and publications anywhere in the world. Fortunately for U.S. inventors, most scientific advances occur in the United States, Europe, and Japan. This section also places a burden on management to be diligent with regard to public presentations by employees (recall management issue number 1 from the beginning of the chapter, under "Managing Intellectual Property"). Many times technical employees attend scientific and trade conferences, submit papers, and make presentations. If those papers and presentations describe what the company later submits to the PTO as a patent application, the firm can lose its right to patent the invention if more than one year elapses between the presentation and the filing of the patent.

Public Uses or Commercial Sales Section 102(b) also starts a one-year clock if the patented item is used publicly or sold commercially more than one year before the patent application has been filed. For commercial sales, the one-year limit applies equally to the applicant and to third parties. In other words, if the item that the applicant wants to patent is sold more than one year before filing, either by the applicant or some third party such as a rival in business, the right to patent the product is lost. Quite often, tests of market acceptability or experimental uses or sales of a new product are necessary (management issue number 2 at the start of the chapter). In such cases, the applicant should obtain nondisclosure agreements (NDAs) from participants in the market tests of products that the firm may seek to patent in the future. Note that even an *offer* to sell a product that the applicant later seeks to patent, if the offer is made more than one year prior to the filing date, can destroy *novelty* under Section 102(b). Consider the facts in Case 12-2.

Case 12-2

TP Laboratories, Inc., an Indiana corporation, Appellant/Cross Appellee v. Professional Positioners, Inc., a Wisconsin corporation, Professional Positioners, Inc.,

United States Court of Appeals for the Federal Circuit 724 F.2d 965 (Fed. Cir. 1984)

BACKGROUND AND FACTS

The plaintiff, TP Laboratories, makes and sells orthodontic supplies and appliances to the dental profession. The plaintiff is closely connected with the professional practice of the Kesling and Rocke Orthodontic Group. The two businesses share a building. The Kesling and Rocke Group developed the invention that is at issue in this case. The invention was first conceived by Kesling in 1956 and reduced to practice in 1962; filing for the patent took place that year. A patent was issued in 1965 and shortly thereafter it was assigned to TP Laboratories. During the 1958–61 period of time, the invention was given to three patients for use, but no fee was ever charged. The patients using the devices never signed nondisclosure agreements. Later, plaintiff sued defendant for using its patented invention and defendant claims the patent was invalid because of public use more than one year before filing. The district court judge ruled that the patent was invalid and plaintiff appeals.

Opinion by Nies, Circuit Judge

The subject matter of the '820 patent is a molded tooth positioning appliance which is to be worn several hours a day by a person undergoing orthodontal treatment. The general type of device is not new. The improvement by Kesling lies in placing wires in the device which fit in the embrasure area between the teeth and keep the appliance in position without the necessity of the patient exerting constant jaw pressure. The wires are referred to as "seating devices," "seating springs," "precision seating springs," "springs," or "metal adjuncts." Because of the shape, as seen below, the invention is also referred to as a tooth positioner with "C's":

* * *

The use of tooth positioners with C's in the treatment of three K&R patients during the period 1958–61 led to the issues under 35 U.S.C. § 102(b). It is undisputed that these three devices fell within the language of the '820 [the patent application] claims and no modification of design was made as a consequence of these uses. The evidence which established these uses was found in the patient records of K&R and the underlying facts are not in dispute. Appellant characterizes these uses as secret and/or experimental; appellees urge that they are, as found by the district court, public uses within the meaning of the statute.

The first use of the claimed invention on a patient occurred on August 25, 1958. Orthodontal treatment of this patient (Furst) spanned the time period between February 1958 and April 1964. Use of the device terminated after approximately two months. During discovery, the device itself was produced, having been retained by K&R in the patient's model box. This patient's mandibular model from the model box was inscribed "experimental wires." Over the six year period of treatment, this patient was also fitted with other devices, retainers as well as positioners not embraced by the '820 claims.

Another patient (Rumely-Brady) who had begun treatment in August 1958 was supplied with a tooth positioner equipped with C's on November 10, 1959. Entry on the record card of this patient indicates "results fair" on December 18, 1959; "results better" on February 5, 1960, and "results good" on August 1, 1960. Nevertheless, use of the device was discontinued on January 16, 1961, in favor of retainers, because certain spacing irregularities were not being corrected. The same positioner with C's was again prescribed on May 5, 1961, and was used in conjunction with various other devices until at least March of 1962. The patient missed a later scheduled appointment which is the last entry on her card.

A positioner with C's was prescribed for a third patient (Spiers-Elliott) on November 1, 1960. Its use apparently was discontinued about three months later, a different device being mailed to the patient on February 2, 1961. During the treatment of this patient, which spanned the period of time between January 21, 1960, and November 24, 1961, three different positioners were prescribed, only one of which was embraced by the '820 claims.

* * *

The evidence in this case clearly establishes use by at least three patients more than one year prior to the application date. Furthermore, these users were "under no limitation, restriction or obligation of secrecy to the inventor." [Citations omitted.] Certainly there is no evidence to the contrary and there is testimony to support such a finding. . . . Consequently, the Court can only conclude that the patients were under no obligations of secrecy or for that matter any restrictions. TP argues that these items were in secret because even the patients were not aware of the "testing." This is not significant. The plain fact is that the claimed invention was not kept secret. It was open to public observation without restriction which is sufficient to constitute "public use." Furthermore, Dr. Furst was aware that the precision seating springs were a new device. . . . In addition, several of Mrs. Spiers Elliott's associates saw the device. Consequently, the feigned secrecy relied upon by TP accords it no aid in claiming that the "use" was not "public."

Decision and Outcome

The Court of Appeals for the Federal Circuit invalidated the '820 patent held by the plaintiff because there was public use of the invention more than one year before filing for the patent application took place. Section 102(b) bars issuance of a patent if more than one year elapses between public use and filing for the patent.

Questions for Analysis

1. Before spending the money to apply for a patent, most companies, the plaintiff included, test their products to see if they work. What could the plaintiff have possibly done to preserve the opportunity to patent his invention? Suppose the plaintiff had required each patient using the invention during the '820 time period to sign a nondisclosure agreement. Would that have been enough?

2. Would the outcome in this case have been different had the patients complained about the device and the plaintiff had modified the design of the device that was later to become the '820 patent? Are the plaintiffs being penalized for getting it right the first time?

3. Just how "public" was the use of this device? Does a device in someone's mouth constitute "public" use?

Section 102(g): Reasonable Diligence

Under Section 102(g), an applicant is entitled to a patent unless

> g. before the applicant's invention thereof the invention was made in this country by another who had not abandoned, suppressed, or concealed it. In determining priority of invention there shall be considered not only the respective dates of conception and reduction to practice of the invention, but also the reasonable diligence of one who was first to conceive and last to reduce to practice, from a time prior to conception by the other.

Abandonment   Section 102(g) establishes priority based on the *date of invention* so long as the invention has not been *abandoned, suppressed, or concealed. Abandonment* has been defined legally as occurring if an inventor has not been reasonably diligent in the transition from the conception of the invention to the actual building of the invention (generally characterized as *reduction to practice*). Clearly, documentation of the steps taken by the inventor after conception of the invention can prove decisive in determining whether the inventor or firm is entitled to priority and thus a patent. There has been a sizeable volume of litigation over the issue of abandonment. A number of cases have held that a lengthy list of activities does not qualify to excuse lengthy delays between conception and reduction to practice.

Referring to the time line in the "Nutz and Boltz" box, to retain priority, the inventor must be reasonably diligent between times x and y. Two examples may suffice to give readers an appreciation of what are not legally excusable delays.

1. A university professor conceives of a patentable invention but does not have funding for his graduate assistant during the summer. The graduate assistant resumes work on the project during the fall, but the professor loses priority because a court finds that he has not been reasonably diligent between conception and reduction to practice. The court held in such a situation that the vagaries of university calendars were not its concern.[3]
2. A firm's R&D department discovers a process for dramatically improving the sharpness of laptop monitors. The firm sells laptops and currently has a large inventory. The firm decides to reduce its inventory of existing laptops before pursuing a patent that is likely to make its inventory largely obsolete. Work on making a prototype of the discovery therefore comes to a halt. Can a firm's marketing strategy be used as an excuse for delay in reducing to practice an innovation that clashes with its current sales efforts? Again the courts have looked at this issue and have answered with an emphatic No.[4]

In determining whether an inventor has been reasonably diligent after conception in reducing an invention to practice, courts have taken into account the economic circumstances of the inventor. If the inventor holds a day job and works out of his garage, courts allow greater leeway in defining "reasonable diligence." Again, it is important to have access to an IP attorney for consultation on this kind of tricky issue.

Case 12-3 combines the issues of prior art under Section 102(a) and reasonable diligence between the time when the invention has taken place and when the inventor actually reduces the invention to practice. Notice that the claim that the invention was not new because of *prior art* (a publication or reference that describes what the applicant is trying to patent) only applies when the anticipatory reference (or prior art) is contained in a *single reference* and not pieced together from several references. Note further that, as with prior case, defendants charged with patent infringement often claim as an affirmative defense that the plaintiff's patent was invalid.

[3] *Griffith v. Kanamaru*, 816 F.2d 624, 2 U.S.P.Q.2d 1361 (Fed. Cir. 1987).

[4] *Christie v. Seybold*, 55 F. 69 (6th Cir. 1893) is an oft-cited case that stands for the proposition that marketing considerations are not sufficient to excuse delays in reducing an invention to practice.

Case 12-3

Dr. Sakharam D. Mahurkar v. C.R. Bard, Inc

United States Court of Appeals for the Federal Circuit
79 F.3d 1572 (Fed. Cir. 1996)

FACTS AND CASE BACKGROUND

Dr. Sakharam D. Mahurkar sued the defendant, Mr. Bard, for patent infringement on a medical device called a double-lumen catheter used to help chronic dialysis patients. The court awarded Dr. Mahurkar damages in excess of $4 million. The case was appealed on the basis of validity and infringement. Mr. Bard argues that Mahurkar's patent is invalid because his work was published in a nationwide catalog, called the Cook catalog.

Opinion by Rader, Circuit Judge

Section 102(g) of title 35 contains the basic rule for determining priority. Section 102(g) also provides basic protection for the inventive process, shielding in particular the creative steps of conception and reduction to practice. In the U.S., the person who first reduces an invention to practice is "prima facie the first and true inventor." However, the person "who first conceives, and, in a mental sense, first invents . . . may date his patentable invention back to the time of its conception, if he connects the conception with its reduction to practice by reasonable diligence on his part, so that they are substantially one continuous act." Stated otherwise, priority of invention "goes to the first party to reduce an invention to practice unless the other party can show that it was the first to conceive the invention and that it exercised reasonable diligence in later reducing that invention to practice."

To have conceived of an invention, an inventor must have formed in his or her mind "a definite and permanent idea of the complete and operative invention, as it is hereafter to be applied in practice." The idea must be "so clearly defined in the inventor's mind that only ordinary skill would be necessary to reduce the invention to practice, without extensive research or experimentation."

* * *

Bard bears the burden of persuasion on the status of the Cook catalog as prior art. Bard must persuade the trier of fact by clear and convincing evidence that the Cook catalog was published prior to Dr. Mahurkar's invention date.

At trial, Dr. Mahurkar offered evidence to demonstrate prior invention in two ways. He offered evidence to show he conceived and reduced to practice his invention before publication of the catalog. He also offered evidence to show that he conceived of his invention prior to the date of publication of the Cook catalog and that he proceeded with reasonable diligence from a date just prior to publication of the catalog to his filing date. Bard, in turn, challenged Dr. Mahurkar's evidence.

With all of the evidence from both sides before the jury, Bard must persuade the jury by clear and convincing evidence that its version of the facts is true. In other words, Bard must persuade the jury that Dr. Mahurkar did not invent prior to publication of the catalog. This is because (1) he did not conceive and reduce his invention to practice before the publication date and (2) he did not conceive and thereafter proceed with reasonable diligence as required to his filing date. If Bard fails to meet this burden, the catalog is not prior art under section 102(a).

Viewing the evidence of record below in the light most favorable to Bard, this court concludes that no reasonable jury could have found clear and convincing evidence that the Cook catalog was prior art. Dr. Mahurkar testified that he conceived and began work on dual-lumen, flexible, hemodialysis catheters, including the '155 catheter, in 1979. From late 1980 through early 1981, Dr. Mahurkar constructed polyethylene prototype catheters in his kitchen. He bought tubing and various machines for making and testing his catheters.

During this time period, he also tested polyethylene prototypes and used them in flow and pressure drop tests in his kitchen. These tests used glycerine to simulate blood. These tests showed, to the limit of their design, the utility of his claimed invention. Dr. Mahurkar designed these tests to show the efficiency of his structure knowing that polyethylene catheters were too brittle for actual use with humans. But, he also knew that his invention would become suitable for its intended purpose by simple substitution of a soft, biocompatible material. Dr. Mahurkar adequately showed reduction to practice of his less complicated invention with tests which "[did] not duplicate all of the conditions of actual use."

Dr. Mahurkar provided corroboration for his testimony. Dr. Mahurkar confidentially disclosed the catheter prototype tips of his '155 invention to Geoffrey Martin, President of Vas-Cath Inc. in 1981, and Brian L. Bates of Cook, Inc. Mr. Martin testified that he received the polyethylene prototype tips from Dr. Mahurkar in 1981. Dr. Mahurkar also produced a letter from Stephen Brushey, an employee of Vas-Cath, dated April 21, 1981, that described several of his catheters. Additionally, Dr. Mahurkar presented a letter from Brian L. Bates of Cook, Inc., dated October 23, 1981. In this letter, Cook was "impressed with the thought and technology which has gone into the fabrication of the prototype material."

In addition to evidence of actual reduction to practice before publication of the Cook catalog, Dr. Mahurkar also showed reasonable diligence from his conception date through the filing of his patent application. From conception to filing, Dr. Mahurkar continuously sought to locate companies capable of extruding his tubing with the soft, flexible materials necessary for human use.

On this record and with the applicable burden of persuasion, no reasonable jury could have found that Bard proved the Cook catalog was prior art. Consequently, the court properly granted Dr. Mahurkar's motion for JMOL [Motion for a Judgment as a Matter of Law] of non-anticipation of claim 1 of the '155 patent.

Decision and Outcome

This court affirms the district court's denial of Bard's motion for JMOL under 35 U.S.C. § 102(a) and affirms the district court's grant of Dr. Mahurkar's cross motion. *Note:* A JMOL is filed by a party who believes that the evidence is so overwhelmingly in his favor that no reasonable jury could find for the other party. In this case, Bard filed a JMOL that was properly denied. The court ruled that a reasonable jury could have ruled for Dr. Mahurkar.

Questions for Analysis

1. How does the court define conception for purposes of Section 102(a) of the Patent Act?
2. What steps taken by the plaintiff indicated to the court that he was reasonably diligent between conception and reduction to practice?
3. Notice that a lot of the work in inventing this medical device was undertaken in the plaintiff's kitchen. If the plaintiff was a large corporation, do you think it would have tolerated such a long delay between conception and reduction to practice so that the inventor could find biocompatible material?
4. Examine this case on the basis of the steps that the plaintiff took to document significant events, such as conception and reasonable diligence. When did the court consider that the plaintiff's invention had been reduced to practice.

Section 103: Nonobviousness

Section 103 precludes the issuance of patents for inventions that only trivially advance knowledge in the field.

> a. A patent may not be obtained though the invention is not identically disclosed or described as set forth in section 102 of this title [35 USCS § 102], if the differences between the subject matter sought to be patented and the prior art are such that the subject matter as a whole would have been obvious at the time the invention was made to a person having ordinary skill in the art to which said subject matter pertains. Patentability shall not be negatived by the manner in which the invention was made.

The acid test for Section 103 is whether, at the time of the invention application, the improvement would have been obvious to one skilled in the industry. If the response to the question "Would this improvement be obvious to one skilled in the industry?" is yes, then a patent should not be issued. In evaluating a challenge to an existing patent based on nonobviousness, courts will look at whether the patent

1. Is a commercial success.
2. Solves some long-felt but unsolved need or needs.
3. Was tried by others who failed to solve the problem.
4. Was copied by others in the field.

Courts reason that the nonobviousness test has been passed if the patent is a commercial success. Otherwise, others would have made the obvious improvement. The fact that others tried to invent the same patent, but failed, also indicates that the creation was not obvious to those skilled in the industry. Given the potentially high cost of being judged an infringer, the fact that a firm copies a patent also indicates that the patent was not obvious to those skilled in the industry.

Obvious Changes   Changes in the form, proportion, degree, or aggregation of old elements have long been held *obvious* and thus not patentable. If old elements are aggregated and produce some synergistic and unexpected results, then it is possible that such an aggregation will survive a challenge based on obviousness. In challenging a patent based on a contention of obviousness, combinations of references in general (scholarly articles, an assemblage of other patents, etc.) are not usable in a skilled combination to show obviousness (see Case 12-3). However, a single reference that revealed the likely outcome of minor changes to a patented item would subject the patent applicant to a Section 103 obviousness challenge and, most probably, would prevent issuance of a patent.

Organizational Issues   Section 103(c) covers situations in large organizations where, over time, each step in the modification of a machine or process may be obvious given the previous steps in the inventive process. Section 103(c) does not allow an obviousness challenge to a patent where the subject matter of the prior art and the claimed invention were, at the time of the invention, owned by the *same* party. In such situations, institutional knowledge cannot be held against the organization for purposes of a challenge based on obviousness, even though the "new" patent applies an obvious next step to inventions previously developed by the organization.

Patentable Subject Matter

statutory subject matter
Things that can be patented, which can involve a process, machine, manufacture, or composition of nature.

Section 101 of the Patent Act mentions "process, machine, manufacture, or composition of matter" as statutory subject matter for patent applications. Imagine a tin container that contains a new pharmaceutical drug. The *process* of making the drug is patentable. The *machines* that make the drug and the tin are patentable. The tin container may be patentable as a *manufacture*. As long as the drug is not naturally occurring, it also is patentable as a *composition of matter*.

There are several categories of nonstatutory subject matter, referring to things that *cannot* be patented:

nonstatutory subject matter
Things that cannot be patented, which, most notably, are things that can be discovered (laws of nature, naturally occurring substances, and so forth) as opposed to invented.

- Perhaps most fundamentally, *ideas* cannot be patented. Patents must be and can only be applied to something that *does something* rather than to an idea, no matter how clever the idea is.
- Moreover, patents are restricted to things that are *created* as opposed to things that are *discovered*. So laws of nature and mathematical formulas cannot be patented. Thus, the famous mass/energy conversion equation deduced (discovered) by Albert Einstein—$E = mc^2$—could not be patented, but the creation of a nuclear reactor could be.
- *Printed material, functions of machines, mental processes* such as total quality management, and *compilations of data* are not patentable subject matter.
- Finally, naturally occurring substances generally cannot be patented, but *artificial life forms,* including genetically altered versions of existing life forms, can be patented. Genetically engineered lab mice have been patented and the process of cloning is patentable unless the subject matter of the cloning is human.

Patent Infringement

patent infringement
The acquisition or use of a patent, without permission, by a party other than the patent holder.

The most basic right that a patentee possesses is the right to exclude others from making, using, or selling the subject matter of a patent. In the U.S. system, a patentee has no obligation to make use of a patent, but retains the right to exclude others from replicating or selling the patent. A patent-holder can permit others to use his or her patent, usually in return for royalty payments. However, if another entity (individual or company) makes use of a patent-holder's invention without permission, that party is guilty of patent infringement. Also

Ethical Challenges   Thickets of Patents

In the United States, the Gillette Co. has been synonymous with razors and razor blades since the 1920s. A few years back, Gillette began a conscious campaign to improve the state of the art in shaving and began to patent a series of improvements to razor blades and razors, culminating with the triple-blade razor that worked with floating springs in the razor itself. As discussed by Kevin Rivette and David Kline in their recent book, *Rembrants in the Attic,* large companies have been able to use patent law not only to give themselves monopolies for their inventions, but also to get so many patents in an area that it creates a thicket that is bound to snare any other firms that attempt to enter the field. The fruits of this strategy are briefly discussed in an abstract of a story from the *America City Business Journal* below.

As Rivette and Kline note, Gillette is not the only large firm to use patent law to ward off competition by obtaining a large number of patents in an area. A question arises as to whether it is ethical for a large firm to use patent law to *suppress* innovation. Many patents are obtained by large firms that have no intention whatsoever of using these "inventions." Large firms have the money to finance obtaining patents whose sole purpose is to foreclose entry by other firms. As a future manager, would you agree with corporate counsel (your firm's attorney) to spend $100,000 obtaining patents whose sole purpose was to create a thicket designed to deter competition from innovating in your firm's niche market?

Rembrandts in the Attic: Unlocking the Hidden Value of Patents, Author: Rivette, Kevin G. and David Kline (1999).
"Rembrandts in the Attic" shows how to utilize intellectual property as both a corporate asset and a strategic business tool to enhance the commercial success of the enterprise. Rivette and Kline present case studies of companies, such as IBM, Avery Dennison, Xerox, Lucent, Gillette, Dell, Texas Instruments, and Hitachi, which have deployed their patents as competitive weapons to capture and defend market share, outflank and out-market rivals, increase R & D effectiveness, and achieve greater results in mergers and acquisitions and joint venture activities.

Source: Book review at http://www.walmart.com/catalog/product.gsp?cat=19398&product_id=715894&type=3&path=0:3920:18600:19398&dept=3920.

GILLETTE ACCUSES VA. RAZOR RIVAL OF PATENT VIOLATIONS

Boston-based Gillette Co. accused Verona, Va.-based American Safety Razor Co. of infringing its patents for disposable three-blade razors and imitating the appearance of Gillette products. In a suit filed in federal court in Boston, Gillette said American Safety Razor's Tri-Flexxx three-blade razor infringes Gillette patents on the Mach3 shaving system. The smaller rival also copied Gillette's packaging design to deceive consumers, Gillette said in the suit. American Safety Razor denied the allegations.

Source: Reprinted with permission of Michael Olivieri, Publisher, *Boston Business Journal.*

included under this section of the Patent Act is the exclusive right to offer for sale and to sell any product made with a patented *process,* including products that are made abroad.

Defenses in Patent Infringement Cases

Courts have devised several conceptual tests regarding what is and what is not a patent infringement. Keep in mind that a first line of defense for defendants in infringement cases is to claim that the patent at issue is invalid. We have spent much of this chapter discussing grounds for invalidity of patents. A defendant may argue that

1. A *patent is invalid* because it was granted in spite of the fact that the knowledge embodied in the patent already existed (in other words, the invention is not *new,* Sections 102(a) and (b)).

2. Anything new in the patent is trivial and obvious to one skilled in the industry (the *nonobviousness* requirement of Section 103).

In addition,

3. A patent can be declared invalid if the patentee *withheld material information* from the examiner.
4. Even if a patent is valid, patentees can lose their patent rights if they *misuse their patent.* This most often occurs if the patentee tries to extend patent monopoly by tying the sale of a patented product to a nonpatented product. Tying contracts involving two products, one patented and the other not, are violations of Section 3 of the Clayton Act, which is one of the antitrust statutes (more discussion of intellectual property and antitrust appears in Chapter 19).

Assuming that the plaintiff in a patent infringement case is able to overcome challenges to the validity of its patent, there are several remaining defenses available to the alleged infringer. Before considering those, make note of the fact that *independent creation is not a defense, unless* the infringer can show that its invention was created prior to the patentee's invention (more than one year prior to filing) and that the infringer employed the invention as a trade secret. This defense, called the *first inventor's defense,* was added by the American Inventors Protection Act of 1999. Finally, if challenges to the validity of the patent or disqualifying conduct on the part of the patentee cannot be proved, the infringer can claim the accused device does not infringe. A defendant would typically attempt to prove this assertion with expert testimony on the differences between the plaintiff's device, process, and so forth, and the defendant's.

Infringement

Recall that a patent applicant must describe his or her invention in the patent application. In their patent applications, applicants who are successful make *claims* (descriptions) regarding what is new about their inventions. In a nutshell, the criteria for determining whether a patent infringement takes place is whether the claims made in the patentee's patent application describe the defendant's allegedly infringing device or process. As with most legal concepts, determining an infringement under patent law can involve enormous complexity even though the conceptual criteria seem reasonably simple and straightforward.

Literal Infringement   The most straightforward patent infringement case involves a claim of *literal infringement*. In a literal infringement case, the claims made in the patentee's patent application are examined. If the infringing device or process of the defendant is described *exactly* in the patent application, the defendant has infringed. If the allegedly infringing (accused) device or process does everything described in the patent application, but also does more, it is also an infringement. An accused device (of the defendant's) could merit an improvement patent, but the infringer would have to obtain permission of the patentee before applying for the improvement patent.

Doctrine of Equivalents   The *doctrine of equivalents* applies, and makes the defendant liable for a patent infringement, when an accused device performs substantially the same function(s), in substantially the same way, to obtain substantially the same result provided by the patented device. In other words, the accused device or process of the defendant is not *literally* described by the claims made in the patent application, but the essence of the accused device accomplishes the same thing as the patented device (in a similar way using similar methods). Quite obviously, when the doctrine of equivalents applies, the defendant's accused device generally competes for sales with the plaintiff's patented device.

Damages

According to Section 284 of the Patent Act,

> Upon finding for the claimant [the patentee] the court shall award the claimant damages adequate to compensate for the infringement, but in no event less than a reasonable royalty for the use made of the invention by the infringer, together with interest and costs as fixed by the court.
>
> When damages are not found by a jury, the court shall assess them. In either event, the court may increase the damages up to three times the amount found or assessed.
>
> The court may receive expert testimony as an aid to the determination of damages or of what royalty would be reasonable under the circumstances.

Section 284 calls for application of a "but for" criterion for determining damages. The question asked is, "*But for* the infringement, what would be the financial position of the patentee?" A number of cases have established, through precedent, the parameters of the "but for" damages test. Among the damages that case law indicates the patentee can recover are

1. *Lost profits on lost sales.* This damage measure attempts to capture for the patent-holder any profits the patentee would have earned on sales it would have made but for the infringement. This category of damages requires the patentee to show that it would have made the sales that the infringer actually captured and to demonstrate what the profitability of those additional sales would have been.

2. *Price erosion.* A patent grants the patentee a monopoly, which enables the inventor to sell at a higher price than if there is competition. Patentees are entitled to recover, not only for lost profits on lost sales, but also for any reduction in price (hence profits) that occurs on sales that they (the patentees) do make or that the defendant made.

3. *Reasonable royalties.* Patentees are entitled to recover reasonable royalties on sales made by the infringer *that the patentee would not have made.* In some cases, patentees cannot show that sales made by the defendant would have been made by the patentee, but for the infringement.

4. *Prejudgment interest.* Continuing with the "but for" test, but for the infringements, the patentee would have had more money at an earlier date—that is, at the time sales would have occurred instead of much later when a court award is received. These funds presumably could have been invested and earned a return over that time lapse.

Adjustments to Court Damages

When Defendants Knowingly Infringe or Plaintiffs Initiate Frivolous Lawsuits   Section 284 also allows judges to triple the computed "compensatory" damages found by the court or by a jury. Tripling of damages occurs when the conduct of the defendant is judged to be particularly egregious—for example, in situations where defendants knew they were infringing and continued the illegal conduct. Section 285 of the Patent Act allows courts in "exceptional cases" to award attorney fees to the prevailing parties. Exceptional cases are, again, those in which the defendant's conduct is egregious, such as when the defendant is knowingly infringing. It is common in cases in which the plaintiff (patentee) is awarded triple damages for attorney fees to be awarded to the plaintiff as well. Note, however, that Section 285 also contemplates *awards of attorney fees to defendants* when the plaintiff initiates a clearly nonmeritorious infringement case.

Requirement to Provide Notice and Statute of Limitations   Under Section 287 a patentee forfeits all damages from infringements if the patentee does not provide notice to an infringer, by placing a sign either on the product or on other selling materials, unless the patentee can prove that the infringer was notified of the infringement and continued to sell

International Perspective/Ethical Challenges
AIDS, Drug Prices, and the Third World

We suspect that the bargain between society and inventors strikes most business students as eminently reasonable: both society and inventors benefit when patentees are granted monopolies for limited periods of time but must disclose the underlying innovation. For those outside the United States, however, this "deal" between U.S. society and inventors can have heart-wrenching consequences. In the Third World, especially Africa, AIDS is running rampant and drug treatments are very expensive, far too expensive for most Africans or African governments to afford. The reason the drugs treating AIDS are too expensive is not because of the cost of production. The cost of producing AIDS-retarding drug treatments is about 1/20th of the price.

The reason the drug prices are so high is because of patent law. Legal monopolies are granted to pharmaceutical companies and they are exploiting their monopoly by fixing prices for these life-saving drugs at prices that enable them to pay for the R & D costs that enabled them to create these drugs, as well as make profits. Once these life-savings drugs are created, should drug companies be allowed to set prices that may be reasonable in Europe and the United States, but are utterly beyond the means of residents of Third World countries? Consider the following story:

> "Many more people will be able to be treated for AIDS"
>
> Daniel Burman, MSF's medicine co-ordinator

INDIAN FIRM OFFERS CHEAP AIDS DRUGS
Many sufferers cannot afford vital drugs. An Indian drug company is planning to supply expensive anti-AIDS drugs to the world's poor for less than a dollar a day. Bombay-based Cipla Ltd is offering the triple-cocktail treatment to international aid agency Medecins Sans Frontieres (MSF). Similar drug therapies can cost between $10,000 and $15,000 per patient per year, far beyond the reach of a huge majority of sufferers. Cipla will sell the anti-retroviral cocktail to MSF at the knock-down price on condition the Paris-based agency distributes the drugs for free.

Three-Tier Pricing
"We are offering the drugs at a humanitarian price," said Cipla chairman Yusuf Hamied. "This is my contribution to fighting AIDS," he said. More than 36m people in the world now live with HIV and AIDS, over 70 percent of whom live in the poverty-stricken countries of Sub-Saharan Africa. Mr Hamied said Cipla had created a three-tier pricing scheme, under which wholesalers would pay $1,200 per patient per year, governments would pay $600, and MSF would get the cheapest rate of $350. An MSF spokesman said a pilot project to distribute the drugs could be operational "very soon." The Indian group makes cheap copies of drugs that are patent-protected elsewhere in the world. The AIDS cocktail comprises three drugs—stavudine, lamivudine and nevirapine. Local laws allow Indian firms to make the drugs as long as they use a process that differs from the original patented process. Leading multinational drug companies recently negotiated deals with some African nations worst affected by AIDS, offering a ninety-percent discount. But the Cipla offer will undercut even that. Phil Thomson, a spokesman for GlaxoSmithKlein—which holds patents on lamivudine—was skeptical. It would appear that the offer is partially one of donation. As a consequence of that, questions have to be raised about sustainability of the offer," he said. "Certainly questions need to be answered."

Drug Companies Accused
Drug companies in rich nations have often been accused of putting profits ahead of any commitment to combating an epidemic which is decimating populations in developing countries. MSF has long campaigned for the cost of anti-AIDS drugs to be reduced. Last weekend, Brazil threatened to copy two of the most expensive AIDS drugs if the makers do not lower their prices. The U.S. said copying the drugs violates patent rules and has complained to the World Trade Organisation (WTO). The involvement in the dispute of the WTO could eventually allow the U.S. to impose sanctions on Brazil for violating patent rules giving the pharmaceuticals exclusive rights to produce the drugs.

Source: From "Many More People Will Be Able to be Treated for AIDS," February 7, 2001. BBC News Online. Reprinted with permission of British Broadcasting Corporation.

We have two ethical questions for business students to answer:

1. Should the United States impose sanctions on Brazil if it persists in allowing copying of

AIDS-treatment drugs and their sale for nominal prices, thus undercutting the monopoly prices of the U.S. drug companies who are patentees on those drugs?

2. If you worked for a U.S. firm that had patents on pharmaceutical drugs for the treatment of AIDS,

what is the strongest argument you could offer that defends patent laws that keep drug prices high enough that most Third World sufferers die without any treatment?

infringing products. Also under Section 286, there is a six-year statute of limitations on damage claims, which means that the patentee cannot recover damages for infringing sales that took place more than six years prior to the filing of the complaint or counterclaim for damages.

STATE TRADE SECRET LAWS

trade secrets
Secret information (of a formula, a device, etc.) kept confidential to maintain a competitive advantage. The formula for Coca-Cola is a trade secret!

Trade secret law is based on a body of common law that predates the Constitution. Although each state has its own common law tradition, 41 states have adopted the Uniform Trade Secrets Act (UTSA). According to Section 1(4) of the UTSA,

"Trade secret" means information, including a formula, pattern, compilation, program, device, method, technique, or process, that:

i. derives independent economic value, actual or potential, from not being generally known to, or not being readily ascertainable by proper means by, other persons who can obtain economic benefits from its disclosure or use, and

ii. is the subject of efforts that are reasonable under the circumstances to maintain its secrecy.

The UTSA definition indicates that the *subject matter* of a trade secret could be very broad, but that

1. The trade secret is not part of the public domain.[5]
2. The trade secret has value because it is not in the public domain.
3. The possessor of the trade secret is using *reasonable security measures* to keep it secret.

Since the subject matter of trade secrets is quite extensive, and since trade secret law has potent protective power, inventors often face a choice of which mechanism(s) to use to protect their inventions: patent law or trade secret law. On the other hand, for ideas, customer lists, and formulas used to develop products, the choice is clear: they are not patentable subject matter and thus can be protected only by treating them as trade secrets.

Trade Secret Protection versus Patent Applications

If we compare the costs of protecting innovation through the use of trade secrets versus patents, the additional costs of patenting a product, process, and so on can be sizeable while the costs of relying on trade secrets are likely to be already incurred as normal security expenses. Moreover, when a patent is awarded, the application becomes part of the public record, which may reveal more about the company (as well as about the invention) than the applicant desires. There are companies throughout the world that have little respect for IP ownership.

---

[5] The term *public domain* refers to what is known in society in each and every field, even though no one person is familiar with more than a small part of the public domain.

Patent litigation is an expensive and stressful way of enforcing IP rights. Small firms may not have the resources to finance patent litigation and can be forced to "settle" with large infringing firms on terms that amount to an involuntary license (remember, the minimum recovery in patent claims is a "reasonable royalty"). For these and other reasons, many firms choose to rely extensively, sometimes entirely, on trade secrets for IP protection, while many other firms rely on trade secrets to protect innovations and inventions in their early phases until they decide to apply for a patent or a copyright.

On the other hand, patents provide more protection than trade secrets. For patents, independent creation is not a defense while it is for trade secrets. In the rapidly changing technological environment, it is rare for a firm to be able to keep a truly important discovery as a trade secret.

Misappropriation of Trade Secrets

Misappropriation of trade secrets is a tort and is prohibited by UTSA. UTSA specifically prohibits two actions:

1. Disclosure or use of a trade secret by someone who is not legally authorized to disclose or use the trade secret.
2. Receipt and use of a trade secret by one who knows or has reason to know that the trade secret was acquired from a source who did what is prohibited in (1).

In plain English, most defendants in misappropriation of trade secret cases are

1. *Employees or ex-employees* who set up their own firms and compete with their former employer using trade secrets acquired from their former employer.
2. *Other employers* who obtain the trade secrets from employees or ex-employees of the original employer/possessor of the trade secret(s) or use some other surreptitious means of obtaining another firm's trade secrets.

Consulting, law, and accounting firms, along with their employees, have been defendants in trade secret cases. These parties acquire trade secrets in connection with their contract work with client firms. Interestingly, these parties are almost always contractually bound by nondisclosure agreements (NDAs) that specifically prohibit acquiring and using trade secrets.

Improper Means of Conducting Business

The UTSA defines "improper means" of obtaining trade secrets as "theft, bribery, misrepresentation, breach or inducement of a breach of duty to maintain secrecy, or espionage through electronic or other means." Many of these terms have obvious meanings. Company A sends an employee to apply (pose) as a secretary for Company B. Company A's employee is trained in espionage and secretly copies plans for a new product that Company B hopes to patent and then market. This is a misappropriation of a trade secret using improper means. Many firms have used ingenious schemes to acquire trade secrets from other firms, often even engaging in criminal actions such as trespass, wiretaps, and computer break-ins. Another source of trade secret theft has been visitors at factories, posing as tourists, who come equipped with hidden cameras. Prostitutes have been used to acquire trade secrets from technical employees, particularly in foreign countries.

reverse engineering
A legal means for discovering trade secrets by analysis of another firm's products, processes, and so forth.

Reverse Engineering

You may find it interesting that **reverse engineering** is *not* an improper means of conducting business. For goods that are not patented, it is perfectly legitimate for a firm to buy the products of a competitor, figure out how the products are made, and reproduce similar or identical products as long as no trademark interest (discussed in the next chapter) is violated. In short, for products that are not patented, *independent creation* is a defense. If the defendant in a trade secret infringement case can demonstrate that it independently created what another firm sought to hold secret, even if the defendant was using the plaintiff's products to learn the secret(s), there is no misappropriation tort. The tort of misappropriation occurs, for example, when the defendant uses ex-employees to gain information about the plaintiff's research and development efforts.

Company Policy or Breakdowns in Management

There are companies willing to engage in such nefarious actions as trade secret misappropriation simply because the stakes are so high. The advantages conferred by trade secrets may be worth millions or even billions in some situations. Independent creation is a defense in trade secret cases, but research and development is very expensive. It may be cheaper to steal trade secrets than to go through the hard work of discovering them honestly. It is also important to recognize that upper-level management at some companies is not always fully apprised of the activities of mid-level managers, who may be under intense pressure to develop new, innovative products. On-the-job actions of employees are attributable to the company and create liability for the company, even if upper management is unaware, and indeed would not approve of the actions of subordinate managers.

The lines are not clearly drawn. Mid-level managers are often promoted from the ranks of technical staff and often have connections with disgruntled employees from other (competing) companies. Such disgruntled employees may have valuable firm-specific information that they are happy to share. A court may later decide that what was shared was trade secret information. So, while it may be true that, in some cases, upper management is active in misappropriating trade secrets from other firms, in other cases it is the undetected actions of mid-level managers that generate liability. In still other cases, honest misunderstandings can generate liability, as could be the case when a new employee brings in skills that both the employee and the new company believe to be general skills, but which a court later views differently.

Economic Espionage Act of 1996

Congressional awareness of the importance of trade secrets resulted in the passage in 1996 of the Economic Espionage Act. Section 1831 of the Act makes it a federal crime to misappropriate a trade secret "that will benefit any foreign government, foreign instrumentality, or foreign agent." Under the act, misappropriation of a trade secret is defined similarly to the language used in the UTSA with a broader scope in terms of what is prohibited. If there is a foreign connection established in the theft (broadly defined) of a trade secret, defendants are subject to a fine of up to $500,000 and imprisonment of not more than 15 years. Organizations are subject to fines up to $10,000,000. Section 1832 prohibits the theft of trade secrets using exactly the same language as Section 1831 to define misappropriation. If there is no foreign entity involved, then defendants stealing trade secrets are subject to 10 years of imprisonment and fines up to $5,000,000. These severe criminal sanctions reflect the seriousness with which lawmakers treat this issue. In addition to federal regulations, most states have their own criminal statutes prohibiting the theft of trade secrets.

Applicable Labor Law

At common law, employees have *fiduciary* duties to their employer(s), which, generally speaking, requires that, while on the job, employees must put the interests of employers above their own. Fiduciary duties include the duty to be loyal. While employed, an employee has a duty to avoid conflicts of interest and, as such, must disclose to his or her employer relevant information acquired on the job. At common law, fiduciary duties to employers also continue after the employment relationship has terminated, no matter what

Nutz and Boltz   Spy vs. Spy Is No Game at High-Techs

When a federal grand jury issued a six-count indictment last week accusing a former General Motors executive of passing design secrets to Volkswagen, it touched on a sore spot in big business.

Companies tend to avoid talking publicly about the threat of industrial espionage, but there's no doubt it has ultracompetitive tech companies on the Eastside worried. . . Companies are constantly striving to find out what their competitors are up to while trying to protect themselves from hacker attacks and frustrated employees with information that could bury a company.

"In our business, a healthy dose of paranoia is well-founded," said Jim Adler, president and CEO of Bellevue-based VoteHere.net.

There's good reason to be suspicious. In industry surveys, the FBI and American Society of Industrial Security estimate U.S. businesses lose between $24 billion and $250 billion a year because of corporate espionage. Some is from computer hacking but much more is from employees tempted to sell information to competitors. . .

[In spite of the magnitude of losses, cases of industrial espionage appearing in court are rare.] Ira Winkler, president of Delaware-based Internet

Security Advisors and author of a book on corporate espionage, said there's a reason for that.

Companies that file lawsuits have to prove they've been harmed and that an employee is responsible. Plus, they may have to reveal even more secrets in court to prove their case. Most often, companies don't want to admit their employees can cripple them.

"Companies are trusting of their own people even though every company has disgruntled employees—which is where most of these cases come from," Winkler said.

That phenomenon has given birth to nondisclosure forms [and to agreements] which limit where a person can work after having access to company secrets.

At VoteHere.net, which provides secure voting on the Internet, . . . the company has nondisclosure agreements and is always testing its computer security to ensure voting information can't be manipulated. The company combats internal threats by keeping sensitive information in only a few brains.

Source: Adapted from a Luke Timmerman article in the *Seattle Times*, May 31, 2000.

the reason for termination. Employees are liable to their former employers for revealing trade secrets, even after their employment relationship has ended.

On the other hand, *general skills* developed by employees while working for one employer can be used in subsequent jobs. Courts do not favor employment practices and policies that prevent ex-employees from being able to use their skills, even if these skills were paid for by the former employer. Firm-specific information can generally be protected by trade secret law, but general skills that are known and valuable in the industry (of employment) cannot.

Employment Contracts

Employers in many industries, and particularly in high-tech industries, are often unwilling to rely on common law protection of trade secrets based on fiduciary duty. Such employers generally make use of refined employment contracts that inform employees of actions that the employer considers a breach of contract. Employment contracts often specifically inform employees that their job exposes them to trade secrets and bind them to a nondisclosure agreement (NDA). Employment contracts are often coupled with exit interviews in which a departing employee is reminded of the NDA and what the employer considers to be trade secrets.

Common Law Shop Rights Doctrine

At common law, employers can make use of the *shop rights* doctrine, which gives employers royalty-free, nonexclusive rights to use any patent or copyright developed on the job by an employee. Employers have been unwilling to accept this common law division of rights. Most typically, employers have used employment contracts to supplement the allocation rights provided under common law. Employment contracts typically require employees to *assign* (transfer rights) to an employer all IP developed while working for that employer. Assignment clauses give employers title not only to all patents and copyrights developed on the job, but also to any discoveries that may lead to patents, copyrights, and/or trade secrets. In addition, employers further augment assignment clauses by requiring employees to *notify* the employer of any prospects for patents or copyrights or of any other IP discovered while working for the employer. Under patent law, if an employee is hired to invent things, then the employing company is entitled to file for a patent under the *company's* name.

Covenant Not to Compete Clauses

noncompete clause
A contract agreement that prohibits an employee from going to work in a competing business for a specified time span.

In addition to requiring notification of all IP employees develop while working for the employer and assignment of all IP developed using company facilities that relates to company business, employers also make use of **covenant not to compete (noncompete) clauses.** These clauses in employment agreements prohibit employees from working for rivals for a period of time. A typical covenant not to compete clause would prohibit an employee from working for another firm in the same business as that of the current employer for a two-year period. Such clauses are often also geographically limited, and so might prohibit employment with competing businesses anywhere in a surrounding three-state area. Courts do not particularly like noncompete clauses and will refuse to enforce them if they are not reasonable. So, to be enforceable, covenant not to compete clauses must be *reasonably limited in time and space.* A five-year covenant not to compete would be deemed unreasonable and hence unenforceable. With the Internet, the geographic area where some companies compete is becoming irrelevant, though it remains germane to many bricks-and-mortar businesses. Historically, covenants not to compete have had to be limited to the area where the employer actually competes to be enforceable. Case 12-4 illustrates difficulties with enforcing covenants not to compete.

Case 12-4

Apac Teleservices, Inc., an Illinois Corporation, Plaintiff v. Shawn M. McRae and Access Direct Telemarketing, Inc., an Iowa Corporation, Defendants

United States District Court for the Northern District of Iowa, Cedar Rapids Division
985 F. Supp. 852 (N.D. Iowa 1997)

FACTS AND CASE BACKGROUND

APAC Teleservices, Inc. (APAC), and Access Direct Telemarketing, Inc. (Access Direct), are competitors in the outsource telemarketing industry. In addition to outsource telemarketing, APAC also provides inbound telemarketing services. Access Direct (the defendant) does not currently have an inbound telemarketing operation, but it plans to have one soon. According to Access Direct's Chief Executive Officer, Thomas Cardella, Access Direct had been searching for someone to head up its

Inbound department for some time before it hired Shawn McRae as Vice-President in charge of Inbound Telemarketing operations. McRae was working for APAC before he left to take this position with Access Direct.

A simple way of explaining "outsource telemarketing" is that it means that one company makes telephone calls on behalf of another company to generate business. For instance, handling telesales for certain long-distance providers is an example of outsource telemarketing. On the flip side, "inbound telemarketing" means that a company receives incoming calls from customers on behalf of another company. An example of inbound telemarketing is receiving and handling customer services inquiries for another company.

Shawn McRae began working as a technology consultant for APAC in late August or September of 1996. By October, he had moved to APAC's office in Cedar Rapids, Iowa, where he worked in the Information Technology (IT) department as a consultant for a specific project called the "G-Prime Advanced Technology Platform Project for AT&T." In January of 1997 he began working as a full-time APAC employee, continuing his work in the IT department as one of the head "architects" for the ATP Project for AT&T, and on another project using Computer Telephony Integration (CTI). When he became a full-time employee he signed a nondisclosure agreement, and four months later, in April of 1997, he signed a restrictive covenant, which contained a noncompetition agreement. In the beginning of September 1997, McRae left APAC to work for Access Direct. APAC has filed for an injunction to prevent McRae from working for Access Direct based on the restrictive covenant he signed while working for APAC.

Opinion by Michael J. Melloy

Most of McRae's work at APAC had focused on these two information technology projects, the ATP and CTI, before he left to work for Access Direct.

As Vice-President of Inbound at Access Direct, McRae asserts that his job is radically different than what he was doing at APAC. At APAC he worked in the information technology department and was primarily focused on outbound telemarketing; at Access Direct, he works in an operations capacity focused exclusively on inbound telemarketing. At APAC he helped to select and adapt off-the-shelf products to meet the joint needs of APAC and APAC's clients; at Access Direct he works with clients to decide what kinds of information the clients need to know and how Access Direct can best forecast their clients' needs and provide information back to them. Instead of testing off-the-shelf products and tailoring those products to meet specific client's needs, now all McRae has to do is to tell the IT department what the Inbound department needs to be able to do, and the IT department has sole responsibility to design the solution. In addition, in his new job McRae will determine demographic locations, attendance policies, scheduling, financial budgets, and profit margins. He will also work with other departments, such as IT and human resources, to decide how the Inbound department is going to train its staff, and he will hire and fire employees.

* * *

1. PROBABILITY THAT APAC WILL SUCCEED ON THE MERITS

In deciding whether to grant a preliminary injunction, the Court's initial estimation of the strength of the plaintiff's case plays a role, but it is not determinative. The probability of success does not require that the party seeking relief prove a greater than fifty percent likelihood that it will succeed on the merits. [Citations omitted.] Instead of a rigid measuring stick, the Court flexibly weighs the particular circumstances of the case to determine "whether the balance of equities so favors the movant that justice requires the court to intervene to preserve the status quo until the merits are determined."

* * *

Before this Court even begins to analyze these criteria, however, this Court must examine whether APAC has made the necessary showing to prove that McRae's new position at Access Direct calls his covenant not to compete into question: that is, whether McRae's new job is similar in capacity to his former job at APAC, or whether he is likely to disclose APAC's proprietary information or client information to Access Direct. If APAC fails to prove that either of these two situations exist, it is unnecessary for this Court to examine whether APAC has otherwise proven each of the next four criteria.

* * *

Even if McRae's job at Access Direct is in a different capacity than what he was doing at his former job, APAC could still prove that McRae violated the noncompetition agreement by showing that in his new job, it is likely that he will disclose APAC's proprietary or client information. See Restrictive Covenant Agreement, Pl.'s Ex. 5, Dep. Ex. 8, P 4 ("Employee covenants that . . . [he] shall not . . . assist anyone in the conduct of a business competitive with that of Employer in which Employee is in . . . a capacity in which it is likely that Employee will disclose Employer's Proprietary Information or Client Information"). APAC argues that McRae's job will inevitably lead to such disclosure, while the defendants assert that it will not.

* * *

What appears most useful about McRae's experience with CTI on the inbound side is that he became familiar with various off-the-shelf products that are currently available on the market. As will be discussed *infra,* McRae would violate both the noncompetition covenant and the nondisclosure agreement if he used his technological knowledge to modify these off-the-shelf products to meet the needs of Access Direct's Inbound operation, but that is not what his job at Access Direct entails. In McRae's new job, he will simply tell the IT department at Access Direct what his department needs, and the IT department will have total responsibility to design the solution. While his knowledge of available off-the-shelf products may make him more articulate in expressing his needs to the IT department, ultimately the technological solution will be in someone else's hands.

* * *

The bottom line is that McRae left a technical position in information technology at APAC to assume an operations position for a competitor company. Although McRae lied to both APAC and Access Direct in order to negotiate a good job at Access Direct, APAC has not demonstrated a probability of success on the merits that either (1) McRae or Access Direct is lying about the job responsibilities that McRae's new position at Access Direct entails, or that (2) McRae's new position will inevitably lead him to disclose proprietary or confidential information.

Decision and Outcome

Accordingly, the court denied plaintiff's request for an injunction preventing McRae from working for defendant, Access Direct, but granted the injunction that prevented him from disclosing plaintiff's trade secrets to Access Direct.

Questions for Analysis

1. The court alludes to the fact that the defendant employee (McRae) lied while working for the plaintiff. Is the court taking into account McRae's lack of honesty when it denies plaintiff's motion to enjoin him from working for his new employer, but does enjoin McRae from disclosing trade secrets?
2. What was the significance of the defendants' (both of them) showing that McRae's new job was substantially dissimilar to his previous job? Since the job was substantially dissimilar, does that mean that McRae was not violating his covenant not to compete clause in his contract with his former employer?

Covenant not to compete clauses are also used in connection with mergers and acquisitions. A company that is buying another company does not want to risk the threat that the owner of the acquired company will start a new company and compete with his former company.

Remedies

Sanctions against Former Employees

In most trade secret misappropriation cases, both an ex-employee and a new employer are defendants. In virtually all cases, the assets of the ex-employee are inadequate to justify a suit for damages associated with trade secret misappropriation. Although there may be two defendants, the ex-employee and new employer, the focus of the case from the perspective of the plaintiff (the holder of the trade secret that is claiming misappropriation) is often on showing that the *new employer knew or should have known* that it was receiving a misappropriated trade secret so that a damage award can be obtained from the employing company. Most certainly, if it can be shown that the new employer explicitly paid the ex-employee for access to trade secrets, liability for misappropriation is established. Such proof is often difficult.

If the new employee is in a new job that breaches a covenant not to compete, liability for that violation is readily established against the employee. With an enforceable covenant not to compete, the job of monitoring for the possible dissemination of trade secrets by ex-employees is lessened as a noncompete suit can be initiated against the former employee immediately.

Injunctions

Since the assets of individual employees rarely provide a damage recovery expectancy that justifies a suit economically, the most effective remedy against a former employee may be an injunction. For injunctive relief, the former employer would have to show the possibility of irreparable damage and the likelihood of winning an accompanying lawsuit. Both requirements are met when a former employee violates an enforceable covenant not to compete. The former employer does not have to show actual misappropriation of a trade secret to bar its ex-employee from working for a competitor. If an ex-employee defies an injunction, he or she can face jail time. In addition, a new employer can be joined in the injunction to prevent appropriation of the trade secret(s) and even to call for dismissal of the employee. Note again, however, that many covenants not to compete have been declared unreasonable and thus not enforceable.

Establishment of Liability

In trade secret misappropriation suits, direct evidence of misappropriation of trade secrets is often impossible to obtain. Indirect proof often comes in the form of a history, first showing that defendant had made a number of attempts to solve "the problem" but was unsuccessful, then showing that the alleged misappropriator made significant progress shortly after hiring the ex-employee who had access to the trade secrets. Product comparisons also provide (more direct) evidence on the likely misappropriation of trade secrets. Consider the case of a software firm that contends that another firm is selling a competing software package based on misappropriated trade secret code. Expert analysis in this situation is likely to compare the alternative software packages' code on a line-by-line basis. Finding code that is identical, even down to errors in lines of code, provides strong evidence in support of a misappropriation claim.

Damages and Remedies for Misappropriation of Trade Secrets

According to UTSA, plaintiffs in misappropriation of trade secret suits are entitled to recover both "actual loss caused by misappropriation and the unjust enrichment caused by misappropriation that is not taken into account in computing actual loss. In lieu of damages measured by other methods, damages caused by misappropriation may be measured by imposition of liability for a reasonable royalty for a misappropriator's unauthorized disclosure or use of a trade secret." Similarities with damages allowed in patent infringement cases are apparent. Plaintiffs are entitled to recover lost profits if they can show they would have made sales enjoyed by the defendant but for the misappropriation. Plaintiffs are entitled to recover profits of the defendant as long as they can show that those profits are due to the trade secret misappropriation. When all else fails, plaintiffs are entitled to a reasonable royalty for the use of their trade secret that was disclosed or used by the defendant.

A significant problem for proof of damages in trade secret cases is the defense that defendant's profits and sales were not due to the misappropriation of the trade secret. Proving that the defendant made sales because of the trade secret that was wrongfully acquired instead of for other reasons often is a difficult task. Injunctions can be beneficially used in some cases where there is a showing that the trade secret was misappropriated but not disseminated. The defendant can be prohibited from using or disclosing the trade secret, even though proof of monetary damages may be lacking.

Security and Trade Secrets

As has been demonstrated by many sports teams, the best offense may be a good defense. Once a trade secret suit begins, it is difficult to keep the secret under wraps. If a plaintiff claims that the defendant made profits and sales as a result of trade secrets, the jury must have some basis for evaluating that claim. In other words, the jury must be shown proof that the trade secret was indeed valuable and was the cause of the defendant's profits and sales. The UTSA calls for courts to use reasonable means to preserve trade secrets, including "granting protective orders in connection with discovery proceedings, holding in-camera hearings (closed), sealing records of the action, and ordering any persons involved in the litigation not to disclose an alleged trade secret without court approval." In spite of the safeguards provided by the UTSA, many trade secrets no longer are secret after litigation.

As the stakes associated with retention and pilferage of trade secrets have increased, security measures taken by firms to protect trade secrets have similarly escalated. Quite obviously the sophistication of industrial espionage has continued to increase. In 1986, Congress addressed the need for greater protection of proprietary information with passage of the Computer Fraud and Abuse Act of 1986, which makes it a federal crime to break into governmental or financial (banks') computer systems.[6] Organizational security has become a major issue not only for private companies but also for governmental and educational institutions. Indeed, an entire industry has sprung up around security and much of its recent growth has been in the high-tech arena.

[6] Pub. L. N. 99-474, codified at 18 U.S.C. § 1030.

Summary

Real Property Is Tangible but Not Moveable; Personal Property Attached to Real Property Becomes Real Property

- Property owned by businesses can be classified as *real* or *personal*.
- Personal property is either *tangible* or *intangible*.
- Real property includes land and anything firmly attached thereto.
- Real property also includes airspace to a reasonable height above the surface and mineral rights below the surface.
- Fixtures are personal property that are attached to real property and become real property.
- In determining whether personal property becomes a fixture, and thus real property, courts consider intent of the party attaching the personal property, the degree of attachment, and the ownership of the property.

Transfers of Ownership of Real Property Are Memorialized by Transfers of Deeds, Which

- Ownership of real property is represented by a *deed* that legally describes the land and is delivered to the purchaser.
- Changes in ownership of real property as well as liens or encumbrances are typically *recorded* and available for public inspection.
- There are three types of deeds: *general warranty, special warranty,* and *quitclaim.* General warranty deeds offer the greatest protection to purchasers because the seller is warranting that there are no liens or encumbrances other than those described on the deed.

Are Recorded as Public Documents; Liens and Encumbrances on Real Property Also Are Recorded so That Purchasers Can Determine Who Owns Real Property; When the Owner of Real Party Leases It to a Tenant, Landlords Are Obligated to Keep the Premises Habitable	• In quitclaim deeds, the seller is not promising that he or she owns the property, but whatever rights he or she owns are transferring to the purchaser. • If a creditor cannot recover funds any other way, the creditor can file a lien on real property. If the property is sold, the lien-holder has higher priority to the proceeds of the sale than the seller. • *Encumbrances* on real property include *easements* and *restrictive covenants.* • Under the recording acts in most states, a subsequent purchaser for value has priority over a previous purchaser who did not record the transfer of ownership at the county recording office. • The recording acts vary from state to state. • When an owner of real property rents to another, the owner becomes the *lessor,* or landlord, and the renter becomes the *lessee* or tenant. • Landlords are responsible for keeping leased premises in habitable condition, giving notice before eviction, and adhering to building codes.
Personal Property Is Normally Owned and Sold without Documents of Title, Except for Motor Vehicles; Leasing Personal Property Is Called a Bailment; Lost Property Is Owned by the Finder, Except Against the True Owner	• Tangible personal property is property that can be touched and moved. Intangible property is property that has no palpable existence. Patent and contract rights are examples. • Except for motor vehicles and a few other kinds of personal property for which pedigree is important, ownership of most personal property is not based on a title, but rather on a bill of sale or sales receipt. • When an owner of personal property gives possession of personal property to another, the owner becomes the *bailor* and the possessor becomes the *bailee.* • Bailees have an obligation to use reasonable care as to the bailed property and must return it. • Bailors must use reasonable care in renting personal property that could harm the bailee if it is not in working order. • Property can be *lost, mislaid,* or *abandoned.* The finder of lost property becomes the owner against the world, except for the original owner. • The finder of mislaid property becomes a bailee of that property until the owner returns to reclaim the property. • Property is considered abandoned when the owner discards the property or it is lost or mislaid and the owner stops searching for the property. • Most states have *estray statutes* that enable the finder of lost or mislaid property to advertise that they found the property but if it is not claimed within a period of time, generally one year, they become the owner of the property.
Patents and Trade Secrets Receive Protection under U.S. Law; the PTO Determines Whether Patents Are Issued; Trade Secret Law Is State Law	• *Patents* provide a reward to inventors that society is willing to pay in order to encourage innovation. In return for a monopoly for 20 years from the filing date, an inventor must be willing to reveal what he has invented. • States protect intellectual property using *trade secret* laws, which make *misappropriation* of trade secrets illegal. The American Inventors Protection Act of 1999 provides protections for those who choose not to patent but, instead, to protect their inventions through trade secret laws. • The Patent and Trademark Office makes patent determinations. A patent application is initially submitted to a PTO *patent examiner.* • Ultimately, all decisions of the PTO are subject to review by the courts.

<table>
<tr>
<td>

To Qualify for a Patent, an Invention Must Be New and Nonobvious; under U.S. Law, Priority Is Given to the First to Invent, Not the First to File

</td>
<td>

- Patents are issued to those whose inventions are *new, useful,* and *nonobvious.*
- Section 102(a) defines what is *new* in terms of what is in the public domain at the time of the invention. If an invention has already been described or patented anywhere in the world, it is not new. Also, if the invention was known or used by someone in the United States, it is not new.
- Section 102(b) defines disqualifying acts that take place more than one year before an applicant applies for a patent with the PTO. If the patented item is described in a publication or patented anywhere in the world, used commercially, or sold in the United States, then the applicant is not entitled to a patent.
- Section 102(g) awards priority to the *first to invent* rather than the *first to file* as long as the invention has not been abandoned, concealed, or suppressed. To maintain priority, applicants must be reasonably diligent after invention until the invention is reduced to practice.
- Section 103 denies a patent to anyone whose invention is obvious to someone skilled in the industry.

</td>
</tr>
<tr>
<td>

To Receive a patent, the Subject Matter Must Be a Process, Manufacture, Machine, or Composition of Matter; an Infringement exists when the Patent Application Describes the Defendant's Device

</td>
<td>

- In order to be patentable, the subject matter in a patent application must be *statutory:* that is, a *process, manufacture, machine,* or *composition of matter.* Ideas, mathematical formulas, and naturally occurring life forms are not patentable.
- Inventors who create new life forms are entitled to patents on those life forms.
- Patent applications must contain a detailed explanation sufficient to allow one skilled in the industry to reproduce the patented item or process.
- The claims made in the patent application form the basis for infringement suits.
- A *literal infringement* occurs when the claims made in the patent application describe the accused device of the defendant.
- The *doctrine of equivalents* applies when the accused device performs substantially the same function(s), in substantially the same way, to obtain substantially the same result provided by the patented device.

</td>
</tr>
<tr>
<td>

Damages in Patent Cases Allow Plaintiffs to Recover Lost Profits and, at a Minimum, Reasonable Royalties Plus Attorney Fees and Court Costs; Damages Are Tripled in Some Cases

</td>
<td>

- The basic rule governing patent damages is that the patentee should recover enough money to be placed in the same position that would have been enjoyed had the patent not been infringed.
- Patentees can recover for infringement based on lost profits on lost sales, lowered prices as a result of competition from the infringing device, and reasonable royalties on sales made by the defendant that the plaintiff would not have made.
- In some (egregious) cases, plaintiffs are able to recover triple damages based on bad conduct by the defendant. Also in egregious cases, the winning party is sometimes awarded court costs and attorney fees.
- Plaintiffs are required to provide *notice* that their products are patented either on the product or in selling materials.

</td>
</tr>
<tr>
<td>

At Common Law, in Each State There Is Protection for Trade Secrets, Which Is Information

</td>
<td>

- A *trade secret* is information that gives a firm a competitive advantage because it is kept secret.
- Trade secret protection is based on common law notions of acceptable and unacceptable methods of competing.
- *Misappropriation* of trade secrets occurs when a firm's trade secrets are obtained by the defendant using illegal methods of gaining information, or when someone who has confidential information breaches his or her fiduciary duty to the plaintiff.
- Ex-employees are the main source of trade secret misappropriation.

</td>
</tr>
</table>

That Gives a Firm an Advantage by Being Secret; the Most Common Source for Loss of Trade Secrets is Former Employees; Employers Make Use of Employment Contracts to Protect Trade Secrets

- Firms have an obligation to use reasonable methods to preserve their trade secrets or else the courts will dismiss claims of trade secret misappropriation.
- The Economic Espionage Act of 1996 imposes severe penalties on anyone guilty of misappropriating trade secrets from a U.S. firm on behalf of a foreign entity.
- *Employment contracts* frequently contain nondisclosure agreements and *covenants not to compete*. Court enforcement of covenants not to compete depends on their reasonableness. Covenants not to compete should be reasonably limited in time and space.
- Remedies against trade secret misappropriators include monetary damage claims and injunctions against former employees and competitors.
- Since damages in trade secret cases are difficult to establish, injunctions are often the best hope for effective remedies.

Key Terms

bailment, *367*
deed, *363*
intellectual property (IP), *369*
noncompete clause, *388*

nonstatutory subject matter, *379*
patent examiner, *371*
patent infringement, *379*

real property, *362*
reverse engineering, *389*
statutory subject matter, *379*
trade secrets, *384*

Questions for Review and Analysis

1. Set up a chart that classifies property as real or personal, tangible or intangible, and then pick five examples of property, such as a house, a bank account, a copyright, money, and an easement, and place each item into the classifications listed above. Pick five more examples of property and do the same thing.

2. Discuss the differences between Sections 102(a) and (b) with respect to "priority." What are the critical dates for each section? What parts of Sections 102(a) and (b) pertain to the United States and what parts pertain to the world?

3. Explain how courts integrate market or economic factors when they make decisions about whether an invention is "obvious" under Section 103.

4. What is the difference between a literal infringement and an infringement based on the doctrine of equivalents?

5. Compare and contrast the protection to intellectual property provided by trade secrets relative to that provided by patents. What important defense is available to defendants in trade secret cases that is not available to patent infringement defendants?

If You Really Understood This Chapter, You Should Be Able to Provide Informed Commentary on the Following:

1. **Bailment or Lease of Space?** Trivial differences sometime have significant legal consequences. We have all parked our cars in parking lots. In some cases, we are given tickets and park the car ourselves. In other situations, we give keys to the parking lot attendant who parks the car. On January 8, 1980, Kirkland Strawder drove his car to a parking lot in Houston owned by Allright, Inc. Strawder placed his car in a line to be parked and gave the keys to a parking lot attendant for Allright. When Strawder returned, his car could not be found, but later it was found stripped and wrecked. When Strawder gave keys to the Allright attendant, that act created a bailment and Allright, as bailee, had an obligation to return the car or else show that the failure to return the car was not due to Allright's negligence. In contrast, when you park your car in a parking deck, you are frequently given a ticket that says, "Park at your own risk" and "We are not responsible for damage or loss of your vehicle." Why are these ticket restrictions legal when you park your car but not legal when you give your keys to a parking lot attendant? [*Allright, Inc. v. Strawder,* 679 S.W.2d 81 (Tex. App. 1984).]

2. **Lost or Abandoned Property.** In 1983, two brothers, Danny Lee and Jeffrey Allen Smith, found a 16-foot fiberglass boat lying beside a highway in Mobile County, Alabama. The boys stopped police officers to discuss the situation and, over the boys' objections, the officers impounded the boat. No one ever claimed the boat and the Smiths want possession and ownership of the boat. Alabama does not have estray statutes, so there was no way to provide public notice to the original owners. The boys indicated that if the true owner did not claim the boat, they wanted it. The county of Mobile wanted to sell the boat and use the proceeds for recreational programs. A local ordinance allows the county to sell lost or abandoned personal property at a public auction if it is not claimed within six months. What would you predict was the result? [*Smith v. Sheriff Purvis,* 474 So. 2d 1131 (Ala. App. 1985).]

3. **Novelty, Date of Invention, and Public Use.** The date of invention claimed by plaintiff is February 10, 1965. In April of 1964, DuPont was trying to find a commercial use for its Surlyn, a recently developed product. Shortly thereafter, Butch Wagner, who was in the business of selling re-covered golf balls, began to experiment with Surlyn as a golf ball cover. He first made some sample balls by hand and then, using a one-iron, determined that the material was almost impossible to cut. He obtained more Surlyn and made several dozen experimental balls, trying different combinations of additives to achieve the proper weight, color, and a texture that could easily be released from an injection-molding machine. By November 5, 1964, he had developed a formula that he considered suitable for commercial production and had decided to sell Surlyn-covered balls in large quantities. The date is established by a memorandum recording his formula, which Wagner wrote in his own hand and gave to his daughter for safekeeping on the occasion of her son's birthday. Wagner was careful not to disclose to anyone why the golf balls he constructed were so tough and difficult to cut. At least three golfers had used the Surlyn-covered balls and Wagner had sold more than 1,000 during the fall of 1964. Did the noninforming, public use of the Surlyn-covered balls in 1964 prevent DuPont from patenting what it claimed it invented on February 10, 1965? Would this situation be evaluated under Section 102(a) or (b). [*Dunlop Holdings Limited v. Ram Golf Corporation,* 524 F.2d 33 (7th Cir. 1975).] (Dunlop Holdings Limited is owned by DuPont.)

4. **Reduction to Practice and Section 102(b).** A defense contractor, UMC, offered to sell the Navy a UMC-B accelerometer in early 1967. In late 1968, UMC filed for a patent on the UMC-B accelerometer. UMC, however, says that, at the time of the offer to sell the UMC-B accelerometer to the Navy, they were not in existence because UMC-B accelerometers had not been reduced to practice. Recall in the chapter the time line that had three points: x (the date of invention), y (when the invention was reduced to practice), and z (when the applicant filed for a patent). Normally, under Section 102(b), an offer to sell the claimed invention more than one year prior to filing with the PTO for a patent disqualifies the patent applicant, in this case UMC. In this case, however, the offer to sell took place more than one year before z, the filing date, but at that time no accelerometers had been built. Can an offer to sell something that is not in existence at the time of the offer trigger the one-year rule under Section 102(b)? See *UMC Electronics Company v. United States,* 816 F.2d 647 (Fed. Cir. 1987).

5. **Nonobviousness.** Question 3 above asks how courts integrate economic and market forces in their analyses of nonobviousness and the validity of patents. Question 3 poses a difficult question, but the case cited in this discussion provides an illuminating answer. Jack Caveney, the founder of Panduit, began a research program in 1961 to develop a cable tie that could bundle cables and insulated wires. The research and development process lasted for nine years and cost several million dollars. Several patents were issued to Caveney, who assigned them to Panduit. Sales began in 1970 and, by 1984, annual sales of Caveney's cable ties reached $50 million. In 1968 Dennison Manufacturing began a research and development program to create a one-piece cable tie. After several years and several millions of dollars of expenses, they had not succeeded. In 1976, Dennison copied Panduit's cable and Panduit sued. A district court ruled that each of Panduit's patents was invalid because of obviousness. The market facts alone suggest that Panduit's patents were not obvious, even to one skilled in the field. In *Panduit Corporation v. Dennison Manufacturing,* 810 F.2d 1561 (Fed. Cir. 1987), the Court of Appeals for the Federal Circuit listed at least six major errors made by the district court. Declarations of invalidity of patents by district and circuit courts were a major factor leading to the creation of the Court of Appeals for the Federal Circuit.

6. **Are Customer Lists Trade Secrets?** Curtis 1000 is a seller of customized stationery, business forms, and printing services to business firms. Curtis is suing Roy Suess, a former employee, for misappropriation of trade secrets and violation of a covenant not to compete. Suess, a sales employee of Curtis for 24 years, quit on September 15, 1993, believing that he was about to be fired by Curtis. During his tenure with Curtis, Suess signed three covenants not to compete, but there was no additional consideration for agreeing not to compete against Curtis for two years after termination of employment. Suess was employed "at-will," which meant that he did not have a fixed employment contract and could be fired or could quit with no notice or reason. American Business Forms (ABF), a company in the same business as Curtis, had been busy hiring salesmen away from Curtis. It hired Suess five days after he left Curtis as its first salesman in the two-county area and promised to advance him the expenses of defending against any suit by Curtis to enforce the covenant not to compete. Suess proceeded to solicit current and recent customers of Curtis in the area, in violation of the covenant. Suess claims that Curtis made no efforts to keep its customer lists secret and that covenants not to compete in Illinois are limited in enforcement to protection of trade secrets. If Curtis made no effort to keep its customer lists secret, they are not trade secrets and therefore the covenants not to compete are meaningless. What do you think? [*Curtis 1000, Inc. v. Roy Suess and American Business Forms, Inc.,* 24 F.3d 941 (7th Cir. 1994).]

Social Responsibility, Policy, and Ethics in a High-Tech World

7. **Patent Laws versus State Trade Secret Laws.** Courts often have struggled with determination of where the supremacy of federal patent law begins and ends, and with determination of the appropriate sphere of authority for state trade secret law. It is clear from the Supremacy Clause in the U.S. Constitution that, in conflicts between patent law and state trade secret laws, patent law has priority. It is also clear that trade secrets can include a much broader array of subjects than patent law. Suppose that the owner of a trade secret was of the opinion that his trade secret could be patented. Can the owner protect his "invention" as a trade secret even though the trade secret is patentable? Suppose another firm comes along, independently discovers the trade secret, and tries to patent that trade secret? Can a state declare that it is statutorily creating a new form of intellectual property based on design? Compare *Kewannee Oil Co. v. Bicron Corp., et al.,* 416 U.S. 470 (1974), with *Bonito Boats, Inc. v. Thunder Craft Boats, Inc.,* 489 U.S. 141 (1989), both Supreme Court cases.

Using the Internet to Your Advantage

1. The first website you may want to look at that deals with patents and patent law is, of course, the U.S. Patent and Trademark Office site (http://www.uspto.gov). The PTO website provides a wealth of materials including a sophisticated patent search engine (http://www.uspto.gov/patft/index.html) for reviewing patents that date back to 1790, when the first three patents were issued by the fledgling U.S. government. The PTO website is among the most sophisticated and user-friendly websites in all of government. Increasingly, companies are setting patent strategy internationally. The European Patent Office (EPO) can be reached at http://www.epo.co.at/index.htm, the Canadian Intellectual Property Office is located at http://cipo.gc.ca/, and the Japan Patent Office is located at http://www.jpo.go.jp/index.htm. The World Intellectual Property Organization (WIPO) is located at http://www.wipo.org/. There are a number of private websites that offer relevant material related to patents, such as patents.com (http://www.patents.com).

2. An example of the Uniform Trade Secrets Act, which has been adopted by 41 states, is located at http://www.cerebalaw.com/utsa.htm. A private attorney, R. Mark Halligan, has assembled 300 trade secret cases and a wealth of other information about trade secrets at http://www.execpc.com/~mhalligin/. Three law and economics scholars have written an economic analysis of trade secrets that was published in the *Journal of Economic Perspectives* and is available at http://www.daviddfriedman.com/Academic/Trade_Secrets/Trade_Secrets.html.

3. Discussion of property law can be found under Findlaw.com at http://www.findlaw.com/01topics/33property. An informative discussion of real property law is available at http://www.intcounselor.com/real-property.html. Bailment law is discussed at http://web.waukesha.tec.wi.us/busocc/law/bailppt/.

Chapter **Thirteen**

Copyright, Trademark, and Protection of Software

Learning Objectives

On completing this chapter, you should

1. Be familiar with what can and cannot be protected by copyright law.
2. Be able to discuss the consequences of copyright infringement and some of the main defenses defendants have used in such cases.
3. Be familiar with the interface between the Internet and copyright law.
4. Understand the basic purpose of trademark law and basic requirements that must be met to get a trademark registered by the PTO.
5. Be able to discuss the clashes that have occurred between trademark owners, celebrities, and established companies and domain name owners.
6. Be able to apply copyright law to the cyberspace debate about downloading copyrighted works, both musical and cinematic.

OVERVIEW

Article 1, Section 8 of the U.S. Constitution delegates to the federal government responsibility for the encouragement of *both* inventors *and authors*. In the last chapter we dealt with how Congress, the Patent and Trademark Office, and courts provide legal protection for inventors through patent law. In the United States, authors are primarily protected through copyright laws passed by Congress, administered by the Office of Copyright, and interpreted by court decisions. As with patent law, the stakes surrounding copyright have become increasingly costly. Mistakes that involve copyright law, especially when the Internet is involved, can easily be multimillion-dollar mistakes.

This chapter examines trademark law and some of the difficulties that the Internet has created for enforcement of trademark law. In particular, trademark law has been challenged by domain names on the Internet, but Congress has passed recent legislation that is very favorable to trademark owners.

NEW YORK (AP)—A federal judge ruled Wednesday that the Internet music-sharing service MP3.com willfully violated the copyrights of record companies, and ordered it to pay Universal Music Group $25,000 per CD, or roughly $118 million. U.S. District Judge Jed S. Rakoff said it was necessary to send a message to the Internet community to deter copyright infringement. Rakoff said he could have awarded as much as $150,000 per CD but chose a considerably smaller amount, in part because MP3.com had acted more responsibly than other Internet startups. Universal Music Group, the world's largest record company, had urged a stiff penalty in the closely watched case. "Music is a media and the next infringement may be very different," said Universal lawyer Hadrian Katz. "It may be video or it may be film or it may be books or it may be something very different." Katz had urged the judge to award the record company up to $450 million because MP3.com had copied 5,000 to 10,000 of the company's CDs. The lawyer said such a penalty would cost MP3.com as much as $3.6 billion once the company was forced to pay all the other companies whose copyrights it had violated when it created an online catalog of 80,000 CDs.

Source: Reprinted with permission of The Associated Press.

Consequences of Ignoring Copyright and Trademark Law

Cyberspace is littered with the corpses of high-flying dot-coms that thought they could ignore copyright and trademark laws. MP3.com, which was one of the darlings of the startup dot-coms, had a cavalier attitude toward copyright law. In contrast, Universal Music Group, which likely had the largest stake in enforcement of copyright laws as they relate to Internet transactions, was very serious about copyright enforcement. The unfortunate consequences of ignoring copyright law for MP3.com are discussed in the "Cyberlaw Developments" box. As we will see later, Napster.com is another Internet startup that basically bet the store on being able to ignore or avoid copyright laws. The *DeCSS* litigation, which involves software designed to undermine the encryption software (CSS) that protected movie DVDs from being duplicated, provides another example for all to see that copyright owners have an arsenal of legal tools to combat unauthorized duplications of copyrighted material.[1]

COPYRIGHT

Overview

copyright
A grant to authors of exclusive rights to reproduce and distribute a protected work.

A **copyright** is given for "original works of authorship fixed in any tangible medium of expression, . . . from which the work can be perceived, reproduced, or otherwise communicated, either directly or with the aid of a machine or device."[2] The *works* for which copyrights are awarded include literary works, including computer software, musical, dramatic, pictorial, and graphic movies; sound recordings; and audiovisual performances

---

[1] *Universal City Studios v. Corley,* 273 F.3d 429 (2nd Cir. 2001).

[2] Section 102(a) of the Copyright Act. The current copyright statute is the Copyright Act of 1976, Pub. L. No. 105-298, codified at §101 et seq.

that have been captured on film.[3] A copyright grants to the author *exclusive rights to reproduce and distribute* the copyrighted work as well as exclusive rights to *prepare derivative* works. A book about, say, former President Clinton would be an original work of authorship and the medium is the pages in the book.[4] A movie made from the book is a derivative work.

Exclusive rights to reproduce, distribute, and make derivative works are the main rights given to copyright owners by U.S. copyright law. There are additional, less important rights given to copyright owners by U.S. copyright law, discussed below.

Impact of the Berne Convention: Copyright Formalities

In 1988 the United States joined most of the rest of the world and became a member of the Berne Convention, which is an organization of most of the nations of the world, the goal of which is to provide for international reciprocity for copyrights. The Berne Convention is based on three principles, which significantly impact U.S. copyright law. The three principles, which all signatory countries must agree to, are

1. *Complete reciprocity.* A copyrighted work from another country must be given the same copyright protections as a work from a "national" citizen.
2. *No formalities required.* A work is considered copyrighted when it is published. Registration or notice of copyright registration is not required for a valid copyright.
3. *A minimum level of protection.* For copyrighted works, signatory nations must agree to provide a minimum level of protection that is independent of the legal protection given by the signatory nation.

As a result of joining the Berne Convention, the United States had to abandon its previous requirement that a copyright holder *register* a new work with the U.S. Copyright Office in order to obtain copyright protection. Additionally, the United States had to abandon its notice requirement (© placed next to the copyrighted work with name of the author or copyright owner and date of publication) in order for a copyright holder to be able to sue for copyright damages. Under current U.S. copyright law, however, a copyright owner who does register and provides notice is entitled to greater damages if there is a copyright infringement suit.

Registration of Copyrighted Work

Although registration is not required, there are still significant advantages to U.S. copyright registration and to the provision of notice of the copyright registration to potential infringers. Registration of copyrighted material is inexpensive, $30 for most registrations, and relatively easy to accomplish, requiring that a copy of the copyrighted work be sent to the Copyright Office in Washington, D.C. (http://www.loc.gov/copyright/).

Risks of Copyright Registration

Registration of a copyright does require that the copyrighted material be part of the public record. If there are trade secrets revealed by the public display of the copyrighted material, then these disclosures impose an additional, possibly prohibitive, nonmonetary cost of copyright registration that management should consider. For computer software, because disregard for U.S. copyrights is a serious problem and infringement enforcement in some Third World countries is spotty at best, the Copyright Office allows for registration

---

[3] Section 102(a) of the Copyright Act. The current copyright statute is the Copyright Act of 1976, Pub. L. No. 105-298, codified at §101 et seq.

[4] Section 106 of the Copyright Act.

of software code when only the first and last 25 pages of code are made available to the public.[5]

Duration of a Copyright

Currently (for works authored after 1978), a copyright lasts for the life of the author, plus 70 years (a result of the Sonny Bono Act).[6] For joint works, the copyright lasts for the life of the last surviving author plus 70 years. A work for hire lasts for 95 years from date of publication or 120 years from creation, whichever expires first. A work for hire results when an employer hires someone to create copyrighted works, such as a screenplay for a movie or an operating manual for a consumer appliance. Once a copyright expires, the protected work becomes part of the public domain, free for all to use as desired, and cannot be copyrighted again.

Scope of Copyright Protection

In defining the scope of protection provided by copyright law, it is important to *distinguish the expression of an idea from the idea itself.* Copyright law protects against copying of copyrightable material. An idea is not copyrightable, but an expression of an idea is copyrightable. The idea of a love story for a movie, play, or novel is often fairly straightforward. The expression of an idea, whether it be *this textbook* or the movie *When Harry Met Sally,* can be copyrighted.[7] Copyrighting either of the works mentioned above protects the authors against having their work copied by others, but does not prevent other authors from using the *idea* of a legal environment text or a love story to create their own expressions of these ideas.

According to Section 102(b) of the Copyright Act, copyrights cannot be used to protect any "idea, procedure, process, system, method of operation, concept, principle, or discovery . . ." As you may note, *some of what is listed in Section 102(b) can be protected by patent law but is explicitly excluded from copyright protection.* Although patent law cannot be used to protect the discovery of an original idea, it can be used to protect a new and useful process. In general, copyright law cannot be used to protect the *functionality* associated with, say, software. Functionality can only be protected with patent law.

Copyright Protection for Databases

Facts, whether or not they are in the public record, cannot be protected under copyright law, but the *arrangement of facts* can be, as long as the arrangement exhibits some minimal level of creativity. Suppose Harry researches landholdings of the Catholic Church in Europe in the seventeenth century and arranges the holdings identified in a country-by-country table, showing acreage and land under cultivation, in a book that is purchased by the library of the local university. Suppose that Mary (1) copies the page that has the table on it with the landholdings of the Catholic Church and (2) writes her own book that also has a table on the landholdings of the Catholic Church in Europe in the seventeenth century. Harry can sue Mary if she copies his table in her book, but not if she merely uses the facts that Harry uncovered.

---

[5] The presumption is that a copier could not operate the software program by just having access to the first and last 25 pages of code. U.S. Copyright Office, Copyright Registration of Computer Programs, Circular 61.

[6] The formal name of the Sonny Bono Act is Copyright Term Extension Act of 1998, Pub. L. No. 105-298, 112 Stat. 2827. The constitutionality of the Copyright Term Extension Act has been challenged by a number of organizations and the Supreme Court has agreed to hear the case, *Eldred v. Ashcroft,* 534 U.S. 1126 (2002).

[7] *When Harry Met Sally* is a movie from 1989 starring Billy Crystal and Meg Ryan.

In order to qualify for copyright protection, there must be a nontrivial level of creativity exhibited. Certainly many databases do involve sufficient creativity to qualify for copyright protection and receive registration from the Office of Copyright. However, if the only creativity exhibited in a database is an alphabetical arrangement of names (such as in a phone book), copyright law will not protect against the copying of those names in the same order by rival phone book companies.[8] Similarly, if the only creativity exhibited in reproducing court cases from the public record is in the creation of a new set of page numbers, that level of creativity is not sufficient to qualify for copyright protection, as is illustrated in Case 13-1.

[8] *Feist Publications, Inc. v. Rural Telephone Service Co., Inc.*, 499 U.S. 340 (1991).

Case 13-1

Matthew Bender & Company, Inc. v. West Publishing Corporation

United States Court of Appeals for the Second Circuit
158 F.3d 693 (2nd Cir. 1998)

FACTS AND CASE BACKGROUND

In this case the logical plaintiffs and defendants are reversed. The defendant is West Publishing Company, which publishes federal and state court opinions. The plaintiffs, Bender & Company, Inc., manufactures and markets CD-ROM disks that cite West compilations of cases. When West publishes federal and state court opinions, which are part of the public record, it makes use of a system of citation that it created, called star pagination. *Star pagination is a computer-created system of page numbers in reported court cases that are part of a page numbering system that West created. When Bender copies court cases published by West, it also copies the West star pagination system. West claims that when Bender copies its star pagination on its CD-ROMs, it is a violation of West's copyright protection. In this case, the plaintiff (Bender) is seeking a declaratory judgment by the courts that copying and otherwise making use of West's star pagination is not a copyright infringement. The U.S. District Court for the Southern District of New York granted summary judgment to the defendant, Bender Company, thereby giving them the declaratory judgment they were seeking, which indicated that they could continue copying cases that included West's star pagination. However, the defendants (West) now appeal with the argument that the star pagination method used by Bender infringes their copyright-protected arrangement of cases.*

Opinion by Jacobs, Circuit Judge

West's primary contention on appeal is that star pagination to West's case reporters allows a user of plaintiffs' CD-ROM discs (by inputting a series of commands) to "perceive" West's copyright-protected arrangement of cases, and that plaintiffs' products (when star pagination is added) are unlawful copies of West's arrangement.

* * *

DISCUSSION

West's case reporters are compilations of judicial opinions. The Copyright Act defines a "compilation" as "a work formed by the collection and assembling of preexisting materials or of data that are selected, coordinated, or arranged in such a way that the resulting work as a whole constitutes an original work of authorship." [Citations omitted] Compilations are copyrightable, but the copyright "extends only to the material contributed by the author of such work, as distinguished from the preexisting material employed in the work." Works of the federal government are not subject to copyright protection, although they may be included in a compilation.

* * *

Under *Feist* [a Supreme Court Decision], two elements must be proven to establish infringement: "(1) ownership of a valid copyright, and (2) copying of constituent elements of the work that are original." Bender and HyperLaw concede that West has proven the first element of infringement, *i.e.,* that West owns a valid copyright in each of its case reporters.

However, as is clear from the second *Feist* element, copyright protection in compilations "may extend only to those components of a work that are original to the author." The "originality" requirement encompasses requirements both "that the work was independently created . . . ," *and* that it possesses at least some minimal degree of creativity. At issue here are references to West's volume and page numbers distributed through the text of plaintiffs' versions of judicial opinions. West concedes that the pagination of its volumes—*i.e.,* the insertion of page breaks and the assignment of page numbers—is determined by an automatic computer program, and West does not seriously claim that there is anything original or creative in that process. As Judge Martin noted, "where and on what particular pages the text of a court opinion appears does not embody any original creation of the compiler." Because the internal pagination of West's case reporters does not entail even a modicum of creativity, the volume and page numbers are not original components of West's compilations and are not themselves protected by West's compilation copyright. "As a constitutional matter, copyright protects only those constituent elements of a work that possess more than a *de minimis* quantum of creativity."

* * *

The Eighth Circuit in *West Publishing Co.* adduces no authority for protecting pagination as a "reflection" of arrangement, and does not explain how the insertion of star pagination creates a "copy" featuring an arrangement of cases substantially similar to West's—rather than a dissimilar arrangement that simply references the location of text in West's case reporters and incidentally simplifies the task of someone who wants to reproduce West's arrangement of cases. It is true that star pagination enables users to locate (as closely as is useful) a piece of text within the West volume. But this location does not result in any proximate way from West's original arrangement of cases (or any other exercise of original creation) and may be lawfully copied.

Decision and Outcome

The appeal by West Publishing Co. is rejected, which means that Bender can continue to reproduce court opinions that make use of West's star pagination system.

Questions for Analysis

1. Briefly explain star pagination? Can a computer arrangement of page numbers constitute creativity sufficient to qualify for a copyright?

2. Does this case affirm the proposition that if a machine creates the copyrightable portion of a copyrighted work, it cannot qualify as a copyright? Don't computer graphic artists make extensive use of computers in creating their works, which are copyrightable?

3. What did the court say was clearly not copyrightable about West Publishing's service? Are facts in the public domain ever copyrightable?

Copyright Infringement

Exclusive Rights

Under Section 106 of the Copyright Act, copyright owners have exclusive rights to *reproduce and distribute* copyrighted works subject to various defenses, most prominently the *fair use* defense. Copyright law also gives owners exclusive rights to distribute and to prepare *derivative* works. Section 106 also states that only copyright holders have the rights

4. in the case of literary, musical, dramatic, and choreographic works, pantomimes, and motion pictures and other audiovisual works, to *perform* the copyrighted work publicly; [Emphasis added]

5. in the case of literary, musical, dramatic and choreographic works, pantomimes, and pictorial, graphic, or sculptural works, including the individual images of a motion picture or other audiovisual work, to *display* the copyrighted work publicly . . . [Emphasis added]

Proof of Copying

A copyright holder that believes its copyright has been infringed can file suit against the suspected infringer. In such suits, defendants in some instances will admit to copying. In other cases, there is indirect evidence of copying. As an example, in most functioning computer programs, there are some mistakes in the source code or object code. If the same mistakes that are present in the plaintiff's software are present in the defendant's allegedly infringing software, chances are very high that the defendant copied some of the plaintiff's software. Some computer vendors have been known to insert "dummy" code in their software just for the purpose of making proof of infringement easier in the event of litigation.

In most cases, in order to prove infringement, the complaining copyright holder must show

- That there is *substantial similarity* between the copyrighted work and the accused work.
- That the defendant had *access* to the copyrighted work.

Access to the Copyrighted Work

independent creation
An effective defense in an infringement case based on the claim that the other user of a copyrighted creation independently developed the same creation.

In copyright law, **independent creation** is a valid defense. Hence, it is critically important to show that the defendant had access to the copyrighted work. If the defendant did not have access to the copyrighted work, then it is likely to be concluded that the accused work is an independent creation. A few years ago, George Harrison, a former member of the Beatles, was sued for a copyright infringement of the song *He's so Fine,* based on Mr. Harrison's song *My Sweet Lord*.[9] In order to deflect the independent creation defense, the plaintiffs showed that *He's so Fine* was a hit in England and that Harrison, a close student of music, undoubtedly heard the song many times. Harrison lost the case, though the judge observed that he thought it was an "unconscious" infringement.

Substantial Similarity as Applied in Software Cases

substantial similarity
Similarities that are so striking as to disprove independent creation.

A standard (test) used in determining **substantial similarity** is that the similarities are so striking as to disprove independent creation. In determining substantial similarity, the idea must be separated from the expression of the idea and facts must be separated from the expression of facts. Ultimately it is for the jury (or the judge in his or her role as finder of facts) to decide whether there is a substantial similarity between an accused work and the copyrighted work. Electronic spreadsheets are composed of ideas and expressions of ideas. Among the ideas embedded in an electronic spreadsheet are the mathematical formulas that allow a user to manipulate standard accounting data in a much more efficient fashion than is possible with paper and pencil. The expression of an idea may be the structure, sequence, and organization of the command structure that appears above the electronic grid lines displayed on a computer monitor. The mathematical formulas cannot be protected by copyright laws and neither can the grid lines, but the structure, sequence, and organization of the command structure can be *if* there are other ways of achieving the same functionality.

---

[9] *Abkco Music, Inc. v. Harrisongs Music, Ltd.*, 508 F. Supp. 708 (S.D.N.Y. 1981).

Literal and Nonliteral   In computer software, both the literal and the nonliteral portions of software are protectible under copyright law. The literal portions of a program are the computer code, both *source code* and *object code*. Object code is only readable by machines, but it is protectible under copyright law. Source code is readable and thus more easily copied, manipulated, or altered by humans. COBOL, Visual Basic, C++, and HTML are all forms of source code. Although source code does not read like a book, it is decipherable by people trained in the programming language and can be altered or copied with relative ease by programmers. Programs are generally written in the form of source code, then transformed (compiled) into object code before being delivered to customers. So most computer software is distributed to customers in the form of object code. Screen displays and user interfaces are considered nonliteral parts of computer software and are also protectible by copyright law.

Infringement: Actual and Statutory Damages

If it is decided that an infringement has occurred, the Copyright Act provides remedies for plaintiffs, including monetary damages. A successful plaintiff in a copyright infringement suit can opt for either actual damages or statutory damages. In addition, a defendant can face criminal sanctions for willful violations of the Copyright Act.

Actual Damages

Section 504(b) of the Copyright Act allows a copyright owner to recover for actual damages incurred as a result of an infringement *and, in addition,* the profits the infringer earned as a result of the infringement(s), but qualified by a statutory prohibition on double counting.[10] Double counting could occur if the plaintiff was able to recover for its lost profits on sales lost to the defendant plus the profits earned by the defendant *on those same sales.*

Burden of Proof

In the claim for profits received by the infringer, the copyright owner need only identify the gross revenue generated by the infringements. The burden of proof is upon the infringer to show company costs, which are then subtracted from gross revenue received from infringing sales. Costs, in most cases, are only *variable* costs without an allocation of fixed costs. Defendants are only entitled to deduct variable costs from gross revenue, with the difference representing *incremental profit* damages recoverable by the plaintiff. For much copyrighted material, such as computer software or musical recordings, variable costs are generally trivial in relation to the gross revenue enjoyed by the infringer.

In the Alternative: Statutory Damages

For *registered* copyright owners, copyright law (Section 504(c)(1)) allows plaintiffs in infringement cases to elect, in the alternative, statutory damages "at any time before final judgment is rendered . . ." This section allows "an award of statutory damages for all infringements involved in the action, with respect to any one work, for which any one infringer is liable individually, or for which any two or more infringers are liable jointly and severally, in a sum of not less than $750 or more than $30,000 as the court considers just." This section limits recovery to the amounts listed above for each copyrighted work, *regardless of the number of infringements.*

If the copyright owner possessed a large number of copyrights and each was infringed by the defendant, then the alternative listed in Section 504(c)(1) could yield greater damages than the "actual damages" provided for in Section 504(b) listed above. In most cases, however, proof of actual damages will yield greater damage awards because actual damages vary according to the number of infringements.

---

[10] Defendants' profits are sometimes referred to as "unjust enrichment."

If the court finds that an infringement was willful, meaning that the defendant knew that he was infringing, Section 504(c)(2) allows the court to raise statutory damages to $150,000 for each infringement. On the other hand, if the infringer is successful in proving that his infringements were innocent—that he did not know and had no reason to know that his actions were infringing the copyright of the plaintiff—the court is entitled to reduce statutory damages to $200 per infringement.

Additional Remedies and Criminal Liability

Section 505 of the Copyright Act allows for recovery of full costs, including "reasonable" attorney fees to the *prevailing* party, plaintiff or defendant. If the infringement suit by a plaintiff is obviously nonmeritorious, then the defendant could be awarded court costs and attorney fees. Court costs and attorney fees are typically awarded to the plaintiff when the defendant willfully infringed and behaved badly during litigation, such as by failing to provide documents that were named in subpoenas and by providing witnesses who were obviously uncooperative during depositions. Also, in egregious cases where it is clear that the defendant was aware the he or she was violating a copyright, as in the case of copying videos or CDs that contain computer software or copyrighted music, *courts can award triple damages.*

As anyone who has rented a video from Blockbuster or like rental stores probably knows, violations of copyright laws are also criminal offenses. Section 506(a) defines "Criminal Infringement," indicating that

> Any person who infringes a copyright willfully . . . for purposes of commercial advantage or private financial gain . . . shall be punished as provided in section 2319 of title 18. . . .
> Section 2319 provides for criminal sanctions against willful infringers ranging from fines to incarceration for up to 10 years. Section 506 also provides for *forfeiture and destruction* of "all infringing copies or phonorecords and all implements, devices, or equipment used in the manufacture of such infringing copies or phonorecords."

Copyright Defenses

First Sale

A copyright owner has exclusive rights to reproduce the protected portions of a copyrighted work. Under the Copyright Act, the copyright owner has exclusive rights to distribute, perform, and display copyrighted works. Copyright owners also have exclusive rights to prepare **derivative works.** Derivative means a transformation or adaptation of protected works. Copyright owners derive their revenue from copyrighted works, primarily by licensing the copyright work. When you buy a CD from a famous musical group, you become a licensee who is entitled to replay the copyrighted work with the CD and a CD player. When you buy a book, you are entitled to read the copyrighted work. In either case, the purchase of a CD or a book does not entitle you to reproduce the copyrighted material and resell it to others. However, under copyright law, there is a *first sale* exception that allows licensees of copyrighted material to resell the CD or book to friends or others.[11] The first sale exception does not allow a licensee to rent or distribute commercially the copyrighted material. Also, *the first sale defense does not apply if the copyrighted work is software,* which means that you can legally resell your CDs if they contain musical works, but not if they contain software programs.

derivative works
Adaptations or transformations of copyrighted works.

Using Software and Making Archival Copies

Section 117 of the Copyright Act indicates that owners of a copy of a computer program do not infringe the copyright if they make, or authorize the making of, a copy or an adaptation

---

[11] Section 109 of the Copyright Act.

of the program, provided that making the copy or adaptation

1. Is an essential step in operating the program, or
2. Is for archival use (a spare) and all archival copies are destroyed when the license to the software program ends.

Fair Use Exception

fair use
Unauthorized use of copyrighted material for teaching, research, criticism, and so forth that is not an infringement.

The **fair use** exception to the copyright laws allows unauthorized parties to reproduce parts or all of copyrighted works if the reproductions are for purposes of criticisms, commentary, news, teaching, or research.[12] The foregoing list is not exhaustive. A copyrighted book can be reviewed by a critic, and parts of the book reproduced in connection with the review, without that reproduction involving an infringement (even if the review is exceedingly negative!). The fair use exception is an affirmative defense in a copyright infringement suit, meaning that the burden of proof to qualify for the exception is borne by the defendant. Courts consider a number of factors when determining whether a defendant's copying qualifies for the fair use defense. When all is said and done, cases seem to be decided based on whether a defendant's reproductions and distributions *foreclose* sales of the copyrighted material in its market. If the answer is yes, indicating that as a result of the reproductions the copyright holder(s) lose sales, then an infringement is likely to be found.

Factors Used by the Courts in Fair Use Cases Factors that courts use in determining whether an unauthorized reproduction or distribution of some or all of a copyrighted work qualifies for the fair use exception include:

1. Whether a claimed infringing use is *commercial*. If the conclusion is yes, then it is very likely, but not universal, that the use will be deemed an infringement.
2. The *nature* of the copyrighted work. If the copying takes place to create compatibility with an operating system or hardware, then it is more likely to be deemed a fair use. Fictional works receive greater protection from the copyright laws than factual works.
3. The *amount* of copying. The more of the copyrighted work reproduced by the defendant, the more likely the reproductions are to be judged infringements.
4. The *market effect*. As stated above, however, this is the most decisive factor. If the market for the copyrighted work of the copyright owner is affected by the defendant's actions, it is very unlikely that fair use will be found.

Types of Infringement In Case 13-2, which involves the fair use exception, entire copyrighted works were copied. Another factor that the court may examine is whether a device or technique has a noninfringing use. In the *Sony* case, the issue was whether time-shifting through the use of video tape recorders (VTRs) is a noninfringing use (that qualified for the fair use exception). Notice in the *Sony* case that *direct infringements* took place due to actions of Sony VTR owners. Sony was a defendant by virtue of being a *contributory infringer*. The claim made by the plaintiff (Universal City Studios, Inc., which owned copyrights to TV programs) was that without VTRs sold by Sony, unauthorized reproductions of copyrighted works (TV programs) would not have taken place. Defendants in contributory infringement cases can generally escape liability if they can show that their devices have significant noninfringing uses, such as time-shifting in the case involving Sony.

Liability also can be established for infringement based on *vicarious* actions. If the defendant has the right to control the infringer, and financially benefits from the infringement, the defendant is *vicariously liable* to the plaintiff for an infringement. So an employer that benefits from infringing actions of employees is likely to be liable for their actions.

---

[12] Section 107 of the Copyright Act.

Case 13-2

Sony Corporation v. Universal City Studios, et al.

United States Supreme Court
464 U.S. 417 (1984)

FACTS AND CASE BACKGROUND

Owners of copyrights on television programs, Universal City Studios et al., sued manufacturers of home video tape recorders (VTRs), including Sony Corporation, in the U.S. District Court for the Central District of California. The plaintiffs alleged that some individuals had used the VTRs to record some of the owners' copyrighted works on television, that these individuals had thereby infringed the copyrights, and that the recorder manufacturers were liable for such infringement because of their sale of the recorders. The district court entered judgment for the manufacturers, but the U.S. Court of Appeals for the Ninth Circuit reversed, holding the manufacturers liable for contributory infringement. The U.S. Supreme Court now decides if the sale of home video tape recorders to the general public constituted contributory infringement of copyrights on television programs.

Opinion: Stevens, Judge

An explanation of our rejection of respondents' [Universal City Studios et al.] unprecedented attempt to impose copyright liability upon the distributors of copying equipment requires a quite detailed recitation of the findings of the District Court. In summary, those findings reveal that the average member of the public uses a VTR principally to record a program he cannot view as it is being televised . . . to watch it once at a later time. This practice, known as "time-shifting," enlarges the television viewing audience. For that reason, a significant amount of television programming may be used in this manner without objection from the owners of the copyrights on the programs. For the same reason, even the two respondents in this case, who do assert objections to time-shifting in this litigation, were unable to prove that the practice has impaired the commercial value of their copyrights or has created any likelihood of future harm. Given these findings, there is no basis in the Copyright Act upon which respondents can hold petitioners liable for distributing VTR's to the general public. The Court of Appeals' holding that respondents are entitled to enjoin the distribution of VTR's, to collect royalties on the sale of such equipment, or to obtain other relief, if affirmed, would enlarge the scope of respondents' statutory monopolies to encompass control over an article of commerce that is not the subject of copyright protection . . .

I.

The two respondents in this action, Universal City Studios, Inc., and Walt Disney Productions, produce and hold the copyrights on a substantial number of motion pictures and other audiovisual works. In the current marketplace, they can exploit their rights in these works in a number of ways: by authorizing theatrical exhibitions, by licensing limited showings on cable and network television, by selling syndication rights for repeated airings on local television stations, and by marketing programs on prerecorded videotapes or videodiscs. Some works are suitable for exploitation through all of these avenues, while the market for other works is more limited.

Petitioner Sony manufactures millions of Betamax video tape recorders and markets these devices through numerous retail establishments, some of which are also petitioners in this action. [Footnotes deleted]

* * *

The respondents and Sony both conducted surveys of the way the Betamax machine was used by several hundred owners during a sample period in 1978. Although there were some differences in the surveys, they both showed that the primary use of the machine for most owners was "time-shifting"—the practice of recording a program to view it once at a later time, and thereafter erasing it. Time-shifting enables viewers to see programs they otherwise would miss because they are not at home, are occupied with other tasks, or are viewing a program on another station at the time of a broadcast that they desire to watch. Both surveys also showed, however, that a substantial number of interviewees had accumulated libraries of tapes. Sony's survey indicated that over 80% of the interviewees watched at least as much regular television as they had before owning a Betamax. Respondents offered no evidence of decreased television viewing by Betamax owners.

* * *

In summary, the record and findings of the District Court lead us to two conclusions. First, Sony demonstrated a significant likelihood that substantial numbers of copyright holders who license their works for broadcast on free television would not object to having their broadcasts time-shifted by private viewers. And second, respondents failed to demonstrate that time-shifting would cause any likelihood of nonminimal harm to the potential market for, or the value of, their copyrighted works. The Betamax is, therefore, capable of substantial noninfringing uses. Sony's sale of such equipment to the general public does not constitute contributory infringement of respondents' copyrights.

Decision and Outcome

The U.S. Supreme Court held that the sale of home videotape recorders did not constitute contributory infringement of television program copyrights because there were noninfringing legitimate uses for VTRs such as time-shifting.

Questions for Review

1. If surveys showed that the predominant use of Sony VTRs was to acquire libraries of copyrighted programming that would be viewed multiple times, would the court's decision have been different? Why do you think it would or wouldn't?
2. How could the use of VTRs result in nonminimal harm to copyright owners?

No Electronic Theft Act, 1997

This legislation is widely viewed as closing a loophole in criminal law sanctions under the Copyright Act. Until the No Electronic Theft (NET) Act was passed, hackers and mischief-makers who *did not profit* monetarily from their copyright infringing activities did not violate federal criminal copyright law.[13] Thus, hackers who sabotaged national security by violating posted copyrights were subject to civil sanctions, but not criminal incarceration. Since most hackers have few assets, levying financial penalties on them for copyright infringements was not much of a deterrent. The NET Act defines criminal infringers as,

Any person who infringes a copyright willfully either—

1. for purposes of commercial advantage or private financial gain, or
2. by the reproduction or distribution, including by electronic means, during any 180-day period, of 1 or more copies or phonorecords of 1 or more copyrighted works, which have a total retail value of more than $1,000.

Violators of the NET Act can be imprisoned for up to three years if there are more than 10 prohibited reproductions. For a second offense, a perpetrator is subject to six years of imprisonment.

Copyright Law and the Internet

The Internet provides access to a huge array of copyrighted material even though most of it is not registered with the Copyright Office. A lot of copyrighted material that does appear

---

[13] In 1997, the No Electronic Theft (NET) Act, Pub. L. No. 105-147, 111 Stat. 2678, again amended Section 506 by amending subsection (a) in its entirety.

on the Internet is being reproduced (uploaded and downloaded) illegally and in ways that would not qualify for the fair use defense under copyright law. For copyright owners with valuable copyrights, there is an important question regarding the means by which whole-sale reproductions of their works can be prevented without spending an excessive amount of money on copyright enforcement. Suits by record companies against individuals (potential customers) who are violating copyright laws generally will not improve the net worth of copyright owners (record companies) because individuals are not likely to have enough assets to justify a suit. So far in the copying wars that have occurred in cyberspace, copyright owners, record companies and movie owners, have focused their legal attention elsewhere from individuals who are performing the *direct* copyright infringements. We briefly discuss the legal battles by the record companies and movie industry against Napster and others who facilitate undermining anticopying software in the pages below.

ISPs: Bookstores or Publishers?

Copyright owners look to choke points as a means to collect royalties or enforce copyrights. One choke point is provided by ISPs. After all, if ISPs did not provide access to the Internet, the illegal uploaders and downloaders could not engage in infringing activity. It is important to note that there are a lot of ISPs in the world. AOL and MindSpring may have large numbers of subscribers, but virtually all universities provide ISPs for faculty and students.

Unknowingly Reproducing Infringing Material In an analysis reminiscent of the discussion of ISP liability (in Chapter 11) for defamatory material uploaded by subscribers, ISP liability for *copyright infringement* depends on whether ISPs are likened to a bookstore (no liability) or a publisher (liability for copyright infringement). As with defamation cases, courts have generally found that *ISPs should be treated like bookstores* and, therefore, not be liable for the copyright infringements of their subscribers. In *Religious Technology Center v. Netcom On-Line Communications Services,* a federal district court ruled that ISPs were to be treated as though they were bookstores, which meant they were not liable for the copyright violations of subscribers, unless they knew or should have known their subscribers were violating copyright laws.[14]

---

[14] *Religious Technology Center v. Netcom On-Line Communications Services, Inc.*, 907 F. Supp. 1361 (N.D. Cal. 1995).

When There Is a Dispute as to Whether the Posted Material Infringes   Similarly to its stance in the ISP/defamation issue, Congress has exempted ISPs from liability for copyright infringement when

1. A copyright owner contacts an ISP and informs it that one of its subscribers is posting infringing material, but
2. The subscriber disagrees and contends that the material it is posting is not an infringement,

as long as the ISP adheres to a procedure prescribed in Title II to the Digital Millennium Copyright Act (DMCA).[15]

The Digital Millennium Copyright Act, Title II: Online Copyright Infringement Liability Limitation

Even though there were several court decisions favorable to ISPs during the 1990s, there was still legal uncertainty, which Congress largely eliminated with passage of the Digital Millennium Copyright Act (DMCA) in 1998. Although the *Netcom* case absolved ISPs for unknowing reproductions of material that violates copyright laws, it did not resolve the issue of ISP copyright liability when the copyright owner specifically informs the ISP that material posted by a subscriber of the ISP violates the copyright owner's copyright.

Title II of the 1998 DMCA addresses possible legal liability of ISPs (along with other transactions on the Internet) by creating a number of **safe harbors.**[16] In this context, a "safe harbor" completely bars a suit for monetary damage as long as ISPs follow the procedures called for in the DMCA.

safe harbors
Legal protection against infringement liability granted to the copying of protected works if the copying is for uses "permitted" by specific regulations.

E-mails and Other Transmissions   Title II of the DMCA adds a new Section 512 to the Copyright Act. Under the DMCA, an ISP is *not liable* for contributory or vicarious infringement when it is simply performing mechanical routing tasks that allow subscribers to transmit files and messages. Section 512(a) of the DMCA labels this transaction a limitation of copyright liability for "transitory communications." The essence of this limitation is that ISPs are not liable for copyright infringements that may be present in e-mails and other transmitted files, as long as the ISP does not have a say in the initiation of the message, the content of the message, and the addressee(s) of the message. This is one of the pigeonholes that Napster unsuccessfully tried to fit into.

Liability for Posting Infringing Material: DMCA Safe Harbor for ISPs   Without knowledge of possible infringement, ISPs are not liable for posting material that infringes someone else's copyrights. On the other hand, if an *ISP receives financial compensation* for the infringing actions of a subscriber, it will be liable as a *vicarious infringer*. In each of these situations liability is clear, but in many cases an ISP can be caught between the claims of copyright owners and allegedly infringing subscribers. The copyright owner may contend that material reproduced by an ISP is infringing, while the subscriber may just as vigorously contend that the material she is posting is *not* a copyright infringement. Under these circumstances, the ISP is potentially liable to the copyright owner if it does not remove the allegedly infringing material, but it could also be liable to the alleged infringer if the material turns out not to be infringing.

Title II of the DMCA provides ISPs with a protective procedure for eliminating the need to guess (about legality) when confronted by countervailing claims of copyright owners and subscribers. If an ISP is informed by a copyright owner that the ISP is storing or posting

[15] Pub. L. No. 105-304, codified at 17 U.S.C. §1201 et seq.

[16] Title II technically adds a new Section 512 to the Copyright Act.

material from a subscriber that the copyright owner alleges infringes his or her copyrights, then the ISP has specific procedures that it must follow to escape liability (to qualify for the *safe harbor*). *To be protected,*

1. If the ISP *knows* that material stored is infringing, then it must act to expeditiously remove the material from its server.
2. If the ISP does not know for certain that the material stored is infringing, but receives notice from the copyright owner that
    a. Identifies the copyrighted material the owner alleges has been infringed,
    b. Identifies the location of the allegedly infringing material, and
    c. States that the copyright owner in good faith believes the material infringes its copyright,

then the ISP can remove the allegedly infringing material without liability from the subscriber (the party supplying the allegedly infringing material). If the subscriber objects to the removal, then the ISP must inform the copyright owner that it is going to reinstate the subscriber's materials unless the copyright owner files suit to obtain a court order against the subscriber's actions. The copyright owner has 10 to 14 days to file suit against the subscriber who has posted the allegedly infringing material or else the ISP can return the subscriber's material to its accessible presence on the Internet.

Copyright Law and the Internet: Continuing Changes

Virtually everything that appears on the Internet is copyrighted. Virtually everything that appears on the Internet is also regularly uploaded and downloaded without obtaining permission from copyright owners, generally without legal repercussions. That is not to say, of course, that there are no suits by copyright owners against unauthorized reproductions of copyrighted works through the Internet, but litigation is a relative rarity and that is so for good reasons. Much of the downloading would qualify for the fair use exception under the Copyright Act, but much of it would not. So a large volume of the downloading that takes place is illegal but involves material for which the stakes are so low that it does not pay copyright owners to pursue the illegal copying done by individuals, who are also potential customers. It is also notable that much of the unauthorized downloading of copyrighted materials occurs innocently; the downloaders may not even be aware of the copyright laws that are being violated.

Certainly the most egregious copyright violations have occurred in connection with downloading of copyrighted music. The *Napster* case was the most prominent, but with the demise of Napster other challenges to the copyright law continue to occur. A number of websites feature peer-to-peer downloading, claiming that they are somehow unlike Napster. Record companies have sued a number of these newer websites also. Hackers have developed and distributed "DeCSS software," aimed at undermining the anticopying protection of digital versatile disks (DVDs). Predictably, this has been followed by a lawsuit brought by motion picture studios.

TRADEMARK LAW

The basic role of a trademark is to identify the *source* of a product. Consumers are concerned about the quality of goods and, by relying on trademarks, their inspection and search costs can be significantly reduced. When consumers develop trust in a trademarked product, they are thereafter freed from incurring the search and inspection costs they would face if there were no trademarks. The function of trademark law is to prevent consumer confusion by prohibiting sellers from offering competing products using trademarks that are

International Perspective   Frequently Asked Questions: Trademarks

Q: Is a federal registration valid outside the United States?

A: No. Certain countries, however, do recognize a United States registration as a basis for registering the mark in those countries. Many countries maintain a register of trademarks. The laws of each country regarding registration must be consulted.

Q: Do I have to be a U.S. citizen to obtain a federal registration?

A: No. However, an applicant's citizenship must be set forth in the record. If an applicant is not a citizen of any country, then a statement to that effect is sufficient. If an applicant has dual citizenship, then the applicant must choose which citizenship will be printed in the Official Gazette and on the certificate of registration.

Source: U.S. Patent and Trademark Office, Frequently Asked Questions, at http://www.uspto.gov/web/offices/tac/tmfaq.htm.

---

confusingly similar trademarks
Two trademarks so similar that large numbers of customers would be confused by the usage of both.

confusingly similar to another's trademark. By preventing **confusingly similar trademarks,** U.S. trademark law protects customer *goodwill* built up by companies that have worked hard to develop a reputation for quality. Federal trademark law is administered under the Lanham Act, originally passed in 1946 and amended several times since then.[17]

Trademarks, Trade Dress, and Trade Names

Most people are familiar with trademarks, designated by the symbol ®, but there are other marks and related distinctions that are protected by federal or state law including service marks, certification marks, collective marks, trade dress, and trade names. Under the Lanham Act, a federal statute, only trademarks, service marks, certification marks, and collective marks can be registered with the Patent and Trademark Office. The legal protection of trade names and trade dress is based on state common law standards against fraud, but the Lanham Act allows for suits based on imitation of trade dress.

Federal versus State Trademarks

Trademarks are registered by both state and federal authorities. Federal trademarks are far more significant, but state trademarks convey important legal advantages in many cases. When a state registers a trademark, it establishes a date of use for that mark. If the same mark is registered at the federal level, the holder of the state trademark is entitled to continue selling its products as long as the registration of the state mark predates the federal registration of the same mark by another party.

Trademarks and Service Marks

Trademarks are used for tangible, physical goods while *service marks* are used for firms that perform services, including restaurants and consulting firms. According to Section 1127 the Lanham Act, "Construction and definition," "the term 'trademark' includes any word, name, symbol, or device, or any combination thereof," used by a person "to identify and distinguish his or her goods, including a unique product, from those manufactured or sold by others and to indicate the source of the goods, even if that source is unknown." The Lanham Act definition of *service mark* is similar to that of a trademark. According to

---

[17] 15 U.S.C. §§1051–1128.

Section 1127 a service mark is any "word, name, symbol, or device, or any combination thereof" that is used "to identify and distinguish the services of one person, including a unique service, from the service of others and to indicate the source of the services, even if the source is unknown."

Certification and Collective Marks

A certification mark is a mark in which the certifying agent is a third party who vouches for the quality of a product. When consumers shop, many look at whether products they are considering purchasing have the "Good Housekeeping Seal of Approval," which is a certification mark. There are numerous other certification marks, including TRUSTe, ICCP (Institute of Certified Computing Professionals), and UL (Underwriters Laboratory). Notably, certification marks are awarded by third parties. In contrast to certification marks, collective marks are awarded by members of an organization to each other. Collective marks signify that the member is one of the group and often the group is known for quality. Associations of engineers or realtors use collective marks to signify who is a member of their group.

Trade Names and Trade Dress

Trade names cannot be registered with the Patent and Trademark Office unless the trade name is also a trademark. Minnesota Mining and Manufacturing Co. is a trade name with a corresponding trademark, which is 3M®. 3M® is a registered trademark, but the name of the company is not. However, if another company would use "Minnesota Mining and Manufacturing" as its company name and that use confuses the public, the original Minnesota Mining and Manufacturing Co. could sue the impersonator under common law.

Trade dress refers to the distinctive appearance of the business such as the interior decorating of a classy restaurant. If another restaurant were to copy the décor of a successful restaurant, Section 43 of the Lanham Act permits the first restaurant to sue if it can show consumer confusion, even though it is not possible to register trade dress.

Broadening the Scope of Marks Eligible for Receiving a Trademark

Even though the Lanham Act definition of trademark mentions "word, name, symbol, or device," in recent years, companies have tried with some success to trademark colors, sounds, and smells. The trend among judicial opinions has been to broaden the scope of what can be trademarked. On the other hand, if a proposed mark is in any way functional, it cannot be trademarked. The Nike swirl is legitimately trademarked, but if that swirl is placed on the bottom of sneakers, and its presence enables athletes to, say, pivot better, then the swirl design could be copied by other shoe companies because a seller cannot trademark a functional feature of a product.

Federal Registration

Registration Formalities

Registration of a trademark begins with an application, based on interstate sales, or a bona fide intention to sell in interstate commerce within six months. Applications are submitted to the Patent and Trademark Office (PTO) and assigned to an examiner. Applicants are required to submit a sample of the mark that they are trying to get registered by the PTO. The trademark examiner will investigate prior registrations at the PTO that are still in force, with an eye toward determining whether the public will be confused by similarities between the applicant's proposed mark and an already registered mark. In the past, a number of law firms located in Washington, D.C., specialized in conducting trademark searches so that applicants would not waste their time applying for marks that were already in use, or very similar to marks already in force. In recent years, the PTO has developed online search

Nutz and Boltz   What Are the Benefits of Federal Trademark Registration?

1. Constructive notice nationwide of the trademark owner's claim.

2. Evidence of ownership of the trademark.

3. Jurisdiction of federal courts may be invoked.

4. Registration can be used as a basis for obtaining registration in foreign countries.

5. Registration may be filed with U.S. Customs Service to prevent importation of infringing foreign goods.

Source: U.S. Patent and Trademark Office, Frequently Asked Questions, at http://www.uspto.gov/web/offices/tac/tmfaq.htm#Basic002

---

engines that enable firms to conduct preliminary trademark searches without specialized assistance.[18] However, trademark applicants should be mindful that exclusive reliance on the PTO's trademark search engines is not wise at this time and that contacting attorneys who specialize in trademarks is still prudent.[19]

Notice to Other Sellers Nationwide and Recovery of Damages

Federal registration of a trademark provides *constructive* notice to other companies that the mark has already been taken. Actual notice can be provided by using the ® symbol on the product or advertising materials. In order to recover monetary damages, according to Section 1111 of the Lanham Act, the trademark registrant must give notice. Per the act, "no profits and no damages shall be recovered under the provisions of this Act unless the defendant had actual notice of the registration." Obviously, the need to prove that the defendant knew the mark was registered, thus entitling the trademark registrant to possible monetary damages, is eliminated by simply displaying the trademark so that there is no issue of notice.

Duration of Trademarks and Incontestability

The duration of a trademark is potentially infinite, subject to requirements to pay fees required by the PTO. Initially, a trademark registration lasts for 10 years with a requirement to pay fees between the fifth and sixth years after the trademark is registered. After the fifth year, a mark becomes *incontestable,* which is a misnomer because most potential challenges to the validity of the trademark survive the period after incontestability takes place. As an example, if a mark becomes generic (as discussed below) after five years, its validity can be challenged in a subsequent infringement suit. A trademark can be lost through nonpayment of fees to the PTO, which are required every 10 years, or through nonuse (abandonment).

PTO Decisions and Appeals

As with patent law, there are internal and external appeals procedures if applicants or other interested parties disagree with officials of the PTO. Internally, the trademark examiner usually renders a decision within three months of a submission, but amendments are common.

---

[18] The search capabilities are very user friendly. Literally, users need only submit a word to see if it is a registered trademark. Online searches can be conducted at http://www.uspto.gov/web/offices/tac/doc/gsmanual/index.html.

[19] The PTO makes this same point, namely, that their search engines are not a substitute for attorneys skilled in trademark law.

A final decision usually is made within 6 to 18 months of submission. If the examiner rejects an application for a trademark, applicants can appeal to the Trademark Trial and Appeal Board and, if unsuccessful, to the federal courts. If a decision of the board is appealed, the appeal goes to the Court of Appeals for the Federal Circuit (CAFC).

What Can and Cannot Be Registered

A registered trademark carries with it prima facie evidence of validity, which means a challenger, typically a defendant in a trademark infringement suit, has the burden of showing that the "word, name, symbol, or device" adopted by the plaintiff is not eligible to receive a trademark. According to Section 1052 of the Lanham Act, "No trademark by which the goods of the applicant may be distinguished from the goods of others shall be refused registration on the principal register on account of its nature unless it—. . ." after which the statute lists a number of disqualifying categories, which are discussed below in the order in which they occur in Section 1052.

The first disqualifying condition occurs when the mark is deemed *generic*.

Generic Marks

Trademarks are supposed to identify the source of a product so that consumer search costs are reduced. If, instead, the mark refers to a class of products rather than to the products of a particular seller, trademark registration is not performing its economic function. For most people, "aspirin" refers to a class of over-the-counter pain relievers that are usually dispensed as little white pills. There are a number of sellers of aspirin and, if one of them were able to use "aspirin" as a trademark, the rest would be prevented from describing their products in that matter. To allow **generic marks** to be registered as trademarks (1) would not identify a particular brand or seller of aspirin and (2) would give monopoly-like advantages to the seller that was able to use that mark to describe its product.

generic marks
Names or other marks that have come to refer to a class of products (e.g., aspirin) rather than to a product of a particular provider.

Genericide   Many generic descriptions of products began as legitimate trademarks. Aspirin, trampolines, shuttles, and cellophane were all originally trademarked products, but later became generic labels. Both Sanka and Xerox are in some danger of becoming generic, that is, descriptive of a class of goods rather than of individual sellers. Firms whose trademarks are possibly dying of "genericide" can spend large sums of money to save their marks from loss of trademark status. Xerox® has spent heavily on advertisements reminding the public, that "there are two R's in the trademark, Xerox®."

Consider in Case 13-3 whether you think a firm should be able to prevent another firm from using the term "Ale House."

Case 13-3

Ale House Management, Inc. v. Raleigh Ale House, Inc.

United States Court of Appeals for the Fourth Circuit
205 F.3d 137 (4th Cir. 2000)

FACTS AND CASE BACKGROUND

The plaintiffs, Ale House Management (AHM), have been serving food and ale since 1988 and have built 21 Ale Houses in various cities in Florida. In each city where an AHM Ale House resides, the Ale House is named for that city. For example, the AHM Ale House in Orlando is called the Orlando Ale

House. AHM filed suit against the Raleigh Ale House for infringement based on the following three marks: (1) the words "ale house," (2) both the exterior and interior appearances of its facilities, and (3) the copyright of its floor plan drawings. The district court rejected Ale House Management's claims and granted Raleigh Ale House summary judgment.

Opinion by Niemeyer, Circuit Judge

A

Addressing first AHM's claim to exclusive use of the words "ale house," we begin by noting that AHM has not registered "ale house." Nevertheless, it may still seek protection under the Lanham Act, which also protects unregistered marks. [Citations omitted] To ascertain whether a mark is protected, we must determine whether it is (1) generic, (2) descriptive, (3) suggestive, or (4) arbitrary or fanciful. A generic mark "refers to the genus or class of which a particular product is a member," and such a mark "can never be protected." In this case, because Raleigh Ale House suggests that the term "ale house" is generic and AHM has not registered it, AHM bears the burden of establishing that it is not generic.

Acknowledging that "ale house" may be generic in some applications—such as in reference to a neighborhood English pub—AHM argues that it is not generic in reference to a facility that serves both food and beer, particularly when it has an extensive food menu. AHM has failed, however, to present any evidence that "ale house" does not refer to institutions that serve both food and beer. What it did provide was evidence that AHM facilities are primarily large restaurants that also serve beer and that food sales generate the majority of their revenue.

On the other hand, Raleigh Ale House presented extensive evidence, including citations to newspapers, dictionaries, books, and other publications, that the term "ale house" is generic, referring to several types of facilities.

* * *

AHM has presented no evidence suggesting that "ale house" is not a generic term that can refer to institutions serving both food and alcohol. Indeed, it conceded at oral argument that other Florida food-and-drink facilities incorporate "ale house" in their names. The fact that the facilities referred to by Raleigh Ale House and the various public data do not offer the same menu as AHM and that some focus more extensively on beer and ale, does not refute the proposition that "ale house" refers to a "genus or class" of facilities that serve both food and drink.

* * *

In short, we conclude that AHM has no protectable interest in the words "ale house." They are generic words for a facility that serves beer and ale, with or without food, just as are other similar terms such as "bar," "lounge," "pub," "saloon," or "tavern." All serve alcohol alone or both food and alcohol.

B

Although AHM devotes less attention to its trade dress argument, it nevertheless maintains that Raleigh Ale House violated AHM's rights in its trade dress, both as to the exterior and interior appearance of its facilities. At oral argument, however, when AHM was confronted with the observation that the exterior appearances of its various facilities differed significantly in shape, size, style, color, and materials, AHM appeared to abandon its claim with respect to the exterior and to press only its claim that it had a proprietary interest in the appearance of the interior of its facilities, including its service.

As with generic trade names, the trademark laws do not protect a generic trade dress. Trade dress should be considered generic if "well-known" or "common," "a mere refinement of a commonly-adopted and well-known form of ornamentation," or a "common basic shape or design," even if it has "not before been refined in precisely the same way."

* * *

III

* * *

A casual comparison between AHM's various architectural floor plans and Raleigh Ale House's floor plans shows, at most, the imitation of an idea or a concept, but not a copying of the plans themselves.

Raleigh Ale House's floor plans are not in the same dimensions or proportions as any of those presented by AHM.

***

For the reasons given, the judgment of the district court is AFFIRMED.

Decision and Outcome

The plaintiff in this case lost on both grounds: (1) the alleged trademark was ruled generic and (2) their trade dress was considered a mere refinement of a commonly adopted floor plan.

Questions for Review

1. Does this opinion mean that the term "ale house" cannot be part of a valid, registered trademark?
2. What other words that are basically synonyms for "ale house" does the court suggest are also unavailable for trademark registration? Pick a product, any product. Name five ways of describing the product that are so generic that the words could not be trademarked.

Confusingly Similar to Previously Registered Marks

The PTO must consider whether a proposed mark is so similar to previously registered marks that it is likely to cause confusion, mistake, or deception. The criterion used by the PTO is exactly the same as used by courts in infringement suits, namely *confusion of the public*. In making a determination concerning possible confusion of the public, the PTO (like a court) is not bound by what the "majority" thinks. The PTO will deny registration of a mark that so resembles a nonabandoned mark, previously registered, that a *substantial number of the public* is likely to be confused.

There are no hard and fast rules concerning whether a proposed mark too closely resembles a previously registered mark, resulting in confusion among the public. At trial, both sides (the trademark registrant and the alleged infringer) often bring in expert witnesses, usually marketing research professors or statisticians, to assist juries in making that factual determination. Demonstrations of confusion among the public, or lack thereof, are provided by results of surveys, time-series analysis of purchasing habits, and focus groups. The trademark owner is not obligated to show that a majority of the public was confused, just a substantial number.

In cyberspace, the principles are the same for determining whether a trademark infringement has taken place. In Case 13-4, the Ninth Circuit Court of Appeals grapples with consumer confusion in cyberspace.

Case 13-4

Brookfield Communications, Inc. v. West Coast Entertainment Corporation

United States Court of Appeals for the Ninth Circuit
174 F.3d 1036 (9th Cir. 1999)

FACTS AND CASE BACKGROUND

The focus of this case is the application of federal trademark law and unfair competition laws in relation to cyberspace. The plaintiff, Brookfield (holder of the trademark "movie buff") seeks an injunction to prohibit the defendant from using the trademarked phrase in their domain name and in the metatag for the website. West Coast Entertainment registered the domain name moviebuff.com, so when Brookfield found the domain taken, they registered moviebuffonline.com. Brookfield uses the website to sell its computer software called "MovieBuff." West Coast Entertainment is one of the largest video rental stores and intended to use the website moviebuff.com to provide, inter alia, a searchable entertainment database similar to "MovieBuff" software.

Opinion by O'Scannlain, Circuit Judge

IV

* * *

The district court classified West Coast and Brookfield as non-competitors largely on the basis that Brookfield is primarily an information provider while West Coast primarily rents and sells videotapes. It noted that West Coast's web site is used more by the somewhat curious video consumer who wants general movie information, while entertainment industry professionals, aspiring entertainment executives and professionals, and highly focused moviegoers are more likely to need or to want the more detailed information provided by "MovieBuff." This analysis, however, overemphasizes differences in principal lines of business, as we have previously instructed that "the relatedness of each company's prime directive isn't relevant." Instead, the focus is on whether the consuming public is likely somehow to associate West Coast's products with Brookfield. Here, both companies offer products and services relating to the entertainment industry generally, and their principal lines of business both relate to movies specifically and are not as different as guns and toys. Thus, Brookfield and West Coast are not properly characterized as non-competitors.

Not only are they not non-competitors, the competitive proximity of their products is actually quite high. Just as Brookfield's "MovieBuff" is a searchable database with detailed information on films, West Coast's web site features a similar searchable database, which Brookfield points out is licensed from a direct competitor of Brookfield. Undeniably then, the products are used for similar purposes. "The rights of the owner of a registered trademark . . . extend to any goods related in the minds of consumers." The relatedness is further evidenced by the fact that the two companies compete for the patronage of an overlapping audience. The use of similar marks to offer similar products accordingly weighs heavily in favor of likelihood of confusion.

In addition to the relatedness of products, West Coast and Brookfield both utilize the Web as a marketing and advertising facility, a factor that courts have consistently recognized as exacerbating the likelihood of confusion. Both companies, apparently recognizing the rapidly growing importance of Web commerce, are maneuvering to attract customers via the Web. Not only do they compete for the patronage of an overlapping audience on the Web, both "MovieBuff" and "moviebuff.com" are utilized in conjunction with Web-based products.

Given the virtual identity of "moviebuff.com" and "MovieBuff," the relatedness of the products and services accompanied by those marks, and the companies' simultaneous use of the Web as a marketing and advertising tool, many forms of consumer confusion are likely to result. People surfing the Web for information on "MovieBuff" may confuse "MovieBuff" with the searchable entertainment database at "moviebuff.com" and simply assume that they have reached Brookfield's web site. In the Internet context, in particular, entering a web site takes little effort—usually one click from a linked site or a search engine's list; thus, Web surfers are more likely to be confused as to the ownership of a web site than traditional patrons of a brick-and-mortar store would be of a store's ownership. Alternatively, they may incorrectly believe that West Coast licensed "MovieBuff" from Brookfield, or that Brookfield otherwise sponsored West Coast's database. Other consumers may simply believe that West Coast bought out Brookfield or that they are related companies.

* * *

The district court apparently assumed that likelihood of confusion exists only when consumers are confused as to the source of a product they actually purchase. It is, however, well established that the Lanham Act protects against the many other forms of confusion that we have outlined.

* * *

Here, we must determine whether West Coast can use "MovieBuff" or "moviebuff.com" in the metatags of its web site at "westcoastvideo.com" or at any other domain address *other than* "moviebuff.com" (which we have determined that West Coast may not use).

* * *

We agree that West Coast can legitimately use an appropriate descriptive term in its metatags. But "MovieBuff" is not such a descriptive term. Even though it differs from "Movie Buff" by only a single space, that difference is pivotal. The term "Movie Buff" is a descriptive term, which is routinely used in the English language to describe a movie devotee. "MovieBuff" is not. The term "MovieBuff" is not in the dictionary. Nor has that term been used in any published federal or state court opinion. In light of the fact that it is not a word in the English language, when the term "MovieBuff" *is* employed, it is used to refer to Brookfield's products and services, rather than to mean "motion picture enthusiast." The proper term for the "motion picture enthusiast" is "Movie Buff," which West Coast certainly *can* use. It cannot, however, omit the space.

* * *

VII

As we have seen, registration of a domain name for a Web site does not trump long-established principles of trademark law. When a firm uses a competitor's trademark in the domain name of its web site, users are likely to be confused as to its source or sponsorship. Similarly, using a competitor's trademark in the metatags of such web site is likely to cause what we have described as initial interest confusion. These forms of confusion are exactly what the trademark laws are designed to prevent.

Accordingly, we reverse and remand this case to the district court with instructions to enter a preliminary injunction in favor of Brookfield in accordance with this opinion.

REVERSED and REMANDED.

Decision and Outcome

The court agreed with the plaintiff and reversed the trial court. The court ruled that the defendant's domain name and use of metatags infringed plaintiff's trademark because they were likely to confuse the public.

Questions for Review

1. What was the nature of the consumer confusion that the court was concerned about in this case? Do trademark owners and domain owners have to be competitors for consumer confusion about trademarks and domain names to exist?

2. Besides confusion over trademarks, what other confusion was the court concerned about? Can a firm use a metatag to describe its product when it is the trademark of another firm?

Marks That Are Merely Descriptive

Words that simply describe a product, such as "car starter" for batteries, do not qualify for trademark registration at the federal level. If the PTO allowed words or phrases that were merely descriptive to be protected as registered trademarks, very quickly other sellers would run out of ways to describe their products because those words would be the registered trademarks of competitors.

Fanciful and Suggestive Marks

fanciful marks
Trademarks that have no direct functional or descriptive relationship with a product subject to the mark.

The concept underlying the existence and use of trademarks is that a trademark (the mark) becomes "distinctive" in the sense that it acquires *secondary* meaning that is important and valuable to the owner(s) of the mark. The *strongest* marks are those that are **fanciful,** having no direct functional or descriptive relationship with the product that is subject to the trademark. Many of these marks make use of distinctive lettering patterns that are well

Nutz and Boltz   Where Can I Conduct a Trademark Search?

Searches may be conducted on-line at http://tess2.uspto.gov/bin/gate.exe?f=tess&state=lbambt.1.1, or by visiting the Trademark Public Search Library, between 8:00 a.m. and 5:30 p.m. at 2900 Crystal Drive, 2nd Floor, Arlington, Virginia 22202. Use of the Public Search Library is free to the public. Also, certain information may be searched at a Patent and Trade-mark Depository Library. These libraries have CD-ROMS containing the database of registered and pending marks. (However, the CD-ROMS do not contain images of the design marks.)

Source: U.S. Patent and Trademark Office, Frequently Asked Questions, at http://www.uspto.gov/web/offices/tac/tmfaq.htm#Search004

known by the public, not for their literal meaning, but for the products they stand for. The Minnesota Mining and Manufacturing Company is better known for its trademarked 3M® products. America Online (AOL) and AT&T have trademarks that are combinations of letterlike symbols and distinctive designs that are easily recognizable. None of the foregoing trademarks in any way describes qualities of the products that are sold by these companies.

The PTO does allow for registration of trademarks that are *suggestive* of the qualities of a product. Cool Whip® is a registered trademark of the Kraft® Food Company for a whipped cream product that is refrigerated. Cool Whip® *suggests* the qualities of the product, but it surely has acquired secondary meaning as a registered trademark. Duracell® is another trademark that is suggestive but not merely descriptive of the underlying product. The message that this battery manufacturer/seller is trying to convey is, quite obviously, that its batteries (which are in fact cells) are *durable* and long lasting. Coca-Cola® was once challenged as being merely descriptive and then, later, as being misdescriptive as it no longer contained cocaine from coca plants that had been used previously to make the product. Both challenges failed.

Remedies

Section 1114(1) of the Lanham Act defines a trademark infringer as

Any person who shall, without consent of the registrant—

a. use in commerce any reproduction, counterfeit, copy, or colorable immitation of a registered mark in connection with the sale, offering for sale, distribution, or advertising of any goods or services . . . [for] which such use is likely to cause confusion, or to cause mistake, or to deceive, or

b. reproduce, counterfeit, copy, or colorably imitate a registered mark and apply such reproduction . . . to labels, signs, prints, packages, wrappers, receptacles or advertisements intended to be used in commerce . . . in connection with the sale . . . of goods or services . . . [for] which such use is likely to cause confusion, or to cause mistake, or to deceive. . .

Anyone guilty of infringing shall be liable in a civil action by the registrant for the remedies provided by the Lanham Act. In ordinary English, a defendant in a trademark infringement suit is liable for using a mark that is so similar to a registered mark *that it causes confusion, mistake, or fraud.* Under (b) above, the registrant cannot recover profits or damages unless the infringement was intentional.

Defenses

As discussed above, when a mark becomes incontestable, it achieves an elevated status. According to Section 1115(b), once a mark becomes incontestable "the registration shall be conclusive evidence of the validity of the registered mark and of the registration of the mark, of the registrant's ownership of the mark, and of the registrant's exclusive right to use the registered mark in commerce." In spite of "incontestability," the act lists eight separate defenses available to defendants in infringement cases, including proof that

1. The mark was fraudulently obtained.
2. The mark was abandoned.
3. The mark was being used by the defendant with permission of the registrant.
4. The name, term, or device charged to be an infringement is a use of the defendant's name in his own business.
5. The mark was in use by the defendant before registration of the registrant's mark took place.
6. The accused mark was registered and in use prior to registration of the registrant's mark.
7. The registrant's mark was used to violate the antitrust laws.
8. The equitable principles of laches, estoppel, or acquiescence are applicable.

This lengthy list of defenses is not exhaustive. Notably, as discussed above, genericity remains a defense. Notice in item 8 of the listed defenses that *acquiescence* is a defense. Acquiescence is claimed when a trademark owner is aware of a use of its mark, or a confusingly similar mark, by a third party, but makes no response to that activity within a reasonable time span. The Lanham Act places the burden of policing a mark upon the registrant. A trademark owner's failure to take action when apparent infringement is taking place can result in loss of ability to enforce the mark. In this situation, the registrant not only loses the right to enjoin use of the mark by infringers but also loses any claims for damages.

Injunctions

A remedy often used in trademark infringement suits is the injunction. An injunction is a court order to cease illegal behavior, in this case, trademark infringement. Trademark owners are often rightly concerned that their reputation for quality can be harmed or lost by infringing sales of products from another seller, which could be of inferior quality. Failure to abide by an injunction is considered contempt of court and can result in jail time. Section 1116 of the Lanham Act allows the court to require a defendant against whom an injunction has been issued to report to the plaintiff the manner in which it has complied with the injunction. Compliance requires cessation of sales with the infringing trademark. In addition, some injunctions require corrective advertising to reduce customer confusion. The injunction or court order could involve publication of statements by the defendant disassociating itself with the plaintiff or the plaintiff's trademarks. Finally, the court order could involve product recalls of sales that were enjoyed using a mark that is confusingly similar to the registrant's mark.

Court-Awarded Damages

Upon a showing that any right of a registered trademark owner has been violated, courts are entitled to award damages equal to (1) the defendant's profits, (2) the harm to the trademark owner, and (3) costs of litigation.[20] As with copyright law, the plaintiff need only show the defendant's sales, with the burden upon the defendant to show costs. Courts can award additional amounts as damages, not to exceed three times *actual damages* incurred by the plaintiff. Again, it is possible that the plaintiff can suffer actual damages that are greater than just the profits of the defendant, especially if the plaintiff's reputation or goodwill is harmed. In exceptional cases, courts can award attorney fees to the prevailing parties,

---

[20] Section 1117 of the Lanham Act.

which also indicates that frivolous suits launched by trademark owners could result in the loss of attorney fees to the defendant.

Counterfeit Marks (Knockoffs)

For *intentional use of counterfeit marks,* Section 1117 requires the court to award triple damages, measured by defendant's profits or damages to the plaintiff, whichever is greater, combined with reasonable attorney fees and possibly prejudgment interest. Again, the targets for intentional use of counterfeit marks are likely to be fly-by-night businesses, many of which are foreign-owned. These businesses are defrauding the public and harming the reputations of the trademark owners. There have been a number of clothing firms that have fraudulently sewn in labels of popular designers, such as Calvin Klein and Ann Taylor, on garments that are often of much lower quality than what these designers are known for.

Section 1124: Importation Forbidden of Goods Bearing Infringing Marks or Names

Because of the problem of foreign counterfeiting of U.S. trademarked goods, Section 1124 forbids importation of such goods and actually allows U.S. trademark owners to collaborate with customs officers in stopping these goods at the border. This section allows trademark owners to give to custom officials trademark registration documentation so that, if knock-off goods bearing that trademark appear during a customs examination of imported goods, those goods can be refused entry into the United States or seized.

The Anti-Dilution Act of 1996

Dilution and Noncompeting Goods

When an applicant applies for registration of a trademark, the PTO requires identification of the class of goods for which the applicant is seeking the trademark. There is a U.S. classification of goods and an international classification. Oddly enough, the PTO uses the international classification (IC) of goods on its website.[21] To determine which class your goods are in, it is necessary merely to go to the PTO website and describe the good. Coats, televisions, computer software, and automobiles are among goods for which trademarks are significant. Coats are in IC 25, television sets are in IC 9, most computer software is in IC 9, and automobiles are in IC 12. Part of the rationale behind classification of goods is the notion that a similar trademark applied in different classes will not necessarily confuse the public whereas a similar mark within the same class will. For example, the PTO has allowed 34 separate registrations of the term "Bad Ass," many of which have been abandoned. Among the active and concurrent registrants for the Bad Ass® trademark are one vendor who sells "sporting goods, namely, wakeboards, wakeboard bindings," and so forth in IC 28 and Bad Ass® studios, which sells both goods and services for "photographic, video and recording studio (audio and video)" in IC 41.

Federal Anti-Dilution Act[22]

Antidilution legislation is designed to deal with companies that name themselves cleverly, using titles such as McDentists, Buick Beer, or DuPont Shoes. McDonald's, Buick, and DuPont have extremely well-known marks, the value of which may be *diluted* by sellers of noncompeting goods that could "free-ride" on the goodwill and reputation built up by these better-known sellers. Dilution is also likely to cause public confusion as to whether famous trademark owners have actually decided to branch out into new lines of commerce, such as dentistry for the McDonald's corporation.

---

[21] http://www.uspto.gov/web/offices/tac/doc/gsmanual/manual.html.

[22] Pub. L. No. 104-98, codified at 15 U.S.C. §1125.

Added protection for a good domain name—even one that has a registered trademark—is essential to keep copycats and cybersquatters from making trouble with a b-to-b's hard-earned name, advised Rob Smith, director of marketing and sales for idNames, a division of Network Solutions Inc.

Once a domain name has been secured, businesses should register as many permutations of the name as they can, Smith said. He encourages b-to-b [business to business] operators to register their names using a variety of misspellings and homonyms, inserting hyphens and adding foreign country names at the end. While there are about 110 countries that have restrictions on who can register domain names, there are dozens where no rules apply, he said.

"In the b-to-b space, companies need to be aware that their domain name is up for grabs in over 70 countries, including the U.K., South Africa, Israel, Mexico, Russia and Switzerland," Smith warned. "Anybody with a computer and a credit card can register your company's name in those unrestricted countries."

Businesses have more name protection in the U.S. To learn about domain name dispute policies in the U.S., companies can log on to Network Solutions www.domainmagistrate.com. The site explains companies' rights under new legislation passed by Congress last year.

B-to-b operators also should register derogatory versions of their own names to prevent others from doing so, Smith said. Network Solutions has data on the most popular insulting names used and reports that a company's name followed by "sucks" is the hands-down leader in the category.

However, employing that strategy is no guarantee. In a widely reported case, Verizon Communications Inc., the newly named company launched by Bell Atlantic Corp. and GTE Corp., registered "verizonsucks.com to preempt others from ridiculing it on a similar site.

Online hacker magazine *2600* registered the domain name "verizonreallysucks.com" to poke fun at the company. Angered by the move, Verizon filed a lawsuit against the magazine, alleging *2600*'s actions posed an infringement on Bell Atlantic's trademark rights under the Anticybersquatting Consumer Protection Act passed by Congress last November. The case is currently in litigation.

Despite the Verizon case, Smith said companies should still do all they can to protect their names. "The core question we ask our customers is whether they are willing to lose their Internet identity because they didn't do enough to protest their domain name," he said.

Source: From Judith Nemes, "Domain Names Have Brand Impact," *BtoB Magazine*, a Crain Communications, Inc. publication. Reprinted with permission.

Section 1125 of the Lanham Act was amended in 1996 to deal with the dilution problem at the federal level. Section 1125(a) provides a civil action for anyone who uses in commerce any "word, term, name, symbol or device, . . . which—(1) is likely to cause confusion, or to cause mistake, or to deceive as to the affiliation . . . or (2) in commercial advertising or promotion, misrepresents the nature, characteristics, qualities, or geographic origin of his or her or another person's goods, services, or commercial activities . . ." This is standard anti-infringement protection for use of marks that are likely to confuse the public.

Famous Marks

Subsection (c) of 1125 was added in 1996. This subsection gives owners of "famous" marks the right to sue for an injunction to stop use of marks that are likely to cause *dilution*. The prohibition only applies to the use of marks that takes place after the famous mark becomes famous. In amending the Lanham Act, Congress has decided that famous marks deserve special treatment because they are targets for free-riding by much smaller firms that want to associate their products with the famous marks. In determining whether a mark is famous, Subsection (c) directs courts to consider the inherent distinctiveness of the mark, its duration, its geographic scope, its advertising, and so on. For many famous marks such as McDonald's, courts have a relatively easy time determining whether the mark is "famous."

Remedies: Injunctions and Monetary Damages

Subsection (c) of the Anti-Dilution Act of 1996 does not allow owners of famous marks to recover monetary damages against the diluter unless there is a showing that there was a willful intent on the part of the diluter to trade on the reputation of the famous mark, in which case the owner of the famous mark is entitled to damages and profits, as discussed above.[23] It is difficult to imagine a diluter nonwillfully using a variation of a famous mark, but, generally, owners of famous marks just want the diluting activity to stop. Many diluters are small firms with few attachable assets and showing intent is often difficult.

Anticybersquatting Consumer Protection Act of 1999

Internet and Domain Names

Until recently the four important sources of IP protection have been patents, copyrights, trademarks, and trade secret laws. With the rise of e-commerce, the World Wide Web has spawned a new form of IP, domain names, prompting the need for additional protections.

As an interesting example of market evolution, the regulation of domain names has actually taken place *privately* (as opposed to by government regulation) and is outside the control of the PTO. Domain names are currently administered by ICAAN, the Internet Corporation for Assigned Names and Numbers (http://www.icann.org). As e-commerce has gained in significance, the importance and economic value of domain names have increased. For an extended time span, enterprising denizens of the Internet recognized an opportunity and exploited that opportunity by taking (and registering) domain names of famous companies with names that are trademarked. When the Internet was just being discovered and legal rights were uncertain, many large companies were willing to pay $10,000 or more to cybersquatters so that they could eliminate the confusion and nuisance issues they caused. Case 13-5 is illustrative of court approaches to cybersquatting cases before the Anticybersquatting Consumer Protection Act was passed. You'll find that Toys "R" Us won the suit, but certainly may wonder whether it can collect any follow-up damage claims.

---

[23] 15 U.S.C. §1125(c).

Case 13-5

Toys "R" Us, Inc. v. Eli Abir

United States District Court for the Southern District of New York
45 U.S.P.Q.2D (BNA) 1944 (S.D.N.Y. 1997)

FACTS AND CASE BACKGROUND

Toys "R" Us is a nationwide retail store and owns a family of trademarks with varying derivations of the "R" Us phrase. The defendant, Abir, purchased the domain name "toysareus.com" and offered it for sale to the Toys "R" Us company. Abir stated that if Toys "R" Us did not purchase the domain name from him, then he would operate a worldwide toy catalog at the toysareus.com website. A month after the court issued a temporary restraining order against Abir, with respect to the "toysareus.com" domain name, plaintiffs allege that they discovered that defendant registered a "kidsareus.com" domain name.

Toys "R" Us claims that the operation of a website "kidsareus.com" will offer irreparable damage to their business and the effect of infringement and dilution is magnified because of the timing with the holiday shopping season.

The plaintiffs seek an injunction to prevent Abir from using the "kidsareus.com" website and a ruling that Abir has violated the Toys "R" Us trademark.

Opinion by John G. Koeltl, District Judge

To prevail on a motion for a preliminary injunction, the party requesting relief must demonstrate: (1) that it is subject to irreparable harm; and (2) either (a) that it will likely succeed on the merits, or (b) there are sufficiently serious questions going to the merits to make them a fair ground for litigation, and that a balance of the hardships tips decidedly in favor of the moving party.

The requirement of irreparable harm is satisfied if the plaintiff can show a likelihood of success in this case. A showing of likelihood of confusion is a required element of trademark infringement and false designation claims. The Second Circuit Court of Appeals has held that such a showing necessarily establishes the requisite irreparable harm in this context. Similarly, the Court of Appeals has also held that a showing of likelihood of dilution, which is a required element under § 43(c) of the Lanham Act, necessarily establishes the requisite irreparable harm with respect to a preliminary injunction in this context.

To prevail on its infringement and false designation of origin claims under §§ 32(1) or 43(a), the plaintiffs must prove that they have a valid mark subject to protection and that the defendants' mark results in a likelihood of confusion. The plaintiffs own federal trademark registrations for marks whose dominant portion is the term, or component, "R" US. The fact that Toys "does not own a registered mark for 'R US' per se, does not prevent the plaintiff[s] from claiming the 'R US' designation as a common component of a 'family of marks.'" Courts have found that the "R" US family of marks is subject to protection under the Lanham Act. Thus, the plaintiffs have satisfied the first prong of their trademark infringement claims.

* * *

First, the "R" US marks have been already adjudicated to be strong marks for purposes of trademark infringement claims, and the record in this case presents no evidence for this Court to find otherwise. The marks are best described as suggestive and thus would be protectable even without proof of secondary meaning. However, other courts have found secondary meaning and the record here supports that finding.

Second, there is a high degree of similarity between the plaintiffs' Toys "R" Us mark and the defendants' "TOYSAREUS.COM" domain name. "There is no evidence that the composite term 'R US' or the phonetic equivalent 'ARE US' existed before it was coined and extensively used by [Toys] . . . . Any visual differences between plaintiffs' and defendants' marks become nonexistent when the marks are spoken."

Third and Fourth, the products at issue in this case—relatively inexpensive toys and other children's items—are identical. As a result, there is no market gap for the defendants to bridge. The distribution channels in this case—cyberspace—are also identical. Further, the cyberspace medium renders it especially difficult for consumers to evaluate any quality differences between the plaintiffs' and the defendants' products.

Fifth, actual confusion is presumed here because the defendants admit they intended to cause confusion and that they acted in bad faith.

Sixth, it is plain that the defendants are guilty of bad faith. Their use of the domain site that copied Toys "R" Us was a deliberate bad faith effort at cyberpiracy.

Seventh, it appears that defendants' products are not thought to be the same quality as the plaintiffs' products.

Finally, it is doubtful that children or parents shopping the Internet for toys are sophisticated buyers.

The defendants are incorrect in suggesting that a disclaimer posted on the "TOYSAREUS.COM" web site can cure any possible confusion.

Having established a likelihood of confusion, the plaintiffs have satisfied the second prong of their trademark infringement claims. Thus, the plaintiffs have successfully proven a likelihood of success on the merits of these claims.

"The owner of a famous mark shall be entitled . . . to an injunction against another person's commercial use in commerce of a mark or trade name, if such use begins after the mark has become famous and causes dilution of the distinctive quality of the mark . . . ." To prevail on its dilution claim under § 43(c), the plaintiffs must show that the "R" US marks are famous and that the defendants' use of the "R" US mark in a commercial manner diluted the marks.

For similar reasons discussed above with respect to the strength of the plaintiffs' "R" US marks, it is plain that the marks are famous. Toys has extensively publicized its marks for almost a forty-year period and continues to do so today. No evidence is presented to contradict the plaintiffs' long history and use of the marks. Other courts have specifically found the "R" US family of marks to be protectable under § 43(c) because of the distinctiveness and fame it enjoys. Thus, having established that the "R" US family of marks is famous, to succeed on the merits of this claim the plaintiffs need only show that the defendants are engaged in a commercial use that will cause dilution of the marks.

* * *

For the foregoing reasons, the plaintiffs' motion for a preliminary injunction is granted. The Court will enter a separate Order incorporating the preliminary injunction. So ordered.

Decision and Outcome

The court granted the plaintiffs' motion for a preliminary injunction that prevents the defendant from using kidsareus.com as a domain name.

Questions for Review

1. What is the difference between trademark infringement and dilution? What is the principal focus of this case?
2. What other factors weighed heavily in favor of Toys "R" Us? Was the mark a famous mark? Was there evidence that the defendant was operating in bad faith?

Cybersquatting

As the Internet became more popular, cybersquatting became more prevalent and it became more and more obvious that cybersquatters were engaged in "shakedown" operations. Congress responded with the Anticybersquatting Consumer Protection Act of 1999, which amends the Lanham Act by providing that any person who, with bad-faith intent to profit from the goodwill of a trademark or service mark of another, registers or uses an Internet domain name that is identical to, confusingly similar to, or dilutive of such a mark shall be liable in a civil action brought by the owner of the mark.[24]

According to Section 2 the 1999 Anticybersquatting Consumer Protection Act,

Congress finds that the unauthorized registration or use of trademarks as Internet domain names or other identifiers of online locations (commonly known as 'cybersquatting')—

1. results in consumer fraud and public confusion as to the true source or sponsorship of products and services;
2. impairs electronic commerce, which is important to the economy of the United States; and
3. deprives owners of trademarks of substantial revenues and consumer goodwill.

This act prohibits the use of domain names or identifiers of online locations that are the trademark of another person, or are sufficiently similar to a trademark so as to cause likely confusion, mistake, deception, or dilution of the distinctive quality of a famous trademark. Note, further, that bad-faith use of domain names can carry criminal penalties as a result

---

[24] Pub. L. No. 106-113, codified at 15 U.S.C. §1117.

of this legislation. In lieu of proof of actual damages from a trademark infringement or dilution, the 1999 act also allows trademark owners to elect statutory damages, which are no less than $1,000 and, for willful damages, can be as high at $300,000 per infringement, plus full costs and reasonable attorney fees.

ICANN's Role

Finally, as discussed in Chapter 4, ICANN has developed its own procedures for reassignment of domain names when bad faith is shown. For domestic websites, U.S. courts can defer to ICANN's dispute resolution procedures, though in at least one case a federal district court maintained that it was not bound by ICANN decisions. For websites that are owned by foreigners, trademark infringement suits by trademark owners may be ineffective because U.S. courts lack jurisdiction. Reassignment of domain names through ICANN's Uniform Domain Name Dispute Resolution Policy may be the most effective procedure for trademark owners aggrieved by websites, owned by those outside the jurisdiction of U.S. courts, that select confusingly similar domain names.

Concluding Remarks about Trademarks

Trademarks are the third leg of statutory intellectual property protection at the federal level. It is easy to underrate the importance of this branch of IP. The fact that so many companies imitate and counterfeit registered trademarks indicates how high the stakes are in trademark law. Ask yourself whether you would buy any nonbranded computer, car, or golf clubs. The rise of the Internet and e-commerce has created a rival, nongovernmental source of IP protection. Clever domain names initially enabled many dot-com companies to experience exponential growth. Congress has resolved the clash between domain names and trademarks on the side of trademarks.

Summary

Copyrights Are Given for Original Works of Authorship That Can Be Reproduced from a Fixed Medium; Registration and Copyright Notice Are No Longer Necessary

- The financial importance of copyright law is enormous. Literally billions of dollars are tied up in copyrighted works and also billions are lost through copyright infringement and piracy.
- Copyrights are given for original works of authorship fixed in any tangible medium of expression.
- Copyrighted works do not have to be registered or provide notice as a result of the Berne Convention, of which the United States became a member in 1988.
- *Registration* of copyrights with the U.S. Copyright Office has benefits if the copyrighted work is infringed because damages are higher and notice is provided to the world.
- Copyrights are long lasting: the life of the author plus 70 years for original works not for hire and 95 to 120 years for works for hire.

Copyrights Protect Expressions of Ideas, Not the Ideas Themselves; to Obtain a Copyright, Arrangements of Facts Must Display Some Originality

- Copyrights protect *expressions of ideas, not the ideas* themselves.
- Copyright law does not protect the functionality of software; only patents can do that.
- Copyrights cannot protect compilations of facts, but can protect against copying the arrangement of facts as long as the author exhibits some minimal level of originality.
- For copyrighted works, copyright law provides the author with exclusive rights to reproduce and distribute such works. Also, copyright law provides that only authors (or owners of the copyrighted work) can prepare derivative works.

Copyright Law Provides Protection from Works That Are Substantially Similar, but Software Developers Cannot Use Copyright Law to Protect the Functionality of Software	• For a claim of infringement, the owner of a copyrighted work must show that the infringer had access to the copyrighted work because *independent creation* is a copyright defense. • The test for copyright infringement is whether the accused work and the copyrighted work are *substantially similar.* • Copyright protects the underlying code, both source and object, of copyrighted software. Also, copyright law can protect user interfaces and command structures of copyrighted software.
For an Infringement, Copyright Law Provides for Recovery of Lost Profits of the CR Owner and the Profits of the Infringer, but with No Double Recovery; in the Alternative, CR Owners Can Recover Statutory Damages	• Copyright law provides for damages in the event of infringement. Actual damages are computed by determining the copyright owner's lost profits on lost sales and the profits of the infringer, with a prohibition on double counting. • Once the copyright owner establishes lost sales due to infringing sales of the infringer, the burden of proof is upon the infringer to establish costs. • In the alternative, the Copyright Act provides for *statutory damages,* which range between $200 and $150,000 per infringement depending on the willfulness of the infringer. • If the defendant's behavior is egregious, courts are empowered to treble damages. • Copyright law also contains criminal sanctions for willful violations including incarceration for up to 10 years.
Copyright Law Allows for a Number of Defenses, Including First Sale, Making of Archival Copies, and Fair Use; Copyright Infringers Can Be Direct, Contributory, or Vicarious	• There are a number of exceptions and defenses available to those who reproduce or distribute copyrighted works without authorization. Among those defenses and exceptions is the *first sale exception,* which allows purchasers of copyrighted material to resell it to others. • Purchasers of copyrighted software are entitled to make archival copies of the software bought. • The *fair use* defense is available to those who copy copyrighted work without permission if the copying is for research, teaching, parody, criticism, and other allowable purposes. • Determination of whether unauthorized copying of a copyrighted work qualifies for the fair use exception depends on a number of factors, but the most important factor is the impact on the market for the copyrighted work. If the market for the copyrighted work is negatively impacted, most likely the copier will not qualify for the fair use exception. • Copyright infringers can be direct infringers, contributory infringers, or vicarious infringers.
Congress Has Responded with a Number of New Laws That Protect Copyrighted Works from Being Copied or Distributed by	• The Digital Millennium Copyright Act of 1999 creates substantial modification of copyright law addressing the manufacture or distribution of products that are designed to circumvent technological measures taken by copyright owners to protect their copyrighted works. Copyright owners are still entitled to make archival copies of their software. • The No Electronic Theft Act of 1997 was passed to provide criminal penalties to those who, for whatever reasons, profit or prank, sabotage computer systems.

Infringers; Most of This New Legislation Pertains to Internet or Online Activities	• If an employee creates a copyrighted work on the job, it is a work for hire and ownership of the copyright resides with the employer.

Congress Has Intervened to Protect ISPs from Liability for Defamation and for Carrying Allegedly Infringing Material as Long as the ISPs Follow Procedures Prescribed by the Digital Millennium Copyright Act	• Courts and Congress have decided that Internet service providers are more like bookstores than publishers for purposes of copyright protection, which means that they are not liable unless they are apprised of the claimed copyright infringement and it is not contested by the content provider. • In general, as long as ISPs merely transmit information, they are not liable for its content according to Title II of the Digital Millennium Copyright Act (DMCA). • The DMCA provides a procedure for dealing with allegedly infringing material. If an ISP is informed that material it has posted infringes a copyright of a third party, the DMCA provides a *safe harbor* to guide the ISP when there is a dispute as to whether the material does infringe a copyright of a third party.

Trademark Law Provides Protection for Distinctive Marks That Manufacturers and Others Use to Identify Their Products or Work	• Trademark law is based on the Lanham Act, which was passed in 1946 but has been amended many times. • The basic role of a trademark is to identify the source of a product. Trademarks represent quality and goodwill and cut down on consumer search costs. • A trademark includes any word, name, symbol, or device used by a person to identify his or her goods. • Federal registration of trademarks takes place through the Patent and Trademark Office. Initial duration of a trademark is 10 years, but, between the fifth and sixth years, fees must be paid. In theory, the duration of a trademark can be forever as long as the mark does not become generic and the owner does not abandon the mark. • Recent decisions by courts have expanded registered trademarks to include colors, sounds, and other symbols that previously would not qualify for a trademark.

As with Patent Law, Everything Submitted to the PTO Is Entitled to a TM Except for Generic Names, Marks That Are Confusingly Similar, and Marks That Are Merely Descriptive or Misdescriptive.	• A mark becomes generic when it no longer signifies the origin of the product but, instead, designates a class of products. Trampoline, escalator, and aspirin are examples of marks that became generic. • Marks that are confusingly similar to previously registered marks cannot be registered if customer confusion would result. Customer confusion is not based on the majority of customers but rather on a demonstration that a significant number of customers are confused. • Registration is denied to marks that are merely descriptive or misdescriptive. • The strongest marks are those that acquire secondary meaning. Marks that are suggestive can acquire secondary meaning, but the strongest marks are fanciful. • After five years on the principal register, a mark becomes *incontestable*. Most challenges remain to incontestable marks, but after five years the mark cannot be challenged for being confusingly similar to a previously registered mark or on the basis that the mark is merely descriptive.

If a Business Uses a Mark That Is Confusingly Similar to a Registered TM, an Infringement Probably Has Occurred; Congress Has Augmented Protection Given to TM Owners through the Anti-Dilution Act and the Anticybersquatting Consumer Protection Act

- The criterion for trademark infringement is that the accused mark is likely to cause confusion among the public or fraud is involved.
- Counterfeit marks are deliberate imitations of registered trademarks and damages are recoverable for intentional infringements.
- Trademark owners often seek *injunctions* to stop infringers from continuing to sell products that are likely to confuse the public and dilute the goodwill they have built up through their reputation for quality.
- For deliberate infringements, trademark owners can seek damages equal to the defendant's profits, the harm to the trademark owner, and, in some cases, the costs of litigation. For egregious cases, damages can be tripled.
- The Anti-Dilution Act of 1996 provides remedies for owners of famous trademarks even if the defendant is selling products not sold by the trademark owner. Again, the criterion for a violation is if the defendant's mark is likely to confuse the public.
- The Anticybersquatting Consumer Protection Act of 1999 provides remedies to trademark owners whose trademarks show up as *domain names* on the WWW. If bad faith is shown, the statute provides for substantial statutory damages, injunctions, and, in some cases, criminal sanctions.

Key Terms

confusingly similar trademarks, *413*
copyright, *399*
derivative works, *406*

fair use, *407*
fanciful marks, *420*
generic marks, *416*
independent creation, *404*

safe harbors, *411*
substantial similarity, *404*

Questions for Review and Analysis

1. Advise your rich uncle on what the U.S. Copyright Office does. What if your uncle tells you that he has heard that you don't have to register with the Copyright Office in order to get a copyright? Can you tell your uncle what the value of registering with the Copyright Office is?

2. What can be protected with respect to a software program and what cannot?

3. In deciding whether someone who has made unauthorized copies of copyrighted works qualifies for the fair use defense, courts look at a number of factors. What are those factors, which is the most important, and why is it the most important?

4. After five years of being registered with the Patent and Trademark Office, a mark is said to be "incontestable." What does incontestable mean in this context?

5. What does the Anticybersquatting Consumer Protection Act do? How does this act cut down on nuisance suits?

If You Really Understood This Chapter, You Should Be Able to Provide Informed Commentary on the Following:

1. **Minimal Levels of Creativity.** The plaintiff, George L. Kregos, in this case appeals a judgment from a district court judge that denied his motion for summary judgment based on copyright claims against the Associated Press (AP). Plaintiff's claims were based on a "pitching form" that contained nine items of information including such vital statistics as won/lost record, earned run average, and other statistics. It is undisputed that, prior to his creation of the form in 1983, such forms did not exist. In 1984 the AP began using a pitching form that was virtually identical to Kregos' 1983 form. The defendant, AP, claims that the plaintiff's form did not display the minimal level of creativity necessary to be copyrightable. The defendant also claims that plaintiff is trying to copyright a blank form, which has not been allowed since *Baker v. Selden,* 101 U.S. (11 Otto) 99, 25 L. Ed. 841 (1879), a case in which the Supreme Court ruled that blank forms were not copyrightable. What do you think? Does a nine-item form providing a list of statistics for baseball pitchers merit a a copyright? [*Kregos v. Associated Press,* 937 F.2d 700 (2nd Cir. 1991).]

2. **Fair Use and Market Impact.** Some of you may have seen the movie *The People vs. Larry Flint.* The movie was loosely based on the life of Larry Flint and his battles with the Reverend Jerry Falwell. In 1983 *Hustler,* a raunchy "adult" magazine, ran a parody of a Campari ad that featured Jerry Falwell, describing his "first time" as being incest with his mother in an outhouse and saying he always gets "sloshed" before his sermons. Falwell sued Larry Flint and *Hustler* magazine for defamation, but that suit was thrown out because it was clear that the story about Falwell was a parody and thus protected by the First Amendment, as the movie joyously recounts. The part of the litigation that should interest students involves the reaction of Jerry Falwell to the parody. Falwell, as part of a fund-raising venture, sent out the entire parody of him in *Hustler* magazine to 500,000 rank-and-file members of the "Moral Majority." In the fund-raiser, Falwell claimed he was "defending his mother's memory" in court. *Hustler* magazine counter-sued Falwell for infringing their copyright. Falwell claims that he is entitled to the fair use defense. Review the four factors that the courts use in deciding whether the fair use defense applies and predict whether Falwell qualified for that defense. [*Hustler Magazine, Inc. v. Moral Majority, Inc.,* 796 F.2d 1148 (9th Cir. 1986).]

3. **Copyright Protection of Software.** The debate about how much protection copyright law should provide for software has been ongoing since software and PCs became popular. Experts agree that the graphical user interfaces (GUIs) developed by the Apple Corporation during the late 1980s were far and away superior to those of MS-DOS developed by the Microsoft Corporation. When Microsoft released Windows 1.0, the similarities were such that Apple first considered suing Microsoft for copyright infringement, but eventually decided to license Microsoft's Windows program. Subsequent versions of Windows incorporated even more of the GUIs that Apple developed, leading Apple to sue for copyright infringement. The major issue in the case was the degree of protection that the GUIs developed by Apple could expect to receive. Apple argued that the "look and feel" of the Windows releases beyond the 1.0 version were strikingly similar to those of Apple's MacIntosh and Lisa computers and, therefore, the copyright protection for its software should extend beyond copying source and object code. Microsoft argued that (a) Apple had licensed away much of the distinctive features of its GUIs and that what was not licensed was either (b) functional or (c) in the public domain. Should the courts protect the "look and feel" of software or just the literal aspects, source code and object code? One answer was provided by the Ninth Circuit Court of Appeals in *Apple Computer, Inc. v. Microsoft Corp.,* 35 F.3d 1435 (9th Cir. 1994).

4. **Damages in Copyright Cases.** Deltak brought suit against ASI for copyright infringement and won on the issue of liability: the trial court found that ASI had reproduced and distributed copyrighted material owned by Deltak. Both Deltak and ASI were in the business of selling books, audios, and videotapes that teach data processing and other computer-related skills. Deltak sold a Career Development System (CDS) that included, on the left side of the form, a manual of forms and a task list that a company might want to teach its programmers. On the right side of Deltak's CDS is a list of specific teaching materials sold by Deltak. ASI copied the left side of Deltak's CDS but substituted materials it sold on the right-hand side of the form. A number of defendant's infringing copies were distributed to Deltak's customers. By the time the suit was filed, defendant had begun retrieving the infringing copies and, by the time of the trial, all of the infringing copies had been retrieved. Deltak claims that it lost profits on lost sales of its CDS products and that it lost profits on sales it would have made to the customers to which ASI distributed its infringing version of the CDS form with ASI's products featured. There are other facts in this case that make resolution of damages a complicated issue. [*Deltak, Inc. v. Advanced Systems, Inc.,* 767 F.2d 357 (7th Cir. 1985).]

5. **Trademark Dilution.** The defendants in this case are dentists who provide dental services under the name "McDental." The defendants advertised their office with an orange sign and obtained a state service mark under the name of "McDental." Plaintiff, McDonald's, claims to have first learned of the defendant's existence in 1987 and quickly communicated their concerns to defendants by letter. In previous cases, McDonald's was successful in enjoining the use of the name "McBagel's" in the case of a restaurant and "McSleep" in the case of a motel. The defendants claim they cannot recall even a single customer associating their services with that of McDonald's. The defendants also claim to have had no intention to associate themselves with the McDonald's

Corporation. Note that the defendants are not selling products that compete with the plaintiffs. Do the plaintiffs have the exclusive right to use the term "Mc" before their products? [*McDonalds's Corporation v. Druck and Gerner, DDS., P.C.,* 814 F. Supp. 1127 (N.D.N.Y. 1993).]

6. **"Suck" Sites, Free Speech, Metatags, and Trademarks.** Can a website that is critical of another business use the trademarked name of the business? In his polite moments, defendant, Andrew S. Faber, claimed that Bally's Total Fitness "sucked." Defendant created a website that was named "Bally's sucks." The plaintiff, Bally's, a federally registered trademark, claimed that customers are likely to be confused by the "Bally's sucks" website. Defendant scoffs at the notion that customers would think that a website whose domain name was "Bally's sucks" would confuse visitors as to whether the website was endorsed by or originated from the plaintiff. Defendant also used metatags of Bally's, which are transparent fonts that use the name "Bally's," generally accomplished by using a white font on a white background. Can those critical of the commercial practices of a business use the business's name and also employ metatags to draw browsers of those who input the business's name in a search engine? [*Bally's Total Fitness Holding Corporation v. Andrew S. Faber,* 29 F. Supp. 2d 1161 (C.D. Cal. 1998).]

Social Responsibility, Policy, and Ethics in a High-Tech World

7. **The Digital Millennium Copyright Act (DMCA) and Free Speech.** In a nutshell, Corley established a website, 2600 Enterprises, that discussed DeCSS, which is a program to undermine the anticopying protection of DVDs (digital versatile disks) that are contained in CSS (content scrambling system) software. In a word, Corley lost the case at the trial court level and was enjoined from posting the DeCSS software on the 2600 Enterprises website and also from posting links to other websites that advertised the availability of DeCSS software. Corley appealed the trial court decision, claiming that the DMCA violates his rights of freedom of expression under the First Amendment. Corley claims that (1) computer code is constitutionally protected free speech and, therefore, (2) the government must demonstrate a compelling state interest in order to interfere. Enforcement of the DMCA is most definitely interfering with his freedom of expression. Corley claims that "in a journalistic world, . . . you have to show your evidence . . . and particularly in the magazine that I work for, people want to see specifically what it is that we are referring to," including "what evidence . . . we have" that there is in fact technology that circumvents CSS. The case was decided in New York on November 28, 2001. Should the courts be in a position to censor articles by Internet "reporters" who claim that the audiences they write for have a particularly "show me the evidence" attitude in order to uphold copyright law? [*Universal City Studios, Inc. et al. v. Eric Corley,* 273 F.3d 429 (2nd Cir. 2001).]

Using the Internet to Your Advantage

1. Of course, the two government entities relevant to this chapter are the U.S. Copyright Office (http://www.loc.gov/copyright/) and the Patent and Trademark Office (http://www.uspto.gov). The Legal Information Institute provides a complete listing of all U.S. Copyright law at http://www4.law.cornell.edu/uscode/17/ch1.html. Title 15 of the U.S. Code, Chapter 22 contains U.S. trademark law and can be accessed at http://www4.law.cornell.edu/uscode/15/ch22.html. International copyrights are enforced under the Berne Convention (http://www.law.cornell.edu/treaties/berne/overview.html). Much of the international enforcement of copyright law has been subsumed by the World Intellectual Property Organization (http://www.wipo.org). International registration of trademarks takes place under the Madrid system at http://www.wipo.org/madrid/en/index.html. Note, however, that the United States is not part of the Madrid Agreement. The United States contends that the standards for obtaining an international trademark under the Madrid system are too loose and too many trademarks are issued. The WIPO has a trademark enforcement branch (http://www.wipo.org/about-ip/en/index.html?wipo_content_frame=/about-ip/en/trademarks.html) and continues to become more and more influential in enforcing intellectual property rights internationally.

2. Of course, there are a number of private websites, mainly sponsored by attorneys, that deal with copyright and trademark issues. An award-winning website on copyright law, called, oddly enough, the "Copyright Website" is at http://www.benedict.com/. A website that assists both

trademark and patent applicants is the American Patent and Trademark Law Center (http://www.patentpending.com/). An article entitled "A Primer on Trademark Law and Internet Addresses" is located at http://www.loundy.com/JMLS-Trademark.html. The Cyberspace Law Institute (http://www.cli.org) offers articles relevant to the interface between trademark, copyright, and the Internet. The Legal Information Institute at Cornell University (http://www.law.cornell.edu/topics/copyright.html) offers links to recent Supreme Court and court of appeals cases dealing with copyright law. Anyone inserting relevant words into Internet search engines can get a number of articles written on just about any copyright or trademark topic. Try, for example, inputting the term "fair use."

Chapter **Fourteen**

Business Organization and Cybercompanies

Learning Objectives

On completing this chapter, you should

1. Be able to recognize and discuss the differences between basic forms of business organization: sole proprietorships, partnerships, and corporations.
2. Understand the structure of ownership and management and other distinctive features of the corporate form of business.
3. Appreciate the advantages of hybrid organizations such as limited liability companies and franchises.
4. Be able to discuss some of the legal consequences of establishing a website.
5. Understand how tax and jurisdictional issues have created legal uncertainty for websites.
6. Recognize the similarities and differences between operating a website and operating a bricks-and-mortar company.

OVERVIEW

Traditional Business Organization

From peddling newspapers, to operating a franchise of a national fast-food chain, to manufacturing airliners, every business activity is conducted within the framework of a *business organization,* informal or formal. Traditionally, there are three basic legal forms of business organizations: *sole proprietorship, partnership,* and *corporation.* More recently, there has been legal recognition of specialized hybrid forms of business organization within these basic categories, with every form having its own special characteristics—rights and obligations. Among the popular forms of hybrids are S corporations, limited liability companies (LLCs), limited liability partnerships, and limited partnerships.[1]

---

[1] An S corporation is referred to as a hybrid because it is a corporation that is taxed as though it was a partnership.

Cybercompanies

In recent years, we have witnessed the emergence of a new form of business, the cyber-company. Increasingly, traditional bricks-and-mortar companies also have created substantial Web presences (making them so-called bricks-and-clicks companies). What is distinctive about cybercompanies is that they are a creation of a contract between a Web host and a cybercompany, whereas traditional corporations (and limited partnerships and other hybrid organizations) are created by compliance with a state incorporation statute by corporate promoters. As we will see, vital aspects of cybercompanies, from their names to their basic capacities, are the result of a contract with a Web host company. Whether competition among Web hosts eventually makes Web hosting agreements routine and commonplace is still to be determined. What is clear is that expanding capabilities made available on the World Wide Web by advances in technology have made Web hosting agreements a *sine qua non* for many companies.[2]

Legal Issues All Companies Must Face

Whether, functionally, a business takes a bricks-and-mortar form or exists as a cybercompany, it still will exist as some variant of the three forms of business organization listed above. Hence, business managers need to understand the characteristics of the alternative organizational structures available. For each form of business organization covered in this chapter, our review will be particularly concerned with legal issues involved in

- The formation of the business.
- The governance of the business once it exists.
- The legal characteristics of its financing obligations, its life, and transferability.
- Dissolution and winding up.
- Other features that are characteristic advantages and/or disadvantages of the particular business form.

We use the same procedure when we consider any novel features of cybercompanies, comparing and contrasting their features with those of the traditional business organization reviewed in this chapter.

SOLE PROPRIETORSHIPS

sole proprietorship
A business owned by one person who is fully responsible for (and liable for) the business.

A **sole proprietorship** is a business owned by one person who operates the business for his or her own profit. About three-quarters of all business firms in the United States are of this simplest form. Sole proprietorships are, by and large, relatively small businesses, operated by an owner, perhaps with a handful of employees. Hair salons, plumbing, electrical and other construction businesses, car dealerships, and professional practices (doctors, lawyers, accountants) are a few of many examples of solely owned and operated businesses. Although generally small in sales volume and scope of operations, some sole proprietorships, such as construction companies and car dealerships, can have millions of dollars of annual sales and dozens of employees.

Benefits of Sole Proprietorships

The sole proprietorship form of business has many advantages that make it popular. To begin with, the legal formation of this type of business is very simple as there are virtually

---

[2] *Sine qua non* is Latin for "without which there is none," indicating here that continued success requires entry into the cyberworld.

no formal business formation paperwork requirements other than, in some instances, registration with local government and the payment of permitting fees.[3] So there are uniquely low organizational costs involved in starting a sole proprietorship. This form of business is also attractive to the entrepreneurially oriented as, in effect, the owner *is* the business—he or she makes the management decisions for the firm. The owner has complete freedom to determine whether to operate or shut down, whether to expand or shrink, what products to provide, when to take a vacation, whom to hire and fire, what benefits to pay, and so forth. As the one owner of the business, the sole proprietor is the recipient of all of the profits the business provides.

For income tax purposes, profits of sole proprietorships are reported as personal income (on Schedule C of the personal tax return) and, hence, are taxed just once as personal income (unlike standard corporate income, which is subject to "double" taxation). Sole proprietors also may shield some portion of their current earnings from taxation by making retirement plan contributions into a Keogh plan or into an SEP-IRA (two forms of retirement savings vehicles that can enjoy interest and capital gains growth exempt from taxes). If the business initially loses money "on paper," a sole proprietorship could provide benefits as a tax shelter. Also, since management knowledge doesn't have to be shared with anyone else, this form of business has the greatest secrecy (privacy) advantage, though income still has to be reported to the IRS.

Disadvantages of Sole Proprietorships

A major disadvantage of the sole proprietorship form of business is *unlimited liability*—the owner is *personally* responsible for any and all debts incurred by the business. Hence, an owner's total wealth, personal as well as business, may be taken to satisfy business debts. A partial respite from limited liability is provided by business insurance. Also, since banks typically require owners of small corporations to personally sign on loans, in reality, the major disadvantage of unlimited liability for sole proprietors applies to involuntary debts—that is, to tort liability to third parties.

A second major weakness of sole proprietorships is its limited ability to raise capital. Financing for sole proprietorships is limited to what can be provided from the private funds of the owner or to what can be borrowed. Outsiders are reluctant to invest in a company that is dependent upon the health and whims of the sole proprietor.

Closely related to this second weakness is concern for the difficulty of selling ownership interest in a proprietorship. Sales of such businesses are often slow, at prices that reflect significant discounts from what the owner thinks the business is worth, and costly in terms of transaction expenses (advertising, brokerage fees). In a related vein, continuity of the business in the event of the death or disability of the owner is also an issue. Technically, these events result in the dissolution of the business. Even if the business is taken over by and transferred to other family members or someone outside the family, a new proprietorship is established.

Of course, since the sole proprietor owner is the manager, free to make all decisions, he or she also faces the burden of having to be a jack-of-all-trades for the business. This can constitute a third major disadvantage in a technology-driven world as the technical expertise and vision needed to develop successful businesses in today's economy can require the brainpower (intellectual capital) of multiple individuals with an ownership interest in the success of the startup enterprise. It also may be difficult to hire and retain high-quality employees when the opportunity for advancement (e.g., to a management position) is typically limited.

[3] In most cities, a business is required to purchase a permit to do business in the city.

PARTNERSHIPS

partnership
A business jointly
owned by two or more
people.

A **partnership** is formed when two or more individuals decide to join together and operate a business together for profit. A partnership, by its very nature, indicates the existence
of an *agreement* between or among partners, whether that agreement is *express* or *implied*.
Partners are co-owners of a business and, as such, are jointly responsible for managerial
control of the firm and entitled to jointly share in its profits. Partners can agree to whatever
terms they want regarding the sharing of responsibility for management decisions, the
shares of profits flowing to each partner, the capital contribution(s) of each partner, and so
on, so long as those terms are not prohibited by law or contrary to public policy. Under their
partnership agreement, then, partners are the managers of a firm, fully entitled to participate in all decisions for the firm. In addition, partners are also *agents* of the partnership,
which means that actions of a single partner legally bind the entire partnership.

The Partnership Agreement

Virtually all states have passed the Uniform Partnership Act (UPA), which defines the
rights and duties of partners in the absence of an agreement.[4] In 1992, the National Conference of Commissioners on Uniform State Laws (NCCUSL) enacted the Revised
Uniform Partnership Act that has been adopted (by the spring of 2003) by 31 states and the
District of Columbia.[5] In the absence of an agreement to the contrary, the laws governing
partnerships are stated in the UPA. The UPA is a codification of common law, which applies
unless the partners agree otherwise.

According to the UPA, if nothing is otherwise contracted for in a partnership agreement,

1. *All partners are entitled to equal shares of profits and losses.* Upon dissolution of the
   partnership, all partners are entitled to equal shares of partnership assets, regardless of
   who contributed what to the partnership.

2. *All partners have an equal say or vote in management decisions.* For most management
   decisions, majority rules. However, some decisions involving fundamental change require unanimous agreement.

3. *Partnerships have entity status,* which means they can sue and be sued, as well as own
   property. A partnership business, however, is *not required to pay income tax.* Earnings
   are allocated to the partners.

4. *Partnerships automatically dissolve upon the death or incapacity of a partner.* It is
   common in many partnerships to have a *continuation agreement* in which survivors of
   the deceased partner are entitled to the value of that partner's pro rata share of the
   business.

Except for very small partnerships that are expected to be of limited duration, it is prudent to
consult an attorney to draw up a *written* partnership agreement. Partnership agreements
drawn up by a competent attorney are particularly useful when the partnership is dissolving,
as that is a time when litigation is common. A partnership agreement can be likened to a
prenuptial agreement: it determines who gets what in the event of dissolution of the
partnership, but it can also deal with other matters, such as management roles, salaries for

---

[4] The Uniform Partnership Act (UPA) was created by the NCCUSL (http://www.nccusl.org) and the text of
the UPA is available at www.law.upenn.edu/bll/ulc/upa/upa1200.pdf.

[5] The NCCUSL discussion of the need for the *Revised* UPA is available at http://www.nccusl.org/nccusl/
pressreleases/pr1-00-5.asp. The number of states listed above refer to those that have adopted the 1994
revision of the UPA together with the 1997 revisions.

partners, distribution of profits, entry of new partners, and other issues pertinent to the particular partnership. Without a written agreement, those decisions are dictated by the UPA.

Types of Partnerships

General Partnerships

Most partnerships, combining two or more businesspeople, are *general partnerships*. Indeed what we have been describing so far is a general partnership. In this type of business organization, each partner is an owner/manager and each partner has unlimited liability for partnership debts. Each partner is also an *agent* of the partnership and has the power to bind the partnership, hence his or her partner(s), by his or her actions in business (agency law is discussed in the next chapter). Also, each partner in a general partnership owes *fiduciary* responsibilities to put the interests of the partnership above his or her own (aspects of partners' fiduciary responsibilities to each other are discussed below).

Limited Partnerships

limited partners
Investors in a limited liability partnership (LLP) who, unlike general partners, are not personally liable for obligations of the business they have invested in.

The other common type of partnership is a *limited partnership* (LLP), which, in actuality, is very different from a general partnership. A limited partnership has general partners who have management responsibilities as described above and who have unlimited liability for partnership debts. **Limited partners** in a limited partnership, however, are investing partners who do not have management responsibilities. The critically important distinguishing characteristic (benefit) of a limited partnership is that the limited partners *do not have unlimited liability*. With regard to liability, they are in the same position as shareholders in a corporation. As is generally the case with a corporation's stockholders, if a limited partnership goes bankrupt, creditors cannot pursue the personal assets of the investing (limited) partners, as long as the limited partners in fact limit their activity to investing and *do not participate in management*.

Advantages of Partnerships

Relative to sole proprietorships, partnerships provide a number of advantages. As a group, partners have more borrowing power with banks and other suppliers of capital. In general, a group also has more of its own capital to contribute than do sole proprietors. With limited partnerships there is a further increased ability to raise capital without the threat of unlimited liability. Partnerships allow for a pooling and specialization of talents.

As indicated above, for all partnerships, profits earned or losses suffered by the partnership are considered personal income of the partners. If organizers anticipate initial losses in a venture, such as is the case in making a movie or drilling for oil, a partnership can yield substantial tax benefits. While the partnership is in production making a movie or searching for oil, "losses" are reported to the IRS and all partners, general and limited, are entitled to deduct their share of these losses when determining their overall tax obligations.

A partnership is required to file an information return with the Internal Revenue Service (IRS) that reports what profits (or losses) accrued to the partner owners during the tax year, but there is no "business" income tax obligation of the partnership itself. Partnerships that make profits are virtually forced to distribute their profits because such income is attributed (and reported to the IRS) *pro rata* to each partner. If partnership income is not distributed, partners are taxed on income that they have not received.

Disadvantages of Partnerships

Partnerships share the main disadvantages of sole proprietorships, foremost of which is the unlimited liability of general partners (but not of limited partners in an LP). Also, while more ownership participants provide for more financing capacity, the ability of partners to personally fund or borrow for the firm's capital needs are still limited as compared to the fund-raising capacity of a publicly owned corporation.[6] Ownership in a partnership is also relatively illiquid if a sale is desired, and the rights of individual partners to exit the partnership through a sale of ownership is often strictly limited by the partnership agreement. Partnerships are often simply dissolved when one of the partners dies, which is required if there is not a clause to the contrary, called a *continuation* agreement, in the partnership agreement.

Fiduciary Duties of Partners to One Another

The essence of the obligations of partners to other members of a partnership is called a *fiduciary duty,* which exists as a requirement of the *fiduciary relationship* between (among) partners. In a fiduciary relationship, partners must put the interest(s) of the partnership above their own. This requires partners to *fully disclose* possible conflicts of interest and to *refrain from voting* on partnership matters when there is such a conflict of interest. For example, if a partner owns real estate that the partnership is considering acquiring, that partner should fully disclose his or her ownership interest and should not vote on whether to acquire the property. Partners should not compete with the partnership, nor should partners take money from third parties in connection with their partnership business without fully disclosing that fact. Any monies so received from their business activities are thus owned by the partnership, not the individual partners.

Although partners have a fiduciary relationship with each other, ultimately a partnership is based on consent. If individuals decide they do not want to be in a partnership with each other, the partnership is dissolved. Partners do not have to justify their decisions to associate or not associate with other individuals. If trust between individuals is lost, then the end of the partnership will follow shortly. Many small businesses, including those organized by professionals, are operated as partnerships. Doubtless, most individuals entering into such business arrangements are not fully informed with regard to problems a partnership can encounter or fully apprised of the obligations borne by members of a partnership. Case 14-1 can fill some of those gaps.

---

[6] In part because they can guarantee investors limited liability, limited partnerships are able to raise substantial funds, much like stock-issuing corporations. General partner "owners" are still unlimitedly liable in a limited partnership, which is not true for owners of a corporation.

Case 14-1

Collete Bohatch v. Butler & Binion

Supreme Court of Texas

977 S.W. 2d 543, 41 Tex. Sup. Ct. J. 308 (Tex. 1998)

FACTS AND CASE BACKGROUND

Collete Bohatch went to work in an office of the Butler & Binion law firm (partnership) in 1986. The managing partner of the office she worked in was John McDonald and that office had one other lawyer, Richard Powers. The office did work almost exclusively for Pennzoil Corporation.

Bohatch became a full partner in February 1990, at which time she began receiving internal firm reports that showed numbers of hours billed by each attorney, the number of hours worked, and so forth. Upon reviewing these reports, Bohatch became concerned that McDonald was overbilling

Pennzoil and discussed this with Powers. On July 15, 1990, Bohatch met with Louis Paine, the overall firm's managing partner, reporting her concerns to him, then described this meeting to Powers.

The following day, McDonald met with Bohatch and informed her that Pennzoil was not satisfied with her work. Bohatch testified that this was the first time she had ever heard criticism of her work for Pennzoil. The next day, Bohatch repeated her concerns in a conference call to a number of Butler & Binion managing partners. Over the next month, the firm engaged in an investigation of the complaint(s). In August, Bohatch was informed that the investigation revealed no basis for her contentions and that she should begin looking for other employment. It was indicated that the firm would continue providing her with office space, a secretary, a monthly draw, and insurance while she conducted this job search.

In January 1991, the firm denied Bohatch a year-end partnership distribution for 1990 and reduced her tentative distribution share for 1991 to zero. In June, the firm paid Bohatch her monthly draw and told her that this draw would be her last. In August, the firm gave Bohatch until November to vacate her office.

By September, Bohatch had found new employment. On October 18, 1991, she filed suit against Butler and Binion for multiple claims including breach of fiduciary duty and breach of partnership agreement. The firm formally voted to expel her from the partnership three days later on October 21, 1991.

The court of appeals ruled that the firm's only duty to Bohatch was not to expel her in bad faith, According to the appeals court, "'[b]ad faith' in this context means only that partners can not expel another partner for self-gain." Finding no evidence that the firm expelled Bohatch for self-gain, the court concluded that Bohatch could not recover for breach of fiduciary duty. However, the court concluded that the firm breached the partnership agreement when it reduced Bohatch's tentative partnership distribution for 1991 to zero without notice, and when it terminated her draw three months before she left. The court concluded that Bohatch was entitled to recover $35,000 in lost earnings for 1991 but none for 1990, and no mental anguish damages. Accordingly, the court rendered judgment for Bohatch for $35,000 plus $225,000 in attorney's fees.

Opinion by Justice Enoch

II. BREACH OF FIDUCIARY DUTY

We have long recognized as a matter of common law that "[t]he relationship between . . . partners . . . is fiduciary in character, and imposes upon all the participants the obligation of loyalty to the joint concern and of the utmost good faith, fairness, and honesty in their dealings with each other with respect to matters pertaining to the enterprise." [Citations omitted] Yet, partners have no obligation to remain partners; "at the heart of the partnership concept is the principle that partners may choose with whom they wish to be associated." The issue presented . . . is whether the fiduciary relationship between and among partners creates an exception to the at-will nature of partnerships; that is, . . . whether it gives rise to a duty not to expel a partner who reports suspected overbilling by another partner.

* * *

[T]he partnership agreement contemplates expulsion of a partner and prescribes procedures to be followed, but it does not specify or limit the grounds for expulsion. . . Therefore, we look to the common law to find the principles governing Bohatch's claim that the firm breached a duty when it expelled her.

Courts in other states have held that a partnership may expel a partner for purely business reasons. Further, courts recognize that a law firm can expel a partner to protect relationships both within the firm and with clients. Finally, many courts have held that a partnership can expel a partner without breaching any duty in order to resolve a "fundamental schism."

The fiduciary duty that partners owe one another does not encompass a duty to remain partners or else answer in tort damages. Nonetheless, Bohatch and several distinguished legal scholars urge this Court to recognize that public policy requires a limited duty to remain partners—i.e., a partnership must retain a whistleblower partner . . . because permitting a law firm to retaliate against a partner who in good faith reports suspected overbilling would discourage compliance with rules of professional conduct and thereby hurt clients.

While this argument is not without some force, we must reject it. A partnership exists solely because the partners choose to place personal confidence and trust in one another . . . [A] partner can be expelled for accusing another . . . of overbilling without subjecting the partnership to tort damages. Such charges, whether true or not, may have a profound effect on the personal confidence and trust essential to the partner relationship. Once such charges are made, partners may find it impossible to continue to work together . . .

* * *

We hold that the firm did not owe Bohatch a duty not to expel her for reporting suspected overbilling by another partner.

III. BREACH OF THE PARTNERSHIP AGREEMENT

The court of appeals concluded that the firm breached the partnership agreement by reducing Bohatch's tentative distribution for 1991 to zero without the requisite notice . . . [T]he firm's right to reduce the bonus was contingent upon providing proper notice to Bohatch . . . Accordingly, the court of appeals did not err in finding the firm liable for breach of the partnership agreement. Moreover, because Bohatch's damages [stem from contract breach], and because she sought attorney's fees at trial under [the] Texas Civil Practice and Remedies Code, we affirm the court of appeals' award of Bohatch's attorney's fees.

Decision and Outcome

The court held that Ms. Bohatch could not sue for her ejection as a partner in the firm even though she was felt she was doing the right thing by alerting the firm to possible overbilling. Bohatch was entitled, according to the court, to recover for damages for breach of the partnership agreement in connection with her status as a partner.

Questions for Analysis

1. What fiduciary duties do partners owe to other partners?
2. Why did the Texas Supreme Court reason that such duties were not breached in this case?
3. Could another conclusion have been reached depending on the sharing of earnings from Pennzoil work?
4. Would this case make you more or less comfortable becoming a partner in a firm? Explain.

Termination of Partnerships

General Partnerships

There is a maxim that "It is easier to get married than to break up." This maxim applies with special force to termination of partnerships, which are often accompanied by some bitterness and unwillingness to compromise. It is a wise investment to have a written partnership agreement that specifies who gets what upon dissolution and termination of the partnership. *Dissolution* of a partnership takes place when the partners can no longer carry on business together. Often partnerships dissolve because of disagreements among the partners, but other reasons include better opportunities elsewhere for some of the partners, unpaid debt, and a decision to become a corporation. If a partner dies, becomes bankrupt, withdraws, or is expelled, the partnership terminates, unless the partnership has a continuation agreement to continue business even though a partner dies or becomes incapacitated. If a partner dies or becomes incapacitated, the survivors of the ex-partner are entitled to fair market value of the partner's interest, but do not become partners unless asked by the remaining partners.

Nutz and Boltz Partnering for a Win-Win Outcome

Once upon a time, there were two consultants who worked for a successful consulting firm. One was six years older than the other and served as head of one of the divisions. The two consultants were a dynamic pair, creating training programs, generating new ideas, and facilitating powerful client sessions. They also deeply enjoyed and were stimulated by each other's thoughts and energy. They became friends, and in the course of working together, decided that they wanted to create their own business. So they left their old employer and created a new company. Their organization thrived and became known for its creativity, high impact training, and personalized consulting.

Yet, three years later, the friendship was gone, and their relationship was strained, painful, and tense. They split up early in the fourth year, one buying the other out.

What happens to the friendship, the synergy, and goodwill so characteristic of the start of a partnership? What happens to destroy friendships and long-standing relationships, be it in the context of business or personal life?

It turns out that every partnership is actually a crucible in which different personalities, perceptions, needs, and drives are mixed under the pressure and heat of daily interaction, work demands, and the friction of time. The result can be a new level of relationship that is tested and tempered to a higher strength and quality.

Or the results can be more destructive, either shattering the crucible (the partnership) or throwing one or more of the partners out of the mix. The failure to attend to the psychological or emotional quotient issues within the relationship, particularly fear, are almost always the root cause of the disruption and loss.

CARING TO CONFRONT

The main reason that the emotional issues are not addressed is usually due to the failure to clearly state—or hear—the needs and feelings we have in relation to each other's actions. More than 90 percent of the failure is to be found in two areas: a lack of courage to confront, or the inability to access the courage to allow ourselves to be confronted.

* * *

For a partnership to thrive over the long term requires attention, focus, and a great deal of work. The work is mostly inner-directed, with manifestations in the ways we listen, confront, invite feed-back, and create emotional safety for the expression of "negative" feelings and problematic emotional states.

* * *

Over the years, some guidelines for success have become clear. The guidelines have their own logic, but it is the more convoluted and demanding logic of the psyche. These psychological, relationship-focused guidelines have proven over time to offer a greater margin of success. They help to create more satisfying and even joyful relationships.

GUIDELINES FOR EFFECTIVE LONG-TERM PARTNERING

1. Get clarity, in writing, as to the purpose of the partnership. Include its ultimate aims and goals.

2. Make an explicit agreement with each other regarding your inner commitment to the integrity of the partnership and your own "truths" within the relationship, exercising both the courage to respectfully confront and to invite respectful confrontation.

3. Clarify expectations and responsibilities as you see them, and also discuss how you expect them to evolve and change over time. Take the time to write them down and revisit them quarterly.

4. Create agreements and a forum for frequent truth-telling check-ins. This means frequently inviting and encouraging both appreciative and corrective feedback, as well as checking in to how your partner is feeling about him or herself, the partnership, and each other.

5. Agree, up front, on a mutually respected and acceptable "honest broker" to help listen, mediate, and offer perspective when things get tense and it is difficult to internally resolve issues.

6. Negotiate, in advance, how you want to be confronted and addressed when there are problems, particularly when it has to do with how you are behaving or interacting with others.

7. Finally, while you are in a positive frame of mind at the very beginning, create a well-researched and thoughtful legal agreement for the worst case scenario on how to end the partnership fairly and respectfully.

Sources: Reprinted with permission from "The Primacy of Courage in Partnering with Others," by Robert E. Staub, *Journal for Quality and Participation,* May/June 2000. Copyright © 2000 Association for Quality and Participation.

Winding Up

Winding up a partnership takes place when the partners pay off their debts to outsiders and liquidate assets. Unless there is an agreement to the contrary, any assets used by the partnership are *partnership assets* and are not returned to the partner that contributed those assets. During the winding up process, partners continue to owe each other fiduciary duties to put the interests of the partnership above their own, even if they are leaving the partnership because of dissatisfaction with the partnership.

Limited Partnerships: Dissolution and Winding Up

Since all limited partnerships have written agreements, those agreements take precedence if either a general partner or limited partner dies or no longer wants to participate. In general, the death of a limited partner has no impact on continuation of the partnership because limited partners are not allowed to participate in management. It is common for limited partnership agreements to make provisions for the death or departure of a general partner and to have *continuation agreements* that state that the business does not terminate with the death or departure of a general partner. For limited partnerships, dissolution and winding up involve similar procedures and legal issues as those for a general partnership. In general, limited partners have a higher priority than general partners to the assets of a limited partnership, while employees and outside creditors have a higher claim to partnership assets than limited partners.

CORPORATIONS

Entity Status

corporation
Form of business in which management (control) is separate from ownership, with stockholder owners free of personal liability for corporate obligations.

A **corporation** is a legal creation of state incorporation statutes and, in law, is a *person* (this is called entity status). By statutory provision, these legal creations (corporations) have powers generally ascribed to individuals: they can own property, can buy and sell, can sue and be sued, and can be parties to contracts. Unlike natural persons, however, the duration or life of a corporation is potentially infinite: as long as there are shareholders, the corporation can continue, even through bankruptcy!

Ownership and Management

The owners of an incorporated business are its stockholders—more specifically, the owners of the corporation's *common stock*. The stockholder owners of a corporation hope (expect) to be rewarded by receiving *dividends*—periodic distributions of earnings—and/or by realizing capital gains in wealth through appreciation of stock prices. The expectation is that these beneficial results will be provided by a firm that has a professional management team—a team of hired managers that works for the stockholder owners of the firm. American business volume is dominated by corporate business transactions, which make up about 90 percent of total business volume reported in the United States. That's probably not surprising as the identities of gigantic corporations—GE, General Motors, Procter & Gamble, Microsoft, Sears, Kroger, Home Depot, and a legion of others—are prominent fixtures in the business world.

The Parties in a Corporation

Large Corporations

In a corporation there are three distinct parties:

- Common shareholders, who own the corporation.

- Directors, who are charged with overseeing the management of the corporation.
- Corporate officers, such as president (chief executive officer or CEO), treasurer (chief financial officer or CFO), and others, who are selected by the directors to manage the day-to-day affairs of the corporation.

For large corporations, these parties are separate; most shareholders are not on the board of directors and are not corporate officers. Although it is common in large corporations for corporate directors and officers to also be stockholders, directors and officers are separate groups and held to different legal obligations. Directors answer to shareholders and are elected by them. Corporate officers are selected by the board of directors and their obligations are generally defined by a contract that they have with the corporation.

Small Corporations

Small corporations also have stockholders, directors, and officers, but there is likely to be considerable overlap between these groups. The stockholders of a small corporation also tend to be on the board of directors, and many are also top-tier corporate officers. Small corporations have much in common with partnerships, both general and limited. As with partnerships, owners of small corporations also are the operators. Small corporations that only have one class of stock and fewer than 75 stockholders, none of whom can be corporations, can elect to be S corporations, which means they are taxed as though they are partnerships. S corporations' earnings are not taxed, but, as with partnerships, profits and losses generated by the company are considered income measures to stockholders. If a small corporation anticipates initial losses in its operations, the S election will save stockholders tax obligations as losses are passed through to stockholders.

Advantages of Corporations

Limited Liability

With the large corporation model in mind, we can easily list a number of specific key advantages and disadvantages that characterize the corporate form of business. Perhaps most importantly, corporations are *limited liability* businesses. Stockholders, although they are owners, with rare exception cannot be held responsible for liabilities incurred by the corporation they own. As a legal entity, a corporation has authority to act (as if it were a natural person) and has liability for its actions, separate and apart from the actual persons who are the corporation's owners.

Transferability of Ownership and Indefinite Longevity

The legal structure of large corporations creates an ability to attract enormous sums of capital for investment purposes. Anyone interested in buying stock in General Electric has only to call a broker, or make a few computer key strokes, and within minutes (even seconds) will have accomplished that goal. Selling is just as easy. Transacting in either direction is also possible at very low cost (numerous Internet sites offer trades of up to 5,000 shares of stock at fees in the $10 range for the entire trade).

So, unlike ownership in partnerships and proprietorships, ownership in a large corporation is readily transferable. This transferability also corresponds to the lack of any natural life of a large corporation. Again, unlike sole proprietorships and partnerships, which technically terminate with the death of a partner/owner, death or incapacity of a stockholder has no impact on the continuation of a corporation. With easy transferability, a potentially unlimited life, and a history of rewarding performance for stockholder owners, corporations attract large volumes of capital in exchange for stock ownership.

Advantages and Disadvantages of the Basic Legal Forms of Business Organization

	Form of Business Organization		
	---	---	---
	Sole Proprietorship	**Partnership**	**Corporation**
Advantages	• Owner has complete control • Owner receives all profits • Low organizational costs • Income reported and taxed on owner's personal tax return • Easily dissolved	• More fund-raising ability than a sole proprietorship • More available managerial skills and time • Able to divide managerial tasks • Income reported and taxed on individual partners' tax returns	• Limited liability for owners; can only lose their investment • Ready access to large amounts of capital • Ownership (stock) is easily transferable • Unlimited life • Professionally managed by a large team of executives
Disadvantages	• Owner has unlimited liability; personal wealth fully exposed • Limited ability to raise capital • Owner must have a broad skill set • Staffing difficult with limited advancement opportunities for employees • Continuity at death of owner and transferability are problems	• Owners have complete liability; liability is joint and several • Still limited in ability to raise capital • Partnership likely to dissolve with death (or other withdrawal) of a partner • Difficult to sell or transfer ownership	• Most costly to organize • Subject to more government oversight • Significant public reporting requirements—limits on maintaining secrecy • Overall taxes generally higher because of double taxation

Some Disadvantages of Corporate Form

Of course, corporations have distinctive disadvantages also. The formation of a corporation is more demanding, hence more costly, than is the case with other forms of business. Moreover, once formed, larger corporations with many shareholders are subject to far greater government oversight (regulation and reporting requirements) than are partnerships and proprietorships.

The corporate form of business can be subject to a significant tax disadvantage. Corporations strive to earn profits for the benefit of stockholders. Any such profits earned by a corporation are subject to a corporate income tax (profits tax) levy. From their after-tax profits, if corporations pay dividends to their stockholders, those dividends are subject to personal income tax obligations at the stockholders' individual ordinary income tax rates that, for many stockholders, can be quite high. Hence, corporate profits (owned by stockholders) are subject to often hefty **double taxation**.

double taxation
Exposure of corporate earnings to taxation once at the corporate level and again at the individual level.

On the other hand, retained earnings—corporate profits that are not distributed to shareholders—are not subject to the same double taxation. Retained earnings add to the value of corporate stock and, when this extra value is received at the time of a stock sale, shareholders will likely only be obligated to pay lower capital gains tax on the additional profits they realize at the time of a sale of stock.

Corporate Formation

Unless a member of the management team has been through the process before, formation of a corporation virtually requires assistance from an attorney. For businesspersons who have gone through incorporations before, increasingly there are useful online incorporation packages that are available at modest prices. For experienced businesspersons who have been involved in previous incorporations, only minimal assistance may be required.

State Incorporation Statutes

Since corporations are a creation of state incorporation statutes, compliance with the relevant statutes is normally required to gain the advantages of being a corporation, including limited liability for shareholders, entity status, and indefinite duration. In order to incorporate, states require that corporate promoters complete forms that supply information about the name of the corporation, initial financing (classes of stock and par value), and the names of incorporators. If the state incorporation statute is complied with, the incorporators will receive a corporate certificate from state authorities and the corporation is ready to do business. Normally, after the certificate of incorporation is received, incorporators will hold their first corporate meeting, at which time stock typically is issued, a board of directors is elected, and corporate bylaws are adopted.

Each state has its own incorporation statute, but many states have adopted a version of the Model Business Corporation Act. The existence of some state-by-state differences in incorporation acts make it prudent for a business to hire an in-state attorney for incorporation purposes. A business need not incorporate in the state where it has the most business. About two-thirds of the largest U.S. businesses incorporate in the state of Delaware because its statutes and courts take a hands-off (pro-management) approach to internal corporate governance.

Corporate Bylaws

The board of directors (discussed below) is charged with broadly managing the corporation. At their first meeting, they typically adopt corporate bylaws that have previously been drawn up by their corporate attorney. Corporate bylaws serve as an *operating manual* for a corporation. In the corporate bylaws, there will be discussion of

- Issuance of stock.
- Possible restrictions on stock transfers.
- Situations in which more than a simple majority of the board of directors is required to approve a change in structure, such as a merger with another firm.
- Mechanisms for resolving deadlocks.
- Many other details of managing the corporation.

Corporate bylaws vary depending on the type of corporation. So corporate bylaws for a professional corporation of lawyers or doctors are typically much different that those for a corporation whose core business is manufacturing.

Management of the Corporation

Stockholders

While stockholders *own* a corporation, they have little or nothing to do directly with its management. Instead, shareholders elect a board of directors, which has legal responsibility to manage the corporation for the benefit of those shareholders. The board delegates actual hands-on management of the corporation to corporate officers, who are expected to be diligent *agents* for the owners, pursuing the economic interests of those owners.

Directors

board of directors
Stockholder-elected board that selects a corporation's chief executive officer and oversees corporate policy.

As discussed above, directors of a corporation are elected by stockholders to manage the corporation for the benefit of stockholders. Elected by stockholder owners, the **board of directors** has ultimate authority to put a senior management team in place and to guide corporate policy. The board is apt to include key company personnel as well as outside individuals who typically are successful and prominent businesspeople. Stockholders vote periodically (generally yearly) for a slate of board candidates. Directors owe a *fiduciary duty* to the corporation, which means that, in their duties as directors, they are obligated to put the interests of the corporation above their own. Fiduciary duties in corporations are discussed in more detail below.

Officers

A corporation's president or chief executive officer (CEO) is responsible for the day-to-day management of the corporation's conduct of business, presumably in conformance with the general policies endorsed by the board. He or she is apt to be instrumental in the appointment of a team of senior-level executives and to work closely with that team in directing the activities of the various functional components of the corporation (ranging from operations to finance functions). Corporate officers are employees of the corporation as well as agents. When they act within their scope of authority, the corporation is legally responsible for their actions. If, for example, a corporate president signs a contract on behalf of the corporation, the corporation is legally bound to perform or is culpable for breach of contract in a court of law.

Fiduciary Duties of Directors and Officers

As with the managing partners in partnerships, both the board of directors and corporate officers have *fiduciary* obligations to the corporation. These obligations are the same as for partnerships; directors and officers of a corporation have an obligation to place the interests of the corporation above their own personal interests. Both are required to avoid secretly competing with the corporation, to reveal conflicts of interests, and, in the case of directors, to refrain from voting on issues when they have a conflict of interest. In addition, directors and officers are legally obligated to protect corporations by not disclosing trade secrets even after their affiliation with the corporation has terminated.

Shareholder Agreements, Proxies, and Voting Trusts

It is common for shareholders in small corporations to form agreements so that the balance of power within the corporation is maintained. Consider the following: A, B, and C each own one-third of the shares of Corporation X. When the corporation was formed, A, B, and C each expected to be elected to the board of directors and each expected to serve, with a salary, as chief corporate officers. After one year, however, A and B decide that they do not think that C is carrying his weight and want him out. As a means of ejecting C, A and B could decide

1. Not to elect C to the board of directors.
2. To fire C from his employed position with Corporation X.
3. Not to issue any dividends, but instead to distribute profits of Corporation X in the form of bonuses to its chief corporate officers.

If all these measures were adopted, it would effectively squeeze out the ownership interests of C without compensation.

Voting Trusts and Proxies

The events described above occur with such frequency that attorneys have devised plans to avoid these contingencies. It is common for shareholders who intend to form a small corporation to create a *voting trust* in which their right to vote for members of the board of directors is held by a trustee. A shareholder's right to vote based on stock ownership is called a *proxy*. In a voting trust, the trustee has proxies for each of the shareholders and instructions on how to vote so that coalitions as described above cannot occur. Often voting trusts are time-limited, or are limited in duration until certain events take place.

Corporate Bylaws

Another way of protecting minority shareholders from being the victim of squeeze-outs of the kind described above is to require certain changes to be approved unanimously. If the corporate bylaws specify that shareholder C is the corporate treasurer and that unanimous approval among shareholders for changing the corporate bylaws is required, then C also has a measure of protection. Also, in the corporate bylaws, deadlocks should be defined and procedures should be elucidated for breaking such deadlocks and for what happens if the deadlock cannot be broken. Deadlocks can occur if management is divided over a fundamental issue such as merger or dissolution of the corporation. Deadlocks often occur in two-person corporations but can also arise in larger corporations. If there is no agreement on resolution of deadlocks in the corporate bylaws, shareholders do have the option to go to court and have the court declare the corporation deadlocked and begin the process of dissolution.

Preemptive Rights

At common law, and in most state incorporation statutes, shareholders are entitled to purchase a proportional share of new issues of stock so that their relative ownership percentage is preserved. If, for example, Corporation X (above) issued new stock, A, B, and C would be entitled to purchase one-third of the stock each. By agreement, generally in the corporate bylaws, the corporate promoters can declare that preemptive rights do not exist. In virtually all publicly traded, large corporations, preemptive rights have been abolished, but for small corporations, preemptive rights maintain the balance of power among shareholders when there is a new issuance of corporate stock for sale.

Impact of Cumulative Voting

As a corporation gets larger, it is common for voting trusts and preemptive rights to be replaced or terminated. As the number of shareholders increases, election of members of the board of directors increasingly resembles a political campaign, especially if there are rivals for spots on the board. If an election to the board of directors is contested, competing candidates will solicit proxies, or the right to vote, from shareholders. *Cumulative voting* is a common feature of corporations that fosters minority representation. If we return to our example of three shareholders, A, B, and C, each with one-third of the stock, C will never have representation on the board of directors if A and B form a coalition and agreement among themselves not to vote for C's candidates. In each election, A and B will unite and vote for their candidate. If cumulative voting is present, then C has three votes, one for each director position, but she can vote all three votes in one of the elections and in this way cumulative voting allows for minority representation on the board of directors.

Mergers, Termination, and Liquidation

Mergers

There are certain *fundamental changes* in corporations that not only require a majority of votes among the board of directors, but also require approval of the majority of the shareholders. *Mergers* are among the changes that require shareholder approval, hence the frenzied rush in takeover attempts to gain a majority of the shareholders from the target corporation. In a typical merger, the *acquiring company* seeks to obtain a majority of the stock of the *target company* so that

1. It can elect its own members to the board of directors and have both the new board of directors and a majority of shareholders vote for merger (refer to the chart). If the merger is a friendly merger, the acquiring firm may make a deal with members of the board of directors of the target firm that they can retire or quit on very attractive terms, often called "golden parachutes."

2. If the tender offer is "adverse," it means that the members of the board of directors for the target firm are going to resist takeover by the acquiring firm. Members of the board of the target firm may propose their own tender offer to their shareholders or

3. The acquiring company may bring in a "white knight," another corporation with financial assets, that will assist in making a more attractive tender offer than that of the original acquiring firm.

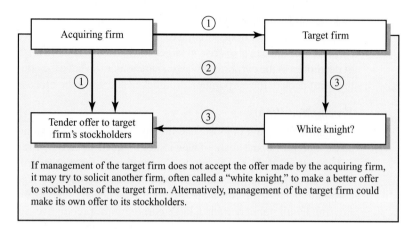

If management of the target firm does not accept the offer made by the acquiring firm, it may try to solicit another firm, often called a "white knight," to make a better offer to stockholders of the target firm. Alternatively, management of the target firm could make its own offer to its stockholders.

Termination of a Corporation

Termination of a corporation is another act that requires approval of a majority of shareholders. In the example above, the target corporation can be terminated by the acquiring corporation, because the acquiring corporation now has a majority of the shares of the target corporation. On the other hand, the acquiring corporation may decide to allow the target corporation to continue to operate as a subsidiary. If the acquiring corporation decides to buy out the remaining shareholders of the target corporation, those shareholders (of the target corporation) can generally assert their common law rights of *appraisal,* which means that they can have the value of their stock independently appraised so that they receive a fair price from the acquiring firm. Where the acquiring firm has more than 90 percent of the shares, minority shareholders can be forced to sell their shares, at fair market value according to an independent appraiser, to the acquiring firm if it wants to operate the target firm as a wholly owned subsidiary.

Dissolution and Winding Up

In general, when a corporation decides to terminate, that decision that must be approved by a majority of both the board of directors and the shareholders. Usually, termination of a corporation is accomplished in two stages: *dissolution* and *winding up*. During a voluntary dissolution, the corporation is still operating but is not taking on new business. An involuntary dissolution takes place when the corporation is unable to pay its bills and a creditor is insisting upon liquidation of corporate assets to satisfy its debt claims. During the winding up phase of corporate termination, the board of directors is responsible for paying off creditors and distributing any remaining assets, pro rata, according to stock ownership. If the corporation is bankrupt, a court may appoint a trustee to supervise paying off creditors and liquidating assets.

Sale of Assets

Conceptually, if a corporation sells all or most of its assets, it is the same as terminating; the corporation is no longer in business and shareholders are entitled to the proceeds of the sale after creditors have been paid. The sale of all, or substantially all, of the assets of a corporation must be approved by a majority of both the board of directors and shareholders. In most states, the sale of more than 50 percent of the assets of a corporation triggers the requirement of management to obtain approval of the majority of both the board of directors and shareholders. From the point of view of the firm selling its assets, the transaction is treated like a merger and termination. For the acquiring firm, it is just an acquisition of assets and therefore does not generally require approval of the shareholders of the acquiring firm.

HYBRID ORGANIZATIONS

Limited Partnerships

As discussed above, a limited partnership is a partnership that provides limited partners with limited liability as long as the limited partners do not participate in management, as defined by the Uniform Partnership Act (discussed below).

Formalities and Prohibitions

A limited partnership must have at least one general partner and at least one limited partner, but the general partner can be a corporation in most states. Unlike a general partnership, a limited partnership must be registered with a state in much the same way that a corporation is. Failure to qualify under the state limited liability act causes limited partners to have unlimited liability.

Maintaining Limited Liability

To maintain his or her protected status, a limited partner must be a passive investor in the partnership, not a participant in management. An investor can be deemed a general partner, hence liable for partnership obligations, by helping in the control of the partnership, or by engaging in conduct or communications that would cause a third party to believe, reasonably, that the investor is a general partner. Because of the sizeable number of disputes over the line between limited and general partner participation, the 1985 Revised Uniform Limited Partnership Act clarifies what activities limited partners can perform and still not be deemed general partners, hence unlimitedly liable for partnership debts.[7] The list includes

1. Guaranteeing partnership debt.
2. Serving as a consultant to the partnership.
3. Acting as an agent or serving as an employee of the partnership.
4. Attending partnership meetings.
5. Voting on various partnership activities.

Limited liability for a limited partner can be lost if, for example, a limited partner interacts with vendors and/or customers of the limited partnership in a way that would reasonably lead such parties to conclude that the limited partner is a general partner.

Limited Liability Companies (LLCs) and More on Limited Liability Partnerships (LLPs)

Limited Liability Companies

All 50 states in the United States have either adopted or proposed legislation authorizing LLCs (limited liability companies). As with S corporations, LLCs offer the joint advantages of corporate limited liability and the favorable tax treatment of a partnership,

---

[7] At this writing, 39 states had adopted the 1976 Uniform Limited Partnership Act with the 1985 amendments. Forty-nine states have adopted the Uniform Limited Partnership Act of 1976.

Nutz and Boltz   Informed Choices on Organizing Your Business

You may recall the Chapter 1 discussion of the plight of the friends who were struggling to retain or regain control of intellectual property they had shared with a potential benefactor. Perhaps some of their other fellow students had commercializable ideas as well and managed to keep control of them. In fact, you and a couple of your friends may have such intellectual property and may be on the threshold of launching a business based on your ideas. If so, you'll have to choose a form of business organization. So consider the following scenario. You and two friends have created software, usable on the Internet, that will provide "lowest cost" purchasing and transport information for manufacturers who must buy inputs worldwide. You have demonstration software in hand and need only a few months of further commercial-scale development to be ready to market your software to manufacturers anywhere in the world. You've consulted with two corporate attorneys in a law firm that is anxious to work with you and, unfortunately, gotten two very different views on what form of organization you should establish.

ADVICE OF ATTORNEY NUMBER ONE

A general partnership does not require the services of expensive legal help to protect against risks that are largely irrelevant for young graduates who have few assets to worry about losing. Not only is incorporating expensive, but failure to comply with corporate formalities could forfeit the alleged advantages of incorporating. Instead of hiring an attorney to dress up the organization as a legitimate business, owner/operators can operate with very informal rules and become more formalized and restrictive as the business grows. For those with few assets, unlimited liability is not a significant risk. Furthermore, business insurance can provide protection for all but enormous risks at a very moderate cost. For closely held corporations in their beginning stages, banks will demand personal signatures of owner/operators, so the advantages of limited liability that corporations provide apply mainly to credit supplied by creditors and tort claims of third parties. Most business ideas, including high-tech ideas, fail. Why get suited up for the major leagues when the owner/operators are still in the minor leagues and may abandon the idea if a great employment offer from an established firm comes along?

ADVICE OF ATTORNEY NUMBER TWO

The advice of attorney two is, in a word, "incorporate." The advantages of incorporation are obvious: limited liability, perpetual existence, and a business structure that can grow with the business. If losses are anticipated, election of S corporation status will generate the tax advantages of a partnership, allowing owners to offset other income with the paper losses that are expected in the first few years of operation for new high-tech startup. A closely held corporation allows owners to exercise all the powers of a general partnership in terms of restricting ownership, guaranteeing jobs for owner/operators, and structuring dividends. Operating as a corporation negates the inference that the business is a hobby of the owner/operators. Getting corporate stationery and other accoutrements of a corporate form will establish credibility with banks and potential suppliers of capital. Ownership of patents, copyrights, and trademarks is facilitated by a corporate business organization. The goal of many high-tech startups is an IPO (initial public offering). IPOs necessitate corporate form; so if an IPO is the goal, why not move things along?

AUTHORS' THOUGHTS

The choice of business organization for young entrepreneurs who may be working at a "day" job should be determined by a number of factors. The further along the "idea" [to make millions] is toward a patent or copyrighted software, the more desirable is the corporate form. At the beginning stages of the development of a viable business idea, incorporation does not make much sense, particularly if finances are tight. If the owner/operators of the high-tech startup do have significant assets, this factor would mitigate toward corporate formation. Partnerships are easy to operate and the initial partnership agreement need only include the factors that the partners deem important, such as who gets what if the partnership dissolves and how to resolve disputes. Limited partnerships are as complicated as corporations to form and are mainly desirable for tax purposes, especially if the owner/operators expect an initial period of losses. Owner/operators who have previously been involved in high-tech startups are probably savvy enough to radically cut down on legal expenses. Increasingly, legal forms are available online and most of the clerical work can be downloaded without need for attorney assistance. In short, our advice for high-tech startups manned by students with few assets is, "It depends!"

with earnings flowing through to individual LLC owners' personal incomes for tax purposes. From this point of departure, LLCs differ from S corporations in a number of advantageous ways. LLCs are permitted to have multiple classes of stock, can have any number of stockholder members, and are not limited in the classes of owners, so LLCs can issue stock that will be owned by corporations and partnerships.

Limited Liability Partnerships

In a number of states, professional service providers (such as doctors and dentists) are not permitted to form LLCs, but are permitted to join together in limited liability partnerships. In these states, professional codes of ethics require professionals to be unlimitedly liable for malpractice to their clients. As with LLCs, LLPs must be registered with the state in which the organization resides in accordance with the statute that authorizes creation of such organizations. Operating as an LLP generally provides partners with protection against claims resulting from the malpractice of *other professional members or employees of the partnership* as well as from torts of employees that they do not supervise. Professional partners in LLPs are still unlimitedly liable for their own malpractice and for torts committed by employees they supervise, though there are variations in liability from state to state.

OTHER FORMS OF BUSINESS ORGANIZATION

It is likely that any business you might start would take one of the forms described above. There are other forms that you likely will have some exposure to in the future, and brief descriptions of the most common of those should provide perspective on their characteristics and reasons for their existence.

Joint Ventures

Innovations in electronics, biology, and other sciences have spurred a proliferation of technologies that have commercial potential. Many innovations are the brainchild of individuals or small groups of individuals with great ideas, but limited access to financing and the other inputs needed to transform discovery into commercial products. It is commonplace for large companies, such as Johnson and Johnson in the pharmaceutical industry, to team up in a joint venture with an early-stage development company to commercialize a particular technology or even a single product. In addition, large companies, from petroleum exploration and refining giants to automobile manufacturers, can team up for specific projects as well.

joint venture
A general partnership with a limited life, formed for a specific purpose by two or more companies.

As described by the U.S. Supreme Court, a **joint venture** is a general partnership created for a specific purpose and having a limited life. Such an arrangement can be viewed as a partnership between or among firms (generally corporations), with terms of participation spelled out by a joint venture agreement that typically defines the rights and obligations of the participants, including sharing of any benefits or costs associated with the joint venture's activities. Such an alliance does not result in the creation of an entity that has legal standing (like a corporation) and, hence, the rights of a person. So income generated by a joint venture typically would not be taxable to the alliance, the alliance would not have the right to own property, and the alliance could not sue and/or be the target of a suit. The individual company participants in the joint venture continue their existences with no alteration of status due to their participation in a joint venture. A distinct advantage of a joint venture is that once the task that caused the joint venture to be created is finished, the parties can go their separate ways with no ongoing legal obligations to each other.

Nutz and Boltz   In the News: Joint Venture

Belo and Time Warner Cable will spend $25 million to launch two new 24-hour cable news channels in Houston and San Antonio in 2002. The 50-50 joint ventures are part of a bigger deal that gives TWC retransmission rights to Belo's TV stations and that commits TWC to carrying Belo's existing Texas Cable News channel across its Texas systems. Like the retrans deal, TWC's commitment to carry TXCN has a 10-year term. The two joint-venture news channels have initial 20-year terms.

Sources: Excerpt from Steve McClellan, "Texas Two-Step," *Broadcasting & Cable* 130, no. 41 (October 2, 2000), p. 34. See also Richard Tedesco, "Retrans Standoff in Houston," *Broadcasting & Cable* 130, no. 11 (March 13, 2000), p. 12; and Paula Rooney, "5 Biggest Investors: Paul Allen," *Computer Reseller News,* no. 860 (September 20, 1999), p. 34.

Franchises

Surely every college student feels familiar with franchise operations from having eaten too many meals at McDonald's, Burger King, or Subway, washed down with Coke or Pepsi products distributed by a local franchised distributor. Most students have shopped at The Gap, The Limited, and Structure; spent late hours at Kinko's; and purchased cars made in a distant location but sold through a local franchised dealer. The retail outlets, at which the transactions linked to the experiences described above take place, may operate as proprietorships, partnerships, corporations, or some other specific form of business—the existence of a franchise does not dictate the form of business. But franchising is so common and pervasive in our economy that it deserves discussion in this chapter, even though it is not a separate *form* of business organization. Indeed, over a third of retail sales in our country take place in franchise outlets.

Successful franchise businesses generally have two prominent features:

- They offer a trademark with widespread brand recognition.
- They offer uniformity in the product or service sold.

Hence, a Big Mac lover can expect a nearly identical hamburger from a McDonald's, whether it's bought in Vancouver or Virginia Beach. As is typical of franchise businesses, a McDonald's franchisee would operate as a semi-independent business (most often of corporate form), subject to standards and requirements specified by the franchisor (McDonald's Corporation).

To become a franchisee, an applicant generally must make an upfront payment to "buy" the franchise, then must pay annual fees that typically are a percentage of gross sales. Franchisees also often are required to make prescribed payments for participation in cooperative advertising—national advertising and promotions for all stores in the chain. In exchange, franchise applicants typically expect to receive

1. Use of a trademark, trade dress, and product line that will bring customers in the door.
2. A plan for the successful conduct of business in which the kinks have been worked out in the past.
3. Provision of the inputs (such as pizza dough, tomato sauce, cheese, etc.) that will ensure the uniformity of product that customers demand.

In fact, franchisees are often required to buy their inputs from the franchisor. Franchisees sometimes complain that this allows franchisors to levy disguised royalty charges in the form of overpriced inputs such as paper wrappers, product ingredients, and specialized inputs such as ice cream dispensers.

Nutz and Boltz Tips for Franchising

Entering a franchise agreement is one option for starting your own business with minimum risk. Although some franchises offer tried and true plans for business opportunities, prospective franchisees must be wary of franchisors who appear to offer sure-fire methods for success while struggling themselves to stay alive in the market. The mere fact that a business is franchised is not a guarantee of its success. If you are considering entering a franchise agreement, be prepared to do the same research and careful planning that go with any start-up venture.

THINGS TO KNOW BEFORE CHOOSING A FRANCHISE

Before you decide that franchising is right for you, consider several factors. Investigating and closely comparing three or four franchises or franchisors will give you an idea of "norms" in the industry. Information about a franchise or franchisor and its expectations can be obtained from the franchisor and various governmental and trade organizations. As a prospective franchisee, you should obtain as much information as possible. The list below is far from being all-inclusive; however, it provides a guide for essential questions to ask.

Just as in any business venture, franchised businesses are subject to market fluctuations and economic trends. You should obtain a thorough analysis of an area's demographics to decide if the potential location is prime for such an operation. Just because a restaurant is successful in southern California does not mean it will be successful in Maryland.

Evaluate your knowledge of the franchise business. How much, if any, experience do you have in the area? If you do not have much experience, decide whether the franchisor's training program will compensate for your lack of experience.

Be willing to devote a great deal of time, effort, and money to the operation. Franchisors often require that the franchisee be personally involved in the day-to-day operations of the business and personally guarantee the financial obligations of the business. Do not be deceived. You will not simply negotiate the deal and wait for the profits to roll in.

Find out how many franchises the franchisor owns. Significant franchisor ownership may show the franchisor's confidence in its product and create common interests between the franchisor and franchisee.

The cash needs for franchise operations are similar to any other start-up business. As a franchisee, you must pay a franchise fee in addition to financing the premises, equipment, advertising, and operation capital. Franchisors will usually provide an estimate of capital required to start, but it is best to obtain an independent evaluation.

As a franchisee, you will be required to follow the franchisor's operational requirements. Often, such requirements are all encompassing. Therefore, if you are an independent person who prefers to do things in your own way, you should evaluate whether you can operate within the structures of the franchise.

Sources: Reproduced with the permission of the Maryland State Bar Association, Inc., publisher of the MSBA Public Awareness Brochure series.

Franchise Agreement

franchise agreement
A contract that spells out the details of the agreement between a franchisor and a franchisee—for example, between Ford Motor Company and a local Ford dealership.

A **franchise agreement** is a contract between a franchisor (the parent company) and a franchisee that spells out the details of the agreement entered into, including the rights and obligations of both parties. These typically will include strict limits on the use of the franchisor's trademark, trade names, and trade dress; the use of the franchisor's operating manual, other instructional and training materials, and even "knowledge" gained from company training programs; identification of the allowable location for a franchised operation; description of the assigned territory acquired by the franchisee; agreements for fee payments; commitments to the company advertising program; and bases and conditions for termination of a franchise agreement.

Franchisee Protection Law

There has been an explosive growth of franchising in the last quarter of a century, resulting in an attendant evolutionary development of franchise law. A primary focus of franchise law, at both the federal and state level, has been on protecting franchisees from unscrupulous actions of franchisors. In general, parent companies (franchisors) are much more powerful than franchisees. At the federal level, the Federal Trade Commission imposes disclosure standards in the form of its *Franchise Rule,* which requires that, well before the exchange of any money for franchise rights, a franchisor provide an applicant with documentation that includes the following:

- Names, addresses, and telephone numbers of other franchisees.
- Information on any litigation brought against the company.
- Audited financial statements of the franchisor.
- Information on any bankruptcy proceedings of the franchisor.
- Information on the background and experience of the franchisor's key executives.
- Detailed description of the rights and obligations of the franchisor and franchisee.
- A sample set of contracts.
- Estimates of the full amount of likely needed initial investment.
- Information on all fees.
- Any restrictions on the geographic territory available to the franchisee.
- A specific indication of whether or not that territory will be exclusive.
- A listing of what must be purchased from the franchisor.
- The number of franchisees in operation.
- The number of franchises that have gone out of business in the preceding three years.[8]

These requirements are intended to assure the availability of relevant information needed by a prospective franchisee to make an informed decision regarding a franchise investment. The FTC Franchise Rule is not a guarantee that a new franchisee will make a profit, but the franchisor is subject to fines and injunctions for violations of the rule. The FTC Franchise Rule is violated when (1) required information is not disclosed by the franchisor to the franchisee or (2) the information disclosed is inaccurate. A number of states also have extensive franchise statutes that are stricter than those in place at the federal level, and franchisors are liable for offering franchises without supplying the information required by the state statutute or for supplying inaccurate information. Even so, there are still frequent "bad experiences" with franchise purchases, even though many other franchises are very successful.

Termination of the Franchise Agreement

There have been many incidents of hardworking franchisees who have built up a franchise only to have the franchisor find some reason to terminate the franchise and install a company employee to manage the business and capture benefits from the franchisee's efforts. Once a franchisee builds up a territory or franchised area of operations, it is often more profitable for the parent company to install an employee of the parent company to operate the previously franchised business.

As discussed above, states as well as the FTC have passed laws to protect the legitimate expectations of franchisees. Generally, a franchise agreement will contain provisions that specify conditions under which the franchise can be terminated. It is legitimate for the franchisor to expect that *quality control* will be maintained by the franchisee and, in some cases, there are objective measures of quality control. In general, protective legislation requires the franchisor to *notify* the franchisee before any anticipated termination. Some

---

[8] The Franchise Rule of the FTC can be accessed at http://www.ftc.gov/bcp/franchise/netrule.htm.

states also require that franchisors state the *reasons* for a termination and provide franchisees an *opportunity to correct* the problem(s). Finally, most franchise agreements have *arbitration clauses* to enable the parties to get faster resolution of disputes. Case 14-2 involves a franchisor/franchisee dispute.

Case 14-2

Cooper Distributing Co., Inc., a New Jersey Corporation v. Amana Refrigeration, Inc., a Delaware Corporation

United States Court of Appeals for the Third Circuit
63 F.3d 262 (3rd Cir. 1995)

CASE BACKGROUND AND FACTS

Defendant Amana Refrigeration, Inc. ("Amana"), a manufacturer of home appliances, appeals a judgment for $9,375,000 in favor of plaintiff Cooper Distributing Co., Inc. ("Cooper"), a distributor of Amana home appliances. After supplying Cooper with its products for approximately 30 years, Amana attempted to terminate its relationship with Cooper. Cooper sued, claiming that the termination and the circumstances surrounding it gave rise to a variety of state law claims.

Amana began to manufacture home appliances in the 1940's. [Citations omitted] Currently, Amana is a "full line" home appliance manufacturer: it offers for sale a full set of home appliances, including refrigerators, cooking and laundry appliances, dishwashers, and air conditioners. For many years, Amana employed a two-step process in the distribution of its products. It would sell its products to a network of independent wholesale distributors, who, pursuant to agreements with Amana, would sell to retail dealers located in the wholesale distributors' contractually recognized sales regions. The retail dealers would then sell the products to consumers.

Cooper began operating as an independent wholesale distributor in 1931. In 1961, Cooper started to distribute Amana products. Cooper and Amana signed an agreement permitting Cooper to distribute Amana's products in New Jersey and New York and have periodically signed new agreements over the years. Their most recent Distribution Agreement (the "Agreement"), which was signed in 1990, allowed Cooper to distribute Amana products in New Jersey, New York, Connecticut, and Pennsylvania.

During its relationship with Amana, Cooper operated a showroom/marketing center, first in Newark and subsequently in Englewood Cliffs, New Jersey. Cooper used this facility for Amana product demonstrations, dealer training in Amana products, and dealer open houses. Cooper's sales managers studied the Amana product line, and in turn gave Amana product training to retail dealers. Cooper also placed Amana advertisements in the yellow pages and newspapers, advertised as an authorized Amana servicer, instructed its servicemen to wear Amana uniforms, distributed promotional items bearing the Amana name, and, pursuant to the Agreement, promised to "use its best efforts to promote sales" of Amana products. Cooper's dealers perceived Amana and Cooper as being one and the same.

In the early 1980's, the marketing of appliances began to change, and by the late 1980's most full-line manufacturers had eliminated the first step in the two-step distribution process. Instead of selling to wholesale distributors, the manufacturers sold directly to retail dealers. Consistent with this trend, Amana started to depart from its previous practice of selling its products to the wholesale distributors. Instead, Amana began to sell directly to certain retail dealers located in the wholesale distributors' sales regions. Amana first sold its appliances directly to "national" retail dealers like Sears. The Agreement explicitly permitted Amana to make such sales to national retailers. Then, in the summer of 1991, Amana went further. Relying on a provision of the Agreement that reserved for

Amana the "right to make sales directly," Amana began to deal directly for the first time with a non-national retail dealer in Cooper's region, P.C. Richard & Son ("P.C. Richard"). P.C. Richard had a chain of 20 retail stores and represented Cooper's largest account. Amana also sold its products directly to other smaller local retail dealers. Until Amana began selling to the national and local retailers, Cooper had been the exclusive distributor in its region for nearly 30 years.

At the same time that the home appliance industry saw the elimination of two-step distribution, Amana's marketing responsibilities changed. Amana's parent company, Raytheon, which also sold other appliance brands such as Speed Queen and Caloric, decided to consolidate the distribution of its brands. The result was that several of the distributors that sold one but not all of Raytheon's brands were eliminated. In November 1991, Amana terminated its relationship with Cooper pursuant to a provision of the Agreement that allowed either party to terminate the Agreement on ten days written notice. At the same time, Amana also terminated its relationships with 20 of the other 23 remaining Amana wholesale distributors across the country.

In response to its termination, Cooper commenced this action in New Jersey state court alleging, among other things, that Amana had (1) violated section 5 of the NJFPA, N.J.S.A. § 56:10-5, by terminating Cooper's franchise without good cause; (2) breached the 1990 Agreement by selling to the local retailers in Cooper's region; (3) breached the Agreement's implied obligation of good faith and fair dealing; and (4) tortiously interfered with Cooper's prospective economic advantage. In November 1991, the state court issued a temporary restraining order prohibiting termination of or interference with Cooper's Amana distributorship. After the case was removed by Amana to federal court, [footnotes deleted] a preliminary injunction was entered on February 10, 1992, enjoining Amana "from taking any action whatsoever to limit . . . or in any way interfere with Cooper's activities as a distributor of Amana products."

Opinion by Alito, Circuit Judge

II. NEW JERSEY FRANCHISE PRACTICES ACT

Prompted in large part by the practices of automobile manufacturers and major oil companies, New Jersey enacted the NJFPA in 1971. [References deleted] The Act protects franchisees against indiscriminate termination by providing that "it shall be a violation of this act for a franchisor to terminate, cancel, or fail to renew a franchise without good cause." N.J.S.A. § 56:10-5. A franchise exists under the NJFPA if: (1) there is a "community of interest" between the franchisor and the franchisee; (2) the franchisor granted a "license" to the franchisee; and (3) the parties contemplated that the franchisee would maintain a "place of business" in New Jersey. N.J.S.A. §§ 56:10-3a, -4. Contending that it was not properly held liable under the NJFPA, Amana argues, first, that as a matter of law Cooper was not a "franchisee" under the Act and second, that the district court gave the jury prejudicially erroneous instructions on the NJFPA claim. We will discuss each of these arguments in turn.

* * *

Amana does not argue that the termination of its business relationship with Cooper was for "good cause," a concept that is "limited to failure by the franchisee to substantially comply with those requirements imposed upon him by the franchise."

* * *

> The Act's concern is that once a business has made substantial franchise-specific investments [which are of minimal utility outside the franchise,] it loses virtually all of its bargaining power. . . . Specifically, the franchisee cannot do anything that would risk termination, because that would result in a loss of much or all of the value of its franchise-specific investments. Thus, the franchisee has no choice but to accede to the demands of the franchisor, no matter how unreasonable these demands may be.

Thus, in order to find a "community of interest," two requirements must be met: (1) the distributor's investments must have been "substantially franchise-specific," and (2) the distributor must have been required to make these investments by the parties' agreement or the nature of the business. In this appeal, Amana has not addressed the second of these requirements, but Amana has strenuously argued that Cooper failed to meet the first of these requirements, i.e., that it failed to show that its investments were substantially franchise-specific.

* * *

Second, and perhaps most important, a reasonable jury could find that one of Cooper's most important assets was franchise-specific goodwill. It is clear that goodwill can constitute a franchise-specific asset. To qualify, however, the goodwill in question must be useful for the alleged franchisee only in the context of its relationship with the alleged franchisor. Moreover, if a distributor sells the products of many manufacturers and creates some goodwill for all or many of these manufacturers, that kind of goodwill "cannot be enough to create a 'community of interest.'"

* * *

Finally, we consider Cooper's investments in tangible assets. The NJFPA protects franchise-specific "tangible capital investments, such as 'a building designed to meet the style of the franchise, special equipment useful only to produce the franchise product, and franchise signs.'" In this case, Cooper introduced evidence showing that it had invested in some tangible items that were of no value outside the Amana-franchise context—for example, the display housing for Cooper's showroom bearing the Amana logo and Amana demonstration models.

We do not mean to imply that all of Cooper's investments were Amana-specific. On the contrary, the record shows that Cooper possessed assets that would clearly be useful outside the Amana context. See, e.g., App. 1041 (electronic mail system), App. 1032-22 (computer system), App. 1036-37 (repair tools). However, the jury was not required to find that Cooper's investments were *entirely* franchise-specific but merely that they were "*substantial[ly]* franchise-specific." ISI, 614 A.2d at 141 [emphasis added]. Looking at all of the evidence of Cooper's investments in the light most favorable to Cooper, we hold that a jury reasonably could conclude that Cooper's assets were substantially franchise-specific.

* * *

Decision and Outcome

The court went on to affirm the trial court verdict that the defendant, Amana, had violated the NJFPA, which requires a showing of good cause before a franchisee is dismissed.

Questions for Analysis

1. Was the defendant arguing that the franchisee (Cooper) deserved to be terminated or simply that Cooper was not a franchisee? What makes a company a franchisee of another company in New Jersey?

2. What is the goal of the New Jersey Franchise Practices Act? What role does franchise-specific investment play in achievement of the goal of the NJFPA?

3. Termination of long-time franchises is fraught with a sense of betrayal by the franchisee, then, later, a call to an attorney, leading to litigation. In the case above, the cost to the franchisor is millions in court-awarded damages plus attorney fees and diverted executive time. As a future manager, possibly of a franchisor, can you think of any measures that you could take to ameliorate franchisee anger and retaliation while still terminating a franchise?

CYBER COMPANIES AND INTERNET AGREEMENTS

Prior to taking this course, and certainly by now in the course, you are aware of the explosive growth that e-commerce and e-businesses have experienced. Even so, a few facts about that expansion may be useful. Before 1990 there was no e-commerce to speak of. By 1996 there were still fewer than 500 websites devoted to e-commerce and total e-commerce revenue for the year is estimated to have been about $2.6 billion. Today, literally trillions of dollars move electronically in Internet transactions.

Exponential growth in e-commerce is expected to continue for some time, but the recent economic slowdown, which began in the last quarter of 2000, considerably dampened enthusiasm for dot-coms and high-tech companies in general. During this period, an inevitable stock market adjustment in valuation of high-tech firms has been occurring, correcting what Alan Greenspan, chairman of the Federal Reserve System, called the "irrational exuberance" afflicting the stock market. Nasdaq, which is heavily weighted toward high-tech firms, dropped more than 50 percent in value, comparing March values in 2000 and 2001, and continued its decline in 2002. By the second quarter of 2001, investors had apparently decided that, while they might still be interested in high-tech companies, their interest would be focused on these companies only if they show promise of yielding profits in the near future.

Bricks and Clicks

bricks-and-mortar (B&M) companies
Traditional companies, the fixed assets of which are predominantly in the form of buildings and fixed equipment.

In the not too distant past, say 1999, companies were often divided between **bricks-and-mortar (B&M)** companies and the dot-coms that had very few physical assets but were known for their presence on the Internet. Perhaps the most widely publicized dot-com is Amazon.com, though there are other famous (or infamous) dot-coms such as Napster, eBay, and Yahoo!, just to name a few. The distinction, however, between the B&Ms and the dot-coms is fast becoming irrelevant. Increasingly, major companies are establishing substantial Web presences that allow customers to shop online. Amazon's archrival, Barnes and Noble, now maintains a website that compares favorably with Amazon.com in terms of completeness and variety. Although Amazon.com originally had almost no physical assets, it recently has been investing in warehouses to facilitate distribution. Each major bookseller has moved toward the other's market position as both seek to find the optimal combination of bricks and clicks.

Legal Liabilities Associated with Establishing a Website

The "bricks" associated with constructing a website are all composed of software. As such, all e-businesses rely extensively on software and, most probably, specialized software developers and website designers. By their nature, e-businesses have to deal extensively with IP legal issues, especially with copyright and trademark law. In addition, all e-businesses have to be familiar with changes in contract law brought about by e-commerce and extensive software development contracts. Of course, e-businesses are also affected by cybertorts and product liability.

All of these issues have been discussed in previous chapters of this book. The focus in this chapter is upon the confluence of contracts and arrangements that an e-business must make with other e-businesses (Web hosting companies) if it is to maximize its revenue and profit opportunities. By necessity, we will be returning to a number of the legal issues that are discussed in other chapters, though such return engagements will not be in depth.

Adequacy of Website Development

Websites should be competent to perform the services they advertise and should be able to meet the orders for the goods that they offer for sale. A website will be expected to have adequate product availability and service capability to meet anticipated consumer demand. If a website is selling high-tech products on which customers are likely to require assistance, there should be adequate service technician staffing available, both by telephone and online, to provide a reasonable level of customer service. Failure to provide such infrastructure could be a breach of contract on the sale of products, which would allow customers to demand refunds. Alternatively, advertising tech support when selling a product, while knowing that tech support availability to customers is virtually nonexistent, can be grounds for fraud claims.

If Susan buys a Palm Pilot from a website, she ought to have some reasonable means of communicating with the website if the Palm Pilot does not work properly or some of the components were not shipped. If the phone number associated with the website is always busy and e-mails are not answered within a reasonable time, Susan does not have a reasonable means of communicating with the website or of getting a reasonable level of service. At a minimum, the website is breaching its contract with Susan. At some point, when the gap between the level of service advertised and that actually provided by the website becomes too great to ignore, a legal issue of fraud arises.

Unfair and Deceptive Advertising: Federal Trade Commission Definition

The FTC has authority to prohibit both *unfair* and/or *deceptive* advertising and this authority extends to websites advertising on the Internet. The FTC has a division dedicated to consumer protection (http://www.ftc.gov/bcp/menu-internet.htm) and provides numerous articles that assist consumers in avoiding becoming online victims of unfair and deceptive advertising.

Reasonable Substantiation

Website advertisers that make unsubstantiated claims are subject to FTC enforcement actions, which are likely to be costly to the advertiser and a public relations disaster. In a successful suit, the FTC will obtain a cease and desist order from the courts, requiring a halt to the deceptive advertising. To cure earlier misrepresentations, the FTC may seek a court order requiring corrective advertisements.

reasonable substantiation
Documentation, using acceptable methodology, of claims made in advertising or other forms of product promotion.

To avoid FTC enforcement actions, a website should have **reasonable substantiation** for the claims it makes in its advertisements. If a website product advertisement claims that "doctors recommend its products relative to other products," there must be a survey that conforms to customary practices for survey takers that confirms these claims. If there is a claim that a celebrity endorses a product sold by a website, the website must verify that the celebrity actually uses the product. It is also important to note that other regulatory bodies can intervene in website advertising. Websites that advertise about the availability or benefits of pharmaceutical products are subject to scrutiny of the Food and Drug Administration (FDA). For other products, additional regulatory agencies may need to be consulted.

Warranties, Refunds, Shipping, Handling, and Credit

There are numerous state and federal laws that apply to warranties, refunds, shipping, and handling charges. Many of the UCC constraints on warranties and disclaimers were discussed in Chapters 7 through 9. There are other laws that regulate acceptable practices on refunds for returned merchandise, packaging, and shipment of ordered goods (discussed in Chapter 18).

Ignorance of applicable laws and regulations can result in costly consequences for a website operator. Examples of costly problems are easy to envision. If a website accepts installment payments, it could inadvertently trigger Truth in Lending Act (TILA) requirements, which necessitate a lengthy list of specific disclosures that are not normally provided by websites. According to the TILA, any payment plan that involves any charge for interest or that requires more than four installments requires TILA disclosures, including a boldface listing of the annual percentage rate of interest, even if the interest charge is zero.

FTC Action to Ensure Fulfillment

Timely merchandise shipments also can create a legal problem for e-businesses. The FTC's Mail or Telephone Order Merchandise Trade Regulation Rule requires on-time shipment of merchandise when a notice is listed conspicuously, or if there is no time listed, then within 30 days of the date when a buyer places his or her order. If an order cannot be fulfilled within 30 days, the seller must obtain customer consent for the delay or offer an immediate refund.

During the summer of 2000, the FTC announced that it had settled several cases involving some of the most prominent e-commerce retail websites, including Toysrus.com, CDNow, and Macys.com, for failing to deliver goods promised during the Christmas shopping rush of 1999. These websites and others had to pay fines ranging between $20,000 and $350,000 for their failures in fulfilling Christmas orders in a timely manner or in complying with backup provisions in the FTC shipping regulation.

Click-Wrap Agreements

Websites should have *terms of use* agreements with their customers that are available in click-wrap form. A term-of-use click-wrap agreement should discuss issues such as

- Copyright content of any software products that may be downloaded and any linking policy that the website has with other websites.
- Privacy policy, which would normally discuss what uses are made of information acquired by the website.
- Dispute resolution procedures in connection with purchases or licenses of information.
- Warranty disclaimers on any of the risks that the website does *not* want to bear.

(Extensive discussion of the enforceability of click-wrap agreements was provided in Chapters 8 and 9.)

Jurisdiction

As discussed in Chapter 2, the question of state jurisdiction over an out-of-state website is not clearly defined. When a political entity has *jurisdiction* over a person or company, it means that court decisions within that political entity can affect the subject person or company. Jurisdiction over out-of-state websites depends on whether the website has "minimum contacts" with in-state residents. In general, states do not have jurisdiction over an out-of-state website if the only activity the website engages in is fulfilling orders from in-state customers. Some courts have held, however, that if there is e-mail interaction between customers and the website, that activity satisfies the minimum contacts test. It follows that a website that provides tech support for the products that it sells would also subject itself to the jurisdiction of any states where residents of that state make use of the tech support.

The other factor to keep in mind is that click-wrap agreements, which are part of e-commerce transactions, almost always have arbitration clauses as well as forum clauses. In most online purchases, customers making the purchase have waived their rights to sue in their home states when they click to buy. In general,

- It is good business for any website to have click-wrap agreements that contain arbitration clauses.
- As long as the website is properly advised by an attorney, such click-wrap arbitration agreements, which waive rights of customers to sue in court, should be enforceable as they will have been prepared to avoid being too one-sided.

Many of the issues introduced above play roles in Case 14-3.

Case 14-3

Lynda Butler v. Beer Across America

United States District Court for the Northern District of Alabama
83 F. Supp. 2d 1261 (N.D. Ala. 2000)

CASE BACKGROUND AND FACTS

The plaintiff in this case is the mother of a minor who the plaintiff alleges purchased an alcoholic beverage from the defendant, Beer Across America, which operates from a website that accepted the credit card of the minor. The plaintiff filed the suit in the Circuit Court of Shelby County, in the State of Alabama. Defendant, an out-of-state corporation, removed the case to Federal District Court based on diversity of citizenship and then moves to have the case dismissed based on lack of personal jurisdiction.

Opinion by Hancock, Senior District Judge

The Court has before it the August 6, 1999 motion of defendants Beer Across America, Merchant Direct, and Shermer Specialties (collectively "Beer Across America") to dismiss the present action for lack of personal jurisdiction. [Footnotes deleted] Pursuant to the Court's October 8, 1999 order, the motion came under submission on December 17, 1999.

* * *

The burden of establishing personal jurisdiction over a nonresident defendant is on the plaintiff. [Citations omitted] To survive a defendant's motion to dismiss for lack of personal jurisdiction, the plaintiff must demonstrate a prima facie case of personal jurisdiction, which requires the presentation of evidence sufficient to withstand a motion for a directed verdict. In considering whether such a showing has been made, the court must accept as true all uncontroverted facts alleged in the complaint and must also draw all reasonable inferences arising from controverted assertions of fact in the light most favorable to the plaintiff.

* * *

Here, the facts are simple. In early April of 1999, plaintiff's minor son, who apparently was left home unsupervised (but with a credit card issued in his name) while his parents vacationed, placed an order for twelve bottles of beer with defendants through Beer Across America's Internet site on the World Wide Web. Under the applicable provisions of the U.C.C., the sale occurred in Illinois. The beer was then shipped to plaintiff's son in Alabama and delivered to the Butler residence by the carrier acting, the entire time, as the agent of the plaintiff's son. The sale was not discovered by plaintiff until she returned home and found several bottles of beer from the shipment remaining in the family's refrigerator. Together, these facts present the following question: whether personal jurisdiction properly may be asserted by a federal court sitting in diversity in Alabama over a nonresident Illinois defendant in an action arising from a sale made in Illinois solely in response to an order placed by an Alabama resident via the Internet?

* * *

As one arm of the due process analysis, the court initially must determine whether at least minimum contacts exist between the defendant and the jurisdiction. The significant question is whether "the defendant's conduct and connection with the forum State are such that he should reasonably anticipate being haled into court there"? . . . General jurisdiction may be exercised when a defendant's contacts with the forum are sufficiently numerous, purposeful, and continuous, as to render fair an assertion of power over the defendant by that state's courts no matter the nature or extent of the relationship to the forum entailed in the particular litigation; if general jurisdiction is established, absolutely no connection need be shown between the state and the claim for the defendant to be summoned constitutionally before that forum's courts . . . Regardless of the specific or general nature of the contacts in question, for purposes of satisfying due process, they must be purposeful on the part of the defendant;

"it is essential in each case that there be some act by which the defendant purposefully avails itself of the privilege of conducting activities within the forum State, thus invoking the benefits and protection of its laws."

* * *

Regarding the minimum contacts element of due process analysis, plaintiff asserts that defendants' contacts with the state of Alabama are sufficient for either general or specific jurisdiction. To support general jurisdiction, the plaintiff cites not only the sale to her son but also the defendants' sales (in Illinois) to other Alabama residents as well as the sale of beer to defendants by two Alabama brewers through a non-party Illinois wholesaler. However, the plaintiff has not offered any competent evidence to seriously controvert the defendants' averments that they are not registered to do business in Alabama; that they own no property in the state; that they maintain no offices in the state; that they have no agents in Alabama; that their key personnel have never even visited the state; and that they do not place advertisements with Alabama media outlets (except for what nationally placed advertisements may reach the state) or engage in any other significant promotions targeting the state, which would rise to such a level as would justify an exercise of general jurisdiction by this state's courts. What plaintiff has offered is simply not sufficient to conclude that Beer Across America can be brought before an Alabama tribunal for any claim that any plaintiff may bring.

Decision and Outcome

The court granted the defendant's motion to dismiss based on lack of jurisdiction. The court ruled that the degree of contacts between the forum state, Alabama, of the plaintiffs and the defendants, located in Illinois, was not sufficient to impose jurisdiction on the defendants.

Questions for Analysis

1. Does this case strongly support the proposition that the mere fact that a website can be accessed in a state does not mean that the website is subject to the jurisdiction of that state?

2. If pornography was offered at a website (say, in Illinois), and it was reachable by citizens of a second state that had strict antipornography laws, would the site be subject to criminal prosecution in that second state? Interstate shipment of pornography using the U.S. mail is clearly illegal. What is the critical difference from the beer sale case?

3. Suppose that the defendants in this case made one trip across the South and into Alabama promoting their products. According to the court in this case, would the "minimum contacts" test be satisfied? Should one promotional trip make that much difference? If one trip does make a difference, then it is clear, is it not, that management should carefully consider whether to promote their products by traveling to states where sales are made?

IP Protection

Who Owns the Copyright to "Your" Website?

We have previously discussed many of the IP issues that confront e-businesses. If an e-business has a website designed by an independent contractor, the copyright to the design is owned by the website designer unless there are provisions to the contrary in the contract between the website and the independent contractor. So a contract for website development should include specification of who gets the copyrights to the computer code, artwork, music, and text. Failure to gain agreement on these issues will hamper the website if it decides to use another website developer for upgrades. In addition, for material that cannot be protected by either patent or copyright law, there should be NDAs required of the website developer to protect valuable trade secrets belonging to the website owner.

How Can You Use IP Law to Protect Yourself from Imitators?

Components of websites such as text and artwork can be protected from imitation by other websites, but the overall "look and feel" of a website will be difficult to protect under current copyright law. Trademark law could be used to protect the overall "look and feel" of a website because trademark infringement is based on consumer confusion, which is inherently a "look and feel" test. Trademark law, however, will not protect the functionality of a website. Websites that have a distinctive appearance also may be able to sue imitators for a *trade dress* infringement, again based on the issue of consumer confusion.

Keep in mind, however, that if the appearance of a website frequently changes, it will be difficult to claim its appearance is "distinctive." Increasingly, websites are using patent law to protect methods of operation (recall the group of patents that Amazon.com has to protect its method of allowing customers to purchase books online). In general, there is little legal protection of the IP used to build a website unless another website *copies* components of artwork or text.

Databases or "facts" that are made available on a website are not protectible, though arrangements of data or facts are protectible under copyright law. Quite obviously, websites should avoid replicating copyrighted material that is owned by third parties, unless they have permission of the third parties. Also, given the number of software patents that have been issued, websites that offer searching or other services should be aware that these methods of operation may infringe the patents of another firm. Finally, suppose that a website makes it clear that it does not like the way you do business. Can Microsoft sue a website entitled "Microsoftsucks"? The answer is no and that is the unpleasant response that a number of other prominent companies have discovered when they have encountered "suck" sites. The high regard the courts have for freedom of expression protects "suck" sites from suits even though these sites are using part of a "famous" site's trademark.

Possible Infringement Suits against Your Website and Protection of Your IP Rights

Websites should not use the name or likeness of anyone, especially celebrities, without formal permission. Posting a name or likeness of a person without permission is a common law invasion of privacy. A number of states recognize a "right of publicity," which means that the name or likeness of a person can be protected even after death. If you use your own trademark on your website, you have an obligation to provide notice if the trademark is registered at the state or federal level. If you use the trademarks of another firm, you should be careful to ensure that no false association, affiliation, or sponsorship is implied by the use of another's mark and, furthermore, you should avoid using language that could *dilute* the value of a famous mark.

Linking to Sites of Third Parties

It is prudent to obtain permission before linking with the website of another business or nonprofit organization. Linking to other websites without permission could imply an affiliation or sponsorship that does not exist and, thus, could be an unfair trade practice under the laws of various states. Porn sites that provide links to "respectable" sites have been sued for unfair trade practices after the porn site was told that its links to, say, beauty contests were not welcome. Similarly, a small firm selling herbal remedies that links its visitors to a Web page of a major pharmaceutical company, such as Smith-Kline, could be sued for an unfair trade practice. Also, if the small firm does some framing, linking to websites minus the website advertising, it could be both a copyright and a trademark infringement. Websites should avoid "deep" links that allow visitors to skip the home page of another website and link with a page of interest deep within the website. This, too, might be an unfair trade practice or a copyright or trademark infringement.

Privacy Policies

Privacy Policies Are Standard

Websites offer a number of advantages relative to B&M establishments. When a person comes into your store, you can observe how the customer is dressed, his or her age, and other characteristics, but you have no idea where the customer came from or where he or she is going. Matters are different with a website as, with cookies and other means of extracting information from website visitors, significant information can be obtained from visitors if desired. At the same time, it's clear that websites are under increasing pressure not to violate privacy rights of visitors to their websites. Quite certainly, it is prudent for a website to post a privacy policy regardless of whether it is collecting information from visitors or members (remember that 97 percent of websites do collect personal information). In addition, it is important to spell out whether this information will be supplied to third parties. Finally, it is imperative for a website to follow its own privacy policy.

If Children Are Involved, Special Care Is Required

If a website is directed toward children under 13, it must comply with the Children's Online Privacy Protection Act, which requires parental permission before collecting information. There are proposals to require mandatory privacy policies at all websites and, therefore, it is prudent for websites to sign up with TRUSTe or BBBOnLine, which require "best practices" in collection and management of personal information from online visitors. Best practices in data collection include the Fair Information Principles of the FTC. Websites that do not adopt a third-party certification (such as TRUSTe) of their adherence to industry standards with respect to the collection and management of personal information may be targets for the FTC.

Web Hosting Agreements

Creation of a cyber business with a suitable website host has some similarities with the creation of a corporation under state incorporation statutes. A company that complies with state incorporation statutes enjoys important legal advantages, most notable among them the limited liability of shareholders. In return, state law controls the internal governance of corporations including resolutions of disputes between shareholders and the board of directors. In a sense, the state's incorporating authority sets the terms and conditions for operation of a corporation.

To exist as a cyber business, a website owner generally must enter into a detailed agreement with a website host regarding terms of service. In this arrangement, the Web host largely dictates the terms and conditions under which the cyber company conducts its business. Some of the terms of service that must be addressed are "technical." These include agreements on

1. Additional disk space, Internet traffic, and e-mail accounts.
2. Email POP accounts.
3. FTP access and anonymous FTP.
4. CGI scripting, telnet access.
5. Domain name registration, design services.
6. Secured credit card transactions.

Although a lot of what appears immediately above may seem tediously technical, anyone with an involvement with a cyber company should pay detailed attention to these points. Fortunately, the Web hosting market provides "turnkey" operations that enable an aspiring cyber company to deal with one company for most of its website preferences. One such company is Webhosters.com (www.webhosters.com). According to Webhosters.com, it is

> [t]he definitive guide to web hosting! Our mission is to provide the most objective, accurate and non-biased information pertaining to web hosting. Use the navigation panel on the left [the text is taken from WebHosters website] to browse the content and the many tools provided. Every day, thousands of web developers use WebHosters.com to find their host . . . Now it's your turn!

Companies that wish to establish a website and are unfamiliar with these terms would do well to contact a business lawyer who has e-commerce experience. For a Web-based business, the appearance of its cyber storefront is more important than the storefronts of most B&M operations. It is vitally important for a website to have an agreement with its Web host that enables the website to accommodate increased traffic if the website becomes much more popular.

Other Web Hosting Issues

Many Web hosting issues are likely to change substantially as Internet technology continues to evolve. At present, the most pressing issues addressed in Web hosting agreements are

1. *Reliability.* Servers sometimes crash, but if crashes occur too often, they severely interfere with activities conducted on the website. Definitions of reliability should be established in the Web hosting agreement.
2. *Domain name integrity.* If a host obtains a domain name, responsibility for enforcing trademark infringements should be addressed. A Web host that obtains a domain name for a website, but then fails to prosecute trademark or domain name infringements, leaves the website with no legal protection for the domain name.
3. *Site updates.* A host's responsibilities for updating a website should be described with specificity in terms of frequency and content.
4. *Legality requirements.* In Web hosting agreements, it is common for hosts to require that any website hosted be used only for lawful purposes. Web hosts generally indicate further that
   a. The host will cooperate with law enforcement.
   b. The host can suspend operation of a website without liability if the host believes that the website is being used for illegal purposes or is creating liability exposure for the host (e.g., because of the publication of defamatory material).
   c. The host will prohibit spamming and impersonations at the website.
5. *IP protection.* A host's contract will indicate that the host can terminate a website if the site is being used to decompile, disassemble, or reverse engineer Web hosting software in order to appropriate trade secrets from the host or create derivative works.

Games and Contests

Faced with intense competition for the attention of Internet travelers, many websites offer games, contests, and sweepstakes to their site users. These activities should be offered with considerable caution because of the inconsistency of state laws dealing with gaming, gambling, and so forth. Compliance with the laws of one state (your home state, perhaps) does not ensure compliance with the applicable laws in other states. Many states require disclosures of the odds of winning a contest and some states require registration statements. Some of the required state disclosure and registration requirements are so onerous that it is not worth the effort of meeting the requirements for the volume of Web traffic to be gained. Websites that do not comply with the most restrictive state laws regarding sweepstakes should exclude participants from those states.

Out-of-Date Offers

Having succeeded in making electronic contracts binding, website owners should be aware of the binding obligations they face for honoring outdated offers that remain present at their websites. Such offers might be for out-of-stock merchandise or for items listed at prices that are no longer accurate. Unlike advertisements, offers made on a website are binding since acceptances of those offers by website visitors are binding also. Website owners should carefully scrutinize and update offers made at their website on a regular basis.

Reasonable Attribution Procedures

As discussed in Chapter 9, if website owners use reasonable attribution procedures, they can accept credit card orders and charge the party identified on the credit card. If use of the card is not authorized by the cardholder, that dispute must be resolved between the credit card issuer and the cardholder. On the other hand, if the website does not use a reasonable attribution procedure, then acceptance of an order using a credit card makes it much more difficult for the website to bind the cardholder if the cardholder repudiates the transaction.

Encryption and Scrambling

Given the current state of security, reasonable attribution procedures involve use of encryption to guard against interception of transmitted information. If encryption is not used, then there must be some cross-referencing of information to verify that the cardholder is indeed placing the order. Additionally, in order to cross-reference information on customers, companies must securely store the requisite information to guard against hackers' access to that information. Lack of success in this task will generate liability based on negligence in secure storage.

Summary

Sole Proprietorships Are the Easiest Type of Company to Manage, but Are Generally Small Because Investors Are Leery of Investing in One Person

- There are three main forms of business organization: *sole proprietorships, partnerships,* and *corporations.*
- Sole proprietorships are owned by one person, who faces unlimited liability for obligations incurred by the company.
- Sole proprietorships are not separate entities from their owner in terms of taxes, liability, and management.
- Sole proprietorships are often at a disadvantage in raising capital because outsiders are generally unwilling to risk money on the life of an individual.
- Similarly, it is often difficult to sell a sole proprietorship and diversification is difficult because of the size of the company.

Partnerships Are Regulated by the Uniform Partnership Act, Adopted in 49 States, which Obligates Partners to Fiduciary Duties to Other Partners and to the Partnership

- Partnerships are formed when two or more partners join together and operate a business for profit.
- Partnership law in the United States largely conforms to the Uniform Partnership Act, which has been adopted in 49 states, while 31 states have adopted the Revised Uniform Partnership Act.
- The UPA and RUPA operate when nothing is said in the partnership agreement regarding a point of law. Partners have great freedom to manage their partnership and divide up profits in any way they agree.
- There are two, very different, types of partnerships: *general* and *limited.* In a general partnership, all partners are unlimitedly liable, while in a limited partnership only the general partners are liable for partnership debts.
- In comparison to sole proprietorships, partnerships have a number of advantages including in the raising of capital. Partnerships are more complicated to manage and disputes among partners are often sources of litigation.
- Profits of both partnerships and sole proprietorships are taxed as ordinary income to the partners or owners.
- Partners owe *fiduciary duties* to each other, requiring that they put the interests of the partners and partnership above their own.

Corporations Are Legal Persons, Owned by Shareholders, Overseen by a Board of Directors That Hires Chief Corporate Officers to Manage the Affairs of the Business; a Distinctive Feature of Corporations Is Limited Liability for Owners	• Corporations are considered *persons in law*. They can contract, can sue and be sued, must pay taxes, and have potentially infinite duration. Corporations are managed by a board of directors that appoint chief corporate officers. • Shareholders of a corporation are its owner and benefit from limited liability. Ownership of a corporation is transferable through the sale of corporate shares. • Corporations are taxed on their income and, if dividends are declared, shareholders are taxed on the dividend distributions. • Both directors and officers are *agents* of a corporation and, as such, owe fiduciary duties to the corporation.
Limited Partners in Limited Partnerships Enjoy Limited Liability; the S Corporate Form Is Often Adopted by Smaller Corporations to Avoid Double Taxation; LLCs and LLPs Are Hybrid Organizations That Offer Desirable Features of Both Partnerships and Corporations	• *Limited partnerships* must be registered with the state in order to qualify for limited liability for the limited partners. • Limited partners must refrain from management activity to qualify for limited liability. The line between what limited partners can do and cannot do to qualify for limited liability is articulated in the Revised Limited Partnership Act. • Limited partners qualify for the attractive tax features of limited partnerships. In addition, transfers of ownership shares are much easier than for general partnerships. • *Closely held corporations* share a lot of characteristics with partnerships. The largest shareholders are generally also on the board of directors and are chief corporate officers of such companies. • Closely held corporations are governed by corporate bylaws and shareholder agreements that resemble those of partnerships. Limits are placed on the transferability of stock ownership, protections for minority interests are included, and generally there are provisions for resolving disputes. • *S corporations* are generally smaller than C corporations. S corporations are taxed as if they are partnerships, but there are restrictions on size that make C corporations the only alternative for corporations with more than 75 shareholders. • *Limited liability companies* and *limited liability partnerships* straddle the lines on advantages of the limited liability of corporations and the tax advantages of partnerships. • LLCs and LLPs are often selected by professionals to protect themselves from acts of negligence of other professionals while still complying with ethical requirements imposed by state licensing boards.
Other Forms of Business Organization Include Joint Ventures and Franchises, Which Are Subject to FTC and State Regulation	• *Joint ventures* are like partnerships of two companies or individuals, organized to accomplish a task, but do not generally have an indefinite life. Joint venture partners are jointly, severally, and unlimitedly liable for obligations of the joint venture. • *Franchises* are very popular, particularly in the retailing of branded products in the United States. Franchises are able to use trademarks of the parent company in return for agreeing to conduct business within the guidelines of a franchise agreement. • The Federal Trade Commission requires that franchisors disclose to franchisees various risks and details of provisions in their franchise agreements. • Often, when a franchise is terminated, there is the potential for litigation.

Establishing a Website Creates Significant Legal Liability Exposure for Owners; Adroit Use of Privacy Statements, Conditions of Use, and Other Legal Records Can Limit Legal Exposure (Both Tax and Product Liability) for Website Owners	• Establishing a website entails exposure to a sizeable array of potential legal liabilities. Businesses should be able to fulfill the commitments made on their websites. The potential legal liability that is associated with a website often can be limited by click-wrap agreements in which customers and members agree to waive their rights to sue and/or submit to other restrictions. • An important legal issue is the exposure of a website to the jurisdictions of other states. The basic test for establishing jurisdiction is the "minimum contacts" test, which looks at whether the website has purposely availed itself of the privileges of operating in the forum state. • There are two important legal issues associated with jurisdiction: taxation and liability for fraud and malfunctioning products. If a state establishes jurisdiction, then the website must travel to that forum state to defend itself in any suit or else lose the pending suit by default. • The more active a website is, the more likely it is that a court will rule that the website is subject to the jurisdiction of another state. • Websites, however, can negate jurisdictional disadvantages by including *arbitration* and *choice of forum* clauses in their terms of service agreements.
Among the Significant Legal Constraints Websites Face Are Those Imposed by Copyright Law and the FTC's Prohibitions on Unfair and Deceptive Trade Practices	• Websites are subject to FTC constraints on *unfair and deceptive* advertising. The FTC has intervened in a number of website cases to require websites to cease and decrease deceptive practices. • There are important copyright issues associated with websites, including ones involving website design and linking to other websites (most often when the linking distorts destination website function). Trademark law can be enlisted to provide protection against trademark imitation. If a trademark is used, it is important to designate it as such. • Linking your website to another site can be an unfair trade practice depending on the facts of the situation. • In general, it is prudent to have a *privacy policy* and to adhere to what is said in the privacy policy.
Websites Sign Web Hosting Contracts That Constrain What Websites Can Do and How Rapidly They Can Grow; Websites Are Subject to Most of the Consumer Protection Laws That Apply to Other (Non-Web) Businesses.	• Web hosting agreements are akin to state charters granted to corporations. The Web host creates the terms of trade for the websites that locate on its server. • Web hosting agreements should discuss reliability, control, and responsibility for domain names. • Website owners should be cognizant of a number of laws that were enacted to protect consumers. Website owners should know when the Truth in Lending Act applies, how the Telephone Order Merchandise Trade Regulation Rule applies to their activities, and when contests are considered sweepstakes.

Key Terms

board of directors, *447*	double taxation, *446*	partnership, *438*
bricks-and-mortar (B&M) companies, *460*	franchise agreement, *455*	reasonable substantiation, *461*
corporation, *444*	joint venture, *453*	sole proprietorship, *436*
	limited partners, *439*	

Questions for Review and Analysis

1. A point that is critical to understanding business organization law is recognition that no one form of business organization is clearly the best. What is best depends on the business, the stage of business, and many other factors. Name five factors that may affect your choice of business organization.

2. One of the factors that should have appeared on your list in Question 1 is tax exposure. Discuss why examination of the tax issue often leads small to medium-sized businesses to select partnership as their form of business organization.

3. Discuss how franchises resemble partnerships and the dissimilarities. Do parent companies owe fiduciary duties to franchisees? Is there a difference between a duty to operate in "good faith" and a fiduciary duty?

4. Is there a way of operating a website and conducting e-commerce without becoming subject to the jurisdictions of states whose residents purchase your products? Aren't e-mails and other contacts inevitable when business is being conducted? What can a website do to negate assertions of jurisdiction by state courts that are located where customers of the website reside? *Hint:* Suppose the customer "agrees" to be bound by the laws of the state designated by the website?

5. The Federal Trade Commission has power to issue cease and desist orders to businesses, including websites, if they engage in unfair or deceptive trade practices. List five ways in which a website can expose itself to claims of unfair or deceptive trade practices.

If You Really Understood This Chapter, You Should Be Able to Provide Informed Commentary on the Following:

1. **Franchise Termination and Good Faith.** An issue that crops up frequently in franchise terminations is good faith. Almost invariably, it is the franchisee that claims the franchisor is violating its obligation to exercise good faith in its treatment of the franchisee. Consider the following facts: Gerardo and LuAnn Perez were franchisees of the McDonald's Corporation beginning in 1988, but by 1995 were disillusioned with their experience with McDonald's. The Perezes wanted to sell their franchise and proposed four prospective purchasers to McDonald's for its approval, each of which McDonald's turned down. In the Franchise Offering Circular that the Perezes agreed to when they became franchisees, McDonald's reserved the right to refuse to consent to the sale if the applicants had not completed an applicant training program administered by McDonald's. Plaintiffs seek a declaration judgment that "a qualified, ready, willing, and able buyer, based on reasonable standards, must be allowed to enter the McDonald's applicant training program for the purpose of further evaluations and a final determination as to whether he or she will be admitted into the [McDonald's] System." There is no term in the Franchise Offering Circular that requires McDonald's to admit anyone to the applicant training program, but plaintiff contends that the covenant of good faith requires that contract discretion be exercised reasonably and not arbitrarily or capriciously. What do you think? [*Gerardo and LuAnn Perez v. McDonald's Corporation,* 60 F. Supp. 2d 1030 (1998).]

2. **Fiduciary Obligations of Directors of a Corporation.** Suppose the only three shareholders of a corporation make an agreement among themselves to elect each other to the board of directors of the corporation. Francis McQuade was one of three shareholders in a corporation that owned the New York Giants baseball team (this was before the team moved to San Francisco) who agreed to use "best efforts" to keep him as a member of the board of directors and corporate treasurer. The agreement was signed in 1919. During the next several years, the other two shareholders clashed with McQuade, who was manager of the baseball team as well. The other two shareholders had joined in an agreement with McQuade that they would also be elected to the board of directors, but in 1928 they refused to vote for McQuade, who was then voted off the board of directors. McQuade sued for specific performance of the agreement between the shareholders. The other shareholders, defendants Charles Stoneham and John McGraw, argued that their agreement was contrary to public policy because, by not voting for McQuade, they were protecting the corporation from McQuade, whom they regarded as incompetent. What do you think? Should the courts enforce a contract that calls for members of the board of directors to take actions that they believe are not in the best interests of the corporation? Also, even if the courts refuse to enforce the

contract, should McQuade retain his right to sue for damages based on breach of contract? [*McQuade v. Stoneham,* 189 N.E. 234 (N.Y. 1934).]

3. **Director Negligence.** An issue raised by the next case is the level of awareness and preparation that directors must devote to their duties in order to fulfill their fiduciary obligations to the corporation. Trans Union was a publicly traded company that engaged in railcar-leasing operations. The chairman of the board of directors, Jerome W. Van Gorkom, was nearing retirement and was of the opinion that Trans Union stock was undervalued. Van Gorkom asked his chief financial officer, Donald Romans, to work out a buyout price for stock owned by Van Gorkom. Romans's estimate of the value of Trans Union stock was $55 per share at a time when Trans Union stock was selling for $37 per share. There were a lot of additional facts involved in the case but, basically, a meeting was called with one day's notice and the board of directors was presented with a buyout figure of $55 per share. The buyout figure was a bid offered by another firm to effect a leveraged buyout of Trans Union. Shareholders formed a class and sued the board of directors for negligence, claiming that the "intrinsic" value of Trans Union could have been even higher than $55 per share, even though it was trading at $37 per share at the time. The defendants, the board of directors, claimed that they relied on presentations by officers of Trans Union. Can a board of directors rely on its chief corporate officers for such an important decision or do they have to do more? [*Smith v. Van Gorkom,* 488 A.2d 858 (Del. 1985).]

4. **Fiduciary Duties of Partners—How Long Do They Last?** Covalt and High were corporate officers and shareholders in CSI. Covalt owned 25 percent of the stock and High owned the remaining 75 percent of the stock. In late 1971, after both High and Covalt had become corporate officers of CSI, they orally agreed to the formation of a partnership. The partnership bought land and constructed an office and warehouse building on the land. In February 1973, CSI leased the building from the partnership for a five-year term. Following expiration of the initial term of the lease, CSI remained a tenant of the building. In December 1978, Covalt resigned his corporate position and was employed by a competitor of CSI. Covalt, however, remained a partner with High in the ownership of the land and the building rented to CSI. On January 9, 1979, Covalt wrote to High demanding that the monthly rent for the partnership real estate leased to CSI be increased from $1,850 to $2,850 per month. Upon receipt of the letter, High informed Covalt he would determine if the rent could be increased. Thereafter, however, High did not agree to the increased rent and took no action to renegotiate the amount of the monthly rent payable. By 1980 the partnership was dissolved. Can one partner sue the other when there are only two partners and they disagree? [*Covalt v. High,* 675 P.2d 999 (N.M. Ct. App. 1983).]

5. **Political Combat in Cyberspace.** We know from a previous chapter that "suck" sites are protected by the First Amendment. In several cases, courts have ruled that rights of freedom of expression allow critics of various companies or governmental actions to use the names of those entities in their websites and in their domain names. Thus, websites such as www.microsoftsucks.com are legal and not subject to suit for a trademark infringement. Richard Bucci, doing business as Catholic Radio, obtained a domain name entitled www.plannedparenthood.com. Bucci was an anti-abortion activist and promoted his anti-abortion book *The Cost of Abortion.* Visitors to Bucci's website saw a banner that read, "Welcome to the Planned Parenthood Homepage!" Bucci claimed that his website was providing the "other side" in the abortion debate and thus his website was protected by the First Amendment. What do you think? Is there any real difference between what Bucci was doing at this website and the "suck" sites? The case itself is available on the Web at http://www.jmls.edu/cyber/cases/planned1.html, but could be looked up on LexisNexis at *Planned Parenthood Federation of America, Inc., v. Bucci,* 1997 U.S. Dist. LEXIS 3338 (S.D.N.Y. 1997).

6. **Doing Business Where?** In 1994, Carleen and Robert Thomas, a couple living in California, operated an Amateur Action Computer Bulletin Board System (AABBS) that allowed subscribers to download sexually explicit material. Also available at the website were options to purchase sexually explicit material via overland mail. The Thomases were prosecuted for interstate transportation of obscene materials in the Western District of Tennessee at the initiation of a postal inspector, based on the postal inspector's view that the Western District of Tennessee was conservative and more likely to return a guilty verdict. An issue that arose in this case was whether community standards as to obscenity in western Tennessee should control what takes place throughout the United States, as websites are generally accessible anywhere in the world. The

issue has relevance not only in the porn industry but also in other quasi-legal activities including online gambling and pharmacies. In some states, contests are legal, while in others, they are not. The question is, can websites limit their offerings to states where what they are selling is legal even though residents located in other states, where what is being offered is illegal, can access the website? What safeguards must the website operators take? For an example of what not to do, look at *United States v. Thomas,* 74 F.3d 701 (6th Cir. 1996).

Social Responsibility, Policy, and Ethics in a High-Tech World

7. **Jurisdiction Based on Internet Presence.** Jurisdiction based on access from the Internet is an issue that continues to plague courts. At present, the standard seems to be that if a website does nothing but make itself accessible on the World Wide Web, this act does not make the website and its owners subject to the jurisdiction of any state whose citizens can access the site. See *Cybersell, Inc. v. Cybersell, Inc.,* 130 F.3d 414 (9th Cir. 1997). On the other, minimal amounts of activity apparently do subject the business to the jurisdiction of courts in states where residents interact with the website. The interaction can be in the form of mail, e-mail, or phone conversations. See *Zippo Manufacturing Co. v. Zippo Dot Com,* 952 F. Supp. 1119 (W.D. Pa. 1997). Both of the cases above are cited in a more recent case in which an ISP is being sued by a copyright owner for acts of a customer of the ISP. Personal jurisdiction became an issue because the copyright owner is located in Maryland and the ISP only operates in Georgia. Again in this case, the plaintiff, the Maryland firm, made the claim that the ISP enabled copyright infringements to take place and, therefore, subjected it to jurisdiction of the Maryland courts. The court in the aforementioned case made the following statement: "We are not prepared at this time to recognize that a State may obtain general jurisdiction over out-of-state persons who regularly and systematically transmit electronic signals into the State via the Internet based solely on those transmissions. Something more would have to be demonstrated. And we need not decide today what that 'something more' is because ALS Scan has shown no more." See *ALS Scan, Inc. v. Digital Service Consultants, Inc., et al.,* 2002 U.S. App. LEXIS 11745 (4th Cir. Md. June 14, 2002), for the latest in the continuing jurisdictional skirmishes in cyberspace.

Using the Internet to Your Advantage

1. Of course, the government has a number of agencies whose missions involve assisting businesses, especially small businesses. The Small Business Administration (SBA) has a wealth of information under the hyperlink Starting Your Business at http://www.sbaonline.sba.gov. Also, the Federal Trade Commission has a number of "Don'ts" for business, but it also has a number of positive messages. For businesspeople considering franchises, the FTC has a Web page (http://www.ftc.gov/bcp/franchise/netfran.htm) that provides links to the FTC Franchise Rule, state laws, and other useful information.

   The U.S. Department of Commerce (http://www.doc.gov) has a lot of useful information, particularly for businesses that are high-tech or are exporting. Also, the Department of Commerce has a Minority Business Development Agency (http://www.mbda.gov/) that assists minorities with start-up business financing and alternative financing. For women, the SBA has online assistance at http://www.onlinewbc.gov/.

2. There is a wealth of information available online from the private sector. The NOLO Legal Center (http://www.nolo.com/index.cfm) has a Small Business hyperlink that provides legal discussion of sole proprietorships, partnerships, corporations, limited liability companies, and other forms of business organization. The article "12 Website Design Decisions Your Business or Organization Will Need to Make," by Dr. Ralph F. Wilson, available at http://www.wilsonweb.com/articles/12design.htm, provides information for businesses that are establishing a Web presence. There is, of course, a wealth of e-business advice available online. An online magazine *E-Business Advisor* (http://www.advisor.com/www/E-BusinessAdvisor) appears to be aimed toward high-tech companies but has a number articles on e-business architecture. Just about any business organization topic, ranging from online incorporation (http://www.inc.com/services/start_biz/13919.html) to special issues associated with franchising (http://www.franchiseresales.com/), are available at most search engines if you input the appropriate keyword.

Government Regulation

Chapter **Fifteen**

Agency, Electronic Agents, and Employment at Will

Learning Objectives

After completing this chapter, you should

1. Have a firm understanding of agency relationships, their formation, and the legal ramifications of such relationships.
2. Be able to clearly distinguish between employees and independent contractors.
3. Be able to describe the array of duties that principals and agents owe to each other.
4. Be familiar with electronic agents and the legal issues that such agents create.
5. Know the evolution of employment and discharge standards for at-will employment.
6. Be mindful of the hazards companies face for wrongful and/or abusive discharges of workers.

OVERVIEW

Although some people work for "themselves," the vast majority of people in the United States work for others. During regular business hours, when they are working for "the company" that employs them, a majority of working-age people have consented to place the interests of the company they work for (their employer) above their own. During their time at work, employees agree to the supervision and control of management (within limits, of course). That relationship is consensual; the employer has agreed to have its employees work for and represent it, and the employees have agreed to do so. Legally, when an employee agrees to work for an employer after receiving a job offer, an *agency relationship* is created.

The employment relationship is probably the most important (economically) legal relationship in which most people will participate. Many of the rights and duties of the parties in an employment relationship are defined by common law principles of *agency law*. Although an employment relationship creates one of the most important agency agreements (between the employee and employer), agency relationships encompass more that just employment. Agency relationships are created whenever a client hires a professional, such as a lawyer or real estate agent, to represent him or her, even though the lawyer or real estate agent is not an employee of the client.

An essential element of an agency relationship is that one party (the *principal*) is exposed to liability to third parties for the actions of an *agent,* who may be a professional agent (such as an attorney), an employee, or even an electronic actor. Most of the time, the principal is not sued or otherwise liable to third parties for the actions of the agent because the agent does what the principal expects him to do and the relationship does not generate any liability for the principal. The focus in this chapter is on situations in which the principal does incur liability as a result of actions taken by an agent who is acting on behalf of the principal.

Basic Principles of Agency Law

Ignoring a number of exceptions and caveats that are discussed below, there are three basic principles of agency law:

1. The principal is liable to third parties for the torts committed by an agent and for performance on contracts entered into by an agent for the principal, as long as the actions at issue were taken within the scope of the agent's authority.
2. The agent is also liable for his or her torts, but not for performance on contracts entered into for the principal if the contracting activities are within the agent's scope of authority.
3. A principal is not liable for the actions of agents who are acting outside their scope of authority.

Two Important Issues

Two important legal questions typically arise in litigation involving principals and agents:

- Does an agency relationship exist?
- If an agency relationship does exist, was the agent acting within his scope of authority?

The three basic principles listed above can be applied to real-world situations, keeping in mind the proposition that, most of the time, the core legal issues courts have to grapple with are *whether an agency relationship exists* and/or *whether the agent was acting within his scope of authority*.

WHAT IS AN AGENCY RELATIONSHIP?

agency
A relationship, based on consent, in which one party (the agent) agrees to act under the direction of and on behalf of another party (the principal).

According the *Restatement (Second) of Agency,* an **agency** is "the fiduciary relation which results from the manifestation of consent by one person to another that the other shall act in his behalf and subject to his control, and consent by the other so to act."[1] Not surprisingly, many (students and others) are rightfully put off by such legalese so additional discussion of this stilted definition is in order.

Fiduciary Relation

A **fiduciary relationship** exists when one person agrees to perform duties to *benefit another*. To illustrate this relationship, consider the arrangement often made for children through which they receive money in trust, typically in the event of an unexpected death of parents. In a trust, an appointed *trustee* is the legal owner of the money held in trust and a particular child is the *beneficiary* of the trust. It is presumed that the child is not

---

[1] As with tort law, the *Restatements* are not binding on courts but are very influential and are generally following by the courts, which frequently quote liberally from the *Restatements* to justify their decisions.

fiduciary relationship
The relationship that exists when one party agrees to perform prescribed duties for the benefit of another. This relationship imposes responsibilities or duties on the party (often a trustee) who has agreed to the assignment.

principal
An employer, business, client, or other party who engages or hires another party (an agent) to perform designated duties.

knowledgeable enough to manage money, so the trustee manages the trust money on the child's behalf. If the trustee performs as required by law, the trustee makes prudent investments so that the money held in trust will grow and benefit the child, until the child becomes an adult and assumes full ownership of the money. If, instead, the trustee benefits himself by borrowing from the trust or by investing in enterprises that he owns, the trustee is breaching his fiduciary duty to the child.

In an agency relationship, the agent agrees to perform certain tasks to benefit the **principal.** While performing these tasks, the agent is required, by virtue of the fiduciary relationship between himself and the principal, to use *best efforts* on behalf of the principal. If, instead, the agent is negligent in performing on behalf of the principal, the agent is breaching his fiduciary relationship with the principal. A more detailed discussion of fiduciary relationship is provided below.

Consent

With very few exceptions, an agency relationship is based on consent. The agent consents to work on behalf of the principal and the principal agrees to have the agent work on his behalf. In the *Restatement* definition of agency, consent on the part of *both* the principal and the agent to the agency relationship is listed as a requirement. In some cases, employment contracts exist between principals and agents. In spite of an employment contract, if consent on the part of either party to the agency relationship ceases to exist, the agency is terminated, even though a breach of contract may be taking place with termination of the employment relationship and, hence, the agency relationship.

Principal

The language of agency is antiquated. Indeed, in the not too distant past, the employment relationship was described as a master–servant relationship. In today's ordinary parlance, "principals" and "masters" are generally referred to as employers, corporations, and clients. The most common example of an agency relationship exists whenever a company hires an individual to work for it as an employee. The hiring company is the *principal* and the employee is the *agent.* As mentioned above, not all agents are employees. However, all employees are agents.

Legal Consequences of Agency

There are two types of third parties who are potentially affected by agency relationships (see Nutz and Boltz box on page 479). On the one hand, there are contracting partners of the principal: customers, suppliers, and other businesses and individuals who enter into contracts with the principal through actions of the agent. When a purchasing agent for a large corporation signs a contract to buy a shipment of carpet on behalf of a corporation for a new showroom it is about to open, the corporation, not the purchasing agent, is liable for making payment, assuming that the carpet company sends conforming goods. On the other hand, a delivery person who is driving a company truck negligently and, as a result, causes a wreck with another motorist commits a tort for which both the company and the delivery person are potentially liable to the injured third party.

independent contractor
A person who contracts to perform a task but maintains autonomy as to performance of that task.

Independent Contractors

Not everyone hired by a company to do a job is either an employee or an agent. If a company has an electrical problem at its plant, it may hire an outside electrician to come in and make needed repairs. In this situation, the electrician would be an **independent contractor,** not an employee. It is common for companies that have temporary needs for additional clerical help to contract with a temporary agency to send temporary workers. It

Nutz and Boltz

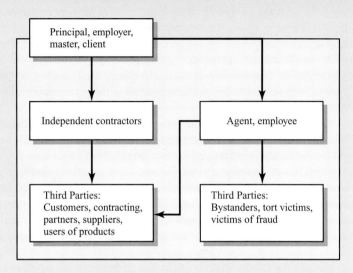

is often much cheaper for companies to "outsource" such temporary needs to independent contractors because the employment relationship can be expensive. If temporary help is hired with full company employment status, the company must withhold taxes, provide benefits, and provide additional health and safety regulation. In Case 15-1, an issue arose as to whether the plaintiff was an employee or an independent contractor. If a court deems a temporary worker to be an employee, the plaintiff qualifies for workers' compensation, which is paid for by the employer. This array of duties and obligations is not required of the company that uses independent contractors to cover its temporary labor needs. In general, when there is doubt about the status of a person who is working for a company, the company often takes the position that the person is an independent contractor because the tax consequences are more favorable, there is less regulation of the independent contractor relationship, and employers are not liable for torts committed by independent contractors.

Tort Liability of Employers

Although, generally, an *employer is not liable if an independent contractor commits a tort while working for the company,* there are several exceptions to this rule. If an electrician is negligent while working for a company, and that negligence causes a damaging power outage to several other companies in the vicinity, the hiring company is not liable for that tort. Independent contractors, such as an outside electrical contractor, are not employees, though they can be agents of the hiring company, as is the case when a real estate agent is hired. Most independent contractors, however, are not agents of the hiring company and, thus, there is a substantially lessened legal exposure to possible tort liability when a company hires an independent contractor.

The Inherently Dangerous Activity Exception

If a company hires an independent contractor to perform *inherently dangerous tasks,* such as working with dynamite or storing hazardous waste, the employing company *is liable* if the independent contractor commits a tort while engaging in such tasks.

Control

Control is the key to determining whether a person hired to perform services for an employer is an independent contractor or an employee. If the employer has the right to control not only what the person hired does but also the way he performs the task, then the hired person is an employee. An independent contractor typically maintains autonomy over the way he or she performs the job he or she was hired to perform. The *Restatement (Second) of Agency* defines an independent contractor as "a person who contracts with another to do something for him but who is not controlled by the other nor subject to the other's right to control with respect to his physical conduct in the performance of the undertaking. He may or may not be an agent."

Given the substantial legal differences that accompany employee status relative to independent contractor status, courts have had to grapple with the task of defining criteria for differentiating between the two. Many court cases have followed when an injurious accident has occurred at a work site and a determination must be made as to whether the person committing the likely tort is an employee or an independent contractor. Typically, individuals do not have the financial wherewithal to satisfy expensive tort claims, particularly if the claim involves personal injury, so tort victims often look to the employing company for compensation. If the person committing the tort is judged to be an independent contractor, the company usually escapes paying for damages caused by the tort.

Among the factors that courts look at in determining whether a person is an employee or independent contractor are

- *The degree of control exercised by the employer.* The more control exercised by the employer, the more likely the person will be deemed an employee.
- *Whether the person has a distinct business from the employer.* Obviously, if the person has his or her own business, the person is generally viewed as being an independent contractor.
- *Which party supplies the tools.* Employers generally supply tools to employees while independent contractors supply their own tools.
- *Method of payment.* In general, employees are paid by the hour while independent contractors are paid by the job.
- *Tax status.* If an employer withholds taxes, it is virtually inevitable that the person will be classified as an employee in court procedures.
- *Level of skill.* The greater the level of skill, the more likely the person is classified as an independent contractor.

Case 15-1

Stephen R. Hemmerling, Appellant v. Happy Cab Co., Appellee

Supreme Court of Nebraska
247 Neb. 919, 530 N.W. 2d 916 (Neb. 1995)

BACKGROUND AND FACTS

It has been the practice of many employers to characterize their relationship with those that work for them as that of employer–independent contractor. This is particularly true in the taxicab industry where cab drivers typically exercise a good deal of discretion during their work hours.

While operating a Happy Cab Co. taxicab, appellant, Stephen R. Hemmerling, was involved in a traffic accident and suffered personal injuries. Hemmerling's claim for workers' compensation benefits was denied, and Hemmerling filed a petition in the Workers' Compensation Court. The Workers' Compensation Court held that Hemmerling was an independent contractor on the date of the accident and not an employee; therefore, Hemmerling was not entitled to workers' compensation.

At the time of the hearing in Workers' Compensation Court, Happy Cab operated approximately 95 cabs. By the terms of the lease, Hemmerling leased the taxicab to Happy Cab for a term of 1 year, thus Hemmerling is the lessor and Happy Cab the lessee. On September 13, 1991, the parties executed two agreements, a rental agreement and an equipment lease agreement . . . The following terms of the equipment lease agreement are pertinent to this issue:

> *4. Possession and control of the equipment during the period of this lease is entirely vested in the Lessee, in such way as to be good against all the world, including the Lessor. Operation of the equipment shall be under the exclusive control and supervision of the Lessee which will be operated by Lessee in the ordinary course of Lessee's business.*

The Court of Appeals in Nebraska affirmed the decision of the Workers' Compensation Court that Hemmerling was an independent contractor.

Opinion by Justice Lanphier

The right of control is the chief factor distinguishing an employment relationship from that of an independent contractor.

> An independent contractor is one who, in the course of an independent occupation or employment, undertakes work subject to the will or control of the person for whom the work is done only as to the result of the work and not as to the methods or means used. Such a person is not an employee within the meaning of the workmen's compensation statutes.

* * *

We have repeatedly stated that although control or the right of control is the chief factor to be considered when identifying one acting on behalf of another as an employee or an independent contractor, it is not the conclusive factor . . .

Ordinarily, when a court is presented with a dispute regarding a party's status as an employee or an independent contractor, there is no contract vesting the right of control in an employer, and in such cases, the party's status is a question of fact . . . However, where the inference is clear that there is, or is not, a master and servant relationship, the matter is a question of law. Here, we are presented with a question of law for the reasons more fully explained below. By contract, Happy Cab had the right to control Hemmerling. Further, an application of the analysis we have used to discern the true nature of an employment versus independent contractor relationship creates a clear inference that a master-servant relationship exists.

* * *

Paragraph 4 of the equipment lease agreement vests the exclusive control, supervision, and possession of the taxicab in Happy Cab. Paragraph 4 gives Happy Cab the right to control the only equipment used by Hemmerling. This language does not denominate the relationship between the parties; rather, it proves the first, and most important, factor, which thus establishes that an employment relationship existed between the parties. According to paragraph 4, Happy Cab had the right to control the methods or means used by Hemmerling in the course of operating the taxicab by virtue of its exclusive control over the taxicab. Although there are ambiguities in the equipment lease agreement arising from the parties' failure to strike the surplus terms, those ambiguities do not detract from the clear right of control possessed by Happy Cab by virtue of paragraph 4.

* * *

Not all of the remaining factors are applicable in this case, but those that are further support the conclusion that an employment relationship existed between the parties. Hemmerling was not engaged in a distinct occupation or business from that of Happy Cab. Happy Cab argues that it was in the business of leasing cabs, but in fact, Happy Cab held the certificate of public convenience to provide cab services, and Hemmerling did that work. The type of work is that which can be done by employees rather than specially skilled independent contractors.

* * *

Decision and Outcome

The Supreme Court of Nebraska reversed the order of the Court of Appeals, which affirmed the review panel's order upholding the trial court's decision, and remanded the matter to the trial court for a determination of the benefits due Hemmerling. The Supreme Court held that Hemmerling was an employee, not an independent contractor, because of the degree of control exercised by the defendant, Happy Cab Co., over the taxicab, the only equipment used in this line of work.

Questions for Analysis

1. Why does the defendant, Happy Cab, want the plaintiff characterized as an independent contractor?
2. What is one fact, besides the control issue, that suggests the relationship between the parties is that of employer–employee rather than employer–independent contractor?

Summary

When one person agrees to perform tasks on behalf of another and both parties are in agreement, an agency relationship is formed. As described above, principals are liable for the actions of agents who are acting within the scope of authority set out in the agency relationship. The employment relationship is one example of an agency relationship, but not all agency relationships are based on employment. If a company hires an independent contractor, its exposure for tort liability is less than if the person hired is classified as an employee. The key difference between employee and independent contractor is the degree of control that the hiring company exerts over the person hired. Courts also look at other factors to determine whether the person hired is an independent contractor or employee.

Formation of an Agency

Even though there are very substantial legal consequences that accompany the existence of an agency relationship, such relationships are very easy to form. The only legal requirement for forming an agency relationship is a consensual agreement between the parties. Most agency agreements need not even be in writing. An exception to this general rule is applicable if an agent is hired to negotiate contracts that themselves must be in writing (such as real estate contracts). This is the so-called equal dignity rule. Also, when a principal conveys power of attorney to another, that agreement must be in writing.

Consideration is not required to form a valid agency relationship. Among relatives, it is not infrequent that an adult child will act as the agent for elderly parents and that agency relationship typically does not involve any payment of fees. In this situation, the agency relationship is gratuitous.

Types of Agency Formation

Consent

As mentioned above, agencies are created when there is consent between the parties. The consent can be *expressed* (by far the most common) or *implied,* based on circumstances that would cause a reasonable person to conclude that an agency relationship exists. Consider Garcia, standing on a corner and seeing several others get on a truck that takes them to a farm to pick fruit. If Garcia also gets on the truck, an agency relationship is created, even though there is no specific agreement between the parties. This implied consent principle is a core issue in Case 15-2.

Ratification

ratification
An action by a principal that indicates acceptance of the actions of another, even if those actions were executed by a party who was not an agent for the principal or was acting outside his or her scope of authority.

Ratification occurs when, after the fact, a principal indicates that he is willing to accept actions of a person who, at the time the act takes place, was not an agent or was acting outside his scope of authority. Suppose James works as a janitor for a large office building and is approached by someone selling cleaning supplies. Suppose that James agrees that the deal offered on supplies is a good one and signs an invoice on behalf of the large office building. Later on when the bill arrives, James's supervisor wants an explanation, which James provides. If the building operator pays the bill, the actions of James and the contract are ratified, even though James did not have authority to negotiate contracts at the time he signed for the cleaning supplies. When a principal ratifies an action of a nonagent or an agent acting outside his scope of authority, the principal must ratify the entire action.

Estoppel

estoppel
Principle under which a party is barred from denying or alleging specific facts, based on prior conduct and/or representations.

Agency by **estoppel** results when a reasonable third party believes that A is acting as an agent for P. Suppose Sam works for Acme Office Supplies Co. and collects money in C.O.D. transactions. Suppose Sam is fired by Acme but arrives at the office of a law firm, delivers a chair while wearing the uniform of the office supply company, and collects the money for the chair. The law firm is entitled to keep the chair and does not have to pay Acme Office Supplies Co. because there was an agency by estoppel between Sam and Acme.

Generally in estoppel cases, the principal must do something, or fail to do something, that leads the third party to believe that this nonagent is an agent. In the example above, by not informing customers that Sam had been fired, Acme allowed customers to reasonably believe that Sam was still an agent/employee.

Agency by estoppel is also characteristic of franchises. In general, franchises (for fast-food restaurants, pizza deliverers, and a wide array of businesses) are separate legal entities from their parent companies. That separateness, however, is often not apparent to the general public. In a number of cases, courts have held that franchisees were agents of the parent companies.

Operation of Law

family car doctrine
Principle that imposes an agency relationship between parents and children drivers by which parents are made financially responsible for torts committed by those children when driving.

For various public policy reasons, agency relationships are sometimes required by law. As an example, the **family car doctrine** prevails in many states. If a minor is involved in an automobile accident in these states, the minor is deemed an agent of the parents by operation of law, so that the victims of the vehicular negligence of the minor will have someone (the parents) to collect from.

Case 15-2

Ginn v. Renaldo, Inc.

Court of Appeals of Georgia
359 S.E.2d 390 (Ga. Ct. App. 1987)

BACKGROUND AND FACTS

Plaintiff Ginn brought this action against defendant Renaldo, Inc. d/b/a Baker Street to recover damages for injuries received at defendant's nightclub. This appeal arises from a directed verdict in favor of defendant at the close of plaintiff's case.

The facts of record, construed most strongly in favor of plaintiff, showed that on the evening in question plaintiff became "silly drunk" at defendant's nightclub and was asked by several patrons and the manager to leave the premises. He initially declined, but upon arrival of the police he voluntarily left the premises, escorted by the manager and an unidentified male patron. While talking with the police in the nightclub's parking lot, plaintiff realized that he had left his jacket inside. Upon his attempt to reenter the premises and retrieve the jacket, he was met at the door by the manager and an unidentified male patron. (Plaintiff was unable to recall if this patron was the same one who had earlier escorted him out.) He repeatedly attempted to persuade the manager to admit him so that he could retrieve his jacket, but she steadfastly refused. Suddenly and without warning, the patron pushed plaintiff, who lost his balance and fell backward. Plaintiff testified, "[T]o break my fall I put my hand against the door frame and he slammed the door on my hand and I pushed it back open with my right hand and before I could get my right hand out of the door he slammed it again and held it shut and was obviously pushing with all his might because it hurt very much and I started screaming at him to open the door, that he had my hand in the door and to let the door open and I would get my hand out, and he held it for several minutes . . . pushing with all his might. . . ."

Opinion by Pope

"Proof of agency and of the nature of the agency may be made by showing circumstances, apparent relations, and the conduct of the parties. . . ." [Citations deleted.] However, "where the only evidence that a person is an agent of another party is the mere assumption that such agency existed, or an inference drawn from the actions of that person that he was an agent of another party, such evidence has no probative value and is insufficient to authorize a finding that such an agency exists. A review of the record in this case persuades us that the unidentified person alleged to have caused plaintiff's injuries was merely an individual patron of defendant's nightclub. Although this person was at the door of the nightclub with the manager, there is no evidence that he had been requested to assist the manager in dealing with plaintiff or that he was in any way concerned with or responsible for the security of the nightclub. The testimony of defendant's president—that on occasion patrons, "without asking them to do anything from me or any of my employees," intercede in altercations or when other patrons become rowdy or unruly and assist in escorting the troublemakers out of the nightclub—provides no evidence of agency and, in any event, is irrelevant to the alleged agency relationship in the case at bar. We accordingly find no probative evidence of agency by implication.

* * *

Likewise, we find no record evidence of agency by ratification. " 'Ratification is the affirmance by a person of a prior act which did not bind him but which was done or professedly done on his account, whereby the act, as to some or all persons, is given effect as if originally authorized by him.' " However, "[t]he doctrine of ratification is not applicable against a principal as to the act of a third person who did not assume to act in the name of or under the authority of the principal." The evidence in this case shows that the unidentified patron acted in an individual capacity and not as one holding himself out as acting in the name of or under the authority of defendant.

Decision and Outcome

On this basis, the court granted summary judgment dismissal of the plaintiff's claims against the bar.

Questions for Analysis

1. What additional fact would the plaintiff have had to allege in order to avoid the granting of a motion for a summary judgment for the defendant?
2. If the plaintiff had evidence that (a) the defendant had allowed the same patron to perform such "escorting" services before and (b) after a successful escort, the defendant allowed the patron to drink free for the rest of the night, would the outcome in this case been different? Don't you suspect that the "helpful" patron was probably rewarded with free drinks after the incident? Would an alert manager charge the helpful patron for drinks afterward to avoid liability?

SCOPE OF AUTHORITY OR EMPLOYMENT

To the extent that principals are *not liable* for the actions of agents or employees unless they are operating within their scope of authority or employment, it is vitally important to determine the boundary lines of that authority. If a traveling salesman gets drunk at a bar at night, then kills another motorist on the road, a lot is at stake in determining whether that salesmen was still on the job or was on his free time. At common law, the authority of an agent is *express, implied,* or *apparent.* There is some overlap between these concepts and the type of agency formed. Since agents by estoppel are not real agents (in the minds of principals), their authority cannot be express because the employer *does not want* agents by estoppel to represent them.

Express Authority

express authority
Clear authority, through written or verbal communication, for an agent to act on behalf of a principal.

Most agency relationships are business relationships and, as such, the **express authority** of the agent (or employee) is articulated with reasonable specificity. If a person is hired as a salesperson, the employer will generally state the contracting authority of the agent. The agent may have limits on the size of contracts he or she can negotiate before being required to get approval of the home office. The salesperson may not have authority to make warranties and that lack of authority may be spelled out in boldface print so that customers will not be in a position to later claim that the salesperson made additional guarantees about the product that do not appear in the contract.

Implied Authority

implied authority
The right of an agent to act on behalf of a principal with all the ramifications of agency status, inferred from prior conduct and/or representations and by what is customary within the industry.

Even though an employment contract may spell out what the company expects of an employee in detail, all agents and employees also have **implied authority** to do things necessary to accomplish what the company expects the agent to do. For example, a rancher may expressly tell a foreman to go to a horse auction, look over what is being offered, and purchase, say, three horses suitable for working on the ranch. In other words, the foreman (an employee) has express authority to purchase three horses for the ranch. The foreman also has implied authority to drive a vehicle to the auction, stay at a hotel where other buyers are staying, get meals, and generally become as familiar as possible with any inside "dope" regarding the horses that are going to be offered for sale at the auction. That inside "dope" may be available only at a bar where ranch hands hang out. If the foreman is driving to the auction and injures another motorist, the foreman and the ranch are liable for damages. On the other hand, there are a number of agency relationships that cannot be implied—they must be expressed. For example, check writing authority cannot be implied; it must be express.

Apparent Authority

apparent authority
The authority a third party, acting as a reasonable person, would believe an apparent agent would possess in light of available information.

Drawing on the discussion above about agency by estoppel, an agent (or nonagent) has **apparent authority** based on the reasonable beliefs of third parties. At least some of the reason for the belief of the third party must be attributable to an action or nonaction of the principal. If a company selects Edward as the company's president, Edward has apparent authority to sign contracts on behalf of the company. It is reasonable for third parties to expect that a company president has authority to sign contracts. Edward has apparent authority to sign contracts even if his employment contract expressly prohibits him from signing contracts on behalf of the company.

LIABILITY OF PRINCIPALS AND EMPLOYERS

Liability of a Principal for Contracts Created by Agents

Most contracts in the United States are negotiated and signed by agents. All employees of corporations are agents of the corporations they work for. Contracts they sign on behalf of that corporation bind their employers, not the employees who signed the contracts. As stated above, there are two caveats: (1) at the time the contract is signed, the employee must be acting within his *scope of authority* and (2) the fact of agency must be known to the third party. In most cases, the agency relationship is *fully disclosed* to the third party, as would be the case when a representative of a large corporation negotiates a contract on behalf of the corporation. The third party clearly knows that the representative of the corporation, often an attorney, is an agent of the corporation. The first basic rule of agency then applies:

- The principal (the corporation) is liable for contracts negotiated by the agent within the agent's scope of authority.
- The agent is not liable to the third party for contracts negotiated on behalf of the principal.

Undisclosed Agency Relationship

In some cases, the agency relationship is not disclosed or is only partially disclosed. If the third party is unaware that the party he is dealing with is an agent for another, the agency relationship is considered *undisclosed*. Under such circumstances:

- The third party is entitled to hold the agent liable for performance under the contract.
- Upon discovering that the agent was representing another party (the principal), the third party is entitled to insist upon performance from the principal as well. In some states, the third party is required to elect whether to hold the agent or the principal liable for nonperformance under a contract.
- Assuming the agent was operating within the scope of his authority, the agent can sue for *indemnification* from the principal, if the principal fails to perform on the contract and the agent is sued by the third party.[2]

Partially Disclosed Agency Relationship

A *partially disclosed* agency relationship exists when the third party is aware that the agent is representing another party but does not know the identity of the principal. Under these circumstances,

- The agent is not liable for nonperformance under the contract unless the agent exceeded his or her authority.
- The third party can hold the principal liable for nonperformance under the contract.
- The principal can hold the third party liable for nonperformance under the contract.

Partial and undisclosed agency relationships are not the norm but make a lot of sense when the identity of the principal would cause third parties to change their positions in ways that are adverse to those of the principal. This phenomenon is especially common

---

[2] Indemnification means to hold harmless. If an agent negotiates a contract for an undisclosed principal and the principal fails to perform as called for in the contract, the agent is entitled to indemnification by the principal. In this case, the indemnification to which the agent is entitled from the principal includes provision of legal representation and payment of any damages that are recovered by the third party at trial for breach of contract.

in real estate, involving property owners in areas where developers plan to build upscale residential or commercial developments. If a landowner knows that a developer is placing a bid for his property, chances are the landowner will raise his asking price. By using an undisclosed agency, or even a partially disclosed agency arrangement, the developer can avoid being squeezed by the last few landowners who know that the developer must acquire all the land in the area to assemble a suitable tract for a planned development.

Liability of Principals and Employers for Torts and Crimes

There are several ways of looking at the liability of principals and employers for torts and crimes of employees. First, the fact that a person is "on the job" does not negate his or her personal liability for torts and crimes. So agents and employees are virtually always liable for crimes and torts they commit. In many cases, the liability of principals for torts and crimes of agents depends crucially on whether, at the time of the tort and/or crime, the agent was *acting within his or her scope of authority*. If the agent is also an employee, the common law doctrine of *respondeat superior* applies, which literally means "let the master respond," reflecting the medieval origins of the common law. A company is vicariously liable for torts of employees committed within their scope of employment—the company is liable even though it was not negligent in the hiring process.

With this standard in mind, let us undertake the task, piece by piece, of delineating the areas in which liability of the employer is clear, migrating then into situations in which the liabilities of the parties are not so clear.

Case I

The employee is negligent and injures a third party. As an example, a stock person at WalMart stacks poorly balanced heavy merchandise on top of some shelves, resulting in falling merchandise and an injury to an unsuspecting shopper when he is looking at some adjacent merchandise. In this situation, liability on the part of the employer is clear. The actions of the employee clearly occurred on the job and within his or her scope of employment. In addition, employers have obligations to make their businesses safe for those that they invite in for shopping.

Case II

An agent or employee is on the job, commits an intentional tort, and harms a third party. In general, employers are *not liable* for intentional torts committed on the job because the employer can rightfully say that the agent or employee is not authorized to violate the law or commit an intentional tort. There are, however, a number of exceptions to this rule. If the exceptions apply, it means that the employer is liable to third parties for intentional torts committed by employees on the job. Exceptions include

- *If there is evidence that management authorized the acts,* then the company is liable along with the employee for the intentional tort.
- *In most cases, if management had knowledge of the intentional torts and did nothing to stop them,* the company is liable for the resulting damages. Suppose a company hires members of a motorcycle gang to collect on overdue accounts. If complaints of heavy-handed collection practices reach management, and nothing is done to investigate or correct the reported problems, then the company will be held liable for any damages resulting from inappropriate collection practices, even if the company manual available to employees warns against intimidation and use of force.

Case III

An employee commits an intentional tort on the job and at the time of the tort, one or more of the following factors are present:

1. *The employee was advancing the interests of the company.* Suppose a deliveryperson raped a woman, but at the time he gained entry, he was carrying in a chair to the woman's apartment. Under such circumstances, the company would most likely be liable to the woman.
2. *The company furnished the means that accomplished the intentional torts,* such as uniforms, identification, or delivery vehicles.
3. *The employer had notice of past aggressive acts of the employee.*
4. *The employer failed to perform due diligence checks before hiring the employee for a position with potential for harm.* In camps that cater to children, camp operators have a duty to check out whether counselors and coaches have any history of complaints at previous places of employment, particularly complaints about sexually inappropriate behavior.

Some of the principles discussed above are applied in Case 15-3. In this case, "P.L." are the initial identifiers of a minor.

Case 15-3

P.L., Respondent v. Lynn Aubert, Respondent, Daniel Brooks, Independent School District No. 306, Petitioners, Appellants

Supreme Court of Minnesota
545 N.W.2d 666 (Minn. 1996)

BACKGROUND AND FACTS

In Lange v. National Biscuit Company, *a 1973 case, the Minnesota Supreme Court established the precedent that an employer could be liable for intentional torts of employees if (1) at the time of the tort, the employee was on the job and furthering the interests of the employer, even though (2) the employee's actions were not reasonably foreseeable.*

Lynn Aubert was a 42-year-old licensed school teacher starting her first year of teaching at La-Porte High School, LaPorte, Minnesota, in September of 1989. She was interviewed for the position by Daniel Brooks, who was the high school principal and school superintendent for School District No. 306 (ISD No. 306), the LaPorte school district. A standard background check was completed and she was found to have good academic credentials and exceptional personal references.

P.L. was a student in three classes that Aubert taught—clerical, business math, and accounting. Early in the school year, Aubert began talking with P.L. about personal problems with her marriage and her family. She also spoke with him about his family's problems and his personal problems with drinking. In November or December of that school year, Aubert began kissing P.L. while they were alone in the classroom. In December, Aubert had a Christmas party at her home for her business math students. During the party, she spent time dancing with P.L., resting her hands on his buttocks. More intimate contact occurred in the months following the party. During times alone with P.L., Aubert would lock the classroom door, and she and P.L. would engage in intimate sexual contact both over and under their clothing. She would also have him sit with her at her desk during class and they would engage in intimate sexual contact hidden only by her desk, while other students were present in the room. Aubert also asked other teachers to excuse P.L. from their classes so that he might receive "extra help." P.L. would meet Aubert in her classroom, she would lock the door, and they would engage in intimate sexual contact consisting of repeated touching of the genitals over and under their clothing, kissing, and hugging.

P.L. and Aubert had a falling out and in the aftermath, P.L. is suing both the teacher and the school district. In December 1992, P.L. filed a complaint alleging several counts of inappropriate behavior on the part of Aubert, and alleging that Brooks and Independent School District (ISD) No. 306 were responsible for Aubert's behavior. The complaint alleged causes of action against Aubert, Brooks, and ISD No. 306 for battery, intentional infliction of emotional distress, sexual harassment, breach of fiduciary duty, negligent supervision, negligent infliction of emotional distress, and negligent hiring. The trial court granted defendants' Brooks (Principal) and ISD No. 306 motion for a summary judgment against P.L., but denied Aubert's motion for a summary judgment.

Opinion by Tomljanovich

In *Marston* the employee was a psychologist who made unwelcome and improper sexual advances to patients during and immediately after therapy sessions in his office. *Marston,* 329 N.W.2d at 308. We noted that the doctor "intentionally departed from the standards of his profession, not . . . to cause harm . . . , but rather to confer a personal benefit on himself." In that situation, we held the employer liable for the employee's actions, because there was a fact issue as to whether the acts were within the scope of the doctor's employment. We stated that "it should be a question of fact whether the acts of [defendant] were foreseeable, related to and connected with acts otherwise within the scope of employment." This issue of foreseeability was raised because of expert testimony at the lower court that sexual relations between doctors and patients was a "well-known hazard and thus . . . foreseeable." It was the foreseeability of the risk that determined the outcome of the *Marston* case.

Here we find no evidence that such relationships between teacher and student are a "well-known hazard"; thus foreseeability is absent. While it is true that teachers have power and authority over students, no expert testimony or affidavits were presented regarding the potential for abuse of such power in these situations; thus there can be no implied foreseeability.

"The master is liable for any such act of the servant which, if isolated, would not be imputable to the master, but which is so connected with and immediately grows out of another act of the servant imputable to the master, that both acts are treated as one indivisible tort . . ." *Lange* at 785–86 [quoting *Gulf. C. & S. F. Ry. Co. v. Cobb,* 45 S.W.2d 323, 326 (Tex. Civ. App. 1931)]. Here, the sexual contact by the teacher toward the student could not be considered an "indivisible" act directly related to her teaching duties. Thus liability of the master cannot be imputed, even though the acts were committed within work related time and place.

* * *

Brooks and ISD No. 306 performed standard teacher evaluations of Aubert. In addition to the evaluations, Brooks and his assistant made several unannounced visits to Aubert's classrooms. Because the school had no public address system, all messages were hand-delivered by staff and students to classrooms throughout the course of the school day. Even with all of this interaction during the school day, the clandestine relationship between teacher and student was never observed.

A school district cannot be held liable for actions that are not foreseeable when reasonable measures of supervision are employed to insure adequate educational duties are being performed by the teachers, and there is adequate consideration being given for the safety and welfare of all students in the school. The safety and welfare of the students in a school setting is paramount. However, in this case, closer vigilance would not have uncovered the relationship because both participants worked hard to conceal it.

* * *

Decision and Outcome

The decision of the trial court to grant a motion for summary judgment to the principal and the school district was affirmed. The school district was not liable because, the court held, the unauthorized actions of the teacher were not reasonably foreseeable and measures to avoid this event would not have prevented it since the principals were both determined to conceal their actions. This case should be thought of as an exception to the holding of the Minnesota Supreme Court in *Lange.*

Questions for Analysis

1. What is the difference between the *Marston* case discussed above by Judge Tomljanovich and this case?
2. If an employee took a gun to work and killed several co-workers, customers, and bystanders, is the employer liable for those injured or killed? What additional facts would you have to know in order to make a determination of liability?
3. If the independent school district did not have student evaluations, could it claim that the actions of Aubert were unforeseeable?

Case IV

The company hires an independent contractor. As mentioned above, if a company hires an independent contractor it is not liable for the torts of the independent contractor if the independent contractor is not an agent. If the independent contractor is hired to perform exceptionally dangerous activities, however, the hiring company is liable if a tort occurs. In most cases the hiring company is liable for the torts of the independent contractor when the activity, such as the storage of hazardous waste, is subject to strict liability.

Case V

The company hires an employee who commits a crime. In many situations, intentional torts are also crimes. In most cases, though, even if an employing company is civilly liable to the third-party victim for an intentional tort, the company is not liable criminally. Employers or principals are liable for criminal activity only if they conspired with the employee in the commission of the crime. There are a few *strict liability crimes* in which violations occur without a showing of intent. In those cases, a company can be criminally liable. It is a crime, for example, to sell pharmaceutical drugs that are contaminated, even if there is no showing that anyone at the selling pharmaceutical company was aware that the drugs were contaminated. It should be noted, however, that if the employer is a corporation, criminal liability does not substantially differ from a civil fine by the government, as a corporation cannot be sent to prison.

RIGHTS AND OBLIGATIONS OF AGENTS (EMPLOYEES) AND PRINCIPALS (EMPLOYERS)

Fiduciary Obligations of Agent to the Principal

fiduciary duties
Duties owed to principals by agents, including the duties to provide best-effort, diligent performance on behalf of the principal; provide notice of material occurrences; avoid conflicts of interest; obey instructions from the principal; and provide accurate accounting of financial flows.

Agents owe a fiduciary duty to principals. They must place the interests of the principal above their own while working on behalf of the principal. There are several dimensions of the **fiduciary duty** agents owe to principals; failure to adhere to all such duties subjects the agent to liability to the principal.

Performance

First and foremost, agents have a duty to use *reasonable diligence* in the performance of their duties on behalf of the principal. If a business hires an attorney to represent it, and the attorney misses a court appearance, the attorney has not used reasonable diligence in the performance of his duties for the company. In general, agents and employees do not guarantee results but, rather, are required to put forward *best efforts* to achieve the desired results. If employees design and build a motor vehicle, then market the product, they are not guaranteeing that the employer will make a profit. If a company wants to pay only for results, they can pay employees on some type of piecework basis, such as paying for production

Nutz and Boltz   Your Tort Liability for the People You Hire

During your life, you will have contact with all three: agents, employees, and independent contractors. The following table summarizes the liabilities associated with hiring one of the three.

Agent	Tort liability of the principal determined by *scope of authority*	Scope of authority may be determined by reasonable beliefs of *third parties*
Employee	Tort liability of the employer determined by *scope of employment*	Scope of employment normally occurs within *regular business hours* with exceptions for traveling salespeople
Independent contractor	Tort liability of employer based on whether the IC is engaging in *ultrahazardous activity*	Tort liability of employer sometimes expanded by *statute*

based on number of items processed and rewarding sales with commissions. Most employees are paid by the hour or are on salary, though companies do encourage performance by providing bonuses in the form of stock options.

Notice

Agents are required to provide notice to principals of events that are relevant to their jobs. In particular, agents are charged with monitoring mail relevant to their jobs, because *notice to the agent is considered notice to the principal as well.* If an employee of a company receives a letter indicating acceptance of a contract offer, that letter is considered notice to the company. Also, employees charged with maintaining a safe working environment are charged with giving notice to the company of unsafe conditions at the work site. Notifying the principal or employer of situations relevant to their jobs is one aspect of rendering reasonably diligent performance to the principal.

Loyalty

In one very widely quoted passage in the Bible, Jesus tells a parable that concludes that "no man can serve two masters," an admonition that is likely common to all organized religions. When an agent works for a principal, the agent owes the principal undivided loyalty, which means that the agent cannot compete with the principal or take money in the performance of his or her duties from other sources. Also, agents are supposed to avoid conflicts of interest. If Ellen, while working as a real estate agent for a developer, comes across some desirable real estate that may interest the developer, Ellen must notify the developer and give him the first opportunity to purchase the real estate. It would be a breach of Ellen's fiduciary duty of loyalty should she secretly acquire the real estate and then resell it to the developer.

Obedience

Within reason, an agent or employee must follow instructions given by the principal. Failure to follow such instructions subjects the agent to liability to the principal if the agent's failure to follow instructions costs the principal money. There are limitations on this fiduciary obligation, such as when the instructions of the principal are contrary to law or when such instructions call for unethical conduct. If an employer instructs an employee to falsify safety reports that are required by a government agency, the employee does not have to follow those instructions. If the employee is fired as a result, the employee can sue the employer for *wrongful discharge* (discussion of this point of law takes place later in the chapter). Suppose an employer instructs a female salesperson to wear a provocative outfit and visit a purchasing agent of a large account with an admonition to "make the sale under any circumstances." Such instructions are unethical and, again, if the female employee refuses to comply and is fired, the company is liable for wrongful discharge (and probably discrimination based on sex). Finally, note that agents can disregard instructions from the principal in emergencies when there is no time to contact the principal.

Accounting

Principals who entrust money to agents are entitled to have an accounting of those funds, which means the agents must keep adequate records so that the principal can determine revenues, expenses, and profits. Agents have a duty to keep separate accounts for the principal's funds. If funds of the principal and agent are commingled, the principal is entitled to all the funds in the commingled accounts necessary to satisfy his or her claims. If the agent fails to provide adequate records, or if there is a suspicion that the records provided are falsified, the principal can take the agent to court for an accounting.

Duties of the Principal to the Agent

In general, the relationship between principal and agent is economic; the agent is willing to represent the principal because the principal is compensating the agent. From another perspective, the principal is willing to pay the agent because the agent has talents that are more efficient to use for assigned tasks than for the principal to perform the tasks himself.

Compensation

The most compelling duty of the principal to the agent is to pay the agent. Most principal–agent relationships occur in connection with employment contracts in which compensation is explicit and subject to significant government regulation (discussed in this and the next two chapters). Moreover, the principal or employer owes a duty to pay the agent or employee in a timely manner.

Reimbursement and Indemnification

If agents or employees incur expenses in connection with performing on behalf of the principal, they are entitled to reimbursement from the principal. If an agent or employee is sued by a third party while acting within his scope of authority, the principal or employer is required by law to *indemnify* the agent or employee. As discussed above, indemnification is provided when the principal or employer pays for all legal expenses incurred by an agent or employee who is sued by a third party due to actions the agent or employee took on behalf of the principal or employer. An agent or employee is entitled to be indemnified only if (s)he was acting within the scope of employment at the time (s)he engaged in the actions that resulted in a lawsuit filed by a third party.

Jane works as website designer for the Jano Corporation. In connection with her duties as a designer, George, Jane's supervisor, gives her an interesting logo that Jane incorporates into the Jano website. Unfortunately for Jane, the logo has been copyrighted by another firm, which now sues Jane personally for copyright infringement. Jane is entitled to indemnification from Jano for both her legal bills and, additionally, any judgment that the other firm is able to receive from the courts for Jane's actions.

Cooperation

Normally the interests of the principal and agent are matched, meaning that both parties want the agent to be successful. There are, however, times when it is actually in the interests of the principal to prevent an agent from completing tasks, particularly when the principal owes substantial commissions upon successful completion of a job by the agent. Imagine a sales representative who is given an area to exploit for sales purposes and who becomes very successful. The hiring company is aware that the sales representative has done a good job, but knows that it will owe a lot of commissions under the current compensation scheme. It is possible that the principal may interfere with successful completion of sales by its sales representative and invade the territory with other sales representatives who are paid according to a different (and cheaper) compensation scheme. Such actions would breach the duties that the principal owes to its employees.

Safe Working Conditions

A common law duty of principals is to provide agents or employees with safe working conditions and equipment with which to work. Employers have affirmative duties under the common law to make sure that the work site is safe. For most employers, this common law duty to provide a safe work environment has been largely superceded by worker safety regulations issued by the Occupational Safety and Health Administration, a federal agency, and by state worker-safety commissions' regulations. If the employer hires an independent contractor, it is the responsibility of the independent contractor to inspect the work site and make arrangements for safety.

ELECTRONIC AGENTS

Note that companies can hire people to negotiate contracts on their behalf and, unless something unusual occurs, the company is liable for the contracts executed even though they are entirely negotiated by agents. Increasingly, now, companies are using electronic agents to create contracts.

The use of electronic agents is a relatively recent technological advance that has required significant legal changes. According to the Uniform Computer Information Transactions Act (UCITA), an **electronic agent** can be defined as "a computer program, or electronic or other automated means, used independently to initiate an action, or to respond to electronic messages or performances, on the person's behalf without review or action by an individual at the time of the action or response to the message or performance."[3] As discussed in Chapters 7–9, a large slice of contract law has been based on intent and yet, increasingly, contracts are being created as a result of interaction between two electronic agents. Electronic agents are used by firms to accomplish all sorts of tasks, including shopping for bargains, creating contracts, and adding terms in a click-wrap program.

electronic agents
Combination of software and computer hardware that engages in transactions, including the execution of contracts, on behalf of a principal (typically, a corporation).

As noted in Chapter 9, UCITA has only been adopted by two states and its ultimate adoption by a substantial number of states is very much in doubt. At this point, UCITA should be viewed as having about the same weight as a *Restatement.* It is not binding on the courts, but it is often very influential.

Scope of Authority

Electronic agents are often equipped with artificial intelligence. With this endowment, such agents are not limited to simply finding the lowest prices on specified items but, indeed, are capable of a series of recursive decisions, which may be prompted by the actions of electronic agents from the other side of a buy-sell situation. Paralleling the situation with a human employee (or agent), it is a significant legal issue to determine what scope of authority

---

[3] Section 102(a)(27) of the Uniform Computer Information Transactions Act.

an electronic agent possesses. Frequently, electronic agents are sent out (into cyberspace) to accomplish a specific task, such as buying a particular product for the lowest price, given other specifications that are built into the search. When the electronic agent engaged in this activity finally selects the lowest-priced item that fits the specifications, the seller, who we'll assume is also employing an electronic agent, requests the buyer's electronic agent to read a click-wrap agreement and agree or not agree with all the terms in total.

Suppose a software product sold by Company S is purchased by an electronic agent acting on behalf of Company B, and the website requires that in order to purchase online, the electronic agent must agree to waive all warranties and agree not to sue Company S under any circumstances. Furthermore, suppose that the click-wrap agreement contains a clause that prohibits B from criticizing S's products under penalty of 50 percent of its profits. Under UCITA, which has been adopted in two states but which could be adopted in all 50 states, Company B is bound by click-wrap terms "agreed to" by its electronic agent. The scope of authority of an electronic agent is tempered under Section 206(a) of UCITA, which states that "a court may grant appropriate relief if the operations resulted from fraud, electronic mistake, or the like."

In addition, Section 111 of UCITA and the accompanying Official Comments indicate that the enforceability of contracts formed by electronic agents is limited by unconscionability constraints.[4] In the hypothetical situation above, the click-wrap agreement waiving all warranties may be enforceable, but forfeiting 50 percent of Company B's profits for criticizing S's software would not be enforceable because the requirement is unconscionable. Most of the limitations on the authority of electronic agents to "agree" to a contract are summarized in Official Comment 3 of Section 111, which states:

> **3. Electronic commerce.** This Act confirms the enforceability of automated contracting involving "electronic agents," but in some cases automation may produce unexpected, potentially oppressive results due to errors in programs, problems in communication, or other unforeseen circumstances in the automation process. Common law concepts of mistake may apply, as may Sections 206 and 213. In addition, in appropriate cases, unconscionability doctrine may invalidate a term because a procedural breakdown in automated contract formation produces unexpected and oppressive results in the terms of the agreement.

Clearly, the authors of UCITA anticipated that computer glitches may cause electronic agents to malfunction and produce bizarre results, such as orders that are numerically improbable. Thus, under Section 111, the employer of an electronic agent is not unlimitedly liable for all the actions of such agents even though, clearly, UCITA "confirms the enforceability of automated contracting involving—'electronic agents . . .'"

Assent by Electronic Agents

Official Comment 3(c) to Section 112 of UCITA explores what is meant by assent by electronic agents. According to the comments, "For electronic agents, assent cannot be based on knowledge or reason to know, since computer programs are capable of neither . . ." Instead, according to the Official Comments, assent by electronic agents is based on the acts of the electronic agent, either in the form of "an authentication or if, in circumstances, the operations indicate assent." Authentication takes place when a party either signs, or takes some other specified action, such as a mouse click, ". . . with the intent to sign a record, otherwise to execute or adopt an electronic symbol, sound, message, or process referring to, attached to, included in, or logically associated or linked with, that record."[5] Buried in the

---

[4] The Official Comments are clarifying remarks made by the authors of UCITA so that the meanings of various sections are made clearer.

[5] Section 102(a)(6)(B) of UCITA.

On my computer screen, a juicy bid pops up—a buyer willing to pay top dollar for an item I'm selling. In the next moment, as I fumble to type and click, the bid flashes away.

A competitor, moving as fast as a computer, has already closed the deal. And, in this case, it probably was a computer.

I'm sitting in a roomful of workstations at I.B.M.'s Thomas J. Watson Research Center in Yorktown Heights, N.Y., participating in an experiment on how well people compete against computers in auctions.

Researchers at the International Business Machines Corporation expect transactions like this to become common, and in a limited way, automated bidding robots or "bots" already exist. Auction sites like eBay allow people to specify the most they are willing to pay for an item, and their bids automatically rise as others bid higher.

But I.B.M. envisions more sophisticated situations and has established an Institute for Advanced Commerce to study them. Automated software, computer scientists at I.B.M. predict, will search different suppliers and negotiate prices with them. "We're wondering what a world looks like when there are a billion of these software agents transacting business on our behalf," said Dr. Steve R. White, who heads the research.

In the future, a purchasing agent looking to order pencils may enter some data—say, quantity, maximum price, date needed—and set the software loose on the Web.

That situation raises questions as well. Do these bidding bots bid differently from people? Could they change the behavior of financial markets? There is some evidence that they may; some blame computerized program trading, in part, for the stock market crash of 1987.

"They're much faster than people," Dr. White said of bidding robots, "and they're much stupider than people."

Pitting the bots against one another, the I.B.M. researchers found they often got into cutthroat price wars, relentlessly undercutting one another until one figures out that it can make more money by selling a few items at high profit and pops the price back up. Then the competitors follow suit, and the cycle repeats."

The first time this kind of roller coaster price war occurred, the researchers thought it was "some dumb artifact of the simulation," Dr. White said. But the same behavior kept on showing up in other simulations with different bidding rules. The bots, it appeared, were doomed to repeat the past, because they did not remember it.

The researchers then cured that self-defeating behavior by having them keep track of past pricing trends. "We're trying to give them enough smarts so that we trust them," Dr. White said.

The next question was, What happens when the bots go up against people? In a series of experiments, the I.B.M. researchers have looked at the fairly simple "double auction" similar to the way stocks are traded.

In a double auction, sellers put in "ask" bids specifying what price they're hoping to receive for their wares. The buyers similarly bid what they're willing to pay, and transactions are completed when a buyer accepts a seller's price, or a seller agrees to a buyer's bid.

In such auctions, the price quickly and almost inevitably converges to an easily calculable ideal. But how to gain the most in the fluctuations is unknown. "You just do the best you can," said Dr. Jason Shachat, a visiting scientist at I.B.M. "We don't know what perfect play is."

* * *

The I.B.M. work is interesting, said Dr. John O. Ledyard, a professor of economics and social science at the California Institute of Technology, but he is skeptical that the bot advantage will play out in "thin" markets where there are only a few buyers or sellers, and where good deals are more a matter of skill than speed.

"That requires another level of intelligence, which is a harder problem," he said. "Speed matters where you can take advantage of mistakes, but speed can hurt in negotiations."

Source: From Kenneth Chang, "New Age Bidding: Against Computers, Humans Usually Lose," *New York Times,* January 2, 2001. Copyright © 2001 by The New York Times Co. Reprinted with permission.

legalese is allowance for adoption "of an electronic symbol," such as the yes button in a typical Internet offer.

Reactions of Electronic Agents

Official Comment 3(c) goes on to note that, "In this Act [UCITA], manifesting assent requires a prior opportunity to review. For an electronic agent, this opportunity occurs only if the record or term was presented in such a way that a reasonably configured electronic agent could react to it." Exactly what is meant by the "reactability" of an electronic agent is not clear. The same comment notes, "The capability of an automated system to react and an assessment of the implications of its actions are the only appropriate measures of assent." The Official Comment seems to envision electronic agents making use of *artificial intelligence* when confronted by offers made on the Internet that are accompanied by click-wrap terms that the electronic agent "reacts" to.

Sound farfetched or commonplace in your own experience? Consider the situation in the "Cyberlaw Developments" box on page 495.

As electronic agents get more sophisticated, it is likely that there will be additional legal issues that will arise regarding the scope of their authority. Great advances have been made in the area of artificial intelligence, which will be incorporated into electronic agents. With some exceptions, businesspeople are bound by agreements that are assented to by electronic agents. As we've seen, the exceptions, according to the Official Comments of the UCITA, rely on common law doctrines regarding mistake and unconscionability that are, by their nature, ambiguous. It remains to be seen how easily the principal represented by an electronic agent can use these doctrines to escape a contract agreed to by a software program that makes use of an electronic agent.

HIRING HUMAN AGENTS: EMPLOYMENT AT WILL

The Thirteenth Amendment to the U.S. Constitution not only abolishes slavery but also prohibits "involuntary servitude." In other words, no person can be forced to work for another person even if the worker owes the employer and promises to work for the employer for a fixed period of time. The right of employees to quit one job (employer) when they decide they want to take a new job, or to simply not work, is unchallenged legally. What is subject to debate is the other side of the equation, which is the right of employers to discharge employees when they want to for any or no reason, or for reasons that violate public policy.

For most people, their jobs are their most valuable economic resources and losing their jobs is a major event. For most employers, hiring and firing a single employee is a routine occurrence. As a result, there is a widespread perception that there is an imbalance in bargaining power between employers and employees. If an employee loses her job, there is generally a major (personal) economic dislocation while, for employers, it is generally relatively easy to find a replacement for any one employee.

Employment at Will

employment at will
Employment standard, in the absence of an employment contract, under which employers may fire and employees may quit without good cause—simply acting on the desire to take the action.

The common law doctrine of **employment at will** means that an employee can quit an employer for any reason, and a parallel principle holds for employers: they can fire an employee without good cause. The employment-at-will doctrine allows employers complete discretion in the termination of employees. Application of the employment-at-will doctrine would allow an employer to fire an employee who has worked for the employer for 15 years, and to do so with no notice or justification. The potential harshness of this doctrine has caused courts and legislatures to limit the free discretion of employers. Little by little, exceptions have been carved into the doctrine of employment at will, both through legislation and through common law rulings of courts.

It still remains the case in the United States that most employees do not have employment contracts and that their relationships with their employers are at-will relationships. But, as noted above, even though most employees work without employment contracts, employers still do not have complete discretion to hire and fire employees at will, as courts and legislatures have intervened in numerous contexts to limit the discretion of employers to fire employees.

Implied Employment Contracts

implied employment contract
An enforceable employment contract formed on the basis of conduct. Manuals, other company documents, and statements of company managers often become part of an implied employment contract.

There have been numerous court cases in which employees have countered seemingly arbitrary firings by claiming that some combination of employee manuals and oral statements by managers have created an **implied employment contract** that contains a term or terms that prohibit arbitrary firings.[6] In some cases, employee manuals guarantee that, if a manager has a complaint about an employee's performance, the manager will notify the employee and give him (or her) time to adjust his performance. In other cases, company manuals state that employees will not be discharged unless there is "good cause." Courts have held that implied employment contracts have been created if the actions of the employer create a reasonable expectation on the part of employees that they will not be fired except for a showing of good cause, such as misconduct on the job, lack of productivity, or a downturn in business for the employer.

Employer Measures Used to Combat Implied Employment Contracts

In most instances, employers can negate a reasonable expectation by employees that they have an employment contract by giving them papers that say, "Your employment with our firm is on an at-will basis. There is no implied employment contract between us and we are not required to show 'good cause' if we decide to terminate your employment with us." In addition, employers who wish to avoid costly wrongful discharge litigation should put a legend on the top of each page of an employee manual that restates the proposition that employment with the company is at will and that no implied employment contract exists between the employer and employee.

Case 15-4 revolves around the existence of an employment contract, even though the employer may not have understood that it was executing such a contract.

---

[6] See, for example, *Duldulao v. St. Mary Nazareth Hospital Center*, 115 Ill.2d 482, 505 N.E. 2d 314 (Ill. 1987).

Case 15-4

Toussaint v. Blue Cross & Blue Shield of Michigan; Ebling v. Masco Corporation

Supreme Court of Michigan

408 Mich. 579 292 N.W.2d 880 (Mich. 1980)

BACKGROUND AND FACTS

Charles Toussaint brought an action for wrongful discharge from his employment by Blue Cross and Blue Shield of Michigan. The plaintiff testified that on the day he was hired in 1967 he was given a "Supervisory Manual" and a pamphlet of "Guidelines", which contained the defendant's personnel policies and procedures, including certain grounds and procedures for discipline of employees and termination of their employment. The plaintiff argues that these documents constitute a written part of his otherwise oral employment contract with the defendant and that, under the terms of the Supervisory Manual, he could be discharged "for just cause only", after warnings, notice, a hearing and other procedures provided in the Supervisory Manual. The plaintiff testified that in 1972 he was called into his supervisor's office and told to resign. His employment with the defendant eventually ended after review of the decision by the defendant's personnel department, company president, and chairman of the board of trustees, but the plaintiff was not given the benefit of all of the procedures in the Supervisory Manual. A jury in Wayne Circuit Court . . . returned a verdict for the plaintiff of approximately $73,000 after the trial court denied the defendant's motion for a directed verdict of no cause of action. The Court of Appeals, D.C. Riley, P.J., and Bashara and Mahinske, JJ., reversed and instructed the trial court to enter a judgment for the defendant. Plaintiff appeals.

Opinion by Levin

Toussaint testified that he had been interviewed by and, on the date of his hire, met with an officer of Blue Cross who "indicated to me that as long as I did my job that I would be with the company" until mandatory retirement at age 65. The officer gave him a Supervisory Manual. Toussaint asked "how secure a job it was and [the officer] said that if I came to Blue Cross, I wouldn't have to look for another job because he knew of no one ever being discharged". On cross-examination he was asked "[did] you have an employment contract?" and responded "I certainly felt I did", and that the pertinent sections of the Supervisory Manual were part of "my contract".

* * *

Toussaint's case is, if anything, stronger because he was handed a manual of Blue Cross personnel policies which reinforced the oral assurance of job security. It stated that the disciplinary procedures applied to all Blue Cross employees who had completed their probationary period and that it was the "policy" of the company to release employees "for just cause only".

Our colleague [in the lower decision] acknowledges that, apart from an express agreement, an employee's legitimate expectations grounded in an employer's written policy statements have been held to give rise to an enforceable contract. He states, however, that the cases so holding are distinguishable because they concern deferred compensation (termination pay, death benefits and profit-sharing benefits) that "the employers should reasonably have expected would induce reliance by the employee in joining or remaining in the employer's service". He does not explain why an employer should reasonably expect that a promise of deferred compensation would induce reliance while a promise of job security would not.

Although the manual of personnel policies was handed to Toussaint in response to his inquiry regarding job security, our colleague concludes that the record is without "any evidence whatever that Mr. Toussaint relied" upon its provisions.

We hold that:

1. a provision of an employment contract providing that an employee shall not be discharged except for cause is legally enforceable although the contract is not for a definite term—the term is "indefinite," and

2. such a provision may become part of the contract either by express agreement, oral or written, or as a result of an employee's legitimate expectations grounded in an employer's policy statements.

3. In *Toussaint*, as in *Ebling*, there was sufficient evidence of an express agreement to justify submission to the jury.

4. A jury could also find for Toussaint based on legitimate expectations grounded in his employer's written policy statements set forth in the manual of personnel policies.

* * *

Decision and Outcome

The court reinstated the jury verdict of the trial court in which the jury found that an implied employment contract existed between Toussaint and Blue Cross Blue Shield.

Questions for Analysis

1. In light of decisions like this one, what should employers do if they want to maintain their discretion to hire and fire at will? Is it realistic to want to maintain that kind of discretion?

2. In many "Employee Manuals," employers copy the following legend: "These materials are not part of an employment contract. The relationship between The Company and The Employee is strictly on an at-will basis." Can employers really contend that they will treat employees fairly but maintain that the relationship is employment at will?

Public Policy: Whistle-Blower Protections

whistle-blower protections
Statutory prohibitions on the firing of workers for reporting hazardous products or law violations or engaging in other specific protected actions in support of public policy.

There are a number of statutes, including the Civil Rights Act of 1964, the Occupational Safety and Health Act of 1971, and the Clean Water Act of 1972, that specifically prohibit employers from retaliating against employees who report what they believe are violations of those statutes—that is, they provide whistle-blower protection. In other cases, courts have made decisions about whether the firing of an employee constitutes the common law tort of *wrongful discharge*. There have been a number of cases in which employees have been fired for reporting that

- The products of a company were unsafe or
- The employer was violating a law.

In addition, employees have been fired for serving on a jury or for having filed a workers' compensation claim. It is important to note that the public policy exception to the employment-at-will doctrine is narrow and is not intended to justify the airing of all sorts of grudges against employers. A plaintiff in a public policy (whistle-blower) exception case must be able to show that (1) the discharge contravenes some well-established public policy expressed in the constitution, statutes, or regulations and (2) no other remedy except for the disclosures was reasonably available. If the company has an internal procedure for handling employee complaints, but the plaintiff opts to go to the media instead to reveal what he or she believes is an unsafe design of a product, the plaintiff in a wrongful discharge suit will not be saved by the public policy exception.

Abusive Discharges

Plaintiffs who were employed at will have nevertheless successfully sued their employers for abusive discharges, particularly when there was evidence of sexual harassment. The

Ethical Challenges

What is the price of following your conscience? Although there have been noted cases where whistle-blowers followed their consciences and were recognized for their courage, there have been far more cases where the person blowing the whistle on misconduct by his or her employer was fired without recognition. It is clear blowing the whistle on your employer is a very high-risk action, though there are some statutes that protect whistle-blowers. For government employees, however, the stakes have recently been raised by the Senate Intelligence Authorization Act of 2001. The new law criminalizes government employees who reveal classified government information, but as is pointed out in the article below, much of the information that the government classifies is merely embarrassing to government officials and is not a threat to national security. The fear is that there will be far fewer disclosures of government boondoggles that should be revealed to taxpayers because the cost of getting caught has just been increased significantly.

A WHISTLEBLOWER'S NIGHTMARE

It now seems likely that President Clinton is going to sign an intelligence bill that, without a shred of public congressional testimony, will codify the most restrictive anti-whistleblowing penalties for government employees the nation has ever seen. If he does, early in the next session Congress should drag this insidious measure out into the public spotlight and repeal it.

The bill would make it a felony for government employees to leak any "properly classified" material. On the surface, that sounds like good common sense. Here's why it isn't:

- "Properly classified" is a term so ambiguous that it is likely to mean, at any given time, whatever the current U.S. attorney general thinks it means. Since the penalties run up to three years in federal prison, at the very least any such law should be codified in a way that can't be subject to individual whim.
- Federal laws already exist to protect material that could directly jeopardize national security.

Espionage statutes make it a criminal offense to disclose without authorization "national defense" information with the intention of helping a foreign power or harming the United States. Other laws make it a crime to release certain types of especially sensitive information. These include names of U.S. undercover intelligence operatives and information derived from intercepted communications.

- Although federal employees are officially the target of this draconian measure, it is really the public that is likely to be harmed. If all classified information has that kind of threat hanging over it, reporters are a lot less likely to get stories like the classics about $400 hammers and $6,000 coffee pots. And journalists who are handed such leaks are likely to be faced with subpoenas and potential jail time of their own if they don't divulge their sources.

This is not some poor-journalists-have-tough-lives lament. Members of Congress with conservative credentials no less impeccable than those of Rep. Henry Hyde, R-Ill., and Bob Barr, R-Ga., have expressed outrage.

Barr, for one, is no pushover when it comes to keeping secrets. The former CIA official and former U.S. attorney said the measure "will create—make no mistake about it, with not one day of hearings, without one moment of public debate, without one witness—an official secrets act."

Hyde, who chairs the House Judiciary Committee, quite rightly contends that a bill of such a sweeping nature should have come before that committee. Early next year, it probably will, even if the Democrats take control of the House. Rep. John Conyers Jr., D-Mich., who in that case would take the chairman's gavel, said he feels just as Hyde does.

This is a bad bill, an anti-public bill. We look forward to seeing Congress put it back under the magnifying glass. In public.

Source: *Omaha World-Herald,* October 26, 2000, available at http://www.freerepublic.com/forum/a39f97e6b19ca.htm.

theory that typically rationalizes an abusive discharge claim is that the employer made working conditions so heinous that an ordinarily reasonable woman could no longer work at that establishment. The other tort claim often used by plaintiffs in abusive discharge cases is that they were victims of *intentional infliction of emotional distress*. In order to prevail with such claims, the plaintiff must show (1) that the employer intentionally engaged in extreme and outrageous behavior and (2) that behavior resulted in severe emotional distress to the victim. The plaintiffs in such cases need not be victims of sexual harassment, but simply could be the object of ridicule and practical jokes on the job.

Other Limitations on the Application of the Employment-at-Will Doctrine

Employment Contracts and Collective Bargaining Agreements

Some private sector employees have employment contracts that do provide protection against arbitrary firings and, in fact, allow an employee to be fired only upon a showing of good cause. Good cause is usually explained in considerable detail in these contracts and some elements of due process are generally incorporated into the termination procedure. For example, an employment contract may require the employer to notify an employee if the company believes the employee's performance is unsatisfactory, then give the employee time to make changes. There may be requirements for documentation of lack of productivity or other "good" causes of separation from employment.

Similarly, in collective bargaining agreements, union members are generally protected from arbitrary firings. Under collective bargaining agreements, a company generally has to justify a firing, but the firing can be due to a downturn in demand for the products of the employer rather than the result of some claimed deficiency on the part of the fired worker. Outsourcing, which replaces jobs that would be held by company employees, along with layoffs, continues to be a significant cause of friction in industrial relations (addressed in some detail in the next chapter).

Government Employees

An employee working for any level of government has a protected interest that courts have held cannot be taken without some *due process* procedures. As a result, federal and state employees are not subject to employment-at-will status; for these workers, there must be a showing that their discharges were due to lack of productivity or for some other valid reasons. When government employees are discharged, they are entitled to be notified in advance and can request a hearing to state their side of the story.

Regulatory Constraints

In the United States today, hiring someone is a highly regulated act, even if the resulting employment relationship is at will. In addition to the prohibited actions listed above, it is important to keep in mind that employers are prohibited from discriminating in any term or condition of employment with respect to race, sex, religion, national origin, color, age, disability, or union status. In a number of states and cities, on-the-job discrimination based on sexual orientation is also illegal.

Even for workers who are employed in an at-will status, it is mandatory, based on numerous statutes, for employers not to be discriminatory on the bases of race, gender, age, or disability with respect to health and retirement benefits. Federal and state governments regulate hours, minimum wages, and overtime pay. There are worker safety acts and a workplace oversight bureaucracy that is very detail-oriented with regard to what constitutes a safe work environment. It is illegal for workers to agree with an employer to work in an unsafe work environment and it is illegal to agree not to file workers' compensation claims, which are administered by state agencies. Workers who are employed without an employment contract are, nevertheless, entitled to extensive benefits if they are terminated by their employers. They are entitled to a continuation of benefits enjoyed in their employment, as long as they pay for them, and also are entitled to unemployment compensation. If an employee works for more than one year for an employer, he or she is entitled to unpaid family medical leave, with a return to the job left at the end of the leave period. All of these regulatory statutes are discussed in the next two chapters.

Illegal Aliens, Guest Workers, and Job Security

Perhaps the most vulnerable sector of the workforce is composed of those who are in the U.S. illegally. Although there are illegal aliens from many countries, many of the *illegal aliens* come from south of the Mexican border. Currently, illegal aliens have little job security. Employers violate the Immigration Reform and Control Act (IRCA) of 1986 when they hire illegal aliens and are subject to fines that begin at $250 and increase to $5,000 for repeated violations. Employers are required by law to ask for identification, but if a prospective employee has a state-issued driver's license and a Social Security card, employers are prohibited from additional inquiries. It is quite obvious that many aliens are employed in the United States and many are working with false identification.

The real question is whether this portion of the workforce will continue working under the current set of rules, or whether they will be accorded guest worker status. Before the September 11, 2001, events, there was serious discussion of another amnesty for illegal aliens who had spent a significant amount of time in the United States. As illegal aliens, they have far fewer rights than working U.S. citizens or legal, resident aliens.

Summary

In an Agency Relationship, Principals Are Liable to Third Parties for the Torts and Contracts of Agents That Arise within the Agent's Scope of Authority

- A *principal* is liable to third parties for the torts committed and contracts executed by an agent acting within the agent's *scope of authority*.
- An agent is liable to third parties for torts committed, but not for contracts executed, within the agent's scope of authority.
- A principal is not liable for torts or contracts of agents that take place outside of the agent's scope of authority.
- An *agency* is the manifestation of consent by one person to act on behalf of and under the control of another.
- A *fiduciary relationship* exists when one person agrees to place the interests of another above his own for the duration of the fiduciary relationship.
- Employees are agents for a company and owe a *fiduciary duty* to their employer.
- An employer business is liable to third parties if an agent of the company is negligent within his or her scope of employment.

In General, Employers Are Not Liable for Torts of Independent Contractors, So It Is Important to Determine Whether a Person Hired Is an Employee or an Independent Contractor; an Agency Relationship Is Based on Consent, Except When

- In general, employers are not liable for torts of independent contractors unless the independent contractor was hired to perform *inherently dangerous* activities.
- There are a number of factors courts look at to determine whether an employer has hired an employee or contracted with an independent contractor. The most important factor is the *degree of control the employer maintains over the person*. The greater the control, the more likely the relationship is to be deemed an employment relationship.
- Among the other factors courts examine in determining whether the person hired is an independent contractor or an employee are the withholding of taxes, the identity of the supplier of needed tools, the industry in which the employer and the person employed are, the method of payment, and the level of required skill.
- An agency is formed if there is *consent* between two parties that one party will work on behalf of the other. An agency relationship does not require consideration.
- An agency can be created after the fact by *ratification*, when one party agrees to accept and be bound by actions performed on his behalf by another person.
- An *agency by estoppel* can exist when a third party *reasonably believes* that a purported agent is working on behalf of a purported principal. The principal must have done something to create the reasonable belief by the third party that the purported agent was working for him or her.

Ratification, Estoppel, or Operation of Law Is Involved	• An agency can be created by operation of law for public policy reasons, such as when a minor drives an automobile owned by his or her parents and is involved in an accident.
An Agent's Authority Is Expressed, Implied, or Apparent; Accompanying Obligations Apply Whether the Agency Is Disclosed, Partially Disclosed, or Undisclosed	• The scope of an agent's authority can be *express, implied,* or *apparent.* • Express authority is defined by the principal. • Implied authority is based on the reasonable belief of the agent supplemented by what is customary within the industry and by prior conduct between the two parties. • Apparent authority is based on reasonable belief of third parties, but must include some actions of the principal to inculcate such a belief. • Principals are liable for the actions of *fully disclosed, partially disclosed,* and *undisclosed* agents acting within their scope of authority. • Third parties are entitled to hold an undisclosed agent liable for actions and contracts of the agent. • Principals are generally liable for nonintentional actions of agents that are committed on the job within the agent's scope of authority.
Principals Can Be Liable for Intentional Torts of Agents if Agents Are Advancing the Interests of the Principal or the Principal Had Notice; Both Principals and Agents Owe Duties to Each Other, Except if the Agent Is Electronic	• A principal can be liable for the intentional torts of an agent if the agent was advancing the interests of the principal at the time of the tort and the principal had some notice that the agent had acted inappropriately in the past. • Other factors courts will consider are whether the principal or employer performed due diligence before hiring the employee and whether the principal supplied the means that enabled the employee to accomplish the intentional tort. • Agents owe *fiduciary duties* to principals, which include a duty to use reasonable diligence when performing on behalf of the principal, a duty to provide notice to the principal of job-related facts, a duty to avoid conflicts of interest, a duty to obey the instructions of the principal, and an accounting for any monies entrusted to or received by the agent. • Principals are obligated to compensate agents according to their agreement, to reimburse agents for expenses, and to indemnify them for any legal liability they incur while working for the principal. Principals also are obligated to cooperate with agents in their performance of their appointed tasks and to provide them with safe working conditions. • In general, principals are likewise liable for actions undertaken by *electronic agents* acting within their scope of authority. Electronic agents can bind companies to contracts unless the other party to the contract has reason to know that the electronic agent is malfunctioning.
Most Employees Do Not Have an Employment Contract, but Instead Work for Their Employers on an At-Will Basis; At-Will Employees Can Sue for Wrongful Discharge, Employment Discrimination, and Violation of Union Agreements and	• Many employment contracts are *at will,* which means that the employee can quit the job for any reason and the employer can fire the employee for any reason. • When companies provide their employees with manuals and other materials, some courts have found that these materials become part of *implied* employment contracts. • Even though an employee is employed on an at-will basis, he or she cannot be fired for *blowing the whistle* on an employer who is violating the law. • Employers can be sued for *wrongful discharge* for firing an employee who reports a violation of law. They can be sued for an *abusive discharge* if they terminate an employee who has been sexually harassed or otherwise mistreated. • Unionized employees are also protected from discharges without cause by *collective bargaining* agreements. • In general, government employees cannot be discharged without cause. • In addition there are regulatory limitations on discharging an employee based on race, sex, national origin, age, or disability.

on the Basis of Protections Granted to Government Workers

- Employers are prohibited by the Immigration Reform and Control Act from hiring illegal aliens, but noncompliance is widespread. If a prospective worker has a driver's license and one other form of ID, employers are required to accept the eligibility of the person for employment.

Key Terms

agency, *477*

apparent authority, *485*

electronic agents, *493*

employment at will, *497*

estoppel, *483*

express authority, *485*

family car doctrine, *483*

fiduciary duties, *490*

fiduciary relationship, *478*

implied authority, *485*

implied employment
   contract, *497*

independent contractor, *478*

principal, *478*

ratification, *483*

whistle-blower
   protections, *499*

Questions for Review and Analysis

1. Discuss the difference between an agent and an employee. What is the difference between an employee and an independent contractor? What is the difference between an agent and an independent contractor? When do these categories overlap, that is, can an employee also be an agent? Can an independent contractor also be an employee?

2. We've again run into the term *fiduciary relationship*. In this chapter, the application is to the duties of employees and agents to their employers. Select and carefully explain one action that a president of a company would or would not take because of her fiduciary duties to the company. Explain one action that a janitor of a company would or would not take because his fiduciary duties to the company.

3. Explain factors that are used by courts to decide the scope of authority of employees and agents. Why is it so important to identify the limit or scope of authority of employees and agents?

4. Explain the difference between implied authority and apparent authority.

5. Name five ways, discussed in the chapter, in which an employer can incur liability by firing an at-will employee.

If You Really Understood This Chapter, You Should Be Able to Provide Informed Commentary on the Following:

1. **Scope of Employment.** In this case, the defendant driver was an employee, negligent while driving, and the defendant's negligence was the cause of the plaintiff's injuries. As with most of the cases in this chapter, the case is not really about the defendant driver as it is clear that the driver was negligent. The important issue presented in this case is whether the driver's employer, Thermal Equipment, can be sued based on the claim that the driver was acting within his scope of employment at the time of the accident. The driver, Richard Lanno, was driving a company truck at the time of the accident, but the collision took place as Lanno was driving home. Thermal Equipment allowed Lanno to take the truck home because he was a trusted employee and patrons of Thermal called Lanno directly when they needed service. Thermal was aware that Lanno occasionally used their vehicle for personal use. When the actual accident occurred, Lanno was going to a store to pick up a few items before going home. For more than a century, however, employers have not been liable to third parties when its employees were coming or going to work. On the other hand, Lanno considered himself on call for Thermal and its customers 24 hours a day and on weekends. What do you think? Should Thermal have to pay for Lanno's negligence while Lanno was on a personal errand? [*Lazar v. Thermal Equipment Corp.,* 148 Cal.App.3d 458, 195 Cal. Rptr. 890 (1983).]

2. **Intentional Torts on the Job.** As with the previous case, this one is really about whether the employer is liable, in this instance, for intentional torts committed by an employee. Jerome Lange was the manager of a small grocery store in Minnesota that carried Nabisco products. Ronnell Lynch was employed by Nabisco as a cookie salesman-trainee and was assigned his own territory, which included Lange's store. Lynch was hired on March 1, 1969. Between his hiring date and

May 1, 1969, Nabisco received numerous complaints about Lynch for being overly aggressive. One of Lynch's favorite tactics was to place Nabisco inventory on shelf space reserved for other companies. In May of 1969, Lynch was called back to the plaintiff's store to rearrange merchandise that had previously been delivered and an argument erupted between plaintiff and Lynch. The plaintiff told Lynch to leave and he did, but not before he beat Lange and trashed the store. Nabisco claims that Lynch was acting outside his scope of employment when he committed the torts because Nabisco specifically prohibits employees from using violence on the job or violating criminal law. Plaintiff claims that the defendant was working for Nabisco at the time and was advancing the interests of Nabisco when the altercation occurred and that the employer had notice that Lynch was not stable. What do you think? [*Lange v. National Biscuit Co.,* 211 N.W.2d 783 (Minn. 1973).]

3. **Independent Contractors.** Whether a person hired by an employer is an independent contractor or an employee can have significant legal implications. As we know from the chapter, in general employers are liable for the torts of employees, but not for the torts of independent contractors. As discussed in the chapter, if an accident occurs that harms a third party, it is unlikely that the employee involved will have sufficient resources to compensate third-party victims for the injuries (or death). Where ambiguity exists, it is common for employers to designate people they hire as independent contractors, not only because of tort law implications but, also, because employees have more rights under law and are more expensive because of employer responsibilities for contributions to social security and for other taxes. Phoenix Newspapers, Inc. (PNI), hired Frausto and others to deliver newspapers under a Delivery Agent Agreement that stated Frausto and his fellow delivery people were "independent contractors." While delivering PNI's newspapers, Frausto struck the plaintiff, William Santiago, who was riding a motorcycle at the time. Frausto was required by his contract with PNI to personally deliver 75 percent of the newspapers he picked up at a central distribution point. If there were complaints, Frausto could be fired by PNI. Santiago claims Frausto is in fact an employee of PNI, but both the trial court and the court of appeals in Arizona dismissed Santiago's claims against PNI. What do you think? In effect, Frausto is an adult "paperboy." Are paperboys employees or independent contractors? [*Santiago v. Phoenix Newspapers, Inc.,* 794 P.2d 138 (Ariz. 1990).]

4. **Apparent Authority.** There are many situations in which an employer seeks to diminish its liability exposure by limiting the actual and implied authority of its employees or agents, only to find that their authority has been stretched by application of the apparent authority standard. Zbigniew Lambo and Scott Kennedy were employees of a securities company that was taken over by the defendant, Paulson Investment Co. Thereafter, both Lambo and Kennedy made sales presentations to Paulson customers, including some of the plaintiffs. Solicitations and sales of the unregistered securities involved in this case were made using Paulson's letterhead. The sale of unregistered securities is illegal under both federal and state securities law and was outside the authority of Lambo and Kennedy. Sales presentations were made at Paulson's office. Between August 11, 1982, and September 9, 1984, the plaintiffs (this is a class-action suit, so there are many plaintiffs) purchased the unregistered securities. The securities proved to be valueless. The defendant moves for a judgment notwithstanding the verdict claiming that it should not be liable for actions of its agents who were acting outside their actual and implied authority by selling unregistered securities. Plaintiffs claim Paulson is liable because Lambo and Kennedy had apparent authority to conduct such business. What do you think? [*Badger v. Paulson Investment Co.,* 803 P.2d 1178 (Or. 1991).]

5. **Negligent Hiring.** Suppose that an employer hires a truck driver who lies on his employment application when asked whether he had ever been arrested. In fact, the employee, Terry Taylor, has been arrested numerous times within the past 10 years for felony theft, assault, and lewd conduct. Altogether, Taylor has been convicted of three felonies in Colorado and also has an extensive arrest record in the state of Washington, where Taylor was employed when the events prompting this case took place. Three months after being hired, Taylor, contrary to company policies, stopped at a Holiday Inn; observed the plaintiff, Gracye Connes, working alone at the Holiday Inn as a night clerk; and sexually assaulted her. Connes sues Taylor's employer, Molalla Transport System, Inc. (Molalla), under the theory of negligent hiring. It is clear that Taylor was acting outside his scope of authority at the time of the assault. Molalla claims that it checked with former employers of

Taylor and checked his driving record. Plaintiff claims that Molalla should have checked Taylor's nonvehicular criminal record before putting someone that unstable out on the road. The Supreme Court of Colorado ruled against the plaintiff in this case [*Connes v. Molalla Transport System, Inc.*, 831 P.2d 1316 (Colo. 1992)], but, since that time, two events have taken place that might change the outcome if the case were to come to trial today:

1. Software is available that enables employers to easily check criminal records of employees and applicants and

2. In light of the scandals that have affected the Catholic Church and other organizations that deal with children, there seems to be much greater awareness of the serial nature of pedophiles and, likely, other sexual predators.

See if you agree with the reasoning of the Supreme Court of Colorado in the *Connes* case.

6. **Negligent Retention.** Mark Livigni, manager of a store owned by National Super Markets, Inc. (NSM), left his store one night but stopped by the store later to check on things. In the interim, Livigni had enjoyed a few alcoholic beverages. Livigni saw what he believed was inappropriate behavior by a 10-year-old boy outside the store. While chasing down the 10-year-old, Livigni pulled a four-year-old from a car and tossed him into the air, causing the boy (Ferris Bryant) to be injured. NSM claims that Livigni was acting outside his scope of employment and, therefore, that it is not liable for his actions. Bryant claims that NSM had notice that Livigni was potentially violent based on two incidents in a 17-year tenure with NSM:

1. Livigni once struck a fellow employee with an empty milk crate during an argument and

2. At the time of the incident, Livigni was on probation for striking his son and causing him to break his collarbone.

NSM claims it did not know about the domestic incident involving Livigni's son, but there is evidence that Livigni discussed the situation with co-workers. NSM claims that the milk crate incident was contested and that it had no reason to believe that Livigni was not an excellent employee. Should a company be imputed with knowledge of a domestic incident based on employee discussions and should this information be useable to infer that the company knew, or should have known, that Livigni was potentially violent? Does this make the company negligent in retaining him? [*Bryant v. Livigni*, 250 Ill. App. 3d 303, 619 N.E. 550 (Ill. App. Ct. 1993).]

Social Responsibility, Policy, and Ethics in a High-Tech World

7. **Responsibility of Principals for Actions Agents Were Told Not to Take.** Real estate agents and agencies are notorious for a form of racial profiling called "racial steering," which is the practice of steering prospective clients to different sections of town based on the race of the client. In 1987, the Leadership Council, a nonprofit organization located in Chicago, suspected the defendant, Matchmaker Real Estate Sales Center, Inc. (Matchmaker), of racial steering. In order to prove its case, the Leadership Council sent five testers, who were matched pairs of prospective clients who differed only by race, to Matchmarker to see how each group would be treated. In each case, the white testers were steered toward areas of Chicago that were primarily inhabited by whites with a like-pattern policy applied to the black testers, that is, they were steered to areas of Chicago where most of the residents were black. The sole stockholder of Matchmaker was Erwin Ernst, who (1) did not approve of racial steering and (2) set up policies and procedures to ensure that Matchmaker's agents complied with fair housing laws. Matchmaker also required its employees to attend fair housing training seminars and had organized support for fair housing laws and practices among real estate firms. Racial steering is illegal under at least two federal statutes, the 1866 Civil Rights Act and the Fair Housing Act of 1968. The City of Chicago, the Leadership Council, and the individuals involved in the testing sued Matchmaker's agents/employees involved in the racial steering. The plaintiffs also sued Ernst and Matchmaker. It is clear that, at the time of the racial steering, Matchmaker's employees were on the job. Should a real estate firm be liable for actions of its employees that it takes specific measures to ensure do not take place? If the employer is liable, what more could such an employer do, under the circumstances? Should an employer be liable for punitive damages for events that the employer does not know about? As a counterpoint, if its employee/agents make more sales by racial steering, who benefits? [*Chicago v. Matchmaker Real Estate Sales Center*, 982 F.2d 1086 (7th Cir. 1992).]

Using the Internet to Your Advantage

1. Some of the practical issues related to agency law are discussed in more detail at http://www.agencylaw.com/ than is available in the chapter. The 'Lectric Law Library provides a definition of *respondeat superior* at http://www.lectlaw.com/def2/q042.htm and of *fiduciary duty* at http://www.lectlaw.com/def/f026.htm. An article entitled "Legal Issues of Electronic Commerce: Activity Policies, Intelligent Agents and Ethical Transactions" appears at http://www.hytime.org/papers/higgins1.html.

2. The NOLO law center has a discussion of the law associated with hiring independent contractors at http://www.nolo.com/lawcenter/index.cfm/catID/EC0EEB1C-16EA-4F81-833ED5890B19383A. The NOLO center also has an article entitled "Proving a Worker Is Not an Employee" at: http://www.nolo.com/lawcenter/auntie/questions.cfm/objectID/2E7C9C67-3011-4CB2-BCE58BCD0B66A93F/catID/561FF7A5-12CD-4059-8EA7DE4254733BE3. The law associated with wrongful discharges is discussed by the SA&S site (sponsored by the law firm of Schmeltzer, Aptaker & Shepard) in an article entitled "Public Policy Wrongful Discharge Law Still in Flux," available at http://www.saspc.com/art_824.htm.

3. The Legal Information Institute at the Cornell University School of Law provides a law school level analysis of agency law at http://www.law.cornell.edu/topics/agency.html. A website dedicated to protecting whistle-blowers is located at http://www.whistleblower.org/. In many cases, whistle-blowers work at jobs on an at-will basis, but are protected by various statutes and the common law from being fired for reporting violations of law by employers.

Chapter **Sixteen**

Employment Law and Protection of Workers

Learning Objectives

After completing this chapter, you should

1. Know the basic legislation that provides protection for worker wages, benefits, and income after retirement or in the event of disability.
2. Be able to discuss worker safety legislation, including workers' compensation statutes and the Occupational Safety and Health Act.
3. Understand the laws that guarantee worker rights to organize and form unions, and procedures that both management and labor have available for filing complaints about unfair labor practices.
4. Understand and be able to cite examples of unfair labor practices.
5. Have a good understanding of legal and illegal techniques for monitoring employee performance. This should include knowledge of laws that deal with drug testing, polygraphs, and the monitoring of phone calls and e-mail.

OVERVIEW

As discussed in the last chapter, employing a worker is a highly regulated act in the United States, even if the person is hired on an employment-at-will basis with no explicit employment contract between the employer and employee. Employment law is a vast topic, so this chapter is restricted to a limited examination of the prominent parts of employment legislation, mainly at the federal level. Among the topics examined in this chapter are worker safety laws and other protective laws that apply to all workers. Attention is then directed to labor-management laws that protect rights of workers to organize and form unions. Finally, on-the-job privacy issues and legislation are addressed. The following chapter focuses on employment discrimination legislation.

INCOME PROTECTION LEGISLATION

Fair Labor Standards Act

During the Great Depression of the 1930s, a sizeable volume of worker protection legislation was enacted by Congress. Among the prominent acts of Congress passed were the Wagner Act, which provided the framework for allowing workers to organize into unions, and the Social Security Act, which provided for pensions for workers once they retire.[1] In 1938, Congress passed the Fair Labor Standards Act (FLSA), which supplied a floor for various dimensions of employment relationships.[2] The FLSA applies to all businesses engaged in interstate commerce or engaged in the production of goods destined for interstate commerce, so its reach is quite broad.

Minimum Wages and Overtime Pay

minimum wage
A legal requirement that employers must pay employees at least a minimum wage—that is, a minimum rate per hour—as defined by the Fair Labor Standards Act. The minimum wage has been adjusted upward numerous times since it began in 1938.

The FLSA provides the structure for setting a **minimum wage** for employees of all businesses subject to the act, effectively setting a floor for wages in the United States, given the breadth of FLSA coverage. Currently, the minimum wage in the United States is $5.15 per hour, but it has been adjusted upward numerous times in the past, as indicated clearly in the chart in the "Nutz and Boltz" box on page 510, and doubtless will continue to be adjusted upward in the future. While most workers are entitled to minimum wages, there are some categories of workers who are exempt. These include executives, administrative employees, professional employees (doctors and lawyers, among others), and outside salespersons. The FLSA also requires that covered employees be paid at "time and a half" for any hours worked in excess of 40 during a week (e.g., if the base wage is $10.00 per hour, the legally required overtime pay rate is $15.00 per hour). As with most federal legislation, the FLSA has been amended numerous times and is quite complicated, so businesspeople subject to FLSA requirements are well advised to have access to a labor lawyer.

Child Labor

The FLSA places severe limits on child labor. Under this act, children under 14 are essentially limited to delivering newspapers, babysitting, working for their parents, and engaging in some forms of agricultural labor. Except for work in these categories (delivering newspapers, etc.), it is illegal to hire a child under 14 to work for you. Children ages 14 to 16 are allowed to work, but only in nonhazardous jobs and with their on-the-job time limited to three hours daily during school days and eight hours during nonschool days. Most states require children under 16 to get work permits. Children between 16 and 18 are not subject to hour limitations, but are prohibited from working in hazardous occupations such as coal mining.

The Social Safety Net: Income Maintenance

In 1935, Congress passed the Social Security Act, which has provided income protection for workers ever since. There are several components to Social Security, including old age retirement income, disability income, and Medicare. The aspect of Social Security that most people are familiar with is the required contribution (tax) that must be paid under the Federal Insurance Contributions Act (FICA).[3] Required contributions are collected from both employees and employers and accumulated in a fund that is expected to pay out income when the covered employee retires.

---

[1] National Labor Relations Act of 1935 (Wagner Act), Pub. L. No. 74-198, codified at 29 U.S.C. §§ 151–169, and Social Security Act of 1935, Pub. L. No. 74-271, codified at 42 U.S.C. §§ 301–1397.

[2] Pub. L. No. 75-718, codified at 29 U.S.C. §§ 201–260.

[3] Codified at 26 U.S.C. §§ 3101–3125.

Nutz and Boltz

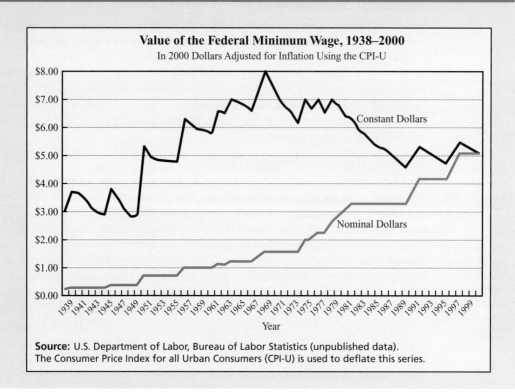

Value of the Federal Minimum Wage, 1938–2000

In 2000 Dollars Adjusted for Inflation Using the CPI-U

Source: U.S. Department of Labor, Bureau of Labor Statistics (unpublished data).
The Consumer Price Index for all Urban Consumers (CPI-U) is used to deflate this series.

Independent Contractors versus Employees

Currently, employees and employers each contribute 6.2 percent of the employee's gross (before tax) income up to an income level of $80,400 (a ceiling that is indexed upward yearly). When covered workers retire, they are entitled to benefits that are mathematically related to their contribution levels while working and are adjusted annually to track increases in the cost of living.[4] Employers do not have to pay Social Security taxes for independent contractors, which is one important economic reason for employers preferring that status for some of the people they hire. The IRS has devised various criteria for determining whether a worker is an employee, rather than an independent contractor. For workers, of course, employers have to contribute to Social Security if, in fact, the person working for them is an employee. Many of the tests devised by the IRS for determining whether a person is an employee or an independent contractor are based on common law principles of agency law, discussed in the previous chapter.

In addition to retirement income, Social Security provides some minimal income for people who become disabled. According to the Social Security Administration, "The definition of disability in the Social Security law is a strict one. To be eligible for benefits, a person must be unable to do any kind of substantial gainful work because of a physical or mental

---

[4] If you contribute more toward Social Security than some lower-income person, you will get higher Social Security checks when you retire, but the increments will not be proportional to the differences in income. If A earned twice as much as B and both were under the Social Security cap during their entire careers, A would have contributed twice what B contributed, but A's Social Security check upon retirement would be well short of twice the amount of B's Social Security check.

impairment (or a combination of impairments), which is expected either: to last at least 12 months, or to end in death." In addition, the Social Security Administration operates the Medicare system for people 65 and older. Both employers and employees contribute 2.9 percent of the employee's gross income to Medicare. In contrast to requirements for retirement and disability contributions under Old-Age, Survivors, and Disability Insurance (OASDI—the formal name for the Social Security Act), however, there is no cap on the salary level subject to required Medicare contributions.

Regulation of Private Pension Plans: Employee Retirement Income Security Act (ERISA)

Social Security retirement income is barely adequate for an austere lifestyle and most workers augment their Social Security retirement income with pension plans. In 1974 Congress passed the Employee Retirement Income Security Act (ERISA) to regulate the administration of private pension plans.[5] ERISA does not require that every employer have a pension plan, but it subjects those employers that do to ERISA regulations, which are quite extensive and complicated. ERISA was created to accomplish two primary objectives:

1. To prevent workers who have been employed by a firm for a long time from having their pensions forfeited by some obscure rule.
2. To protect against the loss of pension funds by preventing fund mismanagement and by providing a backup insurance program for retirement fund losses.

vested
A person's right to retirement benefits is vested when the right to those benefits cannot be terminated even if the employee changes jobs, is laid off, or is fired.

unemployment compensation
A state program that compensates workers who are laid off, usually at a percentage of wages for a period of time. Often, unemployment compensation is established at 50 percent of the former employee's wages for a period of six months.

The first objective, preventing workers from having their pension benefits forfeited, is accomplished largely through regulation of *vesting requirements.* Once an employee is **vested,** the employee has a legal right to pension assets in accordance with the details of his or her pension plan. ERISA requires that (1) an employee have a vested right to all of his or her own contributions to the pension plan immediately and (2) the employee must be vested, and thus entitled to share in employer contributions, within five years of employment. In contrast to Social Security, ERISA requires that private pension plans be *fully funded* so that, if the sponsoring company goes bankrupt, its employees will still have their earned pension benefits. ERISA also requires contributions from pension plans to the government-operated insurance plan (the Pension Benefit Guaranty Corporation) so that, if a pension plan of a company is mismanaged and becomes bankrupt, funds are available for the company's retirees, past and prospective. Finally, ERISA extensively regulates terminations of pension plans.

Protection for Workers after Termination of Employment

Over 96 percent of workers in the United States qualify for **unemployment compensation.** Unemployment compensation is provided through a partnership between the federal

---

[5] Pub. L. No. 93-406, codified at 29 U.S.C. §§ 1001 *et seq.*

and state governments. At the federal level, the Social Security Act provides broad guidelines for the unemployment compensation program. Actual administration of the program is mainly through state agencies. All states have unemployment compensation plans and, typically, these plans provide for a maximum of six months of income payments to unemployed workers. During the prescribed time span, an unemployed worker is entitled to income payments equal to 50 percent of his or her former wages, up to set maximums.[6] Employers are taxed at the state level to fund unemployment compensation and the rates paid are directly proportional to the stability of the workforce for that employer. So employers are taxed lower amounts for unemployment compensation if they have relatively few layoffs and relatively few workers who qualify for unemployment compensation.

misconduct
Willful or wanton conduct on the part of an employee, such as fighting or stealing from the employer, that results in termination of employment and disqualification for unemployment benefits.

Not every unemployed worker is entitled to unemployment benefits. An ex-employee who voluntarily quits a job is not entitled to unemployment compensation. Neither is an ex-employee entitled to those benefits if he or she was terminated for **misconduct**. Misconduct can best be described as willful or wanton behavior, such as getting in a fight on the job or stealing from the employer. Mere incompetence or negligence by an employee, however, will not disqualify that employee from unemployment compensation. If an employee is fired for making a big mistake on the job, that employee is still entitled to unemployment compensation.

RETENTION OF HEALTH BENEFITS

COBRA, 1995

After a worker has been separated from employment, for whatever reason, he or she is in a very vulnerable situation and often does not have the financial means to subscribe to a new health plan. If the former employer had a health plan in which the ex-employee participated, COBRA (Consolidated Omnibus Budget Reconciliation Act of 1985) allows the ex-employee to continue paying premiums to stay on the employer's health plan for a period of 18 to 36 months.[7] There are substantial financial penalties for employers who violate COBRA requirements.

Health Insurance Portability and Accountability Act (HIPAA), 1996

Health care insurers, even those provided through employers, typically exclude coverage for "preexisting" conditions. In other words, if a health care insurer takes on a new client who has, say, a chronic backache, the insurer would not have to pay benefits to the insured (client) for that ailment. The common practice of excluding preexisting medical conditions has had the effect of freezing many workers at their existing jobs because, if they switched jobs, they would lose their health care coverage for the medical conditions that arose during the time they worked for their current employer. The Kennedy-Kassebaum Act, otherwise known as the Health Insurance Portability and Accountability Act (HIPAA), guarantees that if a worker transfers from one health plan to another in connection with changing jobs, he or she will not be excluded from the health plan of the new employer regardless of whether the worker has preexisting health condition.[8]

---

[6] If a professional athlete making $500,000 per year was laid off, unemployment compensation for the six-month period would be nowhere near $125,000 (500000/2 = 250000 * .5 = 125,000) because of maximum income caps on unemployment compensation coverage.

[7] Pub. L. No. 99-272, codified at 29 U.S.C. §§ 1161–68.

[8] Pub. L. No. 104-191, codified at 42 U.S.C. §§ 1329 *et seq.*

Family and Medical Leave Act (FMLA), 1993

The Family and Medical Leave Act (FMLA) allows employees to take unpaid leave for up to three months for certain specified medical and family crisis events, such as births, medical problems, and caring for sick relatives.[9] FMLA applies only to employers who have more than 50 employees and, for such employers, only for full-time employees, defined as those who worked more than one year for that employer and who have worked more than 1,250 hours during the year prior to taking leave. In addition, employees whose salaries are in the top 10 percent of the workforce are not covered by the act, which means they have no legal right to take unpaid leave for three months with a guarantee that they can resume working at their former jobs when they return.

The key provision of FMLA is that an employee is guaranteed his or her same position upon returning from taking time off pursuant to FMLA. In general, the minimum leave allowed under the FMLA is three days, but there are exceptions even for that amount of time if the employee has a chronic condition such as asthma or AIDS. If the medical condition giving rise to a leave is foreseeable, the employer is entitled to 30 days' notice. For employers who violate the FMLA, the employee is entitled to collect unpaid wages plus benefits, and the employer may be required to reinstate the employee. Employees also are entitled to sue for extra medical expenses incurred while not taking leave when qualified under the act, plus court costs and attorney fees. The "damages" incurred can be doubled if a court decides the violation was egregious or willful.

WORKER SAFETY LEGISLATION

Near the beginning of the twentieth century, worker safety became an increasingly visible issue. In part, this was because the common law principles of negligence, contributory negligence, assumption of risk, and related doctrines produced results associated with injuries and deaths that most regarded as unsatisfactory. During this time period few, if any, employers offered health care benefits. Worker injuries on the job often literally caused families to go to the "poor house"—what today we would call homeless shelters. The legal system did not protect such workers because employers could generally defend a claim by the injured worker that the workplace was unsafe by showing that, instead, negligence of the injured worker or of coworkers was the cause of the injuries. In addition, even at that time, lawyers were expensive. Large companies (employers) could afford to hire them, whereas most injured employees could not.

Workers' Compensation Statutes

States took the lead in protecting workers on the job by enacting workers' compensation acts, many of which were passed in the early part of the twentieth century. Every state now has a workers' compensation statute that provides compensation for workers injured on the job. The idea behind workers' compensation is to place full liability for an on-the-job injury on the employer while, in return, with a very few exceptions, eliminating the rights of injured workers to go to civil courts and sue employers for damages. There are several other features of workers' compensation laws that merit noting, including

- *Damages are fixed by statute* so that the variance of damage awards is reduced. So, for example, if a worker loses an arm in an accident on the job, there is a dollar-denominated damage award already established by the commission that administers workers' compensation.

[9] Pub. L. No. 103-3, codified at 29 U.S.C. §§ 2601–2654.

- *Workers' compensation is financed by contributions (taxes collected) from employers* paid to a private insurer or state fund, though most state statutes allow employers to self-finance (self-insure) if they have sufficient financial resources.
- *Employers who have fewer accidents at their work sites are taxed less,* so there is a financial incentive for employers to be safety conscious.
- *The system is supposed to work in a lawyer-free environment,* but lawyers specializing in workers' compensation claims have shown that they can usually raise damage awards substantially. Hence, many claimants (injured workers) choose to be represented by lawyers.

Qualifications for Recovery under Workers' Compensation

In the past, to qualify for workers' compensation, an injury had to occur on the job or in the course of employment, *and* the injury had to be *accidental.* The requirement of *accidental injury* has been relaxed in a number of states, which now *only require that injuries occur on the job* to qualify. Thus, in many states, workers can recover for occupational illnesses that, by and large, do not occur because of accidents on the job but rather are the result of working conditions.

On the Job or in the Course of Employment

Disagreements over whether an accident has occurred on the job or not are another source of litigation. If a worker is going to or from work and an accident occurs, the worker *is not entitled* to compensation from workers' compensation. However, if the employee is performing some kind of special errand for the employer, such as picking up a cake for a company party, then the employee is entitled to file for workers' compensation, even though the accident and injury occur outside the work site. Traveling salespeople have been able to recover for injuries that occurred in bars or at motels, because the courts have held that the injuries arose "in the course of employment."

In general, workers' compensation laws prohibit workers from taking employers to civil court unless there is evidence that the employer *intentionally harmed* the employee, which is rare. In addition, employees are not entitled to recover workers' compensation for injuries that are *self-inflicted,* though workers are entitled to recover if their injuries are due to their own negligence.

Damage Awards

Workers' compensation laws generally call for immediate recovery for medical bills and wage replacement as a percentage of weekly wages. Generally, the percentage of weekly wages awarded as damages by workers' compensation laws does not vary from injury to injury within a state. So, if one worker is blinded on the job while another loses a foot, both will receive, say, 50 percent of their pre-injury wages, but the number of weeks will vary. It is plausible that a worker who is blinded will receive 50 percent of his wages for three years, while a worker who loses a foot will receive compensation for only one year. In some states, workers are entitled to a lump sum as compensation for loss of function, such as loss of a leg or sight. Many states provide vocational retraining if an injured worker is unable to return to a former position.

Statute of Limitations

Generally, to have injury claims covered, workers must notify their employers of their claims within 30 days of injury and must file any claim to a workers' compensation board within a set time span. Generally, the time limit is between 60 days and two years of the time when the accident or injury was first noticed, rather than when the events giving rise to the claim first occurred. Suppose that Sam, loading furniture onto a truck, feels a twinge in his back but continues working that day and for the next six months, during which time the condition of his back deteriorates. Sam visits his doctor at the end of this time span, who tells him that he must quit heavy lifting. If the state workers' compensation statute requires that an employee file a claim within 60 days, Sam would have 8 months (60 days plus the six months before the injuries were evident) from the time of injury, under the facts given, to file a claim.

Occupational Safety and Health Act of 1970

In 1970 Congress passed the Occupational Safety and Health Act (OSH Act), the enabling act that created OSHA (OSH Administration).[10] OSHA is notorious for providing very detailed regulations with regard to on-the-job safety standards, but is also very highly praised for reducing rates of on-the-job injuries. In December of 2000, the U.S. Bureau of Labor Statistics (BLS) indicated that "The incidence rate for on-the-job injuries and illnesses in private industry fell to 6.3 cases per 100 equivalent full-time workers in 1999, down from 6.7 cases in 1998." It further indicated that this was a continuation of an ongoing trend, and that the incidence rate had dropped steadily from 8.5 cases per 100 full-time workers in 1994 to the 1999 value. This trend is reflected in the BLS chart reproduced in the "Nutz and Boltz" box on page 516.

To a substantial degree, the OSH Act is consistent with the common law, which imposes a general duty to provide a safe work environment for employees. However, under the OSH Act, none of the common law defenses against liability, such as contributory negligence or assumption of risk, are allowable. If a worker is injured on the job, employers can be liable under the OSH Act for either violating a specific worker safety regulation promulgated by OSHA or for violating the *general duty* to provide a safe work environment.

Source: Copyright © 1997 Ted Goff.

Reporting (Whistle-Blower) Protections and Reporting Requirements Imposed on Businesses

OSHA normally enforces its regulations by responding to complaints from unions or workers that a work environment is unsafe. The OSH Act has antiretaliation provisions, which

[10] Pub. L. No. 91-596, codified at 29 U.S.C. §§ 553, 651–678.

Nutz and Boltz   Incidence Rate for Workplace Injuries and Illnesses, Private Industry, 1994–99

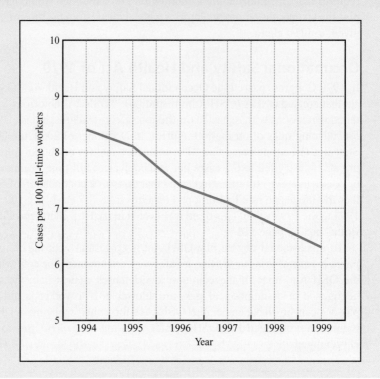

prevent an accused business from firing or otherwise retaliating against an employee who complains to OSHA about unsafe working conditions. In many hazardous situations, there is insufficient time to resolve worker concerns about safety through a complaint process. In such situations, the OSH Act allows workers to refuse orders to work in a setting where the workers, in good faith, believe there is a serious risk of injury or death. Such a refusal is, again, protected from job sanctions.

Businesses are required to maintain injury and illness records for each employee and these reports must be made available to OSHA inspectors. In addition, businesses have self-reporting requirements applicable to significant incidences of injury. If an employee is killed by an on-the-job injury, or if more than five employees are hospitalized in one accident, the employing business must report directly to OSHA within 48 hours.

Generally, for business management students and teachers, worker safety issues may be quite important, but they don't pose a threat to our own personal well-being. Of course, many workers are confronted by on-the-job safety issues in far more threatening ways. Case 16-1 deals with two workers who made up their own minds about the safety conditions they faced on the job, then suffered on-the-job repercussions as a result. The case is about the workers contesting the reprimands they received from their employer for refusing to follow orders when they feared for their lives while working.

Case 16-1

Whirlpool Corp. v. Marshall, Secretary of Labor

Supreme Court of the United States
445 U.S. 1 (1980)

BACKGROUND AND FACTS

Section 11(c)(1) of the Occupational Safety and Health Act of 1970 (Act) prohibits an employer from discharging or discriminating against any employee who exercises "any right afforded by" the Act. Respondent Secretary of Labor promulgated a regulation providing that, among other rights protected by the Act, is the right of an employee to choose not to perform his assigned task because of a reasonable apprehension of death or serious injury coupled with a reasonable belief that no less drastic alternative is available. Claiming that a suspended wire-mesh screen in petitioner's manufacturing plant used to protect employees from objects occasionally falling from an overhead conveyor was unsafe, two employees of petitioner refused to comply with their foreman's order to perform their usual maintenance duties on the screen. They were then ordered to punch out without working or being paid for the remainder of their shift, and subsequently received written reprimands, which were placed in their employment files. Thereafter, OSHA, represented by Secretary of Labor Marshall, brought suit in Federal District Court, alleging that Whirlpool's actions against the two employees constituted discrimination in violation of § 11(c)(1) of the Act, and seeking injunctive and other relief. While finding that the implementing regulation justified the employees' refusals to obey their foreman's order, the District Court nevertheless denied relief, holding that the regulation was inconsistent with the Act and therefore invalid. The Court of Appeals reversed and remanded, agreeing that the employees' actions were justified under the regulation but disagreeing with the conclusion that the regulation was invalid.

Opinion: Mr. Justice Stewart Delivered the Opinion of the Court

* * *

As this case illustrates . . . circumstances may sometimes exist in which the employee justifiably believes that the express statutory arrangement does not sufficiently protect him from death or serious injury. Such circumstances will probably not often occur, but such a situation may arise when (1) the employee is ordered by his employer to work under conditions that the employee reasonably believes pose an imminent risk of death or serious bodily injury, and (2) the employee has reason to believe that there is not sufficient time or opportunity either to seek effective redress from his employer or to apprise OSHA of the danger.

Nothing in the Act suggests that those few employees who have to face this dilemma must rely exclusively on the remedies expressly set forth in the Act at the risk of their own safety. But nothing in the Act explicitly provides otherwise. Against this background of legislative silence, the Secretary has exercised his rulemaking power under 29 U.S.C. § 657 (g)(2) and has determined that, when an employee in good faith finds himself in such a predicament, he may refuse to expose himself to the dangerous condition, without being subjected to "subsequent discrimination" by the employer.

* * *

For these reasons we conclude that 29 CFR § 1977.12 (b)(2) (1979) was promulgated by the Secretary in the valid exercise of his authority under the Act. Accordingly, the judgment of the Court of Appeals is affirmed.

Decision and Outcome

The U.S. Supreme Court held that the Secretary of Labor was within his powers in enacting a regulation that allowed workers, who in good faith believed they were in imminent danger, to refuse a command from a supervisor and not suffer on-the-job punishment.

Questions for Analysis

1. When the court refers to subsequent discrimination by the employer, what is the court talking about? Is the court just using legalese to describe on-the-job sanctions?

2. Does this case ratify the proposition that workers can walk off the job anytime that they believe conditions are unsafe? What limitations did the U.S. Supreme Court place on unilateral actions by employees to prevent abuse?

3. Was the employer contending that that the Secretary of Labor acted outside his scope of authority in enacting a regulation that allowed employees to decide when it was too dangerous to work?

OSHA Inspections

Normally, with a report of an unsafe working condition that appears credible, OSHA will send an inspector. An inspection by an OSHA official is considered a government search and the Fourth Amendment applies. Under this amendment, the company can refuse to allow the OHSA inspector on the premises.[11] If the government can demonstrate probable cause that an OSHA regulation has been violated by the company, it can obtain a search warrant and inspect for violations. In most instances, company management cooperates with OSHA and the parties, including employee representatives, management, and OSHA, to work out a settlement. If the parties cannot agree, OSHA may file a complaint against the company. If the company does not accept an ensuing decision of the administrative law judge of OSHA, it can appeal to OSHRC and, ultimately, to the federal courts.

INDUSTRIAL RELATIONS

Extent of Unionization

Few would doubt the claim that labor–management law is important in the U.S. economy, but a few facts are appropriate to put this claim in perspective. In the 1950s and 1960s, approximately one-fourth of the workforce was unionized; today the figure is about 14 percent. Some of the sectors of the economy that were heavily unionized historically—manufacturing, mining, and transportation—have experienced a prolonged and sizeable decline in the percentage of total employment they account for in the United States. In contrast, the service sector of the private market economy, including the information technology subsector, has been growing rapidly and is largely union-free. The areas of greatest growth for **unions** have been government employees, mainly at the state, county, and city levels. Approximately 37 percent of government workers are unionized. Other occupational classes in which unions continue to be strong include musicians, actors, professional athletes, and a number of professional groups such as nurses, flight attendants, pilots, and airline mechanics.

unions
Organizations of workers that focus on improving wages and other terms and conditions of employment for workers.

In some industries, the influence of unions continues to be strong, but in many others it is largely absent. The future of unionization is anyone's guess, but what is clear is that (1) unions are less a factor today than previously and (2) future trends are not favorable for unions. The South has always had less prevalence of unions than the Northeast and the population in the South has continued to swell relative to that in the Northeast. Producers who rely on unionized manufacturing workers in the United States have a difficult time competing with manufacturing operations in Third World countries, further eroding the impact of unions as this prompts additional flows of jobs from higher-cost U.S. plants to lower-cost

---

[11] Involuntary warrantless searches were held unconstitutional by the U.S. Supreme Court in *Marshall v. Barlow's, Inc.,* 436 U.S. 307 (1978).

foreign plants. Even with a reduced level of clout, it is important to be familiar with organized labor and the labor laws that are the product of decades of labor–management interactions. These laws affect all employers in the United States as "organizing" can take place at any work site. It is also notable that labor laws have the additional role of protecting *concerted activities* by *nonunion employees*. So managers in the twenty-first century still must be cognizant of the main forms of labor laws.

Labor Laws

The history of worker efforts to organize (unionize) is fraught with violence and hard-fought legislative victories. In the early part of the twentieth century, courts often applied antitrust laws (discussed in Chapter 19) against unions, treating them as conspiracies in restraint of trade. Arguably, the first significant labor law was the Railway Labor Act of 1926, which recognized workers' right to organize without interference from employers, though its breadth of application was limited.[12] In 1932, Congress passed the Norris–LaGuardia Act, which was not restricted in its application just to one industry.[13] This act contained several key provisions, including sections that

1. Outlawed yellow dog contracts, which were contracts employers offered to workers that called for them to be fired if they joined a union.
2. Severely restricted the ability of the federal courts to issue injunctions to unions involved in peaceful strikes.
3. Recognized the right of workers to engage in peaceful strikes, boycotts, and pickets.

National Labor Relations Act, 1935

The National Labor Relations Act (NLRA), often called the Wagner Act, is the comprehensive legislation that still regulates industrial relations today, though it has been amended numerous times since 1935. The act established the National Labor Relations Board, which serves as a kind of industrial umpire that labor and management can come to when they think unfair labor practices are occurring. The NLRA statutorily established the right of unions to organize, strike, and engage in collective bargaining agreements in which a union was the sole representative for workers. The act applies to employees and job applicants, but not to management.

Section 7 of the NLRA not only recognizes the right of workers to organize and form unions, but also protects concerted activities of nonunionized workers to organize for "other mutual aid or protection." Section 8 of the act identifies several employer labor practices that are deemed to be "unfair." Among these are

- *Interference* with efforts of employees to form, join, or assist labor organizations or to *engage in concerted activities* for mutual aid or protection.
- *Domination of a labor organization by management.* Management is not allowed to organize a union or participate in any way with union decision making.
- *Discrimination in hiring* or tenure to influence union membership or discourage union activities.
- *Refusal by management to bargain collectively* with duly designated union representatives.

Clearly, the NLRA serves as a foundation for workers to influence the workplace in a structured and organized way.

---

[12] Codified at 45 U.S.C. §§ 151–188.
[13] Codified at 29 U.S.C. §§ 101–115.

Taft-Hartley Act, 1947

By 1947, there was a perception that the NLRA had tipped the balance in industrial relations toward labor, with labor represented as having engaged in widespread abuses. The Taft-Hartley Act addressed this concern by identifying various unfair (hence prohibited) labor practices that could be engaged in by unions, including[14]

- *Closed union shops,* where, in order to be hired, an employee had to be a union member.
- *Secondary boycotts,* through which one union would support another by refusing to handle nonunion goods. Prior to this act, unionized truckers often would refuse to haul goods produced at a plant where a strike was taking place. It also has application to *common situs picketing* on construction sites in which one union would try to shut down all construction at a site until its disagreement with management was resolved.

The Taft-Hartley Act also allowed states to pass so-called right-to-work legislation.[15] Under **right-to-work laws,** even if a union is designated as the sole bargaining agent for employees at a location or for a craft, other workers at the plant do not have to join the union. In states that did not pass right-to-work laws, **union shops** were common, which required new workers to join the union if the union is the designated sole bargaining representative and the union shop is part of the collective bargaining agreement.

Landrum-Griffin Act, 1959

Responding to widespread evidence of union corruption and infiltration by organized crime, Congress passed the Landrum-Griffin Act, which provided for monitoring of the internal affairs of unions to ensure that they were being operated in a democratic manner, free from violence or the threat of violence.[16] Under this act, communists and ex-convicts are prohibited from holding offices in unions. Union management of pension plans and other union funds is strictly regulated and union officials are held accountable to members. Rank-and-file members were guaranteed the right to nominate officers and participate in union meetings. In addition, the ban on secondary boycotts was strengthened and extended, and the practice of picketing for purposes of obtaining recognition was made illegal.

National Labor Relations Board

As mentioned above, the NLRB (Board) operates as an umpire when disputes arise in connection with labor management relations. The NLRB has authority to hear complaints about unfair labor practices from either employees or management of any business that involves or affects interstate commerce, which is almost every sizeable business. Excluded from coverage of the NLRB are airlines and railway companies, which have their own regulatory agencies. Illustratively, there is a Railway Labor Act with provisions very similar to those of the NLRA.

When a complaint is filed with the NLRB, it is adjudicated by an administrative law judge who issues a decision based on his or her finding of facts and interpretation of the NLRA, prior precedents, and relevant court decisions. There is a six-month statute of limitations for complaints of unfair labor practices unless, for some reason, the complaining

right-to-work laws
Under the Taft-Hartley Act of 1947, states have the right to choose to be right-to-work states in which union shops are illegal. If a union wins a certification election, workers in the bargaining unit cannot be forced to join the union.

union shops
In states that do not elect to be right-to-work states, unions that win certification elections can compel all workers they bargain for to join the union and pay dues.

---

[14] Labor Management Relations Act (Taft-Hartley Act), codified at 29 U.S.C. §§ 141–197.

[15] The following states are right-to-work states: Alabama, Arizona, Arkansas, Florida, Georgia, Idaho, Iowa, Kansas, Louisiana, Mississippi, Nebraska, Nevada, North Carolina, North Dakota, Oklahoma, South Carolina, Tennessee, Texas, Utah, Virginia, and Wyoming.

[16] Labor-Management Reporting and Disclosure Act (Landrum-Griffin Act), Pub. L. No. 86-257, codified at 29 U.S.C. § 401 *et seq.*

Nutz and Boltz NLRB Says Temp Workers Can Have a Voice at Work

Temporary workers—who are routinely denied a voice at work—won a major victory Aug. 30 with a National Labor Relations Board ruling that more widely opens the door for temp workers to join unions at their workplaces.

Under earlier rulings, temp workers needed permission from both the employment agency that assigned them to the workplace and the client company before they could join a union. The new ruling allows temp workers to join a union with permanent employees that they work beside without sign-off from the workplace company and the temp agency.

In its ruling, the board wrote that the temporary workers, "are being effectively denied representational rights guaranteed under the National Labor Relations Act."

AFL-CIO President John Sweeney called the ruling "an important step in addressing the rights of contingent workforce employees, who have too often been relegated to second-class status and rights—if any."

Many companies use temporary employees to avoid hiring permanent, full-time workers, yet keep the workers for long periods of time. The temporary workers may be doing the exact same job as permanent employees, but they are paid less, provided with fewer, if any benefits, and until the NLRB ruling, had few rights to choose a voice at work.

The number of temporary jobs is skyrocketing. The U.S. General Accounting Office reported a 577 percent increase in temp jobs between 1982 and 1998, yet overall employment increased by just 47 percent.

Source: http://www.aflcio.org/aboutunions/ns0831a2000.cfm.

party (often a union) did not have knowledge of the alleged unfair labor practice, in which case it has six months from the time it discovered the act.

At a hearing before the NLRB, all sides (unions, management, NLRB inspector) to the dispute can present evidence. The decision of the administrative law judge is final unless either side appeals to members of the NLRB (there are five members of this independent administrative agency). If there is an appeal, the Board then reviews the case and may hear oral arguments from the litigants. Once the Board issues its decision, either side can appeal to the relevant U.S. court of appeals and, ultimately, to the U.S. Supreme Court. Over the years, the U.S. Supreme Court has rendered many opinions on critical issues affecting labor–management issues. The NLRB is a very active institution and its involvement in the workplace is broad and pervasive, as illustrated by the "Nutz and Boltz" box.

Certification and Decertification Elections

The basic purpose of a union organizing effort is to gain *certification* as the sole bargaining agent for workers at a location or for a craft. In order to be certified, the union must get a majority of workers in the relevant category to vote for it to represent them. In recent years, some companies have organized and promoted decertification elections. These are elections by workers to rescind the authority of their union to represent them. As with a certification election, decertification of a union requires a majority of employees' votes. In this set of activities, the primary job of the NLRB is to supervise certification and decertification elections. It is in connection with these elections that most complaints of unfair labor practices occur.

Authorization Cards

The first step in a union organization effort is to get at least 30 percent of the relevant workers to sign an authorization card. The authorization card indicates that the signer agrees that there should be an election to determine whether employees are to be represented by a union. Once union organizers obtain authorizations from more than 30 percent of the workforce, they can present the cards to the regional NLRB office along with a petition for an election.

Appropriate Bargaining Unit

When the NLRB receives authorization cards together with a petition for an election, the NLRB must identify specifically the appropriate bargaining unit. In its petition for an election, the union will propose the contours of the union. The criterion for determining whether a group of workers can be linked together in a union is **mutuality of interest,** which means that groups of workers with conflicting interests cannot be joined together as a union. For example, truckers and railroad workers have conflicting interests because what helps one group harms the other group in terms of demand for their services.

mutuality of interests
A concept the NLRB uses to determine which group of workers belongs in the same bargaining unit. If a group of workers wants a certification election and has a mutuality of interest, then the NLRB will designate the group as a bargaining unit.

Union Elections

Union elections are a lot like political campaigns, which are known for excessive promises, dire predictions, and overblown rhetoric. The competition to represent workers is decided by a majority vote and, if the vote is adverse to the union, there must be a minimum of one year before another election can be held. Of course, unions are expected to abide by labor laws in their pursuit of certification. Prohibited activities that are listed as unfair labor practices under Section 8(a) of the Wagner Act are general and courts have had to interpret the meaning of those prohibitions on a case-by-case basis.

No-Trespass Policies

Access to employees at their work site is often a key to deciding who will win a certification election. If union representatives can gain access to workers on the job, they will have better attendance and more worker interest in their message than if they announce that a meeting will be held after working hours at a different location. Often, a local union that is trying to organize workers will bring in representatives from the affiliated national union who may have developed superior speaking skills, but are not employees of the targeted employer. Imagine that the vice president of the United Mine Workers (UMW) is a particularly gifted speaker and that local organizers want to expose the maximum amount of coal miners to him.[17] A number of questions arise, including the following:

1. Can the employer enforce a no-trespass policy that excludes the vice president of the UMW from the mine and premises owned or leased by the mining company? The answer to this question is a clear yes.

2. Can the employer exclude the vice president of the UMW from grounds controlled by the employer, but still allow other groups such as charities or antiunion speakers to address employees on the job. The answer is a clear no.

As a result of several court decisions, employers can enforce a nondiscriminatory, no-trespass policy. However, if unions are not allowed access to workers, the employer cannot select other groups to address employees on the work site. In addition, if employee/union members circulate pro-union literature during breaks, the employer cannot interfere with that activity nor retaliate against such employees. The core issue in Case 16-2 was management's right to enforce no-trespass policies against nonemployee union representatives.

---

[17] This story is not so farfetched because the first president of the United Mine Workers was the fiery John L. Lewis, who was widely admired and respected for his oratory abilities.

Case 16-2

Lechmere, Inc., Petitioner v. National Labor Relations Board

Supreme Court of the United States
502 U.S. 527, 112 S. Ct. 841 (1992)

BACKGROUND AND FACTS

A retail store was located in a shopping plaza within the metropolitan area of Hartford, Connecticut. All of the store's 200 employees lived in the Hartford metropolitan area; none of them lived on the store owner's property. The store owner was a joint owner of the shopping plaza's parking lot, which was separated from a public highway by a 46-foot-wide grassy strip, almost all of which was public property. In a campaign to organize the store employees, a union inserted a full-page advertisement in a Hartford newspaper, but the advertisement drew little response. Subsequently, union organizers who were not store employees entered the parking lot and placed handbills on the windshields of cars parked in a corner of the lot that was used mostly by the store employees. Each time this occurred, store personnel asked the organizers to leave and the handbills were removed. The organizers relocated to the grassy strip, from where they displayed picket signs over a period of seven months. The organizers were able to secure the names and addresses of 41 employees, approximately 20 percent of the total. The union sent four mailings to these employees and made some attempts to contact them by phone or by home visits. These efforts resulted in only one signed union authorization card. Alleging that the storeowner had violated 8(a)(1) of the National Labor Relations Act (NLRA) (29 U.S.C. § 158(a)(1)) by barring the organizers from the parking lot, the union filed an unfair labor practice charge with the National Labor Relations Board (NLRB). An administrative law judge ruled in the union's favor. The NLRB, affirming, (1) applied a standard under which (a) the employees' rights under Section 7 of the NLRA (29 U.S.C. § 157)—which guarantees employees the right of self-organization—were balanced against the store owner's property rights, and (b) the availability of reasonably effective alternative means of communication was considered; (2) found that the union had no such alternative means available; and (3) held that the store owner was required by Section 7 to grant access to the organizers. On appeal, the United States Court of Appeals for the First Circuit denied the storeowner's petition for review and enforced the NLRB's order (914 F.2d 313).

Opinion by Mr. Justice Clarence Thomas

Alleging that Lechmere had violated the NLRA by barring the nonemployee organizers from its property, the union filed an unfair labor practice charge with respondent National Labor Relations Board (Board). Applying the criteria set forth by the Board in *Fairmont Hotel Co.,* an Administrative Law Judge (ALJ) ruled in the union's favor. [References deleted] He recommended that Lechmere be ordered, among other things, to cease and desist from barring the union organizers from the parking lot and to post in conspicuous places in the store signs proclaiming in part:

> "WE WILL NOT prohibit representatives of Local 919, United Food and Commercial Workers, AFL-CIO ('the Union') or any other labor organization, from distributing union literature to our employees in the parking lot adjacent to our store in Newington, Connecticut, nor will we attempt to cause them to be removed from our parking lot for attempting to do so."

The Board affirmed the ALJ's judgment and adopted the recommended order, applying the analysis set forth in its opinion in *Jean Country,* which had by then replaced the short-lived *Fairmont Hotel* approach. A divided panel of the United States Court of Appeals for the First Circuit denied Lechmere's petition for review and enforced the Board's order. This Court granted certiorari.

* * *

Section 7 of the NLRA provides in relevant part that "employees shall have the right to self-organization, to form, join, or assist labor organizations." 29 U. S. C. § 157. Section 8(a)(1) of the

Act, in turn, makes it an unfair labor practice for an employer "to interfere with, restrain, or coerce employees in the exercise of the rights guaranteed in [§ 7]." 29 U.S.C. § 158(a)(1). By its plain terms, thus, the NLRA confers rights only on *employees,* not on unions or their nonemployee organizers. In *NLRB v. Babcock & Wilcox Co.,* 351 U.S. 105, 100 L. Ed. 975, 76 S. Ct. 679 (1956), however, we recognized that insofar as the employees' "right of self-organization depends in some measure on [their] ability . . . to learn the advantages of self-organization from others," *id.,* at 113, § 7 of the NLRA may, in certain limited circumstances, restrict an employer's right to exclude nonemployee union organizers from his property. It is the nature of those circumstances that we explore today.

* * *

In *Babcock,* as explained above, we held that the Act drew a distinction "of substance," 351 U.S. at 113, between the union activities of employees and nonemployees. In cases involving *employee* activities, we noted with approval, the Board "balanced the conflicting interests of employees to receive information on self-organization on the company's property from fellow employees during nonworking time, with the employer's right to control the use of his property." In cases involving *nonemployee* activities (like those at issue in *Babcock* itself), however, the Board was not permitted to engage in that same balancing (and we reversed the Board for having done so). By reversing the Board's interpretation of the statute for failing to distinguish between the organizing activities of employees and nonemployees, we were saying, in *Chevron* terms, that § 7 speaks to the issue of nonemployee access to an employer's property. *Babcock's* teaching is straightforward: § 7 simply does not protect nonemployee union organizers *except* in the rare case where "the inaccessibility of employees makes ineffective the reasonable attempts by nonemployees to communicate with them through the usual channels." Our reference to "reasonable" attempts was nothing more than a commonsense recognition that unions need not engage in extraordinary feats to communicate with inaccessible employees—*not* an endorsement of the view (which we expressly rejected) that the Act protects "reasonable" trespasses. Where reasonable alternative means of access exist, § 7's guarantees do not authorize trespasses by nonemployee organizers, *even* (as we noted in *Babcock, ibid.*) "under . . . reasonable regulations" established by the Board.

* * *

Decision and Outcome

The U.S. Supreme Court reversed the judgment of the First Circuit and the National Labor Relations Board and allowed Lechmere to continue to enforce no-trespass policies against nonemployee union organizers.

Questions for Analysis

1. Why did the U.S. Supreme Court reverse the decision of the administrative law judge for the National Labor Relations Board? Do the protections of the National Labor Relations Act extend to nonemployees?
2. Under what circumstances would no-trespass policies imposed by management be unfair labor practices?

Threats against Union Membership

Section 8(a) of the NLRA also prohibits employers from threatening to fire workers if they vote for a union, but at the same time assures employers of the right to express their point of view. Often, the distinction between information and threats becomes difficult to decipher when employers bring in speakers to show evidence that, in heavily unionized industries, employment has declined. Employers contend that such presentations are simply examples of an employer exercising its rights to freedom of expression whereas unions see such presentations as thinly disguised threats that, if employees vote for a union, they will lose their jobs.

Discrimination against Union Supporters

Section 8(a) of the Wagner Act prohibits employer sanctions against union supporters simply *because they are union supporters.* Employers, however, are entitled to maintain and enforce rules that make the workforce more efficient. As often occurs, when a discharge of a union supporter occurs, the union may claim that the employee was fired for his pro-union organizing activity. Companies, well aware of Section 8(a), will claim, instead, that they had independent (job performance) grounds for firing the union supporter.

In such mixed motive cases, the NLRB and courts have sided with the union and its supporters when the company

- Gives inconsistent reasons for the discharge.
- Discharges the union supporter on the basis of past deeds that were condoned or disregarded at the time of commission.
- Enforces rules that are generally not enforced.
- Applies disproportionately severe sanctions to union supporters and neglects to give customary warnings.

In these cases, courts also have had to consider whether an employer can fire a pro-union employee who also does one or more of the following:

- Is dishonest on the job.
- Assaults a supervisor or fellow employee.
- Engages in sexual harassment.
- Uses intoxicants on the job.
- Engages in illegal wildcat strikes.
- Is grossly insubordinate on the job.

Each of these acts has been adjudged to be a sufficient basis for dismissal according to the courts or the NLRB, even though the perpetrator was supporting a union at the time.

Decertification Procedures

As is required for certification, in efforts to decertify a union, the petition for a decertification election must be signed by 30 percent of the relevant employees in the bargaining unit. The decertification petition cannot be initiated by the employer, a supervisor, or an agent of the employer. As with a certification election, the petition is submitted to the NLRB for recognition and, if the decertification election fails, no new decertification election can be held for a period of one year.

Actions by Employers

An employer is entitled to request an NLRB-supervised election when the union is requesting a renewal of its existing, collective bargaining agreement. An employer also is entitled to (1) refuse to deal with a union that it believes no longer represents the majority of employees and (2) conduct an informal poll of employees on that issue. Both of the latter two activities will be deemed "unfair labor practices" if the employer is unable to demonstrate to the NLRB that a majority of workers no longer want the union to represent them. Under such circumstances, the employer who refuses to bargain with the union or takes a poll of workers is taking substantial legal and financial risks.

Conduct of the Parties after a Union Is Certified as the Sole Bargaining Agent

Once a union gains certification, Section 8(a) of the NLRA requires that the employer must bargain in *good faith* with the union over wages and working conditions. A definition of good faith bargaining has not been reduced to specific criteria, but the NLRB is frequently summoned to act by complaints of bad faith bargaining. There have been a number of cases that, by precedent, give the parties guidance on the NLRB's views on this issue. To get a sense of its position, it is notable that

- The General Electric Co. was charged with bargaining in bad faith when it adopted, with much publicity, a strategy of bargaining with the union on a take-it-or-leave-it basis and not proposing any changes in response to union proposals.[18]
- It is considered bargaining in bad faith when, in spite of the existence of a collective bargaining agreement, an employer unilaterally changes a term or condition of employment, which includes wages, working conditions, benefits, and other terms. There is an exception if union–management talks have reached an impasse and the employer implements the union's pre-impasse proposals.
- It is considered a case of not bargaining in good faith if an employer bypasses the union and presents its latest offer directly to employees.
- Bargaining in good faith also requires that, when a union makes a request, the employer will provide a written statement of the company's latest offer. The company should include within its latest offer financial data if the employer is claiming it is unable to afford the latest union offer as well as other foundation materials that form the basis for this offer by the employer.

Bargaining Subjects: Mandatory, Permissive, and Illegal

Mandatory Bargaining Subjects

Once a union is certified, there are three categories of bargaining subjects: mandatory, permissive, and illegal. It is important for managers to know what items fall within the mandatory category, as management is required to bargain in good faith over such items. It should come as no surprise that, for such **mandatory bargaining subjects** as "rates of pay, wages, hours of employment, or other conditions of employment," unilateral employer changes are unfair labor practices, subject to sanction by the NLRB.[19] In defining the inclusiveness of what's called mandatory bargaining subject matter, courts and the NLRB have held that the following are also included: shift differentials, incentive plans, severance pay, paid holiday vacations, and profit sharing plans. Also included are seniority provisions, layoff and recall provisions, no-strike-no-lockout clauses, grievance procedures, and work rules. Most of these items are not subject to serious debate and are clearly recognized as mandatory topics for negotiations.

mandatory bargaining subjects
Wages and other terms and conditions of employment that must be set in collective bargaining agreements if there is a union representing workers.

Outsourcing More controversy surrounds classifications of subcontracting, business closings, and the relocation of a bargaining unit. Of course, the effect of these actions by employers is to reduce the number of employees. From the business perspective, it has been contended that these are *management prerogatives* and should not be viewed as mandatory matters. However, the U.S. Supreme Court has held that the *decision to subcontract,* rather than use union employees, is a mandatory subject of collective bargaining. On the other hand, the Supreme Court has agreed with management that the *decision to close down a business is a management decision* and not a mandatory subject for negotiation.[20] The difference between outsourcing and the decision to shut down a branch of the company is not always apparent to the courts or the affected workers.

---

[18] *National Labor Relations Board v. General Electric Company,* 418 F.2d 736 (2nd Cir. 1969).

[19] Section 9(a) of the National Labor Relations Act.

[20] *Fibreboard Paper Products Corp. v. NLRB,* 379 U.S. 203 (1964), and *First National Maintenance Corp. v. NLRB,* 452 U.S. 666 (1981).

Case 16-3

Fibreboard Paper Products Corp. v. National Labor Relations Board et al.

Supreme Court of the United States
379 U.S. 203 (1964)

BACKGROUND AND FACTS

Respondent union, the bargaining representative for a unit of petitioner's maintenance employees, gave timely notice of its desire to modify the existing collective bargaining agreement. Four days before the expiration of the contract, petitioner (Fibreboard) informed the union that it had determined that substantial savings could be effected by contracting out the maintenance work, and that since it had made a definite decision to do so, negotiation of a new agreement would be pointless. On the contract expiration date, the employment of employees represented by the union was terminated and an independent contractor was engaged to do the maintenance work. The union filed unfair labor practice charges against the employer, alleging violations of §§ 8 (a)(1), 8 (a)(3) and 8 (a)(5) of the National Labor Relations Act. The National Labor Relations Board (NLRB) found that, while petitioner's motive was economic rather than antiunion, petitioner's failure to negotiate with the union concerning its decision to contract out the maintenance work violated § 8 (a)(5) of the Act, which requires bargaining with respect to "wages, hours, and other terms and conditions of employment." The NLRB ordered reinstatement of the maintenance employees with back pay, and the Court of Appeals granted the NLRB's petition for enforcement.

Opinion by Chief Justice Earl Warren

The facts of the present case illustrate the propriety of submitting the dispute to collective negotiation. The Company's decision to contract out the maintenance work did not alter the Company's basic operation. The maintenance work still had to be performed in the plant. No capital investment was contemplated; the Company merely replaced existing employees with those of an independent contractor to do the same work under similar conditions of employment. Therefore, to require the employer to bargain about the matter would not significantly abridge his freedom to manage the business.

The Company was concerned with the high cost of its maintenance operation. It was induced to contract out the work by assurances from independent contractors that economies could be derived by reducing the work force, decreasing fringe benefits, and eliminating overtime payments. These have long been regarded as matters peculiarly suitable for resolution within the collective bargaining framework, and industrial experience demonstrates that collective negotiation has been highly successful in achieving peaceful accommodation of the conflicting interests. Yet, it is contended that when an employer can effect cost savings in these respects by contracting the work out, there is no need to attempt to achieve similar economies through negotiation with existing employees or to provide them with an opportunity to negotiate a mutually acceptable alternative. The short answer is that, although it is not possible to say whether a satisfactory solution could be reached, national labor policy is founded upon the congressional determination that the chances are good enough to warrant subjecting such issues to the process of collective negotiation.

* * *

We agree with the Court of Appeals that, on the facts of this case, the "contracting out" of the work previously performed by members of an existing bargaining unit is a subject about which the National Labor Relations Act requires employers and the representatives of their employees to bargain collectively. We also agree with the Court of Appeals that the Board did not exceed its remedial powers in directing the Company to resume its maintenance operations, reinstate the employees with back pay, and bargain with the Union.

Decision and Outcome

The U.S. Supreme Court held that replacement of employees with an outside company to perform maintenance was an unfair labor practice committed by Fibreboard because it was a mandatory subject that the company could not make a decision on without negotiating with the union.

Questions for Analysis

1. The court in this case held that contracting out was a mandatory subject of negotiation in collective bargaining. Why did the U.S. Supreme Court think that the parties should negotiate about contracting out? What kind of decisions did the Court think were solely within management perogatives?
2. What did the independent contractor list as some of the advantages of the defendant hiring it?

Employee Monitoring   In our recent history, there has been a series of cases dealing with whether drug testing and other forms of employee monitoring are mandatory subjects of bargaining under the National Labor Relations Act. Management considers drug testing a health issue and takes the position that this should not be the subject of mandatory negotiations with unions. The NLRB has held, however, that a unilateral imposition of drug testing following accidents on the job is a mandatory subject of negotiations and, thus, is an unfair labor practice.[21] The employer in the prominent test case leading to this decision was the Johnston-Bateman Company, which initiated a drug-and-alcohol-testing program after each on-the-job accident without consulting the union. In another case, the court also held that installation of hidden cameras in the workplace, including in restrooms, is a mandatory subject of negotiations.[22] Finally, the NLRB has held that imposition of mandatory drug testing *for job applicants* is not part of mandatory subjects because such testing does not change terms and conditions of employment for those already employed.[23]

Permissive Subjects of Bargaining

permissive subjects of bargaining
Topics that can be considered in collective bargaining agreements but are not mandatory. The use of union labels on products is a permissive subject of bargaining.

Permissive subjects of bargaining are just that: they may be discussed during collective bargaining negotiations, but they are not mandatory. The refusal to bargain over these topics is not considered an unfair labor practice under Section 8(a) of the NLRA. Furthermore, unilateral employer changes to one of the permissive subjects, such as an increase in benefits for retired union members, is not an unfair labor practice. Prominent among the items commonly included among permissive topics are

- Redefinition of the bargaining unit and segmentation of workers in ways that differ from the NLRB's classifications.
- Benefits of retired members.
- Internal union affairs.
- Use of union labels.
- Indemnification clauses.

This list is not exhaustive.

Illegal Subjects

illegal subjects
It is illegal to consider subjects in collective bargaining such as secondary boycotts, closed shops, and refusals to enforce the civil rights laws.

There are several topics that are **illegal subjects** and, therefore, should not be part of negotiations between a union and the employer. If the union tries to insert a term indicating

---

[21] *Johnston-Bateman Company*, 295 N.L.R.B. 26 (1989).
[22] *Colgate-Palmolive Company*, 323 N.L.R.B. 82 (1997).
[23] *Star Tribune*, 295 N.L.R.B. 63 (1989).

that its members will not carry the cargo of any employer that is currently in a labor dispute in which a strike is occurring, that agreement would be illegal under the Taft-Hartley Act as it is a *secondary boycott.* Similarly, if an employer tried to bargain for *having a management representative on the governing board of the union,* the subject is illegal because such practices are prohibited by the NLRA of 1935. Other illegal subjects include *closed union shops, agreements not to file workers' compensation claims,* and *agreements not to enforce the civil rights laws.*

Strikes, Lockouts, and Work Stoppages

There are three kinds of strikes: economic, unfair labor practice, and illegal strikes. The rules governing each type of strike are different and it behooves managers to know the differences. Strikes generally occur when collective bargaining negotiations break down. They are a serious event in the lives both of most companies and unions, and this seriousness has been magnified lately by increased use of replacement workers, which has considerably raised the ante when a strike occurs. Indeed, strikes are potentially (financial) survival-threatening to one or both of the parties involved.

Economic Strikes

economic strikes
Strikes whose primary aim is to improve wages.

Economic strikes occur when the parties—labor and management—are unable to reach agreement on wages or other terms and conditions of employment. Strikes are a brutal way of resolving differences because they generally hurt both sides. When union leaders decide to call a strike, it is because they think the strike will hurt employers worse than their members and thus will soften bargaining positions of management. Often, economic strikes backfire and result in the union being broken. Striking union workers are sometimes reduced to returning to employers and asking to be allowed to return to work under the conditions proposed by the employer.

Rights of Employers during Economic Strikes

A potent weapon that employers can and do use during and after economic strikes is the hiring of permanent replacement workers. When replacement workers are hired, there is no obligation on the part of an employer to rehire striking workers, unless the strikers make an unconditional offer to return to work and there are vacancies left by departing replacement workers. An employer does not have to reinstate a striking employee if

1. The striking worker has secured equivalent employment elsewhere, or
2. The striker is not rehired for legitimate business reasons, or
3. The striker has engaged in egregious misconduct during the strike.

Economic strikes are far more effective when a large percentage of firms in the industry are unionized so that all employers can be confronted with essentially the same union offer. When only a portion of the firms in an industry are unionized, higher wage demands by unions may result in a competitive disadvantage for the employer of unionized workers and, ultimately, less employment in unionized firms.

unfair labor practice strikes
Strikes that are based on alleged unfair labor practices by employers such as actions that contravene agreements made in collective bargaining.

Unfair Labor Practice Strikes

As opposed to economic strikes, **unfair labor practice strikes** are called to protest actions by employers, such as unjust reprimands or dismissals, use of subcontractors in contravention of the current collective bargaining agreement, or failure to bargain in good faith. In contrast to the situation with an economic strike, after an unfair labor practice strike, if a striker makes an unconditional offer to return to work, he is generally entitled to return to his old job. During the strike, replacement workers may be hired, but these hires are not permanent. Once workers offer to return to work, they are entitled to back pay if their employer does not immediately rehire them.

Illegal Strikes

In the two types of strikes discussed above, economic and unfair labor practice, a certified union is in place and there is a dispute with management. There are a number of types of strikes that are illegal under the NLRA. *In illegal strikes, workers are not protected from being fired by the NLRA.*

Organizational Strike　In an organizational strike, a union is picketing an employer to gain employer recognition of the union, and one of three things has taken place: (1) another union has been certified and the striking union is attacking certification, (2) a certification election took place within the last 12 months and the union did not win recognition, or (3) the union has been picketing but has not filed a petition for an election within 30 days.

Secondary Boycotts　As discussed above, unions cannot gang up and support fellow unions in their battles with employers. A secondary boycott occurs when a union strikes a neutral employer, though there are many variations on this theme. Suppose the Teamsters are striking against Roadway Trucking Company, which buys thousands of tires monthly for operating its fleet of trucks. If the Teamsters strike a tire company in order to put pressure on Roadway, it has engaged in an illegal secondary boycott. At construction sites, where workers for several employers (subcontractors) file in the same gate, a strike by one union could potentially shut the entire site down because of the reluctance of union members to cross picket lines. A convention has been reached in these situations whereby the employer being struck will be given a separate entrance, with the striking union only allowed to picket that entrance.

wildcat strikes
Strikes that are unauthorized by the parent union or are contrary to the terms of a collective bargaining agreement that calls for arbitration of disputes.

Wildcats Strikes　A **wildcat strike** takes place when a local union, without approval from the parent union, goes on strike and by that action violates the collective bargaining agreement currently in place. It is common for collective bargaining agreements to call for arbitration when a local union and an employer cannot agree about such issues as grievances, firings, or worker safety concerns. Typically, wildcat strikes are spontaneous; an incident occurs at the work site, such as an injury of a worker, tempers flare, harsh words are exchanged, threats are made, and the situation erupts into a wildcat strike, which is frequently accompanied by violence.

Strikes That Violate a Collective Bargaining Agreement　There are times when the collective bargaining agreement between a union and management contains a no-strike clause and calls for arbitration of labor disputes. In this situation, strikes are illegal, but, in order to get a court injunction against a strike, both the no-strike clause and the arbitration agreement must be present.

Strikes by Public Employees　Government employees at all levels are denied the legal right to strike. Although employment with the government is often not as high paying as similarly skilled jobs in the private sector, it generally offers more job security and benefits also may be more generous. There are unions that represent public employees, but those unions are not allowed to call for a strike or encourage one. If a strike does occur, all strikers are subject to dismissal, though amnesty often is granted when the strike is called off and the parties settle. When federal air traffic controllers went on strike in 1981 and ignored return-to-work calls, all were fired by then-President Ronald Reagan. As a sequel, the union representing the air traffic controllers, the Professional Air Traffic Controllers Organization (PATCO), was decertified for its encouragement of the strike. Since that time, strikes by federal employees have been nonexistent.

Strikes That the President Believes Threaten National Security or Health   The Taft-Hartley Act provides the president with the right to request an order delaying a strike for an 80-day "cooling off" period. If the president declares that a strike in a key industry creates a national emergency, the courts can issue an injunction, which makes a strike an act in contempt of court, with strikers immediately subject to arrest. During the first months of his presidency, President George W. Bush twice averted strikes by airline employees using provisions of the Taft-Hartley Act to call for a cooling-off period.

Lockouts

lockouts
A tactic used by management when a strike is imminent. They can be legal as long as the purpose is not to break the union.

A **lockout** is an employer's counterpart to a strike by workers. A lockout by employers is a tactic that is normally used when a strike is imminent. It allows employers to be proactive rather than simply reactive during a time of labor turmoil. Sometimes unions single out one employer for a strike with the presumption that the terms negotiated with that employer will then become the industry standard. Not wanting to be picked off individually, employers may decide to enhance their bargaining position by all initiating a lockout. Such lockouts are legal if the purpose of the lockout is to improve the bargaining position of employers. Lockouts also can be classified as unfair labor practices if the purpose of the lockout is to break the union through pressure for employees to vote for decertification of the union.

Public Employers and Employees

As discussed above, the greatest growth for unions recently has been in the public sector. In some sense this growth is ironic because the most potent bargaining tactic available to unions in the private sector is the right to strike, but in the public sector, virtually all strikes are illegal. With regard to labor-management interactions, the NLRA has no authority over public employees. At the federal level, public employees are subject to the Federal Service Labor-Management Relations Statute (FSLMRS), which is part of the Civil Service Reform Act of 1978.[24] The FSLMRS does authorize the formation and recognition of labor unions, but specifically provides that calling for strikes, work stoppages, or encouraging the same is an unfair labor practice. The Federal Labor Relations Authority (FLRA), the federal civil service equivalent to the NLRB, is authorized to revoke a union's certification for calling or encouraging a strike. There are equivalent organizations at the state and local levels to deal with unions of public employees.

Impact of the NLRA on Nonunion Employees

As mentioned earlier, the NLRA not only supports the establishment of unions, but also provides for protection of employees who are engaged in *concerted actions for their mutual benefit*. As the number of unionized workers has decreased as a percentage of the total workforce, the significance of the NLRA protections for nonunion employees has increased. Concerted activity is a loose term that may involve only a single employee, if that employee is acting in concert with other employees who approve of his or her actions. As long as workers are engaged in *concerted activity* for the promotion of safety or some other approved goal, the NLRA provides protection against being fired.

Promotion of Safety

For obvious reasons, all employees are concerned with on-the-job safety. If an employer does not provide a safe work environment, there are two types of actions that employees can take to protect themselves. First, if working conditions are abnormally dangerous, a single employee or group of employees can refuse to perform or can walk off the job and

---

[24] Pub. L. No. 95-454, codified at 5 U.S.C. § 7101 *et seq.*

International Perspective   What Are the Important International Labor Issues?

The International Confederation of Free Trade Unions (ICFTU) was set up in 1949 and has 231 affiliated organisations in 150 countries and territories on all five continents, with a membership of 158 million. It has three major regional organisations, APRO for Asia and the Pacific, AFRO for Africa, and ORIT for the Americas. It also maintains close links with the European Trade Union Confederation (ETUC) (which includes all ICFTU European affiliates) and Global Union Federations, which link together national unions from a particular trade or industry at international level.

MEMBERSHIP

It is a Confederation of national trade union centres, each of which links together the trade unions of that particular country. Membership is open to bone fide trade union organisations, that are independent of outside influence, and have a democratic structure.

According to the ICFTU, the World Trade Organization is seen as a threat to worker rights. According to the ICFTU:

- The vast expansion in trade and investment, particularly in the 1990s, has had equally profound effects on labour standards around the world. While some regions have benefited, the negative effects are most obvious in the 850 export processing zones around the world where minimum labour standards are regularly violated and trade union organisers are forbidden entry. On average, 80% of the workers in the zones are young and unorganised women workers.

- 15 million children work to make items which enter into international trade. Forced or slave labour is used on a massive scale in some countries to produce textiles, gold, diamonds, agricultural exports and other commodities.

- Concurrently, the World Trade Organisation (WTO) has developed unprecedented powers to intervene in what were previously domestic policy concerns. This has been unaccompanied by any social, development, gender or environmental dimension to its actions.

- The ICFTU's work on trade and labour standards includes regular policy statements to the WTO which comment on investment, services, development and many other areas of WTO policy. The ICFTU issues regular reports on the labour policies of particular countries and shows how these impact on trade. And the ICFTU has produced various publications on the links between labour standards and world trade.

Sources: http://www.icftu.org/displaydocument.asp?Index=990916422 and http://www.icftu.org/focus.asp?Issue=trade&Language=EN.

not be subject to reprisal. This protection originates from the OSH Act, as discussed earlier. There are other situations in which working conditions cannot be deemed *abnormally dangerous,* but that nevertheless are unsafe. In one case, eight employees walked off the job when their employer wanted them to work in an unheated warehouse when the temperature was 20 degrees Fahrenheit. The court ruled in this case that the eight employees walking off the job were engaged in a justified concerted activity and, thus, could not be summarily fired by their employer.

Employee Committees

Employee committees dealing with labor–management communication, the creation and enforcement of rules, and disciplinary problems are allowable concerted activities. If employee committees begin to bargain over wages, however, they become the functional equivalent of unions, which becomes a serious problem for management if management participates on these committees as well. It is an unfair labor practice for management to dominate a union and, also, for having a member of management on a committee that "bargains" for wages, hours, or working conditions. Reflecting these "committee" issues, the total quality management movement has become a target for unions in recent years.

ON-THE-JOB PRIVACY ISSUES

The Internet has sharpened the confrontation over protection of privacy, but there are a number of other privacy battles that also are being waged. A sizeable slice of the privacy confrontation arises from on-the-job issues between employers and employees. From the perspective of employers, it is clear that they have a legitimate interest in determining whether employees are coming to work in an impaired state due to the use of drugs or alcohol. Employers are also legitimately concerned about on-the-job theft, inappropriate sexual or harassing behavior, and Internet cruising that has nothing to do with the employer's business.

At the same time, most would agree that what employees do in their off hours is none of an employer's business so long as it does not affect on-the-job productivity. In the past, employers have used information gathered about employees to make illegitimate decisions and have asked for irrelevant information. Obviously objectionable questions such as "Have you ever fantasized sexually about a member of your sex?" have been used to screen applicants. Clearly, skirmishes over privacy on the job can occur in many arenas.

Drug Testing

Drug Testing by Private Companies

As a condition of employment, private employers in virtually all states can require both job applicants and employees to take drug tests that may involve urine, blood, or hair samples. The Fourth Amendment does not apply to private employers, leaving them relatively unfettered in their drug-testing activities. Some employers administer a progression of drug tests that are increasingly accurate (and expensive). If an employee fails the first test, he or she is generally required to retest using procedures that are more precise. In an increasing number of states, there are legal restrictions on testing employees *after* they have been hired.

probable cause
A number of states require employers to have probable cause to test or retest employees for drug use. Probable cause occurs when events take place that make it more likely than not that the person being tested has been impaired by drugs.

These states generally require employers to have **probable cause** to retest an employee after he or she has already been hired. Probable cause is generally established when there is on-the-job evidence of erratic behavior, which indicates possible drug use, or if there are precipitous declines in productivity.

Drug Testing by Public Employers

When the employer is a governmental entity, courts have held that drug testing is *a search* for Fourth Amendment purposes. Generally, the Fourth Amendment requires a showing of probable cause. Hence, to require testing, a governmental employer must have good reason to believe that an individual employee is impaired. Given the transparent disparity of treatment between employees who work for public versus private employers, courts have decided that there are a number of exceptions that allow for drug testing of public employees, even without a showing of individualized probable cause.

At this point, the courts are engaging in ambiguous balancing tests when evaluating testing of public employees for substance abuse. The more serious the potential threat of impairment to public health and safety, the more nonindividualized drug tests of public employees are allowed. Those who carry guns on the job, as police do, can be tested without a showing of individualized probable cause.[25] Public employees who work in public transportation have been tested for drugs in the aftermath of train wrecks, even though there is no individualized showing of probable cause to indicate that a particular employee is a substance abuser.[26]

[25] *National Treasury Employees Union v. Von Raab*, 489 U.S. 602 (1989).
[26] *Skinner v. Railway Labor Executives' Ass'n*, 489 U.S. 656 (1989).

Polygraph Testing

Polygraph tests (lie detectors) have been used by employers to expose employee theft and for other purposes, such as determining whether an employee has criminal tendencies. Many labor groups have petitioned government, state and federal, to end the unrestricted use of polygraphs on the job. In general, employer requirements for employees to take polygraph tests have been outlawed under the Employee Polygraph Protection Act of 1988.[27] This act was a direct response to the frequency of inappropriate uses of polygraphs by employers. Prior to this act, prospective employees were often quizzed about matters unrelated to job performance. As a result of the act, polygraph testing has been largely eliminated. There are, however, exceptions to the Employee Polygraph Protection Act prohibitions. Illustratively, when an employee is accused of stealing, polygraph testing is permissible but must be administered according to specific documented procedures. Employers also can use polygraph testing on employees who work in security jobs, but again with specific procedural requirements.

Psychological Testing and Counseling

Some states, such as California, specifically protect the right of privacy in their constitution. In California there have been cases in which questions on job interview questionnaires have been ruled too intrusive. Most of these cases relate to situations in which prospective applicants must answer questions about matters totally unrelated to the job, such as ones asking about sexual preferences. Employers should carefully consider whether getting the answers to intrusive questions, particularly those that do not clearly relate to job performance, are really worth the effort.

Many employers offer employees job counseling to deal with personal problems. In some cases, substance abuse, marital problems, and other sensitive issues are discussed in counseling sessions. If the counselor is an employee of the firm, employees who go to such counselors *should not assume* that counseling sessions are totally confidential unless the company makes a promise to that effect. Many employment-related decisions are made as a result of consultations with job counselors who are employees as well. Indeed, employees have been fired as a result of disclosures made to counselors provided by employers.

On-the-Job Monitoring by Employers

Employers have increasing capabilities to monitor employee activity on the job and are using these capabilities. There have been abuses when employers have used their monitoring abilities to view members of the opposite sex in situations where the employees (invariably female) had a reasonable expectation of privacy. New technology, especially software, gives employers the ability to monitor on-the-job productivity for word processor users and others whose jobs make heavy use of computer programs. Cameras are also common at most work sites, allowing the monitoring of physical activities. Software has been developed that tracks where employees travel on the Internet and is able to report to employers whether the employee has been visiting "adult" sites on the job. Numerous workers have lost their jobs or have been reprimanded as a result of on-the-job Internet cruising.

---

[27] Pub. L. No. 100-347, codified 29 C.F.R. part 801 *et seq.*

Inform Employees of What Will Be Monitored

In general, there are no federal or state laws that prohibit employer monitoring of employees. In some cases, employer monitoring can be an *unreasonable intrusion* into the private affairs of an employee (and thus an actionable tort for invasion of privacy), particularly if the monitoring is not related to job performance. Employers who monitor employees by camera, through software or other means, should inform employees of that fact. Informing employees that they are subject to monitoring may curb the objectionable behavior that is the target of monitoring. In addition, employees who have been informed of the monitoring will have a reduced expectation of privacy, thus undercutting any tort claim based on an employer's unreasonable intrusion into the private affairs of another.

Employer Monitoring of Phone Calls

Congress passed the Omnibus Crime Control and Safe Streets Act in 1968.[28] This act regulated on-the-job wiretapping by employers for a number of years. Under this act, employers were prohibited from tapping telephone conversations of employees on the job unless

- The telephone monitoring was during the regular course of business or
- The employee had consented to the employer's telephone monitoring.

These exceptional permissions were so broad that employers had no trouble monitoring phone conversations of employees as a matter of course. Even though courts often have been hostile to employer monitoring of employee conversations, prudent managers have been able to insulate themselves from liability by simply informing employees that a condition of employment is acceptance of employer monitoring of phone conversations.

The Electronic Communications Privacy Act of 1986

In 1986 Congress passed the Electronic Communications Privacy Act (ECPA) that amended the 1968 Omnibus Crime Control Act.[29] The protections provided by the ECPA were extended not just to e-mail, but also to cellular and wireless phone communications so that the use of scanners to intercept conversations was made a criminal act (in the same way that the Omnibus Crime Control Act made wiretapping telephone conversations a criminal act in 1968). Unless some exception applies, monitoring or intercepting e-mail or cellular or wireless phone conversations is illegal under the ECPA.

The ECPA provides employers the same access to e-mails that the Omnibus Crime Control Act allowed employers to telephone conversations that take place on the job, along with the same exceptions. Hence, informing employees of possible e-mail monitoring insulates employers from liability for engaging in that monitoring. Of course, if employers expect computers assigned to their workers to be used only for company-related purposes, and not for private (e-mail) conversations, employees should be informed of that expectation. Proper warnings reduce claims that employees have an expectation of privacy with respect to e-mails. So, with considerable confidence, employers can legally monitor phone and e-mail conversations on the job by informing employees that their phone or e-mail conversations are subject to monitoring. Indeed, at least one court has held that, even if employers tell employees that their e-mails will remain confidential, employees do not have a reasonable expectation of privacy with respect to e-mails that are sent on the job (see Case 16-4).

---

[28] Title III of the Omnibus Crime Control and Safe Streets of 1968, Pub. L. No. 90-351, codified at 18 U.S.C. §§ 2510–2520.

[29] Pub. L. No. 99-508, codified at 18 U.S.C. §§ 2510–2521.

Case 16-4

Bill McLaren Jr. v. Microsoft Corporation

Court of Appeals of Texas, Fifth District, Dallas
1999 WL 339015, 1999 Tex. App. LEXIS 4103 (Tex. Ct. App. 1999)

FACTS AND CASE BACKGROUND

McLaren was an employee of Microsoft Corporation. In December 1996, Microsoft suspended McLaren's employment pending an investigation into accusations of sexual harrassment and "inventory questions." McLaren requested access to his electronic mail to disprove the allegations against him. According to McLaren, he was told he could access his e-mail only by requesting it through company officials and telling them the location of a particular message. By memorandum, McLaren requested that no one tamper with his Microsoft office workstation or his e-mail. McLaren's employment was terminated on December 11, 1996.

Following the termination of his employment, McLaren filed suit against the company alleging as his sole cause of action a claim for invasion of privacy. In support of his claim, McLaren alleged that . . . Microsoft had invaded his privacy by "breaking into" some or all of the personal folders maintained on his office computer and releasing the contents of the folders to third parties. According to McLaren, the personal folders were part of a computer application created by Microsoft in which e-mail messages could be stored. Access to the e-mail system was obtained through a network password. Access to personal folders could be additionally restricted by a "personal store" password created by the individual user. McLaren created and used a personal store password to restrict access to his personal folders.

Opinion by Roach, Justice

Texas recognizes four distinct torts, any of which constitutes an invasion of privacy:

1. Intrusion upon the plaintiff's seclusion or solitude or into his private affairs;
2. Public disclosure of embarrassing private facts about the plaintiff;
3. Publicity which places the plaintiff in a false light in the public eye;
4. Appropriation, for the defendant's advantage, of the plaintiff's name or likeness.

[Citations deleted throughout] At issue in this case is whether McLaren's petition states a cause of action under the first recognized tort. There are two elements to this cause of action: (1) an intentional intrusion, physically or otherwise, upon another's solitude, seclusion, or private affairs or concerns, which (2) would be highly offensive to a reasonable person. When assessing the offensive nature of the invasion, courts further require the intrusion to be unreasonable, unjustified, or unwarranted. This type of invasion of privacy is generally associated with either a physical invasion of a person's property or eavesdropping on another's conversation with the aid of wiretaps, microphones, or spying.

In his petition and on appeal, McLaren contends the fact that the e-mail messages were stored under a private password with Microsoft's consent gave rise to "a legitimate expectation of privacy in the contents of the files."

In *Trotti,* the court considered the privacy interest of an employee in a locker provided by the employer to store personal effects during work hours. The court began its analysis by recognizing that the locker was the employer's property and, when unlocked, was subject to legitimate, reasonable searches by the employer. The court further reasoned:

> This would also be true where the employee used a lock provided by [the employer], because in retaining the lock's combination or master key, it could be inferred that [the employer] manifested an interest both in maintaining control over the locker and in conducting legitimate, reasonable searches.

But, the court concluded, when, as in *Trotti,* an employee buys and uses his own lock on the locker, with the employer's knowledge, the fact finder is justified in concluding that the "employee manifested, and the employer recognized, an expectation that the locker and its contents would be free from intrusion and interference."

McLaren urges that the locker in *Trotti* is akin to the e-mail messages in this case, "only the technology is different." We disagree. First, the locker in *Trotti* was provided to the employee for the specific purpose of storing *personal* belongings, not work items. In contrast, McLaren's workstation was provided to him by Microsoft so that he could perform the functions of his job. In connection with that purpose and as alleged in McLaren's petition, part of his workstation included a company-owned computer that gave McLaren the ability to send and receive e-mail messages. Thus, contrary to his argument on appeal, the e-mail messages contained on the company computer were not McLaren's personal property, but were merely an inherent part of the office environment.

Further, the nature of a locker and an e-mail storage system are different. The locker in *Trotti* was a discrete, physical place where the employee, separate and apart from other employees, could store her tangible, personal belongings. The storage system for e-mail messages is not so discrete. As asserted by McLaren in his petition, e-mail was delivered to the server-based "inbox" and was stored there to read. [Footnotes deleted.] McLaren could leave his e-mail on the server or he could move the message to a different location. According to McLaren, his practice was to store his e-mail messages in "personal folders." Even so, any e-mail messages stored in McLaren's personal folders were first transmitted over the network and were at some point accessible by a third-party. Given these circumstances, we cannot conclude that McLaren, even by creating a personal password, manifested—and Microsoft recognized—a reasonable expectation of privacy in the contents of the e-mail messages such that Microsoft was precluded from reviewing the messages.

Decision and Outcome

The Court of Appeals of Texas ruled that dismissal of McLaren's appeal was appropriate. McLaren's expectation of privacy as to his company e-mail file was overruled by the legitimate investigations by Microsoft regarding a sexual harassment claim against McLaren.

Questions for Analysis

1. Of the four invasions of privacy, what kind of invasion was McLaren alleging took place in this case?

2. What is the significance of the claim made by McLaren that he had an expectation that his e-mail messages would remain private because he stored them in a personal locker?

3. Does this case support the proposition that employee purses can be searched? What are its implications for the monitoring of bathrooms and dressing rooms? Was it important that McLaren's e-mails were used on the job and were the subject of the charges lodged against him by a female co-worker?

Summary

At the Federal Level, Legislation Has Been Passed That Sets Minimum Wages and Limits Child Labor; Old-Age Incomes Are Supplemented by Social Security Law While Private Pensions Are Regulated by

- The Fair Labor Standards Act ensures that most workers in the United States receive a *minimum wage* and *time and a half* for overtime (work over 40 hours in a week).

- The FLSA also places severe limits on the use of *child labor*.

- The Old-Age, Survivors, and Disability Insurance Act (the Social Security Act) provides income to retirees and their survivors, as well as those who are disabled. The Social Security Administration also manages Medicare.

- Private pension plans are regulated under the Employee Retirement Income Security Act (ERISA). ERISA ensures that long-term employees will receive a pension and that pension plan characteristics fall within certain guidelines. ERISA also requires that private pension plans be fully funded and provides insurance to workers whose pension plans are not adequately funded.

- After termination of employment, most workers qualify for *unemployment compensation,* with benefits that vary in duration and amount from state to state.

- There are a number of other acts of Congress that provide protection for health benefits, including COBRA (Consolidated Omnibus Budget Reconciliation Act of 1985), HIPAA (Health Insurance Portability and Accountability Act), and the FMLA (Family Medical Leave Act).

ERISA; Post-Employment Benefits Are Protected by COBRA and HIPAA, While the FMLA Protects Worker Leaves	• COBRA allows ex-employees to continue coverage for up to 36 months with employer-provided health benefits if they pay for them. • HIPAA ensures that no worker who is switching jobs will be prevented from obtaining coverage with the health care provider of the new employer because of a preexisting health condition. • The FMLA allows employees to take unpaid leave for up to three months annually when a medical or family crisis event occurs and then return to their jobs.
At the Federal Level, the Occupational Safety and Health Act Protects Worker Safety, but Worker Safety Protection Is Supplemented by State Workers' Compensation Laws	• The mainstays of worker safety legislation are workers' compensation statutes and the Occupational Safety and Health (OSH) Act. • In order to qualify for workers' compensation, an injury must be job-related. A consequence of workers' compensation is that the employer is always liable unless the injury is intentionally self-inflicted by the employee. • Under workers' compensation, damages are established by statute and are not determined by a jury. • In general, acceptance of workers' compensation benefits precludes a civil court suit by an employee against the employer. • The OSH Act established OSHA (Occupational Safety and Health Administration), which issues worker safety regulations. • Under the OSH Act, a worker can refuse an instruction by a supervisor if the worker believes that his or her health or life is in imminent danger on the job. • The Fourth Amendment applies to OSHA inspections of work facilities.
Industrial Relations Regulations Give Workers Rights to Organize Unions but Set Boundaries on the Tactics Used by Both Labor and Management	• Unions are prevalent in some sectors of the economy but have declined in the number of members. • Modern industrial relations are shaped by the National Labor Relations Act (NLRA) of 1935, which recognizes worker rights to *organize* and form *unions*. • The NLRA created the National Labor Relations Board (NLRB), which acts as an industrial umpire. The NLRA designates a number of labor practices engaged in by management as unfair and, hence, illegal. • The Taft-Hartley Act, passed in 1947, identified a number of labor practices that unions have employed as unfair and, hence, illegal. • The Landrum-Griffin Act, passed in 1959, was designed to ensure that labor unions are organized and operated in a democratic manner, free from corruption. • Both unions and management, claiming to be victims of unfair labor practices, can take their complaints to the NLRB, which has the power to issue *cease and desist orders*.
U.S. Labor Law Allows Workers to Decide Whether to Unionize through Certification Elections; During These Elections, the NLRB Supervises the Conduct of the Workers and the Employer	• Unions become sole bargaining representatives of workers when they win *certification* elections. A *decertification* election takes place when workers vote to determine whether they want a union to continue to represent them. • In order to call for a certification election, union representatives must get 30 percent of the workers in the bargaining unit to sign authorization cards. • The NLRB determines the appropriate bargaining unit for certification elections. • Management can enforce no-trespass policies against nonemployee union representatives, but any such policy must be nondiscriminatory. • It is an unfair labor practice for management to threaten the jobs of workers who vote for unions. It is also an unfair labor practice to discriminate against union members. • After a union has been selected as the representative of workers, management must bargain in good faith with the selected union. Take-it-or-leave-it bargaining tactics are evidence of *bad faith* bargaining.

<table>
<tr>
<td>

If a Company Is Unionized, It Must Bargain with the Union about Certain Topics Such as Wages; It May Bargain over Other Topics, Such as Benefits, but It May Not Negotiate with the Union about Forbidden Topics; When Negotiations Break Down, Labor Law Allows Strikes and Lockouts

</td>
<td>

- Rates of pay, wages, hours of employment, and other conditions of employment are *mandatory topics* for collective bargaining. Unilateral changes in mandatory topics for collective bargaining by management are unfair labor practices.
- There are a number of topics that are *permissive topics,* such as benefits of retired members, use of union labels, and indemnification clauses. It is permissible to negotiate about these topics during collective bargaining but not mandatory.
- There are several *illegal topics* that, consequently, cannot be the subjects of collective bargaining. These include closed union shops, agreements not to file workers' compensation claims, and agreements not to enforce the civil rights laws.
- Unions and management can use *strikes* and *lockouts* to enhance their bargaining powers.
- An *economic strike* is based on dissatisfaction with wages or other terms and conditions of employment.
- An *unfair labor practice strike* is based on a claim by a union that management has engaged in an unfair labor practice.
- A number of strikes that unions have called are illegal, including strikes of an employer who has had a union certification election during the last 12 months in which the union failed to gain a majority vote. Worker rights are much different depending on whether a strike is based on economics, unfair labor practices, or is illegal.
- Lockouts are used by management when a strike is imminent. A lockout can be legal so long as it is not for the purpose of breaking a union.
- In general, public employees do not have the right to strike. Public employees who engage in strikes can be fired.
- The NLRA also protects nonunion employees' right to engage in concerted efforts to improve working conditions.

</td>
</tr>
<tr>
<td>

Employee Privacy Law Is in a State of Flux; Employers Have Limited Rights to Test for Drug Usage, but Are Not Allowed to Subject Workers to Lie Detectors; Employers Can Monitor Phone Calls and E-mails if They Have Consent or It Is in the Ordinary Course of Business

</td>
<td>

- In most states, it is legal for employers to test employees for drug use. In some states there are restrictions on retesting employees after they have been hired, unless there is some showing of *probable cause* to believe that the employee has been using drugs or abusing alcohol.
- When a public employer tests employees for drug use, it must have probable cause because such testing is considered a *search.* There are a number of exceptions that allow public employers to drug test employees in sensitive positions without an individualized showing of probable cause.
- With a few exceptions, employers are prohibited from requiring employees to take polygraph tests because of the Employee Polygraph Protection Act.
- Most states allow employers to require employees to take psychological tests, but some states require a showing that the questions used are job-related.
- Employees have privacy rights that can be violated by employer surveillance of employees.
- The Omnibus Crime Control and Safe Streets Act of 1968 prohibits monitoring of phone calls by employers except when (1) the employee consents or (2) it is done in the regular course of business.
- The Electronic Communications Privacy Act of 1986 allows employers to monitor employee e-mails as well as phone calls as long as employees have given consent or the monitoring is conducted in the regular course of business.

</td>
</tr>
</table>

Key Terms

Questions for Review and Analysis

1. *Safety net* is a term that suggests that the government will prevent those in weaker positions from falling too low. Discuss five acts of Congress dealing with employment that are designed to prevent those disadvantaged by poor luck, age, or relationship with their employer(s) from suffering additional harm.

2. Discuss how the common law rule that employers are supposed to provide a safe working environment has been nearly completely displaced by state workers' compensation laws and the OSH Act. Given the comprehensiveness of these acts, is the common law rule irrelevant?

3. The major labor statutes, passed at the federal level, enable workers to organize but also place limits on certain bargaining techniques. How does the Taft-Hartley Act modify the National Labor Relations Act to provide a balance between what unions can do to organize and what management can do to provide its perspective to workers.

4. Strikes are the industrial equivalent of war and, yet, there are rules that the parties must follow in spite of the fact that a strike is occurring. What strikes are legal and what are illegal? What management tactics are allowed during strikes and what tactics are disallowed?

5. In many workplaces, employers can test employees for drugs, subject them to psychological tests, videotape them while working, and listen to and read phone and e-mail communications. Besides polygraphs, can you think of any measures that employers can undertake that would violate employee privacy rights, or is employee privacy an oxymoron (a combination of words that do not belong together)?

If You Really Understood This Chapter, You Should Be Able to Provide Informed Commentary on the Following:

1. **Concerted Activity.** Although the National Labor Relations Act protects workers who join together to form a union from being fired for such organizing, it also protects nonunion concerted action by employees if it is for the purpose of mutual benefit. Suppose that an employee was concerned about whether a product being sold by his employer fits contract specifications and talks with other employees about the suitability of the product. Laurence Schillinger began working in a temporary trainer position for Compuware in early July 1994, working on a project with the state of Michigan. Schillinger discussed work-related problems with other employees from the very beginning of his employment. On August 22, 1994, Compuware terminated Schillinger at the direction of Peat Marwick. Peat Marwick decided to remove Schillinger because Schillinger had threatened, on August 19, 1994, to approach the state with work-related concerns, in violation of a Peat Marwick work rule. Schillinger claims that his actions are protected from employer sanction by Section 8 of the National Labor Relations Act, which makes it an unfair labor practice "to interfere with, restrain, or coerce employees in the exercise of the rights guaranteed in section [7] . . . ." 29 U.S.C. § 158(a)(1). At issue in the case was whether Schillinger was protected even though none of his coworkers deputized Schillinger to represent them. How do you distinguish on-the-job complaining from protected concerted activity? [*Compuware Corporation v. National Labor Relations Board,* 134 F.3d 1285 (6th Cir. 1998).]

2. **When Is an Election Final?** In May 1990, intervenor United Food and Commercial Workers Union, Local 400 (the Union), began organizing at several of Be-Lo's retail grocery stores. In February 1991, following a lengthy recruitment campaign, the Union demanded recognition, advising Be-Lo that a majority of the company's employees had signed union authorization cards designating the Union as their official bargaining representative. Be-Lo challenged the Union's claim of majority and declined to recognize the Union. An election to resolve the matter was scheduled for March 21, 1991. During the weeks preceding the election, the company openly campaigned against unionization, holding meetings, circulating memoranda, showing videotapes, and sending out flyers, including a flyer in the form of a mock "pink slip" purportedly given to employees of unionized stores that had been forced to close following unionization. Be-Lo also took "employment actions" against a number of employees who favored unionization of the company. Following the election, the Union picketed several Be-Lo locations. Be-Lo responded by seeking five separate injunctions to exclude the picketers from its premises under the company's no-solicitation policy. In all five cases, the courts of the Commonwealth of Virginia granted Be-Lo's requested injunctions. Upon review by the NLRB (Board), it was determined that Be-Lo had

violated several provisions of the National Labor Relations Act (NLRA). The Board further determined that Be-Lo's violations were so egregious that a reelection would be tainted and ordered Be-Lo to recognize the Union based on the fact that a majority of workers had signed union authorization cards. In an election tainted by violations of the NLRA, can the Board use signatures on union authorization cards as a proxy for the will of the workers? [*Be-Lo v. National Labor Relations Board,* 126 F.3d 268 (4th Cir. 1997).]

3. **Online Snooping by Employers and the Electronic Communications Privacy Act (ECPA).** The ECPA gives employers access to employee e-mail and phone conversations if (1) employees consent to provide employers access to this information or (2) it is in the ordinary course of business. The ECPA prohibits other interceptions of electronic communications. Robert Konop was a pilot for Hawaiian Airlines, Inc. (Hawaiian), but was not happy with the concessions that his union was granting to his employer. Robert Konop established a website that was password protected and was restricted to fellow employees as a means of airing grievances. James Davis, a vice president of Hawaiian, approached Gene Wong, another pilot, and asked if he could access Konop's website using Wong's name to obtain a password. Davis claimed he was concerned that Konop was providing fraudulent information to other pilots using this website and wanted to see the content of the website. Wong agreed to allow Davis to use his name to gain access to Konop's website and, as a result of information obtained, Konop claims he was subjected to sanctions on his job. Konop claims that Davis and Hawaiian violated the ECPA by gaining access to his website, which was critical of Hawaiian. Hawaiian claims that the ECPA prohibits only interception of contemporaneous electronic communications and that what it accessed was "stored" electronic communication and therefore not illegal. Konop contends that such a distinction makes no sense. What do you think? It is clear that Hawaiian comes to the court with "unclean" hands given its admission of gaining fraudulent access. [*Robert C. Konop v. Hawaiian Airlines, Inc.,* 236 F.3d 1035 (9th Cir. 2001).]

4. **What Constitutes a Search for Public Employees.** As you know from the chapter, public employees, that is, employees of a governmental unit, are protected from being searched on the job by the Fourth Amendment, whereas employees of private firms are not. An issue that has arisen, though, is what constitutes a search? If a public employee's supervisor looks inside the subordinate's desk, is that a search? The answer is no according the U.S. Supreme Court in *O'Connor v. Ortega,* 480 U.S. 709 (1987), because of what the Supreme Court termed the "realities of the workplace." A supervisor, public or private, has to be able to evaluate subordinate employees. In *Ortega,* however, the U.S. Supreme Court held that the right of public employers to search the offices or desks of public employees did not extend to outsiders such as the police or other branches of government. In 1999, the federal government, through the FBI, was conducting an investigation of possible criminal wrongdoing at the San Francisco Human Rights Commission (HRC). The FBI was informed that documents relevant to their investigation were being shredded at the HRC. Federal agents walked with HRC supervisors to the office of Zula Jones, retrieved documents on the floor and from her file cabinets, and obtained samples from her floor of shredded documents. Some of the documents retrieved in Jones's office were relevant to the investigation and Jones filed a motion to suppress the evidence obtained in this manner. If Jones's supervisor okayed the search of her office by FBI agents, does that make the search okay under the Fourth Amendment? [*United States of America v. Zula Jones,* 286 F.3d 1146 (9th Cir. 2002).]

5. **Blurring the Public–Private Distinction.** Richard Drake worked for Delta Air Lines and claimed he was fired because he expressed pro-union sentiments. Delta says Drake was fired because he failed a drug test. Drake demands due process protection so that he can prove his claim that he was singled out because of his pro-union views. Drake demands due process before his termination because the drug test he took was required by Federal Aviation Administration (FAA) and, if he was a public employee, he would be entitled to due process before being terminated. Since drug testing is mandated by federal regulations, Drake contends that it is the same as a government-mandated test, which brings in the Bill of Rights under the U.S. Constitution and due process. What do you think? Does drug testing by a private employer that is mandated by the federal government transform an unregulated activity (drug testing) into something that enables the employee to make use of the protections provided by the U.S. Constitution? [*Richard Drake v. Delta Air Lines, Inc.,* 1997 U.S. Dist. LEXIS 22753 (E.D.N.Y. 1997).]

Social Responsibility, Policy, and Ethics in a High-Tech World

6. **Outsourcing and Employee Retirement Income Security Act (ERISA).** When employees are near retirement, they often qualify for enhanced retirement benefits and their costs to company health care are most likely much greater than average. Section 510 of ERISA specifically makes it unlawful for an employer to discharge any employee "for the purpose of interfering with the attainment of any right to which such participant may become entitled." John Potelicki began working for the defendant, Textron, in 1966, with his most recent job that of a swirl polisher. Potelicki was a member of the United Auto Workers (UAW), who represented employees at the Textron plant under a collective bargaining agreement (CBA) that had been negotiated by the UAW. In February of 1991 Potelicki injured his arm, and in December of that same year Textron began laying off workers because of declines in business. Potelicki was laid off while on disability. According to the CBA, Potelicki had to be reinstated as an employee for Textron within 48 months in order to retain seniority rights and recall rights. Forty-eight months after his layoff, Textron notified the UAW that it considered Potelicki's seniority rights expired because he was not rehired within 48 months of his layoff. During that period of time, Textron had outsourced Potelicki's job to another firm. Potelicki claims that the company has taken an action that interfered with his rights to qualify for a 30-year vested pension. Had Potelicki been reinstated, he was six months away from qualifying for the 30-year pension. Textron claims that it had legitimate reasons for not rehiring Potelicki. Of course, this is a common situation: a disabled, older employee is laid off shortly before qualifying for his or her full pension. Before deciding to outsource certain activities, should companies be required to examine whether any of its employees are unduly harmed by such actions? See *John Potelicki v. Textron, Inc.,* 2000 U.S. App. LEXIS 2428 (6th Cir. 2000).

Using the Internet to Your Advantage

1. Of course, most of the pertinent information about government regulation of labor can be accessed at the U.S. Department of Labor (http://www.dol.gov). Information about the Fair Labor Standards Act, which regulates payment of minimum wages, overtime, and other provisions, can be found at http://www.dol.gov/dol/topic/wages/index.htm. Also, guidance on the Family and Medical Leave Act can be found at http://www.dol.gov/esa/fmla.htm. The official website of the Social Security Administration is titled Social Security Online and can be accessed at http://www.ssa.gov. ERISA and COBRA are discussed in a number of private websites, mainly ones sponsored by law firms but also by industry groups dedicated to reform of these acts. Among the websites that discuss ERISA are http://www.qdro.pair.com/erisa.htm and http://www.mapnp.org/library/legal/emp_law/laws/erisa.htm. Analysis and advice related to COBRA appear at http://consumerlawpage.com/brochure/cobra.shtml and http://www.krautlaw.com/cons/he6.html.

2. Worker safety is regulated by the Occupational Safety and Health Administration (http://www.osha.gov). The governmental industrial umpire is the National Labor Relations Board, which can be accessed at http://www.nlrb.gov/. Workplace privacy is the subject of much debate by a number of worker and privacy advocates. A very informative site is located at http://www.privacyrights.org/fs/fs7-work.htm. Workplace privacy is a concern of the American Civil Liberties Union, which has several Web pages devoted to the issue at http://www.aclu.org/library/pbr5.html. The FindLaw website has compiled a number of cases pertinent to privacy in the workplace and has a link to the Electronic Communications Privacy Act at http://cyber.findlaw.com/privacy/workplace.html. Also, the Electronic Frontier Foundation has Web pages devoted to workplace privacy at http://www.eff.org//Privacy/Workplace/.

Chapter **Seventeen**

Antidiscrimination Legislation

Learning Objectives

After completing this chapter, you should

1. Know the basic legislation that provides protection against employment discrimination based on protected class: race, sex, color, religion, national origin, age, and disability.
2. Know the elements of a prima facie case under the disparate treatment and disparate impact legal standards, the defenses available to defendants, and how plaintiffs attempt to overcome those defenses.
3. Know what constitutes the quid pro quo and hostile environment forms of sexual harassment and what employers can do to defend themselves.
4. Understand what affirmative action plans are likely to be legal or illegal.
5. Know what protection is provided by the Age Discrimination in Employment Act.
6. Know who is protected by the Americans with Disabilities Act, what are reasonable accommodations, and the standards for liability under the act.

OVERVIEW

As was discussed in the last two chapters, most employees do not have fixed-term employment contracts or, in fact, any employment contract at all. The legal status of most employees in the United States is that of employment at will, so that the employee can decide to quit at will, with or without justification, and the employer can decide to terminate the employee's position, again, with or without justification or cause.

In spite of the fact that most employees work without an employment contract providing job security, there are constraints under which employers operate with respect to their ability to hire, fire, and promote employees. Employers are not allowed to retaliate against employees who report violations of various laws including environmental and worker safety laws. Employers cannot require employees to perform unethical acts such as secretly recording conversations under pain of losing one's job. Employers are potentially liable to employees whom they mislead by enticing them to leave their current jobs with the promise of long-term employment that somehow does not materialize.

This chapter examines the most significant constraints on employer actions: those mandated by antidiscrimination statutes. There are three major statutes that prohibit various forms of on-the-job discrimination by employers: the Civil Rights Act of 1964, the Age Discrimination in Employment Act of 1967, and the Americans with Disabilities Act of 1990.[1] Each of these important statutes has been revised several times and court rulings based on these statutes have evolved over time as well.

CIVIL RIGHTS ACT OF 1964

The Civil Rights Act (CRA) of 1964 was the culmination of political and social pressure, reinforced by the organizing efforts of civil rights groups, mainly those representing what were referred to at the time as Negroes (there have been changes, of course, in the way minorities are referred to). The CRA of 1964 has a number of provisions that do not relate to employment and those provisions are not a focus of discussion in this book. Illustratively, Title II of the CRA prohibits discrimination by race, sex, and national origin in public accommodations provided by restaurants.

protected classes
Groups with specific traits or characteristics, such as race, color, gender, religion, or national origin, for whom discrimination based on the traits is prohibited.

Title VII of the CRA prohibits discrimination by employers based on five characteristics or **protected classes,** which are race, color, sex, religion, and national origin. If it is shown that employers exhibit bias with respect to any of these five attributes in their on-the-job actions, the 1964 CRA has been violated, even if there is no employment contract between the employer and employees.

What the CRA Prohibits

According to Section 703(a) of the 1964 CRA,

 a. It shall be an unlawful employment practice for an employer—

 1. to fail or refuse to hire or to discharge any individual, or otherwise to discriminate against any individual with respect to his compensation, terms, conditions, or privileges of employment, because of such individual's *race, color, religion, sex, or national origin;* [emphasis added]

So Section 703 prohibits employers from making employment decisions based on the five classes listed in the section. That means, for example, that employers cannot hire only men in managerial positions, cannot refuse to hire Jews, and cannot prefer to hire light-skinned African Americans over darker-skinned African Americans.[2] A host of other discriminatory practices have been the subject of lawsuits and are discussed in this chapter. In ordinary English, Title VII prohibits employers, unions, and government from discriminating in the terms and conditions of employment, including pay, based on the five protected classes listed above.

Protected Classes and Disparate Treatment

We have made reference to protected classes, and it is important to have a clear understanding of this concept as it is a foundation of antidiscrimination legislation. The idea behind the protected class concept is that the CRA is violated if an employer treats members of a protected class differently from those outside protected classes. Suppose, for example, that an accounting firm was interested in hiring accountants, but maintained the following hiring criteria:

 • It would consider hiring men who had completed an undergraduate degree in accounting and had a GPA above 3.0, but

---

[1] Civil Rights Act of 1964, Pub. L. No. 88-352, codified at 42 U.S.C. §§ 2000e–2000e-17; Age Discrimination in Employment Act of 1967, Pub. L. No. 90-202, codified at 29 U.S.C. §§ 621–634; Americans with Disabilities Act of 1990, Pub. L. No. 101-336, codified at 42 U.S.C. §§ 12101–12118.

[2] We will discuss the justifications for affirmative action later in this chapter.

- It would not consider hiring women for the same position unless they had both an undergraduate degree in accounting and a GPA above 3.5.

In the example above, it is clear that the employer is treating men and woman differently in a term or condition of employment and, since sex or gender is a protected class, Title VII is violated.

If we change the facts slightly, we see how the concept of employment at will interacts with the CRA. If an employer were superstitious and refused to hire job applicants who applied for a job on Fridays, the employer would not be in violation of the CRA because those applying for a job on a Friday do not comprise a protected class. The employer is free to hire or not hire someone who applies for a job on Friday. Other (and more important) classes that are not protected by the CRA of 1964 are *citizenship* and *sexual orientation.* Employers can legitimately refuse to hire anyone who is not an American citizen and thus discriminate based on citizenship. Similarly, an employer can refuse to hire homosexuals, or can fire homosexuals if they are detected, and such discriminatory practices do not violate the 1964 CRA even though there has been intense pressure by some groups to make homosexuality a protected class. There are a number of states and local jurisdictions that have made sexual orientation a protected class. At the federal level, however, that has not occurred.

Prima Facie Evidence of a Violation of the CRA of 1964

disparate treatment
A specific difference in treatment of individuals in different classes that violates a protected class antidiscrimination requirement. Paying lower wages to females than to male workers in identical jobs involves disparate treatment if no applicable exception applies.

Based on the text of the CRA and court decisions, there are two major categories of violations of the CRA. One of these is described as **disparate treatment.** As the name indicates, disparate treatment violations arise from employers applying different employment standards based on a protected characteristic (class). So, in our earlier example, there was disparate treatment of female applicants for accounting positions as, to be considered, they were required to have higher GPAs than male applicants.

Disparate Treatment

In order for a plaintiff in an employment discrimination suit to get a hearing in court, the plaintiff must be able to show four facts. Solid evidence of the four facts establishes a prima facie case. These facts are

1. The plaintiff was a member of a protected class.
2. The plaintiff applied for a job (or promotion or was treated differently on the job, etc.) and must have been qualified.
3. The plaintiff was not hired (or promoted or was treated differently on the job).
4. If an initial employment case, the employer continued to search for new applicants or hired someone outside the plaintiff's protected class.[3]

Impact of a Prima Facie Case in Disparate Treatment Cases   When a plaintiff in a Title VII case proves the elements of a prima facie case, the burden shifts to the defendant to articulate an acceptable reason for not hiring (or promoting, etc.) the member of the protected class. If the defendant offers no justification for the apparent disparate treatment, then the plaintiff is entitled to a judgment. In virtually no cases do defendants fail to defend themselves, usually in one of the following forms. The defendant may claim, for example, that (s)he hired someone outside the protected class because that person was more qualified. If the defendant articulates a valid basis for not hiring the plaintiff (or for treating him or her differently on the job), then the burden shifts back to the plaintiff

---

[3] If the case involved promotions, the fourth prong of establishing a prima facie case is that the employer promoted someone outside the protected class or continued searching.

to prove that defendant's articulated reason for (his) decision was simply a *pretext* for discrimination.

Was the Stated Reason for the Employment Decision a Pretext?   Suppose an employer is sued for employment discrimination based on race under Title VII and the plaintiff has made out a prima facie case in the manner discussed above. Suppose, further, that the defendant/employer claims that, although both the plaintiff and the person (s)he hired were both equally qualified on paper, the (nonminority) person (s)he hired was more outgoing in an interview. The plaintiff/minority then would have the burden of showing that the interview evaluations were just a pretext for discrimination based on race. Suppose the plaintiff subpoenaed the defendant's employment records and found that, for the last 10 hires made by the defendant, each time the deciding factor was the interview, in which white job candidates were rated higher than minority applicants. Although it is statistically possible, it is extremely improbable that otherwise equally qualified minority applicants showed up worse in interviews than their white counterparts on 10 separate occasions. A jury would be entitled to find, and most likely would find, that it is far more probable that the interview evaluations were a pretext for what was actually discrimination based on race.

Disparate Impact Discrimination

disparate impact
Effects of policies that affect (impact) protected classes differently from others, which are illegal even if the intent of the policies is not discriminatory.

The second broad category of violations of the CRA is based on **disparate impact.** The existence of this category reflects the fact that some employer practices, possibly including many that are not intentionally discriminatory, are discriminatory in their impact on employment. As an example, suppose an employer administered strength tests to applicants for accounting jobs. Undoubtedly, reliance on a strength test, with jobs going to the strongest applicants, would favor male relative to female applicants. Meanwhile, most would say that physical strength has little to do with being a successful accountant, so there is no reasonable rationale by which the employer can justify the use of this screening test. Imposing a strength test on applicants for accounting positions, then, could undoubtedly be successfully challenged as constituting *disparate-impact* discrimination.

In order to make out a prima facie case of disparate-impact discrimination, it is not necessary to show discriminatory intent—though certainly such intent may exist in some situations. Although the disparate impact of a strength test for accounting applicants is obvious and clearly unrelated to job performance, there have been many real-world disparate-impact discrimination cases in which it has not been so clear whether the tests or practices used for screening purposes by employers are job-related or not. Reflecting the importance of the issue and the high financial stakes (damages) involved, an entire industry has developed that focuses on creating *employment tests* that are reliable predictors of job applicants' likely productivity on the job and, hence, able to withstand court challenges.

A prima facie case of disparate-impact discrimination exists when a plaintiff can show that

1. The defendant employer used a hiring practice or employment test to screen job applicants that
2. Had a *disparate impact* on members of the plaintiff's protected class, and
3. The employment test or practice was not justified based on *business necessity*.

Each of these phrases has figured prominently in Title VII litigation. In some cases, the conclusion that disparate-impact discrimination has occurred has been inferred from a showing that, with a reasonable degree of statistical reliability (statistical significance), a greater proportion of members of the protected class are screened out by a challenged hiring practice or have failed the employment test than is true of those outside the class. In many situations, sample sizes are too small to perform standard statistical tests. As an alternative to statistical tests, disparate impact has been demonstrated by reliance upon the four-fifths rule. The four-fifths rule is failed when the following ratio is less than .8:

$$\frac{\text{Pass rate of protected group}}{\text{Pass rate of the highest group}}$$

If Hispanic applicants for clerical positions at a large office complex passed an English competency test given to all applicants for such jobs 60 percent of the time, but white applicants passed 90 percent of the time, the English competency test would fail the four-fifths rule (60/90 < .8). The fact that the test fails the four-fifths rule does not mean the test is illegal; it just means that the employer has to demonstrate that the test is justified by **business necessity.** More specifically, the employer would have to demonstrate that most or all of those failing the test could not perform the job applicants were tested for, while most or all of those passing the test could.

business necessity
An advantage to a business that makes the business more efficient as a consequence of reliance on what is deemed the business necessity (often a screening test in an employment situation).

Business Necessity

In the landmark *Griggs v. Duke Power* case, the employer (Duke Power) was challenged over the use of a generalized, industrial IQ test—the Wonderlic test—given to applicants for management positions.[4] The test had never before been given to applicants for management positions at Duke Power, but was instituted shortly after the 1964 Civil Rights Act was passed. Duke Power had never promoted minorities to management positions before 1964 and it used the Wonderlic test to screen applicants for management positions once the Civil Rights Act was in place. The U.S. Supreme Court struck down Duke Power's use of the test, stating that there was no showing that the test successfully screened qualified applicants for management positions. Clearly, in 1964 the Wonderlic test was not justified by business necessity and it was ruled illegal because that test had an adverse impact on minorities because it was clear that a higher proportion of minorities failed the test relative to nonminorities.

Following the *Griggs* decision, height and weight tests were successfully challenged as requirements for police officers. The conclusion was that these tests had disparate impacts on women even though there was no showing that shorter, lighter applicants (who happened, generally, to be women) could not be good police officers.

Not all tests that may have disparate impacts have been struck down. In general, educational requirements have withstood challenge when there are minimum standards of

---

[4] *Griggs v. Duke Power Co.*, 401 U.S. 424 (1971).

"We're looking for people from a wide variety of ethnic, racial, and social backgrounds who can bench press 200 pounds."

Source: Copyright © 2001 by Randy Glasbergen, www.glasbergen.com.

competency required to practice in the field linked to the educational requirement. So employers can refuse to interview anyone who does not possess a medical degree (M.D.) when they are considering hiring for a physician slot at a hospital. The bar examination was challenged, but not successfully, by minority law students who claimed disparate impact. The courts disagreed and held that passing the bar examination was a business necessity to successfully practice law.

Mixed Motives

mixed motive discrimination cases
Cases brought in situations where employers make employment decisions on more than one basis with some consideration given to illegal motives and some to legal motives.

Keep in mind that discrimination in employment cases are likely to be acrimonious affairs in which each side assembles a large volume of evidence. Frequently, **mixed motive discrimination cases** arise, as when an employer uses both legal and illegal criteria for making its employment decision. As an illustration, imagine Jane Smith has been an aggressive but productive employee in her job as an account manager for a large consulting company. Suppose, further, that her employer considered promoting her to partner status and solicited opinions of existing partners. Assume that many of the partners (all male) commented favorably on Jane's ability to work with clients and get the job done, but many others were critical of her aggressive personality, with some suggesting that she should go to "charm" school and wear more feminine outfits.[5] Finally, let us suppose that Jane was told she would not be promoted to partner status and that, as a result, she filed suit, claiming discrimination based on sex.

In the hypothetical above (which is based on an actual case), two factors are possibly at work in the partnership's decision not to make an offer to Jane: (1) she is aggressive and hard to get along with and (2) her demeanor clashes with the traditional feminine attributes that many of the male partners were accustomed to with female colleagues. The first factor is a legal criterion for deciding whether to elevate an associate (junior employee) to partner status, while the second is illegal because it is based on sexual stereotyping. With differing specifics, this type of mixed motive situation arises with sufficient frequency that the courts have devised a standardized decision rule for application to such cases. What courts require for an acceptable defense to a discrimination charge is that the employer demonstrate (prove) that the same employment decision would have been reached had it not used illegal criteria in its employment decision. In the situation Jane faced, the employer would have to demonstrate that it would have denied her partnership status if she was a man and exhibited the same characteristics.

EEOC Regulatory Framework

Title VII of the CRA only applies to employers (and unions and governments) that have more than 15 members and that affect interstate commerce. Title VII has a relatively short statute of limitations of six months, so aggrieved victims of employment discrimination have six months to complain or else they are barred from filing a claim.[6] Plaintiffs in employment discrimination claims must first file their claim(s) with the Equal Employment Opportunity Commission (EEOC) or with a state employment agency that has a cooperative agreement with the EEOC. The EEOC may decide that the case is sufficiently meritorious to file a claim against the employer on behalf of the plaintiff, but in most cases the EEOC does not file a claim. The EEOC may investigate and attempt to persuade the parties, the employee or job applicant and the employer, to reach some kind of compromise or settlement. If the EEOC cannot obtain a settlement, it often chooses not to file on behalf of the plaintiff, even if it believes that the case has merit. The EEOC has scarce resources and

---

[5] *Price Waterhouse v. Hopkins*, 490 U.S. 642 (1989).

[6] The statute of limitations is 300 days in states where there is an Equal Opportunity Office that receives complaints of alleged violations of Title VII.

uses its legal funds in the cases that it believes will have the greatest impact. Of course, many of the claims that the EEOC or state agencies review are not meritorious. In any event, the EEOC has six months in which to decide whether or not to take legal action on behalf of a plaintiff. If the EEOC decides not to file a suit on behalf of the plaintiff and dismisses the plaintiff's claims, the plaintiff has 90 days within which to file a claim in federal or state court.

Of the suits that the EEOC chooses to pursue, a large proportion are *class action* suits in which the practices of a large employer have impacted a large number of employees. The following sampling of suits filed by the EEOC reflects its inclination to take on cases involving what the commission views as wide-ranging employment discrimination:

- The EEOC supported a suit against Domino's Pizza when Domino's tried to enforce a rule against facial hair. The EEOC claimed that this rule was discriminatory against African Americans because more of them suffered from skin diseases that were exacerbated by shaving daily.[7]
- The EEOC supported a suit on behalf of a woman who was excluded from working around dangerous chemicals while men were not excluded. The stated purpose of the exclusion was to prevent lawsuits by deformed offspring of women who worked in such conditions.[8]
- The EEOC supported litigation that ultimately resulted in a high-profile settlement with Mitsubishi (briefly referred to in the "Nutz and Boltz" box on page 550) based on pervasive sexual harassment and a hostile work environment for women.

Discrimination Based on Race

Although there are notable exceptions, by and large, the prominence of disparate treatment cases has faded because no company in the United States can afford to be openly discriminatory. Explicitly racist or sexist signs for employment such as "Whites Only" or "Wanted: A Few Good Men" no longer exist in places of business. Perhaps in part due to legal changes, there is increased tolerance for diversity in the workplace even though there continue to be disturbing exceptions.[9] Given the decline in prominence of disparate treatment cases, for many years now the majority of employment discrimination litigation has focused on disparate-impact violations, particularly in cases that have involved employment tests and practices used to screen job applicants.

In many disparate-impact discrimination cases, the employment practice or test that is the focus of litigation clearly has a disparate impact on women or some minority group. The typical stance of the defendant/employer, however, is that the test or other screening procedure used is justified by business necessity. In other words, it is claimed, employment decision making by the employer is better using the test than without it. Since most employers are not experts at validating employment tests, they typically outsource to other companies the responsibility for (1) devising appropriate tests and screens for job applicants and (2) providing statistical data and test results to back up claims that applicants who do not score well on the test administered will not perform well if offered a job, and vice versa. In recent years, disparate-impact discrimination cases also have diminished in prominence as court rulings have become more predictable. Companies have

[7] *Bradley v. Pizzaco of Nebraska, Inc.,* 7 F. 3d 795 (8th Cir. 1993).

[8] *United Auto Workers v. Johnson Controls, Inc.,* 113 U.S. 158 (1991).

[9] "EEOC Settles Suit against Salomon Smith Barney for Race and National Origin Bias: African-American, Haitian, Nigerian, and West Indian Workers to Receive $635,000," http://www.eeoc.gov/press/7-16-01.html.

Nutz and Boltz

The following is a typical announcement from the EEOC:

$1.8 MILLION CONSENT DECREE ENDS EEOC FEDERAL EMPLOYMENT DISCRIMINATION SUIT IN ROCKFORD AGAINST INGERSOLL

Hundreds May Receive Compensation for Alleged Race and Sex Bias by Leading Area Employer

ROCKFORD, Ill.—Federal District Court Judge Philip G. Reinhard today approved a $1.8 million Consent Decree resolving a major race and sex employment discrimination lawsuit brought by the U.S. Equal Employment Opportunity Commission (EEOC) under Title VII of the Civil Rights Act of 1964 on behalf of blacks and women alleged to have been discriminated against by Ingersoll Milling Machine Company and its related companies (Ingersoll) (Case No. 99 C 50362). Ingersoll is an international employer with plants in Illinois and Michigan, as well as overseas in Germany. Its Rockford facility manufactures machine tools for use in the automotive industry and other industries.

The Consent Decree, entered in Federal District Court in Rockford, Ill., also resolved two private cases which had been consolidated with EEOC's case: *Jefferson, et al. v. Ingersoll, et al.* (Case No. 98 C 50042) and *Smith v. Ingersoll, et al.* (Case No. 00 C 50260).

The cases, filed beginning in 1998, were based upon more than 30 Charges of Discrimination filed against Ingersoll and alleged that the company refused to hire African-Americans because of their race; discriminated against those African-American individuals it did hire in pay, promotion and other terms and conditions of employment; and discriminated against women in pay.

"This $1.8 million settlement is a first step to remedy racial discrimination in hiring and promotions at Ingersoll," said EEOC Chairwoman Ida L. Castro. "We are very pleased that the injunctive relief will permit EEOC to monitor Ingersoll to ensure its employees a discrimination-free workplace. The Commission's comprehensive enforcement approach has been successful in identifying these illegal and systemic practices by bringing investigators and attorneys together at the outset. We hope that employers will review their practices not just their policies on paper and correct illegal actions voluntarily, to avoid increased risk."

In addition to providing an aggregate of almost $2 million in monetary relief, the Consent Decree includes injunctions which bar Ingersoll from discriminating against African-Americans in connection with hiring, promotion, compensation, and other terms and conditions of employment. Ingersoll is also enjoined from discriminating against women, as well as on the bases of age and retaliation against persons who exercise their federally protected right to complain about employment discrimination.

The Decree also establishes a safeguard against future violations. The Court granted EEOC's request to provide for the appointment of an outside consultant to assist the Court with Ingersoll's implementation of the Decree. The consultant will perform duties similar to those of monitors who oversaw the implementation [of] EEOC's landmark $34 million sexual harassment settlement with Mitsubishi Motor Manufacturing of America in June 1998[,] the largest-ever sexual harassment settlement in U.S. history. "We think the EEOC and Ingersoll can capitalize on that experience in this case to the benefit of all parties," said John C. Hendrickson, regional attorney for EEOC's Chicago District Office.

Today's Decree provides that when Ingersoll begins hiring, it will be obligated to "actively encourage" African-Americans entitled to relief under the Decree to apply for jobs. The Court will set the terms for that "active encouragement" at a later date. Ingersoll will be required to consider the African-Americans who apply on a non-discriminatory basis and will be prohibited from waiving announced standards for favored applicants.

The Consent Decree includes a wide range of other injunctive measures, including terms requiring changes in job posting procedures, clarification of grievance procedures, publication of salary ranges and job grades, recruitment of diverse applicants, and conducting equal employment opportunity training.

The $1.8 million settlement fund will be divided among three groups: $1.3 million will be paid to 34 individuals represented by the Chicago law firm of Soule, Bradtke & Lambert; $400,000 will be paid to rejected African-American job applicants who file claims with EEOC; and $100,000 will be paid to certain victims of compensation discrimination at Ingersoll who also file claims. EEOC anticipates payments to approximately 30 compensation discrimination victims and as many as 400 hiring discrimination victims.

EEOC Regional Attorney Hendrickson said: "This Consent Decree providing for $1.8 million, consultant oversight, and other injunctive relief successfully concludes a vigorous enforcement action against one of the leading employers in one of Illinois'[s] leading cities. It signals, once again, that EEOC will challenge employment discrimination wherever and whenever it is found. It should also signal, to any employer who is paying attention, that the costs of employment discrimination are measured in the millions and cannot be justified to any community of employees, stockholders, or others as merely a cost of doing business."

Hendrickson added: "This case and this Consent Decree are also significant because they demonstrate, as we have demonstrated before, that, in appropriate cases, EEOC can work with the private bar in furthering the public interest. Jennifer Soule and the other private attorneys who worked with us on the Ingersoll litigation carried their full share of the load. Moreover, the cooperative working relationship we had with private counsel created a synergy which maximized the result for the taxpayers and the mission of EEOC. The record in this case is unequivocal: Both EEOC and the private plaintiffs achieved more though their consolidated efforts than either would have working alone."

* * *

In addition to enforcing Title VII, which prohibits employment discrimination based on race, color, religion, sex and national origin, EEOC enforces the Age Discrimination in Employment Act; the Equal Pay Act; Title I of the Americans with Disabilities Act, which prohibits employment discrimination against people with disabilities in the private sector and state and local governments; prohibitions against discrimination affecting individuals with disabilities in the federal government; and sections of the Civil Rights Act of 1991. Further information about the Commission is available on the agency's Web site at www.eeoc.gov.

Source: http://www.eeoc.gov/press/7-13-01.html.

determined what must be done to legally administer employment tests and they have generally avoided trouble by carefully following court objections to earlier tests. Courts have rejected generalized IQ-type tests but have allowed tests that closely tie to performance on the job and are validated by field studies conducted by experts in human resource management.

Discrimination Based on National Origin

During recent years, there have been large inflows of immigrants into the United States, some legal and much of it involving illegal aliens. As mentioned above, employers are entitled to discriminate based on citizenship and can refuse to hire noncitizens. Indeed, there are substantial adverse legal consequences associated with hiring illegal aliens, though it is obvious that many illegal aliens are able to find employment in the United States. As mentioned in the previous chapter, the Immigration Reform and Control Act of 1986 (IRCA) provides for substantial sanctions against employers who hire illegal aliens.[10] On the other hand, concerns have been raised that employers discriminate against some foreigners in an illegal manner based on employer investigations of employee identification. The Immigration Act of 1990 strengthened the antidiscrimination sanctions of the IRCA by preventing employers from demanding too much documentation from job applicants.[11] As the law stands now, if the job applicant has two valid IDs, it is illegal for the employer to investigate further.

A number of industries in some regions in the United States employ high concentrations of people who come from Spanish-speaking countries. For many of these workers, English is a second language at best. With our in-migration experience, two civil rights questions have risen to prominence in recent years: (1) can an employer hire and promote on the basis of proficiency in the English language and (2) can an employer prohibit the use of foreign languages at work sites and enforce English-only requirements at work sites. These are prominent issues in Case 17-1.

[10] Pub. L. No. 99-603, codified at 8 U.S.C. § 1324.
[11] Pub. L. No. 101-649, codified at 8 U.S.C. § 1324B(a)(6).

Case 17-1

Manuel T. Fragante, Plaintiff-Appellant v. City and County of Honolulu; Eileen Anderson; Peter Leong; Dennis Kamimura; George Kuwahara; Kalani McCandless, Defendants-Appellees

United States Court of Appeals for the Ninth Circuit
888 F.2d 591 (9th Cir. 1989)

BACKGROUND AND FACTS

Manuel Fragante applied for a clerk's job with the City and County of Honolulu (Defendants). Although he placed high enough on a civil service eligible list to be chosen for the position, he was not selected because of a perceived deficiency in relevant oral communication skills caused by his "heavy Filipino accent." Fragante alleges defendants discriminated against him on the basis of his national origin, in violation of Title VII of the Civil Rights Act. The district court after a trial found the ability to communicate effectively and clearly was a bona fide occupational qualification (BFOQ) [discussed at the end of the chapter] for the job in question. This finding was based on the court's understanding that an important aspect of defendant's business for which a clerk would be responsible involved the providing of services and assistance to the general public. The court found that defendant's failure to hire Fragante was explained by his deficiencies in the area of oral communication, not because of his national origin. Fragante appeals the court's dismissal of his complaint.

Opinion by Stephen S. Trott

In disparate treatment cases, the employer is normally alleged to have "treat[ed] a person less favorably than others because of the person's race, color, religion, sex, or national origin. . . ." [Citations deleted.] The plaintiff has the initial burden in such a case of proving by a preponderance of the evidence a prima facie case of discrimination.

To establish a prima facie case of disparate treatment, the plaintiff must offer evidence that "give[s] rise to an inference of unlawful discrimination." Plaintiffs commonly prove a prima facie case by showing that the four factors set forth in *McDonnell Douglas* [a case cited in the opinion] are present. To accomplish this a plaintiff, such as Fragante, must show: (1) that he has identifiable national origin; (2) that he applied and was qualified for a job for which the employer was seeking applicants; (3) that he was rejected despite his qualifications; and (4) that, after his rejection, the position remained open and the employer continued to seek applicants from persons of complainant's qualifications. "Title VII's nature and purpose require that the *McDonnell Douglas* test be flexible." The burden of establishing a prima facie case for disparate treatment is not onerous. A determination of whether a plaintiff establishes a prima facie case will depend on the facts of each case.

* * *

We turn our discussion to whether defendants articulated a legitimate, nondiscriminatory reason for Fragante's non-selection. We find that they did.

The record conclusively shows that Fragante was not selected because of the deleterious effect his Filipino accent had upon his ability to communicate orally, not merely because he had such an accent. This is a crucial distinction. Employers may lawfully base an employment decision upon an individual's accent when—but only when—it interferes materially with job performance. There is nothing improper about an employer making such an *honest* assessment of a candidate for a job when oral communication skills pertain to a BFOQ. Employers are permitted to base their non-selection on requirements, such as the oral ability to communicate effectively in English, if the requirement is "reasonably necessary to the normal operation of that particular business or enterprise." 42 U.S.C. § 2000e-2(e)(1).

* * *

Decision and Outcome

The U.S. Circuit Court of Appeals affirmed the decision of the U.S. District Court, which was that the defendant had demonstrated a nondiscriminatory reason for the failure to hire Fragante, namely that his communication skills prevented him from performing satisfactorily on the job.

Questions for Analysis

1. Is this a disparate treatment or a disparate impact case? What was the nature of the disparate treatment the plaintiff claims was applied by the defendant?
2. Can ability to communicate in English be based on listener bias? How would your reasoning be altered if the person actually hired in place of Fragante has a grating, hard-to-understand "New York" accent?

If an employer does discriminate in hiring between those who are citizens of the United States and those who are not, the employer cannot decide to hire aliens from one country and not others. So it would be illegal for an employer to hire noncitizens of European origin but refuse to hire noncitizens from the Caribbean. The "International Perspective" box gives an EEOC Guideline for dealing with the issue of discrimination based on national origin. Notice that this issue crops up in a variety of contexts.

Some Important Disparate-Impact Cases

In the *Wards Cove* case, an employer was sued for relying on proficiency in English as part of the criteria for hiring management and sales staff.[12] The employer operated a seafood processing facility and was sued by employees of Asian descent. In *Wards Cove,* the U.S. Supreme Court held that plaintiffs in Title VII cases bear the burden of proof in disparate impact cases to show that (1) a business practice, such as hiring based on proficiency in English, creates a statistical disparity in hiring patterns relative to the makeup of the labor pool and (2) reliance on the business practice objected to was not justified by business necessity. This case appeared to reverse that part of the *Griggs* decision that required businesses (defendants) to bear the burden of proof on the business necessity justification.

Following the *Wards Cove* case, there was a clamor among civil rights groups to reverse this Supreme Court decision with respect to the burden of proof in disparate-impact discrimination cases. Based on the *Griggs* case discussed earlier, it was viewed as clear that, once a plaintiff in a Title VII case demonstrated that an employment test or hiring practice had a disparate impact, the burden of proof was upon the defendant/employer to prove that the employment test or hiring practice was justified by business necessity. With the *Wards Cove* decision reversing this standard, Congress acted to "reverse" this Supreme Court position when it passed the Civil Rights Act of 1991 (sometimes called the Civil Rights Restoration Act).[13] As a result, the current standard is the old standard that, once a plaintiff shows disparate impact, the defendant must justify the employment practice that gave rise to the disparate impact by showing that reliance on the practice enhances business efficiency.

---

[12] *Wards Cove Packing Co. v. Atonio*, 490 U.S. 642 (1989).

[13] Pub. L. No. 102-166, codified in various sections of 42 U.S.C.

International Perspective   Facts about National Origin Discrimination

Title VII of the Civil Rights Act of 1964 protects individuals against employment discrimination on the basis of national origin as well as race, color, religion and sex.

It is unlawful to discriminate against any employee or applicant because of the individual's national origin. No one can be denied equal employment opportunity because of birthplace, ancestry, culture, or linguistic characteristics common to a specific ethnic group. Equal employment opportunity cannot be denied because of marriage or association with persons of a national origin group; membership or association with specific ethnic promotion groups; attendance or participation in schools, churches, temples or mosques generally associated with a national origin group; or a surname associated with a national origin group.

SPEAK-ENGLISH-ONLY RULE

A rule requiring employees to speak only English at all times on the job may violate Title VII, unless an employer shows it is necessary for conducting business. If an employer believes the English-only rule is critical for business purposes, employees have to be told when they must speak English and the consequences for violating the rule. Any negative employment decision based on breaking the English-only rule will be considered evidence of discrimination if the employer did not tell employees of the rule.

ACCENT

An employer must show a legitimate nondiscriminatory reason for the denial of employment opportunity because of an individual's accent or manner of speaking. Investigations will focus on the qualifications of the person and whether his or her accent or manner of speaking had a detrimental effect on job performance. Requiring employees or applicants to be fluent in English may violate Title VII if the rule is adopted to exclude individuals of a particular national origin and is not related to job performance.

HARASSMENT

Harassment on the basis of national origin is a violation of Title VII. An ethnic slur or other verbal or physical conduct because of an individual's nationality constitute harassment if they create an intimidating, hostile or offensive working environment, unreasonably interfere with work performance or negatively affect an individual's employment opportunities.

Employers have a responsibility to maintain a workplace free of national origin harassment. Employers may be responsible for any on-the-job harassment by their agents and supervisory employees, regardless of whether the acts were authorized or specifically forbidden by the employer. Under certain circumstances, an employer may be responsible for the acts of non-employees who harass their employees at work.

IMMIGRATION-RELATED PRACTICES WHICH MAY BE DISCRIMINATORY

The Immigration Reform and Control Act of 1986 (IRCA) requires employers to prove all employees hired after November 6, 1986, are legally authorized to work in the United States. IRCA also prohibits discrimination based on national origin or citizenship. An employer who singles out individuals of a particular national origin or individuals who appear to be foreign to provide employment verification may have violated both IRCA and Title VII. Employers who impose citizenship requirements or give preference to U.S. citizens in hiring or employment opportunities may have violated IRCA, unless these are legal or contractual requirements for particular jobs. Employers also may have violated Title VII if a requirement or preference has the purpose or effect of discriminating against individuals of a particular national origin.

Source: http://www.eeoc.gov/facts/fs-nator.html.

Part of the *Wards Cove* Supreme Court decision did survive the Civil Rights Act of 1991 as plaintiffs in Title VII cases retained the burden of identifying specifically the *particular business practice* that gives rise to an identified statistical disparity. Plaintiffs cannot simply sue an employer because their protected class is underrepresented. In disparate-impact cases, plaintiffs must identify with particularity a specific business practice(s) that is allegedly discriminatory and not justified by business necessity.

Discrimination Based on Religion

Title VII makes it illegal to impose a term or condition of employment based on religious affiliation, with some exceptions allowed in the case of religious organization employers. If a bishop in the Catholic Church dies, church authorities can discriminate in their selection of a replacement to consider only Catholic clerics.[14] Religious schools can discriminate in their hiring practices to select as teachers only those adhering to their particular religion. However, when an employer is not a religious organization, then not only must the employer not discriminate against employees based on the employee's religion, but also the employer must make **reasonable accommodations** for employees' religious practices. Examples of reasonable accommodations include not requiring employees to work during certain times when work is prohibited by their religion and serving a variety of offerings at company cafeterias, rather than just pork, on a particular day. At the same time, companies do not have to accommodate religious preferences of employees when such accommodations would create *undue hardships* for the employer. In some cases, employees whose religions prohibit them from working on Friday nights, Saturdays, or Sundays have to choose between their religions and their jobs if there is no other way for the business to function within its seniority system while accommodating religion-related work time restrictions.

reasonable accommodations
Modifications of requirements, such as working hours assigned, to accommodate the needs of a protected class.

Discrimination Based on Sex (Gender)

Equal Pay Act (EPA) of 1963

The first major piece of antidiscrimination legislation was the Equal Pay Act (EPA) of 1963, which essentially requires "equal pay for equal work."[15] The EPA states that jobs are "equal" if the jobs entail similar "skill, effort, responsibility and working conditions." Although there were some early high-profile and successful suits brought under the Equal Pay Act, there have been few EPA cases recently. The dearth of cases is due in part to the four exceptions that are allowed under EPA, based on (1) seniority, (2) merit, (3) a system that pays based on quality or quantity of work, and (4) any other factor not based on gender. If a man and a woman are working at identical jobs with the same company, but the man has more years of seniority, then it is legal to pay the man more based on a seniority system used by that employer that ties pay to seniority. The fourth exception, factors other than gender, includes differences in shift pay (night shift workers are typically paid more) and training (management trainees often earn more than the person training them). As long as women have equal access to all shifts and training positions, then pay differentials based on these factors are legal. Also, courts have been unwilling to allow comparisons of different jobs for their "worth to the company" and, so, the only possible violations of EPA occur when jobs are substantially similar and none of the exceptions apply.

Title VII Cases Based on Sex (Gender)

As with other protected classes, it is illegal for an employer to treat men and women workers differently. Reserving some jobs for women and some for men is illegal. Firms looking for truck drivers cannot legally advertise that they are "looking for some energetic men to drive trucks." It is illegal to pay women lower wages than men in like jobs *just because they are women*. It is illegal to take into account the known fact that women live longer than men and require that they contribute more to pension plans, since they are expected to be drawing from the plan for a longer post-retirement time span. It is illegal to refuse to hire male flight attendants, even though surveys of passengers indicate that most passengers prefer females. Prohibiting women from working around dangerous chemicals because of concerns about birth defects is also illegal.

---

[14] This is the BFOQ (bona fide occupational qualification) defense that is discussed below.
[15] Pub. L. No. 88-38, codified at 29 U.S.C. § 206.

Pregnancy Discrimination Act of 1978

The Pregnancy Discrimination Act of 1978 prohibits discrimination against women on account of pregnancy.[16] Employee health benefits packages cannot exclude pregnancy if there are coverage provisions for others affected by major medical events. Women who become pregnant while employed are entitled to be treated like others who are temporarily not able to perform certain tasks. For most jobs, firing a woman because she is pregnant is clearly illegal.

Sexual Harassment and Hostile Work Environment

Although there are exceptions, most sexual harassment cases involve women who are targets of unwanted sexual attention from male employees. If a male supervisor tells a female subordinate that he would promote her if she provides sexual favors to him, he has discriminated based on gender in a term or condition of employment. The topic of sexual harassment on the job is quite broad and can include much more than just what are called **quid pro quo** offers in which the employee is offered or coerced to provide sexual services in return for some job-related benefit. According to the EEOC,

> Unwelcome sexual advances, requests for sexual favors, and other verbal or physical contact of a sexual nature constitute sexual harassment when (1) submission to such conduct is made either explicitly or implicitly a term or condition of an individual's employment, (2) submission to or rejection of such conduct by an individual is used as the basis for employment decisions affecting such an individual, or (3) such conduct has the purpose or effect of unreasonably interfering with an individual's work performance or creating an intimidating, hostile, or offensive working environment.[17]

The example described above and the first EEOC designation of requirements that constitute sexual harassment correspond, of course, to the classic quid pro quo situation, which clearly involves disparate treatment discrimination based on sex. But for the fact that the victim was a particular gender, (s)he would not have been treated in that fashion. The second EEOC designation is intended to combat situations in which advancement on the job is affected by willingness to accommodate a supervisor. Clearly, this is really not much different from the first designation except that providing sexual favors *is not necessarily required* as a condition of employment. Legally, there is virtually no ambiguity about the legal status of the first two examples of sexual harassment provided by EEOC. They are both clearly illegal. There may be substantial controversy about whether the boss did, in fact, proposition his secretary (most propositioners take special care to keep the proposition confidential). However, if it is shown that the boss clearly indicated to a subordinate that she would be promoted if she joined him at a local motel, a violation of Title VII has taken place. In most Title VII cases involving a quid pro quo exchange, there is some confirmatory evidence in the form of a note, an eyewitness, or, recently, online evidence preserved as voicemail, as e-mail, or in a digital video format.

Hostile Work Environment and the Reasonable Woman Test

The third form of conduct listed by EEOC is one that creates a **hostile work environment.** This exists when an employee is (employees are) subjected to sexual crudities that unreasonably interfere with job performance. In a hostile work environment case, there is no need to show that a quid pro quo exists; a cause of action occurs if it is unreasonable to expect a women (or man) to work under such conditions. A hostile work environment is created, for example, when a boss or supervisor *continually* uses profanity and sexually

---

quid pro quo
Literally, "this for that." Applicable to sexual harassment cases in which subordinate employees are offered preferential treatment in the workplace in exchange for sexual favors.

hostile work environment
A work environment that unreasonably interferes with an individual's work performance or one that is intimidating, hostile, or offensive to a reasonable person.

---

[16] Pub. L. No. 95-555, 92 Stat. 2076, codified at 42 U.S.C. § 2000e(k).
[17] EEOC Guidelines on Sex Discrimination, 29 CFR 1604. 11(a).

charged language. There are cases that hold that a single outburst by a boss or supervisor is not sufficient to create a hostile work environment. The courts also have taken judicial notice of differences in sensibilities between men and women and have developed the reasonable woman standard, which is not a unisex standard. In general, courts have recognized that in some occupations, mainly dominated by men, sexually tinged profanity is ubiquitous and *is not* a hostile work environment for men, although it is for women. Many hostile work environment cases have involved women entering nontraditional jobs, such as police departments and truck driving, and encountering a work environment that "reasonable" women regard as intimidating, hostile, or offensive.

In determining whether a work environment is sufficiently hostile, courts take into account the severity of the events complained of. A single groping incident is a far more hostile act than a single exposure to offensive language. Courts also have ruled that victims of a hostile work environment do not have to be so rattled that they have to seek professional treatment in order to maintain a cause of action based on a violation of Title VII. Certainly, if a victim (woman) did have to undergo treatment, took prescription drugs, attempted suicide, or took other significant measures to deal with a hostile work environment, evidence of these matters is admissible at a trial and is likely to influence judges and juries.

Employer Liability for Sexual Harassment

Most employees work for an employer who is an artificial person, that is, a corporation. Corporations can only operate through the actions of employees, and yet, when charges of sexual harassment and the creation of a hostile work environment are brought, corporations, speaking through other employees and attorney/agents, have typically claimed that "they did not know" that a mid-level manager was sexually harassing other employees. In at least one case, the U.S. Supreme Court discussed the fact that different standards apply depending on whether a claimed case of harassment was of the quid pro quo variety or one in which the victim was complaining of a hostile work environment. In the *Harris* case, the U.S. Supreme Court seemed to indicate that, for quid pro quo acts of supervisors, employers are always liable for the actions of their supervisors, regardless of whether they had knowledge of the events.[18]

Complaint Procedures

complaint procedure
Procedure and/or mechanisms that allow employee complaints, especially of sexual harassment or of a hostile work environment, to be communicated to management (and not just the complainer's supervisor).

In an era when sexual harassment complaints are frequent, most employers have **complaint procedures** in place to try to address harassment claims and avoid litigation. If a company does not have a complaint procedure that gives employees an opportunity to make their complaints about on-the-job treatment known to someone other than their immediate supervisors, then that employer cannot be protected by the claim that "they did not know" because they were *negligent* in not setting up a procedure that would enable them to find out about on-the-job harassment. With regard to ignorance claims, the following additional conclusions can be tentatively offered:

1. If an employer has a complaint procedure, but ignores its own complaint procedure, the claim that it "did not know" will not be allowed as a defense.
2. If an employer does not have a complaint procedure, it is in the same legal position as if it ignored its existing complaint procedure and cannot claim ignorance.
3. The complaint procedure should make available someone other than the immediate supervisor of the employee to complain to.
4. If an employer has a complaint procedure, it should be publicized, with emphasis on the fact that it handles complaints involving sexual harassment.

---

[18] *Harris v. Forklift Systems*, 510 U.S. 114 (1993).

As the Internet becomes more integrated into the workplace, more and more hostile environment cases have involved the electronic environment. The electronic environment allows for amplification of unevolved worldviews, such as views by men that women are not qualified to do their jobs, as well as more access to co-workers by e-mail, voicemail, and other electronic connections. Certainly, part of the evidence of a hostile work environment can be gathered from e-mails and electronic bulletin boards. In one case, male pilots used a company-supplied electronic bulletin board to make derogatory comments about the only female pilot and such evidence was used against the company in a hostile environment case filed by the female pilot.[1] Companies are potentially liable for allowing a hostile work environment to persist and part of that environment may be created by e-mails among co-workers, particularly those of a sexual nature, authored by male co-workers to females on the job. For most e-mails, employees have an expectation of privacy, but when the company is charged with a hostile work environment, employee privacy may give way to the need to respond to complaints by women that they are targets of lonely male co-workers who persist in contacting these women in spite of being told to stop.[2] Recent cases suggest the following in the hostile environment/privacy interface in cyberspace:

- Companies are potentially liable to female employees for hostile work environment claims if women complain that e-mails and electronic bulletin boards contain material that is intimidating, hostile, or offensive and nothing is done.
- Companies clearly have an obligation to investigate complaints of sexual harassment and hostile work environments.
- Several cases have held that a company can legally breach confidentiality pledges for company e-mail files if the alleged predator was using company computers and its e-mail system.

Although companies may claim that they are between a "rock and a hard spot," the emerging jurisprudence on this issue seems to be that the Title VII claims are worth investigating and are more important than privacy concerns of employees with respect to e-mails and other electronic communications that take place while using company hardware and software.

[1] *Blakey v. Continental Airlines*, 164 N.J. 38, 751 A.2d 538 (N.J. 2000).
[2] *Bill McLaren Jr. v. Microsoft Corp.*, 1999 Tex. App. LEXIS 4103 (Tex. Ct. App. 1999).

In two recent cases, the U.S. Supreme Court made it clear that employers do have an affirmative defense that exonerates them from liability for the hostile environment form of sexual harassment if (1) there is a well-publicized complaint procedure that is adhered to and (2) the victim of the alleged sexual harassment does not make use of the complaint procedure.[19] It should be noted that, in general, companies are responsible for the actions of their employees on the job and it is rare for sexual harassment to occur with top management completely ignorant of its occurrence. If charges of sexual harassment are brought by an employee and the company does not investigate, or if its investigation is half-hearted or slow, it will be liable for a Title VII violation if the allegations turn out to be true.

[19] *Faragher v. City of Boca Raton*, 524 U.S. 725, 118 S. Ct. 2275 (1998); *Burlington Industries, Inc. v. Ellerth*, 524 U.S. 742 118 S. Ct. 2257 (1998).

Case 17-2 below appears to create two different standards for employer liability resulting from sexual harassment, with the relevant standard depending on whether the employer actually carried out threats that were made to an unwilling employee. The first apparent standard makes an employer liable for quid pro quo sexual harassment regardless of whether the victim took advantage of the employer's complaint procedure. Setting the second standard, companies do have a defense if they are charged with creating a hostile environment but the victim fails to make use of the company complaint procedure.

Case 17-2

Burlington Industries, Inc., Petitioner v. Kimberly B. Ellerth

Supreme Court of the United States
524 U.S. 742 (1998)

BACKGROUND AND FACTS

Respondent Kimberly Ellerth quit her job after 15 months as a salesperson in one of petitioner Burlington Industries' many divisions, allegedly because she had been subjected to constant sexual harassment by one of her supervisors, Ted Slowik. Slowik was a mid-level manager who had authority to hire and promote employees, subject to higher approval, but was not considered a policy-maker. Against a background of repeated boorish and offensive remarks and gestures allegedly made by Slowik, Ellerth places particular emphasis on three incidents where Slowik's comments could be construed as threats to deny her tangible job benefits. Ellerth refused all of Slowik's advances, yet suffered no tangible retaliation and was, in fact, promoted once. Moreover, she never informed anyone in authority about Slowik's conduct, despite knowing Burlington had a policy against sexual harassment. In filing this lawsuit, Ellerth alleged Burlington engaged in sexual harassment and forced her constructive discharge, in violation of Title VII of the Civil Rights Act of 1964, 42 U.S.C. § 2000e et seq. The District Court granted Burlington summary judgment, absolving it from liability. The Seventh Circuit en banc reversed in a decision that produced eight separate opinions and no consensus for a controlling rationale. Among other things, those opinions focused on whether Ellerth's claim could be categorized as one of quid pro quo *harassment, and on whether the standard for an employer's liability on such a claim should be vicarious liability or negligence.*

Included in the opinion of Justice Kennedy were the following incidents to illustrate the working conditions that the plaintiff, Ms. Ellerth, was enduring while working for Burlington.

In March 1994, when Ellerth was being considered for a promotion, Slowik expressed reservations during the promotion interview because she was not "loose enough." [References not included.] *The comment was followed by his reaching over and rubbing her knee. Ellerth did receive the promotion; but when Slowik called to announce it, he told Ellerth, "you're gonna be out there with men who work in factories, and they certainly like women with pretty butts/legs."*

In May 1994, Ellerth called Slowik, asking permission to insert a customer's logo into a fabric sample. Slowik responded, "I don't have time for you right now, Kim—unless you want to tell me what you're wearing." Ellerth told Slowik she had to go and ended the call. A day or two later, Ellerth called Slowik to ask permission again. This time he denied her request, but added something along the lines of, "are you wearing shorter skirts yet, Kim, because it would make your job a whole heck of a lot easier."

Opinion: Justice Kennedy Delivered the Opinion of the Court

In October 1994, after receiving a right-to-sue letter from the Equal Employment Opportunity Commission (EEOC), Ellerth filed suit in the United States District Court for the Northern District of Illinois, alleging Burlington engaged in sexual harassment and forced her constructive discharge, in violation of Title VII. The District Court granted summary judgment to Burlington. The Court found Slowik's behavior, as described by Ellerth, severe and pervasive enough to create a hostile work environment, but found Burlington neither knew nor should have known about the conduct. There was no triable issue of fact on the latter point, and *the Court noted Ellerth had not used Burlington's internal complaint procedures.* [Emphasis added.] Although Ellerth's claim was framed as a hostile work environment complaint, the District Court observed there was a *quid pro quo* "component" to the hostile environment. Proceeding from the premise that an employer faces vicarious liability for *quid pro quo* harassment, the District Court thought it necessary to apply a negligence standard because the *quid pro quo* merely contributed to the hostile work environment. The District Court also dismissed Ellerth's constructive discharge claim.

The Court of Appeals en banc reversed in a decision which produced eight separate opinions and no consensus for a controlling rationale. The judges were able to agree on the problem they confronted: Vicarious liability, not failure to comply with a duty of care, was the essence of Ellerth's case against Burlington on appeal. The judges seemed to agree Ellerth could recover if Slowik's unfulfilled threats to deny her tangible job benefits was sufficient to impose vicarious liability on Burlington. With the exception of Judges Coffey and Easterbrook, the judges also agreed Ellerth's claim could be categorized as one of *quid pro quo* harassment, even though she had received the promotion and had suffered no other tangible retaliation.

* * *

Chief Judge Posner, joined by Judge Manion, disagreed. He asserted Ellerth could not recover against Burlington despite having stated a *quid pro quo* claim. According to Chief Judge Posner, an employer is subject to vicarious liability for "acts that significantly alter the terms or conditions of employment," or "company acts." In the emergent terminology, an unfulfilled *quid pro quo* is a mere threat to do a company act rather than the act itself, and in these circumstances, an employer can be found liable for its negligence only. Chief Judge Posner also found Ellerth failed to create a triable issue of fact as to Burlington's negligence.

* * *

At the outset, we assume an important proposition yet to be established before a trier of fact. It is a premise assumed as well, in explicit or implicit terms, in the various opinions by the judges of the Court of Appeals. The premise is: a trier of fact could find in Slowik's remarks numerous threats to retaliate against Ellerth if she denied some sexual liberties. The threats, however, were not carried out or fulfilled. Cases based on threats which are carried out are referred to often as *quid pro quo* cases, as distinct from bothersome attentions or sexual remarks that are sufficiently severe or pervasive to create a hostile work environment. The terms *quid pro quo* and hostile work environment are helpful, perhaps, in making a rough demarcation between cases in which threats are carried out and those where they are not or are absent altogether, but beyond this are of limited utility.

* * *

When we assume discrimination can be proved, however, the factors we discuss below, and not the categories *quid pro quo* and hostile work environment, will be controlling on the issue of vicarious liability. That is the question we must resolve.

* * *

An employer may be liable for both negligent and intentional torts committed by an employee within the scope of his or her employment. Sexual harassment under Title VII presupposes intentional conduct. While early decisions absolved employers of liability for the intentional torts of their employees, the law now imposes liability where the employee's "purpose, however misguided, is wholly or in part to further the master's business." In applying scope of employment principles to intentional torts, however, it is accepted that "it is less likely that a willful tort will properly be held to be in the course of employment and that the liability of the master for such torts will naturally be more limited." The Restatement defines conduct, including an intentional tort, to be within the scope of employment when "actuated, at least in part, by a purpose to serve the [employer]," even if it is forbidden by the employer. Restatement §§ 228(1)(c), 230. For example, when a salesperson lies to a customer to make a sale, the tortious conduct is within the scope of employment because it benefits the employer by increasing sales, even though it may violate the employer's policies.

* * *

In order to accommodate the agency principles of vicarious liability for harm caused by misuse of supervisory authority, as well as Title VII's equally basic policies of encouraging forethought by employers and saving action by objecting employees, we adopt the following holding in this case and in *Faragher v. Boca Raton, post*, also decided today. An employer is subject to vicarious liability to a victimized employee for an actionable hostile environment created by a supervisor with immediate (or successively higher) authority over the employee. When no tangible employment action is taken, a defending employer may raise an affirmative defense to liability or damages, subject to proof by a preponderance of the evidence, see Fed. Rule Civ. Proc. 8(c). The defense comprises two necessary elements: (a) that the employer exercised reasonable care to prevent and correct promptly any sexually harassing behavior, and (b) that the plaintiff employee unreasonably failed to take advantage of any preventive or corrective opportunities provided by the employer or to avoid harm otherwise. While proof that an employer had promulgated an anti-harassment policy with complaint procedure is not necessary in every instance as a matter of law, the need for a stated policy suitable to the employment circumstances may appropriately be addressed in any case when litigating the first element of the defense. And while proof that an employee failed to fulfill the corresponding obligation of reasonable care to avoid harm is not limited to showing any unreasonable failure to use any complaint procedure provided by the employer, a demonstration of such failure will normally suffice to satisfy the employer's burden under the second element of the defense. *No affirmative defense is available, however, when the supervisor's harassment culminates in a tangible employment action, such as discharge, demotion, or undesirable reassignment.* [Emphasis added.]

* * *

For these reasons, we will affirm the judgment of the Court of Appeals, reversing the grant of summary judgment against Ellerth. On remand, the District Court will have the opportunity to decide whether it would be appropriate to allow Ellerth to amend her pleading or supplement her discovery.

The judgment of the Court of Appeals is affirmed.

Decision and Outcome

The U.S. Supreme Court reinstated Ellerth's claim against Burlington Industries by affirming the court of appeals' reversal of the district court's grant of a motion for a summary judgment for Burlington. On remand, Ellerth's claim for sexual harassment can be defeated if it is shown that she did not take advantage of a company-provided grievance procedure and the grievance procedure was reasonable.

Questions for Analysis

1. Why was the plaintiff unable to claim quid pro quo sexual harassment in this case? If the plaintiff is able to show quid pro quo sexual harassment, how does this help the plaintiff?
2. On remand, did the Supreme Court indicate that it was possible for Burlington Industries to escape liability for the actions of Slowik? What are the two elements of the defense that Burlington would have to show for it to have a defense based on ignorance?

Of course, it must be recognized that not all charges of sexual harassment are based on fact and that there have been suits for wrongful discharge brought by male employees, who were presumed to be guilty and fired, when unsubstantiated charges by subordinate employees were leveled against them. In some cases, males were discharged on flimsy evidence and their views were not solicited or reviewed by their employers. When charges of sexual harassment are brought, companies would do well to make available to both parties, the alleged victim and the perpetrator, *due process in the form of notice and a hearing*. It is important to give both parties a chance to explain themselves before precipitous actions are taken.

Harassing Behavior by Co-Workers and Customers

Companies are also liable for sexual harassment by co-workers who are not supervisors if they have notice of the harassment and they do nothing to correct the situation. Clearly, there are numerous claims that are unfounded. Hence, a company must be prepared to investigate, but should not presume out of the gate that a claim is valid. On the other hand, if a female employee claims to be a target of a stalker, an immediate transfer *of the stalker* may be appropriate. There have been cases where victims of stalkers were transferred and later, when litigation ensued, the victims complained that they bore the brunt of the dislocation costs for events that were not their fault. Again, the number of cases being brought in this area of law indicates how important it is for employers to have complaint procedures in place so that they do not simply have to react to the exigencies of a particular case, as this invariably leads to second-guessing by the courts.

Companies also can be liable to their employees for the harassing behavior of customers, again if they have notice. Most of these cases also involve female employees who are required to wear revealing outfits.

"I can't go out with you ANY weekend Mr. Wankley...
I'm too busy researching sexual harassment litigation."

Source: Reprinted with permission of Carol Simpson Productions.

More Harassment Cases

Following the publicity about sexual harassment cases involving hostile work environments, other (than female) members of protected classes have filed essentially the same claims relating to their situations. There have been discrimination cases based on claims that employers have allowed or created work environments that were hostile to people of color, older workers, and workers with disabilities. As mentioned above, under the 1964 Civil Rights Act, sexual orientation is not a protected class. In the *Oncale* case, however, the legal issue that arose had to do with a same-sex hostile environment.[20] In the *Oncale* case, a male employee was the target of repeated harassment of a crude, sexual nature by other male co-workers occurring, the plaintiff claimed, because he was male. The U.S. Supreme Court agreed that the plaintiff in this case was singled out by other males because he was male and, therefore, that he was discriminated against on the job based on sex, which is a violation of Title VII. The fact that his oppressors were male did not negate the validity of his claim. The *Oncale* case did not create a new protected class based on sexual orientation, but it did create liability for companies who employ supervisors that single out employees of the same sex, either for harassment or for sexual favors.

[20] *Oncale v. Sundowner Offshore Services, Inc.*, 523 U.S. 75, 118 S. Ct. 998 (1998).

Ethical Challenges Discrimination Based on Sexual Orientation

For years homosexuals have argued that they should be protected by Title VII from employment discrimination based on sexual orientation. Congress, however, has not been persuaded by such arguments. There have been several local referenda on the issue of nondiscrimination based on sexual orientation conducted by states and localities and there have been some successes by the gay and lesbian communities, and some notable failures, such as the state referendum conducted in the state of Colorado. The *Oncale* case, discussed in the text, may be a slight break at the federal level, but that case appears limited to the facts in that case, namely, that an employee was singled out for discriminatory treatment based on his gender, but not on his sexual orientation.

Although there are exceptions, for the most part there has been increasing acceptance of homosexuals in various walks of life. At the most recent national conventions, both Republicans and Democrats featured gay speakers, though the Democratic Party has been more vigorous in its advocacy of nondiscrimination. As a future manager, you may be called upon to make employment decisions. Is a person's sexual orientation a factor to be taken into account when making employment decisions? The easy answer is no. Should the company go further and enact an official nondiscrimination policy? Should domestic partnership agreements be part of company health plans for companies allowing for health care coverage of "partners"? If a person was being considered for a high-profile position within a company whose customers include many conservative churchgoers, should possible fallout from customers be a factor in whether to promote the person? In considering spokespersons for company products, should the sexual orientation of the celebrity be a factor? Martina Navratilova was possibly the greatest women tennis player of all time, but she was openly gay and received few opportunities to endorse products. After Billie Jean King, another tennis great, was sued by her lesbian partner, her endorsements were all canceled.

Many people have very strong opinions on this issue. Given the low probability of a legal change at the federal level to protect homosexuals as a class from employment discrimination, much of the de facto change will take place through changes in company policies toward the hiring of gays. Do you have an opinion on how strong your views are in this area?

Remedies under Title VII

For violations of Title VII, there are a number of sanctions that can be imposed on employers. Among the remedies available are the following: the victim of illegal discrimination can be reinstated, awarded back pay, retroactively promoted, and entitled to damages. The Civil Rights Act of 1991 included several provisions that strengthened sanctions that can be visited upon employers, including punitive damage awards for violations that are willful or that exhibit a reckless indifference to the rights of employees. Damage awards are capped according to the size of the employer, but can range from $50,000 for employers with fewer than 100 employees to $300,000 for employers with more than 500 employees.

Affirmative Action

affirmative action
Mechanisms implemented to promote diversity (racial, gender, etc.).

For the past 20 years, plaintiffs in many of the most significant legal battles over employment discrimination have involved claims of discrimination by white employees, particularly white males! Of course, the reason for this litigation is a policy called **affirmative action**. Affirmative action is based on the notion that, because women and minorities suffered explicit and disguised discrimination for a long period of time, it is appropriate to correct for past injustice by allowing for various forms of preferences in favor of those previously discriminated against.

Affirmative action does not come in one flavor; when people talk about affirmative action they could be talking about one or more of the following:

1. *Quotas,* which are requirements that a certain number of job incumbents must be of a particular minority group.
2. *Goals and timetables,* which are requirements that a company must make progress toward a goal of a certain percentage of minorities being hired or retained at a job within a time period.
3. Race, national origin, or gender being treated as one *plus factor* among many others that are examined.
4. *Changes in recruiting practices,* which require companies to recruit from different labor pools than previously, with the goal of creating greater diversity at the workplace.

Although affirmative action may have laudable goals, it is difficult to reconcile affirmative action with the explicit language of Title VII (shown earlier), which appears to unambiguously prohibit discrimination based on race, sex, national origin, religion, and color. In spite of the apparent prohibition, in the *Weber* decision, the U.S. Supreme Court said that Title VII *permits* companies to fashion voluntary affirmative action plans if there were racial imbalances when the affirmative action plan was initiated.[21] Such affirmative action programs are voluntary in the sense that they are not compelled by the government.

The *Weber* decision appeared to validate affirmative action plans by private companies, but subsequent court decisions, by both the U.S. Supreme Court and lower courts, have narrowed considerably the range of allowable affirmative action plans. It should be kept in mind that quotas and goals and timetables are also increasingly in disfavor with courts, because the preferences for a particular group are explicit and thus contrary to the language of Title VII. In addition, if the employer is a local government, the Equal Protection Clause of the Fourteenth Amendment applies. This amendment does not contain an affirmative action exception.

Affirmative Action Plans by Private Firms

Of considerable interest to business managers, the *Weber* decision contains language that can serve as the criteria for evaluating the legality of affirmative action plans implemented by *private employers* in the current legal environment. Given the language of Title VII, affirmative action plans are only legal when

1. There is evidence of discrimination in this field, though not necessarily by the particular organization that is initiating the affirmative action plan.
2. There is an affirmative action plan that the parties can refer to.
3. The affirmative action plan is limited in time.
4. The affirmative action plan sets out a goal.
5. The affirmative action plan terminates when the goal is reached.
6. The plan must not trample on the rights of nonminorities.

Private companies appear to place great value on having a diverse workforce and, therefore, they have initiated a number affirmative action plans. Indeed, a firm that is singled out as not being diverse is increasingly vulnerable to the charge that it is not sensitive to minorities and women, which can bring a number of adverse consequences. For instance, if the firm is large enough to qualify for contracts with the federal government, it is subject to Executive Order 11246, which requires that a firm initiate an affirmative action plan for any job category for which it fails the four-fifths rule (discussed earlier).

---

[21] *United Steelworkers of America v. Weber,* 443 U.S. 193 (1979).

AGE DISCRIMINATION IN EMPLOYMENT ACT OF 1967

mandatory retirement
A policy that sets a maximum age for retirement from a company.

The Age Discrimination in Employment Act (ADEA) of 1967 prohibits discrimination in employment based on age for those over 40.[22] Within this protected age class, it is illegal for firms to fire, not hire, or demote an employee because of age. The act has been amended several times since 1967, but currently for firms (and unions, employment agencies, and the federal government) with more than 20 employees, it is illegal to have a **mandatory retirement** age for nonmanagerial employees. As with Title VII, plaintiffs in ADEA cases can sue based on disparate treatment or disparate impact. For disparate treatment cases, the plaintiff must show that he or she (1) was a member of the protected class (over 40 years of age), (2) was qualified, and (3) was discharged or replaced by the employer. Unlike Title VII cases, plaintiffs do not have to show that they were replaced by someone from outside the protected class. It is a violation of the ADEA for an employer to replace or refuse to hire an employee in his or her upper 50s and replace that individual with someone who is in his or her early 40s, if the actions are based on age and not productivity. Consider Case 17-3.

[22] 29 U.S.C. § 623.

Case 17-3

Calvin Rhodes, Plaintiff-Appellee, Cross-Appellant v. Guiberson Oil Tools, Defendant-Appellant, Cross-Appellee

United States Court of Appeals for the Fifth Circuit
75 F.3d 989 (5th Cir. 1996)

BACKGROUND AND FACTS

Calvin Rhodes began his employment with Dresser Industries in 1955 as a salesman of products and services to the oil industry. In 1986, the oil industry was in the throes of a severe economic downturn. In March of that year, in lieu of being laid off from his job at the Atlas Wireline Division of Dresser, Rhodes was offered a job selling oil field equipment at Compac, another Dresser company which subsequently became Guiberson Oil. Seven months later, on October 31, 1986, Guiberson Oil discharged Rhodes. At the time of his termination, Rhodes was fifty-six years old. In the severance report, Guiberson Oil stated that it had discharged Rhodes because of a reduction in work force and that it would consider re-hiring him. Within two months, however, Guiberson Oil hired a forty-two-year-old salesman to do the same job.

Rhodes sued Guiberson Oil for violating the Age Discrimination in Employment Act, 29 U.S.C. §§ 621-634 (1988) ("ADEA"). A jury found that Guiberson Oil terminated Rhodes from his employment because of his age, but also found that Guiberson Oil had not willfully violated the ADEA. [Footnotes deleted.] On remand, the magistrate judge found that Rhodes had sustained damages in the amount of $188,866.70 as a result of Guiberson Oil's unlawful conduct. Guiberson Oil contends that the evidence is insufficient to support the jury's finding of age discrimination and argues that the district court erred in not granting its motions for a directed verdict or judgment notwithstanding the verdict.

Opinion by Davis and Duhe, Circuit Judges

The Age Discrimination in Employment Act (ADEA) makes it "unlawful for an employer . . . to discharge any individual . . . because of such individual's age." 29 U.S.C. § 623(a)(1) (1988). To establish a prima facie case of age discrimination, the plaintiff "must demonstrate that: (1) he was discharged; (2) he was qualified for the position; (3) he was within the protected class at the time of the discharge; and (4) he was either i) replaced by someone outside the protected class, ii) replaced by someone younger, or iii) otherwise discharged because of his age." [Citations omitted.]

Under the Supreme Court's *McDonnell Douglas-Burdine* framework, the plaintiff first must establish a prima facie case by a preponderance of the evidence; once established, the prima facie case raises an inference of unlawful discrimination. [Footnotes omitted.] The burden of production then shifts to the defendant to proffer a legitimate, nondiscriminatory reason for the challenged employment action. The defendant may meet this burden by presenting evidence that, "*if believed by the trier of fact,* would support a finding that unlawful discrimination was not the cause of the employment action." If the defendant meets its burden, the presumption raised by the plaintiff's prima facie case disappears. However, the plaintiff is accorded the opportunity to demonstrate that the defendant's articulated rationale was merely a pretext for discrimination.

* * *

To sustain a finding of discrimination, circumstantial evidence must be such as to allow a rational factfinder to make a reasonable inference that age was a determinative reason for the employment decision. The factfinder may rely on all the evidence in the record to draw this inference of discrimination. In tandem with a prima facie case, the evidence allowing rejection of the employer's proffered reasons will often, perhaps usually, permit a finding of discrimination without additional evidence. Thus, a plaintiff can avoid summary judgment and judgment as a matter of law if the evidence taken as a whole (1) creates a fact issue as to whether each of the employer's stated reasons was what actually motivated the employer and (2) creates a reasonable inference that age was a determinative factor in the actions of which plaintiff complains. The employer, of course, will be entitled to summary judgment if the evidence taken as a whole would not allow a jury to infer that the actual reason for the discharge was discriminatory.

* * *

Guiberson Oil's defense at trial was not that Rhodes was RIF'd, but that he was discharged because of his poor work performance. Here too, Rhodes presented evidence to counter Guiberson's assertion.

Rhodes customers' testified that Rhodes was an excellent salesman who only lost bids when Guiberson's price was too high. Johnny Ford of CNG Producing Company described Rhodes' performance as follows: "I've only known one other salesman in my career that I think equals Calvin's expertise as a salesman." Leroy Lehmann of Odeco Oil and Gas testified that Rhodes called on his company many times, that Odeco had accepted some of his bids, that Rhodes "possessed the technical skills and ability to explain what he was selling," and that he had no complaints about Rhodes' performance. Terrence Oliver of Texaco testified that Rhodes had made several calls on his company, that Rhodes knew what he was doing, performed his job, and had the technical skills necessary to sell his product. Joshua Patterson of LGS Exploration testified that Rhodes explained his product to Patterson's satisfaction, that Patterson had no problems with Rhodes' technical skills or abilities, that Rhodes was doing his job, and that the other Guiberson salesmen had not called on his company. George Armistead of Union Oil testified that Rhodes called on him every three to six weeks, that Rhodes "not only did what I say he should have done, but he'd go beyond the call of duty," that Rhodes would follow up on projects and "dealt with you in a very professional manner." Kerry Allen of Placid Oil testified that Rhodes answered his questions to his satisfaction, explained the product, and "handled himself very professionally."

* * *

Guiberson officials' testimony also provided support for Rhodes' contention that Guiberson's "productivity" justification of his termination was a pretext for age discrimination. Lee Snyder testified that the memo placed in Rhodes' file explaining that Rhodes lacked technical expertise in downhole operations was substantially true but noted that it was also a "CYA . . . (cover your _ss)" letter. Snyder testified that Rhodes was a good salesman with strong customer contacts and noted that Jack Givens—Snyder's boss who instructed Snyder to fire Rhodes—once said that he could hire two young salesmen for what some of the older salesmen were costing. Snyder quickly backed away from this statement and said that Givens had said he could hire two new salesman for what some of the others were costing him. Givens said he was not aware of telling Snyder this. He also admitted that he had never talked to any of Rhodes' customers about Rhodes' performance as a salesman.

James Sewell, Snyder's other supervisor, testified that he had been very impressed with Rhodes' sales plans and that technical ability was not necessary to sell the product. He also testified that Rhodes had a poor customer base, but admitted that he did not know who Rhodes' customers were, had not talked to any of Rhodes' customers, and had no documentation to support his testimony about Rhodes' poor performance.

* * *

After considering all of the evidence in the record under the standard set forth in *Boeing Co. v. Shipman,* we are convinced that the district court properly accepted the jury's verdict on liability and willfulness. Guiberson Oil's motion for JNOV was properly denied.

Decision and Outcome

The court ruled that there was sufficient evidence for a jury to conclude that Rhodes was discharged because of his age. Rhodes presented evidence that rebutted Guiberson's claim that he was fired for other reasons.

Questions for Analysis

1. On what basis did the plaintiff, Calvin Rhodes, establish a prima facie case of discrimination?
2. What defense did Guiberson Oil, the defendant, use to justify firing Rhodes?
3. What evidence did Mr. Rhodes have that indicated that the justification Guiberson offered for firing him was just a pretext and not the real motive?

There have been a number of ADEA cases in which criteria for retention applied by employers had a *disparate impact* on older workers, but which older workers challenged as not dictated by *business necessity*. Keep in mind that older workers have more money than younger workers and are more willing to challenge, and if necessary to sue, if they believe that they have been victims of discrimination. Companies are entitled to set mandatory retirements for upper management at age 65. Upper management has been defined as inclusive of employees who exercise independent judgment on the job. The ADEA also allows employers to set maximum age limits for airline pilots and police officers whose ability to perform on the job is age-related.

In order to avoid costly litigation, and the accompanying negative publicity, many companies have offered older workers early retirement packages, which typically require them to waive their rights to sue under the ADEA in return for accepting the retirement package offered. As might be expected, there have been charges by older workers that they are sometimes rushed by companies into making rapid decisions regarding retirement packages without being given sufficient time to evaluate them. Protective legislation has been passed in the form of the Older Workers Benefit Protection Act of 1990, which gives older workers a number of rights, including[23]

1. Workers have a minimum of 21 days to consider a proposed plan and 7 days to revoke their decision. If retirement packages, with a waiver of all ADEA claims, are made to a group of workers, they are entitled to a 45-day evaluation period.
2. The employer must refer to the ADEA and Title VII by name if the retirement package contains a waiver of rights under that legislation.
3. The employer must advise employees to consult with their attorneys.

---

[23] Pub. L. No. 101-422, codified at 29 U.S.C. § 623.

Unless employers take all the steps listed above, and some others, which are quite technical, ADEA waivers signed by retirees are not enforceable.

AMERICANS WITH DISABILITIES ACT OF 1990

The Americans with Disabilities Act (ADA) dramatically extended the reach of the Rehabilitation Act of 1973.[24] The Rehabilitation Act, which applied only to federal agencies and federally funded programs including universities, prohibited discrimination based on disability and required covered employers to make reasonable accommodations for those with disabilities. The ADA extended that protection to all employees who work for employers (and unions, etc.) with 15 or more employees.

The ADA prohibits employers from discriminating in the terms and conditions of employment against those with disabilities and requires employers to make reasonable accommodations for them. In the language of the ADA, a violation occurs when an employer refuses to hire or promote an otherwise qualified person on account of disability. Key issues in ADA litigation concern the definition of **disabled**, what is meant by *reasonable accommodations,* and whether accommodating the disabled will cause **undue hardship** for the company.

disabled
Physically or mentally impaired in a way and to a degree that qualifies for protection under the Americans with Disabilities Act.

undue hardship
Standard that frees employers from providing accommodation to a protected class because doing so would be unduly burdensome.

Coverage of the ADA

Dating back to the standards used in the Rehabilitation Act of 1973, a person is considered disabled and thus covered under the ADA if any of the following applies:

1. A physical or mental impairment substantially limits one or more of the major life activities of the individual.
2. The person has a record of impairment.
3. The person is regarded as having such an impairment.

Some articles have suggested that the number of potentially qualified individuals under the ADA is over 40,000,000. Quite obviously, a paraplegic is considered disabled, as are blind, deaf, or mute people or people missing a limb. Illnesses that qualify a person for ADA protection include cancer, AIDS, diabetes, alcoholism, and morbid obesity (those who are more than twice the weight of an average person of that height). People who are currently addicted to drugs or alcohol and are impaired as a result are not entitled to the protection of the ADA. Homosexuals, transvestites, and transsexuals are not entitled to protection under the act.

For a number of medical conditions, modern medicine has provided treatments that allow those afflicted to cope with their ailments. A person might be "legally" deaf, but with hearing aids the person may be able to function in a nearly normal fashion. There are treatments for all sorts of mental conditions as well as treatments for poor vision, high blood pressure, and diabetes. The U.S. Supreme Court has held that a person is covered by the ADA "with reference to corrective measures," which means that a person would have to fit under one of the three categories above *after receiving treatment* to qualify as disabled. In *Sutton v. United Airlines, Inc.,* the U.S. Supreme Court held that female plaintiffs were not sight-disabled since their vision while wearing glasses did not qualify for the protections of the ADA, even though, without prescription glasses, these women would not have been able to see well enough to drive a car, let alone pilot an airplane.[25]

---

[24] Americans with Disabilities Act, Pub. L. No. 101-336, codified at 42 U.S.C. §§ 12101–12117; Rehabilitation Act of 1973, Pub. L. No. 93-112, codified at 29 U.S.C. § 791 *et seq.*

[25] *Sutton v. United Airlines, Inc.,* 527 U.S. 471 (1999).

Reasonable Accommodations

If a firm was trying to hire a typist to assist in data entry and processing orders, it's possible that paraplegics in wheelchairs could perform the requisite typing. They would, however, have difficulty applying for the available job if the only access to company headquarters was up two flights of stairs and like difficulty in getting to a job under the same physically limiting conditions. In most instances, having an elevator, or installing ramps, rather than confronting a paraplegic with stairs would be viewed as a reasonable accommodation. The ADA does not require employers to hire disabled people who are not qualified or able to perform essential job functions, but it does require employers to make *reasonable accommodations* for *otherwise qualified* individuals who happen to be disabled in some way.

Section 101(9) of the ADA states that an employer's obligations to make reasonable accommodations include "(1) making existing facilities accessible to or usable by individuals with disabilities and (2) restructuring jobs, providing modified work schedules, and acquiring or modifying equipment or devices." In addition to elevators and ramps, requirement (1) above has been satisfied in many situations by reserving parking spaces for disabled workers near their offices, revamping bathrooms, and clearing paths at work sites for disabled employees to travel unencumbered. In many instances, the result of disability is that the employee is able to effectively perform in his or her job, but not for full 8- to 10-hour periods. In such instances, employers have satisfied the reasonable accommodation standards by allowing employees to work more from home, reducing full-time jobs to part time, and providing for rest facilities at work, including cots.

Undue Hardship

Employers are not required to make reasonable accommodations for disabled employees if the cost or difficulty of making these accommodations would cause *undue hardship* on the company. Determining what is an undue hardship is accomplished on a case-by-case basis. For some jobs, it is relatively easy to imagine reassignments to accommodate for disabilities. So, when a teacher catches a communicable disease, reassigning her to an administrative position so that the risk of infecting others, particularly children, is minimized may be a reasonable accommodation that is not unduly burdensome. In other instances, courts have held that, if an employee goes on indefinite leave because of disability, accommodating the request for that leave would be an undue hardship.[26]

Questions to Job Applicants from Employers and Pre-Employment Examinations of the Disabled

As an overarching rule, employers and potential employers should strive to treat the disabled as they would nondisabled applicants and employees. Although this general rule is useful, it is not an adequate guide to appropriate behavior by employers for purposes of complying with the ADA, as there are a number of specific restrictions on what can be explored. For example, it is illegal to ask applicants in a job interview whether they are disabled. The following are additional illegal questions according to EEOC:

1. Do you have AIDS?
2. Have you ever been treated for drug addiction or drug abuse?
3. Have you ever been treated for mental health problems?

It is not, however, illegal to ask a job applicant whether he or she will need some kind of reasonable accommodation to take an employment test. Quite obviously, the line between legal and illegal behavior in complying with the ADA is a fine one. It is imperative that

---

[26] *Myers v. Hose*, 50 F.3d 278 (4th Cir. 1995).

Nutz and Boltz   Justices Draw Lines on Claims of Disability

In a case *(Toyota Motor Manufacturing v. Ella Williams,* 534 U.S. 184 (2002)) about carpel-tunnel syndrome, the Supreme Court pulls in the boundaries of the Americans With Disabilities Act.

WASHINGTON—The Supreme Court narrowed the scope of the Americans With Disabilities Act on Tuesday, ruling that an impairment must have a substantial effect on a person's daily life to qualify as a disability under the law.

Conditions that only prevent a worker from performing a specific job-related task are not legal disabilities, the court said. "Merely having an impairment does not make one disabled for purposes of the ADA," the court declared. "Claimants also need to demonstrate that the impairment limits a major life activity."

The ruling could affect millions of workers who suffer from repetitive strain injuries or other impairments that affect their jobs. Both sides—labor and management—in the long-running dispute over the scope of the ADA agreed that the ruling will make it more difficult for workers to prove that they are disabled and therefore entitled under the law to an accommodation by their employers.

The case centered on one worker's inability to perform certain manual tasks at an automobile assembly plant because of carpel-tunnel syndrome. The court ruled that the impairment alone did not qualify the worker as disabled under the ADA.

"To be substantially limited in performing manual tasks, an individual must have an impairment that prevents or severely restricts the individual from doing activities that are of central importance to most people's daily lives," Justice O'Connor wrote. "The impairment's impact must also be permanent or long-term."

RULING CHEERED, PANNED

Kathleen Blank, an attorney-adviser with the National Council on Disability, a federal advisory agency, said the decision "is going to affect a lot of people. This decision is going to give employers a lot of confidence that they can challenge workers on whether they are disabled. It's clearly a decision in favor of employers giving them more latitude to refuse to make accommodations."

But Stephen Bokat, general counsel of the U.S. Chamber of Commerce, hailed the ruling as "the definitive opinion on what constitutes a disability under ADA." He said it should reduce the number of "marginal cases" brought against businesses under the 1990 legislation, but denied that it would encourage employers to resist making accommodations for employees.

"The majority of accommodations are not tremendously expensive, and most employers do it," Bokat said. "It happens every day, whether it's covered by the ADA or not."

Source: Adapted from Edward Walsh, *The Washington Post,* January 9, 2002.

---

companies have access to attorneys well versed in employment law as well as knowledgeable HRM staff who are up to speed with the latest EEOC regulations regarding interview techniques that comply with the ADA and other employment discrimination statutes.

Employers cannot require disabled job applicants to submit to physical examinations unless a definite offer of employment has been made to the applicant and then only if all applicants are required to take such examinations. Employers can condition final offers of employment on the results of the physical examination, but only if the failure to pass the physical examination means that the employee cannot perform the essential functions of the job sought.

Drugs, Alcohol, and Exclusions from Coverage

The ADA does not provide legal protection for those currently using illegal drugs, but it does provide protection against employers who refuse to hire former addicts and those who have sought treatment for drug abuse. Casual drug users who at the time of job application are active drug users are not protected by the ADA. In parallel fashion, the ADA does not protect alcoholics who show up to work impaired. Moreover, employees who are arrested for driving while alcohol-impaired off the job can be fired for that reason. The ADA does, however, make refusal to hire former alcoholics an illegal act.

Dangerous Workers

Employers are not required to hire or retain disabled workers who are a danger to co-workers and who cannot be reassigned in ways that remove the threat to co-workers while still performing their jobs. A surgeon who had AIDS would be vulnerable to being fired for that reason, but an orderly would not. In the *Arline* case, a teacher contracted tuberculosis and was thus contagious and a danger to her students as well as other teachers.[27] She was discharged as a result, but sued and the ensuing dismissal of her case was reversed because there was no inquiry made by the trial court as to whether she could be reassigned to another position and not pose a threat to co-workers. In general, for courts to allow a discharge of an employee because he or she is a threat to co-workers, there must be a showing that the threat to co-workers is immediate and substantial and not speculative. In most of the cases involving HIV-positive employees, courts have not been satisfied that reasonable accommodations could not be made to remove threats to co-workers while still allowing the infected employee to continue employment.

Remedies under the ADA

Remedies under the ADA are similar to those available under Title VII. Victims of illegal employment discrimination due to disability may be entitled to reinstatement, back pay, compensatory and punitive damages, and other costs. Employers who are repeat offenders may be fined as much as $100,000 per ADA violation. Claims filed under the ADA must first be filed with the EEOC, with the same procedures as those that apply in Title VII cases.

EMPLOYER DEFENSES TO TITLE VII, ADEA, AND ADA CLAIMS

Competency and Employment Tests

Often, the first defense offered by employer defendants is that they did not discriminate on the basis of protected class characteristics: the plaintiffs in these cases were not qualified, or could not do the jobs required, or did not deserve the promotions at issue. Certainly, in many cases, there are objective, minimum qualifications for job incumbency. Faced with a plaintiff charging disparate treatment, an employer can counter by legitimately claiming that the plaintiff was not qualified and that we (the employer) do not hire people for that position with the qualifications of the plaintiff. Many times the minimum qualifications are educational or based on years of experience, which are objective business reasons that most judges and juries can accept. Indeed, Section 703(h) of Title VII allows the use of "any professionally developed ability test [that is not] designed, intended, or used to discriminate."

Business Necessity and Employment Tests or Screening Procedures

Competency is closely related to the *business necessity* defense in disparate-impact cases. As was discussed earlier, a business violates Title VII (and the ADEA or ADA) if it uses a business practice to screen for hires or promotions that it cannot justify based on business necessity. As a result of the Supreme Court decision in the *Griggs* case and the Civil Rights Act of 1991, businesses bear the burden of proof when they claim that a screening procedure they use is justified by business necessity. In many instances, there are objective

---

[27] *School Board of Nassau County, Florida v. Arline*, 480 U.S. 273 (1987).

The ADA provides that any place of public accommodations must be accessible to people with disabilities. The ADA statute specifically lists 12 categories of public accommodations including hotels, restaurants, shopping centers, universities, and bowling alleys. Access Now, an advocacy group for the blind, and Robert Gumson, a blind person, sued Southwest Airlines because its website was not reasonably accessible to blind people. The defendant, Southwest, filed a motion to dismiss claiming that the ADA does not apply to "virtual space" locations, only to physical spaces (*Access Now, Inc. and Robert Gumson, v. Southwest Airlines, Co.*, 227 F. Supp. 2d 1312 (S.D. Fla. 2002)) and the district court judge agreed. According to Judge Patricia Seitz, "The plain and unambiguous language of the statute and relevant regulations does not include Internet Web sites." The plaintiff, Robert Gumson, admitted that he had a screen reader on his computer that was equipped with a voice synthesizer, which enabled him to order airline tickets, though he claimed it was difficult and that Southwest should have provided additional assistance to make it more user friendly for the sightless. Gumson also asked for attorney fees and costs, which were denied by Judge Seitz.

There were a number of businesses and academics who applauded the verdict. Walter Olson, senior fellow at the Manhattan Institute and editor of overlawyered. com, noted that the websites of the organizations that claim to speak for the disabled were not in compliance with what Gumson and Access Now were requesting of the Southwest Airlines website. Olson noted that the World Wide Web could become a "classic target-rich environment" for lawyers to sue just about any website. Robert Levy of the Cato Institute said that the dismissal reaffirms the definition of public accommodation. "In this day and age, when government has wormed itself into virtually every area of our private lives, it's important to draw the distinction between what's private and what's public," Levy said.

The fact that websites are the subject of a civil rights lawsuit is just another indication that cyberspace creates novel legal issues in every area of law.

Source: http://news.com.com/2100-1023-962761.html.

economic, business, and psychological studies that, in fact, show that the screening procedure in question does identify those most qualified to perform well on the job.

Seniority

For many jobs, promotions, layoffs, and hiring are based on seniority. Although antidiscrimination legislation addresses some very important issues, Congress did not intend for the civil rights laws to overturn seniority systems; reliance on seniority systems is sanctioned within Title VII as well as in other antidiscrimination in employment statutes. It has been claimed that many seniority systems are tainted by the prior effects of discrimination. Even if that is the case, however, unless there is evidence of new, additional discriminatory acts in the rules or administration of a seniority system, such systems are immune from attack and are valid defenses. If, however, there is evidence that new seniority system rules were adopted that were intentionally discriminatory, a violation of Title VII may be found.

Bona Fide Occupational Qualifications (BFOQ)

The BFOQ defense is based on Section 703(e), which states that it shall not be an unlawful practice to hire employees based on sex, national origin, or religion if these categories are bona fide occupational qualifications. Notice that race is not a class that qualifies for the

BFOQ defense. The BFOQ defense allows movie companies to interview only women for female leads in a motion picture and it is used by religious authorities to interview only members of their faith when an opening occurs for a cleric. Historically, courts have narrowly interpreted the BFOQ defense and have rejected its use numerous times when the job at issue might be classified as traditionally male or female. Thus, airlines have been unsuccessful in using the BFOQ defense to justify hiring only female flight attendants.

Summary

Title VII of the Civil Rights Act of 1964 Makes Illegal Acts of Discrimination in Employment Based on Five Protected Classes; Disparate Treatment Is a Violation of Title VII	• Title VII of the Civil Rights Act (CRA) protects against certain types of discrimination based on *race, sex, color, religion,* and *national origin.* • Employers who are subject to the jurisdiction of the CRA are prohibited from making employment decisions based on membership in one of these classes. Sexual orientation and citizenship are not protected classes. • Overt discrimination, or disparate treatment, occurs when a member of a *protected class* is treated differently from nonmembers by an employer. • A plaintiff in a Title VII lawsuit must prove the elements of a *prima facie* discrimination in order to avoid having the suit dismissed. • The elements of a *prima facie* case based on *disparate treatment* are the plaintiff is a member of a protected class, is qualified for the job or promotion, and was not hired, and the employer continued to search or hired outside the protected class. • Once the plaintiff proves the elements of a prima facie case of discrimination, the burden is on the defendant to justify his or her actions. • If the defendant offers a valid defense, the plaintiff has the burden of showing that the defendant's purported reasons are a *pretext* for illegal discrimination.
Employers and Unions Can Violate Title VII of the CRA if They Use an Employment Practice That Has a Disparate Impact on a Protected Class Not Justified by Business Necessity	• The prima facie elements of *disparate-impact* discrimination are (1) the defendant made use of an employment practice that (2) had a disparate impact on members of the protected class of the plaintiff, and (3) the hiring practice was not justified by *business necessity.* • Once elements (1) and (2) are shown, the burden is upon employers to prove business necessity for reliance on the employment practice that has a disparate impact. • In many cases, challenged-employment decisions are based on *mixed motives,* some of which are legal and some of which are illegal. In such cases, the burden is upon the employer to show that the same decision would have been made even if the illegal criteria were not used.
To Pursue a Claim under the CRA of 1964, Victims Must File within Six Months and File First with the EEOC or the State Equivalent	• Victims of alleged employment discrimination under Title VII have six months to file a complaint. • The Equal Employment Opportunity Commission (EEOC) issues regulations, files lawsuits, and generally supervises enforcement of the CRA of 1964 at the federal level. • Plaintiffs in CRA actions are required to file their suits first with the EEOC or with a state equivalent of the EEOC. The EEOC has six months to decide whether to file a suit on behalf of the plaintiff and generally picks the cases that have the largest impact. If the EEOC does not file suit on behalf of the plaintiff, the plaintiff has 90 days to file suit him- or herself.
Discrimination Based on	• Although employment discrimination based on religion is illegal generally, religious organizations can make employment decisions based on religion and only consider hiring members of their religion for certain positions.

Religion or Gender Is Unlawful under Title VII; Gender Discrimination Protection Is Supplemented by the Equal Pay Act and the Pregnancy Discrimination Act	• Also, employers are required by the CRA to make *reasonable accommodations* for the religious beliefs of employees. • The Equal Pay Act requires equal pay for equal work, but recognizes a number of exceptions based on seniority, merit, quantity or quality of work, or factors such as shift times that are not based on gender. • Title VII prohibits discrimination based on gender in employment decisions regardless of whether gender discrimination is disparate treatment or results in disparate impact. • The Pregnancy Discrimination Act of 1978 prohibits discrimination based on pregnancy and requires pregnancy benefits to be included in health packages that cover similarly significant medical events.
Title VII Is the Main Bulwark against Sexual Harassment and the Creation of Hostile Work Environments; It Is Illegal to Condition a Job Benefit on Provision of Sexual Favors and It Is Illegal to Create an Environment That Offends Reasonable Women	• Title VII prohibits *sexual harassment* and *hostile work environments* based on gender. • Title VII prohibits conditioning hiring, promotion, or any other employment-related benefit on the provision of sexual favors to employers, management, or supervisors. • It is illegal to allow a work environment to become hostile. A hostile work environment is one that unreasonably interferes with an individual's work performance or is intimidating, hostile, or offensive to a reasonable person. • Courts have taken judicial notice that women may react differently than men to profanity, sexual jokes, touching, and other events that could create a hostile work environment. • A hostile work environment could be, in part, created by exposure to offensive material online. Companies may have to screen activities of male employees to prevent the existence of a hostile work environment. • Courts have held employers liable for *quid pro quo* sexual harassment even though it took place without knowledge of senior management. • If companies have a reasonable *complaint procedure,* it may provide a defense if the complaining party was aware of the procedure but did not use it. • Employers can be liable for actions of co-workers and customers that create a hostile work environment.
Affirmative Action Can Be Legal but, Increasingly, It Has Been Successfully Challenged in Court	• *Affirmative action* includes a number of different techniques that are designed to diversify the workforce. The more mandatory the action, such as with quotas, the more likely the affirmative action will be held illegal in court. • Affirmative action by private firms can be legal when there is evidence of prior discrimination and when the plan is limited in time, sets out a goal, and terminates when the goal is reached.
Recent Federal Legislation, the Age Discrimination in Employment Act and the Americans with Disabilities Act, Protects Older Workers and Workers Suffering from Disabilities	• The Age Discrimination in Employment Act (ADEA) of 1967 prohibits discrimination against older workers, defined as workers over age 40. Under the ADEA, *mandatory retirement* policies are illegal, except for those applied to senior management. • Discrimination within the class of older workers is also illegal; for example, a preference for workers in their early 40s relative to workers in their late 50s is prohibited. • The Older Workers Benefit Protection Act of 1990 specifies procedural steps that enable older workers to evaluate retirement packages without being rushed into unwise decisions. • The Americans with Disabilities Act (ADA) of 1990 prohibits discrimination based on *disability* as long as the disabled person can perform the essential functions of the job held or applied for. • Employees are considered disabled if a physical or mental impairment limits one or more major life activities, or if the person has a record of impairment or is perceived as having a disabling impairment.

<table>
<tr><td>

from Being Discriminated Against Based on Age or Disability When They Can Do the Job; Employers Do Have Defenses Based on Competency, Seniority, and BFOQ

</td><td>

- Employers must make *reasonable accommodations* so that disabled workers can take employment tests and perform job assignments.
- Employers do not have to make accommodations for disabled workers if those accommodations would entail *undue hardships*.
- Employers cannot require disabled persons to take a physical examination unless they have been offered a job and all job candidates have to take a similar physical examination.
- The ADA does not protect those currently abusing drugs or alcohol. Similarly, employers do not have to hire employees who may be dangerous to other employees.
- Defenses by employers include competency—the person in a protected class is not qualified; seniority—the decision was made pursuant to a bona fide seniority system; or claims that the class of the person hired fitted within a *bona fide occupational qualification* (BFOQ) for the open position.

</td></tr>
</table>

Key Terms

affirmative action, *563*	disparate treatment, *545*	protected classes, *544*
business necessity, *547*	hostile work environment, *556*	quid pro quo, *556*
complaint procedure, *557*	mandatory retirement, *565*	reasonable
disabled, *568*	mixed motive discrimination	accommodations, *555*
disparate impact, *546*	cases, *548*	undue hardship, *568*

Questions for Review and Analysis

1. List the five protected classes under the Civil Rights Act (CRA) of 1964 and explain what it means to be a member of a protected class. Is citizenship or sexual orientation a protected class under the CRA of 1964? What is the consequence of not being a member of a protected class?

2. What must a victim of illegal discrimination show in order to recover? What is the difference between disparate treatment and disparate impact?

3. What is the difference between quid pro quo sexual harassment and the creation of a hostile environment?

4. Your company is very concerned about increasing the diversity of its workforce. What measures can your firm take to increase diversity and what steps are possibly illegal under Title VII?

5. Give three examples of actions that a company can take to reasonably accommodate disabled workers. Can you think of an example when accommodating disabled workers would constitute an undue hardship for a firm?

If You Really Understood This Chapter, You Should Be Able to Provide Informed Commentary on the Following:

1. **Dangerous Working Conditions.** The plaintiff, Pam Armstrong, was a nurse who worked in Home Care Services of Flowers Hospital, Inc., the defendant. In 1990, Ms. Armstrong was assigned to work for a patient who had AIDS as well as meningitis, which is an infectious disease that often affects AIDS sufferers. At that time, Ms. Armstrong was in her first trimester of pregnancy and told her supervisor that she should not treat this patient because she feared that her baby may be harmed by her exposure to meningitis or some other opportunistic disease from the AIDS patient. Her supervisor at Home Care Supervisor told Armstrong that they did not make exceptions and referred her to the "Universal Precautions" developed by the Center for Disease Control for treating patients with infectious diseases. Armstrong was given an ultimatum by her supervisor and was terminated when she refused her assignment to the patient with AIDS. Armstrong sued her employer under Title VII and the Pregnancy Discrimination Act, but EEOC refused to pursue her claim. What do you think? Do you think that at the time there was significantly more uncertainty about how AIDS was spread and that Armstrong was justified in her concerns? [*Pam Armstrong v. Flowers Hospital, Inc.,* 812 F. Supp. 1183 (M.D. Ala. 1993).]

2. **Disparate Treatment and the Statute of Limitations.** In 1993, Myrtle Thomas was laid off from Eastman Kodak based in part on a ranking system that relied on what Thomas claimed were

racially biased performance appraisals that were administered in 1990–92. Thomas filed suit with EEOC claiming that she was a victim of racial discrimination. Kodak filed a motion for a summary judgment claiming that, even if the performance appraisals were racially biased, the statute of limitations had run on them and therefore they could not be used in Thomas's Title VII claim against Kodak. As you know from the chapter, the statute of limitations for a Title VII violation is six months or, in some cases, 300 days. Under either time period rule, if Thomas was a victim of discrimination based on race because of the performance appraisals, her time for complaining had expired. Thomas claimed that the statute of limitations does not begin to run on those performance appraisals until she was negatively impacted on the job, which occurred at the time of her being laid off. What do you think? If Thomas's employment record was tainted by events that occurred more than 300 days prior to when she filed her Title VII claim, is she barred by the statute of limitations? [*Myrtle Thomas v. Eastman Kodak Company,* 183 F.3d 38 (1st Cir. 1999).]

3. **Hostile Environment for Older Workers.** Mary Ann Crawford was employed in the billing department of Medina General Hospital for 28 years when Darla Kermendy, a much younger woman, was appointed as Crawford's supervisor. Crawford claimed that Kermendy made all kinds of comments that Crawford considered inappropriate, including racial and sexual comments. Crawford sued Medina General Hospital and Kermendy personally based on Kermendy's comments about older workers. Kermendy allegedly made the statement that "I don't think that women over 55 should be working." Kermendy claims that she made the comment about herself because she hoped she could retire at age 55 or younger. Crawford claims the billing department became divided based on age, with the younger women generally making the older ladies feel "stupid, useless, dumb." Crawford admits that she continued to work in the billing department and was not demoted. Crawford sued based on the claim that she was forced to work in a work environment that was hostile to her based on her age. There were two issues the court had to address: (a) could the plaintiff file an Age Discrimination in Employment Act (ADEA) suit based on a hostile work environment and (b) did the plaintiff allege facts sufficient to avoid having the case dismissed? How does the court distinguish a personality dispute between women of different ages and a legitimate hostile environment case based on age? See *Mary Ann Crawford v. Medina General Hospital,* 96 F.3d 830 (6th Cir. 1996).

4. **Reasonable Accommodations.** An issue that has arisen involving Americans with Disabilities Act cases is whether there is a relationship between wages earned by a disabled person and the cost of the reasonable accommodations incurred by employers. Beth Lyon was injured outside work and was on disability for four years. When she returned to work, Ms. Lyon had to wear a knee brace and could not walk long distances without great difficulty. Ms. Lyon requested that her employer, the Legal Aid Society, pay for a parking space near where she worked and the courtroom where she frequently appeared on behalf of clients of the Legal Aid Society. The Legal Aid Society balked at paying $520 per month for the parking space she requested because it was 26 percent of her salary. Lyon claims that the parking space enables her to get to work and the courtroom on time. Without a reserved parking space, Lyon claims she may have to hunt for a parking space and, if she is unsuccessful in finding a parking space nearby, she will likely be late for work or the courtroom. What do you think? Should there be a relationship between salary earned by the employee and the amount the employer is required to spend on "reasonable accommodations" under the ADA? See *Beth Lyons v. The Legal Aid Society,* 68 F.3d 1512 (2nd Cir. 1995).

5. **Employer Liability for Sexual Harassment of Co-Workers.** Kerry Ellison, female, worked for the Internal Revenue Service and met Sterling Gray during her training period in 1984. The two were never great friends, but one day Gray asked Ellison to accompany him to lunch, which she did. Following the lunch, Gray was constantly near her desk pestering her with unnecessary questions. Gray asked Ellison out for dates after work, but she refused. Gray handed Ellison a note that revealed Gray was perhaps dangerously fixated on Ellison. Gray sent other notes that indicated stalking behavior. Ellison contacted her supervisor and complained. Ellison's supervisor, Bonnie Miller, contacted Gray and told him that he must not contact Ellison in any manner and Gray was transferred to another office. Gray contacted the union representative and his transfer was rescinded. It is clear in this case that Ellison's supervisor believed Gray's behavior was sexual harassment, but an IRS investigator did not agree. Ellison filed suit claiming that she was forced to work in a hostile work environment. What do you think? How much responsibility does

an employer have for the actions of employees? [*Kerry Ellison v. Nicholas F. Brady, Secretary of Treasury,* 924 F.2d 872 (9th Cir. 1991).]

Social Responsibility, Policy, and Ethics in a High-Tech World

6. **Affirmative Action, Tests, and Reverse Discrimination.** The city of San Francisco signed a consent decree that required it to more intensively recruit women and minorities for their police force and upper management positions. The plaintiffs in this case, the San Francisco Police Officers Association (POA) and several individual officers, were signers of the consent decree. In response, the city of San Francisco developed a three-part criterion for promotions within the police department based on a multiple-choice test, a written examination, and an oral interview. Each of the three parts was weighted, but when the first test results were revealed, there was an adverse impact for both women and minorities from the multiple-choice and written examinations. Based on the results of administering the new tests for promotions, the Police Commission decided to reweight the various components of the examination so that the oral interview was the sole criterion for promotion if applicants simply passed the first two components, the multiple choice and written examinations. The POA filed suit, charging that the Police Commission had manipulated test results to make sure that more minorities and women and less white men were promoted within the San Francisco Police Department. What do you think? Can employers administer a test, determine which parts of the test women and minorities do well on, then more heavily weight those portions? Isn't there pressure across the board to diversify the workforce, but also a concern that only "qualified" job candidates be selected? See how the Ninth Circuit Court of Appeals dealt with this problem. [*San Francisco Police Officers' Association, et al. v. City and County of San Francisco,* 812 F.2d 1125 (9th Cir. 1987).]

Using the Internet to Your Advantage

1. Most claims of employment discrimination begin with filing at the Equal Employment Opportunity Commission (http://www.eeoc.gov/). Of course, the EEOC has a wealth of information on many aspects of employment discrimination, including directions on how to file a lawsuit, statistics of interest, and antidiscrimination laws and regulations regulating employment. The U.S. Commission on Civil Rights (http://www.usccr.gov/) is an allegedly bipartisan government agency established in 1957 to be a fact-finding, investigative government agency. Elections in Florida have attracted the recent attention of the U.S. Commission on Civil Rights. Virtually every government agency in Washington and in the states has its own civil rights or diversity offices. The Stonewall Inn in New York, where a confrontation between gays and police took place in 1969, has become a National Historic Landmark according to the National Park Service (http://www.nps.gov/diversity/stonewall.htm).

2. There are a number of private organizations that advocate positions on employment discrimination and affirmative action. The American Association for Affirmative Action (http://www.affirmativeaction.org/) is one organization that promotes the use of affirmative action, while the Center for Equal Opportunity (http://www.ceousa.org/), headed by Linda Chavez, seems equally dedicated to creation of a colorblind society and abolition of affirmative action. All victims of discrimination have their proponents, including Advocates for the Disabled, Inc. (http://web1.cirs.org/homepage/advocates/). A collection of websites promoting job opportunities for older workers is located at http://www.pcaphl.org/senjobs.html. The ACLU has been an advocate for worker rights in the workplace and has an interesting Web page on the topic at http://www.aclu.org/issues/worker/hmwr.html.

Chapter Eighteen

Consumer Protection Legislation and Electronic Transactions

Learning Objectives

After completing this chapter, you should

1. Be able to discuss what the Federal Trade Commission views as unfair and deceptive trade practices and be able to provide examples of such practices.
2. Be able to recite the main statutes that regulate consumer products, the packaging of products, and highway safety.
3. Have a basic understanding of what the Food and Drug Administration does in terms of approving new pharmaceutical drugs, regulating food additives, and regulating claims that can be made about these products.
4. Know the main statutes regulating the lending of money, the handling of credit records, and the collection of bills.
5. Be able to discuss the steps the FTC has taken to combat fraud in cyberspace.

OVERVIEW

Consumer protection legislation reflects a view of legislative bodies, most importantly Congress, that common law protections for consumers are inadequate. As a result of this perceived inadequacy, Congress and state legislatures have passed legislation that goes beyond the consumer protection provided by the common law. There are many reasons for passing legislation that provides additional protection beyond that available through the common law. Prominent among these are situations in which

- The consequences of making mistakes or being defrauded are so serious that legislators have made a determination that consumers need additional protections to make the playing field more level between sellers and buyers.
- There has been a history of abuse and fraud such that many in the general populace agree that "something ought to be done" to prevent reoccurrences. Indeed, much consumer

protection legislation has been enacted in the wake of well-publicized scandals or tragedies.

- The products or services regulated, such as pharmaceutical drugs and credit, are often very complicated, thus making the products potentially dangerous, regardless of how careful consumers are.

Although consumer protection legislation is focused on protecting people from the consequences of purchasing, using, and being affected by various products, including credit, it is really a hodgepodge collection of laws that extends from general antifraud protections provided by the Federal Trade Commission to tightly targeted legislation that protects consumers against fraud in, say, the sale of funeral products or jewelry. Space does not permit a complete survey of consumer protection legislation, even at the federal level, and it is important to keep in mind that state legislatures have passed many consumer protection laws. This chapter looks at the general antifraud measures taken on behalf on consumers by the Federal Trade Commission and looks at consumer protection provided in the Food, Drug, and Cosmetic Act and in the Consumer Product Safety Commission. We also review the extensive consumer protection legislation that has been passed in the general area of credit, that is, money lending, and collecting.

unfair trade practices
Business practices that cause, or are likely to cause, substantial injury to consumers, not reasonably avoidable by consumers themselves, and not outweighed by countervailing benefits to consumers.

E-commerce has increased opportunities for consumer fraud and **unfair trade practices.** It is notable that the emergence of e-commerce has created additional opportunities for unscrupulous sellers to defraud consumers. Much of the recently enacted consumer protection legislation has been directed toward abuses that typically occur in e-commerce. It is likely that additional legislation will be enacted that is directed toward fraud and other abuses that occur online.

FEDERAL TRADE COMMISSION

Formation of the Federal Trade Commission

The *Federal Trade Commission (FTC)* was created in 1914 and was given broad authority in Section 5(a) of the FTC Act to declare unlawful trade acts or practices that it believes are *unfair* or *deceptive*.[1] The FTC is a bipartisan independent agency that is headed by five commissioners with no more than three being from the same political party. The authority of the FTC is broad-ranging; roughly half of its operations are aimed at enforcing antitrust laws (which will be discussed in the next chapter), while the other half is designated "consumer protection." The authority of the FTC has often been augmented by subsequent acts of Congress that require FTC enforcement. To date, the FTC has been assigned responsibility for enforcing 46 separate statutes passed by Congress including, as examples, the Wool Products Labeling Act, the Truth-in-Lending Act, the Fair Packaging and Labeling Act, the Clayton Act (relating to antitrust), and the Electronic Fund Transfer Act (for a complete list, see the FTC Web page at http://www.ftc.gov/ogc/stats.htm).

Unfair Trade Practices

The FTC has separate definitions of *unfair* trade practices and *deceptive* trade practices. According to the FTC, unfair trade practices are defined to be those that "cause[s] or [are] likely to cause substantial injury to consumers which is not reasonably avoidable by consumers themselves and not outweighed by countervailing benefits to consumers or to competition."[2] Among the many trade practices that the FTC has declared unfair are the

---

[1] 15 U.S.C. § 45(a)(1).
[2] 15 U.S.C. § 45(n).

collection of information from children by websites, the advertising of highly sugared cereals to children, racist advertising, and the use of pornography in television commercials.

Some of the FTC's regulations are quite detailed, such as its prohibition, directed at sellers of cultured pearls, of describing their products as "pearls" "unless it is immediately preceded, with equal conspicuousness, by the word 'cultured' or 'cultivated,' or by some other word or phrase of like meaning, so as to indicate definitely and clearly that the product is not a pearl."[3] The FTC regards it as unfair to "(b) Condition the availability of an eye examination to any person on a requirement that the patient agree to purchase any ophthalmic goods from the ophthalmologist or optometrist."[4]

Deceptive Trade Practices

Much of the work of the FTC is directed toward combating *deceptive trade practices*. The FTC defines a deceptive trade practice as an act that *is likely to mislead the reasonable consumer* involving a deception likely to *affect a decision of consumers*. A focus of the efforts of the FTC has been on what it regards as false advertising. The FTC considers it deceptive for celebrities to endorse products that they do not actually use. When advertisers make claims that "three out of five doctors recommend product X," the FTC requires that the advertiser use technically accurate surveys that are not biased to verify the claims made.

Consider the actions the FTC took against the Warner-Lambert Company, which manufactured and sold Listerine, a mouthwash that Warner-Lambert claimed also had medicinal value in alleviating the symptoms of colds and sore throats. Warner-Lambert had extensively advertised the medicinal value of Listerine, but could not produce a scientific study that backed up its claims. When the FTC intervened, it not only ordered that Warner-Lambert cease and desist what the FTC regarded as false advertising, but it also required the company to pay for corrective advertising to combat misperceptions that had been built up in the minds of members of the consuming public as a result of previous deceptive advertising.[5]

Trade Practices That Do Not Fit Traditional Categories or Require Customized Legal Attention

TV Commercials

Numerous additional examples of unfair and/or deceptive trade practices could be cited, many of which involve advertising and commercials on television. Consider, as an illustration, the allegations the FTC made regarding TV commercials aired by the Campbell Soup Co. In the commercials complained of, a folk singer sang a soothing song about how "Campbell Soup makes good food," while cameras zeroed in on a slow motion shot of Campbell vegetable soup being poured into a bowl. To enhance appearances for the video, technicians had placed marbles in the bottom of the bowl, making the chunks of meat and vegetables in the soup appear more prominent than they would in "real life." The deception that is taking place with the placement of the marbles in the bottom of the soup bowl is akin to fraud but, under common law, there is no remedy. These actions of the Campbell Soup Co. may be a breach of contract, which would be debatable, but any resulting damages associated with an individual's purchase of Campbell's vegetable soup would be insufficient to justify making an appointment to see an attorney en route to filing a lawsuit. Even

---

[3] 16 C.F.R. § 23.19(b).

[4] 16 C.F.R. § 456.2(b).

[5] *Warner-Lambert Company v. Federal Trade Commission*, 562 F.2d 749 (D.C. Cir. 1977).

for class action suits, assuming a class of "victims" could be assembled, damages are likely to be very small for this type of violation.

Finding Proof in the Pudding Is Too Dangerous

Consider another example of the inadequacy of the common law. If a product is misrepresented or breaches a warranty, then the common law is available as a remedy, as it would be when a drug is improperly labeled, improperly designed, or adulterated. However, at common law, the only remedy consumers have is available only *after they are injured or die from the defective drugs*. At common law, there was no mechanism to require sellers to make their products safe *before* they are sold. In effect, under the common law, consumers are like guinea pigs; they are only entitled to take legal action after they are harmed by the products they "test" by usage. For many products, the consequences of this form of Russian roulette are too horrible to tolerate. Consequently, it makes sense for society to require that sellers of products with such potential for harm prove to a regulatory agency that their products are safe and effective before they are allowed on the market. This is what the Food and Drug Administration requires in the sale of pharmaceutical drugs.

Size Matters in Litigation

Another aspect of consumer protection that makes government regulation appropriate is the disparity of resources between consumers and companies. When two companies are involved in litigation, it is likely that each has been advised for an extended period of time by corporate counsel, so the companies can make informed judgments about the value and viability of business litigation. Not so with consumers. Financing a single lawsuit against a company is likely to exceed the financial resources of individual consumers. Contingency fee arrangements are quite common, but, in many consumer protection cases, damages are too small to make contingency fee arrangements viable. Moreover, large companies that can afford expensive legal talent can overwhelm consumer plaintiffs with a blizzard of motions, requests for documents, and other delaying and obfuscating tactics that discourage such lawsuits.

The Common Law and the Lanham Act

The common law is a more effective tool for competitors trying to protect themselves from misrepresentations made by their rivals. If a rival makes untrue statements about the products of another rival, it is *product disparagement,* which is an actionable tort if the victim of the untrue statements suffers financial loss. Also, Section 43(a) of the Lanham Act, a federal statute, prohibits false and misleading advertising and allows private parties, such as business competitors, to obtain injunctions and recover damages against companies that falsely disparage their products. The Lanham Act has been particularly useful when one company engages in comparative advertising and misstates facts about the products of a rival. *Trade defamation* occurs when, for example, one company falsely alleges that another company does not have the financial assets to complete a job that both companies are trying to land. At common law, if one company tries to palm off its products as those made by another company, this act is likely a trademark infringement, but it is also a common law tort. Strictly speaking, lawsuits between companies are not consumer protection suits. The primary objective of litigation between firms is not to protect consumers, but rather to prevent one firm from unfairly competing against another firm. Even so, consumers are presumably benefited by actions that prevent decisions made on the basis of false information.

In Case 18-1, L&F is suing for injunctive relief (taking the contested commercials off the air) and for damages under the Lanham Act. The case illustrates the principle that the plaintiff in Lanham Act lawsuits still has to show that the defendant made false or misleading statements.

Case 18-1

L&F Products, a Division of Sterling Winthrop Inc., Plaintiff-Appellant v. Procter & Gamble Company, Defendant-Appellee

United States Court of Appeals for the Second Circuit
45 F.3d 709 (2nd Cir. 1995)

BACKGROUND AND FACTS

L&F manufactures and markets LYSOL cleaning products, including LYSOL Basin Tub & Tile Cleaner, a bathroom cleanser, and LYSOL Deodorizing Cleaner, for use in bathrooms as well as other rooms. P&G manufactures and sells several Spic and Span household cleaning products, including Spic and Span Basin-Tub-Tile Cleaner, Spic and Span Bathroom Cleaner, and Ultra Spic and Span, a general cleanser.

In July 1993, P&G began a television advertising campaign in which its products were compared to those of an unnamed competitor. There is no dispute that the unnamed product in each commercial represented LYSOL Deodorizing Cleaner, an all-purpose product often employed for bathroom cleaning. Three commercials are challenged. The disputed commercials take similar tacks in portraying three Spic and Span products. Cheerful music is heard. Although there is no dialogue, each closes with a voice-over. In each of the three ads, a Spic and Span product and LYSOL Deodorizing Cleaner are used by two custodians on identical soiled shower stalls, tubs, or tile floors set in a large, white room. The surfaces are visibly dirty when the custodians begin their tasks. Each custodian is shown making one swipe across the dirty surface; the screen then "dissolves." The custodians leave, looking pleased with their work.

Two new characters enter. Each contrives to casually pass a white cloth over the just-cleaned stalls, tubs or floors. The surface cleaned with LYSOL is ultimately revealed to have left a residue that is seen to sully the cloth. The white cloths passed over the tub, shower and floor cleaned with Spic and Span are not similarly dirtied. By way of illustration, in the shower commercial, two women wearing white socks step into the newly-cleaned bathtubs. They each hang a shower curtain before stepping out of the tub. The woman who stepped into the tub cleaned with the LYSOL product reveals a dirty sock. The other woman's sock is still white.

Because P&G videotaped the filming of the commercials, there can be no controversy about how they were produced. The shower and tub commercials employed templates made of the same materials that formed the tubs and showers themselves. P&G explained that use of the templates was required for technical reasons. Like other manufacturers, P&G has developed its own soap scum for use in testing its products. Its formula includes carbon black, a dark pigment used as a laboratory marker. In order to mimic the tenacity of household soap scum, the laboratory-developed product is baked onto a test surface at high temperatures. Because of the impossibility of baking an entire shower stall or tub, templates are used.

The soiled templates were wiped with the competing products off-screen. There is no dispute that the templates were wiped an equal number of times with a comparable degree of force. They were later inserted into the shower and steambath sets and, on-screen, white cloths were drawn against them. However, the initial swipe across the shower and tub tiles by the custodians was performed on tiles dirtied with ordinary soil, rather than the laboratory-developed scum. The as-yet-unbroadcast floor commercial, by contrast, did not require the use of templates. Unlike its soap scum, P&G's laboratory-developed floor grime does not require baking. The laboratory-developed floor soil was applied to actual floor tiles for both on- and off-screen use.

After a four-day bench trial, the district court issued an opinion in which it found that the advertisements were neither false nor misleading. Accordingly, it dismissed the complaint.

Opinion by Altimari, Circuit Judge

Relying on evidence adduced at trial, including a consumer survey commissioned by L&F, the district court determined that the addition of carbon black to P&G's laboratory-developed soap scum was not misleading. The court found that L&F had failed to demonstrate that consumers believed that they were viewing actual cleaning competitions or that consumers were misled into the belief that the cleaning was effected in only one wipe.

The court also found that the commercials did not convey to a statistically significant number of consumers the message that LYSOL was an ineffective cleaner. Finally, despite an admission by a P&G witness that P&G intended to convey this disputed message, the court determined that L&F had failed to show that the commercials conveyed the message that LYSOL merely appeared to clean. Instead it found only that Spic and Span cleaned more efficiently.

L&F's primary contention on appeal is that the district court erred when it determined that the only message conveyed by the commercials was Spic and Span's relative superiority. L&F urges that other false messages were conveyed through deceptive methods. In particular, L&F maintains that the ads imparted the false message that LYSOL merely appears to clean a surface.

* * *

We thus reject what appears to be L&F's chief grievance: that the "rug-pull" effect conveyed the false message that LYSOL merely appears to clean. By "rug-pull" the parties refer to the surprise at the end of each commercial, when it is revealed that LYSOL has not cleaned as effectively as Spic and Span. L&F's argument is, in essence, that, although LYSOL might be less effective than Spic and Span, it nonetheless would not leave a surface looking clean until it was in fact clean. In other words, a real consumer would, unlike the television viewers, never be unpleasantly surprised.

The difficulty with L&F's argument is that L&F did not establish at trial that the message was false. Despite L&F's complaints about the techniques employed to create the commercials, the fact remains that the two products were handled in identical fashions. An equal number of swipes was applied with comparable force to surfaces coated with a laboratory-developed soap scum that fairly represented the tenacity of the soap deposits found in some homes. Finding no fault with the commercials' production, we cannot dispute the ultimate message: that, at the point when Spic and Span has cleaned a surface, a surface cleaned with LYSOL will not yet be as clean. Because the proof at trial did not establish the falsity of this message, the district court did not clearly err.

In reaching our conclusion, we have rejected several of L&F's arguments with respect to the manner in which the district court analyzed the alleged flaws in the commercials. First, L&F claims that the court displayed an impermissible "skepticism" toward L&F's assertion that the visual images projected by the commercials could convey false messages. A reading of Judge Tenney's opinion makes clear that he simply did not find the ads misleading. Surely he appreciated that largely visual images are capable of conveying a false message.

* * *

Decision and Outcome

The Court of Appeals for the Second Circuit found no error in the findings of the trial court that there was no showing by the plaintiff, L&F, that the advertisements in question were either false or misleading. Accordingly, the judgment of the district court was AFFIRMED.

Questions for Analysis

1. What was the main reason that L&F's complaint was dismissed? Were they able to show that any particular claim made by P&G was false?
2. Do you think it was deceptive of P&G to manufacture its own soap scum? If P&G tried to create a false impression, but a survey revealed that viewers did not believe the falsity, is P&G liable?

Actions and Powers of the FTC

As a result of numerous amendments to the original 1914 act that created the FTC, the FTC has various powers that it can use against businesses that it believes are engaging in unfair or deceptive trade practices. Note, however, that the FTC Act does not provide a private right of action, which means that only the FTC can file a suit against a company for an unfair or deceptive trade practice. The FTC does, however, solicit citizens to submit complaints and has recently installed an online system for filing complaints.[6] Based on consumer complaints and complaints from businesses, the FTC targets businesses for investigation of unfair and deceptive trade practices. If an investigation reveals a case that has merit, the first action the FTC will take will be to contact the company to discuss the alleged violation. In most cases, settlements between the FTC and the company are reached in which the company agrees to refrain from doing what the FTC believes violates a law.

FTC Challenges to Trade Practices of an Individual Company

cease and desist order
An order prohibiting activities that have been deemed illegal.

If the company does not agree with the FTC's position, or refuses to change its practices, the FTC has the power to hold a hearing before an administrative law judge of the FTC and formally proceed against the company. The FTC can file a **cease and desist order** against *trade practices of an individual company* that it believes is engaging in unfair or deceptive trade acts or practices and has the power to impose fines of $25,000 per day for continued violations. The FTC also can file for an injunction and can impose fines of $10,000 per violation. Of course, actions taken by the FTC can be challenged in federal court.

Trade Practice Rules

trade practice rules
Rules for the conduct of business issued by the FTC when it determines that the mode of operation of an industry needs reform.

If the FTC finds that *industry practices* are unfair or deceptive, it can issue **trade practice rules.** Trade practice rules are generally industry-specific or pertain to a particular business function or service, such as advertising or the offering of warranties. Trade practice rules are developed by the FTC when it believes that the modes of operating for an entire industry are in need of reform.[7] To date, the FTC has promulgated 16 trade practice rules directed at, for example, providing tire advertising and labeling guides, guides against bait advertising, guides for the furniture industry, and guides for the use of environmental marketing claims.

A Trade Practice Rule Example

Federal Trade Commission Trade Practice Rule Section 250.2, "Describing wood and wood imitations," indicates that, when a manufacturer is describing wood veneered products, "the wood names should be qualified to disclose the fact of the veneered construction." Further down in this section, the FTC Trade Practice Rule Section 250.2(d) indicates that

> When wood names are used merely to describe a color of a stain finish and/or grain design or other simulated finish applied to the exposed surfaces of furniture that is composed of something other than solid wood of the types named, *it must be made clear* that the wood names are merely descriptive of the color and/or grain design or other simulated finish. Terms such as "walnut finish" or "fruitwood" finish will not suffice.

The example above was picked at random from 16 separate FTC Trade Practice Rules, each of which has several sections and subsections. Some have questioned whether government resources should be used to develop and enforce what sellers of furniture products can say in the way they describe the color of furniture stains. Other examples of possible overregulation by the FTC, of course, can be cited.

Other Actions by the FTC

Much of the activity of the FTC has been directed at advertising the FTC regards as deceptive. The FTC has been vigilant in checking out claims made by advertisers, such as the ones made by Warner-Lambert in the Listerine case discussed above. The FTC insists that

[6] The FTC website for filing a complaint online is
https://rn.ftc.gov/dod/wsolcq$.startup?Z_ORG_CODE=PU01.

[7] For examples of trade practice rules of the FTC, see
http://www.access.gpo.gov/nara/cfr/cfrhtml_00/Title_16/16cfrv1_00.html.

there must be a scientific basis for claims made by firms that advertise and the scientific rigor the FTC insists upon is that which is the norm for the scientific community.

A trade practice involving advertising that the FTC has attacked vigorously is currently called **bait advertising** by the FTC (originally it was termed *bait and switch* advertising). The practice attacked by the FTC occurs when a retail store advertises a very low-priced and attractive offer to the public, but, when customers show up in the store, the store has its salespeople explain that the advertised products have been sold out. The original advertised product is the "bait," and the sales staff is directed to try to "switch" customers to purchase other higher-priced products also sold by the store. According to the FTC, "Bait advertising is an alluring but insincere offer to sell a product or service that the advertiser in truth does not intend or want to sell."[8] Of course, all advertising is designed to be "alluring," so the real test of the insincerity of the advertising is, according to the FTC, determined by whether the store does the following:

1. Refuses to show the advertised product.
2. Disparages the advertised product.
3. Has inadequate quantities at stores.
4. Refuses to take orders for the advertised merchandise to be delivered within a reasonable period of time.
5. Shows or demonstrates a product that is defective, unusable, or impractical for the purpose represented or implied in the advertisement.
6. Uses a sales plan or method of compensating sales staff or penalizing sales staff that is designed to prevent or discourage them from selling the advertised product.

Businesspeople can be liable for bait advertising if they underestimate demand for the products they advertise, though reasonable stockouts are permitted. There is no reasonable excuse, however, for devising sales plans that discourage sales staff from selling products that the store advertises or that encourage disparagement of the products advertised. These practices, if detected, carry a high probability of FTC fines or other sanctions.

ELECTRONIC ADVERTISING: TELEMARKETING, FAX, E-MAIL, AND SPAM

Phones and Faxes

Recognition of the abuses possible with automated and electronic means of contacting people in an unsolicited, unwelcome, and exploitive manner predates commercialization of the Internet. In 1991 Congress passed the Telephone Consumer Protection Act (TCPA), which outlaws automatic dialing of phone numbers for the delivery of prerecorded voice messages.[9] By 1991, fax machines were commonplace and systems for obtaining fax numbers were also available. Combining fax number information with automation technology, sellers could literally make customers pay for their advertising, whether it was wanted or unwanted, through automated fax transmissions. Recipients of the transmissions, of course, bore the cost for the paper the advertisements were written on and the ink/toner and electricity consumed by printing the advertising. The TCPA prohibits advertising to fax machines unless the recipient has first given approval. Importantly, the TCPA requires an **opt in** for advertisers to have permission to make use of another's fax machine. In other

bait advertising
A scheme in which one product is advertised at an attractive price (the "bait") followed, when a customer arrives and asks for the product, by an attempt to "switch" the customer to an alternative, higher-priced product, generally accompanied by disparagement of the advertised product or an out-of-stock claim.

opt in
System that allows a target to choose whether to be included or not, prior to an action involving the target.

---

[8] 16 CFR § 238.0.
[9] Pub. L. No. 102-243, codified at 47 U.S.C. § 227.

Nutz and Boltz   Development of a "Do Not Call" Registry

The following is a news release by the Federal Trade Commission about development of a national "do not call" registry for people who do not want to be called by telemarketers.

FTC CHAIRMAN BRIEFS HOUSE COMMITTEE ON ENERGY AND COMMERCE ABOUT THE TELEMARKETING SALES RULE'S "DO NOT CALL" AMENDMENTS

During testimony today before the House Committee on Energy and Commerce, Federal Trade Commission Chairman Timothy J. Muris provided an overview of the Telemarketing Sales Rule (the Rule or TSR) amendment process, discussion of the "Do Not Call" provisions, and an examination of the agency's request for Congressional approval to fund the operation of the "Do Not Call" registry and its related functions through offsetting fee collections. According to his testimony, Muris anticipates that the costs will fall primarily in three broad categories: 1) costs of development and operation of the "Do Not Call" registry, including the handling of complaints; 2) enforcement costs, which include consumer and business education and international coordination; and 3) agency infrastructure and administration costs, including information technology structural supports.

Muris presented the background of the Rule by explaining that the FTC promulgated the "Do Not Call" and other substantial amendments to the TSR under the express authority granted to the Commission by the Telemarketing and Consumer Fraud and Abuse Prevention Act. The Telemarketing Act, which was adopted in 1994, directed the Commission to issue a trade regulation rule defining and prohibiting deceptive or abusive telemarketing acts or practices including prohibitions against any pattern of unsolicited telemarketing calls, as well as restrictions on the hours unsolicited telephone calls can be made to consumers. Accordingly on August 16, 1995, the Commission adopted the TSR, which defined and prohibited certain deceptive telemarketing practices, prohibited calls by telemarketers or sellers to consumers who had previously requested not to receive such calls from that telemarketer or seller, and prohibited calls to consumers before 8:00 a.m. or after 9:00 p.m. local time for the consumer.

Source: http://www.ftc.gov/opa/2003/01/tsrhousebrief.htm.

words, the TCPA requires fax advertisers to obtain permission from owners of fax machines prior to transmitting fax advertising.

Telemarketers and Spammers

Telemarketing

In a cooperative arrangement with the FTC, Congress passed the Telemarketing and Consumer Fraud and Abuse Prevention Act of 1994, which directed the FTC to develop additional rules regulating telemarketing and fraud on the Internet.[10] The FTC responded with the Telemarketing Sales Rule (TSR) of 1995, which requires telemarketers to do the following before making a sales pitch:

- Inform customers that the call is a sales call.
- Identify the seller's name and the products being sold.
- Inform potential customers of the total cost of the items being sold.[11]

The list above does not include all the requirements imposed upon telemarketers as a result of the 1994 act, but is adequate to show that the FTC has sought to impose *opt in* systems, which makes it much harder for telemarketers to trespass on the time of those answering their phones. Still the number of unsolicited telemarketing calls remains a major irritant for many. In early 2003, the FTC took action to further restrict telemarketing activities, as indicated in the "Nutz and Boltz" box.

[10] Pub. L. No. 103-247, codified at 15 U.S.C. §§ 6101–6108.
[11] The FTC Rules are located at 16 C.F.R. Part 310.

Cyberspace is populated by independent people who do not lightly seek government regulation for assistance. However, spam has become an overwhelming and disagreeable fact that is making e-mail a much less effective tool because most of what people receive through e-mail is unwanted spam.

It has been estimated that spam costs U.S. companies $8 to $10 billion per year—and those costs do not include the aggravation endured by ordinary users. A study by the Federal Trade Commission revealed that 66 percent of spam contains false "From" lines, "Subject" lines, or message text. A recent poll by the Harris Interactive group indicated that 80 percent of Internet users found spam "very annoying" and that 74 percent favored making spam illegal.

The actions of spammers have also attracted the attention of Congress, but to date no legislation specific to spam has been enacted. In the 108th Congress (which began in 2003), three significant bills have been introduced:

- Controlling the Assault of Non-Solicited Pornography and Marketing Act of 2003 (commonly referred to as CAN-SPAM, S. 877)
- The Computer Owner's Bill of Rights (S. 563)
- The Wireless Telephone Spam Protection Act (H.R. 122)

CAN-SPAM is the legislation with perhaps the best chance of being enacted. CAN-SPAM defines an "unsolicted commercial electronic message" (UCE) as any commercial electronic mail message that is not a "transactional or relationship message" and that is sent to the recipient without prior consent. Of course, any attempt to regulate spam must be accomplished within the constraints imposed by the free speech protections of the First Amendment. If CAN-SPAM is signed into law, it will be unlawful for any person to initiate the transmission of a commercial electronic message that contains materially or intentionally false or misleading subject heading or origination information. The objective of this legislation is to compel UCEs to provide a functioning return e-mail address or other Internet-based mechanisms to allow recipients to request not to receive any future messages from that source within 30 days of receiving the spam. This method of dealing with unwanted e-mail is referred to as an "opt-out."

If passed, CAN-SPAM would empower the FTC to enforce the Act so that violations would be considered "unfair and deceptive" trade practices. States would also be empowered under this Act to initiate suits through attorney generals' offices and to seek injunctions as well as damages. CAN-SPAM would also make it illegal for spammers to harvest e-mail addresses from websites or ISPs that have posted notices stating they will not give, sell, or otherwise transfer e-mail addresses maintained by the website or the ISP. In addition, CAN-SPAM provides a cause of action for ISPs to bring a civil suit against spammers who violate their Terms of Service agreements, which prohibit e-mail harvesting. Enforcement by the FTC, state attorneys general, or ISPs can be through civil suits that allow for the recovery of actual damages or for statutory damages equal to $10 per violation. Damages from such suits are capped at $500,000, but damages are tripled for defendants that knowingly and willfully commit a violation.

It is obvious that spam diminishes the value of the services provided by ISPs and websites. Several ISPs have not waited for Congress and have initiated a number of high-profile lawsuits against spammers using various legal theories that include trespass to personal property. In addition, a number of states have enacted their own anti-spam laws, which have allowed states to sue spammers. Of course, state challenges to spammers have faced motions to dismiss for lack of jurisdiction, but in at least one case, a Virginia District Court held that the spamming is sufficient to establish minimum contacts in a state (*Verizon Online Services, Inc. v. Ralsky*, 203 F.Supp.2d 601 (E.D. Va. 2002).

spammers
Distributors of Internet "junk mail" or other materials transmitted to Web users without their permission.

opt out
System that places the burden on a target (of advertising, information distribution, etc.) to ask to be removed from a target list.

Spam

In contrast, there has been no legislation or regulatory ruling at the federal level that has been directed at spammers. **Spammers** are advertisers who send their advertisements in the form of unsolicited e-mails. The current system, with no regulation, does not require spammers to obtain permission from recipients in the form of opt in choices. Neither do recipients always have the ability to **opt out** by notifying spammers that they wish to be removed from e-mailing lists. Some spammers do have forms to complete, permitting recipients to be removed from their lists, but many are skeptical as to the uses made of that information. Many regard the current state of affairs as very unsatisfactory; spammers inundate e-mail addresses to the point that many have instituted screening techniques that also may screen out valuable e-mail along with unwanted spam.

CONSUMER PROTECTION: REGULATION OF PHYSICAL PRODUCTS

Introduction

Pharmaceutical Drugs

It is no accident that comprehensive consumer protection dealing with physical products was first applied to pharmaceutical drugs, foods, and food additives. To focus just on pharmaceutical drugs, the inadequacies of the common law were glaringly apparent even at the turn of the twentieth century. At that time, about the only way to identify a company that was selling dangerous drugs was to have a number of people become seriously ill or die as a result of ingesting its products. There is no remedy at common law that allows customers to inspect or requires a seller to prove the safety of a new product prior to its commercial sale. With pharmaceutical drugs, of course, it is difficult or impossible to make any determination as to the safety of a product simply by inspecting it (rather than ingesting it). So it is not mere historical happenstance that the Pure Food and Drugs Act (now called the Food, Drug and Cosmetic Act) was enacted in 1906 and that the Food and Drug Administration was created in 1927 as the U.S. government initiated an activist role in the pursuit of consumer protection.

Food and Food Safety

Problems associated with food and food additives are only slightly less menacing than those tied to pharmaceuticals. The safety of most food, if prepared properly and not adulterated, is not a major issue in developed countries in today's world. At this point in history, we know what foods, including meats, vegetables, grains, and fruits, are safe. However, in a learning process that may be described as torturous, it has become clear that an essential ingredient of food safety in the United States is provided by *physical inspections* of food products in conjunction with extensive regulation of the uses of fertilizers and pesticides.

Food Additives

In turn, food additives are much like pharmaceutical drugs in terms of their potential to cause problems for consumers. Unlike food, there is no general assurance that food additives are safe. Indeed, research has shown that many food additives that were used for a number of years were unsafe and contributed to higher rates of chronic diseases such as cancer. As with the case of pharmaceuticals, consumer inspections of food additives are unlikely to reveal their dangers, whereas seeing, touching, smelling, and tasting food often tips off consumers to products that are unfit for human consumption.

Pharmaceutical Drugs

As mentioned above, the Pure Food and Drugs Act was passed in 1906, but was substantially amended in 1938 by the Federal Food, Drug and Cosmetic Act. The 1906 act, making it illegal to sell dangerous, misbranded, or adulterated drugs, provided an augmentation of the sanctions available under common law product liability remedies. The 1938 legislation was enacted after about 100 people perished when a drug sold on the market was found to be lethal. The 1938 act required that drug manufacturers prove to the Food and Drug Administration that their products were safe *before* they could be sold to the general public. Thus began broad-scale animal testing and human clinical trials, conducted to conform to FDA regulations. The 1938 act also required the FDA to classify all drugs as either *prescription* or *nonprescription,* the latter commonly referred to as over-the-counter drugs. The Kefauver Amendments of 1962 required drug manufacturers to prove to the FDA that their products were both *safe and effective* for their intended use.

Requiring pharmaceutical companies to prove that their products are both safe and effective takes time, in most cases several years. Recognizing this problem, the Food and Drug Modernization Act was passed in 1997 and included provisions for speeding up approvals of new drugs, especially those that have a high potential for therapeutic gain and those for which there are no satisfactory alternatives available on the market. In some cases, drugs that were being tested for effectiveness also have been made available to others, outside the test group, for therapy. Most of the drugs made available in this fashion have been drugs that are used to treat AIDS patients.

There are a number of regulatory issues that the FDA has so far avoided, but which will demand resolution. Perhaps, most notably, many **dietary supplements** are being used as pharmaceutical drugs to treat ailments, including depression, high blood pressure, and even cancer. At present, sellers of "dietary supplements" (herbal remedies) are not allowed to make direct medicinal or health claims but, indirectly, the message gets across to customers that this or that herb is good for digestion, heart irregularities, anxiety, sexual performance, and so forth. Many dietary supplements directly compete with FDA-approved pharmaceutical drugs. However, unlike FDA-approved drug producers, sellers of dietary supplements do not have to prove that their products are either safe or effective through clinical trials or any other tests to which sellers of pharmaceuticals have to submit. Dietary supplements do have to be approved by the FDA before being introduced to the market, but the approval process is not nearly as rigorous as that required for the introduction of new pharmaceutical drugs.[12] A related concern is that, since many herbal compounds are pharmaceutically active, with most herbal remedies taken at the initiative of the patient/user without physician oversight, dangerous drug interactions that would be easily recognized by doctors go unrecognized, with serious injury or death as possible results.

The tension between the largely unregulated availability of herbal supplements and the FDA in its role as a protector of consumers is clear in the CNN news release in the "Nutz and Boltz" box on page 590.

dietary supplements
May be products that are pharmaceutically active, such as herbal remedies, but that avoid the rigorous testing required of drugs by being classified as dietary supplements.

Food Safety

For the same reasons that common law remedies were inadequate for drugs, the common law was not good enough at protecting consumers from unsafe food—the standard common law *remedies* are just inadequate. The 1906 Pure Food and Drugs Act did allow for criminal prosecutions of those who sold misbranded or adulterated food products and permitted tainted food to be seized and destroyed. Generally, however, for a number of years after passage of this act, enforcement still took place only after the fact; people were sick or dying from consumed products before the seller was identified and police raided the vendor's business.

---

[12] See the following website for the steps necessary to gain premarket approval of dietary supplements: http://www.cfsan.fda.gov/~dms/opareorg.html.

Nutz and Boltz   FDA Wants Warning Labels for Some Herbal Supplements

ATLANTA (CNN)—The government is proposing warning labels and intake restrictions for ephedrine-laced herbal supplements, taken for body-building and weight loss and blamed in at least 17 deaths.

The U.S. Food and Drug Administration plans to cut dramatically the dose of the herbal stimulant that can be put into any dietary supplement, and to ban the marketing of ephedrine-containing products as weight-loss or bodybuilding agents.

The chemical ephedrine, found in these herbal supplements, is like an amphetamine, stimulating the heart and nervous system. But the FDA says the evidence indicates the herbs can cause heart attack, stroke and death.

"A lot of people think that because something is made from a plant or an herb, that it's safe and it can't be dangerous," said the FDA's Bill Schultz.

"What I'd like to say to that is, many of our most powerful drugs started out as herbs . . . the fact that's [sic] it's made from an herb doesn't really mean very much in terms of safety."

The herbs are sold under names such as Ma huang, ephedra and epitonin, and can be taken as tablets or as teas. In addition to deaths, there have been some 800 illnesses linked to the ephedrine-laced supplements.

Specifically, the FDA proposes to:

- Ban supplements with more than 8 milligrams of ephedrine or related alkaloids per serving; setting the maximum daily dose at 24 milligrams. An FDA survey last year uncovered some supplements that called for users to ingest up to 109 milligrams in a single dose.
- Prohibit use of ephedrine products for more than seven days. That would essentially ban ephedrine weight-loss or bodybuilding supplements, because getting those purported health effects requires weeks of use.
- Require many supplements to bear the warning: "Taking more than the recommended serving may result in heart attack, stroke, seizure or death."
- Ban caffeine or other stimulants in combination with ephedrine.

The FDA didn't go as far as Florida and New York, which banned ephedrine supplements after pills marketed themselves with the promise of a "natural high." The bans came when a 20-year-old college student died after taking Ultimate Xphoria last year.

The proposal is open for public comment through August 18, when the FDA will develop a final regulation. The new labels could be several months in coming, and thus far, the supplement industry has agreed to cooperate.

Correspondent Elizabeth Cohen and The Associated Press contributed to this report.

Source: Copyright © 2003 Cable News Network LP, LLLP.

FDA Regulation of Food Products, Labeling, and Advertising

The U.S. Department of Agriculture, which inspects much of the beef, pork, poultry, and other products that Americans consume, is also responsible for much of the regulation of food safety. In this role, a great deal of attention has been focused on the information that is provided in the label attached to food products under the Fair Packaging and Labeling Act of 1966. Under this Act, a food label must include the name and address of the manufacturer, packer, or distributor of the product. In addition, it must provide information on the quantity in the food package as a part of the front label, and must describe the quantity in servings while adhering to various restrictions on the ways in which quantities can be specified. For example, the FDA has specific criteria for determining whether a seller is entitled to label the size of a product as "family size" or "jumbo," pursuant to its goal of making customer comparisons intelligible.

nutrition labels
Product labels that provide detailed information on nutrient content.

Nutrition Labeling

The Nutrition Labeling and Education Act of 1990 requires **nutrition labels** on most foods along with lists of ingredients. Nutritional content and health claims are strictly

Nutz and Boltz   Calcium and Osteoporosis

Low calcium intake is one risk factor for osteoporosis, a condition of lowered bone mass, or density. Life-long adequate calcium intake helps maintain bone health by increasing as much as genetically possible the amount of bone formed in the teens and early adult life and by helping to slow the rate of bone loss that occurs later in life.

Typical Foods: Low-fat and skim milks, yogurts, tofu, calcium-fortified citrus drinks, and some calcium supplements.

Requirements: Food or supplement must be "high" in calcium and must not contain more phosphorus than calcium. Claims must cite other risk factors; state the need for regular exercise and a healthful diet; explain that adequate calcium early in life helps reduce fracture risk later

by increasing as much as genetically possible a person's peak bone mass; and indicate that those at greatest risk of developing osteoporosis later in life are white and Asian teenage and young adult women, who are in their bone-forming years. Claims for products with more than 400 mg of calcium per day must state that a daily intake over 2,000 mg offers no added known benefit to bone health.

Sample Claim: "Regular exercise and a healthy diet with enough calcium helps teen and young adult white and Asian women maintain good bone health and may reduce their high risk of osteoporosis later in life."

Source: http://www.cfsan.fda.gov/~dms/fdhclm.html.

regulated. This act applies to all foods that are fortified in some way and to all goods for which manufacturers advertise health benefits, with the exceptions of coffee, tea, some delicatessen items, and bulk foods. Under the act, food manufacturers are required to state the amounts of saturated fat, cholesterol, dietary fiber, sodium, and calories present in their products, on a per-serving basis. Sellers also are required to state the percentages of recommended daily allowances (RDA) of various vitamins and proteins that a serving of the product provides.

Regulatory Definitions of Food Adjectives

The FDA also regulates food advertisements that claim products are "fresh," "light," "low calorie," "low fat," or "fat free" by providing uniform definitions of these terms. For each of these terms, there is a regulatory definition. For example, the following is the FDA's regulatory definition of the word "fresh" when used to describe foods:

> The regulation defines the term "fresh" when it is used to suggest that a food is raw or unprocessed. In this context, "fresh" can be used only on a food that is raw, has never been frozen or heated, and contains no preservatives. (Irradiation at low levels is allowed.) "Fresh frozen," "frozen fresh," and "freshly frozen," can be used for foods that are quickly frozen while still fresh. Blanching (brief scalding before freezing to prevent nutrient breakdown) is allowed.

In describing food, "less" is often viewed as an attractive attribute. According to the FDA, "This term [less] means that a food, whether altered or not, contains 25 percent less of a nutrient or of calories than the reference food. For example, pretzels that have 25 percent less fat than potato chips could carry a 'less' claim. 'Fewer' is an acceptable synonym."

Health Claims

The FDA also regulates the health claims that can be made with regard to food. As an illustration of its role, consider the FDA's statement in the "Nutz and Boltz" box on page 590.

There is ample scientific evidence that calcium losses for older women can lead to osteoporosis and that foods "high" in calcium can ameliorate problems of bone density loss. The language in the "Nutz and Boltz" box indicates what the FDA believes is an acceptable health claim, applicable to foods such as low-fat milk, skim milk, and the other foods listed. Managers must understand clearly that they cannot make extravagant health claims about the benefits of using their products, but must meet FDA requirements for any claims asserted. The FDA has a list of authorized health claims that can be made about various food products at http://www.cfsan.fda.gov/~dms/fdhclm.html.

Regulation of Medical Devices

A 1976 amendment to the Federal Food, Drug and Cosmetic Act also gives the FDA authority to approve or disapprove sales of new medical devices. The FDA also has authority to regulate advertising and labeling of medical devices. Under the 1997 FDA Modernization Act, reduction of the approval times required on new medical devices has been a major priority. Before sellers of medical devices, such as pacemakers for those suffering from heart disease or shunts for circulation assistance, can bring their products to market, they must secure approval of the FDA.

CONSUMER PRODUCT SAFETY COMMISSION

The Consumer Product Safety Commission (CPSC) was created in 1972 with passage of the Consumer Product Safety Act.[13] The CPSC has jurisdiction over all consumer products except for those regulated by other agencies (such as automobiles, tobacco, firearms, food, drugs, cosmetics, and medical devices). For the products over which it has jurisdiction, the Consumer Product Safety Act authorizes the CPSC to *set safety standards* and *to ban* the manufacture and sale of products that are *potentially dangerous*. If the CPSC determines that a product is imminently dangerous to the public, it has authority to seize the product immediately and keep it off the market.

For the CPSC to ban a product from the market, it must show with credible evidence that the product poses an *unreasonable risk* to consumers and/or others in the market. Again, it may be noted that common law tort and contract claims do provide remedies for products with designs that are found to be unreasonable. For many products, however, the consequences of using tort litigation to eliminate improperly designed products are that some number of people will be maimed or killed before the common law remedies impact sellers. For numerous products, the CPSC has conducted research, usually in response to documentation provided by companies that are required to file injury reports with the CPSC, and this research has led to very specific conclusions regarding design standards required of certain products. For example:

> The CPSC conducted research into the designs of cigarette lighters and determined that requiring cigarette lighters to be child resistant could save a significant number of lives. In 1994 the CPSC enacted its follow-up Safety Standard for Cigarette Lighters.[14] According to the CPSC, a cigarette lighter design complies with its requirement for child resistance if 85 percent or more of children, ages 42 to 51 months, are unable to get the lighters to ignite. The Standard requires manufacturers to conduct their own tests and report the results to the CPSC.

recalls
Mandatory vendor calls for the return of defective products for repair or replacement.

In addition to issuing and enforcing mandatory standards and banning consumer products if there is no feasible way to make those products safe, the CPSC arranges for **recalls** of

---

[13] Pub. L. No. 92-573, codified at 15 U.S.C. §§ 2051–2083.
[14] 16 C.F.R. Part 1210.

products that it deems unsafe. The CPSC also conducts investigations, often in response to citizen complaints; collects safety statistics; and provides consumer education on risks associated with various consumer products. Much of its consumer education work takes the form of cooperative efforts with the media, with state and local government agencies, and with private organizations.

REGULATION OF WARRANTIES

As you know from Chapters 7 and 8, express warranties are promises that sellers make about the products they sell and implied warranties are those imposed on sellers as a matter of law unless they are disclaimed. Under the UCC, *implied warranties of merchantability and fitness for use* are promises by sellers that the products they sell will perform according to the expectations of most consumers. The UCC does allow sellers to disclaim implied warranties or to limit damages with some exceptions. Notably, under the UCC as applied to consumer goods, when damages involve personal injury, limitations of liability, that is, limiting liability of sellers for defective consumer goods, are unconscionable and thus unenforceable.[15]

Magnuson-Moss Warranty Act of 1975

When a company mass-markets a product to consumers, warranty language can be a major factor in the mass marketer's costs, marketing practices, and profitability. Courts have shown themselves to be hostile to artfully written warranties that appear to provide extensive protection to consumers but which, in fact, have so many exclusions and exceptions that (1) they are very difficult to read and understand and (2) the protection provided is often not extensive at all. The Magunson-Moss Act is a federal statute that sets minimum standards for written warranties.[16] Its major goal is to make warranty language comprehensible to consumers.

The Magnuson-Moss Act requires written warranties to state in clear English

1. The parts of the products covered or the types of malfunctions covered.
2. The time period of the warranty.

full and limited warranties
Alternative standards for the legal warranty obligations of product suppliers. Most warranties are limited, as the requirements of full warranties are much more stringent.

3. What will be done if the product does not perform and what will not be done by sellers in the event of a nonfunctioning product (e.g., will a loaner be provided or not?).
4. What the customer has to do to get warranty service and how state law may affect the warranty.

Under the Magnuson-Moss Act, all warranties are classified as either full or limited. The requirements for a **full warranty** are so comprehensive that few manufacturers are willing to take on the requisite responsibilities and potential liabilities. As a result, almost all warranties are designated as **limited.**

Limited Warranties

According to the Magnuson-Moss Act, the minimum federal standards for a limited, written warranty include

1. The warrantor must fix a defective product without charge within a reasonable period of time.
2. During the duration of the written warranty, the warrantor cannot impose any limitation on the duration of any implied warranty.

---

[15] U.C.C. § 2-719(3).
[16] Pub. L. No. 93-637, codified at 15 U.S.C. §§ 2301–2312.

3. The warrantor cannot exclude or limit consequential damages for such breach of any written or implied warranty on such product, unless such exclusion or limitation conspicuously appears on the face of the warranty.

4. If the product malfunctions more than a reasonable number of times, the customer is entitled to either a complete refund or a replacement product.

UCC-Magnuson-Moss Interaction

Note that term 2 above prohibits a warrantor (seller) from imposing any limitation on the duration of any implied warranty during the time of the express limited warranty. Note further that even though number 3 above appears to allow exclusions or limitations of liability on warranties that are conspicuous on the face of the warranty, Section 2-719(3) of the UCC prohibits limitations of liability for personal injury on consumer goods.

CONSUMER PROTECTION LEGISLATION: REGULATING LENDING, CREDIT REPORTS, AND BILL COLLECTING

Consumer finance is an area that is particularly complicated and in which consumers often seem powerless when dealing with banks and other financial institutions, credit bureaus, collection agencies, and businesses that make use of these institutions. For many consumers, making comparisons between the offers made by lenders was impossible before the Truth in Lending Act was passed in 1968, which standardized interest calculations. Prior to federal legislation, credit bureaus were resistant to correcting errors in their files that could have devastating effects on individuals. Lenders maintained many discriminatory practices that harmed women in particular before the passage of the Equal Credit Opportunity Act. Bill collectors abused and even terrorized debtors until their activities were substantially restricted by the Fair Debt Collections Practices Act.

Increasingly, money transfers are electronic. Regulation of such transfers is largely provided by the Electronic Funds Transfer Act. Recent banking legislation in the form of the Gramm-Leach-Bliley Act has provided some privacy protection for consumers whose financial records are computerized and sometimes transmitted between banks and other institutions.

Consumer Credit Protection Act of 1968

The Consumer Credit Protection Act (CCPA) is umbrella legislation that includes the Truth in Lending Act and other federal laws regulating consumer finance.[17] The general federal philosophy regarding credit is one of full disclosure, with the idea being that consumers can make intelligent choices if they are presented with accurate information. In contrast to this philosophy, many states regulate lending by setting limits on the interest rates lenders are allowed to charge. State laws that set caps on allowable interest rates are called **usury laws**.

usury laws
State laws that set maximum limits on allowable interest charges.

Truth-in-Lending Act (TILA)

According to the preamble of the TILA [15 U.S.C. § 1601(a)],

> The informed use of credit results from an awareness of the cost thereof by consumers. It is the purpose of this subchapter to assure a meaningful disclosure of credit terms so that the consumer will be able to compare more readily the various credit terms available to him and avoid the uninformed use of credit, and to protect the consumer against inaccurate and unfair credit billing and credit card practices.

---

[17] Pub. L. No. 90-321, codified at 15 U.S.C. § 1601 *et. seq.*

annual percentage rate (APR)
The yearly interest rate on a credit agreement, calculated in a standardized fashion, that must be disclosed to a borrower under the Truth in Lending Act.

The essence of the TILA is the requirement for lenders to conspicuously reveal the cost of borrowed money (interest and other charges) to debtors. The TILA requires lenders to reveal the **annual percentage rate (APR)** of interest charged for credit that is made available in connection with loans, sales, or leases. In addition, there are complicated rules and formulas for revealing other charges imposed by lenders such as points, loan investigation fees, title costs, and the like. The TILA is triggered whenever a lender charges any interest or whenever a seller allows four or more payments for the purchase of goods sold, regardless of whether interest is charged. The TILA does not apply if the borrower is a business or if the amount lent is more than $25,000, except in the case of consumer real estate loans. Over the years, the Truth-in-Lending Act (TILA) has been amended many times.[18] In 1976 Congress added lessees to those provided protection by TILA when it passed the Consumer Leasing Act.

Damages

The TILA places a premium on strict adherence to technical disclosure requirements. In general, for violations of any sort, consumers are entitled to recover twice the finance charge in the transaction, but no more than $1,000 and no less than $100. In addition, if there is a showing that a TILA violation occurred, the consumer victim is entitled to rescind the loan. For attorneys, TILA class action suits became very popular because there was a provision that allowed for recovery of reasonable attorney fees. Attorneys who detected a disclosure error in the loan forms used by a bank, department store, or other financial institution could organize a class action, guaranteeing class members a minimum of $100 if the litigation was successful, with the attorneys able to bill for reasonable attorney fees for their time.

In the years immediately following enactment of the TILA, there was a widespread perception that creditors were being victimized for innocuous technical errors that really did not mislead consumers. Congress then amended the TILA to limit damages in several ways, including

- In the case of a class action, for each single infraction of the TILA, recoverable damages are limited to the lesser of $500,000 or 1 percent of the net worth of the creditor.[19]
- A creditor has no liability for any failure to comply with any requirement imposed by the TILA if, within 60 days after discovering an error and prior to any lawsuit, the creditor notifies the customer and corrects the error.
- If a creditor shows that the TILA violation was not intentional, but rather was due to a computer malfunction or other bona fide error such as clerical, calculation, and printing errors, there is no liability.

By requiring a rigid format for disclosure of interest charges through a uniform computation of the APR, along with disclosures of all other charges, some may claim that the TILA seems too detail-focused. However, prior to enactment of the TILA, it was almost impossible for consumers to make informed comparisons of loan charges because of the large variety of terms banks and other financial institutions used to describe the interest rates applied. Today, when credit cards compete based on low initial APRs, consumers are able to make intelligent choices because of TILA-mandated disclosures. Truth in lending and the TILA are the focus of Case 18-2.

---

[18] 15 U.S.C. § 1601 *et seq.*
[19] 15 U.S.C. § 1640.

Case 18-2

Ruthie Gibson, on behalf of herself and all others similarly situated v. Bob Watson Chevrolet-Geo, Inc., Defendant-Appellee

United States Court of Appeals for the Seventh Circuit
112 F.3d 283 (7th Cir. 1997)

BACKGROUND AND FACTS

Ms. Gibson bought a used car from Bob Watson Chevrolet on credit. The dealer gave her a statement captioned "Itemization of Amount Financed." The statement contains a category referred to as "Amounts Paid to Others on Your Behalf," under which appears an entry that reads: "To North American for Extended Warranty $ 800.00." The dealer admits that a substantial, though at present unknown, amount of the $800 was retained by him rather than paid over to the company that issued the warranty (North American). The question is whether the failure to disclose this retention violates the Truth in Lending Act.

Opinion by Chief Judge Richard Posner

There are two possible violations. First, when the dealer sells cars for cash rather than on credit, it marks up the warranty less (according to the plaintiffs), and hence retains a smaller amount of the warranty charge. Because the charge by the issuer of the warranty is presumably unaffected by the amount of the dealer's mark-up, the dealer is levying an additional charge on its credit customers that plaintiffs call a "finance charge," which must be disclosed to the customer. [Citations omitted.]

Second, the Act requires the lender or creditor to provide "a written itemization of the amount financed," including "each amount that is or will be paid to third persons by the creditor [the dealer here] on the consumer's behalf, together with an identification of or reference to the third person." The argument that Bob Watson Chevrolet (as before, we're using Gibson's case as typical of all three cases) violated this provision is straightforward, and let us start with it. The amount to be paid to North American on Gibson's behalf is not stated correctly in the written itemization of the amount financed that Gibson received. It is true that the consumer is not entitled to the statement unless he makes a written request for it and there is no indication that Gibson did. But the creditor is allowed to skip this stage and simply provide the itemization of the amount financed without being asked for it. That appears to be what Bob Watson Chevrolet did. In any event, it furnished the itemization, and the itemization contains a false representation.

* * *

The defendants argue that the Federal Reserve Board, the oracle of the Truth in Lending Act, has issued an Official Staff Commentary that authorizes the dealers to do what they did here. The commentary (a part of the Federal Reserve Board's Regulation Z) addresses the situation in which the creditor retains a portion of the fee charged to a customer for a service provided by a third party, such as an extended warranty. It provides that "the creditor in such cases may reflect that the creditor has retained a portion of the amount paid to others. For example, the creditor could add to the category 'amount paid to others' language such as '(we may be retaining a portion of this amount).' " The commentary, being limited to the case in which the fee "is payable in the same amount in comparable cash and credit transactions" has no bearing on the claim that the dealers in these cases are hiding a finance charge. But as to the other possible violation, the failure to itemize accurately, the defendants contend that the words "may" and "could" show that they can if they want disclose that they are retaining some of the fee but that they are not required to do so. In other words, they read the commentary to say: "You may conceal the fact that you are pocketing part of the fee that is ostensibly for a third party, but if you are a commercial saint and would *prefer* to tell the truth, you may do that too." So interpreted, however, the commentary not only would be preposterous; it would contradict the statute. The only sensible reading of the commentary is as authorizing the dealer to disclose only the fact that he is retaining a portion of the charge, rather than the exact amount of the retention. Even this is a considerable stretch of the statute; and it is as far as, if not farther than, the statute will stretch.

* * *

Anyway the issue is not whether these violations are technical, or whether technical violations should be actionable, or whether consumer class actions should be discouraged, but whether the complaints in these cases state a claim. And since they do, the dismissal of the plaintiffs' state-law fraud claims on the ground that disclosures that comply with the Truth in Lending Act do not violate the Illinois consumer protection laws, which confer immunity for acts "specifically authorized" by a federal or state agency, was erroneous too. The judgments are therefore reversed with instructions to reinstate the lawsuits. We hope it's not too late for the district court to reassign all the identical Truth in Lending auto dealer class actions to one judge.

Decision and Outcome

Judge Posner held that the complaint by Ms. Gibson was actionable and the case is remanded to the trial court.

Questions for Analysis

1. What exactly was the nature of the violations of the Truth-in-Lending Act by the defendants in this case?
2. What argument did the defendants try to make with respect to the Official Staff Commentary of the Federal Reserve Board? Why did that argument fail?

Liability for Unauthorized Credit Card Charges

For lost or stolen credit cards used to make charges that obviously are not authorized by the credit card holder, the TILA limits cardholder liability to $50.00 for all unauthorized charges made before the credit card company is informed of the loss or theft. For unsolicited credit cards that are intercepted in the mail and used to make charges, there is no liability for the person whose name appears on the card. The TILA outlines a procedure for resolving disputes with credit card companies that does not cause a consumer to sacrifice his or her credit record. The TILA also allows cardholders (consumers) to refuse to pay for faulty goods that are purchased with a credit card for which the merchant refuses to offer a satisfactory replacement. In such situations, the consumer is again able to protect his or her credit record.

Equal Credit Opportunity Act of 1974

Although it may seem inconceivable now, at one time it was the practice of many banks and financial institutions to require the husband's signature on any loan or credit extended to a wife, regardless of whether she independently qualified for the loan or extension of credit. Women often found out to their horror that, if they became divorced or widowed, they did not have credit "in their own name." The Equal Credit Opportunity Act (ECOA) of 1974 prohibits discrimination in lending based on gender, as well as on race, age, marital status, religion, and national origin.[20] The ECOA also prohibits discrimination in lending based on the form of income received, such as when income is derived from public assistance or alimony. The ECOA also prohibits the practice of requiring a spouse's signature on loans or other instruments providing for extensions of credit for which the applicant qualifies on her (or his) own.

[20] Pub. L. No. 93-495, 88 Stat. 1521.

Fair Credit Reporting Act of 1970

When the Fair Credit Reporting Act was passed in 1970,[21] there were large numbers of reports of abuse by credit bureaus, with claims that faulty reports were literally wrecking people's lives. Most probably motivated by cost consideration, the primary abusive practice attributed to credit bureaus was their refusal to investigate allegations of errors. Compounding whatever problems credit record errors caused, credit bureaus made requested reports available to all kinds of businesses, some legitimate (such as businesses that were considering lending money to a named person) and some illegitimate, such as private investigators. The FCRA requires that, any time a consumer is denied credit or insurance because of a credit report, the consumer must be informed of that fact and given the name and address of the credit bureau.

Before the FCRA, probably the most aggravating aspect of dealing with credit bureaus was their unresponsiveness to consumers' allegations of errors. The FCRA allows consumers to request a copy of the information that a credit bureau gives out about them and the names of any creditors or others who have requested the credit report. If a consumer discovers what he or she believes is an error is in his or her files, the credit bureau is required to reinvestigate the information upon written request by the consumer. Often, the cause of inaccurate information in credit bureau records is confusion over the names of the complaining consumer and someone else who does have bad credit. Credit bureaus are required to delete from consumer records any information that is erroneous or not verifiable, but the credit bureau is not required to change the file if its reinvestigation reveals the information is correct. The consumer is entitled, however, to insert his or her version of events if the consumer and the credit bureau do not agree with the results of the reinvestigation.

Fair Debt Collection Practices Act of 1977

The Fair Debt Collection Practices Act (FDCPA) of 1977 was enacted to combat the perceived widespread abuses of collection agencies.[22] It is worth noting that the FDCPA does not apply to banks or other financial institutions that are attempting to collect money that is owed them, but only applies to *collection agencies* that specialize in collecting money from debtors that original creditors were not able to collect. There is an exception, however, if a creditor claims it is a collection agency, in which case it is bound by the restrictions listed below. Attorneys who regularly collect debts on behalf of businesses also are regulated by the FDCPA. Common law suits have been successfully filed against collection agencies, in particular through reliance on the tort of intentional infliction of emotional distress. The problem of abusive debt collections was sufficiently prevalent, however, that Congress clarified and enhanced the rights of consumers with the FDCPA.

The main focus of the FDCPA is on outlawing certain debt collection tactics, including

- Calling employees at work if their employers object.
- Calling third parties about the debtor's debts, other than parents, spouses, or financial advisors.
- Calling debtors at inconvenient times, which are defined in the FDCPA as before 8:00 A.M. or after 9:00 P.M.
- Calling debtors after the collection agency is aware that the debtor is represented by an attorney.

[21] Pub. L. No. 91-508, 84 Stat. 1127, codified at 15 U.S.C. 1681 *et seq.*
[22] Pub. L. No. 95-109, 91 Stat. 874, codified at 15 U.S.C. §§ 1692–1695o.

- Using abusive tactics, such as profanity, or engaging in fraud, such as by impersonating police or immigration officers.
- Communicating with debtors after receiving notice that the debtor is refusing to pay the debt, except to say that legal action may be taken by the collection agency.

validation notice
Notice that credit collectors must provide to purported debtors indicating a 30-day window for disputing a debt claim or for requesting written verification of debt.

As with all of the consumer legislation under the Consumer Credit Protection Act, primary enforcement is provided by the FTC. Within five days of the first time a collection agency contacts a debtor, they are required by the FDCPA to provide a **validation notice** to the debtor. The validation notice states that the debtor has 30 days within which to dispute the amount or existence of the debt and to request written verification of the debt from the collection agency. The collection agency is only required to respond to a request for verification of the debt if the debtor makes the request in writing.

As with the Truth-in-Lending Act, courts typically make very technical rulings on the application of the FDCPA to collection agencies. Consider Case 18-3.

Case 18-3

Michael DeSantis, As Next Friend of John B. DeSantis Sr., Plaintiff-Appellant v. Computer Credit, Inc., Defendant-Appellee

United States Court of Appeals for the Second Circuit
269 F.3d 159 (2nd Cir. 2001)

BACKGROUND AND FACTS

Plaintiff Michael D. DeSantis brought this suit on behalf of John B. DeSantis, Sr., against Computer Credit, Inc., a debt collection agency. At some point prior to April 27, 2000, John B. DeSantis, Sr., apparently incurred a debt of $319.50 to Dr. Jeffrey A. Stahl. Dr. Stahl assigned the debt for collection purposes to Computer Credit, which is a "debt collector" within the meaning of the Act. See 15 U.S.C. §1692a(6).

On April 27, 2000, Computer Credit sent a letter to John DeSantis. That letter is now the subject of this action. The letter reads:

> *This notice will serve to inform you that your overdue balance with Dr. Jeffrey A. Stahl has been referred to Computer Credit, Inc., a debt collector.* [T]he doctor insists on payment or a valid reason for your failure to make payment. *The law prohibits us from collecting any amount greater than the obligation stated above. Unless you notify us to the contrary, we will assume the amount due is correct. This communication is sent to you in an attempt to collect this debt. Any information obtained will be used for that purpose.* In the absence of a valid reason for your failure to make payment, pay the above debt or contact the doctor to settle this matter. *Payment can be sent directly to the doctor. (emphases added)*

The complaint alleges that the letter violated the terms of the Act, notwithstanding the debt validation notice on the reverse side of the letter, by contradicting or confusing the letter's statutorily required message. The complaint focuses on the letter's second and penultimate sentences (those reproduced in italics [rom] above).

Defendant moved to dismiss the action for failure to state a claim on which relief could be granted. The district court granted defendant's motion, finding that the defendant's letter did not contradict or overshadow the message required by the Act. This appeal followed.

Opinion by Leval, Circuit Judge

The Fair Debt Collection Practices Act establishes certain rights for consumers whose debts are placed in the hands of professional debt collectors for collection, and requires that such debt collectors advise the consumers whose debts they seek to collect of specified rights. In relevant part, the Act provides that, within five days of a debt collector's initial communication with the consumer, the debt collector must

> send the consumer a written notice containing . . . a statement that if the consumer notifies the debt collector in writing within [thirty days after receipt of the notice] that the debt, or any portion thereof, is disputed, the debt collector will obtain verification of the debt or a copy of a judgment against the consumer and a copy of such verification or judgment will be mailed to the consumer by the debt collector.

15 U.S.C. § 1692g (a)(4). The Act further provides that

> if the consumer notifies the debt collector in writing within the thirty day period . . . that the debt, or any portion thereof, is disputed . . . the debt collector shall cease collection . . . until the debt collector obtains verification of the debt . . . and a copy of such verification . . . is mailed to the consumer by the debt collector.

* * *

A debt collector violates the Act if it fails to convey the information required by the Act. Even if a debt collector conveys the required information, the collector nonetheless violates the Act if it conveys that information in a confusing or contradictory fashion so as to cloud the required message with uncertainty. Thus, a debt collector violates the Act if its communication is "reasonably susceptible to an inaccurate reading" of the required message. [Citations omitted.]

In determining whether a debt collector violates the Act, we apply "an objective standard, measured by how the 'least sophisticated consumer' would interpret the notice received from the debt collector." The critical question is therefore whether the notice fails to convey the required information "clearly and effectively and thereby makes the least sophisticated consumer uncertain" as to the meaning of the message. (Posner, C.J.) ("The unsophisticated consumer is to be protected against confusion whatever form it takes.")

In our view, the complaint in this case states a claim upon which relief can be granted. Computer Credit's letter to plaintiff states that the creditor "insists on" a valid reason for failure to make payment. The letter further instructs the plaintiff that "in the absence of" such a valid reason, he should either pay the debt or contact the creditor to settle. The Act, however, gives the consumer the right to notify the debt collector that the debt "is disputed," in which event the collector must cease all efforts to collect until it has verified the debt and mailed verification to the consumer. The consumer's right to take the position, at least initially, that the debt is disputed does not depend on whether the consumer has a valid reason not to pay. The consumer, for example, may not recognize the name of the creditor, may not know whether she incurred the debt, may have a question whether the debt (or part of it) has been paid, or may be unsure of the amount. Assuming the debt is in fact owed, these would not be "valid reasons" not to pay it. Nonetheless, regardless of the absence of a valid reason for nonpayment, the collector is obligated by the Act to cease collection, pending verification, if it receives the consumer's written notification of "dispute," and the Act requires the collector to notify the consumer of the collector's obligation to obtain verification upon receipt of such notice.

* * *

The question before us is whether the complaint states an actionable claim. We rule that Computer Credit's dunning letter had sufficient capacity to confuse an unsophisticated consumer on a message required by the Act that the district court erred in ruling as a matter of law that the letter did not violate the Act. We do not reach the further question whether the letter violated the Act as a matter of law.

Decision and Outcome

The judgment of the district court was vacated and the case was remanded to the district court for further proceedings because the letter received by the plaintiff was confusing enough to have a jury or finder of fact rule on whether it violated the FDCPA.

Questions for Analysis

1. Explain precisely how the defendant's letter violated the Fair Debt Collection Practices Act? Rewrite the letter the defendant sent the plaintiff so that it complies with the Act.
2. Does the ruling in this case mean that the defendant loses? What must the plaintiff demonstrate at trial in order to win the case?

REGULATION OF E-COMMERCE

Electronic Funds Transfer Act of 1978

E-commerce predated the Internet by several decades. Responding to novel situations that were created by e-commerce, in 1978 Congress enacted the Electronic Funds Transfer Act (EFTA).[23] Check cards or debit cards, used with automatic teller machines (ATMs), are regulated by the EFTA as are preauthorized electronic fund transfers and automatic debits of consumer bank accounts. In contrast to credit cards, debit cards are password protected so that transfers can only take place with provision of a customer personal identification number (PIN). The EFTA regulation of debit cards is similar to the regulation of credit cards in that, under this act, it is illegal for a bank to send out such cards unless requested by customers. If a customer reports loss of a debit card to the bank that issued the card within two days, consumer liability for unauthorized transfers is limited to $50. If a lost debit card is reported within 60 days of the discovery of the loss, consumer liability is limited to $500. There is unlimited liability, equal to the amount of money in the customer's bank account, for unauthorized transfers if lost cards are not reported within 60 days.

Banks are required by the EFTA to issue receipts for ATM transfers. These transfers also must be reported on monthly banking statements received by consumers. For preauthorized transfers, which often are automatic transfers to a creditor such as a mortgage company, banks are required to provide a written or oral statement that the transfer did or did not take place, or provide a phone number for customers to verify that the pre-authorized transfer took place.

Off-Line Debit Cards

Off-line debit cards have characteristics of both online debit cards, described immediately above, and credit cards. In fact, the logos on many off-line debit cards are MasterCard or Visa, and they can be used without also using PIN numbers. Off-line debit cards can be used by simply signing a slip, as with a credit card, but the result is that the customer's bank account is debited rather than credit being extended by a third party. To make the distinction more ambiguous, many off-line debit cards have cash reserve arrangements so that a debit can be made in excess of the assets currently in the customer's bank account. Currently, there is no legal cap on liability for lost or stolen off-line debit cards, but both VISA and MasterCard have voluntarily imposed a $50 limit.

E-Commerce and the FTC

The FTC has been very active recently in attempting to police the Internet (some of this was discussed in Chapter 11). A major part of the FTC's consumer protection efforts on the Internet concerns privacy. Although a large share of the efforts of the FTC have been directed at enforcing privacy legislation recently passed by Congress, the FTC also has engaged in extensive consumer education and has launched a number of free-lance strikes against

---

[23] Pub. L. No. 95-630, 92 Stat. 3728, codified at 15 U.S.C. §§ 1643–1693r.

Internet fraud. The FTC also has partnered with a number of private firms that are known to be assisting in verifying that websites adhere to their privacy statements.

Combating Internet Fraud and Deception

The FTC has been vigilant in combating Internet scams in the form of get-rich-quick, work-at-home "opportunities." According to FTC sources, the FTC has taken over 140 law enforcement actions against over 490 companies and individuals to halt fraud and deception on the Internet.[24] According to an FTC report entitled "Combating Internet Fraud and Deception," "The FTC has not only attacked traditional schemes that moved on-line, like pyramid and credit repair schemes, but also has brought suit against page jacking, mouse trapping, modern hijacking, fraudulent e-mail marketing, and other hi-tech schemes that take unique advantage of the Internet."

Consumer Fraud Database

The FTC has used the Internet to assemble data and to marshal the forces of state and local governments in alliance with private sector partners to combat fraud on the Internet. Many of the complaints received by the FTC are sent electronically by e-mail. The FTC has assembled what it calls the Consumer Sentinel database (http://www.consumer.gov/sentinel/), which it claims is the largest North American consumer fraud database. At the time of the most recent FTC report on combating Internet fraud, the Consumer Sentinel had over 250 law enforcement offices as members, as well as all 50 attorneys general in the United States, the FBI, the U.S. Attorney's offices, and the Royal Canadian Mounted Police. The Consumer Sentinel is linked to the Internet and allows the FTC to spot trends from the reports of fraud that are received in the Consumer Sentinel database.

FTC Advertising and Marketing Guidelines for Websites

Most websites are created and maintained by legitimate businesses that are interested both in making money and in complying with applicable laws and government regulations. Since e-commerce is relatively new, not all the decisions that e-businesses must make are clear regarding their propriety under existing laws. To provide some guidance for websites engaged in e-commerce, the FTC published "Advertising and Marketing on the Internet: Rules of the Road," which is available at http://www.ftc.gov/bcp/conline/pubs/buspubs/ruleroad.htm. According to this FTC publication, standard trade rules apply in cyberspace, which means that the FTC has authority to prevent deceptive and unfair trade practices on the Internet.

This publication goes on to note that the FTC requires all claims made by websites to be *substantiated.* Not only are *sellers* responsible for claims made by websites but, also, "Third parties—such as advertising agencies or website designers and catalog marketers—may be liable for making or disseminating deceptive representations if they participate in the preparation or distribution of the advertising, or know about the deceptive claims." Accordingly, the group of parties potentially liable is much broader than just sellers. The FTC indicates that advertising agencies and website designers "are responsible for reviewing the information used to substantiate ad claims. They may not simply rely on an advertiser's assurance that the claims are substantiated." Similarly, the FTC publication states that

> To protect themselves [from liability], **catalog marketers** should ask for material to back up claims rather than repeat what the manufacturer says about the product. If the manufacturer doesn't come forward with proof or turns over proof that looks questionable, the catalog marketer should see a yellow "caution light" and proceed appropriately, especially when it comes to extravagant performance claims, health or weight loss promises, or earnings guarantees.

---

[24] See a series of FTC PDF files located at http://www.ftc.gov/bcp/internet/cases-netsum.pdf.

International Perspective

As the Internet compresses distance and eliminates borders, it makes the exposure of U.S. citizens to fraudulent scams perpetrated from any location in the world cheap and easy. One "international" scam, now well known but still drawing in victims into the late 1990s, was the Nigerian Advance Fee Scheme. This fraud apparently grossed hundreds of millions of dollars yearly in the second half of the 1990s.

Targeted at small and medium-sized businesses and charities, this global scam (with victims in Russia, Southeast Asia, Australia, New Zealand, the United States, and other countries) involves a surprise letter from someone claiming to work for the Nigerian Central Bank or the Nigerian government. The letter sender claims that he needs a reputable foreign company into whose account funds can be deposited, in the amount of, say, $30 million, reflecting purported overpayments on a government procurement contract. The proposed payoff for helping with the "problem" is lucrative, and the intended victim is reassured of the legitimacy of the deal by forged or false documents with official Nigerian government letterhead and seals, falsified letters of credit, pay-

ment schedules, bank drafts, and so forth. Meetings also have been arranged between intended victims and "government officials" in "government offices" (real or fake). Once an intended victim buys into the scheme, something goes wrong, requiring a money advance from the victim—possibly a government official has demanded an up-front bribe, an unforeseen tax must be paid, or some other event. The needed money must be advanced by the victim before the lucrative deal can go forward and money transferred. The scam often continues for several months, with a number of "surprises" and needed additional payments.

At the Internet ScamBusters site, you are asked, what should you do if you receive a letter offering such a participation? The answer is, "The U.S. Secret Service has instructed anyone in the U.S. to forward information to U.S. Secret Service, Financial Crimes Division, 950H Street, NW, Washington, D.C. 20001, or e-mail using the Secret Service form or direct to 419.fcd@usss.treas.gov."

For lists of Internet scams, many of international origin, see http://www.scambusters.org/search.html.

Quite clearly, according to the FTC, the rules it applies to bricks-and-mortar businesses to protect consumers will be applied in cyberspace. There is ample evidence of fraud taking place on the Internet, but, up to now, the FTC is using its resources to provide guidance and to foster self-regulation when possible.

STATE CONSUMER PROTECTION LEGISLATION

States have their own consumer protection legislation, which is quite extensive. Not surprisingly, there is considerable variation across states in consumer protection law, so it is impossible to generalize fully. It should be noted, though, that virtually all states have some unfair trade practice statutes that can be used against companies that defraud consumers. Many such laws provide very stiff penalties for consumer fraud and triple damage awards are common.

For some areas of consumer protection, federal preemption applies. As a logical example, states do not have any power to approve or reject the introduction of a new pharmaceutical drug to the market. States do have laws affecting consumer finance, but many of these laws are usury laws that are generally irrelevant except when inflation pushes nominal interest rates to lofty heights. State tort laws can be used in some cases, generally after the fact, to attack the design of various products including pharmaceutical products. State tort laws can be used to reward victims of improperly designed products, but someone has to die or be injured before those laws can be used.

Many would argue that the main way states try to protect consumers is through licensing laws. For many occupations, including electricians, doctors, plumbers, and veterinarians, practitioners have to pass a state-required competency examination. Requiring the passing of such tests is the state's way of ensuring that persons practicing in the tested profession or occupation have the minimal required competency. In the state of North Carolina, there are 35 separate professions or occupations that require a license before a person is entitled to do business. There are criminal penalties for practicing without a license and no consumer is required to pay an unlicensed professional for work performed, even if he or she flawlessly performed the work he or she was hired to do.

States generally do not have jurisdiction to pursue out-of-state businesses that prey on their citizens. The Internet, of course, exacerbates this problem as it allows out-of-state websites to easily engage in transactions with in-state residents without physically entering the state. State authorities rarely have the resources to go chasing after out-of-state websites. Hence, it often makes more sense for state authorities to link up with the FTC when there is evidence of fraud on the Internet. In other cases, states are preempted from regulating in areas that are extensively regulated at the federal level. There are plenty of state prosecutions of fraudulent businesses, but the major protections for consumers against unfair and deceptive trade practices come at the federal level through the Federal Trade Commission. There is no state agency that has the power of the Consumer Product Safety Commission to set product standards for consumer products sold in all of the 50 states. This parallels the existence of the most significant consumer protection legislation in the areas of pharmaceutical drugs, food, and food additives resting at the federal level with the Food and Drug Administration. The same is true of consumer protection in finance, as the major legal constraints lenders, credit bureaus, and collection agencies face are provided by federal laws requiring disclosure of relevant costs of obtaining money, providing remedies for mistakes by credit bureaus, and limiting the tactics used by bill collectors.

Summary

Much Consumer Protection Legislation Was Enacted Because Common Law Remedies for Fraud Were Widely Perceived as Inadequate; the FTC Has Authority to Prohibit Trade Practices That It Considers Deceptive and Unfair and Can Issue Cease and Desist Orders as Well as Trade Practice Rules

- Consumer protection legislation has been enacted where common law remedies are inadequate. This is often the situation when it is difficult to prove intent, preventing consumers from successfully claiming that they were defrauded. In other situations, the consequences of making a mistake are too drastic to rely on the injured-then-sue formula.
- The Internet has expanded opportunities to *defraud* and to take advantage of people.
- Trade practices can be *deceptive,* or *unfair,* or both. The Federal Trade Commission (FTC) has authority to prohibit both deceptive and unfair trade practices.
- According to the FTC, a trade practice is *unfair* if it is likely to cause *substantial injury* to consumers, is *not reasonably avoidable,* and has negative impact *not outweighed by countervailing benefits.*
- *Deceptive* trade practices are those *likely to mislead the reasonable consumer* and that *affect decisions that such a consumer would make.*
- The FTC has, on many occasions, intervened and stopped deceptive and unfair advertising. The FTC has the power to take an advertiser to court and obtain a *cease and desist order* if the administrative law judge for the FTC agrees.
- The FTC also has the power to issue *trade practice rules* for industries in which industry practices are unfair or deceptive.

The Federal Trade Commission Has Authority to

- Under the Lanham Act, it is illegal to make false claims about the goods or services a firm provides and rival firms are entitled to sue firms that make false claims that harm their business.
- The Telephone Consumer Protection Act of 1991 prohibits the automatic dialing of phone numbers for the transmission of prerecorded messages.

Enforce a Wide Array of Consumer Legislation	• The Telemarketing and Consumer Fraud and Abuse Prevention Act of 1994 requires telemarketers to inform consumers that they are making a sales pitch, provide the seller's name, and disclose the total cost of the items being sold. • In 2003 the FTC worked on development of a national "Do Not Call" registry that would provide a list of individuals whom telemarketers cannot call.
The Government Is Proactive in Its Regulation of Food Additives and Drugs through the FDA; It Requires That Companies Selling These Products Prove That Their Products Are Safe and Effective; It Also Regulates Nutritional Advertising	• Among the first products to be regulated at the federal level were food, food additives, and pharmaceutical drugs. The Food and Drug Administration (FDA) is one of the oldest regulatory agencies in the federal government. • In order to market a pharmaceutical drug, the vendor company must prove to the FDA that the product is both *safe and effective*. • Companies have been able to avoid FDA regulation by calling their products "dietary supplements" and by refraining from making explicit health claims for those products. • The Fair Packaging and Labeling Act (FPLA) of 1966 requires sellers to provide information about contents, quantity of servings, and other pertinent information about food products. • The 1990 Nutrition Labeling and Education Act requires nutritional labeling on most foods in addition to ingredients labels. • The FDA provides regulatory definitions for terms such as "low calorie," "fat free," "natural," and "fresh." It also regulates the health claims that can be made about foods. • The Food, Drug and Cosmetic Act of 1976 authorizes the FDA to approve or disapprove new medical devices.
The CPSC Issues Safety Regulations for Products Sold to Consumers; the Magnuson-Moss Act Require Labels and Warranties to Be Accurate and Readable	• The Consumer Product Safety Commission (CPSC) has jurisdiction over all consumer products that are not regulated by some other agency. The CPSC has the power to take off the market products that pose an unreasonable risk to consumers. The CPSC also has the power to issue consumer product safety regulations. • The Magnuson-Moss Act (MMA) requires written warranties to be provided in understandable English. The MMA requires that all warranties be designated as *full* or *limited*. • The MMA requires that all warranty limitations or exclusions be conspicuous. • The effect of UCC rules and the MMA is that sellers cannot limit liability for consumer products that are defective and physically harm consumers.
There Is Extensive Government Regulation of Lending and Transfers of Money; Liability Is Limited for the Loss of Credit and ATM Cards; Discrimination in Lending, the Accuracy of Credit Reports, and Abuses in Collection Tactics Are All Regulated or Prohibited	• The Consumer Credit Protection Act of 1968 is umbrella legislation for federal regulation of lending, credit record reporting, and bill collecting. • The Truth-in-Lending Act (TILA) requires conspicuous disclosure of the costs of borrowing money. TILA applies to consumer loans and requires uniform computation and disclosure of the *annual percentage rate* (APR) charged by lenders. • The TILA is strictly enforced and lenders are liable for very technical violations unless, within 15 days of discovery of a violation, changes are made in the lenders' practices. • For lost or stolen credit cards, liability is limited to $50 for unauthorized charges. • The Equal Credit Opportunity Act prohibits discrimination in lending based on gender, race, and other demographic factors such as marital status, age, religion, and national origin. • The Fair Credit Reporting Act (FCRA) requires credit bureaus to respond to consumer complaints of errors in the their credit records. Under the FCRA, if a consumer contacts a credit bureau and contends that it has made an error, the credit bureau must reinvestigate, correct errors, and include the consumer's version of events, even if the credit bureau does not agree with the consumer. • The Fair Debt Collection Practices Act (FDCPA) applies to collection agencies and limits abusive debt collection tactics such as impersonations, calling debtors at inconvenient times, or contacting third parties about their debts.

- The Electronic Funds Transfer Act (EFTA) regulates check cards and automatic teller transfers. If the consumer promptly reports the loss of a check card within two days, liability is limited to $50, but liabilities are unlimited if lost cards are not reported within 60 days.

Cyberspace Has Opened up New Avenues for Fraud and the FTC Has Taken the Lead in Trying to Police the Internet; Antifraud Efforts by State Authorities Have Been Hampered by Jurisdictional Limitations

- The FTC has taken the lead in prosecuting fraud in cyberspace.
- The FTC has established the Consumer Sentinel to receive complaints from consumers about fraud on the Internet.
- The FTC contends that advertisers, website designers, and catalog providers are all liable for false claims made by sellers who offer their goods for sale on the Internet.
- States have their own consumer protection laws and agencies. In some cases, federal preemption applies, but on most consumer protection subjects, state and federal authorities work together.
- States use *licensing laws* to ensure that practitioners in various professions and occupations have the minimum knowledge necessary to practice in the area. States can revoke licenses if a practitioner engages in fraud. For many Internet activities, states lack resources and authority to pursue out-of-state websites that are defrauding in-state citizens.

Key Terms

annual percentage rate (APR), *595*
bait advertising, *585*
cease and desist order, *584*
dietary supplements, *589*

full and limited warranties, *593*
nutrition labels, *590*
opt in, *585*
opt out, *588*
recalls, *592*

spammers, *588*
trade practice rules, *584*
unfair trade practices, *579*
usury laws, *594*
validation notice, *599*

Questions for Review and Analysis

1. Explain why, in many consumer transactions, common law remedies based on fraud or breach of contract are not realistic. Does it make sense for consumers to join together, in effect, by having an organization like the FTC represent them?

2. Why do you think the earliest forms of consumer protection legislation focused on pharmaceutical drugs and food additives? What are the consequences likely to be when mistakes are made with these products? Can consumers realistically protect themselves?

3. The federal government regulates labels, warranties, and consumer products. Without government regulation, what abuses are likely to occur?

4. Credit extension, interest rates charged, and other details of money lending are complicated and are not subjects that interest most people. Explain how the main thrust of the Truth-in-Lending Act (TILA) addresses this arena. Who is included in the protections afforded by the TILA?

5. It has been said that "A sucker is born every minute." Has the Internet accelerated that rate? Discuss.

If You Really Understood This Chapter, You Should Be Able to Provide Informed Commentary on the Following:

1. **Liability for Mistakes by Credit Agencies.** In the "bad" old days, before the Fair Credit Reporting Act, credit bureaus were unresponsive to consumers because it cost them money to check out consumer complaints. Congress enacted the Fair Credit Reporting Act, recognizing that mistakes by credit bureaus would still occur, but wanting to create a procedure giving credit bureaus an incentive to reinvestigate claims. After all, not every consumer complaint about a credit report is accurate. John M. Stevenson, a successful real estate broker, in 1989 began to receive phone calls about overdue bills. After a period of time, he figured out that the calls came from creditors of his estranged son. Stevenson wrote to TRW, the credit bureau, and explained the situation. After an investigation, most of the son's accounts were expunged from Mr. Stevenson's credit file. After TRW had completed its investigation in February of 1990, it assured Stevenson that all negative credit information had been taken out of his credit record. Unfortunately, Stevenson continued to receive

calls, in part because his estranged son figured out what Stevenson was doing, impersonated his father, and ran up more credit card debt. The Fair Credit Reporting Act requires credit bureaus to use "reasonable procedures to assure maximum possible accuracy." Stevenson filed suit under the Fair Credit Reporting Act and a jury awarded him $100,000 in punitive damages, $30,000 in actual damages, and $20,000 in attorney fees. TRW appeals, arguing that TRW's reinvestigation was complicated by the accounts fraudulently obtained in Stevenson's name and based upon accurate information. The court in this case discussed the level of diligence and accuracy that is required of credit bureaus when a consumer complains that mistakes have occurred. [*John Stevenson v. TRW Inc.,* 987 F.2d 288 (5th Cir. 1993).]

2. **Abusive Debt Collection Tactics.** When a consumer takes a collection agency to court for violations of the Fair Debt Collection Practices Act (FDCPA), the collection agency is not apt to look too good. Often, the debtor was born in another country and does not know his or her rights. Gulendar Ozkaya issued a "stop payment" on a check for an automobile repair because her car still did not work after the services rendered by the repair shop. The amount of the check was over $1,000. Shortly after stopping payment on the check, Ozkaya received a letter from the defendant collection agency, Telecheck Services, which said, among other things, "Telecheck has purchased the check referenced in this notice. As a result, we have entered your name in our NATIONAL COMPUTER FILES. Until this is resolved, we may not approve your checks or the opening of a checking account at over 90,000 merchants and banks who use Telecheck nationally. We have assigned your file to our Recovery Department where it will be given to a professional collection agent. Please be aware that we may take reasonable steps to contact you and secure payment of the balance in full. In order for us to update your file quickly, send a cashier's check or money order for the Total Amount Due in the return envelope provided." Ozkaya filed suit under the FDCPA claiming that Telecheck violated the FDCPA. At issue in this case was whether the plaintiff received a proper validation notice that informed the plaintiff that she had 30 days to contest the validity of the debt. Several courts have held that a validation notice, required under the FDCPA, is invalid if the notice is overshadowed by intimidating language in the rest of the dunning letter. According to the courts, the perspective used in evaluating the language of the collection agency is to assume the debtor is relatively unsophisticated. What do you think? Do the statements above imply that the debtor should ignore his or her rights under the statute and just pay off the debt claimed? See how the court decided this case. [*Gulendar Ozkaya, individually and others similarly situated v. Telecheck Services, Inc.,* 982 F. Supp. 578 (N.D. Ill. 1997).]

3. **Comparative Advertising.** As discussed in the text of the chapter, the Lanham Act makes it unlawful for a firm to misrepresent the qualities of its products or the products of rivals, and provides for a variety of remedies for violations. A typical Lanham Act case involved S.C. Johnson & Son and Clorox. In August 1999, Clorox introduced a 15-second and a 30-second television commercial ("Goldfish I"), each depicting an S.C. Johnson Ziploc Slide-Loc resealable storage bag side-by-side with a Clorox Glad-Lock bag. The bags are identified in the commercials by brand name. Both commercials show an animated, talking goldfish in water inside the competitors' bags. In the commercials, the bags are turned upside-down. The Slide-Loc bag leaks rapidly, while the Glad-Lock bag does not leak at all. In both the 15- and 30-second Goldfish I commercials, the Slide-Loc goldfish says, in clear distress, "My Ziploc Slider is dripping. Wait a minute!" while the Slide-Loc bag is shown leaking at a rate of approximately one drop per one to two seconds. In the 30-second Goldfish I commercial only, the Slide-Loc bag is shown leaking while the Slide-Loc goldfish says, "Excuse me, a little help here," and then, "Oh, dripping, dripping." At the end of both commercials, the Slide-Loc goldfish exclaims, "Can I borrow a cup of water!!!" On November 4, 1999, S.C. Johnson brought an action against Clorox under section 43(a) of the Lanham Act, 15 U.S.C. § 1125(a), for false advertising in the Goldfish I commercials. After S.C. Johnson moved for a preliminary injunction, the district court convened an evidentiary hearing on the motion for a trial on the merits under Fed. R. Civ. P. 65(a)(2). At the evidentiary hearing, Dr. Phillip DeLassus, an outside expert produced by S.C. Johnson, showed, based on samples of Slide-Loc products, that the rate of leakage depicted in the Clorox commercials was literally false. Based on this evidence, the trial court judge issued an injunction against Clorox airing the Goldfish commercials. Clorox revised its commercial in an attempt to make it literally accurate, but the district

court expanded the injunction against Clorox following a motion from S.C. Johnson. The case is fascinating because it shows the detail in which courts are forced to examine implied and explicit claims made by large companies using cartoon commercials. Is this a good use of judicial resources? [*S.C. Johnson v. Clorax Company,* 241 F.3d 232 (2nd Cir. 2001).]

4. **Warnings in English.** As the influx of people from Mexico and other points south continues, bilingual issues confront courts with increasing frequency. In March 1986, when he was less than four months old, plaintiff, Jorge Ramirez, exhibited symptoms of a cold or a similar upper respiratory infection. To relieve these symptoms, plaintiff's mother gave him St. Joseph's Aspirin for Children (SJAC). Although the product label stated that the dosage for a child under two years old was "as directed by doctor," plaintiff's mother did not consult a doctor before using SJAC to treat plaintiff's condition. Over a two-day period, plaintiff's mother gave him three SJAC tablets. Then, on March 15, plaintiff's mother took him to a hospital. There, the doctor advised her to administer Dimetapp or Pedialyte (nonprescription medications that do not contain aspirin), but she disregarded the advice and continued to treat plaintiff with SJAC. Later Jorge developed a severe neurological disorder known as Reyes Syndrome. SJAC contains warnings about Reyes Syndrome, but the warnings are entirely written in English. Through his mother, Jorge files suit against the manufacturer of SJAC, claiming that the warnings about Reyes Syndrome should have been in Spanish since the defendant was aware that a large number of Spanish-speaking people used its product. What do you think? Should a manufacturer incur liability for not providing a Spanish version of the warnings on its products? If Spanish warnings were used, could a Vietnamese family sue because warnings were not in their native tongue? [*Jorge Ramirez v. Plough, Inc.,* 6 Cal. 4th 539, 863 P.2d 167 (Cal. 1993).]

5. **Truth-in-Lending Act and Technical Violations.** The Truth-in-Lending Act requires that each borrower receive two notices of the right to rescind the loan agreements made with the lender. The Elsners, Max and Jacquelyn, were each given a notice of the right to rescind but not two copies of the right to rescind as called for in the TILA statute. There were some other irregularities in this mortgage transaction, but, basically, the Elsners sought to rescind the loan long after the three-day period because the lenders did not provide them each with two copies of the right to rescind, even though each Elsner did receive a copy of their individual right to rescind. Is this violation of the TILA substantive enough for borrowers to rescind the loan long after it was made? [*Max and Jacquelyn Elsner v. Harley and Donna Albrecht,* 460 N.W. 2d 232 (Mich. app. 1990).]

6. **FDA Approval and Adverse Reactions.** An issue that vexes those involved in the production of pharmaceutical drugs is whether their drug designs can be attacked even though they have been approved by the FDA. In the background is a jury, often not skilled in scientific matters; a plaintiff who has died or who has been severely harmed by the defendant's drug; and a plaintiff's attorney, who has an expert, charging sizeable hourly fees, who will testify that the design of the drug is defective. The defendant may have spent millions of dollars getting its drug approved by the FDA, which requires manufacturers to prove that their products are both safe and effective. Kathy Tobin was pregnant with twins and was due in April but was experiencing contractions in January. She was given ritodrine to suppress contractions, but she experienced side effects such as a racing heartbeat. Tobin gave birth to healthy twins in March, but continued to experience heart irregularities and, at age 19, had to have a heart transplant. Tobin files a product liability suit against the manufacturer and its American distributor, Astra Pharmaceutical Products. The defendant moves for a dismissal based on preemption. The defendant claims that because a federal agency, the FDA, has approved the safety and effectiveness of ritodrine, legal attacks on the design of the drug based on state law are preempted. What do you think? How would you like to have your company spend $100 million trying to get a drug approved by the FDA and later get sued in state court based on the claim that the design of the drug is defective in spite of FDA approval? How would you like to be a victim of injury by an "approved drug?" [*Kathy D. Tobin v. Astra Pharmaceutical Products, Inc.,* 993 F.2d 528 (6th Cir. 1993).]

Social Responsibility, Policy, and Ethics in a High-Tech World

7. **Battling Fraud in Cyberspace: The Federal Trade Commission.** Fraud did not begin in cyberspace, but it has blossomed as the Internet medium has enabled those disposed toward committing

fraud to reach more people more cheaply than ever before. In the following case, the district court reviewed the actions of the defendant, Para-Link International, Inc.:

1. Since at least June 1999, and continuing thereafter, defendants have advertised, promoted, and sold paralegal training and other work-at-home employment opportunities to consumers. Defendants, either directly or through third parties, use various advertising media such as Internet Web sites, located at www.para-link.com, taylormadeopportunities.com, and www.thelawclub.com., as well as unsolicited electronic mail and newspaper advertisements to promote their paralegal training and claimed employment opportunities. Through one or more of these advertising media, defendants lure potential purchasers into buying a work-at-home kit, for prices ranging from $395 to $495 that defendants promise will train purchasers to become and earn money as a paralegal. Once consumers pass defendants' qualifying tests, they are then eligible to receive case referrals from defendants. Defendants promise to pay kit purchasers who qualify $25 for each referred completed case, plus $5 per case for expenses.

2. Defendants' unsolicited electronic mail (or "spam") and newspaper advertisements often feature earnings claims and representations such as "Make Over $200 an Hour" and "You Can Process Simple Divorces and Bankruptcies From Home and Make Over $200 an Hour in as little as 30 Days!!!" The text of one e-mail noted that "It's 100% PROVEN! . . . Work When YOU Please!" The unsolicited e-mails often encourage recipients to call a toll-free number to learn more about the opportunity from one of the company's "22 in-house paralegals." Defendants' newspaper advertisements often proclaim "Make $50 per hour working from home." Defendants' Web sites promise that kit buyers will "make serious money" and boast that "you are paid directly by the customer up to $200 an hour!" and that "students can start making money the same day they get their kit!" Finally, defendants promise "your success is guaranteed!"

As a result of an investigation by the FTC, the entire scheme of the defendants was revealed to be a scam. After clients paid their money for their Para-Link kits, their only way of earning money was to rely on Para-Link to send them cases. Para-Link had few cases to send to their paralegal clients. Also, the software that accompanied the Para-Link kits was incompatible with the operating systems of most computers. Often the Para-Legal kits, as delivered, were incomplete and not functional.

Is this what the Federal Trade Commission should be doing? How many other Internet scams have you seen that resemble the one described above where you can allegedly earn "big bucks" while working from your house? Is this an area where trade practice rules are appropriate? Should Congress pass another law regulating the Internet or is this the kind of distraction that we have to live with? The entire case can be found at *Federal Trade Commission v. Para-Link International, Inc.,* 2001 U.S. Dist. LEXIS 17372 (N.D. Fla. 2001).

Using the Internet to Your Advantage

1. The Federal Trade Commission (http://www.ftc.gov) is the federal agency most strongly linked with consumer protection. A major share of the efforts of the FTC has been directed at Internet fraud. Their Web page focusing on e-commerce & the Internet (http://www.ftc.gov/bcp/menu-internet.htm) illustrates the scope of FTC activities in this area. The FTC enforces 46 separate statutes that can be accessed at http://www.ftc.gov/ogc/stats.htm. Another very-high-profile government agency discussed in the chapter is the Food and Drug Administration (http://www.fda.gov). Also, the Consumer Product Safety Commission (http://www.cpsc.gov) has a website that contains a wealth of information about consumer safety issues.

2. A website that explains the Magnuson-Moss Act in more detail is at http://www.mlmlaw.com/library/guides/ftc/warranties/undermag.htm. The Truth-in-Lending Act is explained in (perhaps too much) detail by Regulation Z, which is accessible on the Federal Reserve Board's website at http://www.federalreserve.gov/regulations/regref.htm#z. The texts of the Equal Credit Opportunity Act and the Electronic Funds Transfer Act are reproduced by the Legal Information Institute at Cornell University's law school at http://www4.law.cornell.edu/uscode/15/1691.html and http://www4.law.cornell.edu/uscode/15/1693.html, respectively. The texts of the Fair Credit Reporting Act and the Fair Debt Collection Practices Act appear at the FTC website, http://www.ftc.gov/os/statutes/fcra.htm and http://www.ftc.gov/os/statutes/fdcpa/fdcpact.htm.

Chapter Nineteen

Antitrust and the Interface with Intellectual Property

Learning Objectives

After completing this chapter, you should

1. Be familiar with the two major antitrust laws, the Sherman Act and the Clayton Act, and what is illegal under each act.
2. Know what actions are subject to the per se rule and what are subject to the rule of reason.
3. Know the horizontal trade restraints that are subject to the per se rule.
4. Be able to discuss what constitutes monopolization, what amounts to attempts to monopolize, and the importance of market share.
5. Know what price discrimination, tie-ins, exclusive dealing, and mergers are and when they are likely to be illegal.
6. Understand how courts are attempting to apply existing antitrust laws in high-tech market settings.

OVERVIEW

"Big business" is a shorthand term often pejoratively used to allude to the power that some businesses appear to have, either in competition with other businesses or in their dealings with consumers and other end users of their products. Antitrust law is intended to place some limits on business conduct so that consumers will realize the benefits of efficiency and innovation that are the byproducts of competition between business rivals that actively compete for customers.

Business competition is lessened when one company dominates (*monopolizes*) an entire industry and creates barriers to the entry of other businesses into that industry. Economic studies have shown that in industries that are dominated by a single firm, prices are higher, quantity is lessened, and such industries are less innovative. It can be claimed that consumers are "robbed" of the benefits of competition if business rivals "agree" not to compete on the bases of price (*price-fixing*), of territory, and of product quality, and are able to implement such agreements. Business competition is also generally harmed when all or most of the major businesses in an industry decide to *merge* and form even larger businesses. If a business legitimately achieves "market power" in the sale, say, of product A, through a patent or adroit marketing, then extending its market power into other markets by requiring consumers to purchase product B in order to get product A (a tie-in) unreasonably coerces and restricts consumer choice. All of the forms of conduct (or misconduct) introduced in this paragraph are injurious to competition and are generally illegal acts under antitrust laws.

TENSION BETWEEN ANTITRUST LAW, INNOVATION, AND LOW PRICES

The primary practical goals of antitrust law are to enhance consumer choice and to enable buyers to get the products they want at the lowest possible prices. Of course, firms that produce superior products tend to attract more customers, thus becoming large firms and, as a result, often becoming the possible targets of antitrust authorities. As Learned Hand, a federal court of appeals judge who wrote a number of very influential antitrust opinions, said,

> A single producer may be the survivor out of a group of active competitors, merely by virtue of his superior skill, foresight and industry. In such cases a strong argument can be made that, although the result may expose the public to the evils of monopoly, the [Sherman] Act does not mean to condemn the resultant of those very forces which it is its prime object to foster: finis opus coronat. The successful competitor, having been urged to compete, must not be turned upon when he wins.[1]

As suggested by this quote, a problem of long standing that continues to plague antitrust enforcement is the challenge of *distinguishing* between legitimate competition between business rivals and destructive, illegal competition. Illustratively, when a firm lowers price, there could be a question of whether this is an act of predatory pricing, which can be illegal under the antitrust laws, or simple legitimate competition. Certainly, the goal of antitrust enforcement is not to punish firms that simply lower prices because consumers benefit from lower prices. Yet, large firms that lower prices are often defendants in antitrust suits. While the antitrust laws certainly were not and are not intended to punish product innovation and low prices, distinguishing between legitimate attempts to compete and illegal, anticompetitive conduct is not always easy.

In Antitrust Law, Size Most Definitely Matters

For many students, the most well-known antitrust action is the antitrust suit filed by the U.S. Department of Justice against the Microsoft Corporation in 1998.[2] In recent years, the Microsoft Corporation has had the highest capitalized (stock market) value of any company in the world. There is little doubt that the Microsoft Corporation has enjoyed a near monopoly over operating systems for personal computers (PCs) and that it has used its market power in operating systems in various ways to try to increase sales of Microsoft Office products as well as in promoting its Internet Explorer browser. There is also little doubt that Microsoft has been a highly innovative company and that its products have been a major force propelling the U.S. economy toward its current position of world leadership in information technology. Whether Microsoft has crossed the line of illegality in its conduct vis-à-vis other companies in software and PC hardware markets has been and continues to be the subject of intense legal battles that are not fully resolved at this writing.[3] Other targets of antitrust authorities during the past 100 years have included a large proportion of the largest firms of the time, including Standard Oil Company, U.S. Steel, IBM, AT&T, General Electric, and, most recently, Microsoft.

---

[1] *United States v. Aluminum Co. of America*, 148 F.2d 416 (2nd Cir. 1945).

[2] *United States v. Microsoft Corporation, Inc.*, 253 F.3d 34 (D.C. Cir. 2001).

[3] Although antitrust litigation in the U.S. against Microsoft has been settled for now, EU antitrust authorities have threatened additional legal action.

Size in antitrust law is a relative term. In general, it is large companies that are the targets of antitrust enforcement. The term *large* is a relative term that refers to the size of the company relative to the rest of its industry. In antitrust law, size is typically measured by **market share,** which, in its simplest form, is the percentage of total sales within the relevant market accounted for by sales of a single firm. If one firm makes all the sales in the relevant market, that firm is a **monopoly.** An **oligopoly** exists when a few large firms account for most or all of the sales in an industry. In simple symbolic terms, market share (MS) percent equals firm sales (FS) divided by total sales (TS) in the industry times 100, or

market share
Percent of sales in a defined market accounted for by a firm.

monopoly
A firm has a monopoly if it is the only seller in a market.

oligopoly
An oligopoly exists if there are only a "few" (two, three, four) sellers in a market.

$$MS = (FS/TS)*100$$

A firm with a 100 percent market share would be a monopoly, while four firms, each with a 25 percent market share, would constitute an oligopoly.

High-Tech Products Possess Unique Characteristics That Present Challenges for Antitrust Law

The antitrust difficulties of Microsoft are symptomatic of a troublesome problem that confronts many producers of high-tech products that are used in cyberspace. Many high-tech markets possess what are known as "network externalities." The result of network externalities is that the value of the "network" is further increased the greater the percentage of the total market that uses that particular network. If a seller of a high-tech product, such as an important software product, can gain market acceptance as the industry standard or leader, then makers of hardware and other software products tend to adapt their products to those of the industry leader. As more and more users learn how to operate with the industry leader's products, and as more peripheral products are made compatible with the industry leader's products, market shares of industry leaders tend to become very large.

In high-tech market after market, the twin forces of network externalities and the desire for compatibility between products result in one or a few firms winning very high market shares. Are firms that achieve very high shares in these markets illegal monopolies or are they innovators who deserve the supercompetitive profits that they frequently make? At this point, it is not clear that antitrust authorities have figured out how to determine the good guys from the bad guys—assuming, of course, that there are good guys and bad guys in information technology. To date, antitrust authorities at the U.S. Department of Justice have maintained that traditional antitrust theories apply to high-tech markets without significant modification.

THE SHERMAN ANTI-TRUST ACT, 1890

Before the Civil War, most of American industry consisted of relatively small businesses that, individually, could not control markets over broad geographic areas. Beginning just after the Civil War, the industrial sector of the American economy experienced a dramatic transformation that resulted in a number of markets becoming dominated, nationwide, by a few large firms. By the 1880s, in an era before federal income taxes, huge fortunes were amassed by owners of a handful of hugely successful companies. The captains of these juggernauts had names such as Rockefeller (oil), Carnegie (steel), Mellon (banking), and Morgan (finance and steel), among others. The first antitrust legislation, the Sherman Act, was what may reasonably be labeled populist legislation, designed to prevent large companies from dominating or rigging markets to the detriment of consumers and small businesses.[4]

---

[4] 15 U.S.C. §§ 1 *et seq.*

Antitrust Language and Scope

Per Se and Rule of Reason

Possible antitrust violations are evaluated under two alternative standards, which are typically referred to with the labels *per se rule* and *rule of reason.* There are some agreements between or among firms that rarely, if ever, have benefits for society that are not outweighed by their costs. These would include agreements among several firms at the same level in the market (horizontal competitors) to set price (generally labeled price-fixing). When applying the **per se rule,** courts do not consider whether a price that is "fixed" by agreement of firms involved in the price-fixing was set at a *reasonable level,* but simply conclude that such actions are illegal as a matter of law. If a firm or firms are found guilty of a per se violation, such as price-fixing, dividing up markets, or boycotts (all of which are explained below), courts apply the per se rule and do not consider whether the agreement could have compensating benefits.

per se rule
Antitrust standard under which particular acts, such as agreeing to fix prices, are illegal as a matter of law.

Rule of Reason

Firms make other agreements that may or may not be illegal under the antitrust laws. Some such agreements are subject to judgment under the **rule of reason.** For example, an agreement by a manufacturer to restrict its distributors to carrying only its products and none of the products of competitors is called an *exclusive dealership.* Such agreements are generally legal for small firms, but it may be illegal for very large firms with high market shares to be exclusive dealerships as such agreements could foreclose smaller manufacturers from having outlets for their products. In many cases, there are legitimate business justifications for exclusive dealerships, but, in others, the motives of large manufacturers are clearly to squeeze out smaller competitors. Unlike transactions that are subject to the per se rule, under antitrust law, exclusive dealerships may or may not be illegal. Courts would apply the rule of reason standard and evaluate the costs and benefits of these agreements to the health of competition in the marketplace.

rule of reason
Antitrust standard under which agreements and acts are judged based on their overall effects on competition.

Jurisdiction in the United States

The U.S. antitrust laws are acts of Congress and, as such, are limited in their scope to interstate commerce or anything that affects interstate commerce. Courts have been liberal in their interpretations of conduct that "affects" interstate commerce. Thus, a single hospital in the center of a state was held to affect interstate commerce because some of its financing and insurance originated from out-of-state sources.[5] In addition to U.S. antitrust laws, most states have their own "little Sherman Acts" that closely imitate or exactly replicate the language used in the federal antitrust laws.

Overseas Jurisdiction

Section 8 of the Sherman Act extends liability under U.S. antitrust law to activity by companies that takes place outside the United States and that affects the prices of items imported into the United States. Thus, firms that conspire to raise prices outside the United States can be sued in the United States for violating the Sherman Act. In addition, foreign citizens and firms can sue U.S. firms in the United States for conspiracies hatched in the United States that have the effect of raising prices in their foreign country or countries.

Section 1 of the Sherman Act

According to Section 1 of the Sherman Act, "Every contract, combination in the form of trust or otherwise, or conspiracy, in restraint of trade or commerce among the several

---

[5] *Hospital Building Co. v. Trustees of Rex Hospital et al.,* 425 U.S. 738 (1976).

States, or with foreign nations, is declared to be illegal." In interpreting Section 1 (of the Sherman Act), many courts have noted that every contract restrains trade to some extent. If Farmer A contracts with Processor B to sell all of his corn at the end of the growing season, the contract has restrained A's corn from entering the spot market for corn. The target of Section 1 (of the Sherman Act), however, was not small contracts that were standard operating procedure for most businesses but, rather, contracts that *unreasonably* restrained trade. In early cases in interpreting Section 1, courts looked to common law precedents for guidance. Common law courts would not enforce contracts between competitors that, for example, fixed prices at a certain level. Under the common law, courts considered contracts between competitors preventing competition on price as void and against public policy. Essentially, what Section 1 of the Sherman Act did was make illegal (per se) what were previously unenforceable, void contracts, such as price-fixing agreements, that common law courts would have chosen not to enforce.

Illegal Conduct under Section 1 of the Sherman Act: Agreements between Horizontal Competitors

Using the common law for guidance, several important U.S. Supreme Court decisions identified the following specific kinds of contracts, combinations (agreements), or conspiracies as illegal under Section 1. Each of the following, then, is a per se violation of Section 1 of the Sherman Act.

Horizontal Price-Fixing   When firms at the same level in the market (e.g., all manufacturers) agree not to compete on price, that agreement, whether in the form of a written contract or simply an oral "gentlemen's" agreement, is illegal under Section 1 of the Sherman Act. A price-fixing agreement is considered horizontal if members of the agreement are all manufacturers, all distributors, or all retailers (see the chart in the "Nutz and Boltz" box for a visual demonstration of horizontal competitors and vertical trading partners). Horizontal price-fixing agreements are said to be per se illegal because the act of price-fixing is illegal regardless of whether the price agreed upon by the price fixers is reasonable or not. Virtually any agreement relating to price among horizontal competitors is illegal even if the parties do not agree on a specific price. Generally, an agreement among horizontal competitors to reveal the last price charged is illegal, as is an agreement to allow customers to reveal to competitors the last price charged as part of a reciprocity arrangement among competitors.

horizontal agreements
Agreements between or among firms at the same level of an industry.

Horizontal Agreements Regarding Customers or Territory   If a group of horizontal rival firms agree not to invade each other's territories, the agreement is treated the same as if it were a **horizontal agreement** on price. The same is true of agreements to divide a market by class of customer. If several large distributors of pharmaceutical drugs joined together and divided up the market for drugs between hospitals, drugstores, and doctors, and each firm agreed not to invade the market segment(s) allocated to the other firms, that agreement would be a per se violation of Section 1.

Boycotts   A boycott is an agreement among firms not to deal with another firm or group of firms. In its most raw form, a group of manufacturers could band together and agree not to sell products to a distributor that they did not like. Manufacturers may not like a particular distributor because that distributor fails to maintain quality control over the product. If the goods being distributed are dairy products or beer, temperature control is essential to maintaining the quality of the products. Alternatively, if manufacturers have some kind of price agreement among themselves, that agreement is threatened by distributors who cut prices. Regardless of the reason, an agreement among firms not to deal with another firm or group of firms is a per se violation of Section 1 of the Sherman Act. Boycotts need not be

Nutz and Boltz Horizontal versus Vertical Relationships

Most markets have a common basic structure: Raw materials and component suppliers sell their output to manufacturers, who sell their output to distributors, who in turn sell to retailers, and finally the good is purchased by consumers. Firms at the same level are called horizontal competitors, while firms at different levels in the marketing chain have vertical supplier relationships. If firms linked vertically in the marketing chain merge (e.g., manufacturer–distributor, distributor–retailer, or all three merge), it is called *vertical integration*. The following chart may seem overly simplified, but it does illustrate the difference between a horizontal and a vertical relationship.

With regard to the antitrust laws, any agreement as to price, territory, or customers between horizontal competitors is per se illegal (some exceptions to the application of the per se rule to horizontal agreements are discussed below). That means that an agreement between the first three manufacturers below as to price, territory, or customers would be subject to the per se rule. On the other hand, an agreement between the first manufacturer, a distributor, and a retailer as to territory or customers would be evaluated under the rule of reason and would not be subject to the per se rule, because it is a vertical relationship. Moreover, it would most likely be judged legal unless the market share of this manufacturer was very high.

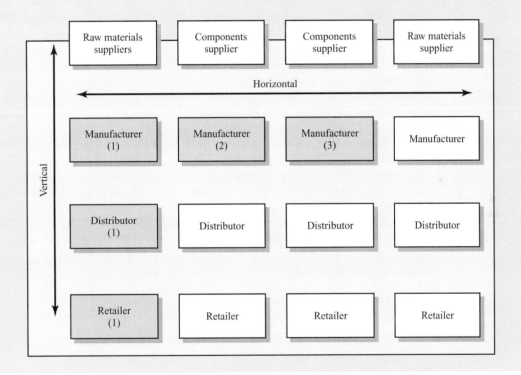

agreements among horizontal competitors to be illegal. Note that, while boycott *agreements* are illegal, unilateral (single firm) refusals to deal with another firm are not illegal, except if the courts decide that a large firm controls an essential facility such as pipelines in a natural gas production area.

Limits on the Application of the Per Se Rule

If the Price-Fixing Is Necessary for a Market to Exist   A prominent line of cases holds that, if a market would not exist but for horizontal agreements among competitors that set or affect price, such collusion is not illegal per se but must be judged under the rule of reason standard. There are a number of markets that have been identified as subject to this doctrine, including those in the music industry and in college athletics.[6] Licensing fees for playing music on television, on radio, and at any gathering or event where money is charged have been set for years by Broadcast Music Inc. (BMI); American Society of Singers, Composers and Publishers (ASCAP); and Society of European Stage Authors and Composers (SESAC). If radio programs had to individually negotiate with composers and recording artists, living and dead, the transaction costs would be far too great and we would not have much music on radio and other media outlets. BMI, for example, sets uniform fees (fixed prices) for the playing of musical compositions on radio, thus significantly eliminating transaction costs for radio stations. By setting uniform royalties for playing musical compositions, BMI creates a market that would not exist otherwise.

Statutes That Authorize Antitrust Exemptions, Particularly Price-Fixing

At both federal and state levels, Congress and state legislatures have allowed price-fixing for various economic and political reasons. There are a number of settings in which business entities attempt to control price. Labor unions attempt to fix wages (prices for work time) for their members. Interestingly, some of the first litigation applications of Section 1 of the Sherman Act were directed at labor unions. Agricultural cooperatives collect the farm output of many farmers and deal collectively with large food processors in order to raise the prices received by members of the cooperatives. At the state level, insurance rates, liquor prices, and prices in several other industries have been exempt from the antitrust laws when the industries are regulated at the state level and are subject to price supervision by state authorities (regulated prices can be fixed prices). Due to one U.S. Supreme Court decision rendered in 1922, *professional baseball is exempt* from the antitrust laws. Interestingly, that precedent has not been followed for other sports, which consequently are not exempt from the antitrust laws.[7] The National Football League, for example, has been sued several times for violating antitrust laws.

Most exemptions from the antitrust laws are exemptions from Section 1 of the Sherman Act for price-fixing. Firms in highly regulated industries often are allowed to fix prices under some form of government supervision, but these firms are not exempt from other sections of the antitrust laws that prohibit monopolization or exclusionary practices such as tie-ins or boycotts. For years telephone rates were fixed, with governmental rate regulation, but that did not prevent AT&T from being a defendant in a major monopolization suit that eventually led to the breakup of the nationwide Bell System.

Fertile Grounds for Antitrust Violations

Trade Shows Studies of violations of Section 1 of the Sherman Act reveal that as many as 40 percent of such violations began with conversations at trade shows. At trade shows, competitors come together to display their products to buyers and to obtain valuable information about what their rivals are offering. Trade shows are also occasions where alcohol is often the beverage of choice. Business rivals who have been vigorously competing throughout the year may have a few drinks together and start discussing industry problems. Often, sooner or later prices are discussed by these industry rivals and this may be followed by a discussion of some scheme to maintain "reasonable" prices or price "stability." These

---

[6] *Broadcast Music, Inc. v. Columbia Broadcasting System, Inc.*, 441 U.S. 1 (1979); *NCAA v. Board of Regents*, 468 U.S. 85 (1985).

[7] *Federal Baseball Club of Baltimore v. National League of Professional Baseball Clubs*, 259 U.S. 200 (1922).

Ethical Challenges The Continuing Justification for Baseball's Antitrust Exemption

When baseball received an exemption from the nation's antitrust laws by a single decision of the U.S. Supreme Court, following a suit by the Federal Baseball Club of Baltimore, the implications were not as clear as they are today. In 1922, following World War I, baseball was the national pastime; neither the NFL nor the NBA existed and no other sport rivaled baseball in fan appeal, with the possible exception of boxing. Since that time, as we all know, professional sports has become big business and there are a number of other professional sports that rival the appeal of baseball. None of these other sports have exemptions from the antitrust laws. Indeed, the sole justification for continuing baseball's antitrust exemption seems to be that the baseball's antitrust exemption was established by precedent and Congress has not acted to eliminate it. Many do not find baseball's antitrust exemption innocuous, as the article below points out.

An ethical principle that most people subscribe to is that similarly situated parties should receive similar treatment. How ethical is it to continue to treat baseball differently than other major professional sports? The following article is quite critical of continuing the antitrust exemption for baseball.

IN ANTITRUST WE TRUST

If baseball's exemption were lifted, real fans might be able to afford tickets, and teams would stop holding cities hostage. Call your congressman.

To be a sports fan these days is to be taking a course in economics: Salary caps, arbitration, revenue sharing and large market are terms probably as well known as hit-and-run and full-court press to sports fans who grew up in the '80s. It's gratifying to see that the sports press is catching up on these things, too. Two recent articles are particularly gratifying. The May 15 issue of Sports Illustrated includes a superb feature by E.M. Swift on the effect that corporations are having on ticket prices, and the May 15 issue of the New Yorker has a piece by James Surowiecki on a possible solution to the problem.

Actually, Surowiecki's piece is about baseball's antitrust exemption and how its removal would benefit fans. This is not a new idea; Marvin Miller, former chief economist for the steelworkers union and the first executive director of the Major League Baseball Players Association, proposed the idea some time ago. In a greatly oversimplified version it was like this: The New York Yankees, or rather, their owner, George Steinbrenner, can hold the city of New York hostage in demand for a new stadium built with public money by threatening to move the Yankees elsewhere.

Miller's and Surowiecki's theory—and again, I'm oversimplifying—is that if Major League Baseball's exemption from the antitrust laws were completely repealed, what or who would stop, say, the Oakland A's or Minnesota Twins (or some other disgruntled so-called small-market team) from saying, "Hey, an old stadium without luxury boxes in New York is fine with us, we'll be arriving on the next plane"?

And the answer to that question is: Nothing, and certainly not the commissioner's office, could prevent such a thing from happening—and that's not oversimplified. Miller's wrinkle was to suggest that absence of the antitrust exemption could only bring about something else that might, in the long run, be more beneficial. What, he suggested, would prevent, say, a new Triple-A minor league franchise from moving into New York, and perhaps another in Brooklyn, and maybe one in Newark, and how about Washington, which has been without big league ball for almost 30 years? And what would prevent them from eventually developing into a competing major league? And, again, the answer to these questions is: If you remove baseball's exemption from antitrust laws, nothing at all could prevent these things from happening.

Swift's story in SI touches on a topic that, judging from radio call-in show traffic, is the hottest in sports right now: the cost of going to a game. I won't bore you with numbers; suffice it to say that every sport has seen a ridiculous rise in ticket prices over the last 10 years. There was a time not too long ago when we could legitimately say that ticket prices shouldn't concern us, that it was simply a case of supply and demand and that if people didn't like the product or didn't think it was worth the price, then they would stop buying and the price would come back down. But with corporations buying up more and more tickets, especially to professional football and basketball games, there are fewer tickets available to average (i.e., "real") fans, and the ones that are available are priced out of the range of working people.

What I'm suggesting is that the removal of all antitrust laws for all professional sports could go a long way toward bringing ticket prices down, as well as saving cities hundreds of millions of dollars on new stadiums. More professional teams, even minor league teams, means more competition for the NFL, NBA and Major League Baseball, and, inevitably, less meat in the corporate-owned seats of big-time professional sports. And that will lower tickets prices faster than the drop in the NBA's Nielsen ratings.

If you're a fan, you're by definition a victim. But that doesn't mean you have to be helpless. You've got a phone, you've got e-mail, you've got stamps and you've got a congressman.

Source: From "In Antitrust We Trust," by Allen Barra, May 19, 2000, Salon.com News. Reprinted with the permission of Salon.com.

topics compose illegal material for conversations or other communications between horizontal competitors and can be illegal subject matter for such interactions among other firms as well. A good rule of thumb to keep in mind is, "Do not drink and talk about prices at trade shows." If your boss starts talking about price within earshot of other executives at a trade show, leave. Violations of Section 1 of the Sherman Act are felonies and the U.S. Department of Justice, when it brings price-fixing actions, has a policy of insisting that all participants in price conspiracies serve some active jail time.

Trade Associations and Professional Codes   It is legitimate for horizontal competitors to form trade associations to deal with common problems facing their industry. For example, a group of firms selling similar products may be concerned about U.S. import policy and may jointly hire a lobbyist to advocate their points of view to Congress. Certainly there are other common problems that face various industries that justify trade associations. At times, trade associations collect and circulate industry data, including data relating to pricing. Such activities are subject to scrutiny for "collusive" content and, in some situations, trade publications have been the subject of antitrust prosecutions under Section 1. As a result of a number of court decisions, the following statements are tentatively offered:

1. It is legal to publish *industry average prices* and costs as long as specific prices are not identified with individual firms.
2. It is legal to publish recorded prices, but it is *not legal for a trade publication to predict future prices* with any degree of specificity. It is legal to suggest that cost increases may cause prices to rise in the industry.
3. It is *not legal to publish formulas* that firms use to compute prices based on geography or cost factors.

Price-Fixing among Licensed Professionals   For professionals such as doctors, attorneys, and dentists, it was common until the 1970s to have prohibitions in professional codes against advertising a willingness to cut prices. Informally, minimum fee schedules were circulated and professionals who undercut minimum prices were targets of "ethical" inquiries by professional boards, leading to possible revocations of their licenses.[8] During the 1970s and 80s, the Justice Department aggressively prosecuted professional associations that suppressed price competition among professionals or actively engaged in price-fixing. Case 19-1 is typical of the price-fixing cases that were directed against professional groups for whom a professional association aided and abetted price-fixing.

[8] In many professions, it was considered unethical by professionals to compete on price.

Case 19-1

Goldfarb et Ux. v. Virginia State Bar et al.

Supreme Court of the United States
421 U.S. 773 (1975)

BACKGROUND AND FACTS

A married couple, unable to retain an attorney willing to perform a real estate title examination for a fee less than that prescribed as the minimum fee for such service in the fee schedule published by the Fairfax, Virginia, County Bar Association, instituted a class action against the County and State Bars in the United States District Court for the Eastern District of Virginia, alleging that the operation of the minimum fee schedule, as applied to fees for legal services relating to residential real estate transactions, constituted price fixing in violation of Section 1 of the Sherman Act (15 U.S.C. § 1). The fee schedule was enforced by the State Bar by its issuance of fee schedule reports and ethical opinions that stated that deviation from minimum fee schedules might lead to disciplinary action. After a trial on the issue of liability only, the District Court held that (1) the minimum-fee schedule violated the Sherman Act and (2) although the actions of the State Bar were exempt from the Sherman Act as constituting state action, the actions of the County Bar were not so exempt. The U.S. Court of Appeals for the Fourth Circuit reversed, holding that (1) the State Bar's actions were immune from Sherman Act proscriptions as constituting state action and (2) the County Bar was also immune since the practice of law was not "trade or commerce" under the act but was a "learned profession" exempt from the act, the challenged activities not having sufficient effect on interstate commerce to support Sherman Act jurisdiction in any event.

Opinion: Mr. Chief Justice Burger Delivered the Opinion of the Court

We granted certiorari to decide whether a minimum-fee schedule for lawyers published by the Fairfax County Bar Association and enforced by the Virginia State Bar violates § 1 of the Sherman Act, 26 Stat. 209, as amended, 15 U.S.C. § 1. The Court of Appeals held that, although the fee schedule and enforcement mechanism substantially restrained competition among lawyers, publication of the schedule by the County Bar was outside the scope of the Act because the practice of law is not "trade or commerce," and enforcement of the schedule by the State Bar was exempt from the Sherman Act as state action as defined in Parker v. Brown, 317 U.S. 341 (1943).

* * *

The fee schedule the lawyers referred to is a list of recommended minimum prices for common legal services. Respondent Fairfax County Bar Association published the fee schedule although, as a purely voluntary association of attorneys, the County Bar has no formal power to enforce it. Enforcement has been provided by respondent Virginia State Bar which is the administrative agency [Footnotes omitted] through which the Virginia Supreme Court regulates the practice of law in that State; membership in the State Bar is required in order to practice in Virginia. Although the State Bar has never taken formal disciplinary action to compel adherence to any fee schedule, it has published reports condoning fee schedules, and has issued two ethical opinions indicating that fee schedules cannot be ignored. The most recent opinion states that "evidence that an attorney *habitually* charges less than the suggested minimum fee schedule adopted by his local bar Association, raises a presumption that such lawyer is guilty of misconduct. . . . "

* * *

A purely advisory fee schedule issued to provide guidelines, or an exchange of price information without a showing of an actual restraint on trade, would present us with a different question. [Citations omitted.] The record here, however, reveals a situation quite different from what would occur under a purely advisory fee schedule. Here a fixed, rigid price floor arose from respondents' activities: every lawyer who responded to petitioners' inquiries adhered to the fee schedule, and no lawyer asked for additional information in order to set an individualized fee. The price information disseminated did not concern past standards, cf. *Cement Mfrs. Protective Assn. v. United States,* 268 U.S. 588 (1925), but rather minimum fees to be charged in future transactions, and those minimum rates were increased over time. The fee schedule was enforced through the prospect of professional discipline from the State Bar, and the desire of attorneys to comply with announced professional norms, see generally *American Column Co., supra,* at 411; the motivation to conform was reinforced by the assurance that other lawyers would not compete by underbidding. This is not merely a case of an agreement that may be inferred from an exchange of price information, *United States v. Container Corp.,* 393 U.S. 333, 337 (1969), for here a naked agreement was clearly shown, and the effect on prices is plain.

Moreover, in terms of restraining competition and harming consumers like petitioners the price-fixing activities found here are unusually damaging. A title examination is indispensable in the process of financing a real estate purchase, and since only an attorney licensed to practice in Virginia may legally examine a title, see n. 1, *supra,* consumers could not turn to alternative sources for the necessary service. All attorneys, of course, were practicing under the constraint of the fee schedule. See generally *United States v. Container Corp., supra,* at 337. The County Bar makes much of the fact that it is a voluntary organization; however, the ethical opinions issued by the State Bar provide that any lawyer, whether or not a member of his county bar association, may be disciplined for "*habitually* [charging] less than the suggested minimum fee schedule adopted by his local bar Association. . . . " These factors coalesced to create a pricing system that consumers could not realistically escape. On this record respondents' activities constitute a classic illustration of price fixing.

* * *

In arguing that learned professions are not "trade or commerce" the County Bar seeks a total exclusion from antitrust regulation. Whether state regulation is active or dormant, real or theoretical, lawyers would be able to adopt anticompetitive practices with impunity. We cannot find support for the proposition that Congress intended any such sweeping exclusion. . . .

The language of § 1 of the Sherman Act, of course, contains no exception. "Language more comprehensive is difficult to conceive." *United States v. South-Eastern Underwriters Assn.,* 322 U.S. 533, 553 (1944). And our cases have repeatedly established that there is a heavy presumption against implicit exemptions, *United States v. Philadelphia National Bank,* 374 U.S. 321, 350–351 (1963); *California v. FPC,* 369 U.S. 482, 485 (1962). Indeed, our cases have specifically included the sale of services within § 1. *E.g., American Medical Assn. v. United States,* 317 U.S. 519 (1943); *Radovich v. National Football League,* 352 U.S. 445 (1957).

* * *

Decision and Outcome

The judgment of the court of appeals was reversed and the case was remanded to that court with orders to remand to the district court. The claim that attorneys or any learned profession was exempt from the antitrust laws was rejected by the U.S. Supreme Court.

Questions for Analysis

1. Why did the U.S. Supreme Court not agree with the contention of the county bar association that the lawyers should be exempt from the antitrust laws?

2. Did the court of appeals believe that applying antitrust laws to the practices of the legal profession was going to harm that profession?

3. The county bar indicated that no attorneys had ever been disbarred for ignoring the recommended minimum-fee schedules. Why did the Supreme Court find that argument unconvincing? Did the Supreme Court find the fee schedule at issue to be a recommendation or mandatory?

Boycotts Revisited   For "professional" groups, ranging from doctors to contractors, there are

1. *Professional codes* that are designed to protect the public from unscrupulous and dangerous practitioners. For example, state professional codes for psychiatrists prohibit them from having sexual contact with their patients.
2. *Certain practices* that stockbrokers and attorneys, as examples, adhere to with regard to their handling of money entrusted to them by clients. It is generally a violation of those "practice codes" for stockbrokers or attorneys to borrow from the funds that have been entrusted to them.
3. A number of professional codes that builders, contractors, and engineers abide by that directly enhance safety for them and the consuming public.

Members of these various group professional associations typically agree to adhere to their association's codes. Often, a part of these codes is a pledge not to do business with those who do not adhere to the applicable codes. An agreement not to do business with another group of businesspeople sounds very much like a boycott, which is a per se violation of the Sherman Act. However, if the purpose of refusing to do business with another group is adherence to a code that directly advances financial integrity or safety, it is not illegal. Even though a professional code advances public safety or integrity, however, adherence to such a code is illegal when that code is used to punish those who cut prices.

Bid-Rigging

In a number of states, state and local governments award contracts for construction and road building to the lowest bidders. In like fashion, contracts to supply milk to schools, state hospitals, and other state facilities are awarded to the lowest bidder. In many of these situations, the same five or six firms are repeatedly bidding against one another. Executives representing these companies often get to know each other, either at trade shows or through joint projects, and often become friends. In friendship or not, the temptation to rig bids (by agreeing not to underbid each other for government contracts) in these settings often appears to be irresistible, though it should be resisted (if, for no other reason, because such collusion is a felony under Section 1 of the Sherman Act). Of course, the collusive rigging of prices (bids) results in agreed-to higher prices, accompanied by agreements with regard to which vendor(s) will get which job(s). These **bid-rigging** arrangements, by their nature, require a good bit of information (on the rigging arrangements) to be shared by a sizeable number of people.

bid-rigging
Price-fixing by supposed competing firms, incorporated into the "bids" they submit for contracts to be awarded to the low bidder(s).

Not surprising, then, in bid-rigging situations, word of collusive agreements often somehow leaks. Not infrequently, shortly thereafter various executives can be found hastily striving to strike plea bargain deals with government prosecutors, hoping to avoid active jail sentences. According to the Justice Department, since 1988 the Antitrust Division has filed 134 milk bid-rigging cases, involving 81 corporations and 84 individuals. Job losses and jail sentences were commonplace in these cases. Bid-rigging occurs in many industries. The "Nutz and Boltz" box on page 622 gives an excerpt from the U.S. Department of Justice that reveals another industry in which a prosecution for bid-rigging has occurred.

Vertical Restraints

vertical restraints
Restrictive agreements between firms at different levels in the marketing chain—e.g., between a manufacturer and a distributor.

Vertical restraints are treated much more leniently under the antitrust laws than are horizontal restraints. Whereas most horizontal agreements are subjected to the per se rule under Section 1 of the Sherman Act, most vertical agreements are evaluated under the rule of reason. Vertical restraints exist between businesses at different levels in the marketing chain. Agreements between manufacturers and distributors are vertical agreements, as are

Nutz and Boltz

CANADIAN COMPANY CHARGED WITH BID RIGGING ON SALES OF TACTILE TILE

WASHINGTON, D.C.—A Canadian company was charged today [September 17, 2001] with rigging bids for the sale of tactile tile to the Long Island Railroad, located in New York, the Department of Justice announced.

In a one-count felony charge, filed in U.S. District Court in Concord, New Hampshire, 1256384 Ontario Limited (Ontario Limited) from Oakville, Ontario, was charged with conspiring with unnamed co-conspirators to submit collusive, noncompetitive, and rigged bids for the sale of tactile tile from the spring of 1998 until the fall of 1998.

Tactile tile is a corrugated tile designed to warn visually impaired persons that they are approaching a dangerous area. It is usually sold to public transportation authorities or to contractors hired to perform construction for public transportation authorities and is typically installed along the edge of train platforms.

According to the charge, Ontario Limited and its co-conspirators carried out the bid-rigging scheme by discussing the price for the bid, agreeing on which corporate co-conspirator would be the low responsive bidder, and submitting a collusive, non-competitive and rigged bid to the railroad.

This is the second case to be filed in an investigation of the tactile tile industry. On August 9, 2000, ADA Fabricators Inc. was also charged with participating in this conspiracy. ADA, after pleading guilty, was sentenced to pay a $48,000 fine.

The maximum penalty for a corporation convicted of violating the Sherman Act is a fine of $10 million. The fine may be increased to twice the gain derived from the crime by the conspirators or twice the loss suffered by the victims of the crime, if either of those amounts is greater than the statutory maximum fine.

The investigation is being conducted by the Antitrust Division's New York Office and the Federal Bureau of Investigation's Bedford, New Hampshire Division. The United States Attorney's Office for the District of New Hampshire assisted in the investigation.

Anyone with information concerning price fixing in the tactile tile industry or bid rigging or price fixing in other industries should contact the New York Office of the Antitrust Division at (212) 264-0383.

Source: http://www.usdoj.gov/atr/public/press_releases/2001/9051.htm.

agreements between distributors and retailers. The following are examples of vertical restraints:

1. *A manufacturer may set territorial boundaries* (see the chart in the "Nutz and Boltz" box on the opposite page) for its distributors or franchisees. It is common for breweries to assign its distributors specific geographic territories and to exclude its distributors from making sales outside of their assigned territories (into another distributor's territory). Franchisees are often limited in the areas where they are allowed to establish outlets and also have agreements with parent companies that limit the parent company from establishing new franchises within a certain proximity of existing franchisees. Each of these agreements is called a *vertical territorial allocation* and each would be examined under the rule of reason.

2. *A manufacturer may divide up responsibilities of its distributors.* Pharmaceutical companies may tell independent sales representatives that they are limited to selling to hospitals, to drugstores, or to physicians. This restriction is called a *vertical customer allocation.*

3. *A manufacturer may establish exclusive dealerships* by requiring distributors not to carry products of competitors. Nike, for example, may tell distributors of sports apparel that they cannot carry products that compete with Nike products and remain Nike distributors. This restriction is called an *exclusive dealing arrangement.*

Nutz and Boltz Vertical Trading Relationships

If the manufacturer in the diagram below sets exclusive territories for its distributors (1), (2), and (3), that restriction is judged under the rule of reason and will most likely be legal unless the market share of the manufacturer is very large. On the other hand, if the three distributors on their own were to agree on territories and not to invade each other's territory, it would be a per se violation of Section 1 of the Sherman Act.

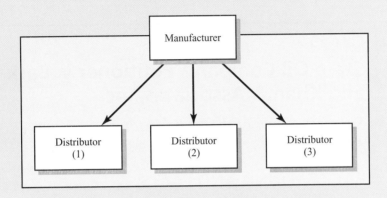

4. *A manufacturer may suggest retail prices.* It is common for manufacturers to put "Manufacturer's suggested retail price" (MSRP) right on boxes that are sold to retailers. Often retailers will display a lower price next to the manufacturer's suggested price so consumers think that they are getting a bargain. If horizontal competitors suggested prices their rivals should select, they would immediately be subject to suit for a per se violation of Section 1 of the Sherman Act.

Vertical Price Fixing

Until recently, it was considered conventional wisdom that vertical price-fixing was per se illegal, based on Supreme Court decisions dating back to 1914.[9] Vertical price-fixing occurs when a seller, by contract, sets not only the price for the product it sells to a buyer, but also the price that the buyer can set for subsequent buyers, usually consumers or other end users. Vertical price-fixing, often called **resale price maintenance**, involves agreements between manufacturers and resellers in which the manufacturers set the prices downstream resellers can charge their customers. An economic justification for making vertical price-fixing illegal is the presumption that, if manufacturers are involved in illegal price-fixing themselves, resale price maintenance reinforces the price structure created by price-fixing at the manufacturing level.

As discussed above, however, vertical pricing restrictions between manufacturers and retailers have been treated much more leniently than price agreements, of any kind, between competitors. Over the years, courts have carved out several exceptions to the per se rule as it applies to vertical price-fixing. A manufacturer can terminate distributors and retailers who are known to be price cutters if they announce in advance that they will not

resale price maintenance
Agreement between a manufacturer and the resellers of its products through which the manufacturer sets the prices the resellers must charge their customers.

---

[9] *Dr. Miles Medical Co. v. John D. Park & Sons*, 220 U.S. 373 (1911).

sell to distributors and retailers who do not adhere to their suggested resale prices.[10] In Case 19-2, Justice O'Conner indicated that the per se rule for vertical price-fixing did not apply when the manufacturer set *maximum* prices. Still, the per se rule for vertical *minimum* price-fixing remains part of antitrust law. A manufacturer whose contract with a distributor requires the distributor to charge at least a specific minimum price, or a price based on a formula set by the manufacturer, is violating Section 1 of the Sherman Act.

[10] *United States v. Colgate & Co.*, 250 U.S. 300 (1919).

Case 19-2

State Oil Company, Petitioner v. Barkat U. Khan and Khan & Associates, Inc.

Supreme Court of the United States
522 U.S. 3 (1997)

BACKGROUND AND FACTS

Respondents' agreement to lease and operate a gas station obligated them to buy gasoline from petitioner State Oil Company at a price equal to a suggested retail price set by State Oil, less a specified profit margin, required them to rebate any excess to State Oil if they charged customers more than the suggested price, and provided that any decrease due to sales below the suggested price would reduce their margin. After they fell behind in their lease payments and State Oil commenced eviction proceedings, respondents brought this suit in federal court, alleging in part that, by preventing them from raising or lowering retail gas prices, State Oil had violated § 1 of the Sherman Act. The District Court entered summary judgment for State Oil on this claim, but the Seventh Circuit reversed on the basis of Albrecht v. Herald Co. *[Citation omitted], in which this Court [the U.S. Supreme Court] held that vertical maximum price fixing is a* per se *antitrust violation. Although the Court of Appeals characterized* Albrecht *as "unsound when decided" and "inconsistent with later decisions," it felt constrained to follow that decision.*

Opinion: Justice O'Connor Delivered the Opinion of the Court

Respondents sued State Oil in the United States District Court for the Northern District of Illinois, alleging in part that State Oil had engaged in price fixing in violation of § 1 of the Sherman Act by preventing respondents from raising or lowering retail gas prices. According to the complaint, but for the agreement with State Oil, respondents could have charged different prices based on the grades of gasoline, in the same way that the receiver had, thereby achieving increased sales and profits. State Oil responded that the agreement did not actually prevent respondents from setting gasoline prices, and that, in substance, respondents did not allege a violation of antitrust laws by their claim that State Oil's suggested retail price was not optimal.

* * *

Thus, our reconsideration of *Albrecht's* continuing validity is informed by several of our decisions, as well as a considerable body of scholarship discussing the effects of vertical restraints. Our analysis is also guided by our general view that the primary purpose of the antitrust laws is to protect interbrand competition. [Citations omitted.] "Low prices," we have explained, "benefit consumers regardless of how those prices are set, and so long as they are above predatory levels, they do not threaten competition." Our interpretation of the Sherman Act also incorporates the notion that condemnation of practices resulting in lower prices to consumers is "especially costly" because "cutting prices in order to increase business often is the very essence of competition."

So informed, we find it difficult to maintain that vertically-imposed maximum prices could harm consumers or competition to the extent necessary to justify their *per se* invalidation.

* * *

After reconsidering *Albrecht's* rationale and the substantial criticism the decision has received, however, we conclude that there is insufficient economic justification for *per se* invalidation of vertical maximum price fixing. That is so not only because it is difficult to accept the assumptions underlying *Albrecht,* but also because *Albrecht* has little or no relevance to ongoing enforcement of the Sherman Act. Moreover, neither the parties nor any of the *amici curiae* have called our attention to any cases in which enforcement efforts have been directed solely against the conduct encompassed by *Albrecht's per se* rule.

* * *

In overruling *Albrecht,* we of course do not hold that all vertical maximum price fixing is *per se* lawful. Instead, vertical maximum price fixing, like the majority of commercial arrangements subject to the antitrust laws, should be evaluated under the rule of reason. In our view, rule-of-reason analysis will effectively identify those situations in which vertical maximum price fixing amounts to anticompetitive conduct.

There remains the question whether respondents are entitled to recover damages based on State Oil's conduct. Although the Court of Appeals noted that "the district judge was right to conclude that if the rule of reason is applicable, Khan loses," its consideration of this case was necessarily premised on *Albrecht's per se* rule. Under the circumstances, the matter should be reviewed by the Court of Appeals in the first instance. We therefore vacate the judgment of the Court of Appeals and remand the case for further proceedings consistent with this opinion.

Decision and Outcome

The U.S. Supreme Court held that the per se rule with regard to *maximum* resale prices was overruled and manufacturers could legally set maximum resale prices for their distributors, subject to a rule-of-reason analysis.

Questions for Analysis

1. Why was Khan suing State Oil since Khan was behind on its payments to State Oil?
2. In overruling the decision in the *Albrecht* case, was the Court saying that vertical price-fixing is legal? If a manufacturer sets minimum resale prices for its distributors, would such agreements be legal?

Section 2 of the Sherman Act

Section 2 of the Sherman Act reads as follows:

> Every person who shall monopolize, or attempt to monopolize, or combine or conspire with any other person or persons, to monopolize any part of the trade or commerce among the several States, or with foreign nations, shall be deemed guilty of a felony, and, on conviction thereof, shall be punished by fine not exceeding $10,000,000 if a corporation, or, if any other person, $350,000, or by imprisonment not exceeding three years, or by both said punishments, in the discretion of the court.

Section 2 of the Sherman Act prohibits (1) monopolization and (2) attempts to monopolize. The standards for violations of these two prohibitions are similar but distinct. It is illegal to *monopolize* an industry, but it is not illegal to be a monopoly. This seeming conundrum reveals the tension between the antitrust laws and innovation. Firms that are innovative may become very large because they are selling superior products, but these same firms may often, then, become targets of antitrust authorities for violating Section 2 of the Sherman Act.

Monopolization

Although the standards for violation of Section 2, as articulated by the courts, have wavered and are still subject to some debate, the Section 2 prohibition against monopolization is violated when

1. A firm possesses monopoly power in a relevant market.
2. The market power is willfully acquired or maintained, as distinguished from being the result of a superior product, business acumen, or luck.[11]

Since the offense is monopolization, often the remedy in successful monopolization cases is a breakup of the defendant firm accused of monopolization.

Monopoly Power

monopoly power
Ability possessed by a firm to be a price maker (to set prices charged) rather than being a price taker (unable to sell at a price higher than the "competitive" market price).

In order for a plaintiff (often the U.S. government) to successfully prosecute a defendant for monopolizing a market, the plaintiff must show that the defendant has monopoly power. In economic terms, **monopoly power** means the firm has some control over price and has the ability to exclude competition. In court cases, evidence of monopoly power is generally demonstrated in large part by showing that the accused monopolist defendant has a *high market share*. Based on numerous antitrust cases, the minimum market share necessary to show that a firm has monopoly power is about 60 percent. A firm that has less than 60 percent market share cannot reasonably be said to monopolize a market, according to these court decisions. Among some of the more famous Section 2 monopolization cases, Standard Oil had about a 90 percent market share of oil refining capacity in 1912 when it was sued, which is about the same market share that Microsoft has with respect to operating systems for personal computers. When AT&T was broken up by the U.S. government in the early 1980s, it had over a 90 percent market share of the telephone long-distance market.

Market Share and Market Definition

Many monopolization cases are won or lost based on market definition. Recall that market share is firm sales divided by total sales in the industry. In general, most plaintiffs in monopolization cases contend that the relevant market is narrow while defendants contend that it is broad because the greater the value for total sales within the relevant market, the lower the apparent market share of the defendant. Since a market share for the defendant of over 60 percent is likely to be required for a prosecution for monopolization, a lot is at stake in market definition.

Product Market A firm cannot exert monopoly power in a relevant market unless it controls most of the product supply in the market. If a firm tries to raise price (to a monopoly level) and there are close substitute products available, customers will simply switch to those lower-priced substitutes. Suppose a firm controls all of the regular whole milk in a market, but does not control the supply of 2% milk, 1% milk, and skim milk. If the firm raised prices significantly on its regular whole milk, undoubtedly many buyers would shift to lower-fat milk. Thus, it makes sense to include all fluid milk products in the dairy market (product market) because all fluid dairy products are *reasonably interchangeable*.

Geographic Extent of the Relevant Market For many markets, the relevant geographic market is composed of the boundaries of the United States. For other markets, such as those for milk, cement, and other products with a low value-to-volume ratio (resulting in

---

[11] *United States v. Grinnell Corp.*, 384 U.S. 563 (1966).

transportation costs that are relatively high), the relevant market is local. Real estate is another industry that is local. For local markets, the geographic extent is defined as the area over which rival firms compete and the area over which a buyer could reasonably look for alternative supplies. A potential home buyer who works in Richmond, Virginia, will not survey housing throughout the entire United States but, instead, will focus on the city of Richmond and surrounding suburbs. Residential construction companies similarly are most often geographically limited.

Impact of Global Markets and the Internet Globalization and the Internet have made many older ways of looking at geographic markets obsolete. Many markets that were formerly national have become international, including the markets for automobiles, industrial metals such as steel, consumer electronic appliances, and computers. Calculating nationwide market shares for the United States can create a misleading image of the intensity of competition. The fact that a "defendant's" market share is over 60 percent in the United States does not mean very much if the U.S. firm sells abroad and there are many large foreign firms that are significant competitors in the United States. For any product sold online, the area over which buyers could reasonably look for alternative supplies may be worldwide. Many retail markets that were formerly considered local no longer are because of the Internet and e-commerce, subject, of course, to constraints imposed by transport costs and political barriers to product flows.

Deliberate Acts to Acquire or Maintain Monopoly Power

In order to successfully sue a firm for monopolization, there must be a showing of the firm's anticompetitive conduct aimed at deliberately acquiring or maintaining its monopoly power. The larger the market share of a defendant, the more likely its conduct will be judged anticompetitive.

There are no limits to the imagination of firms working to gain competitive edges over their competition. If a firm has a superior product, it will seek to expand its competitive edge by continuing to improve the product to better accommodate consumer preferences. At the same time, there are other ways a firm can attain market advantages, many of which may be anticompetitive. Let us suppose that the largest supplier of milk in a local market offers to sell its milk to the large local groceries in the area with the following deal: (1) if the grocery store wants to carry milk provided by the large supplier, it must agree that 80 percent of the dairy product shelf space in the grocery store will be reserved for the large supplier and (2) the grocery store also must agree to carry the entire line of dairy products offered by the large firm. Such a contract has the effect of restricting competing suppliers' access to customers, making it very difficult for them to, in fact, compete.

essential facilities
Portals, typically in processing, distribution, or transmission facilities, through which products must flow to be sold.

In many markets there are choke points, otherwise known as *essential facilities*. **Essential facilities** are portals into which all products in a class must enter in their trip to the marketplace. Such portals are usually owned by the largest firms in the market. Manipulation of access to essential facilities has been at the heart of many antitrust cases.

Consider the only cheese factory in the state of Arizona. If there is not sufficient daily demand for fluid milk products to exhaust the production of Arizona dairy farms, the surplus milk is made into cheese or butter, or else it goes unsold and spoils. Suppose the largest dairy cooperative in the state of Arizona, with a market share of over 75 percent, also owned the only cheese factory. The only way to preserve competition in the sale of milk in Arizona might be to require the largest cooperative to make its cheese factory available to all dairy farmers and other small cooperatives on a nondiscriminatory basis. Absent this requirement, fluid milk producers who don't have access to the essential facility (cheese factory) for converting a part of their production into a salable product would likely have inadequate revenues to stay in business "competing" against the company that does have the factory. Similar situations exist in oil distribution and in telephone networks, where the largest firms also own distribution pipelines or transmission systems.

Microsoft, Essential Facilities and Software Design

Choke points are particularly prevalent in high-tech markets, where one dominant firm may set compatibility standards. At one time, the U.S. government in its suit against Microsoft considered the Windows operating system an essential facility. It follows from such reasoning that under antitrust norms Microsoft would be prevented from changing Windows, or making it incompatible with application software from other software firms, without notifying its rivals and giving them an opportunity to make their software compatible with newer versions of Windows. Such discussions are still taking place.

For much of the 1990s, the U.S. Department of Justice pursued antitrust claims against Microsoft. Following the decision in Case 19-3, a consent decree was signed between the Justice Department and Microsoft, though attorneys general in some of the 19 states that had also sued Microsoft initially did not agree to the settlement.[12] The consent decree signed by Microsoft required it to change certain marketing practices that antitrust authorities claimed stifled competition.

Again, note that the court of appeals decision in this episode of the Microsoft antitrust saga is just one stop on a long sojourn that begins at the district court level but can go up and down, even to the U.S. Supreme Court or a U.S. court of appeals, and finally back down to the district court. This decision, by the U.S. court of appeals, was the last before the Justice Department and Microsoft finally agreed on the terms of a consent decree.

---

[12] Nine of the original 19 states who sued Microsoft on alleged antitrust violations did not agree to the consent decree signed by the U.S. Department of Justice and Microsoft. Eventually, all 19 state attorneys general agreed to a modified consent decree signed by Microsoft.

Case 19-3

United States of America, Appellee v. Microsoft Corporation, Appellant

United States Court of Appeals for the District of Columbia Circuit 253 F.3d 34 (D.C. Cir. 2001)

BACKGROUND AND FACTS

Relying almost exclusively on Microsoft's varied efforts to unseat Netscape Navigator as the preeminent Internet browser, the Justice Department and attorneys general from 19 states charged Microsoft with four distinct violations of the Sherman Act:

- *Unlawful exclusive dealing arrangements in violation of § 1 of the Sherman Act.*
- *Unlawful tying of Internet Explorer to Windows 95 and Windows 98 in violation of § 1.*
- *Unlawful maintenance of a monopoly in the PC operating system market in violation of § 2 of the Sherman Act.*
- *Unlawful attempted monopolization of the Internet browser market in violation of § 2.*

The states also brought pendent claims charging Microsoft with violations of various state antitrust laws.

After a 76-day bench trial, the District Court issued its Findings of Fact. United States v. Microsoft Corp., *84 F. Supp. 2d 9 (D.D.C. 1999)* ("Findings of Fact").

Having found Microsoft liable on all but one count, the district court then asked plaintiffs to submit a proposed remedy. In their proposal, plaintiffs sought specific conduct remedies, plus structural relief that would split Microsoft into an applications company *and an* operating systems *company, which means a breakup of Microsoft. The district court adopted plaintiffs' proposed remedy without substantive change.*

Microsoft appealed the decision of the district court within a week after it issued its Final Judgment.

Judges: Before Edwards, Chief Judge, Williams, Ginsburg, Sentelle, Randolph, Rogers, and Tatel, Circuit Judges

After carefully considering the voluminous record on appeal—including the District Court's Findings of Fact and Conclusions of Law, the testimony and exhibits submitted at trial, the parties' briefs, and the oral arguments before this court—we find that some but not all of Microsoft's liability challenges have merit. Accordingly, we affirm in part and reverse in part the District Court's judgment that Microsoft violated § 2 of the Sherman Act by employing anticompetitive means to maintain a monopoly in the operating system market; we reverse the District Court's determination that Microsoft violated § 2 of the Sherman Act by illegally attempting to monopolize the internet browser market; and we remand the District Court's finding that Microsoft violated § 1 of the Sherman Act by unlawfully tying its browser to its operating system. Our judgment extends to the District Court's findings with respect to the state law counterparts of the plaintiffs' Sherman Act claims.

* * *

[In this portion of the opinion, the court discusses whether Microsoft illegally tied its Windows and IE products.]

Our judgment regarding the comparative merits of the per se rule and the rule of reason is confined to the tying arrangement before us, where the tying product is software whose major purpose is to serve as a platform for third-party applications and the tied product is complementary software functionality. While our reasoning may at times appear to have broader force, we do not have the confidence to speak to facts outside the record, which contains scant discussion of software integration generally. Microsoft's primary justification for bundling IE APIs [Application Programming Interfaces] is that their inclusion with Windows increases the value of third-party software (and Windows) to consumers. *See* Appellant's Opening Br. at 41–43. Because this claim applies with distinct force when the tying product is *platform* software, we have no present basis for finding the per se rule inapplicable to software markets generally. Nor should we be interpreted as setting a precedent for switching to the rule of reason every time a court identifies an efficiency justification for a tying arrangement. Our reading of the record suggests merely that integration of new functionality into platform software is a common practice and that wooden application of per se rules in this litigation may cast a cloud over platform innovation in the market for PCs, network computers and information appliances.

C. On Remand

Should plaintiffs choose to pursue a tying claim under the rule of reason, we note the following for the benefit of the trial court:

First, on remand, plaintiffs must show that Microsoft's conduct unreasonably restrained competition. Meeting that burden "involves an inquiry into the actual effect" of Microsoft's conduct on competition in the tied good market, *Jefferson Parish,* 466 U.S. at 29, the putative market for browsers. To the extent that certain aspects of tying injury may depend on a careful definition of the tied good market and a showing of barriers to entry other than the tying arrangement itself, plaintiffs would have to establish these points. . . .

Of the harms left, plaintiffs must show that Microsoft's conduct was, on balance, anticompetitive. Microsoft may of course offer procompetitive justifications, and it is plaintiffs' burden to show that the anticompetitive effect of the conduct outweighs its benefit.

Second, the fact that we have already considered some of the behavior plaintiffs allege to constitute tying violations in the monopoly maintenance section does not resolve the § 1 inquiry. The two practices that plaintiffs have most ardently claimed as tying violations are, indeed, a basis for liability under plaintiffs' § 2 monopoly maintenance claim. These are Microsoft's refusal to allow OEMs [original equipment manufacturers] to uninstall IE or remove it from the Windows desktop, *Findings of Fact* ¶ ¶ 158, 203, 213, and its removal of the IE entry from the Add/Remove Programs utility in Windows 98, *id.* ¶ 170. *See supra* Section II.B. In order for the District Court to conclude these practices also constitute § 1 tying violations, plaintiffs must demonstrate that their benefits—if any [Citations omitted.]—are outweighed by the harms in the *tied product* market.

In Section II.B we also considered another alleged tying violation—the Windows 98 override of a consumer's choice of default web browser. We concluded that this behavior does not provide a distinct basis for § 2 liability because plaintiffs failed to rebut Microsoft's proffered justification by demonstrating that harms in the operating system market outweigh Microsoft's claimed benefits. *See supra* Section II.B. On remand, however, although Microsoft may offer the same procompetitive justification for the override, plaintiffs must have a new opportunity to rebut this claim, by demonstrating that the anticompetitive effect in the *browser* market is greater than these benefits.

* * *

Decision and Outcome

On remand the court of appeals appointed a new judge to hear the case. Subsequent to this decision, the U.S. Department of Justice and 10 of the 19 states reached a consent decree with Microsoft that left the software giant intact. With a few additional details, including recovery of attorney fees by the states, the attorneys general for the remaining nine states settled their antitrust claims against Microsoft.

Questions for Analysis

1. Did the court believe that the per se rule should be applied to the alleged tie-in in this case? How did the court try to limit the precedential value of this case?

2. On remand, how is the district court supposed to evaluate the legality of the tie between Windows and IE? What are some of the costs and benefits of bundling products, as opposed to selling them separately, according to this court?

Attempts to Monopolize

Large firms that are not yet monopolies violate Section 2 of the Sherman Act if they attempt to monopolize a relevant market. Generally, defendants in attempt-to-monopolize cases are large firms with market shares of greater than 20 percent. Firms charged with attempting to monopolize a market are firms that *engage in anticompetitive acts* and that *have a dangerous probability of success* in creating a monopoly. Among the actions that have been the subject of attempted monopolization cases are

1. *Predatory pricing* through which a large firm tries to drive its competition out of the market with prices that are below its average variable costs. *It is not illegal to price below costs of rivals, but it is illegal to price below your own costs if the purpose is to create a monopoly.* In many industries, very aggressive (low) prices have been used to penetrate a market and create a market standard based on the products provided by the firm charging low prices. Of course, the purpose of lowering price and driving out rivals from the market is to enable the price cutter to later raise prices and realize monopoly profits. Predatory pricing makes sense only when there are some kinds of barriers to reentry as, otherwise, the investment a price-cutting firm makes in winning market share by pricing below its costs will not be worthwhile.

2. Firms attempting to monopolize markets typically engage in *exclusionary tactics* aimed at denying rival firms in the industry access to markets. Firms charged with attempting to monopolize markets often make use of exclusive distributorships or tie-ins (discussed below) to further their market share at the expense of that rival's shares.

International Perspective

Even as Microsoft has made some progress in dealing with the antitrust charges it faces in the United States, it has confronted parallel international problems, as indicated in the following excerpt.

MICROSOFT FACES ANTITRUST HEARING IN EUROPE

Despite Some Recent U.S. Settlements, Cases Continue in European Union

BRUSSELS—In the wake of recent settlement deals in Microsoft antitrust cases in the United States, European Commissioner for Competition Issues Mario Monti confirmed Wednesday [November 21, 2001] that the software company is due to defend itself against European antitrust charges. The European lawsuit is distinct from the case in the United States, but there are similarities. Microsoft must fight accusations that it has violated European antitrust rules by using illegal practices to extend its dominant position in the market for operating systems into the market for low-end server operating systems (defined as cheaper servers usually used as file and print servers as well as Web servers).

It is reported that the European Commission believes that Microsoft has withheld from vendors of alternative server software the key interoperability information they need in order to allow their products to communicate with Microsoft's dominant PC and server software products. Microsoft will have to begin defending itself against the Commission's charges, even as it is having some success in resolving the antitrust charges it has faced in the United States.

The European Commission is the executive body of the European Union. Its responsibilities include regulating competition in the E.U.

Source: From Paul Meller, IDG News Service, November 21, 2001. Reprinted with permission of the IDG News Service.

In virtually every industry, there are ways of excluding competition, not just by selling superior products, but by contracts and other manipulations that create uneven playing fields. Increasingly, defendants in attempt-to-monopolize cases have made use of intellectual property as a lever to break into additional markets using their IP as "bait." Typically, a firm that possesses very valuable IP may use demand for its IP as means of selling other products.

In order to prosecute a firm for attempting to monopolize, the government or other plaintiff (often a firm that has been driven out of or excluded from a market) must show that the defendant *specifically intended* to exclude competitors or to attain monopoly power. While it is easy to articulate a verbal criterion for liability in attempt-to-monopolize cases, in the real world it is not easy to distinguish vigorous competition from attempts to monopolize. Again, the importance of market share should be apparent. The larger the market share of the defendant, the more likely the firm will be found liable for attempting to monopolize, especially if it is successful in excluding most of its actual and potential competition. Determining the relevant market in attempt-to-monopolize cases is just as fraught with uncertainty as it is when the defendant is charged with monopolizing an industry.

THE CLAYTON ACT

By 1914, when the Clayton Act was passed, there were a number of specific practices that were widely perceived as anticompetitive, but which were not specifically outlawed by the Sherman Act. Section 2 of the Clayton Act outlawed price discrimination (defined below) when its effect may be *to substantially lessen competition or tend to create monopoly*.[13] Section 3 of the Clayton Act paralleled Sherman Act Section 2, outlawing tie-ins and exclusive dealerships if they, too, substantially lessen competition or tend to create monopoly, and also accorded the same treatment to mergers that may substantially lessen competition or tend to create monopoly. Notice that each of the practices addressed—price discrimination,

---

[13] 15 U.S.C. § 18.

tie-in sales, exclusive dealerships, and mergers—occurs or exists in our economy every day. *These acts are illegal only when competition may be substantially lessened or if the likelihood of monopoly is increased.* By and large, as a practical matter, these acts are illegal only when the defendant is a firm with an already high market share.

Section 2: Price Discrimination

Price discrimination occurs when a seller sells the same product to different customers at different prices. Local movie theaters price discriminate when they charge senior citizens lower prices based on their age. Physicians are known to charge lower prices to less wealthy patients. Local movie theaters and physicians, however, are not the target of Section 2 of the Clayton Act. The target of Section 2 of the Clayton Act was and is large firms that use price discrimination in a way so as to lessen competition or create a monopoly. One group that was especially supportive of Section 2 was comprised of independent grocers who complained that large grocery chains were charged substantially lower prices for food by large food processors and that, as a consequence, competition was being lessened in retail and wholesale food markets.

The theory underlying Section 2 of the Clayton Act is that a large firm can lower prices in one area of the country, or to a class of customers where it trying to establish itself, and still charge monopolistic prices in other areas or markets where it is the dominant firm. Smaller firms, which do not have a wide geographic range or a diversified customer base, will be driven out of the markets where the large firm charges low prices. Thus would the big (dominant) firms get bigger, with the smaller firms that cannot successfully compete be driven out of the marketplace. A problem with enforcement of Section 2 of the Clayton Act is that it is difficult to distinguish vigorous price competition from illegal price discrimination. Under Section 2 of the Clayton Act, it is also illegal to induce price discrimination from the *buying side,* again where the effect may be to substantially lessen competition or tend to create monopoly.

There are two important defenses frequently relied on by large firms sued for price discrimination. First, if a firm charges a lower price in one area relative to another area to *meet prices charged by rivals* in that (lower price) area so that it will not lose business, the firm can effectively rely on the **meeting-competition defense.** Second, if there are *lower costs* of serving one customer relative to another, the large firm is allowed to charge lower prices accompanying the lower costs, relying on a **cost-justification defense** for the lower prices. Cost savings frequently are available based on quantity sold as the per unit costs of selling to a high-volume customer tend to be lower than those for small purchasers. In general, lower prices charged to high-volume customers must be based on lower costs and the price differences must reflect cost differences. The fact that a firm wants to land a large customer, for which the per unit cost of selling may be slightly less, will not give the seller *carte blanche* freedom to radically reduce prices for that target customer.

Significant reform of Section 2 of the Clayton Act took place in 1936 with passage of the Robinson-Patman Act.[14] Firms can overtly price discriminate by charging lower prices. They also can disguise price discrimination by paying secret rebates to purchasers, by giving them below-cost delivery terms, or by rendering in-kind services, such as providing advertising at zero or very low costs. These practices are outlawed by reforms brought to Section 2 through the Robinson-Patman Act. That act also allowed firms injured by price discrimination to sue for triple damages.

In the real world of antitrust actions, Section 2 of the Clayton Act is often considered a nuisance, and the government rarely initiates Section 2 lawsuits. Frequently, however, firms

meeting-competition defense
Defense against charges of predatorily low prices based on a showing that the low prices were necessary to effectively compete.

cost-justification defense
Defense against charges that prices charged to some (usually large) customers are too low, based on a showing that the lower prices charged are justified by the lower unit costs of serving those customers.

[14] U.S.C. § 13.

Nutz and Boltz Price Discrimination

As with the other conduct that is sometimes prohibited under the Clayton Act, price discrimination is illegal only where the effect may be to lessen competition or tend to create monopoly. Suppose that Seller (1) has a large market share and that it is largely unchallenged in its "home" market and thus sets its price at P_{11}. Suppose further that in market (2), Seller (1) sets its price at P_{12}, which is significantly lower than P_{11}. Thus, Seller (1) is engaging in price discrimination, selling the same product to different customers at different prices, and if such price discrimination enables him to drive Seller (2) out of the market, there may be a substantial lessening of competition.

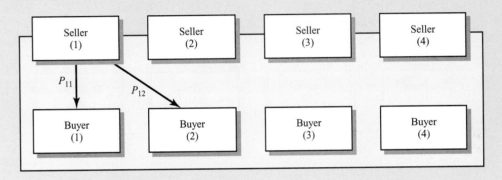

that are defendants in breach of contract cases file a counterclaim against the plaintiffs based on a Section 2 Clayton Act price discrimination suit. Frequently, the threat of a possible triple-damage claim by a defendant in a Section 2 suit is enough to get the plaintiff to settle the breach of contract case for much less than its actual damages.

Section 3: Exclusive Dealerships and Tie-Ins

Exclusive Dealership Contracts

exclusive dealing contract
Agreements between a manufacturer and the distributors or retailers who sell its products prohibiting the sales of products of a rival manufacturer by those resellers.

Exclusive dealing contracts are vertical agreements, usually between manufacturers on the one hand and distributors or retailers on the other, in which the distributor or retailer is prohibited from carrying products of a business rival of the manufacturer. Section 3 of the Clayton Act prohibits exclusive dealerships or tie-ins, but only when their effects may be to substantially lessen competition or to tend to create monopoly. In the language of Section 3, "It shall be unlawful for any person engaged in commerce, in the course of such commerce, to lease or make a sale or contract for sale of goods, . . . on the condition, agreement, or understanding that the lessee or purchaser thereof shall not use or deal in the goods, wares, merchandise, machinery, supplies, or other commodities of a competitor . . ."

Although firms that engage in exclusive dealerships could also be in violation of Section 1 of the Sherman Act for engaging in an unreasonable trade restraint, they are generally sued under Section 3 of the Clayton Act. Again, familiar rules apply when exclusive dealing contracts are evaluated under Section 3 of the Clayton Act. In general, the larger their market share, the more likely defendants are to be found in violation of the Clayton Act. Exclusive dealing contracts for small firms do not substantially lessen competition. Since market share is a critical factor in determining liability, defining the market becomes a significant source of debate in Section 3, Clayton Act, cases and the market definition discussion above under monopolization becomes relevant again. Exclusive dealerships tend to substantially lessen competition when large manufacturing firms tie up most or all of the

Nutz and Boltz   Exclusive Dealerships

Under the rule of reason, an exclusive distributorship could be illegal if it may lessen competition or tend to create monopoly. This could occur if Manufacturer (1) obtained exclusive dealership arrangements with most of the distributors in the industry and other manufacturers were foreclosed from most or all of the market.

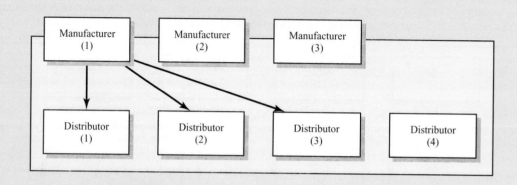

distributors in a market, so that other manufacturers are foreclosed from most or all of the relevant market.

Tying Arrangements

tying contract

A contract requiring a customer to buy a "tied" product in order to be able to buy a "tying" product.

Tying contracts are agreements in which a seller tells buyers that, "in order to purchase my product A, you must also purchase my other product, B." Again, these contracts are illegal only when they may substantially lessen competition or tend to create monopoly, which generally requires that the defendant have a large market share (at least 40 percent or more). A classic tie-in case involved the IBM Corporation during the 1930s when it had more than a 70 percent market share of mainframe computer sales. At that time, IBM offered to lease its computers to businesses, but lessees had to also agree to purchase paper cards from IBM. At that time, paper cards (which were not supposed to be bent, folded, or spindled) were used to input data.[15] IBM sold its brand of cards at higher-than-market prices for equivalent cards from other producers.

tying product

A product in which a producer enjoys monopoly power.

In a tying arrangement, the product over which the defendant has market power is called the **tying product,** and the additional product that buyers must purchase in order to obtain the tying product is the *tied product.* In the IBM case, mainframe computers were the tying product and the paper data cards were the tied product.

In order for a tie-in to be illegal, a plaintiff has to show that (1) the defendant has *market power in the tying product* and (2) purchasers are required to buy both products. IBM had market power in the sale or lease of mainframe computers that was legitimately acquired (they had a superior product). IBM did not have market power or a superior product in the data input card arena. The alleged competitive evil generated by tie-ins is that large firms are able to leverage market power in one market (in the IBM case, in mainframe computers) into another market (cards in the IBM case).

---

[15] *International Business Machines, Inc. v. United States,* 298 U.S. 131 (1936).

Nutz and Boltz Tying Contracts

In typical tie-in cases, the seller will offer to sell (or lease) product A, the tying product, to the buyer so long as the buyer also agrees to buy the tied product, Product B. Again, such contracts are illegal only if they may lessen competition or tend to create monopoly, which events mainly occur when there is a showing that the seller has a high market share in the market for the tying product.

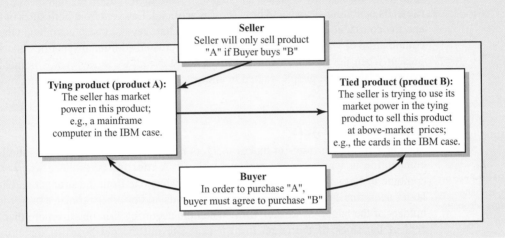

The legal status of tie-ins is not clear at present. At one time, courts applied per se rules to tie-ins if it was clear that the defendant had market power in the tying product. In the case of tying a patented product with an unpatented product, the per se rule probably still applies. There are, however, several defenses available to defendants in tie-in cases, including

1. The *defendant can claim it does not have market power in the market for the tying product,* which brings up the issues of market definition and correct measures of market shares.

2. The *defendant can assert that product A and product B are really one product* and that each is a component of that product. When Microsoft was charged with illegally tying together its Windows operating system with Internet Explorer, its Internet browser, its primary defense was that Internet Explorer was an integral component of the Windows operating system and not a separate or even separable product.

3. The *defendant can claim that the tied products offered on the market by third parties are not of adequate quality.* In the IBM case, IBM claimed that cards offered for sale by other firms jammed the card readers used by its mainframe computers and, thus, decreased demand for the tying product. The evidence IBM offered that cards of sellers caused its machines to jam was weak according to most independent observers of the case.

High-Tech Products and Tie-Ins: Contractual and Technological

The economic success of high-tech products often depends on their compatibility with other high-tech products. When an industry leader introduces a new version of its flagship product, such as an operating system for PCs, it generally will make sure that its peripheral products, such as its Internet browser, are compatible with new versions of the operating system. Making products compatible can create technological tie-ins, which are generally legal. On the other hand, if Microsoft refused to sell Windows unless purchasers also bought MS Word, this clearly would be an illegal tie-in contract given the high market share of Windows in the PC operating system market.

The difference between an illegal *contractual tie-in* and a *technological tie-in* is not completely clear. As indicated before, in its antitrust case with the DOJ Microsoft claimed that its operating system, Windows, and its Internet browser, Internet Explorer, were components of one product. The DOJ, on the other hand, claimed abundant evidence, mainly obtained from internal e-mails between Microsoft executives, that Windows and Internet Explorer were separate products and that the technological tie-in *created* by Microsoft between its operating system and browser was artificial. Lawyers from both sides of this case and the courts, at the trial and again at the appellate level, closely examined whether the combination of Windows and Internet Explorer created additional synergies that were not present when the products were sold separately. Needless to say, it was pointed out on many occasions that people trained in antitrust law probably were not experts in software design.

Section 7: Mergers

merger
A combination of two or more firms, with the merging firms becoming one firm.

Section 7 of the Clayton Act makes mergers between two firms that substantially lessen competition or tend to create monopoly illegal. A **merger** takes place when two firms combine to form one firm. This usually occurs when one firm, the stronger and generally larger acquiring firm, offers its stock, cash, bonds and/or other promises to pay to shareholders of the target, or weaker, firm. When the acquiring firm obtains more than 50 percent of the stock of the target firm, it can vote out the old board of directors of the acquired firm, install its own directors, and either liquidate the firm or continue its operation as a subsidiary owned by the acquiring firm. Of course, it also can operate the acquired assets as an absorbed component of the single firm, eliminating the need for any separate board of directors, accompanied by an exchange of acquirer stock, money, or something else of value for the stock of the acquired company. Also within the scope of Section 7 of the Clayton Act are *consolidations,* which occur when two firms of roughly equal size agree to dissolve and reform as a single "new" firm. As another possibility, an acquiring firm need not purchase common stock of the target firm; it could acquire assets of the target firm directly by making a purchase of those assets. There are rules and formulas that are used to determine when acquisition of the assets of a target firm by an acquiring firm constitute, in substance, a merger. Such acquisitions of all, or nearly all, of the assets of another firm are subject to possible court challenge under Section 7 of the Clayton Act.

Quite obviously, mergers, consolidations, and purchases of assets are commonplace in the economy. As discussed before, as an antitrust policy matter, only mergers that may substantially lessen competition or tend to create monopoly are illegal. So, in practical terms, only mergers (or consolidations or purchases of assets) involving firms with high market shares are illegal. Any time the market share of the defendant(s) is a factor, market definition becomes a decisive issue along the lines discussed above in connection with Section 2 monopolization cases. Once the relevant market is defined, the market shares of the merging companies can be calculated.

Note that there are several kinds of mergers, with differing standards of liability associated with each kind of merger. It should not be surprising that horizontal agreements are treated more harshly in law than are vertical combinations. Mergers between two firms can be usefully classified as

1. *Horizontal*—a merger of two firms at the same level in the market such as manufacturing, distributing, or retailing. Horizontal mergers are regarded as the greatest threat to

competition because they can create a market structure that is conducive to price-fixing or monopoly and, thus, they face the most stringent standards for liability.

2. *Vertical*—a merger of two firms at different levels in the market. Vertical mergers pose several competitive concerns, including possible foreclosure (manufacturers cannot find outlets for their products because of mergers between leading manufacturers and distributors or retailers), and barriers to entry are raised if a new firm has to enter the market as a vertically integrated firm. A fully vertically integrated firm is a firm that owns raw materials and component suppliers, manufacturing, distribution, and retailing facilities.

3. *Product extension*—a merger that takes place if a firm combines with another firm that produces closely related products or produces the same product in a geographically nearby market. For example, a product extension merger occurs when a firm that produces detergents and other kinds of soaps acquires the leading firm in the bleach market. Product extension mergers can harm competition in the bleach industry because potential competition is sometimes diminished. Potential competition can cause leading firms within an industry to charge lower prices so as to avoid entry into the industry by firms producing related products or those located nearby.

4. *Pure conglomerate*—a merger between unrelated firms—that is, ones that before the merger were not competitors, customers of, or suppliers of one another and did not produce related products. Although concern is periodically raised about mergers between any two very large firms, to date no pure conglomerate merger has ever been successfully prosecuted under Section 7 of the Clayton Act.

Hart-Scott-Rodino Antitrust Improvements Act of 1976

Since mergers are an everyday event in our modern economy, the DOJ and the FTC would be hard-pressed to evaluate the competitive consequences of each one. However, since size matters in antitrust law, Congress passed the Hart-Scott-Rodino (HSR) Act, which requires any firm that with more than $100 million in assets or sales to report to the U.S. Department of Justice and to the Federal Trade Commission planned mergers with any other firm that has more than $10 million in assets or sales.[16] The HSR Act requires firms involved in such mergers to give the Justice Department and the FTC 30 days to react. Upon review, these government authorities can decide that the proposed merger does not threaten competition. Alternatively, either the FTC or the Antitrust Division of the U.S. Department of Justice could reach a different conclusion and file suit under Section 7 of the Clayton Act to have the merger declared illegal.

Many times the threat of an antitrust lawsuit is enough to discourage merging firms and have them drop their merger plans. Note that, in many cases, in order to get a merger approved, by either the U.S. Department of Justice or some other regulatory body (national or international), the merging firms have to agree to accept some terms that they may find unacceptable. The most common conditions are requirements to spin off or sell parts of their businesses. This definitely was on the minds of the managers pursuing the proposed merger that was abandoned by America Air and British Air, discussed in the "Nutz and Boltz" box on page 638.

How Much Is Too Much? For business executives, an aggravating feature of law in general, and antitrust law in particular, is lack of specificity. Business executives want to know beforehand whether a merger is likely to be challenged by government antitrust authorities under Section 7 of the Clayton Act. Mergers are very expensive and require

---

[16] Pub. L. No. 94-435, 90 Stat.1390, codified at 16 C.F.R. Parts 801–803.

Nutz and Boltz   American Air, British Air Drop Plans for Venture

AMR Corp.'s American Airlines and British Airways dropped plans for a trans-Atlantic joint venture—and effectively nixed chances for a new U.S.—United Kingdom aviation treaty—after deciding a second time that the price of regulatory approval was too rich. In the short run, the move preserves limits on flying between the U.S. and London's Heathrow Airport, perhaps the world's most important international hub. Longer term, it likely weakens the "one-world" alliance led by American and British Air.

On Friday the U.S. Department of Transportation approved giving the two carriers antitrust immunity to coordinate pricing, schedules, and profits. But it said the two carriers would have to give U.S. competitors enough highly prized takeoff and landing slots at London's Heathrow airport for 16 flights daily.

Competitors had argued that the mega-alliance, joining the world's biggest carrier with Europe's largest, could monopolize air service between New York and Heathrow. American and British Air expected regulators to force them to give up enough slots for 11 or 12 round-trip flights a day, people familiar with the matter said. But when the price came in higher, the two carriers almost immediately decided the status quo [not merging] was better.

* * *

Source: *Wall Street Journal.* Eastern Edition by Scott McCartney and Daniel Michaels. Copyright 2002 by Dow Jones & Co., Inc. Reproduced with permission of Dow Jones & Co., Inc. via Copyright Clearance Center.

---

enormous amounts of time investment by attorneys, accountants, executives from the merging companies, and others. To incur these costs and then be confronted, unexpectedly, by a government challenge to the merger is a risk that businesspeople would certainly want to avoid.

Fortunately, the U.S. Department of Justice and the FTC have established Merger Guidelines addressing the circumstances under which they will challenge a merger between horizontal competitors. The Merger Guidelines are entirely based on combinations of market shares so, as a precursor to gauging the risk of a challenge to a planned merger, the relevant market must be defined. Once the relevant market is defined and market shares of firms in the industry are determined, government officials are in a position to determine whether they will challenge a proposed merger. Many industries are well-defined and firms in such industries often have firm knowledge of what their market share is as well as market shares of other leading firms in the industry.

Vertical Mergers

Foreclosure theories—arguments that a vertical merger will foreclose opportunities to other businesses, lessening competition—have often been used when vertical mergers have been challenged in court by the DOJ or the FTC. Again, quite obviously, foreclosure theories are only relevant if the merging firms are a large part of the relevant market (requiring, of course, that the relevant market be defined and market share computed). Evidence of foreclosure might be offered by small manufacturers, who could claim that a merger between the largest manufacturer and the largest retailer in the industry could foreclose access to one of their key customers. After the proposed merger, these other producers would argue, it is unlikely that the large manufacturer/retailer would purchase from other manufacturers. Vertical mergers could also substantially lessen competition if they set off a chain reaction, inducing other firms in the industry to undertake similar mergers. If a new firm were considering entering an industry in which such vertical integration had become widespread, it would have to consider entering at several levels and this could constitute a significant barrier to entry.

JUSTICE DEPARTMENT ANTITRUST GUIDELINES FOR LICENSING OF INTELLECTUAL PROPERTY

In response to legal uncertainty regarding the licensing of intellectual property, the DOJ and the FTC issued *Antitrust Guidelines for Licensing of Intellectual Property* in 1995.[17] According to these IP Guidelines, "Although there are clear and important differences in the purpose, extent, and duration of protection provided under the intellectual property regimes of patent, copyright, and trade secret, the governing antitrust principles are the same." Although these government agencies claim that the same principles of antitrust law apply with equal force to licensing intellectual property, there is recognition of differences. The most obvious difference is that the primary goal of antitrust is to prevent monopoly, but patent, and to a lesser extent copyright, law creates legal monopolies or, at least, rights to exclude others from replicating the protected IP. Reconciling antitrust and intellectual property standards will be increasingly important as more and more of the assets of large corporations take the form of IP.

The DOJ and FTC IP Guidelines recognize the tension between antitrust and IP by stating that, "[I]f a patent or other form of intellectual property does confer market power, that market power does not by itself offend the antitrust laws." The IP Guidelines recognize that market (or even monopoly) power can be legitimately obtained through a superior product, but they do not presume that a patent or copyright necessarily confers market power on the owner because there are often good substitutes for any particular form of IP. The IP Guidelines list two instances in which a firm's IP can create antitrust liability for it:

1. "An arrangement that effectively merges the research and development activities of two of only a few entities that could plausibly engage in research and development in the relevant field might harm competition for the development of new goods and services."

2. "An acquisition of intellectual property may lessen competition in a relevant antitrust market."

joint venture
Combination of businesses "joined" to accomplish specific tasks, such as conducting a research project, with the combination generally limited in duration.

The first instance listed deals with situations in which two firms are leaders in the same industry and they form a **joint venture** aimed at research and development rather than competing separately in the research arena. Blocking such joint ventures in research and development may sacrifice the synergies that could occur when two leaders in innovation want to join forces on a project. The second competitive concern listed by the IP Guidelines concerns acquisitions, presumably by purchase or lease of IP. Again, it is hard to justify denying a firm the right to purchase innovation except if that firm uses the innovation for anticompetitive purposes. The IP Guidelines also state that owning, but not using, IP will not be considered anticompetitive.

The language used throughout the IP Guidelines reflects the tension between innovation that is protected by some part of IP law and the objective of maintaining competition without undermining IP rights. According to the IP Guidelines, "[I]n the vast majority of cases, restraints in intellectual property licensing arrangements are evaluated under the rule of reason." As we know, under this standard, antitrust authorities will weigh the pro-competitive consequences of the license or other use of the IP against its anticompetitive

---

[17] http://www.usdoj.gov/atr/public/guidelines/ipguide.htm.

consequences. Extensive use of the rule of reason, of course, creates more legal uncertainty than reliance on per se rules.

The IP Guidelines discuss "safety zones," which encompass transactions that the government will not attack under the antitrust laws. According to the IP Guidelines, "[B]ecause licensing arrangements often promote innovation and enhance competition, the Agencies [the FTC and the Antitrust Division of the DOJ] believe that an antitrust 'safety zone' is useful in order to provide some degree of certainty and thus to encourage such activity." In the IP Guidelines an example of a "safety zone" is provided which indicates that a license between an owner of IP and a licensee will not be challenged if there are *at least four other technologies* that are substitutable and are available at comparable cost and if the license is not transparently anticompetitive. Many markets do not meet these exacting standards, but a sizeable number do.

As indicated at the beginning of this chapter, antitrust authorities are trying to apply legal concepts that were shaped in the Industrial Age to products that are creating the Information Age, many of which are IP based and which immediately create some form of monopoly or other market restriction. IP products are intangible and sometimes are accessible with a few clicks of a computer mouse. Traditional geographic boundaries to markets are often not relevant with these products. Substitutability among products is also a questionable concept when the products are subject to patent and copyright restrictions.

Courts have dealt with the interface between IP and antitrust law by developing the notion that IP owners can forfeit rights to enforce IP remedies against infringers if they violate antitrust laws. Such suits are becoming increasingly common, involving both patent and copyright owners.

SANCTIONS AND ENFORCEMENT UNDER THE ANTITRUST LAWS

There are three main ways in which the federal antitrust laws are enforced: (1) criminal and civil enforcement actions brought by the Antitrust Division of the Department of Justice, (2) civil enforcement actions brought by the Federal Trade Commission, and (3) lawsuits brought by private parties asserting damage claims.

Sherman Act Suits

Sherman Act violations can be punished as criminal felonies, though criminal prosecutions are mainly limited to Section 1 Sherman Act violations in which the defendants are clearly aware they are violating the act. The Department of Justice alone is empowered to bring criminal prosecutions under the Sherman Act. Individual violators can be fined up to $350,000 and sentenced to up to three years in federal prison for each offense; corporations can be fined up to $10 million for each offense. Violations of Section 2 of the Sherman Act are sufficiently ambiguous that DOJ officials have chosen not to bring criminal charges against defendants for such violations. As an illustration, Bill Gates, CEO of Microsoft at the time the Justice Department brought Microsoft to court for violations of Section 2 of the Sherman Act, was not the target of a criminal violation claim.

Clayton Act Suits

The Clayton Act is a civil statute, which means that it carries no criminal penalties. Alleged violations of the Clayton Act can be prosecuted by either the Department of Justice or the Federal Trade Commission. If there are possible violations of Section 1 of the Sherman Act also involved, the DOJ normally will be the party filing suit.

Suits by Private Parties and State Attorneys General

A provision in the Clayton Act also permits private parties injured by an antitrust violation to sue in federal court for three times their actual damages plus court costs and attorney fees. State attorney general may bring civil suits under the Clayton Act on behalf of injured consumers in their states, and groups of consumers often bring suits on their own. Such follow-on civil suits, as sequels to criminal enforcement actions, can provide very effective additional deterrents to criminal activity. Victims of price-fixing or monopolization also can file claims for violations of the Sherman Act and, if these plaintiffs are successful, they also are entitled to a triple damage award plus attorney fees and court costs.

Most states also have antitrust laws closely paralleling the federal antitrust laws. The state laws generally apply to violations that occur wholly in one state. These state laws are enforced in parallel fashion to the actions taken under federal laws, generally through the offices of state attorneys general.

Summary

Promotion of Competition Is the Main Objective of Antitrust Law; Firms with High Market Shares Have Been Targets of Most Antitrust Lawsuits

- Antitrust law is intended to promote competition between firms so that consumers benefit from low prices and innovation.
- Often, firms with *high market shares* are defendants in antitrust cases. Firms in high-tech markets also often amass large market shares because of the characteristics of those markets.
- The Sherman Act, passed in 1890, was designed to prevent combinations in restraint of trade and monopolies.
- When a firm is charged with a per se violation of the antitrust laws, it cannot defend itself by claiming that what it is doing has pro-competitive consequences. *Price-fixing, boycotts,* and *dividing* up *markets* by territory or customers are *per se violations* of the Sherman Act.
- Some combinations have both pro-competitive and anticompetitive consequences. These agreements are generally evaluated under the *rule of reason,* which means that they may or may not be illegal.

Section 1 of the Sherman Act Deems Illegal Trade Restraints That Are Judged Unreasonable; Some Trade Restraints, Such as Price-Fixing, Are Subject to the Per Se Rule While Others, Such as Most Vertical Restraints, Are Analyzed under the Rule of Reason

- Section 1 of the Sherman Act prohibits every combination, contract, or conspiracy in restraint of trade. Price-fixing, boycotts, and market divisions allocating territories or customers are per se violations of Section 1.
- Violations of Section 1 of the Sherman Act require a showing that there was some kind of agreement. Mere imitation of the prices of a rival is not a violation.
- There are number of *exemptions* from the antitrust laws, particularly from Section 1 of the Sherman Act. Agricultural cooperatives, unions, and industries regulated by the federal or state governments are exempt from some aspects of the antitrust laws.
- Many violations of Section 1 of the Sherman Act have begun at trade shows or reflect parts of professional association rules or codes.
- It is generally illegal for horizontal competitors to exchange price information.
- Adherence to professional codes is legal as long as the purpose or effect is not to punish firms that cut prices.
- *Bid-rigging* is another activity qualifying as a Section 1 violation. Bid-rigging cases have been numerous in bids on government contracts.
- Under Section 1 of the Sherman Act, *vertical combinations* are treated much more leniently than are *horizontal restraints*. Most vertical combinations are evaluated under the rule of reason and are legal as long as the market share of the defendant is not too large.
- *Vertical price-fixing* is illegal if the manufacturer sets minimum prices for its distributors or retailers.

Section 2 of the Sherman

- Section 2 of the Sherman Act prohibits *monopolization* and *attempts to monopolize.*
- Monopolization occurs when a firm possesses monopoly power and takes deliberate actions to acquire or maintain that monopoly power.

Act Makes Monopolization and Attempts to Monopolize Illegal; Defendants in Section 2 Cases Are Firms with Large Market Shares, Requiring Courts to Define the Relevant Product and Geographic Markets	• Monopoly power is generally evidenced by a market share over 60 percent. • In order to calculate market share, the market must be defined. The *product market* is defined as the cluster of products that are reasonably interchangeable. The *geographic market* is defined as the area within which buyers can reasonably turn to alternative suppliers and the area in which sellers compete. • Being a monopoly is not illegal. The *antitrust laws* are not supposed to penalize a firm with a superior product. Monopolization requires a showing that the defendant took anticompetitive actions that led to the acquisition or maintenance of monopoly power. • In some markets, large firms have *essential facilities* that they may have to allow competitors to use on a nondiscriminatory basis, if they want to escape antitrust enforcement actions. • A firm violates Section 2 of the Sherman Act when its anticompetitive actions have a dangerous probability of creating a monopoly. Only large firms with market shares over 20 percent are defendants in attempt-to-monopolize cases. In attempt-to-monopolize cases, there must be a showing that the defendant specifically intended to gain monopoly power.
The Clayton Act Prohibits Price Discrimination, Tie-Ins, and Exclusive Dealing when Those Acts Substantially Lessen Competition	• Under the Clayton Act, it is illegal *to discriminate in price* when the effect may be to lessen competition or if there is a tendency to create monopoly. Price discrimination exists when a firm offers the same goods to different customers at different prices. • There are two defenses to price discrimination claims: (1) the price differences were due to *meeting competition* or (2) they are the result of *cost differences*. • Section 3 of the Clayton Act prohibits *tie-ins* or *exclusive dealing* when the effects may be to lessen competition or if there is a tendency to create monopoly. • A tie-in exists when a buyer is required to buy product B (the tied good) in order to purchase product A (the tying product). A tie-in is illegal when the seller has market power or a high market share in product A's market. • High-tech products can create tie-ins because many such products are worthless unless they are *compatible* with hardware or operating systems. Many sellers of high-tech products deliberately make their products incompatible with the peripheral products of rivals.
Mergers between Two Firms Can Be Illegal if There Is a Substantial Lessening of Competition, Which Often Is Judged Based on Impacts on Market Shares	• Section 7 of the Clayton Act makes a merger between two firms illegal when the effect may be to lessen competition or to tend to create monopoly. Mergers are illegal only when the merging firms have large market shares. • The Hart-Scott-Rodino Act requires large firms that merge with other large firms to notify the Justice Department. • *Vertical mergers* can be illegal if the effect of the vertical merger is to *foreclose* competitors from obtaining suppliers or outlets for their products. • *Conglomerate mergers* can be illegal if the merger has the effect of reducing potential competition.
The DOJ and FTC Jointly Enforce Antitrust Laws and Often Join Together to Issue Guidelines Such as Those That Apply to Intellectual Property	• The Department of Justice and the Federal Trade Commission jointly issued IP Guidelines on the Licensing of Intellectual Property in 1995. The familiar principles of antitrust policy apply to intellectual property, but there is recognition that patent law grants monopolylike powers to its owners. As in other markets, firms with high market shares are subject to more antitrust scrutiny. • Remedies for violations of the antitrust laws can involve jail time, fines, divestiture, consent decrees, and cease and desist orders. • The antitrust laws are jointly enforced by the Department of Justice and the Federal Trade Commission. In addition, suits brought by private parties are common in antitrust law. If a private party wins an antitrust suit, it is entitled to triple damages, plus attorney fees and court costs.

Key Terms

bid-rigging, *621*
cost-justification defense, *632*
essential facilities, *627*
exclusive dealing
   contract, *633*
horizontal agreements, *614*
joint venture, *639*

market share, *612*
meeting-competition
   defense, *632*
merger, *636*
monopoly, *612*
monopoly power, *626*
oligopoly, *612*

per se rule, *613*
resale price maintenance, *623*
rule of reason, *613*
tying contract, *634*
tying product, *634*
vertical restraints, *621*

Questions for Review and Analysis

1. It is useful to recognize some of the key differences between markets that are competitive and markets that are monopolized. Explain why, in competitive markets, the goods and services produced are more likely to be lower priced and exhibit more variety, and why the rate of innovation is likely to be greater in such markets.

2. Why not apply the rule of reason to all alleged violations of the antitrust laws including price-fixing and boycotts? After all, it is possible that the price selected by members of a price-fixing cartel could be the same as the price that would occur in a competitive market, or is that plausible?

3. Recently, in some critical markets such as those for computer chips, operating systems for PCs, and some in other parts of the communications industry, market shares of the leading firms have become very high by the traditional standards used in antitrust cases. Why might market share be less indicative of market power in high-tech markets than it is in traditional "smokestack" industries such as the steel and oil-producing industries?

4. Tie-ins are at the heart of many recent antitrust cases. What is the difference between a contractual tie-in, which may be illegal, and a technological tie-in, which is much less likely to be prosecuted as an antitrust violation? Discuss tie-ins in relation to the *Microsoft* case.

5. Telecommunications, the Internet, cable, television, Internet radio, and streaming video all seem to blend together. Is it meaningful to talk about the television industry without talking about cable? Are traditional market definitions becoming meaningless as we become more and more connected electronically?

If You Really Understood This Chapter, You Should Be Able to Provide Informed Commentary on the Following:

1. **Economic Rationality and Antitrust: Attempts to Monopolize.** A widely believed myth clashed with economic theory to produce new antitrust law in the form of precedent that has been used to dismiss a number of antitrust lawsuits. The myth was that a number (21) of Japanese firms conspired for about 20 years to depress prices in the U.S. market for televisions. The plaintiff in this was a large U.S. seller of televisions, Zenith Radio Corp. Zenith contended that Japanese firms were competing unfairly and in violation of Sections 1 and 2 of the Sherman Act. The Japanese firms were accused of "predatory" pricing, which is pricing below average variable costs, in an effort to win market share. The case against the Japanese firms collapsed because it was pointed out that

   a. It makes no economic sense to incur losses for 20 years in the hope of one day being able to charge monopoly prices.

   b. Even if one firm was willing to lose money for a period of time, it is inconceivable that a large group of 21 firms would have the discipline to maintain a conspiracy to depress prices for 20 years.

   The case itself gave the term *predatory pricing* a bad name in the sense that after this *Matsushita* case, many claims of violations of Section 2 of the Sherman Act based on predatory pricing were dismissed as being economically implausible. Indeed, the *Matsushita* case has gained even wider impact as the economic plausibility scrutiny has extended to many other antitrust claims. The inquiry made is whether it is economically plausible for a defendant to engage in behavior that is in violation of an antitrust law. If the answer is no, then the case will be dismissed. [*Matsushita Electronic Industries Co., Ltd. et al, v. Zenith Radio Corp.,* 475 U.S. 574 (1986).]

2. **Essential Facilities and Monopolization.** Once upon a time, three (big) hills in Aspen, Colorado, were owned by three different companies and these companies agreed to a joint marketing plan that included an "all Aspen" ticket that was redeemable for skiing on any of the three hills. Later, the Aspen Skiing Company (Aspen) acquired the second hill in Aspen and opened yet another hill for skiing. The joint marketing plan with the all-Aspen ticket continued until 1977, when Aspen stopped honoring the all-Aspen tickets. The plaintiff is the Aspen Highlands Skiing Corporation (Highlands), which owned the fourth hill. After Aspen refused to honor the all-Aspen tickets, the Highlands began marketing its own all-Aspen tickets, but Aspen refused to honor tickets sold by the Highlands and refused to sell lift tickets to its facilities to Highlands customers. The Highlands sued under Section 2 of the Sherman Act and claimed that Aspen's refusal to honor all-Aspen tickets caused it to lose market share and threatened to give Aspen a complete monopoly of the Aspen ski market. The jury was asked to decide whether Aspen (1) possessed monopoly power in a relevant market and (2) willfully acquired, maintained, or used monopoly power for anticompetitive or exclusionary purposes. The case had a number of interesting aspects, such as disagreements over whether the Aspen ski market was indeed a market given the availability of other ski resorts. When it lost at the trial court level, Aspen appealed, claiming that the antitrust decision meant that it had to cooperate with a rival. The U.S. Supreme Court dealt with this issue by considering whether a dominant firm in a market may possess an "essential facility," such as a joint marketing plan, that must be offered to smaller rivals on an equitable basis to assure that there will be competition in the market. See *Aspen Skiing Co. v. Aspen Highlands Skiing Corp.,* 472 U.S. 585 (1985).

3. **Are Sports Different? Part I.** The NCAA, for years, negotiated on behalf of its member institutions with respect to television, radio, and other rebroadcast rights. In effect, the NCAA fixed prices for its members and prevented price competition among colleges and universities in the licensing of their rebroadcast rights. The NCAA also had a revenue-sharing plan that rewarded colleges and universities with less famous football programs relative to the powerhouses. One of the perennial football powerhouses has been the University of Oklahoma. When the University of Oklahoma negotiated directly with a television network, it ran afoul of an NCAA rule, so it went to court seeking an injunction against enforcement of the rule, citing Section 1 of the Sherman Act. The NCAA admits that it sets prices for its members, but says that without some price-fixing, there would be chaos in the market to broadcast college football. According to the NCAA, it is a terrible waste of resources for the networks to negotiate with each college or university, so that some agreement on the rules among competitors through the NCAA is necessary. The NCAA claims that it is inappropriate to apply the per se rule to its price-fixing activity. What do you think? Are sports different or are there other industries for which relaxation of the per se rule is appropriate? [*National Collegiate Athletic Association v. Board of Regents of the University of Oklahoma,* 468 U.S. 85 (1984).]

4. **OEMs, ISOs, and Tie-ins.** Many antitrust cases have pitted an original equipment manufacturer (OEM) against one or more independent service organizations (ISOs). In many industries, large shares of the profits to be earned flow from the servicing of products sold, not just from the original product sales. The issues leading to litigation often are prompted because ISOs have won a large share of the contracts for service support. Generally, an OEM, upon discovering that ISOs are making large profits while it may be struggling, seeks to tie sales of original equipment to service agreements. Illustratively, during the 1980s, Eastman Kodak, which sold photocopiers and micrographic equipment, faced a declining market share for its service division. In 1985 and 1986, Kodak allegedly adopted a policy under which the company (1) sold parts only to buyers of the company's equipment who either used the company's service or repaired their own equipment, (2) limited ISO's access to other sources of parts by forbidding entities that manufactured parts for the company to sell such parts to anyone other than the company, (3) pressured other entities not to sell the company's parts to the ISOs, and (4) took steps to restrict the availability of used equipment. In response, several ISOs sued Kodak for violations of Section 1 of the Sherman Act through an illegal tie-in between Kodak's equipment and its servicing [Section 3 of the Clayton Act could not be used because it prohibits tie-ins between two goods and services are not considered a good]. An issue that arises in these kinds of cases is the relevant market. The ISO plaintiffs contended that the market for what they do (servicing Kodak products) is Kodak products, while Kodak claims that the market is all photographic and micrographic equipment, for which Kodak has only a small

market share. What do you think? Is tying the sale of equipment to a servicing agreement an illegal tie-in? [*Eastman Kodak Company v. Image Technical Services, et al.,* 504 U.S. 451 (1992).]

5. **Price Discrimination and Price Competition.** One of the conceptual problems faced by Section 2 Clayton Act suits, which prohibit price discrimination where the effect may be to lessen competition or create monopoly, is that it is difficult to distinguish illegal price discrimination from legitimate price competition. Typically, the defendant in price discrimination suits is a seller who is pricing its products below those of rivals and is being sued for the act of lowering prices. The goal of antitrust is supposed to be lower prices for consumers and, yet, in many price discrimination suits, the defendant is being sued for lowering prices. Wal-Mart Stores, Inc., has been the target of many smaller pharmacies because Wal-Mart often spends a lot of money advertising how low its prices are. American Drugs, Inc., is a small family-owned pharmacy that sued Wal-Mart in Arkansas for deeply discounting prices for its prescription and nonprescription drugs. The prosecution of firms for low prices has not enjoyed a warm reception from courts. [*Wal-Mart Stores, Inc. v. American Drugs, Inc.,* 319 Ark. 214, 891 S.W. 2d 30 (Ark.1995).]

Social Responsibility, Policy, and Ethics in a High-Tech World

6. **Misuse of Patents and Antitrust.** An increasingly common defense in patent and copyright infringement cases rests on the claim by the defendant that the plaintiff (and owner of intellectual property in the form of a patent or copyright) committed antitrust violations and, thus, is not entitled to pursue an infringement claim. Often, the defense of the defendant is that the patentee or copyright owner has illegally tied its patent or copyright to a nonpatented good or service and, thus, has forfeited its patent or copyright privileges. Such was the case in *Data General v. Grumman Systems.* In response to a copyright infringement suit by Data General (DG), Grumman claimed that DG could not maintain its infringement action because DG had used its ADEX copyrights to violate Sections 1 and 2 of the Sherman Antitrust Act, 15 U.S.C. §§ 1 and 2. Specifically, Grumman charged that DG misused its copyrights by

   a. Tying the availability of ADEX (DG's copyrighted software, named Advanced Diagnostic Executive System) to a consumer's agreement either to purchase Data General support services (a "positive tie") or not to purchase support services from third-party maintainers (TPMs) (a "negative tie").

   b. Willfully maintaining its monopoly in the support services aftermarket by imposing the alleged tie-in and refusing to deal with third-party maintainers.

   The case is complicated factually, but the important part of the opinion is the part that deals with the "misuse" defense. [*Data General Corporation, et al. v. Grumman Systems Support Corporation,* 36 F.3d 1147 (1st Cir. 1994).]

Using the Internet to Your Advantage

1. Federal antitrust laws are jointly enforced by the U.S. Department of Justice Antitrust Division (http://www.usdoj.gov/atr/index.html) and the Antitrust/Competition Division of the Federal Trade Commission (http://www.ftc.gov/ftc/antitrust.htm). The Legal Information Institute at the Cornell University School of Law has a web page devoted to "Antitrust: An Overview" at http://www.law.cornell.edu/topics/antitrust.html. The Section of Antitrust Law of the American Bar Association has a web page (http://www.abanet.org/antitrust/home.html) that has assembled many of the most recent antitrust cases. Abstracts of the *Antitrust Law Journal* are obtainable online at http://www.abanet.org/antitrust/coverpage.html.

2. There are a wealth of private websites that are sponsored by law firms and others concerned with antitrust policy and legal developments. The law firm of Alston & Bird has a web page devoted to antitrust at http://www.antitrust.org/. FindLaw.com has its own set of web pages devoted to antitrust at http://findlaw.com/01topics/01antitrust/. The *Antitrust Law and Economics Review* has its own web page (http://www.metrolink.net/~cmueller), which has a list of what it labels "dirty dozen" recent antitrust cases that it deems contrary to antitrust law (many of these cases are recent and are among the cases listed in the chapter and in the end-of-chapter cases). A history of antitrust law can be found in the West Law Dictionary at http://www.wld.com/conbus/weal/wantitr1.htm.

Chapter Twenty

Government Regulation of Securities and Online Trading

Learning Objectives

After completing this chapter, you should

1. Know what a security is and what the regulatory consequences are of selling securities in a public offering.
2. Understand the consequences of selling a security when the registration statement or prospectus contains a material misstatement or omission.
3. Be able to discuss the ways that smaller firms are able to qualify for an exemption from SEC requirements for a public offering.
4. Understand the reporting requirements for firms that are subject to the 1934 act.
5. Thoroughly understand insider trading, how it occurs, its legal consequences, and the measures firms take to avoid it.
6. Be able to discuss the steps Congress and the SEC have taken to deal with online trading and press conferences of high-tech firms.

OVERVIEW

From the turn of the twentieth century, states had tried to regulate security (stock and bond) fraud, but state **blue sky** laws were widely perceived to be ineffective because of jurisdictional barriers.[1] Regulation of securities by the federal government dates back to the 1930s, following the Great Stock Market Crash that began in 1929. A federal agency, the Securities and Exchange Commission (SEC), was created in 1934 and has been active in regulating stock market transactions for nearly 70 years. At the time of the creation of the SEC, it was widely believed that fraud and a lack of confidence in the integrity of the stock market

---

[1] State securities laws were often called "blue sky" laws because of an alleged case of stock fraud in which the defendant had no other assets for his "company" except the blue sky.

blue sky
A generic term that refers to state securities laws. Around the turn of the last century (1900), several states justified regulation of securities because some of their citizens had invested in companies that had no assets backing up their values, other than the "blue sky."

were factors in the precipitous fall in stock market values in 1929. The Internet, which has allowed investors to bypass stockbrokers and other intermediaries, enables investors to make their own purchases and sales of securities directly in online transactions, creating new opportunities for profit and fraud. The SEC has responded by enacting new regulations that directly apply to the new legal issues that are created by online trading.

This chapter reviews "traditional" securities law that was well-established before the Internet created new investment opportunities and new challenges for the SEC. Included in this examination is discussion of the scope of securities regulation, definitional descriptions of securities, the registration of securities, exemptions from regulation, and prohibitions on "illegal" transactions such as insider trading. In the second part of the chapter, attention is focused on online transactions and examination of the ways in which the Internet has altered the legal landscape for capital formation.

THE SECURITIES ACT OF 1933

securities
Contracts that are subject to regulation by the Securities and Exchange Commission (SEC). Securities generally involve an investment of money in a common enterprise where profits are earned primarily due to the efforts of third parties, not the investor.

stocks
Certificates that certify ownership in a company, generally a corporation. Stockholders are owners of corporations.

bonds
Instruments that represent long-term corporate debt. A bondholder is entitled to interest payments during the life of the bond and the principal value of the bond at maturity.

Briefly defined, **securities** in common experience are mostly **stocks** and **bonds** that are traded on organized markets. Of course, there are lots of pieces of paper (contracts) that represent promises to pay that are traded in some form of market. This would include accounts receivable, mortgages, and insurance contracts, none of which are securities. The distinction is important because the SEC has authority to regulate securities, but it does not have authority to regulate all financial transactions. Securities are subject to extensive and specialized regulation, as we see below. In addition to accounts receivable, mortgages, and insurance contracts, the SEC does not have authority to regulate pension plans, commodities and precious metals trading, or issuance of promissory notes. Each of the foregoing is regulated in some other manner by a federal or state authority.

The Securities Act of 1933 (1933 Act) was the first major federal statute regulating securities.[2] In many ways, all securities regulation can be linked to either the Securities Act of 1933 or the Securities Exchange Act of 1934 (1934 Act).[3] The Securities Act of 1933 regulates a company's initial sale of stock to the investing public, while the 1934 Act regulates the aftermarket, or the stock market. The 1933 Act requires that securities be *registered* with the SEC before sale to the public.

More on the Question of What Is a Security

The statutory definition of a security under the 1933 Act is broad. Section 2 (a) of the 1933 Act states that

> When used in this title, unless the context otherwise requires—
>
> 1. The term "security" means any note, stock, treasury stock, security future, bond, debenture, evidence of indebtedness, certificate of interest or participation in any profit-sharing agreement, collateral-trust certificate, preorganization certificate or subscription, transferable share, investment contract, voting-trust certificate, certificate of deposit for a security, fractional undivided interest in oil, gas, or other mineral rights, any put, call, straddle, option, or privilege on any security, certificate of deposit, or group or index of securities (including any interest therein or based on the value thereof), or any put, call, straddle, option, or privilege entered into on a national securities exchange relating to foreign currency, or, in general, any interest or instrument commonly known as a "security," or any certificate of interest or participation in, temporary or interim certificate for, receipt for, guarantee of, or warrant or right to subscribe to or purchase, any of the foregoing.

---

[2] 48 Stat. 74, codified at 15 U.S.C. §§ 77a *et seq.*
[3] 48 Stat. 881, codified at 15 U.S.C. §§ 78a *et seq.*

The Howey Test for What Is a Security

Given the broad and generally unenlightening statutory definition of a security (immediately above), courts have been required to clarify what is and is not a security. In the landmark *Howey* case, the U.S. Supreme Court was asked to decide whether an investment contract in citrus trees was a security.[4] The contract offered by the Howey Company to investors entailed the sale of a parcel of land that contained citrus trees together with a service contract. The U.S. Supreme Court ruled that this transaction was a sale of a security and, since it was not registered with the SEC, it was an illegal contract and thus rescindable at the option of the purchaser. According to the Court, an investment contract is a security if (1) it is an investment of money (2) in a common enterprise (3) with a reasonable expectation of profits (4) that are *solely* due to the efforts of third parties.

Case 20-1, the *Howey* case, was the definitive guide on what the Supreme Court considered a security in 1946. In subsequent cases, the definition of a security has become even more inclusive.

---

[4] *Securities and Exchange Commission v. W.J. Howey Co.*, 328 U.S. 293 (1946).

Case 20-1

Securities & Exchange Commission v. W. J. Howey Co. et al.

Supreme Court of the United States
328 U.S. 293 (1946)

BACKGROUND AND FACTS

During the 1940s, the Howey Company sold Florida real estate upon which orchard trees were located. When the sale took place, the purchasers were given a piece of paper that entitled them to the real estate and orchard trees. At the same time, the Howey Company also sold a service contract that guaranteed purchasers that the trees would be watered and properly cared for. When the purchase took place, the purchase of the service contract was optional, but over 80 percent of the purchasers of the orchards also purchased the service contracts.

Opinion: Mr. Justice Murphy Delivered the Opinion of the Court

Section 2 (1) of the Act defines the term "security" to include the commonly known documents traded for speculation or investment. [Footnotes omitted.] This definition also includes "securities" of a more variable character, designated by such descriptive terms as "certificate of interest or participation in any profit-sharing agreement," "investment contract" and "in general, any interest or instrument commonly known as a 'security.'" The legal issue in this case turns upon a determination of whether, under the circumstances, the land sales contract, the warranty deed and the service contract together constitute an "investment contract" within the meaning of § 2 (1). An affirmative answer brings into operation the registration requirements of § 5 (a), unless the security is granted an exemption under § 3 (b). The lower courts, in reaching a negative answer to this problem, treated the contracts and deeds as separate transactions involving no more than an ordinary real estate sale and an agreement by the seller to manage the property for the buyer.

The term "investment contract" is undefined by the Securities Act or by relevant legislative reports. But the term was common in many state "blue sky" laws in existence prior to the adoption of the federal statute and, although the term was also undefined by the state laws, it had been broadly construed by state courts so as to afford the investing public a full measure of protection. Form was disregarded for substance and emphasis was placed upon economic reality. An investment contract thus came to mean a contract or scheme for "the placing of capital or laying out of money in a way intended to secure income or profit from its employment." [Citations omitted.] This definition was uniformly applied by state courts to a variety of situations where individuals were led to invest money in a common enterprise with the expectation that they would earn a profit solely through the efforts of the promoter or of some one other than themselves.

By including an investment contract within the scope of § 2 (1) of the Securities Act, Congress was using a term the meaning of which had been crystallized by this prior judicial interpretation. It is therefore reasonable to attach that meaning to the term as used by Congress, especially since such a definition is consistent with the statutory aims. In other words, an investment contract for purposes of the Securities Act means a contract, transaction or scheme whereby a person invests his money in a common enterprise and is led to expect profits solely from the efforts of the promoter or a third party, it being immaterial whether the shares in the enterprise are evidenced by formal certificates or by nominal interests in the physical assets employed in the enterprise. . . . It permits the fulfillment of the statutory purpose of compelling full and fair disclosure relative to the issuance of "the many types of instruments that in our commercial world fall within the ordinary concept of a security." It embodies a flexible rather than a static principle, one that is capable of adaptation to meet the countless and variable schemes devised by those who seek the use of the money of others on the promise of profits.

* * *

This conclusion is unaffected by the fact that some purchasers choose not to accept the full offer of an investment contract by declining to enter into a service contract with the respondents. The Securities Act prohibits the offer as well as the sale of unregistered, non-exempt securities. Hence it is enough that the respondents merely offer the essential ingredients of an investment contract.

Decision and Outcome

The U.S. Supreme Court overruled the court of appeals, holding that the investment contracts offered by the Howey Company were securities and that investors were entitled to get their money back (rescind the contract) because Howey had not registered the contracts with the SEC.

Questions for Analysis

1. According to the U.S. Supreme Court, what are the three elements necessary for an investment contract (a piece of paper) to be a security?
2. Notice that, in the third element of the Supreme Court's definition of a security, the word "solely" is used. In later court definitions of a security, the word "solely" is no longer used. What does this suggest?
3. What three pieces of paper (or contracts) together does the Securities and Exchange Commission allege constitutes a security?

Other Clarifications of What Is a Security

More recently, there have been other cases that have extended and clarified the Supreme Court's holding in the *Howey* case. In subsequent cases, courts have found that an investment contract that satisfies the first three criteria above is a security if profits are *primarily or substantially* due to the efforts of third parties. By changing the word "solely" in the fourth criterion to *primarily* or *substantially,* pyramid schemes, which typically involve some effort on the part of the investor, are now deemed securities because the profitability of the investment is still primarily or substantially due to the efforts of third parties. Sellers of pyramid schemes that do not register them with the SEC are now illegally selling an unregistered security.

In other cases, courts have used the *family resemblance test*. This test focuses on the motivations of the buyer and seller, the plan of distribution, the reasonable expectations of buyer/investors, and whether there are other laws that regulate the transaction, rendering SEC regulation unnecessary.[5] For most transactions, it is very obvious whether the piece of paper being sold is or is not a security. When there is doubt about whether the piece of paper is a security, the consequences can be very substantial because the sale of an unregistered security is illegal and entitles investors to get their money back.

Informing and Protecting Investors

According to the SEC website (http://www.sec.gov), the 1933 Act has, as its two main goals, to

- Require that investors receive financial and other significant information concerning securities being offered for public sale.
- Prohibit deceit, misrepresentations, and other fraud in the sale of securities.

Informing Investors

registration statement
A legal document required by the SEC before an issuer of securities can sell to the public. The registration statement contains descriptive information on the issuer, a recitation of risks associated with the securities to be issued, discussion of management, and other material information that would affect a reasonably prudent investor.

Registration Statements   The SEC accomplishes the first goal by requiring that sellers of securities file **registration statements** with the SEC before they are allowed to sell securities to the public. For an offering of stock to the public, the SEC required registration statement is an involved document requiring the combined efforts of corporate executives, accountants, securities attorneys, and underwriters. The registration statement must contain detailed financial data as well as biographical information about the executives, any "deals" that executives are getting in terms of discounted stock, and other information. Much of the information that would appear in a typical "business plan" appears in registration statements. Among the other information the SEC requires in the registration statement is the following:

1. Disclosure of how the proceeds of the sale of securities are going to be used.
2. Description of the business issuing the stock.
3. An audited financial statement that has been attested to by a certified public accountant.
4. Discussion of the significant features of the particular security being offered for sale such as whether it is redeemable or callable, whether there is a dividend preference if it is stock, whether it has voting rights, and other attributes of the security.

prospectus
A shortened version of the registration statement that must be given to investors before they purchase securities sold by the issuer.

Prospectuses   The 1933 Act also requires that, before the sale of any security, each investor must be given a **prospectus** that contains the same sort of financial and other information that is in the registration statement. The prospectus enables investors to make informed choices when they are deciding whether to invest in the issuer's business. Unless the SEC indicates to issuers (the company offering the securities for sale to the public) that the registration statement is incomplete, issuers can begin selling securities to the public 20 days after filing the registration statement.

material misstatements or omissions
"Mistakes" in the registration statement that are likely to affect the purchase decisions of reasonably prudent investors.

Section 11 of the 1933 Act

Section 11 of the 1933 Act makes all signers of a registration statement liable for **material misstatements or omissions** contained in the registration statement or in prospectuses. Material misstatements are statements of "fact" that are false and would be considered important by a *reasonable investor*, but not necessarily by the plaintiff (or actual investor)

---

[5] *Reves v. Ernst & Young*, 494 U.S. 56 (1990).

in the case. It is also a violation of Section 11 if the registration statement or prospectus *omits a material fact* that the hypothetical reasonable investor would consider important in the decision as to whether to invest.

At common law, fraud was committed when a seller of securities (1) made a material misstatement (2) knowing the statement was false, but (3) made such statement with intent to deceive, and (4) the plaintiff reasonably relied on the material misstatement and (5) damages occurred because of material misstatement and reliance by the plaintiff.

Common law fraud remains a possible remedy in securities fraud cases, but it is often very difficult to prove the two intent elements, (2) and (3) above. To a large extent, what the 1933 Act did was eliminate the need for the plaintiff in a stock fraud case to prove intent. As pointed out above, a prospectus is a condensed version of the registration statement that is filed with the SEC. Since investors are required to have a prospectus provided before purchasing the security being issued, reasonable reliance on a prospectus containing false statements is presumed. That presumption can be overturned by a showing that the investor knew the statements in the prospectus were false, but purchased the securities anyway.

Parties Liable for Violation of Section 11

As mentioned above, if the registration statement contains a material misstatement or omission, *all signers are liable* along with the company issuing the securities. The liability of the signers of a registration statement is joint and several, meaning that each signer who does not have a defense (discussed below) is potentially liable to investors for the entire amount of their losses. The following parties sign registration statements and, thus, have potential liability:

1. In the case of new companies (an initial public offering), *corporate promoters,* but in the case of established companies, the president or CEO, the chief financial officer, and the chief accounting officer. Other corporate officers may also sign.

2. **Underwriters** or investment bankers, who are experts at valuing companies and at selling company securities to stock brokers and dealers, who in turn sell to investors.

3. Members of the board of directors.

4. Accountants and attorneys who deal with the expertise portions of the registration statement.

This list is not exhaustive. If a future member of the board of directors gives consent to be named in the registration statement, then that individual is liable even though he or she has not signed the registration statement. The issuer (the company offering the securities) of the securities is always liable if the registration statement contains a material misstatement or omission.

Success Has 1,000 Fathers, but Failure Is an Orphan

Signing a registration statement, and hence becoming liable for material misstatements or omissions, is a major step that involves substantial legal uncertainty. Of course, if the company issuing the securities does well, no one cares if there was a material misstatement or omission in the registration statement. There will be no lawsuits when the issuer is successful because investors do not want their money back; they want to keep ownership of the securities that have appreciated in value. It is only when the issuer does poorly and the value of the securities sold by the issuer erodes or loses value entirely that securities lawsuits arise. There are insurance companies, however, that provide protection for signers of registration statements that contain material misstatements or omissions that were unknown to signers of the registration statements.

underwriters
Sometimes called investment bankers. Underwriters place a value on securities based on the value of the underlying business that issues the securities. In its full underwriting capacity, an underwriter buys a new issue of securities and resells that issue to investors.

Damages under Section 11 of the 1933 Act

A purchaser of securities from a company that issued a registration statement that contained a material misstatement or omission is entitled to *rescind the sale* and obtain a *return of consideration* paid for the security. If the purchaser has sold the security, the purchaser is entitled to the difference between what he or she paid for the security and what he or she received when it was sold. In addition, the SEC has the power to investigate and prosecute firms and individuals that it believes have violated the 1933 Act. In order to recover, investors harmed by a misleading registration statement must file suit within two years of the effective date of the registration statement. There are criminal sanctions for egregious violations of the 1933 Act that call for imprisonment for up to five years and fines of up to $10,000.

Defenses

For signers of registration statements, there is one primary defense to a Section 11 claim and several other technical defenses that have lesser significance. Among the technical defenses, if the defendant in a Section 11 case can show that the purchaser was aware that there were material misstatements or omissions in the registration statement or prospectus, then it cannot be said that the purchaser relied on the false statements or omissions. This is an affirmative defense that requires the defendant to prove what was in the mind of the plaintiff, which can be very difficult or impossible because, in most public offerings, the defendant has no specific information about purchasers. Another defense potentially available to defendants rests on the claim that *there was no causation* between the material misstatements or omissions and the plaintiff's damages. Again, this is a defense that may be technically available, but it is an affirmative defense that requires a showing that some other factor was the reason why the securities purchased lost value. If a material misstatement or omission was made in the prospectus, and that information becomes known, in most cases it is linked to the causes for the decline in the value of the stock.

due diligence defense

The due diligence defense is effective when the defendant in a Section 11 claim is able to show that he or she conducted an independent investigation of the statements made in the registration statement and was unable to detect an error.

Due Diligence Defense   A signer of a registration statement can avoid liability for material misstatements or omissions if the signer can demonstrate that he or she exercised *due diligence*. The **due diligence defense** is usable if the signer conducted a reasonable investigation of the statements made in the registration statement but was unable to discover the misstatements or omissions. Satisfying the requirements for due diligence defense is not easy as it requires a signer/defendant to not accept statements made by company executives but, instead, to independently verify the content of those statements. For the accounting statements and the legalese that makes up much of the registration statements, signers of registration statements can rely on the statements of professionals (accountants and lawyers) made *within their areas of expertise*. Similarly, accountants and attorneys who sign a registration statement are liable only for the portions of the registration statements that they prepared.

Other Liabilities Associated with Public Offerings   Of course, companies hoping to raise money in the securities markets do not solely rely on prospectuses to sell stock. Companies use a variety of tactics to attract the attention of potential investors and sometimes hold presentations, often called "road shows," that extol the potential profitability of an investment in the security offered for sale. At one time, a road show literally involved management of the issuing company meeting with and answering questions from potential purchasers of the securities being offered for sale. Section 12(2) provides a remedy for an investor who was induced to purchase a security by means of misleading oral or written communications, including a prospectus, but also other communications that may include brochures, videotapes, and live performances by management of the issuer.

The remedies for misleading oral or written communications in connection with the sale of a security in a public offering are the same for Section 12(2) as for Section 11.

Basically, an investor is entitled to get his or her money back or the difference between what was paid for the securities and what they were sold for. Defendants are entitled to mitigate damages by showing that the decline in value of the security was attributable to factors other than those linked to the misleading statements made in connection with the sale of the security.

Exempt Securities and Exempt Transactions

Complying with SEC requirements for a public offering of securities is so expensive that many small companies try to qualify for some kind of exemption. At a minimum, complying with SEC regulations for a public offering requires an outlay of $1 million for legal, accounting, and printing expenses. Obviously, for a company that is trying to raise $500,000, it is uneconomical to raise money in this manner.

Exempt Transactions

exempt transactions
Sales of securities to the investing public that are exempt from most of the requirements of public offerings as set by the 1933 Act, such as a registration statement and prospectus.

For many high-tech startups, there are three typical phases of financing, often labeled Stage I, II, and III. In Stage I, promoters of the business often look for friends and family to support them, but may seek angel financing from investors who are willing to risk a small amount of money on a high-risk venture. Once a firm gets Stage I financing and shows some promise, it will generally need another injection of capital before Stage III, which is an IPO, an initial public offering, which entails all the costs discussed above associated with a public offering under the 1933 Act. A crucial stage for many successful ventures is obtaining Stage II financing. Stage II financing is generally beyond the financial resources of family, friends, and even angel financing, but is not large enough to justify the regulatory costs associated with a public offering. Firms seeking to raise between $500,000 and $5 million in Stage II financing generally rely on a number of **exempt transactions** permitted by the 1933 Act.

Small Offerings: Regulation D

safe harbors
In law, a safe harbor is a procedure that, if followed, will insulate a party from legal liability.

There are four separate transaction exemptions provided by Regulation D. Even though these transactions are exempt from the public offering requirements of the 1933 Act, assistance of a skilled securities attorney is mandatory because a failure to correctly qualify for an exemption results in the issuing firm selling an unregistered security, which of course is illegal under the 1933 Act. The four exemptions provided by Regulation D are **safe harbors,** but the harbors are only safe for a firm that strictly adheres to the requirements of the exemption chosen.

Each of the exemptions listed below has its own set of restrictions on advertising, solicitations, and resales of securities sold. It is important to keep in mind that the exemptions provided by Regulation D were created because those raising capital are *not* making public offerings. In light of that restriction, Regulation D imposes limits on advertising and solicitations, limits access to the securities offered for sale to a restricted or private audience, and imposes limits on resales to prevent purchasers of exempted stock from being conduits for larger distributions to investors.

Rule 504   Rule 504 provides a safe harbor for firms that are seeking to raise up to $1 million in any one year, but again with limitations. Firms seeking to qualify for this exemption must not be development stage companies that have no specific business plans. Neither can they be investment companies seeking funds for investments in other businesses or businesses seeking to merge with or acquire another company. Specifically, Rule 504 was established for small companies seeking Stage II financing that are actual, functioning businesses.

Rule 504a This rule is for firms that do not have business plans but seek to raise up to $500,000 in a one-year period for the purpose of locating or acquiring firms that have business plans or interesting ideas. Compliance with Rule 504a requires the firm to notify the SEC and restricts the firm to no advertising or general solicitation. Resales of securities acquired in 504a sales are generally prohibited, unless the seller qualifies for another exempt transaction under Regulation D, because these securities are unregistered.

Rule 505 Many firms in need of Stage II financing rely on Rule 505, which allows firms to raise up to $5 million within a 12-month period. There are a number of restrictions contained in Rule 505. First, there can be no more than 35 **unaccredited investors.** The antithesis of unaccredited investors, **accredited investors,** include financial institutions and wealthy individuals whose net worth is more than $1 million or whose net income per year exceeds $200,000. In addition, executive officers and directors of the company seeking to raise funds are considered accredited investors. Rule 505 places no limits on the number of accredited investors, but if there is one unaccredited investor, all investors must be provided with the kind of information that would be contained in a registration statement. In practice, complying with state disclosure requirements is usually sufficient to satisfy the requirement of Rule 505 to provide to potential investors information adequate for them to make an informed investment decision. As with most exempt transactions, compliance with Rule 505 is complicated and should only be attempted with the aid of a competent securities attorney.

Rule 506 Unlimited funds can be raised under the **private placement** exemption of the 1933 Act. Section 4(2) of the 1933 Act provides a private placement exemption from the registration requirements of the 1933 Act, but defining *private placements* has not been easy in the face of court decisions that have failed to set a bright line between what is allowed and what is not allowed. As is typical, the legal consequences of making a mistake can be onerous as failure by the issuer of privately placed securities to qualify for the exemption sought may result in sales of an unregistered security, violating Section 11 of the 1933 Act.

There are two requirements that an issuer has to satisfy to qualify for Rule 506:

1. "There are no more than or the issuer reasonably believes that there are no more than 35 purchasers of securities from the issuer in any offering . . ."
2. "Each purchaser who is not an accredited investor either alone or with his purchaser representative(s) has such knowledge and experience in financial and business matters that he is capable of evaluating the merits and risks of the prospective investment, or the issuer reasonably believes immediately prior to making any sale that such purchaser comes within this description."

Since Rule 506 is available for a "private" placement, the first requirement of Rule 506 limits the number of investors to a small group, and thus makes sure that the securities are not offered to "the public." The second requirement is often called the "rich" and "smart" rule. Under Rule 506, each purchaser must be either accredited (rich) or have the experience to evaluate the risks and merits of the prospective investment (smart). Rule 506 can be used by firms in need of Stage II financing, but it more commonly is used by financial firms seeking to raise unlimited amounts of capital by offering unregistered securities to institutional investors who are not in need of the protections offered by government (SEC) regulation.

unaccredited investors
Investors who are not "rich" (a net worth over $1 million or an annual income over $200,000) and are not corporate insiders such as officers or directors.

accredited investors
Investors who can afford to take risks on exempt transactions, either because they meet certain net worth or income requirements or because they are financial institutions, or investors who have access to the type of information that is available in a registration statement because they are corporate insiders.

private placement
An exempt transaction that qualifies for its exemption from the registration requirements of a public offering because it does not involve sales to the general public.

THE SECURITIES EXCHANGE ACT OF 1934

Rather than dealing with the issuance and initial sale of securities, the Securities Exchange Act of 1934 is applicable to the secondary market (after-market) in which securities are resold freely. To that end, the 1934 Act regulates securities exchanges, brokers, dealers, national securities associations (the National Association of Securities Dealers [NASD] is the most prominent), and firms whose securities are traded in organized markets or are otherwise subject to jurisdiction of the 1934 Act. Consistent with the general philosophy of the federal securities laws, the primary thrust of the 1934 Act is *full disclosure,* so that the investing public will be able to make informed choices when making financial investment decisions. The 1934 Act also has some very tough antifraud provisions that can severely penalize those who use insider information to defraud security market participants.

Reporting Requirements for Firms Regulated by the 1934 Act

Under Section 12 of the 1934 Act, an issuer of securities is required to register with the SEC each nonexempt class of securities if the firm is engaged in interstate commerce, has total assets exceeding $5 million and (1) is listed on a national stock exchange or (2) has more than 500 equity owners (shareholders). If the firm is registered with the SEC under Section 12, it must issue regular reports of its financial condition and there are penalties for material misstatements or omissions in these reports. Firms subject to Section 12 are referred to as *public companies,* because they must disclose their financial condition quarterly and annually in 10Q, 10K, and 8Q reports (described below). "Going private" refers to actions firms that have been regulated under Section 12 take to avoid continued regulation. This is generally accomplished by reducing the number of shareholders to fewer than 300.

Both before and after investing in securities issued by a firm, shareholders and potential shareholders need to have some means of evaluating the value of their investments or their investment opportunities. The 1934 Act requires firms to keep investors and the investing public informed by requiring the issuance of various reports. Among the reports required by the SEC for a public corporation are

- 10-Q reports, which are unaudited quarterly statements of operations and financial condition. 10-Q reports must be filed within 45 days of the end of each quarter.
- 10-K reports, which are annual, audited statements of the financial condition of the firm and must be filed with the SEC within 90 days of the end of the firm's fiscal year.[6]
- 8-K reports, which are required when unusual events affect the firm, such as changes in ownership, sales or acquisitions of key assets, resignation of directors, and other events.

An essential feature of the Enron scandal was the apparent deliberate misreporting of revenue and asset values by Enron in its annual (10-K) report. Enron investors were left holding shares of stock of a worthless corporation in part because the true financial condition of the company was not reported. Higher-level executives apparently were aware of the precarious condition of the company's finances and sold their Enron stock before the bad news became public and drove Enron share prices downward.

Section 10(b)

Section 10(b) is a broad antifraud provision that has been applied, most conspicuously, to insider trading (discussed extensively next) on the stock market. Pursuant to its power to enact regulations that are consistent with the 1934 Act, the SEC promulgated Rule 10b-5. The language of Rule 10b-5 is very inclusive and makes frequent use of the word "any."

---

[6] In the wake of the Enron and WorldCom scandals, there are likely to be additional constraints imposed on accounting firms that audit and report the financial condition of Section 12 firms. Among the reforms most often discussed is a prohibition of an accounting firm that performs audits also receiving money in the form of consulting fees.

Rule 10b-5 states:

It shall be unlawful for any person, directly or indirectly, by the use of any means or instrumentality of interstate commerce, or of the mails, or of any facility of any national securities exchange,

a. To employ any device, scheme, or artifice to defraud,

b. To make any untrue statement of material fact or to omit to state a material fact necessary in order to make the statements made, in the light of the circumstances under which they were made, not misleading, or

c. To engage in any act, practice, or course of business which operates or would operate as a fraud or deceit upon any person,

in connection with the purchase or sale of any security.

insider trading
Purchases or sales of securities by corporate insiders, tippees, or others restricted from trading while in possession of material information that is not publicly known.

In short, Rule 10b-5 arms the SEC to root out fraud in the purchase or sale of any security. Although Rule 10b-5 has been most prominently used against **insider trading**, it also has been employed to find that press conferences held by corporate spokespersons have violated Section 10(b) of the Securities Act of 1934. Prosecutions for violations of Section 10(b) have followed when corporate spokespersons have been too optimistic about their company's future prospects, and also have followed comments that have been too dismal about the company's future. Lawsuits based on statements of corporate executives or corporate spokespersons are generally class-action, shareholder derivative suits in which the plaintiffs are making the claim that corporate management is guilty of violating their fiduciary duties to shareholders. Lawyers organizing these class action suits are entitled to recover "reasonable" attorney fees for their efforts. Liability for statements about the future prospects of a corporation by corporate executives was substantially limited by the Private Securities Litigation Reform Act of 1995, which is discussed below.

Insider Trading

Since 1961, the SEC has taken the position that corporate directors, officers, and majority shareholders should not be allowed to trade in their company's stock if they are in possession of material inside information that is not known to the public at the time of the purchases or sales of securities. As in the 1933 Act, information is *material* if it is information that would affect the decision to buy or sell a security made by a *reasonably prudent investor*. Over time, the reach of Rule 10b-5 has expanded to include trading by key employees, **tippees** of insiders, consultants, attorneys, and reporters who are entrusted with material, inside information, along with tippees of consultants, attorneys, and reporters. During the 1980s, Congress passed two major statutes to augment the efforts of the SEC to combat insider trading.

tippees
The recipients of insider information from corporate insiders or others for whom disclosure of such information involves a breach of fiduciary duty.

Application of Rule 10b-5 to Insider Trading

In theory, stock prices on organized exchanges are constantly and quickly adjusting to correct valuations of corporations whose stock is traded daily. The value of a corporation changes for a variety of reasons, which include macroeconomic events, changes in demand for the goods or services produced by the corporation, discovery of new materials, innovations that are protected by patents, mergers with other firms, changes in labor costs, legal changes, and more. Also, investor confidence in the integrity of the market affects stock market prices. If the shares of a corporation are undervalued, there are opportunities for investors to make above-average rates of return by purchasing its shares, but increased demand for shares will raise stock prices until the rate of return offered, adjusted for risk, returns to the average risk-adjusted rate of return. For overvalued stock, the process works in reverse.

insiders
Traditionally, insiders include corporate officers, directors, and greater-than-10-percent shareholders. More recently, the term has been expanded to include key employees such as legal, technical, and financial staff.

Insider Information and Market Integrity   There are some situations when corporate insiders are in possession of inside or private information that enables them, with virtual certainty, to predict the direction of stock price changes for their company. If the firm is in the mineral exploration business and the firm discovers a huge mineral deposit, it is a pretty safe bet that the value of the firm's shares will go up. A firm that previously had a very lucrative contract with the federal government, but is about to lose that contract because of improprieties, will likely lose value. A firm that has a major breakthrough in biotech will very likely increase in value while a firm that is the target of a major strike will lose value.

Executives are likely to be among the first to learn about the aforementioned events. They are in a position to realize windfall profits if they can trade in shares of their company's stock using advanced knowledge of coming events (inside information) while the rest of the investing public is ignorant of these material facts. Rule 10b-5 makes it illegal for insiders who have advance knowledge of material information, not publicly known, to take advantage of that information in stock trades. Quite obviously, executives can avoid liability under Rule 10b-5, when in possession of insider information, by simply not selling or buying their company's stock. Case 20-2 deals with insiders who did not follow this rule.

Case 20-3 supports the contention that some things don't change. Corporate executives are prone to emphasize the positive, but, at some point, such "spinning" becomes deceptive. In Case 20-2, executives became aware of adverse information involving changes in the terms of crucial contracts affecting the involved firms. A question arises as to whether management should refrain from making any press statements. Of course, generally it is quite awkward to not say anything.

Case 20-2

In re Hi/fn, Inc., Securities Litigation; This Document Relates to: All Actions

United States District Court for the Northern District of California
2000 U.S. Dist. LEXIS 11631 (N.D. Cal. 2000)

BACKGROUND AND FACTS

Hi/fn designs and markets semiconductor devices used to provide secure, high-bandwidth connections to the Internet and increased data storage. During all times relevant to this action, Hi/fn was dependent on two companies for 85% of its revenues: Quantum Corporation ("Quantum") and Lucent Technologies, Inc./Ascend Communications (hereinafter "Lucent"). Plaintiffs allege that in June 1999, Hi/fn executives attended a meeting in which defendants learned that Lucent planned to "migrate Lucent's Ascend TNT product from a 48 port modem card to a 96 port card and eventually to a 256 port card," "which would result in a substantial reduction in Lucent's requirements for Hi/fn's 7711 (subsequently 7751) processor chips." Although Hi/fn sales representatives were concerned about the effect of Lucent's proposed new product development and the potential that Lucent would require 50% fewer Hi/fn parts, Farnham and Harrah "remained upbeat." Information also surfaced and was made known to the defendants that its other largest customer was going to substantially reduce its orders from Hi/fn also.

The complaint alleges that the realization that Hi/fn's two largest customers would soon reduce their orders "resulted in growing concerns among Hi/fn's increasingly troubled sales staff." Plaintiffs *assert that these concerns were expressed at the Quarterly Sales Meeting held at the Pruneyard Hotel in Campbell, CA from August 2–5, 1999. At this meeting, Hi/fn's sales staff allegedly forecast revenues of $43 million for fiscal year 2000, a slight increase over the $41 million earned in fiscal year 1999. Plaintiffs contend that Farnham, Hi/fn's Chief Executive Officer, angrily wrote over this forecast, replacing it with a $65 million projection, telling the sales staff that they needed to "make it happen." Plaintiffs state that this projection was made without any actual market or demand analysis, and that the sales staff believed there was no way to exceed its original $43 million projection.*

Plaintiffs also contend that, on July 26, 1999, defendants Farnham and Walker informed analysts, among other things, that Hi/fn expected returns of $65 million in fiscal year 2000 and that Hi/fn's outlook beyond September 1999 was positive. Finally, on September 8, 1999, Farnham allegedly told a CNBC interviewer that the market for data storage (dominated by Quantum) would increase approximately 20% per year, and that the networking market (dominated by Lucent) would more than "double" yearly for "the next 3 to 4 years." Moreover, plaintiffs assert that, equipped with information of an impending revenue decline, the individual defendants collectively sold 105,170 shares of Hi/fn stock at prices as high as $114.88 from July 28, 1999 to August 17, 1999. Defendants as a group received proceeds of over $10 million. The plaintiffs allege that the defendants violated Section 10(b) of the 1934 Act by selling while in possession of inside information that the value of the company would fall once the inside information that Hi/fn's two largest customers were about to radically reduce their orders of Hi/fn's products.

"After word of the leak reached the market place," Hi/fn issued a press release and held a "conference call" regarding the shortfall. The information caused Hi/fn stock to decline from $104-3/4 at the close of trading on October 6, 1999 to $74 on October 7, 1999, and, after a temporary halt in trading, to a low of $37-3/4 at the close of trading on October 8, 1999.

Now before the Court is defendants' motion to dismiss plaintiffs' First Amended Complaint.

Opinion by Susan Illston, United States District Judge

1. Puffery

Defendants also argue that the disputed "general statements of optimism" are not actionable, because they constitute vague and ambiguous "puffery" and "corporate cheerleading." Defendants contend that plaintiffs may not "string" together alleged misrepresentations, but rather must address each allegedly false statement individually and assert why each statement is false. Defendants assert that plaintiffs have not done so. Finally, defendants contend that allegations of historical fact are not actionable. Plaintiffs respond that statements that refer to a company's operations, stock value, revenue forecasts, and other matters of importance to investors are in fact actionable when viewed in the context of other misleading statements or omissions.

"Projections and general expressions of optimism may be actionable" under federal securities laws. A forecast may be actionable if any of the following factors are correct: (1) the statement is not genuinely believed, (2) there is not a reasonable foundation for the belief, or (3) the speaker is aware of undisclosed facts that tend to undermine the accuracy of the projection. . . . Plaintiffs concede that accurate statements of historical fact do not form a basis for liability under federal securities laws. However, assuming the truth of plaintiffs' allegations of knowledge of imminent reductions in orders from Hi/fn's customers, defendants either did not genuinely believe their alleged statements or were aware of undisclosed facts that tended to undermine the accuracy of their statements. Although plaintiffs do not list subsequent to each statement the reasons for their belief that the statement was false, it is apparent that plaintiffs have alleged falsity based on the previously detailed undisclosed information. Accordingly, the Court concludes that the forecasts of significant increases in Hi/fn's business and revenues were not mere puffery and can be actionable.

2. Duty to Make Predictions

Defendants also argue that Hi/fn was under no duty to predict with precision if and when Quantum and Lucent would reduce their orders. Rather defendants assert that Hi/fn was simply obligated to identify and notify of risks within its knowledge. Plaintiffs respond that, even if defendants were not obligated to make predictions about another company's business, defendants' argument is made irrelevant by the fact that defendants in fact made positive predictions about the doubling of its customers' businesses, and should therefore be required to disclose any change in those forecasts.

A company is not charged with the ability to know "to a certainty" the plans of another entity. Defendants argue that *In re Stac* supports the further proposition that here, even if Quantum and Lucent had informed defendants that they soon intended to significantly decrease their orders, Hi/fn "could not have known whether . . . [they] would truly do so."

This argument would be closer to the mark if Hi/fn's management had made no statements at all concerning the strength of the market for its products. Since Hi/fn chose to make such statements, however, and since their actual statements are alleged to have been false and misleading, their duty to disclose becomes academic.

* * *

Here, defendants in fact chose to make predictions, which predictions plaintiffs allege to be false and misleading. Further, the disputed disclosures relate not to predictions as to competitors' behavior, but to statements made by and about customers on whom the bulk of Hi/fn's sales depended. No previous disclosures provided specific information regarding actual inventory build-ups or new product developments by Hi/fn's customers. Accordingly, taking as true plaintiffs' allegations that defendants had information that the predictions they were making were in fact incorrect, plaintiffs have stated a claim for violation of defendant's duty to disclose material information.

* * *

Decision and Outcome

The court denied the defendant's motion to dismiss ruling that a trial was appropriate to determine if the defendants engaged in fraud in violation of Section 10(b) based on their misleading statements made to the public and the huge sales of stock before the negative information about Hi/fn became public.

Questions for Analysis

1. What are the false statements made by the defendants? Did the defendants know for sure that their business was going to decline? Didn't the defendants provide warning that their predictions for future sales were conditional on certain risks not occurring?

2. Why were the cautionary statements of the defendants not enough to insulate them from having to go to trial based on a violation of Section 10(b)?

3. At the trial, what will the plaintiffs have to show in order to recover against the defendants for a violation of Section 10(b)?

Insiders under Rule 10b-5   Corporate officers, directors, and majority shareholders have been deemed *insiders,* who are prohibited from trading securities of their own company while in possession of material insider information. Over the years, there has been an expansion of those deemed to be insiders. Key employees, such as geologists in companies engaged in mineral explorations, have been prosecuted for violating Rule 10b-5 for trading while in possession of insider information.

Tippees   Knowing that they are subject to prosecution for insider trading, some corporate insiders have provided tips to outsiders that the value of their firm is likely to change dramatically once the material information that they are in possession of becomes known. Tippees are also liable under Rule 10b-5 for inside trading if they received inside information from a corporate insider when the tip constitutes a breach of fiduciary duty to the corporation by the insider. Tippees could provide tips of inside information to other tippees, and these remote tippees are also liable under Rule 10b-5 if they knew that the tips were originally received from corporate insiders and the tips constituted a breach of fiduciary duties by the corporate insiders.

The mere possession of inside information by a noninsider is not a violation of Rule 10b-5 so long as the insider information was not obtained as a result of breach of a fiduciary duty by a corporate insider. Suppose, for example, a person who regularly dined at fancy restaurants observed what he recognized as senior executives from two corporations starting to have lunch together on a frequent basis. He might rightly guess that this was because they were contemplating an acquisition or merger. If the person purchased stock from the company that was going to be acquired, it could be argued that he would be trading with insider information (information not generally available to investors) but the purchases would not be illegal because the insider information was not illegally acquired.

Misappropriation Inside information about a corporation often comes into possession of outsiders through their jobs. The outsider may be a financial reporter, an attorney brought in to facilitate a merger, or some other consultant or software expert hired to provide consulting services. If these outsiders obtain inside information, then make use of that information in ways that would amount to a breach of their fiduciary duties to their employers, they are liable for a violation of Section 10(b) of the 1934 Act. If outsiders make use of material inside information by buying or selling securities, and making use of that inside information is a breach of their fiduciary duty to their employer, they have committed fraud in connection with the purchase or sale of a security.

misappropriators
Consultants, reporters, attorneys, and others who are entrusted with confidential information but make use of that information for their own purposes such as engaging in securities transactions.

Tippees of Misappropriators It is also a violation of Section 10(b) if **misappropriators** provide tips to others; these tippees are also liable under Section 10(b). Consider the following situation. A financial reporter working for *The Wall Street Journal* writes a regular column for his employer entitled "Heard on the Street," in which he interviews executives for various firms and then writes positive or negative articles about the firm. Suppose, further, that *The Wall Street Journal* has told its reporters that information they gather in connection with their jobs is confidential and should not be disclosed before publication. Also assume that stock prices move up or down for the firms that are reviewed by the reporter, depending on how favorable the articles written about them appear. If the reporter trades in shares of stock of companies he is writing about before his information appears in print, he is a misappropriater. If, in advance of publication, he tips some of his friends about whether the article he is writing is favorable or unfavorable, he is breaching his fiduciary duty to his employer and the tippee has committed a securities violation if he or she trades the stock of that company.

Limits on Section 10(b)

Although the reach of Section 10(b) (or Rule 10b-5) is very broad, there are limits. In order to violate Section 10(b), there must be a showing that the defendant engaged in some kind of subterfuge beyond simple negligence. Suppose an accounting firm audits the books of a corporation and issues its reports. Suppose, further, that the accounting firm was negligent in its audit and, because of its negligence, the audit report is inaccurate, with the corporation appearing to be in better financial shape than it actually is. Finally, suppose, based on the report of the accounting firm, that a number of investors bought shares of the firm's stock that, shortly thereafter, became valueless as the firm went bankrupt. Is the accounting firm guilty of a violation of Section 10(b)? Courts have answered in the negative. A violation of Section 10(b) requires *scienter,* a Latin word for a "bad heart," or evil intent. Scienter is a requirement for fraud, since the plaintiff must show that the fraudulent party knew he or she was misrepresenting a material fact. With insider trading, defendants are aware that they are not supposed to trade securities while in possession of material inside information and, yet, they go ahead anyway or provide tips to tippees. This satisfies the scienter requirement of Section 10(b).

Section 16(b) of the 1934 Act

Section 16(a) of the 1934 Act requires officers, directors, and greater-than-10-percent shareholders of public companies to report, on a quarterly basis, their holdings of securities of the firm they serve or own. Section 16(b) makes it illegal for officers, directors, or

Nutz and Boltz Martha Stewart and ImClone

Martha Stewart, the well-known doyenne of fashion, cooking, and thrift, has been the subject of an insider trading investigation by the SEC, as indicated by the article below.

SEC KNOCKING ON MARTHA'S DOOR

NEW YORK, Oct. 22, 2002—(CBS) Securities and Exchange Commission lawyers have told Martha Stewart that they are ready to file civil securities fraud charges against the home decor entrepreneur for her alleged role in an insider trading scandal, according to published reports Tuesday.

The SEC gave Stewart a formal notice last month of its intent to file civil charges, and Stewart's attorneys have reportedly responded, which is allowed before the commission makes its final decision.

In most cases, such a notice leads to filing of charges.

The possibility of civil charges represents a potentially devastating scenario for Stewart, who is accused of selling shares of ImClone Systems after getting tipped off about negative news surrounding one of its promising new cancer drugs.

* * *

Stewart is already under investigation by the Justice Department, which is probing whether she lied to lawmakers about her sale of ImClone shares.

She sold nearly 4,000 shares of ImClone on Dec. 27—one day before the Food and Drug Administration announced it would not review the biotechnology company's cancer drug, Erbitux. ImClone's stock subsequently plummeted.

Stewart has maintained that she and her broker Peter Bacanovic had a standing order to sell the shares if the stock dropped below $60.

Stewart is friends with Sam Waksal, founder and former chief executive of ImClone, who pleaded guilty last week to several counts of bank fraud, securities fraud, conspiracy to obstruct justice and perjury.

Waksal did not implicate Stewart, and his plea was not part of an agreement to cooperate with prosecutors—rare in a criminal plea.

Douglas Faneuil, Bacanovic's assistant, initially supported Stewart's and Bacanovic's account, but later admitted he withheld information when first interviewed by investigators from the SEC and the FBI.

Source: "SEC Knocking on Martha's Door," October 22, 2002, CBS News Archives. Copyright © 2002 CBS News. Reprinted with permission.

Author's postscript: In connection with allegations of insider trading, Martha Stewart has been criminally indicted for obstruction of justice and perjury. The government is also suing her civilly for securites fraud (insider trading) under Section 10(b) of the 1934 Act.

---

short-swing profits
Profits made or losses avoided from the purchase and sale, or sale and purchase, of the same securities within a six-month period, when the transactors are corporate officers, directors, or greater-than-10-percent shareholders.

greater-than-10-percent shareholders to make short swing profits, which are profits that are earned from the purchase and sale, or sale and purchase, of the same security within a six-month period. Unlike Rule 10b-5, there is no need for the plaintiff in a Section 16(b) case to show that the trades were motivated by knowledge of insider information. In fact, there is no need to show any intent at all for a violation of Section 16(b); a violation could occur inadvertently if purchases and sales of securities occur too frequently. When a Section 16(b) suit is filed, it is a shareholder derivative suit; the plaintiff is a shareholder and is suing one of the aforementioned parties for misfeasance toward the corporation. If the shareholder is successful in the suit, the **short-swing profits** earned are confiscated from the offending insiders and returned to the corporation. A shareholder bringing a Section 16(b) suit, however, is entitled to recover "reasonable" attorney fees, which is one reason why most plaintiffs in Section 16(b) cases are attorneys, who determine that a violation has occurred by examining the reports required by Section 16(a). Typically, such attorneys then buy one share of stock and initiate a suit.

STATUTORY REFORMS

Insider Trading Sanctions Act of 1984

During the 1980s, there was widespread publicity about insider trading. A number of Wall Street tycoons, such as Ivan Bosky, Michael Millken, and Dennis Levine, made hundreds of millions of dollars based on insider information. At that time, there was a concern that, with insider traders able to make millions from illegal trades, the sanctions against them were woefully inadequate deterrents. In 1984 Congress passed the Insider Trading Sanctions Act (ITSA), which provided for criminal penalties of $100,000 and civil penalties of three times profits earned on trades made based on insider information.[7] The ITSA also included jail terms of up to five years for anyone convicted of insider trading in connection with attempted takeovers of other companies.

Insider Trading and Securities Fraud Enforcement Act of 1988

In 1988, Congress passed additional legislation in the form of the Insider Trading and Securities Fraud Enforcement Act (ITSFEA), which raised the maximum penalty for insider trading from 5 to 10 years in jail and made it more likely that those convicted of insider trading would serve jail time.[8] Maximum fines for insider trading were raised to $1 million and violators of insider trading prohibitions could be liable to victims for triple the profits gained or losses avoided as a result of the wrongful trades. The ITSFEA also placed liability upon brokerage houses to police themselves for violations by employees that the brokerage knew, or should have known had the brokerage house not recklessly disregarded available information, were violating insider trading regulations. Criminal fines could be enforced against brokerage houses for up to $2.5 million. The ITSFEA also relies on dishonor among thieves; it provides for bounties as high as 10 percent of ill-gotten gains for those who turn in insider traders. The act also provides for a private right of action for anyone trading in the same class of securities at the same time that insider trading violations were occurring. Not only are insider traders liable, but tippees, including remote tippees, are jointly and severally liable, though total damages are capped at the amount of profits made or losses avoided by the insider traders.

The Private Securities Litigation Reform Act of 1995

By the mid-1990s, there was a general perception that the regulatory pendulum had likely swung too far in the direction of shareholder protection, with legitimate corporate actions suppressed by the securities laws. High-tech firms, in particular, were being sued based on press releases and statements made at press conferences. Attorneys specializing in securities laws would scrutinize statements made by corporate spokespersons. Unless every statement made turned out to be accurate, corporate management could be sued for "misleading" shareholders and the investing public. High-tech firms, however, tend to be in topsy-turvy market environments, characterized by major uncertainties and change so rapid that just about anything said today may need to be corrected tomorrow.

Over President Clinton's veto, Congress passed the Private Securities Litigation Reform Act (PSLRA) of 1995.[9] The PSLRA allows corporations to hold press conferences and issue forward-looking statements without incurring potential securities liability as long as the firm follows certain procedures that enable it to qualify for "safe harbor" treatment. Essentially, the PSLRA allows a firm to qualify for safe harbor treatment for future market projections as long as

- The forward-looking statements are identified as such
- The statements are accompanied by meaningful cautionary language that calls attention to the fact that there are risks that could cause these forward-looking statements to be inaccurate.

---

[7] Pub. L. No. 98-376, codified at 15 U.S.C. § 78u(d)(2)(A).

[8] Pub. L. No. 100-704, codified at 15 U.S.C. § 78u-1.

[9] Pub. L. No. 104-67, 109 Stat. 737, codified at 15 U.S.C. §§ 77z-2, 78u-5. With the benefit of hindsight, the wisdom of President Clinton's veto of this legislation is being assessed much more favorably.

The cautionary language must actually point to factors that could cause the forward-looking statements to become inaccurate and not just contain boilerplate "generic" language that indicates all forward-looking statements are potentially inaccurate because of overall economic factors. In other words, the cautionary language must focus on the key factors that affect the individual firm that is making the statements. Recent legislation plays a key role in Case 20-3.

Case 20-3

Lawrence M. Greebel, Richard Crane, Brian D. Robinson, and John and Ann Somers on behalf of themselves and all others similarly situated, Appellants v. FTP Software, Inc.; Robert W. Goodnow, Jr.; Penny C. Leavy; Douglas F. Flood; Jonathan Rodin; Charlotte H. Evans; and David H. Zirkle, Appellees

United States Court of Appeals for the First Circuit
194 F.3d 185 (1st Cir. 1999)

BACKGROUND AND FACTS

The complaint alleges the following. FTP Software, Inc. develops, markets, and supports Internet and Intranet software for personal computers and networks. By the beginning of the Class Period [footnotes deleted] (from July 14, 1995 to January 3, 1996), the demand for FTP's software was diminishing because many of FTP's clients were either developing the technology themselves or acquiring competing systems from other manufacturers, such as Microsoft and Netscape. Microsoft, for example, was incorporating networking capabilities into its new Windows 95 software, free of additional charge. In addition, FTP was struggling to keep pace with "revolutionary" technological developments that threatened to render its software obsolete. In response, FTP and several of its directors and officers through fraudulent schemes inflated FTP's stock price and then made various false statements and material omissions. Plaintiffs allege that FTP failed to disclose the threats to its continued success, as well as several "questionable" sales practices. These included the making of "warehouse shipments"—that is, booking a fictitious sale of a product to a non-existent buyer, shipping that product to a warehouse for storage, and then eventually returning it to FTP. According to plaintiffs, one FTP employee who complained about these shipments, and who refused (in at least one instance) to sign for the product return, was dismissed as a result of his protest, all before the Class Period. . . .

FTP also made several statements that the plaintiffs characterize as false or materially misleading. On July 14, 1995, the first day of the Class Period, David Zirkle, FTP's President and Chief Executive Officer, reported FTP's financial performance results for the second fiscal quarter of 1995. Zirkle declared: "We are pleased with our performance for the second quarter. Sales continue to be strong in both our U.S. and international channels." Zirkle also touted the release of several new products, stating that "[t]hese products should help us achieve our revenue objective for the second half of 1995." Plaintiffs argue that these comments "falsely convey[ed] the impression that sales were, and would continue to be, healthy and strong" and that this false impression was deliberately *aided by FTP's failure to disclose that in or around January 1995, the French Post Office canceled its planned purchase of $10 million of FTP products "due to the impending release of 'Windows'95.'"*

* * *

FTP continued the "drumbeat" of misleading positive statements, according to plaintiffs, when Zirkle, speaking in an interview published in the November 27–December 3, 1995 issue of Mass High Tech *said that "the networking business (TCP/IP) is a cash cow that is feeding the development of other businesses, which are feeding back new technology that makes the core business even better." In December 1995, two other securities firms issued positive reports on FTP; after these statements, FTP's stock rose.*

Finally, the complaint alleges, the "truth [began] to emerge" on January 4, 1996, when FTP announced that its earnings for the fourth fiscal quarter of 1995 would be less than the same period in 1994. FTP stated that this decline reflected, in part, the company's investment in its New Ventures Business Unit, but, nonetheless, the company's stock fell $13.375 per share to close at $11.875 per share (a one-day decline of 52%). Plaintiffs emphasize that this decline represented a $27 drop in market value (an approximately 70% decrease) from a Class Period high of $38.875 per share.

Opinion by Lynch

* * *

We review the dismissal of plaintiffs' complaint de novo, giving plaintiffs the benefit of all reasonable inferences, but holding plaintiffs to the standard of showing a strong inference of scienter. We think the claims are either insufficiently particularized or, where particularized, do not permit a strong inference of scienter.

At the heart of plaintiffs' case is the allegation that defendants consistently overstated the earnings of the company by improperly booking as revenue (and inadequately reserving) "sales" that were actually contingent transactions. This was improper, plaintiffs say, under generally accepted accounting principles ("GAAP"), specifically Statement of Financial Accounting Standards No. 48 ("FAS 48"). Plaintiffs claim that the sales were contingent because there were unlimited return rights. Plaintiffs say that they have evidence both tending directly to show conscious wrongdoing on the part of defendants and circumstantial evidence from which such wrongdoing may be inferred, including that the defendants had both motive and opportunity.

* * *

1. The "White-Out" Allegations and the Rule 56(f) Motion

The "white-out" allegations claimed that FTP personnel "whited out" (in a manner undetectable to company auditors) the customers' additions to standard purchase orders; those additions made orders contingent on the customers' unlimited right to return the goods to FTP. The white-out allegations were powerful, as the district court recognized in initially denying the motion to dismiss. If adequately supported, claims that management deliberately altered company records to hide material information from company auditors could well create strong inferences of scienter. But, as the district court correctly ruled on summary judgment, plaintiffs could not produce admissible evidence to support the white-out allegations, and so we disregard these allegations.

2. The Warehousing Allegations

The warehousing allegations remain. In essence, the complaint asserts that at some time before the Class Period, the company made a phony sale or sales and caused to be booked as goods sold certain product that was shipped to a warehouse and not to customers; the company then recognized the revenue from such phony sales. After a period, the product was sent back from the warehouse as "returned" goods. The allegations state that Robert Casa, an employee who refused to sign for the "returned" product and complained about the practice, was fired. If true, such practices by a company are very serious.

The complaint is deficient in not identifying when this took place. The complaint is specific only in saying this occurred before the Class Period. The complaint alleges, on information and belief, that the practice continued into the Class Period but provides no specifics about why the practice is thought to have occurred during the Class Period or why it caused harm to plaintiffs. The defendants say the temporal lag means the allegations are irrelevant and should be disregarded. The allegations are not irrelevant—evidence of past practice may indeed be probative of present practice. But there is scant else from which to infer that this was the company's practice at any pertinent time, and the allegations are not enough to support a strong inference of scienter.

* * *

The district court correctly refused to dismiss the complaint originally and was well within its discretion in limiting the discovery it afforded. The difficult and different balance the Act now requires—testing allegations before little or no discovery, but holding plaintiffs to a strong inference of scienter standard—has been honored in this case. Plaintiffs did not have enough weight on their side of the balance to meet the requirements of the Act, and so we affirm the dismissal. Costs to appellants.

Decision and Outcome

Relying on the PLSRA, the court affirmed the dismissal of this case because the plaintiffs did not specifically state alleged facts that showed fraud or harmed the plaintiffs. In light of the Enron debacle, it would be interesting if the court of appeals would rule the same way. Note that the complaint alleges inflated revenue projects, which figured prominently in the allegations of fraud against Enron executives.

Questions for Analysis

1. Why were the "white-out" allegations not sufficient to prove that the defendants knowingly made false statements? Why did the court dismiss the "white-out" allegations?

2. Why were the warehouse allegations, that the defendant was moving software in and out of its warehouse and recording the transfers as sales, not sufficient to be considered fraud if proved in court? Why were these allegations not particular enough?

The Securities Litigation Uniform Standards Act of 1998

The PSLRA was a congressional response to a clearly perceived abuse, that corporations were being sued for not owning perfectly functioning crystal balls. After the passage of the PSLRA, some attorneys pursued corporations under state "blue sky" laws and Congress responded to this development with the Securities Litigation Uniform Standards Act of 1998.[10] This act amended the 1934 Securities Exchange Act to prevent a private party from initiating a class action suit based on the statutory or common law of any state that prohibits a misrepresentation or omission of a material fact or any manipulative device or contrivance concerning the purchase or sale of a security. The effect of this legislation was to preempt class action lawsuits, based on state law, for alleged fraud by firms whose securities were traded on national exchanges.

Sarbanes-Oxley Act, 2002

The Enron debacle inspired calls for reform and Congress responded with the Sarbanes-Oxley Act, which requires CEOs and CFOs (chief financial officers) to personally attest to the accuracy of annual reports issued by the companies they represent under a possible penalty of 20 years in prison for willful violations.[11] CEOs and CFOs are also subject to fines of up to $5 million for willful violations of the act. As to fostering independence for accounting firms, the Sarbanes-Oxley Act calls for corporations subject to Section 12 of the 1934 Act to establish an independent audit board of review for financial statements issued

---

[10] Pub. L. No. 105-353, 112 Stat. 3227, codified at 15 U.S.C. § 77p(b).

[11] Pub. L. No. 107-204, 116 Stat. 745 (2002).

Ethical Challenges   Aren't These Conflicts of Interest Obvious?

In the aftermath of the Enron declaration of bank-ruptcy, politicians and others are looking for scape-goats and high on the list is Arthur Andersen, the accounting firm that audited the books of Enron. Ide-ally, audits by "independent" accounting firms are supposed to apprise investors as to the financial health of companies through required 10K reports, often called annual reports. The independence of the accounting firm performing the audit becomes an issue when, as in the case of Arthur Andersen, the same accounting firm performing the audit also bills the firm for consulting services to the tune of over $100 million. The theory is that investors are to be in-formed by the audits of a firm's finances by an inde-pendent audit, but that independence is in question when the accounting firm performing the audit could lose millions in consulting fees.

by corporations. In addition, Sarbanes-Oxley prohibits registered certified public account-ing firms from performing nonauditing services for the firms for whom they provide annual report production with a few exceptions. This prohibition is clearly aimed at a fundamen-tal conflict of interest that may have allowed the misrepresentations endemic at Enron to avoid being detected and revealed.

REGULATION OF INVESTMENT COMPANIES AND ADVISORS

The Investment Company Act of 1940

The SEC has power to regulate investment companies as a result of the Investment Com-pany Act of 1940.[12] The most common form of investment company is one that manages mutual funds. A mutual fund investment company hires managers to purchase and sell for (manage) a large portfolio of securities on behalf of small and large shareholders. Such companies are subject to SEC regulation under the 1940 Act. There have been several amendments to the Investment Company Act of 1940, most prominently in 1970 and 1975, with passage of the Securities Act Amendments. By regulatory definition, an investment company is one that (1) engages primarily in the business of investing, reinvesting, and trading of securities or (2) is engaged in such business and has more than 40 percent of its assets in the form of investment securities.

Investment companies must be registered with the SEC and must file annual reports. Dividends issued to mutual fund shareholders must be paid only from accumulated, undis-tributed net income (not from the proceeds of additional sales of mutual fund shares). Purchases of securities by investment companies cannot be on margin (borrowed funds). Mutual funds are not allowed to sell short, which is a sale of securities not already owned for later delivery. Each of these practices is considered "high risk" so, by prohibiting these practices, the SEC seeks to limit the risk borne by mutual fund shareholders.

Investment Advisors Act of 1940

The SEC also has power to regulate investment advisors by virtue of the Investment Advisors Act of 1940.[13] According to Section 202(a)(11) of this act, an investment advisor is ". . . any person who, for compensation, engages in the business of advising others, either

[12] Codified at 15 U.S.C. § 80a-1 *et seq.*
[13] Codified at 15 U.S.C. § 80b-1 *et seq.*

directly or through publications or writings, as to the value of securities or as to the advisability of investing in, purchasing, or selling securities, or who, for compensation and as part of a regular business, issues or promulgates analyses or reports concerning securities . . ." If a person is deemed by the SEC to be an investment advisor, that person is subject to fines and disgorgement of profits in the event of fraudulent advising. Generally, investment advisors are required to register with the SEC. With registration records, if an investment advisor has a history of fraud claims, the SEC can refuse registration. Nonregistered investment advisors cannot render advice on purchases or sales of securities and cannot issue analyses or reports concerning securities. On the Internet, there are many websites and investment advisors who recommend purchases and/or sales of securities. The SEC has already taken action against many such websites and stock "gurus" (see the "Tokyo Joe" case discussed later in the chapter).

STATE SECURITIES LAWS

A major reason for federal securities laws was the apparent inadequacy of state securities laws. State laws were ineffective because out-of-state firms could engage in fraud against in-state residents and often escape jurisdiction under state securities laws. Even so, state securities laws continue to be important, particularly for smaller companies that qualify for exemptions from federal laws. Just because a transaction is exempt from federal securities laws does not mean that the transaction is exempt from state laws. Not surprisingly, skilled securities attorneys are knowledgeable about state as well as federal securities laws.

All states have their own securities (blue sky) laws and there is considerable variation from state to state. State laws typically demand disclosures similar to those required at the federal level and also outlaw fraud in the purchase or sale of securities along the lines of Section 10(b) of the 1934 Act. Unlike the SEC, which generally insists on full disclosure but does not evaluate the merits of securities offerings, some states reserve the right to intervene and prevent the sale of securities that state officials deem too risky. So all states require disclosure of the risks of investing in intrastate securities and some states also allow regulators to evaluate the merits of investments offered and foreclose deals that state officials believe have too slim a chance of becoming profitable.

EFFECTS OF THE INTERNET ON SECURITIES LAW

As with other areas of regulatory law, the Internet has had two effects in the securities industry. In broad terms, the Internet (1) has affected commercial practice and (2) has caused Congress and the SEC to change existing regulation. The first effect is not difficult to observe and is the subject of numerous economic and financial studies. The second effect appears as part of the public record and is the focus of the discussion below.

EDGAR
A creation of the SEC. The acronym stands for Electronic Database Gathering, Analysis, and Retrieval. EDGAR enables firms to post prospectuses online and investors to access those prospectuses.

Prior to the Internet era, large investing entities had decided advantages over small investors based on their superior access to relevant information. With the Internet, information that was previously filed with the SEC, but not widely available, has now become easily accessible as a result of **EDGAR,** an SEC-created corporate database (EDGAR stands for Electronic Database Gathering, Analysis, and Retrieval). Using EDGAR, investors and potential investors can access prospectuses of firms that are trying to raise money through public offerings. Firm data, such as that contained in quarterly and annual reports for firms that are subject to Section 12 of the 1934 Act, are also available at EDGAR. In addition, there are a number of private websites that offer potentially valuable information to investors. Not only has the Internet created a more level playing field between large and small investors, but it also has given smaller firms more access to capital when, previously, printing out large amounts of prospectuses and paying middlemen was a barrier to the capital-raising activities of smaller firms.

National Securities Markets Improvement Act of 1996

In 1996, Congress passed the National Securities Markets Improvement Act (NSMIA).[14] Section 510(a) of the act directed the SEC to conduct a study of the new Internet technology available to investors. In the SEC report to Congress, listed among the changes that the Internet has brought to securities transactions are the observations that

- Most domestic companies now make use of EDGAR for their required filings to the SEC, both with respect to public offerings and for their quarterly and annual reports.
- Electronic trading in secondary markets is becoming the norm.
- Information that, previously, was generally available only to institutional investors has now become accessible to small investors.

As a result of the NSMIA, the SEC undertook major studies of the effects of the Internet on investing in securities (see the "Cyberlaw Developments" box).

Corporate Internet Websites

Corporate Internet websites allow a firm to advertise its products and discuss events that are important to the firm in a public forum. Since the SEC requires quarterly and annual reports, some firms have posted the financial statements required by the SEC on their websites. In addition, firms have posted statements and speeches by corporate leaders. It is sometimes difficult for a CEO or other top officer in a corporation to be downbeat about the prospects of the company they work for. However, just as excessively optimistic press conferences about the future prospects of a company have generated lawsuits by shareholders when those rosy projections did not pan out, the same could occur when optimistic statements appear on corporate websites. In complying with the PSLRA, a firm should apply the same careful scrutiny as discussed earlier, *identifying forward statements as just that* and providing *appropriate disclaimers* indicating that any projections discussed are just that, and may not be realized.

Online Offerings

The Internet offers savings to investors by eliminating many layers of middlemen. In the past, underwriters marketed IPOs to stock dealers, who in turn contacted stockbrokers who had investing clients. With the Internet and online access to prospectuses, any and all of the following can be eliminated: underwriters, stock dealers, and stockbrokers. Of course, investors who use their own judgment instead of relying on stock market professionals may be assuming more risk. With the Internet, day-trading investors can order securities as soon as the "waiting" period (20 days from registration with the SEC) expires. Sometimes called ISOs (Internet securities offerings) or DPOs (direct public offerings), it has been estimated that public offerings using the Internet and thus eliminating middlemen can yield 10 to 15 percent more capital actually received by the firm trying to raise money relative to traditional, paper-based offerings.

Public Offerings and Electronic Distribution

As discussed above, firms trying to raise money using *public offerings* have an obligation to ensure that investors obtain a prospectus before paying money for the securities. Since

---

[14] Pub. L. No. 104-290, 110 Stat. 3416.

Cyberlaw **Developments** SEC Studies Online Trading and Makes Recommendations

OFFICE OF COMPLIANCE INSPECTIONS AND EXAMINATIONS: EXAMINATIONS OF BROKER-DEALERS OFFERING ONLINE TRADING: SUMMARY OF FINDINGS AND RECOMMENDATIONS

JANUARY 25, 2001

Introduction

Given the growth and popularity of online trading, the staff of the Securities and Exchange Commission's ("SEC") Office of Compliance Inspections and Examinations ("Staff") initiated a series of examinations of registered broker-dealers providing customers with the ability to place trades through the Internet ("online trading"). In these examinations, the Staff reviewed: (1) the information that firms provide to customers about trading and making investment decisions; (2) advertising; (3) the execution of customers' transactions; (4) capacity for handling customer trading volumes; (5) security measures; and (6) supervision of employees' use of the Internet.

We believe that by sharing the Staff's general findings and observations from these examinations, we can more broadly heighten awareness of these issues by broker-dealers as they evaluate their own online trading systems. We are publishing this summary to highlight issues in this area and to assist broker-dealers in evaluating their online trading systems.

In summary, based on the examinations, the Staff recommends that broker-dealers offering online trading consider the following issues:

- the information provided to customers online about how orders are executed, how margin works, and the possibility of systems' delays;
- the objectivity of their advertising;
- procedures for ensuring that customers receive best execution;
- procedures for ensuring adequate operational capability to handle customer trading volume;
- security measures to protect customer privacy and funds; and
- procedures to supervise employees' use of Internet communications.

This report describes findings and recommendations in each of these areas.

Source: http://www.sec.gov/news/studies/online.htm, January 25, 2001.

1995, the SEC has accepted *electronic delivery of prospectuses*. To comply with SEC regulations, a firm trying to raise money in an online public offering must

- *Provide notice* that prospectuses are available online—the notice must be through the U.S. mail or by e-mail.
- Make *access to the prospectus relatively easy*.
- *Must provide evidence of delivery* of the required information. If e-mail is used, there must be evidence that the information was actually received in the form of a return receipt.

Firms trying to use the Internet have the option to provide notice that they are making a public offering at their website and of complying with the prospectus delivery requirement by *mailing a CD-ROM*. With CD-ROMs, issuers can make use of multimedia, such as audio and video, that are not available in paper formats. The SEC's EDGAR system will not accept multimedia presentations, but the SEC does allow CD-ROMs to function as a prospectus if there is an "equivalent" disclosure in the paper format of the prospectus. If audio is used in the CD-ROM, then a transcript of the audio portion must be included in the paper format. For visual images, of course, issuers may have to relearn the maxim that "a picture is worth a thousand words."

Electronic Road Shows

electronic road shows
Electronic selling materials that firms provide, in addition to prospectuses, used during the waiting period between the filing of the registration statement and when securities can be sold.

As discussed above, issuers are allowed to put on **electronic road shows,** which are oral presentations, to potential investors during the period of time after prospectuses have been delivered but before the registration statements to the SEC are effective. Road shows are a means of selling securities that are part of the public offering and a means of answering questions potential investors might have about the issuer. Generally, the attendees at these road shows are managers of mutual funds who have tremendous assets to devote to the offering that they find promising. As technology has advanced, the Internet has been used to simultaneously webcast a presentation at several locations around the country. The term *road show* is a holdover from the time when management of the issuer would actually meet with potential investors. With the Internet, management of the issuer no longer needs to "hit the road." It should be noted that even before webcasting on the Internet, closed circuit road show presentations were allowed by the SEC. As with paper records and overland presentations, all materials provided in electronic road shows are subject to Section 12(2) of the 1933 Act, making the firm liable for material misrepresentations or omissions.

Other Uses of the Internet to Sell Securities

When a firm's registration statement is effective (the waiting period is over), issuers and their representatives, such as underwriters, are allowed to use promotional literature to encourage sales, but only if prospectuses accompany that literature. The Internet, of course, can be used not only for electronic road shows during the waiting period, but also after the waiting period to show positive features of the issuer, its management, and its future prospects. The SEC requires that all promotional material provided after the effective period to be accompanied by a prospectus. So an important question is, how can an issuer make use of the Internet to promote the public offering and still comply with the prospectus delivery requirement? The SEC has ruled that if there is a link to a prospectus on the Web pages that are promoting securities being offered for sale, the prospectus delivery requirement is satisfied.

Additional Internet Opportunities

Once it was determined that a *single firm* could use the Internet to raise capital through the sale of securities, websites appeared that would aggregate securities offerings from several websites. So, websites now offer securities from several issuers who may be at several stages of capital fund-raising as well. These sites also facilitate trades of securities, with all of theses activities performed electronically over the Internet. Many of the securities bought and sold through Internet websites are for firms not listed on major stock exchanges. Such securities, historically, have been quite illiquid—difficult to trade. Issuer-based bulletin boards quickly evolved into virtual stock markets in cyberspace. With sizeable volumes of transactions in such securities occurring in cyberspace through securities-dealing websites, the SEC has faced novel situations, forcing it to scramble to provide appropriate regulations (see discussion below).

Private Offerings

At first glance, the Internet and "private offerings" do not seem to go hand in hand. Anything accessible on the Internet is accessible worldwide and, thus, does not seem to be

International Perspective Offshore Offerings

Some knowledgeable observers hold the opinion that one disadvantage of the Internet is its ability to facilitate escapes from regulation, including SEC regulation. Others hold just the opposite view. In the past, offshore offerings of securities to U.S. citizens were much less prevalent, but the Internet dramatically increases visibility of offshore offerings of securities. In the United States, of course, all offerings of securities must go through the registration process with the SEC or qualify for an exemption. For offshore offerings of securities, the immediate legal issue is whether the SEC has jurisdiction.

Effective January 1, 1999, Internet websites can make available off-shore offerings of securities as long as there is compliance with the safe harbor provisions of Regulation S, Offshore Offers and Sales.[1] The idea, of course, is to offer securities offshore without incurring the large expenses associated with registering these securities with the SEC. The new regulations issued by the SEC, effective January 1, 1999, change previous rules that required registration of offshore offerings that were "made available" to U.S. investors. Since everything on the Internet is potentially available to anyone with an Internet connection, the SEC had to change its rules with respect to Internet offerings from offshore websites. Under the new regulations, an issuer can avoid SEC regulations if solicitation and other communications are not "targeted at the United States." This means that the website cannot solicit U.S. investors through e-mails or other communications.

DOMESTIC U.S. FIRMS OFFERING OFFSHORE SECURITIES FOR SALE

A distinction is made between U.S. companies offering offshore opportunities to purchase securities and foreign companies doing the same thing. For U.S. companies seeking to avoid SEC registration requirements for offshore public offerings of securities, the U.S. companies must institute a password-protection system that unlocks access to the securities only after the applicants demonstrate that they are not U.S. citizens. For third-party websites—websites that sell offshore securities on behalf of the issuer—the same password-protection system must be in place. Typically, the third-party website would maintain a hyperlink to the issuer's website, but access to that hyperlink must be blocked until the potential investor provides proof that he or she is not a U.S. citizen.

FOREIGN FIRMS OFFERING OFFSHORE SECURITIES FOR SALE

For foreign firms that provide offshore offerings of securities, SEC regulations require that the firm place a prominent disclaimer on the website that clearly states that this offering is directed toward countries other than the United States. In addition, the website should indicate what countries or regions are the target of these public offerings of securities. Issuers also are required to make best efforts to determine the residence of investors and guard against U.S. investors purchasing securities that have not been registered with the SEC. It is not really clear what power the SEC has over foreign companies that do not follow SEC disclaimer regulations and do not register the offshore offerings with the SEC.

[1] 17 C.F.R. §§ 230 and 249.

"private." However, through the use of passwords, there are ways to constrain accessibility of securities offered in a private offering on the Internet so that security sales in a private offering can be limited to those who meet legal requirements. In most cases, access to private offerings is password-limited to predetermined unaccredited investors so that the issuer can comply with either Rule 505 or 506.

Regulation of Securities in Cyberspace?

As has the FTC, the SEC has discovered plenty of instances of fraud on the Internet. Many of the "investment opportunities" offered on the Internet are, technically, securities within the meaning of the *Howey* test and are not registered with the SEC. Therefore, websites offering such investment opportunities are selling unregistered securities. Many other websites are guilty of making fraudulent offers in which firm assets and liabilities are misrepresented, concealing the identity of the offeror (often because of previous convictions for securities fraud), or engaging in other illegalities such as offering pyramid scheme investments. Many of these websites have short lives, but when they are shut down, they often reemerge under another name in a matter of days.

SEC Office of Internet Enforcement

The problem of Internet fraud involving securities is sufficiently widespread that the SEC opened an Office of Internet Enforcement (OIE) in 1998. As of January 2003, the SEC has brought more than 200 Internet-related enforcement actions, which have been categorized by the SEC as "touting of publicly-traded companies," "the sale of bogus investment opportunities," and "the perpetuation of 'pump and dump' stock schemes."

Typical of SEC Internet actions was the securities fraud action that the SEC took against "Tokyo Joe." Tokyo Joe's real name is Yun Soo Oh Park. Mr. Park was an Internet stock picker who made stock purchase recommendations to his clients of stock that he had previously purchased in hopes that his recommendations would inspire his "clients" to *pump* up the promoted stocks' prices so that he could *dump* them on the market at a profit. The SEC has charged Mr. Park with violating the Investment Advisors Act of 1940 and the Securities Exchange Act of 1934, contending that the advice Park dispensed was fraudulent because he failed to disclose that he owned the stocks that he was recommending for purchase by his clients.

The OIE website (http://www. sec.gov/divisions/enforce/internetenforce.htm) identifies its duties as including, among others,

- Identifying areas of surveillance.
- Formulating investigative procedures.
- Providing strategic and legal guidance to SEC Enforcement staff.
- Conducting Internet investigations and prosecutions.

Among other categories, the OIE has taken legal action against websites that

- Make false promises of imminent IPOs (initial public offerings).
- Provide baseless financial projections.
- Display false track records and résumés.
- Provide analyst coverage that is "bought and paid for."
- Make inflated performance claims and provide fake testimonials.

Viewed broadly, the Internet has provided enhanced information access and efficiencies for many investors, but it also has enabled parties willing to engage in fraud to enjoy expanded access to potential investors. The SEC has expanded its efforts to counter securities fraud on the Internet by establishing the Office of Internet Enforcement, which has found that there are plenty of fraudulent statements appearing on the Internet in violation of SEC rules.

Summary

The Stock Market Crash in 1929 and Inability of States to Effectively Regulate Securities

- Federal regulation of securities markets is due largely to the inability of states to regulate fraud from out-of-state sources. Important legislation was adopted after the Stock Market Crash of 1929 and the country's slide into deep depression.

- Securities regulation is divided between the 1933 Act, which regulates sales of securities by original issuers, and the 1934 Act, which created the Securities and Exchange Commission (SEC) and regulates the after-market for securities transactions.

- The U.S. Supreme Court, in defining a security, contends that it requires an investment of money in a common enterprise where profits are realized solely due to the efforts of third parties. In more recent cases, lower federal courts have changed the word "solely" to "primarily" or "significantly."

Caused the Public to Demand more Effective Regulation Leading to Creation of the Securities and Exchange Commission	• Other court definitions of a security make use of the family resemblance test, which takes into account the motivations and expectations of investors and issuers, the plan of distribution of profits, and whether the transaction is regulated by other laws. • If an instrument or contract is a security, then it is subject to SEC regulation. Conversely, if an instrument is not a security, then the SEC has no authority to regulate.
Registration of Securities with the SEC Is Required before They Can Be Legally Sold; Investors Must Be Given a Prospectus That Apprises Them of the Risks They Incur by Investing	• It is illegal to sell an unregistered security in the United States unless the security qualifies for some type of exemption. • If the piece of paper sold is deemed to represent a security, then its sale to investors must be accompanied by a registration statement that is filed with the SEC. • The registration statement is intended to provide full disclosure to the SEC and investors of the risks involved in owning the security. Among the disclosures required in the registration statement are details of how the proceeds of the sales to investors are to be used, a description of the business of the issuer, an audited financial statement attested to by a certified public accountant, and discussion of particular characteristics of the security. • Before a security can be sold to the public, the issuer must ensure that investors are given a prospectus, which contains a summary of the information in the registration statement.
Signers of Registration Statements Are Liable for Material Misstatements or Omissions; Defenses Available to Signers Include Due Diligence; Those Who Are Not "Experts" Are Entitled to Rely on What Is Provided in the Expertise Portions of the Registration Statement	• Section 11 of the 1933 Act makes all signers of a registration statement liable if it contains a material misstatement or omission. Section 11 does not require a showing that the signers of the registration statement knew that the registration statement contained materially false statements or omissions. • Each signer of the registration statement is liable if there is a material misstatement or omission, unless he or she has a valid defense. The liability of signers is joint and several. • An investor is entitled to rescind a purchase of a security if there is a violation of Section 11. • Although a number of defenses are potentially available to those liable for violations of Section 11 of the 1933 Act, the due diligence defense is the most prominent. To qualify for the due diligence defense, a signer of a registration statement must have conducted an independent investigation of the statements contained in the registration document and not detected the error, even though the signer was duly diligent in his or her investigation. • Signers of registration statements are entitled to rely upon the expertise portions of the registration statement that are composed by accountants and securities attorneys and still retain their right to claim the due diligence defense. • Section 12(2) of the 1933 Act provides remedies for misleading oral or written communications in connection with the sale of a security in a public offering. Section 12(2) allows investors to sue for misleading statements made by the issuer that were not contained in the registration statement or prospectus.
A Number of Securities and Securities Transactions Are Exempt from Fully Complying with SEC Requirements	• The high cost of complying with SEC regulatory requirements for a public offering causes firms trying to raise small amounts of money to seek an exemption from the registration requirements of the 1933 Act. • A number of securities are exempt from registration requirements, including securities with maturity dates of less than nine months, securities offered by charities or by savings and loan companies, those offered by governments and insurance companies, and those subject to a number of other exceptions. • The 1933 Act and the SEC also have defined a number of exempt transactions that enable smaller companies to raise money through securities markets in ways other than public offerings.

<table>
<tr>
<td>

The SEC Has Created a Number of Safe Harbors for Small and Medium-Sized Firms to Raise Money in the Capital Markets without Fully Complying with the Registration Requirements of a Public Offering; These Exempt Transactions Require Firms to Prevent quick Resales

</td>
<td>

- Under Regulation D, there are several ways of raising modest amounts of money with minimal regulatory scrutiny.
- Under Rule 504, companies can raise up to $1 million in a 12-month period with much reduced disclosure requirements.
- Rule 505 allows small to medium-sized companies to raise up to $5 million in a 12-month period if they limit the number of unaccredited investors to no more than 35 and comply with other restrictions on advertising and resales.
- Accredited investors include banks and other financial institutions, plus individuals whose net worth exceeds $1 million or whose annual income is in excess of $200,000.
- Rule 506 provides a safe harbor for firms seeking to qualify for Section 4(2) of the 1933 Act. A firm meets the requirements of Rule 506 if it sells to no more than 35 investors and makes sure that each nonaccredited investor has sufficient knowledge and experience in financial and business matters to make him or her capable of evaluating the merits and risks of the prospective investment.
- Securities sold pursuant to Regulation D generally must not be resold for periods of up to two years so that purchasers are truly investors and not just disguised stock brokers.

</td>
</tr>
<tr>
<td>

Firms That Reach a Certain Size, with Over 500 Equity Owners, Must Publicly Report Their Financial Condition

</td>
<td>

- Under Section 12 of the 1934 Act, an issuer of securities is required to register with the SEC if the firm has total assets in excess of $5 million, if it is listed on a national stock exchange, or if it has more than 500 equity owners.
- Section 12 firms are required to issue 10Q, 10K, and 8K reports, which are quarterly and annual reports and reports of unusual events.

</td>
</tr>
<tr>
<td>

Section 10(b) Is a Broad Antifraud Provision of the 1934 Act That Has Been Directed Toward Insider Trading, Which Occurs when Corporate Insiders and Tippees Trade while in Possession of Information That Is Not Public; Also, Short-Swing Profits Are Illegal

</td>
<td>

- Section 10(b) is a broad antifraud provision of the 1934 Act. A violation of Section 10(b) requires a showing that the defendant acted intentionally and was not simply negligent.
- Firms have been prosecuted for violations of Section 10(b) based on statements made at press conferences that turned out to be too optimistic about a firm's future prospects.
- Insider trading is illegal because of Section 10(b) of the 1934 Act. Insider trading occurs when a corporate insider buys or sells securities while in possession of material insider information or provides such information to a tippee who buys or sells securities.
- Corporate insiders include corporate directors, officers, and large shareholders as well as key employees.
- Tippees are persons who receive material inside information from corporate insiders or others, such as attorneys, accountants, consultants, or reporters, who breach their fiduciary duties to their employers.
- Insider information is material if it would affect the decisions made by a reasonably prudent investor.
- Section 16(b) prohibits officers, directors, or greater-than-10-percent shareholders from making short-swing profits, which are profits gained from purchases and sales or sales and purchases of the same security within a six-month period. There is no requirement to show that the defendant made use of insider information.

</td>
</tr>
<tr>
<td>

During the 1980s, Securities Laws Were Reformed to

</td>
<td>

- In a successful shareholder derivative suit, damages are awarded to the corporation, but the shareholders initiating the suit are entitled to recover reasonable attorney fees.
- During the 1980s, Congress strengthened the sanctions against insider trading with passage of the Insider Trading Sanctions Act of 1984 and the Insider Trading and Securities Fraud Enforcement Act of 1988.

</td>
</tr>
</table>

<table>
<tr><td>

Toughen Sanctions against Insider Trading; in the 1990s, Corporate Officers Were Insulated from Liability as Long as Cautionary Language Was Used

</td><td>

- The Private Securities Litigation Reform Act of 1995 allows firms to make forward-looking statements, as long as those statements are accompanied with meaningful cautionary language that points out with specificity risks that may make the forward statements inaccurate.
- The Securities Litigation Uniform Standards Act of 1998 preempts attorneys from filing class action lawsuits against firms based on state securities laws for misrepresentation of a material fact or omission in connection with the purchase or sale of a security.
- The Sarbanes-Oxley Act of 2002 makes CEOs and CFOs criminally liable for false statements included in annual reports and prohibits accounting firms that prepare auditing statements from performing other duties for their clients.

</td></tr>
<tr><td>

The Internet Has Created New Opportunities to Communicate Information and the SEC Is Increasingly Making Use of the Internet to Ensure That Investors Are Fully Informed

</td><td>

- Investment companies are regulated by the Investment Company Act of 1940, which was significantly amended in 1970 and 1975. The Investment Advisor Act of 1940 regulates those who value, recommend, or analyze securities.
- State securities laws continue to be relevant to issuers, especially for smaller offerings that are not registered with the SEC. Most states not only require full disclosure but also maintain the right to block sales of securities that state authorities think are too risky.
- The National Securities Markets Improvement Act, passed in 1996, envisions electronic trading in secondary markets becoming the norm, with firms increasingly relying on online prospectuses provided through the Electronic Database Gathering, Analysis, and Retrieval (EDGAR) system created by the SEC.
- Online offerings allow investors to eliminate many layers of intermediaries.
- EDGAR is increasingly used to deliver prospectuses.
- Virtual stock markets are developing in cyberspace and are making previously illiquid securities much more tradable.
- The SEC provided safe harbor provisions for offshore offerings of securities in 1999 with Regulation S, Offshore Offers and Sales.
- To deal with the problem of Internet fraud in the sale of securities, in 1998 the SEC opened the Office of Internet Enforcement.

</td></tr>
</table>

Key Terms

accredited investors, *654*
blue sky, *647*
bonds, *647*
due diligence defense, *652*
EDGAR, *667*
electronic road shows, *670*
exempt transactions, *653*
insider trading, *656*

insiders, *657*
material misstatements or omissions, *650*
misappropriators, *660*
private placement, *654*
prospectus, *650*
registration statement, *650*
safe harbors, *653*

securities, *647*
short-swing profits, *661*
stocks, *647*
tippees, *656*
unaccredited investors, *654*
underwriters, *651*

Questions for Review and Analysis

1. Only securities—stocks and bonds—are subject to SEC regulation. Distinguish between stocks and bonds, which are securities, and loans, commodity contracts, and other transactions that do not involve securities.

2. Liability for selling securities to the public is based on material misstatements or omissions in a firm's registration statement and prospectuses. Develop several examples of such misstatements or omissions.

3. Small and medium-sized firms can raise money in capital markets by qualifying for exempt transactions. Look at the fundraising objectives of a firm, determine the right exemption for that firm,

and discuss the areas of vulnerability in terms of ensuring that investors receive appropriate information.

4. It is illegal for a corporate insider to trade securities based on material inside information (not available to the public). Besides corporate insiders, list others, such as tippees, who may be liable for insider trading.

5. The Internet offers the potential for expanded opportunities for communicating with potential investors and for the SEC to inform sellers of securities about the legal constraints imposed by securities laws. Go to the SEC website and find five kinds of information that are readily available to you only because of the Internet.

If You Really Understood This Chapter, You Should Be Able to Provide Informed Commentary on the Following:

1. **Are Stock Options Securities?** In 1962, the well-known news magazine *U.S. News and World Report* was reorganized to provide employees of the company with shares in its ownership and profits. Accordingly, the articles of incorporation authorized the issuance of class A and common stock, each having full and equal voting rights. The employees could not sell or transfer their interests during their employment and, upon termination, were required to offer them to the company at values established through mutual agreement or by outside appraisers. This class action suit is brought against *U.S. News & World Report* magazine (Company) by a group of its former employees who terminated their employment during the period from 1974 through 1981. The litigation was triggered by the sale, in October 1984, of *U.S. News* to real estate magnate and developer Mortimer Zuckerman for approximately $176 million. Plaintiffs complain that the stock of the Company, which constituted the corpus of the employee profit-sharing plan, was wrongfully and grossly undervalued for a number of years prior to the sale and that employees, who retired during the designated class period, are owed unpaid benefits and entitled to damages under various legal theories. At issue in this case is whether stock options given to employees are "an investment of money" as addressed in the *Howey* case. [*Charles S. Foltz v. U.S. News & World Report, Inc.,* 627 F.Supp. 1143 (D.D.C. 1986).]

2. **Material Insider Information.** The defendants are members of the board of directors of Basic Inc., a publicly traded firm. The plaintiffs are shareholders who sold their stock in 1977 at less than $46 per share after Basic made public statements that it was not engaged in negotiations with another company to be acquired. In fact, at the time of the denial, Basic was engaged in merger negotiations. The plaintiffs did not allege that the defendants purchased their stock and resold it at a profit or even that the defendants made a profit selling its own stock shortly before the merger. Instead, the plaintiffs claim the defendants are liable because, under Section 10(b) of the 1934 Act, the defendants committed fraud by releasing misleading statements. What do you think? Do corporate executives have an obligation to reveal whenever merger negotiations are taking place? When, within such negotiations, does the probability of a merger become sufficiently high that the fact of negotiations becomes a material fact? What do you think will happen to stock prices of the target firm if merger negotiations are revealed? Can a corporation refuse to do anything, and neither confirm nor deny that merger negotiations are taking place? [*Basic Incorporated v. Max L. Levinson,* 485 U.S. 224 (1988).]

3. **Back to Determining State of Mind: The Private Securities Litigation Reform Act (PSLRA).** It has been alleged that, prior to the passage of the PSLRA, attorneys representing class action shareholders would sue corporate management anytime management made a statement about future events that turned out not to be true. The passage of PSLRA requires,

> In any private action arising under this chapter in which the plaintiff may recover money damages only on proof that the defendant acted with a particular state of mind, the complaint shall, with respect to each act or omission alleged to violate this chapter, state with particularity facts giving rise to a strong inference that the defendant acted with the required state of mind.

In light of the Enron and Worldcom scandals, former President Clinton's veto of the PSLRA looks prescient, and there have been several calls for repeal of the PSLRA. A typical post-PSLRA action occurred after Deanna Brody filed a securities fraud class action in the U.S. District Court for the Northern District of California alleging that Silicon Graphics, Inc. (SGI) and six of its top officers made a series of misleading statements to inflate the value of SGI's stock while they engaged in "massive" insider trading. Brody's case was dismissed because she could not show that, at the time the misleading statements were made, the defendants knew the statements were false or had a reckless disregard for the truth. What do you think? Should shareholders alleging an issuance of misleading information have to show not only that corporate management made false statements but also that management knew the statements were false or had a reckless disregard for the truth at the time the statements were made? [*Deanna Brody et al. v. Edward McCraken, et al.,* 183 F.3d 970 (9th Cir. 1999).]

4. **Private Placements and Regulation D.** Imagine you have a friend getting a degree in engineering or biology, who is very creative and willing to work very hard, but who knows virtually nothing about business. You graduate with a degree in business administration and get a job as a management trainee for a large corporation. Out of the blue, your friend calls you and says that he has enjoyed a breakthrough and has invented something that is as revolutionary as the personal computer. Knowing your friend, you try to calm him down and point out business realities. First, you point out that trying to sell ideas is a nonstarter; he may as well give away the idea for free, but if the idea was fleshed out in the form of a patent or copyright, then maybe he has something to work with. In startup situations it is common for new firms to try to raise money in three stages: Stage 1 = $100,000 to $1,000,000; Stage 2 = $1,000,000 to $5,000,000; and, finally, Stage 3 = IPO (initial public offering), where the objective is to raise as much money as possible. Explain to your friend how to raise this kind of money while still complying with the securities laws.

5. **Regulation of Broker Dealers.** The National Association of Securities Dealers (NASD) regulates its members. Without a license, brokers/dealers cannot trade stock. For years broker/dealers charged a 5 percent markup fee for transactions they effected on behalf of clients. With the Internet and the possibility of trading directly, "discount" brokers made an appearance and the 5 percent rule as a markup has become a thing of the past. The plaintiffs in this case are unaffiliated investors who claim that the First Independence Group (FIG) charged markups of between 11 and 185 percent for transactions they undertook on behalf of clients. FIG clients placed orders for certain stock and, rather than going out on the over-the-counter (OTC) market and obtaining the securities, FIG sold its clients shares from its own inventory of stock. In ascertaining the appropriate retail sales price, FIG relied on quotations from other dealers rather than on their contemporaneous cost of acquiring the stock. In response to complaints from FIG customers, NASD levied large fines against FIG and against two of its officers individually. FIG appealed to the SEC. What do you think? Is it fraudulent for a broker to sell stock to clients at the price other brokers are selling it for or should the broker be limited to the cost he or she paid for the stock plus 5 percent as a markup? [*First Independence Group, Inc., et al. v. Securities and Exchange Commission,* 37 F.3d 30 (2nd Cir. 1994).]

Social Responsibility, Policy, and Ethics in a High-Tech World

6. **Revenue Recognition and Section 11 of the Securities Act of 1933.** This appeal arises from consolidated securities fraud lawsuits filed against Summit Medical Systems, Inc. (Summit); Summit's officers and directors; and Summit's public accountant–independent auditor, Ernst & Young (E&Y) (collectively "defendants"), by Summit shareholders (plaintiffs) in the U.S. District Court for the District of Minnesota. Summit is a corporation headquartered in Minneapolis, Minnesota, that provides "clinical outcomes" medical database software and related products and services. According to the first amended complaint, 2.5 million shares of Summit common stock began trading publicly on August 4, 1995, at $ 9.00 per share. Following the initial public offering, the Summit stock price increased even though no profit was shown by Summit. A secondary public offering was marketed in June 1996. At the end of 1996, the Summit stock price began to decline, eventually falling below the price at which the stock was initially offered to the public. On March 3, 1997, Summit publicly disclosed that it had been improperly recognizing revenues. Following an investigation, Summit announced that it planned to restate its financial results dating back to 1994. On April 4, 1997, Summit filed revised statements with the SEC showing the total revenues for the years 1994 and 1995, and the first nine months of 1996, to be $5.6 million less than originally reported, representing an 11 percent cumulative shortfall. Some of the plaintiffs

purchased stock directly from the issuer in an IPO, but most purchased subsequently in the secondary market. Plaintiffs contend that the mistakes in revenue recognition affected not only those who purchased stock in the IPO but also those who purchased Summit stock in the after-market. This case is, of course, not exactly on the same footing as the Enron case, as Enron was an established firm while Summit was in the IPO stage. There is a strong similarity, though, as Enron's shareholders were fooled because of complicated rules used by its accounting firm with regard to revenue recognition. [*Jong E. Lee et al. v. Ernst & Young, LLP, and Summit Medical Systems, Inc.,* 2002 U.S. App. LEXIS 11919, 294 F. 3d 969 (8th Cir. 2002).]

Using the Internet to Your Advantage

1. Of course, if the topic is securities law, the first website to visit is the Securities and Exchange Commission site (http://www.sec.gov). Increasingly, the SEC is making use of Electronic Data Gathering, Analysis, and Retrieval, or EDGAR, which can be found at http://www.sec.gov/edgar/aboutedgar.htm. Using EDGAR, various required SEC filings can be located at http://www.sec.gov/edgar/searchedgar/webusers.htm. The SEC website is well-organized and full of other useful information.

2. Other websites that provide relevant securities law information include FindLaw.com (http://findlaw.com/01topics/34securities/) and SEC Law.com (http://www.seclaw.com/Welcome.shtml). Stanford University has a securities law class action website at http://securities.stanford.edu/, which has a wealth of data about securities litigation. The famed or infamous king of class action securities lawsuits is Milberg Weiss, which has a website at http://securities.milberg.com/.

Chapter Twenty-One

Environmental Law

Learning Objectives

After completing this chapter, you should

1. Be familiar with the common law tort claims relied on by victims of pollution before federal antipollution legislation was passed and with the limitations of reliance on such common law torts.
2. Be familiar with the National Environmental Policy Act and how it affects government projects.
3. Know the main features of the Clean Air and Clean Water Acts and of the Resource Recovery and Conservation Act.
4. Be generally familiar with legislation that regulates drinking water quality, ocean dumping, oil spills, pesticides, and toxic chemicals.
5. Know how hazardous waste is regulated and who is potentially liable under the Superfund program.

OVERVIEW

Much of the important environmental law today is federal, even though pollution is most often viewed as primarily a "local" problem. When a factory sends clouds of smoke into the air, or discharges chemicals into a river, the effects generally are most harmful to the flora and fauna in the area near the discharge, which suggests that it is not a national problem. The basic reason that most environmental legislation has been enacted at the federal government level has been that local laws have not produced acceptable results. By the late 1960s, there was a general consensus that federal control was necessary. In response, not only has Congress passed numerous statutes that have had a substantial impact on business and the environment, but also it has created the Environmental Protection Agency (EPA) to enact environmental regulations and enforce those regulations in conjunction with statutes passed by Congress. The EPA is now one of the most prominent administrative agencies in the federal government and it may be the one government agency that has the greatest impact on business.

market failure
Natural free-market results that are suboptimal and can be improved by some form of government regulation.

Federal environmental law is the result of three failures: (1) **market failure,** (2) the failure of common law remedies to adequately handle market failures, and (3) the failure of local and state laws to produce nationally acceptable protection of the environment. The free market fails in efficiently dealing with pollution because the costs of polluting air, water, and land are not expenses naturally borne by the businesses and consumers that do the polluting. In small settings, it is possible for people to negotiate about acceptable ways of dealing with waste and pollution, but as population density increases, negotiations break down. There is an extensive economic literature dealing with market failures associated with pollution, requiring whole courses in "environmental economics" for an introductory review. The generally accepted conclusion from this literature is that, without significant legal sanctions that can be leveled against polluters, the ecosystem would cease to function acceptably, given the huge amount of industrial activity in the United States and in developed countries abroad.

COMMON LAW ACTIONS: NUISANCE

nuisance
At common law, a nuisance exists when actions of a defendant substantially and unreasonably interfere with another's enjoyment of his or her property.

While not adequate for all environmental protection needs, common law suits against pollution are still a potent force, even though there are limits to what common law can accomplish. Under the common law, a victim of pollution can sue for a common law **nuisance** if the plaintiff can show the defendant's use of his or her land *substantially and unreasonably interferes* with the enjoyment of the plaintiff's land. The interference from the defendant's land can be caused by noxious smells, smoke, discharge of chemicals, urinating in public, noise, or any other source that causes an unreasonable interference with others' use and enjoyment of their land. A private nuisance affects one or a few persons and occurs when the harm borne by an individual or small group is distinct from the effects on the general public. A public nuisance affects a larger number of people and, in some states, only a public authority such as a state attorney general can sue to stop a public nuisance.

Shortcomings of the Common Law

Nothing in the more recent federal environmental regulation prevents citizens from pursuing common law nuisance suits against those who substantially interfere with their enjoyment of their land. The main problem with common law nuisance suits is that the remedies are blunt and generally do not *abate* pollution. The primary remedy for a plaintiff in a common law nuisance suit is the award of money. Once the money award has been paid by the defendant to compensate the plaintiff for the diminution in the value of his or her land, there is no incentive for the defendant not to continue polluting, unless the plaintiff is also able to get an injunction, in which case the polluting facility is completely shut down.

To Be or Not to Be

Other than money damages, the only other available remedy for environmental injury at common law was an injunction, which can require a polluting defendant to shut down polluting operations under court order. In many cases, an injunction effectively meant that a factory or mine was shut down by court order, unemploying those who worked there, a result that many courts were loathe to impose. Common law courts did not have either the authority or the expertise to order polluters to install pollution control technology, to supervise the operations of plants, or to direct the modified design of products, such as automobiles, that also caused significant pollution problems.

OTHER COMMON LAW ACTIONS

Before extensive federal regulation was enacted, victims of pollution tried to gain relief with a variety of claims under the common law. Among the claims used by plaintiffs in such suits were

- *Trespass.* If an adjacent landowner causes (permits) smoke to travel from his or her property to the airspace of another, that act may constitute a common law trespass. In

International Perspective Dumping Used Computers and Creating Hazardous Waste in Asia

COMPUTER DUMPING "POLLUTING ASIA"

Old computers are been dumped in Asia where they are releasing toxic materials into the environment, say campaigners. A report, called Exporting Harm: The Hi-Tech Trashing Of Asia, details a group of villages in south-eastern China where computers from America are picked apart and strewn along rivers and fields. The transfer of hazardous waste is restricted by a 1989 treaty known as the Basel Convention, but the United States has not ratified it. "I've seen a lot of dirty operations in Third World countries, but what was shocking was seeing all this post-consumer waste," said one of the report's authors, Jim Puckett of the Seattle-based Basel Action Network.

By publishing their report, the campaigners hope it will increase the pressure on American companies and politicians to do more to recycle computer waste.

Burning Plastics

The report says electronic waste is the most rapidly growing waste problem in the world, with toxic ingredients such as the lead, mercury or cadmium being released into the environment. The campaigners visited the waste sites in Guiyu, China, in December where people were smashing up machines to scavenge for the precious metals inside. The report says that workers, with little or no protection against hazardous materials, burned plastics and circuit boards or poured acid on electronic parts to extract silver and gold. The effect was to fill the air with carcinogenic smoke and pollute the water, said the report. The campaigners said preliminary investigations in both Pakistan and India had revealed that these countries were also receiving and processing waste electronics from the West.

Problem "Ignored"

The growing amount of computer waste is becoming an increasing problem, with millions of devices becoming obsolete each year as the technology industry produces faster, better and less expensive equipment. While there are recycling programmes in the US, campaigners say much of the waste electronics finds it way to the developing world. The report suggested that as much as 80% of the America's electronic waste collected to be recycled is shipped out of the country. "Everybody knows this is going on, but they are just embarrassed and don't really know what to do about it," said Ted Smith, head of the Silicon Valley Toxics Coalition, which also helped prepare the new report. "They would just prefer to ignore it."

Source: From "Computer Dumping Polluting Asia," February 25, 2002, BBC News Online. Reprinted with permission of British Broadcasting Corporation.

---

our courts, there is not a bright line between trespass and nuisance. As a consequence, some courts have held that smoke constitutes a nuisance while others have held that it constitutes a trespass. Thus, depending upon the court, pollutants may be characterized as either trespasses or nuisances. In any event, common law trespass suits suffered from some of the shortcomings that also afflict nuisance suits. As with nuisance remedies, a trespass suit can only be started after the pollution at issue has begun, and there is no way to moderate the actions of the polluter once the damages assessed have been paid. An advantage of common law trespass suits has been that it has been easier to obtain an injunction against continuing intrusions with trespass claims.

- *Water rights.* In the eastern half of the United States, which relies on *riparian* water rights, landowners adjacent to bodies of water have the right to make reasonable use of the water, but cannot substantially harm the rights of those living downstream. In this setting, if an upstream landowner caused significant pollution, such that the condition of the water downstream was seriously depreciated or lowered, a tort was committed and the polluter could be subject to claims for damages and a possible injunction.

- *Negligence.* An owner of land who was negligent in maintaining his or her land to such a degree that he or she created a foreseeable risk of polluting the land of a neighbor could be subject to a negligence suit. For example, a landowner who maintains a dam for a fish pond, but does not take proper precautions to avoid collapse of the dam, has created a foreseeable risk and can be liable for resulting damages if the dam breaks, allowing escaping water to damage or wash away property located on the land of a neighbor.

ultrahazardous
A level of hazard, *unusually dangerous,* such that the law imposes a standard of strict liability on activities exhibiting this characteristic.

- *Strict liability.* More recently, owners of land on which hazardous waste has been stored have been subject to tort claims based on strict liability, as courts have deemed storage of hazardous waste an **ultrahazardous** activity. When it is decided that strict liability applies, the tasks confronting plaintiffs in litigation is much easier. Plaintiffs (victims of injury from hazardous waste) in strict liability cases need only prove that the cause of their illnesses or other damage is the identified hazardous waste. They do not have to show that the defendants were negligent in their handling and treatment of the hazardous waste. In many cases, proving negligence is nearly impossible because the negligence may have occurred years prior to legal claims being brought, when improper precautions were taken and the hazardous waste began seeping through soil and invading an underground waterway.

Although common law tort claims against polluters remain a potent force, the requirements of common law claims are idiosyncratic and often difficult to maintain for plaintiffs. Consider the claims made by the plaintiff in Case 21-1, which applies a variety of common law theories for recovery.

Case 21-1

Tommy Moore, Plaintiff-Appellant v. Texaco, Inc., Defendant-Appellee

United States Court of Appeals for the Tenth Circuit
244 F.3d 1229 (10th Cir. 2001)

BACKGROUND AND FACTS

Plaintiff-appellant Tommy Moore appeals from the district court's order granting summary judgment to defendant-appellee Texaco, Inc. Moore sought to hold Texaco liable for damage caused by oil spills from oil storage tanks previously located on Moore's property. Moore asserted claims of negligence, trespass, public and private nuisance and abatement, and unjust enrichment.

On November 3, 1955, Texaco sold the property to Moore's father, L.A. Moore. In the deed to L.A. Moore, Texaco retained the mineral rights to the property. Moore, the plaintiff in this action, acquired the property when his father L.A. Moore died in 1976.

Prior to the 1955 purchase, L.A. Moore resided on land adjacent to the property. Both Moore and his father L.A. Moore knew that a tank farm had previously been located on the property. There is no evidence of record that Texaco conducted any oil field operations on the property after the sale to L.A. Moore.

Moore alleges that the surface soil, subsurface soil, surface water and groundwater on the property is [sic] contaminated by crude oil, natural gas and other crude oil by-products. He contends that he was unaware of this contamination until 1997. He also alleges that Texaco built large earthen berms and dikes on the property that alter and distort the natural contours of the land and provide a breeding ground for mosquitoes.

Opinion by Kelly

1. PUBLIC NUISANCE

Moore's complaint includes a claim for public nuisance pursuant to Okla. Stat. tit. 27A, § 2-6-105(a). The district court did not expressly consider this claim. Section 2-6-105(a) states that "it shall be unlawful for any person to cause pollution of any waters of the state or to place or cause to be placed any wastes in a location where they are likely to cause pollution of any air, land or waters of this state. Any such action is hereby declared to be a public nuisance."

We have recognized that under Oklahoma law, a successor landowner may be entitled to pursue a claim for public nuisance against a predecessor responsible for groundwater pollution. [Citations omitted.] Here, however, Moore's claim fails because he has failed to show that Texaco caused pollution or damage to the property.

A nuisance "consists in unlawfully *doing* an act, or *omitting* to perform a *duty*." Moore presented no evidence that Texaco did anything to cause the pollution on the property. The affidavits of Moore's experts, Gerald Wollaston and Billy Tucker, recite in conclusory terms that Texaco was responsible for the pollution; however, these affidavits contain no factual basis sufficient to justify this conclusion. *Cf. Tosco* (setting out factual basis for conclusion that defendant was responsible for pollution of property, including defendant's own documents showing it could not account for a significant portion of its daily throughput of hazardous waste products when it operated facility).

In his reply brief, Moore argues that causation may be shown by Texaco's "oil field" operations on the land. Although Texaco retained the mineral rights in Moore's land, Moore did not point to any evidence that the pollution to his land was caused by Texaco's exploitation of those rights; rather, Moore's focus was on Texaco's tank farm operations. *See, e.g.,* Appellant's Br. at 24 ("In fact, it should be enough that pollution was found on Plaintiff's land, that Texaco operated tank farms on the land prior to the pollution being found and that evidence shows that the pollution was caused by the operation of the tank and pipelines.").

Moore's experts flirt with application of a form of "res ipsa loquitur," insisting that Texaco controlled the tank farm and that therefore only Texaco could be responsible for the pollution. Assuming that doctrine applies in the public nuisance context, a necessary element of "res ipsa loquitur" is a showing that "the event was *caused* by an instrumentality in the defendant's *exclusive control*." *Nat'l Tel. Coop. Ass'n v. Exxon Corp.*, 38 F. Supp. 2d 1, 10 n.3 (D.D.C. 1998) (emphasis added). The tank farm existed and was operated on the property before Texaco acquired it in 1915. Since there is no specific evidence that the spills occurred during the time Texaco operated the tank farm, any argument that this element is satisfied begs the question.

* * *

3. NEGLIGENCE

The same factors discussed above require affirmance of summary judgment for Texaco on Moore's negligence claim. Moore cites no Oklahoma authority that would make a landowner liable to a subsequent landowner for negligently polluting land prior to the sale. He contends that Texaco committed negligence per se by violating certain statutes pertaining to water pollution; however, as noted above, there is no proof that Texaco actually violated any statute or caused any pollution. It was Moore's responsibility to provide such proof to avoid the entry of summary judgment against him. Finally, for the same reasons cited above, res ipsa loquitur does not apply to the negligence claim.

4. TRESPASS

Under Oklahoma law, "[t]respass involves an actual physical invasion of the real estate of *another* without the permission of the person lawfully entitled to possession." It is clear that the claimed pollution here does not qualify as a trespass under this standard. Moore has presented no evidence that the pollution occurred after Texaco sold the property. Rather, Moore's argument is that the pollution occurred while Texaco owned the property. This being the case, it did not involve a physical invasion of real estate owned by anyone except Texaco itself. This is not a trespass.

* * *

Decision and Outcome

The Court of Appeals for the Tenth Circuit went on to dismiss the other common law claims made by the plaintiff, including the creation of a private nuisance. The plaintiff did not produce evidence sufficient to satisfy the court that Texaco did something that caused the pollution on the plaintiff's land.

Questions for Analysis

1. How does the doctrine of res ipsa loquitur apply to the plaintiff's claim? Why did the court reject the application of that doctrine to this case?
2. What was the substance of the plaintiff's complaint against Texaco based on negligence?
3. Why did the plaintiff fail on the trespass claim? What additional fact did the plaintiff have to allege in order to maintain a trespass claim for the pollution that he contends was caused by Texaco?

FEDERAL LEGISLATION

During the 1960s, it became more and more apparent that state laws and state common law actions were inadequate to accomplish environmental goals that meshed with the desires of most citizens. Moreover, by this time, there were a number of grotesque environmental situations that could no longer be ignored. In the mid-1960s, Lake Erie was declared dead by environmentalists for 200 years. The Cuyahoga River, which traveled through Cleveland on its way to Lake Erie, periodically caught fire because it was so laden with chemicals. Evidence was mounting that heavily used pesticides were being absorbed by birds and posed a threat to humans. Los Angeles was regularly besieged with smog so thick and hazardous that schools were cancelled and children and older people with respiratory illnesses were warned to stay indoors.

National Environmental Policy Act of 1969

environmental impact statement (EIS)
Analysis required whenever a federal government project is likely to have a substantial impact on the environment.

With rapidly growing political support for an environmental movement, Congress responded. In 1969 Congress passed the National Environmental Policy Act (NEPA), which was mainly directed toward federal government projects that were deemed to have significant environmental impacts.[1] NEPA required an environmental impact statement (EIS) for any government project that had significant environmental impacts. Building new highways, licensing nuclear plans, and building dams are examples of government activities that require preparation of an EIS. Environmental groups have sued government agencies to force them to prepare EISs to halt unwanted government projects, knowing that the delays and adverse publicity that result from the preparation and publication of an EIS often are enough to halt a project.

If a government project requires an EIS, the government agency administering the project must

1. Describe the affected environment.
2. Describe the impact of the proposed federal action on the environment.

---

[1] Pub. L. No. 91-190, codified at 42 U.S.C. §§ 4321–4370d.

3. Identify and discuss alternatives to the proposed action.

4. List the resources that will be committed to the action.

5. Contain a cost–benefit study of the proposed action and alternative actions.

There have been many projects that have been significantly altered or, in fact, halted entirely as a result of the preparation of an EIS. Once the EIS for a project has been prepared, it is part of the public record and the public has an opportunity to make comments to the EPA. Once the EPA has received comments made by the public, it has the authority to determine if the project should proceed, though its decisions are subject to appeal to the U.S. courts of appeals. Note that the NEPA does not apply to projects undertaken by private entities such as corporations unless the federal government pays for the project. Also, the NEPA does not apply to projects undertaken by local and state governments.

Case 21-2

Blue Ocean Preservation Society, a Hawaii non-profit corporation; Sierra Club, a California non-profit corporation; Greenpeace Foundation, a Hawaii non-profit corporation, Plaintiffs v. James D. Watkins, Secretary, Department of Energy, et al., Defendants

United States District Court for the District of Hawaii
767 F. Supp. 1518 (D. Haw. 1991)

BACKGROUND AND FACTS

This lawsuit seeks to compel preparation of a federal Environmental Impact Statement ("EIS") for the Hawaii Geothermal Energy Project (the "Project") and to enjoin any further federal participation in the Project until the EIS is completed.

The Project is a cooperative venture of both the State of Hawaii and the federal government to facilitate the development of geothermal power as an alternative energy source in Hawaii. It involves four distinct stages or phases leading to the private development of a 500 megawatt geothermal power plant on the slopes of the Kilauea crater, an active volcano on the Island of Hawaii. The first two phases, involving (1) the building of a small plant for research and testing, and (2) research regarding the feasibility of transporting the power generated to other islands via underwater cable, have already been completed, and any attempt to obtain an EIS for those phases was deemed moot. [Citations omitted.] Phase III, entitled the Geothermal Resource Verification and Characterization Program, was in progress, and involved the drilling of twenty-five (25) commercial-scale exploration wells throughout the Kilauea East Rift Zone in order to "verify" the geothermal resource. This verification would have cleared the way for Phase IV, the construction of the full 500 megawatt project.

Phase III is proceeding with funds appropriated by the Hawaii state legislature. So far, at least two slim-bore scientific observation holes ("SOHs") have been drilled, and four more are called for. It is anticipated that federal funds will be utilized to drill the 25 full-scale holes in areas "proven" by the SOH drilling.

Phase IV would have involved the construction of up to twenty (20) separate geothermal power plants of about 25 megawatts apiece. Each of these will employ eight to ten working wells. The separate plants will necessarily be connected by a network of roads, plumbing, and power lines throughout the subzone areas. It will also involve the laying of overland and underwater cable to carry the power generated to the islands of Maui and Oahu.

Opinion by David Alan Ezra, United States District Judge

a. THE STATUTORY STANDARD

Where an agency has determined that the proposed action will not significantly affect the human environment, a court must examine that determination for reasonableness. [Citations omitted.] The agency's decision should be upheld if it is reasonable, *i.e.*, if it is "'fully informed and well-considered.'" Because it is the EIS itself which will reveal whether and to what degree the proposed action will affect the human environment, the preliminary decision of whether to do an EIS is necessarily based on incomplete and uncertain information. Accordingly, it is not necessary for plaintiffs to *prove* significant effects on the environment in order to prevail in their suit seeking an EIS. It is sufficient to raise "substantial questions . . . regarding whether the proposed action *may* have a significant effect upon the human environment."

The evidentiary offering on this issue is entirely uncontroverted. As indicated, to carry their burden of proof plaintiffs need only raise questions about whether the Project *may* significantly affect the environment. The court is satisfied that this burden has been met many times over in the series of expert witness affidavits, scientific reports, illustrative maps, correspondence and other documents filed by plaintiffs with their motion.

b. THE EVIDENCE OFFERED TO SHOW "SIGNIFICANCE"

The land-based aspect of the Project itself contemplates a network of geothermal plants, wells, power lines, roads and pipes over 26,000 acres, many of them located in the Wao Kele O Puna forest. In 1981, then Governor Ariyoshi formally designated the Wao Kele O Puna forest a Natural Area Reserve, in recognition of its importance as "an environmental and natural heritage site" as well as a "research site" that would "preserve a gene pool of native plant and animal species, particularly of rare and endangered species." This Natural Area Reserve designation was later revoked in a "land exchange" in order to facilitate the proposed geothermal development.

In the hearings on the land exchange proposal, James Jacobi of the U.S. Fish and Wildlife Service ("FWS", a defendant in this action) testified that the forest is "a unique dynamic ecosystem, valuable for both research on and management of the lowland rain forest habitat on the island of Hawaii." He cautioned against the adverse impact geothermal development would have on the ecosystem, as well as the endangered plant and animal species found there.

In addition, three experts—an ornithologist, a geneticist, and a botanist—all affiliated in some way with the University of Hawaii and intimately acquainted with native Hawaiian species and habitats, have submitted affidavits expressing grave concern for the environmental impact of the Project with respect to each of their respective fields. These affidavits alone, uncontroverted by any evidence submitted by the government, easily raise the "substantial questions" of possible environmental impact sufficient to require an EIS under that provision of the statute.

* * *

Having demonstrated "major federal action" in the previous hearing, and now having established ripeness and "significance," plaintiffs have proven their case on the merits. Accordingly, they are entitled to summary judgment.

* * *

Decision and Outcome

The district court judge found that the plaintiffs had raised enough evidence that the project would have a significant environmental impact such that an EIS was required. The court went on to rule that no further work could take place on the project until an EIS was prepared.

Questions for Analysis

1. According to this court, what is the burden that the plaintiffs have to bear in order to compel an EIS? Do the plaintiffs have to demonstrate that the project will have a major impact on the environment before getting the court to compel an EIS?

2. Why do you think that the plaintiffs wanted the Department of Energy to prepare an EIS? Why do you think that the defendants resisted preparation of an EIS?

Environmental Protection Agency

Environmental Protection Agency (EPA)
The federal agency charged with the lion's share of protecting the environment. The EPA enforces the important federal legislation dealing with the environment.

The **Environmental Protection Agency (EPA)** was created in 1970 by an Executive Order from President Richard Nixon. The EPA is one of the largest agencies in the federal government, with over 17,000 employees and a budget of near $10 billion. The EPA is headed by an administrator and several assistant administrators who are appointed by the president, but must be approved by the Senate. The EPA maintains 10 regional offices that are headed by regional administrators. The EPA also partners with state environmental agencies, which develop environmental programs that are approved by the EPA if they are "equivalent to or more stringent than" federal programs for the state. Although state environmental agencies administer state programs that do many of the same tasks as the EPA, federal EPA officials retain authority to revoke authorization if a state program does not live up to federal standards.

The Clean Air Act of 1970

ambient air quality standards
The EPA establishes and enforces primary and secondary AAQSs. Together, the primary and secondary standards form the NAAQSs, established by the EPA to set legal limits on air pollution, based on human health impacts.

Although there was an earlier act passed with the same name in 1963 to assist states, modern federal environmental legislation began in 1970 with passage of the Clean Air Act (CAA).[2] The act was significantly amended in 1977 and 1990 to give the EPA more power, but the 1970 legislation laid the foundation for modern regulation of air pollution. The 1970 CAA authorized the EPA to set primary and secondary **ambient air quality standards,** with quantification of the standards based on the following six pollutants: carbon monoxide, nitrogen oxide, sulfur oxide, ozone, lead, and particulate matter. Under the CAA, primary ambient air quality standards are set by the EPA to be safe for human beings while secondary ambient air quality standards are supposed to protect vegetation, matter, climate, and economic values.

Stationary Sources of Pollution

nonattainment areas
Areas that are not in compliance with NAAQSs. In these areas, states, supervised by the EPA, must devise SIP plans to reduce pollution and bring air quality into compliance with NAAQSs.

In administering the CAA, the EPA divides the country into two zones: *nonattainment* areas and *prevention of significant deterioration* (PSD) areas. **Nonattaintment areas** are those where the air is too polluted to meet the ambient air quality standards set by the EPA, which means that they are unhealthy to humans or fail the secondary ambient air quality standards. Achieving the air quality standards set by the EPA, however, is a task partially assigned to the states through state implementation plans (SIPs). If the air in a state is not in compliance with national air quality standards, the state is required to fashion a SIP plan to accomplish that goal. SIPs must be approved by the EPA and must include state-selected means of addressing pollution flowing from stationary emission sources that were in existence before 1970 and mobile sources, principally motor vehicles. SIP plans also must establish regulations for significant modifications in the construction or operation of stationary sources of air pollution.

[2] Pub. L. No. 91-604, codified at 42 U.S.C. §§ 7401–7671q.

"*I see the company responded to our toxic emissions grievance.*"

Source: Reprinted with permission of Carol Simpson Productions.

Prevention of Significant Deterioration   For new sources of air pollution (new factories) in areas of the country that are in compliance with the national ambient air quality standards that is, **prevention of significant deterioration (PSD) areas**, the EPA establishes performance standards based on *best available control technology* (BACT) for each category of factory or source of pollution. For major new sources of emissions, the EPA evaluates projects on a case-by-case basis. In pristine areas that have good air quality, the EPA will not allow significant deterioration of air quality. For areas that are moderately polluted, the EPA is more lenient. For areas in which the air, while dirty, is still in compliance with national standards, the EPA will not allow new pollution sources if the new source would cause the area to become a nonattainment area.

Nonattainment Areas: Offset Policy   In nonattainment areas, the air is already so dirty that it does not meet national air quality standards. If the EPA were to allow new sources of air pollution in such areas, it would become increasingly difficult to achieve the clean air goals set forth in its national ambient air quality standards. Businesses seeking to build new factories or other structures that bring new sources of pollution into such areas must agree to strict standards, including requirements that

- The plant must make use of *lowest achievable emissions rate* (LAER) technology, which is generally more effective and expensive than the antipollution control technology required by BACT in PSD areas. Conceptually, LAER is the most effective antipollution technology in use in the country.
- The owner of the new factory or other new source of pollution must be in compliance with the state SIP plan in its other operations.
- The owner of the new plant or other structure must present a plan that shows that pollution from its new facility will be *offset* by reductions in the same pollutants from other facilities in the area. There must be no net increase in the amount of pollution in the area.

In order to comply with the offset regimen, the owner of the new plant or other facility may have to purchase antipollution control technology for other factories or purchase other factories and shut them down. A required result of the **offset policy** is that air quality in the nonattainment area is not allowed to deteriorate further as the result of the construction of a new factory.

prevention of significant deterioration (PSD) areas
Areas in compliance with NAAQSs but in which the EPA will enact and enforce regulations to prevent a significant deterioration of air quality.

offset policy
A policy devised by the EPA for allowing new plants and factories in areas that are not in compliance with NAAQSs. Basically, new sources of pollution must be more than offset by reductions in the area of the same kinds of pollution.

bubble program
A program that allows firms to establish new plants or factories in nonattainment areas by conceptually combining all of the pollution produced by a firm's factories and requiring that there be no net increase in pollution as a result of a new plant or factory.

The Bubble Program   The **bubble program** is similar to the offset policy described above in that the end result of a new factory or plant in a nonattainment area must be no net increase in pollution in the area. In the bubble program, all of a firm's plants in an area are lumped together under one *conceptual* bubble with a single smokestack. As long as the amount of pollution emitted from the smokestack is reduced, a firm can obtain permission from the EPA to erect a new factory in a nonattaintment area. Two significant differences between the bubble program and the offset program are that (1) a firm building a new factory in a nonattainment area under the bubble program is allowed to use its discretion in reducing pollution from its other plants and (2) it does not have to employ LAER technology on the new plant.

Mobile Sources of Air Pollution

Automobiles account for large shares of air pollution. For years there has been behind-the-scenes lobbying by representatives of the automobile industry to forestall the imposition of air pollution restrictions on automobiles. Nonetheless, over the years, various amendments to the Clean Air Act have required nearly universal use of unleaded gasoline, installation of catalytic converters on new cars, and enhanced fuel economy standards. In 1990, substantive amendments were added to the Clean Air Act, which called for sizeable reductions in tailpipe emissions by 1998 and further reductions by the year 2000. The 1990 amendments required car manufacturers to install pollution control equipment focused on reducing emissions of hydrocarbons and nitrogen oxides, with an additional requirement that the equipment be designed to last for 10 years. For the smoggiest cities, cleaner (reformulated) blends of gasoline were required that include methanol and ethanol additives (see the "Nutz and Boltz" box on page 690). Not surprisingly in a world of trade-offs, these "cleaner" gasoline blends are generally more costly and perform less well in various ways than ordinary gasoline. During some months when supplies were tight and refining capacity was pushed to the limit, reformulated gasoline requirements were associated with 50- to 75-cent price spikes in the per-gallon cost of gasoline.

Acid Rain   Acid rain is a particularly invidious form of pollution, formed in clouds when common smokestack pollutants, typically sulfur dioxide and nitrogen oxide, combine with oxygen and moisture to form nitric and sulfuric acids. Sulfur dioxide and nitrogen oxide are emitted in large volumes by coal-burning power plants. Acid rain pollution damages both plants and wildlife, particularly lakes that can be a repository for repeated doses of acid-laden rain. Environmental scientists have determined that the use of low-sulfur (clean) coal and the installation of scrubbers on smokestacks can significantly reduce the volumes of chemical pollutants in the atmosphere that create acid rain. Based on this information, the 1990 amendments to the Clear Air Act required significant changes in standard operating procedures for electric utilities, requiring the use of cleaner coal and the installation of more smokestack scrubbers.

hazardous air pollutants
The EPA is required by the CAA to identify air pollutants that can cause serious illness or death in humans. Through February 2002, the EPA has identified 188 hazardous air pollutants.

Hazardous Air Pollutants   The CAA also requires the EPA to identify **hazardous air pollutants** that can cause serious illness or death to humans. According to its latest count, the EPA has identified 188 toxic air pollutants that meet the criteria the EPA uses to classify a pollutant as hazardous (see the EPA Web page at http://www.epa.gov/ttn/atw/188polls.html). An issue that frequently arises in environmental policy debates is whether zero tolerance is appropriate for pollutants that can cause death. To date, the standard to which the EPA requires producers of hazardous air pollutants to adhere is called MACT, for maximum achievable control technology. In Case 21-3, the plaintiffs, an environmental group, contend that the level of emissions of a particular variety of

Nutz and Boltz   Why Does the EPA Require Reformulated Gasoline?

IMPLEMENTATION OF THE REFORMULATED GASOLINE PROGRAM

Summary

The Clean Air Act (CAA) was amended in 1990 requiring the sale of cleaner-burning reformulated gasoline (RFG) in the nine worst nonattainment areas. Since the program began on January 1, 1995, legislation has been introduced to delay or repeal the requirement. RFG must contain oxygenates and should result in a 15 percent reduction of volatile organic compounds (VOCs) and air toxics. While the CAA was being debated, affected parties (e.g., automobile manufacturers, oil industry, and agricultural interests) did not agree on whether and how gasoline should be reformulated.

Some consumers do not accept the RFG program based on complaints that MTBE causes negative health effects, fuel prices increased, and engines do not perform well using RFG. Reported health effects include headaches, dizziness, nausea, sore eyes and throats, and respiratory irritation. Research about MTBE health effects has been inconclusive; however, most studies have failed to find acute health effects. Some other gasoline components are known or probable human carcinogens, so it is difficult to isolate the risk of exposure to MTBE in RFG. Some contend that media attention and the distinct odor of RFG may have increased health reports. RFG is expected to benefit health by helping areas achieve cleaner air. On average, RFG decreases fuel economy by 2–3 miles per gallon because oxygenates have lower energy content than gasoline. There are reports of much higher fuel economy losses for some vehicles. There are also reports that small engines do not perform well using RFG.

From a distribution viewpoint, implementation of the RFG program was uneventful. There were no supply interruptions, and wholesale RFG costs are about 5 cents per gallon more than conventional gasoline. Legislation to suspend or repeal the RFG program would reduce the demand for high-oxygen content fuel. An effective MTBE ban would increase the demand for ethanol, likely resulting in higher RFG prices and distribution problems because ethanol-blended fuels are difficult to transport because of their technical properties.

In December 1994 and January 1995, a few areas that had voluntarily opted in to the program no longer wished to participate. EPA proposed an opt-out policy that allows most areas where RFG is not needed to meet air quality goals to opt out 30 days after a Governor's request. Opt-outs and proposed legislation create uncertainty for the RFG program. They may discourage additional investment in RFG infrastructure by diminishing the demand for RFG and oxygenates. Opt-outs and proposed legislation also raise the question of how nonattainment areas will achieve CAA compliance without RFG. Areas that cannot attain air quality goals because they do not require RFG create an ozone health risk for residents and may be subject to CAA sanctions.

Two issues related to RFG remain unresolved (i.e., the role of ethanol in the RFG program, and RFG imports from Venezuela). A recent Federal court decision struck down an EPA rule that provided a preference for ethanol over MTBE as the oxygenate to be used in RFG. Also, last year after Congress passed an appropriations limitation, EPA withdrew a proposed rule that would have made Venezuelan gasoline more competitive in the U.S. RFG market. The House Appropriations Committee report accompanying H.R. 2099 contains language instructing EPA not to pursue either of these rules during FY 1996.

Source: Susan L. Mayer, Lawrence Cummins, and Migdon Segal, "Implementation of the Reformulated Gasoline Program," CRS Report No. 95-850ENR, August 1, 1995, *available at* http://www.ncseonline.org/NLE/CRSreports/energy/eng-14.cfm?&CFID=7857241&CFTOKEN=20984683.

hazardous air pollutant should be set at zero. A corollary of zero tolerance emissions rates is that the cost of compliance faced by industry should not be a factor in setting the standard.

Case 21-3

Natural Resources Defense Council, Inc., Petitioner v. U.S. Environmental Protection Agency and Lee M. Thomas, Administrator, U.S. Environmental Protection Agency, Respondents, Vinyl Institute, Intervenor

United States Court of Appeals for the District of Columbia Circuit
824 F.2d 1146 (D. C. Cir. 1987)

BACKGROUND AND FACTS

The Administrator [Head] of the Environmental Protection Agency (EPA) is charged with regulating hazardous pollutants, including carcinogens, under section 112 of the Clean Air Act by setting emission standards "at the level which in his judgment provides an ample margin of safety to protect the public health." Current scientific knowledge does not permit a finding that there is a completely safe level of human exposure to carcinogenic agents. The Natural Resources Defense Council ("NRDC") contends that the Administrator must base a decision under section 112 exclusively on health-related factors and, therefore, that the uncertainty about the effect of carcinogenic agents requires the Administrator to prohibit all emissions, or zero tolerance. Enforcing zero tolerance for many of the pollutants on EPA's hazardous list would require the shutdown of many factories and plants. The Administrator of the EPA argues that in the face of this uncertainty he is authorized to set standards that require emission reduction to the lowest level attainable by best available control technology (BACT) whenever that level is below that at which harm to humans has been demonstrated. This case involves determining the appropriate standard for setting allowable levels of a carcinogenic substance whose lowest level detectable may be unsafe for humans at any level of exposure.

Opinion by Robert Bork, Circuit Judge

Section 112 of the Clean Air Act provides for regulation of hazardous air pollutants, which the statute defines as "air pollutant[s] to which no ambient air quality standard is applicable and which in the judgment of the Administrator cause, or contribute to, air pollution which may reasonably be anticipated to result in an increase in mortality or an increase in serious irreversible, or incapacitating reversible, illness." [Citations deleted.] The statute requires the Administrator to publish a list containing each hazardous pollutant for which he intends to adopt an emission standard, to publish proposed regulations and a notice of public hearing for each such pollutant, and then, within a specified period, either to promulgate an emission standard or to make a finding that the particular agent is not a hazardous air pollutant. The statute directs the Administrator to set an emission standard promulgated under section 112 "at the level which in his judgment provides an ample margin of safety to protect the public health."

This case concerns vinyl chloride regulations. Vinyl chloride is a gaseous synthetic chemical used in the manufacture of plastics and is a strong carcinogen. In late 1975, the Administrator issued a notice of proposed rulemaking to establish an emission standard for vinyl chloride. In the notice, the EPA asserted that available data linked vinyl chloride to carcinogenic, as well as some noncarcinogenic, disorders and that "reasonable extrapolations" from this data suggested "that present ambient levels of vinyl chloride may cause or contribute to . . . [such] disorders." The EPA also noted that vinyl chloride is "an apparent non-threshold pollutant," which means that it appears to create a risk to health at all non-zero levels of emission.

* * *

Thus, the terms of section 112 provide little support for the NRDC's position. The uncertainty about the effects of a particular carcinogenic pollutant invokes the Administrator's discretion under section 112. In contrast, the NRDC's position would eliminate any discretion and would render the standard "ample margin of safety" meaningless as applied to carcinogenic pollutants. Whenever *any* scientific uncertainty existed about the ill effects of a nonzero level of hazardous air pollutants—and we think it unlikely that science will ever yield *absolute* certainty of safety in an area so complicated and rife with problems of measurement, modeling, long latency, and the like—the Administrator would have no discretion but would be required to prohibit all emissions. Had Congress intended that result, it could very easily have said so by writing a statute that states that no level of emissions shall be allowed as to which there is any uncertainty. But Congress chose instead to deal with the pervasive nature of scientific uncertainty and the inherent limitations of scientific knowledge by vesting in the Administrator the discretion to deal with uncertainty in each case.

* * *

Decision and Outcome

Judge Bork held in this case that Section 112 of the Clean Air Act did not require the administrator of the EPA to set the allowable levels of hazardous airborne pollutants at zero just because there was scientific evidence that any exposure to vinyl chloride could be associated with increased risk of cancer.

Questions for Analysis

1. Why did Judge Bork reject the arguments of the National Resources Defense Council?
2. What would be the consequences of using the NRDC's proposed criteria in setting the allowable amounts of hazardous air pollutants?

Violations of the Clean Air Act

Environmental protection acts generally contain a formula for dealing with violations. There are civil penalties for most violations and additional criminal sanctions for intentional violations of the CAA. For exceeding emission limits established under the CAA, the EPA has the power to impose civil penalties of up to $25,000 per day. For most other violations, fines of up to $5,000 can be assessed. If it is determined that violators of the CAA made more money by violating the act, the EPA can sue for damages equal to the gains made from not complying. Private citizens, usually banded together in environmental groups, are entitled under the CAA to bring lawsuits to ensure compliance with the act. If they win such suits, either against a violator or against the EPA for not enforcing the CAA as the citizens interpret it, they can recover "reasonable attorney fees." In many cases, "reasonable attorney fees" have been in the hundreds of thousands of dollars. The EPA also pays bounties to private citizens who uncover violations of the CAA. For making false statements to the EPA in connection with various reporting requirements, criminal sanctions are an option. EPA-imposed penalties can include fines of up to $1 million and imprisonment for up to two years.

Clean Water Act of 1972

Federal regulation of water pollution began much earlier than that of air and land pollution. The federal government and the court system have asserted jurisdiction over navigable waters since 1824, beginning with the famous *Gibbons v. Ogden* case, when the U.S. Supreme Court struck down a New York state law that attempted to grant exclusive rights to ferry passengers in state waters.[3] Gibbons, who had been licensed by the U.S. government to ferry passengers from New Jersey to New York, successfully challenged the New York licensing law that had given exclusive rights to Messrs. Fulton and Livingston, inventors of the steam engine. Based on the precedent established in this case, only the federal government has been allowed to pass laws regarding a body of navigable water in the United States. In 1899 the Rivers and Harbors Act was passed, which prohibited ships and manufacturing plants from discharging refuse into navigable waterways or their tributaries.[4] The modern era of federal regulation of water pollution began in 1972 with passage of the Clean Water Act (CWA), which was significantly amended and broadened in 1977.[5]

The focus of federal regulation of water pollution has been on point source pollution. A **point source** is a discernible, discrete conveyance of pollution such as a pipe, channel, or ditch. As the CWA has become more effective in preventing point source pollution, the relative importance of other nonpoint sources of pollution has grown. It is now generally conceded that the greater amount of water pollution originates from **nonpoint sources,** such as from the wind sweeping pesticides or fertilizers from agricultural lands.

The Permit System

Point source pollution controls are administered under the National Pollutant Discharge Elimination System (NPDES), which regulates both navigable waters and public sewage systems. Under this **permit system,** the *discharge of any pollutant into water from a point source is illegal, unless the polluter has a permit that is issued by the EPA.* The EPA only issues permits that allow point source pollution if the polluter complies with its regulations that require installation of *best conventional technology* (BCT), the specifics of which are designated on an industry-by-industry basis. Not surprisingly, the antipollution measures required of a paper factory may be different from those required of a fish processing plant. For unconventional sources of pollution, owners of point source discharges must comply with BAT, the *best available technology economically achievable.* Under either system (BCT or BAT), the EPA reserves the right to amend permits if there are technological breakthroughs in the treatment of effluents. If a new plant is built or a new source of pollution is emitted, the plant is subject to new source performance standards (NSPS). In addition, if state or local governments have stricter antipollution requirements than are called for in the CWA, those stricter standards are required to be incorporated into the permit. On the other side of the coin of EPA strictures on business conduct, if a firm complies with the requirements of the EPA-issued permit, it cannot be sued by downstream users or by environmental groups. In other words, if a firm complies with its permit, it creates a legal safe harbor for the firm.

Enforcement   Permit owners are required to monitor their own discharges and have to file discharge monitoring reports (DMRs). Firms are subject to fines for exceeding allowable limits of effluents discharged under their permit, but are subject to worse penalties if they do not report their own violations or if they deliberately misrepresent the amount of effluents discharged. Firms that violate the requirements of their permits are subject to

---

point source
Any ditch, pipe, or channel from which pollution is emitted into a navigable body of water.

nonpoint source
Water pollution that originates from land, wind, mines, floods, and sewage systems that is not associated with a particular point source.

permit system
Under the Clean Water Act, the discharge of any pollutant into navigable waters from a point source is a violation unless the polluter has a permit issued by the EPA and is in compliance with the requirements of the permit.

---

[3] *Gibbons v. Ogden,* 22 U.S. 1 (1824).

[4] 30 Stat. 1151, codified at 33 U.S.C. §§ 401–418.

[5] The Clean Water Act of 1972, Pub. L. No. 92-500, 86 Stat. 896, as amended by the Clean Water Act of 1977, Pub. L. No. 95-217, 91 Stat. 1566, codified at 33 U.S.C. §§ 1251–1387. The Clean Water Act amended the Federal Water Pollution Control Act of 1948, Pub. L. No. 845, 80th Cong., 62 Stat. 1155.

citizen suits unless the EPA decides to intervene and pursue litigation on behalf of the citizen (who is usually an environmental group). If the EPA decides not to take over the case pushed by a citizen group, and the group is successful in its litigation against a permit holder for a violation of the CWA, it is entitled to recover "reasonable attorney fees."

Violations of the Clean Water Act   In earlier times, penalties for violations of the CWA were viewed as inadequate to provide effective incentives for achieving widespread compliance with the law. Adjustments were made to strengthen those incentives. Currently, there are both civil and criminal penalties for Clean Water Act violations. On the civil side, penalties can be as high as $25,000 per day for each violation. Criminal penalties range from fines of $2,500 per day and one year in jail to $1,000,000 in fines and imprisonment of up to 15 years. There are also provisions in the CWA for injunctions and for requiring polluting parties to pay for cleanups caused by violations of the CWA. Criminal penalties are reserved for intentional violations of the act, such as "midnight" dumping of dangerous chemicals in secluded waterways.

Nonpoint Sources of Pollution

As described above, nonpoint source pollution has become an increasing problem. More than 50 percent of the total volume of pollutants that eventually find their way into flowing water originate from nonpoint sources such as construction sites, agricultural lands, mines, and runoff from roads and highways. A large share of the runoff is the result of air pollution that eventually lands on the ground and of surface water runoffs that overwhelm city sewage systems during floods or heavy rains. As nonpoint sources, on a relative basis, have become an increasing source of pollution, Congress has passed statutes to control some of the worst resulting contamination.

Wetlands: Section 404 of the CWA

wetlands
Areas protected by the EPA that are saturated by surface or groundwater. A permit is required to drain or alter an area designated as a wetland and the EPA has ultimate authority for approving such permits.

Wetlands are areas that are saturated by surface or groundwater "at a frequency or duration sufficient to support a prevalence of vegetation typically adapted for life in saturated soil conditions." In recent years, there has been an increasing recognition of the importance of wetlands to the ecosystem. As a result, restrictions have been enacted that prevent swamps, bogs, and marshes from being drained without a permit. Normally, a permit for such actions must be issued by the U.S. Army Corps of Engineers. However, the EPA has authority to overrule decisions made by the Army Corps. Draining a wetland without a permit, even on your own property, is a violation of law that can result in severe fines and other penalties. In a typical year, about 10,000 permits are issued for activities that directly and significantly affect wetlands. In addition, some 75,000 permits are issued for activities that have only minimally adverse environmental effects on wetlands.

regulatory taking
A government regulation that has the effect of taking all or nearly all of the value of land from a landowner. If a court agrees that the government regulation has effected a regulatory taking, the government must compensate the landowner for the fair market value of the property.

Not everyone applauds the enforcement of wetland protection. Critics of the EPA's enforcement of wetland regulations assert that there are situations in which the EPA has declared large puddles at construction sites to be protected wetlands. Particularly galling to many farmers have been situations where heavy rains and floods have caused fields to be under water, followed by the EPA appearing and ordering the farmer to refrain from draining his or her own fields. Recent court decisions have held that declaring private property a wetland is a **regulatory taking,** which results in the government having to pay fair market value for the property declared a wetland.[6] Also, recent statutory changes in the CWA have exempted some activities from regulation, including many ongoing farming, ranching, and silviculture practices.

---

[6] *Loveladies Harbor v. U.S.*, 28 F.3d 1171 (Fed. Cir. 1994).

The Endangered Species Act of 1973

endangered species
Species of animals that are in danger of becoming extinct, as determined by the Secretary of the Interior pursuant to the Endangered Species Act.

The Endangered Species Act (ESA), passed in 1973, requires the secretary of the Interior to list the animal and plant species that are either **endangered** or *threatened* and to state the critical habitat of each species on the lists.[7] Identifying a species as *endangered* indicates that the species is nearer extinction than a species that is *threatened*. The act prohibits federal agencies from taking any actions that are "likely to jeopardize the continued existence of any endangered or threatened species or result in the destruction or adverse modification of habitat of such species . . ."

The ESA is a favorite vehicle of environmental groups in their efforts to halt federal activities, such as mining or logging, that they believe harm the environment. The northern spotted owl has been put on the endangered species list. Its habitat is in trees in Oregon. As a result, the Forest Service, a federal agency, has curtailed most logging in federal forests where the spotted owl lives. Among the consequences of these actions are high levels of unemployment for loggers in the Northwest and intensive pressure for regulatory changes. More recently, a moratorium has been declared on naming new endangered species and cost–benefit analysis has been introduced as a tool for analyzing proposals for preserving the habitat of an endangered species when such preservation activities would cause significant economic dislocations.

Ocean Dumping and Oil Spills

Ocean Dumping

In 1972, Congress enacted the Marine Protection, Research, and Sanctuaries Act (MPRSA) to prohibit the dumping of materials into ocean waters, if that dumping would unreasonably degrade water quality, would endanger human health, or would harm the marine environment.[8] The MPRSA was amended in 1988 to ban ocean dumping of industrial waste and sewage sludge. Ocean dumping is not allowed in the United States now unless a permit is issued under the MPRSA. In the case of dredged material, the decision to issue a permit is made by the U.S. Army Corps of Engineers, using the EPA's environmental criteria and subject to the EPA's concurrence. The EPA is also responsible for designating recommended ocean disposal sites for use under such permits. As with all regulatory schemes, there are exemptions if the material being dumped into the ocean

1. Is subject to other pollution regulations.
2. Is waste from structures regulated by other laws.
3. Is sewage or other wastes.

Also, existing legislation authorizes the EPA to establish marine sanctuaries, which are oceanic equivalents of national parks, where no dumping is allowed so as to preserve or restore certain areas for their recreational, ecological, or esthetic values. As an example, the coral reefs off the Florida Keys are in a marine sanctuary.

Oil Spills

The Oil Pollution Act (OPA) was signed into law in August 1990, largely in response to rising public concern following the Exxon *Valdez* incident in which a tanker owned by the Exxon company ran aground, ruptured, and blackened Alaskan shores for more than 1,000 miles.[9] The purpose of the OPA was to improve the nation's ability to prevent and

---

[7] Pub. L. No. 93-205, 87 Stat. 884, codified at 16 U.S.C. §§ 1531–1544.

[8] Pub. L. No. 92-532, 86 Stat. 1052 and 1061, codified at 33 U.S.C. §§ 1401–1445 and 16 U.S.C. §§ 1431–1445.

[9] Pub. L. No. 101-380, 104 Stat. 484, codified at 33 U.S.C. §§ 2701–2961.

respond to oil spills by establishing provisions that expand the federal government's capability, providing money and resources necessary, to respond to oil spills. The OPA also created the national Oil Spill Liability Trust Fund, which is available to provide up to $1 billion per spill incident, for undoing damage to the environment. The OPA increased penalties for regulatory noncompliance by allowing recovery from those responsible for oil spills for damages to natural resources, private property, and the local economy. The act also allows recovery of the increased costs of providing public services in the event of an oil spill.

LAND POLLUTION

Toxic Substances

toxic substances
Materials designated by the EPA as toxic and regulated by the Toxic Substances Control Act.

The Toxic Substances Control Act (TSCA) of 1976 regulates **toxic substances** by requiring the EPA to develop an inventory of existing chemicals and catalog their characteristics and hazards.[10] TSCA requires manufacturers to notify the EPA, 90 days in advance, of the production or importation of new chemicals. The EPA has the power to order tests and analyses of the new chemicals before they can be used commercially and to ban a dangerous chemical entirely or require labeling and restrictions on certain uses. It also can require that manufacturers report adverse effects associated with the production or use of new chemicals. Congress has required that the EPA demonstrate that new TSCA regulations pass a cost–benefit test, which means that the EPA must be able to show a reasonable economic basis for its new regulations, taking into account both the compliance costs of firms subject to the regulations as well as their roles in minimizing risks to the public.

Pesticides and Herbicides

Federal Insecticide, Fungicide, and Rodenticide Act (FIFRA)
The act of Congress that enables the EPA to regulate and, if necessary, ban pesticides that pose an unreasonable risk to humans and the environment.

There has been widespread publicity regarding the possible harm to human health and the environment from usage of pesticides. Probably the first pesticide singled out as a significant threat to humans was DDT, which killed insects, but also was shown to have been absorbed by birds. Scientists determined that DDT was carcinogenic and it was banned. In 1947, Congress passed the **Federal Insecticide, Fungicide, and Rodenticide Act (FIFRA),** which required that both pesticides and herbicides must be[11]

1. Registered before they can be sold.
2. Certified and used only for approved applications.
3. Limited in quantities when applied to food products.

For pesticides such as DDT, the EPA has the power to cancel their registration after a hearing and, if the harm threatened by a pesticide is immediate, the EPA can enjoin (prohibit) use of the pesticide even before a hearing is held. In 1996 the Federal Food, Drug, and Cosmetic Act was amended so that, in order for a pesticide to remain on the market, there must be a reasonable certainty that it does not pose a threat to human health. Of particular concern were pesticides that were possible carcinogenic agents. Nearly all processed foods contain minute residues of pesticides, so completely banning any pesticide content is impracticable. The standard that emerged was that a pesticide could pose no more than a one in a million chance of causing cancer in people.

---

[10] Pub. L. No. 94-469, 90 Stat. 2003, codified at 15 U.S.C. §§ 2601–2692.
[11] Pub. L. No. 80-104, 61 Stat. 163, codified at 7 U.S.C. §§ 136–136y.

FIFRA carries potentially substantial penalties for violators and contains provisions for private rights of action. It is a violation of FIFRA to sell a pesticide or herbicide without registration or if the registration has been suspended or canceled. It is also a violation to sell a pesticide or herbicide that has been mislabeled or adulterated. Labels required by FIFRA include directions for use, warnings about possible threats to people, and directions on what to do in case of accidental poisoning, along with a statement of a product's ingredients.

Private individuals, usually environmental or consumer advocacy groups, can take the EPA to court if it fails to take appropriate action to remove dangerous pesticides or herbicides from the market. For violations of FIFRA by producers and registrants, fines of up to $50,000 as well as imprisonment are possible penalties. Farmers and other users of these products can be subject to lesser penalties, with maximum penalties of fines of $1,000 and imprisonment of 30 days.

Hazardous Waste

hazardous wastes
Solid wastes that, alone or in combination with other substances, have the potential to seriously harm or kill people when improperly stored, treated, transported, or disposed of.

The Resource Conservation and Recovery Act (RCRA) of 1976 was enacted by Congress to deal with the problems of land pollution, principally by hazardous wastes.[12] Hazardous waste is defined by the EPA as including any solid waste or any combinations of solid waste that, when improperly treated, stored, transported, or disposed of, may pose a substantial threat to human health or the environment. The EPA has authority to designate solid waste as hazardous and has identified toxic, radioactive, corrosive, or combustible materials as hazardous.

A Regulatory Paper Trail for Hazardous Waste

manifest
A document that is required by EPA whenever a company subject to the jurisdiction of the EPA stores, treats, transports, or disposes of hazardous waste.

The regulatory scheme maintained under the RCRA involves a "cradle-to-grave" *paper trail,* which makes extensive use of manifests. A producer (or generator) of hazardous waste is required to obtain a manifest informing the EPA that it had produced hazardous waste and that it is storing the waste on-site. The EPA regulates on-site storage of hazardous waste and, depending on the waste, may require certain treatments to make the waste less dangerous. Eventually, of course, generators of hazardous waste usually have to transport the waste for disposal at a dumpsite that is approved for hazardous waste storage and treatment.

When generators contract with a trucking firm to transport hazardous waste to a dumpsite, they are limited in available selections to trucking companies that are qualified to transport hazardous waste. The trucks used to transport such materials are required to conspicuously label the fact that they are carrying hazardous waste (they typically display a large banner that reads *HAZ MAT*). When a trucking firm picks up hazardous waste from a generator, it is given the material manifest and the EPA must be notified that hazardous waste is being shipped. When the hazardous waste is transported to a final disposal site, the operator of the site receives the manifest and is required to notify the generator that it has received the hazardous waste. If the operator of the hazardous waste dump does not notify the generator, then the generator is required to notify the EPA so that the location of the hazardous waste can be determined.

Operators and owners of hazardous waste sites are closely regulated by the EPA, which prescribes standards for construction and operation of disposal plants and storage facilities. Among other requirements, the EPA's standards specify that a dumpsite maintain adequate levels of liability insurance coverage and provide data that show that it has adequate

---

[12] Pub. L. No. 94-580, 90 Stat. 2795, codified at 42 U.S.C. §§ 6901–6986.

financial assets both to close the dumpsite when it is appropriate (or filled) and to continue maintaining the site adequately after closure.

Even though operations of current dumpsites are closely regulated, it is the generators of hazardous waste that are liable if there are problems with on-site storage, transportation, or disposal. If accidents occur involving hazardous waste, a number of parties can be held strictly liable for any damages caused. In the case of generators, they are liable for harm that occurs attributable to hazardous waste that is stored on-site. The company selected to transport the hazardous waste is strictly liable if an accident occurs during transport. The dumpsite is strictly liable if harm occurs when it stores and treats hazardous waste.

The 1984 Hazardous and Solid Waste Amendments Act modified the RCRA so that generators were required to do more to treat hazardous waste, making it less dangerous before its transport to waste dumps.[13] In addition, there were a number of new regulations added to bring regulation to "small" generators of hazardous waste, those generating less than 1,000 kilograms yearly, who had not previously been regulated. Penalties were increased for noncompliance with applicable regulations, with criminal sanctions significantly toughened. The 1984 amendments also authorized citizen suits when the EPA does not act. As a result of the amendments that were enacted in 1984 and 1998, civil penalties can be levied of up to $25,000 per violation, with higher fines to be imposed for more serious violations. Criminal penalties can include fines up to $50,000 per day for violations as well as imprisonment up to two years, with the prospect of doubled sanctions for repeat offenders.

Superfund

Superfund
A fund created through taxes levied on the generators of hazardous waste, particularly companies in the chemical and petroleum industries.

In 1980 Congress passed the Comprehensive Environmental Response, Compensation, and Liability Act (CERCLA), which created the **Superfund**.[14] This law imposed a tax on the chemical and petroleum industries according to the hazardous waste generated by each firm and provided broad federal authority to respond directly to releases or threatened releases of hazardous substances that might endanger public health or the environment. Over a five-year time span, $1.6 billion was collected and placed in a trust fund for cleaning up abandoned or uncontrolled hazardous waste sites. The Superfund was subsequently increased to $10 billion.

The rationale behind creation of the Superfund was that proceeds of the tax on the generators of hazardous waste could be used to clean up abandoned waste dumps that pose a threat to human health.

According to the EPA, CERCLA

- Established prohibitions and requirements concerning closed and abandoned hazardous waste sites.
- Provided for liability of persons responsible for releases of hazardous waste at these sites.
- Established a trust fund to provide for cleanup when no responsible party could be identified.

If a waste dump has been abandoned, and no person responsible for the dumpsite can be identified, Superfund assets are used to clean up and treat the dangerous chemicals at the waste dump. For abandoned waste dumps falling into this category, the EPA has developed

---

[13] Pub. L. No. 98-616, 98 Stat. 3221, codified at 42 U.S.C. § 6901 *et seq.*
[14] Pub. L. No. 96-510, 94 Stat. 2767, codified at 42 U.S.C. §§ 9601–9675.

a National Priorities List, which ranks these abandoned dumps in terms of their threat potential to human health, applying what the EPA calls a *hazard ranking score*. In those situations in which the EPA has had to intervene and use Superfund assets to accomplish a cleanup, the average cost of the response has been estimated to be in the range of $25 million.

potentially responsible persons
Persons that are potentially liable for the cleanup costs of hazardous waste dumps, including generators, transporters, landowners, and dumpsite operators.

Potentially Responsible Persons   The EPA is frequently involved in litigation and a large share of that litigation has been directed toward "**potentially responsible persons** under the CERCLA.**"** If persons responsible for contributing to hazardous waste at a Superfund site can be identified, then the EPA pursues them to pay for the costs of the cleanup. A sizeable share of the assets of the Superfund have actually been used to cover attorney fees and other costs of litigation incurred by the EPA in the pursuit of potentially responsible persons.

The list of potentially responsible persons is a lengthy one and includes the

1. Person(s) (corporations are persons) who generated the wastes disposed of at the site in question.
2. Person who transported the waste to the dumpsite.
3. Person who owned or operated the dumpsite at the time the hazardous waste was received.
4. Person(s) who currently own the land upon which the hazardous waste resides.

joint and several liability
Parties that are jointly and severally liable are each liable to plaintiffs for the entire amount of the damages, though those that are jointly and severally liable may sue each other for contributions.

Joint and Several Liability for Responsible Persons   It is important to note that all responsible persons are jointly and severally liable for environmental cleanup costs, even if an individual "person" is only responsible for a small portion of the hazardous waste. A defendant/responsible person who is **jointly and severally liable** is entitled to sue fellow defendants and others for a *contribution* if all or an inordinate amount of the damages is collected from a single person.

Piercing the Corporate Veil

piercing the corporate veil
Action, with a court disregarding the limited liability protection associated with corporations, that makes a shareholder liable for debts of a corporation owned by the shareholder that exceed the assets of the corporation.

The term **piercing the corporate veil** refers to situations when limited liability for shareholders becomes *unlimited*. In several cases, the EPA has tried to break through a limited liability shield when the "person" engaged in illegal dumping or storage of hazardous waste was a *wholly owned subsidiary* of a parent company. If the EPA disregards limited liability protections, it goes after not only the assets of the subsidiary whose employees generated, stored, or treated targeted hazardous waste, but also the assets of the subsidiary's sole shareholder, the parent company. If all or most of the officers and directors of the subsidiary are also employees of the parent corporation, courts will find liability for the parent corporation if the parent company, in fact, operated a facility that should be cleaned up and was nominally owned by the subsidiary.

Corporate Formalities   When a wholly owned subsidiary works with hazardous waste, it is very important to observe corporate formalities, such as separate bank accounts, logos, and elections of members of the board of directors, to avoid having the corporate veil subject to being pierced by an EPA suit. If, in fact, a parent corporation exercises budgetary control and collects on accounts receivable for a subsidiary, along with making decisions on all government contracts, courts are willing to set aside the limited liability normally attributable to a subsidiary and find that the parent company is liable for the actions of the subsidiary. Finally, EPA is entitled under this law to pursue individuals, corporate officers, directors, and shareholders who were involved in *personally* directing operations that caused hazardous waste cleanups.

Lender Liability

Since current owners of land that contains hazardous waste that the EPA has to clean up are considered potentially liable persons under CERCLA, quite obviously, purchasers of real estate need to take precautions so that they do not buy their way into major liabilities. One area of liability that has been a source of litigation has been the acquisition of real estate by lenders when the borrower defaults on a loan and real estate was security for the loan. Under these circumstances, if the land acquired pursuant to a foreclosure contains an abandoned hazardous waste dump that subsequently is identified as leaking, the lender is liable for the costs of the site's required cleanup.

Congress has recognized that, in many cases in the 1980s and 1990s, lenders became "gun-shy" about making needed loans because of potential CERCLA liability. In 1996 Congress passed the Asset Conservation, Lender Liability and Deposit Insurance Protection Act, which limited potential exposure of lenders when they acquire land through foreclosure.[15] As a result of the 1996 legislation, lenders escape liability for possible hazardous waste *as long as they did not participate in management* of the facility prior to foreclosure. In other words, when the debtor still owned the land upon which the hazardous waste laid, liability of the subsequent owner, the lender, depends on whether the lender participated in management decisions *prior* to the debtor's default on the mortgage. This legislation draws distinctions between lender capacity to make management decisions and actually participation in management. The mere capacity to make decisions does not create liability for a lender, but the participatory activity does. If a lender acquires real estate in a foreclosure proceeding, it must sell or re-lease the facility as soon as possible, even though the lender may still be the "legal" owner.

CERCLA Defenses

innocent landowner defense
This defense is effective if the defendant in a suit brought by the EPA for contributions to clean up hazardous waste can show that no discharge of hazardous waste took place during his or her ownership of the land.

CERCLA allows for an **innocent landowner defense,** which is also known as "third-party defense." To qualify for the third-party defense, a potentially responsible party generally must show that the release of hazardous waste on his land was solely caused by a third party who is neither an employee nor a contracting partner of the responsible party. If the facility was acquired from a third party who caused or allowed hazardous waste to be released during his or her ownership of the property, the purchaser is in a contractual relationship and thus unable to assert the innocent landowner defense. In order to qualify for the innocent owner, third-party defense, the landowner has to establish that

1. He or she did not cause the release of hazardous waste, nor did the seller of the real estate.
2. The owner had no reason to believe that hazardous substances were disposed of at the facility.

due diligence inspections
To qualify for the innocent landowner defense, the landowner must be able to prove that, before purchasing the land, he or she was reasonably diligent in inspecting the land for possible hazardous waste but did not find any.

An owner of real estate can prove that he or she had no reason to be believe that hazardous substances were disposed of at the facility if it can show that, prior to purchase, it undertook an "appropriate inquiry into the previous ownership and uses of the property consistent with good commercial or customary practice, in an effort to minimize liability." In other words, the purchaser performed a *due diligence* check on the history of the real estate it was going to acquire and the investigation did not reveal the presence of hazardous waste. There are now companies that specialize in performing CERCLA **due diligence inspections** of real estate that companies are considering acquiring.

---

[15] Pub. L. No. 104-208, 110 Stat. 3009, codified at 42 U.S.C. § 9601(20).

The only other defenses available to landowners under CERCLA are based on an act of God or war. If the landowner can show that the release of hazardous waste was due to an act of God, such as an earthquake, or the result of a war, then (s)he can escape liability for the costs of cleaning up hazardous wastes that are on or originated from his or her property.

NUCLEAR RADIATION

From its birth, the atomic energy industry has been regulated almost exclusively by the federal government. In 1954 the Atomic Energy Act was enacted, creating the Atomic Energy Commission (AEC).[16] The name of the AEC was changed to the Nuclear Regulatory Commission (NRC) in 1974 with passage of the Energy Reorganization Act.[17] The NRC is responsible for approving permits to build nuclear reactors upon review of construction plans for a proposed facility. After plans for a nuclear plant have been approved and the actual plant's construction is completed, the NRC licenses its startup and continued operation and has the power to suspend its operation if there are breaches of required safety protocols.

Although the NRC licenses the operations of nuclear plants, the EPA has the power to regulate environmental exposure to radiation and the disposal of nuclear waste. In addition, the states are required to regulate low-level discharges of radiation under the Low Level Radioactive Waste Policy Act of 1980.[18] Disposal and storage of nuclear waste materials continue to be vexing issues for regulators because of the universally held NIMBY (not in my back yard) attitude.

STATE AND LOCAL REGULATION OF POLLUTION

As discussed at the beginning of this chapter, pollution is often a local event. Because of that fact, pollution regulations were applied by local and state governments almost from the inception of such governments. In general, state statutes and local ordinances are not preempted by federal environmental regulation. Some states, such as California, have had particularly severe pollution problems, due to geography and the large number of motor vehicles. With its severe pollution problems, California has adopted standards, notably those dealing with automobile emissions, that are stricter than federal standards. Interestingly, state water pollution standards that are stricter than federal standards are, nevertheless, included as requirements applicable to permits that are issued by the EPA under the Clean Water Act.

Local governments typically have their greatest effect on their local environment through zoning ordinances. Prohibitions on commercial buildings in neighborhoods and limits on signs and advertising can have a large impact (many would say not always favorable) on local aesthetics and quality of life. Local governments, as well as state governments, also often operate recycling programs, which are activities that can engage citizens as participants in cleanup efforts on an organized basis.

---

[16] Pub. L. No. 83-703, 68 Stat. 941, codified at 42 U.S.C. §§ 2011–2297g.
[17] Pub. L. No. 93-438, 88 Stat. 1233, codified at 42 U.S.C. § 5801 *et seq.*
[18] Pub. L. No. 96-573, 94 Stat. 3347, codified at 42 U.S.C. § 2021 *et seq.*

Ethical Challenges　Cost–Benefit Analysis versus Stewardship

Environmental law inspires heated debates that often migrate into discussions about environmental ethics. As discussed in Chapter 6, ethics involves analysis of what is right and wrong and ultimately is based on value systems. For some, environmental issues are all about the costs and benefits of various government actions that have dollar values attached to each alternative. Many economists believe that it is possible to measure the value society places on a glorious sunset over a lake with fresh water and plenty of nature. In some of these analyses, economists look at demand for such amenities where they are provided by the private sector and extrapolate a value for government-held "natural" assets in the form of wilderness areas, endangered species, and recreational opportunities.

Others in the environmental advocacy movement base their beliefs on a principle that is often called "stewardship." Stewardship is based on the notion that we should respect the environment and basically pass it on to the next generation in the same or better condition than when we inherited the land we live on. Some environmentalists reject cost–benefit analysis as monetizing things that should be viewed as priceless. However, when real-world environmental debates take place, such as the current debate about whether to drill for oil in the Alaskan Natural Wildlife Refuge (ANWR), it is often impossible to ignore economic issues. Some environmentalists will claim that (1) ANWR is a magnificent national treasure that should not be disturbed by oil companies and (2) the amount of oil that can be procured will not solve our reliance on foreign oil. Once these environmentalists begin addressing economic issues, it is impossible to avoid discussion of costs and benefits.

For those who want to gauge their own and others' ethical environmental compass, it is sometimes useful to examine environmental issues with three maxims:

1. Alternatives should be solely based on economic costs and benefits (which would include the values people are willing to pay for natural recreation).
2. Alternatives should be considered based only on whether they make the physical environment better or worse (an approach based solely on stewardship).
3. Some aspects of the environment can be valued and some cannot.

The moralistic or ethical approach, and the approach taken by some environmental groups, is given by maxim 2 above. The purely business approach, the approach that logging companies and their employees often use, is maxim 1. They think that the value of some endangered species such as the spotted owl is quantifiable and should be weighed against the value to the community of fully employed loggers. Congress is somewhere in between. Certainly the environmentalists have great political power, especially in the Democratic Party, but the Republican Party is often very sympathetic to business interests. There are a number of environmental laws that explicitly call for cost–benefit analyses before a regulation can be enacted, but there are others, such as the Endangered Species Act, that are based on the notion that endangered species should be preserved regardless of the costs. Where is your compass pointing?

Summary

The Inadequacy of Common Law Legal Actions, Such as Nuisance and Trespass Claims, Led to State and Federal Regulation of Pollution; Common Law

- Although environmental concerns are often focused on problems faced in a "local" area, most environmental regulation is the result of federal acts and/or federal agency regulations.

- The dominant role of the federal government in the environmental protection arena is the result of three failures: (1) *market failure*, (2) failure of common law to provide adequate remedies for market failures, and (3) the failure of state and local laws to provide nationally acceptable environmental protection standards.

- Victims of injury from pollution can seek relief under common law principles. Most notably, plaintiffs can lodge claims for *nuisance* injury and for *trespass* under common law, while there are some circumstances under which negligence and strict liability claims can be lodged.

- There are two severe limitations on the effectiveness of common law remedies for pollution offenses: (1) no action against polluting activities is subject to litigation until the offense has been committed (prevention would be better) and (2) as the remedy at common law was generally a

Remedies Remain a Potent Force That Can Be Used to Raise Costs to Polluters	monetary damage award to the injured plaintiff, once the compensation had been awarded, there was no remaining disincentive for the polluter to continue or resume the polluting activities.
Creation of the EPA in 1970 Was Followed by Legislation to Regulate and Reduce Air, Water, and Land Pollution; under NEPA, When a Government Project Imperils the Environment, Government Agencies Must Prepare an Environmental Impact Statement	• From the 1960s forward, rapidly growing political support for an environmental protection movement has resulted in the adoption of a broad array of federal acts aimed at pollution abatement and the creation of a federal agency, the *Environmental Protection Agency (EPA),* authorized to pursue the maintenance and improvement of environmental conditions. • The EPA was created by an executive order of then-President Richard Nixon in 1970. • Modern federal government activism in environmental protection is clearly reflected in the lengthy list of statutes enacted by Congress from the 1960s forward. These include the National Environmental Protection Act (NEPA); the Clean Air Act (CAA); the Clean Water Act (CWA); the Endangered Species Act (ESA); the Marine Protection, Research and Sanctuaries Act (MPRSA); the Oil Pollution Act (OPA); the Toxic Substance Control Act (TSCA); the Federal Insecticide, Fungicide and Rodenticide Act (FIFRA); the Resource Conservation and Recovery Act (RCRA); and the Comprehensive Environmental Response, Compensation and Liability Act (CERCLA). • NEPA requires government agencies to fill out an environmental impact statement (EIS) whenever a government project is likely to have a significant environmental impact. • Currently, the EPA is one of the largest government agencies with more than 17,000 employees.
Under the Clean Air Act, the EPA Sets Legal Limits for Pollution and Divides the Country between Attainment and Nonattainment Areas	• The CAA requires the EPA to set national ambient air quality standards (NAAQS). • The EPA divides areas in the country into two categories: *prevention of significant deterioration* (PSD) areas, where the air is in compliance with the NAAQS but in which the EPA enforces air quality regulations to prevent significant deterioration, and *nonattainment* areas, where air quality does not meet the NAAQS. • The EPA requires new plants and factories located in PSD areas to use best available control technology (BACT). • In nonattainment areas, firms that want to construct new plants and factories have to develop plans that ensure that there will be no net increase in pollutants of the type emitted by the new plant or factory. • 1990 amendments to the CAA call for substantial reductions in emissions of mobile sources of pollution from automobiles.
Under the Clean Water Act, the EPA Issues Permits That Specify the Pollution Control Technology and the Amount of Pollution That a Permit Holder Can Emit; Other Laws Deal with Specific Water Pollution Issues	• The CWA focuses on point sources of water pollution and issues permits to polluters who, in turn, must agree to use antipollution control technology specified in the permit and to limit total amounts of pollution released. • Under the CWA, the EPA has the power to prevent landowners from draining wetlands. If the EPA prevents a landowner from draining a wetland, it must compensate the landowner. • Under the ESA, the secretary of the Interior has the power to list animal or plant species as endangered or threatened and is required to prohibit any actions by federal agencies that harm the habitat of endangered or threatened species. • The MPRSA prohibits dumping into the ocean if the dumping would endanger human health or harm the marine environment. • The OPA created the national Oil Spill Liability Trust Fund to provide a capital reserve available to pay for oil spills. The act also allows the government to sue polluters for the total costs of oil spills.

- The Toxic Substances Control Act regulates toxic materials and requires manufacturers to notify the EPA in advance of the production or importation of new chemicals that may be toxic. The EPA has the power to require manufacturers to conduct tests and has the power to ban dangerous chemicals or restrict their use.

- Pesticides are regulated under FIFRA, which requires sellers to register their products before use. The EPA has the authority to cancel registration of dangerous pesticides such as DDT.

- Hazardous waste is regulated by the RCRA, which requires cradle-to-grave documentation. Generators, transporters, and dumpsite operators are strictly liable for harm that originates from the hazardous wastes they handle.

- The Superfund, created by CERCLA, imposes a tax on the generators of hazardous waste, with the proceeds of the tax used to clean up abandoned hazardous waste dumps. Potentially responsible persons under CERCLA include generators, transporters, landowners, and those who operate hazardous waste facilities. Each of these parties is jointly and severally liable for hazardous waste that causes harm or is cleaned up by the EPA.

- Under CERCLA, the EPA has held corporations liable for actions of subsidiaries. It also has sued lenders who came into possession of land that contained hazardous waste.

- There are defenses available to potentially responsible persons under CERCLA, if these persons can show that third parties were responsible for the harm caused by the hazardous waste.

- Nuclear radiation is regulated by the Nuclear Regulatory Commission, which approves nuclear plant design and construction.

- State and local governments also enact environmental regulations. In general, stricter local standards for pollution control are not deemed to be in conflict with federal statutes and regulations of the EPA.

Key Terms

ambient air quality standards, *687*
bubble program, *689*
due diligence inspections, *700*
endangered species, *695*
environmental impact statement (EIS), *684*
Environmental Protection Agency (EPA), *687*
Federal Insecticide, Fungicide, and Rodenticide Act (FIFRA), *696*

hazardous air pollutants, *689*
hazardous wastes, *697*
innocent landowner defense, *700*
joint and several liability, *699*
manifest, *697*
market failure, *679*
nonattainment areas, *687*
nonpoint source, *693*
nuisance, *680*
offset policy, *688*
permit system, *693*

piercing the corporate veil, *699*
point source, *693*
potentially responsible persons, *699*
prevention of significant deterioration (PSD) areas, *688*
regulatory taking, *694*
Superfund, *698*
toxic substances, *696*
ultrahazardous, *682*
wetlands, *694*

Questions for Review and Analysis

1. You should be able to discuss just what plaintiffs have to show in order to recover in nuisance and trespass cases brought against polluters. What are the different tools available to courts and the EPA to control and reduce pollution?

2. It has been alleged that the goals of pollution control and abatement sometimes clash with those of economic growth. How are both goals accommodated within the Clean Air Act?

3. When the EPA issues permits to firms that pollute water, is it encouraging water pollution? Why doesn't the EPA simply refuse to issue permits to water polluters?

4. The Resource Conservation and Recovery Act requires generators of hazardous waste to create a paper trail. What does this mean and how does creating a paper trail enable the EPA to more effectively regulate hazardous wastes?

5. Pollution occurs at a local level and, yet, the most important pollution control laws are federal. Does this make sense? Explain why or why not.

If You Really Understood This Chapter, You Should Be Able to Provide Informed Commentary on the Following:

1. **Storage of Hazardous Waste and Strict Liability.** In December 1975, Western Petroleum (Western) purchased 40 acres of land in a rural area north of Roosevelt, Utah, that had previously been used as a gravel pit. Western used the property solely for the disposal of formation water, a wastewater produced while drilling for oil. Formation water contains oil, gas, and high concentrations of salt and chemicals, making it unfit for culinary or agricultural uses. In 1976, the Branches purchased a parcel of property immediately adjacent to, and at an elevation of approximately 200 to 300 feet below, Western's property. Two months after purchasing the property, the Branches noticed that their well water began to have a peculiar taste and a distinctive smell of petroleum products. Soap added to the water would no longer form suds. They observed that polluted water from Western's disposal pit was running onto the surface of the Branches' property and, on one occasion, reached their basement, causing damage to food stored there. After testing the well water and finding it unfit for human consumption, and after their rabbits and 100 chickens had died, apparently from the polluted water, the Branches began trucking water to their property from outside sources. The Branches sued Western for polluting their water. An issue that arose at trial was whether Western was strictly liable for polluting the Branches' water. Western claims that, in most states, subterranean pollution is judged based on a negligence standard. If a negligence standard is used, the Branches would have to show that Western's practices were not reasonable and, yet, the evidence shows that Western used methods common in the industry for storing formation water. What do you think? Should it matter that the Branches purchased their property second? [*Lloyd and Jeanne Branch v. Western Petroleum, Inc.,* 657 P.2d 267 (Utah 1982).]

2. **April Showers and Government Regulation.** Although the EPA does a lot of good by protecting the environment, it has been accused of overregulation, with opponents often citing the following case. In preparation for construction of a housing subdivision, Hoffman Homes, a construction company, cleared and graded an area that was about an acre in size. Such clearing and grading operations are common at construction sites. Unfortunately for Hoffman, an April shower caused the area to become a giant mud puddle. The litigation began, literally, when an employee of the U.S. Army Corps of Engineers drove by the construction site and noticed that there was a one-acre pond. The employee told his supervisor, who sent other employees of the Army Corps to investigate. After this check, the Army Corps claimed that the mud puddle was a natural wetland for which Hoffman needed a permit (from the Corps) before draining. Hoffman protests, claiming that there is no evidence that any wildlife treated the mud puddle as a wetland. Hoffman claims that the mud puddle was not connected to any running body of water and therefore it did not affect interstate commerce. The EPA, which took over litigation of the case, claims that migratory birds could decide they wanted to take a break from their travels by resting on the puddle. Is this connection with interstate commerce enough for the EPA to assert authority over a construction site? [*Hoffman Homes, Inc. v. Administrator, United States Environmental Protection Agency,* 999 F.2d 256 (7th Cir. 1993).]

3. **Sharing Cleanup Costs: Is All Hazardous Waste Equal?** Back in 1971, the owners of a landfill that was cleaned up by the EPA had leased it to a predecessor of Browning-Ferris, which operated it until the fall of 1975. Between then and 1988, it was operated by M.I.G. and AAA. In June of that year, after AAA was sold and Ter Maat moved to Florida, M.I.G. abandoned the landfill without covering it properly. Two years after the abandonment, the EPA placed the site on the National Priorities List, the list of toxic waste sites that the Superfund statute requires to be cleaned up; see 42 U.S.C. §§ 9605(8)(B), 9616(d), (e). Shortly afterward, Browning-Ferris and the other plaintiffs, which shared responsibility for some of the pollution at the site, agreed to clean it up. After a judge elucidated a formula for allocating costs, Browning-Ferris appeals. The issues on appeal are whether (1) Ter Maat is personally liable for his part in operating the hazardous waste dump because he is a shareholder also and (2) whether the allocation of costs based on the formula applied by the trial court judge is valid. In the allocation issue, Browning-Ferris claims it is paying too much because it only operated the dump for a short period of time and because the amount of waste it contributed was correspondingly tiny relative to contributions of the other defendants. The district court judge found that the hazardous waste left by Browning-Ferris was particularly toxic and that its management of the dump was particularly irresponsible. Are judges bound to treat all hazardous waste equally? [*Browning-Ferris Industries of Illinois, Inc., et al. v. Richard Ter Maat, et al.,* 195 F.3d 953 (7th Cir. 1999).]

4. **BPT, BAT, BCT, and NSPS Standards.** Environmental litigation often could be viewed as an entertaining three-ring circus if the stakes were not so high. It is common in these battles that the EPA will issue a regulation dealing with the meaning of best practical control technology (BPT), best available technology (BAT), and so on, followed shortly by a lawsuit from an environmental group that contends that the regulations are too lenient. Of course, it is common for the polluter to file its own lawsuit claiming that the EPA's interpretation of BPT or BAT is incorrect or that the EPA does not have authority to issue regulations in the area at issue. In *BP Exploration & Oil, Inc. et al. v. Environmental Protection Company,* 66 F.3d 784 (6th Cir. 1995), the involved oil companies attacked EPA regulations applied to drilling fluids, drill cutting waste, produced water, and produced sand associated with offshore oil and gas drilling. In addition to BPT and BAT, at issue were EPA regulations regarding BCT (best conventional pollutant control technology) and NSPS (new source performance standards). In the same case, the Natural Resources Defense Council (NRDC) claimed that the EPA illegally rejected the zero discharge option and also made other judgments that NRDC claims violated the CWA. Perhaps the EPA is where it should be when it is stationed in the middle ground between oil drilling companies and environmental groups calling for zero discharges. What do you think?

5. **Personal Responsibility.** Case law establishes personal liability for shareholders and corporate officers who personally direct and operate hazardous waste treatment and disposal activities. What about the shareholder of a corporation that owned a subsidiary that dumped waste owned by another company, which later became a Superfund site that was cleaned up by the EPA? According to the facts, that shareholder, Georgoulis, arranged for disposal of the hazardous waste but was not personally involved in the dumping of the waste. EPA contends that Georgoulis had authority to control what the parties did and that he was the sole shareholder. According to the court, "We assume, for purposes of this appeal, that neither Georgoulis nor any employee of the TIC entities had personal knowledge of the contract between WFE and HEC for the disposal of WFE's wastes at the dumpsite. Nor did Georgoulis or any employee of the TIC entities have any personal knowledge of the disposal practices at the dumpsite, nor were they in any way directly involved in waste disposal matters. However, it is beyond genuine dispute that, at all relevant times, Georgoulis had authority to control, and did in fact exert direct control over many significant aspects of the ongoing operations and management of WFE." What do you think? Is the ability to control the same as having personal knowledge such that the person should be personally liable for cleanup costs? [*United States of America, et al. v. TIC Investment Corporation, TIC United Corporation, and Stratton Georgoulis,* 68 F.3d 1082 (8th Cir. 1995).]

Social Responsibility, Policy, and Ethics in a High-Tech World

6. **Environmental Justice.** There is growing attention in the environmental movement to a "social justice" component of pollution and pollution control. The argument is that, not only is the environment harmed by corporations that pollute, but polluters tend to pollute in areas where the politically and economically disadvantaged live. The basic idea is that polluters can more easily get away with damaging pollution if the pollution takes place where poor and minority citizens live. This movement has an international dimension. The claim has been made that U.S., European, and Japanese firms make use of less developed countries, where environmental laws are lax or not enforced, and where country officials are so desperate for business with developed countries that they are willing to incur significant environmental degradation. An organization propounding this point of view is EcoJustice Network (http://www.igc.org/index.html). Note, on their website, that they link workers, minorities, and women's interests together in a "progressive" coalition. As a counterpoint, it has been pointed out that pollution often goes hand in hand with jobs, particularly the type of production jobs that poor people could fill. Lawsuits that block polluters from operating in the vicinity of poor people may block economic opportunities for minorities and other poorer workers. In addition, the professed concern of labor groups in the United States for pollution that occurs in less developed countries has been questioned as no more than a backdoor attempt to keep manufacturing jobs in the United States. Whether the environmental justice movement will move forward and effectively challenge the EPA and major companies to reexamine where pollution takes place, or whether internal conflicts will undermine the cohesiveness of the group, is unclear at this point. The environmental justice movement

is an excellent topic for a term project because examination of the primary focal issues will lead to other issues, some legal and some political, and will reveal how inescapable trade-offs are in this interrelated world.

Using the Internet to Your Advantage

1. Of course, the first government website for this chapter is that of the Environmental Protection Agency (http://www.epa.gov). Virtually all environmental topics and summaries of legislation are accessible at the EPA website (http://www.epa.gov/epahome/topics.html). The EPA has a compilation of the major environmental statutes at http://www.epa.gov/epahome/laws.htm. Note that the EPA also has a global warming Web page at http://www.epa.gov/oar/globalwarming.nsf/content/index.html.

2. There are, of course, many private groups very interested in the environment. The EcoJustice website is provided above. The Environmental Law Institute (http://www.eli.org/) is a group that claims the membership of 50,000 attorneys worldwide. Among environmental groups, certainly the Sierra Club (http://www.sierraclub.com/) has been a leader in initiating lawsuits that have significantly impacted environmental law. Another environmental group that has been active in environmental lawsuits (several of which appear in this chapter) is the Natural Resources Defense Council (http://www.nrdc.org/). On the side opposing environmental groups on most issues is the American Petroleum Institute (http://api-ec.api.org/newsplashpage/index.cfm).

Chapter Twenty-Two

Computer Crime: Pornography, Fraud, Hacking, and Gambling

Learning Objectives

After completing this chapter, you should

1. Recognize the main manifestations of computer and cybercrime.
2. Recognize how the First Amendment protections of freedom of expression pertain to obscenity and pornography laws and be able to predict which laws will withstand constitutional scrutiny by courts.
3. Be able to discuss various ways in which hackers operate and what is legal and illegal hacking.
4. Be familiar with recent legislation that (*a*) inhibits illegal hacking, (*b*) protects IP, and (*c*) is directed at preventing terrorism and espionage.
5. Know the basic rules applicable to Internet gambling and cybermedicine. Both activities are (*a*) prevalent and (*b*) often illegal.

OVERVIEW

Even though the Internet is only a few years old, cyber crime has already become big business, erupting on the Internet in multiple forms. **Hackers** have broken into files that contained credit card accounts and have pilfered millions of dollars in bogus charges. Hackers are also responsible for unleashing viruses, which can wreck havoc on the nation's increasingly linked computers. The Melissa virus, which first appeared on the Internet in March 1999, caused an estimated $80 million in damages to computers worldwide. In the United States alone, Melissa infected 1.2 million computers in one-fifth of the country's largest businesses.[1] The Internet has facilitated rapid growth of activities involving some traditional vices such as gambling and pornography, both of which are billion-dollar industries. The Internet threatens the viability of the regulation of pharmaceutical drugs because of the

[1] http://www.cybercrime.gov/ccpolicy.html#DDSA.

hacker
The *Net Dictionary* defines a hacker as "[a]n expert programmer who likes to spend a lot of time figuring out the finer details of computer systems or networks, as opposed to those who learn only the minimum necessary." Hackers are synonymous with those who gain unauthorized access to inner workings of computer files.

number of websites that offer to sell prescription drugs, with or without a prescription by a "treating" medical doctor, who never comes into physical contact with his or her "patients." The Internet also has facilitated the practice of industrial espionage through which companies (many foreign) attempt to make use of other company's intellectual property. According to Eric Holder, Deputy Attorney General of the U.S. Department of Justice, "It is estimated that U.S. companies lost $200 billion in 1997 due to worldwide copyright, trademark, and trade secret infringement."[2]

The focus of this chapter is crime—specifically, computer crime and cyber crime. In law, a *crime* occurs when (1) a defendant commits a criminal act prohibited by statute and (2) it is shown that there was *criminal intent*. A person who is distracted while driving and ends up in an automobile accident in which someone else is killed has not committed murder, because there was no criminal intent. In some cases, the failure to do something (an omission), such as file your tax returns, can be a criminal act. In a criminal case, the prosecution must prove that the defendant is guilty of the prohibited acts, with the requisite intent. The proof must support the well-known *beyond a reasonable doubt* verdict, which is a higher standard than required for finding the defendant liable in a civil case.

COMPUTER CRIME AND CYBERCRIME

This chapter discusses computer crime and cybercrime. *Computer crime* is crime that involves computers, computer systems, or their applications. *Cybercrime* involves all of the above and occurs in cyberspace. When a hacker penetrates the computer system of a bank, typically hacking into its financial software, the crime committed probably does not involve the Internet. However, the agent involved in this activity certainly makes use of computers and/or a computer system and its applications. The topic of computer and cyber crime already encompasses activities that are too extensive for full coverage in one chapter of a legal environment textbook. Hence, we are selective in the topics explored.

There are a number of areas in which the Internet facilitates crime, fraud, and irresponsible behavior. These include the publishing of **pornography** that is easily accessible by minors. The Internet is regularly plagued by viruses, which may be likened to a cyberspace equivalent of the discharge of harmful biological agents into the human population because the person releasing the virus (biological agents) gets no financial benefit from the act, presumably gaining only the psychic satisfaction of seeing the havoc he or she created. Government and financial institutions are often targets of hackers whose antics run the gamut from pranks, to theft, to international industrial espionage. Hackers have been successful in appropriating trade secrets, with their successes giving birth to a burgeoning cybersecurity industry. In addition, hackers and others have taken huge volumes of intellectual property without paying royalties. Among the IP targets of cybercriminals are software, movies, and records.

pornography
In this book, pornography is sexually oriented, adult material that is constitutionally protected. It may be illegal however, to expose children to pornography, depending on the situation.

More Security, Less Privacy

There is evidence that the terrorists who attacked the World Trade Center in New York and the Pentagon in Washington on September 11, 2001, used the Internet to communicate and coordinate their plans. In response, Congress has passed the 2001 USA PATRIOT Act, which has given significant new powers to federal law enforcement.[3] In

---

[2] Remarks of Eric Holder, Announcing the Intellectual Property Rights Initiative, San Jose, California, July 23, 1999, *available at* http://www.cybercrime.gov/dagipini.htm.

[3] Provide Appropriate Tools Required to Intercept and Obstruct Terrorism (PATRIOT) Act of 2001, H.R. 3162, Pub. L. No. 107-56, 115 Stat. 272.

WHAT DOES CCIPS DO?

The Computer Crime and Intellectual Property Section ("CCIPS") attorney staff consists of about two dozen lawyers who focus exclusively on the issues raised by computer and intellectual property crime. Section attorneys advise federal prosecutors and law enforcement agents; comment upon and propose legislation; coordinate international efforts to combat computer crime; litigate cases; and train all law enforcement groups. Other areas of expertise possessed by CCIPS attorneys include encryption, electronic privacy laws, search and seizure of computers, e-commerce, hacker investigations, and intellectual property crimes.

A large part of CCIPS' strength derives from the diverse skills and the wide variety of experiences its lawyers have had before joining the Section. Before joining CCIPS, its attorneys have been computer scientists, state and federal prosecutors, and associates and partners at law firms. A substantial number of CCIPS' attorneys have received degrees in computer science, engineering, or other technical fields; about half came to CCIPS with prior government service. CCIPS began as the Computer Crime Unit of the former General Litigation and Legal Advice Section of DOJ's Criminal Division in 1991. CCIPS became a Section of the Criminal Division in 1996.

As Attorney General Janet Reno noted in her testimony on "Cybercrime" before the United States Senate Committee on Appropriations on February 16, 2000:

"The cornerstone of our prosecutor cybercrime program is the Criminal Division's Computer Crime and Intellectual Property Section, known as CCIPS. CCIPS was founded in 1991 as the Computer Crime Unit, and was elevated into a Section in 1996. With the help of this Subcommittee, CCIPS has grown from five attorneys in January of 1996, to eighteen attorneys today. CCIPS works closely on computer crime cases with Assistant United States Attorneys known as 'Computer and Telecommunications Coordinators' (CTCs) in U.S. Attorney's Offices around the country. Each CTC is given special training and equipment, and serves as the district's expert in computer crime cases.

The responsibility and accomplishments of CCIPS and the CTC program include:

Litigating Cases:

"CCIPS attorneys have litigating responsibilities, taking a lead role in some computer crime and intellectual property investigations, and a coordinating role in many national investigations, such as the denial of service investigation that is ongoing currently. As law enforcement matures into the Information Age, CCIPS is a central point of contact for investigators and prosecutors who confront investigative problems with emerging technologies. This year, CCIPS assisted with wiretaps over computer networks, as well as traps and traces that require agents to segregate Internet headers from the content of the packet. CCIPS has also coordinated an interagency working group consisting of all the federal law enforcement agencies, which developed guidance for law enforcement agents and prosecutors on the many problems of law, jurisdiction, and policy that arise in the online environment."

"Working with the U.S. Attorney's Office in the District of New Jersey and the FBI, as well as with state prosecutors and investigators, CCIPS attorneys helped ensure that David Smith, the creator of the Melissa virus, pled guilty to a violation of the computer fraud statute and admitted to causing damages in excess of $80 million."

"CCIPS is also a key component in enforcing the "Economic Espionage Act," enacted in 1996 to deter and punish the theft of valuable trade secrets. CCIPS coordinates approval for all the charges under the theft of trade secret provision of this Act, and CCIPS attorneys successfully tried the first jury case ever under the Act, culminating in guilty verdicts against a company, its Chief Executive Officer, and another employee."

"The CTCs have been responsible for the prosecution of computer crimes across the country, including the prosecution of the notorious hacker, Kevin Mitnick, in Los Angeles, the prosecution of the hacker group 'Global Hell' in Dallas, and the prosecution of White House web page hacker, Eric Burns, in Alexandria, Virginia."

* * *

International

"The borderless nature of computer crime requires a large role for CCIPS in international negotiations. CCIPS chairs the G-8 Subgroup on High-tech Crime, which has established a 24 hours a day/7 days a week point of contact with 15 countries for mutual assistance in computer crime. CCIPS also plays a leadership role in the Council of Europe Experts' Committee on Cybercrime, and in a new cybercrime project at the Organization of American States."

Source: http://www.cybercrime.gov/ccips.html.

addition, by executive order, President George W. Bush has expanded the power of federal investigators. There are more proposals for expansion of the powers of law enforcement, most notably at the federal level, particularly in the areas of computer and cyberspace communication and storage of electronic records. Some of the expansions of the powers of the police to monitor what takes place in cyberspace and at your CPU unit are dealt with in this chapter.

The problem of computer crime is sufficiently serious that the U.S. Department of Justice has formed a Computer Crime and Intellectual Property Section (CCIPS) unit, which has been further augmented as a result of the events of September 11, 2001.[4] The "Cyberlaw Developments" box describes the range of activities engaged in by CCIPS.

Particular Challenges to Cybercrime Fighting

Jurisdiction and Sovereignty

The Internet has facilitated the proliferation of two traditional "vices," pornography and gambling. The Internet provides distinct advantages to providers of access to pornography and gambling, in large part because of severe jurisdictional barriers to prosecuting activities deemed to be criminal in those arenas (the next chapter discusses international aspects of cyberlaw in more detail). With various forms of gambling illegal in the United States (or, at least, in most of the United States), jurisdictional barriers enable many small countries to derive significant revenue by licensing websites, readily accessible from any location in the world, that cater to U.S. gamblers. While many of the countries that allow legal gambling are very small, they are sovereign, nonetheless. To date, there is really no way for the United States to declare that its gambling laws are right while the laws regulating gambling in, say, Antigua, are wrong. Lack of a global consensus on what constitutes criminal conduct is a challenge for law enforcement, not only in gambling but also in the distribution of pornography and in the committing of fraud.

Lack of International Cooperation

A large share of the volume of cybercrime is transnational. That is, the alleged criminals are located in one jurisdiction while the victims and participants are located in other jurisdictions. Extradition, the process of getting one jurisdiction to provide an accused party to

[4] http://www.cybercrime.gov/ippolicy.htm#H.

another jurisdiction, is a major barrier to many criminal prosecutions, even when there is consensus on what constitutes criminal behavior. Also, transnational cooperation among law enforcement agencies is far from perfect. There are many institutional and legal barriers to sharing criminal files across borders, even though there are plenty of examples of effective cooperation and sharing. Certainly, for the foreseeable future, extranational interdiction of criminals will continue to be the exception rather than the norm. At the time this text was written, Spain had arrested several members of the terrorist network that was responsible for the September 11, 2001, attacks on the United States. However, under Spanish law it was not legal to extradite the accused terrorists to a country, such as the United States, that applies the death penalty.

The next section of this chapter provides a legal analysis of cyberporn, which is one of the leading moneymakers on the Internet. The chapter then focuses attention on criminal fraud and on cyber "breaking and entering" through illegal hacking. Attention also will be focused on other cybercrimes and the recent government changes that have occurred in the wake of the September 11, 2001, attacks. Because of the terrorist attacks, police are being given much more extensive powers to investigate Internet transmissions. Finally, we examine legal aspects of Internet gambling, cybermedicine, and Internet pharmacies.

PORNOGRAPHY AND OBSCENITY

Pornography is big business. It was big business before the explosive growth of the Internet, but the Internet has opened up new markets, mainly composed of patrons who may have been too embarrassed to be seen in "adult" entertainment establishments, but who can and do anonymously visit porn sites. Studies of the Internet and porn sites have revealed that Americans, mainly men,

- Spent $970 million on adult-content sites in 1998, according to the research firm Datamonitor.[5]
- Accounted for about 8 percent of the more than $18 billion of e-commerce trade in 1999.
- Spent as much on e-porn in 1999 as was spent for all online book purchases and more than was spent on airline tickets.

By one estimate there are over 100,000 adult-oriented websites, with new websites able to be set up and activated with investments of as little as $1,000. The results of one poll indicated that the five most popular websites among men were all porn sites while, for women, the most popular sites were all oriented toward shopping. More statistics could be cited, but the transparent point is that there is a huge demand for pornography, mainly from men, and the Internet has made it much more accessible to customers for whom anonymity is important.

Throughout this chapter, when we use the term *pornography,* we are referring to sexually oriented material (pictures, text, and video) that is constitutionally protected for *adults.* While constitutional guarantees may deem adult access to pornography to be a protected (legal) right, that same access may be deemed criminal if it is provided to children. We use the term *obscene* when referring to material that is not constitutionally protected, even for adults. Obscene material includes child actors involved in pornographic works and extremely bizarre portrayals of sexual conduct. Providing a precise definition for what is obscene has eluded legal scholars, in part because what is obscene has changed through the years as society has changed.

---

[5] Brendan I. Koerner, "A Lust for Profit," *U.S. News & World Report* (March 27, 2000). All of the porn industry statistics are from this *U.S. News & World Report* article.

Constitutional Protection for Freedom of Expression

The First Amendment does not contain a lot of qualifying clauses and exceptions. It says, simply and directly, that "Congress shall make no law . . . abridging the freedom of speech, or of the press . . ." Even though this First Amendment statement appears concrete and absolute, there are in fact significant abridgements of freedom of expression imposed by government (previously discussed in Chapter 5) that reveal that the power of the state can be used to stop, censor, or punish certain types of speech. The targets include speech that involves treason, fraud, copyright infringement, and **obscenity**.

obscenity
Illegal, sexually oriented material that is not constitutionally protected.

Many states and local governments, along with the federal government, have passed laws that outlaw obscene material. As was discussed in Chapter 5, because of a number of U.S. Supreme Court decisions, the First Amendment applies with equal force to limit statutes and police actions both of federal *and* nonfederal (state and local) governments. The standards used by courts to evaluate abridgements of the freedom of expression are very demanding and include the following:

1. The purpose of the government-sponsored limitation on freedom of expression must be to promote a compelling state, or government, interest.
2. The statute or police action must actually promote the compelling state or government interest.
3. The statute or police action must not be overly broad or vague.

Often, statutes that limit freedom of expression based on obscenity standards fail to pass court scrutiny because they are deemed *overly broad*. To this point in time, courts have ruled that they are not going to let the possibility that children may gain access to "adult" material serve as a shield for government-sponsored prohibitions of access to otherwise legal material. Even if the government can demonstrate that the purpose of the anti-obscenity statute is valid, such as protecting youth from exposure to pornography, the courts will declare a statute unconstitutional if they believe that the same objectives could be accomplished through less restrictive means. Furthermore, if there is evidence that children can access the objectionable material through other means, the courts will be skeptical of laws that close off one of several access points.

Children and Adult Materials

Courts certainly are sympathetic to the goal of shielding youth from "adult" material and narrowly tailored statutes passed for that purpose and effect are constitutional, as long as they are not overly broad. State laws that prohibit movie theaters from allowing children under 18 access to X-rated entertainment have been constitutionally upheld. Furthermore, when it is clear that the "actors" are children in explicit entertainment in which sexual acts are taking place, the courts have had no problem declaring such entertainment illegal. Since children are incapable of legally consenting to a sexual act, adults involved in child pornography are committing crimes.

Courts take judicial notice of changes in contemporary mores. During the 1950s, access to novels by James Joyce and Henry Miller was prohibited in certain venues on the basis of the works being labeled obscene and because adult nudity on film or stage was a criminal act in many jurisdictions. Although it is a slight exaggeration, it can be claimed that, in the half century since the 1950s, courts have largely given up on the task of deciding what entertainment is obscene when the entertainers are adults and the audience is of age and is expecting adult entertainment. It is well known that the language used by some nightclub comedians is raw and that what is shown at theaters advertising XXX movies is going to be sexually explicit. In both of these settings, access by children is effectively limited and inadvertent or surprise exposures of children or unsuspecting adults to the adult entertainment offered in these settings is exceedingly unlikely.

Under the standards that have evolved, materials that are displayed in most cities are extremely explicit. However, there have been recent successful prosecutions of vendors displaying material that was deemed to have violated *local obscenity laws*. Illustratively, in Cincinnati, Ohio, a "homoerotic" photographic display has been found to be in violation of local obscenity laws and, in western Tennessee, obscenity laws were deemed to have been violated based on local *community standards* when defendants located in northern California distributed sexually explicit material via an electronic bulletin board (the *Thomas* case is discussed in Case 22-1).

Legal Definition of Obscenity

While defining obscenity successfully is a difficult task, the U.S. Supreme Court has articulated a three-prong criterion for obscenity identification.[6] Under the Supreme Court standard, a court attempting to decide whether material is obscene can inquire whether

1. The average person applying "contemporary community standards" would find that the work, taken as a whole, appeals to the prurient interest.
2. The work "depicts or describes, in a patently offensive way, sexual conduct specifically defined by applicable state law."
3. "[T]he work, taken as a whole, lacks serious literary, artistic, political, or scientific value."

Quite obviously, courts have tried to ensure that laws aimed at restricting obscenity do not prohibit legitimate works of art, many of which may deal extensively with sexual matters. It is clear to anyone who has watched cable TV recently that nudity alone is not legally obscene nor is the presentation of scenes with "strong sexual content."

Federal law prohibits interstate commerce in obscene material and, needless to say, there have been convictions for claimed violations of that law.[7] Of course, an issue in virtually all obscenity cases is whether the material is, in fact, obscene. In Case 22-1, a married couple in northern California was prosecuted for obscenity based on community standards that the prosecution claimed were prevalent in Tennessee. Given the ease of transmission of materials over the Internet, a question arises as to whether the more conservative areas of the United States should be able to set the standards for what is transmitted over the Internet.

[6] *Miller v. California*, 413 U.S. 15 (1973).

[7] 18 U.S.C. § 1465, Transportation of Obscene Matters for Sale or Distribution.

Case 22-1

United States of America, Plaintiff-Appellee v. Robert Alan Thomas and Carleen Thomas, Defendants-Appellants

United States Court of Appeals for the Sixth Circuit
74 F.3d 701, 1996 U.S. App. LEXIS 1069 (6th Cir. 1996)

BACKGROUND AND FACTS

Robert Thomas and his wife Carleen Thomas began operating the Amateur Action Computer Bulletin Board System ("AABBS") from their home in Milpitas, California in February 1991. The AABBS was a computer bulletin board system that operated by using telephones, modems, and personal computers.

Its features included e-mail, chat lines, public messages, and files that members could access, transfer, and download to their own computers and printers. The content of AABBS was pornographic.

In July 1993, a United States Postal Inspector, Agent David Dirmeyer ("Dirmeyer"), received a complaint regarding the AABBS from an individual who resided in the Western District of Tennessee. Dirmeyer dialed the AABBS' telephone number. As a non-member, he viewed a screen that read "Welcome to AABBS, the Nastiest Place On Earth," and was able to select various "menus" and read graphic descriptions of the GIF files and videotapes that were offered for sale.

Subsequently, Dirmeyer used an assumed name and sent in $55 along with an executed application form to the AABBS. Defendant Robert Thomas called Dirmeyer at his undercover telephone number in Memphis, Tennessee, acknowledged receipt of his application, and authorized him to log-on with his personal password. Thereafter, Dirmeyer dialed the AABBS's telephone number, logged-on and, using his computer/modem in Memphis, downloaded the GIF files listed in counts 2–7 of the Defendants' indictments. These GIF files depicted images of bestiality, oral sex, incest, sado-masochistic abuse, and sex scenes involving urination. Dirmeyer also ordered six sexually-explicit videotapes from the AABBS and received them via U.P.S. at a Memphis, Tennessee address. Dirmeyer also had several e-mail and chat-mode conversations with Defendant Robert Thomas.

On January 10, 1994, a search warrant was issued by a U.S. Magistrate Judge for the Northern District of California. The AABBS' location was subsequently searched, and the Defendants' computer system was seized.

On January 25, 1994, a federal grand jury for the Western District of Tennessee returned a twelve-count indictment charging Defendants Robert and Carleen Thomas with the following criminal violations: one count under 18 U.S.C. § 371 for conspiracy to violate federal obscenity laws—18 U.S.C. §§ 1462, 1465 (Count 1), six counts under 18 U.S.C. § 1465 for knowingly using and causing to be used a facility and means of interstate commerce—a combined computer/telephone system—for the purpose of transporting obscene, computer-generated materials (the GIF files) in interstate commerce (Counts 2–7), three counts under 18 U.S.C. § 1462 for shipping obscene videotapes via U.P.S. (Counts 8–10), one count of causing the transportation of materials depicting minors engaged in sexually explicit conduct in violation of 18 U.S.C. § 2252(a)(1) as to Mr. Thomas only (Count 11), and one count of forfeiture under 18 U.S.C. § 1467 (Count 12).

Both Defendants were tried by a jury in July, 1994. Defendant Robert Thomas was found guilty on all counts except count 11 (child pornography). Defendant Carleen Thomas was found guilty on counts 1–10. The jury also found that the Defendants' interest in their computer system should be forfeited to the United States. Robert and Carleen Thomas were sentenced on December 2, 1994 to 37 and 30 months of incarceration, respectively. They filed their notices of appeal on December 9, 1994.

Opinion by Nancy G. Edmunds

Defendants also challenge venue in the Western District of Tennessee for counts 2–7 of their indictments. They argue that even if venue was proper under count 1 (conspiracy) and counts 8–10 (videotapes sent via U.P.S.), counts 2–7 (GIF files) should have been severed and transferred to California because Defendants did not cause the GIF files to be transmitted to the Western District of Tennessee. Rather, Defendants assert, it was Dirmeyer, a government agent, who, without their knowledge, accessed and downloaded the GIF files and caused them to enter Tennessee. We disagree. To establish a Section 1465 violation, the Government must prove that a defendant knowingly used a facility or means of interstate commerce for the purpose of distributing obscene materials. Contrary to Defendants' position, Section 1465 does not require the Government to prove that Defendants had specific knowledge of the destination of each transmittal at the time it occurred.

* * *

Section 1465 is an obscenity statute, and federal obscenity laws, by virtue of their inherent nexus to interstate and foreign commerce, generally involve acts in more than one jurisdiction or state. Furthermore, it is well-established that "there is no constitutional impediment to the government's power to prosecute pornography dealers in any district into which the material is sent." [Citations omitted.]

* * *

2. The Community Standards to Be Applied When Determining Whether the GIF Files Are Obscene

In *Miller v. California,* 413 U.S. 15 (1973), the Supreme Court set out a three-prong test for obscenity. It inquired whether (1) "'the average person applying contemporary community standards' would find that the work, taken as a whole appeals to the prurient interest"; (2) it "depicts or describes, in a patently offensive way, sexual conduct specifically defined by applicable state law"; and (3) "the work, taken as a whole, lacks serious literary, artistic, political, or scientific value."

Under the first prong of the *Miller* obscenity test, the jury is to apply "contemporary community standards." Defendants acknowledge the general principle that, in cases involving interstate transportation of obscene material, juries are properly instructed to apply the community standards of the geographic area where the materials are sent. Nonetheless, Defendants assert that this principle does not apply here for the same reasons they claim venue was improper. As demonstrated above, this argument cannot withstand scrutiny. The computer-generated images described in counts 2–7 were electronically transferred from Defendants' home in California to the Western District of Tennessee. Accordingly, the community standards of that judicial district were properly applied in this case.

3. The Implications of Computer Technology on the Definition of "Community"

Defendants and *Amicus Curiae* appearing on their behalf argue that the computer technology used here requires a new definition of community, i.e., one that is based on the broad-ranging connections among people in cyberspace rather than the geographic locale of the federal judicial district of the criminal trial. Without a more flexible definition, they argue, there will be an impermissible chill on protected speech because BBS [bulletin board services] operators cannot select who gets the materials they make available on their bulletin boards. Therefore, they contend, BBS operators like Defendants will be forced to censor their materials so as not to run afoul of the standards of the community with the most restrictive standards.

The following *Amicus Curiae* submitted briefs on behalf of Defendants in this matter: the American Civil Liberties Union, the Interactive Services Association, the Society for Electronic Access, and The Electronic Frontier Foundation.

Defendants' First Amendment issue, however, is not implicated by the facts of this case. This is not a situation where the bulletin board operator had no knowledge or control over the jurisdictions where materials were distributed for downloading or printing. Access to the Defendants' AABBS was limited. Membership was necessary and applications were submitted and screened before passwords were issued and materials were distributed. Thus, Defendants had in place methods to limit user access in jurisdictions where the risk of a finding of obscenity was greater than that in California. They knew they had a member in Memphis; the member's address and local phone number were provided on his application form. If Defendants did not wish to subject themselves to liability in jurisdictions with less tolerant standards for determining obscenity, they could have refused to give passwords to members in those districts, thus precluding the risk of liability.

This result is supported by the Supreme Court's decision in *Sable Communications of Cal., Inc. v. F.C.C.* where the Court rejected Sable's argument that it should not be compelled to tailor its dial-a-porn messages to the standards of the least tolerant community. The Court recognized that distributors of allegedly obscene materials may be subjected to the standards of the varying communities where they transmit their materials, citing *Hamling,* and further noted that Sable was "free to tailor its messages, on a selective basis, if it so chooses, to the communities it chooses to serve." The Court also found no constitutional impediment to forcing Sable to incur some costs in developing and implementing a method for screening a customer's location and "providing messages compatible with community standards."

Thus, under the facts of this case, there is no need for this court to adopt a new definition of "community" for use in obscenity prosecutions involving electronic bulletin boards. This court's decision is guided by one of the cardinal rules governing the federal courts, i.e., never reach constitutional questions not squarely presented by the facts of a case.

* * *

Decision and Outcome

The Court of Appeals for the Sixth Circuit affirmed the convictions of Robert and Carleen Thomas's convictions and sentences for interstate transportation of obscenity and held that obscenity can be defined in part based on local community standards.

Questions for Analysis

1. Based on the opinion in this case, is it fair to contend that the legal definition of what is obscene varies from community to community? Why did the defendants argue that the government was suing them in the wrong venue? Why would it be to the advantage of the defendants to have a different venue for this case?

2. Do the community standards that are present in rural Western Tennessee determine what is "obscene," and thus illegal, in more liberal areas of the country such as California? Why was the court not troubled by this prospect? How could the defendants in this case have easily avoided jurisdiction of the courts in Western Tennessee?

It could be argued that the *Thomas* decision was an exception, in light of the fact that many obscenity statutes at federal, state, and local levels have been declared unconstitutional, mainly because they have been viewed as being too broad (*Reno v. ACLU* was based on the Communications Decency Act). As the Internet has grown in importance, the main thrust of federal antipornography legislation has been directed at prosecuting purveyors of explicit material that was accessible to minors.

Reasonable Restrictions Based on Time, Place, or Manner

reasonable restrictions
Restrictions governments place on freedom of expression that are not based on content but are based on practical considerations, such as preventing traffic jams when political demonstrations take place or inhibiting the access of children to adult materials.

In previous decisions, the U.S. Supreme Court and other courts have allowed **reasonable restrictions** on the time, place, or manner of freedom of expression. Applying those principles, the Federal Communications Commission (FCC) in past years prohibited network television from showing pornographic, but not obscene, material.[8] In general, courts have upheld the right of governments to pass laws that restrict access by children to "adult" material, while not directly challenging the material itself. Such legally acceptable restrictions may take the form of requiring promoters of pornographic entertainment to limit access to those who can prove that they are over 18 years of age.

Communications Decency Act of 1996

Perhaps emboldened by the *Thomas* decision, Congress passed the Telecommunications Act of 1996, Title V of which became known as the Communications Decency Act (CDA).[9] The CDA made illegal

1. Transmissions in interstate commerce of "any comment, request, suggestion, proposal, image, or other communication which is obscene, knowing that the recipient of the communication is under 18 years of age, regardless of whether the maker of such communication placed the call or initiated the communication."

2. The actions of anyone who "knowingly permits any telecommunications facility under his control to be used for any activity prohibited by paragraph (1) with intent that it be used for such activity."

Shortly after the CDA was passed, it was challenged in court by the ACLU. Since the government was seeking to regulate the content of speech, the court in this case used the strict scrutiny test as well as the three-prong test for illegal, obscene material as articulated in

---

[8] *FCC v. Pacifica Foundation*, 438 U.S. 726 (1978).
[9] Pub. L. No. 104-104, 110 Stat. 56.

Nutz and Boltz   First Amendment Protection of Freedom of Expression

Category of Abridgement	Legal Standard	Comments
Obscenity	Applying contemporary community standards, the average person would find that (1) material appeals to the prurient interest; (2) material depicts or describes, in a patently offensive manner, sexual conduct; or (3) the work lacks serious artistic, political, or scientific value.	At this point, only the most extreme material will be deemed "obscene." Most common application takes place when children are involved.
Content of nonobscene material	There must be a showing that (1) the abridgement is for purposes of promoting a compelling government objective, (2) the abridgement actually promotes the compelling government interest, and (3) the abridgement is not overly broad.	Obscenity, treason, inciting to riot, and protection of minors all have been deemed compelling government objectives. Most abridgements fail because they are deemed too broad.
Time, place, or manner	The courts have allowed governments to place reasonable restrictions on the time, place, or manner of constitutionally protected speech.	Courts have allowed for restrictions on constitutionally protected "adult" material to shield children.

Miller. In *Reno v. American Civil Liberties Union* much of the CDA was declared unconstitutional because its prohibitions were vague and overly broad.

According to Justice Stevens, who wrote the majority opinion in *Reno v. ACLU,* "In order to deny minors access to potentially harmful speech, the CDA effectively suppresses a large amount of speech that adults have a constitutional right to receive. That burden on adult speech is unacceptable if less restrictive alternatives would be at least as effective in achieving the legitimate purpose that the statute [CDA] was enacted to serve."

Other Attempts to Censor the Internet

Following the demise of most of the CDA (some parts were not declared unconstitutional), an unresolved issue remained over whether the government could control websites that *initiate contact* with minors for transmissions that are "obscene, lewd, lascivious, . . ."[10] The same issue was critical in a case involving a New York state statute that made it a crime to disseminate to a minor images that are graphic and that invite or induce a minor to engage in sexual activity. In this case, a New York court ruled that the statute did not violate the First Amendment.[11] So, in this case as well as in the case involving the CDA discussed above (one case federal and the other state), either all or some part of the applicable statute has been upheld in constitutional challenges. The court-endorsed legislation focuses on protecting minors, with both federal and state regulation requiring proof that the defendants accused of illegal conduct initiated contact with the minor.

[10] *Appollomedia Corp. v. Reno,* 19 F. Supp. 2d 1081 (N.D. Cal. 1998).
[11] *People v. Foley,* 620 N.Y.S. 2d 956 (N.Y. App. Div. 1999).

Child Online Protection Act of 1998

In the wake of the Supreme Court's *Reno v. ACLU* decision that discarded much of the CDA, Congress passed the Child Online Protection Act (COPA) in 1998.[12] The focus of the COPA legislation was on requiring website operators to use bona fide methods of identification of visitors to their websites if the websites offered materials that could be deemed harmful to minors. Sanctions for violations of COPA included fines of up to $50,000, along with imprisonment for up to six months in jail for each offense. Material deemed harmful to minors included "any communication, picture, image . . . that is obscene or that" the average person, applying contemporary community standards, would find appeals to the prurient interest, depicts or describes actual or simulated sexual acts, or taken as a whole lacks serious literary value for minors.

The COPA was challenged almost immediately by the ACLU. The federal district court that heard the case issued a temporary injunction restraining the federal government from enforcing the COPA.[13] The district court found that the defenses provided by the COPA were technologically and economically unavailable to many websites and that a large volume of constitutionally protected speech between adults was overly burdened by this legislation. On appeal, the U.S. Court of Appeals for the Third Circuit made the injunction against enforcement of the COPA permanent. According to Senior Circuit Court Judge Garth,

> We base our particular determination of COPA's likely unconstitutionality, however, on COPA's reliance on "contemporary community standards" in the context of the electronic medium of the Web to identify material that is harmful to minors. The overbreadth of COPA's definition of "harmful to minors" applying a "contemporary community standards" clause— although virtually ignored by the parties and the amicus in their respective briefs but raised by us at oral argument—so concerns us that we are persuaded that this aspect of COPA, without reference to its other provisions, must lead inexorably to a holding of a likelihood of unconstitutionality of the entire COPA statute. Hence we base our opinion entirely on the basis of the likely unconstitutionality of this clause, even though the District Court relied on numerous other grounds.

As of the time when this chapter was written, the Department of Justice was appealing (to the Supreme Court) the decision of the Third Circuit Court of Appeals to enjoin enforcement of COPA. At the heart of the appeal, according to news reports, is the phrase "contemporary community standards." Pre-Internet, the term *community* seemed to designate a geographic area. In cyberspace, of course, geographic distance is meaningless. In a case discussed in Question 3 at the end of the chapter, Justice Thomas, writing for the majority of the U.S. Supreme Court, held that the use of "contemporary community standards" to partially define what was obscene was *not* unconstitutional. The case was remanded to the Third Circuit to determine if the injunction against enforcement of COPA should be lifted. Undoubtedly, the Third Circuit opinion on this issue will again be appealed to the U.S. Supreme Court.

In spite of its persistence, attempts by the federal government and by state governments to reduce the amount of pornography on the Internet have been a failure except when the sources of the porn initiate contact with minors. Most websites that feature explicit sexual material contain warnings that state in bold text "You must be 18 to enter." Beyond that, limitations on content are nonexistent, except when participants in the explicit material are children.

---

[12] Pub. L. No. 105-277, tit. XVI, 112 Stat. 2681, 2736–41, codified at 47 U.S.C. § 231.

[13] *ACLU et al. v. Reno* (often referred to as *Reno II*), 31 F. Supp. 2d 473, 1999 U.S. Dist. LEXIS 735 (E.D. Pa. 1999).

Protection of Minors: The Child Pornography Prevention Act of 1996

In 1996, Congress passed the Child Pornography Prevention Act (CPPA) that prohibits and criminalizes the use of computer technology to produce materials that contain depictions of real children involved in sexual activity as well as virtual or fictitious children.[14] Courts have not had problems upholding the constitutionality of laws that decree the transmission of child pornography over the Internet to be illegal. There does remain, however, a split among the circuit courts of appeals regarding the constitutionality of certain language in the CPPA. The language at issue is descriptive of visual depictions that are deemed illegal and include the phrases:

> (B) such visual depiction is, or appears to be, of a minor engaging in sexually explicit conduct;
>
> (C) such visual depiction has been created, adapted, or modified to appear that an identifiable minor is engaging in sexually explicit conduct; or
>
> (D) such visual depiction is advertised, promoted, presented, described, or distributed in such a manner that conveys the impression that the material is or contains a visual depiction of a minor engaging in sexually explicit conduct. . .

The Ninth Circuit Court of Appeal looked at the portion of the CPPA that dealt with computer images not involving real children that portray sexually explicit images. According to the Ninth Circuit, "The question presented in this case is whether Congress may constitutionally proscribe as child pornography computer images that do not involve the use of real children in their production or dissemination. We hold that the First Amendment prohibits Congress from enacting a statute that makes criminal the generation of images of fictitious children engaged in imaginary but explicit sexual conduct."[15] In particular, courts are troubled by the vagueness of CPPA language that prohibits depiction of sexual conduct by persons who "appear to be" minors and by virtual persons that appear to be minors, even though the entire "person" is simply composed of pixels.

The U.S. Supreme Court affirmed the decision of the Ninth Circuit and ruled that two provisions of the CPPA, (B) and (D) above, that prohibited virtual child pornography were unconstitutional under the First Amendment because the language in the CPPA was too broad and unconstitutionally vague.[16] The Supreme Court rejected Congress's contention that the creation of virtual child pornography would encourage attacks against children as not a constitutional basis for prohibiting this form of expression. As a result of the Supreme Court decision, it is still constitutional to prohibit child pornography that makes use of actual child actors, but it is not constitutional to prohibit digital images of child pornography that do not use living child actors.

CYBERSTALKING

According to the U.S. Department of Justice, "Although there is no universally accepted definition of **cyberstalking,** the term is used in this report to refer to the use of the Internet, e-mail, or other electronic communications devices to stalk another person. Stalking

---

[14] Pub. L. No. 104-208, 110 Stat. 3009, codified at 18 U.S.C. § 2256.

[15] *The Free Speech Coalition et al. v. Janet Reno, Attorney General of the United States,* 198 F.3d 1083 (9th Cir. 1999).

[16] *Ashcroft v. The Free Speech Coalition,* 535 U.S. 234 (2002).

In the first successful prosecution under California's new cyberstalking law, prosecutors in the Los Angeles District Attorney's Office obtained a guilty plea from a 50-year-old former security guard who used the Internet to solicit the rape of a woman who rejected his romantic advances. The defendant terrorized his 28-year-old victim by impersonating her in various Internet chat rooms and online bulletin boards, where he posted, along with her telephone number and address, messages that she fantasized of being raped. On at least six occasions, sometimes in the middle of the night, men knocked on the woman's door saying they wanted to rape her. The former security guard pleaded guilty in April 1999 to one count of stalking and three counts of solicitation of sexual assault. He faces up to six years in prison.

A local prosecutor's office in Massachusetts charged a man who, utilizing anonymous remailers, allegedly engaged in a systematic pattern of harassment of a co-worker, which culminated in an attempt to extort sexual favors from the victim under threat of disclosing past sexual activities to the victim's new husband.

An honors graduate from the University of San Diego terrorized five female university students over the Internet for more than a year. The victims received hundreds of violent and threatening e-mails, sometimes receiving four or five messages a day. The graduate student, who has entered a guilty plea and faces up to six years in prison, told police he committed the crimes because he thought the women were laughing at him and causing others to ridicule him. In fact, the victims had never met him.

Source: U.S. Department of Justice, http://www.usdoj.gov/criminal/cybercrime/cyberstalking.htm#.

cyberstalking
Use of electronic means to stalk a person in an intimidating manner. To be illegal, most jurisdictions require a physical threat to accompany the cyberstalking.

generally involves harassing or threatening behavior that an individual engages in repeatedly, such as following a person, appearing at a person's home or place of business, making harassing phone calls, leaving written messages or objects, or vandalizing a person's property." In most states, in order for a person to be prosecuted for the crime of cyberstalking, the stalker must make some kind of credible threat of violence to the victim or to her family (most cyberstalking is conducted by men against women, according to the U.S. Department of Justice).

CYBERCRIME: FRAUD

When existing criminal fraud statutes were written, the transactions that Congress and state legislatures had in mind all involved real people in the physical world. When the Internet was created and acts of fraud started occurring in cyberspace, prosecutors tried to apply existing criminal fraud statutes to apparent violations in cyberspace. The results were not encouraging for foes of fraud. In a number of cases, charges for behavior that appears on its face to be fraudulent were dismissed because the elements of fraud articulated in the statutes were not present. To understand how this is a problem, consider the following situation. Suppose that a skilled hacker did the following:

1. Using pseudonyms, the hacker set up an electronic bulletin board on which he uploaded popular software such as Excel, WordPerfect, and an assortment of computer games.
2. Making use of encryption, he transferred the software to another account and allowed all those with a password to download the software for free.

These actions appear, on their face, to be fraudulent and the perpetrator who actually engaged in these acts, a 21-year-old student at M.I.T., was indicted for wire fraud.[17] The defendant, however, was found not guilty because the wire fraud statute, 18 U.S.C. § 1343, requires that prosecutors prove that the defendant infringed a copyright "willfully and for purpose of commercial advantage or private financial gain." The defendant in this case apparently had some ideological disagreement with copyright law, but did not stand to gain financially from facilitating the widespread duplication of the copyrighted software. As a result, the charges were thrown out.

Computer Antifraud and Antihacking Statutes

Two early statutes passed by Congress in the 1980s are (1) the Counterfeit Access Device and Computer Fraud and Abuse Act of 1984 and (2) the Computer Fraud and Abuse Act of 1986. The Counterfeit Access Device and Computer Fraud and Abuse Act of 1984 makes it a crime if a person[18]

1. knowingly and with intent to defraud produces, uses, or traffics in one or more counterfeit access devices;
2. knowingly and with intent to defraud traffics in or uses one or more unauthorized access devices during any one-year period, and by such conduct obtains anything of value . . .

This act makes hacking a crime if the hacking involves interstate commerce and the motive of the hacker is to make a profit. An *access device* under the act is "any card, plate, code, account number, . . . or other means of account access that can be used, along or in conjunction with another access device, to obtain money, goods, services, or any other thing of value, or that can be used to initiate a transfer of funds (other than a transfer originated solely by paper instrument)." A counterfeit access device is "any access device that is counterfeit, fictitious, altered, or forged, or an identifiable component of an access device or a counterfeit access device." Among the other acts prohibited by this statute are obtaining credit cards with intent to defraud and gaining access to cellular telephone services, without paying for them, by making or altering cellular telephones.

Computer Fraud and Abuse Act of 1986

The Computer Fraud and Abuse Act is aimed directly at computer hackers.[19] Under this act, an individual commits a crime punishable by up to 20 years in prison if he or she has ". . . knowingly accessed a computer without authorization or exceeding authorized access, . . . and thereby obtains—

A. information contained in a financial record of a financial institution, or of a card issuer . . . or contained in a file of a consumer reporting agency on a consumer . . .
B. information from any department or agency of the United States; or
C. information from any protected computer if the conduct involved an interstate or foreign communication . . .

Note that the two kinds of specifically "protected computers" are those owned by government and by financial institutions. Not only does this act prohibit gaining access to restricted information from "protected computers," but it also prohibits using data wrongfully obtained to perpetrate fraud or for other illegal purposes. This statute has been successfully used to punish hacker/pranksters who unleash viruses on government or financial computers. However, just accessing unauthorized files is not enough for a conviction, according to Case 22-2.

---

[17] *United States v. Lamacchia,* 871 F. Supp. 535 (D. Mass. 1994).
[18] Pub. L. No. 98-473, 98 Stat. 2190, codified at 18 U.S.C. §§ 1001 note, 1029.
[19] Pub. L. No. 99-474, codified at 18 U.S.C. § 1030.

Case 22-2

United States, Appellee v. Richard W. Czubinski, Defendant-Appellant

United States Court of Appeals for the First Circuit
106 F.3d 1069 (1st Cir. 1997)

BACKGROUND AND ANALYSIS

For all periods relevant to the acts giving rise to his conviction, the defendant Czubinski was employed as a Contact Representative in the Boston office of the Taxpayer Services Division of the Internal Revenue Service ("IRS"). To perform his official duties, which mainly involved answering questions from taxpayers regarding their returns, Czubinski routinely accessed information from one of the IRS's computer systems known as the Integrated Data Retrieval System ("IDRS"). Using a valid password given to Contact Representatives, certain search codes, and taxpayer social security numbers, Czubinski was able to retrieve, to his terminal screen in Boston, income tax return information regarding virtually any taxpayer—information that is permanently stored in the IDRS "master file" located in Martinsburg, West Virginia. In the period of Czubinski's employ, IRS rules plainly stated that employees with passwords and access codes were not permitted to access files on IDRS outside of the course of their official duties.

In 1992, Czubinski carried out numerous unauthorized searches of IDRS files. He knowingly disregarded IRS rules by looking at confidential information obtained by performing computer searches that were outside of the scope of his duties as a Contact Representative, including, but not limited to, the searches listed in the indictment. Audit trails performed by internal IRS auditors establish that Czubinski frequently made unauthorized accesses on IDRS in 1992. For example, Czubinski accessed information regarding: the tax returns of two individuals involved in the David Duke presidential campaign; the joint tax return of an assistant district attorney (who had been prosecuting Czubinski's father on an unrelated felony offense) and his wife; the tax return of Boston City Counselor Jim Kelly's Campaign Committee (Kelly had defeated Czubinski in the previous election for the Counselor seat for District 2); the tax return of one of his brothers' instructors; the joint tax return of a Boston Housing Authority police officer, who was involved in a community organization with one of Czubinski's brothers, and the officer's wife; and the tax return of a woman Czubinski had dated a few times. Czubinski also accessed the files of various other social acquaintances by performing unauthorized searches.

Opinion by Torruella, Chief Judge

We turn first to Czubinski's conviction on the nine wire fraud counts. [Most footnotes omitted.] The federal wire fraud statute, 18 U.S.C. § 1343, provides in pertinent part:

> Whoever, having devised or intending to devise any scheme or artifice to defraud, or for obtaining money or property by means of false or fraudulent pretenses, representations, or promises, transmits or causes to be transmitted by means of wire . . . communication in interstate or foreign commerce, any writings, signs, signals, pictures, or sounds for the purpose of executing such scheme or artifice, shall be fined under this title or imprisoned not more than five years, or both.

To support a conviction for wire fraud, the government must prove two elements beyond a reasonable doubt: (1) the defendant's knowing and willing participation in a scheme or artifice to defraud with the specific intent to defraud, and (2) the use of interstate wire communications in furtherance of the scheme. *United States v. Sawyer,* 85 F.3d 713, 723 (1st Cir. 1996) (citing *United States v. Cassiere,* 4 F.3d 1006, 1011 (1st Cir. 1993)). Although defendant's motion for judgment of acquittal places emphasis on shortcomings in proof with regard to the second element, by arguing that the wire transmissions at issue were not proved to be interstate, we find the first element dispositive and hold that the government failed to prove beyond a reasonable doubt that the defendant willfully participated in a scheme to defraud within the meaning of the wire fraud statute. That is, assuming the counts accurately describe unauthorized searches of taxpayer returns through interstate wire transmissions, there is insufficient record evidence to permit a rational jury to conclude that the wire transmissions were part of a criminal scheme to defraud under sections 1343 and 1346.

The government pursued two theories of wire fraud in this prosecution: first, that Czubinski defrauded the IRS of its property, under section 1343, by acquiring confidential information for certain intended personal uses; second, that he defrauded the IRS and the public of their intangible right to his honest services, under sections 1343 and 1346 [of the Computer Fraud and Abuse Act].

* * *

A. SCHEME TO DEFRAUD IRS OF PROPERTY

The government correctly notes that confidential information may constitute intangible "property" and that its unauthorized dissemination or other use may deprive the owner of its property rights. [Citations omitted.] Where such deprivation is effected through dishonest or deceitful means, a "scheme to defraud," within the meaning of the wire fraud statute, is shown. Thus, a necessary step toward satisfying the "scheme to defraud" element in this context is showing that the defendant intended to "deprive" another of their protected right.

The government, however, provides no case in support of its contention here that merely accessing confidential information, without doing, or clearly intending to do, more, is tantamount to a deprivation of IRS property under the wire fraud statute. In *Carpenter,* for example, the confidential information regarding the contents of a newspaper column was converted to the defendants's use to their substantial benefit. We do not think that Czubinski's unauthorized browsing, even if done with the intent to deceive the IRS into thinking he was performing only authorized searches, constitutes a "deprivation" within the meaning of the federal fraud statutes.

* * *

Decision and Outcome

The court held that "Mere browsing of the records of people about whom one might have a particular interest, although reprehensible, is not enough to sustain a wire fraud conviction on a 'deprivation of intangible property' theory. Curiosity on the part of an IRS officer may lead to dismissal, but curiosity alone will not sustain a finding of participation in a felonious criminal scheme to deprive the IRS of its property."

Questions for Analysis

1. What additional facts would have to be proven in order for the government to convict Czubinski of a violation of the Computer Fraud and Abuse Act?

2. If the defendant, Czubinski, had sold embarrassing information about the tax forms of celebrities, would he have violated the Computer Fraud and Abuse Act?

3. Is any use of the Internet or computers that are connected to the Internet a "use of interstate wire communications in furtherance of the scheme," which is the required second element of a violation? The court did not answer that question because the government's case failed on the first required element, but what do you think?

Wire Fraud Act, as Amended by the No Electronic Theft Act of 1997

The Wire Fraud Act was passed in 1952, long before the Internet was even a gleam in the eyes of Department of Defense computer scientists who began the project that was later to become the Internet.[20] The Wire Fraud Act requires prosecutors to show that (1) the defendant

---

[20] Act of July 16, 1952, 66 Stat. 722, codified at 18 U.S.C. § 1343.

Ethical Challenges   Ethical Hacking?

It is well known that crime does not "pay," but does this maxim just apply to the "real" world but not to cyberspace? Many hackers begin their "criminal" careers by trying to show how clever they are to their friends. Many are aware that what they are doing is illegal but persist. Apparently, for those who get really good at hacking, there are rewards . . . read on. A question may be asked about how ethical it is for companies who complain about hacking to hire the really good hackers.

"ETHICAL HACKERS" BECOMING MUCH IN DEMAND

BOULDER, Colo.—Hundreds of people spend their days trying to break into your business computer system. They'll find your vulnerable areas, peek inside, and see what kinds of confidential or proprietary information they can pick up.

And you're going to pay them to do it.

Sound scary? It's actually an exploding industry that's becoming more necessary as more computers and individuals get connected. Called "ethical hackers," or the more trendy "white hat hackers," these workers form the front line in the cyberwars, protecting your system from everything and everyone from the "love bug" to internal embezzlers.

"Companies need to have secure networks, and customers need to have confidence in their security," said Michael Puldy, an IBM executive in Boulder. "That confidence is absolutely critical in the e-business market."

Puldy is an executive with the Emergency Response Service and Business Continuity and Recovery Services—the network security divisions of Global Solutions at IBM-Boulder.

Global Solutions, with more than 3,500 employees in Boulder, has become the fastest-growing part of IBM with more than 136,000 employees serving customers in 160 countries. Annual revenues are close to $30 billion.

IBM created the network security segment for business for internal use in 1992. Three years later, the company began offering its customers the service, which includes installing firewalls, intrusion deterrence and detection, security services, system cleanup, and research.

In 1995, 12 people worked in network security full-time. Today, IBM employs hundreds of network security workers in the United States and thousands worldwide.

In addition to computer experts, the security team has workers with backgrounds in the military and law enforcement, Puldy said.

"Our monitors encounter hacking every day," Puldy said. Luckily, most of those efforts are detected on monitors in Boulder before damage is done. "Some are just little probes, people trying to see if they can get in. Sometimes it's worse."

An important part of watching hackers is watching the trends they follow.

IBM's David Chess, a researcher in Westchester County, N.Y., would be considered an old-timer in the information security business, having scribed his first antivirus in 1988. He holds seven patents, and has written several trade articles on viruses.

Chess reports on virus trends for IBM and writes colorful, brief warnings about viruses and hoaxes (anyone remember "How to give a cat a colonic"? It was Chess who said it wasn't a virus).

Chess said the worm viruses—Melissa, the Explore worm, and "I love you"—are the bugs to watch.

"The 'I love you' virus was nothing new. We've seen this type of thing before," Chess said. "But it is a part of a growing trend—this type of virus is around. We're trying to develop an immune system to it."

And as the world gets more wired, the need for ethical hackers and researchers such as Chess has expanded.

"It's growing exponentially. The more people and businesses get connected, the more we need people scanning for vulnerabilities," Puldy said.

New technologies leave people more at risk, too. Puldy said the faster cable connections could actually open files that aren't encrypted to potential snoops who share the connection. . . .

If companies keep antivirus software up to date, they would be immune from about 80 percent of the hacking that is out there, Puldy said. But most companies also need to check the security of their entire systems.

The future of the Internet security industry is wide open, as more schools are starting to train students in safety issues. Purdue University this month approved a new interdisciplinary degree for master's students in information security.

"It is the first interdisciplinary information security program in the United States," said Eugene Spafford, a professor of computer sciences at Purdue. "Instead of offering the program within computer science, we are setting up a program where they can study it with was involved in a scheme to defraud by means of false pretenses, (2) the defendant knew what he or she was doing and willingly participated in a scheme to defraud, and (3) interstate wires or mail communication was used to further the scheme. The Wire Fraud Act was unsuccessfully used in the *LaMacchia* case discussed above because, at the time of prosecution of that case, criminal violation of the Copyright Act required a showing that the defendant gained financially. That loophole was closed by the No Electronic Theft Act of 1997, which made it a felony to do what is prohibited by the Wire Fraud Act, even if there is no financial gain or expectation of financial gain accompanying the illegal activity.[21] The statute still requires that something be taken for a violation to have occurred, so the *Czubinski* decision would not be affected by the No Electronic Theft Act if all the defendant did was browse unauthorized files.

USA PATRIOT Act of 2001

The USA PATRIOT Act was enacted in the wake of the September 11, 2001, terrorist attacks, based in part on evidence that the Internet was used by the terrorists to send messages for the planning and coordination of their attacks. The act amended a number of existing statutes in the following ways:

1. Under previous law, investigators could not obtain a wiretap order to intercept wire communications (involving human voice) when there is evidence only of violations of the Computer Fraud and Abuse Act. Section 202 of the USA PATRIOT Act amends the criminal statute contained in 18 U.S.C § 2516(1) that lists the crimes for which investigators may obtain a wiretap order, adding investigations of felony violations of the Computer Fraud and Abuse Act.

2. Under previous law, the Electronic Communications Privacy Act (ECPA) (discussed below) governed stored electronic communications such as email, but not stored wire communications such as voice mail. To gain access to voice mail, law enforcement agents had to obtain a court order granting permission to place a wiretap while they could gain access to stored email with a search warrant, which is much easier to obtain. The USA PATRIOT Act gives law enforcement access to voice mail authorized by a search warrant and places voice mail in the same category as email.

3. The act also expands the scope of subpoenas for electronic evidence. Under previous law, when the government was investigating a crime, it could not subpoena some records, including credit card number or other form of payment for a communication service. That is, prior to this legislation, the government could not subpoena the way a person paid for the services of an ISP and could not obtain the credit card number employed for card payments.

---

[21] Pub. L. No. 105-147, 111 Stat. 2678, codified at 18 U.S.C. § 506(a).

4. The act also allows for the use of tracking devices (like a phone wiretap) on computer networks. In addition, the USA PATRIOT Act allows law enforcement to intercept the communications of computer hackers. Under the ECPA, employers can monitor conversations by employees and anyone else who uses equipment owned by the employers, including hackers. Previously, their authority to bring in law enforcement was unclear even if they suspected their computers were being used by hackers or trespassers.

5. The USA PATRIOT Act also substantially strengthens jail-time penalties for hackers. For hackers who violate the Computer Fraud and Abuse Act by damaging "protected computers," the act raises maximum sentences from 10 to 20 years. The PATRIOT Act also adds a new offense for hackers who damage computers used for national security. Hackers who release viruses were specifically mentioned by the U.S. Department of Justice in their web page discussion of the USA PATRIOT Act.[22]

The full impact of the USA PATRIOT Act will not be known for some time, but previous discussions of the proper balance between cyber privacy and the rights of government investigators to monitor electronic transmissions are now obsolete. It is clear that, in the future, the government will have a much-enhanced ability to monitor email and other electronic communications. Already, there is talk of software that not only can be used to monitor a suspect's communications across the Internet, but also will report all keystrokes made on a suspect's computer, even when not online. In a pre-Internet context, this is the functional equivalent of the government not only tapping the phone lines of a suspect but also being able to monitor what's typed on his or her typewriter as well.

Other Computer-Related Antifraud Statutes

Identity Theft and Assumption Deterrence Act of 1998

identity theft
occurs when a criminal appropriates personally identifying information and uses that information to commit crimes through impersonation.

Some aspects of the **Identity Theft** and Assumption Deterrence Act of 1998 were discussed in Chapter 11.[23] According to this act, a person who "(7) knowingly transfers or uses, without lawful authority, a means of identification of another person with the intent to commit, or to aid or abet, any unlawful activity that constitutes a violation of Federal law, or that constitutes a felony under any applicable State or local law; shall be punished as provided in subsection (b) of this section." Penalties for violation of the act can range up to 20 years' imprisonment. As discussed in Chapter 11, the FTC has responsibility for enforcement of the act. A hacker who gains access to credit card numbers and misuses them would be violating the act. According to the FTC, the following is a typical modus operandi of an identity thief: "They call your credit card issuer and, pretending to be you, ask to change the mailing address on your credit card account. The imposter then runs up charges on your account. Because your bills are being sent to the new address, it may take some time before you realize there's a problem."[24]

Electronic Communications Privacy Act of 1986

What is likely the most important federal protection of privacy in cyberspace is provided by the Electronic Communications Privacy Act (ECPA).[25] Earlier, in Chapter 16, in connection with on-the-job employment issues, we discussed employer interception of employee phone calls and email. Title I of the ECPA makes unauthorized interception and disclosure of wire, oral, and electronic communication illegal. Among the transmissions that are

---

[22] http://www.cybercrime.gov/PatriotAct.htm.

[23] Pub. L. No. 105-318, 112 Stat. 3007–3009, codified at 18 U.S.C. § 1028.

[24] http://www.ftc.gov/bcp/online/pubs/credit/idtheft.htm#occurs.

[25] Pub. L. No. 99-508, 100 Stat. 1848, codified at 18 U.S.C. §§ 2510–2520.

SOFTWARE PIRATE GUILTY OF COPYRIGHT INFRINGEMENT UNDER NET ACT

CHICAGO—A federal jury here returned a guilty verdict in the nation's first trial under the 1997 No Electronic Theft (NET) Act involving a computer software piracy conspiracy, Scott R. Lassar, United States Attorney for the Northern District of Illinois, announced today. Following a week-long trial, jurors deliberated only 30 minutes late on Friday, May 11, before finding Christian Morley, 28, of Salem, Mass., guilty of conspiracy to infringe software copyrights.

Morley was indicted last year along with 16 other defendants from across the United States and Europe for conspiring to infringe the copyright of more than 5,000 computer software programs that were available through a hidden Internet site that was located at a university in Quebec, Canada. Twelve of the defendants, including an Aurora, Ill., man, allegedly were members or leaders of an international organization of software pirates known as "Pirates with Attitudes," an underground group that disseminated stolen copies of software, including programs that were not yet commercially available. The remaining five defendants were employees of Intel Corp., four of whom allegedly supplied computer hardware to the piracy organization in exchange for obtaining access for themselves and other Intel employees to the group's pirated software, which had a retail value in excess of $1 million. The investigation first became public with the Feb. 3, 2000, arrest of the lead defendant Robin Rothberg, of North Chelmsford, Mass., who was identified as a "council" member, or leader, of PWA. A list of the defendants and their status is attached.

Of the 17 defendants, Rothberg and 12 others pleaded guilty to copyright conspiracy, two remain fugitives, one is still pending and is being evaluated for mental competency, and the last one—Morley—was convicted at trial. The 14 guilty defendants are expected to be sentenced at the end of the summer but no specific dates have been set. Conspiracy to infringe a copyright carries a maximum penalty of five years in prison and a $250,000 fine, or, as an alternative, the Court may impose a fine totaling twice the gross gain to any defendant or twice the gross loss to any victim, whichever is greater. Restitution is mandatory. U.S. District Judge Matthew Kennelly will determine the appropriate sentence to be imposed under the United States Sentencing Guidelines.

"The trial demonstrated law enforcement's commitment to prosecute software piracy cases and the FBI's ability to successfully investigate sophisticated online activity," said Assistant U.S. Attorney James Conway, who represented the government along with Assistant U.S. Attorney Lisa K. Griffin. The case was investigated by the Chicago Field Division of the Federal Bureau of Investigation. The Justice Department's Computer Crime and Intellectual Property Section provided assistance, as did the Business Software Alliance and the Software and Information Industry Association.

The investigation was conducted as part of the Justice Department's nationwide Intellectual Property Initiative, announced in July 1999. The conspiracy and copyright infringement charges in this case were brought under the No Electronic Theft Act, known as the NET Act, which was enacted in 1997 to facilitate prosecutions of Internet copyright piracy. The NET Act makes it illegal to reproduce or distribute such copyrighted works as software programs, *even if the defendant acts without a commercial purpose or for private financial gain.* [Emphasis added.]

Source: http://www.cybercrime.gov/pwa_verdict.htm

subject to the ECPA are email, other computer-generated transmissions, and cellular phone conversations. With some significant exceptions, the ECPA prohibits any person from

1. Intentionally intercepting, or endeavoring to intercept, or procuring "any other person to intercept or endeavor to intercept, any wire, oral, or electronic communication."
2. Intentionally using or disclosing, or endeavoring to use or disclose, "to any other person the contents of any wire, oral, or electronic communication, knowing or having reason to know that the information was obtained through the interception of a wire, oral, or electronic communication in violation of this subsection."

The ECPA can be applied to ISPs, prohibiting them from intentionally disclosing the contents of a communication to any person or entity other than the person for whom the message was intended or the addressee. As mentioned above, there are exceptions to the ECPA, which include

1. The operator of a switchboard (or ISP) can intercept electronic communication in the normal course of employment "while engaged in any activity which is a necessary incident to the rendition of his service or to the protection of the rights or property of the provider of that service."
2. In the *ordinary course of business,* an employer can intercept phone calls as well as email.
3. If either the sender or the recipient of the message *has given prior consent,* the phone call or email can be intercepted.
4. There is a law enforcement exception where the ISP or other service provider inadvertently intercepts a communication that discloses an illegal act. Under these circumstances, the ISP or service provider can disclose to authorities the communication that they intercepted.

Exceptions (2) and (3) above, which were discussed in Chapter 11, enable employers to monitor phone calls and emails of employees if the communication occurs during the ordinary course of business or if the employer has obtained prior consent.

Title I of the ECPA is a generalized prohibition on intercepting communications except when one of the recognized exceptions is applicable. For a first offense, violation of the ECPA that "is not for a tortious or illegal purpose or for purposes of direct or indirect commercial advantage or private commercial gain, and the wire or electronic communication with respect to which the offense under paragraph (a) is a radio communication that is not scrambled or encrypted," maximum punishment is one year of imprisonment and a $500 fine, which is a relatively modest set of sanctions.

Title II of the ECPA is entitled "Unlawful Access to Stored Communications," and the title is indicative of what the act prohibits. Title II of the ECPA makes it a crime to

1. Intentionally access without authorization a facility through which an electronic communication service is provided.
2. Intentionally exceed authorization to access that facility and obtain, alter, or prevent authorized access to a wire or electronic communication while it is in electronic storage in such system.

Title II includes some of the same exceptions as Title I in that an ISP is allowed to do its job, which may involve accessing stored communications, without specific authorization. This act would be violated by a college student who somehow accesses a university computer network and changes his or her grade records. Sanctions for violation of the statute include up to two years in prison, but the sanctions are less if it is a first offense or if the offense was not for commercial gain.

PROTECTION OF INTELLECTUAL PROPERTY

With the increasing importance of intellectual property (IP) as a source of U.S. earning power, Congress has revised several statutes that protect IP in ways that make it a crime any time there is a willful violation of the statutes. In addition, Congress has passed several new statutes that protect IP and carry criminal penalties for violation. Some of these statutes were briefly discussed in Chapters 12 and 13. Violation of these statutes is most often accomplished using a computer, the Internet, or, typically, both. Hence, it is appropriate to discuss these statutes in more detail in this chapter, which focuses attention on cyber crime.

The Economic Espionage Act of 1996

The Economic Espionage Act (EEA) of 1996 makes the misappropriation of trade secrets, using computers or by other means, a crime.[26] Chapter 12 discussed the EEA in connection with the possible consequences of trade secret misappropriation. The EEA is one of several statutes passed by Congress that create criminal liability or augment criminal liability for offenses involving IP. As discussed earlier, this statute makes misappropriation of trade secrets on behalf of a foreign government a much more serious crime than the same acts committed on behalf of U.S. firms. Offenses for violations of the EEA can be as high as 15 years in jail plus fines of up to $10 million and forfeiture of property or proceeds gained by the illegal activities. It is important to recognize that trade secret law has largely been state law and that the EEA federalizes this important component of law. It can be argued that state law enforcement is no match for sophisticated foreign economic espionage agents, rationalizing a growing role for the federal government in trade secret protection.

Criminal Infringement of a Copyright

Most often, a copyright infringer is sued in civil court by the owner of the copyright. There are, however, criminal penalties available for punishing

Any person who infringes a copyright willfully either—

1. for purposes of commercial advantage or for private financial gain, or
2. by the reproduction or distribution, including by electronic means during any 180-day period, of 1 or more . . . copyrighted works, which have a total retail value of more than $1,000,

shall be punished as provided under section 2319 of title 18, United States Code . . .[27]

Under Section 2319, for willful acts, copyright infringers can be imprisoned for up to 10 years as well as being fined and subjected to forfeiture and destruction of "all infringing copies or phonorecords and all implements, devices, or equipment used in the manufacture of such infringing copies or phonorecords."

Digital Millennium Copyright Act of 1998

The Digital Millennium Copyright Act (DMCA) was passed by Congress to deal with the problem of hackers creating software that circumvented protections for copyrighted works.[28] It is common for owners of copyrighted work that is stored on CDs to protect

---

[26] Pub. L. No. 104-294, 110 Stat. 3488, codified at 18 U.S.C. §§ 1831–1839.
[27] 17 U.S.C. § 506(a).
[28] Pub. L. No. 105-304, 112 Stat. 2860, codified at 17 U.S.C. 512.

against duplications by installing software that prevents possessors from duplicating the work. Specifically, it is common for moviemakers to store their copyrighted works on DVDs (digital versatile disks), with the DVD content protected by an encrypted program on the DVD called CSS (Content Scrambling System), which will prevent the work from being duplicated on another CD.

Section 1 of the DMCA makes it illegal to "manufacture, import, offer to the public, [or] provide . . ." any technology or product that is primarily designed for the purpose of circumventing a technological measure that effectively controls access to a copyrighted work. So it is illegal to create software that undermines a system such as CSS aimed at preventing possessors of DVDs from duplicating them. Section 2 of the DMCA prohibits rigging copyright management information to conceal the making of illegal copies of copyrighted software or removing or altering any copyright management system. Section 4 of the DMCA states that "Any person who violates section 1201 (Section 1) or 1202 (Section 2) willfully and for purposes of commercial advantage or private financial gain" shall be fined not more than $500,000 or imprisoned for not more than five years for the first offense, or both, and for any subsequent offense will be subject to fines of up to $1 million and to up to 10 years of incarceration.

INTERNET GAMBLING

Virtually all states have outlawed unlicensed gambling, which may be described as an activity that creates a risk that had no prior existence. During the past 25 years, attitudes toward gambling seem to have shifted toward increased acceptance. There are now 48 states that have legalized or licensed some form of gambling, including state lotteries, and a number of Native American tribes have asserted their sovereignty over reservation territories, exercising their sovereign right to allow gambling on their reservations if they so choose. The Internet has opened up an entire new arena for gamblers with a huge number of websites that offer gambling opportunities. Needless to say, no matter where in the world a gambling site host is physically located, gambling customers have access from any computer that has Internet access. In general, Internet gambling is illegal in the United States but, since most of the gambling website hosts are located offshore and licensed by smaller nations, such as Antigua, the authority of the U.S. government to stop such practices is limited. Gambling in cyberspace is now a billion-dollar business and there appears to be little that can be done by domestic legal authorities to impede its continued growth.

The proliferation of Internet gambling sites raises a number of interesting legal issues. As you likely know, the state of Nevada has long been a home for multiple forms of legal gambling, including sports betting (within the state). For a state like Nevada, an issue that arises is whether legal sports-betting websites housed in that state are subject to the jurisdiction of other states when those Nevada-based websites advertise on the Internet and solicit betting participation by citizens from other states.

In Case 22-3, the State of Minnesota claims that the defendant's website engaged in fraud. The defendant is doing business in the State of Nevada, where gambling is legal. If courts in the State of Minnesota can exert jurisdiction over the defendant, a judgment obtained against the website by a Minnesota court can be enforced against a defendant in Nevada. The defendant in Case 22-3, however, claimed that by gambling at its website, participants agreed to pursue all legal claims in the courts of Belize (a country located in South America).

Case 22-3

State of Minnesota by its Attorney General Hubert H. Humphrey III, Respondent vs. Granite Gate Resorts, Inc., d/b/a On Ramp Internet Computer Services; et al., Appellants

Court of Appeals of Minnesota
568 N.W.2d 715 (Minn. Ct. App. 1997)

BACKGROUND AND FACTS

Rogers, a Nevada resident, is president of Granite Gate, a Nevada corporation that does business as On Ramp. Until August 1995, On Ramp provided Internet advertising on the site located at http://www.vegas.com, which provides Nevada tourist information. Among the sites advertised was WagerNet, an on-line wagering service planned to be available internationally in the fall of 1995, whose page enabled Internet users to subscribe for more information about the service.

The WagerNet site, designed by Rogers, stated:

On-Line sports wagering open to International markets, Fall of 1995

Global Gaming Services Ltd, based in the country of Belize, is pleased to introduce **Wager-Net,** *the first and only on-line sports betting site on the Internet.* **WagerNet** *will provide sports fans with a legal way to bet on sporting events from anywhere in the world . . . 24 Hours a Day!*

Participants have to pay a $100 setup fee, for necessary hardware and software. For security and privacy, all members are issued a card system linked to their personal computer to access WagerNet. Once on-line, the bettor selects the team/s and amount/s they wish to wager. WagerNet then matches the participants's bet with an opposing bettor or bettors to cover the wager. WagerNet charges each bettor a transaction fee of 2.5%. WagerNet claimed that most bookies charged a 10% transaction fee.

The website invited Internet users to put themselves on a mailing list for WagerNet information and included a form for that purpose. It gave a toll-free number for WagerNet and also told Internet users to contact On Ramp at a Nevada telephone number for more information. A note on the page advised users to consult with local authorities regarding restrictions on offshore sports betting by telephone before registering with WagerNet.

A linked web page listed the terms and conditions to which an Internet user assented by applying for the private access card and special hardware and software required to access WagerNet's services. This page stated that any claim against WagerNet by a customer must be brought before a Belizian court, but that WagerNet could sue the consumer in his or her home state to prevent the consumer "from committing any breach or anticipated breach of this Agreement and for consequential relief."

On July 5, 1995, Jeff Janacek, a consumer investigator for the Minnesota Attorney General's office, telephoned the toll-free number shown on an On Ramp site that advertised All Star Sports, a sports handicapping service, and asked how to bet on sports events. An On Ramp employee told Janacek to call Rogers directly. Janacek dialed the number he was given, which was the same number that the WagerNet site directed Internet users to call to receive more information, and spoke with an individual who identified himself as Rogers. Janacek identified himself as a Minnesotan interested in placing bets. Rogers explained how to access WagerNet, told Janacek the betting service was legal, and stated that he hoped the service would be up and running by the 1995 football season.

In July 1995, the attorney general filed a complaint alleging that appellants had engaged in deceptive trade practices, false advertising, and consumer fraud by advertising in Minnesota that gambling on the Internet is lawful. In October 1995, Janacek subscribed to the WagerNet mailing list under a fictitious name and received an on-line confirmation stating that he would be sent updates on the WagerNet service.

The defendants filed a motion to dismiss for lack of personal jurisdiction. The district court al-lowed limited discovery to determine the quantity and quality of defendants' contacts with the state. Rogers refused to produce the names of the persons on the WagerNet mailing list, claiming that the information is the sole property of a Belizian corporation. As a sanction, the court found that it is es-tablished as a fact for this action that the WagerNet mailing list contains the name and address of at least one Minnesota resident. In December 1996, the district court denied appellants' motion to dis-miss for lack of jurisdiction.

Opinion by Willis

This is the first time a Minnesota court has addressed the issue of personal jurisdiction based on Internet advertising. We are mindful that the Internet is a communication medium that lacks histori-cal parallel in the potential extent of its reach and that regulation across jurisdictions may implicate fundamental First Amendment concerns. It will undoubtedly take some time to determine the precise balance between the rights of those who use the Internet to disseminate information and the powers of the jurisdictions in which receiving computers are located to regulate for the general welfare. But our task here is limited to deciding the question of personal jurisdiction in the instant case, and on the facts before us, we are satisfied that established legal principles provide adequate guidance.

* * *

The quantity of contacts here supports the contention that appellants purposefully availed themselves of the privilege of conducting commercial activities in Minnesota. The district court found that (1) computers located throughout the United States, including Minnesota, accessed appellants' web-sites, (2) during a two-week period in February and March 1996, at least 248 Minnesota computers accessed and "received transmissions from" appellants' websites, (3) computers located in Minnesota are among the 500 computers that most often accessed appellants' websites, (4) persons located throughout the United States, including persons in Minnesota, called appellants at the numbers ad-vertised on its websites, and (5) the WagerNet mailing list includes the name and address of at least one Minnesota resident.

In *Maritz, Inc. v. Cybergold, Inc.,* 947 F. Supp. 1328 (E.D. Mo. 1996), a Missouri federal court ex-ercised personal jurisdiction over the California operator of an Internet site that provided information on a forthcoming service that would charge advertisers for access to a mailing list of Internet users. In analyzing the quantity of the defendant's contacts with Missouri, the *Maritz* court found that the defendant "has transmitted information into Missouri regarding its services approximately 131 times," which allowed an inference that the defendant purposefully availed itself of the privilege of conducting activities in Missouri. [Citations omitted.] The quantity of contacts here exceeds that in *Maritz.*

* * *

Even where the quantity of contacts with a state is minimal, the nature and quality of the contacts may be dispositive. *Trident Enters. Int'l, Inc. v. Kemp & George, Inc.,* 502 N.W.2d 411, 415 (Minn. App. 1993); *see also Zippo Mfg. Co. v. Zippo Dot Com, Inc.,* 952 F. Supp. 1119, 1124 (W.D. Pa. 1997) (con-cluding "likelihood that personal jurisdiction can be constitutionally exercised is directly proportion-ate to the nature and quality of commercial activity that an entity conducts over the internet"). Ad-vertising in the forum state, or establishing channels for providing regular advice to customers in the forum state, indicates a defendant's intent to serve the market in that state.

Appellants argue that they "have not directed their activities at the citizens of Minnesota" because they "only placed information on the internet." An Internet site, however, can be viewed as an "ad-vertisement" by which [the foreign corporation] distributes its pictorial images throughout the United States. That the local user "pulls" these images from [the corporation's] computer in [in that case] Italy, as opposed to [the corporation] "sending" them to this country, is irrelevant. By inviting United States users to download these images, [the corporation] is causing and contributing to their distrib-ution within the United States.

* * *

Internet advertisements are similar to broadcast and direct mail solicitation in that advertisers dis-tribute messages to Internet users, and users must take affirmative action to receive the advertised product. Here, the WagerNet site itself stated that it was "open to International markets," indicating an intent to seek customers from a very broad geographic area. The fact that WagerNet had apparently paid for advertising in English on an American commercial site indicates an intent to reach the American market, and by advertising their services with a toll-free number, appellants indicated their intent to solicit responses from all jurisdictions within that market, including Minnesota. A defendant cannot "hide behind the structuring of its distribution system when [the defendant's] intent was to enter the market [in the forum state] and profit thereby." The presence of the disclaimer on the site may be relevant to the merits of the consumer fraud action, but appellants' clear effort to reach and seek potential profit from Minnesota consumers provides minimum contacts of a nature and quality sufficient to support a threshold finding of personal jurisdiction. [Footnote omitted.]

* * *

Appellants, through their Internet advertising, have demonstrated a clear intent to solicit business from markets that include Minnesota and, as a result, have had multiple contacts with Minnesota residents, including at least one successful solicitation. The cause of action here arises from the same advertisements that constitute appellants' contacts with the state and implicates Minnesota's strong interest in maintaining the enforceability of its consumer protection laws. Appellants have not demonstrated that submission to personal jurisdiction in Minnesota would subject them to any undue inconvenience. For these reasons, we hold that appellants are subject to personal jurisdiction in Minnesota because, through their Internet activities, they purposefully availed themselves of the privilege of doing business in Minnesota to the extent that the maintenance of an action based on consumer protection statutes does not offend traditional notions of fair play and substantial justice.

Decision and Outcome

The Court of Appeals of Minnesota upheld a denial of a motion to dismiss based on lack of jurisdiction. The court held that the website solicited business from everywhere, including the State of Minnesota, and therefore it must be prepared to bear the consequences of doing business within the State of Minnesota and was subject to the jurisdiction of Minnesota courts.

Questions for Analysis

1. Does this case support the proposition that, if you establish a website that is accessible in a state, that state can exert jurisdiction over you and your website?
2. What was unfair and deceptive about the WagerNet website? Do you think that when a website says that, if you have a claim against it, you have to go before courts in Belize, but if they have a claim against you, they can sue you in your home state court is unfair?
3. Do you think rulings like the one that occurred in this case will drive all Internet gambling to offshore websites?

State Enforcement of Gambling Debts

Another legal issue that arises within the United States is whether websites can enforce gambling debts in states that do not allow gambling. In one case that was settled, Cynthia Haines used her computer and 12 credit cards to gamble on websites, rather unsuccessfully. Eventually, she was sued by several banks attempting to collect on the credit card debt she had incurred through her gambling activities.[29] In one case she faced, Providian National Bank and Mastercard were the plaintiffs. Ms. Haines countersued and, in the ensuing settlement of the conflicting claims, her credit card debt was erased with Providian and

[29] Charles B. Brundage, "Comment: Playing for Free? The Legality and Enforceability of On-Line Gambling Debts," *Pace International Law Review* 12 (Spring 2000), p. 153.

International Perspective   Offshore Gambling

OFFSHORE GAMBLING CONVICTION UPHELD

WASHINGTON—In a test case for Internet gambling, a federal court in New York on Tuesday upheld the bookmaking conviction of a San Francisco man for illegally operating an offshore gambling site from the Caribbean island of Antigua.

Jay Cohen, who has vowed to appeal his conviction to the U.S. Supreme Court, faces a 21-month prison sentence for violating the 1961 wire act. The act prohibits the use of a telephone and other wire devices to place bets across state lines.

The three-judge panel of the 2nd U.S. Circuit Court of Appeals rejected arguments by Cohen's lawyer, Mark Baker, that his business was no different than off-track betting parlors in New York.

"We need not guess whether the provisions of (the 1961 wire act) apply to Cohen's conduct because it is clear that they do," wrote U.S. District Judge John F. Keenan.

Keenan said the act applied to Cohen's company, World Sports Exchange, because it accepted bets by telephone or Internet.

Melinda Sarafa, another lawyer who represents Cohen, issued a statement expressing disappointment with the decision.

"We believe that the court did not adequately address a number of important issues presented by this case," Sarafa said. "Among those, we maintain that the court ignored legitimate contentions that Mr. Cohen's business operated no differently than various state-run off track betting organizations which accept Interstate wagering instructions by telephone and the Internet."

Cohen, a former stock trader, is the only person who has stood trial and been convicted for running an Internet gambling site in violation of the 1961 wire act.

Source: From Tony Batt, "Offshore Gambling Conviction Upheld," *Las Vegas Review-Journal,* August 1, 2001. Copyright © Las Vegas Review-Journal.

Mastercard agreeing to pay her attorneys' fees of $225,000.[30] Of course, Providian and Mastercard settled the case against Ms. Haines because they were advised by their legal counsel that they would lose if their case against Ms. Haines had gone to trial. California courts have taken the position that, since gambling is illegal in that state, California courts will not enforce illegal contracts. Allowing credit card companies to collect on gambling debts, in effect, enforces illegal gambling contracts.

The impact of the Haines lawsuit was that some credit card banks and issuers became reluctant to be involved in gambling transactions. Providian National Bank announced that it would no longer process gambling transactions. In 1996, the National Gambling Impact Study Commission Act was passed and, after two years of study, the Commission recommended that Internet gambling should be prohibited within the United States.[31] To reinforce its first recommendation, the Commission called for legislation making credit debt incurred while gambling online unrecoverable. Furthermore, the Commission recommended that credit card cash advance machines be banned from casinos or areas where gambling takes place.

At this point in time, common law state and federal court decisions antagonistic to the enforcement of gambling debts, in the form of credit card charges or checks that have insufficient funds, continue to serve as a significant check on the growth of Internet gambling. Of course, enforcement suits only arise if a debtor/gambler is willing to risk his credit by refusing to pay gambling debts.

[30] The case, *Providian National Bank et al. v. Haines,* Case No. CV980858 (Cal. Super. Ct., Marin Cty., July 9, 1999), was discussed in "Mastercard Settles CA Suit over Credit Card Gambling Debt," *Bank & Lender Liability Litigation Reporter* 5, no. 1 (September 1, 1999), p. 4.

[31] Pub. L. No. 104-169, 110 Stat. 1482, codified at 18 U.S.C. § 1955 note.

"That 1,600 pound boulder should keep you from visiting the casinos during work hours. I'm sorry it had to come to this"

Source: Copyright © Jerry King Cartoons, Inc. Reprinted with permission.

Because of adverse court rulings in the United States, offshore websites that feature gambling often require their customers to set up offshore bank accounts in the host country. Our now-familiar example island, Antigua, recognizes and enforces gambling debts without regard to the place of residence of the gambler. According to the U.S. Department of Justice, Internet gambling is illegal under at least four federal statutes. The Wire Act of 1961 makes it illegal for gambling providers to offer or to take bets from gamblers over telephone wires or other wire devices unless the specific act is authorized by a particular state. The Wire Act of 1961 obviously did not mention the Internet and, so, there have been recent congressional proposals specifically aimed at prohibiting Internet gambling. Although some bills have been passed in one House of Congress, to date there is no federal legislation effectively outlawing Internet gambling.

CYBERMEDICINE AND INTERNET PHARMACIES

cybermedicine
The practice of medicine over the Internet, where the doctor and patient are physically separate but generally have electronic communication.

A recent development made possible by the Internet presents a serious challenge to the traditional regulation of the sale of medicine and pharmaceutical drugs. Websites now advertise ready access to various prescription medicines including Viagra, antidepressants, and many other drugs, circumventing the drug sales controls exercised since 1938 by the Federal Drug Administration. Under the Food, Drug and Cosmetic Act, a doctor has to write a prescription for a patient to obtain a prescription drug. The Internet remedy for this obstacle to easy access of drugs is for online drug vendors to contract with doctors to practice **cybermedicine,** prescribing wanted prescription-only drugs on the basis of a cyberexamination of the "patient" (customer). Usually, a cyberexamination requires the patient/customer to simply fill out a questionnaire and, on the basis of the answers provided, the website sells the drugs the patient wants.

Cybermedicine

Obviously, there are legal questions prompted by cybermedicine and accompanying sales of prescription drugs. These include (1) does cybermedicine violate the rules of the state boards that license physicians and (2) can a website legally sell prescription drugs? As to the first issue, video teleconferencing has been used for some time in medicine, so it is hard to claim that there is a requirement for face-to-face examinations before physicians can make diagnoses and prescribe treatments. This is so, even though the Internet is a far more open framework than is closed circuit video teleconferencing. A popular website that practices cybermedicine is Cyberdocs.com. Cyberdocs.com advertises that virtual consultations may be appropriate when patients are away from home, when patients have symptoms of minor ailments, and when patients have relocated and do not have personal relationships with a physician in their new areas of residence.

It is fair to say that many state regulators take a dim view of cybermedicine and Internet pharmacies. The concern of regulators is that, to obtain medicine that a "patient" may have seen advertised on television (such as Viagra), the patient need only fill out a questionnaire and pay for a cyberexamination from a physician with whom the patient has no personal contact. There are several avenues for abuse in this system, with the obvious one being patient falsification of answers on the questionnaire. There is no way to verify the accuracy of the answers provided and, in many (perhaps all) instances, the websites are not really interested in verifying the information as their economic interest is in selling wanted drugs. Indeed, many of the offshore drug vendors sell "prescription drugs" to customers with no prescription required, not even one provided by a cyberdoctor. In addition, many of the offshore Internet pharmacies sell drugs that have not been approved by the FDA.

There are additional legitimate privacy concerns about how the information provided in questionnaires is used and whether that information is sold to third parties who have their own products to peddle. It is notable, too, that state licensing laws for physicians outlaw kickbacks to physicians from sales of drugs. Regulators clearly would like the law to

- Preclude the practice of cybermedicine.
- Prevent any physician who prescribes drugs based on the results of online examinations from having an ownership interest in the business that owns the web vendor site.
- Prevent any sale of prescription medicines without a doctor-provided prescription.
- Outlaw the sale of any drug that is not FDA approved.

Summary

Evidence That the September 11, 2001, Terrorists Made Extensive Use of the Internet Accelerated a Trend Already Underway to Pass Laws Appropriate to Control Cybercrime; to Aid in Its Efforts against Computer and

- Cybercrime is a growth industry. Its volume has expanded explosively with the popularization of the Internet.
- Sizeable volumes of Internet business involve pornography, gambling, and illegal (under U.S. law) drug sales. Other pernicious Internet-focused activities include the spread of computer viruses, disruptive activities of prankster hackers, industrial espionage making use of cybertechnology, and Internet fraud.
- Law developed for a pre-Internet world generally has not been effective in controlling cyberactivities that would be widely viewed as criminal. Consequently, government has responded with legislation and regulation aimed at controlling cybercrime. As is always the case, greater control comes at a cost. In many cases, with laws aimed at controlling cybercrime, the primary cost is a significant loss of privacy.
- Jurisdiction confronts U.S. lawmakers with a difficult challenge in regulating undesirable Internet activities, including the distribution of pornography, the provision of gambling services, the unregulated sales of prescription drugs, and so forth. U.S. customers can readily access websites hosted in countries where activities outlawed in the United States are perfectly legal in the host country, leaving U.S. lawmakers with no acceptable means of regulating the unwanted activities.

Cybercrime, the U.S. DOJ Has Established a Computer Crime and Intellectual Property Section	• To deal with cybercrime, the U.S. Department of Justice has established a Computer Crime and Intellectual Property Section (CCIPS). Members of CCIPS have expertise in encryption, privacy laws, e-commerce, hacker investigations, and intellectual property crimes.
Efforts to Control Pornography in Cyberspace Have Been Thwarted by First Amendment Constraints; Much of the Legislation Passed by Congress and the States Has Been Declared Unconstitutional Because the Legislation Was Too Broad; Courts Have Been More Sympathetic to Antiporn Measures Directed Toward Children	• Pornography is adult-oriented material that is constitutionally protected for adults, while obscene material is not constitutionally protected material even for adults. • Because of the First Amendment, abridgements of rights to freedom of expression imposed by the government must pass a very difficult constitutional test that includes a showing that (1) the purpose of the government-sponsored limitations is to promote a compelling state interest, (2) the abridgement must actually promote the compelling state interest, and (3) it must not be overly broad. • Shielding children from adult material is a compelling state objective that has allowed courts to justify government measures that reduce access to adult material. Also, courts have had no problem declaring obscene, and thus illegal, pornographic material that features children actors. • Obscene material is defined as that which (1) applying contemporary community standards, the average person would find appeals to prurient interest; (2) depicts or describes in a patently offensive manner sexual conduct; and (3) taken as a whole lacks serious literary, artistic, political, or scientific value. • Courts have allowed reasonable restrictions on the time, place, or manner of access to adult material to shield youths from such material. • The Communications Decency Act of 1996 was judged to be unconstitutional because it was overly broad. • The Child Online Protection Act of 1998 was judged to be unconstitutional by a federal court of appeals based on the excessive breadth of application of contemporary standards to define what is harmful to minors. • The part of the Child Pornography Prevention Act, passed by Congress in 1996, that prohibits virtual child pornography has been declared unconstitutional by the U.S. Supreme Court.
Legislators Have Made It Clear That They Consider Misuse of Computers a Serious Crime Whether It Be Stalking or Hacking into Forbidden Areas; Recent Legislation Gives Law Enforcement New Powers to Intercept Email and Other Communication	• Cyberstalking involves use of the Internet to harass or threaten another and is illegal. Most states require a showing that the cyberstalker has physically threatened the victim in some way. • Hacking is making use of a computer in a fraudulent manner. In several cases, criminal statutes have had to be changed to make illegal actions of hackers that have caused havoc and losses of intellectual property. • Two statutes that are directed at hackers are the Counterfeit Access Device and Computer Fraud and Abuse Act of 1984 and the Computer Fraud and Abuse Act of 1986. The former act is aimed at producing or using counterfeit access devices, while the latter act is directed at accessing a computer owned by the government or by financial institutions without authorization. • The USA PATRIOT Act of 2001 gives the government broad new powers to monitor computer communications including email and allows wiretaps in the form of software on computers. • The No Electronic Theft Act of 1997 made it a felony to violate the Wire Fraud Act even if the defendant did not intend to gain financially.
New Legislation Has Been Passed	• The Identity Theft and Assumption Deterrence Act of 1998 makes it illegal to knowingly transfer, without lawful authority, a means of identification of another person with intent to commit illegal activity.

to Deal with Other Cybercrimes Such as Identity Theft, Interception of Electronic Communication, and Undermining of IP Protection	• The Electronic Communications Privacy Act of 1986 makes it illegal to intercept phone and computer communications, including email, but there are two major exceptions for employers who are allowed to monitor both phone and email if it occurs in the regular course of business or if there is consent granted by the employee. • Among the protections of IP is the Economic Espionage Act of 1996, which makes misappropriation of trade secrets a crime with severe penalties, especially if the misappropriator is acting on behalf of a foreign government. • The Digital Millennium Copyright Act of 1998 makes it illegal to break encryption software that protects copyrighted works from being copied.
Offshore Websites Have Opened up Online Gambling That Is Largely beyond the Jurisdiction of the United States; Cybermedicine and Online Pharmacies Are Redefining Access to Medicine and Drugs	• Gambling has been facilitated by the Internet, which allows U.S. gamblers access to websites that are owned by persons who register their websites in countries that have legalized gambling. • In the United States, a number of states refuse to enforce gambling debts incurred by gamblers who make use of the Internet. • U.S. websites that feature gambling and are used by residents in states that do not allow gambling are nevertheless subject to the jurisdiction of the courts in those states for which gambling is illegal. As a result, much of the Internet gambling offered has gone offshore. • Websites have moved into the sale of medical services and pharmaceutical drugs with questionable legal status. In many cases, state licensing boards have made known their hostility toward cybermedicine. • There are a number of websites that sell prescription drugs after a cyberexamination by a physician who reviews answers inserted into a medical questionnaire.

Key Terms

cybermedicine, *736*
cyberstalking, *721*
hacker, *709*

identity theft, *727*
obscenity, *713*

pornography, *709*
reasonable restrictions, *717*

Questions for Review and Analysis

1. There is a lot of activity on the Internet that is criminal. Discuss how privacy rights, jurisdiction, and free speech are being used to shelter criminal activity. Should we give up some of these rights to apprehend and punish cybercriminals?

2. Much of the legislation designed to reduce access to pornography by minors has been declared unconstitutional. What are the main reasons courts have relied on in declaring antiporn laws unconstitutional?

3. At one time, in order to demonstrate their alleged intellectual superiority, a number of teenagers broke into computer systems that guarded records of schools, government generally, and the military. What are the current potential criminal risks associated with hacking illegally into computer systems?

4. Criminal law statutes now protect your name and identity, your communications, and your ideas. Match each of these categories with the appropriate criminal law statute and explain how each statute can be violated.

5. Online gambling and the purchase of pharmaceutical drugs over the Internet are quasi-legal activities that can only take place because the Internet allows the parties offering gambling and drugs access to those who want to be customers. Should law enforcement in the United States tolerate such activity or should it go after small nations that provide shelter for such websites? In addition to policing the physical world, should the United States police all of cyberspace?

If You Really Understood This Chapter, You Should Be Able to Provide Informed Commentary on the Following:

1. **Public Employees on the Job.** Many state and federal statutes dealing with obscenity or sexually explicit themes fail because they are too broad. Can a state limit its employees' access to sexually explicit websites while on the job? The State of Virginia passed a statute that restricted employee access to sexually explicit material while they were working at their jobs using computers owned or leased by the state unless they obtained written approval for bona fide research. Urofsky was one of six state university professors, along with the American Association of University Professors and the ACLU, who challenged the statute. Urofsky argued that the statute violates the First Amendment because it is overly broad. He claims, for example, that the statute could be used to prohibit research related to sexuality, gay and lesbian activity, and sexually explicit poetry. The State of Virginia argued that while working for the government, employees can be restricted as can employees for any employer. The district court decided that the statute violated constitutional protections in part because it was overly broad. The case was appealed to the Fourth Circuit Court of Appeals. [*Melvin I. Urofsky, et al. v. James F. Gilmore, Governor of the State of Virginia,* 167 F.3d 191 (4th Cir. 1999), *cert. den'd,* 531 U.S. 1070 (2001).]

2. **Use of Community Standards in Federal Obscenity Statutes.** The Child Online Protection Act (COPA) (47 U.S.C. § 231) prohibits any person from knowingly, in interstate or foreign commerce by means of the World Wide Web, making any communication for commercial purposes that is available to any minor and that includes any material that is harmful to minors. COPA defines "material that is harmful to minors" as any communication, picture, image, graphic image file, article, recording, writing, or other matter that is obscene or that (1) the average person, applying contemporary community standards, would find, taking the material as a whole and with respect to minors, is designed to appeal or pander to the prurient interest; (2) depicts, describes, or represents, in a manner patently offensive with respect to minors, an actual or simulated sexual act or sexual contact, an actual or simulated normal or perverted sexual act, or a lewd exhibition of the genitals or post-pubescent female breast; and (3) taken as a whole, lacks serious literary, artistic, political, or scientific value for minors (47 U.S.C. § 231(e)(6)). In this case, the U.S. Supreme Court dealt with the issue of whether a federal obscenity statute could be based on community standards. Justice Thomas wrote the opinion of the U.S. Supreme Court. [*John Ashcroft, Attorney General v. America Civil Liberties Union,* 122 S. Ct. 1700 (2002).] Note that the Third Circuit affirmed the district court's decision to prevent enforcement of the Child Online Protection Act because of the Third Circuit's opinion that use of community standards in defining obscenity guaranteed that the statute was overly broad. Does it make any sense to you that local communities have unique, identifiable obscenity standards? See *ACLU et al. v. Reno,* 217 F.3d 162 (3rd Cir. 2000).

3. **Libraries and Protecting Children from Adult Websites on the Internet.** Ignoring some exceptions and qualifiers, the Children's Internet Protection Act (Pub. L. No. 106-554, 114 Stat. 2763) basically requires public school libraries that receive certain forms of federal funds to set up screening systems so that children using the library are shielded from adult sites on the Internet. The full text of the act can be found at http://www.ifea.net/cipa.html. In round one of what is certain to be a dispute that ends up being decided by the U.S. Supreme Court, a federal district court has enjoined enforcement of the act because it is likely that the statute violates the First Amendment. See the decision at http://www.paed.uscourts.gov/documents/opinions/02D0415P.HTM or at 2002 U.S. Dist. LEXIS 9537. What do you think troubled the district court about a requirement that libraries receiving federal funds must set up filtering software to prevent children from encountering obscene or pornographic websites? This is another case that will undoubtedly be appealed to the U.S. Supreme Court.

4. **Electronic Communications Privacy Act.** As we know, employers can monitor on-the-job employee phone and email communications under the ECPA so long as the monitoring occurs in the regular course of business or the employee gives consent. Suppose, however, employees have been assured that the company is not monitoring their conversations. Arias and Albero claim that their employer, an alarm company, recorded their telephone conversations and that the president of the company then overheard the conversations. The company files a motion for a summary judgment claiming that the conversations were recorded in the regular course of business. Not only is the recording of all telephone conversations to which central station employees are parties routine among central station alarm companies, but such recording is recommended or even mandated by

various standard-setting and regulatory bodies in the industry. Is it a violation of the ECPA for a company to record employee conversations in the regular course of business when the employees have been assured that no such recording is taking place? [*Lourdes Arias and Louis Albero v. Mutual Central Alarm Service, Inc.,* 202 F.3d 553 (2nd Cir. 2000).]

Social Responsibility, Policy, and Ethics in a High-Tech World

5. **Economic Espionage Act.** Four Pillars is a Taiwanese company owned by Yang. Avery Dennison Inc. (Avery), an American corporation, is one of Four Pillars' chief competitors in the manufacture of adhesives. Dr. Victor Lee, a native of Taiwan, was employed by Avery in 1986 to do scientific research into adhesives. At all times relevant to this case, Lee was an employee of Avery. In 1989, while Lee was making a presentation in Taiwan, Four Pillars vice president C. K. Kao introduced him to Yang and Sally. Yang asked Lee to serve as a "consultant" to Four Pillars and offered him compensation of $25,000.00 for a year of consultation. The parties agreed that they would keep the arrangement secret. Lee received a check, made out to his sister-in-law, from Four Pillars shortly thereafter. After his return to the United States, Lee corresponded with Yang and Sally, describing the information he would provide them and indicating that some of the information Lee intended to provide the Yangs was confidential to Avery. On August 8, 1989, Lee sent two confidential Avery methodology reports to the Yangs. The Yangs responded that the information was very helpful. Lee continued to supply the Yangs with confidential information, including information that Four Pillars could use in making a new acrylic adhesive developed by Avery. The Yangs sent Lee samples of the adhesives they had created using information he had supplied; Lee tested the samples and offered comparisons with Avery's products derived from the same adhesive formula. The FBI confronted Lee after learning of Lee's industrial espionage. Lee admitted his relationship with the Yangs and Four Pillars and provided the government with materials documenting his activities since 1989. Lee also agreed to cooperate with the government in a sting operation to arrest and prosecute the Yangs. A short time later, Yang told Lee that he would be in the United States during the summer of 1997. Lee volunteered that he had information on a new emulsion coating that he would provide Yang at that time and asked whether Yang might also be interested in information on Avery's operations in Asia. Yang was very interested.

On September 4, 1997, Lee met Yang and Sally in Lee's hotel room in Westlake, Ohio. Lee had consented to the FBI's videotaping of this meeting. In the course of the meeting, Lee showed the Yangs documents provided by the FBI, including an Avery patent application relating to a new adhesive product. The documents were stamped "confidential" and Lee emphasized to the Yangs that the information contained was the confidential property of Avery. Yang and Sally, at Yang's direction, began to tear off the "confidential" stamps. The Yangs discussed with Lee the information Lee had previously provided to Four Pillars. Following the meeting, the Yangs—with the confidential documents in their possession—were arrested by the FBI.

As part of their defense, the Yangs contend that they cannot be criminally prosecuted for something they did not take and they never received: Lee's purported trade secrets at the hotel sting. The Yangs cite *United States v. Hsu,* 155 F.3d 189 (3rd Cir. 1998); claim it was wrongly decided; and contend that they cannot be prosecuted under the Economic Espionage Act (EEA) because it was impossible for them to take something that was nonexistent. What do you think? Can the FBI prosecute for EEA violations when there are no real trade secrets available in the set up "sting" operations for the defendants to take? Should the FBI be setting up sting operations to catch possible violators of the EEA? [*United States of America v. Pin Yen Yang and Four Pillars Enterprise Company, Ltd., et al.,* 281 F.3d 534 (6th Cir. 2002).]

Using the Internet to Your Advantage

1. Two key government agencies in the fight against computer and cybercrime are the U.S. Department of Justice (http://www.usdoj.gov) and, to a lesser extent, the Federal Trade Commission (http://www.ftc.gov). The heart of the cybercrime efforts at the Department of Justice resides in the Computer Crime and Intellectual Property Section (CCIPS) (http://www.cybercrime.gov/index.html). On the CCIPS web page, the U.S. Department of Justice has compiled cybercrime cases and categorized them according to whether they are hacking, IP, or cybercrime document

cases. The Federal Trade Commission enforces the civil sides of several key statutes studied in this chapter. A complete list of the statutes enforced by the FTC is located at http://www.ftc.gov/ogc/stats.htm.

2. A complete text of the USA PATRIOT Act is available at http://personalinfomediary.com/USAPATRIOTACT_Text.htm. A good compilation of cybercrime cases and other information is available at http://www.jonesencyclo.com. The UCLA Online Institute for Cyberspace Law and Policy (http://www.gseis.ucla.edu/iclp/hp.html) "keeps score" on many of the important, recent cases that deal with cybercrime and constitutional rights.

Chapter Twenty-Three

Real Space and Cyberspace: Jurisdiction, Taxation, and International Law Issues

Learning Objectives

After completing this chapter, you should

1. Be able to discuss how jurisdictional principles are applied in cyberspace, particularly with regard to tax jurisdiction.
2. Recognize the effects and importance of the Internet Tax Freedom Act of 1998 and its extension in 2001.
3. Know and be able to discuss the basic principles of international law including comity, sovereign immunity, and the act of state doctrine.
4. Be familiar with the main international organizations that are charged with protecting intellectual property.
5. Know some of the pitfalls of contracting with companies domiciled in other countries and some of the key contractual clauses companies involved in international contracts use to avoid costly litigation.

OVERVIEW

Throughout human existence, geography has exerted dominant influences on human activities. Many of the great empires of antiquity, the middle ages, and modern times grew powerful in part because of their favorable geography. Certainly, access to the sea was a factor in the dominance of England, Phoenicia, Japan and other nations, reflecting the relative ease of traveling and transporting (both things and people) by sea, rather than overland, prior to the existence of modern highway and rail systems. Interestingly, from the perspective of this text, most laws today continue to be based on, or at least strongly influenced by, geography. With very few exceptions, Americans visiting other countries are bound by the laws of those countries when they are in those countries. The same principle applies, of course, when foreigners are in the United States.

With the development of transoceanic air transport, along with cable and wireless international communications, talk about globalization became more prevalent. The Internet can be viewed as an accentuation of the globalization trend that has been ongoing for some time, a trend that acts to reduce the importance of geography. The Internet, however, is more than just a mechanism for acceleration of the demise of geography as a paramount feature of a large array of activities. In fact, for those activities that can occur in cyberspace, geography is not only traversed much more rapidly but, in a very real sense, it is made irrelevant. No website is close to or far away from any other website or browser, as they are all equally accessible. It's not surprising, then, that governments face difficulties as they continue to try to regulate cyberspace using geography as the primary determinant of whether the government in question, foreign or domestic, has the right to regulate or tax a website.

This chapter explores two legal topics that have been discussed in other chapters, jurisdiction and international law, but the context of the analysis in this chapter is mainly the Internet. Specifically, in this chapter, jurisdiction is the legal concept applied to cyberspace taxation within the United States, with international law also explored from the perspective of the Internet.

JURISDICTION

Taxation

Taxes must be collected to pay for all the good things that government provides, such as police, schools, roads, national defense, and social services. At both federal and state levels, the U.S. Constitution constrains the way revenue is raised. At the federal level, until 1913, there were severe constraints on the manner in which taxes could be levied. This was changed with passage of the Sixteenth Amendment. This amendment allowed the federal government to tax income without an **apportionment** among the states according to population, as required by Article 1 of the U.S. Constitution.[1] At the state level, the Interstate Commerce Clause and the Due Process Clause are the principal constitutional constraints on the ways states are permitted to raise tax revenues.

apportionment
The principle of tax law that requires states to allocate tax levies in a manner that does not discriminate against interstate commerce and businesses.

Impact of the Interstate Commerce Clause

The World Wide Web is, by definition, a global phenomenon, but states in the United States have made determined efforts to levy taxes on the Internet and e-commerce. In order to appreciate the legal tax issues created by the Internet, it is necessary to review some basic principles of tax law as they relate to states. Looming over the relevant legal principles is the **Interstate Commerce Clause** (generally referred to as the Commerce Clause) of the U.S. Constitution. To be legal and constitutional, a state tax cannot violate the Commerce Clause, which delegates responsibility for regulating interstate commerce to the federal government. As a general principle, a state tax violates the Commerce Clause if it subjects interstate businesses to higher taxes than in-state businesses.

Interstate Commerce Clause
The authority within the U.S. Constitution for the federal government to regulate interstate commerce. The Interstate Commerce Clause is also the authority for courts to strike down state laws, including tax laws, that discriminate against or place an undue burden on interstate commerce.

[1] The Sixteenth Amendment reads as follows: "The Congress shall have power to lay and collect taxes on incomes, from whatever source derived, without apportionment among the several States, and without regard to any census or enumeration."

Apportionment of State Taxes

States have generally been less fettered than the federal government in the means they have available for generating revenue. Income taxes were being imposed in many states before they were legally permitted at the federal level. Of course, states also have relied heavily on sales and property taxes for revenue generation.

Whether the revenue source is taxes on income or taxes on sales and property, states have been required to *apportion* tax levies. For example, if a person is a resident of a state for only part of the year, then the person's obligation to pay income taxes is prorated according to the time the person is a resident of the state.

Through U.S. history, as businesses expanded from small, local establishments to geographically dispersed national companies, states were required by Supreme Court interpretations of the Commerce Clause to apportion any taxes imposed on multistate businesses according to some formula that reflected geography. Currently, states are allowed to tax income earned by a corporation, but are required to apportion that tax in accordance with the income/revenue generated in-state. The same geographic limitation operates with respect to sales and property taxes. A state can tax the sales of a company that occur within the state, but cannot tax all sales of a multistate or multinational corporation. Property that is located within the state is taxable, but property owned by an in-state company, but located out of state, is not taxable by the "home" state.

Interplay between State and Federal Law

Over time, growing state tax levies started a process that has involved several key players, including company executives, corporate attorneys, state tax authorities, state courts, state legislatures, and, finally, federal courts. In act one of this drama, company executives, advised by company attorneys, would come across some possible loophole in the state tax code that, if properly exploited, would save the company a sizeable sum of money. Suppose State A has a higher sales tax rate than surrounding states and company X determines that it could save tax money if it paid sales tax in the other states rather than in State A. Company X might modify its invoices to reflect a presumption that its sales are not completed until the product is delivered, which would mean that its sales would be taxed at the rates prevalent in the lower-tax states where its buyers were located.

Of course, state tax authorities would notice the loss of tax revenue from company X and could be expected to challenge the validity of company X's invoicing procedures. That challenge could well be contested in a state court if the company does not agree with the tax authorities' demands. If the state tax authorities lose in state court or on appeal to the federal courts, the state legislature may change tax laws to require that all sales made by firms located in State A be recognized as taking place in State A. This law may anger tax authorities in surrounding states, as they would lose sales tax revenue as a result. Eventually, a case emanating from this sequence of events is apt to make its way to federal courts and, perhaps, the U.S. Supreme Court. A likely focus would be on the issue of where sales take place and what state has the right to collect taxes on sales. Tax litigation of this sort, typically involving geography, continued to occupy significant court time through the 1990s when the Internet became a prominent feature of the commerce landscape.

The State of State Sales Tax Law before E-Commerce

Though state tax litigation involving the minutia of tax details has continued, the main corpus of state tax law, based on court precedent, was well established by the time the Internet became important. With regard to the battle over where sales take place, states where buyers are located were generally successful in levying sales taxes based on the location of the

Nutz and Boltz   State Sales Tax Rates (January 1, 2003)

State	Tax Rates	Exemptions Food	Exemptions Prescription Drugs	Exemptions Nonprescription Drugs
Alabama	4		*	
Alaska	none			
Arizona	5.6	*	*	
Arkansas	5.125		*	
California (3)	7.25 (2)	*	*	
Colorado	2.9	*	*	
Connecticut	6	*	*	*
Delaware	none			
Florida	6	*	*	*
Georgia	4	*	*	
Hawaii	4		*	
Idaho	5		*	
Illinois (2)	6.25	1%	1%	1%
Indiana	6	*	*	
Iowa	5	*	*	
Kansas (6)	5.3		*	
Kentucky	6	*	*	
Louisiana	4	2% (4)	*	
Maine	5	*	*	
Maryland	5	*	*	*
Massachusetts	5	*	*	
Michigan	6	*	*	
Minnesota	6.5	*	*	*
Mississippi	7		*	
Missouri	4.225	1.225	*	
Montana	none			
Nebraska (7)	5.5	*	*	
Nevada	6.5	*	*	
New Hampshire	none			
New Jersey	6	*	*	*
New Mexico	5		*	
New York	4	*	*	*
North Carolina	4.5	* (4)	*	
North Dakota	5	*	*	
Ohio	5	*	*	
Oklahoma	4.5		*	
Oregon	none			
Pennsylvania	6	*	*	*
Rhode Island	7	*	*	*
South Carolina	5		*	
South Dakota	4		*	
Tennessee	7	6%	*	
Texas	6.25	*	*	*
Utah	4.75		*	
Vermont	5	*	*	*
Virginia	4.5 (2)	4.0% (5)	*	*

Washington	6.5	*	*	
West Virginia	6		*	
Wisconsin	5	*	*	
Wyoming (3)	4		*	
Dist. of Columbia	5.75	*	*	*

* —indicates exempt from tax, blank indicates subject to general sales tax rate.

Source: Compiled by FTA from various sources.

1. Some state tax food, but allow an (income) tax credit to compensate poor households. They are: ID, KS, SD, and WY.
2. Includes statewide local tax of 1.25% in California and 1.0% in Virginia.
3. Tax rate may be adjusted annually according to a formula based on balances in the unappropriated general fund and the school foundation fund.
4. Food sales are subject to local sales taxes. In LA, food sales scheduled to be exempt on 7/1/03.
5. Tax rate on food is scheduled to decrease to 3.5% on 4/1/03. Statewide local tax is included.
6. Tax rate is scheduled to decrease to 5.2% on 7/1/03.
7. Tax rate scheduled to decrease to 5.0% on 10/1/03.

buyers. In general, states established the right to tax all sales made to in-state residents regardless of where the seller was located, but with mail-order companies being a prominent exception. Additionally, those states where buyers live generally had the right, established through jurisdictional rulings, to make companies selling products to residents of the state collect and remit sales taxes to in-state tax authorities.

Minimum Contacts Test

In general, as long as the *minimum contacts test* for jurisdiction is satisfied, tax authorities can require an out-of-state company, selling products to residents of the state, to collect sales taxes and remit those monies to the customers' state. The minimum contacts test is based on a physical presence of the out-of-state company in the taxing state. Conceptually, however, the minimum contacts test operates based on the answer to the question, "Did the out-of-state company purposely avail itself of the privilege of doing business within the taxing state?" If the answer to that question is yes, the **Due Process Clause** of the U.S. Constitution is not violated if a state court exercises jurisdiction over the out-of-state business. Peeking ahead, you might ask yourself whether establishing a website accessible by residents of other states would be subject to the minimum contacts tests in those states.

Due Process Clause
A basic principle in the American legal system that requires fairness in the government's dealing with persons. In this context, courts have interpreted the Due Process Clause to require that out-of-state businesses must receive some benefit from a state before a state court or taxing authority can exert jurisdiction over the business.

The Mail-Order Exception: The Due Process Clause

In the evolution of state tax collection standards, one prominent exception to the general rule that a state can force out-of-state businesses to both collect sales taxes for them and remit them to the state where the buyers are located emerged. This is in the case of mail-order catalog sales. If a company does nothing but send its catalogs to citizens of a state, that connection alone has been deemed to be insufficient to subject the mail-order company to jurisdiction of the state where buyers live. Hence, mail-order catalog sales escaped sales taxes imposed by states where buyers reside. The U.S. Supreme Court resolved the mail-order sales tax controversy in 1967 in the landmark *Bellas Hess* case, provided as Case 23-1, when it ruled in favor of the mail-order company on the sales tax issue. In the aftermath of that case, the mail-order catalog segment of the retail sales industry blossomed, in part because goods sold in that manner largely escaped state sales taxes. Such was the status of state tax law when e-commerce began expanding rapidly and when state tax authorities started taking notice of lost sales tax revenue on e-commerce sales.

Case 23-1

National Bellas Hess, Inc. v. Department of Revenue of the State of Illinois

Supreme Court of the United States
386 U.S. 753 (1967)

BACKGROUND AND FACTS

The Internet began in 1969. Before the Internet, mail-order companies battled with states over the collection of sales (or use) taxes. In this case, the Illinois Department of Revenue, acting pursuant to an Illinois statute requiring retailers to collect and pay use taxes, brought an action against the defendant in the Circuit Court of Cook County, Illinois, to recover use taxes and penalties with respect to merchandise which the defendant had sold to Illinois customers. The defendant, a mail-order house, was incorporated in Delaware, had its principal place of business in Missouri, and was licensed to do business only in Delaware and Missouri. It did not maintain any places of business in Illinois; did not have in Illinois any agents or representatives to sell or take orders, to deliver merchandise, to accept payments, or to service merchandise it sold; did not own any tangible property, real or personal, in Illinois; had no telephone listing in Illinois; and did not advertise its merchandise for sale in newspapers, on billboards, or by radio or television in Illinois. Orders for its merchandise were mailed to and accepted at its Missouri plant, and its merchandise was sent to customers either by mail or by common carrier. Its catalogues were mailed to its Illinois customers twice a year, its occasional advertising flyers were mailed to past and potential customers in Illinois, and its sales to Illinois customers amounted to $2,174,744 during the approximately 15 months for which the taxes in issue were assessed. The Circuit Court entered a summary judgment in favor of the Department of Revenue, and the Illinois Supreme Court affirmed, rejecting the defendant's contention that the application of the use tax statute to it violated the Due Process and Commerce clauses of the federal Constitution.

Opinion: Mr. Justice Stewart Delivered the Opinion the Court

National [Bellas Hess] argues that the liabilities which Illinois has thus imposed violate the Due Process Clause of the Fourteenth Amendment and create an unconstitutional burden upon interstate commerce. These two claims are closely related. For the test whether a particular state exaction is such as to invade the exclusive authority of Congress to regulate trade between the States, and the test for a State's compliance with the requirements of due process in this area are similar. [Citations omitted.] As to the former, the Court has held that "State taxation falling on interstate commerce . . . can only be justified as designed to make such commerce bear a fair share of the cost of the local government whose protection it enjoys." And in determining whether a state tax falls within the confines of the Due Process Clause, the Court has said that the "simple but controlling question is whether the state has given anything for which it can ask return." The same principles have been held applicable in determining the power of a State to impose the burdens of collecting use taxes upon interstate sales. Here, too, the Constitution requires "some definite link, some minimum connection, between a state and the person, property or transaction it seeks to tax." *Miller Bros. Co. v. Maryland*, 347 U.S. 340, 344–345; *Scripto, Inc. v. Carson*, 362 U.S. 207, 210–211. [Footnotes omitted.] See also *American Oil Co. v. Neill*, 380 U.S. 451, 458.

In applying these principles the [Supreme] Court has upheld the power of a State to impose liability upon an out-of-state seller to collect a local use tax in a variety of circumstances. Where the sales were arranged by local agents in the taxing State, we have upheld such power. We have reached the same result where the mail order seller maintained local retail stores. In those situations the out-of-state seller was plainly accorded the protection and services of the taxing State. The case in this Court which represents the furthest constitutional reach to date of a State's power to deputize an out-of-state retailer as its collection agent for a use tax is *Scripto, Inc. v. Carson*, 362 U.S. 207. There we held that Florida could constitutionally impose upon a Georgia seller the duty of collecting a state use tax upon the sale of goods shipped to customers in Florida. In that case the seller had "10 wholesalers, jobbers, or 'salesmen' conducting continuous local solicitation in Florida and forwarding the resulting orders from that State to Atlanta for shipment of the ordered goods."

But the Court has never held that a State may impose the duty of use tax collection and payment upon a seller whose only connection with customers in the State is by common carrier or the United States mail. Indeed, in the *Sears, Roebuck* case the Court sharply differentiated such a situation from one where the seller had local retail outlets, pointing out that "those other concerns . . . are not receiving benefits from Iowa for which it has the power to exact a price." And in *Miller Bros. Co. v. Maryland,* 347 U.S. 340, the Court held that Maryland could not constitutionally impose a use tax obligation upon a Delaware seller who had no retail outlets or sales solicitors in Maryland. There the seller advertised its wares to Maryland residents through newspaper and radio advertising, in addition to mailing circulars four times a year. As a result, it made substantial sales to Maryland customers, and made deliveries to them by its own trucks and drivers.

In order to uphold the power of Illinois to impose use tax burdens on National in this case, we would have to repudiate totally the sharp distinction which these and other decisions have drawn between mail order sellers with retail outlets, solicitors, or property within a State, and those who do no more than communicate with customers in the State by mail or common carrier as part of a general interstate business. But this basic distinction, which until now has been generally recognized by the state taxing authorities, is a valid one, and we decline to obliterate it.

We need not rest on the broad foundation of all that was said in the *Miller Bros.* opinion, for here there was neither local advertising nor local household deliveries, upon which the dissenters in *Miller Bros.* so largely relied. Indeed, it is difficult to conceive of commercial transactions more exclusively interstate in character than the mail order transactions here involved. And if the power of Illinois to impose use tax burdens upon National were upheld, the resulting impediments upon the free conduct of its interstate business would be neither imaginary nor remote. For if Illinois can impose such burdens, so can every other State, and so, indeed, can every municipality, every school district, and every other political subdivision throughout the Nation with power to impose sales and use taxes. The many variations in rates of tax, in allowable exemptions, and in administrative and record-keeping requirements could entangle National's interstate business in a virtual welter of complicated obligations to local jurisdictions with no legitimate claim to impose "a fair share of the cost of the local government."

The very purpose of the Commerce Clause was to ensure a national economy free from such unjustifiable local entanglements. Under the Constitution, this is a domain where Congress alone has the power of regulation and control.

Decision and Outcome

The U.S. Supreme Court ruled that Illinois did not have authority to impose jurisdiction over National Bellas Hess and require it to collect state sales taxes on its sales to Illinois residents.

Questions for Analysis

1. It would be useful for you to examine the arguments made by the U.S. Supreme Court against the imposition of sales tax requirements on out-of-state mail-order companies and see which of those arguments could apply with equal force to state impositions of jurisdiction and tax requirements on Internet websites.

2. Does it make sense to impose liability for taxes on sales made to residents of a state just because the company does some trivial, unrelated act such as open up an office in the state as a relay station for its trucking operations or for placing ads in local newspapers? Shouldn't the quid pro quo balance be at least somewhat equal between the state imposition of sales tax on all the company's in-state sales and the benefits the company receives from the state?

Cyberlaw **Developments**

The following article appears on the website of the law firm of Satterlee, Stephens, Burke & Burke. At their website there are a number of other articles that discuss state court jurisdiction over out-of-state websites.

WHAT JURISDICTION CONTROLS?

Will on-line publishers find themselves subject to jurisdiction throughout the nation (or the world)? When on-line communications routinely cross state and national borders, whose law will apply?

General Legal Standards for Asserting Jurisdiction

Under the U.S. Constitution, a court cannot assert jurisdiction over a potential defendant unless the defendant has sufficient "minimum contacts" with the forum so as to satisfy traditional notions of fair play and substantial justice. *International Shoe Co. v. Washington,* 326 U.S. 310 (1945). Minimum contacts can consist of either some type of systematic and continuous contact with the forum ("general jurisdiction"), or isolated or occasional contacts purposefully directed toward the forum ("specific jurisdiction"). *Helicopteros Nacionales de Columbia, S.A. v. Hall,* 466 U.S. 408 (1984).

The principal test, for due process purposes, is whether or not the defendant, by its actions, could have reasonably anticipated the possibility of defending a suit in the forum. *World-Wide Volkswagen v. Woodson,* 444 U.S. 286 (1980). In cases in which the litigants are from foreign countries, a court must also consider the policies of the foreign countries, as well as U.S. foreign policy, in determining whether exercising jurisdiction would be fair. *Asahi Metal Ind. Co. v. Superior Court,* 480 U.S. 102 (1987).

It is still too early to determine definitively how most courts will assess jurisdictional questions in the context of entities which have no "real" physical location, but only a "virtual" location on-line. In *Calder v. Jones,* 465 U.S. 783 (1984), the Supreme Court held that the minimum contacts test could be satisfied by speech directed toward the forum, if the speech has sufficient impact within the forum. A similar result was reached in a Canadian case, *Pindling v. National Broadcasting Corp.,* 49 O.R.2d 58 (1984), in which an Ontario court exercised jurisdiction over an American broadcaster whose allegedly libelous broadcasts from the U.S. were received in Canada. These cases may prove to be very important for providing a jurisdictional framework for lawsuits involving on-line communications.

Source: What Jurisdiction Controls? From: http://www.ssb.com/what.html. Copyright © 2000 by Satterlee Stephens Burke & Burke, LLP. Used with permission.

As the Supreme Court indicated in *Bellas Hess,* their ruling that states could not exert jurisdiction for tax purposes over an out-of-state mail-order company was based in part on the (interstate) Commerce Clause and in part on due process requirements. What the U.S. Supreme Court held in *Bellas Hess,* and in many other cases involving attempted extraterritorial exercises of state jurisdiction, is that there must be some *nexus* between the taxing state and the company it is attempting to have collect sales taxes for it. According to the Supreme Court, basic notions of due process are violated if a state can tax a nonresident company that has an insufficient connection or nexus with the taxing state.

State Taxes, Geography, and Websites

When the Internet became "important," states began asserting that websites were subject to their jurisdiction based on a number of concepts. Among the arguments used by states to assert that an out-of-state company that owns a website selling products to its residents owes it sales tax payments, was the argument that websites satisfied the minimum contacts test. So, if a website hires employees within a state, rents office space in, or purposely directs advertising toward a state, the "host" state can be expected to claim that the website is subject to its jurisdiction when it sells products to state residents.

Some states also have asserted that websites pass nexus tests if the websites have used (owned, leased, or rented) a server located within the state and, on that basis, have tried to make websites pay sales taxes on their e-commerce sales. Also, since websites that sell tangible goods often have the goods in inventory somewhere, states have claimed that the location of inventory is enough to enable the repository state to force the website to collect sales tax for its sales to that state's residents.

State and Local Taxing Authorities Threaten the Viability of E-Commerce and the Internet

As e-commerce has enjoyed rapid growth on the Internet in only the last few years, state authorities in charge of taxes have alerted state legislatures to possible losses of tax revenue and, of course, state legislatures have responded by altering tax laws to include e-commerce sales. By 1998, when the Internet Tax Freedom Act was passed, 45 states had passed laws that imposed sales taxes on e-commerce sales. Also, a number of states imposed taxes in the form of

1. Access charges imposed on ISPs or telecommunications companies for connecting customers to the Internet.
2. Downloading charges when software vendors provided electronic delivery of licensed computer software.

Many localities—cities, counties, and townships—also imposed sales taxes and they, too, were claiming the right to impose sales tax on out-of-state websites selling to their jurisdictions. Interestingly, according to one estimate, there are 30,000 taxing authorities in the United States alone, creating a potential for a mass on conflicting claims for tax assessments on e-commerce sales.

Internet Tax Freedom Act of 1998

Internet Tax Freedom Act

This act of Congress imposes a tax moratorium on the imposition of new Internet taxes by states and prohibits discriminatory and multiple taxation of the same Internet transaction by states. State taxes that were in force before October 1998 when the ITFA was enacted can continue to be collected.

In October of 1998, Congress passed the **Internet Tax Freedom Act** (ITFA), which both imposed a moratorium on new state and local taxes on e-commerce sales and banned outright multiple and discriminatory taxes of e-commerce transactions.[2] By that point in time, states were asserting all sorts of bases for imposing taxes on e-commerce. Taxes were being levied on sales of physical products, on connections with ISPs, and on the downloading of computer information, particularly computer software. New websites would be confronted with a bewildering array of tax authorities and most did not have budgets to battle state taxing authorities in state and federal courts. By 1998 it was clear that the viability of e-commerce was threatened by state and local government attempts to levy taxes and exert jurisdiction over websites transacting with in-state and in-locale residents. Congress was determined to give the Internet and e-commerce time to grow before subjecting them to a web of state and local taxes.

To that end, Congress imposed a moratorium on new Internet taxes imposed at the state level when it enacted the ITFA of 1998. Among the highlights of the ITFA are

- *A three-year moratorium on special taxation of the Internet.* The act barred state and local governments from taxing Internet access charges (i.e., the $19.95 or so that many Americans pay monthly to America Online, Mindspring, Earthlink, or other similar services to access the Internet) from October 1, 1998, until October 21, 2001. A limited "grandfather" clause permitted the handful of states that already had taken steps to tax

---

[2] Pub. L. No. 105-277, 112 Stat. 2681–719, codified at 47 U.S.C. §151 note.

Internet access—Connecticut, Iowa, New Mexico, North Dakota, Ohio, South Carolina, South Dakota, Tennessee, Texas, and Wisconsin—to continue if they could demonstrate that their taxes had already been "generally imposed and actually enforced" on Internet access providers prior to October 1, 1998. Not all of the states that were "grandfathered" actually continued collecting taxes applied to Internet access.

- *A three-year moratorium on multiple and discriminatory taxes on electronic commerce.* The act also barred state or local governments from imposing taxes that would subject buyers and sellers of electronic commerce items to taxation in multiple states. It also protected against the imposition of new tax liabilities for consumers and vendors involved in commercial transactions over the Internet, including the application of discriminatory tax collection requirements imposed on out-of-state businesses through strained interpretations of "nexus." It also protected from taxation, for the duration of the moratorium, goods or services that are sold exclusively over the Internet with no comparable offline equivalents.

- *Establishment of a commission to study the question of remote sales.* A temporary Advisory Commission on Electronic Commerce was organized to study electronic commerce tax issues and report back to Congress after 18 months on whether electronic commerce should be taxed and, if so, how it can be taxed in a manner that ensures that such commerce won't be subject to special, multiple, or discriminatory taxes. State and local elected officials were given a prominent voice on this commission. Congress, of course, retained full authority to change or discard the Commission's proposals.

- *Prohibition of federal taxes.* This act formalized the sense of Congress that there should be no federal taxes on Internet access or electronic commerce.

- *A declaration that the Internet should be a tariff-free zone.* This part of the act called on the Clinton administration to work aggressively, through the EU and WTO, to keep electronic commerce free from tariffs and discriminatory taxes. It asked the Commerce Department to report to Congress on barriers hindering the competitiveness of U.S. businesses engaged in electronic commerce abroad.

In short, the ITFA imposed a three-year moratorium (from October 1, 1998, through October 21, 2001) on state and local taxes on Internet access, unless such taxes were generally imposed and actually enforced before October 1, 1998. The moratorium also applied to multiple or discriminatory taxes on e-commerce. There were limited exceptions to the moratorium for certain taxpayers who used the Web to send materials that were harmful to minors and Internet access providers who didn't offer screening software to limit materials harmful to minors.

The ITFA Extension and the Continuing Debate

With the original ITFA scheduled to expire during the fall of 2001, its provisions were reinstated by the Internet Non-Discrimination Act, signed into law in November of that year.[3] The new law extended the state and local tax moratorium through November 1, 2003, on all the taxes that were subject to the moratorium created by the ITFA. The legislation, signed by President George W. Bush, extends through November 1, 2003, the ban on multiple and discriminatory Internet taxes, as well as the ban on Internet access taxes. The legislation also extends the "Sense of the Congress" resolution that there should be no federal taxes on Internet access or electronic commerce, and the U.S. commitment to work aggressively, through the EU and WTO, to keep electronic commerce free from tariffs and discriminatory taxes.

---

[3] Pub. L. No. 107-75, 115 Stat. 703, codified at 47 U.S.C. § 609 note.

Notwithstanding the latest round of legislative protection of the Internet and e-commerce, the debate about taxation of e-commerce continues. On the one side of this debate, opponents of Internet taxation make the claim, eloquently articulated by California Tax Board Chairman Dean Andal, that "Instead of applying traditional legal concepts to the taxation of electronic commerce, state tax bureaucrats are becoming legal contortionists in an attempt to tax Internet sales."[4] According to this view, state and local taxing authorities are using all sorts of ephemeral connections that websites have with their respective states to claim that a sufficient nexus exists to allow all states to force out-of-state websites to collect sales taxes for any state when a website makes a sale to a resident of that state.

On the other hand, an effect of the ITFA and its latest extension is that identical goods in the 45 states that have sales taxes are taxed at different rates, depending on whether sales are made electronically or in person (over-the-counter). The tension produced by this disparate treatment along with the impact on state budgets of growing Internet sales will continue to cause pressure from states for "fair" tax treatment of e-commerce. This tension is especially acute because many states in the early 2000s are struggling to balance their budgets and are desperate to augment their revenues without passing new laws to raise taxes.

INTERNATIONAL LAW

Basic Principles of International Law

sovereignty
The highest political power in a territory. Within their borders, sovereign countries can wield ultimate political power that is answerable to no higher power.

Although there are vast differences in power, each country in the world is sovereign within its borders, which means that, barring war, the laws and rules it enacts cannot be overruled by other countries. Because of the principle of **sovereignty** among nations, international law is somewhat of an oxymoron in that nations choose which parts of international law to adhere to and which parts to ignore. The Berne Convention has attempted to set rules for international enforcement of copyright laws, but the United States was not a member until 1988. Hence, until 1988, the United States was not a member of this convention, which was virtually the only worldwide body enforcing copyrights. The U.S. was reluctant to join because the Berne Convention contained some provisions that were at variance with parts of U.S. copyright law. Other countries also pick and choose which parts of the international law they obey and which they ignore.

From the perspective of individual citizens and companies, of course, there is no freedom of choice with regard to which parts of international law to subscribe to and which to ignore. When their governments sign treaties agreeing to adhere to certain provisions of international law, companies have no choice but to adhere, so the adopted provisions of international law become part of the legal environment for those companies.

There are 15 members of the European Union (EU). The legal environment of the 15 members of the EU is much different than for other countries because countries within the EU have agreed to eliminate many barriers to the movement of goods, capital, services, and people within the territories of member countries. Of course, companies within the EU have a much different legal environment than U.S. companies, at least in part, because the EU has deliberately expanded its geographically open market domain and the accompanying competitive characteristics of EU markets.

International Law Overview

International law is a sizeable topic. As an organizing principle in an introduction to this body of law, we will follow a traditional approach of listing the sources of international law,

[4] http://cox.house.gov/nettax/.

the international organizations that are designed to enforce international laws, and some principles of international law. Finally, we will focus on international Internet issues.

Sources of International Law

Treaties and Conventions

Article I, Section 8, Clause 3 of the Constitution delegates to Congress the power to "regulate Commerce with foreign Nations." Also, Article II, Section 2, Clause 3 indicates that the president "shall have Power, by and with the Advice and Consent of the Senate, to make Treaties, provided two thirds of the Senators present concur." Armed with this constitutional authority, U.S. presidents with concurrence from the Senate have negotiated numerous treaties and conventions with other countries that have the force of law. Formally, a treaty is an agreement between two or more countries that has been agreed to by the highest authorities in each country. A bilateral treaty is a treaty between two countries while a multilateral treaty involves more than two countries. A **convention** is a treaty that has been sponsored by an international organization such as the United Nations. There are a number of important conventions that regulate and enforce international IP law. These include the Paris Convention (Patents and Trademarks), the Berne Convention (Copyrights), and the Madrid Protocol (Trademarks), all of which have many members. Of course, there are treaties and conventions that affect noncommercial issues such as human rights, education, and scientific topics, but the focus in this textbook is on the treaties and conventions that are commerce-related.

convention
A treaty sponsored by an organization such as the United Nations.

Custom

Between nations there are often accepted ways of doing things that eventually harden into law and, thus, become part of the legal environment. When these ways of doing things become part of international law, they are called a *custom* between two or more countries. Customs are part of international law and mainly deal with procedural legal issues. A custom can be defined as a persistent and recurring action or procedure that is used by two or more countries. A custom becomes part of international law when there is recognition that the custom has become binding, which means adherence to the custom is no longer voluntary. Eventually, some customs between countries become codified in the form of treaties.

General Principles of Law

Some general principles of law are recognized by civilized nations as part of international law. A principle of law that is common to the national law of both parties in a dispute makes up part of international law. Due process is an example of a general principle of law. This principle of law can be found in constitutional, statutory, regulatory, or even the common law of most developed countries populated by companies that, on occasion, may be parties to international litigation.

Prior Court Decisions

Although international tribunals are not necessarily bound by prior court decisions dealing with similar legal issues, judges in international cases often cite prior decisions in the rationales for their decisions. If we think of law as a predictor of how decision-makers will resolve disputes, then the prior decisions of judges, and even the teachings of international legal scholars, make up part of international law.

Some Important Legal Principles in International Law

Given the fact that international law is voluntary within the borders of a sovereign country, there are certain legal principles that have been generally adopted by countries to facilitate the cross-border enforcement of laws. All of these principles are based on the idea of *reciprocity,* with separate countries respecting and agreeing to the application of laws of other countries. There certainly are many occasions when the legal actions of one nation are crucially impacted by the legal actions of another country. With reciprocity, a country can expect its legal actions to be treated as it treats the legal actions of other countries. If the legal actions of other countries are respected in the host country, then the host country can expect the same treatment for its legal actions by other countries. Among the generally recognized legal principles of international law are comity, sovereign immunity, and act of state.

Comity

comity
The legal principle that accords deference to the laws and legal actions of the courts of other countries.

Comity is the legal doctrine under which countries recognize and enforce each others' legal decrees. For example, courts generally agree to defer scheduling a trial if the same issues are being tried in a court in another jurisdiction (country). The principle of comity is regularly practiced by courts in this country as they recognize and enforce the valid legal contracts and court orders of other countries.

Sovereign Immunity

sovereign immunity
The principle that other sovereign countries are immune to, or not subject to the jurisdiction of, lawsuits in U.S. courts unless the country is engaging in purely commercial activity or waives its immunity.

Sovereign immunity is one of the oldest principles of international law. This doctrine basically grants immunity to countries from suits in the courts of other countries. Under this doctrine, an action taken by France could not become the subject of a lawsuit brought by a U.S. citizen in a U.S. court. In the United States, this principle has been codified in the Foreign Sovereign Immunity Act that was enacted in 1976.[5] Under this act, most lawsuits against a foreign country are prohibited in both state and federal courts in the United States, though there are two exceptions. The two exceptions that allow lawsuits against foreign governments arise

1. When the foreign government is engaged in *commercial activity* within the United States or taking place outside the United States but having an impact within the United States.
2. When the foreign government *waives* its immunity, either explicitly or by implication.

It is notable that these exceptions have been adopted by a number of other nations. The first exception has generated a sizeable volume of litigation focused on the meaning of "commercial activity." If a foreign government does not pay the company that did the landscaping at its embassy, it is not protected by the doctrine of sovereign immunity. In contrast, if a diplomat has too much to drink and injures a U.S. citizen on his or her drive back to his (her) embassy residence, the diplomat is protected by the doctrine of sovereign immunity. In some such cases of drunk diplomats, foreign nations have waived sovereign immunity and allowed for prosecution, especially in egregious cases.

Act of State

act of state
The legal principle whereby courts in one country will not review the legality of actions of a government from another country.

An **act of state** is a standard that largely prohibits the courts of one country from reviewing another country's legal actions taken within that country's borders. A court in the United States cannot sit in judgment upon an action of another government within its own territory. If a foreign country legalizes a cartel that charges higher prices to U.S. citizens as a result, that act does not allow a U.S. court to apply U.S. antitrust laws to the foreign cartel. Conversely, there are actions of the U.S. government or of state governments within U.S. boundaries that allow domestic business activities that are illegal in other countries.

---

[5] Pub. L. No. 94-583, 90 Stat. 2891, codified at 28 U.S.C. §§ 1330, 1332(a), 1391(f), and 1601–1611.

The act of state doctrine protects U.S. firms operating under U.S. standards from suits in foreign courts.

International and Regional Organizations

United Nations

The importance and relevance of the United Nations (UN) is subject to debate, but for some aspects of international law, the UN continues to play a very significant role. The UN is structured to allow smaller nations to participate in UN activities, including policy making, but reserves the bulk of its power for the larger member nations, such as the United States and China. The legislative body of the UN, called the *General Assembly,* is composed of all member states. Typically, the General Assembly adopts resolutions concerning matters that fall within the purview of the UN Charter, such as trade, finance, and human rights. The *Security Council* is composed of 15 member nations, with five permanent seats reserved to China, England, France, Russia, and the United States. The primary charge of the Security Council is to maintain world peace and security. The Security Council also has authority to dispatch armed forces when appropriate to quell outbreaks of violence. The day-to-day operations of the UN are administered by the Secretariat. The Secretariat is headed by a *secretary-general* who is elected by the General Assembly.

European Union

European Union
The most important regional association of nations and the one that has gone the farthest in substituting international law and authority for national sovereignty.

The **European Union** (EU), formerly called the Common Market and the European Community, is composed of most of the countries of Western Europe.[6] Among its goals are elimination of barriers (such as tariffs and quotas) to movements of goods, services, capital, and labor within the member nations.[7] Accompanying EU's efforts to remove trade barriers between its members has been a blurring of both the line between sovereignty and the relevance of preexisting international treaties. In the EU, decisions that previously were made at the national level are increasingly being made at the Europe-wide level. Reflecting this shift, the EU in recent years has adopted a single currency (called the euro) and, correspondingly, has established one central bank for the EU, equivalent to the U.S. Federal Reserve Bank. A national currency and a national banking system have been two vital attributes that, historically, have characterized nationhood. These functions are now controlled at a higher, Europe-wide level for nations that are members of the EU.

The EU *Council of Ministers,* composed of representatives from each member country, meets regularly to coordinate efforts to fulfill EU objectives. There also is the EU *Commission,* which is independent of the member nations and has been given powers to enact legislation that promotes the interests of the EU as a whole (additional discussion of the EU Commission is provided in the "International Perspective" box). EU countries are slowly, but quite clearly, ceding national sovereignty to an international structure. At each new step, there have been spasms of nationalism, but progress toward unification of the member nations continues.

The North American Free Trade Agreement

Canada, Mexico, and the United States jointly accepted the **North American Free Trade Agreement** (NAFTA) in 1992. NAFTA creates a free trade zone between the three member nations, eliminating most duties, tariffs, quotas, and other trade barriers. As with all

---

[6] There are 15 members of the EU: Austria, Belgium, Denmark, Finland, France, Germany, Greece, Ireland, Italy, Luxembourg, The Netherlands, Portugal, Spain, Sweden, and the United Kingdom.

[7] Imported goods from non-EU countries are subject to tariffs.

International Perspective EU Commission

The European Commission operates at the very heart of the European Union. Its role as the source of policy initiatives is unique; yet this role is not always clearly understood. The Commission has used its right of initiative to transform the framework provided by the treaties establishing the European Communities into today's integrated structures. The benefits for citizens and companies throughout the Union have been considerable: freedom of movement, greater prosperity, much less red tape.

But the Commission has not done this alone. It works in close partnership with the other European institutions and with the governments of the Member States. Although the Commission makes the proposals, all the major decisions on important legislation are taken by the ministers of the Member States in the Council of the European Union, in co-decision (or, in some cases, consultation) with the democratically elected European Parliament.

The Commission consults widely with interested parties from all sectors and all walks of life when preparing draft legislation. In addition to its power of proposal, the Commission acts as the EU executive body and guardian of the Treaties. It represents the common interest and embodies, to a large degree, the personality of the Union. Its main concern is to defend the interests of Europe's citizens. The 20 members of the Commission are drawn from the 15 EU countries, but they each swear an oath of independence, distancing themselves from partisan influence from any source.

The Commission's job is to ensure that the European Union can attain its goal of an ever-closer union of its members. One of the principal tasks here is to secure the free movement of goods, services, capital and persons throughout the territory of the Union. The Commission must also ensure that the benefits of integration are balanced between countries and regions, between business and consumers and between different categories of citizens.

Source: Copyright © European Communities, 1995–2002.

North American Free Trade Agreement
An agreement between Canada, Mexico, and the United States that is working toward abolition of trade barriers among the members.

multilateral trade agreements, there are exceptions, but among the key features of NAFTA are provisions that

- Allow banks and other financial services/securities firms to establish wholly owned subsidiaries in each of the three countries.
- Call for tariffs on most goods, including textiles and apparel, to be phased out over a 10-year period.
- Provide increased protection for intellectual property rights.

"Special interest" provisions still protect the Mexican oil industry from U.S. competition while U.S. sugar interests were able to insert language that will provide protection for their U.S. interests through the continuation of restrictive import quotas. As does the EU, NAFTA maintains tariffs on goods produced outside its member nations.

There are very substantial differences between NAFTA and the EU agreement. Although the definitional goal of NAFTA is free trade, removal of legal barriers to the movement of labor and capital seems a long way off yet there continues to be an enormous inflow of illegal immigrants from Mexico into the United States. The most recent discussions of amnesty for illegal Mexican immigrants in the United States have been derailed by the events of September 11, 2001, but those discussions may resume and could lead to a legalization of this de facto movement of labor into the United States. NAFTA continues to be unpopular with U.S. labor and environmental groups. Labor groups claim that the availability of cheap Mexican labor encourages U.S. businesses to relocate to Mexico, where labor costs are about one-tenth the cost of U.S. labor. Environmental groups complain that, in Mexico, environmental legislation is much more relaxed, enticing U.S. firms to locate polluting facilities there.

Other Regional Economic Associations

There are no other associations of nations that are comparable in function and significance to the EU and NAFTA. In Southeast Asia, the Association of South East Asian Nations (ASEAN) was formed in 1967. It includes, as member countries, Brunei, Cambodia, Darussalam, Indonesia, Laos, Malaysia, Mayanmar, Philippines, Singapore, Thailand, and the Vietnam, but does not include China or Japan. There are also organizations of nations in Latin America and Africa. Probably the most important association of nations in the Third World is the Organization of Petroleum Exporting Countries (OPEC), which exerts a powerful influence on world oil supplies and prices by setting quotas for oil production and sales by its member nations, which include Iran, Iraq, Kuwait, Libya, Saudi Arabia, Nigeria, and Venezuela.

International Courts

The International Court of Justice

International Court of Justice

Also known as the world court, the ICJ resolves disputes among nations, but is limited to those cases for which both nations agree to abide by the judgment of the ICJ.

The United Nations sponsors the **International Court of Justice** (ICJ), also known as the World Court. The only litigants that appear before the ICJ are nations, but some nations sue on behalf of their citizens or industries. The ICJ is a court that focuses on resolution of treaty disputes between nations, though it also passes judgment on countries' "bad acts" that may violate the UN Charter. The ICJ is limited in that its jurisdiction only applies when the countries involved in litigation voluntarily agree to allow the ICJ to hear their case. Even after the ICJ hands down a decision, no nation is bound by such a decision. The ICJ can award monetary damages and issue injunctions, but it can only enforce its decisions if its recommendations to the UN Security Council are considered and affirmed by that body.

The ICJ, located at The Hague in the Netherlands, has 15 judges who serve nine-year terms. No more than two judges can simultaneously be from one member nation of the UN. The ICJ also may be called upon to render advisory opinions on matters of international law by request of the UN or one of its agencies. If a UN member nation is a litigant before the ICJ, it is entitled to appoint one judge who serves on an ad hoc basis for that case. The ICJ is not a common law court and its decisions apply only to the case(s) at hand. They have no precedential value for other cases.

European Court of Justice

European Court of Justice

Enforces EU law among member nations. In cases involving EU law, the ECJ will take appeals from the national courts of member states. It serves as the final arbiter of EU law.

The **European Court of Justice** (ECJ) has jurisdiction to enforce EU law. Each EU member appoints one judge for a six-year term. The basic charge of the ECJ is to enforce the laws of the EU. Member nations, EU institutions, and other interested parties may bring actions before the ECJ. The ECJ is the final authority on EU law. As such, it will take appeals from national courts in EU countries. Paralleling other EU developments, the ECJ is another example of the ceding of authority by sovereign European powers to a Europe-wide organization. Paralleling state judicial systems in the United States, national courts of member nations are the highest authority for national law, but for interpretation and enforcement of EU law, the ECJ is akin to the U.S. Supreme Court. National courts in member nations are responsible for enforcing judgments of the ECJ with respect to EU law, but the ECJ does not have an army at its disposal so it cannot actually force European national courts to comply with its decisions.

International Protection of Intellectual Property

Overview

Protection of intellectual property is an issue that divides the "have" and "have-not" nations of the world. Most of the world's important IP is created in the have nations, while most of the illegal copying and infringing takes place in Third World nations. To address the core of the IP protection issue in stark terms with an ongoing real-world illustration, you may note that it is clear that the enforcement of patent rights held by pharmaceutical companies will effectively result in millions of Africans, affected with AIDS, dying without treatments that have been shown to be effective in extending lives of Americans and Europeans affected with the same disease. Other equally stark issues could be cited. This kind of conundrum is at the heart of many international IP protection confrontations.

Some governments in Third World countries choose not to respect IP rights, in part because their countries derive significant income from infringing or copying materials that are subject to patent, copyright, and trademark laws. In some instances, Third World enterprises make enormous profits by finding ways of smuggling patented and trademarked goods, and copyrighted movies or software, into developed countries. Not surprisingly, these activities have not escaped the notice of inventors, artists, and software developers in developed countries, who have exerted significant pressures on lawmakers. The result has been adoptions of a number of treaties and other forms of legislation aimed at protecting IP from infringements. About the only way to protect IP from infringement by foreign entities is to make the countries where the infringing takes place subject to international trade sanctions that leave them in worse shape tolerating the infringing than they would be in if they acted to prevent it.

The World Trade Organization

World Trade Organization
An organization of over 150 nations that is responsible for enforcing multilateral trade agreements among nations.

The **World Trade Organization** (WTO) was created at the last meeting in Uruguay of the General Agreement on Tariffs and Trade (GATT). GATT has operated as a 130-country organization devoted to lowering tariffs and other barriers to international trade. It has enjoyed a history of significant success in that quest. The WTO is also responsible for enforcing multilateral agreements among nations, including the General Agreement on the Trade in Services (GATS) and the Agreement on Trade-Related Aspects of Intellectual Property Rights (the TRIPS Agreement).

At WTO meetings, a number of issues are typically discussed, generally including tariffs and other restrictions on the free movement of goods and services, trade practices, and enforcement of IP rights and sanctions for nonenforcement of those rights by member nations. When it was formed in 1995, the WTO had 135 member nations. Meetings of WTO representatives have become international events, attracting a widely diverse assortment of protestors, who are concerned that important decisions regarding trade, workers' rights, the environment, and other issues related to technology are being made by the WTO without input from various interest groups they claim to represent.

One of the WTO's several important trade-related functions is that of providing a mechanism for resolving international trade disputes. The WTO is a kind of industrial umpire; nations that believe they have been the victims of violations of trade agreements or trade practices of another nation(s) can take their case before the WTO. Trade disputes that are taken to the WTO first appear before a *panel* of judges from three member nations. Each side presents its evidence to the panel, which then deliberates and provides a decision that includes the panel's findings of fact and law. The report from the panel is then submitted to a WTO *dispute settlement body,* which then can choose to adopt or reject the findings of the panel. The losing party has the right to appeal to an *appellate body,* composed of judges from seven member nations. Appeals are limited to issues of law, with the entire dispute proceeding supposed to be completed within nine months. Once appeals are exhausted, if a trade violation has been found, the WTO can order the offending nation to *cease and desist* and can award damages to the aggrieved nation. If the offending nation refuses to accept the decision of the WTO, the WTO has the power to order trade sanctions in the form of higher tariffs levied on its exports by other member nations.

World Intellectual Property Organization

World Intellectual Property Organization
The organization that has primary responsibility for the international protection of the rights of owners of intellectual property, including patents, copyrights, and trademarks.

As one might expect from the name, the **World Intellectual Property Organization** (WIPO) is responsible for promoting protection of IP throughout the world. The WIPO administers the most important conventions that define and enforce IP rights, including the Berne Convention (copyrights) and the Paris Convention (patents and trademarks). According to the WIPO, intellectual property is divided into two categories:

1. Industrial property, which includes inventions (patents), trademarks, industrial designs, and geographic indications of source.
2. Copyrights, which includes literary and artistic works such as novels; poems and plays; films; musical works; artistic works such as drawings, paintings, photographs, and sculptures; and architectural designs.

Rights related to copyrights include those of performing artists in their performances, producers of phonograms in their recordings, and those of broadcasters in their radio and television programs (separate provisions relating to performing artists and broadcasters are discussed below).

The WIPO is involved in the development of new international treaties that deal with and enforce IP. In addition, the WIPO offers various conflict resolution services for parties that have international disputes involving IP, particularly disputes involving domain name. The WIPO works closely with ICANN to resolve domain name disputes. The WIPO is an ICANN-approved service that follows ICANN's uniform dispute resolution procedure (UDRP) and policy when it receives a referral from ICANN.

Case 23-2 is typical of a WIPO resolution of a domain name–trademark dispute.[8] According to ICANN, if a domain name holder is shown to be a cybersquatter, then it is appropriate to transfer the domain name to the complainant–trademark owner.

[8] http://www.icann.org/udrp/. The case appears at http://www.arbforum.com/domains/decisions/96215.htm.

Case 23-2

Lush Ltd. v. Technology Education Center

Claim Number: FA0012000096215 (2001)

PARTIES

The Complainant is Lush Ltd., Poole, Dorset, United Kingdom ("Complainant") represented by Stephen M. Lane, Sim, Hughes, Ashton & McKay. The Respondent is Technology Education Center, Edmonton, AB, Canada ("Respondent").

REGISTRAR AND DISPUTED DOMAIN NAME(S)

The domain name at issue is "lushcosmetics.com" registered with Network Solutions, Inc.

PROCEDURAL HISTORY

Complainant submitted a Complaint to the National Arbitration Forum (the "Forum") electronically on December 6, 2000; The Forum received a hard copy of the Complaint on December 11, 2000.

On December 8, 2000, Network Solutions, Inc. confirmed by e-mail to the Forum that the domain name **"lushcosmetics.com"** is registered with Network Solutions, Inc. and that the Respondent is the current registrant of the name. Network Solutions, Inc. has verified that Respondent is bound by the Network Solutions, Inc. 4.0 registration agreement and has thereby agreed to resolve domain-name disputes brought by third parties in accordance with ICANN's Uniform Domain Name Dispute Resolution Policy (the "Policy").

On December 14, 2000, a Notification of Complaint and Commencement of Administrative Proceeding (the "Commencement Notification"), setting a deadline of January 3, 2001 by which Respondent could file a Response to the Complaint, was transmitted to Respondent via e-mail, post and fax, to all entities and persons listed on Respondent's registration as technical, administrative and billing contacts, and to postmaster@lushcosmetics.com by e-mail.

Having received no Response from Respondent, using the same contact details and methods as were used for the Commencement Notification, the Forum transmitted to the parties a Notification of Respondent Default.

* * *

RELIEF SOUGHT

The Complainant requests that the domain name be transferred from the Respondent to the Complainant.

PARTIES' CONTENTIONS

A. Complainant alleges the following:

1. Complainant is engaged in the manufacture, distribution and sale of a full range of unique, fresh and handmade soaps, cosmetics and bath products. Complaint registered the trademark **LUSH** in the United States, Canada and numerous other countries throughout the world for use in association with soaps, cosmetics and bath products in International Class 3 and 5.

2. Since at least as early as 1994 and continuously to the present, the complainant has extensively advertised and sold soaps, cosmetics and bath products in a number of countries throughout the world in association with the trademarks **LUSH** and **LUSH COSMETICS.** Complainant presently has 86 retail outlets located in 11 countries throughout the world where its unique, fresh and handmade soaps, cosmetics and bath products are offered for sale and sold in association with the trademarks **LUSH** and **LUSH COSMETICS.**

3. Complainant has expended considerable effort and money in the promotion and advertisement of its fresh and handmade soaps, cosmetics and bath products marked with the trademarks **LUSH** and **LUSH COSMETICS.** These trademarks have become known and recognized by substantial numbers of people throughout the world as serving to identify and distinguish the Complainant's products from the products of others.

4. Respondent has registered the domain name **lushcosmetics.com**, which is identical or confusingly similar to the Complainant's trademarks **LUSH** and **LUSH COSMETICS.** The domain name **lushcosmetics.com** is not being used.

5. Respondent has registered the domain name primarily for the purpose of selling, renting, or otherwise transferring the domain name registration to the Complainant who is the owner of the trade-marks or to a competitor of the Complainant, for valuable consideration in excess of any out of pocket costs directly related to the domain name. After Complainant requested Respondent to voluntarily assign the domain name to Complainant, Respondent refused, and instead offered to sell the domain name to Complainant.

A. Respondent has not submitted a response.

DISCUSSION

Paragraph 15(a) of the Rules instructs this Panel to "decide a complaint on the basis of the statements and documents submitted in accordance with the Policy, these Rules and any rules and principles of law that it deems applicable."

In view of Respondent's failure to submit a response, the Panel shall decide this administrative proceeding on the basis of the Complainant's undisputed representations pursuant to paragraphs 5(e), 14(a) and 15(a) of the Rules.

Paragraph 4(a) of the Policy requires that the Complainant must prove each of the following three elements to obtain an order that a domain name should be cancelled or transferred:

1. the domain name registered by the Respondent is identical or confusingly similar to a trademark or service mark in which the Complainant has rights;

2. the Respondent has no rights or legitimate interests in respect of the domain name; and

3. the domain name has been registered and is being used in bad faith.

Identical and/or Confusingly Similar

The domain name **lushcosmetics.com** incorporates Complainant's entire **LUSH** mark. Therefore, the domain name in question is confusingly similar to the Complainant's mark **LUSH** under Policy # 4(a)(i). *See Quixtar Investments, Inc. v. Smithberger and QUIXTAR-IBO,* D2000-0138 (WIPO Apr. 19, 2000) (finding that because the domain name <quixtar-sign-up.com> incorporates in its entirety the Complainant's distinctive mark, QUIXTAR, the domain name is confusingly similar); *America Online, Inc. v. iDomainNames.com,* FA 93766 (Nat. Arb. Forum Mar. 24, 2000) (finding that Respondent's domain name <go2AOL.com> was confusingly similar to Complainant's mark AOL).

* * *

Rights or Legitimate Interests

Complainant has registered the trademark **LUSH** in the U.S. and all over the world. Further, Complainant has used the **LUSH COSMETICS** mark in connection with its products for five years before registration of the domain name. Such long-standing use and the popularity of the mark throughout the world are sufficient to confer common law trademark rights in **LUSH COSMETICS.** *See Winterson v. Hogarth,* D2000-0235 (WIPO May 22, 2000) (finding that ICANN Policy does not require that Complainant have rights in a registered trademark and that it is sufficient to show common law rights); *Bibbero Systems, Inc. v. Tseu & Assoc.,* FA 94416 (Nat. Arb. Forum May 9, 2000) (finding common law rights in the mark BIBBERO as the Complainant, Bibbero Systems, Inc. had developed brand name recognition with this term by which the Complainant is commonly known).

* * *

Registration and Use in Bad Faith

The fact that Respondent offered to sell the domain name to Complainant evidences Respondent's registration and use of the domain name in bad faith. Policy # 4(b)(i). *See American Anti-Vivisection Society v. "Infa dot Net" Web Services,* FA 95685 (Nat. Arb. Forum Nov. 6, 2000) (finding that "general offers to sell the domain name, even if no certain price is demanded, are evidence of bad faith"); *Banca Popolare Friuladria S.p.A. v. Giovanni Zago,* D2000-0793 (WIPO Sept. 3, 2000) (finding bad faith where the Respondent offered the domain names for sale).

Respondent's passive holding of the domain name further indicates his bad faith in registering the domain name. *See DCI S.A. v. Link Commercial Corp.,* D2000-1232 (WIPO Dec. 7, 2000) (concluding that the Respondent's passive holding of the domain name satisfies the "bad faith" requirement of the Policy); *Clerical Medical Investment Group Ltd. v. Clericalmedical.com,* D2000-1228 (WIPO Nov. 28, 2000) (finding that merely holding an infringing domain name without active use can constitute use in bad faith).

DECISION

Having established all three elements required by the ICANN Policy Rule 4(a), it is the decision of the panel that the requested relief be granted.

Accordingly, for all of the foregoing reasons, it is ordered that the domain name, "**lushcosmetics. com**" be transferred from the Respondent to the Complainant.

Hon. James A. Carmody, Panelist

Dated: January 13, 2001

Decision and Outcome

Based on the WIPO proceedings, the Honorable James Carmody, panelist, determined that the respondent was a cybersquatter and that it was appropriate for ICANN to reassign the domain name to the plaintiff.

Questions for Analysis

1. What is ICANN's three-part criterion for a finding that a domain name should be transferred from the respondent to the complainant? Did the complainant in this situation satisfy the criteria?

2. There are two facts that indicated to the panelist that the respondent held the domain in bad faith. What were those two facts and why do they indicate bad faith on the part of the respondent?

Agreement on Trade-Related Aspects of Intellectual Property Rights

Trade-Related Aspects of Intellectual Property Rights
The organization that establishes minimum legal standards for countries to be members of the Paris Convention for patents and trademarks and the Berne Convention for copyrights.

The Agreement on **Trade-Related Aspects of Intellectual Property Rights** (TRIPS Agreement) is one of the WTO's multilateral agreements. The 135 members of the WTO are automatically members of TRIPS. The essential function of TRIPS is to set minimum standards for protection of intellectual property rights. All WTO members are required by TRIPS to

1. Observe the substantive provisions of the Berne Convention (copyrights), the Paris Convention (patents and trademarks), the Rome Convention (International Convention for the Protection of Performers, Producers of Phonograms, and Broadcasting Organizations), and the IPIC Treaty (Treaty on Intellectual Property in Respect of Integrated Circuits).

2. Adhere to the minimum statutory standards set by TRIPS for various aspects of IP protection. For example, the TRIPS Agreement requires that the minimum duration of copyrights be set at 50 years, patents at 20 years, and trademarks at seven years.

3. Adhere to minimum standards for enforcement of IP regulations. Failure to enforce these minimum standards subjects a member state to a WTO *dispute resolution understanding* claim (discussed above), with possible trade sanctions if found guilty.

4. Treat nationals of other member nations the same as their own (*national treatment*). For example, there should be no discrimination in patent applications depending on whether the applicant is or is not a citizen. Furthermore, member nations are required to publish all relevant IP laws, regulations, and practices. Finally, all foreign nations should be entitled to *most favored nation* treatment, meaning that there should not be discrimination by the host nation against any particular member foreign national.

TRIPS permits a transition period until 2006 for less-developed countries to make their IP laws congruent with TRIPS requirements.

International Contract Law

Convention on Contracts for the International Sale of Goods
A United Nations–sponsored convention that establishes a uniform law of contracts when there is a dispute between companies located in different countries and there is no agreed-upon choice of law clause in the contracts between them.

civil law
The predominant system of law used by countries in Europe. Originally associated with Roman law, civil law relies much more heavily on codes rather than precedents, as is the standard in countries that follow common law systems.

International trade is sufficiently established that there is general awareness of the value of uniformity in contracts so that sellers do not have to be familiar with the contract laws in more than 100 countries. The international equivalent to the Uniform Commercial Code is the United Nations **Convention on Contracts for the International Sale of Goods** (CISG). The CISG has been in place since 1988, but has not actually been adopted internationally. Most international contracts are subject to national contract laws based on choice of law clauses and, in fact, many contracts make use of arbitration clauses that avoid using courts altogether. The CISG is a combination of the principles of contract law in common law countries and contract law in countries that subscribe to the body of **civil law** that is prevalent in Western Europe. *The CISG only applies to business-to-business contracts* in which the businesses are located in different countries.

Also, the provisions of the CISG are only applicable to the formation of sales contracts and the rights and obligations of the parties once they have agreed to a sales contract. There are a number of other contract categories and aspects of contracts that are excluded from the coverage of the CISG, including the following:

1. Sales contracts to consumers.
2. Sales of service contracts.
3. Legal issues related to product liability.
4. Legal issues related to the validity of contracts.
5. Sales contracts that are subject to other regulations, such as sales of securities, auction sales, and sales of ships and vessels.

Although the CISG is closely linked to contract law in civil law countries (discussed below), it does borrow some elements from the UCC. For example, the CISG, like the UCC, does not require that an otherwise valid contract fix price if a reasonable price can be determined based on contemporaneous sales of such goods under comparable circumstances. In other words, under the CISG, as with the UCC, the price term can be left open.

Contract Law in Civil Law Countries

Civil law, the predominant form of law in Western Europe, originated with the Napoleonic Codes in France. Such law has a different mode of creation than does the common law. Civil law relies less on precedent and more on codification of what the parties in a commercial transaction ought to do. Over the years, however, contract law in civil law countries has changed in response to changes in commercial practices, so that the differences that exist in contract law in civil law countries relative to common law countries are less pronounced than previously. The following are some of the features of civil contract law that gave rise to a good bit of litigation. Note that most of these features are not part of the UCC.

Additional terms in the acceptance. Civil contract law treats additional terms in an acceptance as a counteroffer and, thus, a rejection of the offer. This is also the common law rule, but is not part of the UCC, which allows additional terms in an acceptance under certain circumstances without causing the acceptance to be deemed a counteroffer.

Firm offers. Under civil contract law, firm offers, made by either merchants or nonmerchants, are enforceable for the period of time specified in the offer. Of course, in the common law of contracts, an offer can be revoked at any time as long as the other side has not paid consideration to keep the offer open. That rule has been overturned in the UCC, which does make firm, written offers by merchants irrevocable during the period stated by the offer.

Writing requirements. In civil contract law, a merchant can be sued for breach of an oral contract regardless of the amount while, for consumers, the contract must be for less than 5,000 francs (in France) if a party seeks to enforce an oral contract. The UCC limit on enforcement of oral contracts is currently $500, but, when the revised Article 2 is passed, that amount will increase to $5,000.

Case 23-3 illustrates the legal quagmire that can occur when the parties to a sales contract (1) do not have an arbitration clause and (2) are from different countries. See if you can figure out why the defendant in the case wants the federal court in the United States to have jurisdiction.

Case 23-3

Asante Technologies, Inc., Plaintiff v. PMC-Sierra, Inc., Defendant

United States District Court for the Northern District of California, San Jose Division

164 F. Supp. 2d 1142 (N.D. Cal. 2001)

BACKGROUND AND FACTS

This lawsuit arises out of a dispute involving the sale of electronic components. Plaintiff, Asante Technologies Inc., filed the action in the Superior Court for the State of California, Santa Clara County, on February 13, 2001. Defendant, PMC-Sierra, Inc., removed the action to this Court, asserting federal question jurisdiction pursuant to 28 U.S.C. section 1331. Specifically, Defendant asserts that Plaintiff's claims for breach of contract and breach of express warranty are governed by the United Nations Convention on Contracts for the International Sale of Goods ("CISG"). Plaintiff disputes jurisdiction and filed this Motion to Remand and for Attorneys' Fees.

Plaintiff is a Delaware corporation having its primary place of business in Santa Clara County, California. Plaintiff produces network switchers, a type of electronic component used to connect multiple computers to one another and to the Internet. Plaintiff purchases component parts from a number of manufacturers. In particular, Plaintiff purchases application-specific integrated circuits ("ASICs"), which are considered the control center of its network switchers, from Defendant.

Defendant is also a Delaware corporation. Defendant asserts that, at all relevant times, its corporate headquarters, inside sales and marketing office, public relations department, principal warehouse, and most design and engineering functions were located in Burnaby, British Columbia, Canada. Defendant also maintains an office in Portland, Oregon, where many of its engineers are based. Defendant's products are sold in California through Unique Technologies, which is an authorized distributor of Defendant's products in North America. It is undisputed that Defendant directed Plaintiff to purchase Defendant's products through Unique, and that Defendant honored purchase orders solicited by Unique. Unique is located in California. Determining Defendant's "place of business" with respect to its contract with Plaintiff is critical to the question of whether the Court has jurisdiction in this case.

Plaintiff's Complaint focuses on five purchase orders. [Footnotes omitted.] Four of the five purchase orders were submitted to Defendant through Unique as directed by Defendant. However, Plaintiff does not dispute that one of the purchase orders, dated January 28, 2000, was sent by fax directly to Defendant in British Columbia, and that Defendant processed the order in British Columbia. Defendant shipped all orders to Plaintiff's headquarters in California. Upon delivery of the goods, Unique sent invoices to Plaintiff, at which time Plaintiff tendered payment to Unique either in California or in Nevada.

The Parties do not identify any single contract embodying the agreement pertaining to the sale. Instead, Plaintiff asserts that acceptance of each of its purchase orders was expressly conditioned upon acceptance by Defendant of Plaintiff's "Terms and Conditions," which were included with each Purchase Order. Paragraph 20 of Plaintiff's Terms and Conditions provides "APPLICABLE LAW. The validity [and] performance of this [purchase] order shall be governed by the laws of the state shown on Buyer's address on this order." [Citations omitted.] The buyer's address as shown on each of the Purchase Orders is in San Jose, California. Alternatively, Defendant suggests that the terms of shipment are governed by a document entitled "PMC-Sierra TERMS AND CONDITIONS OF SALE." Paragraph 19 of Defendant's Terms and conditions provides "APPLICABLE LAW: The contract between the parties is made, governed by, and shall be construed in accordance with the laws of the Province of British Columbia and the laws of Canada applicable therein, which shall be deemed to be the proper law hereof. . . ."

Plaintiff now requests this Court to remand this action back to the Superior Court of the County of Santa Clara pursuant to 28 U.S.C. section 1447(c), for asserting lack of subject matter jurisdiction. In addition, Plaintiff requests award of attorneys' fees and costs for the expense of bringing this motion.

Opinion by James Ware, United States District Judge

* * *

The CISG only applies when a contract is "between parties whose places of business are in different States." [Footnotes omitted.] If this requirement is not satisfied, Defendant cannot claim jurisdiction under the CISG. It is undisputed that Plaintiff's place of business is Santa Clara County, California, U.S.A. It is further undisputed that during the relevant time period, Defendant's corporate headquarters, inside sales and marketing office, public relations department, principal warehouse, and most of its design and engineering functions were located in Burnaby, British Columbia, Canada. However, Plaintiff contends that, pursuant to Article 10 of the CISG, Defendant's "place of business" having the closest relationship to the contract at issue is the United States.

* * *

Plaintiff next argues that, even if the Parties are from two nations that have adopted the CISG, the choice of law provisions in the "Terms and Conditions" set forth by both Parties reflect the Parties' intent to "opt out" of application of the treaty. Article 6 of the CISG provides that "the parties may exclude the application of the Convention or, subject to Article 12, derogate from or vary the effect of any of its provisions." Defendant asserts that merely choosing the law of a jurisdiction is insufficient to opt out of the CISG, absent express exclusion of the CISG. The Court finds that the particular choice of law provisions in the "Terms and Conditions" of both parties are inadequate to effectuate an opt out of the CISG.

Although selection of a particular choice of law, such as "the California Commercial Code" or the "Uniform Commercial Code" *could* amount to implied exclusion of the CISG, the choice of law clauses at issue here do not evince a clear intent to opt out of the CISG. For example, Defendant's choice of applicable law adopts the law of British Columbia, and it is undisputed that the CISG *is* the law of British Columbia. Furthermore, even Plaintiff's choice of applicable law generally adopts the "laws of" the State of California, and California is bound by the Supremacy Clause to the treaties of the United States. Thus, under general California law, the CISG is applicable to contracts where the contracting parties are from different countries that have adopted the CISG. In the absence of clear language indicating that both contracting parties intended to opt out of the CISG, and in view of Defendant's Terms and Conditions which would apply the CISG, the Court rejects Plaintiff's contention that the choice of law provisions preclude the applicability of the CISG.

* * *

It is undisputed that the Complaint on its face does not refer to the CISG. However, Defendants argue that the preemptive force of the CISG converts the state breach of contract claim into a federal claim. Indeed, Congress may establish a federal law that so completely preempts a particular area of law that any civil complaint raising that select group of claims is necessarily federal in character.

It appears that the issue of whether or not the CISG preempts state law is a matter of first impression. In the case of federal statutes, "the question of whether a certain action is preempted by federal law is one of congressional intent. The purpose of Congress is the ultimate touchstone." Transferring this analysis to the question of preemption by a treaty, the court focuses on the intent of the treaty's contracting parties.

In the case of the CISG treaty, this intent can be discerned from the introductory text, which states that "the adoption of uniform rules which govern contracts for the international sale of goods and take into account the different social, economic and legal systems would contribute to the removal of legal barriers in international trade and promote the development of international trade." The CISG further recognizes the importance of "the development of international trade on the basis of equality and mutual benefit."

The Court concludes that the expressly stated goal of developing uniform international contract law to promote international trade indicates the intent of the parties to the treaty to have the treaty preempt state law causes of action.

* * *

Decision and Outcome

The plaintiff in this case wanted the case remanded to a state court, hoping to pursue its claim under state contract law that, presumably, was expected to be more favorable. The federal district court, however, denied the plaintiff's motion to remand concluding that the CISG preempts the UCC when parties (companies) from different countries sue each other and have not agreed in their original contract(s) on any particular jurisdiction, leaving jurisdiction, according to the court, federal.

Questions for Analysis

1. Does this case support the proposition that, when the parties to a contract are from different countries and both countries have signed the Convention on Contracts for the International Sale of Goods (CISG), choice of law clauses are not effective? What was the court's argument about preemption of state law by federal law?

2. What language in the choice of law provision of the contract between the two parties would have enabled the parties to opt out of the CISG?

The UNCITRAL Model for E-Commerce

United Nations Commission for International Trade Law
The group that is responsible for proposing model acts for national adoption. The CISG is a product of the UNCITRAL. A model act for e-commerce is in the works.

The **United Nations Commission for International Trade Law** (UNICTRAL) proposed a model for e-commerce contract law in 1996 (http://www.uncitral.org/english/texts/electcom/). The UN Model Law was proposed as a supplement to national contract law. The UN hoped that by proposing this law it would influence nations, when they change their contract law, to deal fully with e-commerce. The UNCITRAL Model Law has the following, somewhat familiar, provisions:

1. Electronic messages have legal effect imitating E-SIGN and UETA.
2. Electronic writings are valid legal documents if they can be reproduced and accessed later.
3. An electronic signature occurs if the electronic message identifies the sender and the buyer indicates approval to the information.
4. A contract can be created by an exchange of electronic messages.

The main thrust of this Model Law is to create parity between paper and electronic writings, which is the same thrust as in E-SIGN and UETA. As of October 2001, the following nations had adopted some or all of the proposed Model Law: Australia, Bermuda, Colombia, France, Hong Kong Special Administrative Region of China, Ireland, Philippines, Republic of Korea, Singapore, Slovenia, the States of Jersey (Crown Dependency of the United Kingdom of Great Britain and Northern Ireland), and, within the United States of America, Illinois.

International Jurisdiction

Criminal Jurisdiction

In legal disputes involving jurisdiction, a decisive factor is a familiar one: whether a nexus or a connection exists between the alleged criminal and the jurisdiction that alleges a crime has taken place. There are five general principles that can be used to justify an international exercise of jurisdiction:

1. *Territoriality* principle of jurisdiction; that is, the place where the alleged crime took place is one basis for determining jurisdiction.
2. *Nationality* of the person allegedly committing the crime.
3. *Protective* principle, which provides jurisdiction for a nation when the crime threatens a significant national interest.

4. *Passive personality* principle, which allows for the exercise of jurisdiction based on the nationality of the *victims* of the crime.

5. *Universality* principle, which allows for taking the alleged criminal into custody.

While these five principles for resolving international jurisdictional disputes have broad use, not all of the principles are applicable in every case. The first principle is clearly the most important and, in most cases, the others are not involved. A foreigner who commits a crime generally does so in a particular "territorial" location. That criminal is normally prosecuted for that crime in the jurisdiction where the offense took place. In some instances, the act committed may not necessarily be a crime in other jurisdictions. This is particularly true for "crimes" involving gambling, obscenity, and infringements of IP.

Civil Jurisdiction: Choice of Forum Clauses

choice of forum clause
Clause within a contract in which the contracting parties agree on which courts have jurisdiction to resolve disputes.

choice of law clauses
Clauses that specify which substantive law will be used in the event of a dispute between the contracting parties.

As discussed in Chapter 2, jurisdiction is the authority of a government to resolve disputes between individuals and/or businesses. In many instances in international contracts, jurisdiction is based on *consent*. It is common for contracts between parties of different countries to have a *forum selection*, or **choice of forum, clause,** which specifies what courts have jurisdiction in the event of contract disputes. In addition, these contracts generally have **choice of law clauses** that determine which jurisdiction's substantive laws apply to the contract transaction. Since websites are accessible throughout the world, forum selection and choice of law clauses are prevalent. For example, during the spring of 2002, the last clause in the terms of service at the Yahoo! website contained the following language:

> The TOS and the relationship between you and Yahoo shall be governed by the *laws of the State of California* without regard to its conflict of law provisions. *You and Yahoo agree to submit to the personal and exclusive jurisdiction* of the courts located within the county of Santa Clara, California. [Italics added.]

In addition to actual consent, jurisdiction may be asserted over a person or business by (1) being physically present in the area, (2) having the nationality of the forum or court, (3) being domiciled in the forum, or (4) having minimum contacts with the forum. The first three bases are not controversial, but the fourth basis brings up the issue of whether foreign countries can order websites to comply with their domestic laws. Illustrating this issue, a French court ordered Yahoo! to block access on its auction site to Nazi memorabilia.[9] As we have seen above, Yahoo! claims that all relations between it and people who make use of its website are governed by the laws of California, which include protection of freedom of expression under the First Amendment to the U.S. Constitution. Under that standard, there would be no limits to access for Nazi items.

EU Jurisdiction: Overriding Choice of Forum Clauses

The EU does not recognize jurisdiction based on minimum contacts, but it does have criteria for exerting jurisdiction over consumer sales if (1) the sales take place in the consumer's country of domicile, (2) the seller solicits the sales through advertising directed to consumers or agrees to accept payments in installments, (3) the seller is located in another member state, and (4) the suit is brought in the seller's country of domicile. If consumers can establish all four conditions, courts in the consumer's country will have jurisdiction, even if contracts signed by the consumer have forum selection clauses that grant jurisdiction to other countries.

[9] See Tech Investor, usatoday.com, November 28, 2000.

Choice of Law   In November of 2000, European justice ministers passed a law that will force traders to abide by the laws of all 15 member nations of the EU when they go online. The new law, called the Brussels I regulation, was drawn up by the European Commission to enable consumers, in a dispute with an online seller, to sue the seller in the country where the consumer resides, and to apply the laws of the consumer's country to that dispute. The new law, regarded as highly pro-consumer, has similarities to state long-arm statutes in the United States, in that it makes sellers appear in courts that are located in consumers' jurisdictions. Concerns have been raised by sellers that, with the Brussels I regulation, the EU is taking a step backward. Rather than having one EU standard, it appears under Brussels I that there remain 15 separate European markets (jurisdictions), with different rules for each, all of which sellers will have to adhere to. The burden on larger businesses is not apt to be too onerous as they already have a presence in most of the EU nations. However, smaller websites will be immediately subject to the jurisdictions of 15 separate countries for products sold to consumers throughout the EU.

Note that these rules allow consumers in the EU to disregard choice of forum and law clauses even though they "agree" to them. Of course "agreement" in most cases is clicking an "I Agree" button in a click-wrap agreement, so the extent of conscious agreement is suspect given the way most e-commerce transactions occur.

Jurisdiction over Property

Jurisdiction over property is called *in rem* jurisdiction. This refers to the jurisdiction of a court to decide the disposition and ownership of property. Quite obviously, in rem jurisdiction is tied to geography, as the country's courts where a property is located have the power to resolve disputes involving the property. The location of property is not really a debatable issue if the property is real, but questions can arise if the property is moveable. Even more imprecise is an identification of the location of intangible property, such as software and other forms of IP.

Choice of Law Clauses

In international contracts, not only do contracting partners generally stipulate to jurisdiction, but often there also is a stipulation as to choice of law (see the Yahoo! terms of service clause above). Note that there is no need for the choice of forum clause to agree with the choice of law clause. The choice of forum clause could stipulate the European Court of Justice (ECJ), but the choice of law clause could designate contract law in the State of Illinois. Note, further, that many (probably most) international contracts make use of arbitration services, such as those of the International Chamber of Commerce. If a contract calls for arbitration to resolve disputes rather than litigation, it is a virtual certainty that any court in the United States, Europe, or Japan will grant a motion to dismiss by the defendant as long as there are no allegations of fraud or deception by the plaintiff. As in other settings, then, courts generally enforce arbitration clauses, not just here in the United States but also abroad. If there is an arbitration clause in a contract, the contracting parties must specify the substantive law that is to govern any prospective dispute. For cases that go before the ECJ, if there is no choice of law clause, the ECJ will apply international law.

In the absence of choice of law clauses in contracts, or in a case involving parties from different countries who are not in a contractual relationship, the national court that has jurisdiction also must decide the applicable law governing the dispute. In a dispute involving public issues or public rights, a national court will apply the laws of its nation. In a dispute involving a private claim in tort or contract, the court will apply the laws of the nation most affected by the outcome of the dispute. Determining the applicable law in the absence of a choice of law clause requires a court look at three possible tests:

1. Whether the applicable law is dictated by statute.
2. Which country has the most significant relationship with the outcome of the dispute.
3. Which country has the greatest governmental interest in the outcome of the dispute.

As we have seen above, the EU has consumer protection laws that disregard choice of law clauses. There are other instances when choice of law clauses are in conflict with a statute, too. If there is a conflict between choice of law clauses and a statute in the forum country, clearly courts are going to disregard the choice of law clause and decide the case as called for by statute.

The *most significant relationship* test is complicated and messy. Courts applying this standard look at a number of factors, including the nationalities of the parties, where the action that gave rise to the dispute took place, and so forth, and make decisions on a case-by-case basis. If the opposing parties perceive advantages to the substantive laws of a particular court (jurisdiction), a sizeable sum of legal expense may be expended on the proper forum issue as the attorneys for each side write briefs in support of motions. Such expenses are unnecessary in contract disputes and may be easily avoided. Every such contract should include a choice of law clause. Applying the most significant relationship test to disputes arising from cyberspace activities is even more difficult than it is for bricks-and-mortar companies. If the parties to a cybercommerce dispute are from different countries, and all the action (negotiation, contract, and alleged breach) leading to the dispute took place in cyberspace, then courts are left with the nationality of the litigants to decide on the choice of law issue. In cases involving parties who are both (all) subject to the jurisdiction of member nations, the EU has decided that the applicable law is dictated by statute, which means that the significant relationship or the greatest governmental interest tests are unnecessary.

Summary

Differences between Real Space and Cyberspace Have Made It Increasingly Difficult to Identify Where Tax Events Take Place, upon Which State Governments Rely for Revenue

- Jurisdiction is based on geography, but cyberspace is quite different from real space.
- States are entitled to tax events such as sales, property ownership, and the earning income that take place within their borders. States generally have been able to levy sales tax on sales made to in-state residents by out-of-state sellers.
- If a state taxes a corporation that operates in several states, it must *apportion* the tax to the activities of the corporation within the state.
- It is common for businesses to try to exploit tax loopholes, for tax authorities to take businesses to state court for interpretation of the state tax code, and for the issues to ultimately be appealed to federal courts. If tax authorities lose in court, it is common for state legislatures to change tax laws.

State Taxation of Out-of-State Business Is Based on Establishment of Minimum Contacts,

- Even before the rise of e-commerce, mail-order companies were exempt from state sales tax for sales made to out-of-state consumers. States have been able to assert jurisdiction based on very tenuous ties to the state such as directed advertisements, the hiring of independent sales staff to cover the state, and any other physical presence.
- Courts have ruled that, in order for a state to exert jurisdiction over an out-of-state business, there must be a showing that the business had some *minimum contacts* with the state. Other times, courts have made use of the word "nexus" to describe the minimum contacts that a business must have with a state in order for the state to exert jurisdiction over the business.

Which Can Be Established through Cyberspace Contact, but Congress Has Extended the Internet Tax Freedom Act until 2003, Exempting Most Websites from Having to Pay Sales Tax	• At present, trivial differences can have significant tax consequences at the state level. If a firm sells software by having customers download the software, it escapes taxation while, if the same customer receives a CD in the mail, it may be subject to sales tax depending on where the inventory of CDs is stored. • Some states also have imposed taxes on Internet access and on the downloading of software. • Congress passed the Internet Tax Freedom Act (ITFA) in 1998. The act prohibits the imposition any new state taxes on e-commerce and outlaws multiple and discriminatory state taxes. The ITFA was renewed for two more years in November 2001.
International Law Is Increasingly Important and the United States Is a Party to Many Treaties and Conventions; International Law Relies on Three Principles: Comity, Sovereign Immunity, and the Act of State Doctrine	• International law is voluntary in the sense that sovereign nations can choose which aspects of international law to adhere to. Of course, there are consequences to ignoring international law, which typically take the form of *trade sanctions*. • The United States gives the president, with advice and consent of the Senate, the power to make and consent to treaties. A number of "conventions," particularly those dealing with IP, are actually multilateral treaties. • If law is viewed as a predictor of how officials will resolve disputes, then international law is composed of treaties, customs, and general principles of law that each nation in a dispute subscribes to, along with prior court decisions. • *Comity* is a principle of international law by which courts in one country respect and enforce decisions of courts in another country. • *Sovereign immunity* is a principle of international law that prevents courts in one country from allowing lawsuits against another country. There are two exceptions: one when the foreign government waives diplomatic immunity and the second when it is engaged in commercial activity. • The *act of state* doctrine immunizes the legality of one country's government from the scrutiny of another country's courts.
Much International Law Is Being Created through Multinational Organizations Such as the EU, NAFTA, and Other Regional Organizations; Increasingly, International Courts Are Overturning National Courts	• Worldwide, the United Nations is the most significant international organization. The European Union (EU) is the most significant regional organization and has progressed the farthest in breaking down international barriers to the movement of goods, capital, labor, and services. • Many of the traditional functions of national governments have been or are being taken over by the EU, including issuing currency, setting banking policies, and establishing tariffs on imports into the EU. • The North American Free Trade Agreement (NAFTA) has established a plan for the gradual abolition of tariffs, but at present there are no plans for an EU-style transfer of national governmental powers to an international organization. • Regional organizations in Southeast Asia, Africa, and Latin America are not nearly as organized or significant as the EU or NAFTA. • The UN has established an International Court of Justice to resolve disputes between nations. The European Court of Justice is the highest court among EU members and has the power to overturn decisions of national courts of member nations with respect to EU law.
International Trade Is Linked with Respect for and Enforcement of	• International protection of IP has become increasingly important. The World Trade Organization (WTO) was created in 1995 at the last session of the GATT (General Agreement on Trade and Tariffs). The WTO functions as an industrial umpire, making decisions about international trade disputes, which are often based on failures to enforce IP laws.

Intellectual Property Rights; Minimum Standards for Various Forms of IP Protection Are Established under TRIPS; WIPO Administers Patent, Copyright, and Trademark Conventions	• The World Intellectual Property Organization (WIPO) is responsible for promoting protection of IP throughout the world. The WIPO administers the Paris Convention (patents and trademarks) and the Berne Convention (copyrights). • The Trade-Related Aspects of Intellectual Property Rights (TRIPS) is a WTO multilateral agreement that sets minimum standards for protection of intellectual property rights. Countries that do not adhere to these minimum standards are subject to trade sanctions. • TRIPS sets specific standards for each (patent, copyright, trademark) component of IP. • The Rome Convention for the Protection of Performers, Producers of Phonograms, and Broadcasting Organizations provides additional protection for artists against the unauthorized recordings of their performances and unauthorized uses of authorized recordings of their performances.
Contracts between Firms from Different Countries Should Contain Choice of Law Clauses but, If No Law Is Specified, Then the CISG Applies for Business-to-Business Contracts	• International contract law is relevant only if the parties do not specify in the contract just what jurisdiction's contract law should apply. *Choice of law clauses* are extremely common in international contracts. • In the absence of a choice of law clause, the Contracts for the International Sale of Goods (CISG) applies, but only for transactions between businesses. For transactions between businesses and consumers, the law of the country where the consumer resides governs the transaction unless a choice of law clause is applicable. • The CISG is patterned more on the contract law of nations that subscribe to the *civil system of law,* but it shares many similarities with the UCC. • The UN has fashioned the United Nations Commission for International Trade Law (UNCITRAL), which provides recommendations for nations to fashion changes in their contract laws to accommodate e-commerce. The main thrust of the UNCITRAL recommendations is to treat electronic records the same as paper records.
International Jurisdiction Should Be Selected When the Parties Have a Contract; If There Is No Such Clause and Parties in a Dispute Have No Agreement, Courts Will Look at Applicable Statutory Law or at Which Nation Has the Most Significant Interest in the Outcome of the Dispute	• International criminal jurisdiction is based on several principles, but the most important is territory; that is, where did the crime take place? • Civil jurisdiction is often determined by *forum selection clauses* in which the parties "agree" to a jurisdiction. It is common for websites to get visitors to agree to both *choice of law* and *choice of forum* clauses. • The EU has recently enacted a trade regulation that rejects choice of forum agreements when the seller and the consumer in the transaction are located in different member states and the seller has a standardized "form" *clickwrap agreement* in which the consumer "agrees" to the forum and choice of law of the seller's choosing. • In the absence of choice of law clauses, in a case that involves companies from different countries, courts will look at whether applicable law is dictated by statute. If there is no applicable statute, courts will look at the country with the most significant relationship with the outcome of the dispute or at which country has the greatest government interest in the outcome of the case.

Key Terms

act of state, *755*
apportionment, *744*
choice of forum clause, *768*
choice of law clauses, *768*
civil law, *763*
comity, *755*
convention, *754*
Convention on Contracts for
   the International Sale of
   Goods, *763*
Due Process Clause, *747*

European Court of Justice, *758*
European Union, *756*
International Court of
   Justice, *758*
Internet Tax Freedom Act, *751*
Interstate Commerce
   Clause, *744*
North American Free Trade
   Agreement, *757*
sovereign immunity, *755*
sovereignty, *753*

Trade-Related Aspects of
   Intellectual Property
   Rights, *763*
United Nations Commission
   for International Trade
   Law, *767*
World Intellectual Property
   Organization, *759*
World Trade Organization, *759*

Questions for Review and Analysis

1. Compare the minimum contacts test, as it is applied to the bricks-and-mortar activity of businesses, to their cyberspace activity. If you were a small business, seeking to sell to customers located in other states, what are some things you could do to avoid having states where these customers live require you to collect sales tax?

2. Respect for international law is based on a number of principles that, together, require nations to respect the legal decisions of other nations. Name three exceptions, namely, situations in which U.S. authorities will subject foreign entities to U.S. jurisdiction.

3. Draw boxes and put in those boxes acronyms such as WTO, WIPO, TRIPS, and so forth, and explain how actions taken with respect to one of the boxes affects what's in the other boxes. For example, the DMCA (Digital Millennium Copyright Act) was passed in order to comply with TRIPS minimum standards to protect IP.

4. You are beginning a trade and service relationship with a company from another country. Name three contract issues that you would be especially concerned about because the company is located in another country. What if the company had subsidiaries located in the United States? Any changes?

5. The EU has recently changed its trade laws and now refuses, among member nations, to enforce choice of forum clauses when a consumer is a purchaser. How might this refusal to enforce choice of forum clauses impact websites within the EU?

If You Really Understood This Chapter, You Should Be Able to Provide Informed Commentary on the Following:

1. **Jurisdiction Based on Agreement with ISP.** Anyone who spends a lot of time cruising the Internet is confronted with buttons that state "I Agree" or "I Do Not Agree." If you hit the first button, you gain access while, if you hit the second button, often you are excluded. Richard Patterson lived in Texas but was a subscriber of CompuServe, an ISP based in Ohio. CompuServe was developing a program entitled "Compuserve Navigator." CompuServe maintained a reservoir of shareware, which is donated software that can be downloaded by subscribers. Some of this shareware is priced and Patterson donated 12 files and sold about $650 worth of software through the CompuServe shareware system. The CompuServe Navigator would enable CompuServe subscribers, including Patterson, to access the stored shareware. When CompuServe began to market its CompuServe Navigator, Patterson notified CompuServe that the terms "WinNAV," "Windows Navigator," and "FlashPoint Windows Navigator" were common law trademarks that he and his company owned. Patterson's software products were Internet browsers and, so, the CompuServe Navigator was a potential competitor. Negotiations between CompuServe and Patterson broke down and CompuServe sued Patterson in Ohio for a declaratory judgment that its CompuServe Navigator will not infringe Patterson's common law trademarks. Patterson filed a motion to dismiss for lack of jurisdiction and that motion was granted by the district court. CompuServe appealed, claiming that in Patterson's subscriber contract, he agreed that the contract was "made and performed in Ohio" and would be governed and construed according to Ohio law. In addition, Patterson sold software through CompuServe. What do you think? [*CompuServe, Inc. v. Richard Patterson*, 89 F.3d 1257 (6th Cir. 1996).]

2. **Does Accessibility Satisfy the Minimum Contacts Test?** The plaintiff is based in New York and owns a jazz club in New York called "The Blue Note" along with a federally registered trademark for "The Blue Note." The defendant owns a jazz club in Missouri with the same name. The defendant also had a website that it was using to promote its jazz club. Plaintiff claims that the defendant's website is accessible by New York residents and, therefore, the minimum contacts test is satisfied. At one time, the defendant's website contained a disclaimer that it was not the famous The Blue Note jazz club in New York and, in fact, provided a hyperlink to the plaintiff's website. Both the disclaimer and the hyperlink were removed after plaintiff complained. What do you think? Does establishing a website necessarily subject you to jurisdiction of the courts in all 50 states? [*Bensusan Restaurant Corp. v. Richard B. King,* 937 F. Supp. 295 (S.D.N.Y. 1996).]

3. **CISG—Much Ado about Nothing?** When two companies are from different countries, the CISG normally applies, unless those parties have a contract that specifies a different law applies. However, suppose that it is clear that the CISG applies, but the CISG is silent on the point of law in dispute. What happens then? Schmitz has requested some drapes from Rockland Industries, a Maryland firm. Rockland produced the drapes, which were very unusual in that they (1) totally blocked out light and (2) conformed to European standards for flame resistance. Schmitz performs "transfer printing," which takes material (such as the drapes) and transfers onto them a pattern. The modified goods are then available for later resale to the public or retailers. Representatives of Rockland represented that their drapes were suitable for transfer printing, but when the printing was applied, about 20 percent of the product had to be discarded. Rockland claims that the law of Maryland should govern this case because case law under the CISG is sparse. Rockland further claims that, under Maryland contract law, Schmitz must prove with expert testimony that Rockland's drapes were unsuitable. If these contentions are accurate, what is the point of having a CISG? The court may rely on the UCC anyway. See the surprise ending at *Schmitz-Werke GMBH & Co. v. Rockland Industries, Inc.,* 2002 U.S. App. LEXIS 12336 (4th Cir. 2002).

4. **Whose Law Applies?** As you know, U.S. ISPs are generally insulated from defamation suits by the Communications Decency Act, as long as they do not contribute to the content of the message. On the other hand, British ISPs are not so lucky. On April 1, 2000, Demon Internet paid $25,000 to a physicist, Laurence Godfrey, as well as court costs, which could run several hundred thousand dollars. There are some important implications of this case. First, it is clear under British law that, if the case had gone to trial, Demon would have lost. Demon did not contribute to content, but hosted an electronic bulletin board in which the defamatory messages were placed. Godfrey was very upset about the messages and sent three faxes to Demon to have them take down the offensive postings. When Demon refused, Godfrey sued and, ultimately, the settlement described above occurred. Since U.S. ISPs are virtually insulated from libel suits unless they contribute to content, the issue is whether they are subject to British law if a British subject is libeled and a U.S. ISP carries the libelous comments just the way Demon Internet did. Undoubtedly there will be such a case in the not-too-distant future. An article about the case is located at http://www.nytimes.com/library/tech/00/04/biztech/articles/01britain.html.

5. **The WIPO, ICANN UDRP, and the ACPA.** Someone who went to sleep in 1990 would have a hard time deciphering the acronyms listed here. Basically the first Circuit Court of Appeals reversed a lower-court decision, ruling that a U.S. court, applying the Anticybersquatting Consumer Protection Act (ACPA), may overturn an ICANN UDRP decision. A WIPO panel ruled that the domain name corinthians.com must be transferred from Sallen to a Brazilian soccer team. Sallen filed suit in U.S. federal court seeking a declaration that he was not a cybersquatter under the ACPA, and to have the transfer stopped. Finding that a "certain controversy" existed as to the domain name, the court applied the ACPA. The court held that, under Section 1114(2)(D)(v) of the ACPA, a domain name owner who has lost a domain name under the UDRP has a cause of action for an injuction to return the domain name if such owner can show he is in compliance with the ACPA. The court determined that Sallen was in compliance and issued an injunction. The WIPO decision can be found at http://www.arbiter.wipo.int/domains/decisions/html/2000/d2000-0461.html. The First Circuit decision overruling the Uniform Domain Name Resolution Policy decision can be found at *Sallen v. Corinthians Licenciamentos Ltd.,* 273 F.3d 14 (1st Cir. 2001). Is this a good idea? What will happen to the credibility of the WIPO internationally if courts in countries across the world decide that they can overturn WIPO decisions?

Social Responsibility, Policy, and Ethics in a High-Tech World

6. **Conflict of Laws and Free Speech.** The First Amendment in the United States prohibits the government from blocking virtually any form of freedom of expression that does not involve child pornography, terrorism, or other forms that themselves involve a crime. The rest of the world does not have the same respect for freedom of expression. In France, it is a crime to incite racial hatred. Yahoo! is one of the premier auction websites on the Internet and among the items offered on a recent Yahoo! auction were Nazi memorabilia, which are illegal in France. French authorities took Yahoo! to court and filed criminal charges against the Internet giant (see article at http://news.com.com/2100-1023-845698.html). Several organizations, such as the League Against Racism and Anti-Semitism and the League of Jewish Students, successfully sued Yahoo in France and obtained a judgment against Yahoo. A U.S. federal district court judge, however, refused to enforce the judgment and says that Yahoo is not bound by French speech law (see story at http://news.com.com/2100-1017-275564.html). This appears to be an amplification of the porno wars, where the most conservative community standards dictate what can be shown on the Internet unless some shielding scheme can be arranged. What do you think? Should the speech laws of one country effectively censor what appears on a website owned by citizens of another country?

Using the Internet to Your Advantage

1. There are a number of organizations that have very strong views about Internet Taxation. The "con" view is represented at http://www.nomorenettax.com/?b1. The "pro" position in favor of allowing states to tax e-commerce is represented by the Center on Budget and Policy Priorities at http://www.cbpp.org/512webtax.htm. There is a Cyber-Jurisdiction center that maintains a number of cases that deal with jurisdictional issues involving the Internet at http://www.geocities.com/SiliconValley/Bay/6201/.

2. An excellent collection of international Internet cases is available at http://www.perkinscoie.com/casedigest/icd_results.cfm?keyword1=international&topic=International, which is a website sponsored by the law firm of Perkins Coie. Other cases involving intellectual property can be accessed at the World Intellectual Property Organization website (http://www.wipo.org/). Of course, there are a number of universities that have built up a deserved reputation in international law such as the International Law Institute at Georgetown University (http://www.ili.org/) and, at Pace University Law School, the Institute of International Commercial Law (http://cisgw3.law.pace.edu/). The International Law Section of the Academy of Legal Studies in Business (http://www.wsu.edu/~legal/alsb_ils) provides links to international business law issues.

3. Among the government agencies involved heavily with international trade and law are the U.S. Department of Commerce (http://www.doc.gov), the International Trade Commission (http://www.usitc.gov), and the U.S. Trade Representative (http://www.ustr.gov). The World Trade Organization is accessible at http://www.wto.org.

Appendix **A**

The Constitution of the United States of America

PREAMBLE

We the People of the United States, in Order to form a more perfect Union, establish Justice, insure domestic Tranquility, provide for the common defense, promote the general Welfare, and secure the Blessings of Liberty to ourselves and our Posterity, do ordain and establish this Constitution for the United States of America.

ARTICLE I

Section 1

All legislative Powers herein granted shall be vested in a Congress of the United States, which shall consist of a Senate and House of Representatives.

Section 2

The House of Representatives shall be composed of Members chosen every second Year by the People of the several States, and the Electors in each State shall have the Qualifications requisite for Electors of the most numerous Branch of the State Legislature.

No Person shall be a Representative who shall not have attained to the age of twenty five Years, and been seven Years a Citizen of the United States, and who shall not, when elected, be an Inhabitant of that State in which he shall be chosen.

Representatives and direct Taxes shall be apportioned among the several States which may be included within this Union, according to their respective Numbers, which shall be determined by adding to the whole Number of free Persons, including those bound to Service for a Term of Years, and excluding Indians not taxed, three fifths of all other Persons.[1] The actual Enumeration shall be made within three Years after the first Meeting of the Congress of the United States, and within every subsequent Term of ten Years, in such Manner as they shall by Law direct. The Number of Representatives shall not exceed one for every thirty Thousand, but each State shall have at Least one Representative, and until

---

[1] Changed by the Fourteenth Amendment.

such enumeration shall be made, the State of New Hampshire shall be entitled to choose three, Massachusetts eight, Rhode-Island and Providence Plantations one, Connecticut five, New York six, New Jersey four, Pennsylvania eight, Delaware one, Maryland six, Virginia ten, North Carolina five, South Carolina five, and Georgia three.

When vacancies happen in the Representation from any State, the Executive Authority thereof shall issue Writs of Election to fill such Vacancies.

The House of Representatives shall chuse their Speaker and other Officers; and shall have the sole Power of Impeachment.

Section 3

The Senate of the United States shall be composed of two Senators from each State, chosen by the Legislature thereof,[2] for six Years; and each Senator shall have one Vote.

Immediately after they shall be assembled in Consequence of the first Election, they shall be divided as equally as may be into three Classes. The Seats of the Senators of the first Class shall be vacated at the Expiration of the second Year, of the second Class at the Expiration of the fourth Year, and of the third Class at the Expiration of the sixth Year, so that one third may be chosen every second Year; and if Vacancies happen by Resignation, or otherwise, during the Recess of the Legislature of any State, the Executive thereof may make temporary Appointments until the next Meeting of the Legislature, which shall then fill such Vacancies.[3]

No Person shall be a Senator who shall not have attained to the Age of thirty Years, and been nine Years a Citizen of the United States, and who shall not, when elected, be an Inhabitant of that State for which he shall be chosen.

The Vice President of the United States shall be President of the Senate, but shall have no Vote, unless they be equally divided.

The Senate shall chuse their other Officers, and also a President pro tempore, in the Absence of the Vice President, or when he shall exercise the Office of President of the United States.

The Senate shall have the sole Power to try all Impeachments. When sitting for that Purpose, they shall be on Oath or Affirmation. When the President of the United States is tried, the Chief Justice shall preside: And no Person shall be convicted without the Concurrence of two thirds of the Members present.

Judgment in Cases of Impeachment shall not extend further than to removal from Office, and disqualification to hold and enjoy any Office of honor, Trust or Profit under the United States: but the Party convicted shall nevertheless be liable and subject to Indictment, Trial, Judgment and Punishment, according to Law.

Section 4

The Times, Places and Manner of holding Elections for Senators and Representatives, shall be prescribed in each State by the Legislature thereof; but the Congress may at any time by Law make or alter such Regulations, except as to the Places of chusing Senators.

The Congress shall assemble at least once in every Year, and such Meeting shall be on the first Monday in December, unless they shall by Law appoint a different Day.[4]

Section 5

Each House shall be the Judge of the Elections, Returns and Qualifications of its own Members, and a Majority of each shall constitute a Quorum to do Business; but a smaller

---

[2] Changed by the Seventeenth Amendment.

[3] Changed by the Seventeenth Amendment.

[4] Changed by the Twentieth Amendment.

Number may adjourn from day to day, and may be authorized to compel the Attendance of absent Members, in such Manner, and under such Penalties as each House may provide.

Each House may determine the Rules of its Proceedings, punish its Members for disorderly Behaviour, and with the Concurrence of two thirds, expel a Member.

Each House shall keep a Journal of its Proceedings, and from time to time publish the same, excepting such Parts as may in their Judgment require Secrecy; and the Yeas and Nays of the Members of either House on any question shall, at the Desire of one fifth of those Present, be entered on the Journal.

Neither House, during the Session of Congress, shall, without the consent of the other, adjourn for more than three days, nor to any other Place than that in which the two Houses shall be sitting.

Section 6

The Senators and Representatives shall receive a Compensation for their Services, to be ascertained by Law, and paid out of the Treasury of the United States. They shall in all Cases, except Treason, Felony and Breach of the Peace, be privileged from Arrest during their Attendance at the Session of their respective Houses, and in going to and returning from the same; and for any Speech or Debate in either House, they shall not be questioned in any other Place.

No Senator or Representative shall, during the Time for which he was elected, be appointed to any civil Office under the Authority of the United States, which shall have been created, or the Emoluments whereof shall have been encreased during such time; and no Person holding any Office under the United States, shall be a Member of either House during his Continuance in Office.

Section 7

All Bills for raising Revenue shall originate in the House of Representatives; but the Senate may propose or concur with Amendments as on other Bills.

Every Bill which shall have passed the House of Representatives and the Senate, shall, before it becomes a Law, be presented to the President of the United States; If he approves he shall sign it, but if not he shall return it, with his Objections to that House in which it shall have originated, who shall enter the Objections at large on their Journal, and proceed to reconsider it. If after such Reconsideration two thirds of that House shall agree to pass the Bill, it shall be sent, together with the Objections, to the other House, by which it shall likewise be reconsidered, and if approved by two thirds of that House, it shall become a Law. But in all such Cases the Votes of both Houses shall be determined by Yeas and Nays, and the Names of the Persons voting for and against the Bill shall be entered on the Journal of each House respectively. If any Bill shall not be returned by the President within ten Days (Sundays excepted) after it shall have been presented to him, the Same shall be a Law, in like Manner as if he had signed it, unless the Congress by their Adjournment prevent its Return, in which Case it shall not be a Law.

Every Order, Resolution, or Vote to which the concurrence of the Senate and House of Representatives may be necessary (except on a question of Adjournment) shall be presented to the President of the United States; and before the Same shall take Effect, shall be approved by him, or being disapproved by him, shall be repassed by two thirds of the Senate and House of Representatives, according to the Rules and limitations prescribed in the Case of a Bill.

Section 8

Congress shall have Power To lay and collect Taxes, Duties, Imposts and Excises, to pay the Debts and provide for the common Defence and general Welfare of the United States; but all Duties, Imposts and Excises shall be uniform throughout the United States.

To borrow Money on the credit of the United States;

To regulate Commerce with foreign Nations, and among the several States, and with the Indian Tribes;

To establish an uniform Rule of Naturalization, and uniform Laws on the subject of Bankruptcies throughout the United States;

To coin Money, regulate the Value thereof, and of foreign Coin, and fix the Standard of Weights and Measures;

To provide for the Punishment of counterfeiting the Securities and current Coin of the United States;

To establish Post Offices and post Roads;

To promote the Progress of Science and useful Arts, by securing for limited Times to Authors and Inventors the exclusive Right to their respective Writings and Discoveries;

To constitute Tribunals inferior to the supreme Court;

To define and punish Piracies and Felonies committed on the high Seas, and Offences against the Law of Nations;

To declare War, grant Letters of Marque and Reprisal, and make Rules concerning Captures on Land and Water;

To raise and support Armies, but no Appropriation of Money to that Use shall be for a longer Term than two Years;

To provide and maintain a Navy;

To make Rules for the government and Regulation of the land and naval Forces;

To provide for calling forth the Militia to execute the Laws of the Union, suppress Insurrections and repel Invasions;

To provide for organizing, arming, and disciplining, the Militia, and for governing such Part of them as may be employed in the Service of the United States, reserving to the States respectively, the Appointment of the Officers, and the Authority of training the Militia according to the discipline prescribed by Congress;

To exercise exclusive Legislation in all Cases whatsoever, over such District (not exceeding ten Miles square) as may, by Cession of particular States, and the Acceptance of Congress, become the Seat of the Government of the United States, and to exercise like Authority over all Places purchased by the Consent of the Legislature of the State in which the Same shall be, for the Erection of Forts, Magazines, Arsenals, dock-Yards, and other needful Buildings;—And

To make all Laws which shall be necessary and proper for carrying into Execution the foregoing Powers, and all other Powers vested by this Constitution in the Government of the United States, or in any Department or Officer thereof.

Section 9

The Migration or Importation of such Persons as any of the States now existing shall think proper to admit, shall not be prohibited by the Congress prior to the Year one thousand eight hundred and eight, but a Tax or duty may be imposed on such Importation, not exceeding ten dollars for each Person.

The Privilege of the Writ of Habeas Corpus shall not be suspended, unless when in Cases of Rebellion or Invasion the public Safety may require it.

No Bill of Attainder or ex post facto Law shall be passed.

No Capitation, or other direct, Tax shall be laid, unless in Proportion to the Census of Enumeration herein before directed to be taken.[5]

---

[5] Changed by the Sixteenth Amendment.

No Tax or Duty shall be laid on Articles exported from any State.

No Preference shall be given by any Regulation of Commerce or Revenue to the Ports of one State over those of another: nor shall Vessels bound to, or from, one State, be obliged to enter, clear, or pay Duties in another.

No Money shall be drawn from the Treasury, but in Consequence of Appropriations made by Law; and a regular Statement and Account of the Receipts and Expenditures of all public Money shall be published from time to time.

No Title of Nobility shall be granted by the United States: And no Person holding any Office of Profit or Trust under them, shall, without the Consent of the Congress, accept of any present, Emolument, Office, or Title, of any kind whatever, from any King, Prince, or foreign State.

Section 10

No State shall enter into any Treaty, Alliance, or Confederation; grant Letters of Marque and Reprisal; coin Money; emit Bills of Credit; make anyThing but gold and silver coin a Tender in Payment of Debts; pass any Bill of Attainder, ex post facto Law, or Law impairing the Obligation of Contracts, or grant any Title of Nobility.

No State shall, without the consent of the Congress, lay any Imposts or Duties on Imports or Exports, except what may be absolutely necessary for executing its inspection Laws: and the net Produce of all Duties and Imposts, laid by any State on Imports or Exports, shall be for the Use of the Treasury of the United States; and all such Laws shall be subject to the Revision and Controul of the Congress.

No State shall, without the consent of Congress, lay any Duty of Tonnage, keep Troops, or Ships of War in time of Peace, enter into any Agreement or Compact with another State, or with a foreign Power, or engage in War, unless actually invaded, or in such imminent Danger as will not admit of delay.

ARTICLE II

Section 1

The executive Power shall be vested in a President of the United States of America. He shall hold his Office during the Term of four Years, and, together with the Vice President, chosen for the same Term, be elected, as follows

Each state shall appoint, in such Manner as the Legislature thereof may direct, a Number of Electors, equal to the whole Number of Senators and Representatives to which the State may be entitled in Congress: but no Senator or Representative, or Person holding an Office of Trust or Profit under the United States, shall be appointed an Elector.

The Electors shall meet in their respective States, and vote by Ballot for two Persons, of whom one at least shall not be an inhabitant of the same State with themselves. And they shall make a List of all the Persons voted for, and of the Number of Votes for each; which List they shall sign and certify, and transmit sealed to the Seat of the Government of the United States, directed to the President of the Senate. The President of the Senate shall, in the Presence of the Senate and House of Representatives, open all the Certificates, and the Votes shall then be counted. The Person having the greatest Number of Votes shall be the President, if such Number be a Majority of the whole Number of Electors appointed; and if there be more than one who have such Majority, and have an equal Number of Votes, then the House of Representatives shall immediately chuse by Ballot one of them for President; and if no Person have a Majority, then from the five highest on the List the said House shall in like Manner chuse the President. But in chusing the President, the Votes shall be taken by States, the Representation from each State having one Vote; A quorum for this purpose shall consist of a Member or Members from two thirds of the States, and a Majority of all the States shall be necessary to a Choice. In every Case, after the Choice of the President, the Person having the greatest Number of Votes of the Electors shall be the Vice President. But if there should remain two or more who have equal Votes, the Senate shall chuse from them by Ballot the Vice President.[6]

The Congress may determine the Time of chusing the Electors, and the Day on which they shall give their Votes; which Day shall be the same throughout the United States.

No Person except a natural born Citizen, or a Citizen of the United States, at the time of the Adoption of this Constitution, shall be eligible to the Office of President; neither shall any Person be eligible to that Office who shall not have attained to the Age of thirty five Years, and been fourteen Years a Resident within the United States.

In case of the Removal of the President from Office, or of his Death, Resignation, or Inability to discharge the Powers and Duties of the said Office, the Same shall devolve on the Vice President, and the Congress may by Law provide for the Case of Removal, Death, Resignation or Inability, both of the President and Vice President, declaring what Officer shall then act as President, and such Officer shall act accordingly, until the Disability be removed, or a President shall be elected.[7]

The President shall, at stated Times, receive for his Services, a Compensation, which shall neither be encreased nor diminished during the Period for which he shall have been elected, and he shall not receive within that Period any other Emolument from the United States, or any of them.

Before he enter on the Execution of his Office, he shall take the following Oath or Affirmation:—"I do solemnly swear (or affirm) that I will faithfully execute the Office of President of the United States, and will to the best of my Ability, preserve, protect, and defend the Constitution of the United States."

Section 2

The President shall be Commander in Chief of the Army and Navy of the United States, and of the Militia of the several States, when called into the actual Service of the United States; he may require the Opinion, in writing, of the principal Officer in each of the executive Departments, upon any Subject relating to the Duties of their respective Offices, and he shall have Power to grant Reprieves and Pardons for Offences against the United States, except in Cases of Impeachment.

He shall have Power, by and with the Advice and Consent of the Senate, to make Treaties, provided two thirds of the Senators present concur; and he shall nominate, and by and with the Advice and Consent of the Senate, shall appoint Ambassadors, other public Ministers and Consuls, Judges of the supreme Court, and all other Officers of the United States, whose Appointments are not herein otherwise provided for, and which shall be established by Law; but the Congress may by Law vest the Appointment of such inferior Officers, as they think proper, in the President alone, in the Courts of Law, or in the Heads of Departments.

The President shall have Power to fill up all Vacancies that may happen during the Recess of the Senate, by granting Commissions which shall expire at the End of their next Session.

Section 3

He shall from time to time give to the Congress Information of the State of the Union, and recommend to their Consideration such Measures as he shall judge necessary and expedient; he may, on extraordinary Occasions, convene both Houses, or either of them, and in

[6] Changed by the Twelfth Amendment.

[7] Changed by the Twenty-fifth Amendment.

Case of Disagreement between them, with Respect to the Time of Adjournment, he may adjourn them to such Time as he shall think proper; he shall receive Ambassadors and other public Ministers; he shall take Care that the Laws be faithfully executed, and shall Commission all the Officers of the United States.

Section 4

The President, Vice President and all civil Officers of the United States, shall be removed from Office on Impeachment for, and Conviction of, Treason, Bribery, or other high Crimes and Misdemeanors.

ARTICLE III

Section 1

The judicial Power of the United States, shall be vested in one supreme Court, and in such inferior Courts as the Congress may from time to time ordain and establish. The Judges, both of the supreme and inferior Courts, shall hold their Offices during good Behaviour, and shall, at stated Times, receive for their Services, a Compensation, which shall not be diminished during their Continuance in Office.

Section 2

The judicial Power shall extend to all Cases, in Law and Equity, arising under this Constitution, the Laws of the United States, and Treaties made, or which shall be made, under their Authority;—to all Cases affecting Ambassadors, other public Ministers and Consuls;—to all Cases of admiralty and maritime Jurisdiction;—to Controversies to which the United States shall be a party;—to Controversies between two or more States;—between a State and Citizens of another State;[8]—between Citizens of different States;—between Citizens of the same State claiming Lands under Grants of different States, and between a state, or the Citizens thereof, and foreign States, Citizens or Subjects.

In all Cases affecting Ambassadors, other public Ministers and Consuls, and those in which a State shall be Party, the supreme Court shall have original Jurisdiction. In all the other Cases before mentioned, the supreme Court shall have appellate Jurisdiction, both as to Law and Fact, with such Exceptions, and under such Regulations as the Congress shall make.

The Trial of all Crimes, except in Cases of Impeachment, shall be by Jury; and such Trial shall be held in the State where the said Crimes shall have been committed; but when not committed within any State, the Trial shall be at such Place or Places as the Congress may by Law have directed.

Section 3

Treason against the United States, shall consist only in levying War against them, or in adhering to their Enemies, giving them Aid and Comfort. No Person shall be convicted of Treason unless on the Testimony of two Witnesses to the same overt Act, or on Confession in open Court.

The Congress shall have Power to declare the Punishment of Treason, but no Attainder of Treason shall work Corruption of Blood, or Forfeiture except during the Life of the Person attained.

---

[8] Changed by the Eleventh Amendment.

ARTICLE IV

Section 1

Full Faith and Credit shall be given in each State to the public Acts, Records, and judicial Proceedings of every other State. And the Congress may by general Laws prescribe the Manner in which such Acts, Records and Proceedings shall be proved, and the Effect thereof.

Section 2

The Citizens of each State shall be entitled to all Privileges and Immunities of Citizens in the several States.

A Person charged in any State with Treason, Felony, or other Crime, who shall flee from Justice, and be found in another State, shall on Demand of the executive Authority of the State from which he fled, be delivered up, to be removed to the State having Jurisdiction of the Crime.

No Person held to Service or Labour in one State, under the Laws thereof, escaping into another, shall, in consequence of any Law or Regulation therein, be discharged from such Service or Labour, but shall be delivered up on Claim of the Party to whom such Service or Labour may be due.[9]

Section 3

New States may be admitted by the Congress into this Union; but no new State shall be formed or erected within the Jurisdiction of any other State; nor any State be formed by the Junction of two or more States, or Parts of States, without the Consent of the Legislatures of the States concerned as well as of the Congress.

The Congress shall have Power to dispose of and make all needful Rules and Regulations respecting the Territory or other Property belonging to the United States; and nothing in this Constitution shall be so construed as to Prejudice any Claims of the United States, or of any particular State.

Section 4

The United States shall guarantee to every State in this Union a Republican Forum of Government, and shall protect each of them against Invasion; and on Application of the Legislature, or of the Executive (when the Legislature cannot be convened) against domestic Violence.

ARTICLE V

The Congress, whenever two thirds of both Houses shall deem it necessary, shall propose Amendments to this Constitution, or, on the Application of the Legislatures of two thirds of the several States, shall call a Convention for proposing Amendments, which in either Case, shall be valid to all Intents and Purposes, as Part of this Constitution, when ratified by the legislatures of three fourths of the several States, or by Conventions in three fourths thereof, as the one or the other Mode of Ratification may be proposed by the Congress; Provided that no amendment which may be made prior to the Year One thousand eight hundred and eight shall in any Manner affect the first and fourth Clauses in the Ninth Section of the first

[9] Changed by the Thirteenth Amendment.

Article; and that no State, without its consent, shall be deprived of its equal Suffrage in the Senate.

ARTICLE VI

All Debts contracted and Engagements entered into, before the Adoption of this Constitution, shall be as valid against the United States under this constitution, as under the Confederation.

The Constitution, and the Laws of the United States which shall be made in Pursuance thereof; and all Treaties made, or which shall be made, under the Authority of the United States, shall be the supreme Law of the Land; and the Judges in every State shall be bound thereby, any Thing in the Constitution or Laws of any State to the Contrary notwithstanding.

The Senators and Representatives before mentioned, and the Members of the several State Legislatures, and all executive and judicial Officers, both of the United States and of the several States, shall be bound by Oath or Affirmation, to support this Constitution; but no religious Test shall ever be required as a Qualification to any Office or public Trust under the United States.

ARTICLE VII

The Ratification of the Conventions of nine States, shall be sufficient for the Establishment of this Constitution between the States so ratifying the Same.

Done in Convention by the Unanimous Consent of the States present the Seventeenth Day of September in the Year of our Lord one thousand seven hundred and eighty seven and of the Independence of the United States of America the Twelfth. In witness whereof We have hereunto subscribed our Names.

AMENDMENTS

[The first 10 amendments are known as the "Bill of Rights."]

Amendment 1   (Ratified 1791)

Congress shall make no law respecting an establishment of religion, or prohibiting the free exercise thereof; or abridging the freedom of speech, or of the press; or the right of the people peaceably to assemble, and to petition the Government for a redress of grievances.

Amendment 2   (Ratified 1791)

A well regulated Militia, being necessary to the security of a free State, the right of the people to keep and bear Arms, shall not be infringed.

Amendment 3   (Ratified 1791)

No Soldier shall, in time of peace be quartered in any house, without the consent of the Owner, nor in time of war, but in a manner to be prescribed by law.

Amendment 4   (Ratified 1791)

The right of the people to be secure in their persons, houses, papers, and effects, against unreasonable searches and seizures, shall not be violated, and no Warrants shall issue, but upon probable cause, supported by Oath or affirmation, and particularly describing the place to be searched, and the persons or things to be seized.

Amendment 5   (Ratified 1791)

No person shall be held to answer for a capital, or otherwise infamous crime, unless on a presentment or indictment of a Grand Jury, except in cases arising in the land or naval forces, or in the Militia, when in actual service in time of War or public danger; nor shall any person be subject for the same offence to be twice put in jeopardy of life or limb; nor shall be compelled in any criminal case to be a witness against himself, nor be deprived of life, liberty, or property, without due process of law; nor shall private property be taken for public use, without just compensation.

Amendment 6   (Ratified 1791)

In all criminal prosecutions, the accused shall enjoy the right to a speedy and public trial, by an impartial jury of the State and district wherein the crime shall have been committed, which district shall have been previously ascertained by law, and to be informed of the nature and cause of the accusation; to be confronted with the witnesses against him; to have compulsory process for obtaining Witnesses in his favor, and to have assistance of counsel for his defence.

Amendment 7   (Ratified 1791)

In Suits at common law, where the value in controversy shall exceed twenty dollars, the right of trial by jury shall be preserved, and no fact tried by a jury, shall be otherwise re-examined in any Court of the United States, than according to the rules of the common law.

Amendment 8   (Ratified 1791)

Excessive bail shall not be required, nor excessive fines imposed, nor cruel and unusual punishments inflicted.

Amendment 9   (Ratified 1791)

The enumeration in the Constitution, of certain rights, shall not be construed to deny or disparage others retained by the people.

Amendment 10   (Ratified 1791)

The powers not delegated to the United States by the Constitution, nor prohibited by it to the States, are reserved to the States respectively, or to the people.

Amendment 11   (Ratified 1795)

The Judicial power of the United States shall not be construed to extend to any suit in law or equity, commenced or prosecuted against one of the United States by Citizens of another State, or by Citizens or Subjects of any Foreign State.

Amendment 12   (Ratified 1804)

The Electors shall meet in their respective states, and vote by ballot for President and Vice-President, one of whom, at least, shall not be an inhabitant of the same state with themselves; they shall name in their ballots the person voted for as President, and in distinct ballots the person voted for as Vice-President, and they shall make distinct lists of all persons voted for as President, and of all persons voted for as Vice-President, and of the number of votes for each, which lists they shall sign and certify, and transmit sealed to the seat of the government of the United States, directed to the President of the Senate;—The President of the Senate shall, in the presence of the Senate and House of Representatives, open all the certificates and the votes shall then be counted;—The person having the greatest number of votes for President, shall be the President, if such number be a majority of the whole number of Electors appointed; and if no person have such majority, then from the persons having the highest numbers not exceeding three on the list of those voted for as President, the House of Representatives shall choose immediately, by ballot, the President. But in choosing the President, the votes shall be taken by states, the representation from each state having one vote; a quorum for this purpose shall consist of a member or members from two-thirds of the states, and a majority of all the states shall be necessary to a choice. And if the House of Representatives shall not choose a President whenever the right of choice shall devolve upon them, before the fourth day of March next following, then the Vice-President shall act as president, as in the case of the death or other constitutional disability of the President.[10] —The person having the greatest number of votes as Vice-President, shall be the Vice-President, if such number be a majority of the whole number of Electors appointed, and if no person have a majority, then from the two highest numbers on the list, the Senate shall choose the Vice-President; a quorum for the purpose shall consist of two-thirds of the whole number of Senators, and a majority of the whole number shall be necessary to a choice. But no person constitutionally ineligible to the office of President shall be eligible to that of Vice-President of the United States.

Amendment 13   (Ratified 1865)

Section 1

Neither slavery nor involuntary servitude, except as a punishment for crime whereof the party shall have been duly convicted, shall exist within the United States, or any place subject to their jurisdiction.

Section 2

Congress shall have power to enforce this article by appropriate legislation.

Amendment 14   (Ratified 1868)

Section 1

All persons born or naturalized in the United States, and subject to the jurisdiction thereof, are citizens of the United States and of the State wherein they reside. No State shall make or enforce any law which shall abridge the privileges or immunities of citizens of the United States; nor shall any State deprive any person of life, liberty, or property, without due process of law; nor deny to any person within its jurisdiction the equal protection of the laws.

Section 2

Representatives shall be apportioned among the several States according to their respective numbers, counting the whole number of persons in each State, excluding Indians not taxed. But when the right to vote at any election for the choice of electors for President and Vice President of the United States, Representatives in Congress, the Executive and Judicial officers of a State, or the members of the Legislature thereof, is denied to any of the male inhabitants of such State, being twenty-one[11] years of age, and citizens of the United States, or in any way abridged except for participation in rebellion, or other crime, the basis of representation therein shall be reduced in the proportion which the number of such male citizens shall bear to the whole number of male citizens twenty-one years of age in such State.

Section 3

No person shall be a Senator or Representative in Congress, or elector of President and Vice President, or hold any office, civil or military, under the United States, or under any State, who, having previously taken an oath, as a member of Congress, or as an officer of

---

[10] Changed by the Twentieth Amendment.

[11] Changed by the Twenty-sixth Amendment.

the United States, or as a member of any State legislature, or as an executive or judicial officer of any State, to support the Constitution of the United States, shall have engaged in insurrection or rebellion against the same, or given aid or comfort to the enemies thereof. But congress may by a vote of two-thirds of each House, remove such disability.

Section 4

The validity of the public debt of the United States, authorized by law, including debts incurred for payment of pensions and bounties for services in suppressing insurrection or rebellion, shall not be questioned. But neither the United States nor any State shall assume or pay any debt or obligation incurred in aid of insurrection or rebellion against the United States, or any claim for the loss or emancipation of any slave; but all such debts, obligations and claims shall be held illegal and void.

Section 5

The Congress shall have power to enforce, by appropriate legislation, the provisions of this article.

Amendment 15   (Ratified 1870)

Section 1

The right of citizens of the United States to vote shall not be denied or abridged by the United States or by any State on account of race, color, or previous condition of servitude.

Section 2

The Congress shall have power to enforce this article by appropriate legislation.

Amendment 16   (Ratified 1913)

The Congress shall have power to lay and collect taxes on incomes, from whatever source derived, without apportionment among the several States, and without regard to any census or enumeration.

Amendment 17   (Ratified 1913)

The Senate of the United States shall be composed of two Senators from each State, elected by the people thereof, for six years; and each Senator shall have one vote. The electors in each State shall have the qualifications requisite for electors of the most numerous branch of the State legislatures.

When vacancies happen in the representation of any State in the Senate, the executive authority of such State shall issue writs of election to fill such vacancies: Provided, That the legislature of any State may empower the executive thereof to make temporary appointments until the people fill the vacancies by election as the legislature may direct.

This amendment shall not be so construed as to affect the election or term of any Senator chosen before it becomes valid as part of the Constitution.

Amendment 18   (Ratified 1919; Repealed 1933)

Section 1

After one year from the ratification of this article the manufacture, sale, or transportation of intoxicating liquors within, the importation thereof into, or the exportation thereof from the United States and all territory subject to the jurisdiction thereof for beverage purposes is hereby prohibited.

Section 2

The Congress and the several States shall have concurrent power to enforce this article by appropriate legislation.

Section 3

This article shall be inoperative unless it shall have been ratified as an amendment to the Constitution by the legislatures of the several States, as provided in the Constitution, within seven years from the date of the submission hereof to the States by the Congress.[12]

Amendment 19 (Ratified 1920)

The right of citizens of the United States to vote shall not be denied or abridged by the United States or by any State on account of sex.

Congress shall have power to enforce this article by appropriate legislation.

Amendment 20 (Ratified 1933)

Section 1

The terms of the President and Vice President shall end at noon on the 20th day of January, and the terms of Senators and Representatives at noon on the 3rd day of January, of the years in which such terms would have ended if this article had not been ratified; and the terms of their successors shall then begin.

Section 2

The Congress shall assemble at least once in every year, and such meeting shall begin at noon on the 3rd day of January, unless they shall by law appoint a different day.

Section 3

If, at the time fixed for the beginning of the term of the President, the President elect shall have died, the Vice President elect shall become President. If a President shall not have been chosen before the time fixed for the beginning of his term, or if the President elect shall have failed to qualify, then the Vice President elect shall act as President until a President shall have qualified; and the Congress may by law provide for the case wherein neither a President elect nor a Vice President elect shall have qualified, declaring who shall then act as President, or the manner in which one who is to act shall be selected, and such person shall act accordingly until a President or Vice President shall have qualified.

Section 4

The Congress may by law provide for the case of the death of any of the persons from whom the House of Representatives may choose a President whenever the right of choice shall have devolved upon them, and for the case of the death of any of the persons from whom the Senate may choose a Vice President whenever the right of choice shall have devolved upon them.

Section 5

Sections 1 and 2 shall take effect on the 15th day of October following the ratification of this article.

Section 6

This article shall be inoperative unless it shall have been ratified as an amendment to the Constitution by the legislatures of three-fourths of the several States within seven years from the date of its submission.

Amendment 21 (Ratified 1933)

Section 1

The eighteenth article of amendment to the Constitution of the United States is hereby repealed.

[12] Repealed by the Twenty-first Amendment.

Section 2

The transportation or importation into any State, Territory, or possession of the United States for delivery or use therein of intoxicating liquors, in violation of the laws thereof, is hereby prohibited.

Section 3

This article shall be inoperative unless it shall have been ratified as an amendment to the constitution by conventions in the several States, as provided in the Constitution, within seven years from the date of the submission hereof to the States by the Congress.

Amendment 22   (Ratified 1951)

Section 1

No person shall be elected to the office of the President more than twice, and no person who has held the office of President, or acted as President, for more than two years of a term to which some other person was elected President shall be elected to the office of the President more than once. But this Article shall not apply to any person holding the office of President when this Article was proposed by the Congress, and shall not prevent any person who may be holding the office of President, or acting as President, during the term within which this Article becomes operative from holding the office of President or acting as President during the remainder of such term.

Section 2

This Article shall be inoperative unless it shall have been ratified as an amendment to the Constitution by the legislatures of three-fourths of the several States within seven years from the date of its submission to the States by the Congress.

Amendment 23   (Ratified 1961)

Section 1

The District constituting the seat of Government of the United States shall appoint in such manner as the Congress may direct:

A number of electors of President and Vice President equal to the whole number of Senators and Representatives in Congress to which the District would be entitled if it were a State, but in no event more than the least populous State; they shall be in addition to those appointed by the States, but they shall be considered, for the purposes of the election of President and Vice President, to be electors appointed by a State; and they shall meet in the District and perform such duties as provided by the twelfth article of amendment.

Section 2

The Congress shall have power to enforce this article by appropriate legislation.

Amendment 24   (Ratified 1964)

Section 1

The right of citizens of the United States to vote in any primary or other election for President or Vice President, for electors for President or Vice President, or for Senator or Representative in Congress, shall not be denied or abridged by the United States or any State by reason of failure to pay any poll tax or other tax.

Section 2

The Congress shall have power to enforce this article by appropriate legislation.

Amendment 25   (Ratified 1967)

Section 1

In case of the removal of the President from office or of his death or resignation, the Vice President shall become President.

Section 2

Whenever there is a vacancy in the office of the Vice President, the President shall nominate a Vice President who shall take office upon confirmation by a majority vote of both Houses of Congress.

Section 3

Whenever the President transmits to the President pro tempore of the Senate and the Speaker of the House of Representatives his written declaration that he is unable to discharge the powers and duties of his office, and until he transmits to them a written declaration to the contrary, such powers and duties shall be discharged by the Vice President as Acting President.

Section 4

Whenever the Vice President and a majority of either the principal officers of the executive departments or of such other body as Congress may by law provide, transmit to the President pro tempore of the Senate and the Speaker of the House of Representatives their written declaration that the President is unable to discharge the powers and duties of his office, the Vice President shall immediately assume the powers and duties of the office as Acting President.

Thereafter, when the President transmits to the President pro tempore of the Senate and the Speaker of the House of Representatives his written declaration that no inability exists, he shall resume the powers and duties of his office unless the Vice President and a majority of either the principal officers of the executive department or of such other body as Congress may by law provide, transmit within four days to the President pro tempore of the Senate and the Speaker of the House of Representatives their written declaration that the President is unable to discharge the powers and duties of his office. Thereupon Congress shall decide the issue, assembling within forty-eight hours for that purpose if not in session. If the Congress, within twenty-one days after receipt of the latter written declaration, or, if Congress is not in session, within twenty-one days after Congress is required to assemble, determines by two-thirds vote of both Houses that the President is unable to discharge the powers and duties of his office, the Vice President shall continue to discharge the same as Acting President; otherwise, the President shall resume the powers and duties of his office.

Amendment 26   (Ratified 1971)

Section 1

The right of citizens of the United States, who are eighteen years of age or older, to vote shall not be denied or abridged by the United States or by any State on account of age.

Section 2

The Congress shall have power to enforce this article by appropriate legislation.

Amendment 27   (Ratified 1992)

No law, varying the compensation for the services of the Senators and Representatives, shall take effect, until an election of Representatives shall have intervened.

Appendix B

Excerpts from The Digital Millennium Copyright Act of 1998

SEC. 1201. CIRCUMVENTION OF COPYRIGHT PROTECTION SYSTEMS

(a) Violations regarding circumvention of technological measures—

   (1) (A) No person shall circumvent a technological measure that effectively controls access to a work protected under this title. The prohibition contained in the preceding sentence shall take effect at the end of the 2-year period beginning on the date of the enactment of this chapter.

      (B) The prohibition contained in subparagraph (A) shall not apply to persons who are users of a copyrighted work which is in a particular class of works, if such persons are, or are likely to be in the succeeding 3-year period, adversely affected by virtue of such prohibition in their ability to make noninfringing uses of that particular class of works under this title, as determined under subparagraph (C).

      (C) During the 2-year period described in subparagraph (A), and during each succeeding 3-year period, the Librarian of Congress, upon the recommendation of the Register of Copyrights, who shall consult with the Assistant Secretary for Communications and Information of the Department of Commerce and report and comment on his or her views in making such recommendation, shall make the determination in a rulemaking proceeding on the record for purposes of subparagraph (B) of whether persons who are users of a copyrighted work are, or are likely to be in the succeeding 3-year period, adversely affected by the prohibition under subparagraph (A) in their ability to make noninfringing uses under this title of a particular class of copyrighted works. In conducting such rulemaking, the Librarian shall examine—

SEC. 1202. INTEGRITY OF COPYRIGHT MANAGEMENT INFORMATION

(a) False copyright management information—No person shall knowingly and with the intent to induce, enable, facilitate, or conceal infringement—

    (1) provide copyright management information that is false, or

    (2) distribute or import for distribution copyright management information that is false.

(b) Removal or alteration of copyright management information—No person shall, without the authority of the copyright owner or the law—

    (1) intentionally remove or alter any copyright management information,

    (2) distribute or import for distribution copyright management information knowing that the copyright management information has been removed or altered without authority of the copyright owner or the law, or

    (3) distribute, import for distribution, or publicly perform works, copies of works, or phonorecords, knowing that copyright management information has been removed or altered without authority of the copyright owner or the law, knowing, or, with respect to civil remedies under section 1203, having reasonable grounds to know, that it will induce, enable, facilitate, or conceal an infringement of any right under this title.

(c) Definition—As used in this section, the term 'copyright management information' means any of the following information conveyed in connection with copies or phonorecords of a work or performances or displays of a work, including in digital form, except that such term does not include any personally identifying information about a user of a work or of a copy, phonorecord, performance, or display of a work:

    (1) The title and other information identifying the work, including the information set forth on a notice of copyright.

    (2) The name of, and other identifying information about, the author of a work.

    (3) The name of, and other identifying information about, the copyright owner of the work, including the information set forth in a notice of copyright.

    (4) With the exception of public performances of works by radio and television broadcast stations, the name of, and other identifying information about, a performer whose performance is fixed in a work other than an audiovisual work.

    (5) With the exception of public performances of works by radio and television broadcast stations, in the case of an audiovisual work, the name of, and other identifying information about, a writer, performer, or director who is credited in the audiovisual work.

    (6) Terms and conditions for use of the work.

    (7) Identifying numbers or symbols referring to such information or links to such information.

    (8) Such other information as the Register of Copyrights may prescribe by regulation, except that the Register of Copyrights may not require the provision of any information concerning the user of a copyrighted work.

(d) Law enforcement, intelligence, and other government activities—This section does not prohibit any lawfully authorized investigative, protective, information security, or intelligence activity of an officer, agent, or employee of the United States, a State, or a political subdivision of a State, or a person acting pursuant to a contract with the United States, a State, or a political subdivision of a State. For purposes of this subsection, the term 'information security' means activities carried out in order to identify and address the vulnerabilities of a government computer, computer system, or computer network.

SEC. 1203. CIVIL REMEDIES

(a) Civil actions—Any person injured by a violation of section 1201 or 1202 may bring a civil action in an appropriate United States district court for such violation.

(b) Powers of the court—In an action brought under subsection (a), the court—

(1) may grant temporary and permanent injunctions on such terms as it deems reasonable to prevent or restrain a violation, but in no event shall impose a prior restraint on free speech or the press protected under the 1st amendment to the Constitution;

(2) at any time while an action is pending, may order the impounding, on such terms as it deems reasonable, of any device or product that is in the custody or control of the alleged violator and that the court has reasonable cause to believe was involved in a violation;

(3) may award damages under subsection (c);

(4) in its discretion may allow the recovery of costs by or against any party other than the United States or an officer thereof;

(5) in its discretion may award reasonable attorney's fees to the prevailing party; and

(6) may, as part of a final judgment or decree finding a violation, order the remedial modification or the destruction of any device or product involved in the violation that is in the custody or control of the violator or has been impounded under paragraph (2).

(c) Award of damages—

(1) In general—Except as otherwise provided in this title, a person committing a violation of section 1201 or 1202 is liable for either—

(A) the actual damages and any additional profits of the violator, as provided in paragraph (2), or

(B) statutory damages, as provided in paragraph (3).

(2) Actual damages—The court shall award to the complaining party the actual damages suffered by the party as a result of the violation, and any profits of the violator that are attributable to the violation and are not taken into account in computing the actual damages, if the complaining party elects such damages at any time before final judgment is entered.

(3) Statutory damages—

(A) At any time before final judgment is entered, a complaining party may elect to recover an award of statutory damages for each violation of section 1201 in the sum of not less than $200 or more than $2,500 per act of circumvention, device, product, component, offer, or performance of service, as the court considers just.

(B) At any time before final judgment is entered, a complaining party may elect to recover an award of statutory damages for each violation of section 1202 in the sum of not less than $2,500 or more than $25,000.

(4) Repeated violations—In any case in which the injured party sustains the burden of proving, and the court finds, that a person has violated section 1201 or 1202 within 3 years after a final judgment was entered against the person for another such violation, the court may increase the award of damages up to triple the amount that would otherwise be awarded, as the court considers just.

(5) Innocent violations—

(A) In general—The court in its discretion may reduce or remit the total award of damages in any case in which the violator sustains the burden of proving, and the court finds, that the violator was not aware and had no reason to believe that its acts constituted a violation.

(B) Nonprofit library, archives, or educational institutions—In the case of a non-profit library, archives, or educational institution, the court shall remit damages in any case in which the library, archives, or educational institution sustains the burden of proving, and the court finds, that the library, archives, or educational institution was not aware and had no reason to believe that its acts constituted a violation.

Appendix C

Excerpts from the E-SIGN Act

TITLE 15, CHAPTER 96, SUBCHAPTER I

Sec. 7001.—General Rule of Validity

(a) In general

Notwithstanding any statute, regulation, or other rule of law (other than this sub-chapter and subchapter II of this chapter), with respect to any transaction in or affecting interstate or foreign commerce—

    (1) a signature, contract, or other record relating to such transaction may not be denied legal effect, validity, or enforceability solely because it is in electronic form; and

    (2) a contract relating to such transaction may not be denied legal effect, validity, or enforceability solely because an electronic signature or electronic record was used in its formation.

(b) Preservation of rights and obligations

This subchapter does not—

    (1) limit, alter, or otherwise affect any requirement imposed by a statute, regulation, or rule of law relating to the rights and obligations of persons under such statute, regulation, or rule of law other than a requirement that contracts or other records be written, signed, or in nonelectronic form; or

    (2) require any person to agree to use or accept electronic records or electronic signatures, other than a governmental agency with respect to a record other than a contract to which it is a party.

(c) Consumer disclosures

    (1) Consent to electronic records

Notwithstanding subsection (a) of this section, if a statute, regulation, or other rule of law requires that information relating to a transaction or transactions in or affecting interstate or foreign commerce be provided or made available to a consumer in writing, the use of an electronic record to provide or make available (whichever is required) such information satisfies the requirement that such information be in writing if—

        (A) the consumer has affirmatively consented to such use and has not withdrawn such consent;

        (B) the consumer, prior to consenting, is provided with a clear and conspicuous statement—

            (i) informing the consumer of

(I)   any right or option of the consumer to have the record provided or made available on paper or in nonelectronic form, and

(II) the right of the consumer to withdraw the consent to have the record provided or made available in an electronic form and of any conditions, consequences (which may include termination of the parties' relationship), or fees in the event of such withdrawal;

(ii) informing the consumer of whether the consent applies

(I)   only to the particular transaction which gave rise to the obligation to provide the record, or

(II) to identified categories of records that may be provided or made available during the course of the parties' relationship;

(iii) describing the procedures the consumer must use to withdraw consent as provided in clause (i) and to update information needed to contact the consumer electronically; and

(iv) informing the consumer

(I)   how, after the consent, the consumer may, upon request, obtain a paper copy of an electronic record, and

(II) whether any fee will be charged for such copy;

(C) the consumer—

(i)   prior to consenting, is provided with a statement of the hardware and software requirements for access to and retention of the electronic records; and

(ii) consents electronically, or confirms his or her consent electronically, in a manner that reasonably demonstrates that the consumer can access information in the electronic form that will be used to provide the information that is the subject of the consent; and

(D) after the consent of a consumer in accordance with subparagraph (A), if a change in the hardware or software requirements needed to access or retain electronic records creates a material risk that the consumer will not be able to access or retain a subsequent electronic record that was the subject of the consent, the person providing the electronic record—

(i)   provides the consumer with a statement of

(I)   the revised hardware and software requirements for access to and retention of the electronic records, and

(II) the right to withdraw consent without the imposition of any fees for such withdrawal and without the imposition of any condition or consequence that was not disclosed under subparagraph (B)(i); and

(ii) again complies with subparagraph (C).

(2) Other rights

(A) Preservation of consumer protections

Nothing in this subchapter affects the content or timing of any disclosure or other record required to be provided or made available to any consumer under any statute, regulation, or other rule of law.

(B) Verification or acknowledgment

If a law that was enacted prior to this chapter expressly requires a record to be provided or made available by a specified method that requires verification or acknowledgment of receipt, the record may be provided or made available electronically only if the method used provides verification or acknowledgment of receipt (whichever is required).

(3) Effect of failure to obtain electronic consent or confirmation of consent

The legal effectiveness, validity, or enforceability of any contract executed by a consumer shall not be denied solely because of the failure to obtain electronic consent or confirmation of consent by that consumer in accordance with paragraph (1)(C)(ii).

(4) Prospective effect

Withdrawal of consent by a consumer shall not affect the legal effectiveness, validity, or enforceability of electronic records provided or made available to that consumer in accordance with paragraph (1) prior to implementation of the consumer's withdrawal of consent. A consumer's withdrawal of consent shall be effective within a reasonable period of time after receipt of the withdrawal by the provider of the record. Failure to comply with paragraph (1)(D) may, at the election of the consumer, be treated as a withdrawal of consent for purposes of this paragraph.

(5) Prior consent

This subsection does not apply to any records that are provided or made available to a consumer who has consented prior to the effective date of this subchapter to receive such records in electronic form as permitted by any statute, regulation, or other rule of law.

(6) Oral communications

An oral communication or a recording of an oral communication shall not qualify as an electronic record for purposes of this subsection except as otherwise provided under applicable law.

(d) Retention of contracts and records

(1) Accuracy and accessibility

If a statute, regulation, or other rule of law requires that a contract or other record relating to a transaction in or affecting interstate or foreign commerce be retained, that requirement is met by retaining an electronic record of the information in the contract or other record that—

(A) accurately reflects the information set forth in the contract or other record; and

(B) remains accessible to all persons who are entitled to access by statute, regulation, or rule of law, for the period required by such statute, regulation, or rule of law, in a form that is capable of being accurately reproduced for later reference, whether by transmission, printing, or otherwise.

(2) Exception

A requirement to retain a contract or other record in accordance with paragraph (1) does not apply to any information whose sole purpose is to enable the contract or other record to be sent, communicated, or received.

(3) Originals

If a statute, regulation, or other rule of law requires a contract or other record relating to a transaction in or affecting interstate or foreign commerce to be provided, available, or retained in its original form, or provides consequences if the contract or other record is not provided, available, or retained in its original form, that statute, regulation, or rule of law is satisfied by an electronic record that complies with paragraph (1).

(4) Checks

If a statute, regulation, or other rule of law requires the retention of a check, that requirement is satisfied by retention of an electronic record of the information on the front and back of the check in accordance with paragraph (1).

(e) Accuracy and ability to retain contracts and other records

Notwithstanding subsection (a) of this section, if a statute, regulation, or other rule of law requires that a contract or other record relating to a transaction in or affecting interstate or foreign commerce be in writing, the legal effect, validity, or enforceability of an electronic record of such contract or other record may be denied if such electronic record is not in a form that is capable of being retained and accurately reproduced for later reference by all parties or persons who are entitled to retain the contract or other record.

(f) Proximity

Nothing in this subchapter affects the proximity required by any statute, regulation, or other rule of law with respect to any warning, notice, disclosure, or other record required to be posted, displayed, or publicly affixed.

(g) Notarization and acknowledgment

If a statute, regulation, or other rule of law requires a signature or record relating to a transaction in or affecting interstate or foreign commerce to be notarized, acknowledged, verified, or made under oath, that requirement is satisfied if the electronic signature of the person authorized to perform those acts, together with all other information required to be included by other applicable statute, regulation, or rule of law, is attached to or logically associated with the signature or record.

(h) Electronic agents

A contract or other record relating to a transaction in or affecting interstate or foreign commerce may not be denied legal effect, validity, or enforceability solely because its formation, creation, or delivery involved the action of one or more electronic agents so long as the action of any such electronic agent is legally attributable to the person to be bound.

(i) Insurance

It is the specific intent of the Congress that this subchapter and subchapter II of this chapter apply to the business of insurance.

(j) Insurance agents and brokers

An insurance agent or broker acting under the direction of a party that enters into a contract by means of an electronic record or electronic signature may not be held liable for any deficiency in the electronic procedures agreed to by the parties under that contract if—

   (1) the agent or broker has not engaged in negligent, reckless, or intentional tortious conduct;

   (2) the agent or broker was not involved in the development or establishment of such electronic procedures; and

   (3) the agent or broker did not deviate from such procedures

Glossary

A

accredited investors   Investors who are either rich enough to afford to take risks on exempt transactions, either because they meet certain net worth requirements or because they are financial institutions, or investors who have access to the type of information that is available in a registration statement because they are corporate insiders.

act of interstate commerce   Goods that are moving from one state to another cannot be taxed by a state based on the act of transporting the goods from one state to another.

act of state   The legal principle whereby courts in one country will not review the legality of actions of a government from another country.

additional terms   Terms in the acceptance that are not in the offer and add to the terms in the offer.

adjudication   The process of resolving a legal dispute.

administrative agencies   An inclusive term for government agencies, bureaus, commissions, and boards created by the legislative or executive branches of government that administer and enforce the statutes that regulate society and the economy.

administrative law   Rules and regulations created by administrative agencies that (1) enable the agencies to regulate business and society in accordance with statutes of the legislative body and policies of the chief executive and (2) provide for regulation of their own behavior.

administrative law judge (ALJ)   An agency employee who serves as a judge in suits brought by the employing agency against a business.

Administrative Procedures Act   The part of administrative law that defines the procedure an administrative agency must follow to enact new regulations.

adversarial system   A judicial system, like that in the United States, that permits each side in litigation to have its best factual and/or expert opinion case presented to a court in the belief that courts (juries) will be able to determine truth and deliver justice with vigorous case presentations by both sides.

affirmative action   Mechanisms implemented to promote diversity (racial, gender, etc.).

affirmative defenses   Affirmative defenses are those that rely on facts or conditions that absolve a defendant of liability, even if the facts alleged in a complaint are true.

after-acquired evidence   Evidence acquired after the point in time when an employment decision has been made.

agency   A relationship, based on consent, in which one party (the agent) agrees to act under the direction of and on behalf of another party (the principal).

alternative dispute resolution (ADR)   Means for resolving legal disputes without pursuing litigation remedies in the traditional judicial system. Negotiation, arbitration, and mediation are examples of ADR.

ambient air quality standards   The EPA establishes and enforces primary and secondary AAQSs. Together, the primary and secondary standards form the NAAQSs, established by the EPA to set legal limits on air pollution, based on human health impacts.

annual percentage rate (APR)   The yearly interest rate on a credit agreement, calculated in a standardized fashion, that must be disclosed to a borrower under the Truth in Lending Act.

answer   A defendant's response to a complaint naming the respondent as a (the) defendant in a lawsuit. Answers are often accompanied by motions filed with the court.

antitrust law   Law that protects commerce from illegal restraints on trade that businesses may impose, attempting to assure the public of access to competitive pricing and quality.

apparent authority   The authority a third party, acting as a reasonable person, would believe an apparent agent would possess in light of available information.

appeals   Requests to a higher court that a case tried in a lower court be reviewed and its outcome altered, based on the claim that errors of law were committed in the trial court.

apportionment   The principle of tax law that requires states to allocate tax levies in a manner that does not discriminate against interstate commerce and businesses.

arbitrary and capricious   Actions of administrative agencies, including promulgation of rules and regulations, can be challenged if these regulations are without technical or scientific foundation.

arbitration   A process through which generally binding resolutions of disputes are imposed by disinterested third parties (not courts).

Article 2 (of the UCC)   Deals with the sale of tangible goods that are moveable.

as is   Refers to the sale of a good in which the seller is not making any guarantees about the quality of the good. Caveat emptor (buyer beware) is the rule of law that applies.

attractive nuisance   A man-made structure that attracts attention (as would a backyard swimming pool) and may cause injury.

attribution procedure   Means of identifying and attributing to a specific party a specific electronic event, such as an online purchase.

authenticate   Verify the identity of a party authorizing an electronic agreement and then authorize the electronic event.

B

bailment   A short-term rental of personal property.

bait advertising   A scheme in which one product is advertised at an attractive price (the "bait") followed, when a customer arrives and asks for the product, by an attempt to "switch" the customer to an alternative, higher-priced product, generally accompanied by disparagement of the advertised product or an out-of-stock claim.

bid-rigging   Price-fixing by supposed competing firms, incorporated into the "bids" they submit for contracts to be awarded to the low bidder(s).

bilateral contract   A contract formed when a promise is given in exchange for a promise.

Bill of Rights   Citizen protections and fundamentally important personal rights that are contained in the first 10 amendments to the U.S. Constitution.

biometric identification   Scientific means of identifying an individual by unalterable characteristics such as fingerprints, voice patterns, retina images, and so forth.

blue sky   A generic term that refers to state securities laws. Around the turn of the last century (1900), several states justified regulation of securities because some of their citizens had invested in companies that had no assets backing up their values, other than the "blue sky."

board of directors   Stockholder-elected board that selects a corporations' chief executive officer and oversees corporate policy.

bona fide purchaser for value   A person who pays money or property for a good in good faith believing the seller is the owner of the goods.

bonds   Debt instruments that indicate long-term corporate indebtedness. A bondholder is entitled to interest payments during the life of the bond and the principal value of the bond at maturity.

boxtop licenses or agreements   Intended contract agreements between vendors and customers, with the intended agreement printed on the product box or on documents inside the box. Agreement is authorized by opening the box, barring immediate action to return subject product(s) and take such further actions as are required for avoiding being bound by the agreement.

breach of contract   Under the UCC, if the goods delivered deviate in any way from what is called for in the contract, it is a breach of contract.

bricks-and-mortar (B&M) companies   Traditional companies, the fixed assets of which are predominantly in the form of buildings and fixed equipment.

bubble program   A program that allows firms to establish new plants or factories in nonattainment areas by conceptually combining all of the pollution produced by a firm's factories and requiring that there be no net increase in pollution as a result of a new plant or factory.

business courts   Specialized courts that have subject matter jurisdiction only over "business" cases.

business necessity   An advantage to a business that makes the business more efficient as a consequence of reliance on what is deemed the business necessity (often a screening test in an employment situation).

C

capacity (to contract)   Capacity is required to have legal standing to enter into a valid contract. Capacity requires competency and adult age.

Carnivore   An FBI software program used to snoop into e-mail and other Internet communications.

categorical imperative   Immanuel Kant insisted that any proposed ethical rule be (1) universalizable and (2) reversible in the sense that it applies equally to the person proposing the rule. Widespread adherence would dramatically reduce the need for administrative agencies.

caveat emptor   The Latin for "buyer beware," it means the seller is not guaranteeing the quality of the goods. If there is a defect in the good(s), the buyer bears all liability for not inspecting the good and recognizing the defect.

cease and desist order   An order prohibiting activities that have been deemed illegal.

certification and collective marks   Trademarks licensed by third-party certifiers of quality such as Underwriters Laboratories or marks that members of associations license to members to display.

certification authorities   Agents that serve as electronic notaries, providing identifications of parties engaged in electronic agreements.

choice of forum clause   Clause within a contract in which the contracting parties agree on which courts have jurisdiction to resolve disputes.

choice of law   Identification of what specific law will be applied in the event of a need for dispute resolution.

choice of law clauses   Clauses that specify which substantive law will be used in the event of a dispute between the contracting parties.

civil law   Public and private laws dealing with public and private rights, as opposed to criminal actions. Redress usually involves monetary awards. This is the predominant system of law used by countries in Europe. Originally associated with Roman law, civil law relies much more heavily on codes rather than precedent, as is the standard in countries that follow common law systems.

clickwrap agreements   Intended contract agreements between vendors (often software producers) and customers, authenticated by mouse clicks.

Code of Federal Regulations   A codification of the general and permanent rules published in the *Federal Register* by the executive departments and agencies of the federal government.

comity   The legal principle that accords deference to the laws and legal actions of the courts of other countries.

Commerce Clause   Article I, Section 8 of the U.S. Constitution gives Congress and the federal government the power to regulate interstate and foreign commerce between the states and among the Indian tribes.

commercial impracticability   A contingency takes place, the nonoccurrence of which was a basic assumption of the parties to the contract, or the promisor is, in good faith, complying with a changed law.

common law   Law developed by "court" decision rather than by legislative creation. Early U.S. common law was based on English custom and judicial decision, with continuing development from U.S. court decisions.

comparative negligence   Doctrine under which liability (responsibility for damages) is allocated between plaintiff and defendant in accordance with their relative responsibilities for the injury suffered.

compensatory damages   A damage award intended to compensate for the value of the injury incurred from a tort.

complaint   The first document filed to initiate a lawsuit. The complaint provides notice to the opposing side in litigation that they have been sued and indicates what will be claimed in the ensuing litigation.

complaint procedure   Procedure and/or mechanisms that allow employee complaints, especially of sexual harassment or of a hostile work environment, to be communicated to management (and not just the complainer's supervisor).

confusingly similar trademarks   Two trademarks so similar that large numbers of customers would be confused by the usage of both.

consent is given   Fourth Amendment protections do not prevent police searches or seizures if those searches are consented to by the owner or lawful possessor of the property.

consequential damages   Damages recoverable in court as a result of a breach of contract that the seller should have known about and that could not be avoided by the buyer through cover. Also, damages that do not occur immediately or directly from a contract breach but may be reasonably foreseeable as occurring subsequently "as a consequence" of the breach. Lost profits are a frequently claimed form of consequential damages.

consideration   This is the thing or act of value provided in exchange for a promise, which is required for a valid contract to be formed.

constitutional law   At the federal level, law based on the U.S. Constitution; at the state level, law based on state constitutions.

consumer protection law   Body of law intended to protect consumers in their ordinary usage of financial institutions, their interactions with other sales vendors, the privacy of their records, and their use of computers.

contract   An agreement that can be enforced by law. Not all agreements are contracts.

contributory negligence   Doctrine under which a defendant is immune from liability if a plaintiff contributed to any degree to his or her own injury.

convention   A treaty sponsored by an organization such as the United Nations.

Convention on Contracts for the International Sale of Goods   A United Nations–sponsored convention that establishes a uniform law of contracts when there is a dispute between companies located in different countries and there is no agreed-upon choice of law clause in the contracts between them.

cookies   Small software programs, installed on browsers' hard drives by websites they visit, that allow data to be gathered by the website on the computer users' other web destinations.

copyright   A grant to authors of exclusive rights to reproduce and distribute a protected work.

copyrights, patents, trade secrets, and trademarks   Mechanisms for keeping intellectual property safe from use by others so that the creator of intellectual property can be rewarded for his or her creative efforts.

corporation   Form of business in which management (control) is separate from ownership, with stockholder owners free of personal liability for corporate obligations.

cost–benefit analysis   Analysis of the overall values of costs and benefits associated with a proposed course of action. For some federal agencies, favorable conclusions from a cost–benefit analysis are required to justify the implementation of new regulations.

cost-justification defense   Defense against charges that prices charged to some (usually large) customers are too low, based on a showing that the lower prices charged are justified by the lower unit costs of serving those customers.

counterclaims   Claims filed by a defendant in a civil suit claiming wrongdoing and resulting liability (to the defendant) on the part of the party who had filed the original complaint against the defendant.

course of dealing   Prior conduct between the parties in previous contracts that can be used to define open terms in a contract.

court-annexed arbitration   Court-ordered arbitration that, while not binding, results in the settlement of a large proportion of cases.

courts of appeals   Courts above trial courts to which a trial court's decision can be appealed if the appellant believes the trial court committed reversible error in its application of procedural law.

cover   A buyer who has received notice of breach of contract from a seller can go in good faith out on the market and secure substitute goods.

criminal law   Law that deals with crimes—i.e., with wrongful acts that violate society's rules for which criminal punishments, including jail or even execution, are required.

cross-examination   The questioning of witnesses by the opposing party's attorney(s) for the purpose of undermining a witness's direct testimony.

cryptography   Mechanisms for translating messages into coded form, to prevent their use by unauthorized recipients, while allowing authorized recipients to decode and read the original messages.

cybermedicine   The practice of medicine over the Internet, where the doctor and patient are physically separate but generally have electronic communication.

cyberstalking   Use of electronic means to stalk a person in an intimidating manner. To be illegal, most jurisdictions require a physical threat to accompany the cyberstalking.

D

damage awards   Monetary awards provided through trial, intended to compensate the recipient for economic injury sustained as the result of wrongdoing by a defendant.

deceptive trade practices   Business practices that are likely to mislead the reasonable consumer with the deception likely to affect a consumer decision.

deed   A document of title that describes real property and identifies its owner(s).

defamation   A false statement, spoken or written, that causes harm.

deposition   Sworn testimony of parties to lawsuits or witnesses, taken before trial.

derivative works   Adaptations or transformations of copyrighted works.

design defect   A product defect that results from faulty design.

destination contract   Exists when the contract does specify the location where goods are to be shipped.

dietary supplements   May be products that are pharmaceutically active, such as herbal remedies, but that avoid the rigorous testing required of drugs by being classified as dietary supplements.

different terms   Terms in the acceptance that differ from terms in the offer.

direct testimony   For the plaintiff, evidence provided by testimony of plaintiffs and witnesses for plaintiffs in response to questions asked by plaintiff's attorney or attorneys. For the defendant, evidence provided by testimony of the defendant and witnesses for the defendant in response to questions asked by defendant's attorney(s).

disabled   Physically or mentally impaired in a way and to a degree that qualifies for protection under the Americans with Disabilities Act.

discovery   Part of the litigation process in which the plaintiff(s) and defendant(s) obtain information both from each other and possibly from third parties who can provide information relevant to the issues to be tried.

discriminates against interstate commerce   An unconstitutional state law that taxes, erects a barrier to, or otherwise disadvantages out-of-state businesses and goods relative to in-state businesses and goods.

disparate impact   Effects of policies that affect (impact) protected classes differently from others, which are illegal even if the intent of the policies is not discriminatory.

disparate treatment   A specific difference in treatment of individuals in different classes that violates a protected class antidiscrimination requirement. Paying lower wages to females than to male workers in identical jobs involves disparate treatment if no applicable exception applies.

double taxation   Exposure of corporate earnings to taxation once at the corporate level and again at the individual level.

due diligence defense   The due diligence defense is effective when the defendant in a Section 11 claim is able to show that he or she conducted an independent investigation of the statements made in the registration statement and was unable to detect an error.

due diligence inspections   To qualify for the innocent landowner defense, the landowner must be able to prove that, before purchasing a tract of land, he or she was reasonably diligent in inspecting the land for possible hazardous waste but did not find any.

Due Process Clause   A basic principle in the American legal system that requires fairness in the government's dealing with persons. In this context, courts have interpreted the Due Process Clause to require that out-of-state businesses must receive some benefit from a state before a state court or taxing authority can exert jurisdiction over the business.

duress   Force, the threat of force, or use of some other form of pressure to induce a person to act in a way that he or she would not choose in the absence of the duress.

E

economic strikes   Strikes whose primary aim is to improve wages.

EDGAR   A creation of the SEC. The acronym stands for Electronic Database Gathering, Analysis, and Retrieval. EDGAR enables firms to post prospectuses online and investors to access those prospectuses.

electronic agents   Combination of software and computer hardware that engages in transactions, including the execution of contracts, on behalf of a principal (typically, a corporation).

electronic data interchange (EDI)   Electronic data interchange, as the label indicates, is the electronic exchange of business information in a structured format. Commonly, EDI is used to coordinate activities involving two businesses.

electronic road shows   Electronic selling materials that firms provide, in addition to prospectuses, used during the waiting period between the filing of the registration statement and the date when securities can be sold.

eminent domain   The power of government to take private land for public use upon paying fair compensation.

employment at will   Employment standard, in the absence of an employment contract, under which employers may fire and employees may quit without good cause—simply acting on the desire to take the action.

enabling statute   A statute that authorizes the creation of and, hence, gives power to an administrative agency.

endangered species   Species of animals that are in danger of becoming extinct, as determined by the Secretary of the Interior pursuant to the Endangered Species Act.

environmental impact statement (EIS)   Analysis required whenever a federal government project is likely to have a substantial impact on the environment.

Environmental Protection Agency (EPA)   The federal agency charged with the lion's share of responsibility for protecting the environment. The EPA enforces the important federal legislation dealing with the environment.

equal protection   The Fourteenth Amendment guarantees that citizens will be treated equally under the law. Governments must have strong justifications for actions that treat people differently based on race or gender.

equitable remedy   A court remedy, seeking fairness, when monetary awards are not adequate to achieve that goal.

E-SIGN Act   A federal statute that seeks to provide uniform legal treatment of contracts formed electronically, using specified electronic methods of authentication.

essential facilities   Portals, typically in processing, distribution, or transmission facilities, through which products must flow to be sold.

estoppel   Principle under which a party is barred from denying or alleging specific facts, based on prior conduct and/or representations.

ethics   The study and philosophy of human conduct with an emphasis on right and wrong.

European Court of Justice   Enforces EU law among member nations. In cases involving EU law, the ECJ will take appeals from the national courts of member states. It serves as the final arbiter of EU law.

European Union   The most important regional association of nations and the one that has gone the farthest in substituting international law and authority for national sovereignty.

exceeded its authority   An administrative agency exceeds its authority when a court determines, after examining the enabling statute, that the agency is not empowered by the enabling statute to perform the challenged action, including the enactment of regulations outside the authority given to the agency.

excessive burden on interstate commerce   An unconstitutional state law that treats in-state and out-of-state businesses equally, but places an excessive burden on interstate commerce.

exclusive dealing contract   Agreements between a manufacturer and the distributors or retailers who sell its products prohibiting the sales of products of a rival manufacturer by those resellers.

executed contract   A contract under which the duties called for from the contracting parties have been fully performed.

executive   The branch of government that is headed by the president or governor and enforces laws.

executive, legislative, and judicial branches   The three branches of the federal government, each of which has its own duties and powers. The legislative branch (Congress) writes our laws, the judicial branch (courts) interprets laws, and the executive branch (headed by the president) handles the government's administrative tasks including the enforcement of laws.

executory contract   A contract that calls for future performance, not yet completed.

exempt securities   Securities that are exempt from the requirements of the 1933 Act to prepare a registration statement for the SEC and from the requirement of giving prospectuses to investors.

exempt transactions   Sales of securities to the investing public that are exempt from most of the requirements of public offerings as set by the 1933 Act, such as a registration statement and prospectus.

express authority   Clear authority, through written or verbal communication, for an agent to act on behalf of a principal.

express contract   A contract based on an explicit agreement, written or oral, between contracting parties.

express warranties   Promises made about the quality of goods.

F

fair use   Unauthorized use of copyrighted material for teaching, research, criticism, and so forth that is not an infringement.

family car doctrine   Principle that imposes an agency relationship between parents and children drivers by which parents are made financially responsible for torts committed by those children when driving.

fanciful marks   Trademarks that have no direct functional or descriptive relationship with a product subject to the mark.

federal district courts   District courts are trial courts in the federal court system. As trial courts, district courts serve as the finders of fact in federal court cases.

Federal Insecticide, Fungicide, and Rodenticide Act (FIFRA)   The act of Congress that enables the EPA to regulate and, if necessary, ban pesticides that pose an unreasonable risk to humans and the environment.

Federal Privacy Act   A right, with some significant exceptions, that citizens have against government disclosures of information collected about them by government agencies unless the citizen has given permission for the disclosure.

Federal Register   Federal publication in which all changes in administrative agency regulations must be published.

federalism   Our system of shared government between the federal government and the states. Powers not delegated to the federal government are reserved to the states and citizens.

fiduciary duties   Duties owed to principals by agents, including the duties to provide best-effort, diligent performance on behalf of the principal; provide notice of material occurrences; avoid conflicts of interest; obey instructions from the principal; and provide accurate accounting of financial flow.

fiduciary relationship   The relationship that exists when one party agrees to perform prescribed duties for the benefit of another. This relationship imposes responsibilities or duties on the party (often a trustee) who has agreed to the assignment.

file wrapper estoppel   Applied in patent infringement cases, doctrine that prevents a patent holder from enlarging the scope of claims for a patent in order to establish an infringement claim when a court finds substantial differences between a patented asset and another "competing" asset.

First Amendment   Guarantees, with some exceptions, nongovernmental interference with freedom of expression and religion.

forum selection   The choice of the location in which actions to resolve disputes, including arbitration, will take place.

Fourth Amendment   Guarantees protection from searches and seizures by the government that are not accompanied by a search warrant based on a showing of probable cause.

franchise agreement   A contract that spells out the details of the agreement between a franchisor and a franchisee—for example, between Ford Motor Company and a local Ford dealership.

fraudulent misrepresentation (fraud)   A deliberate misrepresentation of material facts, knowingly provided with the intent of deceiving another and in a form that a reasonable person could rely on to his or her detriment, in order to gain an advantage.

free rider   An economic agent (e.g., a company) that benefits from the socially desirable actions of others while not being a participant in those actions and, hence, avoiding the accompanying costs. Also, a problem that exists when a person is able to receive an economic benefit without paying for it.

Freedom of Information Act (FOIA)   A right, with some significant exceptions, that citizens have to examine the work of government agencies.

full and limited warranties   Alternative standards for the legal warranty obligations of product suppliers. Most warranties are limited, as the requirements of full warranties are much more stringent.

G

gap-filler   Terms in the UCC that are part of a contract if there is no written term in the contract, or the term is left "open."

generic marks   Names or other marks that have come to refer to a class of products (e.g., aspirin) rather than to a product of a particular provider.

good   Under the UCC, goods are all things that are tangible and moveable.

good faith   Merchants are required under the UCC to be honest in fact in their conduct and transactions.

Government in Sunshine Acts   A right, with some significant exceptions, that citizens have to be informed in advance of the agenda of meetings held by government officials.

government regulation   Government establishes laws in the form of statutes or regulations from administrative agencies that define legal and illegal conduct for the entities being regulated, generally businesses.

government takings   An action of the government in which private property is taken from a citizen.

H

hacker   The *Net Dictionary* defines a hacker as "[a]n expert programmer who likes to spend a lot of time figuring out the finer details of computer systems or networks, as opposed to those who learn only the minimum necessary." Hackers are synonymous with those who gain unauthorized access to inner workings of computer files.

hazardous air pollutants   The EPA is required by the CAA to identify air pollutants that can cause serious illness or death in humans. Through February 2002, the EPA has identified 188 hazardous air pollutants.

hazardous wastes   Solid wastes that, alone or in combination with other substances, have the potential to seriously harm or kill people when improperly stored, treated, transported, or disposed of.

Herfindahl-Hirshman Index (HHI)   Measure of industry concentration used by the U.S. Department of Justice in determining what proposed mergers will likely be challenged.

horizontal agreements   Agreements between or among firms at the same level of an industry.

hostile work environment   A work environment that unreasonably interferes with an individual's work performance or one that is intimidating, hostile, or offensive to a reasonable person.

hung jury   A jury that, based on the evidence presented in trial, is unable to agree on a verdict.

I

identification   Takes place under the UCC when a good is in existence and can be distinguished from other goods.

identity theft   The appropriation of one's personal information—name, address, credit card account number and so forth—to commit theft or fraud. Identity theft occurs when a criminal appropriates personally identifying information and uses that information to commit crimes through impersonation.

illegal subjects   It is illegal to consider subjects in collective bargaining such as secondary boycotts, closed shops, and refusals to enforce the civil rights laws.

illusory promise   Agreements that appear to contain consideration but that, in fact, do not because the promises do not impose legal detriments on the promisors.

implied authority   The right of an agent to act on behalf of a principal with all the ramifications of agency status, inferred from prior conduct and/or representations and by what is customary within the industry.

implied contract   A contract formed in part or in whole based on the conduct of the parties.

implied employment contract   An enforceable employment contract formed on the basis of conduct. Manuals, other company documents, and statements of company managers often become part of an implied employment contract.

implied warranties   Under the UCC, goods sold are subject to implied warranties unless those warranties are expressly disclaimed.

implied warranty of merchantability   Unless disclaimed, it is an implied term in the contract that the goods sold are fit for the ordinary uses for which such goods are used.

impossibility   Condition or situation that relieves a party to a contract from performance of the duties called for in the contract when, through no fault of the contracting parties, performance would be objectively impossible or highly impracticable.

incidental damages   The costs incurred by the nonbreaching party in dealing with costs attributable to the breach of contract and the costs of the nonbreaching party having to go to the market an extra time.

independent administrative agencies   These agencies are independent in the sense that they are headed by commissioners who have fixed terms and do not serve at the pleasure of the president. Technically, these agencies are not part of the executive branch of government but rather set policy independently based on their interpretation of the enabling statute that created the agency.

independent contractor   A person who contracts to perform a task but maintains autonomy as to performance of that task.

independent creation   An effective defense in an infringement case based on the claim that the other user of a copyrighted creation independently developed the same creation.

injunction   A court order commanding that a party do something, stop doing something, or not do something that could cause irreversible harm to the other party.

innocent landowner defense   This defense is effective if the defendant in a suit brought by the EPA for contributions to clean up hazardous waste can show that no discharge of hazardous waste took place during his or her ownership of the land.

insider trading   Purchases or sales of securities by corporate insiders, tippees, or others restricted from trading while in possession of material information that is not publicly known.

insiders   Traditionally, insiders include corporate officers, directors, and greater-than-10-percent shareholders. More recently, the term has been expanded to include key employees such as legal, technical, and financial staff.

intellectual property (IP)   Property, often in the form of ideas or knowledge, that can be of great value. Unlike land or a building, intellectual property is an asset that has no physical (tangible) existence. It is the product of a creative (intellectual) process.

intentional tort   An injurious wrongful action in which the perpetrator of the injury engaged in the act with intent, even though the injury was not intended.

intermediate scrutiny   Courts require that, to be legal, actions of state governments that differentiate between the sexes must contribute to the achievement of a substantial governmental objective.

International Court of Justice   Also known as the world court, the ICJ resolves disputes among nations, but is limited to those cases for which both nations agree to abide by the judgment of the ICJ.

Internet Tax Freedom Act   This act of Congress imposes a tax moratorium on the imposition of new Internet taxes by states and prohibits discriminatory and multiple taxation of the same Internet transaction by states. State taxes that were in force before October 1998 when the ITFA was enacted can continue to be collected.

interpretative regulation   Rulings or published discussions from agencies that indicate how the issuing administrative agency interprets the statutes and substantive regulations it oversees.

interrogatory   Written questions submitted to opposing parties or witnesses in litigation, requiring written answers sworn to by the party answering.

Interstate Commerce Clause   The authority within the U.S. Constitution for the federal government to regulate interstate commerce. The Interstate Commerce Clause is also the authority for courts to strike down state laws, including tax laws, that discriminate against or place an undue burden on interstate commerce.

irrevocable (offers)   A written offer by a merchant that cannot be withdrawn during the period of time the offer states it will remain open.

ISPs   Internet service providers such as AOL, Yahoo!, a university Web-server system, and so forth that are generally treated like *distributors* of publications rather than as *publishers*.

J

joint and several liability   Parties that are jointly and severally liable are each liable to plaintiffs for the entire amount of the damages, though those that are jointly and severally liable may sue each other for contributions.

joint venture   A general partnership with a limited life, formed for a specific purpose by two or more companies. This combination of businesses is "joined" to accomplish specific tasks, such as conducting a research project, with the combination generally limited in duration.

judicial   The branch of government charged with presiding over trials and interpreting and applying laws to particular cases.

judicial review   Occurs when judges, typically at the federal court of appeals level, assess appeals from final decisions of administrative agencies as to the constitutionality or legality of agency actions.

jurisdiction   Authority over the persons and subject matter of litigation, entitling a court to hear and adjudicate a specific action.

justiciable   A conflict that is real and of sufficient consequence to be triable. Courts refuse to hear cases that are trivial, moot, political, or merely hypothetical.

L

law   A collection of enforceable rules of conduct, aimed at controlling, or at least placing acceptable limits on, human behavior.

Learned Hand test   A test for identifying a defective product design that involves comparing the costs imposed on society by a particular design to the costs of an alternative and presumably superior (safety) design.

legal detriment   Legal detriment is a real burden that qualifies as consideration provided by a party to a contract. A legal detriment may involve a promise to pay money, to deliver services or products, or to refrain from certain actions (such as suing another designated party).

legal remedy   A court remedy generally providing monetary compensation.

legislative   The law-making branch of government that is composed of elected representatives: senators and members of the House of Representatives.

limitations of liability   Clauses that limit the amount of damages a buyer can be awarded for breach of a warranty.

limited partners   Investors in a limited liability partnership (LLP) who, unlike general partners, are not personally liable for obligations of the business they have invested in.

liquidated damages   A damage amount, agreed to within a contract by the contracting parties, that represents a reasonable value for a damage award in the event of a contract breach.

litigation   The processes through which the legal system is used to resolve legal disputes.

lockouts   A tactic used by management when a strike is imminent. A lockout can be legal as long as the purpose is not to break the union.

long-arm statutes   State laws that allow states to exercise jurisdiction over nonresidents if certain qualifying conditions, usually the existence of minimum contacts, are met.

M

mandatory arbitration   Mandatory arbitration is the acceptable route for dispute resolution (at least initially) when public policy prohibits specific parties from taking their disputes directly to courts.

mandatory bargaining subjects   Wages and other terms and conditions of employment that must be set in collective bargaining agreements if there is a union representing workers.

mandatory retirement   A policy that sets a maximum age for retirement from a company.

manifest   A document that is required by EPA whenever a company subject to the jurisdiction of the EPA stores, treats, transports, or disposes of hazardous waste.

manufacturing defect   A product defect that generally is the result of a mistake in the manufacturing process.

market failure   Natural free-market results that are suboptimal and can be improved by some form of government regulation.

market share   Percent of sales in a defined market accounted for by a firm.

material breach   Failure of a party to a contract, when there is no legal excuse for that failure, to perform his or her duties under the contract so that the essential purpose of the contract is unfulfilled.

material misstatements or omissions   "Mistakes" in the registration statement that are likely to affect the purchase decisions of reasonably prudent investors.

mediator   A neutral third party used by parties seeking an out-of-court resolution of a dispute. The mediator's role is that of facilitating settlement and fashioning an agreement that the parties to the conflict are willing to accept.

meeting-competition defense   Defense against charges of predatorily low prices based on a showing that the low prices were necessary to effectively compete.

merger   A combination of two or more firms, with the merging firms becoming one firm.

minimum contacts   Indicators of whether a nonresident (to a state) firm has taken advantage of the benefits of having a presence of some type within a host state, enabling the host state to exert jurisdiction over the nonresident firm.

minimum wage   A legal requirement that employers must pay employees at least a minimum wage—that is, a minimum rate per hour—as defined by the Fair Labor Standards Act. The minimum wage has been adjusted upward numerous times since it began in 1938.

minitrial   A private (out-of-court), structured process in which each party to a dispute presents its "case," along with supporting information, before a neutral third party in the pursuit of a settlement without going to a court trial.

misappropriaters   Consultants, reporters, attorneys, and others who are entrusted with confidential information but make use of that information for their own purposes such as engaging in securities transactions.

misconduct   Willful or wanton conduct on the part of an employee, such as fighting or stealing from the employer, that results in termination of employment and disqualification for unemployment benefits.

misuse   Use of a product for purposes for which it is not designed.

mitigation of damages   Actions taken, which are reasonable, to offset or minimize damages incurred due to a contract breach.

mixed motive discrimination cases   Cases brought in situations where employers make employment decisions on more than one basis, with some consideration given to illegal motives and some to legal motives.

mobile sources   Sources of pollution that can move. Automobiles are the main mobile source of pollution.

monopoly   A firm has a monopoly if it is the only seller in a market.

monopoly power   Ability possessed by a firm to be a price maker (to set prices charged) rather than being a price taker (unable to sell at a price higher than the "competitive" market price).

motion for a judgment notwithstanding the verdict (J.n.o.v.)   A request of the court, provided by either party, for rejecting a jury verdict and deciding the case in the favor of the party making the request.

motion for summary judgment   A request (motion) of the court that it render a decision without completing the trial process, generally submitted based on the pleadings and other evidence not in the pleadings when no material facts are in dispute.

motions   Request made to the court by the parties involved in litigation that are ruled on by the court, not by jurors.

motions for a directed verdict   Request (motions) to the court (the judge) to issue a verdict, based on information available to the court, without allowing the jury to deliberate or reach a jury verdict.

motions for judgment on the pleadings   Requests (motions) by either party to a lawsuit requesting that the court resolve the legal issue being contested on the basis of the information provided in the pleadings, without proceeding to trial. This can be accomplished if there are no facts that are in dispute in the case.

mutuality of interest   A concept the NLRB uses to determine which groups of workers belong in the same bargaining unit. If a group of workers wants a certification election and has a mutuality of interest, then the NLRB will designate the group as a bargaining unit.

N

natural monopoly   A market/industry with characteristics that make provision of a product-service more efficient with one "monopoly" provider than would be the case with several "competing" providers.

Necessary and Proper Clause   Provision in the U.S. Constitution that grants to Congress the broad-based authority to use all means that are "necessary and proper" to perform its prescribed functions.

nexus tests   Tests that courts use to determine if connections that out-of-state businesses have with a state are sufficient for a state to exert jurisdiction over the business.

nonattainment areas   Areas that are not in compliance with NAAQSs. In these areas, states, supervised by the EPA, must devise SIP plans to reduce pollution and bring air quality into compliance with NAAQSs.

noncompete clause   A contract agreement that prohibits an employee from going to work in a competing business for a specified time span.

nonpoint source   Water pollution that originates from land, wind, mines, floods, and sewage systems that is not associated with a particular point source.

nonstatutory subject matter   Things that cannot be patented, which, most notably, are things that can be discovered (laws of nature, naturally occurring substances, and so forth) as opposed to invented.

North American Free Trade Agreement   An agreement between Canada, Mexico, and the United States that is working toward abolition of trade barriers among the members.

novation   Substitution, by agreement, of a new contract for a previous contract, generally with the substitution of a new party to the contract in place of a previous contracting party.

nuisance   At common law, a nuisance exists when actions of a defendant substantially and unreasonably interfere with another's enjoyment of his or her property.

nutrition labels   Product labels that provide detailed information on nutrient content.

O

obscenity   Illegal, sexually oriented material that is not constitutionally protected.

offset policy   A policy devised by the EPA for allowing new plants and factories in areas that are not in compliance with NAAQSs. Basically, new sources of pollution must be more than offset by reductions in the area of the same kinds of pollution.

oligopoly   An oligopoly exists if there are only a "few" (e.g., two, three, or four) sellers in a market.

online dispute resolution (ODR)   Resolution of dispute in cyberspace that does not involve court litigation, but instead relies upon settlement, mediation, and arbitration services.

open term   Term in a contract about which nothing is stated. If the term is open, a UCC gap-filler will be supplied.

opportunity costs   The cost of lost or forgone opportunities to utilize resources in alternative, potentially very productive, ways.

opt in   System that allows a target to choose whether to be included or not, prior to an action involving the target.

opt out   System that places the burden on a target (of advertising, information distribution, etc.) to ask to be removed from a target list.

output contracts   Contracts in which the buyer agrees to purchase all the output of the seller during a period of time.

overly broad   A term of art in freedom of expression cases. A restriction on freedom of expression will not be upheld if the courts find that there are less restrictive ways of preventing the harm said to accompany the speech at issue.

P

parity with paper   With "parity," electronic records will be treated the same, and be just as legally binding, as paper records.

parol evidence rule   Court rule that excludes evidence on parties' prior or current discussions, negotiations, statements, or oral arguments if that evidence is at odds with the express terms of the particular contested contract.

partnership   A business jointly owned by two or more people.

patent examiner   An employee of the Patent and Trademark Office (PTO) who reviews (examines) applications for patents.

patent infringement   The acquisition or use of a patent, without permission, by a party other than the patent holder.

per se rule   Antitrust standard under which particular acts, such as agreeing to fix prices, are illegal as a matter of law.

perfect tender rule   Sellers are required to deliver goods that conform perfectly to what is called for in the contract for sale.

permissive subjects of bargaining   Topics that can be considered in collective bargaining agreements but are not mandatory. The use of union labels on products is a permissive subject of bargaining.

permit system   Under the Clean Water Act, the discharge of any pollutant into navigable waters from a point source is a violation unless the polluter has a permit issued by the EPA and is in compliance with the requirements of the permit.

personal injury   Loss of an eye, a limb, or some other serious and even debilitating injury due to the wrongful act of another.

piercing the corporate veil   Action, with a court disregarding the limited liability protection associated with corporations, that makes a shareholder liable for debts of a corporation owned by the shareholder that exceed the assets of the corporation.

pleadings   The complaint, answer, and accompanying documents in litigation. The pleadings document the claims, alleged facts, and defenses to be offered in trial.

point source   Any ditch, pipe, or channel from which pollution is emitted into a navigable body of water.

pornography   In this book, pornography is sexually oriented, adult material that is constitutionally protected. It may be illegal, however, to expose children to pornography, depending on the situation.

potentially responsible persons   Persons that are potentially liable for the cleanup costs of hazardous waste dumps, including generators, transporters, landowners, and dumpsite operators.

precedent A case decision that is used to determine decisions in subsequent cases that have similar sets of facts.

preemption Takes place when a whole area of law is occupied by federal law and any state laws in the area are unconstitutional.

preponderance of the evidence Evidence standard under which judgment is to be determined based on whether a claim is *more likely than not* to be valid.

prevention of significant deterioration (PSD) areas Areas in compliance with NAAQSs but in which the EPA will enact and enforce regulations to prevent a significant deterioration of air quality.

principal An employer, business, client, or other party who engages or hires another party (an agent) to perform designated duties.

private law Law governing disputes between citizens.

private placement An exempt transaction that qualifies for its exemption from the registration requirements of a public offering because it does not involve sales to the general public.

privileged speech Speech that is immune to defamation claims, such as statements made by lawyers, judges, and legislators in the course of their work in courts and in legislative debates.

privity of contract Contracting partners are in privity of contract; all others are not.

probable cause Evidence that indicates that it is more likely than not that a crime has been committed. A number of states require employers to have probable cause to test or retest employees for drug use. Probable cause exists when events take place that make it more likely than not that the person being tested has been impaired by drug use.

procedural due process If government takes a protected interest, it must provide notice before anything is taken and a hearing so that the defendant can respond to the claims made against him or her.

procedural law Law that provides the rules for conducting the courtroom and related procedures in the event of a lawsuit.

procedural regulation Rules created by administrative agencies that detail the procedures to be used in the application of regulations, complaints against regulatory actions, and so forth.

product liability The liability borne by vendors for injuries caused by the sales of defective products.

promissory estoppel This is the doctrine that assures that a promise (offer) will be binding as, otherwise, an offeree would be harmed by relying on a promise made.

prospectus A shortened version of the registration statement that must be given to investors before they purchase securities sold by the issuer.

protected classes Groups with specific traits or characteristics, such as race, color, gender, religion, or national origin, for whom discrimination based on the traits is prohibited.

proximate cause For the purpose of establishing liability, the legal cause of a tort injury.

proxy solicitation A solicitation of the right to vote for shareholders who cannot or will not attend the annual shareholders' meeting.

public law Law governing the relationship between government and citizens.

punitive or exemplary damages Court-awarded damages intended to punish or make an example of a defendant in order to deter wrongful conduct. The monetary damages may be awarded to a plaintiff, at the expense of a defendant, to impose punishment and provide a disincentive for future wrongful action.

punitive damages cap Statutes that set upper limits on the amounts that juries can award for punitive damages.

Q

qualified privilege Protection against defamation claims accorded to statements made in good faith, with an absence of malice, and communicated only to those with a legitimate need for the kind of information provided.

quasi-contract An assumed contract, imposed by courts in the interest of fairness, generally to prevent the unjust enrichment of one party at the expense of another.

quid pro quo Literally, "this for that." Applicable to sexual harassment cases in which subordinate employees are offered preferential treatment in the workplace in exchange for sexual favors.

R

random searches A search in which there is no particularized showing of probable cause.

ratification An action by a principal that indicates acceptance of the actions of another, even if those actions were executed by a party who was not an agent for the principal or was acting outside his or her scope of authority.

rational basis test Distinctions in law made by governments that do not involve race or gender must have a plausible rationale.

real property Land and anything firmly attached thereto, such as a house, office building, and so forth.

reasonable accommodations Modifications of requirements, such as working hours assigned, to accommodate the needs of a protected class.

reasonable expectation of privacy The Fourth Amendment protects areas of activity that citizens expect will not be open to public inspection.

reasonable restrictions Restrictions governments place on freedom of expression that are not based on content but are based on practical considerations, such as preventing traffic jams when political demonstrations take place or inhibiting the access of children to adult materials.

reasonable substantiation   Documentation, using acceptable methodology, of claims made in advertising or other forms of product promotion.

recalls   Mandatory vendor calls for the return of defective products for repair or replacement.

reciprocity   The provision of equivalent treatment without regard to national boundaries. With reciprocity, a U.S. inventor would have his patent application treated equivalently in the United States or in a foreign country.

registration statement   A legal document required by the SEC before an issuer of securities can sell to the public. The registration statement contains descriptive information on the issuer, a recitation of risks associated with the securities to be issued, discussion of management, and other material information that would affect a reasonably prudent investor.

regulatory taking   A government regulation that has the effect of taking all or nearly all of the value of land from a landowner. If a court agrees that the government regulation has effected a regulatory taking, the government must compensate the landowner for the fair market value of the property.

requirements contracts   Contracts in which the buyer agrees to purchase all of its requirements for a particular good from a single seller during a period of time.

resale price maintenance   Agreement between a manufacturer and the resellers of its products through which the manufacturer sets the prices the resellers must charge their customers.

rescission   A contract remedy in which each party to the contract, upon cancellation of a contract, must give back what was transferred in the contract to return the contracting parties to their precontract status.

reverse engineering   A legal means for discovering trade secrets by analysis of another firm's products, processes, and so forth.

reversible error   An error in the application of procedural law of sufficient importance in a trial to form a basis for appeal of the trial outcome.

right-to-work laws   Under the Taft-Hartley Act of 1947, states have the right to choose to be right-to-work states in which union shops are illegal. If a union wins a certification election, workers in the bargaining unit cannot be forced to join the union.

ripeness   A dispute is not ripe for judicial resolution if the party appealing to the court has not exhausted all internal remedies available to that party offered by the government agency.

risk of loss   A risk that goods will be damaged or destroyed after the contract is executed.

risk–benefit analysis   A variant of cost–benefit analysis in which the costs of a proposed course of action are weighed against the identified benefits of reduced risks that result from proceeding.

roughly apportioned   State taxes must be apportioned to activities of a multistate business within the state.

rule of reason   Antitrust standard under which agreements and acts are judged based on their overall effects on competition.

S

safe harbors   In law, a safe harbor is a procedure that, if followed, will insulate the party from legal liability. For example, the legal protection against infringement liability granted to the copying of protected works if the copying is for uses "permitted" by specific regulations.

sale   Occurs when title to a good is transferred from seller to buyer for a price.

sanction   Enforcement and/or punishment power possessed by an administrative agency. May include, but not be limited to, fines, revocation or denial of license, seizure of property, and the withholding of benefits.

scope of revised Article 2 of the UCC   Deals with sales of goods in the real world or through e-commerce.

scope of UCITA   UCITA deals with contracts involving computer software, multimedia interactive products, computer data and databases, and Internet and online information. It does not deal with Internet sales of tangible goods.

scope of UETA   UETA deals comprehensively with e-commerce and contract law, addressing the sale of goods, including e-commerce sales of tangible products.

securities   Contracts that are subject to regulation by the Securities and Exchange Commission (SEC). Securities generally involve an investment of money in a common enterprise where profits are earned primarily due to the efforts of third parties, not the investor.

self-incrimination   Being compelled to testify against oneself under some coercion such as prosecution for perjury or police intimidation.

self-regulation   Regulatory arrangement under which cohesive groups, such as doctors, lawyers, and the like, police the professional activities of members of the group, generally through ethical codes, licensure requirements, certification of quality by third parties or associations, and other means.

settlement   Agreement between litigants to settle their dispute without proceeding through trial, usually accompanied by consideration from both sides to the dispute.

shipment contract   Contract that does not specify a location where the goods are to be shipped.

short-swing profits   Profits made or losses avoided from the purchase and sale, or sale and purchase, of the same securities within a six-month period, when the transactors are corporate officers, directors, or greater-than-10-percent shareholders.

shrinkwrap agreements   Intended contract agreements between vendors and customers printed on a product container wrapping with the agreement triggered or authorized by opening the package wrapping.

sole proprietorship   A business owned by one person who is fully responsible for (and liable for) the business.

sovereign immunity   The principle that other sovereign countries are immune to, or not subject to the jurisdiction of, lawsuits in U.S. courts unless the country is engaging in purely commercial activity or waives its immunity.

sovereign   The highest political power in a territory. Within their borders, sovereign countries can wield ultimate political power that is answerable to no higher power.

spammers   Distributors of Internet "junk mail" or other materials transmitted to Web users without their permission.

specially manufactured   Goods that are customized for the buyer and that the seller does not normally sell.

specific performance   A contract remedy in which the court awards the plaintiff what was promised in the contract by the defendant.

spyware   Software that allows sophisticated information retrieval and reporting.

stare decisis   The common law standard under which judges (courts) are bound to follow decisions set by precedents from prior court decisions.

state court systems   Paralleling the federal court system, state court systems have trial courts (generally designated as district, superior, or circuit courts), courts of appeals, and state supreme courts.

statute   Law enacted by a legislative body. Federal statutes are enacted by Congress and state statutes by state legislatures.

Statute of Frauds   Under the UCC, the Statute of Frauds requires contracts that exceed $500 to be in writing.

statutory subject matter   Things that can be patented, which can involve a process, machine, manufacture, or composition of nature.

stocks   Certificates that certify ownership in a company, generally a corporation. Stockholders are owners of corporations.

strict liability   Liability for injury that exists as a matter of law, even when there is no fault in an event that causes injury.

strict scrutiny   Government distinctions based on race can be justified only if they are to achieve a compelling state objective and the objective can only be achieved by treating people differently based on race.

subpoena power   A subpoena is a written court order requiring the attendance of the person named in the subpoena at a specified time and place for the purpose of being questioned under oath concerning a particular matter that is the subject of an investigation, proceeding, or lawsuit. A subpoena also may require the production of a paper, document, or other object relevant to the particular investigation.

substantial similarity   Similarities that are so striking as to disprove independent creation.

substantive law   Law that spells out the rights and duties of parties to a lawsuit.

substantive regulation   New laws or regulations created by agencies and authorized by congressional delegations of power, which have the same force as statutes enacted by Congress.

successor liability   The liability borne by companies that merge with or buy up the assets of a target company.

summary jury trial   A process in which summary evidence from discovery is presented to an "advisory" jury that renders a nonbinding jury decision as an aid in the pursuit of dispute resolution without going to a court trial.

summons   Written notification to a named defendant that a legal proceeding has been started that requires the defendant to come to court at a specified time and location if the named defendant wishes to offer a defense against the claims lodged.

sunset legislation   Legislation that requires the termination of a government agency or program at a date certain unless the legislature decides to reinstate the program or agency.

Superfund   A fund created through taxes levied on the generators of hazardous waste, particularly those companies in the chemical and petroleum industries.

supremacy   The constitutional standard under which federal law is the law of the land, with any state-created laws subordinate to federal laws so that state laws that conflict with federal law are invalid.

Supremacy Clause   The language in the U.S. Constitution that states that federal law is the supreme law of the land, superior to state law.

T

tampering   Alteration of a product after it is out of the control of the manufacturer in a way that makes it potentially injurious.

tender offer   An offer to shareholders of a target firm by a buyer that seeks to gain control of the target firm.

Tenth Amendment   Reserves all powers not delegated to the federal government for the states and citizens. It is the amendment that most explicitly defines what is meant by "federalism."

tippees The recipients of insider information from corporate insiders or others for whom disclosure of such information involves a breach of fiduciary duty.

tort A civil wrong, not involving a contract, that results in injury (physical or economic). A tort results from violation of a legal duty rather than a contract duty, that is, it is a noncontractual wrong that causes injury.

tort damages Compensation in cases involving injury intended to restore the victim to his or her pre-injury state.

toxic substances Materials designated by the EPA as toxic and regulated by the Toxic Substances Control Act.

trade practice rules Rules for the conduct of business issued by the FTC when it determines that the mode of operation of an industry needs reform.

Trade-Related Aspects of Intellectual Property Rights The organization that establishes minimum legal standards for countries to be members of the Paris Convention for patents and trademarks and the Berne Convention for copyrights.

trade secrets Secret information (of a formula, a device, etc.) kept confidential to maintain a competitive advantage. The formula for Coca-Cola is a trade secret!

tying contract A contract requiring a customer to buy a "tied" product in order to be able to buy a "tying" product.

tying product A product in which a producer enjoys monopoly power.

U

ultrahazardous A level of hazard, *unusually dangerous,* such that the law imposes a standard of strict liability on activities exhibiting this characteristic.

unaccredited investors Investors who are not "rich" (a net worth over $1 million or an annual income over $200,00) and are not corporate insiders such as officers or directors.

unconscionable Terms in a contract that are so one-sided as to shock the conscience of the court. Normally takes place when one side is economically powerful and the other side does not have realistic alternatives.

unconscionable contract An agreement that is void at law because it requires one party, generally with limited bargaining power, to accept terms that are unfair and that, symmetrically, unfairly benefit the party with superior bargaining power.

underwriters Sometimes called investment bankers. Underwriters place a value on securities based on the value of the underlying business that issues the securities. In its full underwriting capacity, an underwriter buys a new issue of securities and resells that issue to investors.

undue hardship Standard that frees employers from providing accommodation to a protected class because doing so would be unduly burdensome.

unemployment compensation A state program that compensates workers who are laid off, usually at a percentage of wages for a period of time. Often, unemployment compensation is established at 50 percent of the former employee's wages for a period of six months.

unfair labor practice strikes Strikes that are based on alleged unfair labor practices by employers such as actions that contravene agreements made in collective bargaining.

unfair trade practices Business practices that cause, or are likely to cause, substantial injury to consumers, not reasonably avoidable by consumers themselves, and not outweighed by countervailing benefits to consumers.

uniform domain name dispute resolution policy A policy devised by ICANN to reassign domain names when it is clear that the domain name owner does not have a legal right to use that domain name.

unilateral contract A contract formed when one promisor offers terms that can be accepted only by an offeree's performance.

union shops In states that do not elect to be right-to-work states, unions that win certification elections can compel all workers they bargain for to join the union and pay dues.

unions Organizations of workers that focus on improving wages and other terms and conditions of employment for workers.

United Nations Commission for International Trade Law The group that is responsible for proposing model acts for national adoption. The CISG is a product of the UNCITRAL. A model act for e-commerce is in the works.

U.S. Supreme Court The highest court in the land, serving primarily as an appeals court, but also as a trial court for disputes between states.

usage of trade (trade usage) The ways similar transactions are usually handled within the industry.

usury laws State laws that set ceilings, that is, maximum limits, on the interest rates that can be charged on loan contracts.

V

validation notice Notice that credit collectors must provide to purported debtors indicating a 30-day window for disputing a debt claim or for requesting written verification of debt.

venue The physical location of the courthouse where a suit will be heard.

verdict The outcome of a trial.

vertical restraints Restrictive agreements between firms at different levels in the marketing chain—e.g., between a manufacturer and a distributor.

vested A person's right to retirement benefits is vested when the right to those benefits cannot be terminated even if the employee changes jobs, is laid off, or is fired.

veto A veto is a vote by the president or chief executive officer that overturns a decision of both houses of the legislature with respect to a bill or proposed law.

W

warranty disclaimers Conspicuous clauses informing buyers that the seller is not guaranteeing the express or implied quality of goods sold under contract.

wetlands Areas protected by the EPA that are saturated by surface or groundwater. A permit is required to drain or alter an area designated as a wetland and the EPA has ultimate authority for approving such permits.

whistle-blower protections Statutory prohibitions on the firing of workers for reporting hazardous products or law violations or engaging in other specific protected actions in support of public policy.

wildcat strikes Strikes that are unauthorized by the parent union or are contrary to the terms of a collective bargaining agreement that calls for arbitration of disputes.

World Intellectual Property Organization The organization that has primary responsibility for the international protection of the rights of owners of intellectual property, including patents, copyrights, and trademarks.

World Trade Organization An organization of over 150 nations that is responsible for enforcing multilateral trade agreements among nations.

writ of certiorari Official written notice of a higher court's decision that it wishes to receive the lower court's record of a case. Such a writ serves as notice that the higher court will review the identified case from the lower court.

wrongful death A death resulting from the wrongful act of another.

Case Index

Subject Index